Standard Normal Distribution (continued)

z	.00	.01	.02	.03	.04	.05	.06	.07	.08	.09
0.0	.5000	.5040	.5080	.5120	.5160	.5199	.5239	.5279	.5319	.5359
0.1	.5398	.5438	.5478	.5517	.5557	.5596	.5636	.5675	.5714	.5753
0.2	.5793	.5832	.5871	.5910	.5948	.5987	.6026	.6064	.6103	.6141
0.3	.6179	.6217	.6255	.6293	.6331	.6368	.6406	.6443	.6480	.6517
0.4	.6554	.6591	.6628	.6664	.6700	.6736	.6772	.6808	.6844	.6879
0.5	.6915	.6950	.6985	.7019	.7054	.7088	.7123	.7157	.7190	.7224
0.6	.7257	.7291	.7324	.7357	.7389	.7422	.7454	.7486	.7517	.7549
0.7	.7580	.7611	.7642	.7673	.7704	.7734	.7764	.7794	.7823	.7852
0.8	.7881	.7910	.7939	.7967	.7995	.8023	.8051	.8078	.8106	.8133
0.9	.8159	.8186	.8212	.8238	.8264	.8289	.8315	.8340	.8365	.8389
1.0	.8413	.8438	.8461	.8485	.8508	.8531	.8554	.8577	.8599	.8621
1.1	.8643	.8665	.8686	.8708	.8729	.8749	.8770	.8790	.8810	.8830
1.2	.8849	.8869	.8888	.8907	.8925	.8944	.8962	.8980	.8997	.9015
1.3	.9032	.9049	.9066	.9082	.9099	.9115	.9131	.9147	.9162	.9177
1.4	.9192	.9207	.9222	.9236	.9251	.9265	.9278	.9292	.9306	.9319
1.5	.9332	.9345	.9357	.9370	.9382	.9394	.9406	.9418	.9429	.9441
1.6	.9452	.9463	.9474	.9484	.9495	.9505	.9515	.9525	.9535	.9545
1.7	.9554	.9564	.9573	.9582	.9591	.9599	.9608	.9616	.9625	.9633
1.8	.9641	.9649	.9656	.9664	.9671	.9678	.9686	.9693	.9699	.9706
1.9	.9713	.9719	.9726	.9732	.9738	.9744	.9750	.9756	.9761	.9767
2.0	.9772	.9778	.9783	.9788	.9793	.9798	.9803	.9808	.9812	.9817
2.1	.9821	.9826	.9830	.9834	.9838	.9842	.9846	.9850	.9854	.9857
2.2	.9861	.9864	.9868	.9871	.9875	.9878	.9881	.9884	.9887	.9890
2.3	.9893	.9896	.9898	.9901	.9904	.9906	.9909	.9911	.9913	.9916
2.4	.9918	.9920	.9922	.9925	.9927	.9929	.9931	.9932	.9934	.9936
2.5	.9938	.9940	.9941	.9943	.9945	.9946	.9948	.9949	.9951	.9952
2.6	.9953	.9955	.9956	.9957	.9959	.9960	.9961	.9962	.9963	.9964
2.7	.9965	.9966	.9967	.9968	.9969	.9970	.9971	.9972	.9973	.9974
2.8	.9974	.9975	.9976	.9977	.9977	.9978	.9979	.9979	.9980	.9981
2.9	.9981	.9982	.9982	.9983	.9984	.9984	.9985	.9985	.9986	.9986
3.0	.9987	.9987	.9987	.9988	.9988	.9989	.9989	.9989	.9990	.9990
3.1	.9990	.9991	.9991	.9991	.9992	.9992	.9992	.9992	.9993	.9993
3.2	.9993	.9993	.9994	.9994	.9994	.9994	.9994	.9995	.9995	.9995
3.3	.9995	.9995	.9995	.9996	.9996	.9996	.9996	.9996	.9996	.9997
3.4	.9997	.9997	.9997	.9997	.9997	.9997	.9997	.9997	.9997	.9998

t-Distribution

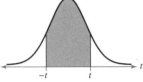

c confidence interval

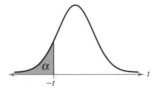

Left-tailed test

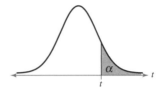

Right-tailed test

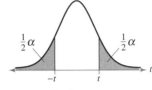

Two-tailed test

	Level of confidence, *c*	0.50	0.80	0.90	0.95	0.98	0.99
	One tail, α	0.25	0.10	0.05	0.025	0.01	0.005
d.f.	**Two tails, α**	0.50	0.20	0.10	0.05	0.02	0.01
1		1.000	3.078	6.314	12.706	31.821	63.657
2		.816	1.886	2.920	4.303	6.965	9.925
3		.765	1.638	2.353	3.182	4.541	5.841
4		.741	1.533	2.132	2.776	3.747	4.604
5		.727	1.476	2.015	2.571	3.365	4.032
6		.718	1.440	1.943	2.447	3.143	3.707
7		.711	1.415	1.895	2.365	2.998	3.499
8		.706	1.397	1.860	2.306	2.896	3.355
9		.703	1.383	1.833	2.262	2.821	3.250
10		.700	1.372	1.812	2.228	2.764	3.169
11		.697	1.363	1.796	2.201	2.718	3.106
12		.695	1.356	1.782	2.179	2.681	3.055
13		.694	1.350	1.771	2.160	2.650	3.012
14		.692	1.345	1.761	2.145	2.624	2.977
15		.691	1.341	1.753	2.131	2.602	2.947
16		.690	1.337	1.746	2.120	2.583	2.921
17		.689	1.333	1.740	2.110	2.567	2.898
18		.688	1.330	1.734	2.101	2.552	2.878
19		.688	1.328	1.729	2.093	2.539	2.861
20		.687	1.325	1.725	2.086	2.528	2.845
21		.686	1.323	1.721	2.080	2.518	2.831
22		.686	1.321	1.717	2.074	2.508	2.819
23		.685	1.319	1.714	2.069	2.500	2.807
24		.685	1.318	1.711	2.064	2.492	2.797
25		.684	1.316	1.708	2.060	2.485	2.787
26		.684	1.315	1.706	2.056	2.479	2.779
27		.684	1.314	1.703	2.052	2.473	2.771
28		.683	1.313	1.701	2.048	2.467	2.763
29		.683	1.311	1.699	2.045	2.462	2.756
∞		.674	1.282	1.645	1.960	2.326	2.576

▼

Elementary Statistics
Picturing the World

Elementary Statistics

Picturing the World

Ron Larson
*Penn State University
at Erie*

Betsy Farber
*Bucks County
Community College*

Annotated Instructor's Edition

Acquisition Editor: *Kathy Boothby Sestak*
Special Projects Manager: *Ann Heath*
Editorial/Production Supervision: *Bayani Mendoza de Leon*
Editor-in-Chief: *Jerome Grant*
Assistant Vice President of Production and Manufacturing: *David W. Riccardi*
Senior Managing Editor: *Linda Mihatov Behrens*
Executive Managing Editor: *Kathleen Schiaparelli*
Development Editor: *Don Gecewicz*
Editor-in-Chief, Development: *Carol Truehart*
Manufacturing Buyer: *Alan Fischer*
Manufacturing Manager: *Trudy Pisciotti*
Marketing Manager: *Melody Marcus*
Marketing Assistant: *Amy Lysik*
Associate Editor, Mathematics/Statistics/Media: *Audra J. Walsh*
Director of Creative Services: *Paula Maylahn*
Associate Creative Director: *Amy Rosen*
Art Director: *Maureen Eide*
Assistant to the Art Director: *John Christiana*
Art Manager: *Gus Vibal*
Art Editor: *Grace Hazeldine*
Cover Designer: *Kiwi Design*
Interior Design: *Meridian Creative Group*
Composition and Art: *Meridian Creative Group*
Editorial Assistant: *Joanne Wendelken*
Cover photos: New York City ©Harvey Loyd/The Stock Market; Child walking ©Roy Corral;
Sunset in the Gorge ©Jay Carroll/Photografix; Asian-American lifting weights ©Tony Stone Images;
Donn Pikop in wheat field ©Chuck Kimmerle/Grand Forks Herald; Space shuttle challenger ©Photo Disk

©2000 by Prentice-Hall, Inc.
Upper Saddle River, New Jersey 07458

Printed in the United States of America

10 9 8 7 6 5 4 3 2 1

ISBN 0-13-010797-2

(Student Edition ISBN 0-13-010734-4)

Prentice-Hall International (UK) Limited, *London*
Prentice-Hall of Australia Pty. Limited, *Sydney*
Prentice-Hall Canada Inc., *Toronto*
Prentice-Hall Hispanoamericana, S.A., *Mexico*
Prentice-Hall of India Private Limited, *New Delhi*
Prentice-Hall of Japan, Inc., *Tokyo*
Prentice-Hall (*Singapore*) Pte. Ltd.
Editora Prentice-Hall do Brasil, Ltda., *Rio de Janeiro*

▶ About the Authors

Ron Larson
*Penn State University
at Erie*

Ron Larson received his Ph.D. in mathematics from the University of Colorado in 1970. At that time he accepted a position with Penn State University, and he currently holds the rank of professor of mathematics at the university. Larson is the lead author of more than two dozen mathematics textbooks that range from sixth grade through calculus levels. Many of his texts, such as the sixth edition of his calculus text, are leaders in their markets. Larson is also one of the pioneers in the use of multimedia and the Internet to enhance the learning of mathematics. He has authored multimedia programs, extending from the elementary school through calculus levels. Larson is a member of several professional groups and is a frequent speaker at national and regional mathematics meetings.

Betsy Farber
*Bucks County
Community College*

Betsy Farber received her Bachelor's degree in mathematics from Penn State University and Master's degree in mathematics from the College of New Jersey. Since 1976, she has been teaching all levels of mathematics at Bucks County Community College in Newtown, Pennsylvania, where she currently holds the rank of professor. She is particularly interested in developing new ways to make statistics relevant and interesting to her students, and has been teaching statistics in many different modes—with TI-83, with MINITAB, and by distance learning as well as in the traditional classroom. A member of the American Mathematical Association of Two-Year Colleges (AMATYC), she is an author of *The Student Edition to Minitab, A Guide to Minitab* and the Study and Solutions guide for *Understandable Statistics*. She served as consulting editor for *Statistics, A First Course* and has written computer tutorials for the CD-ROM correlating to the texts in the Streeter Series in mathematics.

▶ Contents

▶ Chapter 1   Introduction to Statistics

▶ Chapter 2   Descriptive Statistics

▶ Chapter 3   Probability

▶ **Chapter 4   Discrete Probability Distributions**

▶ **Chapter 5   Normal Probability Distributions**

▶ **Chapter 6   Confidence Intervals**

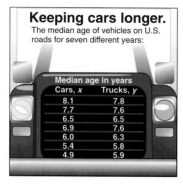

Chapter 10   Chi-Square Tests and the *F*-Distribution

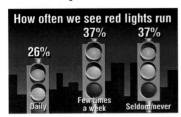

Chapter 11   Nonparametric Tests

▶ Appendices

▶ Preface

Welcome to *Elementary Statistics: Picturing the World*. This book has a variety of pedagogical features, all of which are designed to show students how statistics is used to **picture and describe the world** and to show them that statistics is used to **make informed decisions.** This message—picturing the world— begins with the cover, continues through the chapter openers, sections, exercise sets, and special features.

General Features

Versatile Course Coverage   The table of contents of the text was developed to give instructors **many options.** For instance, by assigning the **Extending the Basics** exercises and spending time on the chapter projects, there is sufficient content to use the text in a two-semester course. More commonly, we expect the text to be used in a three-credit semester course. In such cases, instructors will have to pare down the text's 46 sections. If you want more information on sample syllabi, check the Web site that accompanies the text.

Choice of Table   Our experience has shown that students find a **cumulative density function** (CDF) table easier to use than a "0-to-z" table. Using the CDF table to find the area under a normal curve is the topic of Section 5.2 on pages 202–208. Because we realize that many teachers prefer to use the "0-to-z" table, we have provided an alternative presentation of Section 5.2 using the "0-to-z" table in Appendix A of the book.

Graphical Approach   As with most introductory statistics texts, we begin the descriptive statistics chapter with a survey of different ways to display data graphically. A difference between this text and many others is that **we continue to incorporate the graphical display of data throughout the text.** For example, see the use of stem-and-leaf plots to display data on pages 326 and 329. In all, the text has over 750 graphs—surpassing all other introductory statistics texts.

Variety of Real-Life Applications   We have chosen real-life applications that are representative of the majors of the students taking introductory statistics courses. These include business, psychology, health sciences, sports, computer science, political science, and many others. Choosing meaningful applications for such a diverse audience is difficult. We wanted the applications to be **authentic**—but they also need to be **accessible.**

Data and Source Lines   The data sets in the book were chosen for interest, variety, and their ability to illustrate concepts. Most of the **over 200 data sets** contain actual data with source lines. The remaining data sets contain simulated data that, though not actual, are representative of real-life situations. All data sets containing 20 or more entries are available in a variety of electronic forms, including disk and Internet. In the exercise sets, the data sets that are available electronically are indicated by the icon 🖫 .

Accuracy   Every effort was made to **ensure the mathematical accuracy** of the examples and exercise solutions. The examples and exercises were solved by two people independently. A third person compared the independent solutions and resolved differences. If you encounter errors that we missed, please contact us so that we can correct the problem in a subsequent printing.

Balanced Approach   The text strikes a **balance between computation, decision making, and conceptual understanding.** We have provided many Examples, Exercises, and Try It problems that go beyond mere computation. For instance, look at Exercises 31 and 32 on page 43. Students are not just asked to construct a relative frequency histogram for the given data, they are asked to go a step further and use the histogram to make a decision.

Prerequisites   Statistics contains many formulas and variables, including radicals, summation notation, Greek letters, and subscripts. So, **some familiarity with algebra and evaluation of algebraic expressions** is a prerequisite. Nevertheless, we have made every effort to keep algebraic manipulations to a minimum—often we display informal versions of formulas using words in place of variables. For instance, see the definition of class width on page 30.

Flexible Technology   Although most formulas in the book are illustrated with tabular "hand" calculations, we assume that most students who take this course have access to some form of technology tool, such as Minitab, Excel, or the TI-83. Because the use of technology varies widely, we have made the text flexible. **It can be used in courses with no more technology than a scientific calculator—or it can be used in courses that require frequent use of sophisticated technology tools.** For those who want specific instructions on particular technology tools, separate technology manuals are available to augment the text. Whatever your use of technology, we are sure that you agree with us that the goal of this course is not computation. Rather, it is to gain an understanding of the basic concepts and uses of statistics.

The Cover   Each chapter begins with a photographic introduction that includes real-life data. In keeping with the theme of "picturing the world," **one photo from each of the chapter openers** was used to create the eleven "upper" sides of a dodecahedron. The image was created electronically using a three-dimensional modeling program. On the cover, only 6 of the sides are visible. But on the title screens of electronic versions of the text and supplements, all 11 of the upper sides are visible as the dodecahedron spins. We like this image because it resembles our spinning planet.

Page Layout   We believe that statistics is more accessible to students when it is carefully formatted on each page with a consistent open lay out. This text is the **first college level statistics book to be written to design,** which means that none of its features (Examples, Try It problems, Definitions, or Guidelines) are split from one page to the next. Although this process requires extra planning and work in the development stage, the result is a presentation that is clean and clear.

MAA, AMATYC, NCTM Standards   This text answers the call for a **student-friendly text that emphasizes the uses of statistics** and not just the computation of its myriad of formulas. Our experience indicates that our job as instructors of an introductory course in statistics is not to produce statisticians but to produce informed consumers of statistical reports. For this reason, we have included many exercises that require students to provide written explanations, find patterns, and make decisions.

Chapter Features

Chapter Openers   Each chapter begins with a two-page description of a real-life problem. For example, look at the opener to Chapter 2. The data set contains the ages of the entire population of the fishing village of Akhiok, Alaska. As the chapter is developed, students are asked to return to the data set given in the chapter opener. For instance, on page 32 students are asked to construct a frequency distribution for the ages of the 77 residents of Akhiok. Each chapter opener has two special features called **Where You've Been and Where You're Going.** The first of these shows students how the chapter fits into the bigger picture of statistics, and the second gives students an overview of the chapter.

Chapter Case Study   Each chapter includes a full-page case study with actual data and a series of **thought-provoking questions** that are designed to illustrate the important concepts of the chapter. For instance, the case study on page 329 was taken from the Journal of the American Medical Association and illustrates how hypothesis testing can be used to show that the normal human body temperature is not 98.6 degrees, as is commonly believed. The case studies can be assigned as individual projects or as group projects to be worked in class or outside of class.

Chapter Technology Project   Each chapter has a full-page technology project that gives students additional insight into the way **technology is used to handle large data sets** or complex real-life questions. For instance, the technology project on page 346 shows students how hypothesis testing was used to show gender bias in the selection of jurors in the trial of Dr. Spock.

Chapter Summary   Each chapter concludes with a chapter summary that answers the questions **What did you learn?** and **Why did you learn it?** The chapter summary is designed to be used as a study aid in conjunction with the chapter review exercises. In addition to showing the real-life uses of the material in the chapter, each summary points out one or more common abuses of statistics.

Chapter Review Exercises   Following each chapter summary, we have compiled a set of review exercises that students can use as a **preparation for a chapter test.** The order of the exercises follows the order that the topics were presented in the chapter. The answers to all odd-numbered review exercises are given in the back of the book. The worked out solutions are available in the Student's Solutions Manual.

Chapter Quizzes and Cumulative Tests   The third part of the "end-of-chapter" **self-evaluation** materials is a chapter quiz. In addition, cumulative tests appear after Chapters 3, 6, 9, and 11. The answers to all quiz and test questions are given in the back of the book.

Section Features

Section Organization   Each section is **organized by learning objectives.** These objectives are presented in everyday language in a margin feature called What You Should Learn. The same objectives are then used as subsection titles throughout the section.

Titled Examples   Every concept in the text is clearly illustrated with one or more step-by-step examples. Each of the more than 200 examples is numbered and titled for easy reference. In presenting the examples, we used an **open format with a step-by-step display** that students can use as a model when solving the exercises.

Try Its   Each example in the text is followed by a similar problem called Try It Yourself. The answers to these problems are given in the back of the book, and the worked-out solutions are given in the Student's Solutions Manual. The Try It Yourself questions are a major strength of the text as more than just a collection of exercises, but as a bona fide learning instrument. Few students who take this course understand that one cannot learn statistics by simply reading about it. Instead, **one learns statistics by reading and doing statistics.** Please encourage your students to use this feature—it requires effort, but it pays off in student success.

Study Tips   Most sections contain one or more study tips placed on yellow "sticky notes" in the margin. These tend to be **informal learning aids,** which show how to read a table, use technology, or interpret a result or a graph. For instance, the study tip on page 44 points out that a stem-and-leaf plot has as many leaves as there are entries in the original data set.

Insights   Most sections also contain one or more insights placed on blue "sticky notes" in the margin. The purpose of each insight is to help **drive home an important interpretation or help connect different concepts.** For instance, the insight on page 212 helps students interpret z-scores by pointing out that z-scores that are less than –3 or greater than 3 are very unusual.

Definitions   The critical definitions of statistics are set off with gold screens. In writing the definitions, we strived for two goals—**simplicity and mathematical accuracy.** Consequently, the formal definitions are often followed by student-friendly guidelines that explain, in everyday English, how to apply the definition. For instance, see the definition of population standard deviation on page 70.

Guidelines   Throughout the book, the presentation of a statistical formula is followed by a step-by-step set of guidelines for applying the formula. The guidelines are divided into two columns titled In Words and In Symbols. See page 70 for an example.

Picturing the World   Each section contains a real-life "mini case study" that illustrates the important concept or concepts of the section. Each Picturing the World concludes with a question, and **can be used for general class discussion or group work.** For instance, the Picturing the World on page 88 asks students to interpret a box-and-whisker plot that represents the ages of U.S. presidents.

Technology Examples   Many sections contain a worked example that shows how technology can be used to calculate formulas, perform tests, or display data. For instance, Example 5 on page 72 shows how to use Minitab, Excel, and the TI-83 to find the mean and standard deviation of a data set. Note that this example shows the **screen displays within the presentation of the example.** Additional screen displays are given at the ends of selected chapters. For instance, note the technology reference for Example 7 on page 50.

Section Exercise Sets   Each section concludes with a set of exercises carefully written to nurture student understanding and proficiency.

- **Abundance of Exercises**   The text contains over 1700 exercises, more than twice the number of most introductory statistics books. Our goal is to provide instructors with a versatile teaching instrument that offers a wide range of exercises that **move from basic concepts and skill development to more challenging and interpretive problems.**

- **Exercises are Labeled**   Most exercises are **labeled for easy reference.** For instance, Exercises 9–12 on page 336 are labeled Graphical Analysis because students are asked to use the graphs provided to answer the questions.

- **Paired Format**   Almost all exercises are given in **"paired format"** so that the odd-numbered exercise, whose answer is given in the back of the book, is paired with an even-numbered exercise, whose answer is not given. This paired format is commonly used in mathematics texts, but is less common in statistics texts.

- **Extending the Basics**   Each exercise set ends with a group of exercises called Extending the Basics. These exercises go beyond the material presented in the section—they tend to be more challenging and are not required as prerequisites of subsequent sections.

- **Answers and Solutions**   The answers to all odd-numbered exercises are given in the back of the book, and the worked-out solutions are available in the *Student's Solutions Manual.*

▶ Features

Chapter Openers
Where You've Been

Each chapter begins with a two-page photographic description of a real-life problem. The first page has a feature called Where You've Been. It shows students how the chapter fits into the bigger picture of statistics, by connecting it to topics learned in earlier chapters.

Chapter Openers
Where You're Going

The second page of the chapter opener has a feature called Where You're Going. It gives students an overview of the chapter, exploring concepts in the context of real-world settings.

Section Organization

Each section is organized by learning objectives. These objectives are presented in everyday language in a margin feature called What You Should Learn. The same objectives are then used as subsection titles throughout the section.

Study Tips

Most sections contain one or more study tips placed on yellow "sticky notes" in the margin. These tend to be informal learning aids, which show how to read a table, use technology, or interpret a result or a graph.

The following reproduces a sample textbook page:

44 CHAPTER 2 | Descriptive Statistics

2.2 More Graphs and Displays

Graphing Quantitative Data Sets • Graphing Qualitative Data Sets • Graphing Paired Data Sets

What You Should Learn

* How to graph quantitative data sets using stem-and-leaf plots and dot plots
* How to graph qualitative data sets using pie charts and Pareto charts
* How to graph paired data sets using scatter plots and time series charts

Graphing Quantitative Data Sets

In Section 2.1, you learned several traditional ways to display quantitative data graphically. In this section, you will learn a newer way to display quantitative data, called a **stem-and-leaf plot.** Stem-and-leaf plots are examples of **exploratory data analysis (EDA),** which was developed by John Tukey in 1977.

In a stem-and-leaf plot, each number is separated into a **stem** (the entry's leftmost digits) and a **leaf** (the rightmost digit). A stem-and-leaf plot is similar to a histogram but has the advantage that the graph still contains the original data values. Another advantage of a stem-and-leaf plot is that it provides an easy way to sort data.

EXAMPLE 1 *Constructing a Stem-and-Leaf Plot*

The following are the numbers of league-leading runs batted in (RBIs) for baseball's American League for the last 50 years. Display the data in a stem-and-leaf plot. What can you conclude? *(Source: Major League Baseball)*

```
155 159 144 129 105 145 126 116 130 114 122 112 112 142 126
118 118 108 122 121 109 140 126 119 113 117 118 109 109 119
139 139 122  78 133 126 123 145 121 134 124 119 132 133 124
129 112 126 148 147
```

SOLUTION Because the data entries go from a low of 78 to a high of 159, you should use stem values from 7 to 15. To construct the plot, list these stems to the left of a vertical line. For each data entry, list a leaf to the right of its stem. For instance, the entry 155 has a stem of 15 and a leaf of 5. The resulting stem-and-leaf plot will be unordered. To obtain an ordered stem-and-leaf plot, rewrite the plot with the leaves in increasing order from left to right.

Study Tip

In a stem-and-leaf plot, you should have as many leaves as there are entries in the original data set.

RBIs for American League Leaders

```
 7 | 8              Key: 15|5 = 155
 8 |
 9 |
10 | 58999
11 | 642288937 8992
12 | 96262162 6314496
13 | 0993423
14 | 4520587
15 | 59
```
Unordered Stem-and-Leaf Plot

RBIs for American League Leade

```
 7 | 8              Key: 15|5 = 155
 8 |
 9 |
10 | 58999
11 | 222346788 8999
12 | 112233446 666699
13 | 0233499
14 | 0245578
15 | 59
```
Ordered Stem-and-Leaf Plot

From the ordered stem-and-leaf plot, you can conclude that most of the leaders had between 110 and 130 RBIs.

Titled Examples

Every concept in the text is clearly illustrated with one or more step-by-step examples. Each of the more than 200 examples is numbered and titled for easy reference. In presenting the examples, we used an open format with a step-by-step display that students can use as a model when solving the exercises.

Try Its

Each example in the text is followed by a similar problem called Try It Yourself. The answers to these problems are given in the back of the book, and the worked-out solutions are given in the *Student's Solutions Manual.*

The following reproduces a sample textbook page:

SECTION 2.4 | Measures of Variation **77**

When a frequency distribution has classes, you can estimate the sample mean and standard deviation by using the midpoint of each class.

EXAMPLE 10 *Using Midpoints of Classes*

The circle graph at the right shows the results of a survey in which 100 college students were asked their average monthly earnings during the school year. Make a frequency distribution for the data. Then use the table to estimate the sample mean and the sample standard deviation of the data set.

Working their way through
Two thirds of college students say they have a job. Average monthly earnings:

Copyright 1998, USA TODAY. Reprinted with permission.

Study Tip

When a class is open, as in the last class, you must assign a single value to represent the midpoint. For this example, we selected 600.

SOLUTION Begin by using a frequency distribution to organize the data.

Class	x	f	xf	$x - \bar{x}$	$(x - \bar{x})^2$	$(x - \bar{x})^2 f$
0	0	33	0	-243	59,049	1,948,617
1–99	50	4	200	-193	37,249	148,996
100–199	150	10	1,500	-93	8,649	86,490
200–299	250	13	3,250	7	49	637
300–399	350	12	4,200	107	11,449	137,388
400–499	450	11	4,950	207	42,849	471,339
500+	600	17	10,200	357	127,449	2,166,633
		$\Sigma = 100$	$\Sigma = 24,300$			$\Sigma = 4,960,100$

$$\bar{x} = \frac{\Sigma xf}{n} = \frac{24,300}{100} = 243 \quad \text{Sample mean}$$

Use the sum of squares to find the sample standard deviation.

$$s = \sqrt{\frac{\Sigma(x - \bar{x})^2 f}{n - 1}} = \sqrt{\frac{4,960,100}{99}} \approx 223.8 \quad \text{Sample standard deviation}$$

So, the sample mean is 243 dollars per month and the sample standard deviation is 223.8 dollars per month.

Try It Yourself 10

In the frequency distribution, 600 was chosen to represent the class of $500 and greater. How would the sample mean and standard deviation change if you used 650 to represent this class?

a. Write the first three columns of a *frequency distribution table.*
b. Find the *sample mean.*
c. Complete the *last three columns* of the frequency distribution table.
d. Find the *sample standard deviation.*   *Answer: Page A34*

Insight

The disadvantage with the variance is that its units are usually meaningless. For instance, the variance for the starting salaries is measured in "square dollars." You'll be able to return to the original unit of the data by using the standard deviation.

DEFINITION

The **population standard deviation** of a population data set of N entries is the square root of the variance.

$$\text{Population standard deviation} = \sigma = \sqrt{\sigma^2} = \sqrt{\frac{\Sigma(x - \mu)^2}{N}}$$

GUIDELINES

Finding the Population Variance and Standard Deviation

In Words	In Symbols
1. Find the mean of the population data set.	$\mu = \dfrac{\Sigma x}{N}$
2. Find the deviation of each entry.	$x - \mu$
3. Square each deviation.	$(x - \mu)^2$
4. Add to get the **sum of squares.**	$SS_x = \Sigma(x - \mu)^2$
5. Divide by N to get the **population variance.**	$\sigma^2 = \dfrac{\Sigma(x - \mu)^2}{N}$
6. Find the square root of the variance to get the **population standard deviation.**	$\sigma = \sqrt{\dfrac{\Sigma(x - \mu)^2}{N}}$

▶ **EXAMPLE 3**   *Finding the Population Standard Deviation*

Find the population variance and standard deviation of the starting salaries for Corporation A.

SOLUTION   The table at the left summarizes the steps used to find SS_x.

$$SS_x = 88.5, \qquad N = 10, \qquad \sigma^2 = \frac{88.5}{10} = 8.85, \qquad \sigma = \sqrt{8.85} \approx 2.97$$

So, the population variance is 8.85 and the population standard deviation is about 3.0 or $3000.

Salary x	Deviation $x - \mu$	Squares $(x - \mu)^2$
41	−0.5	0.25
38	−3.5	12.25
39	−2.5	6.25
45	3.5	12.25
47	5.5	30.25
41	−0.5	0.25
44	2.5	6.25
41	−0.5	0.25
37	−4.5	20.25
42	0.5	0.25
	$\Sigma = 0$	$SS_x = 88.5$

Sum of squares of starting salaries for Corporation A

Try It Yourself 3

Find the population standard deviation of the starting salaries for Corporation B.

a. Find the *mean* and each *deviation*, as you did in Try It Yourself 2.
b. *Square* each deviation and *add* to get the sum of squares.
c. *Divide* by N to get the population variance.
d. Find the *square root* of the variance.
e. *Interpret* the results by giving the standard deviation in dollars.

Answer: Page A33

Insights

Most sections also contain one or more insights placed on blue "sticky notes" in the margin. The purpose of each insight is to help drive home an important interpretation or help connect different concepts.

Definitions

The critical statistics definitions are set off with gold screens. Formal definitions are often followed by guidelines that explain, in everyday English, how to apply the definition.

Guidelines

Throughout the book, the presentation of a statistical formula is followed by a set of step-by-step guidelines for applying the formula. The guidelines are divided into two columns titled In Words and In Symbols.

A second type of probability is empirical probability. Empirical probability can be used even if each outcome is not equally likely to occur.

Picturing the World

It seems as if no matter how strange an event is, somebody wants to know the probability that it will occur. The following table lists the probability that some intriguing events will happen.   *(Source: What Are The Chances)*

What are the chances?

Event	Probability
Appearing on *The Tonight Show*	1 in 490,000
Being killed by terrorists overseas	1 in 650,000
Being a victim of serious crime	5%
Writing a best-selling novel	0.00205
Congress will override a veto	4%
Earning a Ph.D.	0.008

Which of these events is most likely to occur? Least likely?

DEFINITION

Empirical (or **statistical probability**) is based on observations obtained from probability experiments. The empirical probability of an event E is the relative frequency of event E.

$$P(E) = \frac{\text{Frequency of event } E}{\text{Total frequency}} = \frac{f}{n}$$

▶ **EXAMPLE 4**   *Finding Empirical Probabilities*

A pond contains three types of fish: bluegills, redgills, and crappies. Each fish in the pond is equally likely to be caught. You catch 40 fish and record the type. Each time, you release the fish back into the pond. The following frequency distribution shows your results.

Fish Type	Number of Times Caught, f
Bluegill	13
Redgill	17
Crappy	10
	$\Sigma f = 40$

If you catch another fish, what is the probability that it is a bluegill?

SOLUTION   The event is "catching a bluegill." In your experiment, the frequency of this event is 13. Because the total of the frequencies is 40, the empirical probability of catching a bluegill is

$$P(\text{bluegill}) = \frac{13}{40}$$

$$= 0.325$$

Try It Yourself 4

An insurance company determines that in every 100 claims, 4 are fraudulent. What is the probability that the next claim the company processes is fraudulent?

a. *Identify* the event. Find the *frequency* of the event.
b. Find the *total frequency* for the experiment.
c. Find the *relative frequency* of the event.

Answer: Page A34

Picturing the World

Each section contains a real-life "mini case study" that illustrates the important concept or concepts of the section. Each Picturing the World concludes with a question.

Technology Examples

Many sections contain a worked example that shows how technology can be used to calculate formulas, perform tests, or display data. Screen displays from Minitab, Excel, and TI-83 are given. Additional screen displays are given at the ends of selected chapters, and detailed instructions are given in separate technology manuals available with the book.

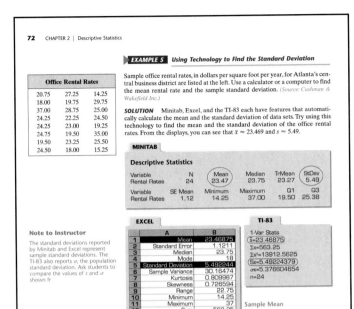

Chapter Technology Project

Each chapter has a full-page technology project that gives students additional insight into the way technology is used to handle large data sets or complex, real-life questions.

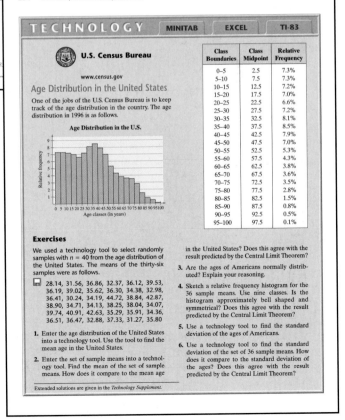

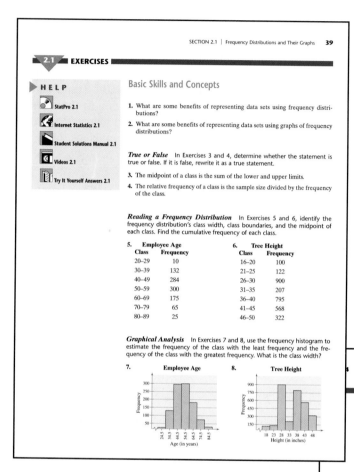

Section Exercise Sets

Each section concludes with a set of exercises carefully written to nurture student understanding and proficiency. They move from basic concepts and skill development to more challenging and interpretive problems.

Labeled Exercises

Most exercises are labeled for easy reference. For instance, exercises labeled Graphical Analysis ask students to use the graphs provided to answer the questions.

Paired Format

Almost all exercises are given in "paired format" so that the odd-numbered exercise, whose answer is given in the back of the book, is paired with an even-numbered exercise, whose answer is not given. This paired format is commonly used in mathematics texts, but is less common in statistics texts.

Extending the Basics

Each exercise set ends with a group of exercises called Extending the Basics. These exercises go beyond the material presented in the section (they tend to be more challenging and are not required as prerequisites of subsequent sections).

Answers and Solutions

The answers to all odd-numbered exercises are given in the back of the book, and the worked-out solutions are available in the *Student's Solutions Manual*.

CHAPTER 7 | Hypothesis Testing with One Sample

35. Writing a Claim Your medical research team is investigating the proper dose of a certain heart medication. The medicine manufacturer thinks that the mean dose should be 10 milligrams. From your point of view, which of the following best represents your claim?

$$\mu = 10, \quad \mu \leq 10, \quad \mu \geq 10$$

36. Writing a Claim A taxicab company claims that the mean travel time between two destinations is about 21 minutes. From the taxicab company's point of view, which of the following best represents this claim?

$$\mu = 21, \quad \mu < 21, \quad \mu > 21$$

37. Writing Hypotheses A refrigerator manufacturer claims that the mean life of its refrigerators is about 15 years. You are asked to test this claim. How would you write the null hypothesis if

(*a*) you represent the manufacturer and want to support the claim?

(*b*) you represent a consumer group and want to reject the claim?

38. Writing Hypotheses An Internet provider is trying to gain advertising deals and claims that the mean time a customer spends on line per day is about 28 minutes. You are asked to test this claim. How would you write the null hypothesis if

(*a*) you represent the internet provider and want to support the claim?

(*b*) you represent an advertiser and want to reject the claim?

Extending the Basics

39. Think About It Why can decreasing the probability of a type I error cause an increase in the probability of a type II error?

40. Think About It Why not use a level of significance of $\alpha = 0$?

Graphical Analysis In Exercises 41 and 42, you are given a null hypothesis and three confidence intervals that represent three samplings. Decide whether each confidence interval indicates that you should reject H_0. Explain your reasoning.

41. $H_0: \mu \geq 70$

(a) $\mu = 68 \pm 1$

(b) $\mu = 69 \pm 2$

(c) $\mu = 71 \pm 1.5$

42. $H_0: \mu \leq 54$

(a) $\mu = 55 \pm 0.5$

(b) $\mu = 53 \pm 1.5$

(c) $\mu = 55 \pm 1.5$

Chapter Case Study

Each chapter has a full-page case study featuring actual data from a real-world context and a series of thought-provoking questions that are designed to illustrate the important concepts of the chapter.

Chapter Summary

Each chapter concludes with a chapter summary that answers the questions What did you learn? and Why did you learn it? This can be used as a study aid in conjunction with the chapter review exercises. In addition to showing the real-life uses of the material in the chapter, each summary points out one or more common abuses of statistics.

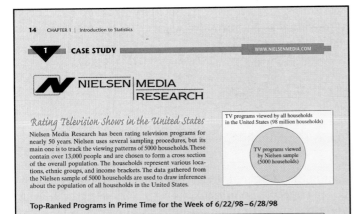

Chapter Review Exercises

A set of review exercises follows each chapter summary. The order of the exercises follows the order that the topics were presented in the chapter. Answers to all odd-numbered review exercises are given in the back of the book. The worked-out solutions are available in the *Student's Solutions Manual*.

Chapter Quizzes and Cumulative Tests

Each chapter ends with a chapter quiz. In addition, cumulative tests appear after Chapters 3, 6, 9, and 11. The answers to all quiz and test questions are given in the back of the book.

---

24   CHAPTER 1 | Introduction to Statistics

1   **CHAPTER SUMMARY**

What did you learn? — *Review Exercises*

• How to distinguish between a population and a sample *(Section 1.1)*	1–4
• How to distinguish between a parameter and a statistic *(Section 1.1)*	5–8
• How to distinguish between qualitative and quantitative data *(Section 1.2)*	9–12
• How to classify data with respect to the four levels of measurement: nominal, ordinal, interval, and ratio *(Section 1.2)*	13–16
• How data are collected: by performing an experiment, using a simulation, taking a census, and using a sampling *(Section 1.3)*	17–20
• How to create a sample using random sampling, stratified sampling, cluster sampling, systematic sampling, and convenience sampling *(Section 1.3)*	21–30

Why did you learn it? Uses and Abuses

Uses Statistics can be used to help you make informed decisions that affect every part of your life, whether personally or on the job. For example, you may never have to conduct a statistical study, but by learning about statistics and experimental design you will be able to detect flaws in other studies. This is important because an improperly designed study can be misleading and result in costing a corporation or the public a lot of money. You will be able to discern between different types of data and know if you can make mathematically meaningful calculations or not.

Abuses Perhaps the greatest single abuse (or misuse) of statistics is in using samples that are biased. In this course, you will learn that if a sample is sufficiently *large* and is truly *random*, then you can be reasonably confident that it is representative of the population from which it was drawn. The problem is that it is occasionally difficult to find a large sample and it is often difficult to choose a random sample. As an example, consider the common technique of conducting a poll by calling random numbers in the telephone book. The results you obtain are from people who have (a) listed phone numbers, (b) are home to answer the phone, and (c) are willing to answer a survey question. People who do not have listed phone numbers, or who work unusual hours and are not home, or who are not willing to participate in a survey will not be represented by your poll.

▶ Supplements

Elementary Statistics: Picturing the World and its ancillary package have been developed in tandem to provide instructors and students with the most comprehensive, supportive package available.

Resources for the Instructor

Annotated Instructor's Edition
Betsy Farber, Bucks County Community College
ISBN 0-13-010797-2

Notes to Instructors appear in the margin of the text to suggest activities that correspond to the example or concept, additional ways to present the material, common pitfalls students encounter, alternate formulas or approaches that may be used, and other helpful teaching tips for instructors. Short answers (numerical, tabular, and/or graphical) to the section and review exercises appear in the margin next to the exercise.

Instructor's Solutions Manual
Jay Schaffer, University of Northern Colorado
ISBN 0-13-040081-5

Complete solutions to all of the exercises, Try It Yourself problems, and case studies are found in a single convenient volume.

Printed Test Bank
Mike McGann, Ventura College
ISBN 0-13-040078-5

Includes more than 1100 additional questions—75% multiple choice and 25% open ended—with an answer key. Computerized versions are available.

Computerized Test Bank
IBM: ISBN 0-13-040082-3   Macintosh: ISBN 0-13-040083-1

Available in both IBM and Macintosh formats.

PowerPoint Presentation
Betsy Farber, Bucks County Community College

Designed to enhance an instructor's classroom presentation, a mini-lecture that corresponds to each chapter of the text has been developed using PowerPoint. Featuring sound, graphics, and numerous additional examples, the PowerPoint presentation is ideal for part-timers or other teachers new to statistics. Most slides include notes offering suggestions for how the material may effectively be presented in class. Each presentation may be edited by the user, as desired, to reflect his or her individual teaching style. In addition, the PowerPoint slides may be printed to use as transparency masters or handed out as note-taking tools for students.

Resources for the Student

Student's Solutions Manual

Jay Shaffer, University of Northern Colorado
ISBN 0-13-040070-X

Complete worked-out solutions to all of the Try It Yourself problems, the odd numbered exercises, and all of the chapter review exercises are included.

Companion Technology Manuals

The TI-83 Manual

Dorothy Wakefield & Kate McLaughlin, University of Connecticut & Manchester Community College
ISBN 0-13-015221-8

The Minitab Manual

Dorothy Wakefield & Kate McLaughlin, University of Connecticut & Manchester Community College
ISBN 0-13-015210-2

The Excel Manual

Beverly Dretzke, University of Wisconsin, Eau Clair
ISBN 0-13-015219-6

Each spiral-bound companion manual works hand-in-glove with the text. Step-by-step keystroke level instructions, with screen captures, provide detailed help for using the technology to work pertinent examples and all of the technology projects in the text. A cross-reference chart indicates which text examples are included and the exact page reference in both the text and technology manual. Output with brief instruction is provided for selected odd-numbered exercises to reinforce the examples.

The Excel Manual includes *PHstat,* a statistics add-in for Microsoft Excel (CD-ROM) featuring a custom menu of choices that lead to dialog boxes to help perform statistical analyses more quickly and easily than off-the-shelf Excel permits.

Text and Minitab Rel. 12.0 Student Version Package

ISBN 0-13-086963-5

Offering exceptional value to the student, a CD-ROM of Minitab Rel. 12.0 Student Version may be packaged with the text for a small additional cost. A similar package is available with **SPSS Student Version.** Consult the publisher for more information.

Media Resources

Data Disk

Packaged free with every copy of the text. Data files for the technology projects, all exercises identified with a 💾 symbol, and selected examples in the book are saved on the data disk as ASCII, Minitab, and Excel files. The data files may also be downloaded from the Web site that accompanies the text.

StatPro

Student CD: ISBN 0-13-014522-X   StatPro Network CD: ISBN 0-13-014524-6

StatPro is a new CD-ROM or network-based tutorial statistics program modeled on Prentice Hall's celebrated MathPro. StatPro features two main components. The first is keyed to the Try It Yourself exercises and provides an example that models the exercise, interactive guided instructions for solving the exercise, and additional problems for practice. Students may use the tutorial section in both a practice or graded-quiz mode. The second component features explorations which help the student's conceptual understanding of the material and promote discovery learning.

Video Tapes

Jim Condor, Manatee Community College
ISBN 0-13-040085-8

A comprehensive set of videos that provide a short lecture and worked examples for almost every section in the book. These videos provide excellent support for students who missed class or need to study the material at their own pace. They are also an invaluable resource for distance learning or self-paced study programs.

Companion Web Site (www.prenhall.com/Larson)

A free Web site provides additional information about the book, access to data base resources, materials for download including the PowerPoint presentation and data files used in the book in multiple formats, an entrance ramp to a demo and our subscription site, Internet Statistics, and more.

Internet Statistics (www.tdlc.com)

This is the first statistics text to appear complete in electronic format. As an alternative or a supplement to the printed text, an enhanced version of the book is available in electronic format via a subscription-based web site. Links built into the web site provide direct access to solutions to the Try It problems and odd exercises. The data files are linked to appropriate examples and exercises. Excel and Minitab files may be accessed directly by users who own those programs. A built-in glossary and formula index encourages context-based access to key terms and formulas. The Syllabus Builder provides the instructor the opportunity to build his or her own syllabus on line and link it directly to the text. Internet Statistics provides a great option for distance learning courses and other "plugged in" students.

▶ Internet Statistics: Picturing the World

Elementary Statistics: Picturing the World is also available on the Internet and on a multimedia CD-ROM. Both versions combine the full text of *Elementary Statistics: Picturing the World* with additional participatory features.

Main Content

The entire text of *Elementary Statistics: Picturing the World* is available in an interactive and easily navigated interface. The interface allows students to quickly jump from one part of the text to another.

An active Table of Contents menu is available at all times. Using this menu, students can easily link to any part of the product.

Complete Solutions

The complete solution for each odd-numbered exercise is incorporated into the product. The solution is linked directly to the exercise.

The complete solution for each *Try It Yourself* exercise is also linked directly to the corresponding exercise.

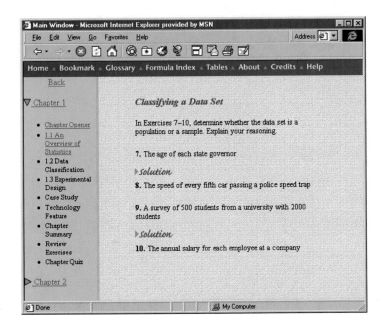

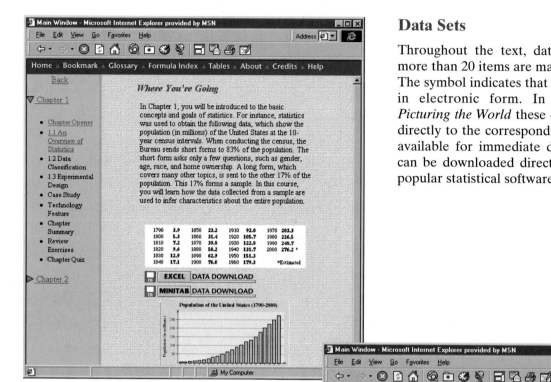

Data Sets

Throughout the text, data sets that contain more than 20 items are marked with a symbol. The symbol indicates that the data is available in electronic form. In *Internet Statistics: Picturing the World* these data files are linked directly to the corresponding data set and are available for immediate download. The data can be downloaded directly into a variety of popular statistical software packages.

Syllabus Manager

The syllabus manager allows instructors to customize the content of the interactive version of the text. Instructors add dates to a syllabus and provide links to particular sections that they would like the students to use. The links can reference any concept, example, exercise or content feature found in *Internet Statistics: Picturing the World.*

Additional Features

- Glossary Index
- Formula Index
- Table Index
- On-line Help
- Bookmarks
- Chat Room

The items listed in the Glossary Index, Formula Index, and Table Index are linked to where they are introduced in the product.

▶ Acknowledgements

We owe a debt of gratitude to the many reviewers who helped us shape and refine *Elementary Statistics: Picturing the World*. In particular we must thank our content advisory panel for their invaluable contribution in carefully reviewing each chapter of the book and making detailed suggestions for improvement.

Content Advisory Panel
Mike McGann, Ventura Community College
Vicki McMillian, Ocean County College
Lindsay Packer, College of Charleston
Carol Shapero, Oakton Community College

Pedagogy and Design Survey Reviewers
John Bernard, University of Texas—Pan American
G. Andy Chang, Youngstown State University
Gary Egan, Monroe Community College
Charles Ehler, Anne Arundel Community College
Douglas Frank, Indiana University of Pennsylvania
Rita Kolb, Catonsville Community College
Jeffrey Linek, St. Petersburg Junior College
Rowan Lindley, Westchester Community College
Diane Long, College of DuPage

Rhonda Magel, North Dakota State University
Aileen Solomon, Trident Technical College
Agnes Tuska, California State University—Fresno
Dex Whittinghill, Rowan University

Reviewers
Marion Baumler, Niagara Community College
Teresa Gauthier, Finger Lakes Community College
Nancy Johnson, Manatee Community College
Robert Kamery, Christian Brothers University
Mike Manesh, Palm Beach Community College
Eric Preibisius, Cuyamaca Community College
Adele Shapiro, Palm Beach Community College

Accuracy Checkers
Aileen Solomon, Trident Technical College
Sarah Streett

We also want to give special thanks to the people at Prentice Hall who worked with us in the development of *Elementary Statistics: Picturing the World*, especially Ann Heath—who worked with us on every aspect of the book, Kathy Boothby Sestak, Jerome Grant, Don Gecewicz, Joanne Wendelken, Melody Marcus, Linda Taft Mackinnon, Bayani Mendoza deLeon, Audra J. Walsh, Linda Behrens, Maureen Eide, Alan Fischer, and Thomas Maksym.

We would also like to thank the staff of Larson Texts, Inc., who assisted with the development and production of the book.

On a personal level, we are grateful to our spouses, Deanna Gilbert Larson and Richard Farber for their love, patience, and support. Also, a special thanks goes to R. Scott O'Neil.

We have worked hard to make *Elementary Statistics: Picturing the World* a clean, clear, and enjoyable text from which to teach and learn statistics. Despite our best efforts to ensure accuracy and ease of use, many users will undoubtedly have suggestions for improvement. We welcome your suggestions.

Ron Larson

Ron Larson

Betsy Farber

Betsy Farber

▶ How to Study Statistics

Studying Statistics Congratulations! You are about to begin your study of statistics. As you progress through the course, you should discover how to use statistics in your everyday life and in your career. The prerequisites for this course are two years of algebra, an open mind, and a willingness to study. When studying statistics, the material you learn each day builds on material you learned previously. There are no shortcuts—-you must keep up with your studies every day. Before you begin, read through the following hints that will help you succeed.

Making a Plan Make your own course plan right now! A good rule of thumb is to study at least two hours for every hour in class. After your first major exam, you will know if your efforts were sufficient. If you did not get the grade you wanted, then you should increase your study time, improve your study efficiency, or both.

Preparing for Class Before every class, review your notes from the previous class and read the portion of the text that is to be covered. Pay special attention to the definitions and rules that are highlighted. Read the examples and work through the Try-Its that accompany each example. Use StatPro for additional practice problems and detailed Try-It explanations. These steps take self-discipline, but pay off because you will benefit much more from your instructor's presentation.

Attending Class Attend every class. Arrive on time with your text, materials for taking notes, and your calculator. If you must miss a class, get the notes from another student, go to a tutor for help, or view the appropriate statistics videotape. Try to learn the material that was covered in the missed class before attending the next class.

Participating in Class When reading the text before class, reviewing your notes from a previous class, or working on your homework, write down any questions you have about the material. Ask your instructor these questions during class. Doing so will help you (and others in your class) understand the material better.

Taking Notes During class, be sure to take notes on definitions, examples, concepts, and rules. Focus on the instructor's cues to identify important material. Then, as soon after class as possible, review your notes and add any explanations that will help to make your notes more understandable to you.

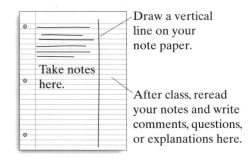

Draw a vertical line on your note paper.

Take notes here.

After class, reread your notes and write comments, questions, or explanations here.

Doing the Homework   Learning statistics is like learning to play the piano or basketball. You cannot develop skills just by watching someone do it; you must do it yourself. The best time to do your homework is right after class, when the concepts are still fresh in your mind. Doing homework at this time increases your chances of retaining the information in long-term memory.

Finding a Study Partner   When you get stuck on a problem, you may find that it helps to work with a partner. Even if you feel you are giving more help than you are getting, you will find that teaching others is an excellent way to learn.

Keeping Up with the Work   Don't let yourself fall behind in this course. If you are having trouble, seek help immediately-from your instructor, a statistics tutor, your study partner, or additional study aids such as videotapes and software tutorials. Remember: If you have trouble with one section of your statistics text, there's a good chance that you will have trouble with later sections unless you take steps to improve your understanding.

Getting Stuck   Every statistics student has had this experience: You work a problem and cannot solve it, or the answer you get does not agree with the one given in the text. When this happens, consider asking for help or taking a break to clear your thoughts. You might even want to sleep on it, or rework the problem, or reread the section in the text. Avoid getting frustrated or spending too much time on a single problem.

Preparing for Tests   Cramming for a statistics test seldom works. If you keep up with the work and follow the suggestions given here, you should be almost ready for the test. To prepare for the chapter test, review the Chapter Summary and work the Review Exercises. Then set aside some time to take the sample Chapter Quiz and the sample Cumulative Test. Analyze the results of your Chapter Quiz and Cumulative Test to locate and correct test-taking errors.

Taking a Test   Most instructors do not recommend studying right up to the minute the test begins. Doing so tends to make people anxious. The best cure for test-taking anxiety is to prepare well in advance. Once the test begins, read the directions carefully and work at a reasonable pace. (You might want to read the entire test first, then work the problems in the order in which you feel most comfortable.) Don't rush! People who hurry tend to make careless errors. If you finish early, take a few moments to clear your thoughts and then go over your work.

Learning from Mistakes   After your test is returned to you, go over any errors you might have made. This will help you avoid repeating some systematic or conceptual errors. Don't dismiss any error as just a "dumb mistake." Take advantage of any mistakes by hunting for ways to improve your test-taking skills.

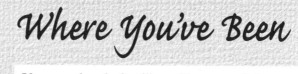

Where You've Been

You are already familiar with many of the practices of statistics, such as taking surveys, collecting data, and describing populations. What you may not know is that collecting accurate statistical data is often difficult and costly. Consider, for instance, the monumental task of counting and describing the entire population of the United States. If you were in charge of such a census, how would you do it? How would you ensure that your results are accurate? These and many more concerns are the responsibility of the United States Census Bureau.

New York City, with a population of over 7 million, has more than twice the population of any other American city. The next four most populated cities in the United States are Los Angeles, Chicago, Houston, and Philadelphia.

Introduction to Statistics

Where You're Going

In Chapter 1, you will be introduced to the basic concepts and goals of statistics. For instance, statistics was used to obtain the following data, which show the population (in millions) of the United States at the 10-year census intervals. When conducting the census, the Bureau sends short forms to 83% of the population. The short form asks only a few questions, such as gender, age, race, and home ownership. A long form, which covers many other topics, is sent to the other 17% of the population. This 17% forms a sample. In this course, you will learn how the data collected from a sample are used to infer characteristics about the entire population.

1790	**3.9**	1850	**23.2**	1910	**92.0**	1970	**203.3**
1800	**5.3**	1860	**31.4**	1920	**105.7**	1980	**226.5**
1810	**7.2**	1870	**39.8**	1930	**122.8**	1990	**248.7**
1820	**9.6**	1880	**50.2**	1940	**131.7**	2000	**276.2***
1830	**12.9**	1890	**62.9**	1950	**151.3**		
1840	**17.1**	1900	**76.0**	1960	**179.3**		*Estimated

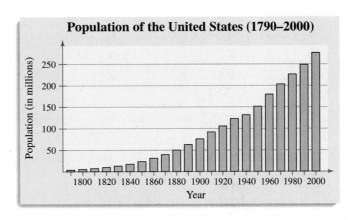

Population of the United States (1790–2000)

An Overview of Statistics

1.1

A Definition of Statistics • Data Sets • Branches of Statistics

What You Should Learn

- *The definition of statistics*
- *How to distinguish between a population and a sample and between a parameter and a statistic*
- *How to distinguish between descriptive statistics and inferential statistics*

A Definition of Statistics

What is statistics? Why should I study statistics? How can studying statistics help me in my profession? These are questions that you may have asked yourself when choosing this course. Almost every day you are exposed to statistics. For example, consider the following excerpts from recent newspapers and journals.

- "A . . . survey of traffic deaths during this past Memorial Day weekend shows a 36% decrease in fatalities compared with last year." *(Source: National Safety Council)*

- " . . . men who eat just two servings of raw tomatoes a week have a 34% less risk of developing prostate cancer." *(Source: Journal of the National Cancer Institute)*

- " . . . more than three-fourths of all college seniors complete at least one internship by graduation and 55% participate in two or more." *(Source: UPI)*

The three statements you just read are based on the collection of **data.**

DEFINITION

Data consist of information coming from observations, counts, measurements, or responses. The singular for data is datum.

Sometimes data are presented graphically. If you have ever read *USA Today,* you have certainly seen one of that newspaper's most popular features—*USA Snapshots.* Graphics such as this present information in a way that is easy to understand.

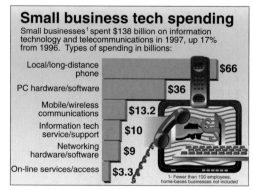

Small business tech spending

Small businesses[1] spent $138 billion on information technology and telecommunications in 1997, up 17% from 1996. Types of spending in billions:

Local/long-distance phone	$66
PC hardware/software	$36
Mobile/wireless communications	$13.2
Information tech service/support	$10
Networking hardware/software	$9
On-line services/access	$3.3

1- Fewer than 100 employees, home-bases businesses not included

Copyright 1998, USA TODAY. Reprinted with permission.

The use of statistics dates back to census taking in ancient Babylonia, Egypt, and later in the Roman Empire, when data were collected about matters concerning the state, such as births and deaths. In fact, the word *statistics* is derived from the Latin word *status*, meaning "state."

But statistics today involves more than collecting data, presenting facts, calculating averages, and drawing graphs. So, what is statistics?

DEFINITION

Statistics is the science of collecting, organizing, analyzing, *and* interpreting data in order to make decisions.

Data Sets

There are two types of data sets you will use when studying statistics. These data sets are called *populations* and *samples*.

DEFINITION

A **population** is the collection of *all* outcomes, responses, measurements, or counts that are of interest.

A **sample** is a subset of a population.

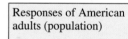 **EXAMPLE 1** *Identifying Data Sets*

In a recent survey, 3002 American adults were asked if they read news on the Internet at least once a week. Six hundred of the adults said yes. Identify the population and the sample. Describe the data set. *(Source: Pew Research Center)*

SOLUTION The population consists of the responses of all American adults and the sample consists of the responses of the 3002 American adults in the survey. The sample is a subset of the responses of all American adults. The data set consists of 600 yes's and 2402 no's.

> Responses of American adults (population)
>
> Responses of adults in survey (sample)

Try It Yourself 1

The U.S. Department of Energy conducts weekly surveys of 800 gasoline stations to determine the average price per gallon of regular gasoline. On July 10, 1998, the average price was $1.066 per gallon. Identify the population and the sample. *(Source: U.S. Department of Energy)*

a. Identify the *population*.
b. Identify the *sample*.
c. What does the data set consist of? *Answer: Page A30*

Whether a data set is a population or a sample usually depends on the context of the real-life situation. For instance, in Example 1, the population was the set of responses of all adult Americans. Depending on the purpose of the survey, the population could have been the set of responses of all adult Americans who live in California or who have telephones or who read a particular newspaper.

Two important terms that are used throughout this course are *parameter* and *statistic*.

DEFINITION

A **parameter** is a numerical description of a *population* characteristic.

A **statistic** is a numerical description of a *sample* characteristic.

▶ **EXAMPLE 2** *Distinguishing between a Parameter and a Statistic*

Decide whether the numerical value describes a population parameter or a sample statistic. Explain your reasoning.

1. A recent survey of a sample of MBAs reported that the average starting salary for an MBA is less than $65,000.
2. Starting salaries for the 667 MBA graduates from the University of Chicago School of Business increased 8.5% from the previous year.

SOLUTION

1. Because the numerical measure of $65,000 is based on a subset of the population, it is a sample statistic.
2. Because the numerical measure of 8.5% is based on all 667 graduates' starting salaries, it is a population parameter.

Picturing the World

How accurate is the U.S. census? According to a post-census evaluation conducted by the Census Bureau, the 1990 census undercounted the U.S. population by an estimated 4.7 million people. The 1990 census was the first census since 1940 to be less accurate than its predecessor.

U.S. Census Undercount

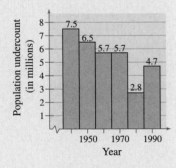

What are some difficulties in collecting population data?

Try It Yourself 2

In 1997, major league baseball teams spent a total of $1,119,537,215 on players' salaries. Does this numerical value describe a population parameter or a sample statistic?

a. Decide whether the numerical value is from a *population* or a *sample*.
b. Specify whether the numerical value is a *parameter* or a *statistic*.

Answer: Page A30 ◀

In this course, you will see how the use of statistics can help you make informed decisions that affect your life. Consider the census that the U.S. government takes every decade. When taking the census, the Census Bureau attempts to contact everyone living in the United States. This is an impossible task. It is important that the census is accurate, because public officials make many decisions based on the census information. Data collected in the 2000 census will determine how to assign congressional seats and how to distribute public funds.

Branches of Statistics

The study of statistics has two major branches—**descriptive statistics** and **inferential statistics.**

> **DEFINITION**
>
> **Descriptive statistics** is the branch of statistics that involves the organization, summarization, and display of data.
>
> **Inferential statistics** is the branch of statistics that involves using a sample to draw conclusions about a population. A basic tool in the study of inferential statistics is probability.

▶ **EXAMPLE 3**   *Descriptive and Inferential Statistics*

A large sample of men, aged 48, was studied for 18 years. For unmarried men, 60% to 70% were alive at age 65. For married men, 90% were alive at age 65. Which part of the study represents the descriptive branch of statistics? What conclusions might be drawn from this study using inferential statistics? *(Source: The Journal of Family Issues)*

SOLUTION   Descriptive statistics involves statements such as "For unmarried men, 60% to 70% were alive at age 65" and "For married men, 90% were alive at 65." A possible inference drawn from the study is that being married is associated with a longer life for men.

> *Try It Yourself 3*
>
> A survey conducted among 1017 men and women by Opinion Research Corporation found that 76% of women and 60% of men had a physical examination within the previous year. *(Source: Men's Health)*
>
> **a.** Identify the descriptive aspect of the survey.
> **b.** What inferences could be drawn from this survey?   *Answer: Page 30* ◀

Throughout this course you will see applications of both branches. A major theme in this course will be how to use sample statistics to make inferences about unknown population parameters.

EXERCISES

HELP

 StatPro 1.1

 Internet Statistics 1.1

 Student Solutions Manual 1.1

 Videos 1.1

Try It Yourself Answers 1.1

1. A sample is a subset of a population.

2. It is usually impractical (too expensive and time consuming) to obtain all the population data.

3. False

4. True

5. True

6. False

7. Population

8. Sample

9. Sample

10. Population

11. Population: Party of registered voters in Bucks County.

 Sample: Party of Bucks County voters responding to phone survey.

12. Population: Major of college students at Central College.

 Sample: Major of college students at Central College who take statistics.

13. Population: Ages of adult Americans who own computers.

 Sample: Ages of adult Americans who own Dell computers.

Basic Skills and Concepts

1. How is a sample related to a population?

2. Why is a sample used more often than a population?

True or False In Exercises 3–6, determine whether the statement is true or false. If it is false, rewrite it as a true statement.

3. A statistic is a measure that describes a population characteristic.

4. A sample is a subset of a population.

5. It is almost impossible for the Census Bureau to obtain all the census data about the population of the United States.

6. Inferential statistics involves using a population to draw a conclusion about a corresponding sample.

Classifying a Data Set In Exercises 7–10, determine whether the data set is a population or a sample. Explain your reasoning.

7. The age of each state governor

8. The speed of every fifth car passing a police speed trap

9. A survey of 500 students from a university with 2000 students

10. The annual salary for each employee at a company

Graphical Analysis In Exercises 11–14, use the Venn diagram to identify the population and the sample.

11. Party of registered voters in Bucks County

 Party of Bucks County voters who responded to phone survey

12. Major of college students at Central College

 Major of college students at Central College who take statistics

13. Ages of adult Americans who own computers

 Ages of adult Americans who own Dell computers

14. Income of all home owners in Ohio

 Income of home owners in Ohio with mortgages

14. Population: Income of all home owners in Ohio.

    Sample: Income of home owners in Ohio with mortgages.

15. Population: Collection of all infants.

    Sample: Collection of the 33,043 infants in the study.

16. Population: Collection of all American households.

    Sample: Collection of the 1023 American households surveyed.

17. Population: Collection of all American women.

    Sample: Collection of the 546 American women surveyed.

18. Population: Collection of all American vacationers.

    Sample: Collection of the 872 American vacationers surveyed.

19. Statistic

20. Statistic

21. Statistic

22. Parameter

23. The statement "56% are the primary investor in their household" is an application of descriptive statistics.

    An inference drawn from the sample is that an association exists between American women and being the primary investor in their household.

24. The statement "spending at least $1800 for their next vacation" is an application of descriptive statistics.

    An inference drawn from the sample is that American vacationers are associated with spending more than $1800 for their next vacation.

25. Answers vary.

26. Answers vary.

Identifying Data Sets   In Exercises 15–18, identify the population and the sample.

15. A study of 33,043 infants in Italy was conducted to find a link between a heart rhythm abnormality and sudden infant death syndrome. *(Source: New England Journal of Medicine)*

16. A survey of 1023 American households found that 65% subscribe to cable television.

17. A survey of 546 American women found that 56% are the primary investor in their household. *(Adapted from: Roper Starch Worldwide for Intuit)*

18. A survey of 872 American vacationers found that they planned on spending at least $1800 for their next vacation.

Distinguishing between a Parameter and a Statistic   In Exercises 19–22, determine whether the numerical value is a parameter or a statistic. Explain your reasoning.

19. The average annual salary for 35 of a company's 1200 accountants is $57,000.

20. In a survey of a sample of high school students, 43% said that their mother has taught them the most about managing money. *(Source: Harris Poll for Girls Incorporated)*

21. In a survey of a sample of computer users, 10% said their computer had a malfunction that needed to be repaired by a service technician.

22. In 1997, the interest category for 12% of all new magazines was sports. *(Source: Oxbridge Communications)*

23. Which part of the survey described in Exercise 17 represents the descriptive branch of statistics? Make an inference based on the results of the survey.

24. Which part of the survey described in Exercise 18 represents the descriptive branch of statistics? Make an inference based on the results of the survey.

Extending the Basics

25. *Identifying Data Sets in Articles*   Find a newspaper or magazine article that describes a survey. Identify the sample used in the survey. What is the sample's population?

26. *Writing*   Write an essay about the importance of statistics for one of the following.

    (a) A study on the effectiveness of a new drug

    (b) An analysis of a manufacturing process

    (c) Making conclusions about voter opinions using surveys

1.2 Data Classification

Types of Data • Levels of Measurement

What You Should Learn

- **How to distinguish between qualitative data and quantitative data**
- **How to classify data with respect to the four levels of measurement: nominal, ordinal, interval, and ratio**

Types of Data

In this section, you will learn how to classify data by type and by level of measurement. Data sets can consist of two types of data: *qualitative data* and *quantitative data.*

DEFINITION

Qualitative data consist of attributes, labels, or nonnumerical entries.

Quantitative data consist of numerical measurements or counts.

EXAMPLE 1 *Classifying Data by Type*

Model	Base Price
Escort LX	$11,430
Ranger 4 × 2 XL	$11,485
Contour LX	$14,460
Taurus LX	$18,445
Windstar	$19,380
Explorer XL 4 × 2	$21,560
Crown Victoria	$21,135
Expedition 4 × 2 XLT	$28,225

The base prices of several vehicles are shown in the table. Which data are qualitative data and which are quantitative data? Explain your reasoning. *(Source: Ford Motor Company)*

SOLUTION   The information shown in the table can be separated into two data sets. One data set contains the names of vehicle models and the other contains the base prices of vehicle models. The names are nonnumerical entries, so these are qualitative data. The base prices are numerical entries, so these are quantitative data.

Try It Yourself 1

The populations of several U.S. cities are shown in the table. Which data are qualitative data and which are quantitative data? *(Source: U.S. Bureau of the Census)*

City	Population	City	Population
Baltimore, MD	702,979	Las Vegas, NV	327,878
Boston, MA	547,725	Lincoln, NE	203,076
Dallas, TX	1,022,830	Seattle, WA	520,947

a. Identify the contents of each *data set.*
b. Decide whether the data consist of *numerical* or *nonnumerical* entries.
c. Specify the *qualitative data* and the *quantitative data.*

Answer: Page A30

Levels of Measurement

Another data characteristic is the data's level of measurement. The level of measurement determines which statistical calculations are meaningful. The four levels of measurement, in order from lowest to highest, are *nominal, ordinal, interval,* and *ratio.*

> **DEFINITION**
>
> Data at the **nominal level of measurement** are qualitative only. Data at this level are categorized using names, labels, or qualities. No mathematical computations can be made at this level.
>
> Data at the **ordinal level of measurement** are qualitative or quantitative. Data at this level can be arranged in order, but differences between data entries are not meaningful.

▶ EXAMPLE 2 *Classifying Data by Level*

Two data sets are shown. Which data set consists of data at the nominal level? Which data set consists of data at the ordinal level? Explain your reasoning. *(Source: Nielsen Media Research)*

Top 5 TV Programs (from Season Premiere to 6/7/98)
1. *Seinfeld*
2. *E.R.*
3. *Veronica's Closet*
4. *Friends*
5. *NFL Monday Night Football*

Network Affiliates in Portland, Oregon
KATU (ABC)
KGW (NBC)
KOIN (CBS)
KPDX (FOX)

SOLUTION The first data set lists the rank of five TV programs. The data consists of the ranks 1, 2, 3, 4, and 5. Because the rankings can be listed in order, these data are at the ordinal level. Note that the difference between a rank of 1 and 5 has no mathematical meaning. The second data set consists of the call letters of each network affiliate in Portland. The call letters are simply the names of network affiliates, so these data are at the nominal level.

Picturing the World

In 1998, the American Film Institute chose the 100 greatest American movies. The institute started with a population of more than 40,000 movies and chose a sample of 400 to put on a ballot. The ballot was mailed to over 1500 film artists and executives. The films were judged on popularity over time, historical significance, cultural impact, and other factors.

The American Film Institute's Top Five American Films
1. *Citizen Kane*
2. *Casablanca*
3. *Gone With the Wind*
4. *The Godfather*
5. *Lawrence of Arabia*

In this list, what is the level of measurement?

Try It Yourself 2

Consider the following data sets. For each data set, decide whether the data are at the nominal level or at the ordinal level.

1. The final standings for the Northeast Division of the National Hockey League
2. A collection of phone numbers

a. *Identify* what each data set represents.
b. Specify the *level of measurement.*

Answer: Page A30 ◀

DEFINITION

Data at the **interval level of measurement** are quantitative. The data can be ordered and you can calculate meaningful differences between data entries. At the interval level, a zero entry simply represents a position on a scale; the entry is not an inherent zero.

Data at the **ratio level of measurement** are similar to data at the interval level, with the added property that a zero entry is an inherent zero. A ratio of two data values can be formed so one data value can be expressed as a multiple of another.

An *inherent* zero is a zero that implies "none." For instance, the amount of money you have in a savings account could be zero dollars. In this case, the zero represents no money—it is an inherent zero. On the other hand, a temperature of 0°C does not represent a condition where no heat is present. The 0°C temperature is simply a position on the Celsius scale; it is not an inherent zero.

New York Yankees' World Series Victories (Years)
1923, 1927, 1928, 1932, 1936, 1937, 1938, 1939, 1941, 1943, 1947, 1949, 1950, 1951, 1952, 1953, 1956, 1958, 1961, 1962, 1977, 1978, 1996, 1998

1997 American League Home Run Totals (by team)	
Anaheim	161
Baltimore	196
Boston	185
Chicago	158
Cleveland	220
Detroit	176
Kansas City	158
Milwaukee	135
Minnesota	132
New York	161
Oakland	197
Seattle	264
Texas	187
Toronto	147

▶ EXAMPLE 3   *Classifying Data by Level*

Two data sets are shown at the left. Which data set consists of data at the interval level? Which data set consists of data at the ratio level? Explain your reasoning. *(Source: Major League Baseball)*

SOLUTION   Both of these data sets contain quantitative data. Consider the dates of the Yankees' World Series victories. It makes sense to find differences between specific dates. For instance, the time between the Yankees' first and last World Series victories is

$$1998 - 1923 = 75 \text{ years.}$$

But it does not make sense to write a ratio using these dates. So, these data are at the interval level. Using the home run totals, you can find differences *and* write ratios. From the data, you can see that New York hit three more home runs than Kansas City hit, and that Seattle hit twice as many home runs as Minnesota hit. So, these data are at the ratio level.

Try It Yourself 3

Decide whether the data are at the interval level or at the ratio level.

1. The body temperatures (°F) of an athlete who is exercising
2. The heart rate, in beats per minute, of an athlete who is exercising

a. *Identify* what each data set represents.
b. Specify the *level of measurement*.   *Answer: Page A30* ◀

The following tables summarize meaningful operations at the four levels of measurement.

Level of measurement	Put data in categories	Arrange data in order	Subtract data values	Determine if one data value is a multiple of another
Nominal	Yes	No	No	No
Ordinal	Yes	Yes	No	No
Interval	Yes	Yes	Yes	No
Ratio	Yes	Yes	Yes	Yes

Summary of Four Levels of Measurement

	Example of a Data Set	Meaningful Calculations
Nominal Level (Qualitative data)	*Major PGA Tournaments* The Masters The U.S. Open The British Open The PGA Championship	*Put in a category.* For instance, these are four categories of major PGA tournaments.
Ordinal Level (Qualitative or quantitative data)	*Motion Picture Association of America Ratings Description* G General Audiences PG Parental Guidance Suggested PG-13 Parents Strongly Cautioned R Restricted NC-17 17 and Under Not Permitted	Put in a category and *put in order.* For instance, a PG rating has a stronger restriction than a G rating.
Interval Level (Quantitative data)	*Average Monthly Temp. (°F) for Sacramento, CA* Jan 45.3 Jul 75.6 Feb 50.3 Aug 74.7 Mar 53.2 Sep 71.7 Apr 58.2 Oct 63.9 May 64.9 Nov 53.0 Jun 71.2 Dec 45.6	Put in a category, put in order, and *find difference in values.* For instance, $50.3 - 45.3 = 5°F$. So, February was 5° warmer than January.
Ratio Level (Quantitative data)	*Average Monthly Precipitation (in inches) for Sacramento, CA* Jan 4.0 Jul 0.1 Feb 2.9 Aug 0.1 Mar 2.1 Sep 0.3 Apr 1.3 Oct 0.9 May 0.3 Nov 2.2 Jun 0.1 Dec 2.9	Put in a category, put in order, find difference in values, and *find ratios of values.* For instance, $\frac{0.3}{0.1} = 3$. So, there was three times as much rain in May as in June.

1.2 ▼ EXERCISES

HELP

 StatPro 1.2

 Internet Statistics 1.2

 Student Solutions Manual 1.2

 Videos 1.2

 Try It Yourself Answers 1.2

1. Nominal and ordinal
2. Ordinal, Interval, and Ratio
3. True
4. False
5. False
6. False
7. Qualitative
8. Quantitative
9. Quantitative
10. Qualitative
11. Ordinal
12. Nominal
13. Ratio
14. Nominal

Basic Skills and Concepts

1. Name each level of measurement for which data can be qualitative.

2. Name each level of measurement for which data can be quantitative.

True or False   In Exercises 3–6, determine whether the statement is true or false. If it is false, rewrite it as a true statement.

3. Data at the nominal level are qualitative only.

4. For data at the ratio level, zero entries represent position only and are not inherent zeros.

5. Data at the ordinal level are quantitative only.

6. For data at the interval level, you cannot calculate meaningful differences between data entries.

Classifying Data by Type   In Exercises 7–10, determine whether the data are qualitative or quantitative.

7. The telephone numbers in a telephone directory

8. The daily high temperatures for the month of June

9. The percentage scores of a class in an exam

10. The player numbers in a baseball team

Classifying Data by Level   In Exercises 11–16, identify the data set's level of measurement. Explain your reasoning.

11. The top five teams in the final college football poll released on January 3, 1998 are listed. *(Source: Associated Press)*

    1. Michigan 2. Nebraska 3. Florida State
    4. Florida   5. UCLA

12. The four major professional tennis tournaments are listed below.

Australian Open   French Open
The Lawn Tennis Championships (Wimbledon)   U.S. Open

13. The total catches (in thousands) for different species of fish in Alabama waters are listed. *(Adapted from National Marine Fisheries Service, Fisheries Statistics and Economics Division)*

    36.3 14.9 48.8 87.3 48.5 17.2 359.0 0.6 32.3 545.9 1.9

14. A corporation's U.S. sales staff is split among the following regions.

Northwest   Southwest   Southeast   Northeast

15. Interval

16. Ratio

17. Ordinal

18. Ordinal

19. Nominal

20. Interval

21. Interval data can be ordered and differences between entries can be calculated. Ratio data has all the properties of interval data with the addition that a ratio of two data values can be formed so one data value can be expressed as a multiple of another.

22. An inherent zero is a zero that implies "none."

15. The average monthly temperatures (in degrees Celsius) at Gulkana Glacier basin in Alaska are listed. *(Source: U.S. Geological Survey, a bureau of the U.S. Department of the Interior)*

−4.6	−11.4	−13.0	−16.7	−13.1	−9.8
−4.6	−0.1	4.7	6.1	2.8	−0.7

16. The lengths (in inches) of a sample of striped bass caught in Maryland waters are listed. *(Adapted from National Marine Fisheries Service, Fisheries Statistics and Economics Division)*

16   17.25   19   18.75   21   20.3   19.8   24   21.82

Graphical Analysis   In Exercises 17–20, identify the level of measurement of the data used in the graph.

17. Does Global Warming Contribute to More Severe El Niños?

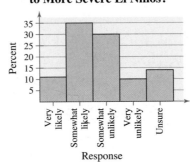

(Source: Yankelovich for the National Science Foundation, American Meteorological Society)

18. Recommendations for a Stock

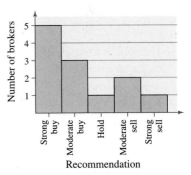

19. Gender Profile of the 105th Congress

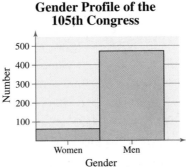

20. State Government Tax Collections by Year

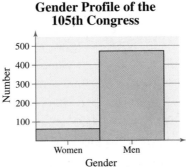

(Source: U.S. Census Bureau)

Extending the Basics

21. *Writing*   Explain how to distinguish between the interval level and the ratio level. Give examples of each.

22. *Writing*   What is an inherent zero? Describe three examples of data sets that have an inherent zero and three that do not.

▼ **1** CASE STUDY

NIELSEN | MEDIA
| RESEARCH

Rating Television Shows in the United States

Nielsen Media Research has been rating television programs for nearly 50 years. Nielsen uses several sampling procedures, but its main one is to track the viewing patterns of 5000 households. These contain over 13,000 people and are chosen to form a cross section of the overall population. The households represent various locations, ethnic groups, and income brackets. The data gathered from the Nielsen sample of 5000 households are used to draw inferences about the population of all households in the United States.

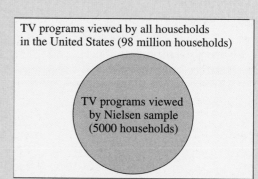
TV programs viewed by all households in the United States (98 million households)

TV programs viewed by Nielsen sample (5000 households)

Top-Ranked Programs in Prime Time for the Week of 6/22/98–6/28/98

Rank	Rank Last Week	Program Name	Network	Day, Time	Rating	Share	Audience
1	7	*60 Minutes*	CBS	Sun., 7:00 P.M.	10.6	23	10,360,000
2	1	*Dateline NBC*	NBC	Tue., 10:00 P.M.	10.3	18	10,100,000
3	5	*E.R.*	NBC	Thu., 10:00 P.M.	10.3	19	10,070,000
4	3	*Just Shoot Me*	NBC	Thu., 9:30 P.M.	10.3	19	10,080,000
5	2	*Seinfeld*	NBC	Thu., 9:00 P.M.	9.7	18	9,550,000
6	7	*20/20*	ABC	Mon., 9:00 P.M.	9.2	16	9,050,000
7	7	*20/20*	ABC	Fri., 10:00 P.M.	8.9	18	8,730,000
8	18	*Frasier*	NBC	Tue., 9:00 P.M.	8.6	15	8,450,000
9	6	*Dateline NBC*	NBC	Mon., 10:00 P.M.	8.4	15	8,250,000
10	10	*Touched by an Angel*	CBS	Sun., 8:00 P.M.	8.3	16	8,120,000

Exercises

1. ***Rating Points*** Each rating point represents 980,000 households or 1% of the households in the United States. Does a program with a rating of 8.4 have twice the number of households as a program with a rating of 4.2? Explain your reasoning.

2. ***Sampling Percent*** What percent of the total number of U.S. households is used in the Nielsen sample?

3. ***Nominal Level of Measurement*** Which columns in the table contain data at the nominal level?

4. ***Ordinal Level of Measurement*** Which columns in the table contain data at the ordinal level? Describe two ways that the data can be ordered.

5. ***Interval Level of Measurement*** Which column in the table contains data at the interval level? How can these data be ordered? What is the unit of measure for the difference of two entries in the data set?

6. ***Ratio Level of Measurement*** Which three columns contain data at the ratio level?

7. ***Share*** The column listed as "Share" gives the percent of televisions in use at a given time. Does the Nielsen rating rank shows by rating or by share? Explain your reasoning.

8. What decisions (inferences) can be made based on the Nielsen ratings?

1.3 Experimental Design

Experimental Design • Data Collection • Sampling Techniques

Experimental Design

The goal of every statistical study is to collect data and then use the data to make a decision. Any decision you make using the results of a statistical study is only as good as the process used to obtain the data. If the process is flawed, then the resulting decision is questionable.

While you may never have to develop a statistical study, it is likely that you will have to interpret the results of one. And before you interpret the results of a study, you should determine whether or not the results are valid. In other words, you should be familiar with how to design a statistical study.

GUIDELINES

Designing a Statistical Study

1. Identify the variable(s) of interest (the focus) and the population of the study.
2. Develop a detailed plan for collecting data. Make sure the data are representative of the population.
3. Collect the data.
4. Describe the data with descriptive statistics techniques.
5. Make decisions using inferential statistics. Identify any possible errors.

Data Collection

There are several ways you can collect data. Often, the focus of the study dictates the best way to collect data. The following is a brief summary of four methods of data collection.

- ***Perform an experiment*** When performing an **experiment,** a treatment is applied to part of a population and responses are observed. A second part of the population is often used as a control group. This group receives no treatment or is given a placebo. After responses from both groups are observed, results are compared. For instance, to test the effect of imposing a new marketing strategy, you could perform an experiment by using the new marketing strategy in a certain region. Each experimental unit is called a *block*. Care must be taken to ensure that the blocks are similar.

- ***Use a simulation*** A **simulation** is the use of a mathematical or physical model to reproduce the conditions of a situation or process. Collecting data often involves the use of computers. Simulations allow you to study situations that are impractical or even dangerous to create in real life and often save time and money. For instance, automobile manufacturers use simulations with dummies to study the effects of crashes on humans.

- **Take a census**   A **census** is a count or measure of an *entire* population. Taking a census provides complete information, but it is often costly and difficult to perform.

- **Use sampling**   A **sampling** is a count or measure of part of a population. The statistics calculated from a sample are used to predict various population parameters. For instance, every year the U.S. Census Bureau samples the U.S. population to update the most recent census data. Using sampling is often more practical than taking a census.

Once you determine which method you will use to collect data, you might decide that a survey can help you. Surveys can be used to take a census or a sampling. A **survey** is an investigation of one or more characteristics of a population. Most often, surveys are carried out on *people* by asking them questions. A disadvantage of using a survey to collect data is that the wording of the questions can lead to biased results.

Picturing the World

The Gallup Organization conducts many polls (or surveys) regarding the president, Congress, and political and nonpolitical issues. A commonly cited Gallup poll is the public approval rating of the President. For example, the approval ratings for President Bill Clinton from 1993 to 1998 are shown in the following graph. (The rating is from the first poll conducted in June of each year.)

President's Approval Ratings, 1993–1998

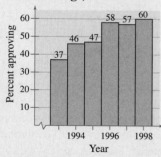

Discuss some ways that Gallup could select a biased sample to conduct a poll. How could Gallup select a sample that is unbiased?

▶ **EXAMPLE 1**   *Deciding Upon Methods of Data Collection*

Consider the following statistical studies. Which method of data collection would you use to collect data for each study? Explain your reasoning.

1. A study of the effect of an asteroid colliding with Earth
2. A study of the effect of aspirin on preventing heart attacks
3. A study of the weights of all linemen in the National Football League
4. A study of Americans' approval rating of the U.S. president

SOLUTION

1. Because it is impractical to create this situation, you would want to use a simulation.
2. In this study, you want to measure the effect a treatment (taking aspirin) has on patients. So, you would want to perform an experiment.
3. Because National Football League teams keep accurate physical records of *all* players, you could take a census.
4. It would be nearly impossible to ask every American whether or not he or she approves of the President's job performance. So, you should use sampling to collect these data.

Try It Yourself 1

Consider the following statistical studies. Which method of data collection would you use to collect data for each study?

1. A study of the effect of exercise on senior citizens
2. A study of the effect of radiation fallout on senior citizens

a. Identify the *focus* and *population* of the study.
b. Choose an appropriate *method of data collection*.   *Answer: Page A30* ◀

Sampling Techniques

To collect data that are unbiased, it is important that you use correct sampling techniques. Remember that when a study is done with faulty data, the results are questionable.

A **simple random sample** is one in which every member of the population has an equal chance of being selected. One way to do this is to assign every member of the population a number and use a random number table like the one in Appendix B.

> **EXAMPLE 2** *Using a Simple Random Sample*

There are 731 students currently enrolled in statistics at your school. You wish to form a sample of eight students to answer some survey questions. Select the students who will belong to the simple random sample.

SOLUTION Assign numbers 1 to 731 to each student in the course. On the table of random numbers, choose a starting place at random and read the digits in the first column in groups of three (because 731 is a three-digit number).

926|307|944|559|654|315|240|634|828|703|681|

Ignoring numbers that are greater than 731, the first eight numbers are 307, 559, 654, 315, 240, 634, 703, and 681. Students who were assigned these numbers will make up the sample.

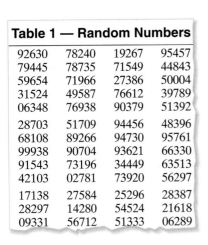

Table 1 — Random Numbers

92630	78240	19267	95457
79445	78735	71549	44843
59654	71966	27386	50004
31524	49587	76612	39789
06348	76938	90379	51392
28703	51709	94456	48396
68108	89266	94730	95761
99938	90704	93621	66330
91543	73196	34449	63513
42103	02781	73920	56297
17138	27584	25296	28387
28297	14280	54524	21618
09331	56712	51333	06289

Try It Yourself 2

A company employs 79 people. Choose a random sample of five to participate in a health habits study.

a. On the table, randomly choose a *starting place.*
b. *Read the digits* in groups of two.
c. Write the five random numbers.   *Answer: Page A30*

Sometimes it is important that your sample contains members from each part (strata) of your population. Using a **stratified sample,** members of the population are separated into groups with similar characteristics such as age, gender, or ethnicity. Then a random sample is selected from each of the strata. For example, if you wished to ensure that your sample had students under 21 years of age, between 21 and 30, and some 30 or more, separate them into three strata according to their age. Choose a sample from each age group.

In a **cluster sample,** the unit for sampling is a naturally occurring subgroup. One or more of the subgroups is selected and each member from that group is used in the sample. Clusters could be the different sections of the course.

In a **systematic sample,** each member of the population is assigned a number. A starting number is randomly selected and then every *k*th (example every 3rd, 5th, 100th, or 1000th) is selected.

A **convenience sample** consists only of the available people. For example, survey the students who come to class early. This often leads to biased studies and is not recommended.

SAMPLING TECHNIQUES

Random sampling

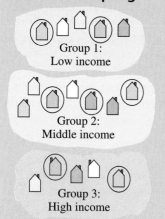

Summary

In a **random sample,** or **simple random sample,** each member of a population has an equal chance of being selected. Each member of the population is assigned a number. You can select a random sample of any population by using a calculator or computer to generate random numbers or by using a table of random numbers. (See Appendix B.)

Example

To use a random sample to measure the number of people who live in Dade County households, you could assign a different number to each household and then use a computer or table of random numbers to generate a sample of numbers. Then count the number of people living in each selected household.

Stratified sampling

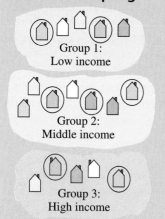

Group 1:
Low income

Group 2:
Middle income

Group 3:
High income

Summary

To select a **stratified sample,** a population is divided into at least two different subsets, called *strata,* that share a similar characteristic. A sample is then randomly selected from each. The defining characteristic can be gender, age, or even political preference. Using a stratified sample ensures that each segment of a population is represented. For this reason, stratified samples are usually preferred over simple random samples.

Example

To collect a stratified sample of the number of people who live in Dade County households, you could divide the households into socioeconomic levels. Then randomly select households from each level.

Cluster sampling

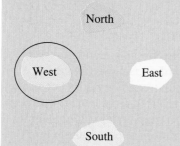

North

West   East

South

Summary

To select a **cluster sample,** divide a population into groups, called clusters, then select *all* of the members in one or more, but not all, of the clusters. This technique is often used because of practical or economical restrictions, but data collected may be less reliable than when a random sample is used.

Example

To collect a cluster sample of the number of people who live in Dade County households, divide the households into groups according to zip codes. Then select all the households in one or more, but not all, zip codes and count the number of people living in each household.

Systematic sampling

Summary

To select a **systematic sample,** a population is ordered in some way and then members of the population are selected at regular intervals. The selection process can start at any randomly chosen point. An advantage of systematic sample is that it is easy to use.

Example

To collect a systematic sample of the number of people who live in Dade County households, you could assign a different number to each household, randomly choose a starting number, and then select every hundredth household and count the number of people living in each.

Convenience sampling	*Summary*	*Example*
	To select a **convenience sample,** simply use any members of a population that are readily available. This method is likely to produce biased results.	To collect a convenience sample of the number of people who live in Dade County households, you could simply question people at a local shopping mall.

▶ **EXAMPLE 3** *Identifying Sampling Techniques*

You are doing a study to determine the opinion of students at your school regarding gun control. Identify the sampling technique you are using if you select the samples listed.

1. You select a class at random and question each student in the class.
2. You divide the student population with respect to majors and randomly select and question some students in each major.
3. You assign each student a number and generate random numbers. You then question each student whose number is randomly selected.

SOLUTION

1. Because each class is a naturally occurring subgroup (a cluster), this is a cluster sample.
2. Because students are divided into strata (majors) and a sample is selected from each major, this is a stratified sample.
3. Each student has an equal chance of being selected, so this is a simple random sample.

Try It Yourself 3

You want to determine the opinion of students at your school regarding gun control. Identify the sampling technique you are using if you select the samples listed.

1. You select students who are in your statistics class.
2. You assign each student a number, and after choosing a starting number, question every 25th student.

a. Determine *how* the sample is *selected*.
b. Identify the corresponding *sampling technique*. *Answer: Page A30* ◀

1.3 ▾ EXERCISES

HELP

 StatPro 1.3

 Internet Statistics 1.3

 Student Solutions Manual 1.3

 Videos 1.3

 Try It Yourself Answers 1.3

1. False
2. False
3. False
4. True
5. Perform an experiment.
6. Use sampling.
7. Use a simulation.
8. Take a census.
9. Simple random sample.
10. Stratified sample.
11. Convenience sample.
12. Cluster sample.
13. Simple random sample.
14. Systematic sample.

Basic Skills and Concepts

True or False   In Exercises 1–4, determine whether the statement is true or false. If it is false, rewrite it as a true statement.

1. Using a systematic sample guarantees that members of each group within a population will be sampled.

2. A census is a count of part of a population.

3. To select a stratified sample, a population is ordered in some way and then members of the population are selected at regular intervals.

4. To select a cluster sample, divide a population into groups and then select all of the members in at least one (but not all) of the groups.

Deciding Upon the Method of Data Collection   In Exercises 5–8, decide which method of data collection you would use to gather data for each study. Explain your reasoning.

5. A study of the effect on the human digestive system of potato chips made with a fat substitute

6. A study of the effect of a product's warning label to determine whether consumers still buy the product

7. A study of how fast a virus would spread in a metropolitan area

8. A study of the salaries of the 535 members of the U.S. Congress

Identifying Sampling Techniques   In Exercises 9–18, identify which sampling technique was used in the study and discuss potential sources of bias (if any). Explain your reasoning.

9. Using random digit dialing, 1599 people were called and asked what obstacles (such as childcare) kept them from exercising. *(Source: Yankelovich Partners, Inc. for Shape Up America!)*

10. Chosen at random, 200 rural and 200 urban persons age 65 or older were asked about their health and experience with prescription drugs.

11. Questioning students as they left a university library, a researcher asked 358 students about their drinking habits.

12. After a hurricane, a disaster area is divided into 200 equal grids. Thirty of the grids are selected and every occupied household in the grid is interviewed to help focus relief efforts on what residents require the most.

13. Chosen at random, 1819 hospital outpatients were contacted and asked their opinion of the care they received.

14. For quality assurance, every twelfth engine part is selected from an assembly line and tested for durability.

15. Stratified sample.

16. Convenience sample.

17. Systematic sample.

18. Simple random sample.

19. Question is biased since it already suggests that drinking fruit juice is good for you. The question might be rewritten as "How does drinking fruit juice affect your health?"

20. Question is biased since it already suggests that drivers who change lanes several times are dangerous. The question might be rewritten as "Are drivers who change lanes several times dangerous?"

21. The households sampled represent various locations, ethnic groups, and income brackets. Each of these variables is considered a stratum.

22. Stratified sampling insures that each segment of the population is represented.

23. (a) Advantage: Allows respondent to express some depth and shades of meaning in the answer.

Disadvantage: Not easily quantified and difficult to compare surveys.

(b) Advantage: Easy to analyze results.

Disadvantage: May not provide appropriate alternatives and may influence the opinion of the respondent.

24. Advantage: Usually results in a savings in the survey cost.

Disadvantage: There tends to be a lower response rate and this can introduce a bias into the sample.

Sampling Technique: Convenience sampling

15. Soybeans are planted on a 48-acre field. The field is divided into one-acre subplots. A sample of plants is taken from each subplot to estimate the harvest.

16. Questioning teachers as they left a faculty lounge, a researcher asked 56 teachers about their teaching styles and grading methods.

17. A list of managers is compiled and ordered. After randomly choosing a starting number, every twentieth name on the list is selected until 1000 managers are selected. Then the managers are questioned about the use of digital media.

18. From calls made with randomly generated telephone numbers, 1012 respondents were asked if they rented or owned their residence.

A Biased Question? In Exercises 19 and 20, determine whether the survey question is biased. If the question is biased, suggest a better wording.

19. Why is drinking fruit juice good for you?

20. Why are drivers who change lanes several times dangerous?

21. *Writing* Nielsen ratings are described in the case study on page 14. Discuss the strata used in the sample.

22. *Writing* Nielsen ratings are described in the case study on page 14. Why is it important to have a stratified sample for these ratings?

Extending the Basics

23. *Open and Closed Questions* Two types of survey questions are open questions and closed questions. An open question allows for any kind of response, while a closed question allows only for a fixed response. For example, an open question and a closed question are given.

Open Question
What can be done to get students to eat healthier foods?

Closed Question
How would you get students to eat healthier foods?
1. Mandatory nutrition course
2. Offer only healthy foods in the cafeteria and remove unhealthy foods
3. Offer more healthy foods in the cafeteria and raise the prices on unhealthy foods

(a) List an advantage and a disadvantage of an open question.

(b) List an advantage and a disadvantage of a closed question.

24. *Who Picked These People?* Sometimes, instead of selecting a sample to survey, some polling agencies ask people to call a telephone number and give their response to a question. List an advantage and a disadvantage of a survey conducted in this manner. What sampling technique is used in such a survey?

TECHNOLOGY

Using Technology in Statistics

Note to Instructor

As an instructor, you can decide the extent to which you want to use technology with this text. Supplements with detailed instructions are available for each of the technology tools shown.

With large data sets, you will find that calculators or computer software programs can help perform calculations and create graphics. Of the many calculators and statistical software programs that are available, we have chosen to incorporate the Minitab and Excel software and TI-83 graphing calculator into this text.

The following example shows how to use these three technologies to generate a list of random numbers.

▶ **EXAMPLE**   *Generating a List of Random Numbers*

A quality control department inspects a random sample of 15 of the 167 cars that are assembled at an auto plant. How should the cars be chosen?

SOLUTION

One way to choose the sample is to number the cars from 1 to 167. To form a list of random numbers from 1 to 167, you can use technology. Each of the technology tools shown requires different steps to generate the list. Each, however, does require that you identify the minimum value as 1 and the maximum value as 167. Check your user's manual for specific instructions.

TI-83

```
randInt(1, 167, 15)
{17 42 152 59 5 116
125 64 122 55 58 60
82 152 105}
```

MINITAB

```
MTB > Random 15 C1;
SUBC > Integer 1 167.

Numbers
81 28 66 95 77 29 132 10
27 124 79 59 136 2 94
```

EXCEL

	A
1	41
2	16
3	91
4	58
5	151
6	36
7	96
8	154
9	2
10	113
11	157
12	103
13	64
14	135
15	90

| **MINITAB** | **EXCEL** | **TI-83** |

When you generate a list of random numbers, you should decide whether it is acceptable to have numbers that repeat. If it is acceptable, then the sampling process is said to be *with replacement*. If it is not acceptable, then the sampling process is said to be *without replacement*.

With each of the three technology tools shown on page 22, you have the capability of sorting the list so that the numbers appear in order. Doing this helps you see whether any of the numbers in the list repeat. If it is not acceptable to have repeats, you should specify that the tool generate more random numbers than you need.

Exercises

1. A CPA is examining the records of a business. The business has 74 major accounts and the CPA decides to audit a random sample of 8 of the accounts. Describe how this could be done. Then use technology to generate a list of 8 random numbers from 1 to 74 and order the list.

2. A quality control department is testing 20 batteries from a shipment of 200 batteries. Describe how this could be done. Then use technology to generate a list of 20 random numbers from 1 to 200 and order the list.

3. Consider the population of ten digits: 0, 1, 2, 3, 4, 5, 6, 7, 8, and 9. Select three random samples of five digits from this list. Find the average of each sample. Compare your results to the average of the entire population. Comment on your results. (*Hint:* To find the average, sum the data entries and divide the sum by the number of entries.)

4. Consider the population of 41 whole numbers from 0 to 40. What is the average of these numbers? Select three random samples of seven numbers from this list. Find the average of each sample. Compare your results to the average of the entire population. Comment on your results. (*Hint:* To find the average, sum the data entries and divide the sum by the number of entries.)

5. Use random numbers to simulate rolling a six-sided die 60 times. Make a tally of your results. How many times did you obtain each number from 1 to 6? Are the results what you expected?

6. Suppose you rolled a six-sided die 60 times and got the following tally.

| 20 ones | 20 twos | 15 threes |
| 3 fours | 2 fives | 0 sixes |

Does this seem like a reasonable result? What inference might you draw from the result?

7. Use random numbers to simulate tossing a coin 100 times. Let 0 represent heads and let 1 represent tails. Make a tally of your results. How many times did you obtain each number? Are the results what you expected?

8. Suppose you tossed a coin 100 times and got 77 heads and 23 tails. Does this seem like a reasonable result? What inference might you draw from the result?

Extended solutions are given in the *Technology Supplement.*
Technical instruction is provided for Minitab, Excel, and the TI-83.

CHAPTER SUMMARY

What did you learn?	*Review Exercises*
• How to distinguish between a population and a sample *(Section 1.1)*	*1–4*
• How to distinguish between a parameter and a statistic *(Section 1.1)*	*5–8*
• How to distinguish between qualitative and quantitative data *(Section 1.2)*	*9–12*
• How to classify data with respect to the four levels of measurement: nominal, ordinal, interval, and ratio *(Section 1.2)*	*13–16*
• How data are collected: by performing an experiment, using a simulation, taking a census, and using a sampling *(Section 1.3)*	*17–20*
• How to create a sample using random sampling, stratified sampling, cluster sampling, systematic sampling, and convenience sampling *(Section 1.3)*	*21–30*

Why did you learn it? Uses and Abuses

Uses Statistics can be used to help you make informed decisions that affect every part of your life, whether personally or on the job. For example, you may never have to conduct a statistical study, but by learning about statistics and experimental design you will be able to detect flaws in other studies. This is important because an improperly designed study can be misleading and result in costing a corporation or the public a lot of money. You will be able to discern between different types of data and know if you can make mathematically meaningful calculations or not.

Abuses Perhaps the greatest single abuse (or misuse) of statistics is in using samples that are biased. In this course, you will learn that if a sample is sufficiently *large* and is truly *random*, then you can be reasonably confident that it is representative of the population from which it was drawn. The problem is that it is occasionally difficult to find a large sample and it is often difficult to choose a random sample. As an example, consider the common technique of conducting a poll by calling random numbers in the telephone book. The results you obtain are from people who have (a) listed phone numbers, (b) are home to answer the phone, and (c) are willing to answer a survey question. People who do not have listed phone numbers, or who work unusual hours and are not home, or who are not willing to participate in a survey will not be represented by your poll.

1 **REVIEW EXERCISES**

1. Population: Collection of all U.S. VCR owners.

Sample: Collection of the 898 VCR owners that were sampled.

2. Population: Collection of all nurses in SF area.

Sample: Collection of 38 nurses in SF area that were sampled.

3. Population: Collection of all U.S. ATM's.

Sample: Collection of 860 ATM's that were sampled.

4. Population: Collection of all U.S. undergraduate English majors.

Sample: Collection of 1420 undergraduate English majors that were sampled.

5. Parameter

6. Statistic

7. Parameter

8. Statistic

9. Quantitative

10. Qualitative

11. Quantitative

12. Qualitative

13. Interval

14. Ordinal

In Exercises 1–4, identify the population and the sample.

1. A survey of 898 U.S. VCR owners found that 16% had VCR clocks that were currently blinking "12:00." *(Source: Wirthlin Worldwide)*

2. Thirty-eight nurses working in the San Francisco area were surveyed concerning their opinions of managed health care.

3. A study of 860 U.S. ATMs (automated teller machines) found that the average surcharge for withdrawals from a competing bank was $1.15. *(Source: Public Interest Research Groups)*

4. A survey of 1420 U.S. undergraduate English majors asked which Shakespearean play was most relevant in the year 2000.

In Exercises 5–8, determine whether the numerical value describes a parameter or a statistic.

5. The 1998 team payroll of the Baltimore Orioles was $68,988,134. *(Source: Major League Baseball)*

6. In a survey of a sample of U.S. adults, 22% owned a portable cellular phone. *(Source: Wirthlin Worldwide)*

7. In the fall of 1997 at the University of Arizona, 89 students were majoring in astronomy. *(Source: University of Arizona Student Research Office)*

8. Nineteen percent of a sample of Indiana ninth graders surveyed smoked cigarettes daily in 1997. *(Source: Indiana University)*

In Exercises 9–12, determine which data are qualitative data and which are quantitative data. Explain your reasoning.

9. The monthly salaries of the employees at an accounting firm

10. The social security numbers of the employees at an accounting firm

11. The ages of a sample of 350 residents of nursing homes

12. The zip codes of a sample of 350 residents of nursing homes

In Exercises 13–16, identify the data set's level of measurement. Explain your reasoning.

13. The daily high temperatures (in degrees Fahrenheit) for Mohave, Arizona, June 10–17, 1998, are listed. *(Source: Arizona Meteorological Network)*

93   91   86   94   103   104   103

14. The EPA size classes for automobiles are listed. *(Source: Carspec)*

subcompact   compact   midsize   fullsize

15. Nominal

16. Ratio

17. Take a census.

18. Perform a simulation.

19. Perform an experiment.

20. Take a sample.

21. Simple random sample.

22. Convenience sample

23. Cluster sample

24. Systematic sample

25. Stratified sample

26. Convenience sample

27. Telephone sampling only samples individuals who have telephones, are available, and are willing to respond.

28. Due to the convenience sample taken, the study may be biased towards the opinions of the students' friends.

29. The selected communities may not be representative of the entire area.

30. In heavy interstate traffic, it may be difficult to identify every tenth car that passed the law enforcement official.

---

15. The four teams in the American League West Division are listed.

Anaheim   Texas   Oakland   Seattle

16. The heights (in inches) of the 1997–1998 Chicago Bulls are listed. *(Source: National Basketball Association)*

74   78   79   78   78   75   83   86   79   78   82   84

In Exercises 17–20, decide which method of data collection you would use to gather data for each study. Explain your reasoning.

17. A study of charitable donations of the judges in Sioux Falls, South Dakota

18. A study of the effect of kangaroos on the Florida Everglades ecosystem

19. A study of the effects of a plant hormone on chrysanthemums

20. A study of the awareness of college students of the ozone layer

In Exercises 21–26, identify which sampling technique was used in the study. Explain your reasoning.

21. Calling randomly generated telephone numbers, a study asked 1001 U.S. adults which medical conditions could be prevented by their diet. *(Source: Wirthlin Worldwide)*

22. A student asks 12 friends to participate in a psychology experiment.

23. A pregnancy study in Cebu, Philippines, randomly selected 33 communities from the Cebu metropolitan area, then interviewed all available pregnant women in these communities. *(Adapted from Cebu Longitudinal Health and Nutrition Survey)*

24. Law enforcement officials use a radar gun to measure the speed of every tenth vehicle on an interstate.

25. Twenty-five students are randomly selected from each grade level at a high school and surveyed about their study habits.

26. A journalist interviews 123 people after they leave a restaurant and asks them how confident they are that the food is safe.

In Exercises 27–30, identify a possible bias or error that might occur in the indicated survey or study.

27. The phone survey in Exercise 21

28. The psychology experiment in Exercise 22

29. The pregnancy study in Exercise 23

30. The vehicle speed sampling in Exercise 24

1 ▼ CHAPTER QUIZ

1. Population: Collection of all individuals with sleep disorders.

Sample: Collection of 163 patients in study.

2. (a) Statistic

(b) Parameter

3. (a) Qualitative

(b) Quantitative

4. (a) Nominal

(b) Ratio

5. (a) Perform an experiment.

(b) Use sampling.

6. (a) Convenience sample

(b) Systematic sample

7. (a) False

(b) False

Take this quiz as you would take a quiz in class. After you are done, check your work against the answers given in the back of the book.

1. Identify the population and the sample in the following study.

A study of 163 patients with sleep disorders was conducted to find a link between obesity and sleep disorders. *(Source: Archives of Internal Medicine 1998)*

2. Determine whether the numerical value is a parameter or a statistic.

(a) In a survey of a sample of parents, 53% said they protect their children from sun exposure using sunscreen. *(Source: Morbidity and Mortality Weekly Report)*

(b) In a union's vote, 67% of all union members voted to ratify a contract proposal.

3. Determine whether the data are qualitative or quantitative.

(a) A database of student identification numbers

(b) The test scores in a statistics class

4. Identify each data set's level of measurement. Explain your reasoning.

(a) A list of the uniform numbers retired by each major league baseball team

(b) The number of products sold by a toy manufacturer each quarter for the current fiscal year

5. Decide which method of data collection you would use to gather data for each study. Explain your reasoning.

(a) A study on the effect of low dietary intake of vitamin C and iron on lead levels in adults

(b) The ages of people living within 500 miles of your home

6. Identify which sampling technique was used in each study. Explain your reasoning.

(a) A journalist goes to a beach to ask people how they feel about water pollution.

(b) For quality assurance, every fifth engine part is selected from an assembly line and tested for durability.

7. Determine whether each statement is true or false. If it is false, rewrite it as a true statement.

(a) A parameter is a numerical measure that describes a sample characteristic.

(b) Ordinal data represent the highest level of measurement.

Where You've Been

In Chapter 1, you learned that there are many ways to collect data. Usually, researchers must work with samples to analyze populations, but occasionally it is possible to collect all the data for a given population. For instance, the following represents census data reporting the ages of the entire population of the 77 residents of Akhiok, Alaska.

28, 6, 17, 48, 63, 47, 27, 21, 3, 7, 12, 39, 50, 54, 33, 45, 15, 24, 1, 7, 36, 53, 46, 27, 5, 10, 32, 50, 52, 11, 42, 22, 3, 17, 34, 56, 25, 2, 30, 10, 33, 1, 49, 13, 16, 8, 31, 21, 6, 9, 2, 11, 32, 25, 0, 55, 23, 41, 29, 4, 51, 1, 6, 31, 5, 5, 11, 4, 10, 26, 12, 6, 16, 8, 2, 4, 28

Akhiok is a small fishing village on Kodiak Island. Pictured here are ten of Akhiok's 77 residents.

Photographs © Roy Corral

Descriptive Statistics

Where You're Going

In Chapter 2, you will learn ways to organize and describe data sets. The goal is to make the data easier to understand and make it easier to see trends, averages, and variations. For instance, in the raw data showing the ages of the residents of Akhiok, it is not easy to see any patterns or special characteristics. Here are some ways you can organize and describe the data.

0,	1,	1,	1,	2,	2,	2,	3,	3,	4,	4,
4,	5,	5,	5,	6,	6,	6,	6,	7,	7,	8,
8,	9,	10,	10,	10,	11,	11,	11,	12,	12,	13,
15,	16,	16,	17,	17,	21,	21,	22,	23,	24,	25,
25,	26,	27,	27,	28,	28,	29,	30,	31,	31,	32,
32,	33,	33,	34,	36,	39,	41,	42,	45,	46,	47,
48,	49,	50,	50,	51,	52,	53,	54,	55,	56,	63

Order the data.

Class	Frequency
0–12	32
13–25	13
26–38	15
39–51	11
52–64	6

Make a frequency distribution table.

Draw a histogram.

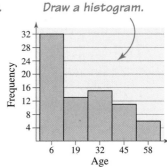

$$\text{Mean} = \frac{0 + 1 + 1 + 1 + 2 + \cdots + 54 + 55 + 56 + 63}{77}$$

$$= \frac{1745}{77}$$

$$\approx 22.7 \text{ years}$$

Find an average.

2.1

Frequency Distributions and Their Graphs

Frequency Distributions • Graphs of Frequency Distributions

What You Should Learn

- **How to construct a frequency distribution including midpoints, relative frequencies, and cumulative frequencies**
- **How to construct frequency histograms, frequency polygons, relative frequency histograms, and ogives**

Frequency Distributions

When a data set has many entries, it can be difficult to see patterns. In this section, you will learn how to organize data sets by grouping the data into intervals called classes and forming a frequency distribution. You will also learn how to use frequency distributions to construct graphs.

DEFINITION

A **frequency distribution** is a table that shows **classes** or **intervals** of data entries with a count of the number of entries in each class. The **frequency, f,** of a class is the number of data entries in the class.

Guidelines for constructing a frequency distribution from a data set are as follows.

GUIDELINES

Constructing a Frequency Distribution from a Data Set

1. Decide on the number of classes to include in the frequency distribution. The number of classes should be between five and twenty; otherwise, it may be difficult to detect any patterns.
2. Find the class width. The **class width** is the difference between the maximum and minimum data entries, divided by the number of classes, and *rounded up to the next convenient number.*

$$\text{Class width} = \frac{\text{Maximum data entry} - \text{Minimum data entry}}{\text{Number of classes}}$$

3. Find the class limits. A **lower class limit** is the least number that can belong to a specific class and an **upper class limit** is the greatest. Use the minimum data entry as the lower limit of the first class. To find the remaining lower limits, add the class width to the lower limit of the preceding class.
4. Use tally marks to sort the data entries into classes.
5. Count the tally marks to find the total frequency, f, for each class.

Study Tip

In a frequency distribution, it is best if each class has the same width.

> ▶ **EXAMPLE 1** *Constructing a Frequency Distribution from a Data Set*

The following sample data set lists the number of minutes 50 Internet subscribers spent on the Internet during their most recent session. Construct a frequency distribution that has seven classes.

50	40	41	17	11	7	22	44	28	21	19	23	37	51	54	42	88
41	78	56	72	56	17	7	69	30	80	56	29	33	46	31	39	20
18	29	34	59	73	77	36	39	30	62	54	67	39	31	53	44	

SOLUTION

1. The number of classes (7) is stated in the problem.

2. The minimum data entry is 7 and the maximum data entry is 88. The class
   width is 12.

$$\text{Class width} = \frac{88 - 7}{7} = \frac{81}{7} \approx 11.57 \qquad \text{Round up to 12.}$$

Lower limit	Upper limit
7	18
19	30
31	42
43	54
55	66
67	78
79	90

3. The minimum data entry is a convenient lower limit for the first class. To
   find the lower limits of the remaining six classes, add the class width of 12
   to the lower limit of each previous class. The upper limit of the first class is
   18, which is one less than the lower limit of the second class. The upper limits of the other classes are $18 + 12 = 30$, $30 + 12 = 42$, and so on. The
   lower and upper limits for all seven classes are shown at the left.

4. Tally the entries for each class.

5. The number of tally marks for a class is the frequency for that class.

The frequency distribution is shown in the following table. The first class, 7–18,
has six tally marks. So the frequency for this class is 6. Notice that the sum of
the frequencies is 50, which is the number of entries in the sample data set. The
sum is denoted by Σf, where Σ is the uppercase Greek letter **sigma.**

Note to Instructor

Let students know that there are
many correct versions for a frequency distribution. To make it
easy to check answers, however,
they should follow the conventions
shown in the text.

Note to Instructor

Be sure that students interpret
the class width correctly as the
distance between lower (or upper)
limits of consecutive classes. A
common error is to use a class
width of 11 for the class 7–18.
Students should be shown that
this class actually has a width
of 12.

Frequency Distribution for Internet Usage (in minutes)

Number of minutes ⟶

Class	Tally	Frequency, f
7–18	⊦⊦⊦ I	6
19–30	⊦⊦⊦ ⊦⊦⊦	10
31–42	⊦⊦⊦ ⊦⊦⊦ III	13
43–54	⊦⊦⊦ III	8
55–66	⊦⊦⊦	5
67–78	⊦⊦⊦ I	6
79–90	II	2
		$\Sigma f = 50$

⟵ Number of subscribers

Check that the sum
of the frequencies
equals the number
in the sample.

$$\frac{63-0}{6} = \frac{63}{6} \approx 11$$

Class	
0 – 10	27
11 – 21	13
22 – 32	16
33 – 43	7
44 – 54	11
55 – 65	3

Try It Yourself 1

Construct a frequency distribution using the ages of the residents of Akhiok given in the chapter opener on page 28. Use six classes.

a. State the *number of classes.* 6
b. Find the minimum and maximum values and the *class width.* 0, 63
c. Find the *class limits.*
d. *Tally* the data entries.
e. Write the *frequency, f,* for each class.   *Answer: Page A30*

After constructing a standard frequency distribution such as the one in Example 1, there are several additional features you can include that will help provide a better understanding of the data. These features are the midpoint, relative frequency, and cumulative frequency of each class.

DEFINITION

The **midpoint** of a class is the sum of the lower and upper limits of the class divided by two. The midpoint is sometimes called the *class mark.*

$$\text{Midpoint} = \frac{(\text{Lower class limit}) + (\text{Upper class limit})}{2}$$

The **relative frequency** of a class is the portion or percent of the data that falls in that class. To find the relative frequency of a class, divide the frequency f by the sample size n.

$$\text{Relative frequency} = \frac{\text{Class frequency}}{\text{Sample size}} = \frac{f}{n}$$

The **cumulative frequency** of a class is the sum of the frequency for that class and all previous classes. The cumulative frequency of the last class is equal to the sample size, n.

After finding the first midpoint, you can find the remaining midpoints by adding the class width to the previous midpoint. For instance, if the first midpoint is 12.5 and the class width is 12, then the remaining midpoints are

$$12.5 + 12 = 24.5, \qquad 24.5 + 12 = 36.5, \qquad 36.5 + 12 = 48.5$$

and so on.

Also, you can write the relative frequency as a decimal or as a percent. The sum of the relative frequencies of all the classes must equal one or 100%.

▶ **EXAMPLE 2**   *Midpoints, Relative and Cumulative Frequencies*

Using the frequency distribution constructed in Example 1, find the midpoint, relative frequency, and cumulative frequency for each class. Identify any patterns.

SOLUTION   The midpoint, relative frequency, and cumulative frequency for the first two classes are calculated as follows.

Class	f	Midpoint	Relative frequency	Cumulative frequency
7–18	6	$\dfrac{7 + 18}{2} = 12.5$	$\dfrac{6}{50} = 0.12$	6
19–30	10	$\dfrac{19 + 30}{2} = 24.5$	$\dfrac{10}{50} = 0.2$	6 + 10 = 16

The remaining midpoints, relative frequencies, and cumulative frequencies are shown in the following expanded frequency distribution.

Frequency Distribution for Internet Usage (in minutes)

Minutes on line ⟶ Class
Number of subscribers ⟶ f

Portion of subscribers

Class	f	Midpoint	Relative frequency	Cumulative frequency
7–18	6	12.5	0.12	6
19–30	10	24.5	0.2	16
31–42	13	36.5	0.26	29
43–54	8	48.5	0.16	37
55–66	5	60.5	0.1	42
67–78	6	72.5	0.12	48
79–90	2	84.5	0.04	50
	$\Sigma f = 50$		$\Sigma \dfrac{f}{n} = 1$	

There are several patterns in the data set. For instance, the most common time span that users stayed on line was 31 to 42 minutes.

Try It Yourself 2

Using the frequency distribution constructed in Try It Yourself 1, find the midpoint, relative frequency, and cumulative frequency for each class. Identify any patterns and characteristics.

a. Use the formulas to *find each midpoint, relative frequency, and cumulative frequency.*
b. *Organize your results* in a frequency distribution.
c. *Identify* patterns that emerge from the data.   *Answer: Page A30* ◀

Handwritten notes:

Class	M.P.	Rel.	
0–10	5	.3506	27
11–21	16	.1688	40
22–32	17	.2078	56
33–43	38	.0909	63
44–54	49	.1429	74
55–65	60	.0390	77

Over 35% of pop. is less than 11 yrs old.

less than 4% of pop is older than 54 years old

Graphs of Frequency Distributions

Sometimes it is easier to identify patterns of a data set by looking at a graph of the frequency distribution. One such graph is a frequency histogram.

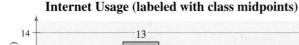

DEFINITION

A **frequency histogram** is a bar graph that represents the frequency distribution of a data set. A histogram has the following properties.

1. The horizontal scale is quantitative and measures the data values.
2. The vertical scale measures the frequencies of the classes.
3. Consecutive bars must touch.

Because consecutive bars of a histogram must touch, bars must begin and end at class boundaries instead of class limits. **Class boundaries** are the numbers that separate classes *without* forming gaps between them. You can mark the horizontal scale at either the midpoints or at the class boundaries.

▶ **EXAMPLE 3**   *Constructing a Frequency Histogram*

Class	Class Boundaries	Frequency, f
7–18	6.5–18.5	6
19–30	18.5–30.5	10
31–42	30.5–42.5	13
43–54	42.5–54.5	8
55–66	54.5–66.5	5
67–78	66.5–78.5	6
79–90	78.5–90.5	2

Draw a frequency histogram for the frequency distribution in Example 2. Describe any patterns.

SOLUTION   First, find the class boundaries. The distance from the upper limit of the first class to the lower limit of the second class is $19 - 18 = 1$. Half this distance is 0.5. So, the lower and upper boundaries of the first class are

$$7 - 0.5 = 6.5 \quad \text{and} \quad 18 + 0.5 = 18.5.$$

The boundaries of the remaining classes are shown in the table at the left. Using the class midpoints or class boundaries for the horizontal scale and choosing possible frequency values for the vertical scale, you can construct the histogram. From the histogram, you can see that most subscribers spent between 19 and 54 minutes on the Internet during their most recent session.

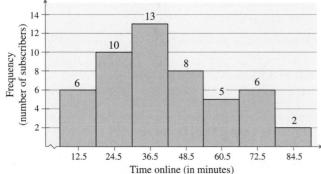

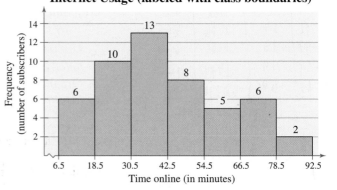

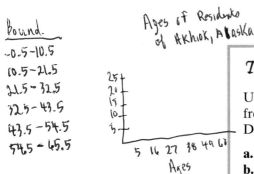

Bound.
-0.5-10.5
10.5-21.5
21.5-32.5
32.5-43.5
43.5-54.5
54.5-65.5

Ages of Residents of Akhiok, Alaska

Try It Yourself 3

Use the frequency distribution from Try It Yourself 1 to construct a frequency histogram that represents the ages of the residents of Akhiok. Describe any patterns.

a. Find the *class boundaries*.
b. Choose appropriate *horizontal and vertical scales*.
c. Use the frequency distribution to *find the height of each bar*.
d. *Describe* any patterns for the data. 32   *Answer: Page A31*

Most residents are less than 32 yrs old.

Another way to graph a frequency distribution is to use a frequency polygon. A **frequency polygon** is a line graph that emphasizes the continuous change in frequencies.

> **EXAMPLE 4**   *Constructing a Frequency Polygon*

Draw a frequency polygon for the frequency distribution in Example 2.

SOLUTION   To construct the frequency polygon, use the same horizontal and vertical scales that were used in the histogram labeled with class midpoints in Example 3. Then plot points that represent the midpoint and frequency of each class and connect the points in order from left to right. Because the graph should begin and end on the horizontal axis, extend the left side to one class width before the first class midpoint and extend the right side to one class width after the last class midpoint. You can see that the frequency of subscribers increases up to 36.5 minutes and then decreases.

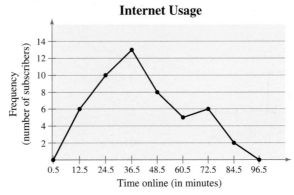

Internet Usage

Study Tip

A histogram and its corresponding frequency polygon are often drawn together. If you have not already constructed the histogram, begin constructing the frequency polygon by choosing appropriate horizontal and vertical scales. The horizontal scale should consist of the class midpoints and the vertical scale should consist of appropriate frequency values.

Try It Yourself 4

Construct a frequency polygon that represents the ages of the residents of Akhiok. Describe any patterns.

a. Choose appropriate *horizontal and vertical scales*.
b. *Plot points* that represent the midpoint and frequency for each class.
c. *Connect the points* and extend the sides as necessary.
d. *Describe* any patterns for the data.   *Answer: Page A31*

pop. is predominantly made up of young people.

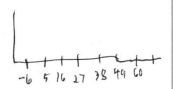

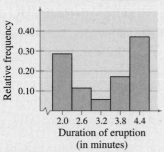
A **relative frequency histogram** has the same shape and the same horizontal scale as the corresponding frequency histogram. The difference is that the vertical scale measures the relative frequencies, not frequencies.

> **EXAMPLE 5**   *Constructing a Relative Frequency Histogram*

Draw a relative frequency histogram for the frequency distribution in Example 2.

SOLUTION   The relative frequency histogram is shown. Notice that the shape of the histogram is the same as the frequency histogram constructed in Example 3. The only difference is the vertical scale.

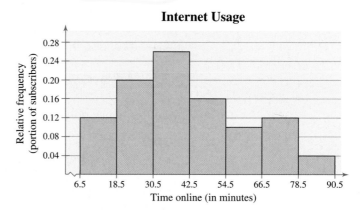

Internet Usage

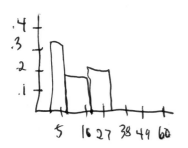

Try It Yourself 5

Construct a relative frequency histogram that represents the ages of the residents of Akhiok.

a. *Use the same horizontal scale* as used in the frequency histogram.
b. *Revise the vertical scale* to reflect relative frequencies.
c. Use the relative frequencies to *find the height of each bar*.

Answer: Page A31

What if you wanted to know how many data entries are above or below a certain value? You could easily find out by constructing a cumulative frequency graph.

DEFINITION

A **cumulative frequency graph,** or **ogive** (pronounce ō′jīve), is a line graph that displays the cumulative frequency of each class at its upper class boundary. The upper boundaries are marked on the horizontal axis and the cumulative frequencies are marked on the vertical axis.

> **GUIDELINES**
>
> ## Constructing an Ogive (Cumulative Frequency Graph)
>
> 1. Construct a frequency table that includes cumulative frequencies.
> 2. Specify the horizontal and vertical scales. The horizontal scale consists of upper class boundaries and the vertical scale measures cumulative frequencies.
> 3. Plot points that represent the upper class boundaries and their corresponding cumulative frequencies.
> 4. Connect the points in order from left to right.
> 5. The graph should start at the lower boundary of the first class (cumulative frequency is zero) and should end at the upper boundary of the last class (cumulative frequency is equal to the sample size).

> **EXAMPLE 6**   *Constructing an Ogive*

Draw an ogive for the frequency distribution in Example 2. Estimate how many subscribers spent less than 60 minutes during their last session.

SOLUTION   Using the frequency distribution, you can construct the ogive shown. The upper class boundaries, frequencies, and the cumulative frequencies are listed in the table. Notice that the graph starts at 6.5, where the cumulative frequency is 0, and the graph ends at 90.5, where the cumulative frequency is 50.

Upper Class Boundaries	f	Cumulative Frequencies
18.5	6	6
30.5	10	16
42.5	13	29
54.5	8	37
66.5	5	42
78.5	6	48
90.5	2	50

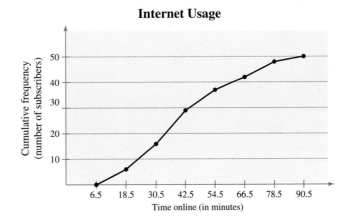

From the ogive, you can see that about 40 subscribers spent less than 60 minutes online during their last session. The greatest increase in usage occurs between 30.5 minutes and 42.5 minutes because the line segment is steepest between these two class boundaries.

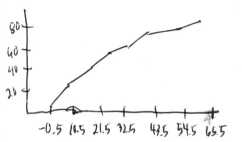

$\cong 63$ resv

$\cong 63$ residents < 45 yrs old.

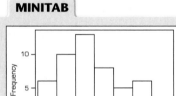

-0.5 11.5 21.5 32.5 42.5 54.5 65.5

Try It Yourself 6

Construct an ogive that represents the ages of the residents of Akhiok. Estimate the number of residents who are less than 45 years old.

a. Specify the *horizontal* and *vertical scales.*
b. *Plot* the points given by the upper class boundaries and the cumulative frequencies.
c. *Construct* the graph.
d. *Estimate* the number of residents who are less than 45 years old.

$\cong 63$ residents < 45 yrs old.

Answer: Page A31

▶ **EXAMPLE 7**   *Using Technology to Construct Histograms*

Use a calculator or a computer to construct a histogram for the frequency distribution in Example 2.

SOLUTION   Minitab, Excel, and the TI-83 each have features for graphing histograms. Try using this technology to draw the histograms as shown.

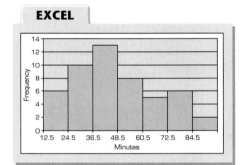

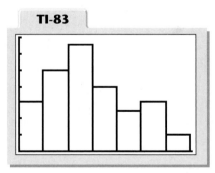

Study Tip

Detailed instructions for using Minitab, Excel, and the TI-83 are shown in the Technology Guide that accompanies this text. For instance, here are instructions for creating a histogram on a TI-83.

STAT ENTER

Enter midpoints in L1.
Enter frequencies in L2.

2nd STATPLOT

Turn on Plot 1.
Highlight Histogram.
Xlist: L1
Freq: L2

ZOOM 9

WINDOW

Xscl=12

GRAPH

Try It Yourself 7

Use a calculator or a computer to construct a histogram that represents the ages of the residents of Akhiok. Use six classes.

a. *Enter* the data.
b. **Construct** the histogram.

Answer: Page A31

2.1 ▬ EXERCISES ▬

HELP

 StatPro 2.1

 Internet Statistics 2.1

 Student Solutions Manual 2.1

 Videos 2.1

 Try It Yourself Answers 2.1

1. By organizing the data into a frequency distribution, patterns within the data may become more evident.

2. Sometimes it is easier to identify patterns of a data set by looking at a graph of the frequency distribution.

3. False

4. False

5. See Odd Answers, page A46

6. See Selected Answers, page A76

7. Least frequency ≈ 10
   Greatest frequency ≈ 300
   Class width = 10

8. Least frequency ≈ 100
   Greatest frequency ≈ 900
   Class width = 5

Basic Skills and Concepts

1. What are some benefits of representing data sets using frequency distributions?

2. What are some benefits of representing data sets using graphs of frequency distributions?

True or False   In Exercises 3 and 4, determine whether the statement is true or false. If it is false, rewrite it as a true statement.

3. The midpoint of a class is the sum of the lower and upper limits.

4. The relative frequency of a class is the sample size divided by the frequency of the class.

Reading a Frequency Distribution   In Exercises 5 and 6, identify the frequency distribution's class width, class boundaries, and the midpoint of each class. Find the cumulative frequency of each class.

5. Employee Age		6. Tree Height	
Class	**Frequency**	**Class**	**Frequency**
20–29	10	16–20	100
30–39	132	21–25	122
40–49	284	26–30	900
50–59	300	31–35	207
60–69	175	36–40	795
70–79	65	41–45	568
80–89	25	46–50	322

Graphical Analysis   In Exercises 7 and 8, use the frequency histogram to estimate the frequency of the class with the least frequency and the frequency of the class with the greatest frequency. What is the class width?

7.

Employee Age

8.

Tree Height

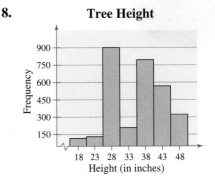

9. (a) 50

   (b) 12.5–13.5 lbs.

   (c) 24

   (d) 19.5 lbs.

10. (a) 50

   (b) 68–70 inches

   (c) 44

   (d) 70 inches

11. (a) Class with greatest relative frequency: 8–9 in.

   Class with least relative frequency: 17–18 in.

   (b) Greatest relative frequency ≈ 0.195

   Least relative frequency ≈ 0.005

   (c) Approximately 0.015

12. (a) Class with greatest relative frequency: 19–20 min.

   Class with least relative frequency: 21–22 in.

   (b) Greatest relative frequency ≈ 40%

   Least relative frequency ≈ 2%

   (c) Approximately 33%

13. Class with greatest frequency: 500–550

   Class with least frequency: 250–300 or 700–750

14. Class with greatest frequency: 4.00–4.10 inches

   Class with least frequency: 4.20–4.30 inches

9. *Graphical Analysis* Use the ogive to approximate (a) the number in the sample, (b) the location of the greatest increase in frequency, (c) the cumulative frequency for a weight of 14.5 pounds, and (d) the weight for which the cumulative frequency is 45.

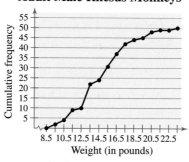

Adult Male Rhesus Monkeys

Weight (in pounds)

10. *Graphical Analysis* Use the ogive to approximate (a) the number in the sample, (b) the location of the greatest increase in frequency, (c) the cumulative frequency for a height of 74 inches, and (d) the height for which the cumulative frequency is 25.

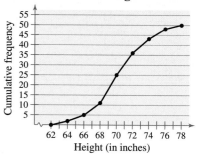

Adult Male Ages 20–29

Height (in inches)

Graphical Analysis In Exercises 11 and 12, use the relative frequency histogram to (a) identify the class with the greatest and the least relative frequency, (b) approximate the greatest and least relative frequency, and (c) approximate the relative frequency of the second class.

11.

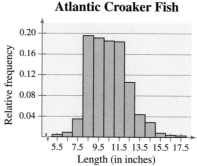

Atlantic Croaker Fish

Length (in inches)

12.

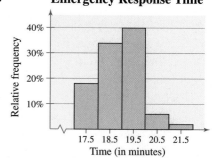

Emergency Response Time

Time (in minutes)

Graphical Analysis In Exercises 13 and 14, use the frequency polygon to identify the class with the greatest and the least frequency.

13.

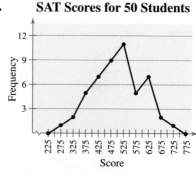

SAT Scores for 50 Students

Score

14.

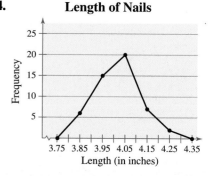

Length of Nails

Length (in inches)

15. See Odd Answers, page A46
16. See Selected Answers, page A76
17. See Odd Answers, page A46
18. See Selected Answers, page A76
19. See Odd Answers, page A46
20. See Selected Answers, page A76

Constructing a Frequency Distribution   In Exercises 15 and 16, construct a frequency distribution for the data set using the indicated number of classes. In the table, include the midpoints, relative frequencies, and cumulative frequencies.

15. Number of classes: 5

Data set: Time (in minutes) spent reading the newspaper in a day

7 39 13 9 25 8 22 0   2 18   2 30 7
35 12 15 8   6 5 29 0 11 39 16 15

16. Number of classes: 6

Data set: Amount (in dollars) spent on books for a semester

91 472 279 249 530 376 188 341 266 199
142 273 189 130 489 266 248 101 375 486
190 398 188 269   43   30 127 354   84

Constructing a Frequency Distribution and a Frequency Histogram
In Exercises 17–20, construct a frequency distribution and a frequency histogram for the data set using the indicated number of classes. Then determine which class has the greatest frequency and which has the least frequency.

17. Number of classes: 6

Data set: July sales (in dollars) for sales representatives at a company

2114 2468 7119 1876 4105 3183 1932 1355 4278 1030 2000
1077 5835 1512 1697 2478 3981 1643 1858 1500 4608 1000

18. Number of classes: 5

Data set: Pungencies (in 1000s of Scoville units) of sixteen tabasco peppers

35 51 44 42 37 38 36 39 44 43 40 40 32 39 41 38

19. Number of classes: 8

Data set: Reaction times (in milliseconds) of a sample of 22 adult females to an auditory stimulus

507 389 305 291 336 310 514 442 307 337 373
428 387 454 323 441 388 426 469 351 411 382

20. Number of classes: 5

Data set: Amount of pressure (in pounds per square inch) at fracture time for 25 samples of brick mortar

2750 2862 2885 2490 2512 2456 2554 2532 2885
2872 2601 2877 2721 2692 2888 2755 2853 2517
2867 2718 2641 2834 2466 2596 2519

Constructing a Frequency Distribution and a Relative Frequency Histogram   In Exercises 21–24, construct a frequency distribution and a relative frequency histogram for the data set. Then determine which class has the greatest relative frequency and which has the least relative frequency.

21. Number of classes: 5

Data set: Bowling scores of a sample of league members

> 154 257 195 220 182 240 177 228 235 146 174 192 165
> 207 185 180 264 169 225 239 148 190 182 205 148 188

22. Number of classes: 5

Data set: A sample of ATM withdrawals (in dollars)

> 35 10 30 25 75 10 30 20 20 10 40 50 40 30 60 70
> 25 40 10 60 20 80 40 25 20 10 20 25 30 50 80 20

23. Number of classes: 7

Data set: Heights (in feet) of a sample of Douglas fir trees

> 40 44 35 49 35 43 35 36 39 37 41 41 48
> 53 37 45 40 36 35 50 42 51 33 34 51 39

24. Number of classes: 5

Data set: Number of acres on a sample of small farms

> 12 9 8 9 8 12 10 9 16 8 13 12
> 10 11 7 14 12 9 8 10 9 11 13 8

Constructing a Cumulative Frequency Distribution and an Ogive   In Exercises 25–28, construct a cumulative frequency distribution and an ogive for the data set. Then describe the location of the greatest increase in frequency.

25. Number of classes: 6

Data set: Retirement ages for a sample of engineers

> 60 65 68 63 66 67 69 67 58 65 67 61
> 63 65 62 64 73 50 61 71 62 69 72 63

26. Number of classes: 5

Data set: Daily saturated fat intakes (in grams) of a sample of people

> 38 32 34 39 40 54 32 17 29 33 57 40 25 36 33 24 42 16 31 33

27. Number of classes: 6

Data set: Gasoline (in gallons) purchased by a sample of drivers during one fill-up

> 7 4 18 4 9 8 8 7 6 2 9 5 9 12
> 4 14 15 7 10 2 3 11 4 4 9 12 5 3

28. Number of classes: 6

Data set: Lengths (in minutes) of a sample of long-distance phone calls

> 1 20 10 20 13 23 3 7 18 7 4 5
> 15 7 29 10 18 10 10 23 4 12 8 6

29. See Odd Answers, page A48

30. See Selected Answers, page A77

31. (a)

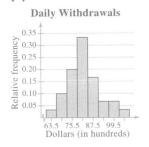

Daily Withdrawals

(b) $9,600

(c) 16.7%

32. (a)

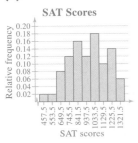

SAT Scores

(b) 698

(c) 48%

33. See Odd Answers, page A48

Constructing a Frequency Distribution and a Frequency Polygon   In Exercises 29 and 30, construct a frequency distribution and a frequency polygon for the data set. Then determine which class has the greatest frequency and which has the least frequency.

29. Number of classes: 5

Data set: Exam scores for all students in a statistics class

83 92 94 82 73 98 78 85 72 90 89 92 96 89 75 85 63 47 75 82

30. Number of classes: 6

Data set: Number of children of the first 41 U.S. Presidents *(Source: The World Almanac and Book of Facts 1998)*

0 5 6 0 2 4 0 4 10 15 0 6 2 3 0 4 5 4 8 5 3

5 3 2 6 3 3 0 2   2   5 1 1 2 2 2 4 4 4 6 1

31. *What Would You Do?*   You work at a bank and are asked to recommend the amount of cash to put in an ATM each day. You don't want to put in too much (security) or too little (customer irritation). Here are the daily withdrawals (in 100s of dollars) for a period of 30 days.

72 84 61 76 104 76 86 92 80 88 98 76 97 82 84

67 70 81 82   89 74 73 86 81 85 78 82 80 91 83

(a) Construct a relative frequency histogram for the data, using eight classes.

(b) If you are willing to run out of cash for 10% of the days, how much cash should you put in the ATM? Explain your reasoning.

(c) If you put $9000 in the ATM, what percent of the days in a month should you expect to run out of cash? Explain your reasoning.

32. *What Would You Do?*   You work in the admissions department for a college and are asked to recommend the minimum SAT scores that the college will accept for a position as a full-time student. Here are the SAT scores for a sample of 50 applicants.

1325 1072   982   996   872   849   785   706   669 1049   885 1367 935

980 1188   869 1006 1127   979 1034 1052 1165 1359   667 1264 727

808   955   544 1202 1051 1173   410 1148 1195 1141 1193   768 812

887 1211 1266   830   672   917   988   791 1035   688   700

(a) Construct a relative frequency histogram for the data, using 10 classes.

(b) If you want to accept the top 88% of the applicants, what should the minimum score be?

(c) If you set the minimum score at 986, what percent of the applicants will you be accepting?

Extending the Basics

33. *Writing*   What happens when the number of classes is increased for a frequency histogram? Use the data set listed and create frequency histograms with 5, 10, and 20 classes. Which graph displays the data best?

2 7 3 2 11 3 15 8 4 9 10 13 9 7 11 10 1 2 12 5 6 4 2 9 15

2.2 More Graphs and Displays

Graphing Quantitative Data Sets • Graphing Qualitative Data Sets • Graphing Paired Data Sets

What You Should Learn

- How to graph quantitative data sets using stem-and-leaf plots and dot plots
- How to graph qualitative data sets using pie charts and Pareto charts
- How to graph paired data sets using scatter plots and time series charts

Graphing Quantitative Data Sets

In Section 2.1, you learned several traditional ways to display quantitative data graphically. In this section, you will learn a newer way to display quantitative data, called a **stem-and-leaf plot.** Stem-and-leaf plots are examples of **exploratory data analysis (EDA),** which was developed by John Tukey in 1977.

In a stem-and-leaf plot, each number is separated into a **stem** (the entry's leftmost digits) and a **leaf** (the rightmost digit). A stem-and-leaf plot is similar to a histogram but has the advantage that the graph still contains the original data values. Another advantage of a stem-and-leaf plot is that it provides an easy way to sort data.

> **EXAMPLE 1**   *Constructing a Stem-and-Leaf Plot*

The following are the numbers of league-leading runs batted in (RBIs) for baseball's American League for the last 50 years. Display the data in a stem-and-leaf plot. What can you conclude? *(Source: Major League Baseball)*

```
155  159  144  129  105  145  126  116  130  114  122  112  112  142  126
118  118  108  122  121  109  140  126  119  113  117  118  109  109  119
139  139  122   78  133  126  123  145  121  134  124  119  132  133  124
129  112  126  148  147
```

SOLUTION   Because the data entries go from a low of 78 to a high of 159, you should use stem values from 7 to 15. To construct the plot, list these stems to the left of a vertical line. For each data entry, list a leaf to the right of its stem. For instance, the entry 155 has a stem of 15 and a leaf of 5. The resulting stem-and-leaf plot will be unordered. To obtain an ordered stem-and-leaf plot, rewrite the plot with the leaves in increasing order from left to right.

Study Tip

In a stem-and-leaf plot, you should have as many leaves as there are entries in the original data set.

RBIs for American League Leaders

```
 7 | 8              Key: 15|5 = 155
 8 |
 9 |
10 | 5 8 9 9 9
11 | 6 4 2 2 8 8 9 3 7 8 9 9 2
12 | 9 6 2 6 2 1 6 2 6 3 1 4 4 9 6
13 | 0 9 9 3 4 2 3
14 | 4 5 2 0 5 8 7
15 | 5 9
```

Unordered Stem-and-Leaf Plot

RBIs for American League Leaders

```
 7 | 8              Key: 15|5 = 155
 8 |
 9 |
10 | 5 8 9 9 9
11 | 2 2 2 3 4 6 7 8 8 8 9 9 9
12 | 1 1 2 2 2 3 4 4 6 6 6 6 9 9
13 | 0 2 3 3 4 9 9
14 | 0 2 4 5 5 7 8
15 | 5 9
```

Ordered Stem-and-Leaf Plot

From the ordered stem-and-leaf plot, you can conclude that most of the RBI leaders had between 110 and 130 RBIs.

Try It Yourself 1

Use a stem-and-leaf plot to organize the Akhiok population data set listed on page 28. What can you conclude?

a. List all possible *stems*.
b. List the leaf of each data entry to the right of its stem.
c. Rewrite the stem-and-leaf plot so that the leaves are ordered.
d. Use the plot to make a conclusion.   *Answer: Page A31*

EXAMPLE 2   *Constructing Variations of Stem-and-Leaf Plots*

Organize the data given in Example 1 using a stem-and-leaf plot that has two lines for each stem. What can you conclude?

SOLUTION   Construct the stem-and-leaf plot as described in Example 1, except now list each stem twice. Use the leaves 0, 1, 2, 3, and 4 in the first stem row and the leaves 5, 6, 7, 8, and 9 in the second stem row. The revised stem-and-leaf plot is shown. From the display, you can conclude that most of the RBI leaders had between 105 and 135 RBIs.

Note to Instructor

If you are using Minitab or Excel, ask students to use this technology to construct a stem-and-leaf plot.

Insight

Compare Examples 1 and 2. Notice that by using two lines per stem, you obtain a more detailed picture of the data.

RBIs for American League Leaders

Key: 15|5 = 155

```
 7 | 8
 8 |
 8 |
 9 |
 9 |
10 |
10 | 5 8 9 9 9
11 | 4 2 2 3 2
11 | 6 8 8 9 7 8 9 9
12 | 2 2 1 2 3 1 4 4
12 | 9 6 6 6 6 9 6
13 | 0 3 4 2 3
13 | 9 9
14 | 4 2 0
14 | 5 5 8 7
15 |
15 | 5 9
```
Unordered Stem-and-Leaf Plot

RBIs for American League Leaders

Key: 15|5 = 155

```
 7 | 8
 8 |
 8 |
 9 |
 9 |
10 |
10 | 5 8 9 9 9
11 | 2 2 2 3 4
11 | 6 7 8 8 8 9 9 9
12 | 1 1 2 2 2 3 4 4
12 | 6 6 6 6 6 9 9
13 | 0 2 3 3 4
13 | 9 9
14 | 0 2 4
14 | 5 5 7 8
15 |
15 | 5 9
```
Ordered Stem-and-Leaf Plot

Try It Yourself 2

Using two rows for each stem, revise the stem-and-leaf plot you constructed in Try It Yourself 1.

a. List each stem *twice*.
b. List all leaves *using the appropriate stem row*.   *Answer: Page A31*

You can also use a dot plot to graph quantitative data. In a **dot plot,** each data entry is plotted, using a point, above a horizontal axis. Like a stem-and-leaf plot, a dot plot allows you to see how data are distributed and to determine specific data entries.

▶ **EXAMPLE 3**   *Constructing a Dot Plot*

Use a dot plot to organize the RBI data given in Example 1.

155	159	144	129	105	145	126	116	130	114	122	112	112	142	126
118	118	108	122	121	109	140	126	119	113	117	118	109	109	119
139	139	122	78	133	126	123	145	121	134	124	119	132	133	124
129	112	126	148	147									

SOLUTION   So that each data entry is included in the dot plot, the horizontal axis should include numbers between 70 and 160. To represent a data entry, plot a point above the entry's position on the axis. If an entry is repeated, plot another point above the previous point.

RBIs for American League Leaders

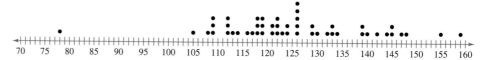

From the dot plot, you can see that most values cluster between 105 and 148.

Try It Yourself 3

Use a dot plot to organize the data listed in the chapter opener on page 28. What can you conclude from the graph?

a. Choose an appropriate scale for the *horizontal axis.*
b. Represent each data entry by *plotting a point.*
c. *Describe* any patterns for the data.   *Answer: Page A31* ◀

Technology can be used to construct stem-and-leaf plots and dot plots. For instance, a Minitab dot plot for the RBI data is shown.

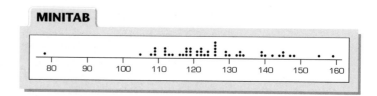

Graphing Qualitative Data Sets

Pie charts provide a convenient way to present qualitative data graphically. A **pie chart** is a circle graph that shows relationships of parts to a whole.

▶ **EXAMPLE 4** *Constructing a Pie Chart*

The numbers of intercity passengers, in millions, traveling by bus, air, subway, and Amtrak in 1995 are listed in the table. Use a pie chart to organize the data. What can you conclude? *(Source: Eno Transportation Foundation Inc.)*

SOLUTION Begin by finding the relative frequency, or percent, of each data entry. Then construct the pie chart using the central angle that corresponds to each data entry. From the pie chart, you can see that very few people chose Amtrak for intercity transportation.

Intercity Passenger Travel

Transportation	Passengers (in millions)
Bus	359
Air	499.1
Subway	351.6
Amtrak	19.7
	$\Sigma = 1229.4$

	f	Relative Frequency	Angle
Bus	359	0.292	105°
Air	499.1	0.406	146°
Subway	351.6	0.286	103°
Amtrak	19.7	0.016	6°

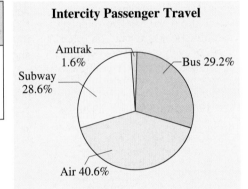

Intercity Passenger Travel

Amtrak 1.6% — Bus 29.2% — Subway 28.6% — Air 40.6%

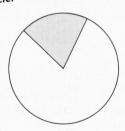
Try It Yourself 4

The numbers of intercity passengers, in millions, traveling by bus, air, subway, and Amtrak in 1985 are listed in the table. Use a pie chart to organize the data. How do the 1985 data compare to the 1995 data? *(Source: Eno Transportation Foundation Inc.)*

Intercity Passenger Travel

Transportation	Passengers (in millions)
Bus	348
Air	363.1
Subway	274.6
Amtrak	20.1

a. Find the *relative frequency* of each data entry.
b. Use the *central angle* to find the portion of the circle that corresponds to each data entry.
c. Compare the 1985 data to the 1995 data. *Answer: Page A32* ◀

Another way to graph qualitative data is to use a Pareto chart. A **Pareto chart** is a vertical bar graph in which the height of each bar represents frequency or relative frequency. The bars are positioned in order of decreasing height, with the tallest bar positioned at the left. Such positioning helps highlight important data and is used frequently in business.

▶ **EXAMPLE 5** *Constructing a Pareto Chart*

Last year, the retail industry lost $40.9 million in inventory shrinkage. The causes of the inventory shrinkage are administrative error ($7.8 million), employee theft ($15.6 million), shoplifting ($14.7 million), and vendor fraud ($2.9 million). If you were a retailer, which causes of inventory shrinkage would you address first? *(Source: National Retail Federation and Center for Retailing Education, University of Florida)*

SOLUTION Using frequencies for the vertical axis, you can construct the Pareto chart as shown. From the graph, it is easy to see that the causes of inventory shrinkage that should be addressed first are employee theft and shoplifting.

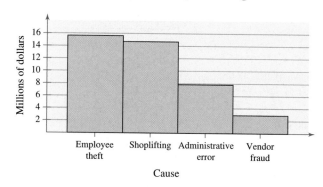

Causes of Inventory Shrinkage

Picturing the World

The five top-selling vehicles in the United States for the first six months of 1998 are shown in the following Pareto chart. Of the top five vehicles, only one was a car. The other four vehicles were trucks. *(Source: Ward's Automotive Reports)*

1998 Top 5 Selling Vehicles

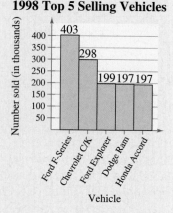

How many vehicles from the top five did Ford sell in the first six months of 1998?

Try It Yourself 5

Every year, the Better Business Bureau (BBB) receives complaints from dissatisfied customers. In a recent year, the BBB received 14,668 complaints about auto dealers, 7792 complaints about home furnishing stores, 5733 complaints about computer sales and service stores, 9728 complaints about auto repair shops, and 4649 complaints about dry cleaning companies. Use a Pareto chart to organize the data. What source is the greatest cause of complaints? *(Source: Council of Better Business Bureaus)*

a. Find the *frequency or relative frequency* for each data entry.
b. *Position the bars in decreasing order* according to frequency or relative frequency.
c. *Interpret the results* in the context of the data. *Answer: Page A32*

Graphing Paired Data Sets

If two data sets have the same number of entries, and each entry in the first data set corresponds to one entry in the second data set, the sets are called **paired data sets.** For instance, suppose a data set contains the costs of an item and a second data set contains sales amounts for the item at each cost. Because each cost corresponds to a sales amount, the data sets are paired. One way to graph paired data sets is to use a **scatter plot,** where the ordered pairs are graphed as points in a coordinate plane.

EXAMPLE 6   *Interpreting a Scatter Plot*

The British statistician Ronald Fisher (see page 274) introduced a famous data set called Fisher's Iris data set. This data set describes various physical characteristics, such as petal length and petal width, for three species of iris. The petal lengths and petal widths for each species are graphed in the scatter plot. What can you conclude? *(Source: Fisher, R. A., 1936)*

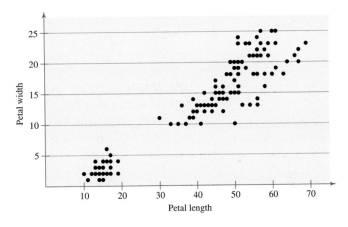

Note to Instructor

A complete discussion of types of correlation occurs in Chapter 9. You may want, however, to discuss positive correlation, negative correlation, and no correlation at this point. Be sure that students do not confuse correlation with causation.

SOLUTION   The horizontal axis represents the petal length and the vertical axis represents the petal width. Each point in the scatter plot represents the petal length and petal width of one flower. From the scatter plot, you can see that for each of the three species, as the petal length increases, the petal width also increases.

Length of Employment (in years)	Salary (in dollars)
5	32,000
4	32,500
8	40,000
4	27,350
2	25,000
10	43,000
7	41,650
6	39,225
9	45,100
3	28,000

Try It Yourself 6

The lengths of employment and the salaries of 10 employees are listed in the table at the left. Graph the data using a scatter plot. What can you conclude?

a. Label the *horizontal and vertical axes.*
b. *Plot* the paired data.
c. Describe any trends.

Answer: Page A32

A data set that is composed of entries taken at regular intervals over a period of time is a **time series.** For instance, the amount of precipitation measured each day for one month is an example of a time series. You can use a **time series chart** to graph a time series.

See *Minitab* and *TI-83* steps on pages 94, 95.

▶ **EXAMPLE 7**   *Constructing a Time Series Chart*

The table lists the number of cellular telephone subscribers, in millions, and a subscriber's average local monthly bill for service, in dollars, for the years 1987 through 1996. Construct a time series chart for the number of cellular subscribers. What can you conclude? *(Source: Cellular Telecommunications Industry Association)*

Year	Subscribers (in millions)	Average Bill (in dollars)
1987	1.2	96.83
1988	2.1	98.02
1989	3.5	89.30
1990	5.3	80.90
1991	7.6	72.74
1992	11.0	68.68
1993	16.0	61.48
1994	24.1	56.21
1995	33.8	51.00
1996	44.0	47.70

SOLUTION   Let the horizontal axis represent the years and the vertical axis represent the number of subscribers, in millions. Then plot the paired data. From the graph, you can see that the number of subscribers has been increasing since 1987. Recent years show greater increases.

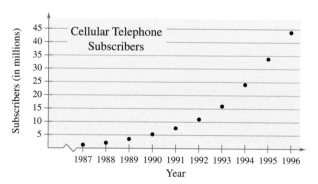

Try It Yourself 7

Use the table in Example 7 to construct a time series chart for a subscriber's average local monthly cellular telephone bill for the years 1987 through 1996. What can you conclude?

a. Label the *horizontal and vertical axes.*
b. *Plot* the paired data.
c. Describe any patterns you see.   *Answer: Page A32* ◀

2.2 ▼ EXERCISES

HELP

 StatPro 2.2

 Internet Statistics 2.2

 Student Solutions Manual 2.2

 Videos 2.2

 Try It Yourself Answers 2.2

1. Quantitative: Stem-and-Leaf Plot, Dot Plot, Histogram, Time Series Chart Qualitative: Pie Chart, Pareto Chart

2. Unlike the histogram, the stem-and-leaf plot still contains the original data values. However, some data are difficult to organize in a stem-and-leaf plot.

3. a   4. c

5. d   6. b

7. 27, 32, 41, 43, 43, 44, 47, 47, 48, 50, 51, 51, 52, 53, 53, 53, 54, 54, 54, 54, 55, 56, 56, 58, 59, 68, 68, 68, 73, 78, 78

   Max: 78   Min: 27

8. 129, 133, 136, 137, 137, 141, 141, 141, 141, 143, 144, 144, 146, 149, 149, 150, 150, 150, 151, 152, 154, 156, 157, 158, 158, 158, 159, 161, 166, 167

   Max: 167   Min: 129

9. 13, 13, 14, 14, 14, 15, 15, 15, 15, 15, 16, 17, 17, 18, 19

   Max: 19   Min: 13

10. 214, 214, 214, 216, 216, 217, 218, 218, 220, 221, 223, 224, 225, 225, 227, 228, 228, 228, 228, 230, 230, 231, 235, 237, 239

   Max: 239   Min: 214

Basic Skills and Concepts

1. Name some ways to display quantitative data graphically. Name some ways to display qualitative graphically.

2. What is an advantage of using a stem-and-leaf plot instead of a histogram? What is a disadvantage?

Putting Graphs in Context   In Exercises 3–6, match the plot with the sample.

(a)
```
2 | 8 9            Key: 2|8 = 28
3 | 2 2 2 3 4 5 7 7 8 9
4 | 0 2 4 5
5 | 1
6 | 5 6
7 | 2
```

(b)
```
6 | 7 8            Key: 6|7 = 67
7 | 4 5 5 8 8 8
8 | 1 3 5 5 8 8 9
9 | 0 0 0 2 4
```

(c)

(d)

3. Prices (in dollars) of a sample of 20 brands of jeans

4. Weights (in pounds) of a sample of 20 first grade students

5. Volumes (in cubic centimeters) of a sample of 20 oranges

6. Ages (in years) of a sample of 20 residents of a retirement home

Graphical Analysis   In Exercises 7–10, use the stem-and-leaf plot or dot plot to list the actual data entries. What is the maximum data entry? What is the minimum data entry?

7.
```
2 | 7              Key: 2|7 = 27
3 | 2
4 | 1 3 3 4 7 7 8
5 | 0 1 1 2 3 3 3 4 4 4 4 5 6 6 8 9
6 | 8 8 8
7 | 3 8 8
```

8.
```
12 | 9             Key: 12|9 = 129
13 | 3 6 7 7
14 | 1 1 1 1 3 4 4 6 9 9
15 | 0 0 0 1 2 4 6 7 8 8 8 9
16 | 1 6 7
```

9.

10.

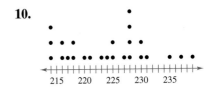

11. Time series chart

12. Pareto chart or pie chart

13. Stem-and-leaf plot or dot plot

14. Pareto chart or pie chart

15. (a) Key: 2| 4 = 24

```
1| 9
2| 11122233444566677
 | 777899
3| 0
```

(b) Key: 2| 4 = 24

```
1| 9
2| 11122233444
2| 566677777899
3| 0
```

It appears that using two rows for each stem displays the data better.

16. See Selected Answers, page A77

17. Key: 3| 3 = 33

```
3| 233459
4| 01134556678
5| 133
6| 0069
```

Most elephant tend to drink less than 55 gallons of water per day.

18. See Selected Answers, page A78

19. Key: 17| 5 = 175

```
16| 48
17| 113455679
18| 13446669
19| 0023356
20| 18
```

It appears that most farmers charge 17 to 19 cents per pound of apples.

20.

Advertisements

It appears that most of the 30 Americans see or hear between 450 and 750 advertisements per week.

Choosing an Appropriate Graph or Display   In Exercises 11–14, determine which types of graphs (stem-and-leaf plot, dot plot, Pareto chart, pie chart, scatter plot, time series chart) would be appropriate to represent the data described by the statement. Explain your reasoning.

11. The quarterly unemployment rate for the past 10 years

12. All state lottery revenues in one year for the following: instant games, three-digit drawings, four-digit drawings, and lottos

13. The price of premium gasoline from a sample of 24 vendors

14. A list of 15 products and their year-to-date sales in thousands of dollars

Stem-and-Leaf Plots   In Exercises 15 and 16, organize the data using (a) a stem-and-leaf plot with one row for each stem and (b) a stem-and-leaf plot with two rows for each stem. Compare the plots and comment on their differences.

15. Ages of a sample of college graduates:

27 24 23 28 25 29 22 26 22 21 21 30 23
27 27 24 22 19 27 24 29 26 21 27 26

16. Math SAT scores for a sample of high school seniors:

490 521 474 538 519 529 560 496 518 489
531 475 525 508 485 492 517 489 507 484

Graphing Data Sets   In Exercises 17–30, organize the data using the indicated type of graph. What can you conclude about the data?

17. Use a stem-and-leaf plot to display the data. The data represent the amount of water (in gallons) consumed by 24 elephants in one day.

33 45 34 47 43 48 35 69 45 60 46 51
41 60 66 41 32 40 44 39 46 33 53 53

18. Use a stem-and-leaf plot to display the data. The data represent the amount of hay (in pounds) eaten by 24 elephants in one day.

449 450 419 448 479 410 446 465 415 455 345 305
491 479 390 393 403 298 503 327 460 351 409 319

19. Use a stem-and-leaf plot to display the data. The data represent the price (in cents per pound) paid to 28 farmers for apples.

19.2 19.6 16.4 17.1 19.0 17.4 17.3 20.1 19.0 17.5 17.6 18.6 18.4 17.7
19.5 18.4 18.9 17.5 19.3 20.8 19.3 18.6 18.6 18.3 17.1 18.1 16.8 17.9

20. Use a dot plot to display the data. The data represent the number of advertisements seen or heard in one week by a sample of 30 Americans.

598 494 441 595 728 690 684 486 735 808 734 590 673 545 702
481 298 135 846 764 317 649 732 582 637 588 540 727 486 703

21.

Housefly Lifespans

4 5 6 7 8 9 10 11 12 13 14
Lifespan (in days)

It appears that the lifespan of a fly tends to be between 4 and 14 days.

22.

Nobel Prize Laureates

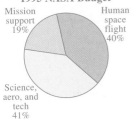

Other 21%
USSR 2%
France 6%
Germany 14%
United States 41%
United Kingdom 16%

It appears that 57% of the Nobel Prize laureates come from either the U.S. or the United Kingdom.

23.

1995 NASA Budget

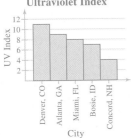

Mission support 19%
Human space flight 40%
Science, aero, and tech 41%

It appears that 40% of NASA's 1995 budget went to human space flight.

24. See Selected Answers, page A78

25.

Ultraviolet Index

UV Index
12
10
8
6
4
2

Denver, CO
Atlanta, GA
Miami, FL
Bosie, ID
Concord, NH

City

It appears that Denver, CO has nearly three times as much UV exposure than Concord, NH.

26. See Selected Answers, page A78

21. Use a dot plot to display the data. The data represent the lifespan (in days) of 40 houseflies.

9	9	4	4	8	11	10	5	8	13	9	6	7	11
13	11	6	9	8	14	10	6	10	10	8	7	14	11
7	8	6	11	13	10	14	14	8	13	14	10

22. Use a pie chart to display the data. The data represent the number of Nobel Prize laureates by country during the years 1901–1993.

United States	170	France	24
United Kingdom	69	USSR	10
Germany	59	Other	88

23. Use a pie chart to display the data. The data represent the 1995 NASA budget (in billions of dollars) divided among three categories. *(Source: NASA)*

Human space flight	5.7
Science, aeronautics, and technology	5.9
Mission support	2.7

24. Use a Pareto chart to display the data. The data represent the 1995 NASA space shuttle operations expenditures (in millions of dollars). *(Source: NASA)*

Orbiter	292.8	Redesigned solid rocket	373.1
System integration	190.5	Solid rocket booster	144.9
External tank	379.6	Launch and landing operations	596.4
Main engine	144.4	Mission and crew operations	298.4

25. Use a Pareto chart to display the data. The data represent the ultraviolet index for five cities at noon on June 30, 1998. *(Source: National Oceanic and Atmospheric Administration)*

| Atlanta, GA | Boise, ID | Concord, NH | Denver, CO | Miami, FL |
| 9 | 7 | 4 | 11 | 8 |

26. Use a scatter plot to display the data. The data represent the hours worked and the hourly wage (in dollars) for a sample of 12 production workers. Describe any trends shown.

Hours	Hourly Wage
33	12.16
37	9.98
34	10.79
40	11.71
35	11.80
33	11.51
40	13.65
33	12.05
28	10.54
45	10.33
37	11.57
28	10.17

27.

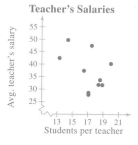

Teacher's Salaries

It appears that a teacher's average salary decreases as the number of students per teacher increases.

28.

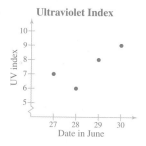

Ultraviolet Index

It appears that the UV index increased through the last days of the month of June.

29. See Odd Answers, page A49

30. See Selected Answers, page A78

31. When data is taken at regular intervals over a period of time, a time series chart should be used.

Sales for Company A

32. See Selected Answers, page A78

---

27. Use a scatter plot to display the data. The data represent the number of students per teacher and the average teacher salary (in thousands of dollars) for a sample of 10 school districts. Describe any trends shown.

Number of Students per Teacher	Average Teacher's Salary
17.1	28.7
17.5	47.5
18.9	31.8
17.1	28.1
20.0	40.3
18.6	33.8
14.4	49.8
16.5	37.5
13.3	42.5
18.4	31.9

28. Use a time series chart to display the data. The data represent the ultraviolet index for Memphis, TN at noon on June 27–30, 1998. *(Source: National Oceanic and Atmospheric Administration)*

June 27	June 28	June 29	June 30
7	6	8	9

29. Use a time series chart to display the data. The data represent the prices of whole milk (in dollars per half gallon) for the indicated years. *(Source: U.S. Bureau of Labor Statistics)*

1990	1991	1992	1993	1994	1995	1996
1.39	1.40	1.39	1.43	1.44	1.48	1.65

30. Use a time series chart to display the data. The data represent the prices of T-bone steak (in dollars per pound) for the indicated years. *(Source: U.S. Bureau of Labor Statistics)*

1990	1991	1992	1993	1994	1995	1996
5.45	5.21	5.39	5.77	5.86	5.92	5.87

Extending the Basics

A Misleading Graph? In Exercises 31 and 32, explain why the graph is misleading. Redraw the graph so that it is not misleading.

31.

Sales for Company A

32.

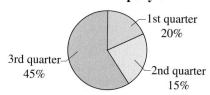

Sales for Company B

	1st quarter	2nd quarter	3rd quarter	4th quarter
	20%	15%	45%	20%

<table>
<tr><td>2.3</td><td># Measures of Central Tendency</td></tr>
</table>

Mean, Median, and Mode • Weighted Mean and Mean of Grouped Data • The Shape of Distributions

What You Should Learn

- *How to find the mean, median, and mode of a population and a sample*
- *How to find a weighted mean and the mean of a frequency distribution*
- *How to describe the shape of a distribution as symmetric, uniform, or skewed*

Mean, Median, and Mode

A **measure of central tendency** is a value that represents a typical, or central, entry of a data set. The three most commonly used measures of central tendency are the mean, the median, and the mode.

> **DEFINITION**
>
> The **mean** of a data set is the sum of the data entries divided by the number of entries. To find the mean of a data set, use one of the following formulas.
>
> $$\text{Population Mean: } \mu = \frac{\Sigma x}{N} \qquad \text{Sample Mean: } \bar{x} = \frac{\Sigma x}{n}$$

Study Tip

Symbol	Description
Σ	The uppercase Greek letter sigma; indicates a summation of values
x	A variable that represents quantitative data entries
N	Number of entries in a population
n	Number of entries in a sample
μ	The lowercase Greek letter mu; the population mean
$\bar{x}$	Read as "x bar;" the sample mean

► EXAMPLE 1   *Finding a Sample Mean*

The prices, in dollars, for a sample of room air conditioners (10,000 Btu/hr) are listed. What is the mean price of the air conditioners? *(Source: Consumer Reports)*

500   840   470   480   420   440   440

SOLUTION   The sum of the air conditioner prices is

$$\Sigma x = 500 + 840 + 470 + 480 + 420 + 440 + 440 = 3590.$$

To find the mean price, divide the sum of the prices by the number of prices in the sample.

$$\bar{x} = \frac{\Sigma x}{n} = \frac{3590}{7} \approx 513$$

So, the mean price for one of the air conditioners is about $513.

> ### *Try It Yourself 1*
>
> Find the mean age of the residents of Akhiok. Use the population data set given in the chapter opener on page 28.
>
> **a.** *Find the sum* of the data entries.
> **b.** *Divide the sum* by the number of data entries.
> **c.** *Interpret the results* in the context of the data.   *Answer: Page A32* ◄

DEFINITION

The **median** of a data set is the middle data entry when the data set is sorted in ascending or descending order. If the data set has an even number of entries, the median is the mean of the two middle data entries.

▶ **EXAMPLE 2**   *Finding the Median*

Find the median of the air conditioner prices given in Example 1.

SOLUTION   To find the median price, first order the data.

420   440   440   470   480   500   840

Because there are seven entries (an odd number), the median is the middle, or fourth, data entry. So, the median air conditioner price is $470.

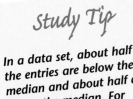

Study Tip

In a data set, about half the entries are below the median and about half are above the median. For instance, in Example 2, three of the prices are below $470 and three are above $470.

> *Try It Yourself 2*
>
> Find the median age of the residents of Akhiok.
>
> **a.** *Order* the data entries.
> **b.** Find the *middle data entry*.
> **c.** *Interpret the results* in the context of the data.   *Answer: Page A32* ◀

▶ **EXAMPLE 3**   *Finding the Median*

The air conditioner priced at $480 is discontinued. What is the median price of the remaining air conditioners?

SOLUTION   The remaining prices, in order, are 420, 440, 440, 470, 500, and 840. Because there are six entries (an even number), the median is the mean of the two middle entries.

$$\text{Median} = \frac{440 + 470}{2} = 455$$

So, the median price of the remaining air conditioners is $455.

Akhiok, Alaska is a fishing village on Kodiak Island.

(Photograph© Roy Corral.)

> *Try It Yourself 3*
>
> Suppose that one of the families of Akhiok relocates to another city. The ages of the family members are 33, 34, 11, 6, and 56. What is the median age of the remaining residents?
>
> **a.** *Order* the data entries.
> **b.** *Find the mean* of the two middle data entries.   *Answer: Page A32* ◀

DEFINITION

The **mode** of a data set is the data entry that occurs with the greatest frequency. If no entry is repeated, the data set has no mode. If two entries occur with the same greatest frequency, each entry is a mode and the data set is called **bimodal.**

> ▶ **EXAMPLE 4**   *Finding the Mode*

Find the mode of the air conditioner prices given in Example 1.

Insight

The mode is the only measure of central tendency that can be used to describe data at the nominal level of measurement.

SOLUTION   To find the mode, it helps to order the data.

420   440   440   470   480   500   840

From the ordered data, you can see that the entry of 440 occurs twice while the other data entries occur only once. So, the mode of the air conditioner prices is $440.

Try It Yourself 4

Find the mode of the ages of the Akhiok residents. Use the data given in the chapter opener on page 28.

a. Find the *frequency* of each data entry.
b. Identify the entry, or entries, that occur with the *greatest frequency*.
c. *Interpret the results* in the context of the data.   *Answer: Page A32*

> ▶ **EXAMPLE 5**   *Finding the Mode*

Political Party	Frequency
Democrat	34
Republican	56
Other	21
Did not respond	9

At a political debate a sample of audience members was asked to name the political party to which they belong. Their responses are summarized in the table at the left. What is the mode of the responses?

SOLUTION   The response occurring with the greatest frequency is "Republican." So, the mode is "Republican," which means that, in this sample, there were more Republicans than people of any other single affiliation.

Try It Yourself 5

In a survey, 250 baseball fans were asked if Mark McGwire's home run record would ever be broken. One hundred sixty-nine of the fans responded "yes," 54 responded "no," and 27 "didn't know." What is the mode of the responses?

a. Identify the entry that occurs with the *greatest frequency*.
b. *Interpret the results* in the context of the data.   *Answer: Page A32*

While the mean, the median, and the mode each describe a typical entry of a data set, there are advantages and disadvantages of using each, especially when the data set contains outliers. An **outlier** is a data entry that is far removed from the other entries in the data set.

EXAMPLE 6   *Comparing the Mean, the Median, and the Mode*

Find the mean, the median, and the mode of the following sample ages of a class. Which measure of central tendency best describes a typical entry?

20   20   20   20   20   20   21   21   21   21
22   22   22   23   23   23   23   24   24   65
                                                    Outlier

SOLUTION

Mean: $\bar{x} = \dfrac{\Sigma x}{n} = \dfrac{475}{20} = 23.75$ years

Median: Median $= \dfrac{21 + 22}{2} = 21.5$ years

Mode: The entry occurring with the greatest frequency is 20 years.

There is no right answer to the question "Which measure of central tendency best describes a typical data entry?" The mean takes every entry into account but is influenced by the outlier of 65. The median also takes every entry into account and it is not affected by the outlier. In this case the mode exists, but it doesn't appear to represent a typical entry. Sometimes a graphical comparison can help you decide which measure of central tendency best represents a data set. The histogram shows the distribution of the data and the location of the mean, the median, and the mode.

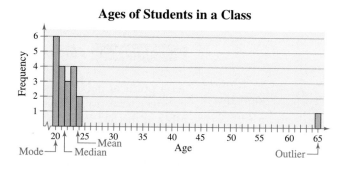

Ages of Students in a Class

Picturing the World

The National Association of Realtors keeps a databank of existing-home sales. One list uses the *median* price of existing homes sold and another uses the *mean* price of existing homes sold. The sales for the first quarter of 1998 are shown in the following graph. *(Source: National Association of Realtors)*

1998 U.S. Existing-Home Sales

Notice in the graph that each month the mean price is about $30,000 more than the median price. What factors would cause the mean price to be greater than the median price?

Try It Yourself 6

Remove the data entry of 65 from the preceding data set. Then rework the example. How does the absence of this outlier change the measures?

a. Find the *mean,* the *median,* and the *mode.*
b. Compare these measures of central tendency with those found in Example 6.

Answer: Page A33

Weighted Mean and Mean of Grouped Data

Sometimes data sets contain entries that have a greater effect on the mean than do other entries. To find the mean of such data sets, you must find the weighted mean.

DEFINITION

A **weighted mean** is the mean of a data set whose entries have varying weights. A weighted mean is given by

$$\bar{x} = \frac{\Sigma(x \cdot w)}{\Sigma w}$$

where w is the weight of each entry x.

▶ **EXAMPLE 7** *Finding a Weighted Mean*

You are taking a class in which your grade is determined from five sources: 50% from your test mean, 15% from your midterm, 20% from your final exam, 10% from your computer lab work, and 5% from your homework. Your scores are 86 (test mean), 96 (midterm), 82 (final exam), 98 (computer lab), and 100 (homework). What is the weighted mean of your scores?

SOLUTION Begin by organizing the scores and the weights in a table.

Source	Score, x	Weight, w	xw
Test Mean	86	0.5	43
Midterm	96	0.15	14.4
Final	82	0.2	16.4
Computer Lab	98	0.1	9.8
Homework	100	0.05	5
		$\Sigma w = 1$	$\Sigma(x \cdot w) = 88.6$

$$\Sigma(x \cdot w) = 88.6$$

$$\bar{x} = \frac{\Sigma(x \cdot w)}{\Sigma w} = \frac{88.6}{1} = 88.6$$

So, your weighted mean for the course is 88.6.

Try It Yourself 7

An error was made in grading your final exam. Instead of getting 82, you scored 98. What is your new weighted mean?

a. Multiply each score by its weight and *find the sum of the weighted entries.*
b. Find the *sum of the weights.*
c. Find the *weighted mean.*
d. *Interpret the results* in the context of the data. *Answer: Page A33* ◀

To find the mean of the grouped data, use the following.

Study Tip

If the frequency distribution represents a population, then the mean of the frequency distribution is approximated by

$$\mu = \frac{\Sigma(x \cdot f)}{N}$$

where $N = \Sigma f$.

DEFINITION

The **mean of a frequency distribution** for a sample is approximated by

$$\bar{x} = \frac{\Sigma(x \cdot f)}{n}$$

Note that $n = \Sigma f$.

where x and f are the midpoints and frequencies of a class, respectively.

GUIDELINES

Finding the Mean of a Frequency Distribution

In Words	*In Symbols*
1. Find the midpoint of each class.	$x = \dfrac{\text{Lower Limit} + \text{Upper Limit}}{2}$
2. Find the sum of the products of the midpoints and the frequencies.	$\Sigma(x \cdot f)$
3. Find the sum of the frequencies.	$n = \Sigma f$
4. Find the mean of the frequency distribution.	$\bar{x} = \dfrac{\Sigma(x \cdot f)}{n}$

Class Midpoint

x	f	$(x \cdot f)$
12.5	6	75.0
24.5	10	245.0
36.5	13	474.5
48.5	8	388.0
60.5	5	302.5
72.5	6	435.0
84.5	2	169.0
	$n = 50$	$\Sigma = 2089.0$

EXAMPLE 8 **Finding the Mean of a Frequency Distribution**

Use the frequency distribution at the left to approximate the mean number of minutes Internet subscribers spent online during their most recent session.

SOLUTION

$$\bar{x} = \frac{\Sigma(x \cdot f)}{n} = \frac{2089}{50} \approx 41.8$$

So, the mean time spent online was approximately 41.8 minutes.

Try It Yourself 8

Use a frequency distribution to approximate the mean age of the residents of Akhiok. (See Try It Yourself 2 on page 33.)

a. Find the *midpoint* of each class.
b. Find the *sum of the products* of each midpoint and corresponding frequency.
c. Find the *sum of the frequencies.*
d. Find the *mean.*

Answer: Page A33

The Shape of Distributions

A graph reveals several characteristics of a frequency distribution. One such characteristic is the shape of the distribution.

> **DEFINITION**
>
> A frequency distribution is **symmetric** when a vertical line can be drawn through the middle of a graph of the distribution and the resulting halves are approximately mirror images.
>
> A frequency distribution is **uniform** (or **rectangular**) when all entries, or classes, in the distribution have equal frequencies. A uniform distribution is also symmetric.
>
> A frequency distribution is skewed if the "tail" of the graph elongates more to one side than to the other. A distribution is **skewed left (negatively skewed)** if its tail extends to the left. A distribution is **skewed right (positively skewed)** if its tail extends to the right.

When a distribution is symmetric, the mean, median, and mode are equal. If a distribution is skewed left, the mean is less than the median and the median is usually less than the mode. If a distribution is skewed right, the mean is greater than the median and the median is usually greater than the mode. Examples of these commonly occurring distributions are shown.

Insight

The mean will always fall in the direction the distribution is skewed. For instance, when a distribution is skewed left, the mean is to the left of the median.

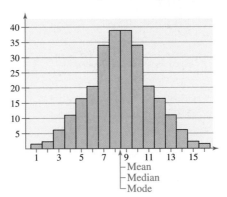

Symmetric Distribution

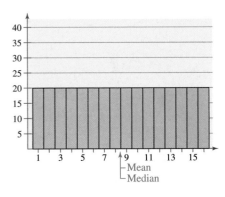

Uniform Distribution

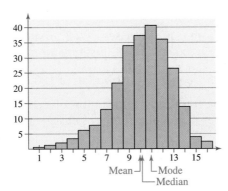

Skewed-Left Distribution

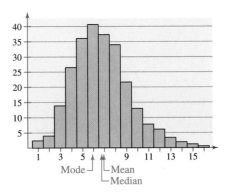

Skewed-Right Distribution

2.3 EXERCISES

HELP

StatPro 2.3

Internet Statistics 2.3

Student Solutions Manual 2.3

Videos 2.3

Try It Yourself Answers 2.3

1. False
2. False
3. False
4. False
5. Skewed right
6. Symmetric
7. Uniform
8. Skewed left
9. (7)
10. (5)
11. (8)
12. (6)

Basic Skills and Concepts

True or False   In Exercises 1–4, determine whether the statement is true or false. If it is false, rewrite it so it is a true statement.

1. The median is the measure of central tendency most likely to be affected by an extreme value (an outlier).

2. Every data set must have a mode.

3. Some quantitative data sets do not have a median.

4. The mean is the only measure of central tendency that can be used for data at the nominal level of measurement.

Graphical Analysis   In Exercises 5–8, determine whether the shape of the distribution in the histogram is symmetric, uniform, skewed left, skewed right, or none of these. Justify your answer.

5.
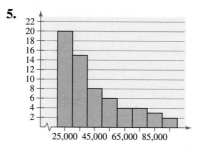

6.
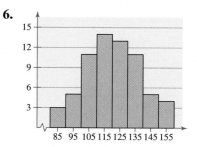

7.
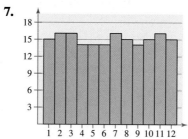

8.
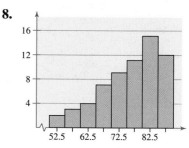

Matching   In Exercises 9–12, match the distribution with one of the graphs in Exercises 5–8. Justify your decision.

9. The frequency distribution of 180 rolls of a dodecagon (a 12-sided die)

10. The frequency distribution of salaries at a company where a few executives make much higher salaries than the majority of employees

11. The frequency distribution of scores on a 90-point test where a few students scored much lower than the majority of students

12. The frequency distribution of weights for a sample of seventh grade boys

13. (a) $\bar{x} = 6.23$
median = 6
mode = 5

(b) median

14. (a) $\bar{x} = 19.6$
median = 19.5
mode = 19, 20

(b) mean

15. (a) $\bar{x} = 4.57$
median = 4.8
mode = 4.8

(b) median

16. (a) $\bar{x} = 184.6$
median = 182.5
mode = not possible

(b) mean

17. (a) $\bar{x} = 97$
median = 97.2
mode = 94.8, 95.4, 97.2, 103.1

(b) median

18. (a) $\bar{x} = 61.15$
median = 55
mode = 80, 125

(b) median

19. (a) $\bar{x}$ = not possible
median = not possible
mode = "Worse"

(b) mode

20. (a) $\bar{x}$ = not possible
median = not possible
mode = "Watchful"

(b) mode

21. (a) $\bar{x} = 170.63$
median = 169.3
mode = not possible

(b) mean

22. (a) $\bar{x}$ = not possible
median = not possible
mode = "Domestic"

(b) mode

23. (a) $\bar{x} = 22.6$
median = 19
mode = 14

(b) median

Mean, Median, and Mode In Exercises 13–26, do the following.

(a) Find the mean, median and mode of the data, if possible. If it is not possible, explain why the measure of central tendency cannot be found.

(b) Which measure of central tendency best represents the data? Explain your reasoning.

13. The maximum number of seats in a sample of sport utility vehicles *(Source: Consumer Reports)*

6 6 9 9 6 5 5 5 7 5 5 5 8

14. The education cost per student (in thousands of dollars) from a sample of ten liberal arts colleges *(Source: U.S. News and World Report)*

22 26 19 20 20 18 21 17 19 14

15. The time (in seconds) for a sample of seven sports cars to go from 0 to 60 miles per hour *(Source: Motor Trend)*

3.7 4.0 4.8 4.8 4.8 4.8 5.1

16. The cholesterol level of a sample of 10 female employees

154 216 171 188 229 203 184 173 181 147

17. The points per game scored by each NBA team during a recent season

94.8 100.6 98.9 103.1 87.5 90.6 97.8 94.2 99.6 100.5
95.4 97.2 100.0 94.8 95.3 96.1 97.2 95.4 100.2 102.8
99.0 96.4 90.5 100.9 95.5 103.1 89.2 99.4

18. The duration (in minutes) of every power failure at a residence in the last 10 years

18 26 45 75 125 80 33 40 44 49
89 80 96 125 12 61 31 63 103 28

19. The responses of a sample of 1040 people who were asked if the air quality in their community is better or worse than it was 10 years ago

Better: 346   Worse: 450   Same: 244

20. The responses of a sample of 1019 people who were asked how they felt when they thought about crime

Unconcerned: 34   Watchful: 672   Nervous: 125   Afraid: 188

21. The top speed (in miles per hour) for a sample of seven sports cars *(Source: Motor Trend)*

187.3 181.8 180.0 169.3 162.2 158.1 155.7

22. The responses of a sample of 1001 people who were asked if their next vehicle purchase will be foreign or domestic

Domestic: 704   Foreign: 253   Don't know: 44

23. The recommended prices for several stocks that analysts predict should produce at least 10% total returns in the 21st century. *(Source: Money)*

41 20 22 14 15 25 18 40 17 14

24. (a) $\bar{x} = 16.6$
median = 15
mode = not possible
(b) mean

25. (a) $\bar{x} = 14.11$
median = 14.25
mode = 2.5
(b) mean

26. (a) $\bar{x} = 316.09$
median = 289
mode = not possible
(b) median

27. A = mode
B = median
C = mean

28. A = mean
B = median
C = mode

29. 85.6

30. $32,640

24. The number of weeks it took to reach a target weight for a sample of five patients with eating disorders treated by psychodynamic psychotherapy *(Source: The Journal of Consulting and Clinical Psychology)*

15.0 31.5 10.0 25.5 1.0

25. The number of weeks it took to reach a target weight for a sample of 14 patients with eating disorders treated by psychodynamic psychotherapy and cognitive behavior techniques *(Source: The Journal of Consulting and Clinical Psychology)*

2.5 20.0 11.0 10.5 17.5 16.5 13.0
15.5 26.5 2.5 27.0 28.5 1.5 5.0

26. The number of aircraft 11 airlines have in their fleets *(Source: Airline Transport Association)*

563 667 443 544 358 178 289 182 105 82 66

Graphical Analysis In Exercises 27 and 28, the letters A, B, and C are marked on the horizontal axis. From these, determine which is the mean, which is the median, and which is the mode. Justify your answers.

27. **Sick Days Used by Employees**

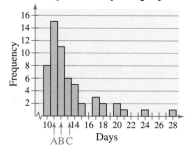

28. **Hourly Wages of Employees**

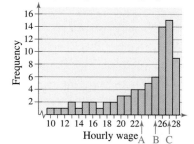

Finding the Weighted Mean In Exercises 29–32, find the weighted mean of the data.

29. The scores and their percent of the final grade for a statistics student are given. What is the student's mean score?

	Score	Percent of final grade
Homework	85	15%
Quiz	80	20%
Quiz	92	20%
Quiz	76	20%
Final Exam	93	25%

30. The average starting salaries (by degree attained) for 25 employees at a company are given. What is the mean starting salary for these employees?

8 with MBAs: $42,500   17 with BAs in business: $28,000

31. 2.8
32. 82
33. 65.5
34. 70.14
35. 35.01
36. 15.28

31. A student receives the following grades, with an A worth 4 points, a B worth 3 points, a C worth 2 points, and a D worth 1 point. What is the student's mean grade point score?

B in two 3-credit classes   D in one 2-credit class

A in one 4-credit class   C in one 3-credit class

32. The mean scores for a statistics course (by major) are given. What is the mean score for the class?

8 engineering majors: 83   5 math majors: 87

11 business majors: 79

Finding the Mean of Grouped Data In Exercises 33–36, approximate the mean of the grouped data.

33. The heights (in inches) of 16 female students in a physical education class

Height (in inches)	Frequency
60–62	3
63–65	4
66–68	7
69–71	2

34. The heights (in inches) of 21 male students in a physical education class

Height (in inches)	Frequency
63–65	2
66–68	4
69–71	8
72–74	5
75–77	2

35. The ages of residents of Medicine Bow, Wyoming, according to the 1990 census *(Source: U.S. Bureau of the Census)*

Age	Frequency
0–9	57
10–19	68
20–29	36
30–39	55
40–49	71
50–59	44
60–69	36
70–79	14
80–89	8

36. The lengths of long-distance calls (in minutes) made by one person in one year

Length of call	Number of calls
1–5	12
6–10	26
11–15	20
16–20	7
21–25	11
26–30	7
31–35	4
36–40	4
41–45	1

Shape of a Distribution In Exercises 37–40, construct a frequency distribution and a frequency histogram of the data using the indicated number of classes. Describe the shape of the histogram as symmetric, uniform, negatively skewed, positively skewed, or none of these.

37. Positively Skewed

38. Positively Skewed

39. Symmetric

40. Uniform

41. (a) $\bar{x} = 6.01$
median $= 6.01$

(b) $\bar{x} = 5.95$
median $= 6.01$

(c) mean

42. (a) $\bar{x} = 26.03$
median $= 14.4$

(b) $\bar{x} = 20.04$
median $= 13.55$

(c) mean

(d) median

37. Number of classes: 6

Data set: The number of days 20 patients remained hospitalized

6 9 7 14 4 5 6 8 4 11 10 6 8 6 5 7 6 6 3 11

38. Number of classes: 5

Data set: The number of beds in a sample of 24 hospitals

149 167 162 127 130 180 160 167 221 145 137 194
207 150 254 262 244 297 137 204 166 174 180 151

39. Number of classes: 5

Data set: The heights (to the nearest inch) of 30 males

67 76 69 68 72 68 65 63 75 69 66 72 67 66 69
73 64 62 71 73 68 72 71 65 69 66 74 72 68 69

40. Number of classes: 6

Data set: The results of rolling a six-sided die 30 times

1 4 6 1 5 3 2 5 4 6 1 2 4 3 5
6 3 2 1 1 5 6 2 4 4 3 1 6 2 4

41. *Coffee Content* During a quality assurance check, the actual coffee content of six jars of instant coffee was recorded as 6.03, 5.59, 6.40, 6.00, 5.99 and 6.02.

(a) Find the mean and the median of the coffee content.

(b) Suppose the third value had been incorrectly measured and was actually 6.04. Find the mean and median of the coffee content again.

(c) Which measure of central tendency, the mean or the median, was affected more by the data entry error?

42. *U.S. Exports* The following data are the U.S. exports (in billions of dollars) to 19 countries for a recent year. *(Source: U.S. Department of Commerce)*

Canada	133.7	Japan	67.5
Mexico	56.8	United Kingdom	30.9
Germany	23.5	South Korea	26.6
Taiwan	18.4	Singapore	16.7
Netherlands	16.6	France	14.4
China	12.0	Brazil	12.7
Australia	12.0	Belgium	12.5
Malaysia	8.5	Italy	8.8
Switzerland	8.4	Thailand	7.2
Saudi Arabia	7.3		

(a) Find the mean and median.

(b) Find the mean and median without the U.S. exports to Canada.

(c) Which measure of central tendency, the mean or the median, was affected more by the elimination of the Canadian export data?

(d) Which of the two measures, the mean or the median, is more appropriate for this list?

43. (a) Mean
   (b) Median
   (c) Mode
44. Car A
45. (a) $\bar{x} = 49.23$
   (b) median $= 46.5$
   (c)
```
1 | 13
2 | 28
3 | 6667778      median
4 | 13467
5 | 1113         mean
6 | 1234
7 | 2246
8 | 5
9 | 0
```
   (d) Positively skewed
46. 49.17
   Using a trimmed mean elimi-
   nates potential outliers that
   may affect the mean of all the
   entries.
47. Two different symbols are
   needed since they describe a
   measure of central tendency
   for two different sets of data
   (sample is a subset of the
   population).

Extending the Basics

43. *Data Analysis*   A consumer testing service obtained the following miles per gallon in five test runs performed with three types of compact cars.

	Run 1	Run 2	Run 3	Run 4	Run 5
Car A:	28	32	28	30	34
Car B:	31	29	31	29	31
Car C:	29	32	28	32	30

(a) If the manufacturer of Car A wants to advertise that their car performed best in this test, which measure of central tendency—mean, median, or mode—should be used for their claim? Explain your reasoning.

(b) If the manufacturer of Car B wants to advertise that their car performed best in this test, which measure of central tendency—mean, median, or mode—should be used for their claim? Explain your reasoning.

(c) If the manufacturer of Car C wants to advertise that their car performed best in this test, which measure of central tendency—mean, median, or mode—should be used for their claim? Explain your reasoning.

44. *Midrange*   The midrange is (maximum entry + minimum entry)/2. Which of the dealers in the previous problem would prefer to use the midrange statistic in their ads? Explain your reasoning.

45. *Data Analysis*   Students in an experimental psychology class did research on depression as a sign of stress. A test was administered to a sample of 30 students. The scores are given.

44 51 11 90 76 36 64 37 43 72 53 62 36 74 51
72 37 28 38 61 47 63 36 41 22 37 51 46 85 13

(a) Find the mean of the data.

(b) Find the median of the data.

(c) Draw a stem-and-leaf display for the data using one line per stem. Locate the mean and median on the display.

(d) Describe the shape of the distribution.

46. *Trimmed Mean*   To find the 10% trimmed mean of a data set, order the data, delete the lowest 10% of the entries and the highest 10% of the entries, and find the mean of the remaining entries. Find the 10% trimmed mean for the data in the previous problem. Compare the four measures of central tendency. What is the benefit of using a trimmed mean versus using a mean found using all data entries? Explain your reasoning.

47. *Writing*   The population mean μ and the sample mean $\bar{x}$ have essentially the same formulas. Explain why it is necessary to have two different symbols.

Measures of Variation

2.4

Range • Deviation, Variance, and Standard Deviation • Interpreting Standard Deviation • Standard Deviation for Grouped Data

What You Should Learn

- **How to find the range of a data set**
- **How to find the variance and standard deviation of a population and of a sample**
- **How to use the Empirical Rule and Chebychev's Theorem to interpret standard deviation**
- **How to approximate the sample standard deviation for grouped data**

Range

In this section, you will learn different ways to measure the variation of a data set. The simplest measure is the range of the set.

> **DEFINITION**
>
> The **range** of a data set is the difference between the maximum and minimum entries in the set.
>
> Range = (Maximum entry) − (Minimum entry)

EXAMPLE 1   *Finding the Range of a Data Set*

Two corporations each hired 10 graduates. The starting salaries for each are as follows.

Starting Salaries for Corporation A (1000s of dollars)

Salary	41	38	39	45	47	41	44	41	37	42

Starting Salaries for Corporation B (1000s of dollars)

Salary	40	23	41	50	49	32	41	29	52	58

Find the range of the starting salaries for Corporation A.

SOLUTION   To find the least and greatest salaries, it helps to order the data.

37   38   39   41   41   41   42   44   45   47

Minimum ⟶   Maximum ⟵

Range = (Maximum salary) − (Minimum salary) = 47 − 37 = 10

So, the range of the starting salaries for Corporation A is 10 or $10,000.

Insight

Both data sets in Example 1 have a mean of 41.5, a median of 41, and a mode of 41. And yet the two sets of 41 differ significantly.

The difference is that the entries in the second set have greater variation. Your goal in this section is to learn how to measure the variation of a data set.

> ### Try It Yourself 1
>
> Find the range of the starting salaries for Corporation B.
>
> **a.** Identify the *minimum* and *maximum* salaries.
> **b.** Find the *range*.
> **c.** Compare your answer with that of Example 1.   *Answer: Page A33*

Deviation, Variance, and Standard Deviation

As a measure of variation, the range has the advantage of being easy to compute. Its disadvantage, however, is that it uses only two entries from the data set. Two measures of variation that use all the entries in a data set are the variance and the standard deviation. However, before you learn about these measures of variation, you need to know what is meant by the deviation of an entry in a data set.

Note to Instructor

Remind students of the reason for the difference between the symbols μ and $\bar{x}$.

DEFINITION

The **deviation** of an entry x in a population data set is the difference between the entry and the mean, μ, of the data set.

$$\text{Deviation of } x = x - \mu$$

▶ **EXAMPLE 2** *Finding the Deviations of a Data Set*

Find the deviation of each starting salary for Corporation A.

SOLUTION The mean starting salary is $\mu = 415/10 = 41.5$. To find out how much each salary deviates from the mean, subtract 41.5 from the salary. For instance, the deviation of 41 is $41 - 41.5 = -0.5$ (or $-\$500$). The table at the left lists the deviations of each of the 10 starting salaries.

Salary x	Deviation $x - \mu$
41	-0.5
38	-3.5
39	-2.5
45	3.5
47	5.5
41	-0.5
44	2.5
41	-0.5
37	-4.5
42	0.5
$\Sigma x = 415$	$\Sigma(x - \mu) = 0$

Deviations of starting salaries
for Corporation A

Try It Yourself 2

Find the deviation of each starting salary for Corporation B.

a. Find the *mean* of the data set.
b. *Subtract* the mean from each salary.
c. *Organize* your results in a table. *Answer: Page A33* ◀

In Example 2, notice that the sum of the deviations is zero. Because this is true for any data set, it doesn't make sense to find the average of the deviations. To overcome this problem, you can square each deviation. In a population data set, the mean of the squares of the deviations is called the **population variance.**

Study Tip

When you add the squares of the deviations, you compute a quantity called the sum of squares, denoted SS_x.

DEFINITION

The **population variance** of a population data set of N entries is

$$\text{Population variance} = \sigma^2 = \frac{\Sigma(x - \mu)^2}{N}$$

The symbol σ is the lowercase Greek letter sigma.

Insight

The disadvantage with the variance is that its units are usually meaningless. For instance, the variance for the starting salaries is measured in "square dollars." You'll be able to return to the original unit of the data by using the standard deviation.

DEFINITION

The **population standard deviation** of a population data set of N entries is the square root of the variance.

$$\text{Population standard deviation} = \sigma = \sqrt{\sigma^2} = \sqrt{\frac{\Sigma(x - \mu)^2}{N}}$$

GUIDELINES

Finding the Population Variance and Standard Deviation

In Words	*In Symbols*
1. Find the mean of the population data set.	$\mu = \dfrac{\Sigma x}{N}$
2. Find the deviation of each entry.	$x - \mu$
3. Square each deviation.	$(x - \mu)^2$
4. Add to get the **sum of squares**.	$SS_x = \Sigma(x - \mu)^2$
5. Divide by N to get the **population variance**.	$\sigma^2 = \dfrac{\Sigma(x - \mu)^2}{N}$
6. Find the square root of the variance to get the **population standard deviation**.	$\sigma = \sqrt{\dfrac{\Sigma(x - \mu)^2}{N}}$

▶ **EXAMPLE 3**   *Finding the Population Standard Deviation*

Find the population variance and standard deviation of the starting salaries for Corporation A.

SOLUTION   The table at the left summarizes the steps used to find SS_x.

$$SS_x = 88.5, \qquad N = 10, \qquad \sigma^2 = \frac{88.5}{10} = 8.85, \qquad \sigma = \sqrt{8.85} \approx 2.97$$

So, the population variance is 8.85 and the population standard deviation is about 3.0 or $3000.

Salary x	Deviation $x - \mu$	Squares $(x - \mu)^2$
41	−0.5	0.25
38	−3.5	12.25
39	−2.5	6.25
45	3.5	12.25
47	5.5	30.25
41	−0.5	0.25
44	2.5	6.25
41	−0.5	0.25
37	−4.5	20.25
42	0.5	0.25
	$\Sigma = 0$	$SS_x = 88.5$

Sum of squares of starting salaries for Corporation A

Try It Yourself 3

Find the population standard deviation of the starting salaries for Corporation B.

a. Find the *mean* and each *deviation,* as you did in Try It Yourself 2.
b. *Square* each deviation and *add* to get the sum of squares.
c. *Divide* by N to get the population variance.
d. Find the *square root* of the variance.
e. *Interpret* the results by giving the standard deviation in dollars.

Answer: Page A33 ◀

Insight

Often the population standard deviation is unknown and the sample standard deviation is used to estimate it. The formulas for the variance and standard deviation of a sample differ slightly from those for populations. Dividing by $n - 1$ rather than n produces higher estimates.

DEFINITION

The **sample variance** and **sample standard deviation** of a sample data set of n entries is

$$\text{Sample variance} = s^2 = \frac{\Sigma(x - \bar{x})^2}{n - 1}$$

$$\text{Sample standard deviation} = s = \sqrt{s^2} = \sqrt{\frac{\Sigma(x - \bar{x})^2}{n - 1}}.$$

GUIDELINES

Finding the Sample Variance and Standard Deviation

In Words	*In Symbols*
1. Find the mean of the sample data set.	$\bar{x} = \dfrac{\Sigma x}{n}$
2. Find the deviation of each entry.	$x - \bar{x}$
3. Square each deviation.	$(x - \bar{x})^2$
4. Add to get the **sum of squares.**	$SS_x = \Sigma(x - \bar{x})^2$
5. Divide by $n - 1$ to get the **sample variance.**	$s^2 = \dfrac{\Sigma(x - \bar{x})^2}{n - 1}$
6. Find the square root of the variance to get the **sample standard deviation.**	$s = \sqrt{\dfrac{\Sigma(x - \bar{x})^2}{n - 1}}$

See *Minitab* and *TI-83* steps on pages 94, 95.

▶ **EXAMPLE 4** *Finding the Sample Standard Deviation*

Suppose that the starting salaries given in Example 1 are for the Chicago branches of Corporations A and B. Each corporation has several other branches, and you plan to use the starting salaries of the Chicago branches to estimate the starting salaries for the larger populations. Find the *sample* standard deviation of the starting salaries for the Chicago branch of Corporation A.

SOLUTION

$$SS_x = 88.5, \qquad n = 10, \qquad s^2 = \frac{88.5}{9} \approx 9.83, \qquad s = \sqrt{9.83} \approx 3.14$$

So, the sample variance is about 9.83 and the sample standard deviation is about 3.1 or $3100.

Try It Yourself 4

Find the sample standard deviation of the starting salaries for the Chicago branch of Corporation B.

a. Find the *sum of squares,* as you did in Try It Yourself 3.
b. *Divide* by $n - 1$ to get the sample variance.
c. Find the *square root* of the variance. *Answer: Page A33* ◀

Office Rental Rates		
20.75	27.25	14.25
18.00	19.75	29.75
37.00	28.75	25.00
24.25	22.25	24.50
24.25	23.00	19.25
24.75	19.50	35.00
19.50	23.25	25.50
24.50	18.00	15.25

> **EXAMPLE 5** **Using Technology to Find the Standard Deviation**

Sample office rental rates, in dollars per square foot per year, for Atlanta's central business district are listed at the left. Use a calculator or a computer to find the mean rental rate and the sample standard deviation. *(Source: Cushman & Wakefield Inc.)*

SOLUTION   Minitab, Excel, and the TI-83 each have features that automatically calculate the mean and the standard deviation of data sets. Try using this technology to find the mean and the standard deviation of the office rental rates. From the displays, you can see that $\bar{x} \approx 23.469$ and $s \approx 5.49$.

MINITAB

Descriptive Statistics

Variable	N	Mean	Median	TrMean	StDev
Rental Rates	24	23.47	23.75	23.27	5.49

Variable	SE Mean	Minimum	Maximum	Q1	Q3
Rental Rates	1.12	14.25	37.00	19.50	25.38

Note to Instructor

The standard deviations reported by Minitab and Excel represent sample standard deviations. The TI-83 also reports σ, the population standard deviation. Ask students to compare the values of s and σ shown from the same data.

EXCEL

	A	B
1	Mean	23.46875
2	Standard Error	1.1211
3	Median	23.75
4	Mode	18
5	Standard Deviation	5.492244
6	Sample Variance	30.16474
7	Kurtosis	0.809987
8	Skewness	0.726594
9	Range	22.75
10	Minimum	14.25
11	Maximum	37
12	Sum	563.25
13	Count	24

TI-83

1-Var Stats
$\bar{x}=23.46875$
$\Sigma x=563.25$
$\Sigma x^2=13912.5625$
$Sx=5.49224379$
$\sigma x=5.376604654$
$n=24$

Sample Mean

Sample Standard Deviation

Try It Yourself 5

Sample office rental rates, in dollars per square foot per year, for Seattle's central business district are listed. Use a calculator or a computer to find the mean rental rate and the sample standard deviation.

19.00	15.50	17.75	24.25	20.50
19.75	18.25	21.75	19.50	29.75
22.75	31.00	21.00	26.50	19.50
22.00	18.75	26.50	18.75	20.00

a. *Enter* the data.
b. *Calculate* the sample mean and the sample standard deviation.

Answer: Page A33

Interpreting Standard Deviation

When interpreting the standard deviation, remember that it is a measure of the typical amount an entry deviates from the mean. The more the entries are spread out, the greater the standard deviation.

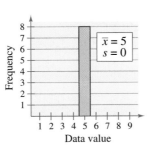

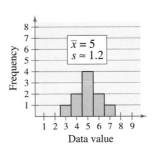

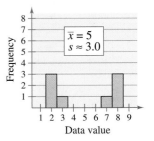

▶ **EXAMPLE 6** **Estimating Standard Deviation**

Without calculating, estimate the population standard deviation of each data set.

1.
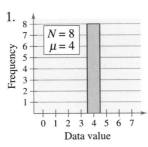

2.
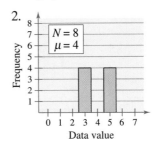

3.
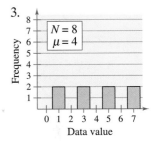

SOLUTION

1. Each of the eight entries is 4. So, each deviation is 0, which implies that $\sigma = 0$.

2. Each of the eight entries has a deviation of ± 1. So, the population standard deviation should be 1. By calculating, you can see that $\sigma = 1$.

3. Each of the eight entries has a deviation of ± 1 or ± 3. So, the population standard deviation should be about 2. By calculating, you can see that $\sigma \approx 2.24$.

Try It Yourself 6

Write a data set that has 10 entries, a mean of 10, and a population standard deviation that is approximately 3. (There are many correct answers.)

a. *Write* a data set that has five entries that are 3 units less than 10 and five entries that are 3 units more than 10.

b. *Calculate* the population standard deviation to check that σ is approximately 3.

Answer: Page A33

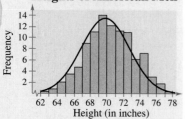
Many real-life data sets have distributions that are approximately bell shaped. Later in the text, you will study this type of distribution in detail. For now, however, the following *Empirical Rule* can help you see how valuable the standard deviation can be as a measure of variation.

Bell-Shaped Distribution

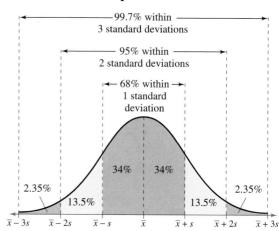

Empirical Rule (or 68-95-99.7 Rule)

For data with a (symmetric) bell-shaped distribution, the standard deviation has the following characteristics.

1. About 68% of the data lies within 1 standard deviation of the mean.
2. About 95% of the data lies within 2 standard deviations of the mean.
3. About 99.7% of the data lies within 3 standard deviations of the mean.

EXAMPLE 7   *Using the Empirical Rule*

In a survey conducted by the National Center for Health Statistics, the sample mean height of American women (ages 20–29) was 64 inches with a sample standard deviation of 2.75 inches. Estimate the percent of the women whose heights are between 64 inches and 69.5 inches.

SOLUTION   The distribution of the women's heights is shown at the left. Because the distribution is bell shaped, you can use the empirical rule. When you add two standard deviations to the mean height, you get

$$\bar{x} + 2s = 64 + 2(2.75) = 69.5.$$

So, the percent of the heights between 64 inches and 69.5 inches is

$$34\% + 13.5\% = 47.5\%.$$

Heights of American Women

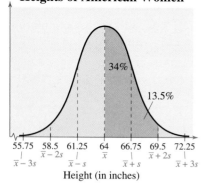

Try It Yourself 7

Estimate the percent of the heights that are between 61.25 and 64 inches.

a. How many standard deviations is 61.25 to the left of 64?
b. Use the Empirical Rule to estimate the percent of the data between $\bar{x} - s$ and $\bar{x}$.
c. *Interpret* the result in the context of the data.   *Answer: Page A33*

The following theorem applies to *all* distributions. It is named after the Russian statistician Pafnuti Chebychev (1821–1894).

Chebychev's Theorem

The portion of any data set lying within k standard deviations ($k > 1$) of the mean is at least

$$1 - \frac{1}{k^2}.$$

- $k = 2$: In any data set, at least $1 - \frac{1}{2^2} = \frac{3}{4}$, or 75%, of the data lie within 2 standard deviations of the mean.

- $k = 3$: In any data set, at least $1 - \frac{1}{3^2} = \frac{8}{9}$, or 88.9%, of the data lie within 3 standard deviations of the mean.

▶ **EXAMPLE 8**   *Using Chebychev's Theorem*

Insight

In Example 8, Chebychev's Theorem tells you that at least 75% of the population of Florida is under the age of 88.8. This is a true statement, but it is not nearly as strong a statement as could be made from reading the histogram.

In general, Chebychev's Theorem gives cautious estimates of the percent lying within k standard deviations of the mean. Remember, the theorem applies to all distributions.

The age distributions for Alaska and Florida are shown in the histograms. Decide which is which. Apply Chebychev's Theorem to the data for Florida using $k = 2$. What can you conclude?

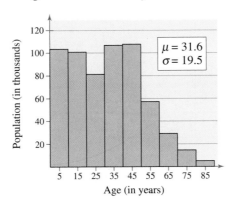
$\mu = 31.6$
$\sigma = 19.5$

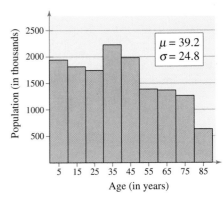
$\mu = 39.2$
$\sigma = 24.8$

SOLUTION   The histogram on the right shows Florida's age distribution. You can tell this because the population is greater and older. Moving two standard deviations to the left of the mean puts you below 0. Moving two standard deviations to the right of the mean puts you at $39.2 + 2(24.8) = 88.8$. So, you can say that at least 75% of the population of Florida is between 0 and 88.8 years old.

Try It Yourself 8

Apply Chebychev's Theorem to the data for Alaska using $k = 2$.

a. *Subtract* two standard deviations from the mean.
b. *Add* two standard deviations to the mean.
c. *Apply* Chebychev's Theorem for $k = 2$.
d. *Interpret* the result in the context of the data.   *Answer: Page A33*

Standard Deviation for Grouped Data

In Section 2.1, you learned that large data sets are usually best represented by a frequency distribution. The formula for the sample standard deviation for a frequency distribution is

$$\text{Sample standard deviation} = s = \sqrt{\frac{\Sigma(x - \bar{x})^2 f}{n - 1}}$$

where $n = \Sigma f$ is the number of entries in the data set.

> **EXAMPLE 9** **Finding the Standard Deviation for Grouped Data**

Number of Children in 50 Households						
1	3	1	1	1	1	2
2	1	0	1	1	0	0
0	1	5	0	3	6	3
0	3	1	1	1	1	6
0	1	3	6	6	1	2
2	3	0	1	1	4	1
1	2	2	0	3	0	2
4						

You collect a random sample of the number of children per household in a region. The results are shown at the left. Find the sample mean and the sample standard deviation of the data set.

SOLUTION These data could be treated as 50 individual entries and you could use the usual formula for mean and standard deviation. Because there are so many repeated numbers, however, it is easier to use a frequency distribution table.

x	f	xf
0	10	0
1	19	19
2	7	14
3	7	21
4	2	8
5	1	5
6	4	24
	$\Sigma = 50$	$\Sigma = 91$

$x - \bar{x}$	$(x - \bar{x})^2$	$(x - \bar{x})^2 f$
-1.8	3.24	32.40
-0.8	0.64	12.16
0.2	0.04	0.28
1.2	1.44	10.08
2.2	4.84	9.68
3.2	10.24	10.24
4.2	17.64	70.56
		$\Sigma = 145.40$

$$\bar{x} = \frac{\Sigma xf}{n} = \frac{91}{50} \approx 1.8 \qquad \text{Sample mean}$$

Use the sum of squares to find the sample standard deviation.

$$s = \sqrt{\frac{\Sigma(x - \bar{x})^2 f}{n - 1}} = \sqrt{\frac{145.4}{49}} \approx 1.7 \qquad \text{Sample standard deviation}$$

So, the sample mean is 1.8 children and the standard deviation is 1.7 children.

Study Tip

Remember that formulas for grouped data require you to multiply by the frequencies.

Try It Yourself 9

Change three of the 6s in the data set to 4s. How does this change the sample mean and sample standard deviation?

a. Write the first three columns of a *frequency distribution table*.
b. Find the *sample mean*.
c. Complete the *last three columns* of the frequency distribution table.
d. Find the *sample standard deviation*. *Solution: Page A33*

When a frequency distribution has classes, you can estimate the sample mean and standard deviation by using the midpoint of each class.

> **EXAMPLE 10** *Using Midpoints of Classes*

The circle graph at the right shows the results of a survey in which 100 college students were asked their average monthly earnings during the school year. Make a frequency distribution for the data. Then use the table to estimate the sample mean and the sample standard deviation of the data set.

Copyright 1998, USA TODAY. Reprinted with permission.

SOLUTION   Begin by using a frequency distribution to organize the data.

Class	x	f	xf	$x - \bar{x}$	$(x - \bar{x})^2$	$(x - \bar{x})^2 f$
0	0	33	0	-243	59,049	1,948,617
1–99	50	4	200	-193	37,249	148,996
100–199	150	10	1,500	-93	8,649	86,490
200–299	250	13	3,250	7	49	637
300–399	350	12	4,200	107	11,449	137,388
400–499	450	11	4,950	207	42,849	471,339
500+	600	17	10,200	357	127,449	2,166,633
		$\Sigma = 100$	$\Sigma = 24,300$			$\Sigma = 4,960,100$

$$\bar{x} = \frac{\Sigma xf}{n} = \frac{24,300}{100} = 243 \qquad \text{Sample mean}$$

Use the sum of squares to find the sample standard deviation.

$$s = \sqrt{\frac{\Sigma(x - \bar{x})^2 f}{n - 1}} = \sqrt{\frac{4,960,100}{99}} \approx 223.8 \qquad \text{Sample standard deviation}$$

So, the sample mean is 243 dollars per month and the sample standard deviation is 223.8 dollars per month.

> *Try It Yourself 10*
>
> In the frequency distribution, 600 was chosen to represent the class of \$500 and greater. How would the sample mean and standard deviation change if you used 650 to represent this class?
>
> **a.** Write the first three columns of a *frequency distribution table*.
> **b.** Find the *sample mean*.
> **c.** Complete the *last three columns* of the frequency distribution table.
> **d.** Find the *sample standard deviation*.   *Answer: Page A34*

2.4 EXERCISES

HELP

 StatPro 2.4

 Internet Statistics 2.4

 Student Solutions Manual 2.4

 Videos 2.4

 Try It Yourself Answers 2.4

1. The range is the difference between the maximum and minimum values of a data set. The advantage of the range is that it is easy to calculate. The disadvantage is that it uses only two entries from the data set.

2. (a) 25.1

(b) 45.1

(c) Changing the maximum value of the data set greatly affects the range. The range is very sensitive to extreme values.

3. 73

4. 10

5. A deviation, $(x - \mu)$, is the difference between an observation, x, and the mean of the data, μ. The sum of the deviations is always zero.

6. The units of variance are squared. Its units are meaningless. (Example: dollars²)

7. See Odd Answers, page A50

8. Graph (a) has a standard deviation of 2.4 and graph (b) has a standard deviation of 5. Graph (b) has more variability.

Basic Skills and Concepts

1. *Range* Explain how to find the range of a data set. What is an advantage of using the range as a measure of variation? What is a disadvantage?

2. *Skill Check*

(a) Find the range of the data set. (Groom's age at first marriage)

24.3 46.6 41.6 32.9 26.8 39.8 21.5 45.7 33.9 35.1

(b) Change 46.6 to 66.6 and find the range of the new data set.

(c) Compare your answer to parts (a) and (b).

Graphical Reasoning In Exercises 3 and 4, find the range of the data set represented by the display or graph.

3.

```
2 | 3 9          Key: 2|3 = 23
3 | 0 0 2 3 6 7
4 | 0 1 2 3 3 8
5 | 0 1 1 9
6 | 1 2 9 9
7 | 5 9
8 | 4 8
9 | 0 2 5 6
```

4.

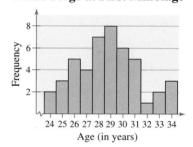

Bride's Age at First Marriage

5. *Deviation* Explain how to find the deviation of an entry in a data set. What is the sum of all the deviations in any data set?

6. *Think About It* Why is the standard deviation used more frequently than the variance? (*Hint:* Consider the units of the variance.)

7. *Think About It* Explain the relationship between variance and standard deviation. Can either of these measures be negative? Explain. Find a data set for which $n = 5$, $\bar{x} = 7$, and $s = 0$.

8. *Graphical Reasoning* Both data sets represented below have a mean of 50. One has a standard deviation of 2.4 and the other has a standard deviation of 5. Which is which? Explain your reasoning.

(a)

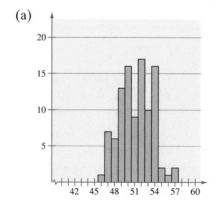

(b)

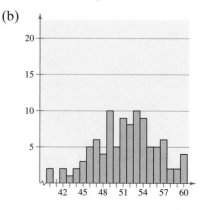

9. When calculating the population standard deviation, you divide the sum of the squared deviations by n, then take the square root of that value. When calculating the sample standard deviation, you divide the sum of the squared deviations by $n - 1$, then take the square root of that value.

When given a data set, one would have to determine if it represented the population or was a sample taken from the population. If the data is a population, then σ is calculated. If the data is a sample, then s is calculated.

10. 7, 8.1, 5.69, 2.39

11. 10, 16.57, 10.25, 3.20

12. 14, 11.11, 21.61, 4.65

13. 19, 17.92, 59.58, 7.72

14. {3, 3, 3, 7, 7, 7}

15. Company B

16. Player B

17. (a) 17.6, 37.35, 6.11
8.7, 8.71, 2.95

   (b) It appears from the data that the annual salaries in LA are more variable than the salaries in Long Beach.

18. (a) 18.1, 37.33, 6.11
13, 12.26, 3.50

   (b) It appears from the data that the annual salaries in Dallas are more variable than the salaries in Houston.

9. *Writing* Describe the difference between the calculation of population standard deviation and sample standard deviation. Given a data set, how do you know whether to calculate σ or s?

Skill Check   In Exercises 10 and 11, find the range, mean, variance, and standard deviation of the population data set.

10. 11 10 8 4 6 7 11 6 11 7

11. 13 23 15 13 18 13 15 14 20 20 18 17 20 13

Skill Check   In Exercises 12 and 13, find the range, mean, variance, and standard deviation of the sample data set.

12. 15 8 12 5 19 14 8 6 13

13. 24 26 27 23 9 14 8 8 26 15 15 27 11

14. *Understanding the Concept*   Find a population data set that contains six entries, has a mean of 5, and has a standard deviation of 2.

15. *Applying the Concept*   You are applying for a job at two companies. Company A offers starting salaries with $\mu = \$31,000$ and $\sigma = \$1000$. Company B offers starting salaries with $\mu = \$31,000$ and $\sigma = \$5000$. From which company are you more likely to get an offer of $33,000 or more? Explain.

16. *Applying the Concept*   An Internet site compares the strokes per round of two professional golfers. Which golfer is more consistent: Player A with $\mu = 71.5$ strokes and $\sigma = 2.3$ strokes, or Player B with $\mu = 70.1$ strokes and $\sigma = 1.2$ strokes? Explain.

17. *Comparing Two Data Sets*   Sample annual salaries, in thousands of dollars, for municipal employees in Los Angeles and Long Beach are listed.

Los Angeles: 20.2 26.1 20.9 32.1 35.9 23.0 28.2 31.6 18.3
Long Beach: 20.9 18.2 20.8 21.1 26.5 26.9 24.2 25.1 22.2

   (a) Find the range, variance, and standard deviation of each data set.
   (b) Interpret the results in the context of the real-life setting.

18. *Comparing Two Data Sets*   Sample annual salaries, in thousands of dollars, for municipal employees in Dallas and Houston are listed.

Dallas: 34.9 25.7 17.3 16.8 26.8 24.7 29.4 32.7 25.5
Houston: 25.6 23.2 26.7 27.7 25.4 26.4 18.3 26.1 31.3

   (a) Find the range, variance, and standard deviation of each data set.
   (b) Interpret the results in the context of the real-life setting.

19. (a) 5.1, 2.95, 1.72
4.2, 1.99, 1.41

(b) It appears from the data that the annual salaries for public teachers are more variable than the salaries for private teachers.

20. (a) 405, 16225.27, 127.38
552, 34575.14, 185.94

(b) It appears from the data that the SAT scores for females are more variable than the SAT scores for males.

21. (a) Greatest sample standard deviation: (ii)
Data set (ii) has more entries that are farther away from the mean.

Least same standard deviation: (iii)
Data set (iii) has more entries that are close to the mean.

(b) The three data sets have the same mean, but have different standard deviations.

22. (a) Greatest sample standard deviation: (i)
Data set (i) has more entries that are farther away from the mean.

Least same standard deviation: (iii)
Data set (iii) has more entries that are close to the mean.

(b) The three data sets have the same mean, median, and mode, but have different standard deviations.

19. *Comparing Two Data Sets* Sample annual salaries, in thousands of dollars, for public and private elementary school teachers are listed.

Public teachers: 38.6 38.1 38.7 36.8 34.8 35.9 39.9 36.2
Private teachers: 21.8 18.4 20.3 17.6 19.7 18.3 19.4 20.8

(a) Find the range, variance, and standard deviation of each data set.
(b) Interpret the results in the context of the real-life setting.

20. *Comparing Two Data Sets* Sample SAT scores for eight males and eight females are listed.

Male SAT scores: 1059 1328 1175 1123 923 1017 1214 1042
Female SAT scores: 1226 965 841 1053 1056 1393 1312 1222

(a) Find the range, variance, and standard deviation of each data set.
(b) Interpret the results in the context of the real-life setting.

21. *Graphical Reasoning*

(a) Without calculating, which data set has the greatest sample standard deviation? Which has the least sample standard deviation? Explain your reasoning.

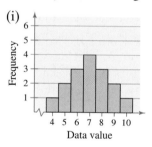 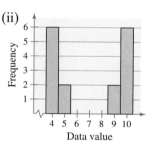 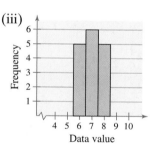

(b) How are the data sets the same? How do they differ?

22. *Graphical Reasoning*

(a) Without calculating, which data set has the greatest sample standard deviation? Which has the least sample standard deviation? Explain your reasoning.

```
(i)  0 | 9              (ii) 0 | 9              (iii) 0 |
     1 | 5 8                 1 | 5                    1 | 5
     2 | 3 3 7 7             2 | 3 3 3 7 7 7          2 | 3 3 3 3 7 7 7 7
     3 | 2 5                 3 | 5                    3 | 5
     4 | 1                   4 | 1                    4 |
 Key: 4 | 1 = 41         Key: 4 | 1 = 41          Key: 4 | 1 = 41
```

(b) How are the data sets the same? How do they differ?

23. (a) Similarities: Both estimate proportions of the data contained within k standard deviations of the mean.
Difference: The empirical rule assumes the distribution is bell-shaped, Chebychev's Theorem makes no such assumption.

(b) You must know that the distribution is bell-shaped.

(c) If $k = 1$, Chebychev's Theorem would return a proportion equal to zero. If $k < 1$, it would return a negative proportion (which is not possible).

24. (a) 68%

(b) (5.7, 24.3)

25. 47.5%

26. ($500, $1900)

27. (.05, 6.59)

28. (48.07, 56.67)

29. 2.075, 1.328

23. *Writing*

(a) Discuss the similarities and the differences between the Empirical Rule and Chebychev's Theorem.

(b) What must you know about a data set before you can use the Empirical Rule?

(c) When using Chebychev's Theorem, why must k be greater than one?

24. *Empirical Rule*   A bell-shaped distribution has a mean of 15 and a standard deviation of 3.1.

(a) What percent of the entries fall between 11.9 and 18.1?

(b) Between what two numbers do 99.7% of the data lie?

25. *Empirical Rule*   The mean value of land and buildings per acre from a sample of farms is $1000 with a standard deviation of $200. The data set has a bell-shaped distribution. Estimate the percent of farms whose land and building values per acre are between $1000 and $1400.

26. *Empirical Rule*   The mean value of land and buildings per acre from a sample of farms is $1200 with a standard deviation of $350. Between what two values does 95% of the data lie? (Assume the data set has a bell-shaped distribution.)

27. *Chebychev's Theorem*   Old Faithful is a famous geyser at Yellowstone National Park. From a sample, the mean duration of Old Faithful's eruptions is 3.32 minutes and the standard deviation is 1.09 minutes. Apply Chebychev's Theorem to the data using $k = 3$. Interpret the results in the context of the real-life setting. *(Source: Yellowstone National Park)*

28. *Chebychev's Theorem*   The mean time in a women's 400-meter dash is 52.37 seconds with a standard deviation of 2.15. Apply Chebychev's Theorem to the data using $k = 2$. Interpret the results in the context of the real-life setting.

29. *Grouped Data*   The results of a random sample of the number of pets per household in a region are shown in the histogram. Estimate the sample mean and the sample standard deviation of the data set.

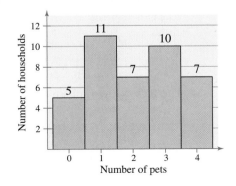

30. See Selected Answers, page A78

31. See Odd Answers, page A50

32.

midpoint, x	f
5	12.8
15	12.2
25	14
35	18.3
45	16.6
55	16.2
65	17.6
75	12.2
85	6
95	1.2
	127.1

$$\bar{x} = \frac{\Sigma xf}{n} = \frac{5558.5}{127.1} \approx 43.73$$

$$s = \sqrt{\frac{\Sigma(x - \bar{x})^2 f}{n - 1}}$$

$$= \sqrt{\frac{70926.06}{127.1 - 1}} \approx 23.72$$

33. $CV_{\text{heights}} \approx 4.73$

$CV_{\text{weights}} \approx 9.83$

It appears that weight is more variable than height.

30. *Grouped Data*   The number of wins for each National Football League team in 1997 are listed. Make a frequency distribution (using five classes) for the data set. Then approximate the population mean and the population standard deviation of the data set. *(Source: National Football League)*

10	9	9	6	3	11	11	8	7	6	13	12	8	4	4
10	8	6	6	4	13	10	9	9	4	13	7	7	6	5

31. *Grouped Data*   The estimated distribution (in millions) of the U.S. population by age for the year 2000 is shown in the circle graph. Make a frequency distribution for the data. Then use the table to estimate the sample mean and the sample standard deviation of the data set. Use 70 as the midpoint for "65 years and over." *(Source: U.S. Census Bureau)*

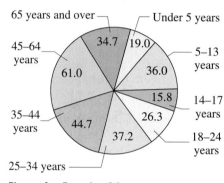

Figure for Exercise 31

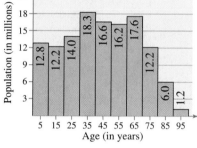

Figure for Exercise 32

32. *Grouped Data*   Japan's estimated population for the year 2010 is given in the bar graph. Make a frequency distribution for the data. Then use the table to estimate the sample mean and the sample standard deviation of the data set. *(Source: U.S. Census Bureau, International Data Base)*

Extending the Basics

33. *Coefficient of Variation*   The coefficient of variation, *CV*, describes the standard deviation as a percent of the mean. Because it has no units, you can use the coefficient of variation to compare data with different units.

$$CV = \frac{\text{Standard deviation}}{\text{mean}} \times 100\%$$

The following data show the heights (in inches) and weights (in pounds) of the members of a basketball team. Find the coefficient of variation for each data set. What can you conclude?

Heights: 72   74   68   76   74   69   72   79   70   69   77   73
Weights: 180   168   225   201   189   192   197   162   174   171   185   210

34. (a) Public: $s = 1.72$
    Private: $s = 1.41$

  (b) Answers are the same.

35. (a) -2.61
    skewed left

  (b) 4.12
    skewed right

  (c) 0
    symmetric

  (d) -8
    skewed left

  (e) 4.79
    skewed right

36. (a) 550, 302.765

  (b) 5500, 3027.65

  (c) 55, 30.2765

  (d) By multiplying each entry by a constant k, the new sample mean is $k \cdot \bar{x}$ and the new sample standard deviation is $k \cdot s$.

37. (a) 550, 302.765

  (b) 560, 302.765

  (c) 540, 302.765

  (d) By adding or subtracting a constant k to each entry, the new sample mean will be $\bar{x} + k$ with the sample standard deviation being unaffected.

34. *Shortcut Formula* You used $SS_x = \Sigma(x - \bar{x})^2$ when calculating variance and standard deviation. An alternate formula that is sometimes more convenient for hand calculations is

$$SS_x = \Sigma x^2 - \frac{(\Sigma x)^2}{n}.$$

To calculate a sample variance, divide the sum of squares by $n - 1$. To calculate the sample standard deviation, find the square root of the variance.

(a) Use the shortcut formula to calculate the sample standard deviation for the following.

| Public teachers: | 38.6 | 38.1 | 38.7 | 36.8 | 34.8 | 35.9 | 39.9 | 36.2 |
| Private teachers: | 21.8 | 18.4 | 20.3 | 17.6 | 19.7 | 18.3 | 19.4 | 20.8 |

(b) Compare your results to those obtained in Exercise 19.

35. *Pearson's Index of Skewness* The English statistician Karl Pearson (1857–1936) introduced a formula for the skewness of a distribution.

$$P = \frac{3(\bar{x} - \text{median})}{s} \qquad \text{Pearson's index of skewness}$$

Most distributions have an index of skewness between -3 and 3. When $P > 0$, the data are skewed right. When $P < 0$, the data are skewed left. When $P = 0$, the data are symmetric. Calculate the coefficient of skewness for each distribution. Describe the shape of each.

(a) $\bar{x} = 17, s = 2.3$, median $= 19$ (b) $\bar{x} = 32, s = 5.1$, median $= 25$

(c) $\bar{x} = 37, s = 6.2$, median $= 37$ (d) $\bar{x} = 45, s = 10.5$, median $= 73$

(e) $\bar{x} = 57, s = 9.4$, median $= 42$

36. *Team Project: Scaling Data* Consider the following sample data set.

  100 200 300 400 500 600 700 800 900 1000

(a) Find $\bar{x}$ and s.
(b) Multiply each entry by 10. Find $\bar{x}$ and s for the revised data.
(c) Divide the original data by 10. Find $\bar{x}$ and s for the revised data.
(d) What can you conclude from the results of (a), (b), and (c)?

37. *Team Project: Shifting Data* Consider the following sample data set.

  100 200 300 400 500 600 700 800 900 1000

(a) Find $\bar{x}$ and s.
(b) Add 10 to each entry. Find $\bar{x}$ and s for the revised data.
(c) Subtract 10 from the original data. Find $\bar{x}$ and s for the revised data.
(d) What can you conclude from the results of (a), (b), and (c)?

2 ▼ CASE STUDY

SUNGLASS ASSOCIATION of AMERICA

Sunglass Sales in the United States

The Sunglass Association of America is a not-for-profit association of manufacturers and distributors of sunglasses. Part of the association's mission is to gather and distribute marketing information about the sale of sunglasses. The data presented here are based on surveys administered by Jobson Optical Research International.

Outlet Type	Number of Locations
Optical Store	34,043
Sunglass Specialty	2,060
Dept. Store	6,866
Discount Dept. Store	10,376
Catalog Showroom	887
General Merchandise	11,868
Supermarket	21,613
Convenience Store	83,613
Chain Drug Store	31,127
Indep. Drug Store	7,034
Chain Apparel Store	26,831
Chain Sports Store	5,760
Indep. Sports Store	14,683

Number (in 1000s) of Pairs of Sunglasses Sold

Price	$0–$10	$11–$30	$31–$50	$51–$75	$76–$100	$101–$150	$151+
Optical Store	0	290	3,164	1,240	3,654	842	478
Sunglass Specialty	192	708	2,515	1,697	1,145	805	378
Dept. Store	1,224	1,464	1,527	488	38	16	5
Discount Dept. Store	8,793	5,284	147	67	16	8	0
Catalog Showroom	153	100	65	35	29	9	0
General Merchandise	6,147	495	0	0	0	0	0
Supermarket	14,108	316	0	0	0	0	0
Convenience Store	19,726	2,985	0	0	0	0	0
Chain Drug Store	17,883	3,432	50	0	0	0	0
Indep. Drug Store	1,352	1,110	12	0	0	0	0
Chain Apparel Store	3,464	1,804	186	112	40	17	7
Chain Sports Store	672	526	430	72	45	18	4
Indep. Sports Store	875	1,997	1,320	528	206	85	11

Exercises

1. *Mean Price* Estimate the mean price of a pair of sunglasses sold at (a) an optical store, (b) a sunglass specialty store, and (c) a department store. Use $200 as the midpoint for $151+.

2. *Revenue* Which type of outlet had the greatest total revenue? Explain your reasoning.

3. *Revenue* Which type of outlet had the greatest revenue per location? Explain your reasoning.

4. *Standard Deviation* Estimate the standard deviation for the number of pairs of sunglasses sold at (a) optical stores, (b) sunglass specialty stores, and (c) department stores.

5. *Standard Deviation* Of the 13 distributions, which has the greatest standard deviation? Explain your reasoning.

6. *Bell-Shaped Distribution* Of the 13 distributions, which is more bell shaped? Explain your reasoning.

2.5 Measures of Position

Quartiles • Percentiles and Other Fractiles

What You Should Learn

- *How to find the first, second, and third quartiles of a data set*
- *How to find the interquartile range of a data set*
- *How to represent a data set graphically using a box-and-whisker plot*
- *How to interpret other fractiles such as percentiles*

Quartiles

In this section, you will learn how to use fractiles to specify the position of a data entry within a data set. **Fractiles** are numbers that partition, or divide, an ordered data set into equal parts. For instance, the median is a fractile because it divides an ordered data set into two equal parts.

DEFINITION

The three **quartiles** Q_1, Q_2, and Q_3 approximately divide an ordered data set into four equal parts. About one quarter of the data falls on or below the **first quartile** Q_1. About one half the data falls on or below the **second quartile** Q_2, and about three quarters of the data falls on or below the **third quartile** Q_3. The second quartile is the same as the median of the data set.

▶ **EXAMPLE 1** *Finding the Quartiles of a Data Set*

The test scores of 15 employees enrolled in a CPR training course are listed. Find the first, second, and third quartiles of the test scores.

13 9 18 15 14 21 7 10 11 20 5 18 37 16 17

SOLUTION   First, order the data set and find the median, Q_2. Once you find Q_2, you can divide the data set into two halves. The first and third quartiles are the medians of the lower and upper halves of the data set.

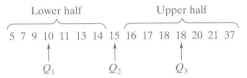

So about one fourth of the employees scored 10 or less, about one half scored 15 or less, and about three fourths scored 18 or less.

Try It Yourself 1

Find the first, second, and third quartiles for the ages of the Akhiok residents. Use the data set given in the chapter opener on page 28.

a. *Order* the data set.
b. Find the median, Q_2.
c. Find the first and third quartiles, Q_1 and Q_3.   *Answer: Page A34*

▶ **EXAMPLE 2** **Using Technology to Find Quartiles**

The tuition costs, in thousands of dollars, for 25 liberal arts colleges are listed. Use a calculator or a computer to find the first, second, and third quartiles. (*Source: U.S. News and World Report*)

23 25 30 23 20 22 21 15 25 24 30 25 30
20 23 29 20 19 22 23 29 23 28 22 28

SOLUTION   Minitab, Excel, and the TI-83 each have features that automatically calculate quartiles. Try using this technology to find the first, second, and third quartiles of the tuition data. From the displays, you can see that $Q_1 = 21.5$, $Q_2 = 23$, and $Q_3 = 28$, which means that about one quarter of these colleges charge tuition of \$21,500 or less, one half charge \$23,000 or less, and about three quarters charge \$28,000 or less.

Study Tip

There are several ways to find the quartiles of a data set. Regardless of how you find the quartiles, the results are rarely off by more than one data entry. For instance, in Example 2, the first quartile, as determined by Excel, is 22 instead of 21.5.

EXCEL

	A	B	C	D
1	23			
2	25		Quartile(A1:A25,1)	
3	30		22	
4	23			
5	20		Quartile(A1:A25,2)	
6	22		23	
7	21			
8	15		Quartile(A1:A25,3)	
9	25		28	
10	24			
11	30			
12	25			
13	30			
14	20			
15	23			
16	29			
17	20			
18	19			
19	22			
20	23			
21	29			
22	23			
23	28			
24	22			
25	28			

TI-83

```
1-Var Stats
↑n=25
minX=15
Q1=21.5
Med=23
Q3=28
maxX=30
```

Note to Instructor

For Minitab and the TI-83, quartiles are found with the following ranks.

Q_1: $\dfrac{1(n + 1)}{4}$

Q_2: $\dfrac{2(n + 1)}{4}$

Q_3: $\dfrac{3(n + 1)}{4}$

MINITAB

Descriptive Statistics

Variable	N	Mean	Median	TrMean	StDev
Tuition	25	23.960	23.000	24.087	3.942

Variable	SE Mean	Minimum	Maximum	Q1	Q3
Tuition	0.788	15.000	30.000	21.500	28.000

Try It Yourself 2

The tuition costs, in thousands of dollars, for 25 universities are listed. Use a calculator or a computer to find the first, second, and third quartiles. *(Source: U.S. News and World Report)*

20 26 28 25 31 14 23 15 12 26 29 24 31
19 31 17 15 17 20 31 32 16 21 22 28

a. *Enter* the data.
b. *Calculate* the first, second, and third quartiles.
c. What can you conclude?   *Answer: Page A34*

After finding the quartiles of a data set, you can find the interquartile range.

DEFINITION

The **interquartile range (IQR)** of a data set is the difference between the first and third quartiles.

$$\text{Interquartile range (IQR)} = Q_3 - Q_1$$

▶ EXAMPLE 3   *Finding the Interquartile Range*

Find the interquartile range of the 15 test scores given in Example 1. What can you conclude from the result?

SOLUTION   From Example 1, you know that $Q_1 = 10$ and $Q_3 = 18$. So, the interquartile range is

$$\text{IQR} = Q_3 - Q_1 = 18 - 10 = 8.$$

This means that the test scores in the middle half of the data set vary by eight points.

Try It Yourself 3

Find the interquartile range for the ages of the Akhiok residents. Use the data set given in the chapter opener on page 28.

a. Find the first and third quartiles, Q_1 and Q_3.
b. *Subtract* Q_1 from Q_3.
c. *Interpret* the result in the context of the data.   *Answer: Page A34*

Another important application of quartiles is to represent data sets using box-and-whisker plots. A **box-and-whisker plot** is an exploratory data analysis tool that highlights the important features of a data set. To graph a box-and-whisker plot, you must know the following values.

Insight

The IQR is a measure of variation that gives you an idea of how much the middle half of the data varies. It can also be used to identify outliers. Any data value that lies more than 1.5 IQRs to the left of Q_1 or to the right of Q_3 is an outlier. For instance, 37 is an outlier of the 15 test scores in Example 1.

1. The minimum entry
2. The first quartile, Q_1
3. The median, Q_2
4. The third quartile, Q_3
5. The maximum entry

These five numbers are called the **five-number summary** of the data set.

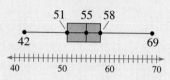
GUIDELINES

Drawing a Box-and-Whisker Plot

1. Find the five-number summary of the data set.
2. Construct a horizontal scale that spans the range of the data.
3. Plot the five numbers above the horizontal scale.
4. Draw a box above the horizontal scale from Q_1 to Q_3 and draw a vertical line in the box at Q_2.
5. Draw whiskers from the box to the minimum and maximum entries.

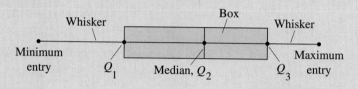

> **EXAMPLE 4** **Drawing a Box-and-Whisker Plot**

See *Minitab* and *TI-83* steps on page 94, 95.

Draw a box-and-whisker plot that represents the 15 test scores given in Example 1. What can you conclude from the display?

SOLUTION The five-number summary of the test scores is as follows.

$$\text{Min} = 5 \qquad Q_1 = 10 \qquad Q_2 = 15 \qquad Q_3 = 18 \qquad \text{Max} = 37$$

Using these five numbers, you can construct the box-and-whisker plot shown. You can make several conclusions from the display. One is that about half the scores are between 10 and 18.

Test Scores in CPR Class

| 5 | 10 | 15 | 18 | | | | | | | | | | | | | | | | | | | | | | | | | | | | | 37 |

5 6 7 8 9 10 11 12 13 14 15 16 17 18 19 20 21 22 23 24 25 26 27 28 29 30 31 32 33 34 35 36 37

Try It Yourself 4

Draw a box-and-whisker plot that represents the ages of the residents of Akhiok. Use the data set given in the chapter opener on page 28.

a. Find the *five-number summary* of the data set.
b. Construct a *horizontal scale* and *plot* the five numbers above it.
c. Draw the *box*, the *vertical line*, and the *whiskers*.
d. Make some conclusions.

Answer: Page A34

Percentiles and Other Fractiles

In addition to using quartiles to specify a measure of position, you can also use percentiles and deciles. These common fractiles are summarized as follows.

Fractiles	Summary	Symbols
Quartiles	Divide a data set into four equal parts.	Q_1, Q_2, Q_3
Deciles	Divide a data set into ten equal parts.	$D_1, D_2, D_3, \ldots, D_9$
Percentiles	Divide a data set into one hundred equal parts.	$P_1, P_2, P_3, \ldots, P_{99}$

Percentiles are often used in education and health-related fields to indicate how one individual compares with others in a group. For instance, test scores and children's growth measurements are often expressed in percentiles.

▶ **EXAMPLE 5** **Interpreting Percentiles**

The graph represents the cumulative frequency distribution for the 1996 SAT test scores of college-bound students. What test score represents the 64th percentile? How should you interpret this?

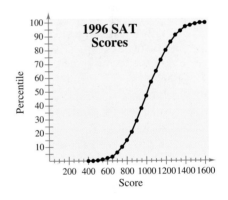

SOLUTION From the graph, you can see that the 64th percentile represents a test score of 1090. This means that 64% of the students had an SAT score of 1090 or less.

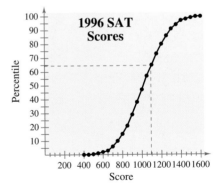

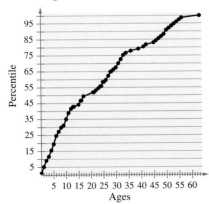

Ages of Residents of Akhiok

Try It Yourself 5

The ages of the residents of Akhiok are represented in the cumulative frequency graph at the left. At what percentile is a resident whose age is 47? How should you interpret this?

a. *Use the graph* to find the percentile that corresponds to the given age.
b. *Interpret* the results in the context of the data. *Answer: Page A34* ◀

▼ 2.5 ▼ EXERCISES

▶ H E L P

⊙ **StatPro 2.5**

🌐 **Internet Statistics 2.5**

🎬 **Student Solutions Manual 2.5**

📼 **Videos 2.5**

📖 **Try It Yourself Answers 2.5**

1. The basketball team scored more points per game than 75% of the teams in the league.

2. The salesperson sold more hardware equipment than 80% of the other sales people.

3. The student scored above 63% of the students who took the ACT placement test.

4. The child is taller than 87% of the other children in the same age group.

5. True

6. False

7. (a) Min = 10
  (b) Max = 21
  (c) $Q_1 = 13$
  (d) $Q_2 = 15$
  (e) $Q_3 = 17$
  (f) IQR = 4

8. See Selected Answers, page A78

9. See Odd Answers, page A50

10. See Selected Answers, page A78

11. See Odd Answers, page A51

12. See Selected Answers, page A78

Basic Skills and Concepts

1. The points scored per game by a basketball team represent the third quartile for all teams in a league. What can you conclude about the team's points scored per game?

2. A salesperson at a company sold $6,903,435 of hardware equipment last year, a figure that represented the eighth decile of sales performance at the company. What can you conclude about the salesperson's performance?

3. A student's score on the ACT placement test for college algebra is in the 63rd percentile. What can you conclude about the student's test score?

4. A doctor tells a child's parents that their child's height is in the 87th percentile for the child's age group. What can you conclude about the child's height?

True or False In Exercises 5 and 6, determine whether the statement is true or false. If it is false, rewrite it as a true statement.

5. The second quartile is the median of an ordered data set.

6. The five numbers you need to graph a box-and-whisker plot are the minimum, the maximum, Q_1, Q_3, and the mean.

Graphical Analysis In Exercises 7–10, use the box-and-whisker plot to identify (a) the minimum entry, (b) the maximum entry, (c), the first quartile, (d) the second quartile, (e) the third quartile, and (f) the interquartile range.

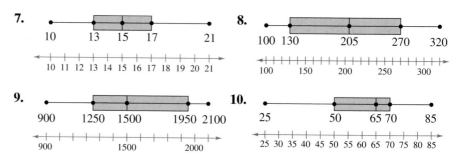

Skill Check In Exercises 11 and 12, (a) find the three quartiles and (b) draw a box-and-whisker plot of the data.

💾 **11.** 4 7 7 5 2 9 7 6 8 5 8 4 1 5 2 8 7 6 6 9

💾 **12.** 2 7 1 3 1 2 8 9 9 2 5 4 7 3 7 5 4 7
    2 3 5 9 5 6 3 9 3 4 9 8 8 2 3 9 5

13. (a) 25, 40 , 47.5

(b) $P_{25} = Q_1 = 25$
$P_{50} = Q_2 = 40$
$P_{75} = Q_3 = 47.5$

(c) **Retirements in the House of Representatives**

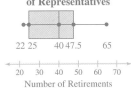

(d) Half of the retirements are between 25 and 47.5.

14. (a) 3.5, 6, 7.5

(b) $P_{25} = Q_1 = 3.5$
$P_{50} = Q_2 = 6$
$P_{75} = Q_3 = 7.5$

(c) **Retirements in the Senate**

(d) Half of the retirements in the Senate are between 3.5 and 7.5.

15. See Odd Answers, page A51

16. See Selected Answers, page A79

17. $Q_1 = B$, $Q_2 = A$, $Q_3 = C$

18. $P_{10} = T$, $P_{50} = R$, $P_{80} = S$

19. See Odd Answers, page A51

20. (a) 15.125, 15.8, 17.65

(b) **Railroad Equipment Manufacturers**

(c) Half of the hourly earnings are between $12.13 and $17.65.

Representing Data with Fractiles and Graphs In Exercises 13–16, (a) find the data set's first, second, and third quartiles, (b) find the values that represent the data set's 25th, 50th, and 75th percentiles, (c) draw a box-and-whisker plot that represents the data set, and (d) interpret the results in the context of the data.

13. The number of retirements in the House of Representatives by election year, 1964–1996

33 22 23 29 40 43 47 49 34 40 22 40 23 27 65 48 50

14. The number of retirements in the Senate by election year, 1964–1996

2 3 6 4 6 7 8 10 5 3 4 6 6 3 7 9 13

15. The hourly earnings (in dollars) of a sample of 19 automotive mechanics

10.65   9.80   9.45 12.20 10.35 14.60   9.95   9.40   9.70 11.50
13.15 14.20 10.40   9.85 13.25 15.35 11.50 11.20 13.55

16. The ages at which 11 secondary school teachers obtained tenure

27 31 26 28 30 28 45 32 29 35 28

17. *Graphical Analysis* The letters A, B, and C are marked on the histogram. Match them to Q_1, the median, and Q_3. Justify your answer.

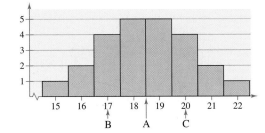

18. *Graphical Analysis* The letters R, S, and T are marked on the histogram. Match them to P_{10}, P_{50}, and P_{80}. Justify your answer.

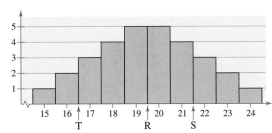

Using Technology to Find Quartiles and Draw Graphs In Exercises 19 and 20, use a calculator or a computer to (a) find the data set's first, second, and third quartiles, (b) draw a box-and-whisker plot that represents the data set, and (c) interpret the results in the context of the data.

19. The number of hours of television watched per day by a sample of 28 people

2 4 1 5 7 2 5 4 4 2 3 6 4 3 5 2 0 3 5 9 4 5 2 1 3 6 7 2

20. The hourly earnings (in dollars) of a sample of 25 railroad equipment manufacturers

15.60 18.75 14.60 15.80 14.35 13.90 17.50 17.55 13.80
14.20 19.05 15.35 15.20 19.45 15.95 16.50 16.30 15.25
15.05 19.10 15.20 16.22 17.75 18.40 15.25

21. 70 inches

22. P_{78}

23. (a) 42, 49, 56

(b)

Ages of Executives

(c) Half of the ages are between 42 and 56 years.

(d) 49

Interpreting Percentiles In Exercises 21 and 22, use the cumulative frequency distribution to answer the questions. The cumulative frequency distribution represents the heights of American males in the 20–29 age group. *(Source: National Center for Health Statistics)*

21. What height represents the 20th percentile? How should you interpret this?

22. What percentile is a height of 76 inches? How should you interpret this?

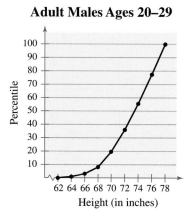

Adult Males Ages 20–29

Extending the Basics

23. *Ages of Executives* The ages of a sample of 100 executives are listed.

```
31 62 51 44 61 47 49 45 40 52 60 51 67 47 63 54 59 43 63 52
50 54 61 41 48 49 51 54 39 54 47 52 36 53 74 33 53 68 44 40
60 42 50 48 42 42 36 57 42 48 56 51 54 42 27 43 43 41 54 49
49 47 51 28 54 36 36 41 60 55 42 59 35 65 48 56 82 39 54 49
61 56 57 32 38 48 64 51 45 46 62 63 59 63 32 47 40 37 49 57
```

(a) Order the data and find the first, second, and fourth quartiles.

(b) Draw a box-and-whisker plot that represents the data set.

(c) Interpret the results in the context of the data.

(d) Based on this sample, at what age would you expect to be an executive? Explain your reasoning.

TECHNOLOGY

| MINITAB | | EXCEL | | TI-83 |

DAIRY FARMERS of AMERICA

The Dairy Farmers of America is an association that provides help to dairy farmers. Part of this help is gathering and distributing statistics on milk production.

Monthly Milk Production

The following data set was supplied by a dairy farmer. It lists the monthly milk production (in pounds) for 50 different Holstein dairy cows. *(Source: Matlink Dairy, Clymer, NY)*

2825	2072	2733	2069	2484
4285	2862	3353	1449	2029
1258	2982	2045	1677	1619
2597	3512	2444	1773	2284
1884	2359	2046	2364	2669
3109	2804	1658	2207	2159
2207	2882	1647	2051	2202
3223	2383	1732	2230	1147
2711	1874	1979	1319	2923
2281	1230	1665	1294	2936

www.dfamilk.com

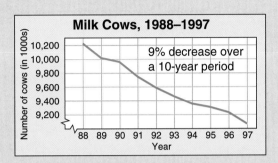

Milk Cows, 1988–1997

9% decrease over a 10-year period

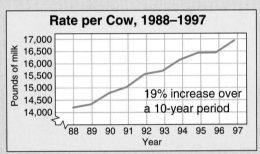

Rate per Cow, 1988–1997

19% increase over a 10-year period

From 1988 to 1997, the number of dairy cows in the United States decreased and the yearly milk production increased.

Exercises

In Exercises 1–4, use a computer or calculator. If possible, print your results.

1. Find the sample mean of the data.

2. Find the sample standard deviation of the data.

3. Make a frequency distribution for the data. Use a class width of 500.

4. Draw a histogram for the data. Does the distribution appear to be bell shaped?

5. What percent of the distribution lies within one standard deviation of the mean? Within two standard deviations of the mean? How do these results agree with the Empirical Rule?

In Exercises 6–8, use the frequency distribution found in Exercise 3.

6. Use the frequency distribution to estimate the sample mean of the data. Compare your results to Exercise 1.

7. Use the frequency distribution to find the sample standard deviation for the data. Compare your results to Exercise 2.

8. *Writing* Use the results of Exercises 6 and 7 to write a general statement about the mean and standard deviation for grouped data. Do the formulas for grouped data give results that are as accurate as the individual entry formulas?

Extended solutions are given in the *Technology Supplement.*
Technical instruction is provided for Minitab, Excel, and the TI-83.

Here are some *Minitab* and *TI-83* printouts for three examples in this chapter.

(See Example 7, page 50)

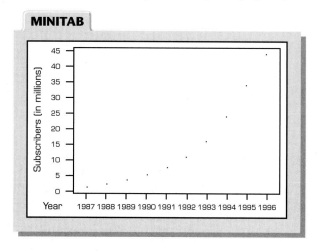

(See Example 4, page 71)

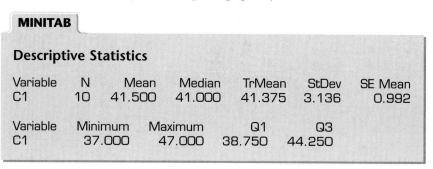

Descriptive Statistics

Variable	N	Mean	Median	TrMean	StDev	SE Mean
C1	10	41.500	41.000	41.375	3.136	0.992

Variable	Minimum	Maximum	Q1	Q3
C1	37.000	47.000	38.750	44.250

(See Example 4, page 88)

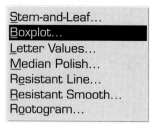

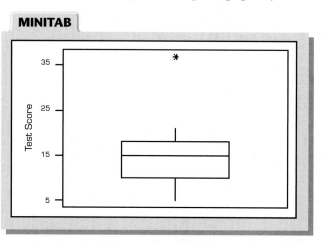

(See Example 7, page 50)   (See Example 4, page 71)   (See Example 4, page 88)

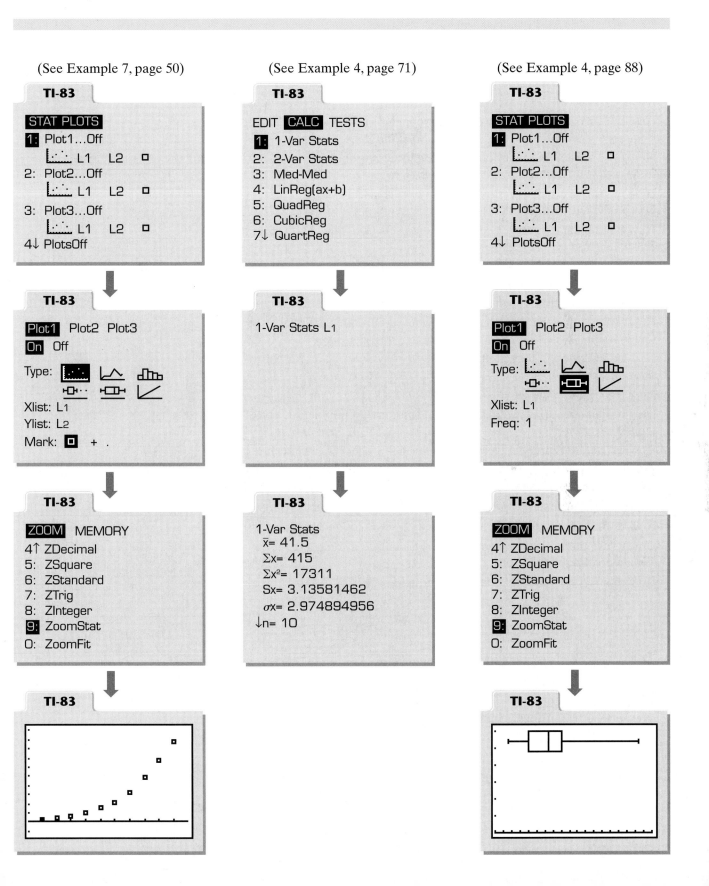

▼ **2**   **CHAPTER SUMMARY**

What did you learn?

	Review Exercises
• How to construct a frequency distribution including midpoints, relative frequencies, and cumulative frequencies *(Section 2.1)*	*1–3*
• How to construct frequency histograms, frequency polygons, relative frequency histograms, and ogives *(Section 2.1)*	*4–7*
• How to graph and interpret quantitative data sets using the exploratory data analysis tools of stem-and-leaf plots and dot plots *(Section 2.2)*	*8, 9*
• How to graph and interpret qualitative data sets using pie charts and Pareto charts *(Section 2.2)*	*10, 11*
• How to graph and interpret paired data sets using scatter plots and time series charts *(Section 2.2)*	*12, 13*
• How to find the mean, median, and mode of a population and a sample *(Section 2.3)*	*14, 15*
• How to find a weighted mean and the mean of a frequency distribution *(Section 2.3)*	*16–19*
• How to describe the shape of a distribution as symmetric, uniform, or skewed *(Section 2.3)*	*20–25*
• How to find the range of a data set *(Section 2.4)*	*26, 27*
• How to find the variance and standard deviation of a population and of a sample *(Section 2.4)*	*28–31*
• How to use the Empirical Rule and Chebyshev's Theorem to interpret standard deviation *(Section 2.4)*	*32–35*
• How to approximate the sample standard deviation for grouped data *(Section 2.4)*	*36, 37*
• How to find the first, second, and third quartiles of a data set *(Section 2.5)*	*38, 39*
• How to find the interquartile range of a data set *(Section 2.5)*	*40, 42*
• How to use the exploratory data analysis tool of describing a data set using a box-and-whisker plot *(Section 2.5)*	*41, 43*
• How to interpret percentiles and other fractiles *(Section 2.5)*	*44, 45*

Why did you learn it? Uses and Abuses

Uses   There are two basic reasons for studying descriptive statistics.

1. It is difficult to see trends or patterns in raw, unorganized data. It is like the old saying, "You can't see the forest for the trees." When you use the techniques presented in this chapter to organize, graph, and summarize data, you make the forest visible.

2. When you read reports, news items, or advertisements prepared by other people, you are seldom given raw data sets. Instead, you are given graphs, measures of central tendency, and measures of variation. To be a discerning reader, you need to understand the terms and techniques of descriptive statistics.

Abuses   Misleading statistical graphs are common in newspapers and news magazines. For instance, see Exercise 31 and 32 on page 54.

2 ▼ REVIEW EXERCISES

1. See Odd Answers, page A51

2. (See problem 1)

3. (See problem 1)

4. Liquid Volume 12 oz Cans

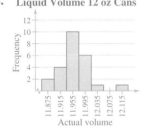

5. Liquid Volume 12 oz Cans

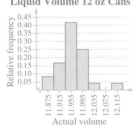

6. See Selected Answers, page A79

7. Meals Purchased

8.
```
1 | 3789
2 | 012333445557889
3 | 11234578
4 | 347
5 | 1
```

9. Average Daily Highs

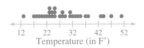

In Exercises 1–3, use the following data set. The data set represents the income (in thousands of dollars) of 20 employees at a small business.

| 30 | 28 | 26 | 39 | 34 | 33 | 20 | 39 | 28 | 33 |
| 26 | 39 | 32 | 28 | 31 | 39 | 33 | 31 | 33 | 32 |

1. Make a frequency distribution of the data set using five classes. Include the class midpoints, limits, frequencies, and boundaries.

2. Find the relative frequency for each class and include it in your table.

3. Find the cumulative frequency for each class and include it in your table.

In Exercises 4 and 5, use the following data set. The data represent the actual liquid volume in 24 twelve-ounce cans.

11.95	11.91	11.86	11.94	12.00	11.93	12.00	11.94
12.10	11.95	11.99	11.94	11.89	12.01	11.99	11.94
11.92	11.98	11.88	11.94	11.98	11.92	11.95	11.93

4. Make a frequency histogram using seven classes.

5. Make a relative frequency histogram of the data set.

In Exercises 6 and 7, use the following data set. The data represent the number of meals purchased during one night's business at a sample of restaurants.

153	104	118	166	89	104	100	79	93	96	116
94	140	84	81	96	108	111	87	126	101	111
122	108	126	93	108	87	103	95	129	93

6. Make a frequency distribution with six classes and draw a frequency polygon.

7. Make an ogive of the data set using six classes.

In Exercises 8 and 9, use the following data set. The data represent the average daily high temperature (in degrees Fahrenheit) during the month of January for Chicago, Illinois. *(Source: National Oceanic and Atmospheric Administration)*

| 33 | 31 | 25 | 22 | 38 | 51 | 32 | 23 | 23 | 34 | 44 | 43 | 47 | 37 | 29 | 25 |
| 28 | 35 | 21 | 24 | 20 | 19 | 23 | 27 | 24 | 13 | 18 | 28 | 17 | 25 | 31 |

8. Make a stem-and-leaf plot of the data set. Use one line per stem.

9. Make a dot plot of the data set.

In Exercises 10 and 11, use the following data set. The data set represents the top seven American Kennel Club registrations (in thousands) in 1996. *(Source: American Kennel Club, New York, NY)*

Breed	Labrador Retriever	Rottweiler	German Shepherd	Golden Retriever	Beagle	Poodle	Dachshund
Number registered (in thousands)	150	90	79	69	57	57	48

10.

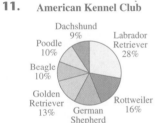

11.

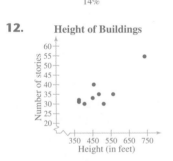

12. **Height of Buildings**

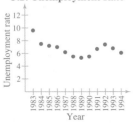

It appears that as height increases, the number of stories increases.

13. **U.S. Unemployment Rate**

10. Make a Pareto chart of the data set.

11. Make a pie chart of the data set.

12. The following are the height (in feet) and the number of stories of nine notable buildings in Miami. Use the data to construct a scatter plot. What type of pattern is shown in the scatter plot? *(Source: 1998 World Almanac and Book of Facts)*

Height (in feet)	738	562	510	484	456	450	405	375	375
Number of stories	55	35	30	35	40	33	30	32	31

13. The U.S. unemployment rate over a 12-year period is given. Use the data to construct a time series chart.

Year	1983	1984	1985	1986	1987	1988
Unemployment rate	9.6	7.5	7.2	7.0	6.2	5.5

Year	1989	1990	1991	1992	1993	1994
Unemployment rate	5.3	5.5	6.7	7.4	6.8	6.1

14. Find the mean, median, and mode of the data set.

9 7 8 6 9 12 11 5 9 10

15. Find the mean, median, and mode of the data set.

28 35 29 29 33 32 29 33 31 29

16. Estimate the mean of the frequency distribution you made in Exercise 1.

17. The following frequency distribution shows the number of magazine subscriptions per household for a sample of 60 households. Find the mean number of subscriptions per household.

Number of magazines	0	1	2	3	4	5	6
Frequency	13	9	19	8	5	2	4

18. Six test scores are given. The first five test scores are 15% of the final grade, and the last test score is 25% of the final grade. Find the weighted mean of the test scores.

75 67 86 77 79 88

19. Four test scores are given. The first three test scores are 10% of the final grade, and the last test score is 70% of the final grade. Find the weighted mean of the test scores.

81 95 89 87

14. 8.6, 9, 9

15. 30.8, 30, 29

16. 31.7

17. 2.083

18. 79.6

19. 87.4

20. Skewed

21. Skewed

22. Skewed left

23. Skewed right

24. Median

25. Mean

26. 2.8

27. 3.84

28. 9, 3.19

29. 63.67, 8.11

30. 2453.47
306.15

31. 38653.5
6762.2

32. (18.50, 33.50)

20. Describe the shape of the distribution in the histogram you made in Exercise 4. Is the distribution symmetric, uniform, or skewed?

21. Describe the shape of the distribution in the histogram you made in Exercise 5. Is the distribution symmetric, uniform, or skewed?

In Exercises 22 and 23, decide if the distribution is skewed right, skewed left, or symmetric.

22.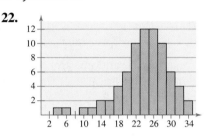

23.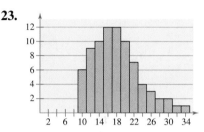

24. For the histogram in Exercise 22, which is greater, the mean or the median?

25. For the histogram in Exercise 23, which is greater, the mean or the median?

26. The data set represents the mean price of a movie ticket (in U.S. dollars) for a sample of 12 U.S. cities. Find the range of the data set.

7.82 7.38 6.42 6.76 6.34 7.44 6.15 5.46 7.92 6.58 8.26 7.17

27. The data set represents the mean price of a movie ticket (in U.S. dollars) for a sample of 12 Japanese cities. Find the range of the data set.

19.73 16.48 19.10 18.56 17.68 17.19
16.63 15.99 16.66 19.59 15.89 16.49

28. The mileage (in thousands) for a rental car company's fleet is listed. Find the population mean and standard deviation of the data.

6 14 3 7 11 13 8 5 10 9 12 10

29. The age of each Supreme Court justice as of May 21, 1998 is listed. Find the population mean and standard deviation of the data.

73 78 68 62 61 58 49 65 59

30. Dormitory room prices (in dollars for one school year) for a sample of four-year universities are listed. Find the sample mean and the sample standard deviation of the data.

2445 2940 2399 1960 2421 2940 2657 2153
2430 2278 1947 2383 2710 2761 2377

31. Sample salaries (in dollars) of public school teachers are listed. Find the sample mean and the standard deviation of the data.

46,098 36,259 35,084 38,617 42,690 26,202 47,169 37,109

32. The mean rate for cable television from a sample of households was $26.00 per month with a standard deviation of $2.50. Between what two values does 99.7% of the data lie? (Assume that the data set has a bell-shaped distribution.)

33. 47.5%

34. The percent of the ages contained between 25 and 91 years is at least 75%.

35. The percent of the flight lengths between 0.11 and 12.59 days is at least 89%.

36. 2.48, 1.24

37. 2.44, 1.73

38. 56

39. 70

40. 14

41.

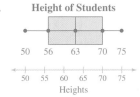

Height of Students

Heights

42. 4

43.

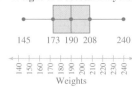

Weight of Football Players

Weights

44. 23%

45. P_{89}

33. The mean rate for cable television from a sample of households was $24.50 per month with a standard deviation of $2.75. Estimate the percent of cable television rates between $24.50 and $30.00. (Assume that the data set has a bell-shaped distribution.)

34. The mean age of a senator in the 105th Congress was 58 and the standard deviation was 16.5. Apply Chebychev's Theorem to the data using $k = 2$. Interpret the results in the context of the real-life setting.

35. The mean length of the first 20 space shuttle flights was 6.35 days and the standard deviation was 2.08 days. Apply Chebychev's Theorem to the data using $k = 3$. Interpret the results in the context of the real-life setting.

36. The results of a random sample of the number of television sets per household in a region are listed. Find the sample mean and standard deviation of the data.

Number of televisions	0	1	2	3	4	5
Number of households	1	8	13	10	5	3

37. The results of a random sample of airplanes and the number of defects found in their fuselages are listed. Find the sample mean and standard deviation of the data.

Number of defects	0	1	2	3	4	5	6
Number of planes	4	5	2	9	1	3	1

In Exercises 38–41, use the following data set. The data represent the heights (in inches) of students in a statistics class.

50 51 54 54 56 59 60 61 61 63
64 65 68 69 70 70 71 71 75

38. Find the height that corresponds to the first quartile.

39. Find the height that corresponds to the third quartile.

40. Find the interquartile range.

41. Make a box-and-whisker plot of the data.

42. Find the interquartile range of the data from Exercise 15.

43. The weights (in pounds) of the defensive players on a high school football team are given. Make a box-and-whisker plot of the data.

173 145 205 192 197 227 156 240 172 185
208 185 190 167 212 228 190 184 195

44. A student's test grade of 68 represents the 77th percentile of the grades. What percent of students scored higher than 68?

45. In 1997 there were 753 "oldies" radio stations in the United States. If one station finds that just 84 stations have a larger daily audience than it does, what percentile does this station come closest to in the daily audience rankings? (*Source: 1998 World Almanac and Book of Facts*)

2 ▼ CHAPTER QUIZ

1. See Odd Answers,
   page A52

2. 125.22, 13.00

3. (a)
U.S. Sporting Goods

Footwear 13%
Recreational transport 34%
Clothing 22%
Equipment 31%

(b)
U.S. Sporting Goods

Sales (in billions of dollars)
16 14 12 10 8 6 4 2

Recreational transport
Equipment
Clothing
Footwear

Sales areas

4. (a) 751.63, 784.5, none

   (b) 575, 48135.13, 219.40

5. $125,000 and $185,000

6. (a) 76, 79, 88

   (b) 12

   (c)
   Wins for Each Team

   65   76 79 88   101

   65   75   85   95   105
   Wins

Take this quiz as you would take a quiz in class. After you are done, check your work against the answers given in the back of the book.

1. The data set is the number of minutes a sample of 25 people exercises each week.

   108 139 120 123 120 132 123 131 131 157 150 124 111
   101 135 119 116 117 127 128 139 119 118 114 127

   (a) Make a frequency distribution of the data set using five classes. Include class limits, midpoints, frequencies, boundaries, relative frequencies, and cumulative frequencies.

   (b) Display the data using a frequency histogram and a frequency polygon on the same axes.

   (c) Display the data using a relative frequency histogram.

   (d) Describe the shape of the distribution as symmetric, uniform, or skewed.

   (e) Display the data using a box-and-whisker plot.

   (f) Display the data using an ogive.

2. Use frequency distribution formulas to approximate the mean and sample standard deviation of the data set in Exercise 1.

3. U.S. sporting goods sales (in billions of dollars) can be classified in four areas: clothing (9.6), footwear (5.9), equipment (13.5), and recreational transport (15.1). Display the data using (a) a pie chart and (b) a Pareto chart. *(Source: National Sporting Goods Association)*

4. Weekly salaries (in dollars) for a sample of registered nurses are listed.

   774 446 1019 795 908 667 444 960

   (a) Find the mean, the median, and the mode of the salaries. Which best describes the average salary?

   (b) Find the range, variance, and standard deviation of the data set. Interpret the results in the context of the real-life setting.

5. The mean price of new homes from a sample of houses is $155,000 with a standard deviation of $15,000. The data set has a bell-shaped distribution. Between what two prices do 95% of the houses fall?

6. The number of wins for each Major League Baseball team in 1997 are listed. *(Source: Major League Baseball)*

   98 96 79 78 76 86 80 78 68 67 90 84 77 65
   101 92 88 78 68 84 79 76 73 68 90 88 83 76

   (a) Find the quartiles of the data set.

   (b) Find the interquartile range.

   (c) Construct a box-and-whisker plot.

Where You've Been

In Chapters 1 and 2, you learned how to collect and describe data. Once the data are collected and described, you can use the results to write summaries, form conclusions, and make decisions. For instance, the Army Corp of Engineers maintains several dams on the Columbia and Snake Rivers. From studies at these dams, researchers have estimated that a hydroelectric turbine in the dams kills about 15% of all fish that pass through it during their downstream migration as juveniles. There are many proposals for solving this problem: bypass channels located near the turbine entrances, spilling water over the dams during downstream migrations, and capturing and transporting juvenile fish downstream.

The Columbia and Snake River system has 18 main-stem hydroelectric dams and dozens of other dams on smaller tributaries. The dams impede juvenile (downstream) and adult (upstream) migrations by their physical presence and by creating reservoirs. The upstream migration is helped greatly by the creation of fish ladders, but the downstream migration has been a tougher problem.

Probability

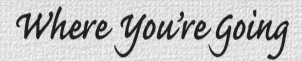

Where You're Going

In Chapter 3, you will learn how to use data to predict the probability that an event will occur. For instance, suppose that you wanted to find the probability that a juvenile salmon will pass unharmed through the turbines of one or more hydroelectric dams on the Columbia and Snake Rivers. After many samplings, you determine that 85 out of 100 juveniles can pass safely through a turbine. So, you can say that the probability of passing through one, two, or three turbines is as follows.

$$\text{Probability of passing through one turbine} = \tfrac{85}{100} = 0.85$$

$$\text{Probability of passing through two turbines} = \tfrac{85}{100} \cdot \tfrac{85}{100} \approx 0.723$$

$$\text{Probability of passing through three turbines} = \tfrac{85}{100} \cdot \tfrac{85}{100} \cdot \tfrac{85}{100} \approx 0.614$$

This process can be continued, and you will learn to calculate the probability of passing through n turbines as

$$\text{Probability of passing through } n \text{ turbines} = \left(\tfrac{85}{100}\right)^{n}.$$

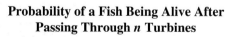

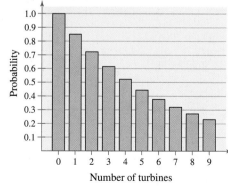

Probability of a Fish Being Alive After Passing Through n Turbines

3.1 Basic Concepts of Probability

Probability Experiments • Types of Probability • Properties of Probability

Probability Experiments

When weather forecasters say that there is a 90% chance of rain or a physician says there is a 35% chance for a successful surgery, they are stating the chance, or *probability,* that a specific event will occur. Decisions such as "should you wash your car" or "should you proceed with surgery" are often based on these probabilities. In the previous chapter, you learned about the role of the descriptive branch of statistics. Since probability is the foundation of inferential statistics, it is necessary to learn about it before proceeding to the second branch—inferential statistics.

DEFINITION

A **probability experiment** is an action through which specific results (counts, measurements, or responses) are obtained. The result of a single trial in a probability experiment is an **outcome.** The set of all possible outcomes of a probability experiment is the **sample space.** An **event** consists of one or more outcomes and is a subset of the sample space.

> **Study Tip**
>
> Here is a simple example of the use of the terms "probability experiment," "sample space," "event," and "outcome."
>
> Probability Experiment:
> Roll a six-sided die.
> Sample Space:
> {1, 2, 3, 4, 5, 6}
> Event:
> Roll an even number, {2, 4, 6}
> Outcome:
> Roll a 2, {2}

> ▶ **EXAMPLE 1**   *Identifying the Sample Space of a Probability Experiment*

A probability experiment consists of tossing a coin and then rolling a six-sided die. Describe the sample space.

SOLUTION

There are two possible outcomes when tossing a coin, a head (H) or a tail (T). For each of these, there are six possible outcomes when rolling a die: 1, 2, 3, 4, 5, or 6. One way to list outcomes for actions occurring in a sequence is to use a **tree diagram.** From the tree diagram, the sample space has 12 outcomes.

{H1, H2, H3, H4, H5, H6, T1, T2, T3, T4, T5, T6}

Tree Diagram for Coin and Die Experiment

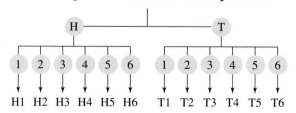

SURVEY

There should be a limit to the number of terms a U.S. senator can serve.

Check one response:

☐ Agree
☐ Disagree
☐ No opinion

Try It Yourself 1

A probability experiment consists of recording a response to the survey statement at the left *and* tossing a coin. Identify the sample space.

a. Start a tree diagram by forming a branch for each possible response to the survey.
b. At the end of each survey response branch, draw a new branch for each possible coin outcome.
c. Find the *number of outcomes* in the sample space.
d. List the *sample space*.   *Answer: Page A34*

In the rest of this chapter, you will learn how to calculate the probability or likelihood of an event. Events are often represented by uppercase letters, such as *A, B,* and *C.* An event that consists of a single outcome is called a **simple event.** For instance, if you determine the blood type of a sample, then a simple event *A* is "the blood is type A." In contrast, the event *E* is "the blood is not type A" and is not simple because it consists of three possible outcomes, {B, AB, O}.

▶ EXAMPLE 2   *Identifying Simple Events*

Decide whether the event is simple or not. Explain your reasoning.

1. For quality control, you randomly select a computer chip from a batch that has been manufactured that day. Event *A* is selecting a specific defective chip.
2. You roll a six-sided die. Event *B* is rolling at least a 4.

SOLUTION

1. Event *A* has only one outcome: choosing the specific defective chip. So, the event is a simple event.
2. *B* has three outcomes: rolling a 4, a 5, or a 6. Because the event has more than one outcome, it is not simple.

Note to Instructor

Ask students to use a tree diagram to develop the sample space that results from rolling two six-sided dice. Emphasize that the outcome {3, 2} is different from the outcome {2, 3} for a statistician, but not for a player. Point out that the event {3, 2} is a simple event. The event "roll a sum of 5" is not simple because it consists of the four outcomes {1, 4}, {2, 3}, {3, 2}, and {4, 1}.

Try It Yourself 2

You ask for a student's age at his or her last birthday. Decide whether each event is simple or not.

1. Event *C*: The student's age is between 18 and 23, inclusive.
2. Event *D*: The student's age is 20.

a. Decide how many outcomes are in the event.
b. State whether the event is *simple* or not.   *Answer: Page A34*

Types of Probability

There are three types of probability: classical probability, empirical probability, and subjective probability. The probability that event E will occur is written as $P(E)$ and is read "the probability of event E."

> ### DEFINITION
>
> **Classical** (or **theoretical**) **probability** is used when each outcome in a sample space is equally likely to occur. The classical probability for an event E is given by
>
> $$P(E) = \frac{\text{Number of outcomes in } E}{\text{Total number of outcomes in sample space}}.$$

▶ **EXAMPLE 3**   *Finding Classical Probabilities*

You roll a six-sided die. Find the probability of the following events.

1. Event A: rolling a 3
2. Event B: rolling a 7
3. Event C: rolling a number less than 5

SOLUTION   When rolling a six-sided die, the sample space consists of six outcomes: $\{1, 2, 3, 4, 5, 6\}$.

1. There is one outcome in event $A = \{3\}$. So,

$$P(3) = \frac{1}{6} \approx 0.167.$$

2. Because 7 is not in the sample space, there are no outcomes in event B. So,

$$P(7) = \frac{0}{6} = 0.$$

3. There are four outcomes in event $C = \{1, 2, 3, 4\}$. So,

$$P(\text{number less than 5}) = \frac{4}{6} = \frac{2}{3} \approx 0.667.$$

Standard Deck of Playing Cards

Hearts	Diamonds	Spades	Clubs
A ♥	A ♦	A ♠	A ♣
K ♥	K ♦	K ♠	K ♣
Q ♥	Q ♦	Q ♠	Q ♣
J ♥	J ♦	J ♠	J ♣
10 ♥	10 ♦	10 ♠	10 ♣
9 ♥	9 ♦	9 ♠	9 ♣
8 ♥	8 ♦	8 ♠	8 ♣
7 ♥	7 ♦	7 ♠	7 ♣
6 ♥	6 ♦	6 ♠	6 ♣
5 ♥	5 ♦	5 ♠	5 ♣
4 ♥	4 ♦	4 ♠	4 ♣
3 ♥	3 ♦	3 ♠	3 ♣
2 ♥	2 ♦	2 ♠	2 ♣

> *Try It Yourself 3*
>
> You select a card from a standard deck. Find the probability of the following.
>
> 1. Event D: Selecting a seven of diamonds
> 2. Event E: Selecting a diamond
> 3. Event F: Selecting a diamond, heart, club, or spade
>
> **a.** Identify the *total number of outcomes* in the sample space.
> **b.** Find the *number of outcomes* in the event.
> **c.** Use the *classical probability formula*.   *Answer: Page A34* ◀

A second type of probability is empirical probability. Empirical probability can be used even if each outcome is not equally likely to occur.

Picturing the World

It seems as if no matter how strange an event is, somebody wants to know the probability that it will occur. The following table lists the probability that some intriguing events will happen. *(Source: What Are The Chances)*

What are the chances?

Event	Probability
Appearing on *The Tonight Show*	1 in 490,000
Being killed by terrorists overseas	1 in 650,000
Being a victim of serious crime	5%
Writing a best-selling novel	0.00205
Congress will override a veto	4%
Earning a Ph.D.	0.008

Which of these events is most likely to occur? Least likely?

DEFINITION

Empirical (or **statistical probability**) is based on observations obtained from probability experiments. The empirical probability of an event E is the relative frequency of event E.

$$P(E) = \frac{\text{Frequency of event } E}{\text{Total frequency}} = \frac{f}{n}.$$

▶ **EXAMPLE 4**   *Finding Empirical Probabilities*

A pond contains three types of fish: bluegills, redgills, and crappies. Each fish in the pond is equally likely to be caught. You catch 40 fish and record the type. Each time, you release the fish back into the pond. The following frequency distribution shows your results.

Fish Type	Number of Times Caught, f
Bluegill	13
Redgill	17
Crappy	10
	$\Sigma f = 40$

If you catch another fish, what is the probability that it is a bluegill?

SOLUTION   The event is "catching a bluegill." In your experiment, the frequency of this event is 13. Because the total of the frequencies is 40, the empirical probability of catching a bluegill is

$$P(\text{bluegill}) = \frac{13}{40}$$

$$= 0.325$$

Try It Yourself 4

An insurance company determines that in every 100 claims, 4 are fraudulent. What is the probability that the next claim the company processes is fraudulent?

a. *Identify* the event. Find the *frequency* of the event.
b. *Find the total frequency for the experiment.*
c. Find the *relative frequency* of the event.

Answer: Page A34 ◀

Note to Instructor

Ask each student in your class to toss a coin 10 times and count the number of heads. Tally the results for the entire class. How close is the total number of heads to 50% of the total number of tosses? Emphasize that variation in experimental results is expected. If your students have a technology tool available in class, ask them to perform a simulation of tossing a coin 1000 times. Use 0 for heads and 1 for tails. Discuss the results.

As you increase the number of times a probability experiment is repeated, the empirical probability (relative frequency) of an event approaches the theoretical probability of the event. This is known as the **law of large numbers.**

Law of Large Numbers

As an experiment is repeated over and over, the empirical probability of an event approaches the theoretical (actual) probability of the event.

As an example of this law, suppose you want to determine the probability of tossing a head with a fair coin. If you toss the coin 10 times and get only 3 heads, you obtain an empirical probability of $\frac{3}{10}$. Because you tossed the coin only a few times, your empirical probability is not representative of the theoretical probability, which is $\frac{1}{2}$. If, however, you toss the coin several thousand times, then the law of large numbers tells you that the empirical probability will be very close to the theoretical or actual probability.

EXAMPLE 5   *Using Frequency Distributions to Find Probabilities*

Employee Ages	Frequency
age 15 to 24	54
age 25 to 34	366
age 35 to 44	233
age 45 to 54	180
age 55 to 64	125
65 and over	42
	$\Sigma f = 1000$

You survey a sample of 1000 employees at a company and record the age of each. The results are shown at the left in the frequency distribution. If you randomly select another employee, what is the probability that the employee is between 25 and 34 years old?

SOLUTION   The event is selecting an employee who is between 25 and 34 years old. In your survey, the frequency of this event is 366. Because the total of the frequencies is 1000, the probability of selecting an employee between the ages of 25 and 34 years old is

$$P(\text{age 25 to 34}) = \frac{366}{1000} = 0.366.$$

Try It Yourself 5

Find the probability that an employee chosen at random is between 15 and 24 years old.

a. Find the *frequency* of the event.
b. Find the *total of the frequencies.*
c. Find the *relative frequency* of the event.   *Answer: Page A34*

The third type of probability is **subjective probability.** Subjective probabilities result from intuition, educated guesses, and estimates. For instance, given a patient's health and extent of injuries, a doctor may feel that the patient has a 90% chance of a full recovery. Or a business analyst may predict that the chance of the employees of a certain company going on strike is 0.25.

Type	Summary	Formula
Classical (Theoretical) Probability	The number of outcomes in the sample space is known and each outcome is equally likely to occur.	$P(E) = \dfrac{\text{Number of outcomes in event } E}{\text{Number of outcomes in sample space}}$
Empirical Probability	The frequency of outcomes in the sample space is estimated from experimentation.	$P(E) = \dfrac{\text{Frequency of event } E}{\text{Total frequency}} = \dfrac{f}{n}$
Subjective Probability	Probabilities result from intuition, educated guesses, and estimates.	None

A probability cannot be negative or greater than 1. So, the probability of an event E is between 0 and 1, inclusive. That is, $0 \le P(E) \le 1$.

EXAMPLE 6　*Classifying Types of Probability*

Classify each statement as an example of classical probability, empirical probability, or subjective probability. Explain your reasoning.

1. The probability of your phone ringing during dinner is 0.5.
2. The probability that a voter chosen at random will vote Republican is 0.45.
3. The probability of winning a 1000-ticket raffle with one ticket is $\frac{1}{1000}$.

SOLUTION

1. This probability is most likely based on an educated guess. It is an example of subjective probability.
2. This statement is most likely based on a survey of voters, so it is an example of empirical probability.
3. Because you know the number of outcomes and each is equally likely, this is an example of classical probability.

Insight

If $P(E) = 0$, event E is impossible. If $P(E) = 1$, then event E is certain.

Unlikely　Likely

Impossible　Even　Certain

0　0.5　1

Try It Yourself 6

Based on previous counts, the probability of a salmon successfully passing through a dam on the Columbia River is 0.85. Is this statement an example of classical, empirical, or subjective probability?

a. Identify the *event*.
b. Decide whether the probability is *determined* by knowing all possible outcomes, whether the probability is *estimated* from the results of an experiment, or whether the probability is an *educated guess*.
c. Make a *conclusion*.
Answer: Page A34

Properties of Probability

The sum of the probabilities of all outcomes in a sample space is 1 or 100%. An important result of this fact is that if you know the probability of an event E, you can find the probability of the *complement of event E*.

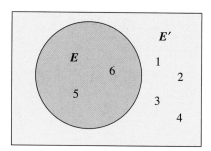

The area of the rectangle represents the total probability of the sample space (1 = 100%). The area of the circle represents the probability of event E, while the area outside the circle represents the probability of the complement of event E.

For instance, if you roll a die and let E be the event "the number is at least 5," then the complement of E is the event "the number is less than 5." In other words, $E = \{5, 6\}$ and $E' = \{1, 2, 3, 4\}$.

Using the definition of the complement of an event and the fact that the sum of the probabilities of all outcomes is 1, you can determine the following formulas:

$$P(E) + P(E') = 1 \qquad P(E) = 1 - P(E') \qquad P(E') = 1 - P(E)$$

The Venn diagram illustrates the relationship between the sample space, an event E, and its complement E'.

▶ **EXAMPLE 7**   *Finding the Probability of the Complement of an Event*

Use the frequency distribution given in Example 5 to find the probability of randomly choosing an employee who is not between 25 and 34 years old.

SOLUTION   From Example 5, you know that

$$P(\text{age 25 to 34}) = \frac{366}{1000} = 0.366.$$

So, the probability that an employee is not between 25 and 34 years old is

$$P(\text{age is not 25 to 34}) = 1 - \frac{366}{1000} = \frac{634}{1000} = 0.634.$$

Note to Instructor

Discuss other events (and complements) from the roll of a die. Ask students to calculate probabilities of the event and of the complement to see the relationship.

    Event *A*: Roll a 4.
    Event *B*: Roll an odd number.
    Event *C*: Roll a 7.
    Event *D*: Roll a 2 or greater.

Try It Yourself 7

Use the frequency distribution in Example 4 to find the probability that a fish that is caught is *not* a redgill.

a. *Find the probability* that the fish is a redgill.
b. *Subtract* the resulting probability from 1.
c. State the probability as a fraction and as a decimal.

Answer: Page A34 ◀

3.1 EXERCISES

HELP

 StatPro 3.1

 Internet Statistics 3.1

 Student Solutions Manual 3.1

 Videos 3.1

 Try It Yourself Answers 3.1

1. (a) Yes
   (b) No
   (c) No
   (d) Yes
   (e) Yes
2. It is impossible to have more than a 100% chance of rain.
3. {0, 1, 2, 3, 4, 5, 6, 7, 8, 9}
4.

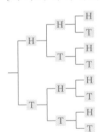

{HHH, HHT, HTH, HTT, THH, THT, TTH, TTT}

5. See Odd Answers, page A52
6. See Selected Answers, page A79
7. Simple event
8. Not a simple event
9. Empirical probability
10. Classical probability
11. 0.508
12. 0.513

Basic Skills and Concepts

1. Determine which of the numbers (a) 0, (b) 1.5, (c) −1, (d) 50%, and (e) $\frac{2}{3}$ could represent the probability of an event. Explain your reasoning.

2. Explain why the following statement is incorrect:
The probability of rain tomorrow is 120%.

Identifying a Sample Space   In Exercises 3–6, identify the sample space of each probability experiment. Draw a tree diagram if it is appropriate.

3. Guessing the last digit in a telephone number

4. Tossing three coins

5. Determining a person's blood type (A, B, AB, O) and gender (M, F)

6. Rolling two dice

Simple Events   In Exercises 7 and 8, decide whether the event is a simple event or not. Explain your reasoning.

7. A computer is used to select randomly a number between 1 and 2000. Event A is selecting 359.

8. A computer is used to select randomly a number between 1 and 2000. Event B is selecting a number less than 200.

Classifying Types of Probability   In Exercises 9 and 10, classify the statement as an example of classical probability, empirical probability, or subjective probability. Explain your reasoning.

9. According to company records, the probability that a washing machine will need repairs during a six-year period is 0.10.

10. The probability of choosing six numbers from 1 to 40 that match the six numbers drawn by a state lottery is 1/3,838,380 ≈ 0.00000026.

Graphical Analysis   In Exercises 11 and 12, use the diagram to answer the question. (*Source: Congressional Quarterly, Inc., Washington D.C.. America at the Polls 2, 1965, and America Votes, biennial, (copyright)*)

11. What is the probability that a voter chosen at random did not vote for Bill Clinton in the 1996 election?

12. What is the probability that a voter chosen at random did not vote for a Republican representative in the 1996 election?

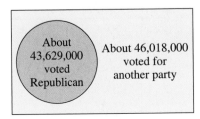

13. 0.159
14. 0.841
15. 0.000953
16. 0.999
17. 0.072
18. 0.224
19. 0.944
20. 0.793
21. (a) 0.5
    (b) 0.25
    (c) 0.25
22. 0.5

Finding Probabilities In Exercises 13–16, consider a company that selects employees for random drug tests. The company uses a computer to select randomly employee numbers that range from 1 to 6296.

13. Find the probability of selecting a number less than 1000.

14. Find the probability of selecting a number greater than 1000.

15. Find the probability of selecting a number divisible by 1000.

16. Find the probability of selecting a number that is not divisible by 1000.

Voting Ages In Exercises 17–20, use the following frequency distribution. The distribution shows the number of American voters (in millions) according to age. *(Source: U.S. Bureau of the Census)*

Ages of Voters	Frequency (in millions)
18 to 20 years old	10.8
21 to 24 years old	13.9
25 to 34 years old	40.1
35 to 44 years old	43.3
45 to 64 years old	53.7
65 years old and over	31.9

Find the probability that a voter chosen at random is

17. between 21 and 24 years old.

18. between 35 and 44 years old.

19. not between 18 and 20 years old.

20. not between 25 and 34 years old.

21. *Genetics* When two pink snapdragon flowers (RW) are crossed, there are four equally likely possible outcomes for the genetic makeup of the offspring: red (RR), pink (RW), pink (WR), and white (WW). If two pink snapdragons are crossed, what is the probability that the offspring is (a) pink?, (b) red?, and (c) white?

22. *Genetics* There are six basic types of coloring in registered collies: sable (SSmm), tricolor (ssmm), trifactored sable (Ssmm), blue merle (ssMm), sable merle (SSMm), and trifactored sable merle (SsMm). The *Punnett square* shows the possible coloring of the offspring of a trifactored sable merle collie and a trifactored sable collie. What is the probability that the offspring has the same coloring as one of its parents?

	R	W
R	RR	RW
W	RW	WW

	SM	Sm	sM	sm
Sm	SSMm	SSmm	SsMm	Ssmm
Sm	SSMm	SSmm	SsMm	Ssmm
sm	SsMm	Ssmm	ssMm	ssmm
sm	SsMm	Ssmm	ssMm	ssmm

Parents
Ssmm and SsMm

23. 0.747

24. 0.160

25. 0.253

26. 0.972

27. The probability of choosing a tea drinker who does not have a college degree.

28. The probability of choosing a smoker whose mother did not smoke.

29. (a) 0.506

   (b) 0.117

   (c) 0

Employment by Industry   In Exercises 23–26, use the following pie chart. The pie chart shows the number of workers (in thousands) by industry for the United States. *(Source: U.S. Department of Labor)*

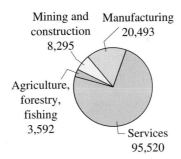

23. Find the probability that a worker chosen at random was employed in the services industry.

24. Find the probability that a worker chosen at random was employed in the manufacturing industry.

25. Find the probability that a worker chosen at random was not employed in the services industry.

26. Find the probability that a worker chosen at random was not employed in the agriculture, forestry, or fishing industry.

Writing   In Exercises 27 and 28, write a statement that represents the complement of the given probability.

27. The probability of randomly choosing a tea drinker who has a college degree (Assume that you are choosing from the population of all tea drinkers.)

28. The probability of randomly choosing a smoker whose mother also smoked (Assume that you are choosing from the population of all smokers.)

Extending the Basics

29. *Back to Akhiok*   A stem-and-leaf display for the ages of all 77 residents of Akhiok, Alaska is shown.

```
0 | 0 1 1 1 2 2 2 3 3 4 4 4 5 5 5 6 6 6 6 7 7 8 8 9
1 | 0 0 0 1 1 1 2 2 3 5 6 6 7 7
2 | 1 1 2 3 4 5 5 6 7 7 8 8 9
3 | 0 1 1 2 2 3 3 4 6 9
4 | 1 2 5 6 7 8 9
5 | 0 0 1 2 3 4 5 6
6 | 3
```

If a resident is selected at random, find the probability he or she will be (a) at least 21 years old, (b) between 40 and 50 years old inclusive, and (c) older than 65.

30. (a) {(SSS), (SSR), (SRS), (SRR),
(RSS), (RSR), (RRS),
(RRR)}

(b) {(RRR)}

(c) {(SSR), (SRS), (RSS)}

(d) {(SSR), (SRS), (SRR), (RSS),
(RSR), (RRS), (RRR)}

31. No, 1:5

32. (a) 0.444

(b) 0.556

33. 1:3

34. 3:1

30. *Wet or Dry?* You are planning a three-day trip to Seattle, Washington in October. Use the following tree diagram to answer the questions.

(a) List the sample space.

(b) List the event(s) "It rains all three days."

(c) List the event(s) "It rains on exactly one day."

(d) List the event(s) "It rains on at least one day."

Tree Diagram for Rainy Days

Day 1 Day 2 Day 3

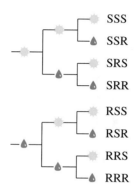

Odds

SSS
SSR
SRS
SRR
RSS
RSR
RRS
RRR

Odds In Exercises 31–34, use the following information. In gambling, the chances of winning are often expressed in terms of odds rather than probabilities. The odds of winning is the ratio of the number of successful outcomes to the number of unsuccessful outcomes. The odds of losing is the ratio of the number of unsuccessful outcomes to the number of successful outcomes. For example, if the number of successful outcomes is 2 and the number of unsuccessful outcomes is 3, the odds are 2:3 (read "2 to 3") or $\frac{2}{3}$. (*Note:* The *probability* of success is $\frac{2}{5}$.)

31. A beverage company puts game pieces under the caps of its drinks and claims that one in six game pieces wins a prize. The official rules of the contest state that the odds of winning a prize are 1:6. Is this correct? Explain your reasoning.

32. The odds of an event occurring are 4:5. Find (a) the probability that the event will occur and (b) the probability that the event will not occur.

33. If a card is picked at random from a standard deck of 52 playing cards, find the odds that it is a spade.

34. If a card is picked at random from a standard deck of 52 playing cards, find the odds that it is not a spade.

Conditional Probability and the Multiplication Rule

3.2

Conditional Probability • Independent and Dependent Events • The Multiplication Rule

Conditional Probability

In this section, you will learn how to find the probability that two events occur in sequence. Before you can find this probability, however, you must know how to find conditional probabilities.

DEFINITION

A **conditional probability** is the probability of an event occurring, given that another event has already occurred. The conditional probability of event B occurring, given that event A has occurred, is denoted by $P(B|A)$ and is read as "probability of B, given A."

▶ **EXAMPLE 1** *Finding Conditional Probabilities*

	Gene present	Gene not present	Total
High IQ	33	19	52
Normal IQ	39	11	50
Total	72	30	102

1. Two cards are selected in sequence from a standard deck. Find the probability that the second card is a queen, given that the first card is a king. (Assume that the king is not replaced.)
2. The table at left shows the results of a study in which researchers examined a child's IQ and the presence of a specific gene in the child. Find the probability that a child has a high IQ, given that the child has the gene. *(Source: Psychological Science)*

SOLUTION

1. Because the first card is a king and is not replaced, the remaining deck has 51 cards, 4 of which are queens. So, $P(B|A) = \frac{4}{51} \approx 0.078$.
2. There are 72 children who have the gene. So, the sample space consists of these 72 children. Of these, 33 have a high IQ. So, $P(B|A) = \frac{33}{72} \approx 0.458$.

Try It Yourself 1

1. Find the probability that a child does not have the gene.
2. Find the probability that a child does not have the gene, given that the child has a normal IQ.

a. Find the *number of outcomes* in the event and in the sample space.
b. *Divide* the number of outcomes in the event by the number of outcomes in the sample space. *Answer: Page A34* ◀

Independent and Dependent Events

The question of the independence of two or more events is important to researchers in fields such as marketing, medicine, and psychology. You can use conditional probabilities to determine whether events are independent or dependent.

DEFINITION

Two events are **independent** if the occurrence of one of the events does not affect the probability of the occurrence of the other event. Two events A and B are independent if

$$P(B|A) = P(B) \quad \text{or if} \quad P(A|B) = P(A).$$

Events that are not independent are **dependent.**

▶ **EXAMPLE 2**   *Classifying Events as Independent or Dependent*

Decide whether the events are independent or dependent.

1. Selecting a king from a standard deck (A), not replacing it, and then selecting a queen from the deck (B)
2. Tossing a coin and getting a head (A), and then rolling a six-sided die and obtaining a 6 (B)
3. Practicing the piano (A), and then becoming a concert pianist (B)

SOLUTION

1. $P(B|A) = \frac{4}{51}$ and $P(B) = \frac{4}{52}$. The occurrence of A changes the probability of the occurrence of B, so the events are dependent.
2. $P(B|A) = \frac{1}{6}$ and $P(B) = \frac{1}{6}$. The occurrence of A does not change the probability of the occurrence of B, so the events are independent.
3. If you practice the piano, the chances of becoming a concert pianist are greatly increased, so these events are dependent.

Try It Yourself 2

Decide whether the events are independent or dependent events. Explain your reasoning.

1. A salmon swims successfully through a dam (A) and then swims successfully through a second dam (B).
2. Exercising frequently (A) and having a low resting heart rate (B)

a. *Decide* whether the occurrence of the first event affects the probability of the second event.
b. *State* if the events are *independent* or *dependent*.
c. *Explain* your reasoning.   *Answer: Page A34* ◀

The Multiplication Rule

To find the probability of two events occurring in sequence, you can use the multiplication rule.

> ### The Multiplication Rule for the Probability of *A* and *B*
>
> The probability that two events *A* and *B* will occur in sequence is
>
> $$P(A \text{ and } B) = P(A) \cdot P(B|A).$$
>
> If events *A* and *B* are independent, then the rule can be simplified to $P(A \text{ and } B) = P(A) \cdot P(B)$. This simplified rule can be extended for any number of events.

EXAMPLE 3 — *Using the Multiplication Rule to Find Probabilities*

1. Two cards are selected, without replacement, from a standard deck. Find the probability of selecting a king and then selecting a queen.
2. A coin is tossed and a die is rolled. Find the probability of getting a head and then rolling a 6.

SOLUTION

1. Because the first card is not replaced, the events are dependent.

$$P(K \text{ and } Q) = P(K) \cdot P(Q|K) = \frac{4}{52} \cdot \frac{4}{51} = \frac{16}{2652} \approx 0.006$$

So, the probability of selecting a king and then a queen is about 0.006.

2. The events are independent.

$$P(H \text{ and } 6) = P(H) \cdot P(6) = \frac{1}{2} \cdot \frac{1}{6} = \frac{1}{12} \approx 0.083$$

So, the probability of tossing a head and then rolling a 6 is about 0.083.

Study Tip

If you are not sure if the events are independent, use the formula for dependent events.

Try It Yourself 3

1. The probability that a salmon swims successfully through a dam is 0.85. Find the probability that a salmon successfully swims through two dams.
2. Consider the table shown in Example 1. Find the probability that a child has a normal IQ but does not have the gene.

a. Decide if the events are *independent* or *dependent*.
b. Use the *Multiplication Rule* to find the probability.

Answer: Page A34

To determine if A and B are independent, calculate $P(B)$ and $P(B|A)$. If the values are equal, the events are independent and the multiplication rule is simplified.

> **EXAMPLE 4**   *Using the Multiplication Rule to Find Probabilities*

1. A coin is tossed and a die is rolled. Find the probability of getting a head and then rolling a 2.
2. The probability that a salmon swims successfully through a dam is 0.85. Find the probability that three salmon swim successfully through the dam.
3. Find the probability that none of the three salmon is successful.
4. Find the probability that at least one of the salmon is successful in swimming through the dam.

SOLUTION

1. $P(H) = \frac{1}{2}$. Whether or not the coin is a head, $P(2) = \frac{1}{6}$. The events are independent.

$$P(H \text{ and } 2) = P(H) \cdot P(2) = \frac{1}{2} \cdot \frac{1}{6} = \frac{1}{12} = 0.083$$

So, the probability of tossing a head and then rolling a 2 is about 0.083.

2. The probability that each salmon is successful is 0.85. One salmon's chance of success is independent of the others.

$$P(3 \text{ salmon are successful}) = (0.85)(0.85)(0.85) = 0.614$$

So, the probability that all three are successful is about 0.614.

3. Because the probability of success is 0.85, the probability of failure is $1 - 0.85 = 0.15$.

$$P(\text{none of the three is successful}) = (0.15)(0.15)(0.15) = 0.003$$

So, the probability that none are successful is about 0.003.

4. The phrase "at least one" means one or more. The complement to the event "at least one is successful" is the event "none are successful." Using the rule of complements,

$$P(\text{at least 1 is successful}) = 1 - P(\text{none are successful}) = 1 - 0.003$$
$$= 0.997.$$

There is a 0.997 probability that at least one salmon is successful.

Try It Yourself 4

Suppose engineers can increase the probability of a salmon successfully swimming through a dam to 0.90.

1. Find the probability that three salmon swim successfully through the dam.
2. Find the probability that at least one salmon swims successfully through the dam.

a. Determine whether to find the probability of the event or its complement.
b. Use the *Multiplication Rule* to find the probability. If necessary, use the *Complement Rule*.   *Answer: Page A34*

EXERCISES

HELP

 StatPro 3.2

 Internet Statistics 3.2

 Student Solutions Manual 3.2

 Videos 3.2

Try It Yourself Answers 3.2

Basic Skills and Concepts

1. What is the difference between independent and dependent events?

2. List examples of (a) two events that are independent and (b) two events that are dependent.

True or False In Exercises 3 and 4, determine whether the statement is true or false. If it is false, rewrite it so that it is a true statement.

3. If two events are not independent, $P(A|B) = P(B)$.

4. If events A and B are dependent, then $P(A \text{ and } B) = P(A) \cdot P(B)$.

Classifying Events In Exercises 5–8, decide whether the events are independent or dependent. Explain your reasoning.

5. Selecting a king from a standard deck, *replacing it,* and then selecting a queen from the deck

6. Getting 1.2 inches of rain on Monday night and having the Monday night baseball game cancelled

7. A numbered ball between 1 and 40 is selected from a bin, and then a second numbered ball is selected from the remaining balls in the bin.

8. A numbered ball between 1 and 52 is selected from a bin, *replaced,* and then a second numbered ball is selected from the bin.

9. ***BRCA Gene*** In the general population, one woman in nine will develop breast cancer. Research has shown that one woman in 250 carries a mutation of the BRCA gene. Eight out of 10 women with this mutation develop breast cancer. *(Source: Journal of National Cancer Institute)*

(a) Find the probability that a woman will develop breast cancer, given that she has a mutation of the BRCA gene.

(b) Find the probability that a woman will carry the mutation of the BRCA gene and will develop breast cancer.

(c) Are the events of carrying this mutation and developing breast cancer independent or dependent? Explain.

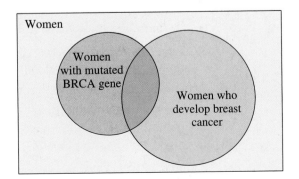

1. Two events are independent if the occurrence of one of the events does not affect the probability of the occurrence of the other event.

If $P(B|A) = P(B)$ or $P(A|B) = P(A)$, then Events A and B are independent.

2. (a) Roll a die twice. The outcome of the 2nd toss is independent of the outcome of the 1st toss.

(b) Draw two cards (without replacement) from a standard 52 card deck. The outcome of the 2nd card is dependent on the outcome of the 1st card.

3. False. If two events are independent, $P(A|B) = P(A)$.

4. False. If events A and B are independent, then $P(A \text{ and } B) = P(A) \cdot P(B)$.

5. Independent

6. Dependent

7. Dependent

8. Independent

9. (a) 0.8

(b) 0.0032

(c) Dependent

10. **(a)** 0.740
  (b) 0.822
  (c) Dependent
11. **(a)** 0.0168
  (b) 0.93
12. **(a)** 0.24
  (b) 0.6
13. **(a)** 0.109
  (b) 0.382
  (c) 0.618

10. *Summer Vacation*   The following table shows the results of a survey in which 104 families were asked if they own a computer and if they will be taking a summer vacation this year.

		Summer Vacation This Year		
		Yes	No	Total
Own a Computer	**Yes**	37	8	45
	No	40	19	59
	Total	77	27	104

(a) Find the probability a family is taking a summer vacation this year.

(b) Find the probability a family is taking a summer vacation this year, given that they own a computer.

(c) Are the events of owning a computer and taking a summer vacation this year independent or dependent events? Explain.

11. *Assisted Reproductive Technology*   A study found that 24% of the assisted reproductive technology (ART) cycles resulted in a pregnancy. Seven percent of the ART pregnancies resulted in multiple births. *(Source: U.S. Department of Health and Human Services)*

ART cycles

Pregnancies

Multiple births

(a) Find the probability that an ART cycle resulted in a pregnancy *and* produced a multiple birth.

(b) Find the probability that an ART cycle that resulted in a pregnancy did not produce a multiple birth.

12. *Race Relations*   A survey found that 60% of American adults think race relations have improved since the death of Martin Luther King, Jr. Of these 60%, 4 out of 10 said the rate of civil rights progress is too slow. *(Source: Marist Institute for Public Opinion)*

(a) Find the probability that an adult thinks race relations have improved since the death of Martin Luther King, Jr. *and* thinks the rate of civil rights progress is too slow.

(b) Given that an adult thinks race relations have improved since the death of Martin Luther King, Jr., find the probability that he or she thinks the rate of civil rights progress is not too slow.

13. *Defective Parts*   In a box of 11 parts, four of the parts are defective. Two parts are selected at random without replacement.

(a) Find the probability that both parts are defective.

(b) Find the probability that both parts are not defective.

(c) Find the probability that at least one part is defective.

14. 0.083

15. (a) 0.839

   (b) 0.167

   (c) 0.506

   (d) Dependent

16. (a) 0.556

   (b) 0.525

   (c) 0.167

   (d) Dependent

14. *Coin and Die* A coin is tossed and a six-sided die is rolled. Find the probability of getting a head and then rolling a 5.

15. *Emergency Savings* The following table shows the results of a survey in which 102 men and 103 women workers ages 25 to 64 were asked if they have at least one month's income set aside for emergencies. *(Adapted from Merrill Lynch)*

	Men	Women	Total
Less than one month's income	17	16	33
One month's income or more	85	87	172
Total	102	103	205

(a) Find the probability that a worker has one month's income or more set aside for emergencies.

(b) Given that a worker is a male, find the probability that the worker has less than one month's income.

(c) Given that a worker has one month's income or more, find the probability that the worker is a female.

(d) Are the events of having less than one month's income saved and being male independent or dependent? Explain.

16. *Health Care for Dogs* The following table shows the results of a survey in which 90 dog owners were asked how much they have spent in the last year for their dog's health care and whether their dogs were purebred or mixed breeds.

		Type of Dog		
		Purebred	Mixed Breed	Total
Health Care	**Less than $100**	19	21	40
	$100 or more	35	15	50
	Total	54	36	90

(a) Find the probability that $100 or more was spent on a dog's health care in the last year.

(b) Given that a dog owner spent less than $100, find the probability that the dog was a mixed breed.

(c) Find the probability that a dog owner spent $100 or more on health care and the dog was a mixed breed.

(d) Are the events "spending $100 or more on health care" and "having a mixed breed dog" independent or dependent? Explain.

17. **(a)** 0.0000000243
    (b) 0.859
    (c) 0.141
18. **(a)** 0.055
    (b) 0.238
    (c) 0.762
19. **(a)** 0.2
    (b) 0.04
    (c) 0.008
    (d) 0.512
    (e) 0.488
20. **(a)** 0.985
    (b) 0.015
    (c) 0.000000125
21. 0.954
22. 0.933

17. ***Blood*** The probability that a person in the United States has type AB$^+$ blood is 3%. Five unrelated Americans are selected at random. *(Source: American Association of Blood Banks)*

    (a) Find the probability that all five have type AB$^+$ blood.
    (b) Find the probability that none of the five has type AB$^+$ blood.
    (c) Find the probability that at least one of the five has type AB$^+$ blood.

18. ***Blood*** The probability that a person in the United States has type O$^+$ blood is 38%. Three unrelated Americans are selected at random. *(Source: American Association of Blood Banks)*

    (a) Find the probability that all three have type O$^+$ blood.
    (b) Find the probability that none of the three has type O$^+$ blood.
    (c) Find the probability that at least one of the three has type O$^+$ blood.

19. ***Guessing*** A multiple-choice quiz has three questions, each with five choices for the answer. Only one of the choices is correct. You have no idea what the answer is to any of the questions, and you have to guess each answer.

    (a) Find the probability of answering the first question correctly.
    (b) Find the probability of answering the first two questions correctly.
    (c) Find the probability of answering all three questions correctly.
    (d) Find the probability of answering none of the questions correctly.
    (e) Find the probability of answering at least one of the questions correctly.

20. ***Bookbinding Defects*** A printing company's bookbinding machine has a probability of 0.005 of producing a defective book. If this machine is used to bind three books, find the probability that (a) none of the books are defective, (b) at least one of the books is defective, and (c) all of the books are defective.

Extending the Basics

By rewriting the formula for the Multiplication Rule, you can write a formula for finding conditional probabilities. The conditional probability of event B occurring, given that event A has occurred, is

$$P(B|A) = \frac{P(A \text{ and } B)}{P(A)}.$$

In Exercises 21 and 22, use the following information. The probability that an airplane flight departs on time is 0.89. The probability that a flight arrives on time is 0.87, and the probability that a flight departs and arrives on time is 0.83.

21. Find the probability that a flight departed on time given that it arrives on time.

22. Find the probability that a flight arrives on time given that it departed on time.

23. (a) 0.444
(b) 0.4
24. (a) 0.074
(b) 0.999
25. (a) 0.462
(b) 0.538
(c) Yes
(d) Answers will vary.

Another way to find conditional probability is to use **Bayes's Theorem.** The probability of event A, given that event B has occurred, is

$$P(A|B) = \frac{P(A) \cdot P(B|A)}{P(A) \cdot P(B|A) + P(A') \cdot P(B|A')}.$$

23. Use Bayes's Theorem to find $P(A|B)$ for the following.
(a) $P(A) = \frac{2}{3}$, $P(A') = \frac{1}{3}$, $P(B|A) = \frac{1}{5}$, and $P(B|A') = \frac{1}{2}$
(b) $P(A) = \frac{3}{8}$, $P(A') = \frac{5}{8}$, $P(B|A) = \frac{2}{3}$, and $P(B|A') = \frac{3}{5}$

24. *Reliability of Testing* A certain virus infects one in every 200 people. A test used to detect the virus in a person is positive 80% of the time if the person has the virus and 5% of the time if the person does not have the virus. (This 5% result is called a *false positive*.) Let A be the event "the person is infected" and B be the event "the person tests positive."
(a) If a person tests positive, what is the probability that the person is infected?
(b) If a person tests negative, what is the probability that the person is not infected?

25. *Birthday Problem* You are in a class that has 24 students. You want to find the probability that at least two of the students share the same birthday.
(a) First, find the probability that each student has a different birthday.

$$P(\text{different birthdays}) = \overbrace{\frac{364}{365} \cdot \frac{363}{365} \cdot \frac{362}{365} \cdots \frac{343}{365} \cdot \frac{342}{365}}^{23 \text{ factors}}$$

(b) The probability that at least two students have the same birthday is the complement of the probability in part (a). What is this probability?
(c) We used a technology tool to generate 24 random numbers between 1 and 365. Each number represents a birthday. Did we get at least two people with the same birthday?

228, 348, 181, 317, 81, 183, 52, 346, 177, 118, 315, 273
252, 168, 281, 266, 285, 13, 118, 360, 8, 193, 57, 107

(d) Use a technology tool to simulate the "Birthday Problem." Repeat the simulation 10 times. How many times did you get "at least two people" with the same birthday?

The Addition Rule

3.3

Mutually Exclusive Events • The Addition Rule • A Summary of Probability

What You Should Learn

- *How to determine if two events are mutually exclusive*
- *How to use the addition rule to find the probability of two events*

Mutually Exclusive Events

In Section 3.2, you learned how to find the probability of two events, *A* and *B*, occurring in sequence. Such probabilities are denoted by $P(A \text{ and } B)$. In this section, you will learn how to find the probability that at least one of two events will occur. Probabilities such as these are denoted by $P(A \text{ or } B)$ and depend on whether the events are mutually exclusive.

> **DEFINITION**
>
> Two events *A* and *B* are **mutually exclusive** if *A* and *B* cannot occur at the same time.

Study Tip

In probability and statistics the word "or" is usually used as an "inclusive or" rather than an "exclusive or." For instance, there are three ways for "Event A or B" to occur.

(1) A occurs and B does not occur.

(2) B occurs and A does not occur.

(3) A and B both occur.

The Venn diagrams below show the relationship between events that are mutually exclusive and events that are not mutually exclusive.

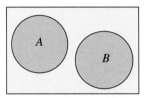

A and B are mutually exclusive.

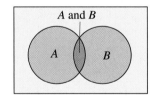

A and B are not mutually exclusive.

EXAMPLE 1 *Mutually Exclusive Events*

Decide if the events are mutually exclusive. Explain your reasoning.

1. Roll a die. *A*: Roll a 3. *B*: Roll a 4.
2. Select a student. *A*: Select a male student. *B*: Select a nursing major.
3. Select a blood donor. *A*: The donor's blood is type O. *B*: The donor is a female.

SOLUTION

1. The first event has one outcome, a 3. The second event also has one outcome, a 4. These outcomes cannot occur at the same time, so the events are mutually exclusive.
2. Because the student can be a male nursing major, the events are not mutually exclusive.
3. Because the donor can be a female with type O blood, the events are not mutually exclusive.

Note to Instructor

Students often confuse the concept of independent events with the concept of mutually exclusive events. Ask students whether the pairs of events in Example 1 are independent or dependent.

The Addition Rule

The Addition Rule for the Probability of *A* or *B*

The probability that events *A or B* will occur, *P*(*A* or *B*), is given by

$$P(A \text{ or } B) = P(A) + P(B) - P(A \text{ and } B).$$

If events *A* and *B* are mutually exclusive, then the rule can be simplified to $P(A \text{ or } B) = P(A) + P(B)$. This rule can be extended to any number of events.

Study Tip

By subtracting P(A and B), you avoid double counting the probability of outcomes that occur in both A and B.

Deck of 52 Cards

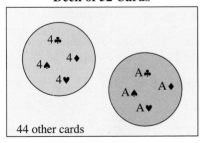

44 other cards

Roll a Die

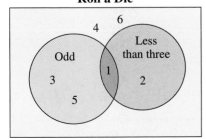

▶ **EXAMPLE 2** *Using the Addition Rule to Find Probabilities*

1. You select a card from a standard deck. Find the probability that the card is a 4 or an ace.
2. You roll a die. Find the probability of rolling a number less than three or rolling an odd number.

SOLUTION

1. If the card is a 4, it cannot be an ace. So, the events are mutually exclusive. The probability of selecting a 4 or an ace is

$$P(4 \text{ or ace}) = P(4) + P(\text{ace}) = \frac{4}{52} + \frac{4}{52} = \frac{8}{52} = \frac{2}{13} \approx 0.154.$$

2. The events are not mutually exclusive because 1 is an outcome of both events. So, the probability of rolling a number less than 3 or an odd number is

$$P(\text{less than 3 or odd}) = P(\text{less than 3}) + P(\text{odd}) - P(\text{less than 3 and odd})$$

$$= \frac{2}{6} + \frac{3}{6} - \frac{1}{6} = \frac{4}{6} = \frac{2}{3} \approx 0.667.$$

Try It Yourself 2

1. A die is rolled. Find the probability of rolling a 6 or an odd number.
2. A card is selected from a standard deck. Find the probability that the card is a face card or a heart.

a. Decide whether the events are *mutually exclusive.*
b. Find $P(A)$, $P(B)$, and, if necessary, $P(A \text{ and } B)$.
c. Use the *Addition Rule* to find the probability.   *Answer: Page A35*

EXAMPLE 3   *Finding Probabilities of Mutually Exclusive Events*

The following frequency distribution shows the volume of sales, in dollars, and the number of months a sales representative reached each sales level during the past three years. If this sales pattern continues, what is the probability that the sales representative will sell between $75,000 and $124,999 next month?

Sales Volume	Months
0–24,999	3
25,000–49,999	5
50,000–74,999	6
75,000–99,999	7
100,000–124,999	9
125,000–149,999	2
150,000–174,999	3
175,000–199,999	1

SOLUTION   To solve this problem, define events A and B as follows.

A = monthly sales between $75,000 and $99,999
B = monthly sales between $100,000 and $124,999

Because events A and B are mutually exclusive, the probability that the sales representative will sell between $75,000 and $124,999 next month is

$$P(A \text{ or } B) = P(A) + P(B) = \frac{7}{36} + \frac{9}{36} = \frac{16}{36} = \frac{4}{9} \approx 0.444.$$

Try It Yourself 3

Find the probability that the sales representative will sell between $0 and $49,999.

a. *Identify* events A and B.
b. Verify that A and B are *mutually exclusive.*
c. Find the *probability* of each event.
d. Use the *Addition Rule* to find the probability.   *Answer: Page A35*

> **EXAMPLE 4** **Using the Addition Rule to Find Probabilities**

A blood bank catalogs the types of blood, including positive or negative Rh-factor, given by donors during the last five days. The number of donors who gave each blood type is listed in the following table. A donor is selected at random.

1. Find the probability that the donor has type O or type A blood.
2. Find the probability that the donor has type B blood or is Rh-negative.

<table>
<tr><td rowspan="2"></td><td colspan="5">Blood Type</td></tr>
<tr><td>O</td><td>A</td><td>B</td><td>AB</td><td>Total</td></tr>
<tr><td>Positive</td><td>156</td><td>139</td><td>37</td><td>12</td><td>344</td></tr>
<tr><td>Negative</td><td>28</td><td>25</td><td>8</td><td>4</td><td>65</td></tr>
<tr><td>Total</td><td>184</td><td>164</td><td>45</td><td>16</td><td>409</td></tr>
</table>

(Rh-factor labels the Positive / Negative rows)

SOLUTION

1. Because a donor cannot have type O blood and type A blood, these events are mutually exclusive. So, using the Addition Rule, the probability that a randomly chosen donor has type O or type A blood is

$$P(\text{type O or type A}) = P(\text{type O}) + P(\text{type A})$$
$$= \frac{184}{409} + \frac{164}{409}$$
$$= \frac{348}{409}$$
$$\approx 0.851$$

2. Because a donor can have type B blood and be Rh-negative, these events are not mutually exclusive. So, using the Addition Rule, the probability that a randomly chosen donor has type B blood or is Rh-negative is

$$P(\text{type B or Rh-neg}) = P(\text{type B}) + P(\text{Rh-neg}) - P(\text{type B and Rh-neg})$$
$$= \frac{45}{409} + \frac{65}{409} - \frac{8}{409}$$
$$= \frac{102}{409}$$
$$\approx 0.249$$

> *Try It Yourself 4*
>
> 1. Find the probability that the donor has type B or type AB blood.
> 2. Find the probability that the donor has type O blood or is Rh-positive.
>
> **a.** Decide if the events are *mutually exclusive*.
> **b.** Use the *Addition Rule*. *Answer: Page A35*

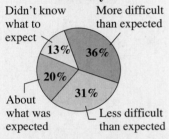

Picturing the World

In a survey conducted by National Family Organization, new mothers were asked to rate the difficulty of delivering their first child compared with what they expected.

How Difficult was the Delivery?

Didn't know what to expect — 13%
More difficult than expected — 36%
About what was expected — 20%
Less difficult than expected — 31%

If you randomly selected a new mother and asked her to compare the difficulty of her delivery to what she expected, what is the probability that she would say that it was the same or more difficult than what she expected?

A Summary of Probability

Type of Probability	Formula
Classical Probability	$P(E) = \dfrac{\text{Number of outcomes in event } E}{\text{Number of outcomes in sample space}}$
Empirical Probability	$P(E) = \dfrac{\text{Frequency of event } E}{\text{Total frequency}} = \dfrac{f}{n}$
Complementary Events	$P(E) + P(E') = 1, \ P(E) = 1 - P(E')$ $P(E') = 1 - P(E)$
Multiplication Rule	$P(A \text{ and } B) = P(A) \cdot P(B|A)$ $P(A \text{ and } B) = P(A) \cdot P(B)$ *Independent events*
Addition Rule	$P(A \text{ or } B) = P(A) + P(B) - P(A \text{ and } B)$ $P(A \text{ or } B) = P(A) + P(B)$ *Mutually exclusive events*

> **EXAMPLE 5**   *Finding Probabilities*

Use the graph at the right to find the probability that a randomly selected draft pick is not a running back or a wide receiver.

SOLUTION   Define events A and B as follows.

    A: Draft pick is a running back.
    B: Draft pick is a wide receiver.

These events are mutually exclusive, so the probability that the draft pick is a running back or wide receiver is

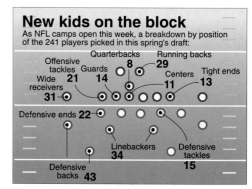

Copyright 1998, USA TODAY. Reprinted with permission.

$$P(A \text{ or } B) = P(A) + P(B) = \frac{29}{241} + \frac{31}{241} = \frac{60}{241}.$$

By taking the complement of $P(A \text{ or } B)$, you can determine that the probability of randomly selecting a draft pick who is not a running back or wide receiver is

$$1 - P(A \text{ or } B) = 1 - \frac{60}{241} = \frac{181}{241} \approx 0.751.$$

Try It Yourself 5

Find the probability that a randomly selected draft pick is not a linebacker or a quarterback.

a. Find the *probability* that the draft pick is a linebacker or a quarterback.

b. Find the *complement* of the event.

Answer: Page A35

3.3 EXERCISES

HELP

StatPro 3.3

Internet Statistics 3.3

Student Solutions Manual 3.3

Videos 3.3

Try It Yourself Answers 3.3

1. $P(A$ and $B) = 0$ because A and B cannot occur at the same time.

2. (a) Toss coin once: $A = \{head\}$ and $B = \{tail\}$

   (b) Draw one card: $A = \{ace\}$ and $B = \{spade\}$

3. True

4. False

5. Not mutually exclusive

6. Mutually exclusive

7. Not mutually exclusive

8. Not mutually exclusive

9. Mutually exclusive

10. Not mutually exclusive

11. (a) No

   (b) 0.432

Basic Skills and Concepts

1. If two events are mutually exclusive, why is $P(A$ and $B) = 0$?

2. List examples of (a) two events that are mutually exclusive and (b) two events that are not mutually exclusive.

True or False In Exercises 3 and 4, determine whether the statement is true or false. If it is false, explain why.

3. If two events are mutually exclusive, they have no outcomes in common.

4. The probability that event A or event B will occur is $P(A$ or $B) = P(A) + P(B) - P(A$ or $B)$.

Graphical Analysis In Exercises 5 and 6, decide if the events shown in the Venn diagram are mutually exclusive. Explain your reasoning.

5.
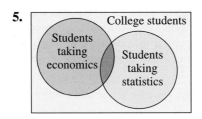

6.
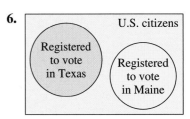

Mutually Exclusive Events In Exercises 7–10, decide if the events are mutually exclusive. Explain your reasoning.

7. Event A: Randomly select a female worker.
   Event B: Randomly select a worker with a college degree.

8. Event A: Randomly select a male worker.
   Event B: Randomly select a worker employed part-time.

9. Event A: Randomly select a person between 18 and 24 years old.
   Event B: Randomly select a person between 25 and 34 years old.

10. Event A: Randomly select a person between 18 and 24 years old.
   Event B: Randomly select a person earning between $20,000 and $29,999.

11. *Audit* During a 52-week period, a company paid overtime wages for 18 weeks and hired temporary help for 9 weeks. During 5 weeks, the company paid overtime *and* hired temporary help.

   (a) Are the events "selecting a week that contained overtime wages" and "selecting a week that contained temporary help wages" mutually exclusive? Explain.

   (b) If an auditor randomly examined the payroll records for only one week, what is the probability that the payroll for that week contained overtime wages or temporary help wages?

12. (a) Not mutually exclusive
   (b) 0.639
13. (a) Not mutually exclusive
   (b) 0.126
14. (a) Not mutually exclusive
   (b) 0.9972
15. (a) 0.069
   (b) 0.874
   (c) 0.232

12. *Newspaper Survey*   A college has an undergraduate enrollment of 3500. Of these, 860 are business majors and 1800 are women. Of the business majors, 425 are women.

(a) Are the events "selecting a woman student" and "selecting a business major" mutually exclusive? Explain.

(b) If a college newspaper conducts a poll and selects students at random to answer a survey, find the probability that a selected student is a woman or a business major.

13. *Carton Defects*   A company that makes cartons finds that the probability of producing a carton with a puncture is 0.05. The probability that a carton has a smashed corner is 0.08. The probability that a carton has a puncture and has a smashed corner is 0.004.

(a) Are the events "selecting a carton with a puncture" and "selecting a carton with a smashed corner" mutually exclusive? Explain.

(b) If a quality inspector randomly selects a carton, find the probability that the carton has a puncture or has a smashed corner.

14. *Can Defects*   A company that makes soda pop cans finds that the probability of producing a can without a puncture is 0.96. The probability that a can does not have a smashed edge is 0.93. The probability that a can does not have a puncture and does not have a smashed edge is 0.893.

(a) Are the events "selecting a can without a puncture" and "selecting a can without a smashed edge" mutually exclusive? Explain.

(b) If a quality inspector randomly selects a can, find the probability that the can does not have a puncture or does not have a smashed edge.

15. *U.S. Age Distribution*   The estimated percent distribution of the U.S. population for 2000 is shown in the following pie chart. Find the following probabilities. *(Source: U.S. Census Bureau)*

(a) Randomly selecting someone under five years old

(b) Randomly selecting someone who is not 65 years or over

(c) Randomly selecting someone who is between 18 and 34 years old

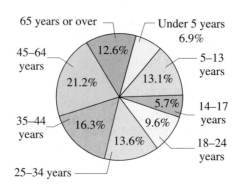

Figure for 15

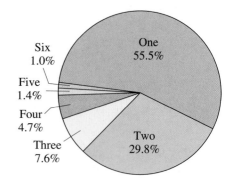

Figure for 16

16. (a) 0.298
(b) 0.445
(c) 0.435
17. (a) 0.014
(b) 0.226
(c) 0.774
(d) b and c
18. (a) 0.0039
(b) 0.0025
(c) 0.213
(d) 0.0032
(e) 0.0063
19. Answers will vary.

Conclusion: If two events, {A} and {B}, are independent, $P(A \text{ and } B) = P(A) \cdot P(B)$. If two events are mutually exclusive, $P(A \text{ and } B) = 0$. The only scenario when two events can be independent and mutually exclusive is if $P(A) = 0$ or $P(B) = 0$.

16. *Tacoma Narrows Bridge* The percent distribution of the number of occupants in vehicles crossing the Tacoma Narrows Bridge in Washington is shown in the pie chart. Find the following probabilities. *(Source: Washington State Department of Transportation)*

(a) Randomly selecting a car with two occupants

(b) Randomly selecting a car with two or more occupants

(c) Randomly selecting a car with between two and five occupants, inclusive

17. *Left-Handed People* In a sample of 1000 people, 120 are left-handed. If two unrelated people are selected at random from the sample, find the probability of the following.

(a) Both people are left-handed.

(b) At least one of the two people is left-handed.

(c) Neither person is left-handed.

(d) Two of the events from (a), (b), and (c) are complementary events. Which two are they? Explain.

18. *Left-Handed People* In a sample of 1000 people (500 men and 500 women), 113 are left-handed (63 men and 50 women). If two unrelated people are selected at random from the sample, find the probability of the following.

(a) Both people are left-handed men.

(b) Both people are left-handed women.

(c) At least one of the two people is left-handed.

(d) The first person is a left-handed man and the second person is a left-handed woman.

(e) One of the two people is a left-handed man and the other is a left-handed woman.

Extending the Basics

19. *Writing* Is there a relationship between independence and mutual exclusivity? To decide, find examples of the following, *if possible*.

(a) Describe two events that are dependent and mutually exclusive.

(b) Describe two events that are independent and mutually exclusive.

(c) Describe two events that are dependent and not mutually exclusive.

(d) Describe two events that are independent and not mutually exclusive.

Use your results to write a conclusion about the relationship between independence and mutual exclusivity.

3   **CASE STUDY**   WWW.INFORMS.ORG

   *Institute for Operations Research and the Management Sciences*

Pick a Lane	**Cycling**
Choose a lane. Enter it and select the closest available space.	Enter the closest lane. Park in any of the 20 closest spaces. If all are full, cycle to next row.

Probability and Parking Lot Strategies

The Institute for Operations Research and the Management Sciences (INFORMS) is an international scientific society with over 12,000 members. It is dedicated to the application of scientific methods to improve decision making, management, and operations. Members of the institute work primarily in business, government, and education. They represent fields as diverse as airlines, health care, law enforcement, the military, the stock market, and telecommunications.

One study published by INFORMS was the result of research conducted by Richard Cassady of Mississippi State University and John Kobza of Virginia Polytechnic Institute. The parking space study was conducted at a mall that has four entrances, seven rows with 72 spaces each, and directional restrictions. The researchers compared several parking lot strategies to see which strategy saves the most time. The two best strategies are called *Pick a Lane* and *Cycling*. The results are listed below.

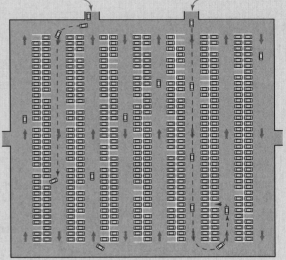

Store entrance

Time or Distance	Pick a Lane	Cycling
Time from lot entrance to parking space	37.7 sec	52.5 sec
Time from lot entrance to store's door	61.3 sec	70.7 sec
Average walking distance to store	257 feet	208 feet

Exercises

1. In a parking lot study, is each parking space equally likely to be empty? Explain your reasoning.

2. According to the results of the study, are you more likely to spend less time using the Pick-a-Lane strategy or the Cycling strategy? Explain.

3. According to the results of the study, are you more likely to walk less using the Pick-a-Lane strategy or the Cycling strategy? Explain.

4. A key assumption in the study was that the drivers can see which spaces are available as soon as they enter a lane. Why is that important?

5. The parking lot is completely full, and one car leaves. What is the probability that the car was in the first row? Explain your reasoning.

6. A person is leaving from a row that is full. What is the probability that the person was parked in one of the 20 spaces that are closest to the store?

7. Draw a diagram of the parking lot. Color code the parking spaces into three categories of 168 spaces each: most desirable, moderately desirable, and least desirable. Assume that the parking lot is half full. Estimate the probability that you can find a parking space in the most desirable category. Explain your reasoning.

Counting Principles

3.4

The Fundamental Counting Principle • Permutations • Combinations • Applications of Counting Principles

The Fundamental Counting Principle

In this section, you will study several techniques for counting the number of ways an event can occur. One is the Fundamental Counting Principle. You can use this principle to find the number of ways two or more events can occur in sequence.

The Fundamental Counting Principle

If one event can occur in m ways and a second event can occur in n ways, the number of ways the two events can occur in sequence is $m \cdot n$. This rule can be extended for any number of events occurring in sequence.

▶ **EXAMPLE 1** *Using the Fundamental Counting Principle*

You are purchasing a new car. Using the following manufacturers, car sizes, and colors, how many different ways can you select one manufacturer, one car size, and one color?

Manufacturer: Ford, GM, Chrysler
Car size: small, medium
Color: white (W), red (R), black (B), green (G)

SOLUTION   There are three choices of manufacturers, two car sizes, and four colors. So, the number of ways to select one manufacturer, one car size, and one color is

$$3 \cdot 2 \cdot 4 = 24 \text{ ways.}$$

A tree diagram can help you see why there are 24 options.

Tree Diagram for Car Selections

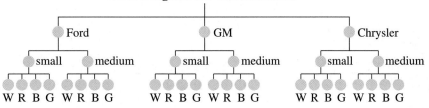

Try It Yourself 1

You increase your choices to include a Toyota, a large car, or a tan or gray car. How many different ways can you select one manufacturer, one car size, and one color now?

a. Find the *number of ways* each event can occur.
b. Use the *Fundamental Counting Principle*.   *Answer: Page A35*

▶ **EXAMPLE 2**   *Using the Fundamental Counting Principle*

The access code for a car's security system consists of four digits. Each digit can be 0 through 9. How many access codes are possible if

1. each digit can be used only once and not repeated?

2. each digit can be repeated?

SOLUTION

1. Because each digit can be used only once, there are 10 choices for the first digit, 9 choices left for the second digit, 8 choices left for the third digit, and 7 for the fourth digit. Using the Fundamental Counting Principle, you can conclude that there are $10 \cdot 9 \cdot 8 \cdot 7 = 5040$ possible access codes.

2. Because each digit can be repeated, there are 10 choices for each of the four digits. So, there are $10 \cdot 10 \cdot 10 \cdot 10 = 10^4 = 10,000$ possible access codes.

Try It Yourself 2

How many license plates can you make if a license plate consists of

1. six (out of 26) alphabetical letters each of which can be repeated?
2. six (out of 26) alphabetical letters each of which cannot be repeated?

a. *Identify* each event and the *number of ways* each event can occur.
b. Use the *Fundamental Counting Principle*.   *Answer: Page A35*

Permutations

An important application of the Fundamental Counting Principle is determining the number of ways that n objects can be arranged in order or in a permutation.

Study Tip

The six permutations for the letters A, B, and C are

ABC, ACB, BAC
BCA, CAB, CBA.

DEFINITION

A **permutation** is an ordered arrangement of objects. The number of different permutations of n distinct objects is $n!$.

The expression **n!** is read as **n factorial** and is defined as follows.

$$n! = n \cdot (n-1) \cdot (n-2) \cdot (n-3) \cdots 3 \cdot 2 \cdot 1$$

As a special case, $0! = 1$.

▶ **EXAMPLE 3**   *Finding the Number of Permutations of n Objects*

The starting lineup for a baseball team consists of nine players. How many different batting orders are possible using the starting lineup?

SOLUTION

The number of permutations is $9! = 9 \cdot 8 \cdot 7 \cdot 6 \cdot 5 \cdot 4 \cdot 3 \cdot 2 \cdot 1 = 362{,}880$. So, there are 362,880 different batting lineups.

Try It Yourself 3

	National League Central Division

The teams in the National League Central Division are listed at the right. How many different final standings are possible?

National League Central Division	
Chicago Cubs	Cincinnati Reds
Houston Astros	Milwaukee Brewers
Pittsburgh Pirates	St. Louis Cardinals

a. Determine *how many teams, n,* are in the Central Division.
b. Evaluate *n!*.   *Answer: Page A35* ◀

Suppose you want to choose some of the objects in a group and put them in order. Such an ordering is called a **permutation of *n* objects taken *r* at a time.**

Permutations of *n* Objects Taken *r* at a Time

The number of permutations of *n* objects taken *r* at a time is

$$_{n}P_{r} = \frac{n!}{(n-r)!}, \qquad \text{where } r \le n.$$

▶ **EXAMPLE 4**   *Finding $_{n}P_{r}$*

Find the number of ways of forming three-digit codes in which no digit is repeated.

SOLUTION

$$_{n}P_{r} = {_{10}P_{3}} = \frac{10!}{(10-3)!} = \frac{10!}{7!} = \frac{10 \cdot 9 \cdot 8 \cdot 7 \cdot 6 \cdot 5 \cdot 4 \cdot 3 \cdot 2 \cdot 1}{7 \cdot 6 \cdot 5 \cdot 4 \cdot 3 \cdot 2 \cdot 1} = 720$$

So, there are 720 possible three-digit codes that do not have repeating digits.

Try It Yourself 4

In a race with eight horses, how many ways can three of the horses finish in first, second, and third place? Assume that there are no ties.

a. *Find* the *quotient* of $n!$ and $(n - r)!$. (List the factors and cancel.)
b. *Write* the result as a sentence.   *Answer: Page A35* ◄

▶ **EXAMPLE 5**   *Permutations of n Objects Taken r at a Time*

Forty-three race cars started the 1998 Daytona 500. How many ways can the cars finish first, second, and third?

SOLUTION   Because there are 43 race cars and order is important, the number of ways the cars can finish first, second, and third is

$$_{43}P_3 = \frac{43!}{(43 - 3)!} = \frac{43!}{40!} = 43 \cdot 42 \cdot 41 = 74,046.$$

Try It Yourself 5

The board of directors for a company has twelve members. One member is the president, another is the vice-president, another is the secretary, and another is the treasurer. How many ways can can these positions be assigned?

a. *Identify* the total number of objects, n, and the number of objects, r, being chosen in order.
b. *Evaluate* $_nP_r$.   *Answer: Page A35* ◄

Suppose you want to order a group of n objects where some of the objects are the same. For instance, consider a group of letters consisting of four A's, two B's, and one C. How many ways can you order such a group? Using the previous formula, you might conclude that there are $_7P_7 = 7!$ possible orders. However, because some of the objects are the same, not all of these permutations are *distinguishable*. How many distinguishable permutations are possible? The answer can be found using the following formula.

Study Tip

The letters AAAABBC can be rearranged in 7! orders, but many of these are not distinguishable. The number of distinguishable orders is

$$\frac{7!}{4! \cdot 2! \cdot 1!} = \frac{7 \cdot 6 \cdot 5}{2}$$
$$= 105.$$

Distinguishable Permutations

The number of **distinguishable permutations** of n objects where n_1 are one type, n_2 are of another type, and so on is

$$\frac{n!}{n_1! \cdot n_2! \cdot n_3! \cdots n_k!}, \text{ where } n_1 + n_2 + n_3 + \cdots + n_k = n.$$

> **EXAMPLE 6** *Distinguishable Permutations*

A building contractor is planning to develop a subdivision. The subdivision is to consist of six one-story houses, four two-story houses, and two split-level houses. In how many distinguishable ways can the houses be arranged?

SOLUTION There are to be twelve houses in the subdivision, six of which are of one type (one-story), four of another type (two-story), and two of a third type (split-level). So, there are

$$\frac{12!}{6! \cdot 4! \cdot 2!} = 13,860$$

distinguishable ways to arrange the houses in the subdivision.

Try It Yourself 6

The contractor wants to plant six oak trees, nine maple trees, and five poplar trees along the subdivision street. If the trees are spaced evenly apart, in how many distinguishable ways can they be planted?

a. *Identify* the total number of objects, n, and the number of each type of object in the group, n_1, n_2, and n_3.

b. *Evaluate* $\dfrac{n!}{n_1! \cdot n_2! \cdots n_k!}$.

Answer: Page A35

Combinations

Suppose you want to buy three CDs from a selection of five CDs. There are 10 ways to make your selections.

ABC, ABD, ABE, ACD, ACE, ADE, BCD, BCE, BDE, CDE

In each selection, order does not matter (*ABC* is the same set as *BAC*). The number of ways to choose r objects from n objects without regard to order is called the number of **combinations of n objects taken r at a time.**

Note to Instructor

You can think of a combination of n objects chosen r at a time as a permutation in which the r selected objects are alike and the remaining $n - r$ (not selected) objects are alike.

Combination of n Objects taken r at a Time

A **combination** is a selection of r objects from a group of n objects without regard to order and is denoted by $_nC_r$. The number of combinations of r objects selected from a group of n objects is

$$_nC_r = \frac{n!}{(n-r)!r!}.$$

3.4 ▲ EXERCISES

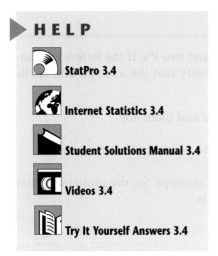

HELP

StatPro 3.4

Internet Statistics 3.4

Student Solutions Manual 3.4

Videos 3.4

Try It Yourself Answers 3.4

1. You are counting the number of ways two or more events can occur is sequence.
2. Permutation: Order matters
   Combination: Order does not matter
3. False, a permutation is an ordered arrangement of objects.
4. True
5. Permutation
6. Combination
7. 6240
8. 30
9. 4500
10. 64
11. 40,320
12. 720
13. 3,628,800
14. 24

Basic Skills and Concepts

1. When you use the Fundamental Counting Principle, what are you counting?

2. What is the difference between a permutation and a combination?

True or False In Exercises 3 and 4, determine whether the statement is true or false. If it is false, rewrite it so it is a true statement.

3. A combination is an ordered arrangement of objects.

4. The number of different ordered arrangements of *n* objects is *n*!.

In Exercises 5 and 6, decide if the situation involves permutations, combinations, or neither. Explain your reasoning.

5. The number of ways 10 people can line up in a row for concert tickets

6. The number of ways a four-member committee can be chosen from 15 people

7. ***Space Shuttle Menu*** Space shuttle astronauts each consume an average of 3000 calories per day. One meal normally consists of a main dish, a vegetable dish, and two different desserts. The astronauts can choose from 10 main dishes, 8 vegetable dishes, and 13 desserts. How many different meals are possible? *(Source: NASA)*

8. ***Menu*** A menu has three choices for salad, five main dishes, and two desserts. How many different meals are available if you select a salad, a main dish, and a dessert?

9. ***Security System*** The access code for a car's security system consists of four digits. The first digit cannot be zero and the last digit must be odd. How many different codes are available?

10. ***True or False Quiz*** Assuming that no questions are omitted, in how many ways can a six-question true-false quiz be answered?

11. ***Horse Race*** A horse race has eight entries. Assuming that there are no ties, in how many different orders can the horses finish?

12. ***Security Code*** In how many ways can the letters A, B, C, D, E, and F be arranged for a six-letter security code?

13. ***Starting Lineup*** The starting lineup for a softball team consists of 10 players. How many different batting orders are possible using the starting lineup?

14. ***Assembly Process*** There are four processes involved in assembling a certain product. These processes can be performed in any order. If management wants to find which order is the least time consuming, how many different orders will have to be tested?

Applications of Counting Principles

> **EXAMPLE 8** *Finding Probabilities*

A word consists of one M, four I's, four S's, and two P's. If the letters are randomly arranged in order, what is the probability that the arrangement spells the word *Mississippi*?

SOLUTION There is one favorable outcome and there are

$$\frac{11!}{1! \cdot 4! \cdot 4! \cdot 2!} = 34{,}650 \qquad \text{11 letters with 1, 4, 4, and 2 like letters}$$

distinguishable permutations of the word *Mississippi*. So, the probability that the arrangement spells the word *Mississippi* is

$$P(\text{Mississippi}) = \frac{1}{34{,}650} \approx 0.000029.$$

> ### Try It Yourself 8
>
> A word consists of one L, two E's, two T's, and one R. If the letters are randomly arranged in order, what is the probability that the arrangement spells the word *Letter*?
>
> **a.** *Find* the number of favorable outcomes and the number of distinguishable permutations.
> **b.** *Divide* the number of favorable outcomes by the number of distinguishable permutations. *Answer: Page A35*

> **EXAMPLE 9** *Finding Probabilities*

Find the probability of being dealt five diamonds from a standard deck of playing cards. (In poker, this is a diamond flush.)

SOLUTION The possible number of ways of choosing 5 diamonds out of 13 is $_{13}C_5$. The number of possible 5-card hands is $_{52}C_5$. So, the probability of being dealt 5 diamonds is

$$P(\text{diamond flush}) = \frac{_{13}C_5}{_{52}C_5} = \frac{1287}{2{,}598{,}960} \approx 0.0005.$$

> ### Try It Yourself 9
>
> A jury consists of five men and seven women. Three are selected at random for an interview. Find the probability that all three are men.
>
> **a.** *Find* the number of ways to choose three men from five and zero women from seven.
> **b.** *Find* the number of ways to choose 3 jury members from 12.
> **c.** *Divide* the result of Part a by the result of Part b. *Answer: Page A35*

3.4 EXERCISES

HELP

 StatPro 3.4

 Internet Statistics 3.4

 Student Solutions Manual 3.4

 Videos 3.4

 Try It Yourself Answers 3.4

1. You are counting the number of ways two or more events can occur is sequence.

2. Permutation: Order matters
   Combination: Order does not matter

3. False, a permutation is an ordered arrangement of objects.

4. True

5. Permutation

6. Combination

7. 6240

8. 30

9. 4500

10. 64

11. 40,320

12. 720

13. 3,628,800

14. 24

Basic Skills and Concepts

1. When you use the Fundamental Counting Principle, what are you counting?

2. What is the difference between a permutation and a combination?

True or False   In Exercises 3 and 4, determine whether the statement is true or false. If it is false, rewrite it so it is a true statement.

3. A combination is an ordered arrangement of objects.

4. The number of different ordered arrangements of n objects is $n!$.

In Exercises 5 and 6, decide if the situation involves permutations, combinations, or neither. Explain your reasoning.

5. The number of ways 10 people can line up in a row for concert tickets

6. The number of ways a four-member committee can be chosen from 15 people

7. *Space Shuttle Menu*   Space shuttle astronauts each consume an average of 3000 calories per day. One meal normally consists of a main dish, a vegetable dish, and two different desserts. The astronauts can choose from 10 main dishes, 8 vegetable dishes, and 13 desserts. How many different meals are possible? *(Source: NASA)*

8. *Menu*   A menu has three choices for salad, five main dishes, and two desserts. How many different meals are available if you select a salad, a main dish, and a dessert?

9. *Security System*   The access code for a car's security system consists of four digits. The first digit cannot be zero and the last digit must be odd. How many different codes are available?

10. *True or False Quiz*   Assuming that no questions are omitted, in how many ways can a six-question true-false quiz be answered?

11. *Horse Race*   A horse race has eight entries. Assuming that there are no ties, in how many different orders can the horses finish?

12. *Security Code*   In how many ways can the letters A, B, C, D, E, and F be arranged for a six-letter security code?

13. *Starting Lineup*   The starting lineup for a softball team consists of 10 players. How many different batting orders are possible using the starting lineup?

14. *Assembly Process*   There are four processes involved in assembling a certain product. These processes can be performed in any order. If management wants to find which order is the least time consuming, how many different orders will have to be tested?

▶ **EXAMPLE 6** *Distinguishable Permutations*

A building contractor is planning to develop a subdivision. The subdivision is to consist of six one-story houses, four two-story houses, and two split-level houses. In how many distinguishable ways can the houses be arranged?

SOLUTION There are to be twelve houses in the subdivision, six of which are of one type (one-story), four of another type (two-story), and two of a third type (split-level). So, there are

$$\frac{12!}{6! \cdot 4! \cdot 2!} = 13{,}860$$

distinguishable ways to arrange the houses in the subdivision.

Try It Yourself 6

The contractor wants to plant six oak trees, nine maple trees, and five poplar trees along the subdivision street. If the trees are spaced evenly apart, in how many distinguishable ways can they be planted?

a. *Identify* the total number of objects, n, and the number of each type of object in the group, n_1, n_2, and n_3.

b. *Evaluate* $\dfrac{n!}{n_1! \cdot n_2! \cdots n_k!}$.   *Answer: Page A35* ◀

Combinations

Suppose you want to buy three CDs from a selection of five CDs. There are 10 ways to make your selections.

ABC, ABD, ABE, ACD, ACE, ADE, BCD, BCE, BDE, CDE

In each selection, order does not matter (*ABC* is the same set as *BAC*). The number of ways to choose r objects from n objects without regard to order is called the number of **combinations of *n* objects taken *r* at a time.**

Note to Instructor

You can think of a combination of n objects chosen r at a time as a permutation in which the r selected objects are alike and the remaining $n - r$ (not selected) objects are alike.

Combination of *n* Objects taken *r* at a Time

A **combination** is a selection of r objects from a group of n objects without regard to order and is denoted by $_nC_r$. The number of combinations of r objects selected from a group of n objects is

$$_nC_r = \frac{n!}{(n - r)!\,r!}.$$

▶ **EXAMPLE 7**   *Finding the Number of Combinations*

A state's department of transportation plans to develop a new section of inter-state highway and receives 16 bids for the project. The state plans to hire four of the bidding companies. How many different combinations of four compa-nies can be selected from the 16 bidding companies?

SOLUTION   Because order is not important, there are

$$_{16}C_4 = \frac{16!}{(16-4)!4!}$$

$$= \frac{16!}{12!4!}$$

$$= 1820$$

different combinations.

Try It Yourself 7

The manager of an accounting department wants to form a three-person advisory committee from the 16 employees in the department. In how many ways can the manager do this?

a. *Identify* the number of objects in the group, n, and the number of objects to be selected, r.
b. *Evaluate* $_nC_r$.
c. *Write* the results as a sentence.   *Answer: Page A35* ◀

The following table summarizes the counting principles.

Principle	Description	Formula
Fundamental Counting Principle	If one event can occur in m ways and a second event can occur in n ways, the number of ways the two events can occur in sequence is $m \cdot n$.	$m \cdot n$
Permutations	The number of different ordered arrangements of n objects	$n!$
	The number of permutations of n objects taken r at a time, where $r \le n$	$_nP_r = \frac{n!}{(n-r)!}$
	The number of distinguishable permu-tations of n objects where n_1 are of one type, n_2 are of another type, and so on	$\frac{n!}{n_1! \cdot n_2! \cdots n_k!}$
Combinations	The number of combinations of r objects selected from a group of n objects without regard to order	$_nC_r = \frac{n!}{(n-r)!r!}$

15. 720

16. 741,354,768,000

17. 32,760

18.
20! = 2,432,902,008,176,640,000

19. 9,189,180

20. 50,400

21. 5,586,853,480

22. 4845

23. 56

24. 20,358,520

25. (a) 70
    (b) 16

26. (a) 120
    (b) 12
    (c) 12

27. (a) 56
    (b) 56
    (c) 112

28. (a) 6,760,000
    (b) 5,760,000

15. *Horse Race* A horse race has 10 entries. Assuming that there are no ties, in how many different ways can these horses finish first, second, and third?

16. *Starting Lineup* The starting lineup for a baseball team consists of nine players. Assuming that each member of a team with 25 players can play each position, in how many different ways can the starting lineup be filled?

17. *Officers* From a pool of 15 candidates, the offices of president, vice-president, secretary, and treasurer will be filled. In how many different ways can the offices be filled?

18. *Class Photo* In how many ways can a class of 20 students line up in a row to pose for a photo?

19. *Planting Trees* A landscaper wants to plant four oak trees, eight maple trees, and six poplar trees along the border of a lawn. If the trees are evenly spaced apart, in how many distinguishable ways can they be planted?

20. *Letters* In how many distinguishable ways can the letters in the word *Statistics* be written?

21. *Selecting a Jury* From a group of 40 people, a jury of 12 people is selected. In how many different ways can a jury of 12 people be selected?

22. *Experimental Group* In order to conduct an experiment, four subjects are randomly selected from a group of 20 people. How many different groups of four subjects are possible?

23. *Pizza Toppings* A pizza shop offers eight toppings. If no topping is used twice, in how many different ways can a three-topping pizza be formed?

24. *Selecting Lottery Numbers* A lottery has 52 numbers. In how many different ways can six of the numbers be selected? (Assume that order of selection is not important.)

25. *Employee Selection* Four sales representatives for a company are to be chosen to participate in a training program. The company has eight sales representatives, two in each of four regions. In how many ways can the four sales representatives be chosen if (a) there are no restrictions and (b) the selection must include a sales representative from each region?

26. *Repairs* In how many orders can three broken computers and two broken printers be repaired if (a) there are no restrictions, (b) the printers must be repaired first, and (c) the computers must be repaired first?

27. *Defective Units* A shipment of 10 microwave ovens contains two defective units. In how many ways can a restaurant buy three of these units and receive (a) no defective units, (b) one defective unit, and (c) at least two good units?

28. *License Plates* In a certain state, each automobile license plate number consists of two letters followed by a four-digit number. How many distinct license plate numbers can be formed if (a) there are no restrictions and (b) the letters "O" and "I" are not used?

29. (a) 658,008

　　 (b) 0.00000152

30. (a) $1.46294163538 \times 10^{22}$

　　 (b) $8.53230870865 \times 10^{19}$

　　 (c) 0.00583

　　 (d) Yes

31. 0.00153

32. 1.067×10^{-8}

29. *Probability*   In a state lottery, you must select 5 numbers out of 40 correctly to win the top prize.

(a) How many ways can 5 numbers be chosen from 40 numbers?

(b) If you purchase one lottery ticket, what is the probability of winning the top prize?

30. *Probability*   A company that has 200 employees chooses a committee of 15 to represent employee retirement issues. When the committee was formed, none of the 56 minority employees were selected.

(a) Use a technology tool to find the number of ways 15 employees can be chosen from 200.

(b) Use a technology tool to find the number of ways 15 employees can be chosen from 144 nonminorities.

(c) If the committee was chosen randomly (without bias), what is the probability that it contained no minorities?

(d) Does your answer to part (c) indicate that the committee selection was biased? Explain your reasoning.

Extending the Basics

Retirement Savings   In Exercises 31 and 32, use the following information. The graph shows the chances that an adult with an annual household income over $35,000 will open a Roth IRA.

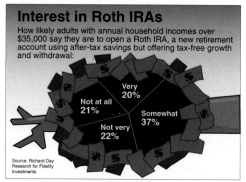

Copyright 1998, USA TODAY. Reprinted with permission.

31. Suppose four people are chosen at random from a group of 100. What is the probability that all four have no interest in opening a Roth IRA? (Assume that the 100 people are represented by the pie chart.)

32. Suppose 10 people are chosen at random from a group of 100. What is the probability that all 10 are very interested in opening a Roth IRA? (Assume that the 100 people are represented by the pie chart.)

TECHNOLOGY MINITAB EXCEL TI-83

Composing Mozart Variations with Dice

Wolfgang Mozart (1756–1791) composed a wide variety of musical pieces. In his Musical Dice Game, he wrote a Wiener minuet with an almost endless number of variations. Each minuet has 16 bars. In the eighth and sixteenth bars, the player has a choice of two musical phrases. In each of the other 14 bars, the player has a choice of 11 phrases.

To create a minuet, Mozart suggested that the player toss 2 six-sided dice 16 times. For the eighth and sixteenth bars, choose Option 1 if the dice total is odd and Option 2 if it is even. For each of the other 14 bars, subtract 1 from the dice total. The following minuet is the result of the following sequence of numbers.

5	7	1	6	4	10	5	1
6	6	2	4	6	8	8	2

Exercises

1. How many phrases did Mozart write to create the Musical Dice Game minuet? Explain.

2. How many possible variations are there in Mozart's Musical Dice Game minuet? Explain.

3. Use technology to select randomly a number from 1 to 11.

    (a) What is the theoretical probability of each number from 1 to 11?

    (b) Use this procedure to select 100 integers between 1 and 11. Tally your results and compare them with the probabilities in part a.

4. What is the probability of randomly selecting options 6, 7, or 8 for the first bar? For all 14 bars? Find each probability using (a) theoretical probability and (b) the results of Exercise 3b.

5. Use technology to select randomly two numbers from 1, 2, 3, 4, 5, and 6. Find the sum and subtract 1 to obtain a total.

    (a) What is the theoretical probability of each total from 1 to 11?

    (b) Use this procedure to select 100 totals between 1 and 11. Tally your results and compare them with the probabilities in part a.

6. What is the probability of randomly selecting options 6, 7, or 8 for the first bar? For all 14 bars? Find each probability using (a) theoretical probability and (b) the results of Exercise 5b.

Extended solutions are given in the *Technology Supplement.*
Technical instruction is provided for Minitab, Excel, and the TI-83.

▼3 CHAPTER SUMMARY

What did you learn?	*Review Exercises*
• How to identify the sample space of a probability experiment and distinguish between simple and compound events *(Section 3.1)*	*1, 2*
• How to distinguish among classical probability, empirical probability, and subjective probability *(Section 3.1)*	*3–8*
• How to identify and use several properties of probability *(Section 3.1)*	*9, 10, 14*
• How to find conditional probabilities *(Section 3.2)*	*11, 12*
• How to distinguish between independent and dependent events *(Section 3.2)*	*15, 16*
• How to use the multiplication rule to find the probability of two events occurring in sequence *(Section 3.2)*	*17, 18*
• How to determine if two events are mutually exclusive *(Section 3.3)*	*19, 20*
• How to use the addition rule to find the probability of two events *(Section 3.3)*	*13, 21, 22*
• How to use the Fundamental Counting Principle to find the number of ways two or more events can occur *(Section 3.4)*	*23, 24*
• How to find the number of ways a group of objects can be arranged in order and the number of ways to choose several objects from a group without regard to order *(Section 3.4)*	*25–29*
• How to use counting principles to find probabilities *(Section 3.4)*	*30, 31*

Why did you learn it? Uses and Abuses

Uses People use probability in almost all fields. Of the three types of probability you studied in this chapter (classical, empirical, and subjective), it might surprise you to know that subjective probability is the most often used—people tend to develop an intuition for the likelihood that an event will occur. The message of this chapter is that your intuition can be sharpened by applying some simple rules of classical and empirical probability. Suppose for instance, you work for a real estate company and are asked to estimate the likelihood that a particular house will sell for its asking price within the next 90 days. You can use your intuition, but you can sharpen your intuition by looking at sales records for similar houses. In doing this, you would be using empirical probability.

Abuses One common abuse of probability is thinking that probabilities have "memories." For example, if a certain three-digit number is drawn (from the numbers 000 through 999) in a state lottery, some people might think there is no chance that the number will be selected in the next drawing. This is not true. No matter how many lottery drawings there are, the probability that a specific three-digit number will be selected is always $\frac{1}{1000}$ or 0.001.

▼3▼ REVIEW EXERCISES

1. Sample space:
{HHHH, HHHT, HHTH, HHTT,
HTHH, HTHT, HTTH, HTTT,
THHH, THHT, THTH, THTT,
TTHH, TTHT, TTTH, TTTT}

Event: Getting three heads
{HHHT, HHTH, HTHH, THHH}

2. Sample space:
{(1, 1), (1, 2), (1, 3), (1, 4),
(1, 5), (1, 6), (2, 1), (2, 2),
(2, 3), (2, 4), (2, 5), (2, 6),
(3, 1), (3, 2), (3, 3), (3, 4),
(3, 5), (3, 6), (4, 1), (4, 2),
(4, 3), (4, 4), (4, 5), (4, 6),
(5, 1), (5, 2), (5, 3), (5, 4),
(5, 5), (5, 6), (6, 1), (6, 2),
(6, 3), (6, 4), (6, 5), (6, 6)}

Event: sum of 4 or 5
{(1, 3), (1, 4), (2, 2), (2, 3),
(3, 1), (3, 2), (4, 1)}

3. Empirical probability
4. Classical probability
5. Subjective probability
6. Empirical probability
7. Classical probability
8. Empirical probability
9. 0.71
10. 0.83

In Exercises 1 and 2, identify the sample space of each probability experiment and list the outcomes of the event.

1. *Experiment:* Tossing four coins, *Event:* Getting three heads

2. *Experiment:* Rolling two six-sided dice, *Event:* Getting a sum of 4 or 5

In Exercises 3–8, classify each statement as an example of classical, empirical, or subjective probability.

3. Based on prior counts, a quality control officer says there is a 0.05 probability that a randomly chosen part is defective.

4. The probability of randomly selecting five cards of the same suit (a flush) from a standard deck is about 0.002.

5. The chance that Corporation A's stock price will fall today is 75%.

6. The probability of a person from the United States being left-handed is 11%.

7. The probability of rolling two six-sided dice and getting a sum greater than nine is $\frac{1}{6}$.

8. The chance that a randomly selected person in the United States is between 15 and 24 years old is 14%. *(Source: U.S. Census Bureau)*

In Exercises 9 and 10, the table shows the U.S. age distribution (in millions) from the 1990 Census. Use the table to determine the probability of the event. *(Source: U.S. Census Bureau)*

Age	0–19	20–39	40–59	60–79	80 and over
Population	29%	33%	21%	14%	3%

9. What is the probability that a randomly selected person in the United States will be at least 20 years old?

10. What is the probability that a randomly selected person in the United States will be less than 60 years old?

In Exercises 11 and 12, the list shows the results of a study on the use of plus/minus grading at North Carolina State University. It shows the percent of students who received grades with pluses and minuses (for example, C+, A–, etc.). *(Source: North Carolina State University)*

- Of all students who received one or more plus grades, 92% were undergraduates and 8% were graduates.
- Of all students who received one or more minus grades, 93% were undergraduates and 7% were graduates.

11. 0.92
12. 0.07
13. 0.60
14. 0.40
15. Independent
16. Dependent
17. 0.0417
18. 0.25
19. Mutually exclusive
20. Not mutually exclusive

11. Find the probability that a student is an undergraduate student, given that the student received a plus grade.

12. Find the probability that a student is a graduate student, given that the student received a minus grade.

13. A random sample of 250 working adults found that 37% access the Internet at work, 44% access the Internet at home, and 21% access the Internet at both work and home. What is the probability that a person in this sample accesses the Internet at home or at work?

14. Using the information in Exercise 13, find the probability that a person does not access the Internet from home or work.

In Exercises 15 and 16, decide whether the events are independent or dependent.

15. Tossing a coin four times, getting four heads, and tossing it a fifth time and getting a head

16. Taking a driver's education course and passing the driver's license exam

In Exercises 17 and 18, find the probability of the sequence of events.

17. You are shopping, and your roommate has asked you to pick up toothpaste and dental rinse. However, your roommate did not tell you which brands to get. The store has six brands of toothpaste and four brands of dental rinse. What is the probability that you will purchase the correct brands of both products?

18. Your sock drawer has nine folded pairs of socks, with three pairs each of white, black, and blue. What is the probability, without looking in the drawer, that you will first select and remove a black pair, then select either a blue or white pair?

In Exercises 19 and 20, decide if the events are mutually exclusive.

19. Event A: Randomly select a person who uses the Internet at least twice a week.

Event B: Randomly select a person who has not used the Internet in seven days.

20. Event A: Randomly select a person who loves cats.

Event B: Randomly select a person who owns a dog.

21. 0.538

22. 0.583

23. 144

24. 1,679,616

25. 84

26. 792

27. 2730

28. 120

29. 2380

30. 0.00000923

31. **(a)** 0.955

   (b) 0.000000761

   (c) 0.045

   (d) 0.999999239

In Exercises 21 and 22, determine the probability.

21. A card is randomly selected from a standard deck. Find the probability that the card is between four and eight (inclusive) or is a club.

22. A twelve-sided die, numbered 1–12, is rolled. Find the probability that the roll results in an odd number or a number less than four.

In Exercises 23 and 24, use the Fundamental Counting Principle.

23. Until recently, with the advent of cellular phones, modems, and pagers, the area codes in the United States and Canada followed a certain system. The first number could not be 0 or 1, the second could only be 0 or 1, and the third could not be 0. Under this system, how many area codes are possible?

24. Assuming that each character can be either a letter or digit, how many four-character license plates are possible?

In Exercises 25–29, use combinations and permutations.

25. A baseball card collector has six identical Mark McGwire cards and three identical Mike Schmidt cards. The collector's album has nine slots per page. In how many distinguishable ways can the collector arrange the nine cards on one page?

26. A florist has 12 different flowers from which floral arrangements can be made. If a centerpiece is to be made using five different flowers, how many different centerpieces could be made?

27. Fifteen cyclists enter a race. In how many ways can they finish first, second, and third?

28. Five players on a basketball team must choose a player on the opposing team to defend. In how many ways can they choose their defensive assignments?

29. A literary magazine editor must choose four short stories for this month's issue from 17 submissions. In how many ways can the editor choose this month's stories?

In Exercises 30 and 31, use counting principles to find the probabilities.

30. In poker, a full house consists of a three-of-a-kind and a two-of-a-kind. Find the probability of a full house consisting of three kings and two queens.

31. A batch of 200 calculators contains three defective calculators. What is the probability that a sample of three calculators will have (a) no defective calculators, (b) all defective calculators, (c) at least one defective calculator, and (d) at least one nondefective calculator?

▼ **3**   **CHAPTER QUIZ**

1. (a) 0.539
  (b) 0.537
  (c) 0.543
  (d) 0.786
  (e) 0.0292

2. Not mutually exclusive
    Dependent

3. (a) 518,665
  (b) 32,193
  (c) 550,858

4. 4500

5. 303,600

Take this quiz as you would take a quiz in class. After you are done, check your work against the answers given in the back of the book.

1. The following table shows the estimated number (in thousands) of earned degrees conferred in the year 2000 by level and gender. *(Source: National Center for Education Statistics)*

		Gender		
		Male	**Female**	**Total**
Level of Degree	**Associate**	209	323	532
	Bachelor	502	659	1161
	Master	187	227	414
	Doctor	27	19	46
	Total	925	1228	2153

A person who earned a degree in the year 2000 is randomly selected. Find the probability of selecting someone who earned

(a) a bachelor's degree.

(b) a bachelor's degree given that the person is a female.

(c) a bachelor's degree given that the person is not a female.

(d) an associate's degree or a bachelor's degree.

(e) a doctorate given that the person is a male.

2. Decide if the events are mutually exclusive. Then decide if the events are independent or dependent. Explain your reasoning.

Event *A*: A golfer scoring the best round in a four-round tournament
Event *B*: Losing the golf tournament

3. A shipment of 150 television sets contains three defective units. In how many ways can a vending company buy three of these units and receive (a) no defective units, (b) one defective unit, and (c) at least two good units?

4. The access code for a car's security system consists of four digits. The first digit cannot be zero and the last digit must be even. How many different codes are available?

5. From a pool of 25 candidates, the offices of president, vice-president, secretary, and treasurer will be filled. In how many different ways can the offices be filled?

1. Quantitative, Ratio

2. Use the sampling method of data collection. The sampling technique should be a simple random sample because it would be difficult to collect this information from the entire population of students.

3. See Odd Answers, page A53

4.

Book Expenses

5. See Odd Answers, page A54

6. Key: 10|3 = 103

```
 9| 0138
10| 349
11| 0016789
12| 037
13| 26
14|
15| 036
16| 02
17| 08
18| 17
19| 15
```

7. Skewed

8. See Odd Answers, page A54

9. $\bar{x} \approx 133.7$
median = 121.5
mode = 110

Statistics

10. range = 105
$s^2 \approx 1036.185$
$s \approx 32.257$

The sample standard deviation is $32.26.

11. See Odd Answers, page A54

12. 0.467
0.5

13. 0.7   **14.** 0.627

15. 142,506

Take this test as you would take a test in class. After you are done, check your work against the answers given in the back of the book.

Refer to the following data set as you take this test. The data set is the number of dollars a sample of 30 people spent in one year on books.

156	150	109	98	136	170	178	195	110	191
187	119	104	160	132	117	111	120	103	123
153	91	162	93	118	127	90	181	110	116

1. Does the data set represent qualitative data or quantitative data? What is the data set's level of measurement?

2. Which method of data collection would you use to gather these data? Which sampling technique would you use? Explain your reasoning.

3. Make a frequency distribution of the data set using five classes. Include class limits, midpoints, frequencies, boundaries, relative frequencies, and cumulative frequencies.

4. Display the data using a frequency histogram and a frequency polygon on the same axes.

5. Display the data using a relative frequency histogram.

6. Display the data using a stem-and-leaf plot.

7. Describe the shape of the distribution as symmetric, uniform, or skewed.

8. Display the data using an ogive.

9. Find the mean, median, and mode of the data set. Are these values parameters or statistics? Explain.

10. Find the range, variance, and standard deviation of the data set. Interpret the results in the context of the real-life setting.

11. Find the quartiles and the interquartile range of the data set and construct a box-and-whisker plot.

12. Find the probability of randomly selecting someone who spent less than $120 on books. What is the probability of randomly selecting someone who spent more than $120?

13. Find the probability of randomly selecting someone who spent less than $120 or more than $160 on books.

14. Five people are selected at random. Find the probability that at least one person spent more than $175.

15. Assume that the 30 people in the data set were contacted through a telephone survey. After performing the survey, five of the respondents are randomly chosen for a more extensive survey. In how many ways can the five respondents be chosen?

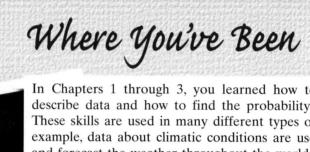

Where You've Been

In Chapters 1 through 3, you learned how to collect and describe data and how to find the probability of an event. These skills are used in many different types of careers. For example, data about climatic conditions are used to analyze and forecast the weather throughout the world. On a typical day, 5000 weather stations, 800 to 1100 upper-air balloon stations, 2000 ships, 600 aircraft, several polar-orbiting and geostationary satellites, and a variety of other data collection devices work together to provide meteorologists with data that are used to forecast the weather. Even with this much data, meteorologists cannot forecast the weather with certainty. Instead, they assign probabilities to certain weather conditions. For instance, a meteorologist might determine that there is a 40% chance of rain (based on the relative frequency of rain under similar weather conditions).

The National Center for Atmospheric Research (NCAR) is located in Boulder, Colorado. It is part of the complex system of organizations that gathers and analyzes data about weather and other climatic conditions.

Discrete Probability Distributions

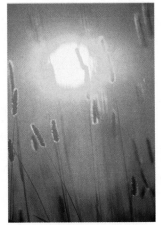

Where You're Going

In Chapter 4, you will learn how to create and use probability distributions. Suppose you are a meteorologist working on a three-day forecast. You have determined that there is a 40% probability of rain on each of the three days. What is the probability that it will rain on 0, 1, 2, or 3 of the days? To answer this, you can create a probability distribution for the possible outcomes.

Day 1 Day 2 Day 3	Probability	Days of Rain
$P(\text{☀},\text{☀},\text{☀}) = 0.216$		0
$P(\text{☀},\text{☀},\text{💧}) = 0.144$		1
$P(\text{☀},\text{💧},\text{☀}) = 0.144$		1
$P(\text{☀},\text{💧},\text{💧}) = 0.096$		2
$P(\text{💧},\text{☀},\text{☀}) = 0.144$		1
$P(\text{💧},\text{☀},\text{💧}) = 0.096$		2
$P(\text{💧},\text{💧},\text{☀}) = 0.096$		2
$P(\text{💧},\text{💧},\text{💧}) = 0.064$		3

From this tree diagram, you can determine the probability of having rain on various numbers of days.

Probability Distribution		
Days of Rain	Tally	Probability
0	1	0.216
1	3	0.432
2	3	0.288
3	1	0.064

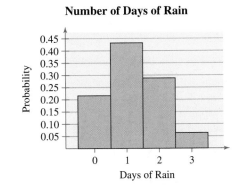

Number of Days of Rain

Probability Distributions

4.1

Random Variables • Discrete Probability Distributions •
Mean, Variance, and Standard Deviation • Expected Value

What You
Should Learn

- *How to distinguish between discrete random variables and continuous random variables*
- *How to construct a discrete probability distribution and its graph*
- *How to determine if a distribution is a probability distribution*
- *How to find the mean, variance, and standard deviation of a discrete probability distribution*
- *How to find the expected value of a probability distribution*

Study Tip

If a random variable is discrete, you can list the possible values it can assume. However, it is impossible to list all values for a continuous random variable.

Note to Instructor

In more advanced texts, the random variable is denoted X while x represents particular values of the random variable. To simplify the discussion, we use x to represent both the random variable and its values.

Random Variables

The outcome of a probability experiment is often a count or a measure. When this occurs, the outcome is called a random variable.

DEFINITION

A **random variable, x,** represents a numerical value assigned to an outcome of a probability experiment.

The word *random* indicates that x is determined by chance. There are two types of random variables: discrete and continuous.

DEFINITION

A random variable is **discrete** if it has a finite or countable number of possible outcomes that can be listed.

A random variable is **continuous** if it has an infinite number of possible outcomes, represented by an interval on the number line.

Suppose you conduct a study of the number of calls a salesperson makes in one day. The possible values of the random variable x are 0, 1, 2, 3, 4, and so on. Because the set of possible outcomes {0, 1, 2, 3 ...} can be listed, x is a discrete random variable. You can represent its values as points on a number line.

Number of Sales Calls (Discrete)

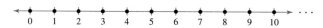

x can have only whole number values: 0, 1, 2, 3, ...

A different way to conduct the study would be to measure the time (in hours) a salesperson spends making calls in one day. Because the time spent making sales calls can be any number from 0 to 24 (including fractions and decimals), x is a continuous random variable. You can represent its values with an interval on a number line, but you cannot *list* all the possible values.

Hours Spent on Sales Calls (Continuous)

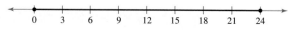

x can have any value between 0 and 24.

▶ **EXAMPLE 1** *Discrete Variables and Continuous Variables*

Decide whether the random variable, x, is discrete or continuous. Explain your reasoning.

1. x represents the number of stocks in the Dow Jones Industrial Average that have share price increases on a given day.

2. x represents the volume of bottled water in a 32-ounce container.

SOLUTION

1. The number of stocks whose share price increases can be counted $\{0, 1, 2, 3, \dots, 30\}$. So x is a *discrete* random variable.

2. The amount of water in the container can be any volume between 0 ounces and 32 ounces. So x is a *continuous* random variable.

Try It Yourself 1

Decide whether the random variable, x, is discrete or continuous.

1. x represents the length of time it takes to complete a test.
2. x represents the number of home runs hit during a baseball game.

a. Decide if x represents *counted* data or *measured* data.
b. Make a conclusion and *explain* your reasoning.   *Answer: Page A35* ◀

It is important that you can distinguish between discrete and continuous random variables because different statistical techniques are used to analyze each. The remainder of this chapter focuses on discrete random variables and their probability distributions. You will study continuous distributions later.

Discrete Probability Distributions

Each value of a discrete random variable can be assigned a probability. By listing each value of the random variable with its corresponding probability, you are forming a probability distribution.

DEFINITION

A **discrete probability distribution** lists each possible value the random variable can assume, together with its probability. A probability distribution must satisfy the following conditions.

1. The probability of each value of the discrete random variable is between 0 and 1, inclusive. That is, $0 \le P(x) \le 1$.

2. The sum of all the probabilities is 1. That is, $\Sigma P(x) = 1$.

Because probabilities represent relative frequencies, a discrete probability distribution can be graphed with a relative frequency histogram.

GUIDELINES

Constructing a Discrete Probability Distribution

Let x be a discrete random variable with possible outcomes $x_1, x_2, \ldots, x_n$.
1. Make a frequency distribution for the possible outcomes.
2. Find the sum of the frequencies.
3. Find the probability of each possible outcome by dividing its frequency by the sum of the frequencies.
4. Check that each probability is between 0 and 1 and that the sum is 1.

▶ **EXAMPLE 2** **Constructing a Discrete Probability Distribution**

An industrial psychologist administered a personality inventory test for passive-aggressive traits to 150 employees. Individuals were rated on a score from 1 to 5, where 1 was extremely passive and 5 extremely aggressive. A score of 3 indicated neither trait. The results are shown at the left. Construct a probability distribution for the random variable x. Then graph the distribution.

Frequency Distribution

Score, x	Frequency, f
1	24
2	33
3	42
4	30
5	21

SOLUTION   Divide the frequency of each score by the total number of individuals in the study to find the probability for each value of the random variable.

$$P(1) = \frac{24}{150} = 0.16 \quad P(2) = \frac{33}{150} = 0.22 \quad P(3) = \frac{42}{150} = 0.28$$

$$P(4) = \frac{30}{150} = 0.2 \quad P(5) = \frac{21}{150} = 0.14$$

The discrete probability distribution is shown in the following table. Note that each probability is between 0 and 1 and that the sum of the probabilities is 1.

x	1	2	3	4	5
$P(x)$	0.16	0.22	0.28	0.2	0.14

The relative frequency histogram is shown at the right. The area of each bar represents the probability of a particular outcome.

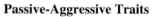

Passive-Aggressive Traits

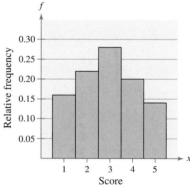

Frequency Distribution

Sales per Day, x	Number of Days, f
0	16
1	19
2	15
3	21
4	9
5	10
6	8
7	2

Try It Yourself 2

A company tracks the number of sales new employees make each day during a 100-day probationary period. The results for one new employee are shown at the left. Construct and graph a probability distribution.
a. *Find* the probability of each outcome.
b. *Organize* the probabilities in a probability distribution.
c. *Graph* the probability distribution.   *Answer: Page A35* ◀

Probability Distribution

Days of Rain	Probability
0	0.216
1	0.432
2	0.288
3	0.064

EXAMPLE 3   *Verifying Probability Distributions*

Verify that the distribution at the left (see page 151) is a probability distribution.

SOLUTION   If the distribution is a probability distribution, then (1) each probability is between 0 and 1, inclusive and (2) the sum of the probabilities equals 1.

1. Each probability is between 0 and 1.
2. $\Sigma P(x) = 0.216 + 0.432 + 0.288 + 0.064 = 1$

Because both conditions are met, the distribution is a probability distribution.

Try It Yourself 3

Verify that the distribution you constructed in Try It Yourself 2 is a probability distribution.

a. Verify that the *probability* of each outcome is between 0 and 1.
b. Verify that the *sum* of all the probabilities is 1.
c. Make a *conclusion*.   *Answer: Page A35*

Picturing the World

In a recent year in the United States, nearly 12 million accidents were reported to the police. A graph of the probability distribution of traffic accidents for various age groups from 15 to 64 is shown . *(Source: U.S. National Highway Traffic Safety Administration)*

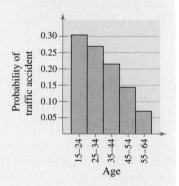

Estimate the probability that a randomly selected person involved in a traffic accident is in the 15 to 34 age groups.

EXAMPLE 4   *Probability Distributions*

Decide whether each distribution is a probability distribution.

1.
x	5	6	7	8
P(x)	0.28	0.21	0.43	0.15

2.
x	1	2	3	4
P(x)	$\frac{1}{2}$	$\frac{1}{4}$	$\frac{5}{4}$	-1

SOLUTION

1. Each probability is between 0 and 1, but the sum of the probabilities is 1.07, which is greater than 1. So, it is *not* a probability distribution.
2. The sum of the probabilities is equal to one, but $P(3)$ and $P(4)$ are not between 0 and 1. So, it is *not* a probability distribution. Probabilities can never be negative or greater than 1.

Try It Yourself 4

Decide whether the distribution is a probability distribution. Explain your reasoning.

1.
x	5	6	7	8
P(x)	$\frac{1}{16}$	$\frac{5}{8}$	$\frac{1}{4}$	$\frac{3}{16}$

2.
x	1	2	3	4
P(x)	0.09	0.36	0.49	0.06

a. Verify that the *probability* of each outcome is between 0 and 1.
b. Verify that the *sum* of all the probabilities is 1.
c. Make a *conclusion*.   *Answer: Page A35*

Mean, Variance, and Standard Deviation

You can measure the central tendency of a probability distribution with its mean and measure the variability with its variance and standard deviation.

Mean of a Discrete Random Variable

The **mean** of a discrete random variable is given by

$$\mu = \Sigma xP(x).$$

Each value of x is multiplied by its corresponding probability and the products are added.

The mean of the random variable represents the "theoretical average" of a probability experiment and sometimes is not a possible outcome. If the experiment were performed many thousands of times, the mean of all the outcomes would be close to the mean of the random variable.

> **EXAMPLE 5** **Finding the Mean of a Probability Distribution**

x	P(x)
1	0.16
2	0.22
3	0.28
4	0.20
5	0.14

The probability distribution for the personality inventory test for passive-aggressive traits discussed in Example 2 is given at the left. Find the mean score. What can you conclude?

SOLUTION Use a table to organize your work, as shown at the right. From the table, you can see that the mean score is 2.94.

x	P(x)	xP(x)
1	0.16	1(0.16) = 0.16
2	0.22	2(0.22) = 0.44
3	0.28	3(0.28) = 0.84
4	0.20	4(0.20) = 0.80
5	0.14	5(0.14) = 0.70
	$\Sigma P(x) = 1$	$\Sigma xP(x) = 2.94$

Mean

A score of 3 represents an individual who exhibits neither passive nor aggressive traits. The mean is slightly under 3 so, you can conclude that the mean personality trait is neither extremely passive nor extremely aggressive, but is slightly closer to passive.

Try It Yourself 5

Find the mean of the probability distribution you constructed in Try It Yourself 2. What can you conclude?

a. *Find the product* of each outcome and its corresponding probability.
b. *Find the sum* of the products.
c. *What* can you conclude?   *Answer: Page A35*

While the mean of the random variable of a probability distribution describes a typical outcome, it gives no information about how the outcomes vary. To study the variation of the outcomes, you can use the variance and standard deviation of the random variable of a probability distribution.

Standard Deviation of a Discrete Random Variable

The **variance** of a discrete random variable is

$$\sigma^2 = \Sigma (x - \mu)^2 P(x).$$

The **standard deviation** is

$$\sigma = \sqrt{\sigma^2}.$$

Study Tip

A shortcut formula for the variance of a probability distribution is

$$\sigma^2 = [\Sigma x^2 P(x)] - \mu^2.$$

▶ **EXAMPLE 6** *Finding the Variance and Standard Deviation*

x	P(x)
1	0.16
2	0.22
3	0.28
4	0.20
5	0.14

The probability distribution for the personality inventory test for passive-aggressive traits discussed in Example 2 is given at the left. Find the variance and standard deviation of the probability distribution.

SOLUTION From Example 5, you know that the mean of the distribution is $\mu = 2.94$. Use a table to organize your work, as shown below.

x	P(x)	x − μ	(x − μ)²	P(x)(x − μ)²
1	0.16	−1.94	3.764	0.602
2	0.22	−0.94	0.884	0.194
3	0.28	0.06	0.004	0.001
4	0.20	1.06	1.124	0.225
5	0.14	2.06	4.244	0.594
	$\Sigma P(x) = 1$			$\Sigma P(x)(x - \mu)^2 = 1.616$

Variance

So, the variance is $\sigma^2 = 1.616$, and the standard deviation is

$$\sigma = \sqrt{\sigma^2} = \sqrt{1.62} \approx 1.27.$$

Try It Yourself 6

Find the variance and standard deviation for the probability distribution constructed in Try It Yourself 2.

a. *For each value of x, find the square* of the deviation from the mean and multiply that by the corresponding probability of *x*.
b. *Find the sum* of the products for the variance.
c. *Take the square root* of the variance for the standard deviation.

Answer: Page A35 ◀

Expected Value

Note to Instructor

Tell students that expected value plays a role in decision theory. Point out that although probabilities can never be negative, the expected value can be negative.

DEFINITION

The **expected value** of a discrete random variable is equal to the mean of the random variable.

$$\text{Expected Value} = E(x) = \mu = \Sigma xP(x)$$

▶ **EXAMPLE 7**   *Finding an Expected Value*

At a raffle, 1500 tickets are sold at $2 each for four prizes of $500, $250, $150, and $75. You buy one ticket. What is the expected value of your gain?

SOLUTION   To find the gain for each prize, subtract the price of the ticket from the prize. For instance, your gain for the $500 prize is $500 − 2 = $498. Then write a probability distribution for the possible gains (or outcomes).

Gain, x	$498	$248	$148	$73	−$2
Probability, $P(x)$	$\frac{1}{1500}$	$\frac{1}{1500}$	$\frac{1}{1500}$	$\frac{1}{1500}$	$\frac{1496}{1500}$

Then, using the probability distribution, you can find the expected value.

$$E(x) = \Sigma xP(x)$$
$$= \$498 \cdot \frac{1}{1500} + \$248 \cdot \frac{1}{1500} + \$148 \cdot \frac{1}{1500} + \$73 \cdot \frac{1}{1500} + (-\$2) \cdot \frac{1496}{1500}$$
$$= -\$1.35$$

Because the expected value is negative, you can expect to lose an average of $1.35 for each ticket you buy.

Insight

In most applications, an expected value of 0 has a practical interpretation. For instance, in gambling games, an expected value of 0 implies that a game is a fair game (an unlikely occurrence!). In a profit and loss analysis, an expected value of 0 represents the breakeven point.

Try It Yourself 7

During a one-year selling period (225 days), a sales representative made between 0 and 9 sales per day, as shown in the table. If this pattern continues, what is the expected value for the number of sales per day for the sales representative?

Number of sales, x	0	1	2	3	4	5	6	7	8	9
Frequency, in days	25	48	60	45	20	10	8	5	3	1

a. *Identify the possible outcomes* and *find the probability* of each.
b. *Find the product* of each outcome and its corresponding probability.
c. *Find the sum* of the products.
d. *Interpret* the results.   *Answer: Page A35* ◀

4.1 ▼ EXERCISES

HELP

 StatPro 4.1

 Internet Statistics 4.1

 Student Solutions Manual 4.1

 Videos 4.1

 Try It Yourself Answers 4.1

1. A random variable represents a numerical value assigned to an outcome of a probability experiment.
   Examples: Answers will vary.
2. A random variable is discrete if it has a finite or countable number of possible outcomes that can be listed.
   Condition 1: $0 \leq P(x) \leq 1$
   Condition 2: $\Sigma P(x) = 1$
3. False
4. True
5. True
6. True
7. Discrete
8. Continuous
9. Discrete
10. Continuous
11. Continuous
12. Discrete
13. Discrete
14. Continuous

Basic Skills and Concepts

1. What is a random variable? Give an example of a discrete random variable and a continuous random variable. Justify your answer.

2. What is a discrete probability distribution? What are the two conditions that determine a probability distribution?

True or False In Exercises 3–6, determine whether the statement is true or false. If it is false, rewrite it so that it is a true statement.

3. In most applications, continuous random variables represent counted data, while discrete random variables represent measured data.

4. For a random variable, x, the word *random* indicates that the value of x is determined by chance.

5. The mean of a random variable represents the "theoretical average" of a probability experiment and sometimes is not a possible outcome.

6. The expected value of a discrete random variable is equal to the mean of the random variable.

Graphical Analysis In Exercises 7 and 8, decide whether the graph represents a discrete random variable or a continuous random variable. Explain your reasoning.

7. The home attendance for football games at a university

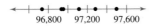

8. The length of time students use a computer each week

Discrete or Continuous? In Exercises 9–14, decide whether the random variable, x, is discrete or continuous. Explain your reasoning.

9. x represents the number of highway fatalities in one year in California.

10. x represents the length of time it takes to get to work.

11. x represents the volume of blood drawn for a blood test.

12. x represents the number of rainy days in the month of July in Florida.

13. x represents the number of books sold per quarter at a book store.

14. x represents the weight of a chemical compound.

15. 0.22
16. 0.15
17. Yes
18. No
19. No
20. Yes

Determining a Missing Probability In Exercises 15 and 16, determine the probability distribution's missing probability value.

15. A sociologist surveyed the households in a small town. The random variable x represents the number of dependent children in the households.

x	0	1	2	3	4
$P(x)$	0.07	0.20	0.38	?	0.13

16. The sociologist in Exercise 15 surveyed the households in a neighboring town. The random variable x represents the number of dependent children in the households.

x	0	1	2	3	4	5	6
$P(x)$	0.05	?	0.23	0.21	0.17	0.11	0.08

Distributions In Exercises 17–20, decide whether the distribution is a probability distribution. If it is not a probability distribution, identify the property (or properties) that are not satisfied.

17. A company gave psychological tests to prospective employees. The random variable x represents the possible test scores.

x	0	1	2	3	4
$P(x)$	0.05	0.25	0.35	0.25	0.10

18. A survey asked a sample of people how many vehicles each owns. The random variable x represents the number of vehicles owned.

x	0	1	2	3
$P(x)$	0.005	0.435	0.555	0.206

19. A quality inspector checked for imperfections in rolls of fabric. The random variable x represents the number of imperfections found.

x	0	1	2	3	4	5
$P(x)$	$\frac{3}{4}$	$\frac{1}{10}$	$\frac{1}{20}$	$\frac{1}{25}$	$\frac{1}{50}$	$-\frac{1}{100}$

20. A survey asked a sample of people how many times they donate blood each year. The random variable x represents the number of donations for one year.

x	0	1	2	3	4	5	6
$P(x)$	0.30	0.25	0.25	0.10	0.05	0.03	0.02

21. (a) 2.1
 (b) 1.09
 (c) 1.044
22. (a) 1.52
 (b) 2.110
 (c) 1.452
23. See Odd Answers, page A54
24. See Selected Answers, page A79
25. See Odd Answers, page A54
26. See Selected Answers, page A79

21. For the probability distribution in Exercise 17, find the (a) mean, (b) variance, and (c) standard deviation for the test score.

22. For the probability distribution in Exercise 20, find the (a) mean, (b) variance, and (c) standard deviation for the number of blood donations in a year.

Constructing Probability Distributions In Exercises 23–26, (a) use the frequency distribution to construct a probability distribution, find the (b) mean, (c) variance, and (d) standard deviation of the probability distribution, and (e) interpret the results in the context of the real-life situation.

23. The number of dogs per household in a small town. *(Adapted from American Veterinary Medical Association Center for Information Management)*

Dogs	Households
0	316
1	425
2	168
3	48
4	29
5	14

24. The number of cats per household in a small town. *(Adapted from American Veterinary Medical Association Center for Information Management)*

Cats	Households
0	273
1	349
2	203
3	78
4	57
5	40

25. The number of computers per household in a small town.

Computers	Households
0	300
1	280
2	95
3	20

26. The number of motor vehicle accidents per student in a recent year at college.

Accidents	Students
0	260
1	500
2	425
3	305
4	175
5	45

27. (a) 18.375

   (b) 41.734

   (c) 6.460

   (d) 18.375

   (e) The publisher can anticipate an average of $72,581.25 (18,375 × $3.95) per week to be generated by magazine sales.

28. (a) −270

   (b) 15227100

   (c) 3902.19

   (d) −270

   (e) The insurance company can anticipate an average loss of $270 per claim.

29. (a) 0.35

   (b) 0.90

30. (a) 0.45

   (b) 0.80

Expected Value In Exercises 27 and 28, use the given probability distribution to find the (a) mean, (b) variance, (c) standard deviation, and (d) expected value of the probability distribution, and (e) interpret the results in the context of the real-life situation.

27. A publisher introduces a new weekly magazine that sells for $3.95. The company's marketers estimate that sales x (in thousands) will be approximated by the following probability distribution.

x	10	15	20	25	30	35
$P(x)$	0.200	0.300	0.250	0.150	0.075	0.025

28. An insurance company offers fire protection policies with a face value of $90,000. The company analyzes claims x of $30,000, $60,000, and $90,000 and obtains the following probability distribution.

x	0	−30,000	−60,000	−90,000
$P(x)$	0.994	0.004	0.001	0.001

29. ***Finding Probabilities*** A company gave psychological tests to prospective employees. The random variable x represents the possible test scores. Use the relative frequency histogram to find the probability that a person selected at random from the survey's sample had a test score of (a) more than two and (b) less than four.

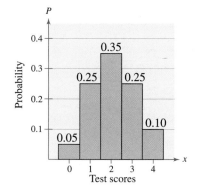

30. ***Finding Probabilities*** A survey asked a sample of people how many times they donate blood each year. The random variable x represents the number of donations for one year. Use the relative frequency histogram to find the probability that a person selected at random from the survey's sample donated blood (a) more than once in a year and (b) less than three times in a year.

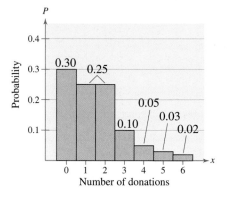

Extending the Basics

31. *Finding Probabilities*   Use the probability distribution you made for Exercise 23 to find the probability of randomly selecting a household that has

(a) less than two dogs.

(b) at least two dogs.

(c) between two and four dogs, inclusive.

32. *Finding Probabilities*   Use the probability distribution you made for Exercise 25 to find the probability of randomly selecting a household that has

(a) no computers.

(b) at least one computer.

(c) between one and three computers, inclusive.

Games of Chance   In Exercises 33 and 34, find the expected net gain to the player for one play of the game. If *x* is the net gain to a player in a game of chance, then *E(x)* is usually negative. This value gives the average amount per game the player can expect to lose.

33. In American roulette, the wheel has the 38 numbers $00, 0, 1, 2, \ldots, 34, 35$, and 36, marked on equally spaced slots. If a player bets $1 on a number and wins, then the player keeps the dollar and receives an additional 35 dollars. Otherwise, the dollar is lost.

34. A charity organization is selling $4 raffle tickets as part of a fund-raising program. The first prize is a boat valued at $3150, and the second prize is a camping tent valued at $450. The rest of the prizes are 15 $25 gift certificates. The number of tickets sold is 5000.

Binomial Distributions

4.2

Binomial Experiments • Binomial Probabilities • Graphing Binomial Distributions • Mean, Variance, and Standard Deviation

What You Should Learn

- *How to determine if a probability experiment is a binomial experiment*
- *How to find binomial probabilities using the binomial probability formula, a binomial probability table, and technology*
- *How to construct a binomial distribution and its graph*
- *How to find the mean, variance, and standard deviation of a binomial probability distribution*

Binomial Experiments

There are many probability experiments for which the results of each trial can be reduced to two outcomes: success and failure. For instance, when a basketball player attempts a free throw, he or she either makes the basket or does not. Probability experiments such as these are called binomial experiments.

> **DEFINITION**
>
> A **binomial experiment** is a probability experiment that satisfies the following conditions.
>
> 1. The experiment is repeated for a fixed number of trials, where each trial is independent of the other trials.
> 2. There are only two possible outcomes of interest for each trial. The outcomes can be classified as a success (S) or as a failure (F).
> 3. The probability of a success, $P(S)$, is the same for each trial.
> 4. The random variable, x, counts the number of successful trials.

The following notation is used for binomial experiments.

Note to Instructor

Emphasize that *p* represents the probability of success on a single trial. Students often have trouble with this concept.

Notation for Binomial Experiments

Symbol	Description
n	The number of times a trial is repeated
$p = P(S)$	The probability of success in a single trial
$q = P(F)$	The probability of failure in a single trial ($q = 1 - p$)
x	The random variable represents a count of the number of successes in n trials: $x = 0, 1, 2, 3, \ldots n$.

Here is a simple example of a binomial experiment. From a standard deck of cards, you pick a card, note whether it is a club or not, and replace the card. You repeat the experiment 5 times, so $n = 5$. The outcomes for each trial can be classified in two categories: $S =$ selecting a club and $F =$ selecting another suit. The probabilities of success and failure are

$$p = P(S) = \tfrac{1}{4} \qquad \text{and} \qquad q = P(F) = \tfrac{3}{4}.$$

The random variable x represents the number of clubs selected in the 5 trials. So, the possible values of the random variable are 0, 1, 2, 3, 4, and 5. Note that x is a discrete random variable because its possible values can be listed.

> **EXAMPLE 1** *Binomial Experiments*

Decide whether the experiment is a binomial experiment. If it is, specify the values of $n, p,$ and q and list the possible values of the random variable x. If it is not, explain why.

1. A certain surgical procedure has an 85% chance of success. A doctor performs the procedure on eight patients. The random variable represents the number of successful surgeries.

2. A jar contains five red marbles, nine blue marbles, and six green marbles. You randomly select three marbles from the jar, *without replacement*. The random variable represents the number of red marbles.

SOLUTION

1. The experiment is a binomial experiment because it satisfies the four conditions of a binomial experiment. In the experiment, each surgery represents one trial. There are eight surgeries, and each surgery is independent of the others. Also, there are only two possible outcomes for each surgery— either the surgery is a success or it is a failure. Finally, the probability of success for each surgery is 0.85.

$$n = 8$$
$$p = 0.85$$
$$q = 1 - 0.85 = 0.15$$
$$x = 0, 1, 2, 3, 4, 5, 6, 7, 8$$

2. The experiment is not a binomial experiment because it does not satisfy all four conditions of a binomial experiment. In the experiment, each marble selection represents one trial and selecting a red marble is a success. When selecting the first marble, the probability of success is 5/20. However, because the marble is not replaced, the probability of success is no longer 5/20. So, the trials are not independent, and the probability of a success is not the same for each trial.

Picturing the World

A recent survey of registered voters in the United States asked whether public school teachers should be required to take drug tests. The respondents answers were either yes or no. *(Source: Family Research Council)*

Survey question: Should public school teachers be required to take drug tests?

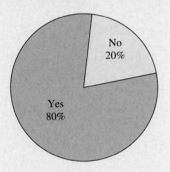

No 20%

Yes 80%

Why is this a binomial experiment? Identify the probability of success, p. Identify the probability of failure, q.

Try It Yourself 1

Decide whether the following is a binomial experiment. If it is, specify the values of $n, p,$ and q and list the possible values of the random variable x. If it is not, explain why.

You take a multiple choice quiz that consists of 10 questions. Each question has four possible answers, only one of which is correct. To complete the quiz, you randomly guess the answer to each question. The random variable represents the number of correct answers.

a. Identify a *trial* of the experiment and what is a "success."
b. Decide if the experiment *satisfies the four conditions* of a binomial experiment.
c. *Make a conclusion and identify* $n, p, q,$ and the possible values of x.

Answer: Page A36

Binomial Probabilities

There are several ways to find the probability of x successes in n trials of a binomial experiment. One way is to use the binomial probability formula.

Binomial Probability Formula

In a binomial experiment, the probability of exactly x successes in n trials is

$$P(x) = {_nC_x}\, p^x q^{n-x} = \frac{n!}{(n-x)!x!} p^x q^{n-x}.$$

EXAMPLE 2 · *Finding Binomial Probabilities*

A six-sided die is rolled 3 times. Find the probability of rolling exactly one 6.

SOLUTION One way to answer the question is to draw a tree diagram.

			Roll 1	Roll 2	Roll 3	Frequency	Number of 6's	Probability
						$(1)(1)(1) = 1$	3	1/216
						$(1)(1)(5) = 5$	2	5/216
						$(1)(5)(1) = 5$	2	5/216
						$(1)(5)(5) = 25$	1	25/216
						$(5)(1)(1) = 5$	2	5/216
						$(5)(1)(5) = 25$	1	25/216
						$(5)(5)(1) = 25$	1	25/216
						$(5)(5)(5) = 125$	0	125/216

There are three outcomes that have exactly one 6, and each has a probability of 25/216. So, the probability of rolling exactly one 6 is $3(25/216) \approx 0.347$. Another way to answer the question is to use the binomial probability formula. In this binomial experiment, rolling a 6 is a success while rolling any other number is a failure. The values for n, p, q, and x are $n = 3$, $p = \frac{1}{6}$, $q = \frac{5}{6}$, and $x = 1$. The probability of rolling exactly one 6 is

$$P(1) = \frac{3!}{(3-1)!1!}\left(\frac{1}{6}\right)^1\left(\frac{5}{6}\right)^2 = 3\left(\frac{1}{6}\right)\left(\frac{25}{36}\right) = 3\left(\frac{25}{216}\right) = \frac{25}{72} \approx 0.347.$$

Note to Instructor

Point out that the probability of a six on the first die, a nonsix on the second, and a nonsix on the third is calculated by multiplying

$\left(\frac{1}{6}\right)\left(\frac{5}{6}\right)\left(\frac{5}{6}\right) = \frac{25}{216}$.

For a nonsix on the first, a six on the second, and a nonsix on the third, the probability is also $\frac{25}{216}$ and likewise for a nonsix on the first and second then a six on the third.

Try It Yourself 2

A card is selected from a deck and replaced. If this experiment is repeated a total of five times, find the probability of selecting exactly three clubs.

a. *Identify* a trial, a success, and a failure.
b. *Identify* n, p, q, and x.
c. Use the *binomial probability formula*. *Answer: Page A36*

By listing the possible values of x with the corresponding probability of each, you can construct a **binomial probability distribution.**

EXAMPLE 3 *Constructing a Binomial Distribution*

In a survey, American workers and retirees were asked to name their expected sources of retirement income. The results are shown in the graph. Seven workers who participated in the survey are asked whether they expect to rely on social security for retirement income. Create a binomial probability distribution for the number of workers who respond yes.

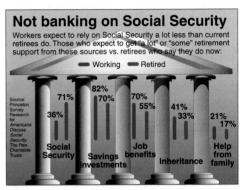

Not banking on Social Security

Workers expect to rely on Social Security a lot less than current retirees do. Those who expect to get "a lot" or "some" retirement support from these sources vs. retirees who say they do now:

● Working   ● Retired

Source: Princeton Survey Research for Americans Discuss Social Security, The Pew Charitable Trusts

Social Security 36% 71% · Savings investments 82% 70% · Job benefits 70% 55% · Inheritance 41% 33% · Help from family 21% 17%

Copyright 1998, USA TODAY. Reprinted with permission.

SOLUTION   From the graph, you can see that 36% of working Americans expect to rely on social security for retirement income. So, $p = 0.36$ and $q = 0.64$. Because $n = 7$, the possible values of x are 0, 1, 2, 3, 4, 5, 6, and 7.

$$P(0) = {_7}C_0(0.36)^0(0.64)^7 \approx 0.044$$

$$P(1) = {_7}C_1(0.36)^1(0.64)^6 \approx 0.173$$

$$P(2) = {_7}C_2(0.36)^2(0.64)^5 \approx 0.292$$

$$P(3) = {_7}C_3(0.36)^3(0.64)^4 \approx 0.274$$

$$P(4) = {_7}C_4(0.36)^4(0.64)^3 \approx 0.154$$

$$P(5) = {_7}C_5(0.36)^5(0.64)^2 \approx 0.052$$

$$P(6) = {_7}C_6(0.36)^6(0.64)^1 \approx 0.010$$

$$P(7) = {_7}C_7(0.36)^7(0.64)^0 \approx 0.001$$

x	$P(x)$
0	0.044
1	0.173
2	0.292
3	0.274
4	0.154
5	0.052
6	0.010
7	0.001
	$\Sigma P(x) = 1$

Study Tip

When probabilities are rounded to a fixed number of decimal places, the sum of the probabilities may differ slightly from 1.

Notice that all the probabilities are between 0 and 1 and that the sum of the probabilities is 1.

Try It Yourself 3

Seven retirees who participated in the survey are asked whether they rely on social security for retirement income. Create a binomial distribution for the number of retirees who respond yes.

a. *Identify* a trial, a success, and a failure.
b. *Identify* n, p, q, and possible values for x.
c. Use the *binomial probability formula* for each value of x.
d. *Organize your results in a table.*   *Answer: Page A36*

Finding binomial probabilities with the binomial probability formula can be a tedious and mistake-prone process. To make this process easier, you can use a binomial probability table. Table 2 in Appendix B lists the binomial probability for selected values of n and p.

▶ **EXAMPLE 4**   *Finding a Binomial Probability Using a Table*

Fifty percent of working adults spend less than 20 minutes commuting to their jobs. If you randomly select six working adults, what is the probability that exactly three of them spend less than 20 minutes commuting to work? Use a table to find the probability. *(Source: Maritz AmeriPoll)*

SOLUTION   A portion of Table 2 is shown here. Using the distribution for $n = 6$, $p = 0.5$, you can find the probability that $x = 3$, as shown by the highlighted areas in the table.

Note to Instructor

Discuss limitations on the use of the table. It can only be used for particular values of p and particular values of n up to 20. Later in the course students will learn how to calculate probabilities for $n > 20$ using the normal approximation to the binomial.

| | | | | | | | | | p | | | | | |
n	x	.01	.05	.10	.15	.20	.25	.30	.35	.40	.45	.50	.55	.60
2	0	.980	.902	.810	.723	.640	.563	.490	.423	.360	.303	.250	.203	.160
	1	.020	.095	.180	.255	.320	.375	.420	.455	.480	.495	.500	.495	.480
	2	.000	.002	.010	.023	.040	.063	.090	.123	.160	.203	.250	.303	.360
3	0	.970	.857	.729	.614	.512	.422	.343	.275	.216	.166	.125	.091	.064
	1	.029	.135	.243	.325	.384	.422	.441	.444	.432	.408	.375	.334	.288
	2	.000	.007	.027	.057	.096	.141	.189	.239	.288	.334	.375	.408	.432
	3	.000	.000	.001	.003	.008	.016	.027	.043	.064	.091	.125	.166	.216
6	0	.941	.735	.531	.377	.262	.178	.118	.075	.047	.028	.016	.008	.004
	1	.057	.232	.354	.399	.393	.356	.303	.244	.187	.136	.094	.061	.037
	2	.001	.031	.098	.176	.246	.297	.324	.328	.311	.278	.234	.186	.138
	3	.000	.002	.015	.042	.082	.132	.185	.236	.276	.303	(.312)	.303	.276
	4	.000	.000	.001	.006	.015	.033	.060	.095	.138	.186	.234	.278	.311
	5	.000	.000	.000	.000	.002	.004	.010	.020	.037	.061	.094	.136	.187
	6	.000	.000	.000	.000	.000	.000	.001	.002	.004	.008	.016	.028	.047

So, the probability that exactly three of the six workers spend less than 20 minutes commuting to work is 0.312.

Try It Yourself 4

Twenty-five percent of all small U.S. businesses have a Web site. If you randomly select 10 small business, what is the probability that exactly four of them have a Web site? Use a table to find the probability. *(Source: U.S. Chamber of Commerce)*

a. *Identify* a trial, a success, and a failure.
b. *Identify* n, p, and x.
c. *Use Table 2* to find the binomial probability.   *Answer: Page A36* ◀

An even more efficient way to find binomial probabilities is to use a calculator or a computer. For instance, you can find binomial probabilities using Minitab, Excel, and the TI-83.

> ### ▶ EXAMPLE 5 *Using Technology to Find a Binomial Probability*

The results of a recent survey indicate that 58% of American households own a gas grill. If you randomly select 100 households, what is the probability that exactly 65 households will own a gas grill? Use a calculator or a computer to find the probability. *(Source: Leo Shapiro Research for Weber GrillWatch)*

SOLUTION   Minitab, Excel, and the TI-83 each have features that allow you to find binomial probabilities automatically.

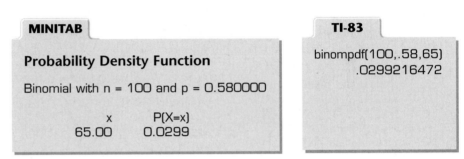

MINITAB

Probability Density Function

Binomial with n = 100 and p = 0.580000

x	P(X=x)
65.00	0.0299

TI-83

binompdf(100,.58,65)
                .0299216472

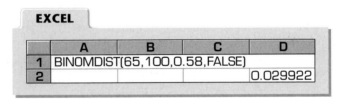

EXCEL

	A	B	C	D
1	BINOMDIST(65,100,0.58,FALSE)			
2				0.029922

From the displays, you can see that the probability that exactly 65 households will own a gas grill is about 0.03.

▷ Try It Yourself 5

The results of a recent survey indicate that 71% of Americans use more than one topping on their hotdogs. If you randomly select 250 Americans, what is the probability that exactly 178 of them will use more than one topping? Use a calculator or a computer to find the probability. *(Source: Leo Shapiro Research for Weber GrillWatch)*

a. *Identify* $n, p,$ and x.
b. *Calculate* the binomial probability.
c. *Interpret* the results.   *Answer: Page A36* ◀

> ▶ **EXAMPLE 6** *Finding Binomial Probabilities*

A survey indicates that 41% of American women consider reading as their favorite leisure-time activity. You randomly select four women and ask them if reading is their favorite leisure-time activity. Find the probability that (1) exactly two of them respond yes, (2) at least two of them respond yes, and (3) fewer than two of them respond yes. (*Source: Louis Harris & Associates*)

SOLUTION

1. Using $n = 4$, $p = 0.41$, $q = 0.59$, and $x = 2$, the probability that exactly two women will respond yes is

    $$P(2) = {}_4C_2(0.41)^2(0.59)^2$$
    $$\approx 0.351.$$

2. To find the probability that at least two women will respond yes, you can find the sum of $P(2)$, $P(3)$, and $P(4)$.

    $$P(2) = {}_4C_2(0.41)^2(0.59)^2 \approx 0.351093$$
    $$P(3) = {}_4C_3(0.41)^3(0.59)^1 \approx 0.162653$$
    $$P(4) = {}_4C_4(0.41)^4(0.59)^0 \approx 0.028258$$

    So, the probability that at least two will respond yes is

    $$P(x \geq 2) = P(2) + P(3) + P(4)$$
    $$\approx 0.542.$$

3. To find the probability that fewer than two women will respond yes, you must find the sum of $P(0)$ and $P(1)$.

    $$P(0) = {}_4C_0(0.41)^0(0.59)^4 \approx 0.121174$$
    $$P(1) = {}_4C_1(0.41)^1(0.59)^3 \approx 0.336822$$

    So, the probability that fewer than two will respond yes is

    $$P(x < 2) = P(0) + P(1)$$
    $$\approx 0.458.$$

Study Tip

The complement of "x is at least 2" is "x is less than 2". So, another way to find the probability in part (3) is

$$P(x < 2) = 1 - P(x \geq 2)$$
$$= 1 - 0.542$$
$$= 0.458.$$

Note to Instructor

Remind students to decide for each question whether it is easier to calculate a probability as given or use the complement rule to get their answer.

Try It Yourself 6

A survey indicates that 21% of American men consider fishing as their favorite leisure-time activity. You randomly select five men and ask them if fishing is their favorite leisure-time activity. Find the probability that (1) exactly two of them respond yes, (2) at least two of them respond yes, and (3) fewer than two of them respond yes. (*Source: Louis Harris & Associates*)

a. Determine the appropriate *values of x* for each situation.
b. Find the *binomial probability* for each value of x. Then find the sum, if necessary.
c. *Interpret* the results.

Answer: Page A36 ◀

Graphing Binomial Distributions

In Section 4.1, you learned how to construct and graph discrete probability distributions. Because a binomial distribution is a discrete probability distribution, you can use the same process.

> ▶ **EXAMPLE 7**   *Constructing and Graphing a Binomial Distribution*

Sixty-five percent of American households subscribe to cable TV. You randomly select six households and ask each if they subscribe to cable TV. Construct a probability distribution for the random variable x. Then graph the distribution. *(Source: Polk)*

SOLUTION   To construct the binomial distribution, find the probability for each value of x. Using $n = 6$, $p = 0.65$, and $q = 0.35$, you can obtain the following.

$$P(0) = {_6}C_0(0.65)^0(0.35)^6 \approx 0.002$$

$$P(1) = {_6}C_1(0.65)^1(0.35)^5 \approx 0.020$$

$$P(2) = {_6}C_2(0.65)^2(0.35)^4 \approx 0.095$$

$$P(3) = {_6}C_3(0.65)^3(0.35)^3 \approx 0.235$$

$$P(4) = {_6}C_4(0.65)^4(0.35)^2 \approx 0.328$$

$$P(5) = {_6}C_5(0.65)^5(0.35)^1 \approx 0.244$$

$$P(6) = {_6}C_6(0.65)^6(0.35)^0 \approx 0.075$$

x	0	1	2	3	4	5	6
$P(x)$	0.002	0.020	0.095	0.235	0.328	0.244	0.075

Subscribing to Cable TV

Because each probability is a relative frequency, you can graph the probability distribution using a relative frequency histogram as shown at the left.

Try It Yourself 7

Forty-one percent of American households own a computer. You randomly select six households and ask each if they own a computer. Construct a probability distribution for the random variable x. Then graph the distribution. *(Source: Electronic Industries Association)*

a. *Find* the binomial probability for each value of the random variable x.
b. *Organize* the values of x and their corresponding probability in a binomial distribution.
c. Use a relative frequency histogram to *graph* the binomial distribution.

Answer: Page A36 ◀

Notice in Example 7 that the histogram is skewed left. The graph of a binomial distribution with $p > 0.5$ is skewed left, while the graph of a binomial distribution with $p < 0.5$ is skewed right. The graph of a binomial distribution with $p = 0.5$ is symmetric.

Mean, Variance, and Standard Deviation

Although you can use the formulas learned in Section 4.1 for mean, variance, and standard deviation of a probability distribution, the properties of a binomial distribution enable you to use much simpler formulas.

Population Parameters of a Binomial Distribution

$$\text{Mean:} \quad \mu = np$$

$$\text{Variance:} \quad \sigma^2 = npq$$

$$\text{Standard deviation:} \quad \sigma = \sqrt{npq}$$

EXAMPLE 8 Finding Mean, Variance, and Standard Deviation

Note to Instructor

It is useful to have students calculate the mean, variance, and standard deviation for a binomial experiment using the general formulas for probability distributions given in Section 4.1. A quick example (and good review) would be to use the distribution for $n = 4$ and $p = 0.3$.

x	$P(x)$	$xP(x)$
0	.240	0
1	.412	.412
2	.265	.530
3	.076	.228
4	.008	.032
	$\Sigma = 1.001$	$\Sigma = 1.202$

Point out that the formula $\mu = np$ gives the same result rounded to two decimal places.

In Pittsburgh, Pennsylvania, 57% of the days in a year are cloudy. Find the mean, variance, and standard deviation for the number of cloudy days during the month of June. What can you conclude? *(Source: National Climatic Data Center)*

SOLUTION   There are 30 days in June. Using $n = 30$, $p = 0.57$, and $q = 0.43$, you can find the mean, variance, and standard deviation as shown below.

$$\mu = np = 30 \cdot 0.57 = 17.1$$

$$\sigma^2 = npq = 30 \cdot 0.57 \cdot 0.43 = 7.353$$

$$\sigma = \sqrt{npq} = \sqrt{7.353} \approx 2.71$$

So, you can conclude that, on the average, there are 17.1 cloudy days during the month of June. The standard deviation is about 2.71 days.

Try It Yourself 8

In San Diego, California, 38% of the days in a year are clear. Find the mean, variance, and standard deviation for the number of clear days during the month of May. What can you conclude? *(Source: National Climatic Data Center)*

a. *Identify a success and the value of n, p, and q.*
b. *Find the product of n and p to calculate the mean.*
c. *Find the product of n, p, and q for the variance.*
d. *Find the square root of the variance for the standard deviation.*
e. What can you conclude?   *Answer: Page A36*

4.2 EXERCISES

HELP

 StatPro 4.2

 Internet Statistics 4.2

 Student Solutions Manual 4.2

 Videos 4.2

 Try It Yourself Answers 4.2

1. (a) $p = 0.50$
   (b) $p = 0.20$
   (c) $p = 0.80$
2. (a) $n = 12$
   (b) $n = 4$
   (c) $n = 8$
   As n increases, the probability distribution widens.
3. Is a binomial experiment. Success: baby recovers $n = 5$, $p = 0.80$, $q = 0.20$, $x = 0, 1, 2, \ldots, 5$
4. Is a binomial experiment. Success: person does not make a purchase $n = 15$, $p = 0.70$, $q = 0.30$, $x = 0, 1, 2, \ldots, 15$
5. Is not a binomial experiment because there are more than 2 possible outcomes for each trial.

Basic Skills and Concepts

1. *Graphical Analysis* The following histograms each represent binomial distributions. Each distribution has the same number of trials n, but different probabilities of success p. Match the following probabilities with the correct graph: $p = 0.20$, $p = 0.50$, and $p = 0.80$. Explain your reasoning.

(a) 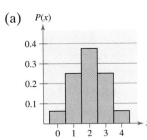 (b) 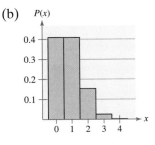 (c)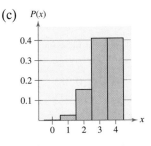

2. *Graphical Analysis* Each histogram shown represents part of a binomial distribution. Each distribution has the same probability of success p, but different numbers of trials n. Match the following values of n with the correct graph: $n = 4$, $n = 8$, and $n = 12$. Explain your reasoning. What happens as the value of n increases?

(a) 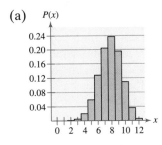 (b) 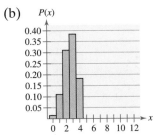 (c)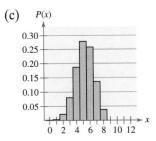

Binomial Experiments In Exercises 3–6, decide whether the experiment is a binomial experiment. If it is, identify a success, specify the values of n, p, and q, and list the possible values of the random variable x. If it is not, explain why.

3. Cyanosis is the condition of having bluish skin due to insufficient oxygen in the blood. About 80% of babies born with cyanosis recover fully. A hospital is caring for five babies born with cyanosis. The random variable represents the number of babies that fully recover. (*Source: The World Book Encyclopedia*)

4. From past records, a clothing store finds that 30% of the people who enter the store will make a purchase. During a one-hour period, 15 people enter the store. The random variable represents the number of people who do *not* make a purchase.

5. A political pollster calls 1012 people and asks, "Do you approve, disapprove, or have no opinion of the way the president is handling his job?" The random variable represents the number of people who approve of the way the president is handling his job.

6. Is not a binomial experiment because the probability of a success is not the same for each trial.

7. (a) 0.088

  (b) 0.104

  (c) 0.896

8. (a) 0.318

  (b) 0.647

  (c) 0.353

9. (a) 0.069

  (b) 0.089

  (c) 0.911

10. (a) 0.021

  (b) 0.026

  (c) 0.974

11. (a) 0.301

  (b) 0.653

  (c) 0.347

6. A state lottery randomly chooses six balls numbered from 1 to 40. You choose six numbers and purchase a lottery ticket. The random variable represents the number of matches on your ticket to the numbers drawn in the lottery.

Finding Binomial Probabilities   In Exercises 7–12, find the indicated probabilities.

7. You are taking a multiple-choice quiz that consists of five questions. Each question has four possible answers, only one of which is correct. To complete the quiz, you randomly guess the answer to each question. Find the probability of guessing

  (a) exactly three answers correctly.

  (b) at least three answers correctly.

  (c) less than three answers correctly.

8. A surgical technique is performed on seven patients. You are told there is a 70% chance of success. Find the probability that the surgery is successful for

  (a) exactly five patients.

  (b) at least five patients.

  (c) less than five patients.

9. Fifty four percent of men consider themselves basketball fans. You randomly select 10 men and ask each if he considers himself a basketball fan. *(Source: Bruskin-Goldring Research)* Find the probability that the number who consider themselves basketball fans is

  (a) exactly eight.

  (b) at least eight.

  (c) less than eight.

10. Ten percent of adults say oatmeal raisin is their favorite cookie. You randomly select 12 adults and ask each to name his or her favorite cookie. *(Source: WEAREVER)* Find the probability that the number who say oatmeal raisin is their favorite cookie is

  (a) exactly four.

  (b) at least four.

  (c) less than four.

11. Twenty one percent of vacationers say the primary purpose of their vacation is outdoor recreation. You randomly select 10 vacationers and ask each to name the primary purpose of his or her vacation. *(Source: Travel Industry Association)* Find the probability that the number who say outdoor recreation is the primary purpose of their vacation is

  (a) exactly two.

  (b) at least two.

  (c) less than two.

12. **(a)** 0.000000158
   (b) ≈ 1
   (c) ≈ 0
13. **(a)** $n = 6, p = 0.36$

x	P(x)
0	0.069
1	0.232
2	0.326
3	0.245
4	0.103
5	0.023
6	0.002

(b)

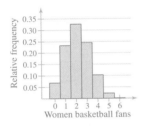

Basketball Fans

(c) 2.16

(d) 1.382

(e) 1.176

(f) On average 2.16, out of 6, women would consider themselves basketball fans. The standard deviation is 1.176 women.

$X = 0, 5,$ or 6 would be uncommon due to their low probabilities.

14. See Selected Answers, page A79
15. See Odd Answers, page A55
16. See Selected Answers, page A80
17. See Odd Answers, page A55
18. 0.124

12. Seventy percent of married couples paid for their honeymoon themselves. You randomly select thirty married couples and ask each if they paid for their honeymoon themselves. *(Source: Bride's Magazine)* Find the probability that the number of couples who say they paid for their honeymoon themselves is

(a) exactly seven.

(b) at least seven.

(c) less than seven.

Constructing Binomial Distributions In Exercises 13–16, (a) construct a binomial distribution, (b) graph the binomial distribution using a relative frequency histogram, find the (c) mean, (d) variance, and (e) standard deviation of the binomial distribution, and (f) interpret the results in the context of the real-life situation. What values of the random variable *x* would you consider unusual? Explain your reasoning.

13. Thirty-six percent of women consider themselves basketball fans. You randomly select six women and ask each if she considers herself a basketball fan. *(Source: Bruskin-Goldring Research)*

14. One in four adults says he or she has no trouble sleeping at night. You randomly select five adults and ask each if he or she has no trouble sleeping at night. *(Source: Marist Institute for Public Opinion)*

15. Five percent of Americans eligible to donate blood actually do. You randomly select four eligible blood donors and ask if they donate blood. *(Source: American Association of Blood Banks)*

16. Thirty-eight percent of Americans have type O⁺ blood. You randomly select five Americans and ask them if their blood type is O⁺. *(Source: American Association of Blood Banks)*

Striking It Rich In Exercises 17 and 18, use the following information. The graph shows the results of a survey of Americans who were asked what they would spend money on first if they suddenly became wealthy. You ask seven people who participated in the survey what they would spend money on first if they suddenly became wealthy. Let *x* represent the number who would vacation.

Copyright 1998, USA TODAY. Reprinted with permission.

17. Construct a binomial distribution.

18. Find the probability that two people will respond "vacation."

19. 0.033

20. 0.002

Extending the Basics

Multinomial Experiments In Exercises 19 and 20, use the following information.

A multinomial experiment is a probability experiment that satisfies the following conditions.

1. Experiment is repeated a fixed number of times.

2. Each trial has k mutually exclusive outcomes: $E_1, E_2, E_3, \ldots, E_k$.

3. Each outcome has a fixed probability. Therefore, $P(E_1) = p_1$, $P(E_2) = p_2$, $P(E_3) = p_3, \ldots, P(E_k) = p_k$. The sum of the probabilities for all outcomes is $p_1 + p_2 + p_3 + \cdots + p_k = 1$.

4. x_1 is the number of times E_1 will occur, x_2 is the number of times E_2 will occur, x_3 is the number of times E_3 will occur, and so on. n is the total number of occurrences.

5. The discrete random variable x counts the number of times $x_1, x_2, x_3, \ldots, x_k$ occurs in a single trial where $x_1 + x_2 + x_3 + \cdots + x_k = n$. The probability that x will occur is

$$P(x) = \frac{n!}{x_1! x_2! x_3! \cdots x_k!} p_1^{x_1} p_2^{x_2} p_3^{x_3} \cdots p_k^{x_k}.$$

19. According to a theory in genetics, if tall and colorful plants are crossed with short and colorless plants, four types of plants will result: tall and colorful, tall and colorless, short and colorful, and short and colorless, with corresponding probabilities of $\frac{9}{16}$, $\frac{3}{16}$, $\frac{3}{16}$, and $\frac{1}{16}$. If 10 plants are selected, find the probability that five will be tall and colorful, two will be tall and colorless, two will be short and colorful, and one will be short and colorless.

20. Another proposed theory in genetics gives the corresponding probabilities for the four types of plants described as $\frac{5}{16}$, $\frac{4}{16}$, $\frac{1}{16}$, and $\frac{6}{16}$. If 10 plants are selected, find the probability that five will be tall and colorful, two will be tall and colorless, two will be short and colorful, and one will be short and colorless.

Air Transport Association

Binomial Distribution of Airplane Accidents

The Air Transport Association of America (ATA) is a support organization for the principal U.S. airlines. Some of the ATA's activities include promoting the air transport industry and conducting industry-wide studies.

The ATA also keeps statistics about commercial airline flights, including those that involve accidents. From 1969 through 1998 for aircraft with 10 or more seats, there were 112 fatal commercial airplane accidents involving U.S. airlines. The distribution of these accidents is shown in the histogram at the right.

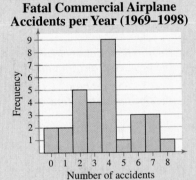

Fatal Commercial Airplane Accidents per Year (1969–1998)

Year	1969	1970	1971	1972	1973	1974	1975	1976	1977	1978	1979	1980	1981	1982	1983
Accidents	7	2	6	7	6	7	2	2	3	5	4	0	4	4	4

Year	1984	1985	1986	1987	1988	1989	1990	1991	1992	1993	1994	1995	1996	1997	1998
Accidents	1	4	2	4	3	8	6	4	4	1	4	2	3	3	0

Exercises

1. In 1997, there were about 8 million commercial flights in the United States. If one is selected at random, what is the probability that it involved a fatal accident?

2. Suppose that the probability of a fatal accident in a given year is 0.0000004. A binomial probability distribution for $n = 8,000,000$ and $p = 0.0000004$ with $x = 0$ to 10 is shown.

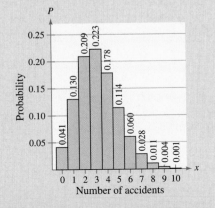

What is the probability that there will be (a) 4 fatal accidents in a year? (b) 10? (c) between 1 and 5, inclusive?

3. Construct a binomial distribution for $n = 8,000,000$ and $p = 0.0000008$ with $x = 0$ to 10. Compare your results to the distribution in Exercise 2.

4. Is a binomial distribution a good model for determining the probability of various numbers of fatal accidents during a year? Explain your reasoning and include a discussion of the four criteria for a binomial experiment.

5. The Federal Aviation Administration says that air flight is so safe that "a person could fly around the clock for over 438 years before being involved in a fatal accident." How can such a statement be justified?

More Discrete Probability Distributions

4.3

The Geometric Distribution • The Poisson Distribution • Summary of Discrete Probability Distributions

- *How to find probabilities using the geometric distribution*
- *How to find probabilities using the Poisson distribution*

Note to Instructor

If you choose, this section can be omitted. None of the material included here will be needed in later sections.

The Geometric Distribution

In this section, you will study two more discrete probability distributions—the geometric distribution and the Poisson distribution.

Many actions in life are repeated until a success occurs. For instance, a CPA candidate might take the CPA exam several times before receiving a passing score, or you might have to dial your Internet connection several times before successfully logging on. Situations such as these can be represented by a geometric distribution.

DEFINITION

A **geometric distribution** is a discrete probability distribution of a random variable x that satisfies the following conditions.

1. A trial is repeated until a success occurs.
2. The repeated trials are independent of each other.
3. The probability of success, p, is constant for each trial.

The **probability that the first success will occur on trial number x** is

$$P(x) = p(q)^{x-1}, \text{ where } q = 1 - p.$$

▶ **EXAMPLE 1**   *Finding Probabilities Using the Geometric Distribution*

From experience, you know that the probability that you will make a sale on any given telephone call is 0.23. Find the probability that your first sale on any given day will occur on your fourth or fifth sales call.

SOLUTION   To find the probability that your first sale will occur on the fourth or fifth call, first find the probability that the sale will occur on the fourth call and the probability that the sale will occur on the fifth call. Then find the sum of the resulting probabilities. Using $p = 0.23$ and $q = 0.77$,

$$P(4) = 0.23 \cdot (0.77)^3 \approx 0.105003$$

and

$$P(5) = 0.23 \cdot (0.77)^4 \approx 0.080852.$$

So, the probability that your first sale will occur on the fourth or fifth sales call is

$$P(\text{sale on fourth or fifth call}) = P(4) + P(5) \approx 0.186.$$

If the first success occurs on the fourth trial, the outcome is FFFS and the probability is

$$P = \overset{F}{(0.77)}\overset{F}{(0.77)}\overset{F}{(0.77)}\overset{S}{(0.23)}.$$

If the first success occurs on the fifth trial, the outcome is FFFFS and the probability is

$$P = \overset{F}{(0.77)}\overset{F}{(0.77)}\overset{F}{(0.77)}\overset{F}{(0.77)}\overset{S}{(0.23)}.$$

> ## Try It Yourself 1
>
> Find the probability that your first sale will occur before your fourth sales call.
>
> **a.** *Use the geometric distribution* to find $P(1)$, $P(2)$, and $P(3)$.
> **b.** *Find the sum* of $P(1)$, $P(2)$, and $P(3)$.
> **c.** *Interpret* the results.   *Answer: Page A36*

The Poisson Distribution

In a binomial experiment you are interested in finding the probability of a specific number of success in a given number of trials. Suppose instead that you want to know the probability that a specific number of occurrences takes place within a given unit of time or space. For instance, to determine the probability that an employee will take 15 sick days within a year, you can use the Poisson distribution.

DEFINITION

The **Poisson distribution** is a discrete probability distribution of a random variable x that satisfies the following conditions.

1. The experiment consists of counting the number of times, x, an event occurs in a given interval. The interval can be an interval of time, area, or volume.
2. The probability of the event occurring is the same for each interval.
3. The number of occurrences in one interval is independent of the number of occurrences in other intervals.

The probability of exactly x occurrences in an interval is

$$P(x) = \frac{\mu^x e^{-\mu}}{x!}$$

where e is an irrational number ≈ 2.71828 and μ is the mean number of occurrences per interval unit.

► EXAMPLE 2   *Using the Poisson Distribution*

The mean number of accidents per month at a certain intersection is 3. What is the probability that in any given month 4 accidents will occur at this intersection?

SOLUTION   Using $x = 4$ and $\mu = 3$, the probability that 4 accidents will occur in any given month at the intersection is

$$P(4) = \frac{3^4 (2.71828)^{-3}}{4!} \approx 0.168.$$

Study Tip

You can also use technology tools, such as Minitab, Excel, and the TI-83, to find Poisson probabilities.

Try It Yourself 2

What is the probability that more than four accidents will occur in any given month at the intersection?

a. *Use the Poisson distribution* to find $P(0)$, $P(1)$, $P(2)$, $P(3)$, and $P(4)$.
b. *Find the sum* of $P(0)$, $P(1)$, $P(2)$, $P(3)$, and $P(4)$.
c. *Subtract* the sum from 1.
d. *Interpret* the results.   *Answer: Page A36*

You can also use a table to find Poisson probabilities. Table 3 in Appendix B lists the Poisson probability for selecting values of x and μ.

EXAMPLE 3   *Finding Poisson Probabilities Using a Table*

A population count shows that there is an average of 3.6 rabbits per acre living in a field. Use a table to find the probability that 2 rabbits are found on any given acre of the field.

SOLUTION   A portion of Table 3 is shown here. Using $\mu = 3.6$ and $x = 2$, you can find the Poisson probability as shown by the highlighted areas in the table.

					μ		
x	3.1	3.2	3.3	3.4	3.5	3.6	3.7
0	.0450	.0408	.0369	.0334	.0302	.0273	.0247
1	.1397	.1304	.1217	.1135	.1057	.0984	.0915
2	.2165	.2087	.2008	.1929	.1850	.1771	.1692
3	.2237	.2226	.2209	.2186	.2158	.2125	.2087
4	.1734	.1781	.1823	.1858	.1888	.1912	.1931
5	.1075	.1140	.1203	.1264	.1322	.1377	.1429
6	.0555	.0608	.0662	.0716	.0771	.0826	.0881
7	.0246	.0278	.0312	.0348	.0385	.0425	.0466
8	.0095	.0111	.0129	.0148	.0169	.0191	.0215

So, the probability that 2 rabbits are found on any given acre is 0.1771.

Picturing the World

The first suspension bridge built in the United States, the Tacoma Narrows Bridge, spans the Tacoma Narrows in Washington state. The average occupancy of vehicles that travel across the bridge is 1.6. The following probability distribution represents the vehicle occupancy on the bridge during a five-day period. *(Source: Washington State Department of Transportation)*

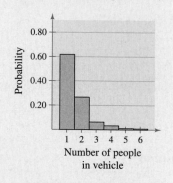

What is the probability that a randomly selected vehicle has two occupants or fewer?

Try It Yourself 3

Two thousand brown trout are introduced into a small lake. The lake has a volume of 20,000 cubic meters. Use a table to find the probability that three brown trout are found in any given cubic meter of the lake.

a. *Find the average* number of brown trout per cubic meter.
b. *Identify* μ and x.
c. *Use Table 3* to find the Poisson probability.   *Answer: Page A36*

Summary of Discrete Probability Distributions

The following table summarizes the discrete probability distributions discussed in this chapter.

Distribution	Summary	Formulas
Binomial Distribution	A binomial experiment satisfies the following conditions. 1. The experiment is repeated for a fixed number (n) of independent trials. 2. There are only two possible outcomes for each trial. Each outcome can be classified as a success or as a failure. 3. The probability of a success must remain constant for each trial. 4. The random variable x counts the number of successful trials out of the n trials. The parameters of a binomial distribution are n and p.	$x =$ the number of successes in n trials $p =$ probability of success on a single trial $q =$ probability of failure on a single trial $q = 1 - p$ The probability of exactly x successes in n trials is $$P(x) = {}_nC_x p^x q^{n-x}$$ $$= \frac{n!}{(n-x)!x!} p^x q^{n-x}.$$
Geometric Distribution	A geometric distribution is a discrete probability distribution of the random variable x that satisfies the following conditions. 1. A trial is repeated until a success occurs. 2. The repeated trials are independent of each other. 3. The probability of success p is constant for each trial. 4. The random variable x represents the number of the trial in which the first success occurs. The parameter of a geometric distribution is p.	$x =$ the number of the trial in which the first success occurs $p =$ probability of success on a single trial $q =$ probability of failure on a single trial $q = 1 - p$ The probability that the first success occurs on the xth trial is $$P(x) = p(q)^{x-1}.$$
Poisson Distribution	The Poisson distribution is a discrete probability distribution that gives the probability of x occurrences of an event over a specified interval of time, area, or volume. The parameter of a Poisson distribution is μ.	$x =$ the number of occurrences in the given interval $\mu =$ the average number of occurrences in a given time or space unit. The probability of x occurrences in an interval is $$P(x) = \frac{\mu^x e^{-\mu}}{x!}.$$

4.3 EXERCISES

HELP

 StatPro 4.3

 Internet Statistics 4.3

 Student Solutions Manual 4.3

 Videos 4.3

 Try It Yourself Answers 4.3

1. Geometric

2. Poisson

3. Poisson

4. Binomial

5. (a) 0.082
   (b) 0.469
   (c) 0.531

6. (a) 0.105
   (b) 0.578
   (c) 0.317

7. (a) 0.249
   (b) 0.784
   (c) 0.216

8. (a) 0.009
   (b) 0.030
   (c) 0.904

Basic Skills and Concepts

Deciding on a Distribution In Exercises 1–4, decide which probability distribution—binomial, geometric, or Poisson—applies to the question. You do not need to answer the question. Instead, justify your choice.

1. *Given:* The probability that a student passes the written test for a private pilot's license is 0.75. *Question:* What is the probability that a student will fail the test on the first trial and pass it on the second trial?

2. *Given:* In Rapid City, South Dakota, the mean number of wet days for May is 12. *Question:* What is the probability that Rapid City has 18 wet days next May? *(Source: The Weather Almanac)*

3. *Given:* The mean number of oil tankers at a port city is 8 per day. The port has facilities to handle up to 12 oil tankers in a day. *Question:* What is the probability that too many tankers will arrive on a given day?

4. *Given:* Forty percent of American adults exercise at least 30 minutes a week. In a survey of 120 randomly chosen adults, people were asked, "Do you exercise at least 30 minutes a week?" *Question:* What is the probability that exactly 50 of the people answer yes?

Geometric Distribution In Exercises 5–8, find the indicated probabilities using the geometric distribution. If convenient, use technology to find the probability.

5. From experience, you know that the probability that you will make a sale on any given telephone call is 0.19. Find the probability that you
   (a) make your first sale on the fifth call.
   (b) make your first sale on the first, second, or third call.
   (c) do not make a sale on the first three calls.

6. A cereal maker places a game piece in its cereal boxes. The probability of winning a prize in the game is one in four. Find the probability that you
   (a) win your first prize with your fourth purchase.
   (b) win your first prize with your first, second, or third purchase.
   (c) do not win a prize with your first four purchases.

7. Basketball player Shaquille O'Neal makes a free throw shot about 53.5% of the time. *(Source: SportsLine USA, Inc.)* Find the probability that
   (a) the first shot O'Neal makes is the second shot.
   (b) the first shot O'Neal makes is the first or second shot.
   (c) O'Neal does not make two shots.

8. An auto parts seller finds that one in every 100 parts sold is defective. Find the probability that
   (a) the first defective part is the tenth part sold.
   (b) the first defective part is the first, second, or third part sold.
   (c) none of the first 10 parts sold are defective.

9. (a) 0.057
   (b) 0.9577
   (c) 0.9004
10. (a) 0.1954
    (b) 0.4335
    (c) 0.5665
11. (a) 0.3293
    (b) 0.8781
    (c) 0.1219
12. (a) 0.130
    (b) 0.653
    (c) 0.347
13. (a) 1000
    999000
    999.50

    On average you would
    have to play 1000 times
    until you won the lottery.
    The standard deviation is
    999.50.

    (b) 1000 times

    Lose money. On average
    you would win $500
    every 1000 times you
    play the lottery. Hence,
    the net gain would be
    − $500.

Poisson Distribution   In Exercises 9–12, find the indicated probabilities using the Poisson distribution. If convenient, use a Poisson probability table or technology tool to find the probability.

9. The mean number of business failures per hour in the United States in a recent year was about 8. *(Source: The Wall Street Journal Almanac)* Find the probability that
   (a) exactly 4 businesses will fail in any given hour.
   (b) at least 4 businesses will fail in any given hour.
   (c) more than 4 businesses will fail in any given hour.

10. A newspaper finds that the mean number of typographical errors per page is four. Find the probability that
    (a) exactly three typographical errors will be found on a page.
    (b) at most three typographical errors will be found on a page.
    (c) more than three typographical errors will be found on a page.

11. A major hurricane is a hurricane with wind speeds of 111 miles per hour or greater. From 1900 to 1999, the mean number of major hurricanes to strike the U.S. mainland per year was about 0.6. *(Source: National Hurricane Center)* Find the probability that in a given year
    (a) exactly one major hurricane will strike the U.S. mainland.
    (b) at most one major hurricane will strike the U.S. mainland.
    (c) more than one major hurricane will strike the U.S. mainland.

12. The mean number of wet days per month for Lewistown, Idaho, is 8.5. Find the probability that in a given month (a) there are exactly 9 wet days, (b) there are at most 9 wet days, and (c) there are more than 9 wet days. *(Source: The USA Today Weather Almanac)*

Extending the Basics

Geometric Distribution: Mean and Variance   In Exercises 13 and 14, use the fact that the mean of a geometric distribution is $\mu = 1/p$ and the variance is $\sigma^2 = q/p^2$.

13. A daily number lottery chooses three balls numbered 0 to 9. The probability of winning the lottery is 1/1000. Let x be the number of times you play the lottery before winning the first time.
    (a) Find the mean, variance, and standard deviation. Interpret the results.
    (b) How many times would you expect to have to play the lottery before winning? Assume that it costs $1 to play and winners are paid $500. Would you expect to make or lose money playing this lottery? Explain.

14. (a) 200
39800
199.50

On average 200 records will be examined before finding one that has been miscalculated. The standard deviation is 199.50.

(b) 200

15. (a) 70
2.0
The standard deviation is 2.0 strokes.

(b) 0.199

16. (a) 7
2.646
The standard deviation is 2.646 inches.

(b) 0.401

17. (a) 0.629

(b) 0.343

(c) 0.029

18. (a) 0.145

(b) 0.1454

14. A company assumes that 0.5% of the paychecks for a year were calculated incorrectly. The company has 200 employees and examines the payroll records from one month.

(a) Find the mean, variance, and standard deviation. Interpret the results.

(b) How many employee payroll records would you expect to examine before finding one with an error?

Poisson Distribution: Variance   In Exercises 15 and 16, use the fact that the variance of a Poisson distribution is $\sigma^2 = \mu$.

15. At one point in a recent year, the mean number of strokes per hole for golfer Tiger Woods was about 3.9. *(Source: PGATour.com)*

(a) Find the variance and standard deviation. Interpret the results.

(b) How likely is Woods to play an 18-hole round and have more than 72 strokes?

16. The mean snowfall in January for Evansville, Indiana, is seven inches. *(Source: The USA Today Weather Almanac)*

(a) Find the variance and standard deviation. Interpret the results.

(b) Find the probability that the snowfall in January for Evansville, Indiana, will exceed seven inches.

17. *Hypergeometric Distribution*   Binomial experiments require that any sampling be done with replacement because each trial must be independent of the others. The hypergeometric distribution also has two outcomes—success and failure. However, the sampling is done without replacement. Given a population of N items having k successes and $N - k$ failures, the probability of selecting a sample of size n that has x successes and $n - x$ failures is given by

$$P(x) = \frac{(_kC_x)(_{N-k}C_{n-x})}{_NC_n}.$$

In a shipment of 15 microchips, two are defective and 13 are not defective. A sample of three microchips is chosen at random. Find the probability that

(a) all three microchips are not defective.

(b) one microchip is defective and two are not defective.

(c) two microchips are defective and one is not defective.

18. *Approximating the Binomial Distribution*   A glass manufacturer finds that 1 in every 1000 glass items produced is warped.

(a) Use a binomial distribution to find the probability of finding five defective glass items in a random sample of 6500 glass items.

(b) The Poisson distribution can be used to approximate the binomial distribution for large values of n and small values of p. Repeat (a) using a Poisson distribution and compare the results.

TECHNOLOGY   MINITAB   EXCEL   TI-83

Using Poisson Distributions as Queuing Models

Queuing means waiting in line to be served. There are many examples of queuing in everyday life: waiting at a traffic light, waiting in line at a grocery check-out counter, waiting for an elevator, being put on hold for a telephone call, and so on.

Poisson distributions are used to model and predict the number of people (calls, computer programs, vehicles) arriving at the line. In the following exercises, you are asked to use Poisson distributions to analyze the queues at a grocery store check-out counter.

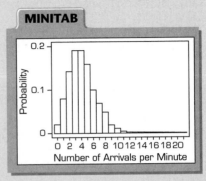

MINITAB

Number of Arrivals per Minute

Exercises

In Exercises 1–6, consider a grocery store that can process a total of four customers at its check-out counters each minute.

1. Suppose that the mean number of customers who arrive at the check-out counters each minute is 4. Create a Poisson distribution with $\mu = 4$ for $x = 0$ to 20. Compare your results with the histogram shown at the upper right.

2. We used Minitab to generate 20 random numbers with a Poisson distribution for $\mu = 4$. Let the random number represent the number of arrivals at the check-out counter each minute for 20 minutes.

   3 3 3 3 5 5 6 7 3 6
   3 5 6 3 4 6 2 2 4 1

   During each of the first four minutes, only three customers arrived. These customers could all be processed, so there were no customers waiting after four minutes.

   (a) How many customers were waiting after 5 minutes? 6 minutes? 7 minutes? 8 minutes?

   (b) Create a table that shows the number of customers waiting at the end of 1 through 20 minutes.

3. Generate a list of 20 random numbers with a Poisson distribution for $\mu = 4$. Create a table that shows the number of customers waiting at the end of 1 through 20 minutes.

4. Suppose that the mean increases to five arrivals per minute. If you can still only process four per minute, how many would you expect to be waiting in line after 20 minutes?

5. Simulate the setting in Exercise 4. Do this by generating a list of 20 random numbers with a Poisson distribution with $\mu = 5$. Then create a table that shows the number of customers waiting at the end of 20 minutes.

6. Suppose that the mean number of arrivals per minute is 5. What is the probability that 10 customers will arrive during the first minute?

7. Suppose that the mean number of arrivals per minute is 4.

   (a) What is the probability that three, four, or five customers will arrive during the third minute?

   (b) What is the probability that more than four customers will arrive during the first minute?

   (c) What is the probability that more than four customers will arrive during each of the first four minutes?

Extended solutions are given in the *Technology Supplement.*
Technical instruction is provided for Minitab, Excel, and the TI-83.

4 ▼ CHAPTER SUMMARY

What did you learn?

	Review Exercises
• How to distinguish between discrete random variables and continuous random variables *(Section 4.1)*	*1–4*
• How to determine if a distribution is a probability distribution *(Section 4.1)*	*5–8*
• How to construct a discrete probability distribution and its graph, and find the mean variance and standard deviation of a discrete probability distribution *(Section 4.1)*	*9–12*
• How to find the expected value of a probability distribution *(Section 4.1)*	*13, 14*
• How to determine if a probability experiment is a binomial experiment *(Section 4.2)*	*15, 16*
• How to find binomial probabilities using the binomial probability formula, a binomial probability table, and technology *(Section 4.2)*	*17–19*
• How to construct a binomial distribution and its graph, and find the mean, variance, and standard deviation of a binomial probability distribution *(Section 4.2)*	*20–22*
• How to find probabilities using the geometric distribution *(Section 4.3)*	*23, 24*
• How to find probabilities using the Poisson distribution *(Section 4.3)*	*25, 26*

Why did you learn it?   Uses and Abuses

Uses   Discrete probability distributions are common in business, science, engineering, and many other occupations. Knowing the characteristics of such distributions is of utmost importance in statistics. For example, suppose you are trying to determine the percent of the population that has a certain characteristic, such as a willingness to vote for your candidate. To determine the percent, you take a random sample of 200 and find that 40% of the sample plans to vote for your candidate. Is it possible that the actual proportion for the population is 50%? As you can see, this question is similar to questions relating to binomial probability distributions. Such questions are critical to the understanding of statistical sampling. By the time you have completed this course, you will be able to answer this type of question.

Abuses   A common misuse of binomial probabilities is to think that the "most likely" outcome is the outcome that will occur most of the time. For instance, suppose you randomly choose a committee of four from a large population that is 50% men and 50% women. The most likely composition of the committee is that it will contain 2 men and 2 women. Although this is the most likely outcome, the probability that it will occur is only 0.375. There is 0.5 chance that the committee will have 1 man and 3 women *or* 3 men and 1 woman. So, if either of these outcomes occur, you should not assume that the selection was biased.

▼ 4 REVIEW EXERCISES

1. Discrete
2. Continuous
3. Continuous
4. Discrete
5. No
6. Yes
7. Yes
8. No

In Exercises 1–4, decide whether the random variable x is discrete or continuous.

1. x represents the number of pumps in use at a gas station.

2. x represents the weight of a truck at a weigh station.

3. x represents the amount of gas pumped at a gas station.

4. x represents the number of defects on a microchip.

In Exercises 5–8, decide whether the distribution is a probability distribution. If it is not, identify the property that is not satisfied.

5. The daily limit for catching red snappers in Florida is four. The random variable x represents the number of fish caught. *(Source: Division of Marine Resources, Florida Department of Environmental Protection)*

x	0	1	2	3	4
$P(x)$	0.36	0.23	0.08	0.14	0.29

6. The vending machine at a workplace holds 48 bottles of iced tea. The random variable x represents the number of days until the iced tea is gone.

x	1	2	3	4	5	6
$P(x)$	0.05	0.15	0.40	0.25	0.10	0.05

7. A greeting card shop keeps records of customers' buying habits. The random variable x represents the number of cards sold to an individual customer.

x	1	2	3	4	5	6	7
$P(x)$	0.68	0.14	0.08	0.05	0.02	0.02	0.01

8. The random variable x represents the number of classes in which a student is enrolled at a university.

x	1	2	3	4	5	6	7	8
$P(x)$	$\frac{1}{80}$	$\frac{2}{75}$	$\frac{1}{10}$	$\frac{12}{25}$	$\frac{27}{20}$	$\frac{1}{5}$	$\frac{2}{25}$	$\frac{1}{120}$

9. (a)

x	Freq	$P(x)$
2	3	0.005
3	12	0.018
4	72	0.111
5	115	0.177
6	169	0.260
7	120	0.185
8	83	0.128
9	48	0.074
10	22	0.034
11	6	0.009
	650	1

(b)

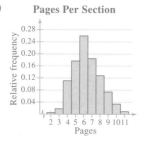

Pages Per Section

(c) 6.377
2.858
1.691

10. See Selected Answers, page A80
11. See Odd Answers, page A56
12. See Selected Answers, page A80
13. 3.37

In Exercises 9–12, (a) use the frequency distribution table to construct a probability distribution, (b) graph the probability distribution using a relative frequency histogram, and (c) find the mean, variance, and standard deviation of the probability distribution.

9. The number of pages in a section from 10 statistics texts

Pages	Sections
2	3
3	12
4	72
5	115
6	169
7	120
8	83
9	48
10	22
11	6

10. The number of goals scored by a soccer team during a 32-game season

Goals	Games
0	7
1	8
2	10
3	3
4	3
5	1

11. A survey asked 200 households how many televisions they owned.

Televisions	Households
0	3
1	38
2	83
3	52
4	18
5	5
6	1

12. A television station sells advertising in 15-, 30-, 60-, 90-, and 120-second blocks. The distribution for one 24-hour day is given.

Length (in seconds)	Number
15	76
30	445
60	30
90	3
120	12

In Exercises 13 and 14, find the expected value of the random variable.

13. A person has shares of eight different stocks. The random variable x represents the number of stocks showing a loss on a selected day.

x	0	1	2	3	4	5	6	7	8
$P(x)$	0.02	0.11	0.18	0.32	0.15	0.09	0.05	0.05	0.03

14. 2.5

15. Yes, $n = 12$, $p = 0.30$,
$q = 0.70$, $x = 0, 1, \ldots, 12$

16. No, the experiment is not
repeated for a fixed number
of trials.

17. **(a)** 0.208

   (b) 0.322

   (c) 0.114

18. **(a)** 0.142

   (b) 0.225

   (c) 0.225

19. **(a)** 0.294

   (b) 0.518

   (c) 0.518

20. **(a)**

x	$P(x)$
0	0.007
1	0.059
2	0.201
3	0.342
4	0.291
5	0.099

(b)

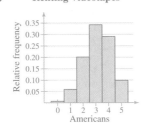

Renting Videotapes

(c) 3.15
1.1655
1.080

21. See Odd Answers, page A56

14. A local pub has a chicken wing special on Tuesdays. The pub owners purchase wings in cases of 300. The random variable x represents the number of cases used during the special.

x	1	2	3	4
$P(x)$	$\frac{1}{9}$	$\frac{1}{3}$	$\frac{1}{2}$	$\frac{1}{18}$

In Exercises 15 and 16, determine whether the experiment is a binomial experiment. If it is not, identify the property that is not satisfied. If it is, list the values of n, p, and q, and the values that x can assume.

15. Bags of plain M&M's contain 30% brown candies. One candy is selected from each of 12 bags. The random variable represents the number of brown candies selected. *(Source: Mars, Inc.)*

16. A fair coin is tossed repeatedly until 15 heads are obtained. The random variable x counts the number of tosses.

In Exercises 17–19, find the indicated probabilities.

17. One in four adults is currently on a diet. Of a random sample of eight adults, what is the probability that the number currently on a diet is (a) exactly three, (b) at least three, and (c) more than three? *(Source: Wirthlin Worldwide)*

18. Three in five adults own an answering machine. Of a random sample of 12 adults, what is the probability that the number owning answering machines is (a) exactly nine, (b) at least nine, and (c) nine or more? *(Source: Wirthlin Worldwide)*

19. Forty-three percent of adults receive fewer than five phone calls a day. Of a random sample of six adults, what is the probability that the number receiving fewer than five calls a day is (a) exactly three, (b) at least three, and (c) three or more? *(Source: Wirthlin Worldwide)*

In Exercises 20–22, (a) construct a binomial distribution, (b) graph the binomial distribution using a relative frequency histogram, and (c) find the mean, variance, and standard deviation of the probability distribution.

20. Sixty-three percent of Americans rent videotapes at least once a month. Consider a random sample of five Americans who are asked if they rent at least one videotape a month. *(Source: TELENATION/Market Facts, Inc.)*

21. Fifty-seven percent of families say that their children have an influence on their vacation destinations. Consider a random sample of six families who are asked if their children have an influence on their vacation destinations. *(Source: YP&B/Yandelovich 1997 Travel Monitor)*

22. (a)

x	P(x)
0	0.012
1	0.096
2	0.293
3	0.397
4	0.202

(b)

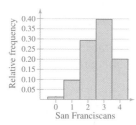

Went to a Movie

(c) 2.68
0.8844
0.940

23. (a) 0.096
(b) 0.518
(c) 0.606

24. (a) 0.432
(b) 0.245
(c) 0.677
(d) 0.816

25. (a) 0.604
(b) 0.305
(c) 0.091

26. (a) 0.9972
(b) 0.8754
(c) 1

22. During the past three months, 67% of San Franciscans went out to the movies. Consider a random sample of four San Franciscans who are asked if they went to the movies in the past three months. *(Source: Scarborough Research)*

In Exercises 23 and 24, find the indicated probabilities using the geometric distribution. If convenient, use technology to find the probabilities.

23. During a promotional contest, a soft drink company places winning caps on one of every six bottles. If you purchase one bottle a day, find the probability that you find your first winning cap (a) on the fourth day, (b) within four days, (c) sometime after three days.

24. In 1998, Mark McGwire hit 70 home runs in the 162 games he played. Imagine that his home run production stayed at that level the following season. What is the probability that he would hit his first home run (a) on the first game of the season, (b) on the second game of the season, (c) on the first or second game of the season, and (d) within the first three games of the season?

In Exercises 25 and 26, find the indicated probabilities using the Poisson distribution. If convenient, use a Poisson probability table or technology to find the probabilities.

25. From 1940 to 1981 (42 years), lightning killed 7741 people in the United States. Assume that this rate holds true today and is constant throughout the year. Find the probability that tomorrow (a) no one in the United States will be struck and killed by lightning, (b) one person will be struck and killed, and (c) more than one person will be struck and killed. *(Source: National Lightning Safety Institute)*

26. It is estimated that sharks kill 10 people each year worldwide. Find the probability that at least three people are killed by sharks this year (a) assuming that this rate is true, (b) if the rate is actually five people a year, and (c) if the rate is actually fifteen people a year. *(Source: International Shark Attack File)*

4 ◣ CHAPTER QUIZ

1. (a) Discrete

  (b) Continuous

2. (a)

x	Freq	P(x)
1	57	0.361
2	37	0.234
3	47	0.297
4	15	0.095
5	2	0.013
	158	1

  (b)

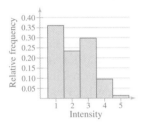

Hurricane Intensity

  (c) 2.165
    1.125
    1.061

    On average the intensity
    of a hurricane will be
    2.165. The standard
    deviation is 1.061.

  (d) 0.108

3. See Odd Answers, page A56

4. (a) 0.1755

  (b) 0.4405

  (c) 0.0067

Take this quiz as you would take a quiz in class. After you are done, check your work against the answers given in the back of the book.

1. Decide if the random variable, x, is discrete or continuous. Explain your reasoning.

  (a) x represents the number of times Yellowstone Park's Old Faithful geyser erupts in one day.

  (b) x represents the amount of sugar (in pounds) eaten each day in the United States

2. The following table lists the number of U.S. mainland hurricane strikes (since 1900) for various intensities according to the Saffir-Simpson Hurricane Scale. *(Source: National Hurricane Center)*

Intensity	Number of Hurricanes
1	57
2	37
3	47
4	15
5	2

  (a) Construct a probability distribution of the data.

  (b) Graph the probability distribution using a relative frequency histogram.

  (c) Find the mean, variance, and standard deviation of the probability distribution and interpret the results.

  (d) Find the probability that a hurricane selected at random for further study has an intensity of at least 4.

3. A surgical technique is performed on eight patients. You are told there is an 80% chance of success.

  (a) Construct a binomial distribution.

  (b) Graph the binomial distribution using a relative frequency histogram.

  (c) Find the mean, variance, and standard deviation of the probability distribution and interpret the results.

  (d) Find the probability that the surgery is successful for exactly six patients.

  (e) Find the probability that the surgery is successful for fewer than six patients.

4. A newspaper finds that the mean number of typographical errors per page is five. Find the probability that

  (a) exactly five typographical errors will be found on a page.

  (b) fewer than five typographical errors will be found on a page.

  (c) no typographical errors will be found on a page.

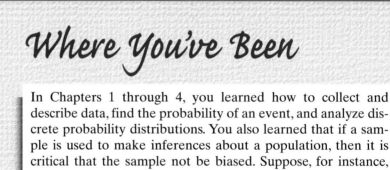

Where You've Been

In Chapters 1 through 4, you learned how to collect and describe data, find the probability of an event, and analyze discrete probability distributions. You also learned that if a sample is used to make inferences about a population, then it is critical that the sample not be biased. Suppose, for instance, that you wanted to measure the serum cholesterol levels of adults in the United States. How would you organize the study? When the National Center for Health Statistics performed this study, it used random sampling and then classified the results according to the gender, ethnic background, and age of the participants. One conclusion from the study was that women's cholesterol levels tended to increase throughout their lives, whereas men's increased to age 65, and then decreased.

In 1990, the National Center for Health Statistics, located in Hyattsville, Maryland, began a 10-year program called *Healthy People 2000* to promote health through changes in people's lifestyles. During the decade, some of the goals were met. For instance, heart disease and stroke death rates were down. Other goals were not met. For instance, although more adults were exercising, a quarter of all adults still engage in no physical activity.

Normal Probability
Distributions

Where You're Going

In Chapter 5, you will learn how to recognize normal (bell-shaped) distributions and how to use their properties in real-life applications. Suppose that you worked for the National Center for Health Statistics and were collecting data about various physical traits of Americans. Which of the following would you expect to have bell-shaped, symmetric distributions: height, weight, cholesterol level, age, blood pressure, shoe size, reaction times, lung capacity? Of these, all except weight and age have distributions that are approximately normal. For instance, the four graphs below show the height and weight distributions for American men and women aged 20 to 29. Notice that the height distributions are bell shaped, but the weight distributions are skewed right.

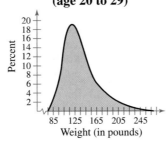

Women's Weights
(age 20 to 29)

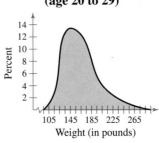

Men's Weights
(age 20 to 29)

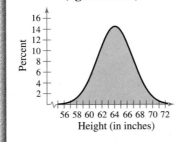

Women's Heights
(age 20 to 29)

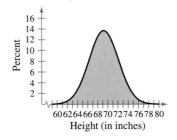

Men's Heights
(age 20 to 29)

5.1 Introduction to Normal Distributions

Properties of a Normal Distribution • Normal Curves and Probability

What You Should Learn

• *How to interpret graphs of normal probability distributions*

• *How to find areas under a normal curve, and use them to find probabilities for random variables with normal distributions*

Note to Instructor

Draw several different continuous probability curves. Then point out that the normal (or Gaussian) curve is graphed using the formula shown in the insight box. Have students discuss measures in nature that are normally distributed. Mention that often grades in a statistics class are not normally distributed.

Insight

If x is a continuous random variable having a normal distribution with mean μ and standard deviation σ, you can graph the normal curve using the equation

$$y = \frac{e^{-\frac{(x-\mu)^2}{2\sigma^2}}}{\sigma\sqrt{2\pi}}.$$

Because e and π are constants, the normal curve depends completely on μ and σ.

Properties of a Normal Distribution

In Section 4.1, you learned that a **continuous random variable** has an infinite number of values that can be represented by an interval on the number line. Its probability distribution is called a **continuous probability distribution.** In this chapter, you will study the most important continuous probability distribution in statistics—the normal distribution. Normal distributions can be used to model many sets of measurements in nature, industry, and business. For instance, the systolic blood pressure of humans, the lifetime of television sets, and even housing costs are all normally distributed random variables.

GUIDELINES

Properties of a Normal Distribution

A **normal distribution** is a continuous probability distribution for a random variable x. The graph of a normal distribution is called the **normal curve.** A normal distribution has the following properties.

1. The mean, median, and mode are equal.
2. The normal curve is bell shaped and is symmetric about the mean.
3. The total area under the normal curve is equal to one.
4. The normal curve approaches, but never touches, the x-axis as it extends farther and farther away from the mean.
5. Between $\mu - \sigma$ and $\mu + \sigma$ (in the center of the curve) the graph curves downward. The graph curves upward to the left of $\mu - \sigma$ and to the right of $\mu + \sigma$. The points at which the curve changes from curving upward to curving downward are called *inflection points*.

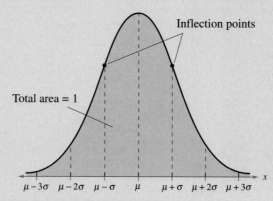

A normal distribution can have any mean and any positive standard deviation. These two parameters, μ and σ, completely determine the shape of the normal curve. The mean gives the location of the line of symmetry and the standard deviation describes how much the data are spread out.

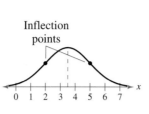

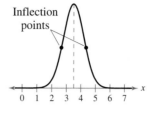

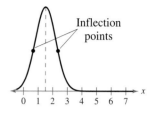

Mean: $\mu = 3.5$
Standard deviation:
$\sigma = 1.5$

Mean: $\mu = 3.5$
Standard deviation:
$\sigma = 0.7$

Mean: $\mu = 1.5$
Standard deviation:
$\sigma = 0.7$

▶ **EXAMPLE 1**   *Understanding Mean and Standard Deviation*

1. Which normal curve has a greater mean?
2. Which normal curve has a greater standard deviation?

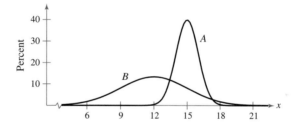

SOLUTION

1. The line of symmetry of curve A occurs at $x = 15$. The line of symmetry of curve B occurs at $x = 12$. So, curve A has a greater mean.
2. Curve B is more spread out than curve A, so curve B has a greater standard deviation.

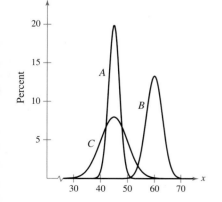

Try It Yourself 1

Consider the normal curves shown at the left. Which normal curve has the greatest mean? Which normal curve has the greatest standard deviation? Justify your answers.

a. Find the location of the *line of symmetry* of each curve. Make a conclusion about which mean is greatest.
b. Determine which normal curve is *more spread out*. Make a conclusion about which standard deviation is greatest.

Answer: Page A36 ◀

▶ **EXAMPLE 2** *Interpreting Graphs of Normal Distributions*

The heights (in feet) of fully grown white oak trees are normally distributed. The normal curve shown below represents this distribution. What is the mean height of a fully grown white oak tree? Estimate the standard deviation of this normal distribution.

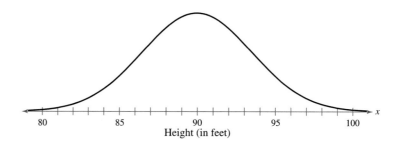
Height (in feet)

SOLUTION

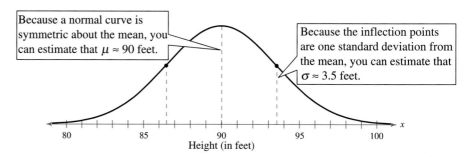

Because a normal curve is symmetric about the mean, you can estimate that $\mu \approx 90$ feet.

Because the inflection points are one standard deviation from the mean, you can estimate that $\sigma \approx 3.5$ feet.

Height (in feet)

So the heights of the oak trees are normally distributed with a mean of about 90 feet and a standard deviation of about 3.5 feet.

Picturing the World

The amount of dissolved oxygen is important in judging the quality of stream water. Acceptable dissolved oxygen levels range from 5 mg/L to 12 mg/L. Students from Strong Vincent High School in Erie, Pennsylvania conducted a study of dissolved oxygen at Cascade Creek. The normal curve shows the students' results.

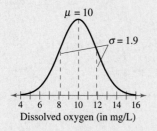
Dissolved oxygen (in mg/L)

Are these dissolved oxygen levels acceptable? If not, are they too high or too low?

Try It Yourself 2

The diameters of fully grown white oak trees are normally distributed. The normal curve shown below represents this distribution. What is the mean diameter of a fully grown white oak tree? Estimate the standard deviation of this normal distribution.

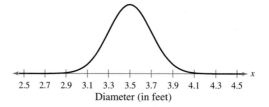
Diameter (in feet)

a. Find the *line of symmetry* and identify the mean.
b. Estimate the *inflection points* and identify the standard deviation.

Answer: Page A36 ◀

Normal Curves and Probability

The total area under a probability curve is equal to 1. The *area of a region under a probability curve* gives the probability that the random variable will have a value in the corresponding interval. In this chapter, you will learn several ways to find areas under normal curves. You have already studied one of these ways in Section 2.4—the *Empirical Rule.*

Empirical Rule

In a normal distribution with mean μ and standard deviation σ, you can approximate areas under the normal curve as follows.

1. About 68% of the area lies between $\mu - \sigma$ and $\mu + \sigma$.
2. About 95% of the area lies between $\mu - 2\sigma$ and $\mu + 2\sigma$.
3. About 99.7% of the area lies between $\mu - 3\sigma$ and $\mu + 3\sigma$.

Note to Instructor

To tie this material to earlier chapters, ask students how many adults in a sample of 1000 would be expected to have an IQ between 70 and 115.

If $\mu = 20$ and $\sigma = 4$, the area between $20 - 4 = 16$ and $20 + 4 = 24$ is 0.68. So, the probability that x is between 16 and 24 is 0.68.

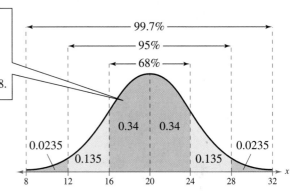

> **EXAMPLE 3** *Estimating a Probability for a Normal Curve*

Adult IQ scores are normally distributed with $\mu = 100$ and $\sigma = 15$. Estimate the probability that a randomly chosen adult has an IQ between 70 and 115.

SOLUTION A score of 70 is two standard deviations below the mean, and a score of 115 is one standard deviation above the mean. Using the Empirical Rule, the area under the normal curve between these two values is

$$\text{Area} = 0.135 + 0.34 + 0.34 = 0.815.$$

So, the probability the adult has an IQ between 70 and 115 is about 0.815.

The probability that a randomly chosen adult has an IQ between 70 and 115 is

$$P(70 < x < 115) = 0.815.$$

Try It Yourself 3

Estimate the probability that a randomly chosen adult has an IQ between 85 and 145.

a. *How many standard deviations* are the scores from the mean?
b. Use the *Empirical Rule* to find the area.   *Answer: Page A36*

HELP

 StatPro 5.1

 Internet Statistics 5.1

 Student Solutions Manual 5.1

 Videos 5.1

 Try It Yourself Answers 5.1

1. Answers will vary.
2. False
3. Answers will vary.
   Similarities: Both curves will have the same line of symmetry.
   Differences: One curve will be more spread out than the other.
4. Answers will vary.
   Similarities: Both curves will have the same shape (i.e. equal standard deviations)
   Differences: The two curves will have different lines of symmetry.
5. No
6. No
7. Yes
8. No
9. 2
10. Mean and standard deviation
11. (9, 21)
12. (14, 24)

Basic Skills and Concepts

1. Find three real-life examples of a continuous variable. Which do you think may be normally distributed? Why?

2. Determine whether the following statement is true or false. If it is false, explain why.

   The total area under the normal curve is 0.997.

3. Draw two normal curves that have the same mean but different standard deviations. Describe the similarities and differences.

4. Draw two normal curves that have different means but the same standard deviations. Describe the similarities and differences.

Graphical Analysis   In Exercises 5–8, decide whether the graph could represent a variable with a normal distribution. Explain your reasoning.

5.
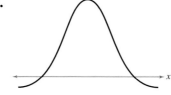

6.

7.
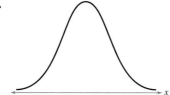

8.
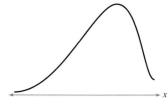

9. If a random variable is normally distributed, approximately 95% of the population values will lie between how many standard deviations from the mean?

10. Name the two parameters that are necessary to determine probabilities for a particular normal distribution curve.

Skill Check   In Exercises 11 and 12, you are given the mean and standard deviation of a continuous random variable that is normally distributed. Find an interval that contains about 95% of the distribution.

11. $\mu = 15, \sigma = 3$

12. $\mu = 19, \sigma = 2.5$

13. 0.68

14. 0.95

15. B

16. A

17. 0.997

18. (3.7, 4.7)

19. (19.86, 20.14)

20. (14.83, 15.17)

Skill Check In Exercises 13 and 14, *x* is a random variable with a normal distribution. Find the probability that *x* falls in the indicated interval.

13. $\mu = 7$, $\sigma = 1.75$, find $P(5.25 < x < 8.75)$

14. $\mu = 20$, $\sigma = 5.4$, find $P(9.2 < x < 30.8)$

15. ***Graphical Analysis*** A company manufactures engine parts. The diameters of the engine parts are normally distributed with a mean of 3 inches and a standard deviation of 0.02 inch. Which of the following normal curves represents this distribution? Justify your conclusion.

(a)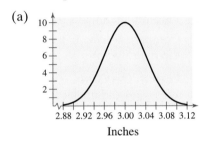

Inches

(b)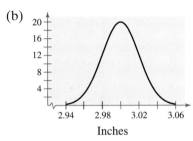

Inches

16. ***Graphical Analysis*** An instruction manual claims that the mean assembly time for a product is 4.2 hours and the standard deviation is 0.25 hour. Which normal curve represents this distribution? Justify your conclusion.

(a)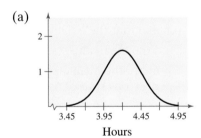

Hours

(b)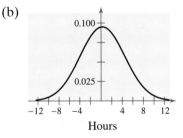

Hours

17. ***Understanding the Concept*** Use the information in Exercise 15 to estimate the probability that an engine part is between 2.94 inches and 3.06 inches.

18. ***Understanding the Concept*** Use the information in Exercise 16 to determine the interval in which 95% of the assembly times will fall.

19. ***Determining Intervals*** The contents of a cereal box are normally distributed, with a mean weight of 20 ounces and a standard deviation of 0.07 ounce. Determine an interval of values into which 95% of the cereal box weights will fall.

20. ***Determining Intervals*** The weights of bags of cookies are normally distributed, with a mean of 15 ounces and a standard deviation of 0.085 ounce. Determine an interval of values into which 95% of the bags of cookies will fall.

21. (a)

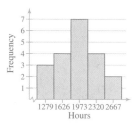

Light Bulb Lifespans

It is reasonable to assume that the lifespan is normally distributed since the histogram is nearly symmetric and bell-shaped.

(b) 1941.35, 432.385

(c) The sample mean of 1941.35 hours is less than the claimed mean, so on the average the bulbs in the sample lasted for a shorter time. The sample standard deviation of 432 hours is greater than the claimed standard deviation, so the bulbs in the sample had a greater variation in lifespan than the manufacturer's claim.

22. (a)

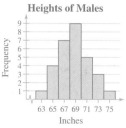

Heights of Males

It is reasonable to assume that the heights are normally distributed since the histogram is nearly symmetric and bell-shaped.

(b) 68.751, 2.855

(c) The mean of your sample is 0.45 inch less than that of the previous study. The standard deviation is nearly identical.

23. 0.68   **24.** 0.475

25. (a) 320 **(b)** 1360 **(c)** 320

21. *Making a Decision*   You work for a consumer watchdog publication and are testing the advertising claims of a light bulb manufacturer. The manufacturer claims that the lifespan of the bulb is normally distributed, with a mean of 2000 hours and a standard deviation of 250 hours. You test 20 light bulbs and get the following lifespans.

2210,   2406,   2267,   1930,   2005,   2502,   1106,
2140,   1949,   1921,   2217,   2121,   2004,   1397,
1659,   1577,   2840,   1728,   1209,   1639

(a) Draw a histogram to display these data. Use five classes. Is it reasonable to assume that the lifespan is normally distributed? Why?

(b) Find the mean and standard deviation of your sample.

(c) Compare the mean and standard deviation of your sample to those in the manufacturer's claim. Discuss the differences.

22. *Making a Decision*   You are performing a study about the height of 20- to 29-year-old males. A previous study found the height to be normally distributed, with a mean of 69.2 inches with a standard deviation of 2.9 inches. You randomly sample 30 males and find their heights to be

72.1,   71.2,   67.9,   67.3,   69.5,   68.6,   68.8,   69.4,   73.5,   67.1,
69.2,   75.7,   71.1,   69.6,   70.7,   66.9,   71.4,   62.9,   69.2,   64.9,
68.2,   65.2,   69.7,   72.2,   67.5,   66.6,   66.5,   64.2,   65.4,   70.0.

(Source: National Center for Health Statistics)

(a) Draw a histogram to display these data. Use seven classes with midpoints of 65.0, 66.5, 68.0, 69.5, 71.5, 73.0, and 74.5. Is it reasonable to assume that the heights are normally distributed? Why?

(b) Find the mean and standard deviation of your sample.

(c) Compare the mean and standard deviation of your sample to those in the previous study. Discuss the differences.

23. *Estimating a Probability*   The lifespan of a battery is normally distributed, with a mean of 2000 hours and a standard deviation of 30 hours. Estimate the probability that a battery's lifespan is between 1970 and 2030 hours.

24. *Estimating a Probability*   The lifespan of a tire is normally distributed, with a mean of 30,000 miles and a standard deviation of 2000 miles. Estimate the probability that a tire's lifespan is between 30,000 and 34,000 miles.

25. *Applying the Concept*   The time per week a student uses a lab computer is normally distributed, with a mean of 6.2 hours and a standard deviation of 0.9 hour. You are planning the schedule for the computer lab. Of 2000 students, estimate the number of students who will use a lab computer for the given number of hours.

(a) Less than 5.3 hours

(b) Between 5.3 hours and 7.1 hours

(c) More than 7.1 hours

26. (a) 12.5
(b) 67.5
(c) 170

27.

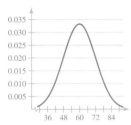

The normal distribution curve is centered at its mean (60) and has 2 points of inflection (48 and 72) representing $\mu \pm \sigma$.

28.

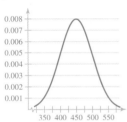

The normal distribution curve is centered at its mean (450) and has 2 points of inflection (400 and 500) representing $\mu \pm \sigma$.

29. (a) 1
(b) 0.25
(c) 0.4

30. (a)

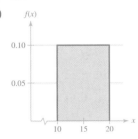

(b) 0.3
(c) 0.5

26. *Applying the Concept* The time per workout an exerciser uses a stair climber is normally distributed, with a mean of 20 minutes and a standard deviation of 5 minutes. You are planning the schedule for a health club. Of 500 members who use a stair climber, estimate the number of people who will use a stair climber for the given number of minutes.

(a) Less than 10 minutes

(b) Between 10 and 15 minutes

(c) Between 15 and 20 minutes

Extending the Basics

27. *Writing* Draw a normal curve with a mean of 60 and a standard deviation of 12. Describe how you constructed the curve and discuss its features.

28. *Writing* Draw a normal curve with a mean of 450 and a standard deviation of 50. Describe how you constructed the curve and discuss its features.

29. *Uniform Distribution* Another continuous distribution is the **uniform distribution.** An example is $f(x) = 1$ for $0 \le x \le 1$. The mean of this distribution is 0.5 and the standard deviation is approximately 0.29. The graph of this distribution is a square with the height and width both equal to 1 unit. In general, the density function for a uniform distribution on the interval from $x = a$ to $x = b$ is given by $f(x) = 1/(b - a)$. The mean is $(a + b)/2$ and the variance is $(b - a)^2/12$.

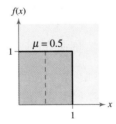

(a) Verify that the area under the curve is 1.

(b) Find the probability that x falls between 0.25 and 0.5.

(c) Find the probability that x falls between 0.3 and 0.7.

30. *Uniform Distribution* Consider the uniform density function $f(x) = 0.1$ for $10 \le x \le 20$. The mean of this distribution is 15 and the standard deviation is 2.89.

(a) Draw a graph of the distribution and show that the area under the curve is 1.

(b) Find the probability that x falls between 12 and 15.

(c) Find the probability that x falls between 13 and 18.

The Standard Normal Distribution

5.2

The Standard Score • The Standard Normal Distribution

The Standard Score

In Section 5.1, you learned to calculate areas under a normal curve when values of the random variable x corresponded to $-3, -2, -1, 0, 1, 2,$ or 3 standard deviations from the mean. In this section, you will learn to calculate areas corresponding to other x-values. To do that you will use the standard score.

DEFINITION

The **standard score,** or **z-score,** represents the number of standard deviations a random variable, x, falls from the mean, μ. To transform the random variable to a z-score, use the following formula:

$$z = \frac{\text{value} - \text{mean}}{\text{standard deviation}} = \frac{x - \mu}{\sigma}$$

Note to Instructor

Mention that a standard score is a measure of position and can be used for any type of distribution. In theory, a z-score can be any real number. In practice, however, almost all z-scores will fall between -3 and $+3$ because almost all data values fall within 3 standard deviations of the mean.

> ▶ **EXAMPLE 1**   *Finding z-Scores*

The mean speed of vehicles along a stretch of highway is 56 mph with a standard deviation of 4 mph. You measure the speed of three cars traveling along this stretch of highway as 62 mph, 47 mph, and 56 mph. Find the z-score that corresponds to each speed. What can you conclude?

SOLUTION   The z-score that corresponds to each speed is calculated below.

$x = 62$ mph	$x = 47$ mph	$x = 56$ mph
$z = \dfrac{62 - 56}{4} = 1.5$	$z = \dfrac{47 - 56}{4} = -2.25$	$z = \dfrac{56 - 56}{4} = 0$

From the z-scores, you can conclude that a speed of 62 mph is 1.5 standard deviations above the mean, a speed of 47 mph is 2.25 standard deviations below the mean, and a speed of 56 mph is equal to the mean.

Insight

A z-score can be negative, positive, or zero. If z is negative, the corresponding x value is below the mean. If z is positive, the corresponding x-value is above the mean. And if z = 0, the corresponding x-value is equal to the mean.

> *Try It Yourself 1*
>
> The monthly utility bills in a city have a mean of $70 and a standard deviation of $8. Find the z-scores that correspond to utility bills of $60, $71, and $92. What can you conclude?
>
> **a.** *Identify* μ and σ of the nonstandard normal distribution.
> **b.** *Transform* each value of the random variable, x, to a z-score.
> **c.** *Interpret* the results.   *Answer: Page A36* ◀

The formula on page 202 gives z in terms of x. If you solve this formula for x, you get a new formula that gives x in terms of z.

$$z = \frac{x - \mu}{\sigma} \qquad \text{Formula for } z \text{ in terms of } x$$

$$z\sigma = x - \mu \qquad \text{Multiply each side by } \sigma.$$

$$\mu + z\sigma = x \qquad \text{Add } \mu \text{ to each side.}$$

$$x = \mu + z\sigma \qquad \text{Interchange sides.}$$

Picturing the World

Each year the Centers for Disease Control and Prevention and the National Center for Health Statistics jointly publish a report summarizing the vital statistics from the previous year. According to one publication, the number of births in a recent year was 3,899,589. The weights of the newborns can be approximated by a normal distribution, as shown by the following graph.

Weights of Newborns

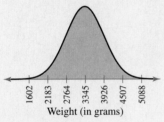

Weight (in grams)

The weights of three newborns are 2000 grams, 3000 grams, and 4000 grams. Find the z-score that corresponds to each weight. Are any of these unusually heavy or light?

Transforming a z-Score to an x-Value

To transform a standard z-score to a data value x in a given population, use the formula

$$x = \mu + z\sigma.$$

▶ **EXAMPLE 2** *Finding an x-Value*

The speeds of vehicles along a stretch of highway have a mean of 56 mph and a standard deviation of 4 mph. Find the speeds x corresponding to z-scores of 1.96, −2.33, and 0. Interpret your results.

SOLUTION The x-value that corresponds to each standard score is calculated as follows.

$$z = 1.96: \qquad x = 56 + 1.96(4)$$
$$= 63.84 \text{ mph}$$

$$z = -2.33: \qquad x = 56 + (-2.33)(4)$$
$$= 46.68 \text{ mph}$$

$$z = 0: \qquad x = 56 + 0(4)$$
$$= 56 \text{ mph}$$

You can see that 63.84 mph is above the mean, 46.68 is below the mean, and 56 is equal to the mean.

Try It Yourself 2

The monthly utility bills in a city have a mean of $70 and a standard deviation of $8. Find the x-*values* that correspond to z-scores of −0.75, 4.29, −1.82. What can you conclude?

a. *Identify μ and σ of the nonstandard normal distribution.*
b. *Transform each z-score to an x-value.*
c. *Interpret the results.* *Answer: Page A37* ◀

The Standard Normal Distribution

There are infinitely many normal distributions, each with its own mean and standard deviation. The normal distribution with a mean of 0 and a standard deviation of 1 is called **the standard normal distribution.**

If each data value of a normally distributed random variable x is transformed into a standard z-score, the result will be the standard normal distribution. When this transformation takes place, the area that falls in the interval of the nonstandard normal curve is the *same* as that under the standard normal curve within the corresponding z-boundaries.

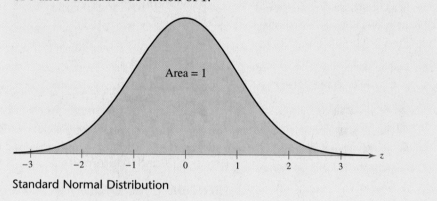

DEFINITION

The **standard normal distribution** is a normal distribution with a mean of 0 and a standard deviation of 1.

Area = 1

Standard Normal Distribution

It is important that you know the difference between x and z. The random variable x is sometimes called a raw score and represents values in a *nonstandard* normal distribution, while z represents values in the *standard* normal distribution.

Because every normal distribution can be transformed to the standard normal distribution, you can use z-scores and the standard normal curve to find areas under any normal curve. The Standard Normal Table in Appendix B lists the cumulative area under the standard normal curve to the left of z for z-scores from -3.49 to 3.49. As you examine the table, notice the following.

Properties of the Standard Normal Distribution

1. The cumulative area is close to 0 for z-scores close to -3.49.
2. The cumulative area increases as the z-scores increase.
3. The cumulative area for $z = 0$ is 0.5000.
4. The cumulative area is close to 1 for z-scores close to $z = 3.49$.

Insight

Because every normal distribution can be transformed to the standard normal distribution, you can use z-scores and the standard normal curve to find areas under any normal curve.

Note to Instructor

Mention that the formula for a normal probability density function on page 194 is greatly simplified when $\mu = 0$ and $\sigma = 1$.

$$y = \frac{e^{-\frac{x^2}{2}}}{\sqrt{2\pi}}$$

The cumulative density function (CDF) table presented in this text might be a slight change from previous texts you have used. The results are consistent with software outputs (CDF in *Minitab* and *Excel*) and can be shown compatible with *TI-83* outputs by using normal CDF and entering (-1E-10,z) for the interval endpoints. Students find this table easier to use than the 0-to-z table. If you prefer to use a 0-to-z table, we have included an alternative presentation of Section 5.2 in Appendix A.

▶ **EXAMPLE 3** *Using the Standard Normal Table*

1. Find the cumulative area that corresponds to a z-score of 1.15.
2. Find the z-score that corresponds to a cumulative area of 0.4052.

SOLUTION

1. Find the area that corresponds to $z = 1.15$ by finding 1.1 in the left column and then moving across the row to the column under 0.05. The number in that row and column is 0.8749. So, the area to the left of $z = 1.15$ is 0.8749.

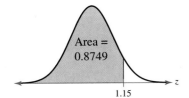

Area = 0.8749

1.15

z	.00	.01	.02	.03	.04	.05	.06
0.0	.5000	.5040	.5080	.5120	.5160	.5199	.5239
0.1	.5398	.5438	.5478	.5517	.5557	.5596	.5636
0.2	.5793	.5832	.5871	.5910	.5948	.5987	.6026
0.9	.8159	.8186	.8212	.8238	.8264	.8289	.8315
1.0	.8413	.8438	.8461	.8485	.8508	.8531	.8554
1.1	.8643	.8665	.8686	.8708	.8729	(.8749)	.8770
1.2	.8849	.8869	.8888	.8907	.8925	.8944	.8962
1.3	.9032	.9049	.9066	.9082	.9099	.9115	.9131
1.4	.9192	.9207	.9222	.9236	.9251	.9265	.9279

2. Find the z-score that corresponds to an area of 0.4052 by locating 0.4052 in the table. The values at the beginning of the corresponding row and at the top of the column give the z-score. For an area of 0.4052, the row value is -0.2 and the column value is 0.04. So, the z-score is -0.24.

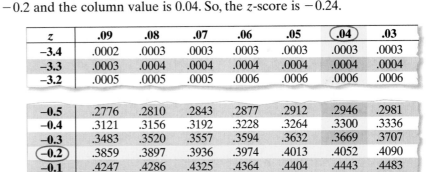

Area = 0.4052

−0.24

z	.09	.08	.07	.06	.05	(.04)	.03
−3.4	.0002	.0003	.0003	.0003	.0003	.0003	.0003
−3.3	.0003	.0004	.0004	.0004	.0004	.0004	.0004
−3.2	.0005	.0005	.0005	.0006	.0006	.0006	.0006
−0.5	.2776	.2810	.2843	.2877	.2912	.2946	.2981
−0.4	.3121	.3156	.3192	.3228	.3264	.3300	.3336
−0.3	.3483	.3520	.3557	.3594	.3632	.3669	.3707
(−0.2)	.3859	.3897	.3936	.3974	.4013	.4052	.4090
−0.1	.4247	.4286	.4325	.4364	.4404	.4443	.4483
−0.0	.4641	.4681	.4721	.4761	.4801	.4840	.4880

Note to Instructor

Have students note that as the z-scores increase, the cumulative areas increase. The CDF is one to one and as such has an inverse. Discuss how this inverse function (INVCDF) can be used when a cumulative area (percentile) is known and the z-score must be found.

Try It Yourself 3

1. Find the area under the curve to the left of a z-score of -2.19.
2. Find the z-score that has an area of 0.985 falling to its left.

a. Locate the given z-score and *find the area* that corresponds to it in the Standard Normal Table.
b. Locate the given area and *find the z-score* that corresponds to it.

Answer: Page A37 ◀

You can use the following guidelines to find various types of areas under the standard normal curve.

GUIDELINES

Finding Areas Under the Standard Normal Curve

1. Sketch the standard normal curve and shade the appropriate area under the curve.
2. Find the area by following the directions for each case shown.

   a. To find the area to the *left* of z, find the area that corresponds to z in the Standard Normal Table.

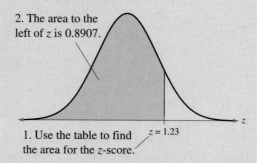

   2. The area to the left of z is 0.8907.

   1. Use the table to find the area for the z-score. $z = 1.23$

   b. To find the area to the *right* of z, use the Standard Normal Table to find the area that corresponds to z. Then subtract the area from 1.

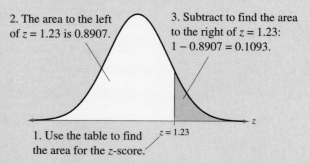

   2. The area to the left of $z = 1.23$ is 0.8907.

   3. Subtract to find the area to the right of $z = 1.23$: $1 - 0.8907 = 0.1093$.

   1. Use the table to find the area for the z-score. $z = 1.23$

   c. To find the area *between* two z-scores, find the area corresponding to each z-score in the Standard Normal Table. Then subtract the smaller area from the larger area.

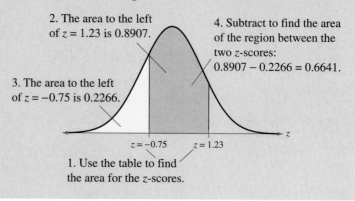

   2. The area to the left of $z = 1.23$ is 0.8907.

   4. Subtract to find the area of the region between the two z-scores: $0.8907 - 0.2266 = 0.6641$.

   3. The area to the left of $z = -0.75$ is 0.2266.

   $z = -0.75$ $z = 1.23$

   1. Use the table to find the area for the z-scores.

> ▶ **EXAMPLE 4** *Finding Area Under the Standard Normal Curve*

Find the area under the standard normal curve to the left of $z = -0.99$.

SOLUTION The area under the standard normal curve to the left of $z = -0.99$ is shown.

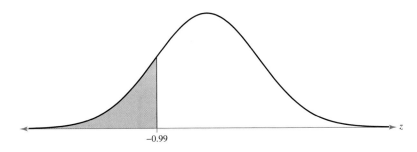

From the Standard Normal Table, this area is equal to 0.1611.

Try It Yourself 4

Find the area under the standard normal curve to the left of $z = 2.13$.

a. *Draw* the standard normal curve and shade the area under the curve and to the left of $z = 2.13$.
b. Use the Standard Normal Table to *find the area* that corresponds to $z = 2.13$.

Answer: Page A37

> ▶ **EXAMPLE 5** *Finding Area Under the Standard Normal Curve*

Find the area under the standard normal curve to the right of $z = 1.06$.

SOLUTION The area under the standard normal curve to the right of $z = 1.06$ is shown.

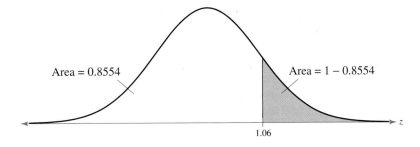

From the Standard Normal Table, the area to the left of $z = 1.06$ is 0.8554. Since the total area under the curve is 1, the area to the right of $z = 1.06$ is

$$\text{Area} = 1 - 0.8554 = 0.1446.$$

Try It Yourself 5

Find the area under the standard normal curve to the right of $z = -2.16$.

a. *Draw* the standard normal curve and shade the area below the curve and to the right of $z = -2.16$.
b. Use the Standard Normal Table to *find the area* to the left of $z = -2.16$.
c. *Subtract* the area from 1.

Answer: Page A37

▶ **EXAMPLE 6**   *Finding Area Under the Standard Normal Curve*

Find the area under the standard normal curve between $z = -1.5$ and $z = 1.25$.

SOLUTION   The area under the standard normal curve between $z = -1.5$ and $z = 1.25$ is shown.

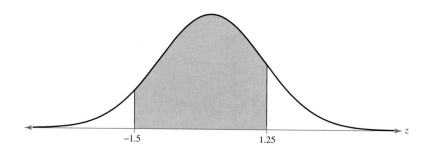

From the Standard Normal Table, the area to the left of $z = 1.25$ is 0.8944 and the area to the left of $z = -1.5$ is 0.0668. So, the area between $z = -1.5$ and $z = 1.25$ is

    Area $= 0.8944 - 0.0668 = 0.8276$.

So, 82.76% of the area under the curve falls between $z = -1.5$ and $z = 1.25$.

Try It Yourself 6

Find the area under the standard normal curve between $z = -2.16$ and $z = -1.35$.

a. Use the Standard Normal Table to *find the area* to the left of $z = -1.35$.
b. Use the Standard Normal Table to *find the area* to the left of $z = -2.16$.
c. *Subtract* the smaller area from the larger area.

Answer: Page A37

5.2 EXERCISES

HELP

StatPro 5.2

Internet Statistics 5.2

Student Solutions Manual 5.2

Videos 5.2

Try It Yourself Answers 5.2

1. $\mu = 0$, $\sigma = 1$

2. $z = \dfrac{x - \mu}{\sigma}$

3. "The" standard normal distribution is used to describe one specific normal distribution ($\mu = 0$, $\sigma = 1$). "A" normal distribution is used to describe a normal distribution with any mean and standard deviation.

4. (c)

5. (a) 1.2
     −2.1
     0

(b) 26,800 miles

6. (a) 0.5
     −1.5
     −1
     2.5

(b) 10560

7. (a) 1.29
     2.14
     −0.86
     −1.29

(b) The scores seem typical.

Basic Skills and Concepts

1. What is the mean of the standard normal distribution? What is the standard deviation of the standard normal distribution?

2. Describe how you can transform a nonstandard normal distribution to a standard normal distribution.

3. *Think About It* Why is it correct to say "a" normal distribution and "the" standard normal distribution?

4. *Think About It* If a z-score is zero, which of the following must be true? Explain your reasoning.

  (a) The mean is 0.

  (b) The corresponding x-value is 0.

  (c) The corresponding x-value is equal to the mean.

5. *Applying z-Scores* A brand of automobile tire has a life expectancy that is normally distributed, with a mean life of 30,000 miles and a standard deviation of 2500 miles.

  (a) The lifespans of three randomly selected tires are 33,000 miles, 24,750 miles, and 30,000 miles. Find the z-score that corresponds to each lifespan.

  (b) You sell this brand of tire and you want to give a guarantee for free replacement of tires that don't wear well. How should you word your guarantee if you are willing to replace approximately 10% of the tires you sell?

6. *Applying z-Scores* Your company manufactures ball bearings. The diameters of the ball bearings are normally distributed, with a mean of 3 inches and a standard deviation of 0.02 inch.

  (a) The diameters of four randomly selected ball bearings are 3.01, 2.97, 2.98, and 3.05. Find the z-score that corresponds to each diameter.

  (b) You are filling an order for 50,000 ball bearings. You agree to replace any whose diameters differ from 3 inches by more than 0.025 inch. About how many do you think you will have to replace?

7. *Applying z-Scores* The scores on a statewide, standardized test are normally distributed with a mean of 76 and a standard deviation of 7.

  (a) The scores of four randomly selected tests are 85, 91, 70, and 67. Find the z-score for each of these.

  (b) You randomly sample the z-scores of 20 students from a local high school. The scores are as follows.

$$-0.31, \quad 0.16, \quad 2.19, \quad 1.35, \quad -0.46, \quad 0.95, \quad -0.15,$$
$$0.46, \quad 0.93, \quad 0.17, \quad -0.86, \quad -0.76, \quad -1.58, \quad -0.45,$$
$$-0.14, \quad 0.81, \quad -0.44, \quad -0.17, \quad 0.73, \quad 1.21$$

Do these scores seem typical? Below average? Above average? Explain your reasoning.

8. **(a)** −1
−0.25
0
1.5
   (b) 48 days
9. **(a)** 167.4
   (b) 124.2
10. **(a)** 18.325
   (b) 20.325
11. −0.67, 0, 0.67
12. −1.28, −0.39, 0.39, 1.28
13. 0.33
14. −0.33
15. 1.29
16. 2.575
17. 0.3849
18. 0.4878
19. 0.6247
20. 0.0228

8. *Applying z-Scores*   The lifespans of a species of fruit fly are normally distributed, with a mean of 36 days and a standard deviation of 4 days.

   (a) The lifespans of four randomly selected fruit flies are 32 days, 35 days, 36 days, and 42 days. Find the *z*-score for each of these.

   (b) You are planning a study to obtain data for the lifespan of 200 fruit flies. For how many days should you plan to conduct the study? (Assume you want to include all data that lies within three standard deviations of the mean.)

9. *Finding Test Scores*   A test has a mean of 153 and a standard deviation of 12. Find the test scores that correspond to (a) $z = 1.2$ and (b) $z = -2.4$.

10. *Finding an x-Value*   Given a normal distribution with $\mu = 20$ and $\sigma = 2.5$, find the value of x that has (a) 25% of the distribution's area to the left and (b) 45% of the distribution's area to the right. (*Hint:* $x = \mu + z\sigma$.)

11. *Quartiles*   Find *z*-scores that correspond to the first, second, and third quartiles.

12. *Percentiles*   Find *z*-scores that correspond to the 10th, 35th, 65th, and 90th percentiles.

Finding a z-Score   In Exercises 13–16, find the indicated *z*-score.

13. Find the *z*-score that has 62.8% of the distribution's area to its left.

14. Find the *z*-score that has 62.8% of the distribution's area to its right.

15. Find the *z*-score for which 80% of the distribution's area lies between $-z$ and z.

16. Find the *z*-score for which 99% of the distribution's area lies between $-z$ and z.

Graphical Analysis   In Exercises 17–20, find the area of the indicated region under the standard normal curve.

17.

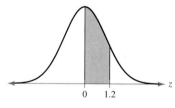

18.

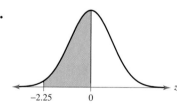

19.

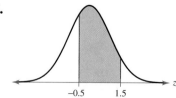

20.

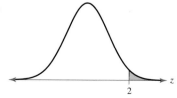

21. 0.9382
22. 0.5987
23. 0.8289
24. 0.9599
25. 0.005
26. 0.0010
27. 0.05
28. 0.006
29. 0.475
30. 0.499
31. 0.437
32. 0.195
33. 0.551
34. 0.832
35. 0.05
36. 0.203
37. 0.9265
38. 0.6736
39. 0.9744
40. 0.5987
41. 0.2912
42. 0.0016
43. 0.1469
44. 0.0054
45. 0.4798
46. 0.4495
47. 0.3133
48. 0.4812
49. 0.7540
50. 0.7748
51. 0.0098
52. 0.05
53. 0.9544
54. Subtract 0.5 from the areas corresponding to $z = 0$ through $z = 3.49$.

Finding Area In Exercises 21–36, find the indicated area under the standard normal curve.

21. To the left of $z = 1.54$

22. To the left of $z = 0.25$

23. To the right of $z = -0.95$

24. To the right of $z = -1.75$

25. To the left of $z = -2.575$

26. To the left of $z = -3.08$

27. To the right of $z = 1.645$

28. To the right of $z = 2.51$

29. Between $z = 0$ and $z = 1.96$

30. Between $z = 0$ and $z = 3.09$

31. Between $z = -1.53$ and $z = 0$

32. Between $z = -0.51$ and $z = 0$

33. Between $z = -0.44$ and $z = 1.18$

34. Between $z = -2.88$ and $z = 0.97$

35. To the left of $z = -2.97$ or to the right of $z = 1.66$

36. To the left of $z = -0.84$ or to the right of $z = 2.81$

Finding Probabilities In Exercises 37–52, find the indicated probability using the standard normal distribution.

37. $P(z < 1.45)$

38. $P(z < 0.45)$

39. $P(z > -1.95)$

40. $P(z > -0.25)$

41. $P(z < -0.55)$

42. $P(z < -2.95)$

43. $P(z > 1.05)$

44. $P(z > 2.55)$

45. $P(0 < z < 2.05)$

46. $P(0 < z < 1.64)$

47. $P(-0.89 < z < 0)$

48. $P(-2.08 < z < 0)$

49. $P(-0.95 < z < 1.44)$

50. $P(-2.95 < z < 0.76)$

51. $P(z < -2.58 \text{ or } z > 2.58)$

52. $P(z < -1.96 \text{ or } z > 1.96)$

Extending the Basics

53. *Chebychev's Theorem vs. the Normal Distribution* Recall from Chebychev's theorem that for an arbitrary probability distribution, it must be true that $1 - (1/4)$, or 75%, of the distribution must fall within two standard deviations of the mean. For normal distributions, approximately how much of the total region under a normal curve lies within two standard deviations of the mean? Explain your reasoning.

54. *Making a Table* The Standard Normal Table in Appendix B lists the area under the standard normal curve to the left of z for z-scores between -3.49 and 3.49. Describe how to construct a standard normal table for the area under the standard normal curve to the left of z for z-scores between 0 and z, as shown in the figure.

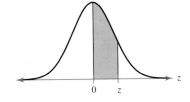

Applications of Normal Distributions

5.3

Comparing Normal Distributions • Probability and Normal Distributions

What You Should Learn

- **How to compare data from two normal distributions**
- **How to find probabilities for normally distributed variables using a table and using technology**
- **How to find a specific data entry of a normal distribution given the probability**

Comparing Normal Distributions

In Section 5.2, you learned how to transform a normally distributed variable x to a z-score using the equation

$$z = \frac{\text{value} - \text{mean}}{\text{standard deviation}} = \frac{x - \mu}{\sigma}.$$

You also learned how to find areas under the standard normal curve. In this section, you will learn how to apply those skills. For instance, transforming x-values to z-scores allows you to compare variables in two normal distributions, as shown in the following example.

> **EXAMPLE 1** *Comparing Scores from Two Distributions*

The Graduate Record Exam (GRE) and the Miller Analogy Test (MAT) are tests that graduate schools use to evaluate applicants. GRE scores are normally distributed, with $\mu = 1500$ and $\sigma = 300$, while MAT scores are normally distributed, with $\mu = 50$ and $\sigma = 5$. You decide to take both tests. You score 1875 on the GRE and 57 on the MAT. On which test did you score better? Explain.

SOLUTION You can transform each score to a standard z-score to determine which is better. The area to the left of the z-score is the percentile.

GRE score: $z = \dfrac{x - \mu}{\sigma} = \dfrac{1875 - 1500}{300} = 1.25$ The area to left of $z = 1.25$ is 0.8944.

MAT score: $z = \dfrac{x - \mu}{\sigma} = \dfrac{57 - 50}{5} = 1.4$ The area to left of $z = 1.4$ is 0.9222.

The MAT z-score (92nd percentile) is greater than the GRE z-score (89th percentile). So, you scored better on the MAT.

Insight

Values that lie more than two standard deviations from the mean are considered unusual. Values that lie more than three standard deviations from the mean are considered very unusual. So if a z-score is greater than 2 or less than -2, it is unusual. If it is greater than 3 or less than -3, it is very unusual.

Try It Yourself 1

You take both tests again and score 1775 on the GRE and 54 on the MAT. On which test did you score better this time? Explain.

  a. *Transform* each test score to a z-score.
  b. *Find* a percentile for each score.
  c. *Decide* which score is better.   *Answer: Page A37*

Probability and Normal Distributions

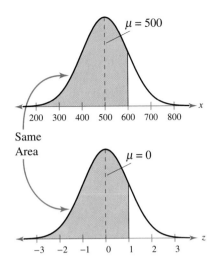

$\mu = 500$

Same Area

$\mu = 0$

If a random variable x is normally distributed, you can find the probability that x will fall in a given interval by calculating the area under the normal curve for the given interval.

To find the area under any normal curve, first convert each data value to a z-score. Then use the standard normal distribution. For instance, consider a normal curve with $\mu = 500$ and $\sigma = 100$, as shown at the upper left. The value of x one standard deviation above the mean is $\mu + \sigma = 500 + 100 = 600$. Now consider the standard normal curve shown at the lower left. The value of z one standard deviation above the mean is $\mu + \sigma = 0 + 1 = 1$. Because a z-score of 1 corresponds to an x-value of 600 and areas are not changed with a transformation to a standard normal curve, the shaded areas in the graphs are equal.

> ▶ **EXAMPLE 2** *Finding Probabilities for Normal Distributions*

A survey indicates that people use their computers an average of 2.4 years before upgrading to a new machine. The standard deviation is 0.5 year. If a computer owner is selected at random, find the probability that he or she will use it for less than 2 years before upgrading. Assume that the variable x is normally distributed.

SOLUTION The graph shows a normal curve with $\mu = 2.4$ and $\sigma = 0.5$ and a shaded area for x less than 2. The z-score that corresponds to 2 years is

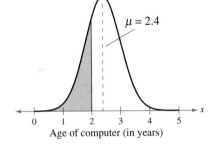

$\mu = 2.4$

Age of computer (in years)

$$z = \frac{x - \mu}{\sigma} = \frac{2 - 2.4}{0.5} = -0.8.$$

Using the Standard Normal Table, $P(z < -0.8) = 0.2119$. The probability that the computer will be upgraded in less than 2 years is 0.2119. So 21.19% of new owners will upgrade in less than two years.

Study Tip

Another way to write the answer to Example 2 is $P(x < 2) = 0.2119$.

Try It Yourself 2

A Ford Escort gets an average of 28 miles per gallon (mpg) with a standard deviation of 1.6 mpg. If an Escort is selected at random, what is the probability that it will get more than 31 mpg? Assume that gas mileage is normally distributed.

a. *Sketch* a graph.
b. *Find the z-score* that corresponds to 31 miles per gallons.
c. Use the Standard Normal Table to *find the area* to the left of z. Subtract from 1 to find the area to the right of that z-score.
d. *Write the result as a sentence.*   *Answer: Page A37* ◀

Note to Instructor

For technology users, have students do Examples 2 and 3 using a technology tool and compare results.

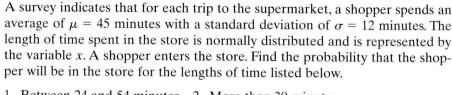

EXAMPLE 3 *Finding Probabilities for Normal Distributions*

A survey indicates that for each trip to the supermarket, a shopper spends an average of $\mu = 45$ minutes with a standard deviation of $\sigma = 12$ minutes. The length of time spent in the store is normally distributed and is represented by the variable x. A shopper enters the store. Find the probability that the shopper will be in the store for the lengths of time listed below.

1. Between 24 and 54 minutes   2. More than 39 minutes

SOLUTION

1. The graph at the left shows a normal curve with $\mu = 45$ minutes and $\sigma = 12$ minutes. The area for x between 24 and 54 minutes is shaded. The z-scores that correspond to 24 minutes and to 54 minutes are

$$z_1 = \frac{24 - 45}{12} = -1.75 \quad \text{and} \quad z_2 = \frac{54 - 45}{12} = 0.75.$$

So, the probability that a shopper will be in the store between 24 and 54 minutes is

$$
\begin{aligned}
P(24 < x < 54) &= P(-1.75 < z < 0.75) \\
&= P(z < 0.75) - P(z < -1.75) \\
&= 0.7734 - 0.0401 \\
&= 0.7333.
\end{aligned}
$$

Another way of interpreting this probability is to say that 77.33% of the shoppers will be in the store between 24 and 54 minutes.

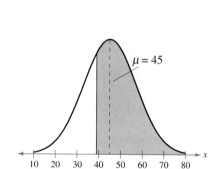

2. The graph at the left shows a normal curve with $\mu = 45$ minutes and $\sigma = 12$ minutes. The area for x greater than 39 minutes is shaded. The z-score that corresponds to 39 minutes is

$$z = \frac{39 - 45}{12} = -0.5.$$

So, the probability that a shopper will be in the store more than 39 minutes is

$$
\begin{aligned}
P(x > 39) &= 1 - P(z < -0.5) \\
&= 1 - 0.3085 \\
&= 0.6915.
\end{aligned}
$$

Try It Yourself 3

What is the probability that the shopper will be in the supermarket between 33 and 60 minutes?

a. *Sketch* a graph.
b. *Find z-scores* that correspond to 60 minutes and 33 minutes.
c. *Find the cumulative area* for each z-score.
d. *Subtract the smaller area from the larger.*   *Answer: Page A37*

Another way to find normal probabilities is to use a calculator or a computer. You can find normal probabilities using Minitab, Excel, and the TI-83.

> **EXAMPLE 4** *Using Technology to Find Normal Probabilities*

Cholesterol levels of American men are normally distributed, with a mean of 215 and a standard deviation of 25. If you randomly select an American man, what is the probability that his cholesterol level is less than 175? Use a calculator or a computer to find the probability.

SOLUTION   Minitab, Excel, and the TI-83 each have features that allow you to find normal probabilities without first converting to standard *z*-scores. For each, you must specify the mean and standard deviation of the population, as well as the *x*-value(s) that determine the interval.

MINITAB

Cumulative Distribution Function

Normal with mean = 215.000 and standard deviation = 25.0000

x	P(X <= x)
175.0000	0.0548

EXCEL

	A	B	C
1	NORMDIST(175,215,25,TRUE)		
2			0.054799

TI-83

normalcdf(0,175,215,25)
.0547992894

From the displays, you can see that the probability that his cholesterol level is less than 175 is about 0.055, or 5.5%.

> *Try It Yourself 4*
>
> If an American man is selected at random, what is the probability that his cholesterol is between 190 and 225? Use a calculator or a computer.
>
> **a.** *Read the user's guide* for the technology tool you are using.
> **b.** *Enter the appropriate data* to obtain the probability.
> **c.** *Write* the result as a sentence.   *Answer: Page A37* ◀

Example 4 shows only one of several ways to find normal probabilities using Minitab, Excel, and the TI-83.

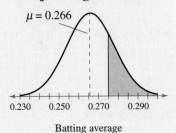

You can also use the normal distribution to find a specific data value (x-value) for a given probability, as shown in Example 5.

▶ EXAMPLE 5   Finding a Specific Data Value

Note to Instructor

Mention that to use the cumulative table to find a z-score, the area given must first be expressed as a cumulative area. It helps to explain these as percentiles. For example, the score in the top 20% represents the 80th percentile. Point out that if students are using a technology tool to find an x-value that corresponds to an area, it is not necessary first to find a z-score.

Scores for a civil service exam are normally distributed, with a mean of 75 and a standard deviation of 6.5. To be eligible for civil service employment, you must score in the top 5%. What is the lowest score you can earn and still be eligible for employment?

SOLUTION   Exam scores in the top 5% correspond to the shaded region shown.

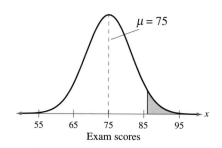

Exam scores

An exam score in the top 5% is any score above the 95th percentile. To find the score that represents the 95th percentile, you must first find the z-score that corresponds to a cumulative area of 0.95. From the Standard Normal Table, you can find that the areas closest to 0.95 are 0.9495 ($z = 1.64$) and 0.9505 ($z = 1.65$). Because 0.95 is halfway between the two areas in the table, use the z-score that is halfway between 1.64 and 1.65. That is, $z = 1.645$. Using the equation $x = \mu + z\sigma$, you have

$$x = \mu + z\sigma$$
$$= 75 + 1.645(6.5)$$
$$\approx 85.69.$$

So, the lowest score you can earn and still be eligible for employment is 86.

> *Study Tip*
>
> In most cases, the given area will not be found in the table, so use the entry closest to it. If the given area is exactly midway between two area entries, use the z-score midway between the corresponding z-scores. For instance, in Example 5, the z-score between 1.64 and 1.65 is 1.645.

Try It Yourself 5

The length of time employees have worked at a corporation is normally distributed, with a mean of 11.2 years and a standard deviation of 2.1 years. In a company cutback, the lowest 10% in seniority are laid off. What is the maximum length of time an employee could have worked and still be laid off?

a. *Sketch* a graph.
b. *Find the z-score* that corresponds to the given area.
c. *Find x* using the equation $x = \mu + z\sigma$.
d. *Write* the result as a sentence.   *Answer: Page A37* ◀

H E L P

 StatPro 5.3

Internet Statistics 5.3

Student Solutions Manual 5.3

Videos 5.3

Try It Yourself Answers 5.3

1. ACT
2. ACT
3. (a) 0.1357
   (b) 0.6983
   (c) 0.1660
4. (a) 0.0668
   (b) 0.9270
   (c) 0.0062
5. (a) 0.1539
   (b) 0.7147
   (c) 0.1314
6. (a) 0.2514
   (b) 0.4972
   (c) 0.2514

Basic Skills and Concepts

Comparing SAT and ACT Scores The Scholastic Assessment Test (SAT) and the ACT are exams used by colleges and universities to evaluate undergraduate applicants. SAT scores are normally distributed, with a mean of 1000 and a standard deviation of 200. ACT scores are normally distributed, with a mean of 20 and a standard deviation of 5. In Exercises 1 and 2, assume that a student takes both tests and gets the indicated scores. On which test did the student score better? Explain.

1. SAT score of 1115 and an ACT score of 23

2. SAT score of 1225 and an ACT score of 26

Finding Probabilities In Exercises 3–8, find the indicated probabilities. If convenient, use technology to find the probabilities.

3. A survey was conducted to measure the height of American males. In the survey, respondents were grouped by age. In the 20–29 age group, the heights were normally distributed, with a mean of 69.2 inches and a standard deviation of 2.9 inches. A study participant is randomly selected. *(Source: National Center for Health Statistics)*

  (a) Find the probability that his height is less than 66 inches.

  (b) Find the probability that his height is between 66 and 72 inches.

  (c) Find the probability that his height is more than 72 inches.

4. The lengths of Atlantic croaker fishes are normally distributed, with a mean of 10 inches and a standard deviation of 2 inches. An Atlantic croaker fish is randomly selected. *(Adapted from National Marine Fisheries Service, Fisheries Statistics and Economics Division)*

  (a) Find the probability that the length of the fish is less than 7 inches.

  (b) Find the probability that the length of the fish is between 7 and 15 inches.

  (c) Find the probability that the length of the fish is more than 15 inches.

5. In a recent year, the ACT scores for high school students with a 3.50 to 4.00 grade point average were normally distributed, with a mean of 24.3 and a standard deviation of 4.2. A student who took the ACT during this time is randomly selected. *(Source: ACT, Inc.)*

  (a) Find the probability that the student's ACT score is less than 20.

  (b) Find the probability that the student's ACT score is between 20 and 29.

  (c) Find the probability that the student's ACT score is more than 29.

6. The weights of adult male rhesus monkeys are normally distributed, with a mean of 15 pounds and a standard deviation of 3 pounds. A rhesus monkey is randomly selected.

  (a) Find the probability that the monkey's weight is less than 13 pounds.

  (b) Find the probability that the monkey's weight is between 13 and 17 pounds.

  (c) Find the probability that the monkey's weight is more than 17 pounds.

7. (a) 0.0062
   (b) 0.9876
   (c) 0.0062
8. (a) 0.0475
   (b) 0.8469
   (c) 0.1056
9. (a) 2.28%
   (b) 83.4
   (c) 72.912
   (d) 67.257
10. (a) 30.85%
   (b) 31.74
   (c) 11.34
   (d) 7.44
11. (a) 43.24%
   (b) 10.02
   (c) 31.209
   (d) 21.486

7. The number of hours per week American adults spend on home computers is normally distributed, with a mean of 5 hours and a standard deviation of 1 hour. An American adult is randomly selected. *(Adapted from American Demographics)*

(a) Find the probability that the hours spent on the home computer by the adult are less than 2.5 hours per week.

(b) Find the probability that the hours spent on the home computer by the adult are between 2.5 and 7.5 hours per week.

(c) Find the probability that the hours spent on the home computer by the adult are more than 7.5 hours per week.

8. The monthly utility bills in a certain city are normally distributed, with a mean of $100 and a standard deviation of $12. A utility bill is randomly selected.

(a) Find the probability that the utility bill is less than $80.

(b) Find the probability that the utility bill is between $80 and $115.

(c) Find the probability that the utility bill is more than $115.

Normal Distributions   In Exercises 9–14, answer the questions about the specified normal distribution.

9. Use the normal distribution in Exercise 3. ($\mu = 69.2$ in., $\sigma = 2.9$ in.)

(a) What percent of the men in the survey have a height that is greater than 75 inches?

(b) If 100 men in the 20–29 age group are randomly selected, about how many will have a height less than 72 inches?

(c) What height represents the 90th percentile?

(d) What height represents the first quartile?

10. Use the normal distribution in Exercise 4. ($\mu = 10$ in., $\sigma = 2$ in.)

(a) What percent of the fish are longer than 11 inches?

(b) If 200 Atlantic croakers are randomly selected, how many will be shorter than 8 inches?

(c) What length represents the third quartile?

(d) What length represents the tenth percentile?

11. Use the normal distribution in Exercise 5. ($\mu = 24.3$, $\sigma = 4.2$)

(a) What percent of the students have an ACT score that is greater than 25?

(b) If 150 students are randomly selected, how many will have an ACT score that is less than 18?

(c) What score represents the 95th percentile?

(d) What score represents the first quartile?

12. (a) 0.0475
   (b) 7.935
   (c) 16.59
   (d) 11.16
13. (a) 99.87%
   (b) 0.798
   (c) 5.67
   (d) 3.96
14. (a) 1.88%
   (b) 60.99
   (c) 106.36
   (d) 89.92
15. (a) 8.024
   (b) 7.684
16. (a) 26.523
   (b) 180
   (c) 25.324

12. Use the normal distribution in Exercise 6. ($\mu = 15$ lb, $\sigma = 3$ lb)

(a) What percent of the monkeys have a weight that is greater than 20 pounds?

(b) If 50 rhesus monkeys are randomly selected, how many will weigh less than 12 pounds?

(c) What is the lightest weight that would still place a rhesus monkey in the top 30% of the weights?

(d) What is the heaviest weight that would still place a rhesus monkey in the bottom 10% of the weights?

13. Use the normal distribution in Exercise 7. ($\mu = 5$ hr, $\sigma = 1$ hr)

(a) What percent of the adults spend more than 2 hours per week on a home computer?

(b) If 35 American adults are randomly selected, how many will say they spend less than 3 hours per week on a home computer?

(c) What is the least number of hours per week an adult can spend on a home computer and be in the top 25% of the times?

(d) What is the greatest number of hours per week an adult can spend on a home computer and be in the bottom 15% of the times?

14. Use the normal distribution in Exercise 8. ($\mu = \$100$, $\sigma = \$12$)

(a) What percent of the utility bills are more than $125?

(b) If 300 utility bills are randomly selected, how many will be less than $90?

(c) What is the smallest utility bill that can be in the top 30% of the bills?

(d) What is the highest utility bill that can be in the bottom 20% of the bills?

15. *Guarantee Period* The lifespan of a machine is normally distributed, with a mean of 10.2 years and a standard deviation of 1.7 years. The manufacturer will replace a machine if it breaks before the guarantee period is over.

(a) If the manufacturer is willing to replace no more than 10%, find the length of time the manufacturer should set for the guarantee.

(b) If the manufacturer is willing to replace no more than 7%, find the length of time the manufacturer should set for the guarantee.

16. *Test Score Requirement* A college requires applicants to have an ACT score in the top 12% of all test scores. The ACT scores are normally distributed, with a mean of 21 and a standard deviation of 4.7.

(a) Find the lowest test score that a student could get and still meet the college's requirement.

(b) If 1500 students are randomly selected, how many would be expected to have a test score that would meet the college's requirement?

(c) How does the answer to part (a) change if the college decides to accept the top 18% of all test scores?

Extending the Basics

Control Charts   When individual measurements of a variable *x* are normally distributed, a control chart can be used to detect processes that are possibly out of statistical control. Three warning signals that a control chart uses to detect a process that may be out of control are as follows.

(1) A point lies beyond three standard deviations of the mean.

(2) There are nine consecutive points that fall on one side of the mean.

(3) At least two of three consecutive points lie more than two standard deviations from the mean.

In Exercises 17–20, a control chart is shown. Each chart has horizontal lines drawn at the mean μ, at $\mu \pm 2\sigma$, and at $\mu \pm 3\sigma$. Determine if the process shown is in control or out of control. Explain.

17. A gear has been designed to have a diameter of 3 inches. The standard deviation of the process is 0.2 inch.

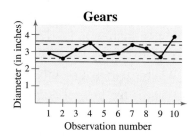

18. A nail has been designed to have a length of 4 inches. The standard deviation of the process is 0.12 inch.

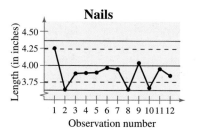

19. A liquid-dispensing machine has been designed to fill bottles with 1 liter of liquid. The standard deviation of the process is 0.1 liter.

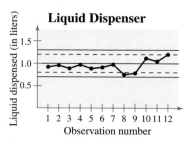

20. An engine part has been designed to have a diameter of 55 millimeters. The standard deviation of the process is 0.001 millimeter.

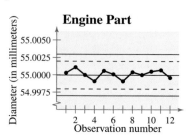

National Center for Health Statistics

NCHS

..Monitoring the Nation's Health

National Center for Health Statistics

Birth Weights in America

The National Center for Health Statistics keeps records of many health-related aspects of people, including the birth weights of all babies born in the United States.

The birth weight of a baby is related to its gestation period (the time between conception and birth). For a given gestation period, the birth weights are normally distributed. The means and standard deviations of the birth weights for various gestation periods are shown at the right.

One of the many goals of NCHS is to reduce the percent of babies born with low birth weights. As you can see from the graph at the upper right, the problem of low birth weights increased from 1981 to 1994.

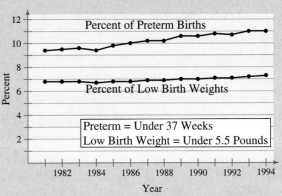

Gestation Period	Mean Birth Weight	Standard Deviation
Under 28 Weeks	2.01 lb	1.32 lb
28 to 31 Weeks	4.77 lb	2.38 lb
32 to 35 Weeks	5.82 lb	1.51 lb
36 Weeks	6.54 lb	1.22 lb
37 to 39 Weeks	7.31 lb	1.11 lb
40 Weeks	7.74 lb	1.07 lb
41 Weeks	7.89 lb	1.09 lb
Over 42 Weeks	7.75 lb	1.14 lb

Exercises

1. The distributions of birth weights for three gestation periods are shown. Match the curves with the gestation periods. Explain your reasoning.

(a)

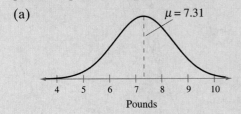

(b)

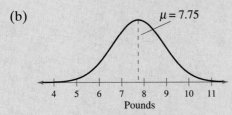

(c)

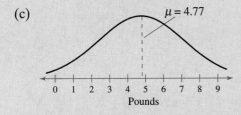

2. What percent of the babies born with each gestation period have a low birth weight (under 5.5 pounds)? Explain your reasoning.

   (a) Under 28 weeks　(b) 32 to 35 weeks

   (c) 37 to 39 weeks　(d) Over 42 weeks

3. Describe the weights of the top 10% of the babies born with each gestation period. Explain your reasoning.

   (a) 37 to 39 weeks　(b) Over 42 weeks

4. For each gestation period, what is the probability that a baby will weigh between 6 and 9 pounds at birth?

   (a) 32 to 35 weeks　(b) 37 to 39 weeks

   (c) Over 42 weeks

5. A birth weight of 2.5 pounds or less is classified by NCHS as a "very low birth weight." What is the probability that a baby has a very low birth weight for each gestation period?

   (a) Under 28 weeks　(b) 32 to 35 weeks

   (c) 37 to 39 weeks

The Central Limit Theorem

5.4

Sampling Distributions • The Central Limit Theorem • Probability and the Central Limit Theorem

What You Should Learn

- *How to find sampling distributions and verify their properties*
- *How to interpret the Central Limit Theorem*
- *How to apply the Central Limit Theorem to find the probability of a sample mean*

Sampling Distributions

In previous sections, you studied the relationship between the mean of a population and values of a random variable. In this section, you will study the relationship between a population mean and the means of samples taken from the population.

> **DEFINITION**
>
> A **sampling distribution** is the probability distribution of a sample statistic that is formed when samples of size n are repeatedly taken from a population. If the sample statistic is the sample mean, then the distribution is the **sampling distribution of sample means.**

Note to Instructor

A good exercise that can be used in conjunction with the Venn diagram is to have each student randomly select a place in the random number table and write down the next five digits horizontally. Students can verify that the population of digits {0, 1, 2, . . . , 9} is uniform and has a mean of 4.5 and standard deviation of 2.87. Have each student calculate the mean of his or her sample and write that result on the board. Students can easily see that the sample means vary but are not dispersed as much as the population (range 0 to 9) is. Construct a histogram of the sample means, find the mean of these means and the standard deviation of the means. (With a TI-83, this takes little time even if only one student does the calculations.) Because the population standard deviation is known for this simulation, the results will be approximately normal.

For instance, consider the following Venn diagram. The rectangle represents a large population, and each circle represents a sample of size n. Because the sample entries can differ, the sample means can also differ. The mean of Sample 1 is $\bar{x}_1$, the mean of Sample 2 is $\bar{x}_2$, and so on. The sampling distribution of the sample means of size n for this population consists of $\bar{x}_1, \bar{x}_2, \bar{x}_3$, and so on. If the samples are drawn with replacement, an infinite number of samples can be drawn from the population.

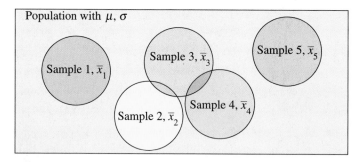

Population with μ, σ

Sample 1, $\bar{x}_1$

Sample 2, $\bar{x}_2$

Sample 3, $\bar{x}_3$

Sample 4, $\bar{x}_4$

Sample 5, $\bar{x}_5$

Properties of Sampling Distributions of Sample Means

1. The mean of the sample means, $\mu_{\bar{x}}$, is equal to the population mean, μ.
2. The standard deviation of the sample means, $\sigma_{\bar{x}}$, is equal to the population standard deviation, σ, divided by the square root of n.

$$\sigma_{\bar{x}} = \frac{\sigma}{\sqrt{n}}$$

The standard deviation of the sampling distribution is called the **standard error of the mean.**

EXAMPLE 1   *A Sampling Distribution of Sample Means*

You write the population values {1, 3, 5, 7} on slips of paper and put them in a box. Then you randomly choose two slips of paper, with replacement. List all possible samples of size $n = 2$ and calculate the mean of each. These means form the sampling distribution of the sample means. Find the mean, variance, and standard deviation of the sample means. Compare your results with the mean $\mu = 4$, variance $\sigma^2 = 5$, and standard deviation $\sigma = \sqrt{5} \approx 2.236$ of the population.

SOLUTION   List all 16 samples of size 2 from the population and the mean of each sample.

Relative Frequency Histogram of Population

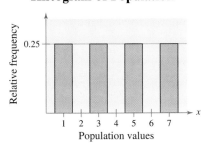

Population values

Relative Frequency Distribution of Sample Means

$\bar{x}$	f	Relative frequency
1	1	0.0625
2	2	0.1250
3	3	0.1875
4	4	0.2500
5	3	0.1875
6	2	0.1250
7	1	0.0625

Sample	Mean	Sample	Mean
1, 1	1	5, 1	3
1, 3	2	5, 3	4
1, 5	3	5, 5	5
1, 7	4	5, 7	6
3, 1	2	7, 1	4
3, 3	3	7, 3	5
3, 5	4	7, 5	6
3, 7	5	7, 7	7

After constructing a relative frequency distribution of the sample means, you can graph the sampling distribution using a relative histogram as shown at the left. Notice that the shape of the histogram is bell shaped and symmetric, similar to a normal curve. The mean, variance, and standard deviation of the 16 sample means are

$$\mu_{\bar{x}} = 4, \ (\sigma_{\bar{x}})^2 = \frac{5}{2} = 2.5, \text{ and } \sigma_{\bar{x}} = \sqrt{\frac{5}{2}} = \sqrt{2.5} \approx 1.581.$$

These results satisfy the properties of sampling distributions because

$$\mu_{\bar{x}} = \mu \text{ and } \sigma_{\bar{x}} = \frac{\sigma}{\sqrt{n}} = \frac{\sqrt{5}}{\sqrt{2}} \approx \frac{2.236}{\sqrt{2}} \approx 1.581.$$

Relative Histogram of Sampling Distribution

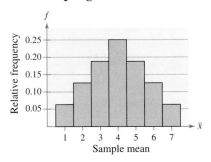

Sample mean

Study Tip

Review Sections 2.3 and 2.4 to find the mean and standard deviation of a frequency distribution.

Try It Yourself 1

List all possible samples of $n = 2$, with replacement, from the population {1, 2, 3, 5, 6, 7}. Calculate the mean, variance, and standard deviation of the sample means. Compare these values to the corresponding population parameters.

a. *Form* all possible samples of size 2 and find the mean of each.
b. *Find* the mean, variance, and standard deviation of the frequency distribution of the sample means.
c. *Compare* the means, variances, and standard deviations with those for the population.   *Answer: Page A37*

The Central Limit Theorem

The Central Limit Theorem is one of the most important and useful theorems in statistics. This theorem forms the foundation for the inferential branch of statistics. The Central Limit Theorem describes the relationship between the sampling distribution of sample means and the population that the samples are taken from.

Note to Instructor

The sample mean, $\bar{x}$, varies from sample to sample and is a random variable. As a random variable, it has a probability distribution, called the sampling distribution of the mean. Mention that other sample statistics, such as s^2, s, and $\hat{p}$, have different sampling distributions that will be studied in the next chapter.

The Central Limit Theorem

1. If samples of size n, where $n \geq 30$, are drawn from any population with a mean μ and a standard deviation σ, then the sampling distribution of sample means approximates a normal distribution. The greater the sample size, the better the approximation.

2. If the population itself is normally distributed, the sampling distribution of sample means is normally distributed for *any* sample size n.

In either case, the sampling distribution of sample means has a mean equal to the population mean.

$$\mu_{\bar{x}} = \mu \qquad \text{Mean}$$

And the sampling distribution of sample means has a variance equal to $1/n$ times the variance of the population and a standard deviation equal to the population standard deviation divided by the square root of n.

$$\sigma_{\bar{x}}^2 = \frac{\sigma^2}{n} \qquad \text{Variance}$$

$$\sigma_{\bar{x}} = \frac{\sigma}{\sqrt{n}} \qquad \text{Standard deviation}$$

Insight

The distribution of sample means has the same mean as the population. But its standard deviation is less than the standard deviation of the population. This tells you that the distribution of sample means has the same center as the population, but it is not as spread out.

Moreover, the distribution of sample means becomes less and less spread out (tighter concentration about the mean) as the sample size n increases.

1. Any Population Distribution

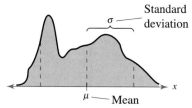

Distribution of Sample Means, $n \geq 30$

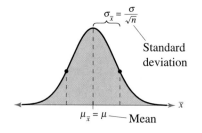

2. Normal Population Distribution

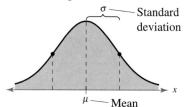

Distribution of Sample Means (any n)

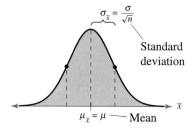

> ▶ **EXAMPLE 2** *Interpreting the Central Limit Theorem*

Phone bills for residents of Cincinnati have a mean of $64 and a standard deviation of $9, as shown in the following graph. Random samples of 36 phone bills are drawn from this population and the mean of each sample is determined. Find the mean and standard error of the mean of the sampling distribution. Then sketch a graph of the sampling distribution.

Distribution for all Phone Bills

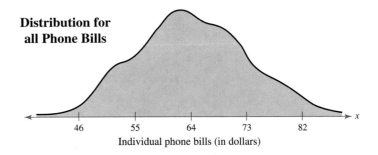

Individual phone bills (in dollars)

SOLUTION   The mean of the sampling distribution is equal to the population mean, and the standard error of the mean is equal to the population standard deviation divided by $\sqrt{n}$. So,

$$\mu_{\bar{x}} = \mu = 64 \quad \text{and} \quad \sigma_{\bar{x}} = \frac{\sigma}{\sqrt{n}} = \frac{9}{\sqrt{36}} = 1.5.$$

From the Central Limit Theorem, because the sample size is greater than 30, the sampling distribution can be approximated by a normal distribution with $\mu = \$64$ and $\sigma = \$1.50$.

Distribution of Sample Means

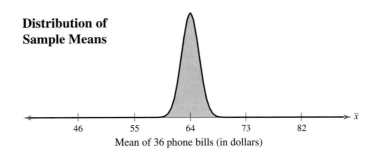

Mean of 36 phone bills (in dollars)

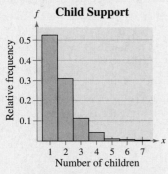

Try It Yourself 2

Suppose random samples of size 100 are drawn from the population in Example 2. Find the mean and standard error of the mean of the sampling distribution. Sketch a graph of the sampling distribution and compare it to the sampling distribution in Example 2.

a. *Find* $\mu_{\bar{x}}$ and $\sigma_{\bar{x}}$.
b. *Identify* the sample size. If $n \geq 30$, *sketch* a normal curve with mean $\mu_{\bar{x}}$ and standard deviation $\sigma_{\bar{x}}$. *Answer: Page A37* ◀

> **EXAMPLE 3** *Interpreting the Central Limit Theorem*

The heights of fully grown white oak trees are normally distributed, with a mean of 90 feet and standard deviation of 3.5 feet. Random samples of size 4 are drawn from this population, and the mean of each sample is determined. Find the mean and standard error of the mean of the sampling distribution. Then sketch a graph of the sampling distribution.

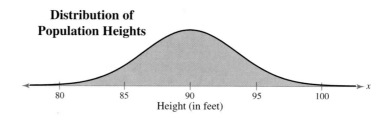

Distribution of Population Heights

Height (in feet)

SOLUTION The mean of the sampling distribution is equal to the population mean and the standard error of the mean is equal to the population standard deviation divided by $\sqrt{n}$. So,

$$\mu_{\bar{x}} = \mu = 90 \text{ feet and } \sigma_{\bar{x}} = \frac{\sigma}{\sqrt{n}} = \frac{3.5}{\sqrt{4}} = 1.75 \text{ feet.}$$

From the Central Limit Theorem, because the population is normally distributed, the sampling distribution is also normally distributed.

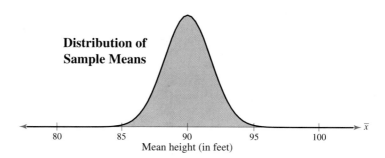

Distribution of Sample Means

Mean height (in feet)

Try It Yourself 3

The diameters of fully grown white oak trees are normally distributed, with a mean of 3.5 feet and a standard deviation of 0.2 foot. Random samples of size 16 are drawn from this population, and the mean of each sample is determined. Find the mean and standard error of the mean of the sampling distribution. Then sketch a graph of the sampling distribution.

a. *Find* $\mu_{\bar{x}}$ and $\sigma_{\bar{x}}$.
b. *Sketch* a normal curve with mean $\mu_{\bar{x}}$ and standard deviation $\sigma_{\bar{x}}$.

Answer: Page A37

Distribution of Population Diameters

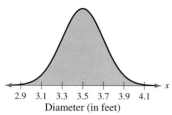

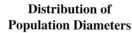

Diameter (in feet)

Probability and the Central Limit Theorem

Note to Instructor

For technology users, students need only calculate the standard error before using the normal CDF.

In Sections 5.2 and 5.3, you learned how to find the probability that a random variable, x, will fall in a given interval of population values. In a similar manner, you can find the probability that a sample mean, $\bar{x}$, will fall in a given interval of the $\bar{x}$ sampling distribution. To transform $\bar{x}$ to a z-score, you can use the equation

$$z = \frac{\text{value} - \text{mean}}{\text{standard error}} = \frac{\bar{x} - \mu_{\bar{x}}}{\sigma_{\bar{x}}} = \frac{\bar{x} - \mu}{\dfrac{\sigma}{\sqrt{n}}}.$$

▶ **EXAMPLE 4** *Finding Probabilities for Sampling Distributions*

The graph at the right lists the length of time adults spend reading newspapers. You randomly select 50 adults ages 18 to 24. What is the probability that the mean time they spend reading the newspaper is between 8.7 and 9.5 minutes? Assume that $\sigma = 1.5$ minutes.

Speed readers
The average adult surveyed who said they read a newspaper the previous day spent about 18 minutes doing so. Minutes spent by age:

18-24	9
25-29	11
30-34	11
35-49	16
50-64	21
65-up	33

Copyright 1998, USA TODAY. Reprinted with permission.

SOLUTION   Because the sample size is greater than 30, you can use the Central Limit Theorem to conclude that the distribution of sample means is approximately normal with a mean and a standard deviation of

Distribution of Sample Means

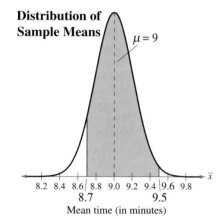

$\mu = 9$

Mean time (in minutes)

$$\mu_{\bar{x}} = \mu = 9 \text{ minutes}$$

$$\sigma_{\bar{x}} = \frac{\sigma}{\sqrt{n}} = \frac{1.5}{\sqrt{50}} \approx 0.212 \text{ minutes}.$$

The graph of this distribution is shown at the left with a shaded area between 8.7 and 9.5 minutes.

The z-scores that correspond to sample means of 8.7 and 9.5 minutes are

$$z_1 = \frac{8.7 - 9}{1.5/\sqrt{50}} \approx -1.41 \text{ and } z_2 = \frac{9.5 - 9}{1.5/\sqrt{50}} \approx 2.36.$$

z-score Distribution of Sample Means

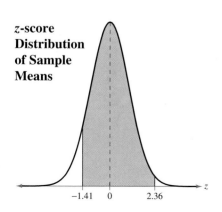

So, the probability that the mean time the adults spend reading the newspaper is between 8.7 and 9.5 minutes is

$$
\begin{aligned}
P(8.7 < \bar{x} < 9.5) &= P(-1.41 < z < 2.36) \\
&= P(z < 2.36) - P(z < -1.41) \\
&= 0.9909 - 0.0793 \\
&= 0.9116.
\end{aligned}
$$

So, 91.16% of adults aged 18 to 24 spend between 8.7 and 9.5 minutes reading the newspaper.

Try It Yourself 4

You randomly select 45 adults aged 65 and up. What is the probability that the mean time they spend reading the newspaper is between 27 and 35 minutes? Use $\mu = 33$ and $\sigma = 4$ minutes.

a. Use the Central Limit Theorem and find $\mu_{\bar{x}}$ and $\sigma_{\bar{x}}$ and sketch the sampling distribution.
b. *Find z-scores* that correspond to 27 minutes and 35 minutes.
c. *Find the cumulative area* that corresponds to each z-score.
d. *Subtract* the smaller area from the larger.   *Answer: Page A38*

▶ **EXAMPLE 5**   *Finding Probabilities for Sampling Distributions*

The mean rent of an apartment in a professionally managed apartment building is $780. You randomly select nine professionally managed apartments. What is the probability that the mean rent is less than $825? Assume that the rents are normally distributed, with a standard deviation of $150. *(Source: M/PH Research)*

SOLUTION   Because the population is normally distributed, you can use the Central Limit Theorem to conclude that the distribution of sample means is normally distributed, with a mean of $780 and a standard deviation of $50.

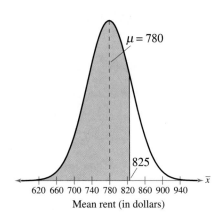

$$\mu_{\bar{x}} = \mu = 780 \quad \text{and} \quad \sigma_{\bar{x}} = \frac{\sigma}{\sqrt{n}} = \frac{150}{\sqrt{9}} = 50$$

The graph of this distribution is shown at the left. The area to the left of $825 is shaded. The z-score that corresponds to $825 is

$$z = \frac{825 - 780}{150/\sqrt{9}} = 0.9.$$

So, the probability that the mean rent is less than $825 is

$$P(\bar{x} < 825) = P(z < 0.9) = 0.8159.$$

$\mu = 780$

825

620 660 700 740 780 820 860 900 940
Mean rent (in dollars)

Try It Yourself 5

The average sales price of an existing single-family house in the United States is $125,700. You randomly select 16 single-family houses. What is the probability that the mean sales price is more than $80,000? Assume that the sales prices are normally distributed with a standard deviation of $26,000. *(Source: National Association of Realtors)*

a. Use the Central Limit Theorem and find $\mu_{\bar{x}}$ and $\sigma_{\bar{x}}$ and sketch the sampling distribution.
b. *Find the z-score* that corresponds to $80,000.
c. *Find the cumulative area* that corresponds to the z-score. Subtract the cumulative area from 1.   *Answer: Page A38*

> **EXAMPLE 6** **Finding Probabilities for x and x̄**

Credit card balances are normally distributed, with a mean of $2870 and a standard deviation of $900.

1. What is the probability that a randomly selected credit card holder has a credit card balance less than $2500?

2. You randomly select 25 credit card holders. What is the probability that their mean credit card balance is less than $2500?

3. Compare the probabilities from (1) and (2).

SOLUTION

1. In this case, you are asked to find the probability associated with a certain value of the random variable x. The z-score that corresponds to $x = \$2500$ is

$$z = \frac{x - \mu}{\sigma} = \frac{2500 - 2870}{900} \approx -0.41.$$

So, the probability that the card holder has a balance less than $2500 is

$$P(x < 2500) = P(z < -0.41) = 0.3409.$$

2. Here, you are asked to find the probability associated with a sample mean, $\bar{x}$. The z-score that corresponds to $\bar{x} = \$2500$ is

$$z = \frac{\bar{x} - \mu}{\sigma/\sqrt{n}} = \frac{2500 - 2870}{900/\sqrt{25}} \approx -2.06.$$

So, the probability that the mean credit card balance of the 25 card holders is less than $2500 is

$$P(\bar{x} < 2500) = P(z < -2.06) = 0.0197.$$

3. Where there is a 34% chance that an *individual* will have a balance less than $2500, there is only a 2% chance that *the mean of a sample* of 25 will have a balance less than $2500.

Study Tip

To find probabilities for individual members of a population with a normally distributed random variable x, use the formula

$$z = \frac{x - \mu}{\sigma}.$$

To find probabilities for the mean x̄ of a sample size n, use the formula

$$z = \frac{\bar{x} - \mu_{\bar{x}}}{\sigma_{\bar{x}}}.$$

Note to Instructor

You may want to tell students that the second formula can also be used to calculate z-scores for individual values. Consider a sample of n = 1 for an individual value.

Try It Yourself 6

Prices for sound-system receivers are normally distributed, with a mean of $625 and a standard deviation of $150. (1) What is the probability that a randomly selected receiver costs less than $700? (2) You randomly select 10 receivers. What is the probability that their mean cost is less than $700? (3) Compare these two probabilities.

a. *Find* the z-scores that correspond to x and x̄.
b. Use the Standard Normal Table to *find the probability* associated with each z-score.
c. *Compare* the probabilities.   *Answer: Page A38*

5.4 EXERCISES

1. False

2. True

3. See Odd Answers, page A57

4. {120 120, 120 140, 120 180, 120 220, 140 120, 140 140, 140 180, 140 220, 180 120, 180 140, 180 180, 180 220, 220 120, 220 140, 220 180, 220 220}

   $\mu_{\bar{x}} = 165$, $\sigma_{\bar{x}} \approx 27.157$

   $\mu = 165$, $\sigma \approx 38.406$

5. 87.5, 1.804

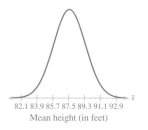

82.1 83.9 85.7 87.5 89.3 91.1 92.9
Mean height (in feet)

6. See Selected Answers, page A80

7. See Odd Answers, page A58

8. See Selected Answers, page A80

9. See Odd Answers, page A58

Basic Skills and Concepts

True or False In Exercises 1 and 2, determine whether the statement is true or false. If it is false, rewrite it so that it is a true statement.

1. The sampling distribution of sample means for sample size 40 has a mean equal to the population mean and a standard deviation equal to the population standard deviation.

2. If a population is normally distributed, the sampling distribution of sample means is also normally distributed for any sample size n.

Verifying Properties of Sampling Distributions In Exercises 3 and 4, find the mean and standard deviation of the population. List all samples (with replacement) of the given size from that population. Find the mean and standard deviation of the sampling distribution and compare them to the mean and standard deviation of the population.

3. The number of movies that all five people in a family have seen in the past month is 4, 2, 8, 0, and 6. Use a sample size of 3.

4. Four people in a carpool paid the following amounts for textbooks this semester: $120, $140, $180, and $220. Use a sample size of 2.

Central Limit Theorem In Exercises 5–8, use the Central Limit Theorem to find the mean and standard error of the mean of the indicated sampling distribution. Then sketch a graph of the sampling distribution.

5. The heights of fully grown sugar maple trees are normally distributed, with a mean of 87.5 feet and a standard deviation of 6.25 feet. Random samples of size 12 are drawn from the population.

6. The number of eggs a female house fly lays during her lifetime is normally distributed, with a mean of 800 eggs and a standard deviation of 100 eggs. Random samples of size 15 are drawn from this population.

7. The per capita consumption of red meat by Americans in a recent year was normally distributed, with a mean of 114.7 pounds and a standard deviation of 38 pounds. Random samples of size 20 are drawn from this population. *(Adapted from U.S. Department of Agriculture)*

8. The per capita consumption of soft drinks by Americans in a recent year was normally distributed, with a mean of 51.2 gallons and a standard deviation of 17.1 gallons. Random samples of size 25 are drawn from this population. *(Adapted from U.S. Department of Agriculture)*

9. ***Increasing the Sample Size*** Repeat Exercise 5 for samples of size 24 and 36. What happens to the mean and standard deviation of the distribution of sample means as the size of the sample increases?

10. 800, 18.257
800, 14.907
As the sample size increases,
the standard error decreases.

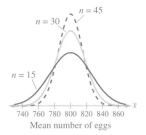

Mean number of eggs

10. *Increasing the Sample Size*   Repeat Exercise 6 for samples of size 30 and 45. What happens to the mean and to the standard deviation of the distribution of sample means as the size of the sample increases?

Graphical Analysis   In Exercises 11 and 12, the graph of a population distribution is shown with its mean and standard deviation. Assume that a sample size of 100 is drawn from each population. Decide which of the graphs labeled (a)–(c) would most closely resemble the sampling distribution of the sample means for each graph. Explain your reasoning.

11. The waiting time (in seconds) at a traffic signal during a red light

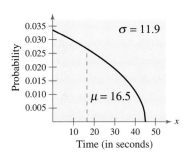

Time (in seconds)

(a)   (b)   (c)

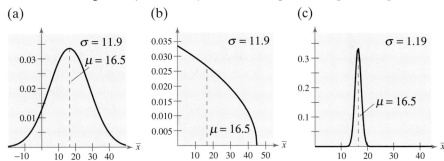

12. The annual snowfall (in feet) for a central New York state county

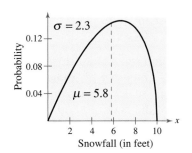

Snowfall (in feet)

(a)   (b)   (c)

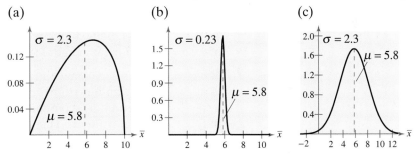

11. (c)

12. (b)

13. ≈ 1

14. 0.0019

Finding Probabilities   In Exercises 13–18, find the probabilities for the indicated sampling distributions.

13. The population mean annual salary for registered nurses is $\mu = \$28{,}000$. A sample of 35 registered nurses is randomly selected. What is the probability that the mean annual salary of the sample, $\bar{x}$, is less than $29,500? Assume $\sigma = \$1700$. *(Adapted from Jobs Rated Almanac)*

14. The population mean annual salary for plumbers is $\mu = \$32{,}500$. A random sample of 42 plumbers is drawn from this population. What is the probability that the mean salary of the sample, $\bar{x}$, is less than $30,000? Assume $\sigma = \$5600$. *(Adapted from Jobs Rated Almanac)*

15. 0.6319

16. 0.2349

17. 0

18. 0.0162

19. Sample of 20 women with mean height less than 70 inches.

20. One man with a height less than 65 inches.

21. Yes

22. Yes

15. During a certain week the mean price of gasoline in the New England region was $\mu = \$1.080$ per gallon. What is the probability that the mean price $\bar{x}$ for a sample of 32 randomly selected gas stations in that area was between $1.075 and $1.090 that week? Assume $\sigma = \$0.045$. *(Adapted from U.S. Department of Energy)*

16. During a certain week the mean price of gasoline in California was $\mu = \$1.164$ per gallon. A random sample of 38 gas stations is drawn from this population. What is the probability that $\bar{x}$, the mean price for the sample, was between $1.169 and $1.179? Assume $\sigma = \$0.049$. *(Adapted from U.S. Department of Energy)*

17. The mean height of American women (ages 20–29) is $\mu = 64$ inches. If a random sample of 60 women (ages 20–29) is selected, what is the probability that $\bar{x}$, the mean height of the sample, is greater than 68 inches? Assume $\sigma = 2.75$ inches. *(Source: National Center for Health Statistics)*

18. The mean height of American men (ages 20–29) is $\mu = 69.2$ inches. If a random sample of 60 men in this age group is selected, what is the probability that $\bar{x}$, the mean height for the sample, is greater than 70 inches? Assume $\sigma = 2.9$ inches. *(Source: National Center for Health Statistics)*

19. *Which Is More Likely?* Assume that the heights given in Exercise 17 are normally distributed. Are you more likely to select randomly one woman with a height less than 70 inches or are you more likely to select a sample of 20 women with a mean height less than 70 inches? Explain.

20. *Which Is More Likely?* Assume that the heights given in Exercise 18 are normally distributed. Are you more likely to select randomly one man with a height less than 65 inches or are you more likely to select a sample of 15 men with a mean height less than 65 inches? Explain.

21. *Make a Decision* A machine used to fill gallon-sized paint cans is regulated so that the amount of paint dispensed has a mean of 128 ounces and a standard deviation of 0.20 ounce. You randomly select 40 cans and carefully measure the contents. The sample mean of the cans is 127.9 ounces. Does the machine need to be reset? Explain your reasoning.

22. *Make a Decision* A machine used to fill pint-sized milk containers is regulated so that the amount of milk dispensed has a mean of 64 ounces and a standard deviation of 0.11 ounce. You randomly select 40 containers and carefully measure the contents. The sample mean of the containers is 64.05 ounces. Does the machine need to be reset? Explain your reasoning.

23. 0.0436
24. 1
25. 1
26. 0.0885

Extending the Basics

Finite Correction Factor   The formula for the standard error of the mean

$$\sigma_{\bar{x}} = \frac{\sigma}{\sqrt{n}}$$

given in the Central Limit Theorem is based on an assumption that the population has infinitely many members. This is the case whenever sampling is done with replacement (each member is put back after it is selected) because the sampling process could be continued indefinitely. The formula is also valid if the sample size is small in comparison to the population. However, when sampling is done without replacement and the sample size, n, is more than 5% of the finite population of size N, there is a finite number of possible samples. A **finite correction factor,**

$$\sqrt{\frac{N - n}{N - 1}},$$

should be used to adjust the standard error. The sampling distribution of the sample means will be normal with a mean equal to the population mean, and the standard error of the mean will be

$$\sigma_{\bar{x}} = \frac{\sigma}{\sqrt{n}} \sqrt{\frac{N - n}{N - 1}}.$$

In Exercises 23–26, determine if the finite correction factor should be used. If so, use it in your calculations when you find the probability.

23. In a sample of 800 stations, the mean cash price for regular gasoline at the pump was $1.007 per gallon and the standard deviation was $0.009 per gallon. A random sample of size 55 is drawn from this population. What is the probability that the mean price per gallon is less than $1.005? *(Adapted from U.S. Department of Energy)*

24. In a sample of 600 farms, the mean value of land and buildings per acre was $1200 and the standard deviation was $200. A random sample of size 32 is drawn from this population. What is the probability that the mean value of land and buildings per acre is less than $1500?

25. In a sample of 500 eruptions of the Old Faithful geyser at Yellowstone National Park, the mean duration of the eruptions was 3.32 minutes and the standard deviation was 1.09 minutes. A random sample of size 30 is drawn from this population. What is the probability that the mean duration of eruptions is between 2.5 minutes and 4 minutes? *(Adapted from Yellowstone National Park)*

26. In a sample of 1200 police officers, the mean annual salary was $33,000 and the standard deviation was $3200. A random sample of size 70 is drawn from this population. What is the probability that the mean annual salary is between $30,000 and $32,500? *(Adapted from Jobs Rated Almanac)*

TECHNOLOGY   MINITAB   EXCEL   TI-83

 U.S. Census Bureau

www.census.gov

Age Distribution in the United States

One of the jobs of the U.S. Census Bureau is to keep track of the age distribution in the country. The age distribution in 1996 is as follows.

Age Distribution in the U.S.

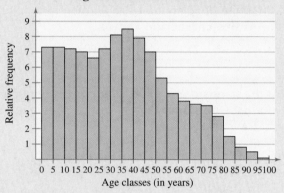

Class Boundaries	Class Midpoint	Relative Frequency
0–5	2.5	7.3%
5–10	7.5	7.3%
10–15	12.5	7.2%
15–20	17.5	7.0%
20–25	22.5	6.6%
25–30	27.5	7.2%
30–35	32.5	8.1%
35–40	37.5	8.5%
40–45	42.5	7.8%
45–50	47.5	6.9%
50–55	52.5	5.2%
55–60	57.5	4.3%
60–65	62.5	3.8%
65–70	67.5	3.6%
70–75	72.5	3.5%
75–80	77.5	2.8%
80–85	82.5	1.5%
85–90	87.5	0.8%
90–95	92.5	0.5%
95–100	97.5	0.1%

Exercises

We used a technology tool to select randomly samples with $n = 40$ from the age distribution of the United States. The means of the thirty-six samples were as follows.

28.14, 31.56, 36.86, 32.37, 36.12, 39.53, 36.19, 39.02, 35.62, 36.30, 34.38, 32.98, 36.41, 30.24, 34.19, 44.72, 38.84, 42.87, 38.90, 34.71, 34.13, 38.25, 38.04, 34.07, 39.74, 40.91, 42.63, 35.29, 35.91, 34.36, 36.51, 36.47, 32.88, 37.33, 31.27, 35.80

1. Enter the age distribution of the United States into a technology tool. Use the tool to find the mean age in the United States.

2. Enter the set of sample means into a technology tool. Find the mean of the set of sample means. How does it compare to the mean age

in the United States? Does this agree with the result predicted by the Central Limit Theorem?

3. Are the ages of Americans normally distributed? Explain your reasoning.

4. Sketch a relative frequency histogram for the 36 sample means. Use nine classes. Is the histogram approximately bell shaped and symmetrical? Does this agree with the result predicted by the Central Limit Theorem?

5. Use a technology tool to find the standard deviation of the ages of Americans.

6. Use a technology tool to find the standard deviation of the set of 36 sample means. How does it compare to the standard deviation of the ages? Does this agree with the result predicted by the Central Limit Theorem?

Extended solutions are given in the *Technology Supplement*.

5.5 Normal Approximations to Binomial Distributions

Approximating a Binomial Distribution • Correction for Continuity • Approximating Binomial Probabilities

What You Should Learn

- *How to decide when the normal distribution can approximate the binomial distribution*
- *How to find the correction for continuity*
- *How to use the normal distribution to approximate binomial probabilities*

Approximating a Binomial Distribution

In Section 4.2, you learned how to find binomial probabilities. For instance, if a surgical procedure has an 85% chance of success and a doctor performs the procedure on 10 patients, it is easy to find the probability of exactly two successful surgeries.

But what if the doctor performs the surgical procedure on 150 patients and you want to find the probability of *fewer than 100* successful surgeries? To do this using the techniques described in Section 4.2, you would have to use the binomial formula 100 times and find the sum of the resulting probabilities. This approach is not practical, of course. A better approach is to use a normal distribution to approximate the binomial distribution.

Normal Approximation to a Binomial Distribution

If $np \geq 5$ and $nq \geq 5$, then the binomial random variable x is approximately normally distributed, with mean $\mu = np$ and standard deviation $\sigma = \sqrt{npq}$.

To see why this result is valid, look at the following binomial distributions for $p = 0.25$ and $n = 4, 10, 25,$ and 50. Notice that as n increases, the histogram approaches a normal curve.

Study Tip

Properties of a binomial experiment
- n independent trials
- Two possible outcomes: success or failure
- Probability of success is p; probability of failure is $1 - p = q$
- p is constant for each trial

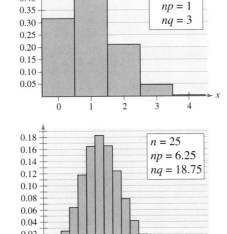

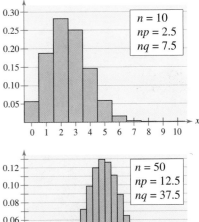

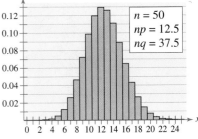

> **EXAMPLE 1**   *Approximating the Binomial Distribution*

Two binomial experiments are listed. Decide whether you can use the normal distribution to approximate x, the number of people who reply yes. If so, find the mean and standard deviation. If not, explain why. *(Source: Marist Institute of Public Opinion, July 1998)*

1. Thirty-seven percent of Americans say that they always fly an American flag on the Fourth of July. You randomly select 15 Americans and ask each if he or she always flies an American flag on the Fourth of July.

2. Ninety-three percent of Americans want the national anthem to remain the same. You randomly select 65 Americans and ask each if he or she wants the national anthem to remain the same.

SOLUTION

1. In this binomial experiment, $n = 15$, $p = 0.37$, and $q = 0.63$. So,

$$np = 5.55 \text{ and } nq = 9.45.$$

Because $np \geq 5$ and $nq \geq 5$, you can use the normal distribution with

$$\mu = 5.55$$

and

$$\sigma = \sqrt{npq} = \sqrt{15 \cdot 0.37 \cdot 0.63} \approx 1.87$$

to approximate the distribution of x.

2. In this binomial experiment, $n = 65$, $p = 0.93$, and $q = 0.07$. So,

$$np = 60.45 \text{ and } nq = 4.55.$$

Because $nq < 5$, you cannot use the normal distribution to approximate the distribution of x.

Try It Yourself 1

Consider the following binomial experiment. Decide whether you can use the normal distribution to approximate x, the number of people who reply yes. If so, find the mean and standard deviation. If not, explain why. *(Source: Marist Institute of Public Opinion, July 1998)*

Only 8% of Americans feel that the nation is more patriotic today than it was decades ago. You randomly select 70 Americans and ask each if he or she feels the nation is more patriotic today than it was decades ago.

a. *Identify* n, p, and q.
b. *Find* the products np and nq.
c. *Decide* whether you can use the normal distribution to approximate x.
d. *Find* the mean μ and standard deviation σ, if appropriate.

Answer: Page A38

Correction for Continuity

Note to Instructor

For technology users who are not limited to $n = 20$ in the table, many more binomial problems can be calculated without using a normal distribution approximation. However, students should be shown that even technology has limitations. The TI-83 cannot calculate the cumulative binomial probability for $n = 10,000$, $p = 0.4$, and $x = 9000$, but that probability can be calculated using a normal approximation. Likewise, depending on the version of Minitab or Excel you are using, there are memory limitations for the binomial distribution.

The binomial distribution is discrete and can be represented by a probability histogram. To calculate *exact* binomial probabilities, you can use the binomial formula for each value of x and add the results. Geometrically, this corresponds to adding the areas of bars in the probability histogram. When you do this, remember that each bar has a width of one unit and x is the midpoint of the interval.

When you use a *continuous* normal distribution to approximate a binomial probability, you need to move 0.5 units to the left and right of the midpoint to include all possible x-values in the interval. When you do this, you are making a **correction for continuity.**

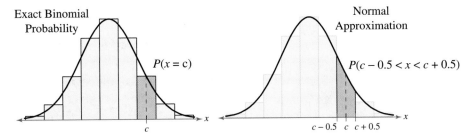

EXAMPLE 2   Using a Correction for Continuity

Use a correction for continuity to convert each of the following binomial intervals to a normal distribution interval.

1. The probability of getting between 270 and 310 successes, inclusive
2. The probability of getting more than 157 and less than 420 successes
3. The probability of getting less than 63 successes

SOLUTION

1. The midpoint values are $270, 271, \ldots, 310$. The boundaries for the normal distribution are $269.5 < x < 310.5$.
2. The midpoint values are $158, 159, \ldots, 419$. The boundaries for the normal distribution are $157.5 < x < 419.5$.
3. The midpoint values are $\ldots, 60, 61, 62$. The boundary for the normal distribution is $x < 62.5$.

Study Tip

To use a correction for continuity, simply subtract 0.5 from the lowest value and add 0.5 to the highest.

Try It Yourself 2

Use a correction for continuity to convert each of the following binomial intervals to a normal distribution interval.

1. The probability of getting between 57 and 83 successes, inclusive
2. The probability of getting at most 54 successes

a. List the *midpoint values* for the binomial probability.
b. Use a *correction for continuity* to write the normal distribution interval.

Answer: Page A38

Picturing the World

In a survey of American adults, people were asked if the law should allow doctors to aid dying patients who want to end their lives. The results of the survey are shown in the following pie chart. *(Source: Harris Poll)*

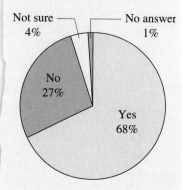

No answer 1%
Not sure 4%
No 27%
Yes 68%

Assume that this Harris Poll is a true indication of the proportion of the population who believe in assisted death for terminally ill patients.
If you sampled 50 adults at random, what is the probability that between 32 and 36, inclusive, would believe in assisted death?

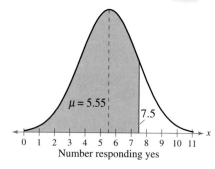

μ = 5.55
7.5
0 1 2 3 4 5 6 7 8 9 10 11
Number responding yes

Approximating Binomial Probabilities

GUIDELINES

Using the Normal Distribution to Approximate Binomial Probabilities

In Words	*In Symbols*
1. Verify that the binomial distribution applies.	Specify n, p, and q.
2. Determine if you can use the normal distribution to approximate x, the binomial variable.	Is $np \geq 5$? Is $nq \geq 5$?
3. Find the mean μ and standard deviation σ for the distribution.	$\mu = np$ $\sigma = \sqrt{npq}$
4. Apply the appropriate continuity correction. Shade the corresponding area under the normal curve.	Add or subtract 0.5 from endpoints.
5. Find the corresponding z-score(s).	$z = \dfrac{(x - \mu)}{\sigma}$
6. Find the probability.	Use the Standard Normal Table.

▶ **EXAMPLE 3** *Approximating a Binomial Probability*

Thirty-seven percent of Americans say that they always fly an American flag on the Fourth of July. You randomly select 15 Americans and ask each if he or she flies an American flag on the Fourth of July. What is the probability that fewer than eight of them respond yes?

SOLUTION   From Example 1, you know that you can use a normal distribution with $\mu = 5.55$ and $\sigma \approx 1.87$ to approximate the binomial distribution. By applying the continuity correction, you can rewrite the discrete probability $P(x < 8)$ as $P(x < 7.5)$ The graph at the left shows a normal curve with $\mu = 5.55$ and $\sigma \approx 1.87$ and a shaded area to the left of 7.5. The z-score that corresponds to $x = 7.5$ is

$$z = \frac{7.5 - 5.55}{1.87} \approx 1.04.$$

Using the Standard Normal Table,

$$P(z < 1.04) = 0.8508.$$

So, the probability that fewer than eight people respond yes is 0.8508.

Try It Yourself 3

Only 8% of Americans feel that the nation is more patriotic today than it was decades ago. You randomly select 70 Americans and ask each if he or she feels the nation is more patriotic today than it was decades ago. What is the probability that more than 10 respond yes?

a. *Apply* the appropriate continuity correction and sketch a graph.
b. *Find* the corresponding *z*-score.
c. *Use* the Standard Normal Table to find the area to the left of *z*.
d. *Subtract* the area from 1.
e. *What* is the probability?   *Answer: Page A38*

EXAMPLE 4   *Approximating a Binomial Probability*

Twenty-nine percent of Americans say they are confident that passenger trips to the moon will occur in their lifetime. You randomly select 200 Americans and ask each if he or she thinks passenger trips to the moon will occur in his or her lifetime. What is the probability that at least 50 will say yes? *(Source: Harper's Index, July 1998)*

SOLUTION   Because $np = 200 \cdot 0.29 = 58$ and $nq = 200 \cdot 0.71 = 142$, the binomial variable x is approximately normally distributed with

$$\mu = np = 58 \text{ and } \sigma = \sqrt{200 \cdot 0.29 \cdot 0.71} \approx 6.42.$$

Using the correction for continuity, you can rewrite the discrete probability $P(x \geq 50)$ as the continuous probability $P(x \geq 49.5)$. The graph shows a normal curve with $\mu = 55$ and $\sigma = 6.42$ and a shaded area to the right of 49.5. The *z*-score that corresponds to 49.5 is

$$z = \frac{49.5 - 58}{6.42} \approx -1.32.$$

So, the probability that at least 50 will say yes is

$$P(x \geq 49.5) = 1 - P(z \leq -1.32)$$
$$= 1 - 0.0934$$
$$= 0.9066.$$

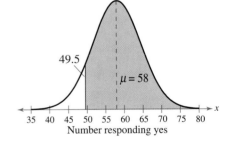
Number responding yes

Try It Yourself 4

What is the probability that at most 65 people will say yes?

a. *Apply* a continuity correction to rewrite $P(x \leq 65)$ and sketch a graph.
b. *Find* the corresponding *z*-score.
c. *Use* the Standard Normal Table to *find the area* to the left of *z*.
d. *What* is the probability?   *Answer: Page A38*

> **EXAMPLE 5** *Approximating a Binomial Probability*

A survey reports that 48% of Internet users use Netscape as their browser. You randomly select 125 Internet users and ask each whether he or she uses Netscape as his or her browser. What is the probability that exactly 63 will say yes? *(Source: Decision Analyst, September 1998)*

SOLUTION Because $np = 125 \cdot 0.48 = 60$ and $nq = 125 \cdot 0.52 = 65$, the binomial variable x is approximately normally distributed with

$$\mu = np = 60 \text{ and } \sigma = \sqrt{125 \cdot 0.48 \cdot 0.52} \approx 5.59.$$

Using the correction for continuity, you can rewrite the discrete probability $P(x = 63)$ as the continuous probability $P(62.5 < x < 63.5)$ The following graph shows a normal curve with $\mu = 60$ and $\sigma = 5.59$ and a shaded area between 62.5 and 63.5.

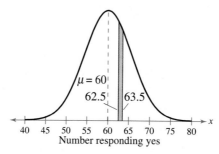

The z-scores that correspond to 62.5 and 63.5 are

$$z_1 = \frac{62.5 - 60}{5.59} \approx 0.45 \quad \text{and} \quad z_2 = \frac{63.5 - 60}{5.59} \approx 0.63.$$

So, the probability that exactly 63 will say they use Netscape is

$$
\begin{aligned}
P(62.5 < x < 63.5) &= P(0.45 < z < 0.63) \\
&= P(z < 0.63) - P(z < 0.45) \\
&= 0.7357 - 0.6736 \\
&= 0.0621.
\end{aligned}
$$

So, there is a probability of about 0.06 that exactly 63 of the Internet users will say they use Netscape.

Note to Instructor

You may want to have students calculate the probability using the binomial formula from Chapter 4 and compare results.

$P(x = 63) = {}_{125}C_{63}(0.48)^{63}(0.52)^{62}$

The TI-83 gives 0.0616662899.

Try It Yourself 5

What is the probability that exactly 61 people will say yes?

a. *Apply* a continuity correction to rewrite $P(x = 61)$ and sketch a graph.
b. *Find* the corresponding z-scores.
c. *Use* the Standard Normal Table to *find the area* to the left of each z-score.
d. *Find* the difference between the areas.
e. *What* is the probability? *Answer: Page A38*

▼ 5.5 ■ EXERCISES ■

▶ HELP

 StatPro 5.5

 Internet Statistics 5.5

 Student Solutions Manual 5.5

 Videos 5.5

Try It Yourself Answers 5.5

1. Use normal distribution.
   70, 4.583
2. Use normal distribution.
   15, 1.936
3. Cannot use normal
   distribution
4. Cannot use normal
   distribution
5. d
6. b
7. a
8. c
9. a
10. d
11. c
12. b

Basic Skills and Concepts

Approximating a Binomial Distribution In Exercises 1–4, a binomial experiment is given. Decide whether you can use the normal distribution to approximate the binomial distribution. If so, find the mean and standard deviation. If not, explain why.

1. A survey of adults found that 70% think public schools need metal detectors. You randomly select 100 adults and ask each if he or she thinks public schools need metal detectors. *(Source: Marist Institute for Public Opinion)*

2. A survey of Internet users found that 75% favored government regulation of unsolicited or "junk" e-mail. You randomly select 20 Internet users and ask each if he or she is in favor of government regulation of junk e-mail. *(Source: www.decisionanalyst.com/publ_data/1998/browse.htm)*

3. In a recent year, the American Cancer Society predicted that the five-year survival rate for new cases of prostate cancer would be 89%. You randomly select 10 men who were new prostate cancer cases this year and calculate their survival rate. *(Source: American Cancer Society)*

4. A survey of American workers found that 8.6% work fewer than 40 hours per week. You randomly select 30 American workers and ask each if he or she works fewer than 40 hours per week.

Matching In Exercises 5–8, match the binomial probability with the correct statement.

Probability	Statement
5. $P(x \geq 45)$	(a) P(there are fewer than 45 successes)
6. $P(x \leq 45)$	(b) P(there are at most 45 successes)
7. $P(x < 45)$	(c) P(there are more than 45 successes)
8. $P(x > 45)$	(d) P(there are at least 45 successes)

Matching In Exercises 9–12, use the correction for continuity and match the binomial probability statement with the corresponding normal distribution statement.

Binomial Probability	Normal Probability
9. $P(x > 89)$	(a) $P(x > 89.5)$
10. $P(x \geq 89)$	(b) $P(x < 88.5)$
11. $P(x \leq 89)$	(c) $P(x \leq 89.5)$
12. $P(x < 89)$	(d) $P(x \geq 88.5)$

13. Binomial: 0.549
Normal: 0.5463

14. Binomial: 0.19
Normal: 0.1875

15. (a) 0.0000199
(b) 0.000023
(c) 0.999977
(d) 0.1635

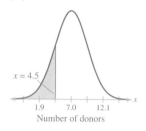

16. See Selected Answers, page A80

17. See Odd Answers, page A58

Graphical Analysis   In Exercises 13 and 14, write the binomial probability that represents the shaded region of the graph. Then write the normal probability that approximates the shaded region of the graph. Find the value of each probability and compare the results.

13.

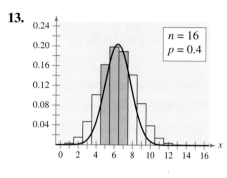

14.

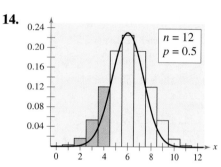

Approximating Binomial Probabilities   In Exercises 15–18, decide whether you can use the normal distribution to approximate the binomial distribution. If so, use the normal distribution to approximate the indicated probabilities and sketch their graphs. If not, explain why and use the binomial distribution to find the indicated probabilities.

15. Seven percent of Americans have type O⁻ blood. You randomly select 30 Americans and ask them if their blood type is O⁻. *(Source: American Association of Blood Banks)*

   (a) Find the probability that exactly 10 people say they have O⁻ blood.

   (b) Find the probability that at least 10 people say they have O⁻ blood.

   (c) Find the probability that fewer than 10 people say they have O⁻ blood.

   (d) A blood drive would like to get at least five donors with O⁻ blood. If there are 100 donors, what is the probability that there will not be enough O⁻ blood donors?

16. Thirty-four percent of Americans have type A⁺ blood. You randomly select 32 Americans and ask them if their blood type is A⁺. *(Source: American Association of Blood Banks)*

   (a) Find the probability that exactly 12 people say they have A⁺ blood.

   (b) Find the probability that at least 12 people say they have A⁺ blood.

   (c) Find the probability that fewer than 12 people say they have A⁺ blood.

   (d) A blood drive would like to get at least 60 donors with A⁺ blood. If there are 150 donors, what is the probability that there will not be enough A⁺ blood donors?

17. Fifty-two percent of adults say chocolate chip is their favorite cookie. You randomly select 40 adults and ask each if chocolate chip is his or her favorite cookie. *(Source: Wearever)*

   (a) Find the probability that at most 15 people say chocolate chip is their favorite cookie.

   (b) Find the probability that at least 15 people say chocolate chip is their favorite cookie.

17. See Odd Answers, page A58

18. (a) 0.99987

  (b) 0.00251

  (c) 0.00013

  (d) 0.230

19. Highly unlikely; no

20. Probable; yes

21. 0.1020

22. 0.1736

17. *continued*

  (c) Find the probability that more than 15 people say chocolate chip is their favorite cookie.

  (d) A community bake sale has prepared 350 chocolate chip cookies. If the bake sale attracts 650 customers and they each buy one cookie, what is the probability there will not be enough chocolate chip cookies?

18. A survey of American workers found that 2.9% work more than 70 hours per week. You randomly select 10 American workers and ask each if he or she works more than 70 hours per week.

  (a) Find the probability that at most three people say they work more than 70 hours per week.

  (b) Find the probability that at least three people say they work more than 70 hours per week.

  (c) Find the probability that more than three people say they work more than 70 hours per week.

  (d) A large company is concerned about overworked employees who work more than 70 hours per week. If the company randomly selects 50 employees, what is the probability there will be no employee working more than 70 hours?

Extending the Basics

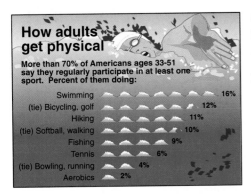

Copyright 1998, USA TODAY. Reprinted with permission.

Getting Physical   In Exercises 19 and 20, use the following information. The graph shows the results of a survey of Americans ages 33 to 51 who were asked if they participated in a sport.

19. You randomly select 250 Americans ages 33 to 51 and ask each if he or she regularly participates in at least one sport. You find that 60% say no. How likely is this result? Do you think the sample is a good one? Explain your reasoning.

20. You randomly select 300 Americans ages 33 to 51 and ask each if he or she regularly participates in at least one sport. Of the 200 who say yes, 9% say they participate in hiking. How likely is this result? Is the sample a good one? Explain your reasoning.

Testing a Drug   In Exercises 21 and 22, use the following information. A drug manufacturer claims that a certain drug cures a rare skin disease 75% of the time. To check the claim, the drug is tested on 100 patients. If at least 70 patients are cured, the claim will be accepted.

21. Find the probability that the claim will be rejected assuming that the manufacturer's claim is true.

22. Find the probability that the claim will be accepted assuming that the actual probability that the drug cures the skin disease is 65%.

5 ▼ CHAPTER SUMMARY

Why did you learn it? Uses and Abuses

Uses The normal distribution is the most important probability distribution of statistics. It can be used to describe many real-life situations as well as approximate other distributions, such as the binomial distribution. The Central Limit Theorem tells you that the distribution of sample means will be normally distributed provided that either the population is normally distributed or the size of the sample is at least 30. So the normal distribution is essential to sampling theory. Sampling theory forms the basis of statistical inference, which you will begin to study in the next chapter.

Abuses A common abuse of normal probability distributions is to confuse the concept of likelihood with the concept of certainty. For instance, if you randomly select a member of a population that is normally distributed, you know that you have a 95% probability of obtaining a result that lies within two standard deviations of the mean. This does not imply, however, that you cannot get an unusual result. In fact, 5% of the time you should expect to get a result that is more than two standard deviations from the mean.

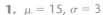

5   **REVIEW EXERCISES**

1. $\mu = 15$, $\sigma = 3$

2. $\mu = -3$, $\sigma = 5$

3. (540, 800)

4. (475, 865)

5. 0.68

6. 0.0015

7. -2.25
    0.5
    2
    3.5

8. 1.54 is more likely to

9. 0.2005

10. 0.9946

11. 0.3936

12. 0.8962

13. 0.0465

14. 0.7967

15. 0.4495

16. 0.2224

17. 0.3519

In Exercises 1 and 2, use the graph to estimate μ and σ.

1.
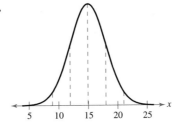

2.
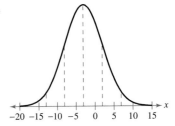

In Exercises 3–6, use the following information and the Empirical Rule to answer the questions. A certain light bulb's lifespan is normally distributed, with a mean of 670 hours and a standard deviation of 65 hours.

3. Between what two lifespans will about 95% of these bulbs fall?

4. Between what two lifespans will about 99.7% of these bulbs fall?

5. Estimate the probability that a randomly selected bulb will last between 605 hours and 735 hours.

6. Estimate the probability that a randomly selected bulb will last more than 865 hours.

In Exercises 7 and 8, use the following information and standard scores to investigate observations about a normal population. A batch of 2500 resistors is normally distributed, with a mean resistance of 1.5 ohms and a standard deviation of 0.08 ohm. Four resistors are randomly selected and tested. Their resistances were measured at 1.32, 1.54, 1.66, and 1.78 ohms.

7. How many standard deviations from the mean are these observations?

8. Do any of these observations seem more or less likely than the others?

In Exercises 9–20, use the Standard Normal Table to find areas under the standard normal curve.

9. Find the area to the left of $z = -0.84$.

10. Find the area to the left of $z = 2.55$.

11. Find the area to the left of $z = -0.27$.

12. Find the area to the left of $z = 1.26$.

13. Find the area to the right of $z = 1.68$.

14. Find the area to the right of $z = -0.83$.

15. Find the area between $z = -1.64$ and the mean.

16. Find the area between $z = -1.22$ and $z = -0.43$.

17. Find the area between $z = 0.15$ and $z = 1.35$.

18. 0.95

19. 0.1336

20. 0.5905

21. 0.8997

22. 0.7704

23. 0.9236

24. 0.3364

25. 0.0124

26. 0.5465

27. The first participant had the lower reading.

28. (a) 62 participants

   (b) 136 participants

29. (a) 0.3156

   (b) 0.3099

   (c) 0.3446

30. (a) 0.9544

   (b) 0.3426

   (c) 0.0026

18. Find the area between $z = -1.96$ and $z = 1.96$.

19. Find the area to the left of $z = -1.5$ and to the right of $z = 1.5$.

20. Find the area to the left of $z = 0.12$ and to the right of $z = 1.72$.

In Exercises 21–26, find the indicated probabilities.

21. $P(z < 1.28)$ **22.** $P(z > -0.74)$

23. $P(-2.15 < z < 1.55)$ **24.** $P(0.42 < z < 3.15)$

25. $P(z < -2.50 \text{ or } z > 2.50)$ **26.** $P(z < 0 \text{ or } z > 1.68)$

In Exercises 27 and 28, use the standard normal distribution to compare two other normal distributions.

27. Blood pressure is described by two numbers: systolic pressure and diastolic pressure (measured in mmHg, or millimeters of mercury). For example, a blood pressure of 120/80 denotes a systolic pressure of 120 mmHg and a diastolic pressure of 80 mmHg. A study of 625 persons ages 26 to 45 finds that their blood pressures are normally distributed. Their systolic pressure had a mean of 122 and a standard deviation of 14, and their diastolic pressure had a mean of 83 and a standard deviation of 9. Two study participants are randomly selected and their blood pressures are measured again. The first participant had a systolic reading of 99 mmHg, while the second had a diastolic reading of 70 mmHg. Which participant had the lower reading with regard to the study population?

28. Health experts often consider blood pressure to be elevated if systolic pressure is 140 or greater or the diastolic pressure is 90 or greater. (a) How many participants in the study in Exercise 27 would you expect to have elevated systolic blood pressure? (b) How many would you expect to have elevated diastolic blood pressure?

In Exercises 29 and 30, find the indicated probabilities.

29. The green turtle migrates across the Southern Atlantic in the winter, swimming great distances. A study found that the mean migration distance was 2200 kilometers and the standard deviation was 625 kilometers. Assuming that the distances are normally distributed, find the probability that a randomly selected green turtle migrates a distance of (a) less than 1900 kilometers, (b) between 2000 kilometers and 2500 kilometers, and (c) greater than 2450 kilometers.

30. The world's smallest mammal is the Kitti's hog-nosed bat, with a mean weight of 1.5 grams and a standard deviation of 0.25 gram. Assuming that the weights are normally distributed, find the probability of randomly selecting a bat that weighs (a) between 1.0 gram and 2.0 grams, (b) between 1.6 grams and 2.2 grams, and (c) more than 2.2 grams.

31. (a) 1.608

   (b) 1.729

32. (a) 112.62

   (b) 75.44, 90.56

33. See Odd Answers, page A58

34. {00, 01, 02, 03, 10, 11, 12, 13, 20, 21, 22, 23, 30, 31, 32, 33}

   1.5, 1.118

   1.5, 0.791

35. (a) 0.0485

   (b) 0.8180

   (c) 0.0823

36. (a) 1

   (b) 0.1446

   (c) 0

37. 154.8, 8.72

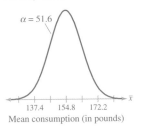

38. 154.8, 4.36

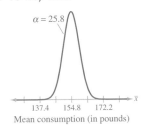

In Exercises 31 and 32, use the Standard Normal Table to locate measurements based on their probability.

31. A zoo is looking for an unusually large jaguar for its "Big Cats" display. The body length (excluding the tail) of jaguars is known to have a mean of 1.4 meters and a standard deviation of 0.20 meter. (a) Suppose the zoo defines "unusually large" as the top 15% of jaguars in body length. Assuming that the body lengths are normally distributed, what requirement would you place on their body length? (b) Redefine "unusually large" as the top 5% and repeat part (a).

32. Refer to the study in Exercise 27. Find (a) the systolic measurement that you would expect one fourth of the participants to fall below and (b) the diastolic measurements that you would expect to contain the middle 60% of the participants.

In Exercises 33–36, use the given population to find the sampling distribution of the sample means for the indicated sample sizes. Find the mean and standard deviation of the population and the mean and standard deviation of the sampling distribution. Compare the values.

33. A corporation has five executives. The number of minutes each exercises a week is reported as 40, 200, 80, 0, and 600. Draw three executives' names from this population, with replacement, and form a sampling distribution of the sample mean of the minutes they exercise.

34. There are four residents sharing a house. The number of times each washes his or her car each month is 1, 2, 0, and 3. Draw two names from this population, with replacement, and form a sampling distribution for the sample mean of the number of times their cars are washed each month.

35. Refer to Exercise 29. If 12 green turtles are randomly selected, find the probability that the sample mean of the distance migrated is (a) less than 1900 kilometers, (b) between 2000 kilometers and 2500 kilometers, and (c) greater than 2450 kilometers. Compare your answers to those in Exercise 29.

36. Refer to Exercise 30. If a sample of 7 Kitti's hog-nosed bats is randomly selected, find the probability that the sample mean is (a) between 1.0 gram and 2.0 grams, (b) between 1.6 and 2.2 grams, and (c) more than 2.2 grams. Compare your answers to those in Exercise 30.

In Exercises 37 and 38, use the Central Limit Theorem to find the mean and standard error of the mean of the indicated sampling distribution. Then sketch a graph of the sampling distribution.

37. The consumption of processed fruits by Americans in a recent year was normally distributed, with a mean of 154.8 pounds and a standard deviation of 51.6 pounds. Random samples of size 35 are drawn from this population. *(Adapted from U.S. Department of Agriculture)*

38. Repeat Exercise 37, assuming that the standard deviation was 25.8 pounds.

39. (a) 0
   (b) 0

40. (a) 0.9918
   (b) 0.9998

41. Do not use normal distribution.

42. Use normal distribution. 5.52, 1.726

43. $P(x > 24.5)$

44. $P(44.5 < x < 45.5)$

45. Use normal distribution. 0.0032

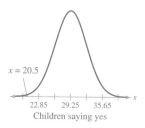

46. 0.171

In Exercises 39 and 40, find the probabilities for the sampling distributions.

39. The mean annual salary for chauffeurs is $21,000. A random sample of size 45 is drawn from this population. What is the probability that the mean annual salary is (a) less than $20,000 and (b) more than $22,500? Assume $\sigma = \$1500$. *(Adapted from Jobs Rated Almanac)*

40. The mean value of land and buildings per acre for a sample of farms is $1300. A random sample of size 36 is drawn from this population. What is the probability that the mean value of land and buildings per acre is (a) less than $1400 and (b) more than $1150? Assume $\sigma = \$250$.

In Exercises 41 and 42, a binomial experiment is given. Decide whether you can use the normal distribution to approximate the binomial distribution. If so, find the mean and standard deviation. If not, explain why.

41. In a recent year, the American Cancer Society predicted that the five-year survival rate for new cases of kidney cancer would be 59%. You randomly select 12 men who were new kidney cancer cases this year and calculate their survival rate. *(Source: American Cancer Society)*

42. A survey found that 46% of women who take at least one vacation a year pack too much. You randomly select 12 women who take at least one vacation a year and ask them if they pack too much. *(Source: USA Today)*

In Exercises 43 and 44, write the binomial probability as a normal probability using the continuity correction.

43. $P(x \geq 25)$

44. $P(x = 45)$

In Exercises 45 and 46, decide whether you can use the normal distribution to approximate the binomial distribution. If so, use the normal distribution to approximate the indicated probabilities and sketch their graphs. If not, explain why and use the binomial distribution to find the indicated probabilities.

45. Sixty-five percent of children aged 12 to 17 keep their savings in a savings account. You randomly select 45 children and ask each if he or she keeps his or her savings in a savings account. Find the probability that at most 20 children will say yes. *(Source: USA Today)*

46. Thirty-three percent of adults graded public schools as excellent or good at preparing students for college. You randomly select 12 adults and ask them if they think public schools are excellent or good at preparing students for college. Find the probability that more than five adults will say yes. *(Source: Marist Institute for Public Opinion)*

▼ **5** ▬▬ **CHAPTER QUIZ** ▬▬▬▬

1. (a) 0.9821
   (b) 0.9994
   (c) 0.9802
   (d) 0.8135
2. (a) 0.9198
   (b) 0.1940
   (c) 0.0456
3. 0.1292
4. 0.5759
5. 77.64%
6. 1509.8
7. 332.688
8. 253.052
9. 0
10. More likely to select one student with a test score greater than 300.
11. Use normal distribution 16.32, 2.285
12. 0.3594

Take this quiz as you would take a quiz in class. After you are done, check your work against the answers given in the back of the book.

1. Find the following standard normal probabilities.
   (a) $P(z > -2.10)$ (b) $P(z < 3.22)$
   (c) $P(-2.33 < z < 2.33)$ (d) $P(z < -1.75 \text{ or } z > -0.75)$

2. Find the following normal probabilities for the given parameters.
   (a) $\mu = 5.5$, $\sigma = 0.08$, $P(5.36 < x < 5.64)$
   (b) $\mu = -8.2$, $\sigma = 7.84$, $P(-5.00 < x < 0)$
   (c) $\mu = 18.5$, $\sigma = 9.25$, $P(x < 0 \text{ or } x > 37)$

In Exercises 3–10, use the following information. In a recent year, grade 8 Washington State public school students taking a mathematics assessment test had a mean score of 276.1 with a standard deviation of 34.4. Possible test scores could range from 0 to 500. Assume that the scores are normally distributed. *(Source: National Center for Educational Statistics)*

3. Find the probability that a student had a score higher than 315.

4. Find the probability that a student had a score between 250 and 305.

5. What percent of the students had a test score that is greater than 250?

6. If 2000 students are randomly selected, how many will have a test score that is less than 300?

7. What is the lowest score that would still place a student in the top 5% of the scores?

8. What is the highest score that would still place a student in the bottom 25% of the scores?

9. A random sample of 60 students is drawn from this population. What is the probability that the mean test score is greater than 300?

10. Are you more likely to select randomly one student with a test score greater than 300 or are you more likely to select a sample of 15 students with a mean test score of 305? Explain.

In Exercises 11 and 12, use the following information. In a survey of adults, 68% thought that DNA tests for identifying an individual were very reliable. You randomly select 24 adults and ask each if he or she thinks DNA tests for identifying an individual are very reliable. *(Source: CBS News)*

11. Decide whether you can use the normal distribution to approximate the binomial distribution. If so, find the mean and standard deviation. If not, explain why.

12. Find the probability that at most 15 people say DNA tests for identifying an individual are very reliable.

Where You've Been

In Chapters 1 through 5, you studied descriptive statistics (how to collect and describe data) and probability (how to find probabilities and analyze discrete and continuous probability distributions). For instance, the Wheat Quality Council uses descriptive statistics to analyze the data collected during its annual crop tour.

In the 1998 crop tour, 444 wheat fields were sampled. Of the 288 fields of spring wheat, the mean yield was 32.5 bushels per acre with a standard deviation of 10.9 bushels per acre. Of the 156 fields of durum wheat, the mean yield was 26.8 bushels per acre with a standard deviation of 8.0 bushels per acre.

Donn Pikop, a buyer for a milling company, checks a wheat spike in a Minnesota field.

The Wheat Quality Council has its headquarters in Pierre, South Dakota. Its primary function is to encourage the development and production of new and better varieties of wheat. The Council also assesses the yield and quality of wheat crops. For instance, in the 1998 crop survey, the wheat averaged about 61 pounds per bushel with a 14% protein content.

Confidence Intervals

Where You're Going

In this chapter, you will begin your study of inferential statistics—the second major branch of statistics. For instance, from the mean of the sample in the 1998 crop survey, the Wheat Quality Council can estimate the mean crop yield to be 32.5 bushels per acre for *all* spring wheat that year. Because this estimate consists of a single number represented by a point on a number line, it is called a point estimate. The problem with using a point estimate is that it is rarely equal to the exact parameter (mean, standard deviation, proportion) of the population.

In this chapter, you will learn how to make a more meaningful estimate by specifying an interval of values on a number line, together with a statement of how confident you are that your interval contains the population parameter. Suppose the Wheat Council wanted to be 90% confident of its estimate for the mean yield of all spring wheat. Here is an overview of how it could construct an interval estimate.

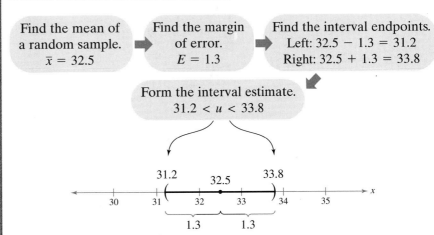

Find the mean of a random sample.
$\bar{x} = 32.5$

Find the margin of error.
$E = 1.3$

Find the interval endpoints.
Left: $32.5 - 1.3 = 31.2$
Right: $32.5 + 1.3 = 33.8$

Form the interval estimate.
$31.2 < u < 33.8$

So, the Wheat Quality Council can be 90% confident that the mean yield for all 1998 spring wheat is between 31.2 and 33.8 bushels per acre.

What You Should Learn

- **How to find a point estimate and a maximum error of estimate**
- **How to construct and interpret confidence intervals for the population mean**
- **How to determine the required minimum sample size when estimating μ**

Estimating Population Parameters

In this chapter, you will learn an important technique of statistical inference—to use sample statistics to estimate the value of an unknown population parameter. In this section, you will learn how to use sample data to make an estimate of the population parameter μ when the sample size is at least 30 or the standard deviation σ is known. To make such an inference, begin by finding a point estimate.

DEFINITION

A **point estimate** is a single value estimate for a population parameter. The most unbiased point estimate of the population mean μ is the sample mean $\bar{x}$.

Note to Instructor

Point out that the sample mean $\bar{x}$ is just as likely to underestimate the population mean as overestimate it and the mean (expected value) of all sample means of size n is equal to the population mean μ. (The Central Limit Theorem)

▶ **EXAMPLE 1**   *Finding a Point Estimate*

Market researchers use the number of sentences per advertisement as a measure of readability for magazine advertisements. The following represents a random sample of the number of sentences found in 54 advertisements. Find a point estimate of the population mean μ. *(Source: Journal of Advertising Research)*

9	20	18	16	9	16	16	9	11	13	22	16	5	18	6	6	5	12
25	17	23	7	10	9	10	10	5	11	18	18	9	9	17	13	11	7
14	6	11	12	11	15	6	12	14	11	4	9	18	12	12	17	11	20

SOLUTION   The sample mean of the data is

$$\bar{x} = \frac{\Sigma x}{n} = \frac{671}{54} \approx 12.4.$$

So, your point estimate for the mean length of all magazine advertisements is 12.4 sentences.

Sample Statistics

Number of Sentences					
16	9	14	11	17	12
99	18	13	12	5	9
17	6	11	17	18	20
6	14	7	11	12	12
5	11	18	6	4	13

Try It Yourself 1

Another random sample of the number of sentences found in 30 magazine advertisements is listed at the left. Use this sample to find another point estimate for μ.

a. Find the sample mean.
b. Estimate the mean sentence length of the population.

Answer: Page A38 ◀

In Example 1, the probability that the population mean is exactly 12.4 is virtually zero. So, instead of estimating μ to be exactly 12.4, you can increase your accuracy by estimating that it lies in an interval. This is called *making an interval estimate.*

DEFINITION

An **interval estimate** is an interval, or range of values, used to estimate a population parameter.

Although you can assume that the point estimate in Example 1 is not equal to the actual population mean, it is probably close to it. To form an interval estimate, use the point estimate as the center of the interval, then add and subtract a margin of error. For instance, if the margin of error is 2.1, then an interval estimate would be given by 12.4 ± 2.1 or $10.3 < \mu < 14.5$. The point estimate and interval estimate are as follows.

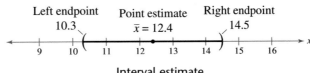

Interval estimate

Before finding an interval estimate, you should first determine how confident you need to be that your interval estimate contains the population mean μ.

DEFINITION

The **level of confidence, c,** is the probability that the interval estimate contains the population parameter.

You know from the Central Limit Theorem that when $n \geq 30$, the sampling distribution of sample means is a normal distribution. The level of confidence, c, is the area under the standard normal curve between the **critical values,** $-z_c$ and z_c. You can see from the graph that c is the percent of the area under the normal curve between $-z_c$ and z_c. The area remaining is $1 - c$, so the area in each tail is $\frac{1}{2}(1 - c)$. For instance, if $c = 90\%$, then 5% of the area lies to the left of $-z_c = -1.645$ and 5% lies to the right of $z_c = 1.645$.

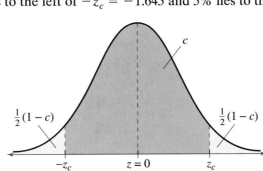

Note to Instructor

Work through the details of finding z_c with different values of c. Point out to students that there is a natural variation from one sample to another, but c is the percent of these sample means that will be between $-z_c$ and z_c.

The distance between the point estimate and the actual parameter value is called the **error of estimate.** When estimating μ, the error of estimate is the distance $|\bar{x} - \mu|$. In most cases, of course, μ is unknown and $\bar{x}$ varies from sample to sample. However, you can calculate a maximum value for the error if you know the level of confidence and the sampling distribution.

DEFINITION

Given a level of confidence c, the **maximum error of estimate** (or error tolerance), E, is the greatest possible distance between the point estimate and the value of the parameter it is estimating.

$$E = z_c \sigma_{\bar{x}} = z_c \frac{\sigma}{\sqrt{n}}$$

When $n \geq 30$, the sample standard deviation s can be used in place of σ.

Picturing the World

During the 1990s, stocks and mutual funds produced some outstanding returns for investors. To estimate the mean annual rate of return for mutual funds, a random sample was taken of 35 mutual funds. The mean annual rate of return for the sample was 25.20%, with a standard deviation of 9.64%. *(Source: Fidelity Investments)*

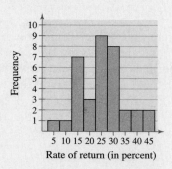

For a 95% confidence interval, what would be the maximum error of estimate for the rate of return?

▶ **EXAMPLE 2** *Finding the Maximum Error of Estimate*

Use the data in Example 1 and a 95% confidence level to find the maximum error of estimate for the number of sentences in a magazine advertisement.

SOLUTION The z-score that corresponds to a 95% confidence level is 1.96. This implies that 95% of the area under the curve falls within 1.96 standard deviations of the mean. You don't know the population standard deviation σ. But because $n \geq 30$, you can use s in place of σ.

$$s = \sqrt{\frac{\Sigma(x - \bar{x})^2}{n - 1}} \approx \sqrt{\frac{1333.2}{53}} \approx 5.0$$

Using the values $z_c = 1.96$, $s \approx 5.0$, and $n = 54$,

$$E = z_c \frac{s}{\sqrt{n}} = 1.96 \cdot \frac{5.0}{\sqrt{54}}$$

$$\approx 1.3.$$

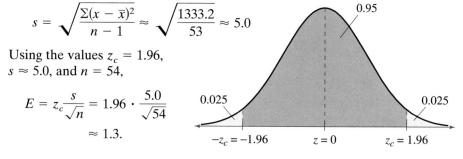

So, you are 95% confident that the maximum error of estimate is about 1.3 sentences per magazine advertisement.

Try It Yourself 2

Use the data given in Try It Yourself 1 and a 95% confidence level to find the maximum error of estimate for the mean number of sentences in a magazine advertisement.

a. *Identify* z_c, n, and s.
b. *Find* E using z_c, s, and n.
c. *State* the maximum error of estimate.   *Answer: Page A38* ◀

Confidence Intervals for the Population Mean

Using a point estimate and a maximum error of estimate, you can construct an interval estimate of a population parameter such as μ. This interval estimate is called a confidence interval.

> ### DEFINITION
>
> A **c-confidence interval** for the population mean μ is
>
> $$\bar{x} - E < \mu < \bar{x} + E.$$
>
> The probability that the confidence interval contains μ is c.

Note to Instructor

Although formulas for $\bar{x}$ and s are shown, we like to encourage students to use technology tools to calculate these statistics. Complete solutions using Minitab or a TI-83 are shown for indicated examples on pages 290 and 291.

GUIDELINES

Finding a Confidence Interval for a Population Mean
($n \geq 30$ or σ known)

In Words	*In Symbols*
1. Find the sample statistics, n and $\bar{x}$.	$\bar{x} = \dfrac{\Sigma x}{n}$
2. Specify σ, if known. Otherwise, if $n \geq 30$, use the sample standard deviation, s.	$s = \sqrt{\dfrac{\Sigma(x - \bar{x})^2}{n - 1}}$
3. Find the critical value, z_c, that corresponds to the given level of confidence.	Use the Standard Normal Table.
4. Find the maximum error of estimate, E.	$E = z_c \dfrac{\sigma}{\sqrt{n}}$
5. Find the left and right endpoints and form the confidence interval.	Left endpoint: $\bar{x} - E$ Right endpoint: $\bar{x} + E$ Interval: $\bar{x} - E < \mu < \bar{x} + E$

Study Tip

The left and right endpoints of a confidence interval are $\bar{x} - E$ and $\bar{x} + E$, respectively. Other ways to represent a confidence interval are $(\bar{x} - E, \bar{x} + E)$ and $\bar{x} \pm E$.

> See *Minitab* steps on page 290.

▶ **EXAMPLE 3** *Constructing a Confidence Interval*

Construct a 95% confidence interval for the mean number of sentences in a magazine advertisement.

SOLUTION In Examples 1 and 2, you found that $\bar{x} = 12.4$ and $E = 1.3$. The confidence interval is as follows.

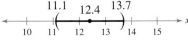

Left Endpoint	Right Endpoint
$\bar{x} - E = 12.4 - 1.3 = 11.1$	$\bar{x} + E = 12.4 + 1.3 = 13.7$

$$11.1 < \mu < 13.7$$

So, with 95% confidence, you can say that the mean number of sentences is between 11.1 and 13.7.

Insight

A larger sample size tends to give you a narrower confidence interval—for the same level of confidence.

Try It Yourself 3

Use the data given in Try It Yourself 1 to construct a 95% confidence interval for the mean number of sentences in a magazine advertisement. Compare your result to the interval found in Example 3.

a. *Find* $\bar{x}$ and E.
b. *Find* the left and right endpoints of the confidence interval.
c. *State* the 95% confidence interval for the mean number of sentences in a magazine advertisement and compare it to Example 3.

Answer: Page A38

▶ **EXAMPLE 4**   *Constructing a Confidence Interval Using Technology*

Use a computer or graphing calculator to construct a 99% confidence interval for the mean number of sentences in a magazine advertisement, using the sample in Example 1.

SOLUTION   To use a technology tool to solve the problem, enter the data and find that the sample standard deviation is $s \approx 5.0$. Then, use the confidence interval command to calculate the confidence interval (ZInterval for *TI-83*, 1-Sample Z for *Minitab*). The display should look like the ones shown here.

TI-83

ZInterval
(10.673, 14.179)
$\bar{x}$=12.42592593
Sx=5.015454801
n=54

MINITAB

Z Confidence Intervals

The assumed sigma = 5.00

Variable	N	Mean	StDev	SE Mean	99.0 % CI
C1	54	12.426	5.015	0.680	(10.673, 14.179)

So, a 99% confidence interval for μ is (10.7, 14.2). With 99% confidence, you can say that the mean number of sentences is between 10.7 and 14.2.

Try It Yourself 4

Use a computer or graphing calculator to construct 75% and 85% confidence intervals for the mean number of sentences in a magazine advertisement. (Use the sample in Try It Yourself 1.) How does the width of the confidence interval change as the level of confidence increases?

a. *Enter* the data.
b. *Use* the appropriate command to construct each confidence interval.
c. *Compare* the confidence intervals.

Answer: Page A38

In Example 4 and Try It Yourself 4, the same sample data was used to construct confidence intervals with different levels of confidence. Notice that as the level of confidence increases, the width of the confidence interval also increases. In other words, using the same sample data, *the greater the level of confidence, the wider the interval.*

In Example 5, notice that if σ is known, then the sample size can be less than 30.

See *TI-83* steps on page 291.

> **EXAMPLE 5**   *Constructing a Confidence Interval, σ Known*

A college admissions director wishes to estimate the mean age of all students currently enrolled. In a random sample of 20 students, the mean age is found to be 22.9 years. From past studies, the standard deviation is known to be 1.5 years. Construct a 90% confidence interval of the population mean age.

SOLUTION   Using $n = 20$, $\bar{x} = 22.9$, $\sigma = 1.5$, and $z_c = 1.645$, the maximum error of estimate at the 90% confidence interval is

$$E = z_c \frac{\sigma}{\sqrt{n}} = 1.645 \cdot \frac{1.5}{\sqrt{20}} \approx 0.55.$$

The 90% confidence interval is as follows.

Left Endpoint	Right Endpoint
$\bar{x} - E = 22.9 - 0.55 = 22.35$	$\bar{x} + E = 22.9 + 0.55 = 23.45$

$$22.35 < \mu < 23.45$$

So, with 90% confidence, you can say that the mean age of the students is between 22.35 and 23.45 years.

So, with 90% confidence, you can say that the mean age of the students is between 22.35 and 23.45 years.

Try It Yourself 5

Construct an 80% confidence interval of the population mean age.

a. *Identify* $n, \bar{x}, \sigma,$ and z_c.
b. *Find* E.
c. *Find* the left and right endpoints of the confidence interval.
d. *Specify* the 80% confidence interval.   *Answer: Page A38*

The horizontal segments represent 90% confidence intervals. In the long run, nine of every ten such intervals will contain μ.

After constructing a confidence interval, it is important that you interpret the results correctly. Consider the 90% confidence interval constructed in Example 5. Because μ already exists, it is either in the interval or not. It is not correct to say "There is a 90% probability that the actual mean is in the interval (22.51, 23.29)." The correct way to interpret your confidence interval is "There is a 90% probability that the confidence interval you described contains μ." This also means, of course, that there is a 10% probability that your confidence interval will not contain μ.

Sample Size

As the level of confidence increases, the confidence interval widens. As the confidence interval widens, the precision of the estimate decreases. One way to improve the precision of an estimate without decreasing the level of confidence is to increase the sample size. But how large a sample size is needed to guarantee a certain level of confidence for a given maximum error of estimate?

Find a Minimum Sample Size to Estimate μ

Given a c-confidence level and a maximum error of estimate E, the minimum sample size, n, needed to estimate μ the population mean is

$$n = \left(\frac{z_c \sigma}{E}\right)^2.$$

If σ is unknown, you can estimate it using s, provided you have a preliminary sample with at least 30 members.

▶ **EXAMPLE 6** *Determining a Minimum Sample Size*

You want to estimate the mean number of sentences in a magazine advertisement. How many magazine advertisements must be included in the sample if you want to be 95% confident that the sample mean is within one sentence of the population mean?

SOLUTION   Using $c = 0.95$, $z_c = 1.96$, $s \approx 5.0$ (from Example 2), and $E = 1$, you can solve for the minimum sample size, n.

$$n = \left(\frac{z_c s}{E}\right)^2 = \left(\frac{1.96 \cdot 5.0}{1}\right)^2 = 96.04$$

When necessary, round up to obtain a whole number. So, you should include at least 97 magazine advertisements in your sample. (You already have 54, so you need 43 more.)

Try It Yourself 6

How many magazine advertisements must be included in the sample if you want to be 95% confident that the sample mean is within two sentences of the population mean? Compare your answer to Example 6.

a. *Identify* z_c, E, and s.
b. *Use* z_c, E, and s to find the minimum sample size n.
c. *State* how many magazine advertisements must be included in the sample and compare your answer to Example 6.

Answer: Page A38 ◀

6.1 ▰ EXERCISES

▶ HELP

StatPro 6.1

Internet Statistics 6.1

Student Solutions Manual 6.1

Videos 6.1

Try It Yourself Answers 6.1

1. You are more likely to be correct using an interval estimate since it is unlikely that a point estimate will equal the population mean exactly.

2. b

3. d

4. b

5. 1.28

6. 1.44

7. 0.47

8. 0.74

9. 1.76

10. 1.56

11. 0.685

12. 0.759

13. (14.775, 15.625)

14. (31.217, 31.563)

15. (4.179, 4.361)

16. (13.114, 13.886)

Basic Skills and Concepts

1. When estimating a population mean, are you more likely to be correct if you use a point estimate or an interval estimate? Explain your reasoning.

2. Which statistic is the best unbiased estimator for μ?
  (a) s (b) $\bar{x}$ (c) the median   (d) the mode

3. Given the same sample statistics, which level of confidence would produce the widest confidence interval? Explain your reasoning.
  (a) 90%   (b) 95%   (c) 98%   (d) 99%

4. What is the effect on the width of the confidence interval when the sample size is increased? Explain your reasoning.
  (a) The width increases   (b) The width decreases   (c) No effect

Critical Values   In Exercises 5 and 6, find the critical value z_c necessary to form a confidence interval at the given level of confidence.

5. $c = 0.80$

6. $c = 0.85$

Graphical Analysis   In Exercises 7–10, use the values on the number line to find the error of estimate.

7. $\bar{x} = 3.8$ $\mu = 4.27$

  3.4 3.6 3.8 4.0 4.2 4.4 4.6

8. $\mu = 8.76$ $\bar{x} = 9.5$

  8.6 8.8 9.0 9.2 9.4 9.6 9.8

9. $\mu = 24.67$ $\bar{x} = 26.43$

  24   25   26   27

10. $\bar{x} = 46.56$ $\mu = 48.12$

  46   47   48   49

Maximum Error of Estimate   In Exercises 11 and 12, find the maximum error of estimate for the given values of c, s, and n.

11. $c = 0.90, s = 2.5, n = 36$

12. $c = 0.95, s = 3.0, n = 60$

Constructing Confidence Intervals   In Exercises 13–16, construct the indicated confidence interval for the population mean, μ.

13. $c = 0.90, \bar{x} = 15.2, s = 2.0, n = 60$

14. $c = 0.95, \bar{x} = 31.39, s = 0.8, n = 82$

15. $c = 0.95, \bar{x} = 4.27, s = 0.3, n = 42$

16. $c = 0.99, \bar{x} = 13.5, s = 1.5, n = 100$

17. (244.928, 316.872)
    (238.040, 323.760)
18. (24.285, 24.975)
    (24.218, 25.042)
19. (25.746, 27.854)
    (25.545, 28.055)
20. (21.163, 24.837)
    (20.811, 25.189)
21. (94.577, 105.423)
22. (70.448, 79.552)
23. (96.165, 103.835)
    $n = 40$ CI is wider
24. (71.607, 78.393)
    $n = 50$ CI is wider
25. (9.719, 11.185)
26. (0.184, 0.216)
27. (8.687, 12.217)
    $s = 5.130$ CI is wider

Applying the Concept In Exercises 17–20, you are given the sample mean and the sample standard deviation. Use this information to construct the 90% and 95% confidence intervals for the population mean. Which interval is wider?

17. A random sample of 32 gas grills has a mean price of $280.90 and a standard deviation of $123.70.

18. From a random sample of 36 days in a recent year, the closing stock prices for Hasbro had a mean of $24.63 and a standard deviation of $1.26. *(Adapted from Financial World)*

19. A random sample of 156 fields of durum wheat has a mean yield of 26.8 bushels per acre and standard deviation of 8.0 bushels per acre. (See page 250.)

20. In 36 randomly selected seawater samples, the mean sodium chloride concentration was 23 cc/cubic meter and the standard deviation was 6.7 cc/cubic meter. *(Adapted from Dorling Kindersley Visual Encyclopedia)*

21. ***Applying the Concept*** You work for a consumer advocate agency and want to find the mean repair cost of a washing machine. As part of your study, you randomly select 40 repair costs and find the mean to be $100.00. The sample standard deviation is $17.50. Construct a 95% confidence interval for the population mean. *(Adapted from Consumer Reports)*

22. ***Applying the Concept*** In a random sample of 50 VCRs, the mean repair cost was $75 and the standard deviation was $12.50. Construct a 99% confidence interval for the population mean. *(Adapted from Consumer Reports)*

23. ***Increasing the Sample Size*** Repeat Exercise 21, changing the sample size to $n = 80$. Which confidence interval is wider? Explain.

24. ***Increasing the Sample Size*** Repeat Exercise 22, changing the sample size to $n = 90$. Which confidence interval is wider? Explain.

25. ***Applying the Concept*** A random sample of 56 American beech trees has a mean height of 10.452 meters and a standard deviation of 2.130 meters. Construct a 99% confidence interval for the population mean height.

26. ***Applying the Concept*** In a random sample of 56 American beech trees, the mean diameter was 0.20 meter and the standard deviation was 0.06 meter. Construct a 95% confidence interval for the population mean.

27. ***Increasing the Standard Deviation*** Repeat Exercise 25, using a standard deviation of $s = 5.130$ meters. Which confidence interval is wider? Explain.

28. *Increasing the Standard Deviation* Repeat Exercise 26, using a standard deviation of $s = 0.1$ meter. Which confidence interval is wider? Explain.

29. *Writing* How does the indicated change affect the confidence interval?

(a) Increase the level of confidence

(b) Increase the sample size

(c) Increase the standard deviation

30. *Writing* Describe how you would form a 90% confidence interval to estimate the population mean age for students at your college.

Applying the Concept In Exercises 31 and 32, you are given the sample mean and the population standard deviation. Use this information to construct the 90% and 99% confidence intervals for the population mean. Which interval is wider?

31. A publisher wants to estimate the mean length of time adults spend reading newspapers. To do this, the publisher takes a random sample of 15 people and gets the following results.

  11, 9, 8, 10, 10, 9, 7, 11, 11, 7, 6, 9, 10, 8, 10

From past studies, the publisher assumes σ is 1.5 minutes.

32. A computer company wants to estimate the hours per week adults use computers at home. In a random sample of 21 adults, the mean length of time a computer was used at home was 5.3 hours. From past studies, the company assumes σ is 0.9 hour. *(Adapted from American Demographics)*

33. *Determining Sample Size* Determine the minimum required sample size if you want to be 95% confident that the sample mean is within one unit of the population mean given $\sigma = 4.8$.

34. *Determining Sample Size* Determine the minimum required sample size if you want to be 99% confident that the sample mean is within two units of the population mean given $\sigma = 1.4$.

35. *Sample Size and Confidence Intervals* A cheese processing company wants to estimate the mean cholesterol content of one-ounce servings of cheese. The estimate must be within 0.5 milligram of the population mean. (a) Determine the minimum required sample size to construct a 95% confidence interval for the population mean. Assume the population standard deviation is 2.8 milligrams. (b) Repeat part (a) using a 99% confidence interval. Which level of confidence requires a larger sample size? Explain.

36. (a) 4

(b) 10

99% CI requires larger sample because more information is needed from the population to be 99% confident.

37. (a) 32

(b) 87

$E = 0.15$ requires a larger sample size. As the error size decreases, a larger sample must be taken to obtain enough information from the population to ensure desired accuracy.

38. (a) 35

(b) 9

$E = 1$ requires a larger sample size. As the error size decreases, a larger sample must be taken to obtain enough information from the population to ensure desired accuracy.

39. (a) 42

(b) 60

$\sigma = 0.30$ requires a larger sample size. Due to the increased variability in the population, a larger sample size is needed to ensure the desired accuracy.

36. *Sample Size and Confidence Intervals* An admissions director wants to estimate the mean age of students enrolled at a college. The estimate must be within 1 year of the population mean. (a) Determine the minimum required sample size to construct a 90% confidence interval for the population mean. Assume the population standard deviation is 1.2 years. (b) Repeat part (a) using a 99% confidence interval. Which level of confidence requires a larger sample size? Explain.

37. *Sample Size and Error Tolerances* A paint manufacturer uses a machine to fill gallon cans with paint. (a) The manufacturer wants to estimate the mean volume of paint the machine is putting in the cans within 0.25 ounce. Determine the minimum sample size required to construct a 90% confidence interval for the population mean. Assume the population standard deviation is 0.85 ounce. (b) Repeat part (a) using an error tolerance of 0.15 ounce. Which error tolerance requires a larger sample size? Explain.

Error tolerance = 0.25 oz   Error tolerance = 1 ml

Figure for Exercise 37   Figure for Exercise 38

38. *Sample Size and Error Tolerances* A beverage company uses a machine to fill 1-liter bottles with water. (a) The company wants to estimate the mean volume of water the machine is putting in the bottles within 1 milliliter. Determine the minimum sample size required to construct a 95% confidence interval for the population mean. Assume the population standard deviation is 3 milliliters. (b) Repeat part (a) using an error tolerance of 2 milliliters. Which error tolerance requires a larger sample size? Explain.

39. *Sample Size and Standard Deviations* A soccer ball manufacturer wants to estimate the mean circumference of soccer balls within 0.1 inch. (a) Determine the minimum required sample size to construct a 99% confidence interval for the population mean. Assume the population standard deviation is 0.25 inch. (b) Repeat part (a) using a standard deviation of 0.3 inch. Which standard deviation requires a larger sample size? Explain.

40. (a) 12
   (b) 3
   $\sigma = 0.20$ requires a larger sample size. Due to the decreased variability in the population, a smaller sample size is needed to ensure the desired accuracy.

41. (a) An increase in the level of confidence will increase the minimum sample size required.
   (b) An increase (larger E) in the error tolerance will decrease the minimum sample size required.
   (c) An increase in the population standard deviation will increase the minimum sample size required.

42. A 99% CI may not be practical to use in all situations. It may produce a CI so wide that it has no practical application.

43. (303.498, 311.252)
44. (99.554, 103.988)
45. (13.680, 15.200)

40. *Sample Size and Standard Deviations* A soccer ball manufacturer wants to estimate the mean circumference of mini-soccer balls within 0.15 inch. (a) Determine the minimum required sample size to construct a 99% confidence interval for the population mean. Assume the population standard deviation is 0.20 inch. (b) Repeat part (a) using a standard deviation of 0.10 inch. Which standard deviation requires a larger sample size? Explain.

41. *Writing* How does the indicated change affect the minimum sample size requirement?
   (a) Increase the level of confidence
   (b) Increase the error tolerance
   (c) Increase the standard deviation

42. *Writing* When estimating the population mean, why not construct a 99% confidence interval every time?

Using Technology In Exercises 43–46, you are given a data sample. Use a computer or graphing calculator to construct a 95% confidence interval for the population mean.

43. A random sample of airfare prices (in dollars) for a one-way ticket from New York to Houston *(Adapted from Newsweek)*

28	8	Key: 29|2 = 292
29	0 2 3 3 5 6 8	
30	0 2 3 4 5 5 5 5 6 6 7 7	
31	3 4 4 6	
32	0 0 1 1 2 2 6 7	

44. A random sample of airfare prices (in dollars) for a one-way ticket from Atlanta to Chicago *(Adapted from Newsweek)*

8	7 7	Key: 8|7 = 87
9	0 4 4	
9	5 6 8 8 8 9	
10	0 1 1 1 1 2 3 3 3 4 4 4	
10	5 5 5 5 6 7 7 8 9	
11	1 4	
11	7	

45. A random sample of the annual precipitation (in inches) for Anchorage, Alaska *(Source: Alaska Climate Research Center)*

14.62	14.66	12.76	16.10	13.09	12.87	14.93	19.48	12.49	15.44
13.67	11.49	15.89	15.17	14.63	13.42	11.81	15.46	12.25	14.97
14.20	16.73	17.64	14.75	14.51	16.89	17.06	13.06	8.61	14.54

46. (16.663, 19.611)

47. **(a)** 0.707

  (b) 0.949

  (c) 0.962

  (d) 0.975

  (e) The finite population correction factor approaches 1 as the sample size decreases while the population size remains the same.

48. **(a)** 0.711

  (b) 0.937

  (c) 0.964

  (d) 0.975

  (e) The finite population correction factor approaches 1 as the population size increases while the sample size remains the same.

49. $n = \left(\dfrac{z_c\sigma}{E}\right)^2 \Rightarrow \sqrt{n} = \dfrac{z_c\sigma}{E} \Rightarrow E$

  $= \dfrac{z_c\sigma}{\sqrt{n}}$

46. A random sample of the annual precipitation (in inches) for Nome, Alaska (*Source: Alaska Climate Research Center*)

16.69	11.17	17.47	18.31	13.41	19.04	29.49	19.27	25.61	20.66
19.91	15.24	19.78	22.15	24.25	15.54	21.66	20.80	14.30	13.56
18.74	7.42	14.41	20.09	12.59	14.97	18.06	22.06	16.96	19.25
19.18	20.22	16.27							

Extending the Basics

Finite Population Correction Factor   In Exercises 47 and 48, use the following information. In this section you studied the formation of a confidence interval to estimate a population mean when the population is large or infinite. When a population is finite, the formula that determines the standard error of the mean, $\sigma_{\bar{x}}$, needs to be adjusted. If N is the size of the population and n is the size of the sample (where $n \geq 0.05N$), the standard error of the mean is

$$\sigma_{\bar{x}} = \frac{\sigma}{\sqrt{n}}\sqrt{\frac{N-n}{N-1}}.$$

The expression $\sqrt{(N-n)/(N-1)}$ is called the **finite population correction factor.** The maximum error of estimate is

$$E = z_c\frac{\sigma}{\sqrt{n}}\sqrt{\frac{N-n}{N-1}}.$$

47. Determine the finite population correction factor for each of the following.

  (a) $N = 1000$ and $n = 500$

  (b) $N = 1000$ and $n = 100$

  (c) $N = 1000$ and $n = 75$

  (d) $N = 1000$ and $n = 50$

  (e) What happens to the finite population correction factor as the sample size n decreases but the population size N remains the same?

48. Determine the finite population correction factor for each of the following.

  (a) $N = 100$ and $n = 50$

  (b) $N = 400$ and $n = 50$

  (c) $N = 700$ and $n = 50$

  (d) $N = 1000$ and $n = 50$

  (e) What happens to the finite population correction factor as the population size N increases but the sample size n remains the same?

49. ***Sample Size***   The equation for determining the sample size, $n = [(z_c\sigma)/E]^2$, can be obtained by solving the equation for the maximum error of estimate, $E = (z_c\sigma)/\sqrt{n}$, for n. Show that this is true and justify each step.

6 CASE STUDY

National Marine Fisheries Services

Shell Lengths of Loggerhead Sea Turtles

The National Marine Fisheries Services is part of the National Oceanic and Atmospheric Administration. NMFS's programs support the conservation and management of living marine resources.

There are six species of sea turtles in the United States and all are protected as endangered species. Rarely does a hatchling sea turtle live to maturity. In fact, it is believed that only 1 in 10,000 hatchlings lives long enough to reproduce.

In a study by Hays and Marsh reported in the *Canadian Journal of Zoology* (75: 40–46, 1997), 71 loggerhead sea turtles were captured and measured off the coast of Britain. The shell lengths of the turtles are shown in the stem-and-leaf plot at the right.

Part of the purpose of the study was to estimate the growth rate of juvenile turtles. The turtles were hatched off the coast of Florida and their drifting time in the Atlantic Ocean was estimated to be between 1.8 and 3.75 years. From this and the fact that a typical hatchling has a shell length of 4.5 centimeters, Hays and Marsh estimated that juvenile loggerhead sea turtles grow at a rate of between 4.3 and 8.9 centimeters per year.

```
 1 | 5 5 6 6 6 7 7 7 7 8 8 8 8 8 8 8 9 9 9 9 9
 2 | 0 0 0 0 0 0 0 0 0 1 1 1 2 2 2 2 2 2 3 4 4
 2 | 5 5 5 6 6 7
 3 | 0 0 0 3 4
 3 | 8                    Key: 1 | 5 = 15 cm
 4 | 0
 4 | 5 9
 5 | 1 4
 5 |
 6 | 0 1 1 4
 6 |
 7 |
 7 | 5 8
 8 |
 8 | 8 8
 9 | 0 0
 9 | 6
10 | 4
```

|←— Shell length —→|

Exercises

1. A loggerhead sea turtle is classified as a juvenile if its shell length is less than 40 centimeters. How many of the turtles in the sample were juveniles?

2. Use the sample to make a point estimate of the mean shell length of juvenile loggerhead sea turtles that drift from their hatching site to the coast of Britain.

3. Find the standard deviation of the sample of juveniles.

4. Use the sample to make an interval estimate of the mean shell length of juvenile loggerhead sea turtles that drift from their hatching site to the coast of Britain.

   (a) Use a 90% confidence level.

   (b) Use a 95% confidence level.

   (c) Use a 99% confidence level.

5. How would your results have differed if you had used all the turtles in the sample instead of just the juvenile turtles? Explain your reasoning.

6. Complete the following table.

Juvenile Turtles	Length at Hatching	Length at Capture	Shell Growth
Minimum	4.5 cm	15 cm	?? cm
Maximum	4.5 cm	40 cm	?? cm

Use the table to estimate the rate of growth for juvenile loggerhead sea turtles under the following assumptions.

(a) Drift time = 1.8 years, minimum shell growth

(b) Drift time = 3.75 years, maximum shell growth

6.2 Confidence Intervals for the Mean (Small Samples)

The *t*-Distribution • Confidence Intervals and *t*-Distributions

What You Should Learn

- *How to interpret the t-distribution and use a t-distribution table*

- *How to construct confidence intervals when n < 30 and σ is unknown*

Historical Reference

William S. Gosset (1876–1937) developed the *t*-distribution while employed by the Guinness Brewing Company in Dublin, Ireland. Gosset published his findings using the pseudonym Student. The *t*-distribution is sometimes referred to as Student's *t*-distribution. (See page 274 for others who were important in the history of statistics.)

The *t*-Distribution

In many real-life situations, the population standard deviation is unknown. Moreover, because of various constraints such as time and cost, it is often not practical to collect samples of size 30 or more. So, how can you construct a confidence interval for a population mean given such circumstances? If the random variable is normally distributed (or approximately normally), the sampling distribution for $\bar{x}$ is a *t*-distribution.

DEFINITION

If the distribution of a random variable x is approximately normal, then the sampling distribution of $\bar{x}$ is a *t*-distribution, where

$$t = \frac{\bar{x} - \mu}{\frac{s}{\sqrt{n}}}.$$

Critical values of t are denoted by t_c. Several properties of the *t*-distribution are as follows.

1. The *t*-distribution is bell shaped and symmetric about the mean.

2. The *t*-distribution is a family of curves, each determined by a parameter called the degrees of freedom. The **degrees of freedom** are the number of free choices left after a sample statistic such as $\bar{x}$ is calculated. When you use a *t*-distribution to estimate a population mean, the degrees of freedom are equal to one less than the sample size.

   d.f. = $n - 1$ Degrees of Freedom

3. The total area under a *t*-curve is 1 or 100%.

4. The mean, median, and mode of the *t*-distribution are equal to zero.

5. As the degrees of freedom increase, the *t*-distribution approaches the normal distribution. After 30 d.f. the *t*-distribution is very close to the standard normal *z*-distribution.

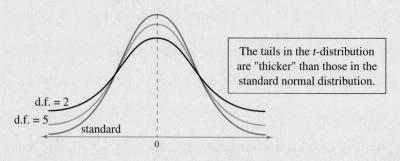

The tails in the *t*-distribution are "thicker" than those in the standard normal distribution.

d.f. = 2
d.f. = 5
standard
0

Table 5 of Appendix B lists critical values of t for selected confidence intervals and degrees of freedom.

▶ EXAMPLE 1   *Finding Critical Values of t*

Find the critical value, t_c, for a 95% confidence when the sample size is 15.

SOLUTION   Because $n = 15$, the degrees of freedom are

$$\text{d.f.} = n - 1 = 15 - 1 = 14.$$

A portion of Table 5 is shown. Using d.f. $= 14$ and $c = 0.95$, you can find the critical value, t_c, as shown by the highlighted areas in the table.

		Level of confidence, c	0.50	0.80	0.90	0.95	0.98
		One tail, α	0.25	0.10	0.05	0.025	0.01
d.f.	Two tails, α		0.50	0.20	0.10	0.05	0.02
1			1.000	3.078	6.314	12.706	31.821
2			.816	1.886	2.920	4.303	6.965
3			.765	1.638	2.353	3.182	4.541
4			.741	1.533	2.132	2.776	3.747
5			.727	1.476	2.015	2.571	3.365
11			.697	1.363	1.796	2.201	2.718
12			.695	1.356	1.782	2.179	2.681
13			.694	1.350	1.771	2.160	2.650
14			.692	1.345	1.761	2.145	2.624
15			.691	1.341	1.753	2.131	2.602
16			.690	1.337	1.746	2.120	2.583

From the table, you can see that $t_c = 2.145$. The graph shows the t-distribution for 14 degrees of freedom, $c = 0.95$, and $t_c = 2.145$.

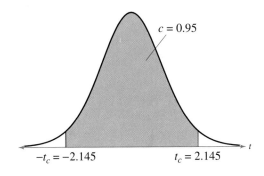

$c = 0.95$

$-t_c = -2.145$ $t_c = 2.145$

Study Tip

Unlike the z-table, critical values for a specific confidence interval can be found in the column headed by c in the appropriate d.f. row. (The symbol α will be explained in Chapter 7.)

Note to Instructor

Point out that after 30 d.f., the t-values are close to the z-values. Moreover, the values in the table that show ∞ d.f. correspond *exactly* to the normal distribution values.

Try It Yourself 1

Find the critical value, t_c, for a 90% confidence when the sample size is 22.

a. Identify the degrees of freedom.
b. Identify the level of confidence, c.
c. Use Table 5 of Appendix B to find t_c.

Answer: Page A38

Confidence Intervals and *t*-Distributions

Constructing a confidence interval using the *t*-distribution is similar to constructing a confidence interval using the normal distribution—both use a point estimate $\bar{x}$ and a maximum error of estimate, E.

GUIDELINES

Constructing a Confidence Interval for the Mean: *t*-Distribution

In Words	*In Symbols*
1. Identify the sample statistics n, $\bar{x}$, and s.	$\bar{x} = \dfrac{\Sigma x}{n}, \quad s = \sqrt{\dfrac{\Sigma(x - \bar{x})^2}{n - 1}}$
2. Identify the degrees of freedom, the level of confidence c, and the critical value t_c.	d.f. $= n - 1$
3. Find the maximum error of estimate, E.	$E = t_c \dfrac{s}{\sqrt{n}}$
4. Find the left and right endpoints and form the confidence interval.	Left endpoint: $\bar{x} - E$ Right endpoint: $\bar{x} + E$ Interval: $\bar{x} - E < \mu < \bar{x} + E$

See *Minitab* steps on page 290.

▶ **EXAMPLE 2** **Constructing a Confidence Interval**

You randomly select 16 restaurants and measure the temperature of the coffee sold at each. The sample mean temperature is 162°F with a sample standard deviation of 10°F. Find the 95% confidence interval for the mean temperature. Assume the temperatures are approximately normally distributed.

SOLUTION Because the sample size is less than 30, σ is unknown, and the temperatures are approximately normally distributed, you can use the *t*-distribution. Using $n = 16$, $\bar{x} = 162$, $s = 10$, $c = 0.95$, and d.f. $= 15$, you can use Table 5 to find that $t_c = 2.131$. The maximum error of estimate at the 95% confidence interval is

$$E = t_c \frac{s}{\sqrt{n}} = 2.131 \cdot \frac{10}{\sqrt{16}} = 5.3275.$$

The confidence interval is as follows.

$\bar{x} - E = 156.6725 \qquad \bar{x} + E = 167.3275$
$\bar{x} = 162$
156 158 160 162 164 166 168

Left Endpoint	Right Endpoint
$\bar{x} - E = 162 - 5.3275 = 156.6725$	$\bar{x} + E = 162 + 5.3275 = 167.3275$

$156.6725 < \mu < 167.3275$

So, with 95% confidence, you can say that the mean temperature of coffee sold is between 156.7°F and 167.3°F.

Try It Yourself 2

Find the 90% and 99% confidence intervals for the mean temperature.

a. *Find t_c and E for each level of confidence.*
b. Use $\bar{x}$ and E to find the *left and right endpoints.*
c. *State* the 90% and 99% confidence intervals for the mean temperature. *Answer: Page A38*

See *TI-83* steps on page 291.

► **EXAMPLE 3**   ***Constructing a Confidence Interval***

You randomly select 20 mortgage institutions and determine the current mortgage interest rate at each. The sample mean rate is 6.93% with a sample standard deviation of 0.42%. Find the 99% confidence interval for the mean mortgage interest rate. Assume the interest rates are approximately normally distributed.

SOLUTION   Because the sample size is less than 30, σ is unknown, and the interest rates are approximately normally distributed, you can use the *t*-distribution. Using $n = 20$, $\bar{x} = 6.93$, $s = 0.42$, $c = 0.99$, and d.f. $= 19$, you can use Table 5 to find that $t_c = 2.861$. The maximum error of estimate at the 99% confidence interval is

$$E = t_c \frac{s}{\sqrt{n}} = 2.861 \cdot \frac{0.42}{\sqrt{20}} \approx 0.269.$$

The confidence interval is as follows.

$\bar{x} - E = 6.661$ $\bar{x} + E = 7.199$
$\bar{x} = 6.93$

6.4   6.6   6.8   7.0   7.2   7.4

Left Endpoint	Right Endpoint
$\bar{x} - E = 6.93 - 0.269 = 6.661$	$\bar{x} + E = 6.93 + 0.269 = 7.199$

$$6.661 < \mu < 7.199$$

So, with 99% confidence, you can say that the mean mortgage interest rate is between 6.66% and 7.20%.

Try It Yourself 3

Find the 90% and 95% confidence intervals for the mean mortgage interest rate. Compare the widths of the intervals.

a. Find t_c and E for each level of confidence.
b. Use $\bar{x}$ and E to find the left and right endpoints.
c. State the 90% and 95% confidence intervals for the mean mortgage interest rate and compare their widths. *Answer: Page A38*

Picturing the World

Two footballs, one filled with air and the other filled with helium, were kicked on a windless day at Ohio State University. The footballs were alternated with each kick. After 10 practice kicks, each football was kicked 29 more times. The distances (in yards) are listed. *(Source: OSC Scientists Get a Kick Out of Sports Controversy, "The Columbus Dispatch," November 21, 1993.)*

Air Filled

1	9
2	0 0 2 2 2
2	5 5 5 5 6 6
2	7 7 7 8 8 8 8 8 9 9 9
3	1 1 1 2
3	3 4 Key: 1	9 = 19

Helium Filled

1	1 2
1	3
1	
2	2
2	3 4 6 6 6
2	7 8 8 8 9 9 9 9
3	0 0 0 0 1 1 2 2
3	3 4 5
3	9

Assume that the distances are normally distributed for each football. Apply the flowchart at the right to each sample. Find a 95% confidence interval for the mean distance each football traveled. Do the confidence intervals overlap? What does this tell you?

The flowchart describes when to use the normal distribution to construct a confidence interval and when to use a *t*-distribution.

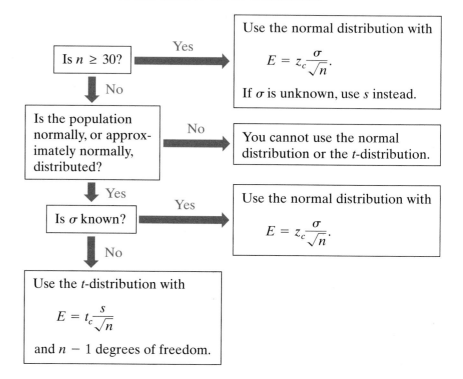

Is $n \geq 30$? — Yes → Use the normal distribution with $E = z_c \dfrac{\sigma}{\sqrt{n}}$. If σ is unknown, use s instead.

No ↓

Is the population normally, or approximately normally, distributed? — No → You cannot use the normal distribution or the *t*-distribution.

Yes ↓

Is σ known? — Yes → Use the normal distribution with $E = z_c \dfrac{\sigma}{\sqrt{n}}$.

No ↓

Use the *t*-distribution with $E = t_c \dfrac{s}{\sqrt{n}}$ and $n - 1$ degrees of freedom.

► **EXAMPLE 4**   *Choosing the Normal or t-Distribution*

You randomly select 25 newly constructed houses. The sample mean construction cost is $181,000 and the population standard deviation is $28,000. Assuming construction costs are normally distributed, should you use the normal distribution, the *t*-distribution, or neither to construct a 95% confidence interval for the mean construction cost? Explain your reasoning.

SOLUTION   Because the population is normally distributed and the population standard deviation is known, you should use the normal distribution.

Try It Yourself 4

You randomly select 18 adult male athletes and measure the resting heart rate of each. The sample mean heart rate is 64 beats per minute with a sample standard deviation of 2.5 beats per minute. Assuming the heart rates are normally distributed, should you use the normal distribution, the *t*-distribution, or neither to construct a 90% confidence interval for the mean heart rate? Explain your reasoning.

a. Use the flowchart to determine which distribution you should use to construct the 90% confidence interval for the mean heart rate.

Answer: Page A38 ◄

6.2 EXERCISES

HELP

StatPro 6.2

Internet Statistics 6.2

Student Solutions Manual 6.2

Videos 6.2

Try It Yourself Answers 6.2

1. 1.833

2. 2.201

3. 2.947

4. 2.539

5. (a) 2.450

   (b) 2.664

6. (a) 3.154

   (b) 4.938

7. (a) (10.855, 14.145)

   (b) (11.157, 13.843)
      t-CI is wider.

8. (a) (12.689, 14.111)

   (b) (12.811, 13.989)
      t-CI is wider.

9. (a) (4.059, 4.541)

   (b) (4.089, 4.511)
      t-CI is wider.

10. (a) (11.945, 16.055)

    (b) (12.371, 15.629)
      t-CI is wider.

11. (59.482, 90.518)
   15.518

12. (60.693, 139.307)
   39.307

13. (61.852, 88.148)
   13.148
   t-CI is wider.

14. (62.959, 137.041)
   37.041
   t-CI is wider.

Basic Skills and Concepts

Finding Critical Values of t In Exercises 1–4, find the critical value, t_c, for the given confidence level c and sample size n.

1. $c = 0.90$, $n = 10$

2. $c = 0.95$, $n = 12$

3. $c = 0.99$, $n = 16$

4. $c = 0.98$, $n = 20$

Maximum Error of Estimate In Exercises 5 and 6, suppose you incorrectly used the normal distribution to find the maximum error of estimate for the given values of c, s, and n. (a) Find the value of E using the normal distribution and (b) then find the correct value using a t-distribution. Compare the results.

5. $c = 0.95$, $s = 5$, $n = 16$

6. $c = 0.99$, $s = 3$, $n = 6$

Constructing Confidence Intervals In Exercises 7–10, construct the indicated confidence interval for the population mean, μ, using (a) a t-distribution. (b) If you had incorrectly used a normal distribution, which interval would be wider?

7. $c = 0.90$, $\bar{x} = 12.5$, $s = 2.0$
   $n = 6$

8. $c = 0.95$, $\bar{x} = 13.4$, $s = 0.85$,
   $n = 8$

9. $c = 0.98$, $\bar{x} = 4.3$, $s = 0.34$,
   $n = 14$

10. $c = 0.99$, $\bar{x} = 14$, $s = 2.0$
   $n = 10$

Repair Costs In Exercises 11 and 12, you are given the sample mean and the sample standard deviation. Assume the variable is normally distributed and use a t-distribution to construct a 95% confidence interval for the population mean, μ. What is the maximum error of estimate of μ?

11. In a random sample of five microwave ovens, the mean repair cost was $75.00 and the standard deviation was $12.50. *(Adapted from Consumer Reports)*

12. In a random sample of seven computers, the mean repair cost was $100.00 and the standard deviation was $42.50. *(Adapted from Consumer Reports)*

13. Suppose you did some research on repair costs of microwave ovens and found that the standard deviation is $\sigma = 15. Repeat Exercise 11, using a normal distribution with the appropriate calculations for a standard deviation that is known. Compare the results.

14. Suppose you did some research on repair costs of computers and found that the standard deviation is $\sigma = 50. Repeat Exercise 12, using a normal distribution with the appropriate calculations for a standard deviation that is known. Compare the results.

15. **(a)** (3.604, 4.996)
    (b) (4.212, 4.388)
    t-CI is wider.

16. **(a)** (1.044, 1.356)
    (b) (1.180, 1.220)
    t-CI is wider.

17. **(a)** 2174.75
    (b) 100.341
    (c) (2071.626, 2277.874)

18. **(a)** 3418.817
    (b) 389.294
    (c) (3105.439, 3732.195)

19. **(a)** 909.083
    (b) 305.266
    (c) (635.374, 1182.792)

20. **(a)** 2.087
    (b) 1.024
    (c) (1.300, 2.874)

Waste Management In Exercises 15 and 16, you are given the sample mean and the sample standard deviation. Assume the variable is normally distributed and use a *t*-distribution to construct a 90% confidence interval for the population mean, μ.

15. (a) In a random sample of 10 American adults, the mean waste generated per person per day was 4.3 pounds and the standard deviation was 1.2 pounds. (b) Repeat part (a), assuming the same statistics came from a sample size of 500. Compare the results. *(Adapted from U.S. Environmental Protection Agency)*

16. (a) In a random sample of 12 American adults, the mean waste recycled per person per day was 1.2 pounds and the standard deviation was 0.3 pound. (b) Repeat part (a), assuming the same statistics came from a sample size of 600. Compare the results. *(Adapted from U.S. Environmental Protection Agency)*

Sample Data In Exercises 17–20, a data set is given. For each data set, find (a) the sample mean and (b) the sample standard deviation, and (c) construct a 99% confidence interval for the population mean, μ. Assume the population of each data set is normally distributed.

17. The monthly incomes for 10 randomly selected people, each with a bachelor's degree in biology *(Adapted from U.S. Bureau of the Census)*

    2148.51   1978.27   2093.63   2091.95   2282.18   2223.64   2276.50
    2207.41   2285.69   2159.72

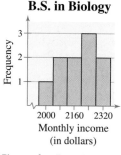

B.S. in Biology

Figure for Exercise 17

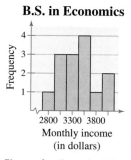

B.S. in Economics

Figure for Exercise 18

18. The monthly incomes for 14 randomly selected people, each with a bachelor's degree in economics *(Adapted from U.S. Bureau of the Census)*

    3450.66   3596.73   3366.66   3455.40   3151.70   2727.08   3283.76
    3527.64   3407.34   4036.64   4083.73   2946.47   3023.41   3806.22

19. The SAT scores for 12 randomly selected senior high school students

    1424   1223   987   692   947   723   837   721   747   540   623   1445

20. The grade point averages for 15 randomly selected college students

    2.3   3.3   2.6   1.8   0.2   3.1   4.0   0.7   2.3   2.0   3.1   1.4   1.3   1.6   1.6

21. use normal distribution
(1.248, 1.252)

22. use *t*-distribution
(21.758, 43.302)

23. use *t*-distribution
(22.762, 25.238)

24. use normal distribution
(18.828, 22.772)

25. Cannot use normal or
t-distribution

26. use *t*-distribution
(21.934, 34.326)

27. $n = 25$, $\bar{x} = 56.0$, $s = 0.25$

$\pm t_{0.99} \Rightarrow$ 99% *t*-CI

$\bar{x} \pm t_c \dfrac{s}{\sqrt{n}} = 56.0 \pm 2.797 \dfrac{0.25}{\sqrt{25}}$

$\approx (55.860, 56.140)$

They are not making good tennis balls since desired bounce height of 55.5 inches is not contained between 55.850 and 56.140 inches.

28. $n = 16$, $\bar{x} = 1015$, $s = 25$

$\pm t_{0.99} \Rightarrow$ 99% *t*-CI

$\bar{x} \pm t_c \dfrac{s}{\sqrt{n}} = 1015 \pm 2.947 \dfrac{25}{\sqrt{16}}$

$\approx (996.581, 1033.419)$

They are making good light bulbs since the desired bulb life of 1000 hours is contained between 996.581 and 1033.419 hours.

Choosing a Distribution In Exercises 21–26, use a normal distribution or a *t*-distribution to construct a 95% confidence interval for the population mean. Justify your decision. If neither distribution can be used, explain why not.

21. In a random sample of 70 bolts, the mean length was 1.25 inches and the standard deviation was 0.01 inch.

22. You took a random sample of 15 two-slice toasters and found the mean price was $32.53 and the standard deviation was $19.45. Assume the prices are normally distributed. *(Adapted from Consumer Reports)*

23. You take a random survey of 25 sports cars and record the miles per gallon for each. The data are listed below. Assume the miles per gallon are normally distributed. *(Adapted from Consumer Reports)*

24	24	27	20	26	23	18	29	24	22	22	27	26
20	28	30	23	24	19	22	24	26	23	24	25	

24. In a recent year, the standard deviation of ACT scores for all students was 4.7. You take a random survey of 20 students and determine the ACT score of each. The scores are listed below. Assume the test scores are normally distributed. *(Source: ACT, Inc.)*

26	22	23	12	19	25	23	21	25	10
17	26	23	24	20	14	21	23	20	22

25. In a random sample of 19 patients at a hospital's minor emergency department, the mean waiting time (in minutes) before seeing a medical professional was 23 minutes and the standard deviation was 11 minutes. Assume the waiting times are not normally distributed.

26. In a random sample of 17 shoppers at a grocery store, the mean amount spent was $28.13 and the standard deviation was $12.05. Assume the amounts spent are normally distributed.

Extending the Basics

27. ***Is It Acceptable?*** A company manufactures tennis balls. When its tennis balls are dropped onto a concrete surface from a height of 100 inches, the company wants the mean height the balls bounce upward to be 55.5 inches. To maintain this average, random samples of 25 tennis balls are periodically tested. If the *t*-value falls between $-t_{0.99}$ and $t_{0.99}$, the company will be satisfied that it is manufacturing acceptable tennis balls. A sample of 25 balls is randomly selected and tested. The mean bounce height of the sample is 56.0 inches and the standard deviation is 0.25 inch. Is the company making acceptable tennis balls? Explain your reasoning.

28. ***Is It Acceptable?*** A company manufactures light bulbs. The company wants the bulbs to have a mean lifespan of 1000 hours. To maintain this average, random samples of 16 light bulbs are periodically tested. If the *t*-value falls between $-t_{0.99}$ and $t_{0.99}$, the company will be satisfied that it is manufacturing acceptable light bulbs. A sample of 16 light bulbs is randomly selected and tested. The mean lifespan of the sample is 1015 hours and the standard deviation is 25 hours. Is the company making acceptable light bulbs? Explain your reasoning.

HISTORY OF STATISTICS - TIMELINE

CONTRIBUTOR	TIME	CONTRIBUTION

John Graunt (1620–1674)

17th century

Studied records of deaths in London in the early 1600s. The first to make extensive statistical observations from massive amounts of data (Chapter 2), his work laid the foundation for modern statistics.

Blase Pascal (1632–1692)

Pierre Fermat (1601–1695)

Pascal and Fermat corresponded about basic probability problems (Chapter 3)—especially those dealing with gaming and gambling.

Pierre Laplace (1749–1827)

18th century

Studied probability (Chapter 3) and is credited with putting probability on a sure mathematical footing.

Carl Gauss (1777–1855)

Studied regression and the method of least squares (Chapter 9) through astronomy. In his honor, the normal distribution is sometimes called the Gaussian distribution.

Lambert Quetelet (1796–1874)

19th century

Used descriptive statistics (Chapter 2) to analyze crime and mortality data and studied census techniques. Described normal distributions (Chapter 5) in connection with human traits such as height.

Francis Galton (1822–1911)

Used regression and correlation (Chapter 9) to study genetic variation in humans. He is credited with discovery of the Central Limit Theorem (Chapter 5).

Karl Pearson (1857–1936)

20th century

Studied natural selection using correlation (Chapter 9). Formed first academic department of statistics, and helped develop chi-square analysis (Chapter 6).

William Gosset (1876–1937)

Studied process of brewing and developed *t*-test to correct problems connected with small sample sizes (Chapter 6).

Ronald Fisher (1890–1962)

Studied biology and natural selection and developed ANOVA (Chapter 10), stressed the importance of experimental design (Chapter 1), and was the first to identify the null and alternative hypotheses (Chapter 7).

Charles Spearman (1863–1945)

20th century (later)

British psychologist who was one of the first to develop intelligence testing using factor analysis (Chapter 10).

Frank Wilcoxon (1892–1965)

Biochemist who used statistics to study plant pathology. He introduced two-sample tests (Chapter 8), which led the way to the development of nonparametric statistics.

John Tukey (1915–)

Worked at Princeton during World War II. Introduced exploratory data analysis techniques such as stem-and-leaf plots (Chapter 2). Also, worked at Bell Laboratories and is best known for his work in inferential statistics (Chapters 6–11).

David Kendall (1918–)

Worked at Princeton and Cambridge. Is a leading authority on applied probability and data analysis (Chapters 2 and 3).

<table>
<tr><td>

6.3

Confidence Intervals for Population Proportions

</td></tr>
</table>

Sample Proportions • Confidence Intervals for a Population Proportion p • Increasing Sample Size to Increase Precision

What You Should Learn

- *How to find a sample proportion*
- *How to construct a confidence interval for a population proportion*
- *How to determine a minimum sample size when estimating a population proportion*

Sample Proportions

Recall from Section 4.2 that the probability of success in a single trial of a binomial experiment is p. This probability is a population **proportion.** In this section, you will learn how to estimate a population proportion p using a confidence interval. As with confidence intervals for μ, you will start with a point estimate.

DEFINITION

The point estimate for p, the population proportion of successes, is given by the proportion of successes in a sample and is denoted by

$$\hat{p} = \frac{x}{n}$$

where x is the number of successes in the sample and n is the number in the sample. The point estimate for the number of failures is $\hat{q} = 1 - \hat{p}$. The symbols $\hat{p}$ and $\hat{q}$ are read as "p hat" and "q hat."

▶ **EXAMPLE 1** *Finding a Point Estimate for p*

In a survey of 883 American adults, 380 said that their favorite sport is football. Find a point estimate for the population proportion of adults who say their favorite sport is football. *(Source: Marist Institute for Public Opinion)*

SOLUTION   Using $n = 883$ and $x = 380$,

$$\hat{p} = \frac{x}{n} = \frac{380}{883} \approx 0.43 \approx 43\%.$$

Insight

In the first two sections, estimates were made for quantitative data. In this section, sample proportions are used to make estimates for qualitative data.

Try It Yourself 1

In a survey of 1470 American adults, 98 said that of all the presidents in our nation's history, they most admire Abraham Lincoln. Find a point estimate for the population proportion of adults who admire Lincoln over all other American presidents. *(Source: Marist Institute for Public Opinion)*

a. *Identify x and n.*
b. *Use x and n to find $\hat{p}$.*

Answer: Page A39 ◀

Confidence Intervals for a Population Proportion p

Constructing a confidence interval for a population proportion p is similar to constructing a confidence interval for a population mean. You start with a point estimate and calculate a maximum error of estimate.

DEFINITION

A *c-confidence interval* for the population proportion p is

$$\hat{p} - E < p < \hat{p} + E \qquad \text{where } E = z_c \sqrt{\frac{\hat{p}\hat{q}}{n}}.$$

The probability that the confidence interval contains p is c.

In Section 5.5, you learned that a binomial distribution can be approximated by the normal distribution if $np \geq 5$ and $nq \geq 5$. When $n\hat{p} \geq 5$ and $n\hat{q} \geq 5$, the sampling distribution for $\hat{p}$ is approximately normal with a mean of $\mu_{\hat{p}} = p$ and a standard error of

$$\sigma_{\hat{p}} = \sqrt{\frac{pq}{n}}.$$

GUIDELINES

Constructing a Confidence Interval for a Population Proportion

In Words	*In Symbols*
1. Identify the sample statistics, n and x.	
2. Find the point estimate, $\hat{p}$.	$\hat{p} = \dfrac{x}{n}$
3. Verify that the sampling distribution of $\hat{p}$ can be approximated by the normal distribution.	Is $n\hat{p} > 5$ and $n\hat{q} > 5$?
4. Find the critical value, z_c, that corresponds to the given level of confidence c.	Use the Standard Normal Table.
5. Find the maximum error of estimate, E.	$E = z_c \sqrt{\dfrac{\hat{p}\hat{q}}{n}}$
6. Find the left and right endpoints and form the confidence interval.	Left endpoint: $\hat{p} - E$ Right endpoint: $\hat{p} + E$ Interval: $\hat{p} - E < p < \hat{p} + E$

Minitab and *TI-83* steps are shown on pages 290 and 291.

▶ EXAMPLE 2 *Constructing a Confidence Interval for p*

Construct a 95% confidence interval for the proportion of American adults who say that their favorite sport is football.

Note to Instructor

Point out that the value for *E* is calculated by multiplying the *z*-score (the number of standard deviations from the mean) times the standard error of the mean. The *z*-scores are found the same way they were found in Section 6.1.

SOLUTION From Example 1, $\hat{p} \approx 0.43$. So, $\hat{q} = 1 - 0.43 = 0.57$. Using $n = 883$, you can verify that the sampling distribution of $\hat{p}$ can be approximated by the normal distribution.

$$n\hat{p} \approx 883 \cdot 0.43 \approx 380 > 5$$

and

$$n\hat{q} \approx 883 \cdot 0.57 \approx 503 > 5$$

Using $z_c = 1.96$, the maximum error of estimate is

$$E = z_c \sqrt{\frac{\hat{p}\hat{q}}{n}} \approx 1.96 \sqrt{\frac{(0.43)(0.57)}{883}} \approx 0.033.$$

The 95% confidence interval is as follows.

Left Endpoint	Right Endpoint
$\hat{p} - E = 0.43 - 0.033 = 0.397$	$\hat{p} + E = 0.43 + 0.033 = 0.463$

$$0.397 < p < 0.463$$

So, with 95% confidence, you can say that the proportion of adults who say football is their favorite sport is between 39.7% and 46.3%.

Try It Yourself 2

Construct a 90% confidence interval for the proportion of adults who say that of all the presidents in our nation's history, they most admire Abraham Lincoln.

a. *Find $\hat{p}$ and $\hat{q}$.*
b. *Find z_c and E.*
c. *Use $\hat{p}$ and E to find the left and right endpoints.*
d. *Specify the 90% confidence interval for the proportion of adults who say Abraham Lincoln over all other American presidents.*

Answer: Page A39 ◀

The confidence level of 95% used in Example 2 is typical of opinion polls. The result, however, is usually not stated as a confidence interval. Instead, the result of Example 2 would usually be stated as "43% with a margin of error of ±3.3%."

> ▶ **EXAMPLE 3**   *Constructing a Confidence Interval for p*

The graph shown at the right is from a survey of 935 adults. Construct a 99% confidence interval for the proportion of adults who think that airplanes are the safest mode of transportation.

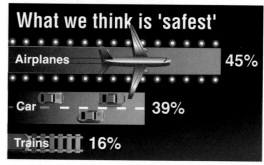

What we think is 'safest'

Airplanes   45%

Car   39%

Trains   16%

Copyright 1997, USA TODAY. Reprinted with permission.

SOLUTION   From the graph, $\hat{p} = 0.45$. So, $\hat{q} = 1 - 0.45 = 0.55$. Using these values and the values $n = 935$ and $z_c = 2.575$, the maximum error of estimate is

$$E = z_c \sqrt{\frac{\hat{p}\hat{q}}{n}} \approx 2.575 \sqrt{\frac{(0.45)(0.55)}{935}} \approx 0.042.$$ Use Table 4 to estimate that z_c is halfway between 2.57 and 2.58.

The 99% confidence interval is as follows.

        Left Endpoint   Right Endpoint

$\hat{p} - E = 0.45 - 0.042 = 0.408$ $\hat{p} + E = 0.45 + 0.042 = 0.492$

$$0.408 < p < 0.492$$

With 99% confidence, you can say that the proportion of adults who think that airplanes are the safest mode of transportation is between 40.8% and 49.2%.

Try It Yourself 3

Use the survey information in Example 3 to construct a 99% confidence interval for the proportion of adults who think that trains are the safest mode of transportation.

a. *Identify* n and $\hat{p}$.
b. *Use* $\hat{p}$ to find $\hat{q}$.
c. *Verify* that the sampling distribution of $\hat{p}$ is approximately normal.
d. *Identify* the critical value, z_c, that corresponds to the given level of confidence.
e. *Find* the left and right endpoints of the confidence interval.
f. *Specify* the 99% confidence interval for the proportion of adults who think that trains are the safest mode of transportation.

Answer: Page A39

Increasing Sample Size to Increase Precision

One way to increase the precision of the confidence interval without decreasing the level of confidence is to increase the sample size.

Finding a Minimum Sample Size to Estimate p

Given a c-confidence level and a maximum error of estimate E, the minimum sample size, n, needed to estimate p is

$$n = \hat{p}\hat{q}\left(\frac{z_c}{E}\right)^2.$$

This formula assumes that you have a preliminary estimate for $\hat{p}$ and $\hat{q}$. If not, use $\hat{p} = 0.5$ and $\hat{q} = 0.5$.

EXAMPLE 4 | Determining a Minimum Sample Size

You are running a political campaign and wish to estimate, with 95% confidence, the proportion of registered voters who will vote for your candidate. What is the minimum sample size needed if you are to be accurate within 3% of the population proportion?

SOLUTION Because you do not have a preliminary estimate for $\hat{p}$, use $\hat{p} = 0.5$ and $\hat{q} = 0.5$. Using $z_c = 1.96$, and $E = 0.03$, you can solve for n.

$$n = \hat{p}\hat{q}\left(\frac{z_c}{E}\right)^2 = (0.5)(0.5)\left(\frac{1.96}{0.03}\right)^2 \approx 1067.11$$

Because n is a decimal, round up to the nearest whole number. So, at least 1068 registered voters should be included in the sample.

Try It Yourself 4

You wish to estimate, with 90% confidence, the proportion of adults age 18 to 29 who have high blood pressure. In a previous survey, 4% of adults in this age group had high blood pressure. What is the minimum sample size needed if you are to be accurate within 5% of the population proportion?

a. *Identify* $\hat{p}$ and $\hat{q}$. If $\hat{p}$ is unknown, use 0.5.
b. *Identify* z_c and E.
c. Use $\hat{p}, \hat{q}, z_c$, and E to *find* the minimum sample size n.
d. *How many* adults should be included in the sample?

Answer: Page A39

6.3 ■ EXERCISES ■

HELP

 StatPro 6.3

 Internet Statistics 6.3

 Student Solutions Manual 6.3

 Videos 6.3

 Try It Yourself Answers 6.3

1. 0.080, 0.920
2. 0.500, 0.500
3. 0.120, 0.880
4. 0.235, 0.765
5. 0.066, 0.934
6. 0.082, 0.918
7. 0.691, 0.309
8. 0.230, 0.770
9. (0.064, 0.096)
   (0.058, 0.102)
10. (0.469, 0.531)
   (0.459, 0.541)
11. (0.117, 0.123)
   (0.115, 0.125)
12. (0.216, 0.254)
   (0.210, 0.260)
13. (0.053, 0.079)
   (0.049, 0.083)
14. (0.065, 0.099)
   (0.060, 0.104)
15. (0.635, 0.747)
   (0.617, 0.765)
16. (0.212, 0.248)
   (0.206, 0.254)
17. (a) 1068
   (b) 822
   (c) Having an estimate of the proportion reduces the minimum samples size needed.

Basic Skills and Concepts

Finding $\hat{p}$ and $\hat{q}$ In Exercises 1–8, let p be the population proportion for the given condition. Find point estimates for p and q.

1. In a survey of 1040 American adults, 83 said they were not confident that the food they eat in the United States is safe. *(Source: Wirthlin Worldwide)*

2. In a survey of 1001 American adults, 501 believed the role of unions in protecting workers' rights is as important today as it was in years past. *(Source: Wirthlin Worldwide)*

3. A study of 34,000 American adults found 4080 had low levels of iodine. *(Adapted from The Centers for Disease Control and Prevention)*

4. A study of 1907 fatal traffic accidents found 449 of the fatalities were alcohol related. *(Adapted from The Centers for Disease Control and Prevention)*

5. Of 1418 high school baseball players, 93 suffered an injury while playing the sport. *(Source: The Pennsylvania Athletic Trainers' Society, Inc.)*

6. Of 1012 high school softball players, 83 suffered an injury while playing the sport. *(Source: The Pennsylvania Athletic Trainers' Society, Inc.)*

7. 181 smokers, in a survey of 262 smokers, considered themselves addicted to cigarettes. *(Source: The Gallup Organization)*

8. 461 adults, in a survey of 2001 adults, would prefer to have a girl if they could only have one child. *(Source: The Gallup Organization)*

Constructing a Confidence Interval In Exercises 9–16, construct the 95% and 99% confidence intervals for the population proportion, p, using the indicated sample statistics. Which interval is wider?

9. Use the statistics in Exercise 1.   **10.** Use the statistics in Exercise 2.

11. Use the statistics in Exercise 3.   **12.** Use the statistics in Exercise 4.

13. Use the statistics in Exercise 5.   **14.** Use the statistics in Exercise 6.

15. Use the statistics in Exercise 7.   **16.** Use the statistics in Exercise 8.

17. *Sample Size* You are a travel agent and wish to estimate, with 95% confidence, the proportion of vacationers who plan to travel outside the United States in the next 12 months. Your estimate must be accurate within 3% of the true proportion.

(a) Find the minimum sample size needed if no preliminary estimate is available.

(b) Find the minimum sample size needed, using a prior study that found that 26% of the respondents said they planned to travel outside the United States in the next 12 months.

(c) Compare the results from (a) and (b). *(Source: Wirthlin Worldwide)*

18. (a) 846
  (b) 305
  (c) Having an estimate of the proportion reduces the minimum sample size needed.

19. (a) 1688
  (b) 1266
  (c) Having an estimate of the proportion reduces the minimum sample size needed.

20. (a) 961
  (b) 592
  (c) Having an estimate of the proportion reduces the minimum sample size needed.

18. *Sample Size* You are a travel agent and wish to estimate, with 98% confidence, the proportion of vacationers who use an online service or the Internet to make reservations for lodging. Your estimate must be accurate within 4% of the population proportion.

(a) If no preliminary estimate is available, find the minimum sample size needed.

(b) Find the minimum sample size needed, using a prior study that found that 10% of the respondents said they used an online service or the Internet to make reservations for lodging.

(c) Compare the results from (a) and (b). *(Source: Wirthlin Worldwide)*

19. *Sample Size* You wish to estimate, with 96% confidence, the proportion of camcorders that need repairs or have problems by the time the product is five years old. Your estimate must be accurate within 2.5% of the true proportion.

(a) If no preliminary estimate is available, find the minimum sample size needed.

(b) Find the minimum sample size needed, using a prior study that found that 25% of camcorders needed repairs or had problems by the time the product was five years old.

(c) Compare the results from (a) and (b). *(Source: Consumer Reports)*

20. *Sample Size* You wish to estimate, with 97% confidence, the proportion of computers that need repairs or have problems by the time the product is five years old. Your estimate must be accurate within 3.5% of the true proportion.

(a) If no preliminary estimate is available, find the minimum sample size needed.

(b) Find the minimum sample size needed, using a prior study that found that 19% of computers needed repairs or had problems by the time the product was five years old.

(c) Compare the results from (a) and (b). *(Source: Consumer Reports)*

Food Irradiation In Exercises 21 and 22, use the following information. The graph shows the results of 500 men, 500 women, 350 people who use microwaves often, and 350 people who rarely use microwaves who were asked if they favored irradiation of red meat to kill disease microbes.

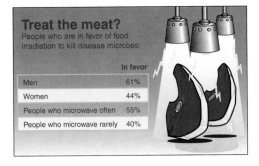

Treat the meat? People who are in favor of food irradiation to kill disease microbes:	In favor
Men	61%
Women	44%
People who microwave often	55%
People who microwave rarely	40%

21. (a) (0.554, 0.666)
(b) (0.383, 0.497)
(c) It is unlikely that the two proportions are equal because the confidence intervals estimating the proportions do not overlap.

22. (a) (0.482, 0.618)
(b) (0.333, 0.467)
(c) It is unlikely that the two proportions are equal because the confidence intervals estimating the proportions do not overlap.

23. (30.4%, 32.4%) is approximately a 95.2% CI.

24. (24%. 30%) is approximately a 96.8% CI.

25. If $n\hat{p} < 5$ or $n\hat{q} < 5$, the sampling distribution of $\hat{p}$ may not be normally distributed; therefore preventing the use of z_c when calculating the confidence interval.

26. $E = z_c\sqrt{\dfrac{\hat{p}\hat{q}}{n}} \Rightarrow \dfrac{E}{z_c} = \sqrt{\dfrac{\hat{p}\hat{q}}{n}} \Rightarrow \left(\dfrac{E}{z_c}\right)^2 = \dfrac{\hat{p}\hat{q}}{n} \Rightarrow n = \hat{p}\hat{q}\left(\dfrac{z_c}{E}\right)^2$

27. See Odd Answers, page A60

21. Construct a 99% confidence interval for (a) the proportion of men who favor irradiation of red meat and (b) the proportion of women who favor irradiation of red meat. Is it possible that these two proportions are equal? Explain your reasoning.

22. Construct a 99% confidence interval for (a) the proportion of frequent microwave users who favor irradiation of red meat and (b) the proportion of infrequent microwave users who favor irradiation of red meat. Is it possible that these two proportions are equal? Explain your reasoning.

Extending the Basics

Newspaper Surveys In Exercises 23 and 24, translate the newspaper excerpt into a confidence interval for p.

23. In a survey of 8451 adults, 31.4% said they were taking Vitamin E as a supplement. The survey's margin of error is plus or minus 1%. (*Source: Decision Analyst, Inc.*)

24. In a survey of 1001 adults, 27% said they had smoked a cigarette in the past week. The survey's margin of error is plus or minus 3%. (*Source: The Gallup Organization*)

25. *Why Check It?* Why is it necessary to check that $n\hat{p} \geq 5$ and $n\hat{q} \geq 5$?

26. *Sample Size* The equation for determining the sample size, $n = \hat{p}\hat{q}[(z_c)/E]^2$, can be obtained by solving the equation for the maximum error of estimate, $E = z_c\sqrt{(\hat{p}\hat{q})/n}$, for n. Show that this is true and justify each step.

27. *Maximum Value of $\hat{p}\hat{q}$* Complete the tables for different values of $\hat{p}$ and $\hat{q} = 1 - \hat{p}$. From the table, which value of $\hat{p}$ appears to give the maximum value of the product $\hat{p}\hat{q}$?

$\hat{p}$	$\hat{q} = 1 - \hat{p}$	$\hat{p}\hat{q}$
0.1	0.9	0.09
0.2	0.8	
0.3		
0.4		
0.5		
0.6		
0.7		
0.8		
0.9		
1.0		

$\hat{p}$	$\hat{q} = 1 - \hat{p}$	$\hat{p}\hat{q}$
0.45		
0.46		
0.47		
0.48		
0.49		
0.50		
0.51		
0.52		
0.53		
0.54		
0.55		

TECHNOLOGY MINITAB EXCEL TI-83

THE GALLUP ORGANIZATION
PRINCETON

WWW.GALLUP.COM

Most Admired Polls

From 1946 to 1997 the Gallup Organization has conducted a "most admired" poll. The methodology for the 1997 poll is described at the right.

> **Survey Question**
> What man* that you have heard or read about, living today in any part of the world, do you admire most?

*Survey respondents are asked an identical question about most admired woman.

"The results are based on telephone interviews with a randomly selected national sample of 1005 adults, 18 and over, conducted December 18–21, 1997. For results based on samples of this size, one can say with 95 percent confidence that the error attributable to sampling and other random effects could be plus or minus 3 percentage points. In addition to sampling error, question wording and practical difficulties in conducting surveys can introduce error or bias into the findings of public opinion polls."

Exercises

1. In 1997, 141 people named President Clinton as their most admired man. Use a technology tool to find a 95% confidence interval for the proportion that would have chosen President Clinton.

2. Does the confidence interval you obtained in Exercise 1 agree with the statement issued by the Gallup Organization that the proportion is 14% plus or minus 3%? Explain.

3. The most named woman was Hillary Clinton. The second named woman was Oprah Winfrey, who was named by 6% of the people in the sample. Use a technology tool to find a 95% confidence interval for the proportion of the population that would have chosen Oprah Winfrey.

4. Use a technology tool to simulate a most admired poll. Assume that the actual population proportion who most admire Oprah Winfrey is 7%. Run the simulation several times using $n = 1005$.

(a) What was the least value you obtained for $\hat{p}$?

(b) What was the greatest value you obtained for $\hat{p}$?

> **MINITAB**
>
> Generate 200 rows of data
>
> Store in column(s): C1
>
> Number of trials: 1005
> Probability of success: .07

5. The Gallup Organization said that the 1997 results were a rarity because in the poll's 52-year history, it was unusual that no one (other than the president and first lady) received more than 6% of the vote. Is it possible, however, that the actual proportion of the population that most admired Oprah Winfrey was 7% or greater? Explain your reasoning.

Extended solutions are given in the *Technology Supplement.*
Technical instruction is provided for Minitab, Excel, and the TI-83.

What You Should Learn

- *How to interpret the chi-square distribution and use a chi-square distribution table*
- *How to use the chi-square distribution to construct a confidence interval for the variance and standard deviation*

Study Tip

The Greek letter χ is pronounced "kì," which rhymes with the more familiar Greek letter π.

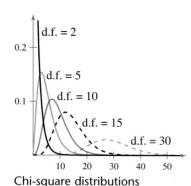

Chi-square distributions

Note to Instructor

If you are short of time, this section can be omitted. Or, if you prefer, it can be covered with Chapter 10 when additional chi-square applications are presented.

The Chi-Square Distribution

In many manufacturing processes, it is necessary to control the amount that the process varies. For instance, an automobile part manufacturer must produce thousands of parts that can be used in the manufacturing process. It is important that the parts vary little or not at all. How can you measure, and consequently control, the amount of variation in the car parts? You can start with a point estimate.

DEFINITION

The **point estimate for σ^2** is s^2 and the **point estimate for σ** is s. s^2 is the most unbiased estimate for σ^2.

You can use a *chi-square distribution* to construct a confidence interval for the variance and standard deviation.

DEFINITION

If the random variable x has a normal distribution, then the distribution of

$$\chi^2 = \frac{(n-1)s^2}{\sigma^2}$$

forms a **chi-square distribution** for samples of any size $n > 1$. Several properties of the chi-square distribution are as follows.

1. All chi-square values, χ^2, are greater than or equal to zero.
2. The chi-square distribution is a family of curves, each determined by the degrees of freedom. To form a confidence interval for σ^2, use the χ^2-distribution with degrees of freedom equal to one less than the sample size.

    d.f. $= n - 1$ Degrees of Freedom

3. The area under each curve of the chi-square distribution is equal to one.
4. Chi-square distributions are positively skewed.

Study Tip

For chi-square critical values with a c confidence level, the following values are what you look up in Table 6 in Appendix B.

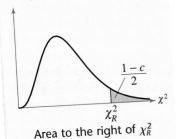

Area to the right of χ_R^2

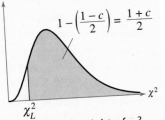

Area to the right of χ_L^2

The result is that you can conclude that the area between the left and right critical values is c.

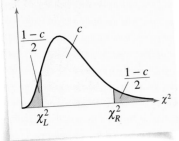

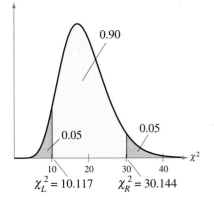

$\chi_L^2 = 10.117$ $\chi_R^2 = 30.144$

There are two critical values for each level of confidence. The value χ_R^2 represents the right-tail critical value and χ_L^2 represents the left-tail critical value. Table 6 in Appendix B lists critical values of χ^2 for various degrees of freedom and areas. Each area in the table represents the region under the chi-square curve to the *right* of the critical value.

> **EXAMPLE 1** *Finding Critical Values for* χ^2

Find the critical values, χ_R^2 and χ_L^2, for a 90% confidence interval when the sample size is 20.

SOLUTION   Because the sample size is 20, there are d.f. $= n - 1 = 20 - 1 = 19$ degrees of freedom. The areas to the right of χ_R^2 and χ_L^2 are

$$\text{Area to right of } \chi_R^2 = \frac{1 - c}{2} = \frac{1 - 0.90}{2} = 0.05$$

and

$$\text{Area to right of } \chi_L^2 = \frac{1 + c}{2} = \frac{1 + 0.90}{2} = 0.95.$$

Part of Table 6 is shown. Using d.f. $= 19$ and the areas 0.95 and 0.05, you can find the critical values, as shown by the highlighted areas in the table.

Degrees of freedom	α						
	0.995	0.99	0.975	0.95	0.90	0.10	0.05
1	—	—	0.001	0.004	0.016	2.706	3.841
2	0.010	0.020	0.051	0.103	0.211	4.605	5.991
3	0.072	0.115	0.216	0.352	0.584	6.251	7.815
15	4.601	5.229	6.262	7.261	8.547	22.307	24.996
16	5.142	5.812	6.908	7.962	9.312	23.542	26.296
17	5.697	6.408	7.564	8.672	10.085	24.769	27.587
18	6.265	7.015	8.231	9.390	10.865	25.989	28.869
19	6.844	7.633	8.907	10.117	11.651	27.204	30.144
20	7.434	8.260	9.591	10.851	12.443	28.412	31.410

χ_L^2 χ_R^2

From the table, you can see that $\chi_R^2 = 30.144$ and $\chi_L^2 = 10.117$. So, 90% of the area under the curve lies between 10.117 and 30.144.

> ## Try It Yourself 1
>
> Find the critical values, χ_R^2 and χ_L^2, for a 95% confidence interval when the sample size is 25.
>
> **a.** *Identify* the degrees of freedom and the level of confidence.
> **b.** *Find* the area to the right of χ_R^2 and χ_L^2.
> **c.** *Use* Table 6 of Appendix B to find χ_R^2 and χ_L^2.   *Answer: Page A39*

Confidence Intervals

You can use the critical values χ_R^2 and χ_L^2 to construct confidence intervals for a population variance and standard deviation. As you would expect, the best point estimate for the variance is s^2 and the best point estimate for the standard deviation is s.

DEFINITION

A c-confidence interval for a population variance and standard deviation is as follows.

$$\frac{(n-1)s^2}{\chi_R^2} < \sigma^2 < \frac{(n-1)s^2}{\chi_L^2}$$
Confidence Interval for σ^2

$$\sqrt{\frac{(n-1)s^2}{\chi_R^2}} < \sigma < \sqrt{\frac{(n-1)s^2}{\chi_L^2}}$$
Confidence Interval for σ

The probability that the confidence intervals contain σ^2 or σ is c.

GUIDELINES

Constructing a Confidence Interval for a Variance and Standard Deviation

In Words	*In Symbols*
1. Verify that the population has a normal distribution.	
2. Identify the sample statistic n and the degrees of freedom.	d.f. $= n - 1$
3. Find the point estimate, s^2.	$s^2 = \dfrac{\Sigma(x - \bar{x})^2}{n - 1}$
4. Find the critical values, χ_R^2 and χ_L^2, that correspond to the given level of confidence c.	Use Table 6 in Appendix B.

	Left Endpoint	Right Endpoint
5. Find the left and right endpoints and form the confidence interval for the population variance.	$\dfrac{(n-1)s^2}{\chi_R^2} < \sigma^2 <$	$\dfrac{(n-1)s^2}{\chi_L^2}$

6. Find the confidence interval for the population standard deviation by taking the square root of each endpoint.

$$\sqrt{\frac{(n-1)s^2}{\chi_R^2}} < \sigma < \sqrt{\frac{(n-1)s^2}{\chi_L^2}}$$

> **EXAMPLE 2** **Constructing a Confidence Interval**

You randomly select and weigh 30 samples of an allergy medicine. The sample standard deviation is 1.2 milligrams. Assuming the weights are normally distributed, construct 99% confidence intervals for the population variance and standard deviation.

SOLUTION   The areas to the right of χ_R^2 and χ_L^2 are

$$\text{Area to right of } \chi_R^2 = \frac{1 - c}{2} = \frac{1 - 0.99}{2} = 0.005$$

and

$$\text{Area to right of } \chi_L^2 = \frac{1 + c}{2} = \frac{1 + 0.99}{2} = 0.995.$$

Using the values $n = 30$, d.f. $= 29$, and $c = 0.99$, the critical values, χ_R^2 and χ_L^2, are

$$\chi_R^2 = 52.366 \qquad \text{and} \qquad \chi_L^2 = 13.121.$$

Using these critical values and $s = 1.2$, the confidence interval for σ^2 is as follows.

Note to Instructor

Point out that the left endpoint requires using χ_R^2 and the right endpoint requires using χ_L^2. This is true because $\chi_R^2 > \chi_L^2$ and dividing the same numerator by a larger value will produce a smaller quotient.

Left Endpoint	Right Endpoint
$\dfrac{(n - 1)s^2}{\chi_R^2} = \dfrac{(30 - 1)(1.2)^2}{52.336} \approx 0.798$	$\dfrac{(n - 1)s^2}{\chi_L^2} = \dfrac{(30 - 1)(1.2)^2}{13.121} \approx 3.183$

$$0.798 < \sigma^2 < 3.183$$

The confidence interval for σ is

$$\sqrt{0.798} < \sigma < \sqrt{3.183}$$
$$0.89 < \sigma < 1.78.$$

So, with 99% confidence, you can say that the population variance is between 0.798 and 3.183. The population standard deviation is between 0.89 and 1.78 milligrams.

Try It Yourself 2

Find the 90% and 95% confidence intervals for the population variance and standard deviation of the medicine weights.

a. *Find* the critical values, χ_R^2 and χ_L^2, for each confidence interval.
b. *Use* n, s, χ_R^2, and χ_L^2 to find the left and right endpoints of the confidence for the variance.
c. *Find* the square roots of the endpoints.
d. *Specify* the 90% and 95% confidence intervals for the population variance and standard deviation. *Answer: Page A39*

▼6.4 ▬ EXERCISES ▬

▶ HELP

 StatPro 6.4

 Internet Statistics 6.4

 Student Solutions Manual 6.4

 Videos 6.4

 Try It Yourself Answers 6.4

1. 16.919, 3.325

2. 28.299, 3.074

3. 35.479, 10.283

4. 44.314, 11.524

5. 52.336, 13.121

6. 37.916, 18.939

7. (a) (0.0000413, 0.000157)

   (b) (0.00643, 0.0125)

8. (a) (0.000609, 0.00220)

   (b) (0.0247, 0.0469)

9. (a) (0.0305, 0.191)

   (b) (0.175, 0.437)

10. (a) (0.00467, 0.0195)

   (b) (0.0683, 0.140)

Basic Skills and Concepts

Finding Critical Values for χ^2   In Exercises 1–6, find the critical values, χ_R^2 and χ_L^2, for the given confidence c and sample size n.

1. $c = 0.90$, $n = 10$ **2.** $c = 0.99$, $n = 13$

3. $c = 0.95$, $n = 22$ **4.** $c = 0.98$, $n = 26$

5. $c = 0.99$, $n = 30$ **6.** $c = 0.80$, $n = 29$

Constructing Confidence Intervals   In Exercises 7–16, construct the indicated confidence intervals for (a) the population variance, σ^2, and (b) the population standard deviation, σ. Assume each sample is taken from a normally distributed population.

7. To analyze the variation of vitamin supplement tablets, you randomly select and weigh 14 tablets. The results (in milligrams) are shown. Use a 90% level of confidence.

500.000	499.995	500.010	499.997	500.015	499.988	500.000
499.996	500.020	500.002	499.998	499.996	500.003	500.000

8. You randomly select and measure the contents of 15 bottles of cough syrup. The results (in fluid ounces) are shown. Use a 90% level of confidence.

4.211	4.246	4.269	4.241	4.260	4.293	4.189	4.248
4.220	4.239	4.253	4.209	4.300	4.256	4.290	

9. The number of hours of reserve capacity of 18 randomly selected automotive batteries is shown. Use a 99% level of confidence. *(Adapted from Consumer Reports)*

1.70	1.60	1.94	1.58	1.74	1.60	1.86	1.72	1.38
1.46	1.64	1.49	1.55	1.70	1.75	0.88	1.77	2.07

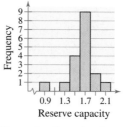

Figure for Exercise 9

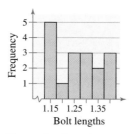

Figure for Exercise 10

10. You randomly select and measure 17 bolts. The results (in inches) are shown. Use a 95% level of confidence.

1.286	1.138	1.240	1.132	1.381	1.137	1.300	1.167	1.240
1.401	1.241	1.171	1.217	1.360	1.302	1.331	1.383	

11. (a) (4.342, 44.636)
   (b) (2.084, 6.681)

12. (a) (13839, 42873.476)
   (b) (117.639, 207.059)

13. (a) (359.596, 1829.774)
   (b) (18.963, 42.776)

14. (a) (128.465, 492.042)
   (b) (11.334, 22.182)

15. (a) (6621.545, 24422.477)
   (b) (81.373, 156.277)

16. (a) (20.547, 150.849)
   (b) (4.533, 12.282)

17. Yes

18. No

11. A lawn mower manufacturer is trying to determine the standard deviation of the mean life of one of its lawn mower models. To do this, it randomly selects 12 lawn mowers that were sold several years ago and finds that the sample standard deviation is 3.25 years. Use a 99% level of confidence. *(Adapted from Consumer Reports)*

12. A magazine includes a report on the prices of CD players. The article states that 26 randomly selected CD players had a standard deviation of $150. Use a 95% level of confidence. *(Source: Consumer Reports)*

13. As part of your vacation planning, you randomly contact 10 hotels in your destination area and record the room rate of each. The results are shown in the stem-and-leaf plot. Use $c = 0.90$. *(Adapted from Smith Travel Research)*

```
 6 | 0 3      Key: 8|3 = 83
 7 |
 8 | 3
 9 | 0
10 | 2 8
11 | 3 8
12 | 2
13 |
14 | 1
```
Data for Exercise 13

Water quality survey

$n = 19$
$s = 15$ grains/gallon

Sample statistics for Exercise 14

14. As part of a water quality survey, you test the water hardness in several randomly selected streams. The results are shown above. Use $c = 0.95$.

15. The monthly incomes of 20 randomly selected individuals who have recently graduated with a bachelor's degree in social science have a sample standard deviation of $107. Use a 95% level of confidence. *(Adapted from U.S. Bureau of the Census)*

16. The sodium chloride concentrations of 13 randomly selected seawater samples have a standard deviation of 6.7 cc/cubic meter. Use a 98% level of confidence. *(Adapted from Dorling Kindersley Visual Encyclopedia)*

Extending the Basics

17. *Is It Acceptable?* You are analyzing the sample of vitamin supplement tablets in Exercise 7. The population standard deviation of the tablet's weights should be less than 0.015 milligram. Does the confidence interval you constructed for σ suggest that the variation in the tablet's weights is at an acceptable level? Explain your reasoning.

18. *Is It Acceptable?* You are analyzing the sample of cough syrup bottles in Exercise 8. The population standard deviation of the bottle's contents should be less than 0.025 fluid ounce. Does the confidence interval you constructed for σ suggest that the variation in the bottle's contents is at an acceptable level? Explain your reasoning.

6 USING TECHNOLOGY TO CONSTRUCT CONFIDENCE INTERVALS

Here are some *Minitab* and *TI-83* printouts for three examples in this chapter. To duplicate the Minitab results, you need the original data. For the TI-83, you can simply enter the descriptive statistics. Answers may be slightly different due to rounding.

(See Example 3, page 255)

Display Descriptive Statistics...
Store Descriptive Statistics...

1-Sample Z...
1-Sample t...
2-Sample t...
Paired t...

1 Proportion...
2 Proportions...

Correlation...
Covariance...

Normality Test...

9	20	18	16	9	16	16	9	11	13	22	16	5	18	6	6	5	12
25	17	23	7	10	9	10	10	5	11	18	18	9	9	17	13	11	7
14	6	11	12	11	15	6	12	14	11	4	9	18	12	12	17	11	20

MINITAB

Z Confidence Intervals

The assumed sigma = 5.00

Variable	N	Mean	StDev	SE Mean	95.0 % CI
C1	54	12.426	5.015	0.680	(11.092, 13.760)

(See Example 2, page 268)

Display Descriptive Statistics...
Store Descriptive Statistics...

1-Sample Z...
1-Sample t...
2-Sample t...
Paired t...

1 Proportion...
2 Proportions...

| 159°F | 173°F | 162°F | 151°F | 173°F | 162°F | 148°F | 172°F |
| 167°F | 170°F | 151°F | 153°F | 172°F | 143°F | 166°F | 170°F |

MINITAB

T Confidence Intervals

Variable	N	Mean	StDev	SE Mean	95.0 % CI
C3	16	162.00	10.00	2.50	(156.67, 167.33)

(See Example 2, page 277)

Display Descriptive Statistics...
Store Descriptive Statistics...

1-Sample Z...
1-Sample t...
2-Sample t...
Paired t...

1 Proportion...
2 Proportions...

MINITAB

Test and Confidence Interval for One Proportion

Test of p = 0.43 vs p not = 0.43

Sample	X	N	Sample p	95.0 % CI	Z-Value	P-Value
1	380	883	0.430351	(0.397694, 0.463009)	0.02	0.983

(See Example 5, page 257) (See Example 3, page 269) (See Example 2, page 277)

TI-83

EDIT CALC **TESTS**
1: Z–Test...
2: T–Test...
3: 2–SampZTest...
4: 2–SampTTest...
5: 1–PropZTest...
6: 2–PropZTest...
7↓ ZInterval...

TI-83

EDIT CALC **TESTS**
2↑ T–Test...
3: 2–SampZTest...
4: 2–SampTTest...
5: 1–PropZTest...
6: 2–PropZTest...
7: ZInterval...
8↓ TInterval...

TI-83

EDIT CALC **TESTS**
5↑ 1–PropZTest...
6: 2–PropZTest...
7: ZInterval...
8: TInterval...
9: 2–SampZInt...
0: 2–SampTInt...
9↓ 1–PropZInt...

TI-83

ZInterval
 Inpt: Data **Stats**
 σ: 1.5
 $\bar{x}$: 22.9
 n: 20
 C–Level: .9
 Calculate

TI-83

TInterval
 Inpt: Data **Stats**
 $\bar{x}$: 6.93
 Sx: .42
 n: 20
 C–Level: .99
 Calculate

TI-83

1–PropZInt
 x: 380
 n: 883
 C–Level: .95
 Calculate

TI-83

ZInterval
 (22.348, 23.452)
 $\bar{x}$= 22.9
 n= 20

TI-83

TInterval
 (6.6613, 7.1987)
 $\bar{x}$= 6.93
 Sx= .42
 n= 20

TI-83

1–PropZInt
 (.39769, .46301)
 $\hat{p}$= .4303510759
 n= 883

▼ 6 **CHAPTER SUMMARY**

What did you learn?

Why did you learn it? Uses and Abuses

Uses Complete information is often unavailable for determining the value of a population parameter such as μ, p, σ^2, or σ. The techniques of estimation you learned in this chapter will help you make accurate estimates of these parameters so that you can make informed decisions.

From what you learned in this chapter, you know that point estimates of population parameters are rarely exact. Remembering this can help you make good decisions in your career, as a consumer, and as a citizen. Here is an example. Suppose the results of a survey tell you that 52% of the population plan to vote for a certain item on a ballot. You now know that this is only a point estimate of the actual proportion that will vote for the item. The interval estimate could be something like $0.49 < p < 0.55$, which means that it is possible that the item will not receive a majority vote.

Abuses When you read the results of a survey, be sure you understand the terminology that is used. For instance, consider the statement *"Unemployment Rate Drops for 3rd Consecutive Month."* One might think that this implies that more people are working and fewer are unemployed. This might not be true, however. As defined by the Bureau of Labor and Statistics, a person is only "unemployed" if he or she is not working *and* has made specific efforts to find work during the previous 4 weeks. People who quit seeking work are not counted as unemployed.

▼6 REVIEW EXERCISES

1. **(a)** 103.5
   (b) 9.016
2. **(a)** 9.469
   (b) 2.064
3. (10.246, 10.354)
4. (0.0922, 0.0928)
5. 47
6. 1992
7. 1.415
8. 1.323

In Exercises 1 and 2, find (a) the point estimate of the population mean and (b) the maximum error of estimate for a 90% confidence interval.

1. Waking times of 40 people who start work at 8:00 A.M. (in minutes past 5:00 A.M.)

135	145	95	140	135	95	110	50	90	165	110	125
80	125	130	110	25	75	65	100	60	125	115	135
95	90	140	40	75	50	130	85	100	160	135	45
135	115	75	130								

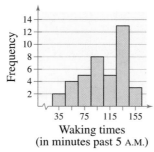

Waking times
(in minutes past 5 A.M.)

Figure for Exercise 1

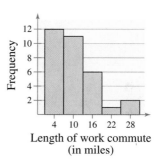

Length of work commute
(in miles)

Figure for Exercise 2

2. Length of work commute of 32 people (in miles)

| 12 | 9 | 7 | 2 | 8 | 7 | 3 | 27 | 21 | 10 | 13 | 3 | 7 | 2 | 30 | 7 |
| 6 | 13 | 6 | 14 | 4 | 1 | 10 | 3 | 13 | 6 | 2 | 9 | 2 | 12 | 16 | 18 |

In Exercises 3 and 4, construct the indicated confidence interval for the population mean, μ.

3. $c = 0.95, \bar{x} = 10.3, s = 0.277,$
   $n = 100$

4. $c = 0.90, \bar{x} = 0.0925,$
   $s = 0.0013, n = 45$

In Exercises 5 and 6, determine the minimum sufficient sample size.

5. Use the point estimate for σ from Exercise 1. Determine the minimum survey size that is necessary to be 95% confident that the sample mean waking time is within 10 minutes of the actual mean waking time.

6. Now, suppose you want 99% confidence with a maximum error of 2 minutes. How many people would it be necessary to survey?

In Exercises 7 and 8, find the critical value, t_c, for the given confidence level c and sample size n.

7. $c = 0.80, n = 8$

8. $c = 0.80, n = 22$

In Exercises 9 and 10, find the maximum error of estimate for μ.

9. $c = 0.90$, $s = 23.4$, $n = 16$, $\bar{x} = 52.8$

10. $c = 0.95$, $s = 0.05$, $n = 25$, $\bar{x} = 3.5$

11. Construct the confidence interval for μ using the statistics in Exercise 9.

12. Construct the confidence interval for μ using the statistics in Exercise 10.

13. In a random sample of 15 CD players brought in for repair, the average repair cost was \$80 and the standard deviation was \$14. Construct a 90% confidence interval for μ. Assume the repair costs are normally distributed. *(Adapted from Consumer Reports)*

14. Repeat Exercise 13 using a 99% confidence interval.

In Exercises 15–18, let p be the proportion of the population who respond yes. Use the given information to find $\hat{p}$ and $\hat{q}$.

15. In a survey of 850 college students, 357 balanced their checkbooks monthly. *(Adapted from Bruskin Goldring)*

16. In a survey of 900 American adults, 81 felt that alcoholism was a reasonable excuse for criminal conduct. *(Adapted from Fox News/Opinion Dynamics)*

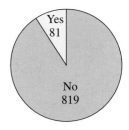

17. In a survey of 209 Montana residents, 61 felt their financial status was worse than a year ago. *(Source: StatLib/Bureau of Business and Economic Research, U. of Montana)*

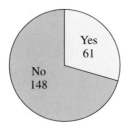

18. In a survey of 1400 American adults, 546 had seen information comparing the quality of health plans, doctors, or hospitals. *(Adapted from Deloitte & Touche)*

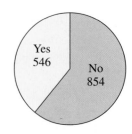

19. (0.387, 0.453)

20. (0.065, 0.115)

21. (0.240, 0.344)

22. (0.360, 0.420)

23. 273

24. 1879

25. 23.377, 4.404

26. 42.980, 10.856

27. 14.067, 2.167

28. 23.589, 1.735

29. (0.003, 0.013)
(0.055, 0.114)

30. (0.002, 0.017)
(0.045, 0.130)

In Exercises 19–22, construct the indicated confidence interval for the population proportion p.

19. Use the sample in Exercise 15 with $c = 0.95$.

20. Use the sample in Exercise 16 with $c = 0.99$.

21. Use the sample in Exercise 17 with $c = 0.90$.

22. Use the sample in Exercise 18 with $c = 0.98$.

23. A study of Pennsylvania high school wrestlers found that 23% had sustained an injury while wrestling that year. Suppose you want to conduct a similar study on New York high school wrestlers, and you wish to estimate (with 95% confidence) the proportion of injured wrestlers within 5%. Use the prior study's proportion to find the minimum required sample size. *(Source: The Pennsylvania Athletic Trainers' Society, Inc.)*

24. Repeat Exercise 23, using a 99% confidence level and a maximum error of estimate of 2.5%. How does this sample size compare to your answer from Exercise 23?

In Exercises 25–28, find the critical values, χ_R^2 and χ_L^2, needed to estimate σ^2 for the given confidence level c and sample size n.

25. $c = 0.95, n = 13$

26. $c = 0.98, n = 25$

27. $c = 0.90, n = 8$

28. $c = 0.99, n = 10$

In Exercises 29 and 30, construct the indicated confidence intervals for σ^2 and σ. Assume the samples are each taken from a normally distributed population.

29. A random sample of the liquid content (in fluid ounces) of 16 beverage cans is shown. Use a 95% level of confidence.

| 14.816 | 14.863 | 14.814 | 14.998 | 14.965 | 14.824 | 14.884 | 14.838 |
| 14.916 | 15.021 | 14.874 | 14.856 | 14.860 | 14.772 | 14.980 | 14.919 |

30. Repeat Exercise 29 using a 99% level of confidence.

▼
6 ▼   **CHAPTER QUIZ**

1. (a) 100.057
   (b) 11.101
   (c) (88.956, 111.158)
2. 34
3. (a) 6.610
   (b) 3.376
   (c) (4.653, 8.567)
   (d) (4.789, 8.431)
4. (3231.737, 4178.263)
5. (a) 0.660
   (b) (0.643, 0.677)
   (c) 930
6. (a) (417.374, 1359.563)
   (b) (20.430, 36.872)

Take this quiz as you would take a quiz in class. After you are done, check your work against the answers given in the back of the book.

1. The following data set represents the repair costs (in dollars) for a random sample of 24 dishwashers. *(Adapted from Consumer Reports)*

41.82	52.81	68.16	73.48	78.88	88.13	88.79	90.07
90.35	91.72	95.34	96.50	101.32	103.59	105.62	111.32
117.14	118.42	118.77	119.01	120.70	140.52	141.84	147.06

(a) Find the point estimate of the population mean.

(b) Find the maximum error of estimate for a 95% level of confidence.

(c) Construct a 95% confidence interval for the population mean and interpret the results.

2. You want to estimate the mean repair cost for dishwashers. The estimate must be within $10 of the population mean. Determine the required sample size to construct a 99% confidence interval for the population mean. Assume the population standard deviation is $22.50. *(Adapted from Consumer Reports)*

3. The following data set represents the time (in minutes) for a random sample of phone calls made by employees at a company.

7.5   2.0   12.1   8.8   9.4   7.3   1.9   2.8   7.0   7.3

(a) Find the sample mean.

(b) Find the sample standard deviation.

(c) Use the t-distribution to construct a 90% confidence interval for the population mean and interpret the results. Assume the population of the data set is normally distributed.

(d) Repeat part (c), assuming $\sigma = 3.5$ minutes. Compare the results.

4. In a random sample of eight people with advanced degrees in biology, the mean monthly income was $3705 and the standard deviation was $566. Assume the monthly incomes are normally distributed and use a t-distribution to construct a 95% confidence interval for the population mean monthly income for people with advanced degrees in biology. *(Adapted from U.S. Bureau of the Census)*

5. In a survey of 2000 American adults age 65 and over, 1320 received a flu shot. *(Source: The Centers for Disease Control and Prevention)*

(a) Find a point estimate for the population proportion p of those receiving flu shots.

(b) Construct a 90% confidence interval for the population proportion.

(c) Find the minimum sample size needed to estimate the population proportion at the 99% confidence level in order to ensure that the estimate is accurate within 4% of the population proportion.

6. Refer to the data set in Question 1.

(a) Construct a 95% confidence interval for the population variance.

(b) Construct a 95% confidence interval for the population standard deviation.

CUMULATIVE TEST

1. 0.770
(0.732, 0.808)

2. 2936

3. 0.455

4. 364.980
83.945
9.162

You would expect 364.98 women to say that the media have a negative effect on women's health. The standard deviation is 9.162.

5. Use normal distribution
364.980
9.162

6. (25.336, 25.864)

7. Normal distribution was used since $n \geq 30$ and σ was unknown.

8. 0.05548
≈ 0

You are more likely to select one woman with a BMI less than 20.

9. (a) (6.495, 18.506)
(b) (2.549, 4.302)

Take this test as you would take a test in class. After you are done, check your work against the answers given in the back of the book.

Refer to the following information as you take this test. In a survey of 474 American women, 365 said that the media have a negative effect on women's health because they set unattainable standards for appearance. *(Source: Shape Up America!)*

1. Find a point estimate for p. Construct a 95% confidence interval for the population proportion, p.

2. Find the minimum sample size needed to estimate the population proportion, p, with 99% confidence. The estimate must be accurate within 2% of p.

3. You randomly select 12 women. Use $\hat{p}$ from Question 1 to find the probability that at least 10 women will agree that the media have a negative effect on women's health because they set unattainable standards for appearance.

4. Use $\hat{p}$ from Question 1 to find the mean, variance, and standard deviation of the binomial distribution and interpret the results.

5. Decide whether you can use the normal distribution to approximate this binomial distribution. If so, find the mean and standard deviation and compare the results to Question 4. If not, explain why.

6. A mathematical way to measure a person's body fat is to use the body mass index (BMI). A person's BMI can be found by dividing weight (in kilograms) by the square of the height (in meters). Assume the 474 women in the survey had a mean BMI of 25.6 and a standard deviation of 3.5. Construct a 90% confidence interval for the mean BMI for all American women.

7. Which distribution did you use to construct the confidence interval in Question 6? Why?

8. Assume that women's BMIs are normally distributed. Are you more likely to randomly select one woman with a BMI less than 20 or are you more likely to select a sample of 15 women with a mean BMI less than 20? Explain.

9. You randomly select and record the BMIs of 30 women. The sample standard deviation is 3.2. Using a 95% level of confidence, construct the confidence intervals for (a) the population variance, σ^2, and (b) the population standard deviation, σ. Assume the sample is taken from a normally distributed population.

Where You've Been

In Chapter 6, you began your study of inferential statistics. There, you learned how to form a confidence interval estimate about a population parameter, such as the proportion of Americans who agree with a certain statement. For instance, in a poll taken for *USA Today*, Americans aged 18 and older were asked several questions about extraterrestrial life. Here are some of the results.

Survey Question	Number Surveyed	Number Who Said Yes
Do you believe UFOs really exist?	614	229
Have you ever seen a UFO?	229	28
Do extraterrestrial beings exist?	614	237
Have you ever seen one?	180	9

Fire in the Sky is Travis Walton's account of alien-UFO abduction that he claims to have happened on November 5, 1975.

UFO sightings have been reported throughout the world, but some of the more famous ones were reported in the southwestern United States. Travis Walton reported his encounter to have taken place in northeastern Arizona, and the famous Roswell encounter was reported to have occurred in Roswell, New Mexico.

Hypothesis Testing with One Sample

Where You're Going

In this chapter, you will continue your study of inferential statistics. But now, instead of making an estimate about a population parameter, you will learn how to test a claim about a parameter.

For instance, suppose that you work for *USA Today* and are asked to test a claim that the proportion of American adults who believe UFOs really exist is $p = 0.30$. To test the claim, you take a random sample of $n = 614$ American adults and find that 229 of them believe that UFOs really exist. Your sample statistic is $\hat{p} = \frac{229}{614} \approx 0.373$.

Is your sample statistic different enough from the claim ($p = 0.30$) to decide that the claim is false? The answer lies in the sampling distribution of sample proportions taken from a population in which $p = 0.30$. The graph below shows that your sample statistic is almost 4 standard errors from the claim value. If the claim is true, this is extremely unlikely. Something is wrong! If your sample was truly random, then you can conclude that the actual proportion of the population is not 0.30. In other words, you tested the original claim (hypothesis) and you decided to reject it.

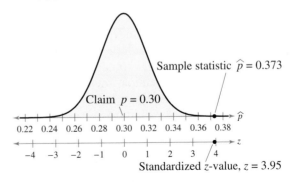

Sample statistic $\hat{p} = 0.373$

Claim $p = 0.30$

Standardized z-value, $z = 3.95$

Sampling Distribution

This scene was added to *Close Encounters of the Third Kind* after the original Spielberg film was released.

Hypothesis Tests • Stating a Hypothesis • Types of Errors and Level of Significance • Statistical Tests and Rejection Regions • Making a Decision and Interpreting the Decision • Strategies for Hypothesis Testing

What You Should Learn

- A practical introduction to hypothesis tests
- How to state a null hypothesis and an alternative hypothesis
- How to identify type I and type II errors and interpret the level of significance
- How to know whether to use a one-tailed or two-tailed statistical test
- How to make a decision based on the results of a statistical test
- How to write a claim for a hypothesis test

Insight

As you study this chapter, don't get confused regarding concepts of certainty and importance. For instance, even if you were very certain that the mean life of a type of AA battery is not 300 minutes, the actual mean life might be very close to this value and the difference might not be important.

Note to Instructor

Because hypothesis testing is a difficult topic for students, we are beginning Chapter 7 with an overview of the terminology and goal of hypothesis testing. Actual testing is described in detail in Sections 7.2 through 7.5.

Hypothesis Tests

Throughout the remainder of this course, you will study an important technique in inferential statistics called hypothesis testing. A **hypothesis test** is a process that uses sample statistics to test a claim about the value of a population parameter. Researchers in fields ranging from medicine to politics rely on hypothesis testing to make informed decisions about new medicines and the outcome of elections.

For instance, suppose a battery manufacturer claims that the mean life of its AA batteries is 300 minutes. If you suspect that this claim is not valid, how could you show that the claim is wrong?

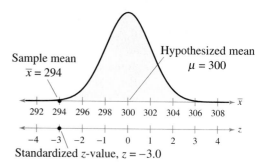

The average life of our new Ultra AA battery is 300 minutes.

Obviously, you can't test all the batteries. But you can still make a reasonable decision about the validity of the claim by taking a random sample from the population. If the sample mean differs enough from the claim, you can decide that the claim is wrong.

For example, to test the battery manufacturer's claim that the mean life of all batteries of this type is $\mu = 300$ minutes, you could take a random sample of $n = 100$ batteries and measure the life of each. Suppose you obtain a sample mean of $\bar{x} = 294$ minutes with a sample standard deviation of $s = 20$ minutes. Does this indicate that the manufacturer's claim is wrong?

To decide, you do something unusual—*you assume the claim is correct!* Then, you examine the sampling distribution of sample means (with $n = 100$) taken from a population in which $\mu = 300$ and $\sigma = 20$. From the Central Limit Theorem, you know this sampling distribution is normal with a mean of 300 and standard error of $20/\sqrt{100} = 2$. In the following graph, notice that your sample mean of $\bar{x} = 294$ minutes is highly unlikely—it is 3 standard errors from the claimed mean! Your assumption that the manufacturer's claim is correct has led you to an improbable result. So, either you had a very unusual sample, or the claim is false. The logical conclusion is that the claim is probably false.

Sampling Distribution

Sample mean $\bar{x} = 294$

Hypothesized mean $\mu = 300$

292 294 296 298 300 302 304 306 308 $\bar{x}$

−4 −3 −2 −1 0 1 2 3 4 z

Standardized z-value, $z = -3.0$

Note to Instructor

Some texts use H_1 to denote the alternative hypothesis. We use H_a because we think it is more intuitive.

Insight

The term "null hypothesis" was introduced by Ronald Fisher (see page 274). If the statement in the null hypothesis is not true, then the alternative hypothesis must be true.

Picturing the World

In a study performed at the Cleveland Clinic, a sample of 50 randomly chosen adults who developed symptoms of the common cold were given five zinc gluconate throat lozenges. The sample mean duration of nasal congestion was four days. So, the researchers claimed that the mean duration of nasal congestion of all adults who take zinc lozenges after developing cold symptoms is four days. (*Source: Annals of Internal Medicine*)

Determine a null hypothesis and alternative hypothesis for this claim.

Stating a Hypothesis

A claim about a population parameter is called a **statistical hypothesis.** To test a statistical hypothesis, you should carefully state a pair of hypotheses—one that represents the claim and the other, its complement. When one of these hypotheses is false, the other must be true. Of these two hypotheses, the one that contains a statement of *equality* is the *null hypothesis*. The complement of the null hypothesis is the *alternative hypothesis*. Either hypothesis—the null or the alternative—may represent the original claim.

> **DEFINITION**
>
> 1. A **null hypothesis, H_0,** is a statistical hypothesis that contains a statement of equality, such as $\leq$, $=$, or $\geq$.
> 2. The **alternative hypothesis, H_a,** is the complement of the null hypothesis. It is a statement that must be true if H_0 is false and it contains a statement of inequality, such as $>$, $\neq$, or $<$.
>
> H_0 is read as "H sub-zero" or "H naught" and H_a is read as "H sub-a."

To write the null and alternative hypotheses, translate the claim made about the population parameter from a verbal statement to a mathematical statement. Then, write its complement. For instance, if the claim value is k and the population parameter is μ, then some possible pairs of null and alternative hypotheses are

$$\begin{cases} H_0\colon \mu \leq k \\ H_a\colon \mu > k \end{cases} \qquad \begin{cases} H_0\colon \mu \geq k \\ H_a\colon \mu < k \end{cases} \qquad \begin{cases} H_0\colon \mu = k \\ H_a\colon \mu \neq k. \end{cases}$$

The following table shows the relationship between possible verbal statements about the parameter μ and the corresponding null and alternative hypotheses. Similar statements can be made to test other population parameters, such as p, σ, or σ^2.

Verbal Statement H_0	Mathematical Statements	Verbal Statement H_a
The mean is . . . greater than or equal to k at least k not less than k	$\begin{cases} H_0\colon \mu \geq k \\ H_a\colon \mu < k \end{cases}$	The mean is . . . less than k below k fewer than k
less than or equal to k at most k not more than k	$\begin{cases} H_0\colon \mu \leq k \\ H_a\colon \mu > k \end{cases}$	greater than k above k more than k
equal to k k exactly k	$\begin{cases} H_0\colon \mu = k \\ H_a\colon \mu \neq k \end{cases}$	not equal to k different from k not k

> ▶ **EXAMPLE 1**   *Stating the Null and Alternative Hypotheses*

Note to Instructor

Begin with a hypothesis statement and ask students to state its logical complement. Some students will have difficulty with the fact that the complement of $\mu \neq k$ is $\mu = k$. Discuss the role of double negative in English. The important point is that if you conclude that H_0 is false, then you are also concluding that H_a is true.

Write the claim as a mathematical sentence. State the null and alternative hypotheses, and identify which represents the claim.

1. A university claims that the proportion of its students who graduate in four years is 82%.

2. A water faucet manufacturer claims that the mean flow rate of a certain type of faucet is less than 2.5 gallons per minute.

3. A cereal company claims that the mean weight of the contents of its 20-ounce size cereal boxes is more than 20 ounces.

SOLUTION

1. The claim "the proportion . . . is 82%" can be written as $p = 0.82$. Its complement is $p \neq 0.82$. Because $p = 0.82$ contains the statement of equality, it becomes the null hypothesis.

$$H_0 \colon p = 0.82 \text{ (Claim)} \qquad \text{and} \qquad H_a \colon p \neq 0.82$$

In this case, the null hypothesis represents the claim.

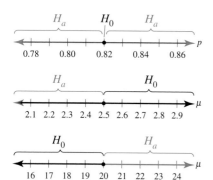

In each of these graphs, notice that each point on the number line is in H_0 or H_a, but no point is in both.

2. The claim "the mean . . . is less than 2.5 gpm" can be written as $\mu < 2.5$. Its complement is $\mu \geq 2.5$. Because $\mu \geq 2.5$ contains the statement of equality, it becomes the null hypothesis.

$$H_0 \colon \mu \geq 2.5 \text{ gpm} \qquad \text{and} \qquad H_a \colon \mu < 2.5 \text{ gpm (Claim)}$$

In this case, the alternative hypothesis represents the claim.

3. The claim "the mean . . . is more than 20 ounces" can be written as $\mu > 20$. Its complement is $\mu \leq 20$. Because $\mu \leq 20$ contains the statement of equality, it becomes the null hypothesis.

$$H_0 \colon \mu \leq 20 \text{ ounces} \qquad \text{and} \qquad H_a \colon \mu > 20 \text{ ounces (Claim)}$$

In this case, the alternative hypothesis represents the claim.

Try It Yourself 1

Write the claim as a mathematical sentence. State the null and alternative hypotheses, and identify which represents the claim.

1. A automobile battery manufacturer claims that the mean life of a certain type of battery is 74 months.

2. A television manufacturer claims that the variance of the life of a certain type of television is less than or equal to 3.5.

3. A radio station claims that its proportion of the local listening audience is greater than 39%.

a. *Identify* the verbal claim and *write* it as a mathematical statement.
b. *Write* the complement of the claim.
c. *Identify* the null and alternative hypotheses and *determine* which one represents the claim.

Answer: Page A39

Types of Errors and Level of Significance

No matter which hypothesis represents the claim, you always test the null hypothesis. So, when you perform a hypothesis test, you make one of two decisions:

1. reject the null hypothesis or

2. fail to reject the null hypothesis.

Because your decision is based on incomplete information (a sample rather than the entire population), there is always the possibility you will make the wrong decision.

For instance, suppose your friend claims that a certain coin is fair. To test your friend's claim, you flip the coin 100 times and get 49 heads and 51 tails. You would probably agree that you do not have enough evidence to reject the claim. Even so, it is possible that the coin is actually not fair and you had an unusual sample.

But what if you flip the coin 100 times and get 21 heads and 79 tails? It is very unlikely that you would get only 21 heads out of 100 tosses with a fair coin. So, you have obtained sufficient evidence to reject your friend's claim that the coin is fair. You can't be 100% sure that the claim is false. It is possible that the coin is fair and you had an unusual sample.

If p represents the proportion of heads, the claim that "the coin is fair" can be written as the mathematical statement $p = 0.5$. Its negation is written as $p \neq 0.5$. So, your null hypothesis and alternative hypothesis are

$$H_0\colon p = 0.5 \text{ (Claim)} \quad \text{and} \quad H_a\colon p \neq 0.5.$$

Remember, the only way to be certain of whether H_0 is true or false is to test the entire population. Because your decision (to reject H_0 or fail to reject H_0) is based on a sample, you must accept the fact that your decision might be incorrect. You might have rejected the null hypothesis when it is actually true. Or, you might have failed to reject the null hypothesis when it is actually false.

D E F I N I T I O N

A **type I error** occurs if the null hypothesis is rejected when it is actually true.

A **type II error** occurs if the null hypothesis is not rejected when it is actually false.

The following table shows the four possible outcomes of a hypothesis test.

	Actual Truth of H_0	
Decision	H_0 *is true.*	H_0 *is false.*
Do not reject H_0	Correct decision	Type II error
Reject H_0	Type I error	Correct decision

Hypothesis testing is sometimes compared to the legal system used in the United States. Under this system, the following steps are used.

	Defendant is innocent.	Defendant is guilty.
Not guilty verdict	Justice	Type II error
Guilty verdict	Type I error	Justice

1. A carefully worded accusation is written.

2. The defendant is assumed innocent (H_0) until proven guilty. The burden of proof lies with the prosecution. If the evidence is not strong enough, there is no conviction. A "not guilty" verdict does not prove that a defendant is innocent.

3. The evidence needs to be conclusive beyond a reasonable doubt. The system assumes that more harm is done by convicting the innocent (type I error) than by not convicting the guilty (type II error).

► EXAMPLE 2 *Identifying Type I and Type II Errors*

The USDA limit for salmonella contamination for chicken is 20%. A meat-packing company claims that its chicken falls within the limit. You perform a hypothesis test to determine whether the company's claim is true. When will a type I or type II error occur? Which is more serious? *(Source: United States Department of Agriculture)*

SOLUTION   Let p represent the proportion of the chicken that is contaminated. The company's claim is "less than or equal to 20% is contaminated." You can write the null and alternative hypotheses as follows.

Chicken meets USDA limits. → $H_0: p \leq 0.2$

Chicken exceeds USDA limits. → $H_a: p > 0.2$

0.16   0.18   0.20   0.22   0.24 p

$H_0: p \leq 0.2$ (Claim)   The proportion is less than or equal to 20%.

$H_a: p > 0.2$ The proportion is greater than 20%.

A type I error will occur if the actual proportion of contaminated chickens is less than or equal to 0.2, but you decide to reject H_0. A type II error will occur if the actual proportion of contaminated chickens is greater than 0.2, but you do not reject H_0.

In this particular context, it is difficult to say which type of error is more serious. With a type I error, you might create a health scare and hurt the sales of chicken producers who were actually meeting the USDA limits. With a type II error, you could be allowing chicken that exceeded the USDA contamination limit to be sold to consumers. A type II error could result in sickness or even death.

Try It Yourself 2

A company specializing in parachute assembly claims that its main parachute failure rate is not more than 1%. You perform a hypothesis test to determine whether the company's claim is true. When will a type I or type II error occur? Which is more serious?

a. *State* the null and alternative hypotheses.
b. *Write* the possible type I and type II errors.
c. *Determine* which error is more serious.

Answer: Page A39 ◄

Because there is variation from sample to sample, there is always a possibility that you will reject a null hypothesis when it is actually true. You can decrease the probability of doing so by lowering the *level of significance*.

DEFINITION

In a hypothesis test, the **level of significance** is your maximum allowable probability of making a type I error. It is denoted by α, the lowercase Greek letter alpha.

The probability of a type II error is denoted by β, the lowercase Greek letter beta.

Insight

When you decrease α (the maximum allowable probability of making a type I error), you are likely to be increasing β.

By setting the level of significance at a small value, you are saying that you want the probability of rejecting a true null hypothesis to be small. Three commonly used levels of significance are $\alpha = 0.10$, $\alpha = 0.05$, and $\alpha = 0.01$.

Statistical Tests and Rejection Regions

Note to Instructor

You can use an example of "false positive" and "false negative" results for a medical test (say diabetes) to discuss type I and type II errors. You might also want to point out that computation of β is beyond the scope of an introductory statistics text.

After stating the null and alternative hypotheses and specifying the level of significance, the next stop in a hypothesis test is to obtain a random sample from the population and calculate sample statistics such as the mean and the standard deviation. The statistic that is compared to the parameter in the null hypothesis is called the **test statistic.** The type of test used and the sampling distribution is based on the test statistic.

In this chapter, you will learn about several one-sample statistical tests. The following table shows the relationships between population parameters and their corresponding test statistics, sampling distributions, and standardized test statistics.

Study Tip

Rejection regions fall in the tails of the sampling distribution. When a test statistic falls in a rejection region, the probability of making a type I error is less than the level of significance.

Population parameter	Test statistic	Sampling distribution	Standardized test statistic
μ	$\bar{x}$	*Normal* ($n \geq 30$) *Student t* ($n < 30$)	*z (Section 7.2)* *t (Section 7.3)*
p	$\hat{p}$	*Normal*	*z (Section 7.4)*
σ^2	s^2	Chi-square	χ^2 (Section 7.5)

One way to decide whether to reject the null hypothesis is to determine whether the standardized test statistic falls within a range of values called the rejection region of the sampling distribution.

DEFINITION

A **rejection region** (or **critical region**) of the sampling distribution is the range of values for which the null hypothesis is not probable. If a test statistic falls in this region, the null hypothesis is rejected. A **critical value** separates the rejection region from the nonrejection region.

The nature of the rejection region depends on whether the hypothesis test is a left-, right-, or two-tailed test. The following graphs show the standard normal distribution. The critical values are denoted by z_0 and the area of the rejection region is equal to α, the level of significance. Similar graphs could be drawn using a t-sampling distribution or a χ^2-sampling distribution.

DEFINITION

1. If the alternative hypothesis H_a contains the less-than inequality symbol (<), the hypothesis test is a **left-tailed test.**

2. If the alternative hypothesis H_a contains the greater-than inequality symbol (>), the hypothesis test is a **right-tailed test.**

3. If the alternative hypothesis H_a contains the not-equal-to symbol ($\neq$), the hypothesis test is a **two-tailed test.** In a two-tailed test, each tail has an area of $\frac{1}{2}\alpha$.

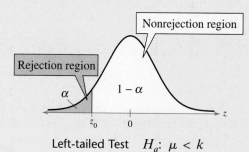

Left-tailed Test $H_a\!: \mu < k$

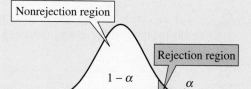

Right-tailed Test $H_a\!: \mu > k$

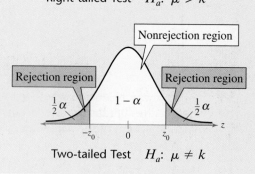

Two-tailed Test $H_a\!: \mu \neq k$

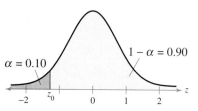

10% Level of Significance

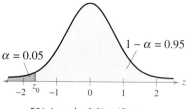

5% Level of Significance

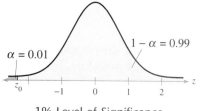

1% Level of Significance

The size of the rejection region depends on the level of significance. The smaller the level of significance, the smaller the size of the rejection region and the lower the probability of rejecting the null hypothesis when it is true. Remember, however, that even a very low level of significance does not constitute proof.

> **EXAMPLE 3** *Identifying the Nature of a Hypothesis Test*

For each claim, state H_0 and H_a in words and in symbols. Then determine whether the hypothesis test is a left-tailed test, right-tailed test, or two-tailed test. Sketch a normal sampling distribution and shade the rejection region.

1. A university claims that the proportion of its students who graduate in 4 years is 82%.

2. A water faucet manufacturer claims that the mean flow rate of a certain type of faucet is less than 2.5 gallons per minute.

3. A cereal company claims that the mean weight of the contents of its 20-ounce size cereal boxes is more than 20 ounces.

SOLUTION

	In Symbols	*In Words*

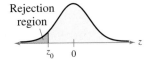

1. H_0 $p = 0.82$ The proportion of students who graduate in 4 years is 82%.
   H_a $p \neq 0.82$ The proportion of students who graduate in 4 years is not 82%.

Because H_a contains the $\neq$ symbol, the test is a two-tailed hypothesis test.

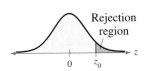

2. H_0 $\mu \geq 2.5$ gpm   The mean flow rate of a certain type of faucet is greater than or equal to 2.5 gallons per minute.
   H_a $\mu < 2.5$ gpm   The mean flow rate of a certain type of faucet is less than 2.5 gallons per minute.

Because H_a contains the $<$ symbol, the test is a left-tailed hypothesis test.

3. H_0 $\mu \leq 20$ oz   The mean weight of the contents of the cereal boxes is less than or equal to 20 ounces.
   H_a $\mu > 20$ oz   The mean weight of the contents of the cereal boxes is greater than 20 ounces.

Because H_a contains the $>$ symbol, the test is a right-tailed hypothesis test.

Try It Yourself 3

For each claim, determine whether the hypothesis test is a left-tailed, right-tailed, or two-tailed test. Sketch a normal sampling distribution and shade the rejection region.

1. An automobile battery manufacturer claims that the mean life of a certain type of battery is 74 months.

2. A radio station claims that its proportion of the local listening audience is greater than 39%.

a. *Write* H_0 and H_a.
b. *Determine* whether the test is left-tailed, right-tailed, or two-tailed.
c. *Sketch* the sampling distribution and shade the rejection region.

Answer: Page A39

Making a Decision and Interpreting the Decision

To conclude a hypothesis test, you make a decision and interpret that decision. There are only two possible outcomes to a hypothesis test: (1) reject the null hypothesis, and (2) fail to reject the null hypothesis.

Decision Rule Based on Rejection Region

To use a rejection region to conduct a hypothesis test, calculate the standardized test statistic (z, t, or χ^2). If the standardized test statistic

1. is in the rejection region, then reject H_0.
2. is *not* in the rejection region, then fail to reject H_0.

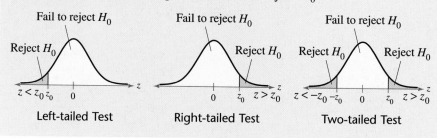

If you fail to reject the null hypothesis, it does not mean that you have accepted the null hypothesis as true. It simply means that there is not enough evidence to reject the null hypothesis.

> **EXAMPLE 4** *Interpreting a Decision*

You perform a hypothesis test for the following claim. How should you interpret your decision if you reject H_0? If you fail to reject H_0?

H_0 (Claim): A university claims that the proportion of its students who graduate in four years is 82%.

SOLUTION If you reject H_0, then you should conclude "there is sufficient evidence to indicate that the university's 4-year graduation rate is not 82%." If you fail to reject H_0, then you should conclude "there is insufficient evidence to indicate that the university's claim (of a 4-year graduation rate of 82%) is false."

Try It Yourself 4

Consider the following claim. You perform a hypothesis test that leads to the rejection of the null hypothesis. How should you interpret your decision? How should you interpret your decision if you fail to reject H_0?

H_a (Claim): A radio station claims that its proportion of the local listening audience is greater than 39%.

a. Interpret your decision if you reject the null hypothesis.
b. Interpret your decision if you do not reject the null hypothesis.

Answer: Page A39

The general steps for a hypothesis test are summarized below.

1. State the claim mathematically and verbally. Identify the null and alternative hypotheses.

$$H_0: \quad \boxed{?} \qquad H_a: \quad \boxed{?}$$

2. Specify the level of significance.

$$\alpha = \boxed{?}$$

3. Determine the type of test and make a rough sketch of the corresponding standardized sampling distribution.

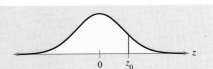

This sampling distribution is based on the assumption that H_0 is true.

Study Tip

The graphs at the right show a right-tailed test. However, the same basic steps also apply to left-tailed and two-tailed tests.

4. Determine any critical values. Add them to your sketch.

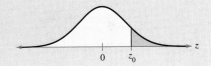

5. Determine any rejection regions. Shade them in your sketch.

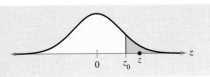

6. Calculate the test statistic and its standardized value. Add it to your sketch.

7. Use the following decision rule.

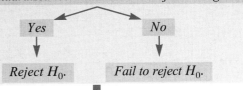

Is the standardized test statistic in the rejection region?

Yes → Reject H_0.

No → Fail to reject H_0.

8. Write a statement to interpret the decision in the context of the original claim.

Strategies for Hypothesis Testing

When you are making a claim or testing someone else's claim, you need to consider the context of the claim and decide whether it is "one-tailed" or "two-tailed."

> ▶ **EXAMPLE 5**   *Writing a Claim as One-Tailed or Two-Tailed*

Consider the claim described at the beginning of this section by a battery manufacturer that the mean life of its AA battery is 300 minutes. You work for a consumer advocate magazine and are asked to test the battery manufacturer's claim. From your point of view, which of the following best represents the manufacturer's claim?

$$\mu = 300, \qquad \mu \leq 300, \qquad \mu \geq 300$$

SOLUTION   To answer this question, you need to think about the context of the manufacturer's claim. As a consumer advocate, your concern is that consumers will get at least 300 minutes of use out of a battery. It would be fine with you if the mean life of the battery turned out to be greater than 300 minutes. So, from your point of view, the manufacturer's claim is best stated as $\mu \geq 300$.

Try It Yourself 5

1. You represent a chemical company that is being sued for paint damage to automobiles. You believe the mean cost of repair per automobile is about $650. From your point of view, which of the following would best express your claim?

$$\mu = 650, \qquad \mu \leq 650, \qquad \mu \geq 650$$

2. You are on a research team that is investigating the mean temperature of adult humans (see page 329). The commonly accepted claim is that the mean temperature is 98.6°F. From your point of view, which of the following best represents this claim?

$$\mu = 98.6, \qquad \mu \leq 98.6, \qquad \mu \geq 98.6$$

a. *Think* about the context of the claim.
b. *Choose* the statement that best represents your point of view.

Answer: Page A39 ◀

In a courtroom, the strategy used by an attorney depends on whether the attorney is representing the defense or the prosecution. In a similar way, the strategy that you will use in hypothesis testing should depend on whether you are trying to support or reject a claim.

▶ EXAMPLE 6 *Writing Hypotheses*

An employee group for a national retailer claims that the mean time spent by employees on personal phone calls is about 10 minutes per day. You are asked to test this claim.

1. How would you write the null hypothesis if you represent the employee group and want to support the claim?
2. How would you write the null hypothesis if you represent the employer and want to reject the claim?

SOLUTION

1. To support a claim, it must be written so that it becomes the alternative hypothesis (using a statement of inequality). In this case, the claim would be "the mean time spent by employees on personal phone calls is less than 10 minutes per day." So, the null and alternative hypotheses are as follows.

$$H_0: \mu \geq 10 \qquad H_a: \mu < 10 \; \text{(Claim)}$$

If the results of the hypothesis test allow you to reject the null hypothesis, then you will have supported the employees' claim.

2. To reject a claim, it must be written so that it becomes the null hypothesis (using a statement of equality). In this case, the claim would be "the mean time spent by employees on personal phone calls is less than or equal to 10 minutes per day." So, the null and alternative hypotheses are as follows.

$$H_0: \mu \leq 10 \; \text{(Claim)} \qquad H_a: \mu > 10$$

If the results of the hypothesis test allow you to reject the null hypothesis, then you will have indicated that the employees spent more than 10 minutes per day on personal phone calls.

Study Tip

Remember that you cannot use a hypothesis test to support your claim if your claim is the null hypothesis. So, as a researcher, if you want a conclusion that supports your claim, word your claim so it is the alternative hypothesis.

Try It Yourself 6

A light bulb manufacturer claims that the mean life of its halogen headlamps is about 2400 hours. You are asked to test this claim. How would you write the null hypothesis if you represent (1) the manufacturer and want to support the claim, and (2) a consumer advocate group and want to reject the claim?

a. *Decide* whether you want to support or reject the claim.
b. If you want to *support the claim*, write it as the alternative hypothesis. If you want to *reject the claim*, write it as the null hypothesis.

Answer: Page A39 ◀

7.1 ▼ EXERCISES

▶ **HELP**

 StatPro 7.1

 Internet Statistics 7.1

 Student Solutions Manual 7.1

 Videos 7.1

 Try It Yourself Answers 7.1

1. H_0: $\mu \leq 645$, H_a: $\mu > 645$
2. H_0: $\mu \geq 128$, H_a: $\mu < 128$
3. H_0: $\sigma = 5$, H_a: $\sigma \neq 5$
4. H_0: $\sigma^2 \geq 1.2$, H_a: $\sigma^2 < 1.2$
5. H_0: $p \geq 0.45$, H_a: $p < 0.45$
6. H_0: $p = 0.21$, H_a: $p \neq 0.21$
7. c $\quad H_a$: $\mu < 3$

8. See Selected Answers, page A81
9. b $\quad H_a$: $\mu \neq 3$

10. See Selected Answers, page A81
11. $\mu > 750$
$\quad H_0$: $\mu \leq 750$ and H_a: $\mu > 750$
$\quad$(Claim: H_a)
12. See Selected Answers, page A81
13. $\sigma \leq 1220$
$\quad H_0$: $\sigma \leq 1220$ and H_a: $\sigma > 1220$
$\quad$(Claim: H_0)
14. See Selected Answers, page A81
15. H_0: $p = 0.44$
$\quad H_0$: $p = 0.44$ and H_a: $p \neq 0.44$
$\quad$(Claim: H_0)
16. See Selected Answers, page A81
17. Type I: Rejecting H_0: $p \geq 0.24$
$\quad$when actually $p \geq 0.24$
$\quad$Type II: Not rejecting H_0:
$\quad p \geq 0.24$ when actually $p < 0.24$.
18. See Selected Answers, page A81

Basic Skills and Concepts

Stating Hypotheses In Exercises 1–6, use the given statement to represent a claim. Write its complement and state which is H_0 and which is H_a.

1. $\mu \leq 645$

2. $\mu < 128$

3. $\sigma \neq 5$

4. $\sigma^2 \geq 1.2$

5. $p < 0.45$

6. $p = 0.21$

Graphical Analysis In Exercises 7–10, match the null hypothesis with its graph. Then state the alternative hypothesis and sketch its graph.

7. H_0: $\mu \geq 3$

(a) ![graph with bold line from 2 to right] μ
$\qquad$ 1 $\quad$ 2 $\quad$ 3 $\quad$ 4

8. H_0: $\mu \leq 3$

(b) ![graph with point at 3] μ
$\qquad$ 1 $\quad$ 2 $\quad$ 3 $\quad$ 4

9. H_0: $\mu = 3$

(c) ![graph with bold line from 3 to right] μ
$\qquad$ 1 $\quad$ 2 $\quad$ 3 $\quad$ 4

10. H_0: $\mu \geq 2$

(d) ![graph with bold line from left to 3] μ
$\qquad$ 1 $\quad$ 2 $\quad$ 3 $\quad$ 4

Stating the Hypotheses In Exercises 11–16, state the claim mathematically. Write the null and alternative hypotheses. Identify which is the claim.

11. A light bulb manufacturer claims that the mean life of a certain type of light bulb is more than 750 hours.

12. As stated by a company's shipping department, the number of shipping errors per million shipments has a standard deviation that is less than 3.

13. The standard deviation of the base price of a certain type of car is no more than \$1220. *(Adapted from Consumer Reports)*

14. A research organization reports that 9% of all grocery shoppers never buy the store brand. *(Source: Wirthlin Worldwide)*

15. The results of a recent study examining the proportion of clinically misdiagnosed cancer cases indicate that 44% of all cancer cases are misdiagnosed. *(Source: The Journal of the American Medical Association)*

16. A study claims that the mean survival time for certain cancer patients treated immediately with chemotherapy and radiation is 24 months.

Identifying Errors In Exercises 17–22, write sentences describing type I and type II errors for a hypothesis test of the indicated claim.

17. A car dealer claims that at least 24% of its new customers will return to buy their next car.

18. A study claims that the proportion of adults with rudimentary literary skills is 21%. *(Source: U.S. Department of Education)*

19. Type I: Rejecting H_0: $\sigma \le 23$ when actually $\sigma \le 23$.

Type II: Not rejecting H_0: $\sigma \le 23$ when actually $\sigma > 23$.

20. Type I: Rejecting H_0: $p = 0.02$ when actually $p = 0.02$.

Type II: Not rejecting H_0: $p = 0.02$ when actually $p \ne 0.02$.

21. Type I: Rejecting H_0: $p \le 0.60$ when actually $p \le 0.60$.

Type II: Not rejecting H_0: $p \le 0.24$ when actually $p > 0.24$.

22. Type I: Rejecting H_0: $\sigma \ge 5$ when actually $\sigma \ge 5$.

Type II: Not rejecting H_0: $\sigma \ge 5$ when actually $\sigma < 5$.

23. Left-tailed

24. Right-tailed

25. Two-tailed

26. Left-tailed

27. Two-tailed

28. Right-tailed

29. (a) There is enough evidence to reject the company's claim.

(b) There is not enough evidence to decide that the company's claim is false.

30. See Selected Answers, page A81

31. (a) There is enough evidence to support the Dept of Labor's claim.

(b) There is not enough evidence to decide that the Dept of Labor's claim is true.

32. See Selected Answers, page A81

33. (a) There is enough evidence to reject the manufacturer's claim.

(b) There is not enough evidence to reject the manufacturer's claim.

34. See Selected Answers, page A81

19. A local chess club claims that the length of time to play a game has a standard deviation of more than 23 minutes.

20. A hospital spokesperson states that 2% of emergency room visits by college undergraduates are for alcohol-related health problems.

21. According to a recent consumer magazine report, more than 60% of all personal cell phone calls are made during evenings and weekends. *(Source: Consumer Reports)*

22. A battery manufacturer guarantees that the standard deviation of the life of its wristwatch batteries is less than 5 months.

Identifying Tests In Exercises 23–28, determine whether the hypothesis test for each claim is left-tailed, right-tailed, or two-tailed. Explain your reasoning.

23. At least 14% of all homeowners have a home security alarm.

24. A manufacturer of grandfather clocks claims that the mean time its clocks lose is no more than 0.02 second per day.

25. A government report claims the proportion of lung cancer cases that are due to smoking is 90%.

26. The mean life of a certain tire is no less than 50,000 miles. *(Source: Goodyear)*

27. A financial analyst claims that the return rate of a 15-year U.S. bond has a standard deviation of 5.3%.

28. A research institute claims the mean length of most dreams is greater than 10 minutes. *(Source: The Lucidity Institute)*

Interpreting a Decision In Exercises 29–34, consider each claim. If a hypothesis test is performed, how should you interpret a decision that (a) rejects the null hypothesis and (b) does not reject the null hypothesis?

29. The mean number of pictures developed for a standard roll of film with 24 exposures is at least 22.

30. The standard deviation of the mean weight of all U.S. Postal Service shipments is 0.40 pound.

31. The U.S. Department of Labor claims the proportion of hourly workers earning over $10.00 per hour is greater than 42%. *(Adapted from U.S. Department of Labor)*

32. An automotive manufacturer claims the standard deviation for the gas mileage of its models is 3.9 miles per gallon.

33. The mean price of a new model year car is $20,440. *(Source: Dodge)*

34. A soft-drink maker claims the mean calorie content of its beverages is 26 calories per serving.

35. $\mu = 10$

36. $\mu < 21$

37. (a) $H_0: \mu \le 15$
   (b) $H_0: \mu \ge 15$

38. (a) $H_0: \mu \le 28$
   (b) $H_0: \mu \ge 28$

39. If you decrease α, you are decreasing the probability that you reject H_0. Therefore, you are increasing the probability of failing to reject H_0. This could increase β, the probability of failing to reject H_0 when H_0 is false.

40. There are no z-values that corresponds to $\alpha = 0$. If $\alpha = 0$, the null hypothesis cannot be rejected and the hypothesis test is useless.

41. (a) Reject H_0
   (b) Do not reject H_0
   (c) Do not reject H_0

42. (a) Reject H_0
   (b) Do not reject H_0
   (c) Do not reject H_0

35. *Writing a Claim* Your medical research team is investigating the proper dose of a certain heart medication. The medicine manufacturer thinks that the mean dose should be 10 milligrams. From your point of view, which of the following best represents your claim?

$$\mu = 10, \qquad \mu \le 10, \qquad \mu \ge 10$$

36. *Writing a Claim* A taxicab company claims that the mean travel time between two destinations is about 21 minutes. From the taxicab company's point of view, which of the following best represents this claim?

$$\mu = 21, \qquad \mu < 21, \qquad \mu > 21$$

37. *Writing Hypotheses* A refrigerator manufacturer claims that the mean life of its refrigerators is about 15 years. You are asked to test this claim. How would you write the null hypothesis if

(*a*) you represent the manufacturer and want to support the claim?

(*b*) you represent a consumer group and want to reject the claim?

38. *Writing Hypotheses* An Internet provider is trying to gain advertising deals and claims that the mean time a customer spends on line per day is about 28 minutes. You are asked to test this claim. How would you write the null hypothesis if

(*a*) you represent the internet provider and want to support the claim?

(*b*) you represent an advertiser and want to reject the claim?

Extending the Basics

39. *Think About It* Why can decreasing the probability of a type I error cause an increase in the probability of a type II error?

40. *Think About It* Why not use a level of significance of $\alpha = 0$?

Graphical Analysis In Exercises 41 and 42, you are given a null hypothesis and three confidence intervals that represent three samplings. Decide whether each confidence interval indicates that you should reject H_0. Explain your reasoning.

41.

$H_0: \mu \ge 70$

(a) $\mu = 68 \pm 1$

(b) $\mu = 69 \pm 2$

(c) $\mu = 71 \pm 1.5$

42.

$H_0: \mu \le 54$

(a) $\mu = 55 \pm 0.5$

(b) $\mu = 53 \pm 1.5$

(c) $\mu = 55 \pm 1.5$

Hypothesis Testing for the Mean (Large Samples)

Critical Values in a Normal Distribution • The z-Test for a Mean μ •
Using P-values for a z-Test

What You Should Learn

- *How to find critical values in a normal distribution*
- *How to use the z-test to test a mean μ*
- *How to find P-values and use them to test a mean μ*

Critical Values in a Normal Distribution

In Chapter 5, you learned that when the sample size is at least 30, the sampling distribution for $\bar{x}$ (the sample mean) is normal.

GUIDELINES

Finding Critical Values in a Normal Distribution

1. Specify the level of significance, α.
2. Decide whether the test is left-tailed, right-tailed, or two-tailed.
3. Find the critical value(s), z_0. If the hypothesis test is
   a. *left-tailed*, find the z-score that corresponds to an area of α.
   b. *right-tailed*, find the z-score that corresponds to an area of $1 - \alpha$.
   c. *two-tailed*, find the z-scores that correspond to $\frac{1}{2}\alpha$ and $1 - \frac{1}{2}\alpha$.
4. Sketch the standard normal distribution. Draw a vertical line at each critical value and shade the rejection region(s).

> ### EXAMPLE 1 *Finding a Critical Value for a Left-Tailed Test*

Find the critical value and rejection region for a left-tailed test with $\alpha = 0.01$.

SOLUTION The graph at the right shows a standard normal curve with a shaded area of 0.01 in the left tail. Using Table 4, the z-score that corresponds to an area of 0.01 is -2.33. So, the critical value is $z_0 = -2.33$. The rejection region is to the left of this critical value.

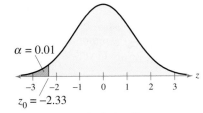

$\alpha = 0.01$

$z_0 = -2.33$

1% Level of Significance

> *Try It Yourself 1*
>
> Find the critical value and rejection region for a left-tailed test with $\alpha = 0.10$.
>
> a. *Draw* a standard normal curve with an area of α in the left tail.
> b. *Use* Table 4 to locate the area that is closest to α.
> c. *Find* the z-score that corresponds to this area. *Answer: Page A39*

> ▶ **EXAMPLE 2** **Finding a Critical Value for a Right-Tailed Test**

Find the critical value and rejection region for a right-tailed test with $\alpha = 0.04$.

SOLUTION The graph at the right shows a standard normal curve with a shaded area of 0.04 in the right tail. The area to the left of z_0 is $1 - \alpha = 1 - 0.04 = 0.96$. Using Table 4, the z-score that corresponds to an area of 0.96 is 1.75. So, the critical value is $z_0 = 1.75$.

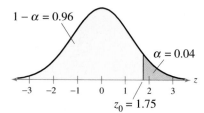

4% Level of Significance

Try It Yourself 2

Find the critical value and rejection region for a right-tailed test with $\alpha = 0.06$.

a. *Draw* a graph of the standard normal curve with an area of α in the right tail.
b. *Use* Table 4 to locate the area that is closest to $1 - \alpha$.
c. *Find* the z-score that corresponds to this area. *Answer: Page A39* ◀

> ▶ **EXAMPLE 3** **Finding Critical Values for a Two-Tailed Test**

Find the critical values and rejection regions for a two-tailed test with $\alpha = 0.05$.

SOLUTION The graph at the right shows a standard normal curve with shaded areas of $\frac{1}{2}\alpha = 0.025$ in each tail. The area to the left of $-z_0$ is $\frac{1}{2}\alpha = 0.025$. and the area to the left of z_0 is $1 - \frac{1}{2}\alpha = 0.975$. Using Table 4, the z-scores that correspond to the areas 0.025 and 0.975 are -1.96 and 1.96, respectively. So, the critical values are $-z_0 = -1.96$ and $z_0 = 1.96$.

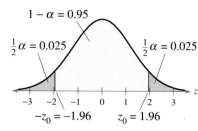

5% Level of Significance

Study Tip

Notice in Example 3 that the critical values are opposites. This is always true for two-tailed z-tests.

The table lists the critical values for commonly used levels of significance.

Alpha	Tail	z
0.10	Left	-1.28
	Right	1.28
	Two	± 1.645
0.05	Left	-1.645
	Right	1.645
	Two	± 1.96
0.01	Left	-2.33
	Right	2.33
	Two	± 2.575

Try It Yourself 3

Find the critical values and rejection regions for a two-tailed test with $\alpha = 0.08$.

a. *Draw* a graph of the standard normal curve with an area of $\frac{1}{2}\alpha$ in each tail.
b. *Use* Table 4 to locate the areas that are closest to $\frac{1}{2}\alpha$ and $1 - \frac{1}{2}\alpha$.
c. *Find* the z-scores that correspond to these areas. *Answer: Page A39* ◀

The z-Test for a Mean μ

The z-test for the mean is used in populations for which the sampling distribution of sample means is normal. To use the z-test, you need to find the standardized value for your test statistic, $\bar{x}$.

$$z = \frac{(\text{Sample mean}) - (\text{Hypothesized mean})}{\text{Standard error}}$$

z-Test for a Mean

The **z-test** is a statistical test for a population mean. The z-test can be used when the population is normal and σ is known, or for any population when the sample size, n, is at least 30. The **test statistic** is the sample mean $\bar{x}$ and the **standardized test statistic** is z.

$$z = \frac{\bar{x} - \mu}{\sigma/\sqrt{n}}, \qquad \frac{\sigma}{\sqrt{n}} = \text{standard error} = \sigma_{\bar{x}}$$

When $n \geq 30$, you can use the sample standard deviation s in place of σ.

Study Tip

With all hypothesis tests, it is helpful to sketch the sampling distribution. Your sketch should include any critical values, rejection regions, and the standardized test statistic.

GUIDELINES

Using a z-Test for a Mean μ

In Words	In Symbols
1. State the claim mathematically and verbally. Identify the null and alternative hypotheses.	State H_0 and H_a.
2. Specify the level of significance.	Identify α.
3. Sketch the sampling distribution.	
4. Determine the critical value(s).	Use Table 4.
5. Determine the rejection region(s).	
6. Find the standardized test statistic.	$z = \dfrac{\bar{x} - \mu}{\sigma/\sqrt{n}}$ or $z = \dfrac{\bar{x} - \mu}{s/\sqrt{n}}$
7. Make a decision to reject or fail to reject the null hypothesis.	If z is in the rejection region, reject H_0. Otherwise, do not reject H_0.
8. Interpret the decision in the context of the original claim.	

Note to Instructor

We use the same format for all hypothesis testing throughout the text. This makes it easier for students to understand the logic of the test. Emphasize that the sampling distribution and consequently the logic of the test is based on the assumption that the equality condition of the null hypothesis is true.

> **EXAMPLE 4**   *Testing μ with a Large Sample*

See *TI-83* steps on page 359.

Picturing the World

Each year, the Environmental Protection Agency (EPA) publishes reports of gas mileage for all makes and models of passenger vehicles. In 1999, compact cars with automatic transmissions that posted the best mileage were the Chevrolet Prizm and Toyota Corolla. Each had a mean mileage of 28 mpg (city) and 36 mpg (highway). Suppose that Chevrolet believes a Prizm exceeds 36 mpg on the highway. To support its claim, it tested 34 cars on highway driving and got a sample mean of 37.2 mpg with a standard deviation of 2.3 mpg. *(Source: EPA)*

Is the evidence strong enough to prove that Prizm's highway mpg exceeds the EPA estimate? Use a z-test with $\alpha = 0.01$.

Employees in a large accounting firm claim that the mean salary of the firm's accountants is less than that of its competitor's, which is \$45,000. A random sample of 30 of the firm's accountants has a mean salary of \$43,500 with a standard deviation of \$5200. At $\alpha = 0.05$, test the employees' claim.

SOLUTION   The claim is "the mean salary is less than \$45,000." So, the null and alternative hypotheses can be written as

$$H_0: \mu \geq \$45,000 \quad \text{and} \quad H_a: \mu < \$45,000. \text{ (Claim)}$$

Because the test is a left-tailed test and the level of significance is $\alpha = 0.05$, the critical value is $z_0 = -1.645$ and the rejection region is $z < -1.645$. Because the sample size is at least 30, the standardized test statistic for the z-test is

$$z = \frac{\bar{x} - \mu}{s/\sqrt{n}} = \frac{43,500 - 45,000}{5200/\sqrt{30}} \approx -1.58.$$

The graph shows the location of the rejection region and the standardized test statistic, z. Because z is not in the rejection region, you fail to reject the null hypothesis. In other words, there is not enough evidence at the 5% level of significance to support the employees' claim that the mean salary is less than \$45,000.

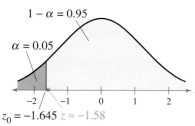

5% Level of Significance

Be sure you understand the decision made in Example 4. Even though your sample has a mean of \$43,500, you cannot (at a 5% level of significance) support the claim that the mean of all the accountants' salaries is less than \$45,000. The difference between your test statistic and the hypothesized mean is probably due to sampling error.

Try It Yourself 4

The CEO of the firm claims that the mean work day of the firm's accountants is less than 8.5 hours. A random sample of 35 of the firm's accountants has a mean work day of 8.2 hours with a standard deviation of 0.5 hours. At $\alpha = 0.01$, test the CEO's claim.

a. *Identify* the claim and state H_0 and H_a.
b. *Identify* the level of significance α.
c. *Find* the critical value, z_0, and identify the rejection region.
d. *Find* the standardized test statistic z.
e. Sketch a graph. *Decide* whether to reject the null hypothesis.
f. Is there enough evidence to support the claim that the mean work day is less than 8.5 hours?

Answer: Page A40

▶ EXAMPLE 5   *Testing μ with a Large Sample*

The U.S. Department of Agriculture reports that the mean cost of raising a child from birth to age 2 in a rural area is $8390. You believe this value is incorrect, so you select a random sample of 900 children (age 2) and find that the mean cost is $8275 with a standard deviation of $1540. At $\alpha = 0.05$, is there enough evidence to conclude that the mean cost is different from $8390? *(Source: U.S. Department of Agriculture Center for Nutrition Policy and Promotion)*

SOLUTION   You want to support the claim that "the mean cost is different from $8390." So, the null and alternative hypotheses are

$$H_0: \mu = \$8390 \qquad \text{and} \qquad H_a: \mu \neq \$8390. \text{ (Claim)}$$

Because the test is a two-tailed test and the level of significance is $\alpha = 0.05$, the critical values are $-z_0 = -1.96$ and $z_0 = 1.96$. The rejection regions are $z < -1.96$ and $z > 1.96$. Because $n \geq 30$, the standardized test statistic for the z-test is

$$z = \frac{\bar{x} - \mu}{s/\sqrt{n}} = \frac{8275 - 8390}{1540/\sqrt{900}} \approx -2.24.$$

The graph shows the location of the rejection regions and the standardized test statistic, z. Because z is in the rejection region, you should decide to reject the null hypothesis. In other words, you have enough evidence to conclude that the mean cost of raising a child from birth to age 2 in a rural area is significantly different from $8390 at the 5% level of significance.

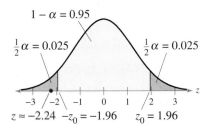

5% Level of Significance

Try It Yourself 5

Using the information and results of Example 5, is there enough evidence to support the claim that the mean cost of raising a child from birth to age 2 in a rural area is different from $8390 at $\alpha = 0.01$?

a. *Identify* the level of significance α.
b. *Find* the critical values, $\pm z_0$, and identify the rejection regions.
c. Sketch a graph. *Decide* whether to reject the null hypothesis.
d. Is there enough evidence to support the claim that the mean cost is significantly different from $8390 at the 1% level of significance?

Answer: Page A40

Using *P*-values for a *z*-Test

Another way to reach a conclusion in a hypothesis test is to use a *P*-value for the sample statistic. Many people prefer this method when using technology.

DEFINITION

Assuming the null hypothesis is true, a **P-value** (or **probability value**) of a hypothesis test is the probability of obtaining a sample statistic with a value as extreme or more extreme than the one determined from the sample data.

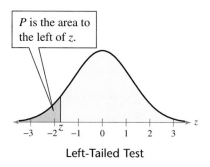

Left-Tailed Test

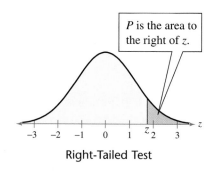

Right-Tailed Test

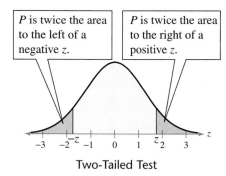

Two-Tailed Test

Note to Instructor

If a *P*-value is less than 0.01, the null hypothesis will be rejected at the common levels of 0.01, 0.05, and 0.10. If the *P*-value is greater than 0.10, then you would fail to reject H_0 for these common levels. Make sure students know that the same conclusion will be reached regardless of whether they use the critical value method or the *P*-value method.

Decision Rule Based on *P*-value

To use a *P*-value to make a conclusion in a hypothesis test, compare the *P*-value to α.

1. If $P \leq \alpha$, then reject H_0.
2. If $P > \alpha$, then fail to reject H_0.

▶ **EXAMPLE 6** *Interpreting a P-value*

The *P*-value for a hypothesis test is $P = 0.0237$. What is your decision if the level of significance is (1) $\alpha = 0.05$ and (2) $\alpha = 0.01$?

SOLUTION

1. Because $0.0237 < 0.05$, you should reject the null hypothesis.
2. Because $0.0237 > 0.01$, you should fail to reject the null hypothesis.

Try It Yourself 6

The *P*-value for a hypothesis test is $P = 0.0347$. What is your decision if the level of significance is (1) $\alpha = 0.01$ and (2) $\alpha = 0.05$?

a. *Compare* the *P*-value to the level of significance.
b. *Make* your decision.

Answer: Page A40 ◀

Study Tip

The lower the P-value, the more evidence there is in favor of rejecting H_0. The P-value gives you the lowest level of significance for which the sample statistic allows you to reject the null hypothesis. In Example 6, you would reject H_0 at any level of significance greater than 0.0237.

> ▶ **EXAMPLE 7** *Using a Technology Tool to Interpret a z-Test*

What decision should you make for the following Minitab printout, using a level of significance of $\alpha = 0.05$?

Study Tip

For this test, a sample of 53 values was entered into a column called "Sample." The hypotheses are

H_0: $\mu = 6.2$

H_a: $\mu \neq 6.2$.

MINITAB

Test of mu = 6.200 vs mu not = 6.2000
The assumed sigma = 0.470

Variable	N	Mean	StDev	SE Mean	Z	P
Sample	53	6.0666	0.4146	0.0646	–2.07	0.039

SOLUTION   The *P*-value for this test is given as 0.039. Because the *P*-value is less than 0.05, reject the null hypothesis.

Try It Yourself 7

For the Minitab hypothesis test shown in Example 7, make a decision at the $\alpha = 0.01$ level of significance.

a. *Compare* the *P*-value to the level of significance.
b. *Make* your decision.   *Answer: Page A40* ◀

GUIDELINES

Using P-values for a z-Test for Mean μ

In Words	*In Symbols*
1. State the claim mathematically and verbally. Identify the null and alternative hypotheses.	State H_0 and H_a.
2. Specify the level of significance.	Identify α.
3. Determine the standardized test statistic.	$z = \dfrac{\bar{x} - \mu}{\sigma/\sqrt{n}}$ or $z = \dfrac{\bar{x} - \mu}{s/\sqrt{n}}$
4. Find the area that corresponds to z.	Use Table 4.

5. Find the *P*-value.
    a. For a left-tailed test, $P =$ (Area in left tail).
    b. For a right-tailed test, $P =$ (Area in right tail).
    c. For a two-tailed test, $P = 2$(Area in tail of test statistic).

| **6.** Make a decision to reject or fail to reject the null hypothesis. | Reject H_0 if *P*-value is less than or equal to α. Otherwise, fail to reject H_0. |

7. Interpret the decision in the context of the original claim.

In an advertisement, a pizza shop claims that its mean delivery time is less than 30 minutes. A random selection of 36 delivery times has a sample mean of 28.5 minutes and a standard deviation of 3.5 minutes. Is there enough evidence to support the claim at $\alpha = 0.01$? Use a *P*-value.

SOLUTION   The claim is "the mean delivery time is less than 30 minutes." So, the null and alternative hypotheses are

$$H_0: \mu \geq 30 \text{ minutes} \quad \text{and} \quad H_a: \mu < 30 \text{ minutes. (Claim)}$$

Using the *z*-test, the standardized test statistic is

$$z = \frac{\bar{x} - \mu}{s/\sqrt{n}} = \frac{28.5 - 30}{3.5/\sqrt{36}} \approx -2.57.$$

Using Table 4, the area corresponding to $z = -2.57$ is 0.0051. Because this test is a left-tailed test, the *P*-value is equal to the area to the left of $z = -2.57$. So, $P = 0.0051$. Because the *P*-value is less than $\alpha = 0.01$, you should decide to reject the null hypothesis. So, at the 1% level of significance, you have sufficient evidence to conclude that the mean delivery time is less than 30 minutes.

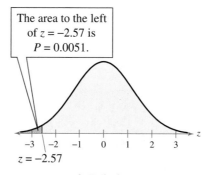

The area to the left of $z = -2.57$ is $P = 0.0051$.

$z = -2.57$

Left-Tailed Test

Try It Yourself 8

Home owners claim that the mean speed of automobiles traveling on their street is greater than the speed limit of 35 miles per hour. A random sample of 100 automobiles has a mean speed of 36 miles per hour and a standard deviation of 4 miles per hour. Is there enough evidence to sup- port the claim at $\alpha = 0.05$? Use a *P*-value.

a. *Identify* the claim. Then *state* the null and alternative hypotheses.
b. *Identify* the level of significance.
c. *Find* the standardized test statistic *z*.
d. *Find* the *P*-value.
e. *Decide* whether to reject the null hypothesis.
f. *Interpret* the decision in the context of the original claim.

Answer: Page A40 ◄

> See *Minitab* steps on page 358.

▶ **EXAMPLE 9** *Hypothesis Testing Using P-values*

You think that the average franchise investment information given in the graph is incorrect, so you randomly select 30 franchises and determine the necessary investment for each. The sample mean investment is $135,000 with a standard deviation of $30,000. Is there enough evidence to support your claim at $\alpha = 0.05$? Use a *P*-value.

Franchise Investment

Average investment is $143,260

43%   41%

14%

Percent responding

Less than $100,000 $100,000 and up   Don't know/ did not answer

SOLUTION   The claim is "the mean is different from $143,260." So, the null and alternative hypotheses are

$$H_0:\ \mu = \$143{,}260 \quad \text{and} \quad H_a:\ \mu \neq \$143{,}260.\ \text{(Claim)}$$

The level of significance is $\alpha = 0.05$. Using the z-test, the standardized test statistic is

$$z = \frac{\bar{x} - \mu}{s/\sqrt{n}} = \frac{135{,}000 - 143{,}260}{30{,}000/\sqrt{30}} \approx -1.51.$$

Using Table 4, the area corresponding to $z = -1.51$ is 0.0655. Because the test is a two-tailed test, the *P*-value is equal to twice the area to the left of $z = -1.51$. So,

$$P = 2(0.0655) = 0.1310.$$

Because the *P*-value is greater than α, you should fail to reject the null hypothesis. So, there is not enough evidence at the 5% level of significance to conclude that the mean franchise investment is not $143,260.

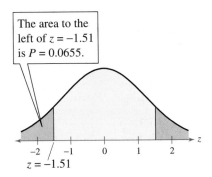

The area to the left of $z = -1.51$ is $P = 0.0655$.

$z = -1.51$

Two-Tailed Test

Try It Yourself 9

One of your distributors reports an average of 150 sales per day for the distributorship. You suspect that this average is not accurate, so you randomly select 35 days and determine the number of sales each day. The sample mean is 143 daily sales with a standard deviation of 15 sales. At $\alpha = 0.01$, is there enough evidence to doubt the distributor's reported average? Use a *P*-value.

a. *Identify* the claim. Then *state* a null and alternative hypotheses.
b. *Identify* the level of significance.
c. *Find* the standardized test statistic z.
d. *Find* the *P*-value.
e. *Decide* whether to reject the null hypothesis.
f. *Interpret* the decision in the context of the original claim.

Answer: Page A40 ◀

7.2 EXERCISES

HELP

 StatPro 7.2

 Internet Statistics 7.2

 Student Solutions Manual 7.2

 Videos 7.2

 Try It Yourself Answers 7.2

1. Specify the level of significance, α. Decide whether the test is left-tailed, right-tailed, or two-tailed. Find the critical value(s), z_0, as follows: (a) Left-tailed: find z_0 that corresponds to an area of α. (b) Right-tailed: find z_0 that corresponds to an area of $1 - \alpha$. (c) Two-tailed: find $\pm z_0$ that corresponds to $\frac{1}{2}\alpha$ and $1 - \frac{1}{2}\alpha$.
2. See Selected Answers, page A81
3. 1.645
4. 1.41
5. -1.88
6. -1.34
7. ± 2.33
8. ± 1.645
9. Right-tailed ($\alpha = 0.01$)
10. Two-tailed ($\alpha = 0.05$)
11. Two-tailed ($\alpha = 0.10$)
12. Left-tailed ($\alpha = 0.05$)
13. **(a)** Fail to reject H_0
    (b) Reject H_0
    (c) Fail to reject H_0
    (d) Reject H_0

Basic Skills and Concepts

1. Explain how to find critical values in a normal sampling distribution.

2. Explain how to use the z-test to test a hypothesized mean μ given a large sample ($n \geq 30$).

Finding Critical Values In Exercises 3–8, find the critical value(s) for the indicated type of test and level of significance α.

3. Right-tailed test, $\alpha = 0.05$
4. Right-tailed test, $\alpha = 0.08$
5. Left-tailed test, $\alpha = 0.03$
6. Left-tailed test, $\alpha = 0.09$
7. Two-tailed test, $\alpha = 0.02$
8. Two-tailed test, $\alpha = 0.10$

Graphical Analysis In Exercises 9–12, (a) state whether the graph shows a left-tailed, right-tailed, or two-tailed test and (b) state whether $\alpha = 0.01$, 0.05, or 0.10.

9.
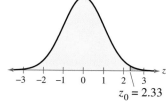
$z_0 = 2.33$

10.
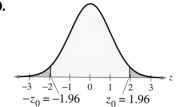
$-z_0 = -1.96 \quad z_0 = 1.96$

11.
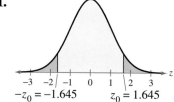
$-z_0 = -1.645 \quad z_0 = 1.645$

12.
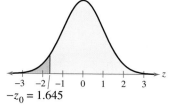
$-z_0 = 1.645$

Graphical Analysis In Exercises 13–16, state whether each standardized test statistic z allows you to reject the null hypothesis. Explain your reasoning.

13. (a) $z = 1.631$
    (b) $z = 1.723$
    (c) $z = -1.464$
    (d) $z = -1.655$

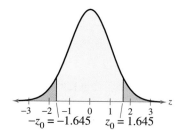
$-z_0 = -1.645 \quad z_0 = 1.645$

14. (a) Reject H_0
   (b) Fail to reject H_0
   (c) Fail to reject H_0
   (d) Reject H_0
15. (a) Fail to reject H_0
   (b) Fail to reject H_0
   (c) Fail to reject H_0
   (d) Reject H_0
16. (a) Fail to reject H_0
   (b) Reject H_0
   (c) Reject H_0
   (d) Fail to reject H_0
17. Reject H_0
18. Fail to reject H_0
19. Reject H_0
20. Reject H_0
21. (a) $H_0: \mu = 40$ $H_a: \mu \neq 40$
   (Claim: H_0)
   (b) ± 2.575
   (c) -0.584
   (d) Fail to reject H_0

14. (a) $z = 1.98$
   (b) $z = -1.89$
   (c) $z = 1.65$
   (d) $z = -1.99$

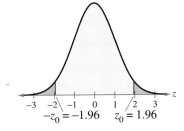

15. (a) $z = -1.301$
   (b) $z = 1.203$
   (c) $z = 1.280$
   (d) $z = 1.286$

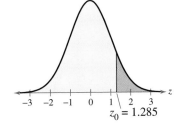

16. (a) $z = 2.557$
   (b) $z = -2.755$
   (c) $z = 2.585$
   (d) $z = -2.475$

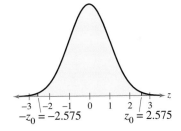

Using the z-Test   In Exercises 17–20, test the claim about the population mean μ at the given level of significance using the given sample statistics.

17. Claim: $\mu = 40$; $\alpha = 0.05$. Sample statistics: $\bar{x} = 39.2$, $s = 3.23$, $n = 75$

18. Claim: $\mu > 1030$; $\alpha = 0.05$. Sample statistics: $\bar{x} = 1035$, $s = 23$, $n = 50$

19. Claim: $\mu \neq 6000$; $\alpha = 0.01$. Sample statistics: $\bar{x} = 5800$, $s = 350$, $n = 35$

20. Claim: $\mu \leq 22{,}500$; $\alpha = 0.01$. Sample statistics: $\bar{x} = 23{,}250$, $s = 1200$, $n = 45$

Testing Claims   In Exercises 21–26, (a) write the claim mathematically and identify H_0 and H_a, (b) find the critical values and identify the rejection regions, (c) find the standardized test statistic, and (d) decide whether to reject or fail to reject the null hypothesis. Then interpret the decision in the context of the original claim.

21. A company that makes cola drinks states that the mean caffeine content per one 12-ounce bottle of cola is 40 milligrams. Suppose you work as a quality control manager and are asked to verify this claim. During your tests, you find that a random sample of thirty 12-ounce bottles of cola has a mean caffeine content of 39.2 milligrams with a standard deviation of 7.5 milligrams. At $\alpha = 0.01$, can you reject the company's claim? *(Adapted from Reader's Digest Eating for Good Health)*

22. (a) H_0: $\mu = 80$ H_a: $\mu \neq 80$
(Claim: H_0)
(b) ± 1.96
(c) 0.555
(d) Fail to reject H_0

23. (a) H_0: $\mu \geq 750$ H_a: $\mu < 750$
(Claim: H_0)
(b) -2.05
(c) -0.500
(d) Fail to reject H_0

24. (a) H_0: $\mu \leq 230$ H_a: $\mu > 230$
(Claim: H_0)
(b) 1.75
(c) 1.442
(d) Fail to reject H_0

25. (a) H_0: $\mu \leq 28$ H_a: $\mu > 28$
(Claim: H_a)
(b) 1.55
(c) 1.318
(d) Fail to reject H_0

26. (a) H_0: $\mu \geq 10$ H_a: $\mu < 10$
(Claim: H_0)
(b) -1.88
(c) -0.510
(d) Fail to reject H_0

22. A coffee shop claims that its fresh-brewed drinks have a mean caffeine content of 80 milligrams per five ounces. You work for a city health agency and are asked to test this claim. You find that a random sample of 42 five-ounce servings has a mean caffeine content of 83 milligrams and a standard deviation of 35 milligrams. At $\alpha = 0.05$, do you have enough evidence to reject the shop's claim? *(Adapted from Reader's Digest Eating for Good Health)*

23. A light bulb manufacturer guarantees that the mean life of a certain type of light bulb is at least 750 hours. If a random sample of 36 light bulbs has a mean life of 745 hours with a standard deviation of 60 hours, do you have enough evidence to reject the manufacturer's claim? Use $\alpha = 0.02$.

24. In your work for a national health organization, you are asked to monitor the amount of sodium in a certain brand of cereal. You find that a random sample of 52 cereal servings has a mean sodium content of 232 milligrams with a standard deviation of 10 milligrams. At $\alpha = 0.04$, can you conclude that the mean sodium content per serving of cereal is no more than 230 milligrams?

25. A scientist estimates that the mean nitrogen dioxide level in West London is greater than 28 parts per billion. You want to test this estimate. To do so, you determine the nitrogen dioxide levels for 36 randomly selected days. The results (in parts per billion) are listed below. At $\alpha = 0.06$, can you support the scientist's estimate? *(Adapted from National Environmental Technology Centre)*

27 29 53 31 16 47 22 17 13 46 99 15 20 17 28 10 14 9
35 29 32 67 24 31 43 29 12 39 65 94 12 27 13 16 40 62

26. A weight loss program claims that program participants have a mean weight loss of at least 10 pounds after one month. You work for a medical association and are asked to test this claim. A random sample of 30 program participants and their weight losses (in pounds) after one month is listed at the right. At $\alpha = 0.03$, do you have enough evidence to reject the program's claim?

Weight Loss (in pounds) after One Month

5	7 7 Key: 5 | 7 = 5.7
6	6 7
7	0 1 9
8	2 2 7 9
9	0 3 5 6 8
10	2 5 6 6
11	1 2 5 7 8
12	0 7 8
13	8
14	
15	0

27. (a) Fail to reject H_0

    (b) Reject H_0

28. (a) Fail to reject H_0

    (b) Fail to reject H_0

29. (a) H_0: $\mu \le 260$ H_a: $\mu > 260$
    (Claim: H_a)

    (b) 0.838

    (c) 0.2005

    (d) Fail to reject H_0

30. (a) H_0: $\mu \le 1.5$ H_a: $\mu > 1.5$
    (Claim: H_a)

    (b) 1.105

    (c) 0.1335

    (d) Fail to reject H_0

31. (a) H_0: $\mu \le 7$ H_a: $\mu > 7$
    (Claim: H_a)

    (b) 2.996

    (c) 0.0013

    (d) Reject H_0

32. (a) H_0: $\mu = 3.4$ H_a: $\mu \ne 3.4$
    (Claim: H_0)

    (b) -1.371

    (c) 0.1706

    (d) Fail to reject H_0

27. *Using P-values* Given H_0: $\mu = 100$, H_a: $\mu \ne 100$, and $P = 0.0461$.

    (a) Do you reject or fail to reject H_0 at the 0.01 level of significance?

    (b) Do you reject or fail to reject H_0 at the 0.05 level of significance?

28. *Using P-values* Given H_0: $\mu \ge 8.5$, H_a: $\mu < 8.5$, and $P = 0.0691$.

    (a) Do you reject or fail to reject H_0 at the 0.01 level of significance?

    (b) Do you reject or fail to reject H_0 at the 0.05 level of significance?

Testing Claims Using P-values In Exercises 29–34, (a) write the claim mathematically and identify H_0 and H_a, (b) find the standardized test statistic z and its corresponding area, (c) find the P-value, and (d) decide whether to reject or fail to reject the null hypothesis. Then interpret the decision in the context of the original claim.

29. In Illinois, a random sample of 85 eighth-grade students has a mean score of 265 with a standard deviation of 55 on a national mathematical assessment test. This prompts a state school administrator to declare that the mean score for the state's eighth-graders on the examination is more than 260. At $\alpha = 0.04$, is there enough evidence to support the administrator's claim? *(Adapted from National Center for Education Statistics)*

30. An automotive battery manufacturer guarantees that the mean reserve capacity of a certain battery is greater than 1.5 hours. To test this claim, you randomly select a sample of 50 batteries and find the mean reserve capacity to be 1.55 hours with a standard deviation of 0.32 hour. At $\alpha = 0.10$, do you have enough evidence to support the manufacturer's claim?

31. A tea drinker's association estimates that the mean consumption of tea by Americans is more than 7 gallons per year. In a sample of 100 people, you find that the mean consumption of tea is 7.8 gallons per year with a standard deviation of 2.67 gallons. At $\alpha = 0.07$, can you support the association's claim? *(Adapted from U.S. Department of Agriculture)*

32. A sample of 60 people shows that the mean tuna consumption by Americans is 3.2 pounds per year with a standard deviation of 1.13 pounds. A nutritionist considers this information and claims that the mean tuna consumption by Americans is 3.4 pounds per year. At $\alpha = 0.8$, can you reject the nutritionist's claim? *(Adapted from U.S. Department of Agriculture)*

33. (a) H_0: $\mu = 15$ H_a: $\mu \neq 15$ (Claim: H_0)
   (b) -0.219
   (c) 0.8258
   (d) Fail to reject H_0

34. (a) H_0: $\mu \geq \$69{,}000$
       H_a: $\mu < \$69{,}000$ (Claim: H_0)
   (b) 0.238
   (c) 0.5948
   (d) Fail to reject H_0

35. Fail to reject H_0

36. (a) Fail to reject H_0
   (b) Reject H_0
   (c) Reject H_0
   (d) Reject H_0

37. Using the classical z-test, the test statistic is compared to critical values. The z-test using a P-value compares the P-value to the level of significance α.

33. The number of years it took a random sample of 32 former smokers to quit permanently is listed. At $\alpha = 0.05$, test the claim that the mean time it takes smokers to quit smoking permanently is 15 years. *(Adapted from The Gallup Organization)*

15.7	13.2	22.6	13.0	10.7	18.1	14.7	7.0	17.3	7.5	21.8
12.3	19.8	13.8	16.0	15.5	13.1	20.7	15.5	9.8	11.9	16.9
7.0	19.3	13.2	14.6	20.9	15.4	13.3	11.6	10.9	21.6

34. An Alabama politician claims that the mean annual salary for engineering managers in Alabama is at least the national mean, $69,000. The annual salary (in dollars) for a random sample of 34 engineering managers in Alabama is listed. At $\alpha = 0.03$, test the politician's claim. *(Adapted from America's Career Infonet)*

65,612	67,610	60,739	76,997	82,977	65,692	81,732	83,302	71,772
82,978	79,608	66,402	67,331	83,160	74,074	55,055	79,496	47,938
65,828	76,414	82,449	71,593	53,018	67,836	46,160	74,877	60,823
71,044	64,214	75,162	64,075	63,056	74,005	57,142

35. *Electric Usage* You believe the mean annual kilowatt usage of American residential customers is less than 10,000. You do some research and find that a random sample of 30 residential customers has a mean kilowatt usage of 9900 with a standard deviation of 280. You conduct a statistical experiment where H_0: $\mu \geq 10{,}000$ and H_a: $\mu < 10{,}000$. At $\alpha = 0.01$, explain why you cannot reject H_0. *(Adapted from Edison Electric Institute)*

36. *Using Different Values of α and n* In Exercise 35, you believe that H_0 is not valid. Which of the following allows you to reject H_0?

(a) Use the same values but increase α from 0.01 to 0.02.

(b) Use the same values but increase α from 0.01 to 0.03.

(c) Use the same values but increase n from 30 to 50.

(d) Use the same values but increase n from 30 to 100.

Extending the Basics

37. *Writing* Explain the difference between the classical z-test for μ and the z-test for μ using a P-value.

7 **CASE STUDY**   WWW.STAT.NCSU.EDU/INFO/JSE

Journal of Statistics Education

Human Body Temperature: What's Normal?

In an article in the *Journal of Statistics Education* (vol. 4, no. 2, 1996), Allen Shoemaker describes a study that was reported in the *Journal of the American Medical Association.** It is generally accepted that the mean body temperature of adult humans is 98.6°F. In his article, Shoemaker uses the data from the JAMA article to test this hypothesis. Here is a summary of his test.

Claim: The body temperature of adults is 98.6°F.

H_0: $\mu = 98.6°F$ (Claim) H_a: $\mu \neq 98.6°F$

Sample Size: $n = 130$

Population: Adult human temperatures (Fahrenheit)

Distribution: Approximately normal

Test Statistics: $\bar{x} = 98.25$, $s = 0.73$

* Data for the JAMA article was collected from healthy men and women, aged 18 to 40, at the University of Maryland Center for Vaccine Development, Baltimore.

Men's Temperatures

96	3
96	7 9
97	0 1 1 1 2 3 4 4 4 4
97	5 5 6 6 6 7 8 8 8 8 9 9
98	0 0 0 0 0 0 1 1 2 2 2 2 3 3 4 4 4 4
98	5 5 6 6 6 6 6 6 7 7 8 8 8 9
99	0 0 0 1 2 3 4
99	5
100	
100	

Key: 96 | 3 = 96.3

Women's Temperatures

96	4
96	7 8
97	2 2 4
97	6 7 7 8 8 8 9 9 9
98	0 0 0 0 0 1 2 2 2 2 2 2 3 3 3 4 4 4 4 4
98	5 6 6 6 6 7 7 7 7 7 7 8 8 8 8 8 8 8 9
99	0 0 1 1 2 2 3 4
99	9
100	0
100	8

Key: 96 | 4 = 96.4

Exercises

1. Complete the hypothesis test by performing the following steps. Use a level of significance of $\alpha = 0.05$.

   (a) Sketch the sampling distribution.

   (b) Determine the critical values and add them to your sketch.

   (c) Determine the rejection regions and shade them in your sketch.

   (d) Find the standardized test statistic. Add it to your sketch.

   (e) Make a decision to reject or fail to reject the null hypothesis.

   (f) Interpret the decision in the context of the original claim.

2. If you lower the level of significance to $\alpha = 0.01$, does your decision change? Explain your reasoning.

3. Test the hypothesis that the mean temperature of men is 98.6°F. What can you conclude at a level of significance of $\alpha = 0.01$?

4. Test the hypothesis that the mean temperature of women is 98.6°F. What can you conclude at a level of significance of $\alpha = 0.01$?

5. Use the sample of 130 temperatures to form a 99% confidence interval for the mean body temperature of adult humans.

6. The conventional "normal" body temperature was established by Carl Wunderlich over 100 years ago. What, in Wunderlich's sampling procedure, do you think might have led him to an incorrect conclusion?

Hypothesis Testing for the Mean (Small Samples)

7.3

Critical Values in a *t*-Distribution • The *t*-Test for a Mean μ • Using *P*-values with *t*-Tests

What You Should Learn

- **How to find critical values in a t-distribution**
- **How to use the t-test to test a mean μ**
- **How to use technology to find P-values and use them to test a mean μ**

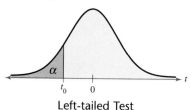

Left-tailed Test

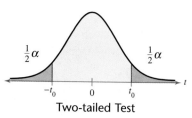

Right-tailed Test

Two-tailed Test

Note to Instructor

A thoughtful student might ask what would be done if the sample size is small, the standard deviation is not known, and you cannot assume that the population is normally distributed. Chapter 11 will cover this case (see nonparametric tests.) You can cover these tests immediately after this section if desirable.

Critical Values in a *t*-Distribution

In real life, it is often not practical to collect samples of size 30 or more. However, if the population has a normal, or nearly normal, distribution, you can still test the population mean μ. To do so, you can use the *t*-sampling distribution with $n - 1$ degrees of freedom.

GUIDELINES

Finding Critical Values in a *t*-Distribution

1. Identify the level of significance, α.
2. Identify the degrees of freedom, d.f. $= n - 1$.
3. Find the critical value(s) using Table 5 in Appendix B in the row with $n - 1$ degrees of freedom. If the hypothesis test is
   a. *left-tailed,* use "One Tail α" column with a negative sign.
   b. *right-tailed,* use "One Tail α" column with a positive sign.
   c. *two-tailed,* use "Two Tail α" column with a negative and a positive sign.

▶ EXAMPLE 1 *Finding Critical Values for t*

Find the critical value, t_0, for a left-tailed test given $\alpha = 0.05$ and $n = 21$.

SOLUTION   The degrees of freedom are

$$\text{d.f.} = n - 1 = 21 - 1 = 20.$$

To find the critical value, use Table 5 with d.f. $= 20$ and 0.05 in the "One Tail α" column. Because the test is a left-tailed test, the critical value is negative. So, $t_0 = -1.725$.

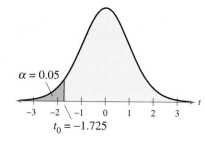

Try It Yourself 1

Find the critical value, t_0, for a left-tailed test with $\alpha = 0.01$ and $n = 14$.

a. *Find* the *t*-value in Table 5. Use d.f. $= 13$ and $\alpha = 0.01$ in the "One Tail α" column.
b. *Use* a negative sign.

Answer: Page A40 ◀

> **EXAMPLE 2** *Finding Critical Values for t*

Find the critical value, t_0, for a right-tailed test with $\alpha = 0.01$ and $n = 17$.

SOLUTION The degrees of freedom are

d.f. $= n - 1 = 17 - 1 = 16$.

To find the critical value, use Table 5 with d.f. $= 16$ and $\alpha = 0.01$ in the "One Tail α" column. Because the test is right-tailed, the critical value is positive. So, $t_0 = 2.583$.

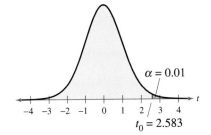

Try It Yourself 2

Find the critical value, t_0, for a right-tailed test with $\alpha = 0.05$ and $n = 9$.

a. *Find* the *t*-value in Table 5 using d.f. $= 8$ and $\alpha = 0.05$ in the "One Tail α" column.
b. *Use* a positive sign.

Answer: Page A40

> **EXAMPLE 3** *Finding Critical Values for t*

Find the critical values, t_0 and $-t_0$, for a two-tailed test with $\alpha = 0.05$ and $n = 26$.

SOLUTION The degrees of freedom are

d.f. $= n - 1 = 26 - 1 = 25$.

To find the critical value, use Table 5 with d.f. $= 25$ and $\alpha = 0.05$ in the "Two Tail α" column. Because the test is two-tailed, one critical value is negative and one is positive. So, $-t_0 = -2.060$ and $t_0 = 2.060$.

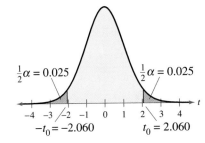

Try It Yourself 3

Find the critical values, $\pm t_0$, for a two-tailed test with $\alpha = 0.01$ and $n = 16$.

a. *Find* the *t*-value in Table 5 using d.f. $= 15$ and 0.01 in the "Two Tail α" column.
b. *Use* a negative and a positive sign.

Answer: Page A40

The t-Test for a Mean μ

To test a claim about a mean μ using a small sample $(n < 30)$ from a normal, or nearly normal, distribution, you can use a t-sampling distribution.

t-Test for a Mean μ

The **t-test for the mean** is a statistical test for a population mean. The t-test can be used when the population is normal or nearly normal, σ is unknown, and $n < 30$. The test statistic is $\bar{x}$ and the **standardized test statistic** is t.

$$t = \frac{\bar{x} - \mu}{s/\sqrt{n}}$$

The degrees of freedom are d.f. $= n - 1$.

$$t = \frac{(\text{Sample mean}) - (\text{Hypothesized mean})}{\text{Standard error}}$$

GUIDELINES

Using the t-Test for a Mean μ (Small Sample)

In Words	*In Symbols*
1. State the claim mathematically and verbally. Identify the null and alternative hypotheses.	State H_0 and H_a.
2. Specify the level of significance.	Identify α.
3. Identify the degrees of freedom and sketch the sampling distribution.	d.f. $= n - 1$
4. Determine any critical values.	Use Table 5.
5. Determine any rejection regions.	
6. Find the standardized test statistic.	$t = \dfrac{\bar{x} - \mu}{s/\sqrt{n}}$
7. Make a decision to reject or fail to reject the null hypothesis.	If t is in the rejection region, reject H_0. Otherwise, fail to reject H_0.
8. Interpret the decision in the context of the original claim.	

Remember that when you make a decision, the possibility of a type I or a type II error exists.

> See *Minitab* steps on page 358.

▶ **EXAMPLE 4** *Testing μ with a Small Sample*

A used car dealer says that the mean price of a 1995 Ford F-150 Super Cab is at least $16,500. You suspect this claim is incorrect and find that a random sample of 14 similar vehicles has a mean price of $15,700 and a standard deviation of $1250. Is there enough evidence to reject the dealer's claim at $\alpha = 0.05$? Assume the population is normally distributed.

SOLUTION   The claim is "the mean price is at least $16,500." So, the null and alternative hypotheses are

$$H_0: \ \mu \geq \$16,500 \ \text{(Claim)} \qquad \text{and} \qquad H_a: \ \mu < \$16,500.$$

Because the test is a left-tailed test, the level of significance is $\alpha = 0.05$. There are d.f. $= 14 - 1 = 13$ degrees of freedom and the critical value is $t_0 = -1.771$. The rejection region is $t < -1.771$. Using the *t*-test, the standardized test statistic is

$$t = \frac{\bar{x} - \mu}{s/\sqrt{n}} = \frac{15,700 - 16,500}{1250/\sqrt{14}} \approx -2.39.$$

The graph shows the location of the rejection region and the standardized test statistic, *t*. Because *t* is in the rejection region, you should decide to reject the null hypothesis. There is enough evidence at the 5% level of significance to reject the claim that the mean price of a 1995 Ford F-150 Super Cab is at least $16,500.

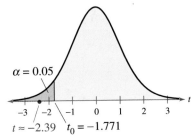

$\alpha = 0.05$

$t \approx -2.39 \quad t_0 = -1.771$

5% Level of Significance

Try It Yourself 4

An insurance agent says that the mean cost of insuring a 1995 Ford F-150 Super Cab is at least $875. A random sample of nine similar insurance quotes has a mean cost of $825 and a standard deviation of $62. Is there enough evidence to reject the agent's claim at $\alpha = 0.01$? Assume the population is normally distributed.

a. *Identify* the claim and state H_0 and H_a.
b. *Identify* the level of confidence α and the degrees of freedom d.f.
c. *Find* the critical value, t_0, and identify the rejection region.
d. *Use* the *t*-test to find the standardized test statistic *t*.
e. Sketch a graph. *Decide* whether to reject the null hypothesis.
f. Is there enough evidence to reject the claim that the mean cost of insuring a 1995 Ford F150 Super Cab is at least $875?

Answer: Page A40 ◀

See *TI-83* steps
on page 359.

> **EXAMPLE 5**   *Testing μ with a Small Sample*

An industrial company claims that the mean pH level of the water in a nearby river is 6.8. You randomly select 19 water samples and measure the pH of each. The sample mean and standard deviation are 6.7 and 0.24, respectively. Is there enough evidence to reject the company's claim at $\alpha = 0.05$? Assume the population is normally distributed.

SOLUTION   The claim is "the mean pH level is 6.8." So, the null and alternative hypotheses are

$$H_0: \mu = 6.8 \text{ (Claim)} \quad \text{and} \quad H_a: \mu \neq 6.8.$$

Because the test is a two-tailed test, the level of significance is $\alpha = 0.05$. There are d.f. $= 19 - 1 = 18$ degrees of freedom and the critical values are $-t_0 = -2.101$ and $t_0 = 2.101$. The rejection regions are $t < -2.101$ and $t > 2.101$. Using the t-test, the standardized test statistic is

$$t = \frac{\bar{x} - \mu}{s/\sqrt{n}} = \frac{6.7 - 6.8}{0.24/\sqrt{19}} \approx -1.82.$$

The graph shows the location of the rejection region and the standardized test statistic, t. Because t is not in the rejection region, you should decide not to reject the null hypothesis. There is not enough evidence at the 5% level of significance to reject the claim that the mean pH is 6.8.

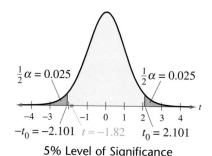

$\frac{1}{2}\alpha = 0.025$ $\frac{1}{2}\alpha = 0.025$

$-t_0 = -2.101$ $t \approx -1.82$ $t_0 = 2.101$

5% Level of Significance

Try It Yourself 5

The company also claims that the mean conductivity of the river is 1890 mg/L. The conductivity of a water sample is a measure of the total dissolved solids in the sample. You randomly select 19 water samples and measure the conductivity of each. The sample mean and standard deviation are 2500 mg/L and 700 mg/L, respectively. Is there enough evidence to reject the company's claim at $\alpha = 0.01$?

a. *Identify* the claim and state H_0 and H_a.
b. *Identify* the level of confidence α and the degrees of freedom d.f.
c. *Find* the critical values, $\pm t_0$, and identify the rejection regions.
d. *Use* the t-test to find the standardized test statistic t.
e. Sketch a graph. *Decide* whether to reject the null hypothesis.
f. Is there enough evidence to reject the company's claim?

Answer: Page A40

Using *P*-values with *t*-Tests

Suppose you wanted to find a *P*-value given $t = 1.98$, 15 degrees of freedom, and a right-tailed test. Using Table 5, you can determine that *P* falls between $\alpha = 0.025$ and $\alpha = 0.05$, but you cannot determine an exact value for *P*. In such cases, you can use technology to perform a hypothesis test and find exact *P*-values.

▶ **EXAMPLE 6**   *Using P-values with a t-Test*

The American Automobile Association claims that the mean daily meal cost for a family of four traveling on vacation in California is $124. A random sample of 11 such families has a mean daily meal cost of $135 with a standard deviation of $20. Is there enough evidence to reject the claim at $\alpha = 0.05$?

SOLUTION   The TI-83 display at the far left shows how to set up the hypothesis test. The two displays on the right show the possible results, depending on whether you select "CALCULATE" or "DRAW."

TI-83
T–Test
Inpt:Data Stats
μ_0:124
x:135
Sx:20
n:11
μ: $\neq \mu_0$ $<\mu_0$ $>\mu_0$
Calculate Draw

TI-83
T–Test
$\mu \neq$ 124
t=1.824143635
$\bar{p}$=.0981105275
x:135
Sx:20
n:11

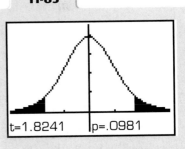

t=1.8241   p=.0981

From the displays you can see that $P \approx 0.0981$. Because $P > 0.05$, there is not enough evidence to reject the claim at the 5% level of significance. In other words, you should not reject the null hypothesis.

Try It Yourself 6

The American Automobile Association claims that the mean nightly lodging rate for a family of four traveling on vacation in California is at least $134. A random sample of six such families has a mean nightly lodging rate of $126 with a standard deviation of $12. Is there enough evidence to reject the claim at $\alpha = 0.05$?

a. *Use* a TI-83 to find the *P*-value.
b. *Compare* the *P*-value to the level of significance α.
c. *Make* a decision.
d. Is there enough evidence to reject the claim?   *Answer: Page A40* ◀

7.3 EXERCISES

HELP

 StatPro 7.3

 Internet Statistics 7.3

 Student Solutions Manual 7.3

 Videos 7.3

 Try It Yourself Answers 7.3

1. Identify the level of significance, α, and the degrees of freedom, $df = n - 1$. Find the critical value(s) using the t-distribution table in the row with $n - 1$ df. If the hypothesis test is:

   (1) left-tailed, use "One Tail α" column with a negative sign.

   (2) right-tailed, use "One Tail α" column with a positive sign.

   (3) two-tailed, use "Two Tail α" column with a negative and a positive sign.

2. See Selected Answers, page A81

3. 1.717

4. 2.764

5. -2.101

6. -1.771

7. ± 2.779

8. ± 2.262

9. **(a)** Fail to reject H_0

   (b) Fail to reject H_0

   (c) Fail to reject H_0

   (d) Reject H_0

10. See Selected Answers, page A81

11. **(a)** Fail to reject H_0

    (b) Fail to reject H_0

    (c) Reject H_0

    (d) Reject H_0

12. See Selected Answers, page A81

Basic Skills and Concepts

1. Explain how to find critical values for a t sampling distribution.

2. Explain how to use a t-test to test a hypothesized mean μ given a small sample ($n < 30$). What assumption about the population is necessary?

Finding Critical Values for t In Exercises 3–8, find the critical value(s) for the indicated test, level of significance α, and sample size n.

3. Right-tailed test, $\alpha = 0.05, n = 23$

4. Right-tailed test, $\alpha = 0.01, n = 11$

5. Left-tailed test, $\alpha = 0.025, n = 19$

6. Left-tailed test, $\alpha = 0.05, n = 14$

7. Two-tailed test, $\alpha = 0.01, n = 27$

8. Two-tailed test, $\alpha = 0.05, n = 10$

Graphical Analysis In Exercises 9–12, state whether the standardized test statistic t indicates that you should reject the null hypothesis. Explain.

9. (a) $t = 2.091$
   (b) $t = 0$
   (c) $t = -1.086$
   (d) $t = -2.096$

10. (a) $t = 1.308$
    (b) $t = -1.389$
    (c) $t = 1.650$
    (d) $t = -0.998$

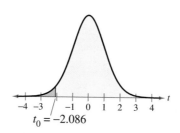

$t_0 = -2.086$

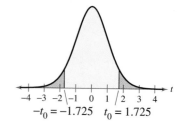

$-t_0 = -1.372$ $t_0 = 1.372$

11. (a) $t = -2.502$
    (b) $t = 2.203$
    (c) $t = 2.680$
    (d) $t = -2.703$

12. (a) $t = 1.705$
    (b) $t = -1.755$
    (c) $t = -1.585$
    (d) $t = 1.745$

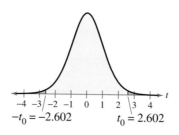

$-t_0 = -2.602$ $t_0 = 2.602$

$-t_0 = -1.725$ $t_0 = 1.725$

13. $H_0: \mu = 15$ (claim)
$H_a: \mu \neq 15$
$t_0 = \pm 4.032$
$t = -0.834$
Fail to reject H_0

14. $H_0: \mu \leq 25$
$H_a: \mu > 25$ (claim)
$t_0 = 1.746$
$t = 2.133$
Reject H_0

15. $H_0: \mu \geq 8000$ (claim)
$H_a: \mu < 8000$
$t_0 = -2.492$
$t = -3.333$
Reject H_0

16. $H_0: \mu = 52,000$
$H_a: \mu \neq 52,200$ (claim)
$t_0 = \pm 3.182$
$t = 2.033$
Fail to reject H_0

17. (a) $H_0: \mu \geq 100$
$H_a: \mu < 100$ (claim)
(b) $t_0 = -3.747$
(c) $t = -4.472$
(d) Reject H_0

18. (a) $H_0: \mu \leq 95$
$H_a: \mu > 95$ (claim)
(b) $t_0 = 3.143$
(c) $t = 0.311$
(d) Fail to reject H_0

19. (a) $H_0: \mu \leq 1$
$H_a: \mu > 1$ (claim)
(b) $t_0 = 1.796$
(c) $t = 2.309$
(d) Reject H_0

20. See Selected Answers, page A81

21. (a) $H_0: \mu = \$24,600$ (claim)
$H_a: \mu \neq \$24,600$
(b) $t_0 = \pm 2.262$
(c) $t = -0.572$
(d) Fail to reject H_0

Using a t-Test In Exercises 13–16, use a t-test to test the claim about the population mean μ for the given level of significance α and sample statistics. For each claim, assume the distribution is approximately normal.

13. Claim: $\mu = 15$; $\alpha = 0.01$. Sample statistics: $\bar{x} = 13.9$, $s = 3.23$, $n = 6$

14. Claim: $\mu > 25$; $\alpha = 0.05$. Sample statistics: $\bar{x} = 26.2$, $s = 2.32$, $n = 17$

15. Claim: $\mu \geq 8000$; $\alpha = 0.01$. Sample statistics: $\bar{x} = 7700$, $s = 450$, $n = 25$

16. Claim: $\mu \neq 52,200$; $\alpha = 0.05$. Sample statistics: $\bar{x} = 53,220$, $s = 1200$, $n = 4$

Testing Claims In Exercises 17–22, (a) write the claim mathematically and identify H_0 and H_a, (b) find the critical values and identify the rejection regions, (c) find the standardized test statistic, and (d) decide whether to reject or fail to reject the null hypothesis. Then interpret the decision in the context of the original claim. For each claim, assume the distribution of the population is approximately normal.

17. A microwave oven repairer says that the mean repair cost for damaged microwave ovens is less than $100. You work for the repairer and want to test this claim. You find that a random sample of five microwave ovens has a mean repair cost of $75 and a standard deviation of $12.50. At $\alpha = 0.01$, do you have enough evidence to support the repairer's claim? *(Adapted from Consumer Reports)*

18. A computer repairer believes that the mean repair cost for damaged computers is more than $95. To test this claim, you determine the repair costs for seven randomly selected computers and find that the mean repair cost is $100 per computer with a standard deviation of $42.50. At $\alpha = 0.01$, do you have enough evidence to support the repairer's claim? *(Adapted from Consumer Reports)*

19. An environmentalist estimates that the mean waste recycled by American adults is more than 1 pound per person per day. You want to test this claim. You find that the mean waste recycled per person per day for a random sample of 12 American adults is 1.2 pounds and the standard deviation is 0.3 pound. At $\alpha = 0.05$, can you support the claim? *(Adapted from U.S. Environmental Protection Agency)*

20. As part of your work for an environmental awareness group, you want to test a claim that the mean waste generated by American adults is more than 4 pounds per day. In a random sample of 10 American adults, you find that the mean waste generated per person per day is 4.3 pounds with a standard deviation of 1.2 pounds. At $\alpha = 0.05$, can you support the claim? *(Adapted from U.S. Environmental Protection Agency)*

21. An employment information service claims that the mean annual pay for full-time male workers over age 25 and without high school diplomas is $24,600. The annual pay for a random sample of 10 full-time male workers without high school diplomas is listed. At $\alpha = 0.05$, test the claim that the mean salary is $24,600. *(Adapted from U.S. Bureau of the Census)*

22,954 23,438 24,655 23,695 25,275 19,212 21,456 25,493 26,480 28,585

22. (a) H_0: $\mu = \$17,100$ (claim)

H_a: $\mu \neq \$17,100$

(b) $t_0 = \pm 2.201$

(c) $t = 0.948$

(d) Fail to reject H_0

23. (a) H_0: $\mu \geq 3.0$

H_a: $\mu < 3.0$ (claim)

(b) 0.130

(c) Fail to reject H_0

24. (a) H_0: $\mu \geq 5.0$

H_a: $\mu < 5.0$ (claim)

(b) 0.001

(c) Reject H_0

25. (a) H_0: $\mu \geq 32$

H_a: $\mu < 32$ (claim)

(b) 0.034

(c) Fail to reject H_0

26. (a) H_0: $\mu = 11.0$ (claim)

H_a: $\mu \neq 11.0$

(b) 0.316

(c) Fail to reject H_0

22. An employment information service says the mean annual pay for full-time female workers over age 25 and without high school diplomas is $17,100. The annual pay for a random sample of 12 full-time female workers without high school diplomas is listed. At $\alpha = 0.05$, test the claim that the mean salary is $17,100. *(Adapted from U.S. Bureau of the Census)*

16,009 16,790 17,328 18,161 16,631 21,028
16,114 17,176 17,503 19,764 15,316 18,801

Testing Claims Using P-values In Exercises 23–26, (a) write the claim mathematically and identify H_0 and H_a, (b) use technology to find the P-value, and (c) decide whether to reject or fail to reject the null hypothesis. Then interpret the decision in the context of the original claim.

23. As part of your study on the food consumption habits of teenage males, you randomly select 20 teenage males and ask each how many 12-ounce servings of soda they drink per day. The results are listed below. At $\alpha = 0.05$, is there enough evidence to claim that teenage males drink less than 3.0 twelve-ounce servings of soda per day? *(Adapted from Center for Science in the Public Interest)*

3.3 2.1 2.5 2.1 3.4 3.3 4.4 3.4 2.5 3.2
2.5 3.8 2.0 2.9 1.9 1.3 1.9 2.8 4.2 2.2

24. A bottled water association says that the mean number of 8-ounce glasses of water American adults drink each day is less than 5.0. The number of 8-ounce glasses of water a random sample of 24 American adults drank in one day is listed. At $\alpha = 0.05$, is there enough evidence to support the association's claim? *(Adapted from USA Today)*

3.6 4.5 5.9 5.3 3.1 4.1 3.9 4.3 4.5 3.6 2.5 5.2
4.7 5.6 3.0 2.6 4.0 2.7 3.9 6.5 5.4 3.1 6.0 2.9

25. You receive a brochure from a large university. The brochure indicates that the mean class size for full-time faculty is less than 32. You want to test this claim. You randomly select 18 classes taught by full-time faculty and determine the class size of each. The results are listed below. At $\alpha = 0.01$, can you support the university's claim? *(Adapted from National Center for Education Statistics)*

35 28 29 33 32 40 26 25 29 28 30 36 33 29 27 30 28 25

26. The dean of a university estimates that the mean number of classroom hours per week for full-time faculty is 11.0. As a member of the student council, you want to test this claim. A random sample of the number of classroom hours for full-time faculty for one week is listed below. At $\alpha = 0.01$, can you reject the dean's claim? *(Adapted from National Center for Education Statistics)*

11.8 8.6 12.6 7.9 6.4 10.4 13.6 9.1

27. P-value $= 0.096 > 0.01 = \alpha$, fail to reject H_0.

28. (a) Fail to reject H_0

(b) Reject H_0

(c) Fail to reject H_0

(d) Reject H_0

29. Use the t-distribution

H_0: $\mu \geq 21$ (claim) and
H_a: $\mu < 21$

$t = -1.118$

P-value $= 0.163$

Fail to reject H_0

30. Use the z-distribution

H_0: $\mu = 337$ (claim)
H_a: $\mu \neq 337$

$z = -3.536$

P-value $= 0.0004$

Reject H_0

31. Use the z-distribution

H_0: $\mu \geq 21$ (claim) and
H_a: $\mu < 21$

$z = -0.894$

P-value $= 0.1867$

Fail to reject H_0

32. Use the t-distribution

H_0: $\mu = 337$ (claim)
H_a: $\mu \neq 337$

$t = -1.118$

P-value $= 0.326$

Fail to reject H_0

33. It is not necessary to a hypothesis test to test the repairer's claim.

$t = \dfrac{\bar{x} - \mu}{\dfrac{s}{\sqrt{n}}} = \dfrac{75 - 50}{\dfrac{12.50}{\sqrt{5}}} = 4.472$

Recall from #17 that:

$t = \dfrac{\bar{x} - \mu}{\dfrac{s}{\sqrt{n}}} = \dfrac{75 - 100}{\dfrac{12.50}{\sqrt{5}}} = -4.472$

27. *Credit Card Balances* To test the claim that the mean credit card balance of cardholders is greater than $1500, you do some research and find that a random sample of six cardholders has a mean credit card balance of $1700 with a standard deviation of $325. You conduct a statistical experiment where H_0: $\mu \leq \$1500$ and H_a: $\mu > \$1500$. At $\alpha = 0.01$, explain why you cannot reject H_0. *(Adapted from Board of Governors of the Federal Reserve System)*

28. *Using Different Values of α and n* In Exercise 27, you believe that H_0 is not valid. Which of the following allows you to reject H_0?

(a) Use the same values but increase α from 0.01 to 0.05.

(b) Use the same values but increase α from 0.01 to 0.10.

(c) Use the same values but increase n from 6 to 12.

(d) Use the same values but increase n from 6 to 24.

Extending the Basics

Deciding on a Distribution In Exercises 29 and 30, decide whether you should use a normal sampling distribution or a t-sampling distribution to perform the hypothesis test. Justify your decision. Then use the distribution to test the hypothesis. Write a short paragraph about the results of the test and what you can conclude about the hypothesis.

29. A car company says that the mean gas mileage for its luxury sedan is at least 21 miles per gallon (mpg). You believe the claim is incorrect and find that a random sample of 5 cars has a mean gas mileage of 19 mpg and a standard deviation of 4 mpg. Assume the gas mileage is normally distributed. At $\alpha = 0.05$, test the company's claim. *(Adapted from Consumer Reports)*

30. An administrator of a state university system says that the mean time full-time faculty spend with students outside of class is 337 hours. The mean time a random sample of 50 full-time faculty members spent with students outside of class was 332 hours and the standard deviation was 10 hours. At $\alpha = 0.01$, test the claim that the mean time is 337 hours. *(Adapted from National Center for Education Statistics)*

31. Repeat Exercise 29, but assume the population standard deviation is $\sigma = 5$ miles per gallon. Compare the results.

32. Repeat Exercise 30, but assume the sample size is 5 and the amount of time is normally distributed. Compare the results.

33. *Is a Test Necessary?* In Exercise 17, suppose the repairer's claim was that the mean repair cost was at least $50. Assuming the same sample statistics, is it necessary to use a hypothesis test to test the repairer's claim? Why or why not?

7.4 Hypothesis Testing for Proportions

Hypothesis Test for Proportions

Hypothesis Test for Proportions

What You Should Learn

- *How to use the z-test to test a population proportion p*

Hypothesis Test for Proportions

In this section, you will learn how to test a population proportion p. If $np \geq 5$ and $nq \geq 5$ for a binomial distribution, then the sampling distribution for $\hat{p}$ is normal with $\mu_{\hat{p}} = p$ and $\sigma_{\hat{p}} = \sqrt{pq/n}$.

z-Test for a Proportion p

Given a binomial distribution such that $np \geq 5$ and $nq \geq 5$, you can use a z-test to test a population proportion p. The **test statistic** is the sample proportion $\hat{p}$ and the **standardized test statistic** is z.

$$z = \frac{\hat{p} - p}{\sqrt{pq/n}}$$

GUIDELINES

Using a z-Test for a Proportion p

Verify that $np \geq 5$ and $nq \geq 5$.

In Words	*In Symbols*
1. State the claim mathematically and verbally. Identify the null and alternative hypotheses.	State H_0 and H_a.
2. Specify the level of significance.	Identify α.
3. Sketch the sampling distribution.	
4. Determine any critical values.	Use Table 4.
5. Determine any rejection regions.	
6. Find the standardized test statistic.	$z = \dfrac{\hat{p} - p}{\sqrt{pq/n}}$
7. Make a decision to reject or fail to reject the null hypothesis.	If z is in the rejection region, reject H_0. Otherwise, fail to reject H_0.
8. Interpret the decision in the context of the original claim.	

See *TI-83* steps on page 359.

> **EXAMPLE 1** *Hypothesis Test for a Proportion*

A medical researcher claims that less than 20% of American adults are allergic to a medication. In a random sample of 100 adults, 15% say they have such an allergy. Test the researcher's claim at $\alpha = 0.01$.

SOLUTION The products $np = 100(0.20) = 20$ and $nq = 100(0.80) = 80$ are both greater than 5. So, you can use a z-test. The claim is "less than 20% are allergic to a medication." So, the null and alternative hypotheses are

$$H_0\text{: } p \geq 0.2 \quad \text{and} \quad H_a\text{: } p < 0.2. \text{ (Claim)}$$

Because the test is a left-tailed test and the level of significance is $\alpha = 0.01$, the critical value is $z_0 = -2.33$ and the rejection region is $z < -2.33$. Using the z-test, the standardized test statistic is

$$z = \frac{\hat{p} - p}{\sqrt{pq/n}} = \frac{0.15 - 0.2}{\sqrt{(0.2)(0.8)/100}} \approx -1.25.$$

The graph shows the location of the rejection region and the standardized test statistic, z. Because z is not in the rejection region, you should decide not to reject the null hypothesis. In other words, there is not enough evidence to support the claim that less than 20% of Americans are allergic to the medication.

Study Tip

Remember that when you fail to reject H_0, a type II error is possible. For instance, in Example 1 the null hypothesis, $p \geq 0.20$, may be false.

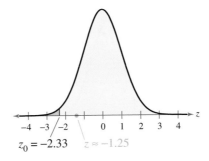

$z_0 = -2.33$ $z \approx -1.25$

Try It Yourself 1

A researcher claims that less than 30% of American adults are allergic to trees, weeds, flowers, and grasses. In a random sample of 86 adults, 20% say they have such an allergy. At $\alpha = 0.05$, is there enough evidence to support the researcher's claim?

a. *Identify* the claim and state H_0 and H_a.
b. *Identify* the level of confidence α.
c. *Find* the critical value, z_0, and *identify* the rejection region.
d. *Use* the z-test to find the standardized test statistic z.
e. *Decide* whether to reject the null hypothesis. Use a graph if necessary.
f. Is there enough evidence to support the researcher's claim?

Answer: Page A40

> See *Minitab* steps
> on page 358.

▶ **EXAMPLE 2**   **Hypothesis Test for a Proportion**

Harper's Index claims that 23% of Americans are in favor of outlawing cigarettes. You decide to test this claim and ask a random sample of 200 Americans whether they are in favor of outlawing cigarettes. Of the 200 Americans, 27% are in favor. At $\alpha = 0.05$, is there enough evidence to reject the claim? *(Source: Harper's Index)*

SOLUTION   The products $np = 200(0.23) = 46$ and $nq = 200(0.77) = 154$ are both greater than 5. So, you can use a z-test. The claim is "23% of Americans are in favor of outlawing cigarettes." So, the null and alternative hypotheses are

$$H_0: p = 0.23 \text{ (Claim)} \quad \text{and} \quad H_a: p \neq 0.23.$$

Because the test is a two-tailed test and the level of significance is $\alpha = 0.05$, the critical values are $-z_0 = -1.96$ and $z_0 = 1.96$. The rejection regions are $z < -1.96$ and $z > 1.96$. Using the z-test, the standardized test statistic is

$$z = \frac{\hat{p} - p}{\sqrt{pq/n}} = \frac{0.27 - 0.23}{\sqrt{(0.23)(0.77)/200}} \approx 1.34.$$

The graph shows the location of the rejection regions and the standardized test statistic, z.

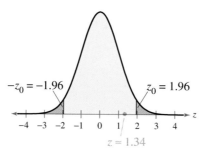

Because z is not in the rejection region, you should fail to reject the null hypothesis. At the 5% level of significance, there is not enough evidence to reject the claim that 23% of Americans are in favor of outlawing cigarettes.

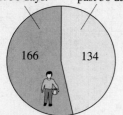

Picturing the World

A recent study claimed that 53.7% of 3-year-olds were given over-the-counter drugs (such as Tylenol) in a period of 30 days. To test this claim you conduct a random telephone survey of 300 parents of 3-year-olds. In the survey, you find that 166 of the 3-year-olds were given an over-the-counter drug during the past 30 days. *(Source: JAMA)*

Given OTC drugs in the past 30 days.   Not given OTC drugs in the past 30 days.

166   134

At $\alpha = 0.05$, is there enough evidence to support the study's findings?

Try It Yourself 2

USA Today reports that 5% of American adults have seen a UFO. You decide to test this claim and ask a random sample of 250 Americans whether they have ever seen a UFO. Of those surveyed, 8% reply yes. At $\alpha = 0.01$, is there enough evidence to reject the claim?

a. *Identify* the claim and state H_0 and H_a.
b. *Identify* the level of confidence α.
c. *Find* the critical values, $-z_0$ and z_0, and identify the rejection regions.
d. *Use* the z-test to find the standardized test statistic z.
e. *Decide* whether to reject the null hypothesis. Use a graph if necessary.
f. *Is* there enough evidence to support the claim?   *Answer: Page A40*

▶ EXAMPLE 3   *Using a Hypothesis Test to Test a Proportion*

The Pew Research Center claims that more than 55% of American adults regularly watch a network news broadcast. You decide to test this claim and ask a random sample of 425 Americans whether they regularly watch a network news broadcast. Of the 425 Americans, 255 respond yes. At $\alpha = 0.05$, is there enough evidence to support the claim? *(Source: Pew Research Center for the People and the Press)*

SOLUTION   The products $np = 425(0.55) \approx 234$ and $nq = 425(0.45) \approx 191$ are both greater than 5. So, you can use a z-test. The claim is "more than 55% of Americans watch a network news broadcast." So, the null and alternative hypotheses are

$$H_0\text{: } p \leq 0.55 \quad \text{and} \quad H_a\text{: } p > 0.55. \text{ (Claim)}$$

Because the test is a right-tailed test and the level of significance is $\alpha = 0.05$, the critical value is $z_0 = 1.645$ and the rejection region is $z > 1.645$. Using the z-test, the standardized test statistic is

$$z = \frac{\hat{p} - p}{\sqrt{pq/n}} = \frac{(x/n) - p}{\sqrt{pq/n}} = \frac{(255/425) - 0.55}{\sqrt{(0.55)(0.45)/425}} \approx 2.07.$$

The graph shows the location of the rejection region and the standardized test statistic, z. Because z is in the rejection region, you should decide to reject the null hypothesis. There is enough evidence at the 5% level of significance to support the claim that more than 55% of American adults regularly watch a network news broadcast.

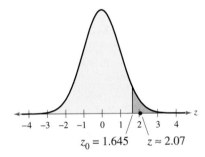

$z_0 = 1.645 \qquad z \approx 2.07$

Try It Yourself 3

The Pew Research Center claims that more than 38% of American adults regularly watch a cable news broadcast. You decide to test this claim and ask a random sample of 75 Americans whether they regularly watch a cable news broadcast. Of the 75 Americans, 33 respond yes. At $\alpha = 0.01$, is there enough evidence to support the claim? *(Source: Pew Research Center for the People and the Press)*

a. *Identify* the claim and state H_0 and H_a.
b. *Identify* the level of confidence α.
c. *Find* the critical value, z_0, and *identify* the rejection region.
d. *Use* the z-test to find the standardized test statistic z.
e. *Decide* whether to reject the null hypothesis. Use a graph if necessary.
f. Is there enough evidence to support the claim?   *Answer: Page A40* ◀

7.4 EXERCISES

HELP

StatPro 7.4

Internet Statistics 7.4

Student Solutions Manual 7.4

Videos 7.4

Try It Yourself Answers 7.4

1. Verify that $np \geq 5$ and $nq \geq 5$. State H_0 and H_a. Specify the level of significance, α. Determine the critical value(s) and rejection region(s). Find the standardized test statistic. Make a decision and interpret in the context of the original claim.

2. If $np \geq 5$ and $nq \leq 5$, the normal distribution can be used.

3. Use normal distribution

   H_0: $p = 0.25$
   H_a: $p \neq 0.25$ (claim)

   $z_0 = \pm 1.96$

   $z = -0.260$

   Fail to reject H_0

4. See Selected Answers, page A81

5. Use normal distribution

   H_0: $p \geq 0.60$
   H_a: $p < 0.60$ (claim)

   $z_0 = -2.33$

   $z = -0.242$

   Fail to reject H_0

6. See Selected Answers, page A81

7. See Odd Answers, page A62

8. See Selected Answers, page A81

9. See Odd Answers, page A62

10. See Selected Answers, page A81

Basic Skills and Concepts

1. Explain how to test a population proportion p.

2. Explain how to decide when a normal distribution can be used to approximate a binomial distribution.

Using the z-Test In Exercises 3–6, decide whether the normal sampling distribution can be used. Test the claim about the population proportion p for the given values and level of significance α.

3. Claim: $p \neq 0.25$; $\alpha = 0.05$. Sample statistics: $\hat{p} = 0.239$, $n = 105$

4. Claim: $p \leq 0.30$; $\alpha = 0.05$. Sample statistics: $\hat{p} = 0.35$, $n = 500$

5. Claim: $p < 0.60$; $\alpha = 0.01$. Sample statistics: $\hat{p} = 0.58$, $n = 35$

6. Claim: $p > 0.125$; $\alpha = 0.01$. Sample statistics: $\hat{p} = 0.2325$, $n = 45$

Testing Claims In Exercises 7–12, (a) write the claim mathematically and identify H_0 and H_a, (b) find the critical values and identify the rejection regions, (c) find the standardized test statistic, and (d) decide whether to reject or fail to reject the null hypothesis. Then interpret the decision in the context of the original claim.

7. A medical researcher says that at least 25% of American adults are smokers. In a random sample of 200 adults, 24.5% say that they are smokers. At $\alpha = 0.01$, do you have enough evidence to reject the researcher's claim? *(Adapted from U.S. National Center for Health Statistics)*

8. A medical researcher estimates that no more than 55% of American adults eat breakfast every day. In a random sample of 250 adults, 56.4% say that they eat breakfast every day. At $\alpha = 0.01$, is there enough evidence to reject the researcher's claim? *(Adapted from U.S. National Center for Health Statistics)*

9. You are employed by an environmental conservation agency that recently claimed more than 30% of American consumers have stopped buying a certain product because the manufacturing of the product pollutes the environment. You want to test this claim. To do so, you randomly select 1050 American consumers and find that 32% have stopped buying this product because of pollution concerns. At $\alpha = 0.03$, can you support the claim? *(Adapted from Wirthlin Worldwide)*

10. An environmentalist claims that more than 50% of British consumers want supermarkets to stop selling genetically modified foods. You want to test this claim. You find that in a random sample of 100 British consumers, 53% say that they want supermarkets to stop selling genetically modified foods. At $\alpha = 0.10$, can you support the environmentalist's claim? *(Adapted from Friends of the Earth)*

11. (a) H_0: $p = 0.60$ (claim)
H_a: $p \neq 0.60$

(b) $z_0 = \pm 2.33$

(c) $z = -2.571$

(d) Reject H_0.

12. (a) H_0: $p = 0.70$ (claim)
H_a: $p \neq 0.70$

(b) $z_0 = \pm 1.96$

(c) $z = -4.469$

(d) Reject H_0.

13. H_0: $p \geq 0.52$ (claim)
H_a: $p < 0.52$

$z_0 = -1.645$

$z = -0.439$

Fail to reject H_0.

14. The company should continue the use of giveaways since there is not enough evidence to say that less the 52% of the attendees would be more likely to stop at the exhibit.

15. P-values are calculated in the same manner as when using the z-test for testing the mean.

H_0: $p \geq 0.25$ (claim)
H_a: $p < 0.25$

$z = -0.103$

P-value $= 0.4602$

Fail to reject H_0

16. H_0: $p = 0.60$ (claim)
H_a: $p \neq 0.60$

$z_0 = \pm 2.33$

$z = -2.587$

Reject H_0

11. In your work for a business regulatory agency, you find that in a sample of 1762 Americans, 1004 of them believe that government regulation of business does more harm than good. At $\alpha = 0.02$, can you reject the claim that 60% of Americans have this view? *(Adapted from Pew Research Center for the People and the Press)*

12. A government watchdog association claims that 70% of Americans agree that the government is inefficient and wasteful. You work for a government agency and are asked to test this claim. You find that in a random sample of 1165 Americans, 746 agreed with this view. At $\alpha = 0.05$, do you have enough evidence to reject the association's claim? *(Adapted from Pew Research Center for the People and the Press)*

Trade Show Giveaways In Exercises 13 and 14, use the following information. The graph shows what attendees think about the effectiveness of giveaways at trade shows.

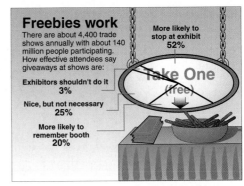

Copyright 1998, USA TODAY. Reprinted with permission.

13. You work for a company that exhibits at trade shows. Using figures from the last 30 trade shows, you find that 48% of the attendees visited your company's exhibit when there was a giveaway. Conduct a hypothesis test of the claim that at least 52% of the attendees at trade shows are more likely to visit an exhibit when there is a giveaway. Use a level of significance of $\alpha = 0.05$.

14. Use your conclusion in Exercise 13 to write a paragraph on the use of giveaways at trade shows. Do you think your company should continue to use giveaways to get people to visit the company's exhibits? Explain.

Extending the Basics

15. *P-values* Explain how you could use P-values to test a hypothesis about a population proportion. Use your explanation and repeat Exercise 7. Compare the results.

16. *Alternate Formula* Repeat Exercise 11, but find the standardized test statistic using the formula

$$z = \frac{x - np}{\sqrt{npq}},$$

where x is the number of successes. Compare the results.

TECHNOLOGY
MINITAB   **EXCEL**   **TI-83**

The Case of the Vanishing Women

53% ➡ 29% ➡ 9% ➡ 0%

In 1968, Dr. Benjamin Spock and others were tried for conspiracy to violate the Selective Service Act by encouraging resistance to the Vietnam War. By a series of three selections, there ended up being no women on the jury. The next year, Hans Zeisel wrote an article in *The University of Chicago Law Review* using statistics and hypothesis testing to argue that the jury selection was biased against Dr. Spock. Dr. Spock was a well-known pediatrician and author of books about raising children. Millions of mothers had read his books and followed his advice. By keeping women off the jury, Zeisel argued that the court prejudiced the verdict.

The jury selection process for Dr. Spock's trial is shown in the flowchart at the right.

Stage 1. The clerk of the Federal District Court selected 350 people "at random" from the Boston City Directory. The directory contained several hundred names, 53% of whom were women. However, only 102 of the 350 people selected were women.

Stage 2. The trial judge, Judge Ford, selected 100 people "at random" from the 350 people. This group was called a venire and it contained only nine women.

Stage 3. The court clerk assigned numbers to the members of the venire and one by one, they were interrogated by the attorneys for the prosecution and defense until 12 members of the jury were chosen. At this stage, only one potential female juror was questioned and she was eliminated by the prosecutor under his quota of peremptory challenges (for which he did not have to give a reason).

Exercises

1. The Minitab display below shows a hypothesis test for a claim that the proportion of women in the city directory is $p = 0.53$. In the test, $n = 350$ and $\hat{p} = 0.2914$. Should you reject the claim? What is the level of significance? Explain.

2. In Exercise 1, you rejected the claim that $p = 0.53$. But this claim was true. What type of error is this?

3. If you reject a true claim with a level of significance that is virtually zero, what does this tell you about the randomness of your sampling process?

4. Describe a hypothesis test for Judge Ford's "random" selection of the venire. Use a claim of

$$p = \frac{102}{350} \approx 0.2914.$$

   (a) Write the null and alternative hypotheses.
   (b) Use a technology tool to perform the test.
   (c) Make a decision.
   (d) Interpret the decision in the context of the original claim. Could Judge Ford's selection of 100 venire members have been random?

MINITAB

Test and Confidence Interval for One Proportion

Test of p = 0.53 vs p not = 0.53

Sample	X	N	Sample p	99.0 % CI	Z-Value	P-Value
1	102	350	0.291429	(0.228862, 0.353995)	-8.94	0.000

Extended solutions are given in the *Technology Supplement*.
Technical instruction is provided for Minitab, Excel, and the TI-83.

7.5

Hypothesis Testing for the Variance and Standard Deviation

7.5

Critical Values • The Chi-Square Test

What You Should Learn

- *How to find critical values for a χ^2-test*
- *How to use the χ^2-test to test a variance or a standard deviation*

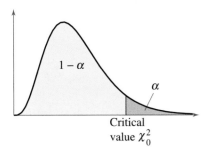

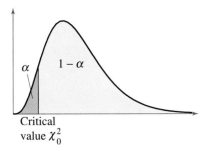

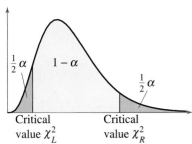

Critical Values

In real life, it is often important to produce consistent predictable results. For instance, consider a company that manufactures golf balls. The manufacturer must produce millions of golf balls each having the same size and the same weight. There is a very low tolerance for variation. If the population is normal, you can test the variance and standard deviation of the process using the chi-square distribution with $n - 1$ degrees of freedom.

GUIDELINES

Finding Critical Values for the χ^2-Test
1. Specify the level of significance, α.
2. Determine the degrees of freedom, d.f. $= n - 1$.
3. The critical values for the χ^2-distribution are found in Table 6 of Appendix B. To find the critical value(s) for a
   a. *right-tailed test,* use the value that corresponds to d.f. and α.
   b. *left-tailed test,* use the value that corresponds to d.f. and $1 - \alpha$.
   c. *two-tailed test,* use the values that correspond to d.f. and $\frac{1}{2}\alpha$ and d.f. and $1 - \frac{1}{2}\alpha$.

▶ **EXAMPLE 1** *Finding Critical Values for χ^2*

Find the critical χ^2-value for a right-tailed test when $n = 26$ and $\alpha = 0.10$.

SOLUTION The degrees of freedom are d.f. $= n - 1 = 26 - 1 = 25$. The graph at the right shows a χ^2-distribution with 25 degrees of freedom and a shaded area of $\alpha = 0.10$ in the right tail. Using Table 6 with d.f. $= 25$ and $\alpha = 0.10$, the critical value is $\chi_0^2 = 34.382$.

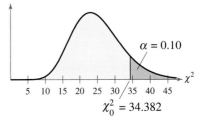

Try It Yourself 1

Find the critical χ^2-value for a right-tailed test when $n = 18$ and $\alpha = 0.01$.
a. Find the value using Table 6 with d.f. $= n - 1$ and the area α.

Answer: Page A40

Note to Instructor

This section can be omitted or covered later (with Chapter 10) without loss of continuity.

▶ **EXAMPLE 2**   *Finding Critical Values for χ^2*

Find the critical χ^2-value for a left-tailed test when $n = 11$ and $\alpha = 0.01$.

SOLUTION   The degrees of freedom are
d.f. $= n - 1 = 11 - 1 = 10$. The graph at
the right shows a χ^2-distribution with 10
degrees of freedom and a shaded area of
$\alpha = 0.01$ in the left tail. The area to the
right of the critical value is $1 - \alpha =$
$1 - 0.01 = 0.99$. Using Table 6 with
d.f. $= 10$ and the area $1 - \alpha = 0.99$, the
critical value is $\chi_0^2 = 2.558$.

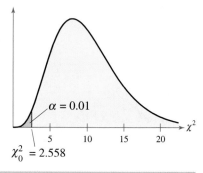

$\chi_0^2 = 2.558$

Try It Yourself 2

Find the critical χ^2-value for a left-tailed test when $n = 30$ and $\alpha = 0.05$.

a. *Find* the value using Table 6 with d.f. $= n - 1$ and the area $1 - \alpha$.

Answer: Page A40 ◀

▶ **EXAMPLE 3**   *Finding Critical Values for χ^2*

Find the critical χ^2-values for a two-tailed test when $n = 13$ and $\alpha = 0.01$.

SOLUTION   The degrees of freedom are d.f. $= n - 1 = 13 - 1 = 12$. The
graph at the left shows a χ^2-distribution with 12 degrees of freedom and a
shaded area of $\frac{1}{2}\alpha = 0.005$ in each tail. The areas to the right of the critical
values are

$$\frac{1}{2}\alpha = 0.005 \quad \text{and} \quad 1 - \frac{1}{2}\alpha = 0.995.$$

Using Table 6 with d.f. $= 12$ and the areas 0.005 and 0.995, the critical values
are $\chi_L^2 = 3.074$ and $\chi_R^2 = 28.299$.

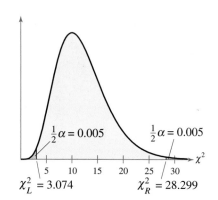

$\frac{1}{2}\alpha = 0.005$ $\frac{1}{2}\alpha = 0.005$

$\chi_L^2 = 3.074$ $\chi_R^2 = 28.299$

Note to Instructor

Because chi-square distributions are
not symmetric (like normal or
t-distributions), in a two-tailed
test the two critical values are not
opposites. Each critical value must
be calculated separately.

Try It Yourself 3

Find the critical χ^2-values for a two-tailed test when $n = 19$ and
$\alpha = 0.05$.

a. *Find* the first critical value using Table 6 with d.f. $= n - 1$ and the
area $\frac{1}{2}\alpha$.
b. *Find* the second critical value using Table 6 with d.f. $= n - 1$ and the
area $1 - \frac{1}{2}\alpha$.

Answer: Page A40 ◀

The Chi-Square Test

To test a variance σ^2 or a standard deviation σ of a population that is normally distributed, you can use the χ^2-test.

χ^2-Test for a Variance or Standard Deviation

The **χ^2-test** is a statistical test for a population variance or standard deviation. The χ^2-test can be used when the population is normal. The **test statistic** is s^2 and the **standardized test statistic** is χ^2. The sampling distribution for s^2 is a chi-square distribution with $n - 1$ degrees of freedom.

$$\chi^2 = \frac{(n - 1)s^2}{\sigma^2}$$

Note to Instructor

Review the properties of chi-square distributions. Tell students that this family of distributions will be used in later chapters, but the degrees of freedom for those tests are not necessarily $n - 1$.

Note to Instructor

Although other methods of testing hypotheses have also required that data come from normally distributed populations, the tests for variances and standard deviations can be misleading if the populations are not normal. Explain that the condition for a normal distribution is more important for tests of variances or standard deviations.

GUIDELINES

Using the χ^2-Test for a Variance or Standard Deviation

In Words	*In Symbols*
1. State the claim mathematically and verbally. Identify the null and alternative hypotheses.	State H_0 and H_a.
2. Specify the level of significance.	Identify α.
3. Determine the degrees of freedom and sketch the sampling distribution.	d.f. $= n - 1$
4. Determine any critical values.	Use Table 6.
5. Determine any rejection regions.	
6. Find the standardized test statistic.	$\chi^2 = \frac{(n - 1)s^2}{\sigma^2}$
7. Make a decision to reject or fail to reject the null hypothesis.	If χ^2 is in the rejection region, reject H_0. Otherwise, fail to reject H_0.
8. Interpret the decision in the context of the original claim.	

> **EXAMPLE 4**   *Using a Hypothesis Test for the Population Variance*

A dairy processing company claims that the variance of the amount of fat in the whole milk processed by the company is no more than 0.25. You suspect this is wrong and find that a random sample of 41 milk containers has a variance of 0.27. At $\alpha = 0.05$, is there enough evidence to reject the company's claim? Assume the population is normally distributed.

SOLUTION   The claim is "the variance is no more than 0.25." So, the null and alternative hypotheses are

$$H_0: \sigma^2 \leq 0.25 \ \text{(Claim)} \quad \text{and} \quad H_a: \sigma^2 > 0.25.$$

Because the test is a right-tailed test, the level of significance is $\alpha = 0.05$. There are d.f. $= 41 - 1 = 40$ degrees of freedom and the critical value is $\chi_0^2 = 55.758$. The rejection region is $\chi^2 > 55.758$. Using the χ^2-test, the standardized test statistic is

$$\chi^2 = \frac{(n-1)s^2}{\sigma^2} = \frac{(41-1)(0.27)}{0.25} = 43.2.$$

The graph shows the location of the rejection region and the standardized test statistic, χ^2. Because χ^2 is not in the rejection region, you should decide not to reject the null hypothesis. You don't have enough evidence to reject the company's claim at the 5% level of significance.

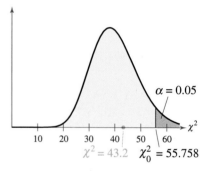

$\chi^2 = 43.2$ $\chi_0^2 = 55.758$

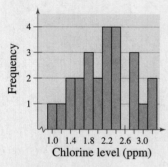

Try It Yourself 4

A bottling company claims that the variance of the amount of sports drink in a 12-ounce bottle is no more than 0.40. A random sample of 31 bottles has a variance of 0.75. At $\alpha = 0.01$, is there enough evidence to reject the company's claim? Assume the population is normally distributed.

a. *Identify* the claim and state H_0 and H_a.
b. *Identify* the level of confidence α and the degrees of freedom d.f.
c. *Find* the critical value and *identify* the rejection region.
d. *Use* the χ^2-test to find the standardized test statistic χ^2.
e. *Decide* whether to reject the null hypothesis. Use a graph if necessary.
f. Is there enough evidence to reject the claim?

Answer: Page A40

> **EXAMPLE 5**   *Using a Hypothesis Test for the Standard Deviation*

A restaurant claims that the standard deviation in the length of serving times is less than 2.9 minutes. A random sample of 23 serving times has a standard deviation of 2.1 minutes. At $\alpha = 0.10$, is there enough evidence to support the restaurant's claim? Assume the population is normally distributed.

SOLUTION   The claim is "the standard deviation is less than 2.9 minutes." So, the null and alternative hypotheses are

$$H_0\colon \sigma \geq 2.9 \text{ minutes} \qquad \text{and} \qquad H_a\colon \sigma < 2.9 \text{ minutes. (Claim)}$$

Because the test is a left-tailed test, the level of significance is $\alpha = 0.10$. There are d.f. $= 23 - 1 = 22$ degrees of freedom and the critical value is 14.042. The rejection region is $\chi^2 < 14.042$. Using the χ^2-test, the standardized test statistic is

$$\chi^2 = \frac{(n-1)s^2}{\sigma^2} = \frac{(23-1)(2.1)^2}{2.9^2} \approx 11.54.$$

The graph shows the location of the rejection region and the standardized test statistic, χ^2. Because χ^2 is in the rejection region, you should decide to reject the null hypothesis. So, there is enough evidence at the 10% level of significance to support the claim that the standard deviation for the length of serving times is less than 2.9 minutes.

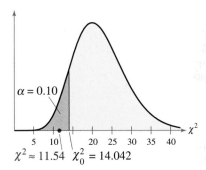

$\alpha = 0.10$

$\chi^2 \approx 11.54$ $\chi_0^2 = 14.042$

Study Tip

Although you are testing a standard deviation in Example 5, the χ^2 statistic requires variances. Don't forget to square the given standard deviations to calculate these variances.

Try It Yourself 5

A police chief claims that the standard deviation in the length of response times is less than 3.7 minutes. A random sample of nine response times has a standard deviation of 3.0 minutes. At $\alpha = 0.05$, is there enough evidence to support the police chief's claim? Assume the population is normally distributed.

a. *Identify* the claim and state H_0 and H_a.
b. *Identify* the level of confidence α and the degrees of freedom d.f.
c. *Find* the critical value and *identify* the rejection region.
d. *Use* the χ^2-test to find the standardized test statistic χ^2.
e. *Decide* whether to reject the null hypothesis. Use a graph if necessary.
f. Is there enough evidence to support the claim?

Answer: Page A40

▶ **EXAMPLE 6** *Using a Hypothesis Test for the Population Variance*

A sporting goods manufacturer claims that the variance of the strength in a certain fishing line is 15.9. A random sample of 15 fishing line spools has a variance of 21.8. At $\alpha = 0.05$, is there enough evidence to reject the manufacturer's claim? Assume the population is normally distributed.

SOLUTION The claim is "the variance is 15.9." So, the null and alternative hypotheses are

$$H_0\text{: } \sigma^2 = 15.9 \text{ (Claim)} \qquad \text{and} \qquad H_a\text{: } \sigma^2 \neq 15.9.$$

Because the test is a two-tailed test, the level of significance is $\alpha = 0.05$. There are d.f. $= 15 - 1 = 14$ degrees of freedom and the critical values are 5.629 and 26.119. The rejection regions are $\chi^2 < 5.629$ and $\chi^2 > 26.119$. Using the χ^2-test, the standardized test statistic is

$$\chi^2 = \frac{(n-1)s^2}{\sigma^2} = \frac{(15-1)(21.8)}{15.9} \approx 19.19.$$

The graph shows the location of the rejection regions and the standardized test statistic, χ^2. Because χ^2 is not in the rejection regions, you should decide not to reject the null hypothesis. At the 5% level of significance, there is not enough evidence to reject the claim that the variance is 15.9.

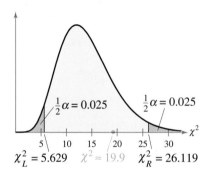

Try It Yourself 6

A tire manufacturer claims that the variance of the diameters in a certain tire model is 8.6. A random sample of 10 tires has a variance of 4.3. At $\alpha = 0.01$, is there enough evidence to support the manufacturer's claim? Assume the population is normally distributed.

a. *Identify* the claim and state H_0 and H_a.
b. *Identify* the level of confidence α and the degrees of freedom d.f.
c. *Find* the critical values and *identify* the rejection regions.
d. *Use* the χ^2-test to find the standardized test statistic χ^2.
e. *Decide* whether to reject the null hypothesis. Use a graph if necessary.
f. Is there enough evidence to reject the claim?

Answer: Page A40 ◀

7.5 EXERCISES

HELP

 StatPro 7.5

 Internet Statistics 7.5

 Student Solutions Manual 7.5

 Videos 7.5

 Try It Yourself Answers 7.5

1. Specify the level of significance, α. Determine the degrees of freedom. Determine the critical values using the χ^2 distribution. If (a) right-tailed test, use the value that corresponds to df and α. (b) left-tailed test, use the value that corresponds to df and $1 - \alpha$. (c) two-tailed test, use the value that corresponds to df and $\frac{1}{2}\alpha$ and $1 - \frac{1}{2}\alpha$.

2. See Selected Answers, page A81

3. 38.885

4. 14.684

5. 0.872

6. 13.091

7. 7.261, 24.996

8. 12.461, 50.993

9. (**a**) Fail to reject H_0
   (**b**) Fail to reject H_0
   (**c**) Fail to reject H_0
   (**d**) Reject H_0

10. See Selected Answers, page A81

11. (**a**) Fail to reject H_0
   (**b**) Reject H_0
   (**c**) Reject H_0
   (**d**) Fail to reject H_0

12. See Selected Answers, page A81

Basic Skills and Concepts

1. Explain how to find critical values in a χ^2 sampling distribution.

2. Explain how to test a population variance or a population standard deviation.

Finding Critical Values In Exercises 3–8, find the critical values for the indicated test for a population variance, sample size n, and level of significance α.

3. Right-tailed test,
   $n = 27, \alpha = 0.05$

4. Right-tailed test,
   $n = 10, \alpha = 0.10$

5. Left-tailed test,
   $n = 7, \alpha = 0.01$

6. Left-tailed test,
   $n = 24, \alpha = 0.05$

7. Two-tailed test,
   $n = 16, \alpha = 0.10$

8. Two-tailed test,
   $n = 29, \alpha = 0.01$

Graphical Analysis In Exercises 9–12, state whether the standardized test statistic χ^2 allows you to reject the null hypothesis.

9. (a) $\chi^2 = 2.091$
   (b) $\chi^2 = 0$
   (c) $\chi^2 = 1.086$
   (d) $\chi^2 = 6.3471$

10. (a) $\chi^2 = 0.771$
   (b) $\chi^2 = 9.486$
   (c) $\chi^2 = 0.701$
   (d) $\chi^2 = 9.508$

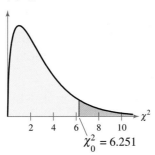

$\chi_0^2 = 6.251$

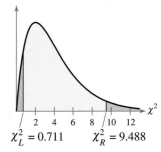

$\chi_L^2 = 0.711$ $\chi_R^2 = 9.488$

11. (a) $\chi^2 = 22.302$
   (b) $\chi^2 = 23.309$
   (c) $\chi^2 = 8.457$
   (d) $\chi^2 = 8.577$

12. (a) $\chi^2 = 10.065$
   (b) $\chi^2 = 10.075$
   (c) $\chi^2 = 10.585$
   (d) $\chi^2 = 10.745$

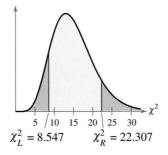

$\chi_L^2 = 8.547$ $\chi_R^2 = 22.307$

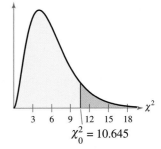

$\chi_0^2 = 10.645$

13. H_0: $\sigma^2 = 0.52$
H_a: $\sigma^2 \neq 0.52$
$\chi_L^2 = 7.564$ $\chi_R^2 = 30.191$
$\chi^2 = 16.608$
Fail to reject H_0.

14. H_0: $\sigma^2 \geq 3.5$
H_a: $\sigma^2 < 3.5$
$\chi_0^2 = 10.851$
$\chi^2 = 19.543$
Fail to reject H_0.

15. H_0: $\sigma \geq 40$
H_a: $\sigma < 40$ (claim)
$\chi_0^2 = 3.053$
$\chi^2 = 11.444$
Fail to reject H_0.

16. H_0: $\sigma \geq 0.12$
H_a: $\sigma < 0.12$ (claim)
$\chi_0^2 = 10.865$
$\chi^2 = 13.261$
Fail to reject H_0.

17. (a) H_0: $\sigma^2 = 3$ (claim)
H_a: $\sigma^2 \neq 3$
(b) $\chi_L^2 = 13.844$ $\chi_R^2 = 41.923$
(c) $\chi^2 = 24.267$
(d) Fail to reject H_0.

18. (a) H_0: $\sigma^2 = 5$ (claim)
H_a: $\sigma^2 \neq 5$
(b) $\chi_L^2 = 10.982$ $\chi_R^2 = 36.781$
(c) $\chi^2 = 19.800$
(d) Fail to reject H_0.

19. (a) H_0: $\sigma \geq 29$
H_a: $\sigma < 29$ (claim)
(b) $\chi_0^2 = 13.240$
(c) $\chi^2 = 19.159$
(d) Fail to reject H_0.

20. See Selected Answers, page A81

21. (a) H_0: $\sigma \leq 0.5$ (claim)
H_a: $\sigma > 0.5$
(b) $\chi_0^2 = 33.196$
(c) $\chi^2 = 47.040$
(d) Reject H_0.

Using the χ^2-Test In Exercises 13–16, use a χ^2-test to test the claim about the population variance σ^2 or standard deviation σ for the given values and level of significance α. Assume the population is normal.

13. Claim: $\sigma^2 = 0.52$; $\alpha = 0.05$. Sample statistics: $s^2 = 0.508$, $n = 18$

14. Claim: $\sigma^2 \geq 3.5$; $\alpha = 0.05$. Sample statistics: $s^2 = 3.42$, $n = 21$

15. Claim: $\sigma < 40$; $\alpha = 0.01$. Sample statistics: $s = 40.8$, $n = 12$

16. Claim: $\sigma < 0.12$; $\alpha = 0.10$. Sample statistics: $s = 0.103$, $n = 19$

Testing Claims In Exercises 17–24, (a) write the claim mathematically and identify H_0 and H_a, (b) find the critical values and identify the rejection region, (c) use the χ^2-test to find the standardized test statistic, and (d) decide whether to reject or fail to reject the null hypothesis. Then interpret the decision in the context of the original claim. Assume the populations are normally distributed.

17. A large appliance company estimates that the variance of the life of its appliances is 3. You work for a consumer advocacy group and are asked to test this claim. You find that a random sample of the lives of 27 of the company's appliances has a variance of 2.8. At $\alpha = 0.05$, do you have enough evidence to reject the company's claim? *(Adapted from Consumer Reports)*

18. An automotive manufacturer believes that the variance of the gas mileage for its luxury sedans is 5. You work for an energy conservation agency and want to test this claim. You find that a random sample of the miles per gallon of 23 of the manufacturer's sedans has a variance of 4.5. At $\alpha = 0.05$, do you have enough evidence to reject the manufacturer's claim? *(Adapted from Consumer Reports)*

19. On a mathematical assessment test, the scores of a random sample of 22 eighth-grade students have a standard deviation of 27.7. This prompts a test administrator to claim that the mean score for eighth-graders on the examination is less than 29. At $\alpha = 0.10$, is there enough evidence to support the administrator's claim? *(Adapted from National Center for Educational Statistics)*

20. A state school administrator says that the standard deviation of test scores for eighth-grade students who took a life-science assessment test is less than 30. You work for the administrator and are asked to test this claim. To do so, you randomly select 10 tests and find that the tests have a standard deviation of 28.8. At $\alpha = 0.01$, is there enough evidence to support the administrator's claim? *(Adapted from National Center for Educational Statistics)*

21. A hospital spokesperson claims that the standard deviation of the waiting times experienced by patients in its minor emergency department is no more that 0.5 minute. You doubt the validity of this claim. If a random sample of 25 waiting times has a standard deviation of 0.7 minute, can you reject the spokesperson's claim? Use $\alpha = 0.10$.

22. (a) H_0: $\sigma \leq \$25$ (claim)
  H_a: $\sigma < \$25$
  (b) $\chi_0^2 = 26.217$
  (c) $\chi^2 = 14.520$
  (d) Fail to reject H_0.

23. (a) H_0: $\sigma^2 \leq 20{,}000$
  H_a: $\sigma^2 > 20{,}000$ (claim)
  (b) $\chi_0^2 = 24.996$
  (c) $\chi^2 = 16.011$
  (d) Fail to reject H_0.

24. (a) H_0: $\sigma^2 \geq 14{,}500$ (claim)
  H_a: $\sigma^2 < 14{,}500$
  (b) $\chi_0^2 = 10.085$
  (c) $\chi^2 = 15.985$
  (d) Fail to reject H_0.

25. P-value $= 0.381$
  Fail to reject H_0.

26. P-value $= 0.475$
  Fail to reject H_0.

22. A travel agency estimates that the standard deviation of the room rates of hotels in a certain city is no more than $25. You work for a consumer advocacy group and are asked to test this claim. You find that a random sample of 13 hotels has a standard deviation of $27.50. At $\alpha = 0.01$, do you have enough evidence to reject the agency's claim? *(Adapted from Smith Travel Research)*

23. The annual salaries of 16 randomly chosen actuaries are listed below. At $\alpha = 0.05$, can you conclude that the variance of the annual salaries is greater than 20,000? *(Adapted from America's Career Infonet)*

45,018	34,952	85,517	45,553	41,900	76,384	48,862	37,615
61,104	96,710	97,875	68,245	39,945	53,582	65,252	72,522

24. An employment information service says that the variance of the annual salaries for public relations managers is at least 14,500. The annual salaries for 18 randomly chosen public relations managers are listed. At $\alpha = 0.10$, can you reject the claim? *(Adapted from America's Career Infonet)*

37,517	50,217	29,177	51,744	69,422	60,770	50,549	50,263
62,939	62,372	65,014	49,164	34,811	55,413	51,310	80,433
34,185	31,805						

Extending the Basics

P-values You can calculate the P-value for a χ^2-test using technology. After calculating the χ^2-test value, you can use the cumulative density function (CDF) to calculate the area under the curve. From Example 4 on page 350, $\chi_0^2 = 55.758$. Using a TI-83 (choose 7 from the DISTR menu), enter 0 for the lower bound, 55.758 for the upper bound, and 40 for the degrees of freedom as shown.

TI-83

χ^2 cdf (0, 55.758, 40)
.9499955637

The P-value is $1 - 0.9499955637 = 0.0500044363$. Because $P > \alpha = 0.05$, the conclusion is to fail to reject H_0.

25. Use the P-value method to perform the hypothesis test for Exercise 23.

26. Use the P-value method to perform the hypothesis test for Exercise 24.

7

A SUMMARY OF HYPOTHESIS TESTING

With hypothesis testing, perhaps more than any other area of statistics, it can be difficult to see the forest for all the trees. To help you see the forest—the overall picture—we provide a summary of what you studied in this chapter.

▶ **Writing the Hypotheses**
- You are given a claim about a population parameter μ, p, σ^2, or σ.
- Rewrite the claim and its complement using $\leq$, $\geq$, $=$ and $>$, $<$, $\neq$.
$$\underbrace{}_{H_0} \qquad \underbrace{}_{H_a}$$
- Identify the claim. Is it H_0 or H_a?

▶ **Specifying a Level of Significance**
- Specify α, the maximum acceptable probability of rejecting a valid H_0 (a type I error).

▶ **Specifying the Sample Size**
- Specify your sample size n.

▶ **Choosing the Test** ■ Any population ■ Normally distributed population
- **Mean:** H_0 describes a hypothesized population mean μ.
  - ■ Use a **z-test** for *any* population if $n \geq 30$.
  - ■ Use a **z-test** if the population is normal and σ is known for any n.
  - ■ Use a **t-test** if the population is normal and $n < 30$, but σ is unknown.

- **Proportion:** H_0 describes a hypothesized population proportion p.
  - ■ Use a **z-test** for *any* population if $np \geq 5$ and $nq \geq 5$.

- **Variance or Standard Deviation:** H_0 describes a hypothesized population variance σ^2 or standard deviation σ.
  - ■ Use a **χ^2-test** if the population is normal.

▶ **Sketching the Sampling Distribution**
- Use H_a to decide if the test is left-tailed, right-tailed, or two-tailed.

▶ **Finding the Standardized Test Statistic**
- Take a random sample of size n from the population.
- Compute the test statistic $\bar{x}$, p, or s^2.
- Find the standardized test statistic z, t, or χ^2.

▶ **Making a Decision**

Option 1. Decision based on rejection region
- Use α to find the critical value(s) z_0, t_0, or χ_0^2 and rejection region(s).
- **Decision Rule:**
  Reject H_0 if the standardized test statistic is in the rejection region.
  Fail to reject H_0 if the standardized test statistic is not in the rejection region.

Option 2. Decision based on P-value
- Use the standardized test statistic or a technology tool to find the P-value.
- **Decision Rule:**
  Reject H_0 if $P \leq \alpha$.
  Fail to reject H_0 if $P > \alpha$.

z-Test for a Hypothesized Mean μ *(Section 7.2)*

Test Statistic: $\bar{x}$

Standardized Test Statistic: z

Critical value: z_0 (Use Table 4.)

If $n \geq 30$, s can be used in place of σ.
Sampling distribution of sample means is a normal distribution.

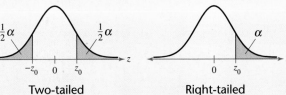

$$z = \frac{\bar{x} - \mu}{\sigma / \sqrt{n}}$$

Sample mean · Hypothesized mean · Population standard deviation · Sample size

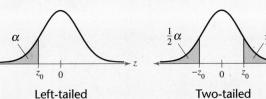

Left-tailed   Two-tailed   Right-tailed

z-Test for a Hypothesized Proportion p *(Section 7.4)*

Test Statistic: $\hat{p}$

Standardized Test Statistic: z

Critical value: z_0 (Use Table 4.)

Sampling distribution of sample proportions is a normal distribution.

$$z = \frac{\hat{p} - p}{\sqrt{pq/n}}$$

Sample proportion · Hypothesized proportion · $q = 1 - p$ · Sample size

t-Test for a Hypothesized Mean μ *(Section 7.3)*

Test Statistic: $\bar{x}$

Standardized Test Statistic: t

Critical value: t_0 (Use Table 5.)

Sampling distribution of sample means is a t-distribution with d.f. $= n - 1$.

$$t = \frac{\bar{x} - \mu}{s / \sqrt{n}}$$

Sample mean · Hypothesized mean · Sample standard deviation · Sample size

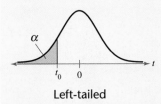

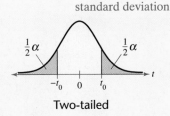

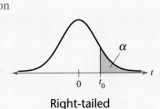

Left-tailed   Two-tailed   Right-tailed

χ^2-Test for a Hypothesized Variance σ^2 or Standard Deviation σ *(Section 7.5)*

Test Statistic: s^2

Standardized Test Statistic: χ^2

Critical value: χ_0^2 (Use Table 6.)
Sampling distribution is a chi-square distribution with d.f. $= n - 1$.

$$\chi^2 = \frac{(n - 1)s^2}{\sigma^2}$$

Sample size · Sample variance · Hypothesized variance

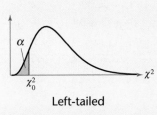

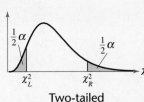

Left-tailed   Two-tailed   Right-tailed

USING TECHNOLOGY TO PERFORM HYPOTHESIS TESTS

Here are some *Minitab* and *TI-83* printouts for some of the examples in this chapter. To duplicate the *Minitab* results, you need the original data. For the *TI-83,* you can simply enter the descriptive statistics.

(See Example 9, page 323)

Data for Investments for 30 Franchises

$70,700	$69,400	$90,600	$85,500	$97,100	$100,800
$114,700	$119,600	$123,600	$127,200	$131,200	$132,000
$134,400	$136,700	$138,500	$140,900	$143,300	$143,900
$151,100	$151,700	$157,200	$159,800	$163,000	$163,500
$169,300	$167,400	$168,800	$168,800	$159,100	$170,200

Display Descriptive Statistics...
Store Descriptive Statistics...

1-Sample Z...
1-Sample t...
2-Sample t...
Paired t...

1 Proportion...
2 Proportions...

Correlation...
Covariance...

Normality Test...

MINITAB

Z-Test

Test of mu = 143260 vs mu not = 143260
The assumed sigma = 30000

Variable	N	Mean	StDev	SE Mean	Z	P
C1	30	135000	30000	5477	−1.51	0.13

(See Example 4, page 333)

Data for prices of 14 Ford Pickups

$14,500	$13,790	$13,800	$14,030	$15,400
$15,560	$15,855	$15,935	$16,150	$16,300
$17,100	$17,100	$17,070	$17,210	

Display Descriptive Statistics...
Store Descriptive Statistics...

1-Sample Z...
1-Sample t...
2-Sample t...
Paired t...

1 Proportion...
2 Proportions...

MINITAB

T-Test of the Mean

Test of mu = 16500 vs mu < 16500

Variable	N	Mean	StDev	SE Mean	T	P
C1	14	15700	1250	334	−2.39	0.016

Display Descriptive Statistics...
Store Descriptive Statistics...

1-Sample Z...
1-Sample t...
2-Sample t...
Paired t...

1 Proportion...
2 Proportions...

MINITAB (See Example 2, page 342)

Test and Confidence Interval for One Proportion

Test of p = 0.23 vs p not = 0.23

Sample	X	N	Sample p	95.0 % CI	Z-Value	P-Value
1	54	200	0.270000	(0.208471, 0.331529)	1.34	0.179

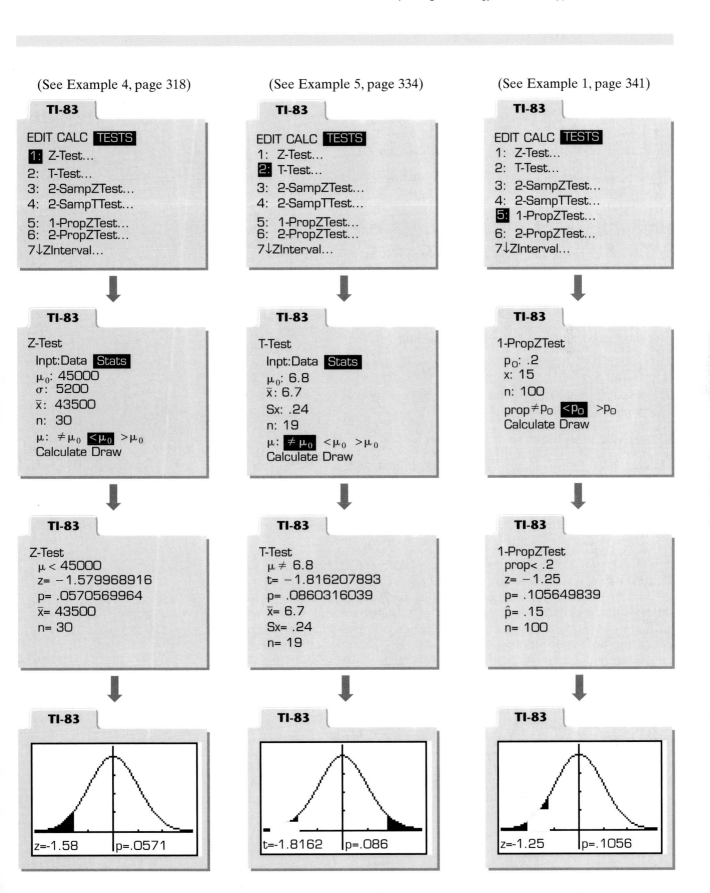

(See Example 4, page 318)

(See Example 5, page 334)

(See Example 1, page 341)

7   **CHAPTER SUMMARY**

What did you learn?

Why did you learn it? Uses and Abuses

Uses Hypothesis testing is important in many different fields, because it gives a scientific procedure for assessing the validity of a claim about a population.

Some of the concepts in hypothesis testing are intuitive, but some are not. For instance, in this chapter you learned that a test statistic does not have to differ much from a hypothesized parameter to conclude that the hypothesis is incorrect. The reason for this is given in the Central Limit Theorem—as n increases, the standard deviation of the sampling distribution gets smaller and smaller.

Suppose, for example, that you are testing a claim that the mean age of Internet users is $\mu = 35.1$ years old. If in a random sample, you obtained a test statistic of $\bar{x} = 33.0$ years and a standardized test statistic of $z = -3.5$, then you can be almost certain that the claim is incorrect. It is the power of the Central Limit Theorem and hypothesis testing that allows you to reach this decision.

Abuses The most common abuse connected with hypothesis testing is not using a random sample. Remember that the entire theory of hypothesis testing is based on the fact that the sample is randomly selected. If the sample is not random, then you cannot use it to imply anything about a population parameter.

7 ▼ REVIEW EXERCISES

1. H_0: $\mu \leq 1593$ (claim)
H_a: $\mu > 1593$

2. H_0: $\mu = 35$ (claim)
H_a: $\mu \neq 35$

3. H_0: $\mu = 150{,}020$
H_a: $\mu \neq 150{,}020$ (claim)

4. H_0: $\mu \geq 0.205$
H_a: $\mu < 0.205$ (claim)

5. (a) H_0: $p = 0.85$ (claim)
H_a: $p \neq 0.85$

(b) Type I error will occur if H_0 is rejected when the actual proportion of American adults who use nonprescription pain relievers is 0.85.

Type II error if H_0 is not rejected when the actual proportion of American adults who use nonper-scription pain relievers is not 0.85.

(c) Two-tailed

(d) There is enough evidence to reject the claim.

(e) There is not enough evidence to reject the claim.

6. See Selected Answers, page A82

7. See Odd Answers, page A63

8. See Selected Answers, page A82

9. $z_0 = -2.05$

10. $z_0 = \pm 2.81$

11. $z_0 = 1.96$

12. $z_0 = \pm 1.75$

13. H_0: $\mu \leq 45$ (claim)
H_a: $\mu > 45$

$z_0 = 1.645$

$z = 2.128$

Reject H_0.

14. See Selected Answers, page A82

15. H_0: $\mu \geq 5.500$
H_a: $\mu < 5.500$ (claim)

$z_0 = -2.33$

$z = -1.636$

Fail to reject H_0

16. See Selected Answers, page A82

In Exercises 1–4, use the given claim to state a null and an alternative hypothesis. Identify which hypothesis represents the claim.

1. Claim: $\mu \leq 1593$

2. Claim: $\mu = 35$

3. Claim: $\mu \neq 150{,}020$

4. Claim: $\mu < 0.205$

In Exercises 5–8, do the following.

(a) State the null and alternative hypotheses.
(b) Determine when a type I or type II error occurs for a hypothesis test of the claim.
(c) Determine whether the hypothesis test is a left-tailed test, a right-tailed test, or a two-tailed test. Explain your reasoning.
(d) How should you interpret a decision that rejects the null hypothesis?
(e) How should you interpret a decision that fails to reject the null hypothesis?

5. An organization believes that the proportion of American adults who use nonprescription pain relievers is 85%. *(Source: American Pharmaceutical Association)*

6. A tire manufacturer guarantees that the mean life of a certain type of tire is at least 30,000 miles.

7. A soup maker says that the standard deviation of the sodium content in one serving of a certain soup is no more than 50 milligrams. *(Adapted from Consumer Reports)*

8. A cereal maker claims that the mean number of fat calories in one serving of its cereal is less than 20.

In Exercises 9–12, find the critical value(s) for the indicated z-test with level of significance α.

9. Left-tailed test, $\alpha = 0.02$

10. Two-tailed test, $\alpha = 0.005$

11. Right-tailed test, $\alpha = 0.025$

12. Two-tailed test, $\alpha = 0.08$

In Exercises 13–16, test the claim about the population mean μ with a z-test using the given sample statistics and level of significance α.

13. Claim: $\mu \leq 45$; $\alpha = 0.05$. Statistics: $\bar{x} = 47.2$, $s = 6.7$, $n = 42$

14. Claim: $\mu \neq 0$; $\alpha = 0.05$. Statistics: $\bar{x} = -0.69$, $s = 2.62$, $n = 60$

15. Claim: $\mu < 5.500$; $\alpha = 0.01$. Statistics: $\bar{x} = 5.497$, $s = 0.011$, $n = 36$

16. Claim: $\mu = 7450$; $\alpha = 0.05$. Statistics: $\bar{x} = 7512$, $s = 243$, $n = 57$

17. H_0: $\mu \leq 0.05$ (claim)
    H_a: $\mu > 0.05$

    $z = 2.200$

    P-value $= 0.0139$

    $\alpha = 0.10 \Longrightarrow$ Reject H_0
    $\alpha = 0.05 \Longrightarrow$ Reject H_0
    $\alpha = 0.01 \Longrightarrow$ Fail to reject H_0

18. H_0: $\mu = 230$
    H_a: $\mu \neq 230$ (claim)

    $z = -5.406$

    P-value ≈ 0

    $\alpha = 0.10 \Longrightarrow$ Reject H_0
    $\alpha = 0.05 \Longrightarrow$ Reject H_0
    $\alpha = 0.01 \Longrightarrow$ Reject H_0

19. $t_0 = \pm 2.093$

20. $t_0 = 2.998$

21. $t_0 = -1.345$

22. $t_0 = 2.201$

23. H_0: $\mu = 95$
    H_a: $\mu \neq 95$ (claim)

    $t_0 = \pm 2.201$

    $t = -2.038$

    Fail to reject H_0

24. H_0: $\mu \leq 12{,}700$ and
    H_a: $\mu > 12{,}700$ (claim)

    $t_0 = 1.725$

    $t = 1.922$

    Reject H_0

25. H_0: $\mu \geq 0$ (claim) and
    H_a: $\mu < 0$

    $t_0 = -1.341$

    $t = -1.304$

    Fail to reject H_0.

26. See Selected Answers, page A82

27. H_0: $\mu = \$25$ (claim)
    H_a: $\mu \neq \$25$

    $t_0 = \pm 1.740$

    $t = 1.642$

    Fail to reject H_0.

28. See Selected Answers, page A82

In Exercises 17 and 18, use a P-value to test the claim about the population mean μ using the given sample statistics. State your decision for $\alpha = 0.10$, $\alpha = 0.05$, and $\alpha = 0.01$ levels of significance.

17. Claim: $\mu \leq 0.05$; Statistics: $\bar{x} = 0.057$, $s = 0.018$, $n = 32$

18. Claim: $\mu \neq 230$; Statistics: $\bar{x} = 216.5$, $s = 17.3$, $n = 48$

In Exercises 19–22, find the critical value(s) for the t-test with the indicated sample size n and level of significance α.

19. Two-tailed test, $n = 20$, $\alpha = 0.05$

20. Right-tailed test, $n = 8$, $\alpha = 0.01$

21. Left-tailed test, $n = 15$, $\alpha = 0.10$

22. Two-tailed test, $n = 12$, $\alpha = 0.025$

In Exercises 23–26, test the claim about the population mean μ using the given sample statistics and level of significance α. Assume the population is normally distributed.

23. Claim: $\mu \neq 95$; $\alpha = 0.05$. Statistics: $\bar{x} = 94.1$, $s = 1.53$, $n = 12$

24. Claim: $\mu > 12{,}700$; $\alpha = 0.05$. Statistics: $\bar{x} = 12{,}804$, $s = 248$, $n = 21$

25. Claim: $\mu \geq 0$; $\alpha = 0.10$. Statistics: $\bar{x} = -0.45$, $s = 1.38$, $n = 16$

26. Claim: $\mu = 4.20$; $\alpha = 0.02$. Statistics: $\bar{x} = 4.41$, $s = 0.26$, $n = 9$

In Exercises 27 and 28, use a t-test to investigate the claim. Assume each population is normally distributed.

27. A fitness magazine advertises that the average monthly cost of joining a health club is $25. You work for a consumer advocacy group and are asked to test this claim. You find that a random sample of 18 clubs has a mean monthly cost of $26.25 and a standard deviation of $3.23. At $\alpha = 0.10$, do you have enough evidence to reject the advertisement's claim?

28. A certain restaurant claims that its hamburgers have no more than 10 grams of fat. You work for a nutritional health agency and are asked to test this claim. You find that a random sample of nine hamburgers has a mean fat content of 13.5 grams and a standard deviation of 5.8 grams. At $\alpha = 0.10$, do you have enough evidence to reject the restaurant's claim?

In Exercises 29 and 30, use a t-statistic and its P-value to test the claim about the population mean μ using the given sample statistics. Assume the population is normally distributed.

29. H_0: $\mu \geq 4$ (claim)
H_a: $\mu < 4$
$t_0 = -2.539$
$t = -0.510$
Fail to reject H_0.

30. H_0: $\mu \leq 9$
H_a: $\mu > 9$ (claim)
$t_0 = 1.812$
$t = 1.533$
Fail to reject H_0.

31. H_0: $p = 0.15$ (claim)
H_a: $p \neq 0.15$
$z_0 = \pm 1.96$
$z = -1.063$
Fail to reject H_0.

32. H_0: $p \geq 0.15$
H_a: $p < 0.70$ (claim)
$z_0 = -2.33$
$z = -3.599$
Reject H_0.

33. Because $np = 3.6$ is less than 5, the normal distribution cannot be used to approximate the binomial distribution.

34. H_0: $p = 0.50$ (claim)
H_a: $p \neq 0.50$
$z_0 = \pm 1.645$
$z = 4.770$
Reject H_0.

35. H_0: $p \leq 0.40$
H_a: $p > 0.40$ (claim)
$z_0 = 1.282$
$z = 2.628$
Reject H_0.

36. H_0: $p = 0.50$ (claim)
H_a: $p \neq 0.50$
$z_0 = \pm 1.96$
$z = 0.160$
Fail to reject H_0.

29. A bottled water association says that the mean number of 8-ounce glasses of water American adults drink each day is at least 4. The number of 8-ounce glasses of water a random sample of 20 American adults drank in one day is listed. At $\alpha = 0.01$, test the association's claim. *(Adapted from USA Today)*

4.7	5.4	3.2	3.9	4.3	4.5	2.5	5.2	4.5	5.3
3.2	2.2	4.1	2.3	3.7	5.1	4.1	3.6	3.1	2.8

30. A large university says the mean number of classroom hours per week for full-time faculty is more than 9. A random sample of the number of classroom hours for full-time faculty for one week is listed. At $\alpha = 0.05$, test the university's claim. *(Adapted from National Center for Education Statistics)*

10.7	9.8	11.6	9.7	7.6	11.3	14.1	8.1	11.5	8.5	6.9

In Exercises 31–34, decide whether the normal distribution can be used to approximate the binomial distribution. If it can, use the z-test to test the claim about the population proportion p for the given values and level of significance α.

31. Claim: $p = 0.15$; $\alpha = 0.05$. Statistics: $\hat{p} = 0.09$, $n = 40$

32. Claim: $p < 0.70$; $\alpha = 0.01$. Statistics: $\hat{p} = 0.50$, $n = 68$

33. Claim: $p < 0.08$; $\alpha = 0.05$. Statistics: $\hat{p} = 0.03$, $n = 45$

34. Claim: $p = 0.5$; $\alpha = 0.10$. Statistics: $\hat{p} = 0.71$, $n = 129$

In Exercises 35 and 36, test the claim about the population proportion p.

35. A communications industry spokesperson claims that over 40% of Americans either own a cellular phone or have a family member that does. In a random survey of 1036 Americans, 456 said that they or a family member owned a cellular phone. Test the spokesperson's claim at the $\alpha = 0.10$ level. What can you conclude? *(Adapted from Wirthlin Worldwide)*

36. The Western blot assay is a blood test for the presence of HIV. It has been found that this test sometimes gives false positive results for HIV; specifically, when it does not find a certain antibody called p-31 antibody. A medical researcher claims that the rate of false positives in this case is 50%. A recent study of 39 randomly selected blood donors who tested positive for HIV but did not have p-31 antibodies in their blood found that 20 were actually HIV negative. Test the researcher's claim of a 50% false positive rate at the $\alpha = 0.05$ level. What can you conclude? *(Source: The Journal of the American Medical Association)*

37. $\chi_0^2 = 30.144$

38. $\chi_L^2 = 3.565$ $\chi_R^2 = 29.819$

39. $\chi_0^2 = 33.196$

40. $\chi_0^2 = 1.145$

41. H_0: $\sigma^2 \le 2$
H_a: $\sigma^2 > 2$ (claim)
$\chi_0^2 = 24.769$
$\chi^2 = 20.230$
Fail to reject H_0.

42. H_0: $\sigma^2 \le 60$ (claim)
H_a: $\sigma^2 > 60$
$\chi_0^2 = 26.119$
$\chi^2 = 16.963$
Fail to reject H_0.

43. H_0: $\sigma^2 = 1.25$ (claim)
H_a: $\sigma \ne 1.25$
$\chi_L^2 = 0.831$
$\chi_R^2 = 12.833$
$\chi^2 = 3.395$
Fail to reject H_0.

44. H_0: $\sigma = 0.035$
H_a: $\sigma \ne 0.035$ (claim)
$\chi_L^2 = 4.601$
$\chi_R^2 = 32.801$
$\chi^2 = 8.278$
Fail to reject H_0.

45. H_0: $\sigma^2 \le 0.01$ (claim)
H_a: $\sigma^2 > 0.01$
$\chi_0^2 = 49.645$
$\chi^2 = 172.800$
Reject H_0.

46. H_0: $\sigma \le 0.0025$ (claim)
H_a: $\sigma > 0.0025$
$\chi_0^2 = 27.688$
$\chi^2 = 19.989$
Fail to reject H_0.

In Exercises 37–40, find the critical value(s) for the χ^2-test with the indicated sample size n and level of significance α.

37. Right-tailed test, $n = 20$, $\alpha = 0.05$

38. Two-tailed test, $n = 14$, $\alpha = 0.01$

39. Right-tailed test, $n = 25$, $\alpha = 0.10$

40. Left-tailed test, $n = 6$, $\alpha = 0.05$

In Exercises 41–44, test the claim about the indicated population parameter (σ or σ^2) with a χ^2-test using the given sample statistics and level of significance α. Assume the population is normally distributed.

41. Claim: $\sigma^2 > 2$; $\alpha = 0.10$. Statistics: $s^2 = 2.38$, $n = 18$

42. Claim: $\sigma^2 \le 60$; $\alpha = 0.025$. Statistics: $s^2 = 72.7$, $n = 15$

43. Claim: $\sigma = 1.25$; $\alpha = 0.05$. Statistics: $s = 1.03$, $n = 6$

44. Claim: $\sigma \ne 0.035$; $\alpha = 0.01$. Statistics: $s = 0.026$, $n = 16$

In Exercises 45 and 46, test the claim about the population variance. Assume each population is normally distributed.

45. A bolt manufacturer makes a type of bolt to be used in airtight containers. The manufacturer needs to be sure that all of its bolts are very similar in width, so it sets an upper tolerance limit for the variance of bolt width at 0.01. A random sample of 28 bolts yields a variance of 0.064 for bolt width. Test the manufacturer's claim that the variance is at most 0.01 at the $\alpha = 0.005$ level. What can you conclude?

46. A bottler needs to be sure that its liquid dispensers are set properly. The standard deviation of liquid dispensed must be no more than 0.0025 liter. A random sample of 14 bottles has a standard deviation of 0.0031 liter. Test the bottler's claim that the standard deviation is no more than 0.0025 liter at the $\alpha = 0.01$ level. What can you conclude?

7 CHAPTER QUIZ

1. (a) H_0: $\mu \geq 94$ (claim)
H_a: $\mu < 94$

(b) Type I error occurs if the H_0 is rejected when actually the mean consumption is at least 94 pounds.

Type II error occurs if the H_0 has not been rejected when actually the mean consumption is less than 94 pounds.

(c) Left tailed
z-test

(d) $z_0 = -2.05$

(e) $z = -0.169$

(f) Fail to reject H_0.

2. See Odd Answers, page A64

3. (a) H_0: $p \leq 0.10$ (claim)
H_a: $p > 0.10$

(b) Type I error occurs if the H_0 is rejected when actually the production of microwaves needing repair is no more than 0.10.

Type II error occurs if the H_0 has not been rejected when actually the production of microwaves needing repair is more than 0.10.

(c) Right tailed
z-test

(d) $z_0 = 1.75$

(e) $z = 0.755$

(f) Fail to reject H_0.

4. See Odd Answers, page A64

5. See Odd Answers, page A64

Take this quiz as you would take a quiz in class. After you are done, check your work against the answers given in the back of the book.

For this quiz, do the following.

(a) State the claim mathematically. Identify H_0 and H_a.
(b) Determine when a type I or type II error occurs.
(c) Determine whether the hypothesis test is a one-tailed or a two-tailed test and whether to use a z-test, a t-test, or a χ^2-test. Explain your reasoning.
(d) Find the critical value(s) and identify the rejection region(s).
(e) Find the appropriate test statistic.
(f) Decide whether to reject or fail to reject the null hypothesis. Then interpret the decision in the context of the original claim.

1. A citrus grower's association believes that the mean consumption of fresh citrus fruits by Americans is at least 94 pounds per year. A random sample of 103 Americans has a mean consumption of fresh citrus fruits of 93.5 pounds per year and a standard deviation of 30 pounds. At $\alpha = 0.02$, can you reject the association's claim that the mean consumption of fresh citrus fruits by Americans is at least 94 pounds per year? *(Adapted from U.S. Department of Agriculture)*

2. An auto maker estimates that the mean gas mileage of its luxury sedan is at least 25 miles per gallon. A random sample of eight cars had a mean of 23 miles per gallon and a standard deviation of 5 miles per gallon. At $\alpha = 0.05$, can you reject the auto maker's claim that the mean gas mileage of its luxury sedan is at least 25 miles per gallon? *(Adapted from Consumer Reports)*

3. A maker of microwave ovens advertises that no more than 10% of its microwaves need repair during the first five years of use. In a random sample of 57 microwaves five years old or less, 13% needed repairs. At $\alpha = 0.04$, can you reject the maker's claim that no more than 10% of its microwaves need repair during the first five years of use? *(Adapted from Consumer Reports)*

4. A state school administrator says that the standard deviation of SAT verbal test scores is 105. A random sample of 14 SAT verbal test scores has a standard deviation of 113. At $\alpha = 0.01$, test the administrator's claim. What can you conclude? *(Adapted from National Center for Educational Statistics)*

5. An employment information service reports that the mean annual salary for full-time male workers over the age of 25 with a bachelor's degree is $53,102. You doubt the validity of this claim. If a random sample of 12 full-time male worker's with bachelor's degrees has a mean annual salary of $52,201 with a standard deviation of $6500, can you reject the service's claim. Use a *P*-value and $\alpha = 0.05$. *(Adapted from U.S. Bureau of the Census)*

Where You've Been

In Chapter 6, you were introduced to inferential statistics and you learned how to form confidence intervals to estimate a parameter. Then, in Chapter 7, you learned how to test a claim about a population parameter, basing your decision on sample statistics and their distributions.

A study reported in the *Journal of the American Medical Association (JAMA)* describes a random sample of 7924 enlisted men who entered the Army from 1965 to 1971 and served in Vietnam. The following proportions were found.

Army Vets Who Served in Vietnam ($n = 7924$)

Condition	Number	Proportion
Depression	357	$\hat{p}_1 = 0.045$
Anxiety	388	$\hat{p}_1 = 0.049$
Alcohol abuse or dependence	1085	$\hat{p}_1 = 0.137$

Vets With a Mission doing volunteer work on a classroom in Vietnam.

Universal Pictures presents an A. Kitman Ho & Ixtlan production, an Oliver Stone picture. Tom Cruise, "Born on the Fourth of July". Kyra Sedgwick, Raymond J. Barry, Jerry Levine, Frank Whaley, and Willem Dafoe. Music by John Williams. Production designer, Bruno Rubeo. Director of Photography, Robert Richardson. Based on the novel by Ron Kovic. Screenplay by Oliver Stone & Ron Covic. Produced by A. Kitman Ho & Oliver Stone. Directed by Oliver Stone. A Universal Release.

The Vietnam War was the longest and most unpopular war the United States ever fought. More than 2 million Americans fought in the war—fifty-eight thousand of them were killed. Since the war, there have been many studies about the effects on Vietnam veterans returning to a country that was so divided in its support of the war.

Hypothesis Testing with Two Samples

Where You're Going

In this chapter, you will continue your study of inferential statistics and hypothesis testing. Now, however, instead of testing a hypothesis about a single population, you will learn how to test a hypothesis that compares two populations.

For instance, in the *JAMA* study a second random sample of 7364 enlisted men who entered the Army from 1965 to 1971 was taken. These men were similar to the Vietnam veteran sample in terms of level of education, employment, income, marital status, and satisfaction with personal relationships. The second group, however, had *not* served in Vietnam. Here are the study's findings for the second group.

Army Vets Who Did Not Serve in Vietnam ($n = 7364$)

Condition	Number	Proportion
Depression	169	$\hat{p}_2 = 0.023$
Anxiety	236	$\hat{p}_2 = 0.032$
Alcohol abuse or dependence	678	$\hat{p}_2 = 0.092$

From these two samples, can you conclude that there was a significantly greater proportion of depression, anxiety, or alcohol abuse or dependence among Army vets who served in Vietnam than among those who did not serve in Vietnam? Or, might the differences in the proportions be due to chance?

In this chapter, you will learn that you can answer these questions by testing the hypothesis that the two proportions are equal. For the proportions of depression, the P-value for the hypothesis that $p_1 = p_2$ is about 0.0000. So, it is almost impossible that the two groups experienced the same proportions of depression.

8.1 Testing the Difference Between Means (Large Independent Samples)

An Overview of Two-Sample Hypothesis Testing • Two-Sample z-Test for the Difference Between Means

What You Should Learn

- *An introduction to two-sample hypothesis testing for the difference between two population parameters*
- *How to perform a two-sample z-test for the difference between two means, μ_1 and μ_2, using large independent samples*

An Overview of Two-Sample Hypothesis Testing

In Chapter 7, you studied methods for testing a claim about the value of a population parameter. In this chapter, you will learn how to test a claim comparing parameters from two populations.

For instance, suppose you are developing a marketing plan for an Internet service provider and want to determine whether there is a difference in the amount of time male and female college students spend online each day. The only way you could conclude with certainty that there is a difference is to take a census of all college students, calculate the mean daily times male students and female students spend online, and find the difference. Of course, it is not practical to take such a census. However, you can still determine with some degree of certainty whether such a difference exists.

You can begin by assuming that there is no difference in the mean times of the two populations. That is, $\mu_1 - \mu_2 = 0$. Then by taking a random sample from each population, and using the resulting two-sample test statistic $\bar{x}_1 - \bar{x}_2$, you can perform a two-sample hypothesis test. Suppose you obtain the following results.

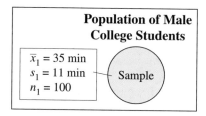

Population of Male College Students

$\bar{x}_1 = 35$ min
$s_1 = 11$ min
$n_1 = 100$

Sample

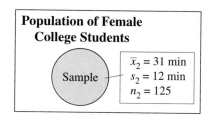

Population of Female College Students

Sample

$\bar{x}_2 = 31$ min
$s_2 = 12$ min
$n_2 = 125$

The graph below shows the sampling distribution of $\bar{x}_1 - \bar{x}_2$ for many similar samples taken from each population. From the graph, you can see that it is quite unlikely to obtain sample means that differ by 4 minutes when the actual difference is 0. The difference of the sample means is more than 2.5 standard errors from the hypothesized difference of 0! So, you can conclude that there is a significant difference in the amount of time male college students and female college students spend online each day.

Sampling Distribution

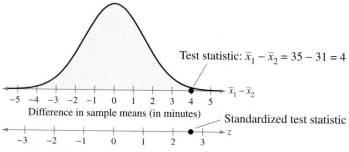

Test statistic: $\bar{x}_1 - \bar{x}_2 = 35 - 31 = 4$

$\bar{x}_1 - \bar{x}_2$

Difference in sample means (in minutes)

Standardized test statistic

z

Note to Instructor

In this chapter, students will primarily use hypothesis tests for which the null hypothesis states that there is no difference in the population parameters. The opportunity to conduct tests for differences other than zero, however, is discussed in the Extending the Basics exercises.

It is important to remember that when you perform a two-sample hypothesis test, you are testing a claim concerning the difference between the parameters in two populations, not the values of the parameters themselves.

> **DEFINITION**
>
> For a two-sample hypothesis test,
> 1. the **null hypothesis, H_0,** is a statistical hypothesis that usually states there is no difference between the parameters of two populations. The null hypothesis always contains the symbol $\leq$, $=$, or $\geq$.
> 2. the **alternative hypothesis, H_a,** is a statistical hypothesis that is true when H_0 is false. The alternative hypothesis contains the symbol $>$, $\neq$, or $<$.

To write a null and an alternative hypothesis for a two-sample hypothesis test, translate the claim made about the population parameters from a verbal statement to a mathematical statement. Then, write its complementary statement. For instance, if the claim is about two population parameters μ_1 and μ_2, then some possible pairs of null and alternative hypotheses are

$$\begin{cases} H_0\text{: } \mu_1 = \mu_2 \\ H_a\text{: } \mu_1 \neq \mu_2 \end{cases} \quad \begin{cases} H_0\text{: } \mu_1 \leq \mu_2 \\ H_a\text{: } \mu_1 > \mu_2 \end{cases} \quad \begin{cases} H_0\text{: } \mu_1 \geq \mu_2 \\ H_a\text{: } \mu_1 < \mu_2 \end{cases}.$$

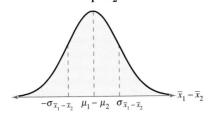

Study Tip

You can also write the null and alternative hypotheses as follows.

$$\begin{cases} H_0\text{: } \mu_1 - \mu_2 = 0 \\ H_a\text{: } \mu_1 - \mu_2 \neq 0 \end{cases}$$

$$\begin{cases} H_0\text{: } \mu_1 - \mu_2 \leq 0 \\ H_a\text{: } \mu_1 - \mu_2 > 0 \end{cases}$$

$$\begin{cases} H_0\text{: } \mu_1 - \mu_2 \geq 0 \\ H_a\text{: } \mu_1 - \mu_2 < 0 \end{cases}$$

Two-Sample z-Test for the Difference Between Means

In the remainder of this section, you will learn how to perform a z-test for the difference between two population means μ_1 and μ_2. To perform such a test, two conditions are necessary.

1. The samples must be independent. Two samples are **independent** if the sample selected from one population is not related to the sample selected from the second population. (You will study the distinction between independent samples and dependent samples in Section 8.3.)

2. Each sample size must be at least 30 or, if not, each population must have a normal distribution with a known standard deviation.

Sampling Distribution for $\bar{x}_1 - \bar{x}_2$

If these requirements are met, then the sampling distribution for $\bar{x}_1 - \bar{x}_2$ (the difference of the sample means) is a normal distribution with mean and standard error of

$$\mu_{\bar{x}_1 - \bar{x}_2} = \mu_1 - \mu_2$$

and

$$\sigma_{\bar{x}_1 - \bar{x}_2} = \sqrt{\frac{\sigma_1^2}{n_1} + \frac{\sigma_2^2}{n_2}}.$$

Notice that the variance of the sampling distribution, $\sigma_{\bar{x}_1 - \bar{x}_2}^2$, is the sum of the variances of the individual sampling distributions for $\bar{x}_1$ and $\bar{x}_2$.

Note to Instructor

Point out the similarities in conducting two-sample hypothesis tests with one-sample tests presented in Chapter 7. Also, point out that *P*-values can be used in this chapter in much the same way they were used in Chapter 7.

Picturing the World

There are about 28,000 civilian federal employees working in Michigan and about 23,000 in Massachusetts. In a survey, 200 federal employees in each state were asked to report their salary. The results were as follows.

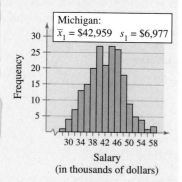

Michigan:
$\bar{x}_1 = \$42,959 \quad s_1 = \$6,977$

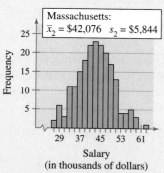

Massachusetts:
$\bar{x}_2 = \$42,076 \quad s_2 = \$5,844$

Is there enough evidence to conclude that there is a difference in the mean incomes of civilian federal employees in Michigan and Massachusetts using $\alpha = 0.05$?

Because the sampling distribution for $\bar{x}_1 - \bar{x}_2$ is a normal distribution, you can use the *z*-test to test the difference between two population means μ_1 and μ_2. Notice that the standardized test statistic takes the form of

$$z = \frac{(\text{Observed difference}) - (\text{Hypothesized difference})}{(\text{Standard error})}.$$

Two-Sample *z*-Test for the Difference Between Means

A **two-sample *z*-test** can be used to test the difference between two population means μ_1 and μ_2 when a large sample (at least 30) is randomly selected from each population and the samples are *independent*. The **test statistic** is $\bar{x}_1 - \bar{x}_2$, and the **standardized test statistic** is

$$z = \frac{(\bar{x}_1 - \bar{x}_2) - (\mu_1 - \mu_2)}{\sigma_{\bar{x}_1 - \bar{x}_2}}, \quad \text{where} \quad \sigma_{\bar{x}_1 - \bar{x}_2} = \sqrt{\frac{\sigma_1^2}{n_1} + \frac{\sigma_2^2}{n_2}}.$$

When the samples are large, you can use s_1 and s_2 in place of σ_1 and σ_2. If the samples are not large, you can still use a two-sample *z*-test, provided the populations are normally distributed and the population standard deviations are known.

If the null hypothesis states that $\mu_1 = \mu_2$, then the expression $\mu_1 - \mu_2$ is equal to 0 in the preceding test.

GUIDELINES

Using a Two-Sample *z*-Test for the Difference Between Means (Large Independent Samples)

In Words	*In Symbols*
1. Identify the claim. State the null and the alternative hypotheses.	State H_0 and H_a.
2. Specify the level of significance.	Identify α.
3. Sketch the sampling distribution.	
4. Find the critical value(s).	Use Table 4.
5. Determine the rejection region(s).	
6. Find the standardized test statistic.	$z = \dfrac{(\bar{x}_1 - \bar{x}_2) - (\mu_1 - \mu_2)}{\sigma_{\bar{x}_1 - \bar{x}_2}}$
7. Make a decision to reject or fail to reject the null hypothesis.	If z is in the rejection region, reject H_0. Otherwise, do not reject H_0.
8. Interpret the decision in the context of the original claim.	

See *TI-83* steps on page 409.

▶ **EXAMPLE 1**   *A Two-Sample z-Test for the Difference Between Means*

Sample Statistics for Household Incomes

Visa Gold	MasterCard Gold
$\bar{x}_1 = \$60,900$	$\bar{x}_2 = \$64,300$
$s_1 = \$12,000$	$s_2 = \$15,000$
$n_1 = 100$	$n_2 = 100$

An advertising executive claims that there is a difference in the mean household income for credit card holders of Visa Gold and of MasterCard Gold. The results of a random survey of 100 customers from each group are shown at the left. The two samples are independent. Do the results support the executive's claim? Use $\alpha = 0.05$. *(Source: Claritas Inc.)*

SOLUTION   You want to test the claim that there is a difference in the mean household incomes for Visa Gold and MasterCard Gold credit card holders. So, the null and alternative hypotheses are

$$H_0: \mu_1 = \mu_2 \quad \text{and} \quad H_a: \mu_1 \neq \mu_2. \text{ (Claim)}$$

Because the test is a two-tailed test and the level of significance is $\alpha = 0.05$, the critical values are -1.96 and 1.96. The rejection regions are $z < -1.96$ and $z > 1.96$. Because both samples are large, s_1 and s_2 are used to calculate the standard error.

$$\sigma_{\bar{x}_1 - \bar{x}_2} = \sqrt{\frac{s_1^2}{n_1} + \frac{s_2^2}{n_2}} = \sqrt{\frac{12,000^2}{100} + \frac{15,000^2}{100}} \approx 1921$$

Using the z-test, the standardized test statistic is

$$z = \frac{(\bar{x}_1 - \bar{x}_2) - (\mu_1 - \mu_2)}{\sigma_{\bar{x}_1 - \bar{x}_2}} \approx \frac{(60,900 - 64,300) - 0}{1921} \approx -1.770.$$

Study Tip

In Example 1, the P-value is 0.0767. Because this is greater than 0.05, you should fail to reject H_0.

The graph at the left shows the location of the rejection regions and the standardized test statistic, z. Because z is not in the rejection region, you should fail to reject the null hypothesis. At the 5% level, there is not enough evidence to conclude that there is a significant difference in the mean household incomes of Visa Gold and MasterCard Gold credit card holders.

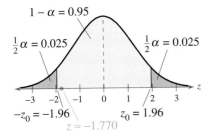

$1 - \alpha = 0.95$
$\frac{1}{2}\alpha = 0.025$
$\frac{1}{2}\alpha = 0.025$
$-z_0 = -1.96$
$z_0 = 1.96$
$z \approx -1.770$

Try It Yourself 1

A survey indicates that the mean credit card charge for residents of New Hampshire and New York is $3900 and $3500, respectively. The survey included a sample of size 50 from each state and sample standard deviations are $900 (NH) and $500 (NY). At $\alpha = 0.01$, is there enough evidence to conclude that there is a difference in the mean credit-card charges? *(Source: Card Management Information Services and the U.S. Census Bureau)*

a. *Identify* the claim and state H_0 and H_a.
b. *Specify* the level of significance α.
c. *Find* the critical values and identify the rejection regions.
d. *Use* the z-test to find the standardized test statistic z.
e. *Decide* whether to reject the null hypothesis. Use a graph if necessary.
f. *Interpret* your decision.   *Answer: Page A41* ◀

▶ **EXAMPLE 2** *Using Technology to Perform a Two-Sample z-Test*

The American Automobile Association claims that the average daily cost for meals and lodging when vacationing in Texas is less than the same average costs when vacationing in Washington state. The table at the left shows the results of a survey of vacationers in each state. At $\alpha = 0.01$, is there enough evidence to support the claim? ($H_0: \mu_1 \geq \mu_2$ and $H_a: \mu_1 < \mu_2$)

SOLUTION The first two displays show how to set up the hypothesis test using a TI-83. The remaining displays show the possible results, depending on whether you select "Calculate" or "Draw."

Sample Statistics for Daily Cost of Meals and Lodging

Texas	Washington
$\bar{x}_1 = \$184$	$\bar{x}_2 = \$195$
$s_1 = \$15$	$s_2 = \$28$
$n_1 = 50$	$n_2 = 35$

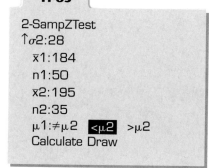

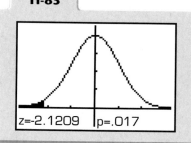

Study Tip

Note that the TI-83 displays $P \approx 0.017$. Because $P > \alpha$, you should fail to reject the null hypothesis.

To use Minitab to perform a two-sample z-test, you must use raw data.

Note to Instructor

Students might be confused about designating Texas as population 1 and Washington as population 2. Explain that the final result of the test would be identical if the subscripts were reversed. Show that reversing the subscripts would produce a right-tailed test for which the test statistic is 2.1209, the critical value is $z = 2.33$, and the rejection region is $z > 2.33$.

Because the test is a left-tailed test and $\alpha = 0.01$, the rejection region is $z < -2.33$. The standardized test statistic, $z \approx -2.12$, is not in the rejection region, so you should fail to reject the null hypothesis. At the 1% level, there is not enough evidence to support the American Automobile Association's claim.

Try It Yourself 2

The American Automobile Association claims that the average daily meal and lodging costs while vacationing in Florida are greater than the same average costs while vacationing in Maryland. The table at the left shows the results of a survey of vacationers in each state. At $\alpha = 0.05$, is there enough evidence to support the claim?

a. *Use* a TI-83 to find the test statistic or the *P*-value.
b. *Determine* whether the test statistic is in the rejection region or *compare* the *P*-value to the level of significance α.
c. *Make* a decision.

Answer: Page A41 ◀

Sample Statistics for Daily Cost of Meals and Lodging

Florida	Maryland
$\bar{x}_1 = \$252$	$\bar{x}_2 = \$244$
$s_1 = 22$	$s_2 = 18$
$n_1 = 150$	$n_2 = 200$

8.1 ▬ EXERCISES ▬▬▬▬▬▬▬▬▬▬▬▬▬▬▬

► HELP

StatPro 8.1

Internet Statistics 8.1

Student Solutions Manual 8.1

**
Videos 8.1**

Try It Yourself Answers 8.1

1. State the hypotheses and identify the claim. Specify the level of significance and find the critical value(s). Find the standardized test statistic. Make a decision and interpret in the context of the claim.

2. (1) The samples must be independent. (2) $\{n_1 \geq 30$ and $n_2 \geq 30\}$ or $\{$each population must be normally distributed with known standard deviations$\}$

3. (a) 2

  (b) 7.603

  (c) z is in the rejection region.

  (d) Reject the claim

4. See Selected Answers, page A82

5. (a) 30

  (b) $z = 1.84$

  (c) z is not in the rejection region.

  (d) Fail to reject H_0.

6. (a) 109

  (b) 5.289

  (c) z is in the rejection region.

  (d) Reject the claim

Basic Skills and Concepts

1. Explain how to perform a two-sample z-test for the difference between the means of two populations using large independent samples.

2. What two conditions are necessary in order to use the z-test to test the difference between two population means?

Testing a Claim In Exercises 3–6, (a) find the test statistic, (b) find the standardized test statistic, (c) decide whether the standardized test statistic is in the rejection region, and (d) decide whether you should reject or fail to reject the claim.

3. Claim: $\mu_1 = \mu_2$, $\alpha = 0.05$
Sample statistics: $\bar{x}_1 = 16$, $s_1 = 1.1$, $n_1 = 50$,
and $\bar{x}_2 = 14$, $s_2 = 1.5$, $n_2 = 50$

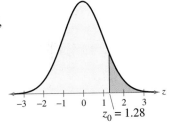

4. Claim: $\mu_1 > \mu_2$, $\alpha = 0.10$
Sample statistics: $\bar{x}_1 = 500$, $s_1 = 30$, $n_1 = 100$,
and $\bar{x}_2 = 510$, $s_2 = 15$, $n_2 = 75$

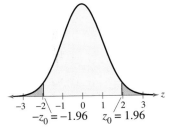

5. Claim: $\mu_1 < \mu_2$, $\alpha = 0.01$
Sample statistics: $\bar{x}_1 = 1225$, $s_1 = 75$, $n_1 = 35$,
and $\bar{x}_2 = 1195$, $s_2 = 105$, $n_2 = 105$

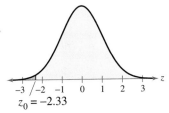

6. Claim: $\mu_1 \leq \mu_2$, $\alpha = 0.03$
Sample statistics: $\bar{x}_1 = 5004$, $s_1 = 136$,
$n_1 = 144$, and $\bar{x}_2 = 4895$, $s_2 = 215$, $n_2 = 156$

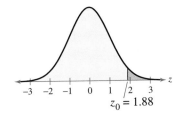

7. (a) $H_0: \mu_1 = \mu_2$ (claim)
  $H_1: \mu_1 \neq \mu_2$
  (b) $z_0 = \pm 1.645$
  (c) $z \approx -2.786$
  (d) Reject H_0

8. (a) $H_0: \mu_1 \leq \mu_2$
  $H_1: \mu_1 > \mu_2$ (claim)
  (b) $z_0 = 1.28$
  (c) $z \approx 3.919$
  (d) Reject H_0

9. (a) $H_0: \mu_1 \geq \mu_2$
  $H_1: \mu_1 < \mu_2$ (claim)
  (b) $z_0 = -2.33$
  (c) $z \approx -1.536$
  (d) Fail to reject H_0

10. (a) $H_0: \mu_1 = \mu_2$ (claim)
  $H_1: \mu_1 \neq \mu_2$
  (b) $z_0 = \pm 2.575$
  (c) $z \approx -3.165$
  (d) Reject H_0

11. (a) $H_0: \mu_1 = \mu_2$ (claim)
  $H_1: \mu_1 \neq \mu_2$
  (b) $z_0 = \pm 2.575$
  (c) $z \approx 0.310$
  (d) Fail to reject H_0

12. (a) $H_0: \mu_1 \leq \mu_2$
  $H_1: \mu_1 > \mu_2$ (claim)
  (b) $z_0 = 1.28$
  (c) $z = 2.349$
  (d) Reject H_0

Testing the Difference Between Two Means   In Exercises 7–16, (a) identify the claim and state H_0 and H_a, (b) use Table 4 to find the critical value(s) and identify the rejection region(s), (c) find the standardized test statistic z, and (d) decide whether to reject or fail to reject the null hypothesis. Then interpret the decision in the context of the original claim. If convenient, use technology to solve the problem.

7. A safety engineer records the breaking distances of two types of tires. Each randomly selected sample has 35 tires. The mean braking distance for Tire Type A is 42 feet with a standard deviation of 4.7 feet. The mean braking distance for Tire Type B is 45 feet with a standard deviation of 4.3 feet. At $\alpha = 0.10$, can the engineer support the claim that the mean braking distance is the same for both types of tires? *(Adapted from Consumer Reports)*

8. To compare the braking distances for two types of tires, a safety engineer conducts 50 breaking tests for each of two types of tires. The mean braking distance for Type C is 55 feet with a standard deviation of 5.3 feet, and the mean braking distance for Type D is 51 feet with a standard deviation of 4.9 feet. At $\alpha = 0.10$, can the engineer support the claim that the mean braking distance for Type C is greater than the mean braking distance for Type D? *(Adapted from Consumer Reports)*

9. You want to buy a microwave oven and will choose Model A if its repair costs are lower than Model B's. For 47 Model A ovens, the mean repair cost was $75 and the standard deviation was $12.50. For 55 Model B ovens, the mean repair cost was $80 and the standard deviation was $20. At $\alpha = 0.01$, would you buy Model A? *(Adapted from Consumer Reports)*

10. You want to buy a vacuum cleaner, and a salesperson tells you the repair costs for Model A and Model B are equal. For 34 Model A vacuum cleaners, the mean repair cost is $50 and the standard deviation is $10. For 46 Model B vacuum cleaners, the mean repair cost is $60 and the standard deviation is $18. At $\alpha = 0.01$, can you reject the salesperson's claim? *(Adapted from Consumer Reports)*

11. The mean ACT score for 43 male high school students is 21.2 and the standard deviation is 4.9. The mean ACT score for 56 female high school students is 20.9 and the standard deviation is 4.6. At $\alpha = 0.01$, do male and female high school students have equal ACT scores? *(Adapted from ACT Inc.)*

12. A guidance counselor claims high school students in a college prep program have higher ACT scores than those in a general program. The mean ACT score for 49 high school students who are in a college prep program is 22.1 and the standard deviation is 4.8. The mean ACT score for 44 high school students who are in a general program is 19.6 and the standard deviation is 5.4. At $\alpha = 0.10$, can you support the guidance counselor's claim that the mean score for college prep students is greater than that for general program students? *(Adapted from ACT Inc.)*

13. (a) H_0: $\mu_1 \leq \mu_2$
H_1: $\mu_1 > \mu_2$ (claim)

(b) $z_0 = 1.96$

(c) $z \approx 4.988$

(d) Reject H_0

14. (a) H_0: $\mu_1 \geq \mu_2$
H_1: $\mu_1 < \mu_2$ (claim)

(b) $z_0 = -1.88$

(c) $z = -6.389$

(d) Reject H_0

15. (a) H_0: $\mu_1 = \mu_2$ (claim)
H_1: $\mu_1 \neq \mu_2$

(b) $z_0 = \pm 2.575$

(c) $z \approx 66.172$

(d) Reject H_0

13. A sociologist claims that children ages 3–12 spent more time watching television in 1981 than children ages 3–12 do today. A study was conducted in 1981 to find the time that children ages 3–12 watched television on weekdays. The results (in hours per weekday) are given below.

2.0	2.5	2.1	2.3	2.1	1.6	2.6	2.1	2.1	2.4	2.1	2.1	1.5
1.7	2.1	2.3	2.5	3.3	2.2	2.9	1.5	1.9	2.4	2.2	1.2	3.0
1.0	2.1	1.9	2.2									

Recently, a similar study was conducted. The results are given below.

1.9	1.8	0.9	1.6	2.0	1.7	1.1	1.1	1.6	2.0	1.4	1.5	1.7
1.6	1.6	1.7	1.2	2.0	2.2	1.6	1.5	2.0	1.6	1.8	1.7	1.3
1.1	1.4	1.2	2.0									

At $\alpha = 0.025$, can you support the sociologist's claim? (*Adapted from University of Michigan's Institute for Social Research*)

14. A sociologist thinks middle school boys spent less time studying in 1981 than middle school boys do today. A study was conducted in 1981 to find the time that middle school boys spent studying on weekdays. The results (in minutes per weekday) are given below.

13.9	17.3	10.0	21.2	12.8	13.7	15.0	11.9	17.3	12.1	13.5
17.9	19.1	18.2	14.8	19.1	6.2	10.6	10.7	23.1	15.7	14.1
10.7	17.2	18.6	16.3	17.8	16.2	15.8	7.5	9.7	3.7	5.3
18.8	8.9									

Recently, a similar study was conducted. The results are given below.

17.5	27.9	14.1	19.9	20.9	19.6	15.9	21.8	23.0	20.6	20.5
31.0	24.0	14.4	22.5	24.6	12.0	18.6	22.8	27.6	20.1	18.5
25.5	22.5	20.0	27.8	13.2	18.4	21.6	23.0	24.5	28.0	17.4
15.2	25.0									

At $\alpha = 0.03$, can you support the sociologist's claim? (*Adapted from University of Michigan's Institute for Social Research*)

15. A production engineer claims that there is no difference in the mean washer diameter manufactured by two different methods. The first method produces washers with the following diameters (in inches).

0.861	0.864	0.882	0.887	0.858	0.879	0.887	0.876	0.870
0.894	0.884	0.882	0.869	0.859	0.887	0.875	0.863	0.887
0.882	0.862	0.906	0.880	0.877	0.864	0.873	0.860	0.866
0.869	0.877	0.863	0.875	0.883	0.872	0.879	0.861	

The second method produces washers with the following diameters (in inches).

0.705	0.703	0.715	0.711	0.690	0.720	0.702	0.686	0.704
0.712	0.718	0.695	0.708	0.695	0.699	0.715	0.691	0.696
0.680	0.703	0.697	0.694	0.714	0.694	0.672	0.688	0.700
0.715	0.709	0.698	0.696	0.700	0.706	0.695	0.715	

At $\alpha = 0.01$, can you reject the production engineer's claim?

16. (a) $H_0: \mu_1 = \mu_2$ (claim)
$H_1: \mu_1 \neq \mu_2$

(b) $z_0 \approx \pm 2.05$

(c) -69.346

(d) Reject H_0

17. They are equivalent through algebraic manipulation of the equation.
$\mu_1 = \mu_2 \Longrightarrow \mu_1 - \mu_2 = 0$

18. They are equivalent through algebraic manipulation of the equation.
$\mu_1 \geq \mu_2 \Longrightarrow \mu_1 - \mu_2 \geq 0$

19. $H_0: \mu_1 - \mu_2 = -9$ (claim)
$H_1: \mu_1 - \mu_2 \neq -9$

Fail to reject H_0. There is not enough evidence to reject the claim.

20. $H_0: \mu_1 - \mu_2 = -1$ (claim)
$H_1: \mu_1 - \mu_2 \neq -1$

Fail to reject H_0. There is not enough evidence to reject the claim.

16. A production engineer claims that there is no difference in the mean nut diameter manufactured by two different methods. The first method produces nuts with the following diameters (in centimeters).

3.330 3.337 3.329 3.354 3.325 3.343 3.333 3.347 3.332 3.358
3.353 3.335 3.341 3.331 3.327 3.326 3.337 3.336 3.323 3.347
3.329 3.345 3.329 3.338 3.353 3.339 3.338 3.338 3.350 3.320
3.364 3.340 3.348 3.339 3.336 3.321 3.316 3.352 3.320 3.336

The second method produces nuts with the following diameters (in centimeters).

3.513 3.490 3.498 3.504 3.483 3.512 3.494 3.514 3.495 3.489
3.493 3.499 3.497 3.495 3.496 3.485 3.506 3.517 3.484 3.498
3.522 3.505 3.501 3.491 3.500 3.499 3.475 3.486 3.501 3.496
3.504 3.513 3.511 3.501 3.487 3.508 3.515 3.505 3.496 3.505

At $\alpha = 0.04$, can you reject the production engineer's claim?

17. *Think About It* Explain why the null hypothesis $H_0: \mu_1 = \mu_2$ is equivalent to the null hypothesis $H_0: \mu_1 - \mu_2 = 0$.

18. *Think About It* Explain why the null hypothesis $H_0: \mu_1 \geq \mu_2$ is equivalent to the null hypothesis $H_0: \mu_1 - \mu_2 \geq 0$.

Extending the Basics

Testing a Difference Other than Zero Sometimes a researcher is interested in testing a difference in means other than zero. In Exercises 19–22, you will test the difference between two means using a null hypothesis of $H_0: \mu_1 - \mu_2 = k$, $H_0: \mu_1 - \mu_2 \geq k$, or $H_0: \mu_1 - \mu_2 \leq k$. The formula for the z-test is still

$$z = \frac{(\bar{x}_1 - \bar{x}_2) - (\mu_1 - \mu_2)}{\sigma_{\bar{x}_1 - \bar{x}_2}}, \qquad \text{where} \qquad \sigma_{\bar{x}_1 - \bar{x}_2} = \sqrt{\frac{\sigma_1^2}{n_1} + \frac{\sigma_2^2}{n_2}}.$$

19. In 1981, a study of 70 children (under 3 years old) found that the mean length of time spent in day care or preschool per week was 11.5 hours with a standard deviation of 3.8 hours. A recent study of 65 children (under 3 years old) found that the mean length of time spent in day care or preschool per week was 20 hours and the standard deviation was 6.7 hours. At $\alpha = 0.01$, test the claim that children spend 9 hours a week more in day care or preschool today than they did in 1981. *(Adapted from University of Michigan's Institute for Social Research)*

20. A recent study of 48 children (ages 6–8) found that the mean length of time spent watching television each week was 12.63 hours and the standard deviation was 4.21 hours. The mean time 56 children (ages 9–12) watched television each week was 13.60 hours and the standard deviation was 4.53 hours. At $\alpha = 0.05$, test the claim that the mean time per week children ages 6–8 watch television is one hour less than that of children ages 9–12. *(Adapted from University of Michigan's Institute for Social Research)*

21. H_0: $\mu_1 - \mu_2 \le 6000$
H_1: $\mu_1 - \mu_2 > 6000$ (claim)

Fail to reject H_0. There is not enough evidence to support the claim.

22. H_0: $\mu_1 - \mu_2 \ge -20{,}500$
H_1: $\mu_1 - \mu_2 < -20{,}500$ (claim)

Fail to reject H_0. There is not enough evidence to support the claim.

23. $-2.45 < \mu_1 - \mu_2 < 0.65$

24. $1.47 < \mu_1 - \mu_2 < 2.13$

21. Is the difference between the mean annual salaries of statisticians in California and Pennsylvania more than $6000? To decide, you select a random sample of statisticians from each state. You find that the mean annual salary for 45 statisticians in California is $43,300 with a standard deviation of $7800 and the mean annual salary for 37 statisticians in Pennsylvania is $37,400 with a standard deviation of $7400. At $\alpha = 0.10$, what should you conclude? *(Adapted from America's Career InfoNet)*

22. A study finds that the mean annual salary for 33 photographers working in North Carolina is $22,800 and the standard deviation is $3600. Another study finds that the mean annual salary for 31 computer programmers working in North Carolina is $43,700 and the standard deviation is $7750. At $\alpha = 0.05$, test the claim that the difference between the mean salary for photographers and the mean salary for computer programmers in North Carolina is less than $20,500. *(Adapted from America's Career InfoNet)*

Confidence Intervals for $\mu_1 - \mu_2$ You can construct a confidence interval for the difference in two population means, $\mu_1 - \mu_2$, by using the following.

$$(\bar{x}_1 - \bar{x}_2) - z_c\sqrt{\frac{\sigma_1^2}{n_1} + \frac{\sigma_2^2}{n_2}} < \mu_1 - \mu_2 < (\bar{x}_1 - \bar{x}_2) + z_c\sqrt{\frac{\sigma_1^2}{n_1} + \frac{\sigma_2^2}{n_2}}$$

In Exercises 23 and 24, construct the indicated confidence interval for $\mu_1 - \mu_2$.

23. A study was conducted to see if an herbal supplement helped to reduce weight. After 12 weeks, 42 subjects using the herbal supplement and a high-fiber, low-calorie diet had a mean weight loss of 3.2 kilograms and a standard deviation of 3.3 kilograms. During the same time period, 42 subjects using a placebo and a high-fiber, low-calorie diet had a mean weight loss of 4.1 kilograms and a standard deviation of 3.9 kilograms. Construct a 95% confidence interval for $\mu_1 - \mu_2$, where μ_1 is the mean weight loss for the group using the herbal supplement and μ_2 is the mean weight loss for the group using the placebo. *(Source: The Journal of the American Medical Association)*

24. Two groups of patients with colorectal cancer are treated with a different drug. Group A's 140 patients are treated using the drug Irinotecan and Group B's 127 patients are treated using the drug Fluorouracil. The mean number of months that Group A reported no cancer-related pain was 10.3 and the standard deviation was 1.2. The mean number of months that Group B reported no cancer-related pain was 8.5 and the standard deviation was 1.5. Construct a 95% confidence interval for $\mu_1 - \mu_2$, where μ_1 is the mean number of months that Group A reported no cancer-related pain and μ_2 is the mean number of months that Group B reported no cancer-related pain. *(Adapted from The Lancet)*

25. There is not enough evidence to support the claim.

26. There is enough evidence to support the claim.

27. $H_0: \mu_1 - \mu_2 \leq 0$ and $H_1: \mu_1 - \mu_2 > 0$ (claim)

    Since 0 is contained in the 95% CI for $\mu_1 - \mu_2$, fail to reject H_0. There is not enough evidence to support the claim.

28. $H_0: \mu_1 - \mu_2 \leq 0$ and $H_1: \mu_1 - \mu_2 > 0$ (claim)

    Since only positive numbers are contained in the 95% CI for $\mu_1 - \mu_2$, reject H_0. There is enough evidence to support the claim.

25. *Make a Decision* Refer to the study in Exercise 23. At $\alpha = 0.05$, test the claim that the mean weight loss for the group using the herbal supplement is greater than the mean weight loss for the group using the placebo. Would you recommend using the herbal supplement with a high-fiber, low-calorie diet to lose weight? Explain your reasoning.

26. *Make a Decision* Refer to the study in Exercise 24. At $\alpha = 0.05$, test the claim that the mean number of months of cancer-related pain relief with Irinotecan is greater than the mean number of months of cancer-related pain relief obtained with Fluorouracil. Would you recommend using Irinotecan over Fluorouracil to relieve cancer-related pain? Explain your reasoning.

27. *Think About It* Compare the confidence interval you constructed in Exercise 23 to the hypothesis test result in Exercise 25. Explain why you would fail to reject the null hypothesis if the confidence interval contains 0.

28. *Think About It* Compare the confidence interval you constructed in Exercise 24 to the hypothesis test result in Exercise 26. Explain why you would reject the null hypothesis if the confidence interval contains only positive numbers.

8 to 10% Saturated
Up to 10% Polyunsaturated
Up to 15% Monounsaturated

Fat
Protein
Carbohydrate

Oat Bran and Cholesterol Level

In an article in the *Journal of Family Practice*, (December 1991, vol. 33, no. 6, pp. 600–608), a study about cholesterol level is described. In the study, men and women (ages 20 to 70) were randomly divided into three groups. Each group was asked to follow the American Heart Association Step I Diet. In addition, the first group was asked to eat two 1-ounce servings of oat bran each day and the second group was asked to eat two 1-ounce servings of wheat cereal each day.

Before the study, each group had mean total cholesterol levels of 238 mg/dL and LDL cholesterol levels of 164 mg/dL. The cholesterol levels of each group after the six-week study are shown in the table at the right.

Step I Diet

Total Fat	30% or less
Carbohydrate	55% or more
Protein	About 15%
Cholesterol	Less than 300 mg per day
Total Calories	To achieve or maintain desired weight

	Oat Bran and Diet $n_1 = 145$	Wheat Cereal and Diet $n_2 = 145$	Diet Alone $n_3 = 176$
Total Cholesterol	$\bar{x}_1 = 224$ $s_1 = 26.7$	$\bar{x}_2 = 231$ $s_2 = 30.5$	$\bar{x}_3 = 236$ $s_3 = 30.2$
LDL Cholesterol	$\bar{x}_1 = 148$ $s_1 = 26.7$	$\bar{x}_2 = 158$ $s_2 = 23.6$	$\bar{x}_3 = 162$ $s_3 = 27.5$

Cholesterol is measured in milligrams per deciliter.

Exercises

In Exercises 1–4, perform a two-sample z-test to determine whether the cholesterol levels of the two indicated groups are different. For each exercise, write your conclusion as a sentence. Use $\alpha = 0.05$.

1. Test the total cholesterol levels of people who ate oat bran while on the Step I Diet against those who ate wheat cereal while on the Step I Diet.

2. Test the total cholesterol levels of people who ate oat bran while on the Step I Diet against those who were on the Step I Diet alone.

3. Test the LDL cholesterol levels of people who ate oat bran while on the Step I Diet against those who ate wheat cereal while on the Step I Diet.

4. Test the LDL cholesterol levels of people who ate oat bran while on the Step I Diet against those who were on the Step I Diet alone.

5. In a different study, reported in the *Annals of the Internal Medicine*, 91 people were given a cholesterol-reducing drug called Pravastatin. The mean level of total cholesterol before the study was 214 mg/dL and the mean level of LDL cholesterol was 140 mg/dL. After the study, the mean levels were 167 mg/dL and 91 mg/dL.

   (a) Test the total cholesterol level of this group with the oat bran group described previously. Use $\alpha = 0.01$ and assume $s = 20$ mg/dL for the Pravastatin group.

   (b) Test the LDL cholesterol level of this group with the oat bran group described previously. Use $\alpha = 0.01$ and assume $s = 20$ mg/dL for the Pravastatin group.

6. In which comparisons did you find a difference in cholesterol levels? Write a summary of your findings.

8.2 Testing the Difference Between Means (Small Independent Samples)

The Two-Sample *t*-Test for the Difference Between Means

What You Should Learn

- **How to perform a t-test for the difference between two population means μ_1 and μ_2 using small independent samples**

The Two-Sample *t*-Test for the Difference Between Means

As you have learned, in real life, it is often not practical to collect samples of size 30 or more from each of two populations. However, if both populations have a normal distribution, you can still test the difference between their means. In this section, you will learn how to use a *t*-test to test the difference between two population means μ_1 and μ_2 using a sample from each population. To use a *t*-test for small independent samples, the following conditions are necessary.

1. The samples must be independent. Recall that two samples are independent if the sample selected from one population is not related to the sample selected from the second population.

2. Each population must have a normal distribution.

When these conditions are met, the sampling distribution for $\bar{x}_1 - \bar{x}_2$, the difference between the sample means, is a *t*-distribution with mean $\mu_1 - \mu_2$. The standard error and the degrees of freedom of the sampling distribution depend on whether the population variances, σ_1^2 and σ_2^2, are equal.

If the population variances are equal, information from both samples is combined to calculate a **pooled estimate of the standard deviation.**

$$\hat{\sigma} = \sqrt{\frac{(n_1 - 1)s_1^2 + (n_2 - 1)s_2^2}{n_1 + n_2 - 2}} \qquad \text{Pooled estimate of } \sigma$$

The standard error for the sampling distribution of $\bar{x}_1 - \bar{x}_2$ is

$$\sigma_{\bar{x}_1 - \bar{x}_2} = \hat{\sigma}\sqrt{\frac{1}{n_1} + \frac{1}{n_2}} \qquad \text{Variances are equal.}$$

and d.f. $= n_1 + n_2 - 2$.

If the variances are not equal, the standard error is

$$\sigma_{\bar{x}_1 - \bar{x}_2} = \sqrt{\frac{s_1^2}{n_1} + \frac{s_2^2}{n_2}} \qquad \text{Variances are not equal.}$$

and d.f. = smaller of $n_1 - 1$ or $n_2 - 1$.

The requirements for the *z*-test described in Section 8.1 and the *t*-test described in this section are compared below.

Study Tip

You will learn to test for differences in variances in two populations in Chapter 10. In this chapter, each example and exercise will state whether the variances are equal.

Note to Instructor

If you choose, you can cover tests for equal variances (Section 10.3) before doing these *t*-tests. In case you cover Section 10.3 later or do not have time to cover it at all, students will be informed whether to assume equal variances in each example and exercise in this section.

	z-Test	*t*-Test
Samples	Must be independent	Must be independent
Distribution and sample size	Both samples must have at least 30 members *or* the populations must be normal with known standard deviations.	The population must be normal. (One or both of the samples can have less than 30 members.)

If the sampling distribution for $\bar{x}_1 - \bar{x}_2$ is a t-distribution, you can use a two-sample t-test to test the difference between two population means μ_1 and μ_2.

Two-Sample t-Test for the Difference Between Means

A **two-sample t-test** is used to test the difference between two population means μ_1 and μ_2 when a sample is randomly selected from each population. To perform this test, each population must be normally distributed, the samples should be independent, and the size of at least one of the samples must be less than 30. The standardized test statistic is

$$t = \frac{(\bar{x}_1 - \bar{x}_2) - (\mu_1 - \mu_2)}{\sigma_{\bar{x}_1 - \bar{x}_2}}.$$

If the population variances are equal, then d.f. $= n_1 + n_2 - 2$ and

$$\sigma_{\bar{x}_1 - \bar{x}_2} = \sqrt{\frac{(n_1 - 1)s_1^2 + (n_2 - 1)s_2^2}{n_1 + n_2 - 2}} \sqrt{\frac{1}{n_1} + \frac{1}{n_2}}.$$

If the population variances are not equal, then d.f. is the smaller of $n_1 - 1$ or $n_2 - 1$ and

$$\sigma_{\bar{x}_1 - \bar{x}_2} = \sqrt{\frac{s_1^2}{n_1} + \frac{s_2^2}{n_2}}.$$

GUIDELINES

Using a Two-Sample t-Test for the Difference Between Means (Small Independent Samples)

In Words	*In Symbols*
1. Identify the claim. State the null and alternative hypotheses.	State H_0 and H_a.
2. Specify the level of significance.	Identify α.
3. Determine the degrees of freedom.	d.f. $= n_1 + n_2 - 2$ or d.f. $=$ smaller of $n_1 - 1$ or $n_2 - 1$
4. Find the critical value(s).	Use Table 5.
5. Identify the rejection region(s).	
6. Find the standardized test statistic.	$t = \dfrac{(\bar{x}_1 - \bar{x}_2) - (\mu_1 - \mu_2)}{\sigma_{\bar{x}_1 - \bar{x}_2}}$
7. Make a decision to reject or fail to reject the null hypothesis.	If t is in the rejection region, reject H_0. Otherwise, do not reject H_0.
8. Interpret the decision in the context of the original claim.	

See *Minitab* steps on page 408.

EXAMPLE 1 A Two-Sample t-Test for the Difference Between Means

Sample Statistics for Stopping Distances

Winterfire	Alpin
$\bar{x}_1 = 51$	$\bar{x}_2 = 55$
$s_1 = 8$	$s_2 = 3$
$n_1 = 10$	$n_2 = 12$

Consumer Reports tested several types of snow tires to determine how well each performed under winter conditions. When traveling on ice at 15 mph, 10 Firestone Winterfire tires had a mean stopping distance of 51 feet with a standard deviation of 8 feet. The mean stopping distance for 12 Michelin XM+S Alpin tires was 55 feet with a standard deviation of 3 feet. Can you conclude that there is a difference in the stopping distances of the two types of tires? Use $\alpha = 0.01$. Assume the populations are normally distributed and the population variances are not equal.

SOLUTION You want to test whether the mean stopping distances are different. So, the null and alternative hypotheses are

$$H_0: \mu_1 = \mu_2 \quad \text{and} \quad H_a: \mu_1 \neq \mu_2. \text{ (Claim)}$$

Because the variances are not equal and the smaller sample size is 10, use d.f. $= 10 - 1 = 9$. Because the test is a two-tailed test with d.f. $= 9$, and $\alpha = 0.01$, the critical values are -3.250 and 3.250. The rejection regions are $t < -3.250$ and $t > 3.250$. The standard error is

$$\sigma_{\bar{x}_1 - \bar{x}_2} = \sqrt{\frac{s_1^2}{n_1} + \frac{s_2^2}{n_2}} = \sqrt{\frac{8^2}{10} + \frac{3^2}{12}} \approx 2.674.$$

Using the *t*-test, the standardized test statistic is

$$t = \frac{(\bar{x}_1 - \bar{x}_2) - (\mu_1 - \mu_2)}{\sigma_{\bar{x}_1 - \bar{x}_2}} \approx \frac{(51 - 55) - 0}{2.674} \approx -1.496.$$

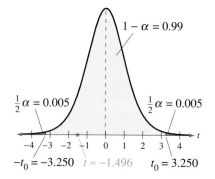

$1 - \alpha = 0.99$

$\frac{1}{2}\alpha = 0.005$ $\frac{1}{2}\alpha = 0.005$

$-t_0 = -3.250$ $t \approx -1.496$ $t_0 = 3.250$

The graph at the left shows the location of the critical regions and the standardized test statistic, *t*. Because *t* is not in a rejection region, you should fail to reject the null hypothesis. At the 1% level, there is not enough evidence to conclude that the mean stopping distances of the tires are different.

Try It Yourself 1

Sample Statistics for Stopping Distances

Winterfire	Alpin
$\bar{x}_1 = 102$	$\bar{x}_2 = 94$
$s_1 = 10$	$s_2 = 4$
$n_1 = 10$	$n_2 = 12$

When traveling on wet pavement at 40 mph, Winterfire had a mean stopping distance of 102 feet with a standard deviation of 10 feet. The mean stopping distance for the Alpin was 94 feet with a standard deviation of 4 feet. If 10 Winterfire tires and 12 Alpin tires were used in the test, can you conclude that the mean stopping distances are different? Use $\alpha = 0.05$. (Assume the populations are normally distributed and the population variances are not equal.)

a. *Identify* the claim and state H_0 and H_a.
b. *Specify* the level of significance α.
c. *Determine* the degrees of freedom.
d. *Find* the critical values and *identify* the rejection regions.
e. *Use* the *t*-test to find the standardized test statistic *t*.
f. *Decide* whether to reject the null hypothesis. Use a graph if necessary.
g. Is there enough evidence to conclude that the mean stopping distances are different?

Answer: Page A41

See *TI-83* steps on page 409.

▶ EXAMPLE 2   *A Two-Sample t-Test for the Difference Between Means*

A manufacturer claims that the calling range (in miles) of its 900-MHz cordless telephone is greater than that of its leading competitor. You perform a study using 14 phones from the manufacturer and 16 similar phones from its competitor. The results are shown at the left. At $\alpha = 0.05$, is there enough evidence to support the manufacturer's claim? Assume the populations are normally distributed and the population variances are equal.

Sample Statistics for Calling Range

Manufacturer	Competition
$\bar{x}_1 = 1275$	$\bar{x}_2 = 1250$
$s_1 = 45$	$s_2 = 30$
$n_1 = 14$	$n_2 = 16$

SOLUTION   The claim is "the mean range of our cordless phone is greater than the mean range of yours." So, the null and alternative hypotheses are

$$H_0: \mu_1 \leq \mu_2 \quad \text{and} \quad H_a: \mu_1 > \mu_2. \text{ (Claim)}$$

Because the variances are equal, d.f. $= n_1 + n_2 - 2 = 14 + 16 - 2 = 28$. Because the test is a right-tailed test, d.f. $= 28$, and $\alpha = 0.05$, the critical value is 1.701. The rejection region is $t > 1.701$. The standard error is

$$\sigma_{\bar{x}_1 - \bar{x}_2} = \sqrt{\frac{(13)(45^2) + (15)(30^2)}{14 + 16 - 2}} \sqrt{\frac{1}{14} + \frac{1}{16}} \approx 13.802.$$

Using the *t*-test, the standardized test statistic is

$$t = \frac{(\bar{x}_1 - \bar{x}_2) - (\mu_1 - \mu_2)}{\sigma_{\bar{x}_1 - \bar{x}_2}} \approx \frac{(1275 - 1250) - 0}{13.802} \approx 1.811.$$

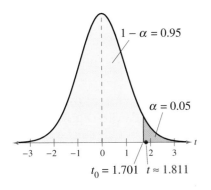

$1 - \alpha = 0.95$

$\alpha = 0.05$

$t_0 = 1.701 \quad t \approx 1.811$

The graph at the left shows the location of the rejection region and the standardized test statistic, *t*. Because *t* is in the rejection region, you should decide to reject the null hypothesis. At the 5% level, there is enough evidence to support the manufacturer's claim that its phone has a greater calling range than its competitor's.

Try It Yourself 2

A manufacturer claims that the watt usage of its 17-inch monitors is less than that of its leading competitor. You perform a study and obtain the results shown at the left. At $\alpha = 0.10$, is there enough evidence to support the manufacturer's claim? Assume the populations are normally distributed and the population variances are equal.

Sample Statistics for Watt Usage

Manufacturer	Competition
$\bar{x}_1 = 73$	$\bar{x}_2 = 74$
$s_1 = 2.4$	$s_2 = 3.2$
$n_1 = 12$	$n_2 = 15$

a. *Identify* the claim and state H_0 and H_a.
b. *Specify* the level of significance α.
c. *Determine* the degrees of freedom.
d. *Find* the critical value and *identify* the rejection region.
e. *Use* the *t*-test to find the standardized test statistic *t*.
f. *Decide* whether to reject the null hypothesis. Use a graph if necessary.
g. Is there enough evidence to support the manufacturer's claim?

Answer: Page A41 ◀

HELP

StatPro 8.2

Internet Statistics 8.2

Student Solutions Manual 8.2

Videos 8.2

Try It Yourself Answers 8.2

---

1. State hypotheses and identify the claim. Specify the level of significance. Determine the degrees of freedom. Find the critical value(s) and identify the rejection region(s). Find the standardized test statistic. Make a decision and interpret in the context of the original claim.

2. See Selected Answers, page A82

   3. (a) $t_0 = \pm 1.725$
   (b) $t_0 = \pm 1.833$

4. **(a)** $t_0 = 2.485$
   (b) $t_0 = 2.718$

5. **(a)** $t_0 = -2.074$
   (b) $t_0 = -2.306$

6. **(a)** $t_0 = \pm 1.96$
   (b) $t_0 = \pm 2.101$

7. $H_0: \mu_1 = \mu_2$
   $H_a: \mu_1 \neq \mu_2$

   (a) -1.8

   (b) $t \approx -1.199$

   (c) t is not in the rejection region.

   (d) Fail to reject H_0. There is not enough evidence to reject the claim.

8. See Selected Answers, page A82

9. See Odd Answers, page A65

Basic Skills and Concepts

1. Explain how to perform a two-sample t-test for the difference between the means of two populations.

2. What conditions are necessary in order to use a t-test to test the difference between two population means?

Finding Critical Values   In Exercises 3–6, use Table 5 to find the critical value(s) for the indicated test, level of significance α, and sample sizes n_1 and n_2. Assume the population variances are (a) equal and (b) not equal.

3. Two-tailed, $\alpha = 0.10$, $n_1 = 10$, $n_2 = 12$

4. Right-tailed, $\alpha = 0.01$, $n_1 = 12$, $n_2 = 15$

5. Left-tailed, $\alpha = 0.025$, $n_1 = 15$, $n_2 = 9$

6. Two-tailed, $\alpha = 0.05$, $n_1 = 19$, $n_2 = 22$

Testing a Claim   In Exercises 7–10, (a) find the test statistic, (b) find the standardized test statistic, (c) decide whether the standardized test statistic is in the rejection region, and (d) decide whether you should reject or fail to reject the claim.

7. Claim: $\mu_1 = \mu_2$, $\alpha = 0.01$
   Sample statistics: $\bar{x}_1 = 33.7$, $s_1 = 3.5$,
   $n_1 = 10$, and $\bar{x}_2 = 35.5$, $s_2 = 2.2$, $n_2 = 7$
   Assume $\sigma_1^2 = \sigma_2^2$

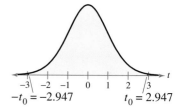

8. Claim: $\mu_1 \geq \mu_2$, $\alpha = 0.10$
   Sample statistics: $\bar{x}_1 = 0.515$, $s_1 = 0.305$,
   $n_1 = 11$, and $\bar{x}_2 = 0.475$, $s_2 = 0.215$, $n_2 = 9$
   Assume $\sigma_1^2 = \sigma_2^2$

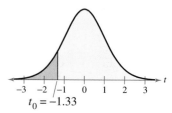

9. Claim: $\mu_1 \leq \mu_2$, $\alpha = 0.05$
   Sample statistics: $\bar{x}_1 = 2250$, $s_1 = 175$,
   $n_1 = 13$, and $\bar{x}_2 = 2305$, $s_2 = 52$, $n_2 = 10$
   Assume $\sigma_1^2 \neq \sigma_2^2$

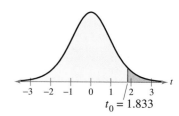

10. $H_0: \mu_1 \le \mu_2$
$H_a: \mu_1 > \mu_2$

(a) -5

(b) $t \approx -4.025$

(c) t is not in the rejection region.

(d) Fail to reject H_0. There is not enough evidence to reject the claim.

11. (a) $H_0: \mu_1 = \mu_2$ (claim)
$H_a: \mu_1 \ne \mu_2$

(b) d.f. = 35
$t_0 = \pm 1.645$

Footwell Intrusion

(c) $t \approx -0.833$

(d) Fail to reject H_0. There is not enough evidence to reject the claim.

12. See Selected Answers, page A82

13. (a) $H_0: \mu_1 \ge \mu_2$
$H_a: \mu_1 < \mu_2$ (claim)

(b) d.f. = 13
$t_0 = -1.350$

(c) $t = -1.912$

(d) Reject H_0. There is enough evidence to support the claim.

14. (a) $H_0: \mu_1 \le \mu_2$
$H_a: \mu_1 > \mu_2$ (claim)

(b) d.f. = 11
$t_0 = 1.363$

(c) $t \approx 2.624$

(d) Reject H_0. There is enough evidence to support the claim.

10. Claim: $\mu_1 \le \mu_2$, $\alpha = 0.01$
Sample statistics: $\bar{x}_1 = 45$, $s_1 = 4.8$,
$n_1 = 16$, and $\bar{x}_2 = 50$, $s_2 = 1.2$, $n_2 = 14$
Assume $\sigma_1^2 \ne \sigma_2^2$

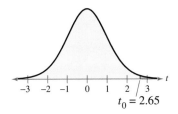

$t_0 = 2.65$

Testing the Difference Between Two Means In Exercises 11–20, (a) write the claim mathematically and identify H_0 and H_a, (b) find the critical value(s) and identify the rejection region(s), (c) find the standardized test statistic, and (d) decide whether to reject or fail to reject the null hypothesis and interpret the decision in the context of the original claim. Assume the populations have approximately normal distributions.

11. An insurance actuary claims that the mean footwell intrusion for small and midsize cars is equal. Crash tests at 40 miles per hour were performed on 14 small cars and 23 midsize cars. The amount that the footwell intruded on the driver's legs was measured. The mean footwell intrusion for the small cars was 23.1 centimeters and the standard deviation was 8.69 centimeters. The mean footwell intrusion for the midsize cars was 25.3 centimeters and the standard deviation was 7.21 centimeters. At $\alpha = 0.10$, can you reject the insurance actuary's claim? Assume the population variances are equal. *(Adapted from Insurance Institute for Highway Safety)*

12. In order to compare the footwell intrusion for small pickups and utility vehicles, several crash tests at 40 miles per hour were performed. For the five pickups that were crashed, the mean footwell intrusion was 20.0 centimeters with a standard deviation of 4.24 centimeters. For the eight utility vehicles that were crashed, the mean footwell intrusion was 19.1 centimeters with a standard deviation of 3.72 centimeters. At $\alpha = 0.05$, can you reject the claim that the mean footwell intrusion for these vehicle types are equal? Assume the population variances are equal. *(Adapted from Insurance Institute for Highway Safety)*

13. In crash tests at five miles per hour, the mean bumper repair cost for 14 small cars is $574 with a standard deviation of $185. In similar tests of 23 midsize cars, the mean bumper repair cost is $734 with a standard deviation of $268. At $\alpha = 0.10$, can you conclude that the mean bumper repair cost is less for small cars that it is for midsize cars? Assume that the population variances are not equal. *(Adapted from Insurance Institute for Highway Safety)*

14. Crash tests at 5 miles per hour were performed on 5 small pickups and 8 small utility vehicles. For the small pickups, the mean bumper repair cost was $1520 and the standard deviation was $403. For the small utility vehicles, the mean bumper repair cost was $937 and the standard deviation was $382. At $\alpha = 0.10$, is there enough evidence to conclude that the mean bumper repair cost is greater for small pickups than for small utility vehicles? Assume the population variances are equal. *(Adapted from Insurance Institute for Highway Safety)*

15. (a) H_0: $\mu_1 \leq \mu_2$
H_a: $\mu_1 > \mu_2$ (claim)
(b) d.f. = 14
t_0 = 1.761
(c) t = 2.098
(d) Reject H_0. There is enough evidence to support the claim.

16. (a) H_0: $\mu_1 = \mu_2$ (claim)
H_a: $\mu_1 \neq \mu_2$
(b) d.f. = $n_1 + n_2 - 2 = 33$
t_0 = ±2.576
(c) $t \approx 0.663$
(d) Fail to reject H_0. There is not enough evidence to resist the claim.

17. (a) H_0: $\mu_1 = \mu_2$
H_a: $\mu_1 \neq \mu_2$ (claim)
(b) d.f. = 21
t_0 = ±2.831
(c) $t \approx -6.410$
(d) Reject H_0. There is enough evidence to support the claim.

18. (a) H_0: $\mu_1 \leq \mu_2$
H_a: $\mu_1 > \mu_2$ (claim)
(b) d.f. = 13
t_0 = 1.350
(c) $t \approx 3.429$
(d) Reject H_0. There is enough evidence to support the claim and to recommend using the new treatment.

15. A personnel director claims that the mean annual wage is greater in Allegheny County than it is in Erie County. In Allegheny County, a random sample of 19 residents has a mean annual income of $30,800 and a standard deviation of $8600. In Erie County, a random sample of 15 residents has a mean annual income of $25,700 and a standard deviation of $5500. At $\alpha = 0.05$, can you support the personnel director's claim? Assume the population variances are not equal. *(Adapted from U.S. Bureau of Labor Statistics, Pennsylvania Department of Labor and Industry)*

16. Test the claim at $\alpha = 0.01$ that the mean annual incomes in Delaware and Greene Counties are the same. A random sample of 17 residents of Delaware County has a mean annual income of $31,200 and a standard deviation of $7800. In Greene County, a random sample of 18 residents has a mean annual income of $29,500 and a standard deviation of $7375. Assume the population variances are equal. *(Adapted from U.S. Bureau of Labor Statistics, Pennsylvania Department of Labor and Industry)*

17. The tensile strength of a metal is a measure of its ability to resist tearing when it is pulled lengthwise. Using a new experimental type of treatment, steel bars were produced with the following tensile strengths (in newtons per square millimeter).

363 355 305 350 340 373 311 348 338 320

With the old method, steel bars were produced with the following tensile strengths (in newtons per square millimeter).

362 382 368 398 381 391 400 410 396 411 385 385 395

At $\alpha = 0.01$, does the new treatment make a difference in the tensile strength of steel bars? Assume the population variances are equal.

18. An engineer wants to compare the tensile strengths of steel bars that are produced using a conventional method and an experimental method. (The tensile strength of a metal is a measure of its ability to resist tearing when pulled lengthwise.) To do so, the engineer randomly selects steel bars that are manufactured using each method and records the following tensile strengths in newtons per square millimeter.

Experimental method:

395 389 421 394 407 411 389 402 422
416 402 408 400 386 411 405 389

Conventional method:

362 352 380 382 413 384 400 378 419
379 384 388 372 383

At $\alpha = 0.10$, can the engineer claim that the experimental method produces steel with greater mean tensile strength? Should the engineer recommend using the experimental method? Assume the population variances are not equal.

19. (a) $H_0: \mu_1 \geq \mu_2$
  $H_a: \mu_1 < \mu_2$ (claim)
  (b) d.f. = 42
  $t_0 = -1.282$
  (c) $t \approx -4.295$
  (d) Reject H_0. There is enough evidence to support the claim and to recommend changing to the new method.

20. (a) $H_0: \mu_1 \geq \mu_2$
  $H_a: \mu_1 < \mu_2$ (claim)
  (b) d.f. = 39
  $t_0 = -1.645$
  (c) $t \approx -1.721$
  (d) Reject H_0. There is enough evidence to support the claim.

19. A new method of teaching reading is being tested on third-grade students. A group of randomly selected students is taught using the experimental curriculum. A control group of randomly selected students is taught using the old curriculum. The reading test scores of the two groups are given in the stem-and-leaf plot.

Old Curriculum		New Curriculum
9	3	
9 9	4	3
9 8 8 4 3 3 2 1	5	2 4
7 6 4 2 2 1 0 0	6	0 1 1 4 7 7 7 7 8 9 9
	7	0 1 1 2 3 3 4 9
	8	2 4

Key:
9|4 = 49 (old curriculum)
4|3 = 43 (new curriculum)

At $\alpha = 0.10$, is there enough evidence to conclude that the new method of teaching reading produces higher reading test scores than the old method? Would you recommend changing to the new method? Assume the population variances are equal.

20. Two teaching methods and their effects on science test scores are being reviewed. A randomly selected group of students is taught in traditional lab sessions. A second randomly selected group of students is taught using interactive simulation software. The science test scores of the two groups are given in the stem-and-leaf plot.

Traditional Lab		Interactive Simulation Software
	6	
9 9 8 8 7 6 6 3 2 1 0	7	0 4 5 5 7 7 8
9 8 5 1 1 1 0 0	8	0 0 3 4 7 8 8 9 9
2 0	9	1 3 9

Key:
0|9 = 90 (traditional)
9|1 = 91 (interactive)

At $\alpha = 0.05$, can you support the claim that the mean science test score is lower for students taught using the lab method than it is for students taught using the interactive simulation software? Assume the population variances are equal.

Extending the Basics

Confidence Intervals for $\mu_1 - \mu_2$ If the populations have equal variances, you can construct a confidence interval for $\mu_1 - \mu_2$ using the following.

$$(\bar{x}_1 - \bar{x}_2) - t_c \hat{\sigma}\sqrt{\frac{1}{n_1} + \frac{1}{n_2}} < \mu_1 - \mu_2 < (\bar{x}_1 - \bar{x}_2) + t_c \hat{\sigma}\sqrt{\frac{1}{n_1} + \frac{1}{n_2}}$$

where $\hat{\sigma} = \sqrt{\dfrac{(n_1 - 1)s_1^2 + (n_2 - 1)s_2^2}{n_1 + n_2 - 2}}$ and d.f. = $n_1 + n_2 - 2$

In Exercises 21 and 22, construct a confidence interval for $\mu_1 - \mu_2$. Assume the populations are approximately normal with equal variances.

21. $-15.664 < \mu_1 - \mu_2 < -4.336$
22. $-5.575 < \mu_1 - \mu_2 < -2.425$
23. $-0.849 < \mu_1 - \mu_2 < 2.849$
24. $1.695 < \mu_1 - \mu_2 < 4.305$

21. In a study of various fast foods, you find that the mean calorie content of 15 grilled chicken sandwiches from Arby's is $\bar{x}_1 = 230$ calories with a standard deviation of $s_1 = 6.2$ calories. You also find that the mean calorie content of 12 similar chicken sandwiches from McDonald's is $\bar{x}_2 = 240$ calories with a standard deviation of $s_2 = 8.1$ calories. Construct a 95% confidence interval for the difference in mean calorie content of grilled chicken sandwiches. *(Adapted from Fast Food Facts, Minnesota Attorney General's Office)*

22. A nutritionist wants to compare the mean protein content of grilled chicken sandwiches from Arby's and McDonald's. To do so, you randomly select several grilled chicken sandwiches from each restaurant and measure the protein content of each. The results are listed below. Construct a 95% confidence interval for the difference in mean protein content of grilled chicken sandwiches. *(Adapted from Fast Food Facts, Minnesota Attorney General's Office)*

Restaurant	Mean protein content	Standard deviation	Sample size
Arby's	$\bar{x}_1 = 23$ grams	$s_1 = 2.1$ grams	$n_1 = 15$
McDonald's	$\bar{x}_2 = 27$ grams	$s_2 = 1.8$ grams	$n_2 = 12$

Confidence Intervals for $\mu_1 - \mu_2$ If the population variances are not equal, you can construct a confidence interval for $\mu_1 - \mu_2$, using the following.

$$(\bar{x}_1 - \bar{x}_2) - t_c\sqrt{\frac{s_1^2}{n_1} + \frac{s_2^2}{n_2}} < \mu_1 - \mu_2 < (\bar{x}_1 - \bar{x}_2) + t_c\sqrt{\frac{s_1^2}{n_1} + \frac{s_2^2}{n_2}},$$

and d.f. is the smaller of $n_1 - 1$ or $n_2 - 1$

In Exercises 23 and 24, construct the indicated confidence interval for $\mu_1 - \mu_2$. Assume the population variances are not equal.

23. To compare the mean cholesterol content of grilled chicken sandwiches from Arby's and McDonald's, you randomly select several sandwiches from each restaurant and measure their cholesterol contents. The results are listed below. Construct a 90% confidence interval for the difference in cholesterol content of grilled chicken sandwiches. *(Adapted from Fast Food Facts, Minnesota Attorney General's Office)*

Restaurant	Mean cholesterol content	Standard deviation	Sample size
Arby's	$\bar{x}_1 = 61$ mg	$s_1 = 3.59$ mg	$n_1 = 15$
McDonald's	$\bar{x}_2 = 60$ mg	$s_2 = 2.41$ mg	$n_2 = 12$

24. A study of fast food found that the mean carbohydrate content of 15 grilled chicken sandwiches from Arby's is $\bar{x}_1 = 41$ grams with a standard deviation of $s_1 = 2.42$ grams. The study also found that the mean carbohydrate content of 12 grilled chicken sandwiches from McDonald's is $\bar{x}_2 = 38$ grams with a standard deviation of $s_2 = 1.65$ grams. Construct a 90% confidence interval for the difference in mean carbohydrate content. *(Adapted from Fast Food Facts, Minnesota Attorney General's Office)*

Testing the Difference Between Means (Dependent Samples)

8.3

Independent and Dependent Samples • The *t*-Test for the Difference Between Means

What You Should Learn

- *How to decide whether two samples are independent or dependent*
- *How to perform a t-test to test the mean of the differences for a population of paired data*

Independent and Dependent Samples

In Sections 8.1 and 8.2, you studied two-sample hypothesis tests in which the samples were independent. In this section, you will learn how to perform two-sample hypothesis tests using dependent samples.

> **DEFINITION**
>
> Two samples are **independent** if the sample selected from one population is not related to the sample selected from the second population. The two samples are **dependent** if each member of one sample corresponds to a member of the other sample. Dependent samples are also called **paired samples** or **matched samples.**

▶ **EXAMPLE 1** *Independent and Dependent Samples*

Dependent Samples

Sample 1   Sample 2

Classify each pair of samples as independent or dependent.

1. Sample 1: Resting heart rates of 35 individuals before drinking coffee
   Sample 2: Resting heart rates of the same individuals after drinking two cups of coffee
2. Sample 1: Test scores for 35 statistics students
   Sample 2: Test scores for 42 biology students who do not study statistics

SOLUTION

1. These samples are dependent. Because the resting heart rates of the same individuals are taken, the samples are related. The samples can be paired with respect to each individual.
2. These samples are independent. It is not possible to form a pairing between the members of samples—the sample sizes are different and the data represent test scores for different individuals.

> *Try It Yourself 1*
>
> Classify each pair of samples as independent or dependent.
>
> 1. Sample 1: Heights of 27 adult females
>   Sample 2: Heights of 27 adult males
> 2. Sample 1: Midterm exam scores of 14 chemistry students
>   Sample 2: Final exam scores of the same 14 chemistry students
>
> **a.** Determine whether the samples are related.   *Answer: Page A41*

Note to Instructor

Dependent samples often involve identical twins, before and after results for the same person or object, or results of individuals matched for specific characteristics.

The *t*-Test for the Difference Between Means

In Sections 8.1 and 8.2, you performed two-sample hypothesis tests with independent samples using the test statistic $\bar{x}_1 - \bar{x}_2$ (the difference in the means of the two samples). To perform a two-sample hypothesis test with dependent samples, you will use a different technique. You will first find the difference for each data pair, $d = x_1 - x_2$. The test statistic is the mean of these differences, $\bar{d} = (\Sigma d)/n$. To conduct the test, the following conditions are required.

1. The samples must be dependent (paired) and randomly selected.
2. Both populations must be normally distributed.

If these requirements are met, then the sampling distribution for $\bar{d}$, the mean of the differences of the paired data entries in the dependent samples, has a *t*-distribution with $n - 1$ degrees of freedom, where n is the number of data pairs.

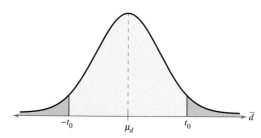

The following symbols are used for the *t*-test for μ_d.

Symbol	Description
n	The number of pairs of data
d	The difference between entries for a data pair, $d = x_1 - x_2$
μ_d	The hypothesized mean of the differences of paired data in the population
$\bar{d}$	The mean of the differences between the paired data entries in the dependent samples $$\bar{d} = \frac{\Sigma d}{n}$$
s_d	The standard deviation of the differences between the paired data entries in the dependent samples $$s_d = \sqrt{\frac{n(\Sigma d^2) - (\Sigma d)^2}{n(n - 1)}}$$

Although formulas are given for the mean and standard deviation of differences, we suggest that you use a technology tool to calculate these statistics.

Because the sampling distribution for $\overline{d}$ is a t-distribution, you can use a t-test to test a claim about the mean of the differences for a population of paired data.

---

t-Test for the Difference Between Means

A t-test can be used to test the difference of two population means when a sample is randomly selected from each population. To perform the test, each population must be normal and each member of the first sample is paired with a member of the second sample. The **test statistic** is $\overline{d}$ and the **standardized test statistic** is

$$t = \frac{\overline{d} - \mu_d}{s_d / \sqrt{n}}.$$

The degrees of freedom are d.f. $= n - 1$.

GUIDELINES

Using the t-Test for the Difference Between Means (Dependent Samples)

In Words	*In Symbols*
1. Identify the claim. State the null and the alternative hypotheses.	State H_0 and H_a.
2. Specify the level of significance.	Identify α.
3. Identify the degrees of freedom.	d.f. $= n - 1$
4. Find the critical value(s).	Use Table 5.
5. Identify the rejection region(s).	

6. Calculate $\overline{d}$ and s_d. Use a table.

$$\overline{d} = \frac{\Sigma d}{n},$$

$$s_d = \sqrt{\frac{n(\Sigma d^2) - (\Sigma d)^2}{n(n - 1)}}$$

7. Calculate the standardized test statistic.

$$t = \frac{\overline{d} - \mu_d}{s_d / \sqrt{n}}$$

8. Make a decision to reject or fail to reject the null hypothesis.

If t is in the rejection region, reject H_0. Otherwise, do not reject H_0.

9. Interpret the decision in the context of the original claim.

See *Minitab* steps on page 408.

▶ **EXAMPLE 2** **The t-Test for the Difference Between Means**

A golf club manufacturer claims that golfers can lower their scores by using the manufacturer's newly designed golf clubs. Eight golfers are randomly selected and each is asked to give his or her most recent score. After using the new clubs for one month, the golfers are again asked to give their most recent score. The scores for each golfer are given in the table below. Assuming the golf scores are normally distributed, is there enough evidence to support the manufacturer's claim at $\alpha = 0.10$?

Golfer	1	2	3	4	5	6	7	8
Score (old design)	89	84	96	82	74	92	85	91
Score (new design)	83	83	92	84	76	91	80	91

SOLUTION The claim is that "golfers can lower their scores." In other words, the manufacturer claims that the score using the old clubs will be greater than the score using the new clubs. Each difference is given by

$$d = (\text{old score}) - (\text{new score}).$$

The null and alternative hypotheses are

$$H_0: \mu_d \leq 0 \quad \text{and} \quad H_a: \mu_d > 0. \text{ (Claim)}$$

Because the test is a right-tailed test, $\alpha = 0.10$, and d.f. $= 8 - 1 = 7$, the critical value is $t_0 = 1.415$. The rejection region is $t > 1.415$. Using the table at the left, you can calculate $\overline{d}$ and s_d as follows.

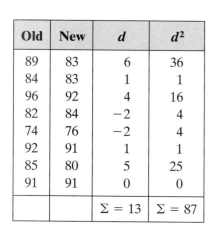

Old	New	d	d^2
89	83	6	36
84	83	1	1
96	92	4	16
82	84	−2	4
74	76	−2	4
92	91	1	1
85	80	5	25
91	91	0	0
		$\Sigma = 13$	$\Sigma = 87$

$$\overline{d} = \frac{\Sigma d}{n} = \frac{13}{8} = 1.625$$

$$s_d = \sqrt{\frac{n(\Sigma d^2) - (\Sigma d)^2}{n(n-1)}} = \sqrt{\frac{8(87) - (13)^2}{8(8-1)}} \approx 3.07$$

Using the t-test, the standardized test statistic is

$$t = \frac{\overline{d} - \mu_d}{s_d/\sqrt{n}} = \frac{1.625 - 0}{3.07/\sqrt{8}} \approx 1.50.$$

$P = .08887 < .10$
Reject

The graph below shows the location of the rejection region and the standardized test statistic, t. Because t is in the rejection region, you should decide to reject the null hypothesis. There is enough evidence to support the golf club manufacturer's claim at the 10% level. The results of this test indicate that after using the new clubs, golf scores were significantly lower.

Note to Instructor

Discuss the fact that cause and effect cannot be assumed. It is possible that the score improved because of other reasons. Many advertisements misuse statistical results by implying a cause and effect that was not substantiated by testing.

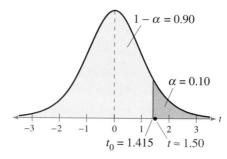

Before	After
72	73
81	80
76	79
74	76
75	76
80	80
68	74
75	77
78	75
76	74
74	76
77	78

Try It Yourself 2

A physician claims that an experimental medication increases an individual's heart rate. Twelve test subjects are randomly selected and the heart rate of each is measured. The subjects are then injected with the medication and, after one hour, the heart rate of each is measured again. The results are listed at the left. Assuming the heart rates are normally distributed, is there enough evidence to support the physician's claim at $\alpha = 0.05$?

a. *Identify* the claim and state H_0 and H_a.
b. *Specify* the level of significance α and the degrees of freedom d.f.
c. *Find* the critical value, t_0, and *identify* the rejection region.
d. *Calculate* $\bar{d}$ and s_d.
e. *Use* the t-test to find the standardized test statistic t.
f. *Decide* whether to reject the null hypothesis. Use a graph if necessary.
g. Is there enough evidence to support the physician's claim?

Answer: Page A41

EXAMPLE 3 The t-Test for the Difference Between Means

A state legislator wants to determine whether her voter's performance rating (0—100) has changed from last year to this year. The following table shows the legislator's performance rating for the same 16 randomly selected voters for last year and this year. At $\alpha = 0.01$, is there enough evidence to conclude that the legislator's performance rating has changed? Assume the performance ratings are normally distributed.

Voter	1	2	3	4	5	6	7	8
Rating (last year)	60	54	78	84	91	25	50	65
Rating (this year)	56	48	70	60	85	40	40	55

Voter	9	10	11	12	13	14	15	16
Rating (last year)	68	81	75	45	62	79	58	63
Rating (this year)	80	75	78	50	50	85	53	60

SOLUTION If there is a change in the legislator's rating, there will be a difference between "this year's" ratings and "last year's" ratings. Because the legislator wants to see if there is a difference, the null and alternative hypotheses are

$$H_0: \mu_d = 0 \quad \text{and} \quad H_a: \mu_d \neq 0. \text{ (Claim)}$$

Because the test is a two-tailed test, $\alpha = 0.01$, and d.f. $= 16 - 1 = 15$, the critical values are -2.947 and 2.947. The rejection regions are $t < -2.947$ and $t > 2.947$.

Before	After	d	d²
60	56	4	16
54	48	6	36
78	70	8	64
84	60	24	576
91	85	6	36
25	40	−15	225
50	40	10	100
65	55	10	100
68	80	−12	144
81	75	6	36
75	78	−3	9
45	50	−5	25
62	50	12	144
79	85	−6	36
58	53	5	25
63	60	3	9
		$\Sigma = 53$	$\Sigma = 1581$

Using the table at the left, you can calculate $\bar{d}$ and s_d as shown below.

$$\bar{d} = \frac{\Sigma d}{n} = \frac{53}{16} = 3.3125$$

$$s_d = \sqrt{\frac{n(\Sigma d^2) - (\Sigma d)^2}{n(n-1)}} = \sqrt{\frac{16(1581) - (53)^2}{16(16-1)}} \approx 9.68$$

Using the t-test, the standardized test statistic is

$$t = \frac{\bar{d} - \mu_d}{s_d/\sqrt{n}} = \frac{3.3125 - 0}{9.68/\sqrt{16}} \approx 1.369. \quad \checkmark \qquad p = .1911 \quad \text{Fail to reject.}$$

The graph at the right shows the location of the rejection region and the standardized test statistic, t. Because t is not in the rejection region, you should fail to reject the null hypothesis at the 1% level. There is not enough evidence to conclude that the legislator's approval rating has changed.

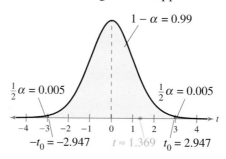

Try It Yourself 3

A medical researcher wants to determine how a drug changes the body's temperature. Seven test subjects are randomly selected and the body temperature of each is measured. The subjects are then given the drug and, after 20 minutes, the body temperature of each is measured again. The results are listed below. At $\alpha = 0.05$, is there enough evidence to conclude that the drug changes the body's temperature? Assume the body temperatures are normally distributed.

Subject	1	2	3	4	5	6	7
Initial Temperature	101.8	98.5	98.1	99.4	98.9	100.2	97.9
Second Temperature	99.2	98.4	98.2	99	98.6	99.7	97.8

a. *Identify* the claim and state H_0 and H_a.
b. *Specify* the level of significance α and the degrees of freedom d.f.
c. *Find* the critical values and the rejection regions.
d. *Calculate* $\bar{d}$ and s_d.
e. *Use* the t-test to find the standardized test statistic t.
f. *Decide* whether to reject the null hypothesis. Use a graph if necessary.
g. Is there enough evidence to support the physician's claim?

Answer: Page A41

Study Tip

If you prefer to use a technology tool for this type of test, enter the data in two columns and form a third column in which you calculate the difference for each pair. You can now perform a one-sample t-test on the difference column as shown in Chapter 7.

8.3 ▬ EXERCISES ▬

HELP

 StatPro 8.3

 Internet Statistics 8.3

 Student Solutions Manual 8.3

 Videos 8.3

 Try It Yourself Answers 8.3

1. Two samples are dependent if each member of one sample corresponds to a member of the other sample. Example: The weights of 22 people before starting an exercise program and the weights of the same 22 people six weeks after starting the exercise program. Two samples are independent if the sample selected from one population is not related to the sample selected from the second population. Example: The weights of 25 cats and the weights of 20 dogs.

2. (1) Each sample must be randomly selected from a normal population. (2) Each member of the first sample must be paired with a member of the second sample.

3. Independent

4. Dependent

5. Dependent

6. Independent

7. Independent

8. Dependent

9. Dependent

10. Dependent

Basic Skills and Concepts

1. What is the difference between two samples that are dependent and two samples that are independent? Give an example of two dependent samples and two independent samples.

2. What conditions are necessary in order to use the dependent samples *t*-test for the mean of the difference of two populations?

Classifying Samples In Exercises 3–10, classify the two given samples as independent or dependent. Explain your reasoning.

3. Sample 1: The SAT scores for 35 high school students who did not take an SAT preparation course

   Sample 2: The SAT scores for 40 high school students who did take an SAT preparation course

4. Sample 1: The SAT scores for 44 high school students

   Sample 2: The SAT scores for the same 44 high school students after taking an SAT preparation course

5. Sample 1: The weights of 51 adults

   Sample 2: The weights of the same 51 adults after participating in a diet and exercise program for one month

6. Sample 1: The weights of 40 females

   Sample 2: The weights of 40 males

7. Sample 1: The average speed of 23 powerboats using an old hull design

   Sample 2: The average speed of 14 powerboats using a new hull design

8. Sample 1: The fuel mileage of 10 cars

   Sample 2: The fuel mileage of the same 10 cars using a fuel additive

9. The table shows the braking distances (in feet) for each of four different sets of tires with the car's antilock braking system (ABS) on and with ABS off. The tests were done on ice with cars traveling at 15 miles per hour. *(Source: Consumer Reports)*

Tire Set	1	2	3	4
Braking distance with ABS	42	55	43	61
Braking distance without ABS	*58*	*67*	*59*	*75*

10. The table shows the heart rates (in beats per minute) of five people before exercising and after.

Person	1	2	3	4	5
Heart rate before exercising	65	72	85	78	93
Heart rate after exercising	*127*	*135*	*140*	*136*	*150*

11. H_0: $\mu_d \geq 0$
 H_a: $\mu_d < 0$ (claim)
 $\alpha = 0.05$, d.f. $= 9$
 $t_0 = -1.833$
 $t \approx 21.082$
 Fail to reject H_0.

12. H_0: $\mu_d = 0$ (claim)
 H_a: $\mu_d \neq 0$
 $\alpha = 0.01$, d.f. $= 7$
 $t_0 = \pm 3.499$
 $t \approx 36.204$
 Reject H_0.

13. H_0: $\mu_d \leq 0$ (claim)
 H_a: $\mu_d > 0$
 $\alpha = 0.10$, d.f. $= 15$
 $t_0 = 1.341$
 $t \approx 67.778$
 Reject H_0.

14. H_0: $\mu_d \leq 0$
 H_a: $\mu_d > 0$ (claim)
 $\alpha = 0.05$, d.f. $= 34$
 $t_0 = 1.645$
 $t \approx 76.476$
 Reject H_0.

15. (a) H_0: $\mu_d \geq 0$
 H_a: $\mu_d < 0$ (claim)
 (b) $t_0 = -2.650$
 (c) $\bar{d} \approx -33.714$
 $s_d \approx 42.034$
 (d) $t \approx -3.001$
 (e) Reject H_0. There is enough evidence to support the claim that the second SAT scores are improved.

16. (a) H_0: $\mu_d \geq 0$
 H_a: $\mu_d < 0$ (claim)
 (b) $t_0 = -3.143$
 (c) $\bar{d} \approx -65.429$
 $s_d \approx 28.530$
 (d) $t \approx -6.068$
 (e) Reject H_0. There is enough evidence to support the claim that the SAT prep course improves verbal SAT scores.

Testing a Claim   In Exercises 11–14, test the claim about the mean of the difference of two populations. Use a t-test for dependent samples at the given level of significance with the given statistics. Is the test right-tailed, left-tailed, or two-tailed? Assume the populations are normally distributed.

11. Claim: $\mu_d < 0$, $\alpha = 0.05$. Statistics: $\bar{d} = 10$, $s_d = 1.5$, $n = 10$

12. Claim: $\mu_d = 0$, $\alpha = 0.01$. Statistics: $\bar{d} = 3.2$, $s_d = 0.25$, $n = 8$

13. Claim: $\mu_d \leq 0$, $\alpha = 0.10$. Statistics: $\bar{d} = 6.1$, $s_d = 0.36$, $n = 16$

14. Claim: $\mu_d > 0$, $\alpha = 0.05$. Statistics: $\bar{d} = 5.3$, $s_d = 0.41$, $n = 35$

Testing the Difference Between Two Means   In Exercises 15–22, (a) identify the claim and state H_0 and H_a, (b) find the critical value(s) and identify the rejection region(s), (c) calculate $\bar{d}$ and s_d, (d) use the t-test to find the standardized test statistic t, and (e) decide whether to reject or fail to reject the null hypothesis and interpret the decision in the context of the original claim. For each sample, assume the distribution of the population is normal.

15. The table shows the scores for 14 students the first two times they took the verbal SAT. At $\alpha = 0.01$, is there enough evidence to conclude that the students' verbal SAT scores improved the second time they took the verbal SAT?

Student	1	2	3	4	5	6	7
Score on first SAT	445	510	429	452	629	433	551
Score on second SAT	446	571	517	478	610	453	516

Student	8	9	10	11	12	13	14
Score on first SAT	358	477	325	513	636	571	442
Score on second SAT	478	532	399	531	648	603	461

16. An SAT prep course claims to improve the test scores of students. The table shows the scores for seven students the first two times they took the verbal SAT. Before taking the SAT for the second time, each student took a course to try to improve his or her verbal SAT scores. Test the claim at $\alpha = 0.01$.

Student	1	2	3	4	5	6	7
Score on first SAT	308	456	352	433	306	471	422
Score on second SAT	400	524	409	491	348	583	451

17. (a) $H_0: \mu_d \geq 0$
$H_a: \mu_d < 0$ (claim)

(b) $t_0 = -1.415$

(c) $\bar{d} \approx -1.125$
$s_d \approx 0.871$

(d) $t \approx -3.653$

(e) Reject H_0. There is enough evidence to support the claim that the fuel additive improved gas mileage.

18. (a) $H_0: \mu_d \geq 0$
$H_a: \mu_d < 0$ (claim)

(b) $t_0 = -1.397$

(c) $\bar{d} \approx -1.611$
$s_d \approx 0.770$

(d) $t \approx -6.277$

(e) Reject H_0. There is enough evidence to support the claim that the fuel additive improved gas mileage.

19. (a) $H_0: \mu_d \leq 0$
$H_a: \mu_d > 0$ (claim)

(b) $t_0 = 1.796$

(c) $\bar{d} \approx 16.833$
$s_d \approx 6.952$

(d) $t \approx 8.388$

(e) Reject H_0. There is enough evidence to support the claim that the new drug reduces systolic blood pressure.

17. The table shows the gas mileage (in miles per gallon) of eight cars with and without using a fuel additive. At $\alpha = 0.10$, is there enough evidence to conclude that the fuel additive improved gas mileage?

Car	1	2	3	4	5
Gas mileage without additive	35.8	37.7	39.4	36.8	36.6
Gas mileage with fuel additive	36.2	39.8	40.1	39.3	36.9

Car	6	7	8
Gas mileage without additive	33.7	38.4	37.3
Gas mileage with fuel additive	34.5	38.8	39.1

18. To test whether a fuel additive improves gas mileage, the gas mileage of nine cars was measured with and without the fuel additive. The results are given below. At $\alpha = 0.10$, can you conclude that the fuel additive improved gas mileage?

Car	1	2	3	4	5
Gas mileage without additive	34.5	36.7	34.4	39.8	33.6
Gas mileage with fuel additive	36.4	38.8	36.1	40.1	34.7

Car	6	7	8	9
Gas mileage without additive	35.4	38.4	35.3	37.9
Gas mileage with fuel additive	38.3	40.2	37.2	38.7

19. A pharmaceutical company guarantees that its new drug reduces systolic blood pressure. The table shows the systolic blood pressure (in millimeters of mercury) for 12 patients before taking the new drug and 3 hours after taking the drug. At $\alpha = 0.05$, can you conclude that the new drug reduces systolic blood pressure?

Patient	1	2	3	4	5	6
Systolic blood pressure (before)	201	171	186	162	165	167
Systolic blood pressure (after)	192	165	167	155	148	144

Patient	7	8	9	10	11	12
Systolic blood pressure (before)	175	148	172	204	188	145
Systolic blood pressure (after)	152	134	151	178	175	121

20. (a) $H_0: \mu_d \leq 0$
$H_a: \mu_d > 0$ (claim)

(b) $t_0 = 1.833$

(c) $\bar{d} \approx 5.300$
$s_d \approx 6.019$

(d) $t \approx 2.785$

(e) Reject H_0. There is enough evidence to support the claim that the new drug reduces diastolic blood pressure.

21. (a) $H_0: \mu_d \leq 0$
$H_a: \mu_d > 0$ (claim)

(b) $t_0 = 2.764$

(c) $\bar{d} \approx 1.255$
$s_d \approx 0.441$

(d) $t \approx 9.438$

(e) Reject H_0. There is enough evidence to support the claim that soft tissue therapy and spinal manipulation help reduce the length of time patients suffer from headaches.

22. (a) $H_0: \mu_d \leq 0$
$H_a: \mu_d > 0$ (claim)

(b) $t_0 = 2.681$

(c) $\bar{d} \approx 1.469$
$s_d \approx 0.494$

(d) $t \approx 10.722$

(e) Reject H_0. There is enough evidence to support the claim that the new drug helps to reduce the number of daily headache hours.

20. A pharmaceutical company claims that its new drug reduces diastolic blood pressure. The diastolic blood pressure (in millimeters of mercury) for 10 patients before taking the new drug and 2 hours after taking the drug is shown in the table below. At $\alpha = 0.05$, is there enough evidence to support the company's claim?

Patient	1	2	3	4	5	6
Diastolic blood pressure (before)	103	122	106	112	125	97
Diastolic blood pressure (after)	98	121	107	105	108	89

Patient	7	8	9	10
Diastolic blood pressure (before)	107	118	112	104
Diastolic blood pressure (after)	102	114	101	108

21. A physical therapist suggests that soft tissue therapy and spinal manipulation help to reduce the length of time patients suffer from headaches. The table shows the number of hours per day a sample of 11 patients suffered from headaches, before and after seven weeks of receiving soft tissue therapy and spinal manipulation. At $\alpha = 0.01$, is there enough evidence to support the therapist's claim? *(Adapted from The Journal of the American Medical Association)*

Patient	1	2	3	4	5	6
Daily headache hours (before)	2.8	2.4	2.8	2.6	2.7	2.9
Daily headache hours (after)	1.6	1.3	1.6	1.4	1.5	1.6

Patient	7	8	9	10	11
Daily headache hours (before)	3.2	2.9	4.1	1.6	2.5
Daily headache hours (after)	1.7	1.6	1.8	1.2	1.4

22. The table shows the number of hours per day a sample of 13 patients suffered from headaches before and after seven weeks of receiving a new drug. At $\alpha = 0.01$, test the claim that the new drug helps to reduce the number of daily headache hours. *(Adapted from The Journal of the American Medical Association)*

Patient	1	2	3	4	5	6	7
Daily headache hours (before)	4.1	3.9	3.8	4.5	2.4	3.6	3.4
Daily headache hours (after)	2.2	2.8	2.5	2.6	1.9	1.8	2.0

Patient	8	9	10	11	12	13
Daily headache hours (before)	3.4	3.5	2.7	3.7	4.4	3.2
Daily headache hours (after)	1.6	1.5	2.1	1.8	3.0	1.7

23. $-1.762 < \mu_d < -1.172$

24. $-1.112 < \mu_d < -0.008$

Extending the Basics

Confidence Intervals for μ_d To construct a confidence interval for μ_d, use the following inequality.

$$\overline{d} - t_{\alpha/2} \frac{s_d}{\sqrt{n}} < \mu_d < \overline{d} + t_{\alpha/2} \frac{s_d}{\sqrt{n}}$$

In Exercises 23 and 24, construct the indicated confidence interval for μ_d.

23. A sleep disorder specialist wants to test the effectiveness of a new drug that is reported to increase the number of hours of sleep patients get during the night. To do so, the specialist randomly selects 12 patients and records the number of hours of sleep each gets with and without the new drug. The results of the two-night study are listed below. Construct a 90% confidence interval for μ_d.

Patient	1	2	3	4	5	6
Hours of sleep without the drug	1.8	2.0	3.4	3.5	3.7	3.8
Hours of sleep using the new drug	3.0	3.6	4.0	4.4	4.5	5.2

Patient	7	8	9	10	11	12
Hours of sleep without the drug	3.9	3.9	4.0	4.9	5.1	5.2
Hours of sleep using the new drug	5.5	5.7	6.2	6.3	6.6	7.8

24. An herbal medicine is tested on 10 patients with sleeping disorders. The table shows the hours of sleep patients got during one night without using the herbal medicine and the hours of sleep the patients got on another night after the herbal medicine was administered. Construct a 95% confidence interval for μ_d.

Patient	1	2	3	4	5
Hours of sleep without medicine	1.0	1.4	3.4	3.7	5.1
Hours of sleep using the herbal medicine	2.9	3.3	3.5	4.4	5.0

Patient	6	7	8	9	10
Hours of sleep without medicine	5.1	5.2	5.3	5.5	5.8
Hours of sleep using the herbal medicine	5.0	5.2	5.3	6.0	6.5

Testing the Difference Between Proportions

8.4

Two-Sample z-Test for the Difference Between Proportions

What You Should Learn

• How to perform a z-test for the difference between two population proportions p_1 and p_2

Two-Sample z-Test for the Difference Between Proportions

In this section, you will learn how to use a z-test to test the difference between two population proportions p_1 and p_2 using a sample proportion from each population. For instance, suppose you want to determine whether the proportion of female college students who earn a bachelor's degree in four years is different from the proportion of male college students who earn a bachelor's degree in four years. To use a z-test to test such a difference, the following conditions are necessary.

1. The samples must be independent.
2. The samples must be large enough to use a normal sampling distribution.

   That is,

$$n_1 p_1 \geq 5, \qquad n_1 q_1 \geq 5, \qquad n_2 p_2 \geq 5, \qquad \text{and} \qquad n_2 q_2 \geq 5.$$

If these conditions are met, then the sampling distribution for $\hat{p}_1 - \hat{p}_2$, the difference between the sample proportions, is a normal distribution with mean

$$\mu_{\hat{p}_1 - \hat{p}_2} = p_1 - p_2$$

and standard error

$$\sigma_{\hat{p}_1 - \hat{p}_2} = \sqrt{\frac{p_1 q_1}{n_1} + \frac{p_2 q_2}{n_2}}.$$

Notice that you need to know the population proportions to calculate the standard error. Because a hypothesis test for $p_1 - p_2$ is based on the condition of equality that $p_1 = p_2$, you can calculate a weighted estimate of p using

$$\bar{p} = \frac{x_1 + x_2}{n_1 + n_2}, \qquad \text{where } x_1 = n_1 \hat{p}_1 \text{ and } x_2 = n_2 \hat{p}_2.$$

Using the weighted estimate $\bar{p}$, the standard error of the sampling distribution for $\hat{p}_1 - \hat{p}_2$ is

$$\sigma_{\hat{p}_1 - \hat{p}_2} = \sqrt{\bar{p}\,\bar{q}\left(\frac{1}{n_1} + \frac{1}{n_2}\right)}, \qquad \text{where } \bar{q} = 1 - \bar{p}.$$

Also, when determining whether the z-test can be used for the difference between proportions, you should use $\bar{p}$ in place of p_1 and p_2 and use $\bar{q}$ in place of q_1 and q_2.

Study Tip

The following symbols are used in the z-test for $p_1 - p_2$. See Sections 4.2 and 5.5 to review the binomial distribution.

Symbol	Description
p_1, p_2	Population proportions
x_1, x_2	Number of successes in each sample
n_1, n_2	Size of each sample
$\hat{p}_1, \hat{p}_2$	Sample proportions of successes
$\bar{p}$	Weighted estimate for p

If the sampling distribution for $\hat{p}_1 - \hat{p}_2$ is normal, you can use a two-sample z-test to test the difference between two population proportions p_1 and p_2.

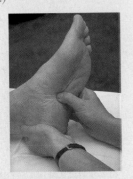
Two-Sample z-Test for the Difference Between Proportions

A two-sample z-test is used to test the difference between two population proportions p_1 and p_2 when a sample is randomly selected from each population. The **test statistic** is $\hat{p}_1 - \hat{p}_2$ and the **standardized test statistic** is

$$z = \frac{(\hat{p}_1 - \hat{p}_2) - (p_1 - p_2)}{\sqrt{\bar{p}\,\bar{q}\left(\frac{1}{n_1} + \frac{1}{n_2}\right)}}, \quad \text{where} \quad \bar{p} = \frac{x_1 + x_2}{n_1 + n_2}.$$

Note: $n_1\bar{p}$, $n_1\bar{q}$, $n_2\bar{p}$, and $n_2\bar{q}$ must be at least 5.

If the null hypothesis states that $p_1 = p_2$, then the expression $p_1 - p_2$ is equal to 0 in the preceding test.

GUIDELINES

Using a Two-Sample z-Test for the Difference Between Proportions

In Words	*In Symbols*
1. Identify the claim. State the null and alternative hypotheses.	State H_0 and H_a.
2. Specify the level of significance.	Identify α.
3. Find the critical value(s).	Use Table 4.
4. Identify the rejection region(s).	
5. Find the weighted estimate of p_1 and p_2.	$\bar{p} = \dfrac{x_1 + x_2}{n_1 + n_2}$
6. Find the standardized test statistic.	$z = \dfrac{(\hat{p}_1 - \hat{p}_2) - (p_1 - p_2)}{\sqrt{\bar{p}\,\bar{q}\left(\frac{1}{n_1} + \frac{1}{n_2}\right)}}$
7. Make a decision to reject or fail to reject the null hypothesis.	If z is in the rejection region, reject H_0. Otherwise, do not reject H_0.
8. Interpret the decision in the context of the claim.	

▶ **EXAMPLE 1**   **A Two-Sample z-Test for the Difference Between Proportions**

See *TI-83* steps on page 409.

In a study of 200 adult female and 250 adult male Internet users, 30% of the females and 38% of the males said that they plan to shop online at least once during the next month. At $\alpha = 0.10$, test the claim that there is a difference in the proportion of female Internet users who plan to shop online and the proportion of male Internet users who plan to shop online.

SOLUTION   You want to determine whether there is a difference in the proportions. So, the null and alternative hypotheses are

$$H_0: p_1 = p_2 \quad \text{and} \quad H_a: p_1 \neq p_2. \text{ (Claim)}$$

Because the test is two-tailed and the level of significance is $\alpha = 0.10$, the critical values are -1.645 and 1.645. The rejection regions are $z < -1.645$ and $z > 1.645$. The weighted estimate of the population proportion is

$$\bar{p} = \frac{x_1 + x_2}{n_1 + n_2} = \frac{60 + 95}{200 + 250} = \frac{155}{450} \approx 0.344$$

and $\bar{q} = 1 - \bar{p} = 1 - 0.344 = 0.656$. Because 200(0.344), 200(0.656), 250(0.344), and 250(0.656) are at least 5, you can use a two-sample z-test. The standardized test statistic is

$$z = \frac{(\hat{p}_1 - \hat{p}_2) - (p_1 - p_2)}{\sqrt{\bar{p}\,\bar{q}\left(\frac{1}{n_1} + \frac{1}{n_2}\right)}} = \frac{(0.30 - 0.38) - 0}{\sqrt{(0.344)(0.656)\left(\frac{1}{200} + \frac{1}{250}\right)}} \approx -1.775.$$

The graph at the left shows the location of the rejection regions and the standardized test statistic. Because z is in the rejection region, you should decide to reject the null hypothesis. You have enough evidence at the 10% level to conclude that there is a difference in the proportion of female and the proportion of male Internet users who plan to shop online.

Sample Statistics for Internet Users

Female	Male
$n_1 = 200$	$n_2 = 250$
$\hat{p}_1 = 0.30$	$\hat{p}_2 = 0.38$
$n_1\hat{p}_1 = 60$	$n_2\hat{p}_2 = 95$

Study Tip

To find x_1 and x_2, use $x_1 = n_1\hat{p}_1$ and $x_2 = n_2\hat{p}_2$.

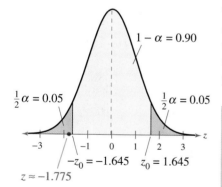

$1 - \alpha = 0.90$

$\frac{1}{2}\alpha = 0.05$ $\frac{1}{2}\alpha = 0.05$

$-z_0 = -1.645$ $z_0 = 1.645$

$z \approx -1.775$

Try It Yourself 1

Consider the results of the *JAMA* study discussed in the Chapter Opener. At $\alpha = 0.05$, is there a difference between the proportion of Vietnam Army veterans who suffer from anxiety and the proportion of non-Vietnam Army veterans who suffer from anxiety?

a. *Identify* the claim and state H_0 and H_a.
b. *Specify* the level of significance α.
c. *Find* the critical values and *identify* the rejection regions.
d. *Find* $\bar{p}$ and $\bar{q}$.
e. *Use* the two-sample z-test to find the standardized test statistic z.
f. *Decide* whether to reject the null hypothesis.
g. Is there enough evidence to conclude that there is a difference between the two groups?

Answer: Page A41 ◀

Sample Statistics for Cholesterol Reducing Medication

Received medication	Received placebo
$n_1 = 4700$	$n_2 = 4300$
$x_1 = 301$	$x_2 = 357$
$\hat{p}_1 = 0.064$	$\hat{p}_2 = 0.083$

EXAMPLE 2 *Two-Sample z-Test for the Difference Between Proportions*

A medical research team conducted a study to test the effect of a cholesterol-reducing medication. At the end of the study, the researchers found that of the 4700 subjects who took the medication, 301 died of heart disease. Of the 4300 subjects who took a placebo, 357 died of heart disease. At $\alpha = 0.01$, can you conclude that the death rate is lower for those who took the medication than for those who took the placebo? *(Source: New England Journal of Medicine)*

SOLUTION You want to determine whether there is a difference in the proportions. So, the null and alternative hypotheses are

$$H_0: p_1 \geq p_2 \quad \text{and} \quad H_a: p_1 < p_2. \text{ (Claim)}$$

Because the test is left-tailed and the level of significance is $\alpha = 0.01$, the critical value is -2.33. The rejection region is $z < -2.33$. The weighted estimate of p_1 and p_2 is

$$\bar{p} = \frac{x_1 + x_2}{n_1 + n_2} = \frac{301 + 357}{4700 + 4300} = \frac{658}{9000} \approx 0.073$$

and $\bar{q} = 1 - \bar{p} = 1 - 0.073 = 0.927$. Because $4700(0.073)$, $4700(0.927)$, $4300(0.073)$, and $4300(0.927)$ are at least 5, you can use a two-sample z-test.

$$z = \frac{(\hat{p}_1 - \hat{p}_2) - (p_1 - p_2)}{\sqrt{\bar{p}\,\bar{q}\left(\dfrac{1}{n_1} + \dfrac{1}{n_2}\right)}} = \frac{(0.064 - 0.083) - 0}{\sqrt{(0.073)(0.927)\left(\dfrac{1}{4700} + \dfrac{1}{4300}\right)}} \approx -3.461$$

The graph at the left shows the location of the rejection region and the standardized test statistic. Because z is in the rejection region, you should decide to reject the null hypothesis. At the 1% level, there is enough evidence to conclude that the death rate is lower for those who took the medication than for those who took the placebo.

Study Tip

To find $\hat{p}_1$ and $\hat{p}_2$, use

$$\hat{p}_1 = \frac{x_1}{n_1} \text{ and}$$

$$\hat{p}_2 = \frac{x_2}{n_2}.$$

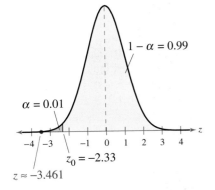

$1 - \alpha = 0.99$

$\alpha = 0.01$

$z_0 = -2.33$

$z \approx -3.461$

Try It Yourself 2

Consider the results of the *JAMA* study discussed in the Chapter Opener. At $\alpha = 0.05$, can you conclude that the proportion of Vietnam Army veterans who suffer from alcohol abuse or dependence is greater than the proportion of non-Vietnam Army veterans who suffer from alcohol abuse or dependence?

a. *Identify* the claim and state H_0 and H_a.
b. *Specify* the level of significance α.
c. *Find* the critical value and *identify* the rejection region.
d. *Find* $\bar{p}$ and $\bar{q}$.
e. *Use* the two-sample z-test to find the standardized test statistic z.
f. *Decide* whether to reject the null hypothesis.
g. Is there enough evidence to conclude that alcohol abuse or dependence is greater for Vietnam Army veterans? *Answer: Page A41*

8.4 EXERCISES

HELP

StatPro 8.4

Internet Statistics 8.4

Student Solutions Manual 8.4

Videos 8.4

Try It Yourself Answers 8.4

1. State the hypotheses and identify the claim. Specify the level of significance. Find the critical value(s) and rejection region(s). Find $\bar{p}$ and $\bar{q}$. Find the standardized test statistic. Make a decision and interpret in the context of the claim.

2. (1) The sample must be independent. (2) $n_1p_1 \geq 5$, $n_1q_1 \geq 5$, $n_2p_2 \geq 5$, and $n_2q_2 \geq 5$

3. $H_0: p_1 = p_2$
   $H_a: p_1 \neq p_2$ (claim)

   The test is a two-tailed test. Fail to reject H_0. There is not enough evidence to support the claim.

4. See Selected Answers, page A82

5. $H_0: p_1 \leq p_2$ (claim)
   $H_a: p_1 > p_2$

   The test is a right-tailed test. Fail to reject H_0. There is not enough evidence to reject the claim.

6. See Selected Answers, page A82

7. (a) $H_0: p_1 = p_2$ (claim)
      $H_a: p_1 \neq p_2$

   (b) $z_0 = \pm 1.96$

   (c) $z = -5.060$

   (d) Reject H_0

8. See Selected Answers, page A82

Basic Skills and Concepts

1. Explain how to perform a two-sample z-test for the difference between two population proportions.

2. What conditions are necessary in order to use the z-test to test the difference between two population proportions?

Testing a Claim In Exercises 3–6, test the claim about the differences between two population proportions p_1 and p_2 at the given level of significance α and the given sample statistics. Is the test right-tailed, left-tailed, or two-tailed? Assume the sample statistics are from independent samples.

3. Claim: $p_1 \neq p_2$, $\alpha = 0.01$. Sample statistics: $x_1 = 35$, $n_1 = 70$, and $x_2 = 36$, $n_2 = 60$

4. Claim: $p_1 < p_2$, $\alpha = 0.05$. Sample statistics: $x_1 = 471$, $n_1 = 785$, and $x_2 = 372$, $n_2 = 465$

5. Claim: $p_1 \leq p_2$, $\alpha = 0.10$. Sample statistics: $x_1 = 344$, $n_1 = 860$, and $x_2 = 304$, $n_2 = 800$

6. Claim: $p_1 \leq p_2$, $\alpha = 0.04$. Sample statistics: $x_1 = 27$, $n_1 = 50$, and $x_2 = 45$, $n_2 = 85$

Testing the Difference Between Two Proportions In Exercises 7–12, (a) identify the claim and state H_0 and H_a, (b) find the critical value(s) and identify the rejection region(s), (c) find the standardized test statistic, and (d) decide whether to reject or fail to reject the null hypothesis and interpret the decision in the context of the original claim. Assume the samples are independent. If convenient, use technology to solve the problem.

7. In a 1990 study of 1539 adults, 520 said they used alternative medicines (for example, folk remedies and homeopathy) in the previous year. In a recent study of 2055 adults, 865 said they used alternative medicines in the previous year. At $\alpha = 0.05$, can you reject the claim that the proportion of adults using alternative medicines has not changed since 1990? *(Source: The Journal of the American Medical Association)*

8. A medical research team studied patients using an antidepressant drug to recover from chronic depression. Of 77 patients who used the drug for two years, five suffered a new bout of depression. Of 84 patients who used the drug for six months, 19 suffered a new bout of depression. At $\alpha = 0.10$, can you reject the claim that the proportions of patients suffering new bouts of depression are the same for both groups? *(Source: The Journal of the American Medical Association)*

9. (a) $H_0: p_1 \geq p_2$
$H_a: p_1 < p_2$ (claim)

(b) $z_0 = -2.33$

(c) $z = -2.859$

(d) Reject H_0

10. (a) $H_0: p_1 \geq p_2$
$H_a: p_1 < p_2$ (claim)

(b) $z_0 = -1.645$

(c) $z = -1.428$

(d) Fail to reject H_0

11. (a) $H_0: p_1 = p_2$ (claim)
$H_a: p_1 \neq p_2$

(b) $z_0 = \pm 1.645$

(c) $z = -9.832$

(d) Reject H_0

12. (a) $H_0: p_1 \geq p_2$
$H_a: p_1 < p_2$ (claim)

(b) $z_0 = -2.33$

(c) $z = -2.514$

(d) Reject H_0

13. $H_0: p_1 \geq p_2$
$H_a: p_1 < p_2$ (claim)

$z_0 = -2.33$

$z = -0.881$

Fail to reject H_0

9. A state-by-state survey found that the proportion of adults who are smokers in Alabama and Missouri was 24.7% and 28.7%, respectively. (Suppose the number of respondents from each state was 2000.) At $\alpha = 0.01$, can you support the claim that the proportion of adults who are smokers is lower in Alabama than in Missouri? *(Adapted from The Centers for Disease Control and Prevention)*

10. In a random survey of 1500 adults in California and 1000 adults in Oregon, you find that the percent who are smokers are 18.4% and 20.7%, respectively. At $\alpha = 0.05$, is there enough evidence to conclude that the proportion of adults who are smokers is lower in California than in Oregon? *(Adapted from The Centers for Disease Control and Prevention)*

11. In a survey of 10,572 college students, 2358 said they had smoked in the last 30 days. In another survey of 8551 college students taken four years later, 2437 said they had smoked in the last 30 days. At $\alpha = 0.10$, can you support the claim that the proportion of college students who said they had smoked in the last 30 days has not changed? *(Source: The Journal of the American Medical Association)*

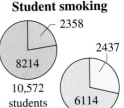

Student smoking

2358

2437

8214

10,572 students

6114

8551 students

12. In a survey of 3420 college students attending private schools, 917 said they had smoked in the last 30 days. In a survey of 5131 college students attending public schools, 1503 said they had smoked in the last 30 days. At $\alpha = 0.01$, can you support the claim that the proportion of college students who said they had smoked in the last 30 days in the private schools is less than the proportion in the public schools? *(Adapted from The Journal of the American Medical Association)*

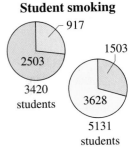

Student smoking

917

1503

2503

3420 students

3628

5131 students

Utility Satisfaction In Exercises 13–16, refer to the survey in the figure. Assume the samples are independent.

13. At $\alpha = 0.01$, can you support the claim that the proportion of customers completely satisfied with their local telephone service is greater in the Midwest than in the Northeast? Assume the survey got responses from 1020 midwestern residents and 900 northeastern residents.

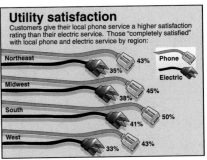

Utility satisfaction
Customers give their local phone service a higher satisfaction rating than their electric service. Those "completely satisfied" with local phone and electric service by region:

Northeast — 43% **Phone**
35% **Electric**

Midwest — 45%
38%

South — 50%
41%

West — 43%
33%

Copyright 1998, USA TODAY. Reprinted with permission.

14. $H_0: p_1 \le p_2$
$H_a: p_1 > p_2$ (claim)
$z_0 = 2.33$
$z = 3.194$
Reject H_0

15. $H_0: p_1 = p_2$ (claim)
$H_a: p_1 \ne p_2$
$z_0 = \pm 1.96$
$z = 3.797$
Reject H_0

16. $H_0: p_1 = p_2$ (claim)
$H_a: p_1 \ne p_2$
$z_0 = \pm 1.96$
$z = -1.400$
Fail to reject H_0

17. $0.028 < p_1 - p_2 < 0.030$

18. $-0.039 < p_1 - p_2 < -0.037$

14. A telephone service representative believes that the proportion of customers completely satisfied with their local telephone service is greater in the South than in the West. If the representative's belief is based on the results of the survey, is there enough evidence to support the representative's belief? Assume the survey included 978 southern residents and 1100 western residents. Use $\alpha = 0.01$.

15. Based on the survey, a consumer advocate reports that the proportion of customers completely satisfied with their electric service is the same in the South and in the West. If the survey included 1000 southern residents and 1100 western residents, can you reject the advocate's claim? Use $\alpha = 0.05$.

16. At $\alpha = 0.05$, can you reject the claim that the proportion of customers completely satisfied with their electric service is the same in the Midwest and in the Northeast? Assume the survey got responses from 1000 midwestern residents and 1020 northeastern residents.

Extending the Basics

Confidence Intervals for $p_1 - p_2$ You can construct a confidence interval for the difference of two population means, $p_1 - p_2$, by using the following.

$$(\hat{p}_1 - \hat{p}_2) - z_c \sqrt{\frac{\hat{p}_1 \hat{q}_1}{n_1} + \frac{\hat{p}_2 \hat{q}_2}{n_2}} < (p_1 - p_2) < (\hat{p}_1 - \hat{p}_2) + z_c \sqrt{\frac{\hat{p}_1 \hat{q}_1}{n_1} + \frac{\hat{p}_2 \hat{q}_2}{n_2}}$$

In Exercises 17 and 18, construct the indicated confidence interval for $p_1 - p_2$. Assume the samples are independent.

17. Several years ago, a survey of 977,000 students taking the SAT revealed that 11.7% of the students were planning to study engineering in college. In a recent survey of 1,085,000 students taking the SAT, 8.8% of the students were planning to study engineering. Construct a 95% confidence interval for the difference in proportions, $p_1 - p_2$. *(Source: College Entrance Examination Board)*

18. In a certain year, the percent of students taking the SAT who said they intended to study social science in college was 7.5%. Ten years later, 11.3% said they intended to study social science in college. Construct a 95% confidence interval for the difference in proportions $p_1 - p_2$. Assume 997,000 students were surveyed the first year and 1,085,000 students were surveyed ten years later. *(Source: College Entrance Examination Board)*

TECHNOLOGY   MINITAB   EXCEL   TI-83

Tails Over Heads

In the article "Tails Over Heads" in the *Washington Post* (Oct. 13, 1996), journalist William Casey describes one of his hobbies—keeping track of every coin he finds on the street! From January 1, 1985 until the article was written, Casey found 11,902 coins.

As each coin is found, Casey records the time, date, location, value, mint location, and whether the coin is lying heads up or tails up. In the article, Casey notes that 6130 coins were found tails up and 5772 were found heads up. Of the 11,902 coins found, 43 were minted in San Francisco, 7133 were minted in Philadelphia, and 4726 were minted in Denver.

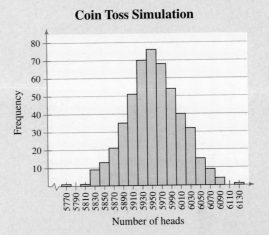

Coin Toss Simulation

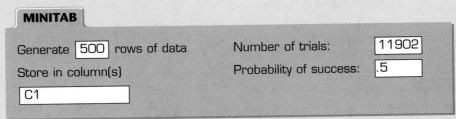

MINITAB

Generate [500] rows of data   Number of trials: [11902]

Store in column(s)   Probability of success: [.5]

[C1]

Calc, Random Data, Binomial Distribution

Exercises

1. Use a technology tool to perform a one-sample z-test to test the hypothesis that the probability of a "found coin" lying heads up is 0.5. Use $\alpha = 0.01$. Use Casey's data as your sample and write your conclusion as a sentence.

2. Does Casey's data differ significantly from chance? If so, what might be the reason?

3. In the simulation shown above, what percent of the trials had heads less than or equal to the number of heads in Casey's data? Use a technology tool to repeat the simulation. Are your results comparable?

In Exercises 4 and 5, use a technology tool to perform a two-sample z-test to decide whether there is a difference in the mint dates and in the values of coins found on a street from 1985 through 1996. Write your conclusion as a sentence. Use $\alpha = 0.05$.

4. Mint dates of coins (years)

   Philadelphia: $\bar{x}_1 = 1984.8$
   $s_1 = 8.6$

   Denver: $\bar{x}_2 = 1983.4$
   $s_2 = 8.4$

5. Value of coins (dollars)

   Philadelphia: $\bar{x}_1 = \$0.034$
   $s_1 = \$0.054$

   Denver: $\bar{x}_2 = \$0.033$
   $s_2 = \$0.052$

Extended solutions are given in the *Technology Supplement*.
Technical instruction is provided for Minitab, Excel, and the TI-83.

8 USING TECHNOLOGY TO PERFORM TWO-SAMPLE HYPOTHESIS TESTS

Here are some *Minitab* and *TI-83* printouts for several examples in this chapter. To duplicate the Minitab results, you need the original data. For the TI-83, you can simply enter the descriptive statistics.

(See Example 1, page 382)

Stopping Distances for 10 Firestone Winterfire Tires, in feet

63   48   57   42   54   58   45   55   37   51

Stopping Distances for 12 Michelin XM+S Alpin Tires, in feet

49   52   52.5   53   54.5   55   55.5   56   57   57.5   58.5   59.5

| Display Descriptive Statistics... |
| Store Descriptive Statistics... |
| 1-Sample Z... |
| 1-Sample t... |
| **2-Sample t...** |
| Paired t... |
| 1 Proportion... |
| 2 Proportions... |
| Correlation... |
| Covariance... |
| Normality Test... |

MINITAB

Two Sample T-Test and Confidence Interval

Two sample T for C1 vs C2

	N	Mean	StDev	SE Mean
C1	10	51.00	8.00	2.5
C2	12	55.00	3.01	0.87

99% CI for mu C1 − mu C2: (−12.3, 4.31)
T-Test mu C1 = mu C2 (vs not =): T = −1.50 P = 0.16 DF = 11

(See Example 2, page 392)

Golf Scores, Old and New Club Design

Golfer	1	2	3	4	5	6	7	8
Score (old design)	89	84	96	82	74	92	85	91
Score (new design)	83	83	90	84	76	91	80	91

| Display Descriptive Statistics... |
| Store Descriptive Statistics... |
| 1-Sample Z... |
| 1-Sample t... |
| 2-Sample t... |
| **Paired t...** |
| 1 Proportion... |
| 2 Proportions... |

MINITAB

Paired T-Test and Confidence Interval

Paired T for C1 − C2

	N	Mean	StDev	SE Mean
C1	8	86.62	6.89	2.43
C2	8	85.00	5.81	2.05
Difference	8	1.62	3.07	1.08

90% CI for mean difference: (−0.43, 3.68)
T-Test of mean difference = 0 (vs > 0): T-Value = 1.50 P-Value = 0.089

(See Example 1, page 371)

TI-83

EDIT CALC **TESTS**
1: Z–Test…
2: T–Test…
3: 2–SampZTest…
4: 2–SampTTest…
5: 1–PropZTest…
6: 2–PropZTest…
7↓ZInterval…

TI-83

2–SampZTest
Inpt:Data **Stats**
σ1: 12000
σ2: 15000
$\bar{x}$1: 60900
n1: 100
$\bar{x}$2: 64300
↓n2: 100

TI-83

2–SampZTest
↑σ2: 15000
$\bar{x}$1: 60900
n1: 100
$\bar{x}$2: 64300
n2: 100
μ1: **≠μ2** < μ2 > μ2
Calculate Draw

TI-83

2–SampZTest
μ1 ≠ μ2
z= −1.769969301
p= .0767321594
$\bar{x}$1= 60900
$\bar{x}$2= 64300
↓n1= 100

(See Example 2, page 383)

TI-83

EDIT CALC **TESTS**
1: Z–Test…
2: T–Test…
3: 2–SampZTest…
4: 2–SampTTest…
5: 1–PropZTest…
6: 2–PropZTest…
7↓ZInterval…

TI-83

2–SampTTest
Inpt:Data **Stats**
$\bar{x}$1: 1275
Sx1: 45
n1: 14
$\bar{x}$2: 1250
Sx2: 30
↓n2: 16

TI-83

2–SampTTest
↑n1: 14
$\bar{x}$2: 1250
Sx2: 30
n2: 16
μ1: ≠μ2 < μ2 **>μ2**
Pooled: No **Yes**
Calculate Draw

TI-83

2–SampTTest
μ1 > μ2
t= 1.811358919
p= .0404131295
df= 28
$\bar{x}$1= 1275
↓$\bar{x}$2= 1250

(See Example 1, page 402)

TI-83

EDIT CALC **TESTS**
1: Z–Test…
2: T–Test…
3: 2–SampZTest…
4: 2–SampTTest…
5: 1–PropZTest…
6: 2–PropZTest…
7↓ZInterval…

TI-83

2–PropZTest
x1: 60
n1: 200
x2: 95
n2: 250
p1: **≠p2** < p2 > p2
Calculate Draw

TI-83

2–PropZTest
p1 ≠ p2
z= −1.774615984
p= .0759612188
$\hat{p}$1= .3
$\hat{p}$2= .38
↓$\hat{p}$= .3444444444

CHAPTER SUMMARY

What did you learn?

- How to perform a two-sample z-test for the difference between two means, μ_1 and μ_2, using large independent samples *(Section 8.1)* —

- How to perform a t-test for the difference between two population means, μ_1 and μ_2, using small independent samples *(Section 8.2)* —

- How to decide whether two samples are independent or dependent *(Section 8.3)* —

- How to perform a t-test to test the mean of the differences for a population of paired data *(Section 8.3)* —

- How to perform a z-test for the difference between two population proportions p_1 and p_2 *(Section 8.4)* —

Two Sample Hypothesis Testing for Population Means

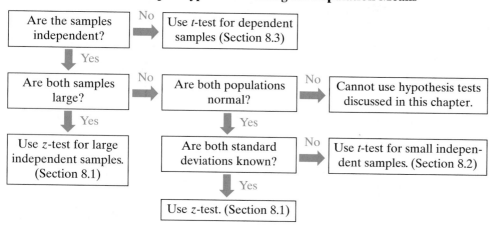

Why did you learn it? Uses and Abuses

Uses You will often want to determine whether there is a difference between two populations. Using the methods for hypothesis testing discussed in this chapter, you will be able to decide whether differences in samples are merely due to sampling error or whether these differences are significant and due to actual differences in the two populations.

Abuses There are many abuses connected with the statistics you studied in Chapter 8. To see why, think of the importance of being able to compare some trait of two different populations, "our product lasts longer, is cheaper, tastes better, is recommended by more doctors," and so on. When you are evaluating such a claim, remember to ask how the claim was determined. What were the sample sizes? Were the samples random? Were they independent? Was the sampling conducted by an unbiased researcher?

8 ▼ REVIEW EXERCISES

1. H_0: $\mu_1 \geq \mu_2$ (claim)
H_1: $\mu_1 < \mu_2$
$z_0 = -1.645$
$z = -1.862$
Reject H_0

2. H_0: $\mu_1 = \mu_2$ (claim)
H_1: $\mu_1 \neq \mu_2$
$z_0 = \pm 2.575$
$z = 3.213$
Reject H_0

3. H_0: $\mu_1 \geq \mu_2$
H_1: $\mu_1 < \mu_2$ (claim)
$z_0 = -1.282$
$z = -2.060$
Reject H_0

4. H_0: $\mu_1 = \mu_2$
H_1: $\mu_1 \neq \mu_2$ (claim)
$z_0 = \pm 1.96$
$z = -10.422$
Reject H_0

5. H_0: $\mu_1 \geq \mu_2$
H_1: $\mu_1 < \mu_2$ (claim)
$z_0 = -1.645$
$z = -2.713$
Reject H_0

6. H_0: $\mu_1 = \mu_2$
H_1: $\mu_1 \neq \mu_2$ (claim)
$z_0 = \pm 1.645$
$z = 1.799$
Reject H_0

7. H_0: $\mu_1 = \mu_2$ (claim)
H_a: $\mu_1 \neq \mu_2$
$t_0 = \pm 1.96$
$t = 1.121$
Fail to reject H_0

8. H_0: $\mu_1 = \mu_2$ (claim)
H_a: $\mu_1 \neq \mu_2$
$t_0 = \pm 1.782$
$t = -0.843$
Fail to reject H_0

9. H_0: $\mu_1 \leq \mu_2$ (claim)
H_a: $\mu_1 > \mu_2$
$t_0 = 1.711$
$t = -1.460$
Fail to reject H_0

In Exercises 1–4, use the given sample statistics (independent samples) to test the claim about the difference between two population means, μ_1 and μ_2, at the given level of significance α.

1. Claim: $\mu_1 \geq \mu_2$, $\alpha = 0.05$. Sample statistics: $\bar{x}_1 = 1.28$, $s_1 = 0.28$, $n_1 = 76$, and $\bar{x}_2 = 1.36$, $s_2 = 0.23$, $n_2 = 65$

2. Claim: $\mu_1 = \mu_2$, $\alpha = 0.01$. Sample statistics: $\bar{x}_1 = 5595$, $s_1 = 52$, $n_1 = 156$, and $\bar{x}_2 = 5575$, $s_2 = 68$, $n_2 = 216$

3. Claim: $\mu_1 < \mu_2$, $\alpha = 0.10$. Sample statistics: $\bar{x}_1 = 0.28$, $s_1 = 0.11$, $n_1 = 41$, and $\bar{x}_2 = 0.33$, $s_2 = 0.10$, $n_2 = 34$

4. Claim: $\mu_1 \neq \mu_2$, $\alpha = 0.05$. Sample statistics: $\bar{x}_1 = 82$, $s_1 = 11$, $n_1 = 410$, and $\bar{x}_2 = 90$, $s_2 = 10$, $n_2 = 340$

In Exercises 5 and 6, (a) identify the claim and state H_0 and H_a, (b) identify the rejection region(s), (c) find the standardized test statistic, (d) decide whether to reject, or fail to reject, the null hypothesis, and (e) interpret this decision in the context of the original claim.

5. In a fast food study, a nutritionist finds that the mean calorie content of 36 Arby's fish sandwiches is 529 calories with a standard deviation of 43 calories. The mean calorie content of 41 McDonald's fish sandwiches is 560 calories with a standard deviation of 57 calories. At $\alpha = 0.05$, is there enough evidence for the nutritionist to conclude that the Arby's sandwich has fewer calories than the McDonald's sandwich? *(Adapted from Fast Food Facts, Minnesota Attorney General's Office)*

6. A study of fast food nutrition compared the caloric content of french fries. Thirty-eight servings of Burger King medium french fries had a mean of 370 calories and a standard deviation of 50 calories, while 35 servings of Hardee's medium french fries had a mean of 350 calories and a standard deviation of 45 calories. At $\alpha = 0.10$, can you support the claim that the caloric content of the two types of french fries is different? *(Adapted from Fast Food Facts, Minnesota Attorney General's Office)*

In Exercises 7–10, use the given sample statistics to test the claim about the differences between two population means, μ_1 and μ_2, at the given level of significance α. Assume the populations are approximately normally distributed.

7. Claim: $\mu_1 = \mu_2$, $\alpha = 0.05$. Sample statistics: $\bar{x}_1 = 250$, $s_1 = 26$, $n_1 = 21$, and $\bar{x}_2 = 240$, $s_2 = 22$, $n_2 = 12$. Assume equal variances.

8. Claim: $\mu_1 = \mu_2$, $\alpha = 0.10$. Sample statistics: $\bar{x}_1 = 0.015$, $s_1 = 0.011$, $n_1 = 8$, and $\bar{x}_2 = 0.019$, $s_2 = 0.004$, $n_2 = 6$. Assume equal variances.

9. Claim: $\mu_1 \leq \mu_2$, $\alpha = 0.05$. Sample statistics: $\bar{x}_1 = 183.5$, $s_1 = 1.3$, $n_1 = 25$, and $\bar{x}_2 = 184.7$, $s_2 = 3.9$, $n_2 = 25$. Assume variances are not equal.

10. H_0: $\mu_1 \geq \mu_2$ (claim)
H_a: $\mu_1 < \mu_2$
$t_0 = -2.326$
$t = 1.295$
Fail to reject H_0

11. (a) H_0: $\mu_1 \leq \mu_2$
H_a: $\mu_1 > \mu_2$ (claim)
(b) $t_0 = 1.645$
(c) $t = 2.266$
(d) Reject H_0

12. (a) H_0: $\mu_1 = \mu_2$
H_a: $\mu_1 \neq \mu_2$ (claim)
(b) $t_0 = \pm2.086$
(c) $t = 1.600$
(d) Fail to reject H_0

13. Independent

14. Dependent

10. Claim: $\mu_1 \geq \mu_2$, $\alpha = 0.01$. Sample statistics: $\bar{x}_1 = 25.6$, $s_1 = 8.25$, $n_1 = 15$, and $\bar{x}_2 = 22.4$, $s_2 = 7.85$, $n_2 = 34$. Assume equal variances.

In Exercises 11 and 12, (a) identify the claim and state H_0 and H_a, (b) identify the rejection region(s), (c) find the standardized test statistic, (d) decide whether to reject, or fail to reject, the null hypothesis, and (e) interpret this decision in the context of the original claim.

11. A study of methods for teaching reading in the third grade was conducted. One classroom of 21 students participated in directed reading activities for eight weeks. Another classroom of 23 students followed the same curriculum without the activities. Students in both classrooms then took the same reading test.

The following are reading scores for the first (treated) classroom.

24   43   58   71   43   49   61   44   67   49   53
56   59   52   62   54   57   33   46   43   57

The following are reading scores for the second (control) classroom.

42   43   55   26   62   37   33   41   19   54   20   85
46   10   17   60   53   42   37   42   55   28   48

Diagnostics suggest that the data are sampled from a normal population and the population variances are equal. Test the claim that third graders taught with the directed reading activities score higher than those taught without the activities. Use $\alpha = 0.05$. *(Source: StatLib/Schmitt, Maribeth C., The Effects of an Elaborated Directed Reading Activity on the Metacomprehension Skills of Third Graders)*

12. A real estate agent claims that there is no difference between the mean household incomes of two neighborhoods. The mean income of 12 households from the first neighborhood was $18,250 with a standard deviation of $1200. In the second neighborhood, 10 households had a mean income of $17,500 with a standard deviation of $950. Assume normal distributions and equal population variances. Test the claim at $\alpha = 0.05$.

In Exercises 13 and 14, classify the samples as independent or dependent. Explain your reasoning.

13. Sample 1: Maze completion times for 14 standard laboratory mice

Sample 2: Maze completion times for 14 laboratory mice bred for higher metabolic rate

14. Sample 1: Maze completion times for 43 mice

Sample 2: Maze completion times for those 43 mice after two weeks of maze practice

15. $H_0: \mu_d = 0$ (claim)
$H_a: \mu_d \neq 0$
$t_0 = \pm 1.96$
$t = 8.065$
Reject H_0

16. $H_0: \mu_d \geq 0$
$H_a: \mu_d < 0$ (claim)
$t_0 = -2.492$
$t = 11.594$
Fail to reject H_0

17. $H_0: \mu_d \leq 6$ (claim) and
$H_a: \mu_d > 6$
$t_0 = 1.282$
$t = 19.921$
Reject H_0

18. $H_0: \mu_d = 15$
$H_a: \mu_d \neq 15$ (claim)
$t_0 = \pm 1.96$
$t = 3.755$
Reject H_0

19. (a) $H_0: \mu_d \leq 0$ and
$H_a: \mu_d > 0$ (claim)
(b) $t_0 = 1.383$
(c) $\bar{d} = 5$
$s_d \approx 8.743$
(d) $t \approx 1.808$
(e) Reject H_0.
(f) There is enough evidence to support the claim.

20. (a) $H_0: \mu_d \leq 0$
$H_a: \mu_d > 0$ (claim)
(b) $t_0 = 1.372$
(c) $\bar{d} = -0.636$
$s_d = 5.870$
(d) $t = -0.359$
(e) Fail to reject H_0
(f) There is not enough evidence to support the claim.

In Exercises 15–18, using a test for paired data, test the claim about the mean of the difference of the two populations at the given level of significance using the given statistics. Is the test right-tailed, left-tailed, or two-tailed? Assume the sample statistics are from populations that are normally distributed.

15. Claim: $\mu_d = 0$, $\alpha = 0.05$. Statistics: $\bar{d} = 10$, $s_d = 12.4$, $n = 100$

16. Claim: $\mu_d < 0$, $\alpha = 0.01$. Statistics: $\bar{d} = 3.2$, $s_d = 1.38$, $n = 25$

17. Claim: $\mu_d \leq 6$, $\alpha = 0.10$. Statistics: $\bar{d} = 10.3$, $s_d = 1.24$, $n = 33$

18. Claim: $\mu_d \neq 15$, $\alpha = 0.05$. Statistics: $\bar{d} = 17.5$, $s_d = 4.05$, $n = 37$

In Exercises 19 and 20, (a) identify the claim and state H_0 and H_a, (b) find the critical value(s) and identify the rejection region(s), (c) calculate $\bar{d}$ and s_d, (d) use the t-test to find the standardized test statistic, (e) decide whether to reject, or fail to reject, the null hypothesis, and (f) interpret the decision in the context of the original claim. For each sample, assume the distribution of the population is normal.

19. A medical researcher wants to test the effects of calcium supplements on men's blood pressure. As part of the study, 10 men are given a calcium supplement for 12 weeks. The researcher measures the men's systolic blood pressure at the beginning and at the end of the 12-week study and records the results shown below. At $\alpha = 0.10$, can the researcher claim that the men's systolic blood pressure decreased? *(Source: The Journal of American Medicine)*

Patient	1	2	3	4	5	6	7	8	9	10
Before	107	110	123	129	112	111	107	112	136	102
After	100	114	105	112	115	116	106	102	125	104

20. In a study testing the effects of an herbal supplement on blood pressure in men, 11 men were given an herbal supplement for 15 weeks. The following measurements are for each subject's systolic blood pressure taken before and after the 15-week treatment period.

Patient	1	2	3	4	5	6	7	8	9	10	11
Before	123	109	112	102	98	114	119	112	110	117	130
After	124	97	113	105	95	119	114	114	121	118	133

At $\alpha = 0.10$, can you reject the claim that systolic blood pressure was lowered?

21. $H_0: p_1 = p_2$
$H_a: p_1 \neq p_2$ (claim)

$z_0 = \pm 1.96$

$z = -1.198$

Fail to reject H_0

22. $H_0: p_1 \leq p_2$ (claim)
$H_a: p_1 > p_2$

$z_0 = 2.33$

$z = -1.249$

Fail to reject H_0

23. $H_0: p_1 \leq p_2$
$H_a: p_1 > p_2$ (claim)

$z_0 = 1.282$

$z = -1.971$

Fail to reject H_0

24. $H_0: p_1 \geq p_2$
$H_a: p_1 < p_2$ (claim)

$z_0 = -1.645$

$z = 0.501$

Fail to reject H_0

25. **(a)** $H_0: p_1 = p_2$ (claim)
$H_a: p_1 \neq p_2$

(b) $z_0 = \pm 1.645$

(c) $z = -0.776$

(d) Fail to reject H_0

(e) There is not enough evidence to reject the claim.

26. **(a)** $H_0: p_1 - p_2 \geq 0.10$ (claim)
$H_a: p_1 - p_2 < 0.10$

(b) $z_0 = -1.645$

(c) $z = 12.430$

(d) Fail to reject H_0

(e) There is not enough evidence to reject the claim.

In Exercises 21–24, test the claim about the difference between two population proportions p_1 and p_2 at the given level of significance α and the given sample statistics. Is the test right-tailed, left-tailed, or two-tailed? Assume the sample statistics are from independent samples.

21. Claim: $p_1 = p_2$, $\alpha = 0.05$. Sample statistics: $x_1 = 375$, $n_1 = 720$, and $x_2 = 365$, $n_2 = 660$

22. Claim: $p_1 \leq p_2$, $\alpha = 0.01$. Sample statistics: $x_1 = 15$, $n_1 = 100$, and $x_2 = 42$, $n_2 = 200$

23. Claim: $p_1 > p_2$, $\alpha = 0.10$. Sample statistics: $x_1 = 227$, $n_1 = 556$, and $x_2 = 198$, $n_2 = 420$

24. Claim: $p_1 < p_2$, $\alpha = 0.05$. Sample statistics: $x_1 = 86$, $n_1 = 900$, and $x_2 = 107$, $n_2 = 1200$

In Exercises 25 and 26, (a) identify the claim and state H_0 and H_a, (b) use Table 4 to find the critical value(s) and identify the rejection region(s), (c) find the standardized test statistic, (d) decide whether to reject, or fail to reject, the null hypothesis, and (e) interpret the decision in the context of the original claim. Assume the samples are independent.

25. In 1991, in a random sample of 200 Canadians, 22 had college degrees. Out of 300 Canadians who were sampled in 1996, 40 had college degrees. At $\alpha = 0.10$, can you reject the claim that the proportion of Canadians with college degrees was the same for both years? *(Adapted from Statistics Canada)*

26. In 1998, of 90,634 students taking the SAT I who were planning to major in education, 68,882 were female. That year, of the 58,135 students planning to major in biological sciences, 36,625 were female. At $\alpha = 0.05$, test the claim that the difference between the percentages of females with intended education majors and intended biological sciences majors is at least 10%. *(Source: College Board)*

8 ▼ CHAPTER QUIZ

1. (a) $H_0: \mu_1 \le \mu_2$
$H_1: \mu_1 > \mu_2$ (claim)

(b) Right tailed z-test

(c) $z_0 = 1.645$

(d) $z = 28.387$

(e) Reject H_0

2. (a) $H_0: \mu_1 = \mu_2$ (claim)
$H_a: \mu_1 \ne \mu_2$

(b) Two tailed t-test (assume vars are equal)

(c) $t_0 = \pm 2.779$

(d) $t = 4.285$

(e) Reject H_0

3. (a) $H_0: p_1 \le p_2$
$H_a: p_1 > p_2$ (claim)

(b) Right tailed z-test

(c) $z_0 = 1.282$

(d) $z \approx 158.471$

(e) Reject H_0

4. (a) $H_0: \mu_d \le 0$
$H_a: \mu_d > 0$ (claim)

(b) Dependent t-test

(c) $t_0 = 1.796$

(d) $t = 9.016$

(e) Reject H_0

Take this quiz as you would take a quiz in class. After you are done, check your work against the answers given in the back of the book.

For this quiz, do the following.
(a) Write the claim mathematically and identify H_0 and H_a.
(b) Determine whether the hypothesis test is a one-tailed test or a two-tailed test and whether to use a z-test or a t-test. Explain your reasoning.
(c) Find the critical value(s) and identify the rejection region(s).
(d) Use the appropriate test to find the appropriate test statistic.
(e) Decide whether to reject or fail to reject the null hypothesis. Then interpret the decision in the context of the original claim.

1. The mean score on a science assessment for 49 male high school students was 299.5 and the standard deviation was 2.0. The mean score on the same test for 50 female high school students was 288.9 and the standard deviation was 1.7. At $\alpha = 0.05$, can you support the claim that the mean scores on the science assessment for male high school students were higher than for the female high school students? *(Adapted from National Center for Educational Statistics)*

2. A science teacher suggests that the mean scores on a science assessment test for nine-year-old boys and girls are equal. If the mean score for 13 boys is 232.2 with a standard deviation of 1.3 and the mean score for 15 girls is 230 with a standard deviation of 1.4, can you reject the teacher's suggestion? Assume the variances are equal and use $\alpha = 0.01$. *(Adapted from National Center for Educational Statistics)*

3. Of 1,296,000 accidents involving drivers aged 21 to 24, 5% involved alcohol. Of 856,000 accidents involving drivers aged 65 years and over, 1% involved alcohol. At $\alpha = 0.10$, can you support the claim that the proportion of accidents involving alcohol is higher for drivers in the 21 to 24 age group than for drivers aged 65 and over? *(Source: U.S. Highway Safety Administration)*

4. The table shows the scores for 12 students the first and second times they took the mathematics SAT. At $\alpha = 0.05$, is there enough evidence to conclude that the student's SAT scores improved on the second test?

Student	1	2	3	4	5	6
Score on first SAT	457	419	343	539	394	413
Score on second SAT	532	523	427	607	444	490

Student	7	8	9	10	11	12
Score on first SAT	392	421	439	340	493	339
Score on second SAT	428	524	532	397	550	357

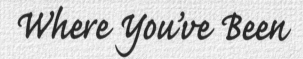

Where You've Been

In Chapters 1–8, you studied descriptive statistics, probability, and inferential statistics. One of the techniques you learned in descriptive statistics was graphing paired data with a scatter plot (Section 2.2). For instance, the winning times for the men's and women's 100-meter run in the summer Olympics from 1928 through 1996 are given in tabular form at the right and in graphical form below.

Year	Men x	Women y
1928	10.80	12.20
1932	10.30	11.90
1936	10.30	11.50
1948	10.30	11.90
1952	10.40	11.50
1956	10.50	11.50
1960	10.20	11.00
1964	10.00	11.40
1968	9.95	11.00
1972	10.14	11.07
1976	10.06	11.08
1980	10.25	11.60
1984	9.99	10.97
1988	9.92	10.54
1992	9.96	10.82
1996	9.84	10.94

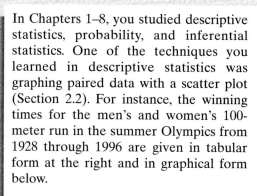

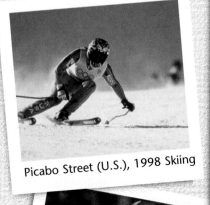

Picabo Street (U.S.), 1998 Skiing

Dan O'Brien (U.S.), 1996 Decathlon

The modern summer Olympic games began in Athens, Greece in 1896. The winter Olympic games began in Chamonix, France in 1924. The games have been held (or scheduled) in the United States eight times: St. Louis (S 1904), Lake Placid (W 1932), Los Angeles (S 1932), Squaw Valley (W 1960), Lake Placid (W 1980), Los Angeles (S 1984), Atlanta (S 1996), and Salt Lake City (W 2002).

Karen Kraft & Missy Schwen (U.S.), 1996 Rowing

Correlation and Regression

Where You're Going

In this chapter, you will study how to describe and test the significance of relationships between two variables when data are presented as ordered pairs. For instance, in the scatter plot for the 100-meter run, it appears that women's fast times tend to correspond to men's fast times and women's slow times tend to correspond to men's slow times. This relationship is described by saying the women's times are positively correlated to the men's times. Graphically, the relationship can be described by drawing a line, called a regression line, that fits the points as closely as possible. The second scatter plot below shows a similar result—the women's running high jump heights are positively correlated to the men's running high jump heights.

Michael Johnson (U.S.)
1996 200-Meter Run

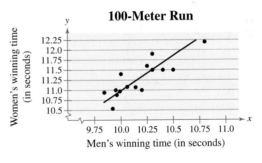

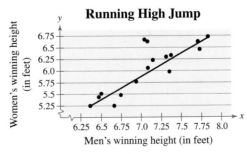

Amy Acuff (U.S.)
1996 Running High Jump

417

9.1

Correlation

An Overview of Correlation • Correlation Coefficient • Hypothesis Testing for a Population Correlation Coefficient • Correlation and Causation

What You Should Learn

- *An introduction to linear correlation, independent and dependent variables, and the types of correlation*
- *How to find a correlation coefficient*
- *How to perform a hypothesis test for a population correlation coefficient ρ*

An Overview of Correlation

Suppose a safety inspector wants to determine whether a relationship exists between the number of hours of training for an employee and the number of accidents involving that employee. Or suppose a psychologist wants to know whether a relationship exists between the number of hours a person sleeps and that person's reaction time. How would you help them determine if any relationship exists?

In this section, you will study how to describe what type of relationship, or correlation, exists between two variables, and how to determine whether the correlation is significant.

DEFINITION

A **correlation** is a relationship between two variables. The data can be represented by the ordered pairs (x, y) where x is the **independent,** or **explanatory, variable** and y is the **dependent,** or **response, variable.**

Note to Instructor

You can begin Chapter 9 using an intuitive approach. Ask students what type of relationship exists between variables such as scores and college grades, height, and IQ. Also, throughout the chapter, emphasize interpretation rather than calculation. Many of the calculations can be performed using technology.

One way to determine whether a linear (straight line) correlation exists between two variables is to use a **scatter plot** in which the ordered pairs (x, y) are graphed as points in a coordinate plane. The independent variable x is measured by the horizontal axis and the dependent variable y is measured by the vertical axis. The following scatter plots show several types of correlation.

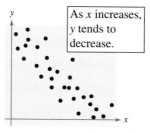

As x increases, y tends to decrease.

Negative Linear Correlation

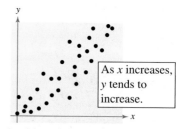

As x increases, y tends to increase.

Positive Linear Correlation

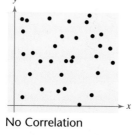

No Correlation

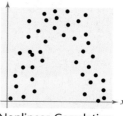

Nonlinear Correlation

Advertising Expenses (1000s of $), x	Company Sales (1000s of $), y
2.4	225
1.6	184
2.0	220
2.6	240
1.4	180
1.6	184
2.0	186
2.2	215

> ▶ **EXAMPLE 1** *Constructing a Scatter Plot*

A marketing manager conducted a study to determine whether there is a linear relationship between money spent on advertising and company sales. The data are listed in the table at the left. Display the data in a scatter plot and determine whether there appears to be a positive or negative linear correlation or no linear correlation.

SOLUTION The scatter plot is shown at the right. From the scatter plot, it appears that there is a positive linear correlation between the variables. Reading from left to right, as the advertising expenses increase, the sales tend to increase.

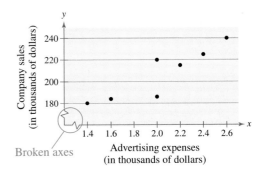

Broken axes

Income Level (in 1000s), x	Donating Percent, y
42	9
48	10
50	8
59	5
65	6
72	3

Try It Yourself 1

A sociologist conducted a study to determine whether there is a linear relationship between family income level (in thousands of dollars) and percent of income donated to charities. The data are listed in the table at the left. Display the data in a scatter plot and determine the type of correlation.

a. *Draw* and *label* the x- and y-axes.
b. *Plot* each ordered pair on the graph.
c. Does there appear to be a correlation?

Answer: Page A41 ◀

Note to Instructor

Have students try to picture a line going through the points. If the line clearly has a positive slope, the correlation is positive. If the slope is clearly negative, the correlation is negative. If they have trouble picturing a line through the points, there is probably no linear correlation. Also, mention that other nonlinear types of correlation exist—quadratic, exponential, etc.—but only linear correlation is discussed in this chapter.

> ▶ **EXAMPLE 2** *Constructing a Scatter Plot*

A student nurse conducts a study to determine whether there is a linear relationship between an individual's weight (in pounds) and daily water consumption (in ounces). The data are listed in the following table. Organize the data in a scatter plot and describe the type of correlation.

Weight, x	102	119	124	141	142	154	201	220
Water, y	50	32	82	64	54	21	86	39

SOLUTION The scatter plot is shown at the right. From the scatter plot it appears that there is no linear correlation between the variables. A person's weight does not appear to be related to the amount of water that person consumes.

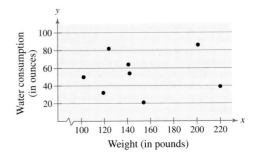

Note to Instructor

Advise students to save any data put into a technology tool as these data will be used throughout the chapter.

Try It Yourself 2

A marketing manager conducts a study to determine whether there is a linear relationship between a person's age and the number of magazines to which that person subscribes. The data are listed in the following table. Display the data in a scatter plot and determine the type of correlation.

Age, x	21	26	33	35	48	50	55	64
Subscriptions, y	4	0	3	1	3	0	2	6

a. *Draw* and *label* the x- and y-axes.
b. *Plot* each ordered pair on the graph.
c. Does there appear to be a correlation?   *Answer: Page A41*

EXAMPLE 3   *Constructing a Scatter Plot Using Technology*

Duration, x	Time, y	Duration, x	Time, y
1.80	56	3.78	79
1.82	58	3.83	85
1.88	60	3.87	81
1.90	62	3.88	80
1.92	60	4.10	89
1.93	56	4.27	90
1.98	57	4.30	84
2.03	60	4.30	89
2.05	57	4.43	84
2.13	60	4.43	89
2.30	57	4.47	86
2.35	57	4.47	80
2.37	61	4.53	89
2.82	73	4.55	86
3.13	76	4.60	88
3.27	77	4.60	92
3.65	77	4.63	91
3.70	82		

Old Faithful, located in Yellowstone National Park, is the world's most famous geyser. The duration (in minutes) of several of Old Faithful's eruptions and the times (in minutes) until the next eruption are listed in the table at the left. Using a TI-83, display the data in a scatter plot. Determine the type of correlation.

SOLUTION   Begin by entering the x-values into List 1 and the y-values into List 2. Use Stat Plot to construct the scatter plot. The plot should look similar to the one shown below. From the scatter plot it appears that the variables have a positive linear correlation. In other words, you can conclude that the longer the duration of the eruption, the longer the time before the next eruption begins.

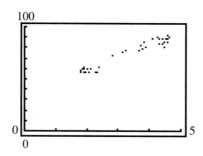

Study Tip

You can also use Minitab and Excel to construct scatter plots.

Try It Yourself 3

Consider the data from the Chapter Opener on women's and men's winning times in the 100-meter run. Use a technology tool to display the data in a scatter plot. Determine the type of correlation.

a. *Enter* the data into List 1 and List 2.
b. *Construct* the scatter plot.
c. Does there appear to be a correlation?   *Answer: Page A41*

Correlation Coefficient

Interpreting correlation using a scatter plot can be subjective. A more precise way to measure the type and strength of a linear correlation between two variables is to calculate the correlation coefficient.

> **DEFINITION**
>
> The **correlation coefficient** is a measure of the strength and the direction of a linear relationship between two variables. The symbol *r* represents the sample correlation coefficient. The formula for *r* is
>
> $$r = \frac{n\Sigma xy - (\Sigma x)(\Sigma y)}{\sqrt{n\Sigma x^2 - (\Sigma x)^2}\sqrt{n\Sigma y^2 - (\Sigma y)^2}}$$
>
> where *n* is the number of pairs of data. The population correlation coefficient is represented by ρ (the lowercase Greek letter rho).

The range of the correlation coefficient is -1 to 1. If *x* and *y* have a strong positive linear correlation, *r* is close to 1. If *x* and *y* have a strong negative linear correlation, *r* is close to -1. If there is no linear correlation or a weak linear correlation, *r* is close to 0. Several examples are shown below.

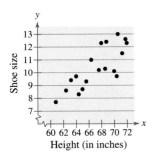

Strong positive correlation
$r = 0.81$

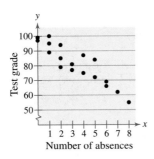

Strong negative correlation
$r = -0.92$

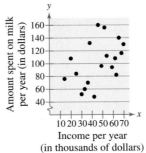

Weak positive correlation
$r = 0.45$

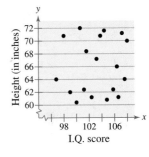

No correlation
$r = 0.04$

> **GUIDELINES**
>
> ## Calculating a Correlation Coefficient
>
> | *In Words* | *In Symbols* |
> |---|---|
> | 1. Find the sum of the *x*-values. | Σx |
> | 2. Find the sum of the *y*-values. | Σy |
> | 3. Multiply each *x*-value by its corresponding *y*-value and find the sum. | Σxy |
> | 4. Square each *x*-value and find the sum. | Σx^2 |
> | 5. Square each *y*-value and find the sum. | Σy^2 |
> | 6. Use these five sums to calculate the correlation coefficient. | $r = \dfrac{n\Sigma xy - (\Sigma x)(\Sigma y)}{\sqrt{n\Sigma x^2 - (\Sigma x)^2}\sqrt{n\Sigma y^2 - (\Sigma y)^2}}$ |

> **EXAMPLE 4** | *Finding the Correlation Coefficient*

Note to Instructor

It helps students if you emphasize the interpretation of the correlation coefficient *r* in each example.

Calculate the correlation coefficient for the advertising expenditures and company sales data given in Example 1. What can you conclude?

SOLUTION   Use a table to help calculate the correlation coefficient.

Advertising Expenses (1000s of $), x	Company Sales (1000s of $), y	xy	x^2	y^2
2.4	225	540	5.76	50,625
1.6	184	294.4	2.56	33,856
2.0	220	440	4	48,400
2.6	240	624	6.76	57,600
1.4	180	252	1.96	32,400
1.6	184	294.4	2.56	33,856
2.0	186	372	4	34,596
2.2	215	473	4.84	46,225
$\Sigma x = 15.8$	$\Sigma y = 1634$	$\Sigma xy = 3289.8$	$\Sigma x^2 = 32.44$	$\Sigma y^2 = 337{,}558$

Using these sums and $n = 8$, the correlation coefficient is

$$r = \frac{n\Sigma xy - (\Sigma x)(\Sigma y)}{\sqrt{n\Sigma x^2 - (\Sigma x)^2}\sqrt{n\Sigma y^2 - (\Sigma y)^2}}$$

$$= \frac{8(3289.8) - (15.8)(1634)}{\sqrt{8(32.44) - 15.8^2}\sqrt{8(337{,}558) - 1634^2}}$$

$$= \frac{501.2}{\sqrt{9.88}\sqrt{30{,}508}}$$

$$\approx 0.913.$$

Because *r* is close to 1, there is a strong positive linear correlation. As the amount spent on advertising increases, the company sales also increase.

Try It Yourself 4

Calculate the correlation coefficient for the income level and donating percent data given in Try It Yourself 1. What can you conclude?

Income Level (in 1000s), x	Donating Percent, y
42	9
48	10
50	8
59	5
65	6
72	3

a. *Identify n.*
b. *Use a table* to calculate Σx, Σy, Σxy, Σx^2, and Σy^2.
c. *Use the resulting sums* to calculate *r*.
d. What can you conclude?   *Answer: Page A41*

▶ **EXAMPLE 5**   *Using Technology to Find a Correlation Coefficient*

Use a technology tool to calculate the correlation coefficient for the Old Faithful data given in Example 3. What can you conclude?

SOLUTION   Minitab, Excel, and the TI-83 each have features that allow you to calculate a correlation coefficient for paired data sets. Try using this technology to find *r*. You should obtain results similar to the following.

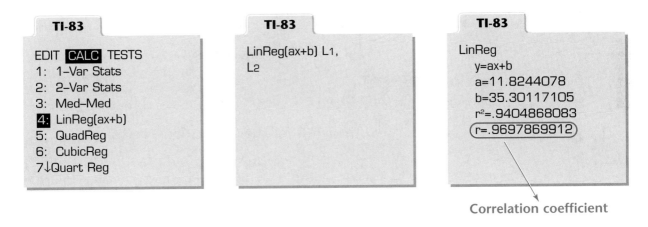

MINITAB
Correlations (Pearson)
Correlation of C1 and C2 = 0.970

EXCEL			
	A	B	C
36	CORREL(A1:A35,B1:B35)		
37			0.969787

Before using the TI-83 to calculate *r*, you must enter the Diagnostic On command. To do so, enter the following keystrokes: [2nd] [0], cursor to *DiagnosticOn*, [ENTER] [ENTER].

The following screens describe how to find *r* using a TI-83 with the data stored in List 1 and List 2.

TI-83
EDIT **CALC** TESTS
1: 1–Var Stats
2: 2–Var Stats
3: Med–Med
4: LinReg(ax+b)
5: QuadReg
6: CubicReg
7↓Quart Reg

TI-83
LinReg(ax+b) L1, L2

TI-83
LinReg
y=ax+b
a=11.8244078
b=35.30117105
r²=.9404868083
(r=.9697869912)

Correlation coefficient

The result, $r \approx 0.970$, suggests a strong positive linear correlation.

Try It Yourself 5

Calculate the correlation coefficient for the data given in the Chapter Opener on page 416. What can you conclude?

a. *Enter* the data.
b. Use the appropriate feature to *calculate r.*
c. What can you conclude?   *Answer: Page A42* ◀

Hypothesis Testing for a Population Correlation Coefficient

Once you have calculated the sample correlation coefficient, r, you will want to determine whether the population correlation, ρ, is significant. You can do this by performing a hypothesis test. A hypothesis test for ρ can be one tailed or two tailed. The null and alternative hypotheses for these tests are as follows.

$\begin{cases} H_0\colon \rho \geq 0 & \text{(no significant negative correlation)} \\ H_a\colon \rho < 0 & \text{(significant negative correlation)} \end{cases}$ **Left-tailed test**

$\begin{cases} H_0\colon \rho \leq 0 & \text{(no significant positive correlation)} \\ H_a\colon \rho > 0 & \text{(significant positive correlation)} \end{cases}$ **Right-tailed test**

$\begin{cases} H_0\colon \rho = 0 & \text{(no significant correlation)} \\ H_a\colon \rho \neq 0 & \text{(significant correlation)} \end{cases}$ **Two-tailed test**

The *t*-Test for the Correlation Coefficient

A *t*-test can be used to test whether the correlation between two variables is significant. The **test statistic** is r and the **standardized test statistic** is

$$t = \frac{r}{\sigma_r} = \frac{r}{\sqrt{\dfrac{1 - r^2}{n - 2}}}.$$

The sampling distribution for r is a t-distribution with $n - 2$ degrees of freedom.

GUIDELINES

Using the *t*-Test for the Correlation Coefficient ρ

In Words	*In Symbols*
1. State the null and the alternative hypotheses.	State H_0 and H_a.
2. Specify the level of significance.	Specify α.
3. Determine the degrees of freedom.	d.f. $= n - 2$
4. Find the critical value(s) and identify the rejection region(s).	Use Table 5 from Appendix B.
5. Find the standardized test statistic.	$t = \dfrac{r}{\sqrt{\dfrac{1 - r^2}{n - 2}}}$
6. Make a decision to reject or fail to reject the null hypothesis.	If t is in the rejection region, reject H_0. Otherwise, do not reject H_0.
7. Interpret the decision in the context of the original claim.	

> **EXAMPLE 6** **The t-Test for a Correlation Coefficient**

In Example 4, you used eight pairs of data to find $r \approx 0.913$. Test the significance of this correlation coefficient. Use $\alpha = 0.05$.

SOLUTION   The null and alternative hypotheses are

$$H_0: \rho = 0 \text{ (no correlation)} \quad \text{and} \quad H_a: \rho \neq 0 \text{ (significant correlation)}.$$

Because there are eight pairs of data in the sample, there are $8 - 2 = 6$ degrees of freedom. Because the test is a two-tailed test, $\alpha = 0.05$, and d.f. $= 6$, the critical values are -2.447 and 2.447. The rejection regions are $t < -2.447$ and $t > 2.447$. Using the t-test, the standardized test statistic is

$$t = \frac{r}{\sqrt{\dfrac{1 - r^2}{n - 2}}} = \frac{0.913}{\sqrt{\dfrac{1 - (0.913)^2}{8 - 2}}} \approx 5.482.$$

The following graph shows the location of the critical regions and the standardized test statistic.

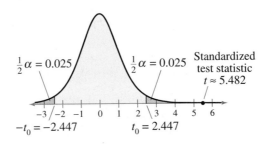

Because t is in the rejection region, you should decide to reject the null hypothesis. At the 5% level, there is enough evidence to conclude that there is a significant correlation between advertising expenditures and company sales.

Study Tip

Be sure you see in Example 6 that when you reject the null hypothesis, it means that there is sufficient evidence that the correlation is significant.

> *Try It Yourself 6*
>
> In Example 5, you calculated the correlation coefficient of the Old Faithful data to be $r \approx 0.970$. Test the significance of this correlation coefficient. Use $\alpha = 0.01$.
>
> **a.** *State* the null and alternative hypotheses.
> **b.** *Specify* the level of significance.
> **c.** *Determine* the degrees of freedom.
> **d.** *Find* the critical values and identify the rejection regions.
> **e.** *Find* the standardized test statistic.
> **f.** *Make a decision* to reject or fail to reject the null hypothesis.
> **g.** Is there enough evidence to conclude that there is a significant correlation between the duration of Old Faithful's eruptions and the time between eruptions?   *Answer: Page A42*

Correlation and Causation

The fact that two variables are strongly correlated does not in itself imply a cause-and-effect relationship between the variables. More in-depth study is usually needed to determine whether there is a causal relationship between the variables.

If there is a significant correlation between two variables, a researcher should consider the following possibilities.

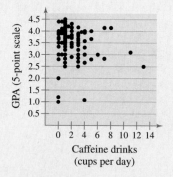
1. **Is there a direct cause-and-effect relationship between the variables?**

   That is, does x cause y? For instance, consider the relationship between advertising expenditures and company sales that has been discussed throughout this section. It is reasonable to conclude that spending more money on advertising will result in more sales.

2. **Is there a reverse cause-and-effect relationship between the variables?**

   That is, does y cause x? For instance, consider the Old Faithful data that have been discussed throughout this section. These variables have a positive linear correlation, and it is possible to conclude that the duration of an eruption affects the time before the next eruption. However, it is also possible that the time between eruptions affects the duration of the next eruption.

3. **Is it possible that the relationship between the variables can be caused by a third variable or perhaps a combination of several other variables?**

   For instance, consider the men's and women's winning times listed in the Chapter Opener. While these variables have a positive linear correlation, it is doubtful that just because the men's winning time decreases the women's winning time will also decrease. The relationship is probably due to several other variables, such as training techniques, improvements in athletic equipment, or climate conditions at the Olympic location.

4. **Is it possible that the relationship between two variables may be a coincidence?**

   For instance, while it may be possible to find a significant correlation between the number of animal species living in certain regions and the number of people who own more than two cars in those regions, it is highly unlikely that the variables are directly related. The relationship is probably due to coincidence.

Determining which of the above cases is valid for a data set can be difficult. For instance, consider the following example. Suppose a person breaks out in a rash each time he eats shrimp at a certain restaurant. The natural conclusion is that the person is allergic to shrimp. However, upon further study by an allergist, it is found that the person is not allergic to shrimp, but to a type of seasoning the chef is putting into the shrimp.

9.1 ▬ EXERCISES ▬

1. Positive linear correlation
2. No linear correlation
3. No linear correlation (but there is a nonlinear correlation between the variables)
4. Negative linear correlation
5. c
6. d
7. b
8. a

Basic Skills and Concepts

Graphical Analysis In Exercises 1–4, the scatter plots of paired data sets are given. Determine whether there is a positive linear correlation, negative linear correlation, or no linear correlation between the variables.

1.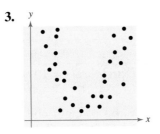

2.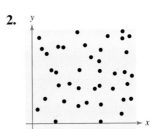

3.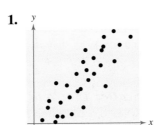

4.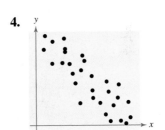

Graphical Analysis In Exercises 5–8, the scatter plots show the results of a survey of 20 randomly selected males ages 24–35. Using age as the explanatory variable, match each scatter plot to the appropriate description. Explain your reasoning.

(a) Age and body temperature
(b) Age and balance on student loans
(c) Age and income
(d) Age and height

5.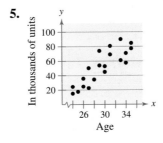

6.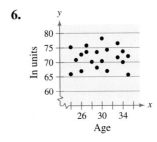

7.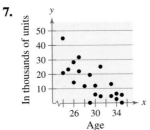

8.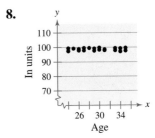

9. Explanatory variable: Amount of water consumed. Response variable: Weight loss.

10. Explanatory variable: Hours of safety classes. Response variable: Number of accidents.

11. (a)

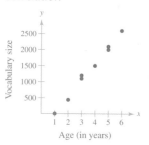

(b) 0.883

(c) Strong positive linear correlation

12. (a)

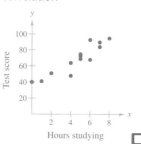

(b) 0.996

(c) Strong positive linear correlation

13. (a)

Test score vs Hours studying scatter plot

(b) 0.923

(c) Strong positive linear correlation

14. See Selected Answers, page A82

Explanatory and Response Variables   In Exercises 9 and 10, identify the explanatory variable and the response variable.

9. A nutritionist wants to determine if the amount of water consumed each day by persons of the same weight and on the same diet can be used to predict individual weight loss.

10. An insurance company hires an actuary to determine whether the number of hours of safety driving classes can be used to predict the number of driving accidents for each driver.

Constructing a Scatter Plot and Determining Correlation   In Exercises 11–18, (a) display the data in a scatter plot, (b) calculate the correlation coefficient, r, and (c) make a conclusion about the type of correlation.

11. The ages (in years) of seven men and their systolic blood pressures

Age, x	16	25	39	45	49	64	70
Systolic blood pressure, y	109	122	143	132	199	185	199

12. The ages (in years) of eight children and the number of words in their vocabulary

Age, x	1	2	3	4	5	6	3	5
Vocabulary size, y	3	440	1200	1500	2100	2600	1100	2000

13. The number of hours 13 students spent studying for a test and their scores on that test

Hours spent studying, x	0	1	2	4	4	5	5
Test score, y	40	41	51	48	64	69	73

Hours spent studying, x	5	6	6	7	7	8
Test score, y	75	68	93	84	90	95

14. The number of hours 12 students watched television during the weekend and the scores of each student who took a test the following Monday

Hours spent watching TV, x	0	1	2	3	3	5
Test score, y	96	85	82	74	95	68

Hours spent watching TV, x	5	5	6	7	7	10
Test score, y	76	84	58	65	75	50

15. (a)

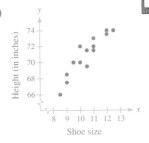

(b) 0.926

(c) Strong positive linear correlation

16. See Selected Answers, page A82

17. (a)

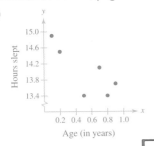

(b) −0.789

(c) Negative linear correlation

18. See Selected Answers, page A83

19. $r = -0.84$

20. b

21. State the null and alternative hypotheses. Specify the level of significance and determine the degrees of freedom. Identify the rejection regions and calculate the standardized test statistic. Make a decision and interpret in the context of the original claim.

22. See Selected Answers, page A83

23. Fail to reject H_0. There is not enough evidence to support the claim a significant linear correlation exists.

24. Reject H_0. There is enough evidence to conclude that a significant linear correlation exists.

15. The shoe sizes and heights (in inches) for 14 men

Shoe size, x	8.5	9.0	9.0	9.5	10.0	10.0	10.5
Height, y	66.0	68.5	67.5	70.0	70.0	72.0	71.5

Shoe size, x	10.5	11.0	11.0	11.0	12.0	12.0	12.5
Height, y	69.5	71.5	72.0	73.0	73.5	74.0	74.0

16. The high temperature (in °F) and coffee sales (in hundreds of dollars) for a coffee shop for eight randomly selected days

Temperature, x	32	39	51	60	65	72	78	81
Coffee sales, y	26.2	24.8	19.7	20.0	13.3	13.9	11.4	11.2

17. The age (in years) and the number of hours slept in a day by six infants

Age, x	0.1	0.2	0.5	0.7	0.8	0.9
Hours slept, y	14.9	14.5	13.4	14.1	13.4	13.7

18. The earnings per share and dividends per share for 10 electric utility companies in a recent year *(Source: The Value Line Investment Survey)*

Earnings per share, x	1.67	1.73	1.77	1.79	1.84
Dividend per share, y	1.73	1.46	1.48	1.42	1.63

Earnings per share, x	1.90	1.92	1.97	1.99	2.00
Dividend per share, y	1.60	1.83	1.46	1.67	1.72

19. Which value of r indicates a stronger correlation: $r = 0.73$ or $r = -0.84$? Explain your reasoning.

20. Which of the following values could not represent a correlation coefficient? Explain why.

(a) $r = 0.92$ (b) $r = 1.05$ (c) $r = -0.73$ (d) $r = -0.05$

21. Explain how to perform a hypothesis test for a population correlation coefficient ρ.

22. Discuss the difference between r and ρ.

Testing a Claim In Exercises 23–26, test the significance of the correlation coefficient r using the given level of significance α and sample size n. Use a two-tailed test.

23. $r = 0.50$, $\alpha = 0.05$, $n = 7$ **24.** $r = 0.75$, $\alpha = 0.10$, $n = 18$

25. Reject H_0. There is enough evidence to conclude that a significant linear correlation exists.

26. Reject H_0. There is enough evidence to support the claim that a significant linear correlation exists.

27. (a) H_0: $\rho = 0$ and H_a: $\rho \neq 0$
 (b) $t_0 = \pm 1.796$
 (c) $t \approx 7.955$
 (d) Reject H_0. There is enough evidence to conclude that a significant linear correlation exists.

28. (a) H_0: $\rho = 0$ and H_a: $\rho \neq 0$
 (b) $t_0 = \pm 1.812$
 (c) $t \approx -4.724$
 (d) Reject H_0. There is enough evidence to conclude that a significant linear correlation exists.

29. (a) H_0: $\rho = 0$ and H_a: $\rho \neq 0$
 (b) $t_0 = \pm 2.179$
 (c) $t \approx 8.497$
 (d) Reject H_0. There is enough evidence to conclude that a significant linear correlation exists.

25. $r = -0.83$, $\alpha = 0.01$, $n = 25$

26. $r = -0.60$, $\alpha = 0.05$, $n = 11$

Testing Claims In Exercises 27–30, (a) identify the claim and state H_0 and H_a, (b) find the critical value(s) and identify the rejection region(s) using Table 5 from Appendix B, (c) find the standardized test statistic, and (d) decide whether to reject the null hypothesis. Then interpret the decision in the context of the original claim. If convenient, use technology to solve the problem.

27. The number of hours 13 students spent studying for a test and their scores on that test are shown in the table. Is there enough evidence to conclude that there is a significant linear correlation between the data? Use $\alpha = 0.10$. (Use the value of r found in Exercise 13.)

Hours spent studying, x	0	1	2	4	4	5	5
Test score, y	40	41	51	48	64	69	73

Hours spent studying, x	5	6	6	7	7	8
Test score, y	75	68	93	84	90	95

28. An instructor wants to show students that there is a linear correlation between the number of hours they watch television during a certain weekend and their scores on a test taken the following Monday. The number of study hours and the test scores for 12 randomly selected students are listed in the table. At $\alpha = 0.10$, is there enough evidence for the instructor to conclude that there is a significant linear correlation between the data? (Use the value of r found in Exercise 14.)

Hours spent watching TV, x	0	1	2	3	3	5
Test score, y	96	85	82	74	95	68

Hours spent watching TV, x	5	5	6	7	7	10
Test score, y	76	84	58	65	75	50

29. You randomly select 14 men and measure the height (in inches) and shoe size of each. The data are listed below. At $\alpha = 0.05$, can you conclude that there is no significant linear correlation between the men's shoe sizes and heights? (Use the value of r found in Exercise 15.)

Shoe size, x	8.5	9.0	9.0	9.5	10.0	10.0	10.5
Height, y	66.0	68.5	67.5	70.0	70.0	72.0	71.5

Shoe size, x	10.5	11.0	11.0	11.0	12.0	12.0	12.5
Height, y	69.5	71.5	72.0	73.0	73.5	74.0	74.0

30. (a) H_0: $\rho = 0$ and
H_a: $\rho \neq 0$

(b) $t_0 = \pm 3.355$

(c) $t \approx 0.822$

(d) Fail to reject H_0. There is not enough evidence to conclude that a significant linear correlation exists.

31. The correlation coefficient remains unchanged when the x-values and y-values are switched.

32. The correlation coefficient remains unchanged when the x-values and y-values are switched.

33. Answers will vary.

30. The following table lists the earnings per share and dividends per share for 10 electric utility companies in a recent year. At $\alpha = 0.01$, can you conclude that there is no significant linear correlation between earnings per share and dividends per share? (Use the value of r found in Exercise 18.)
(Source: The Value Line Investment Survey)

Earnings per share, x	1.67	1.73	1.77	1.79	1.84
Dividend per share, y	1.73	1.46	1.48	1.42	1.63

Earnings per share, x	1.90	1.92	1.97	1.99	2.00
Dividend per share, y	1.60	1.83	1.46	1.67	1.72

Extending the Basics

Interchanging x and y In Exercises 31 and 32, calculate the correlation coefficient *r*, letting Row 1 represent the x-values and Row 2 the y-values. Then calculate the correlation coefficient *r*, letting Row 2 represent the x-values and Row 1 the y-values. What effect does switching the explanatory and response variables have on the correlation coefficient?

31.

Row 1	16	25	39	45	49	64	70
Row 2	109	122	143	132	199	185	199

32.

Row 1	0	1	2	3	3	5	5	5	6	7
Row 2	96	85	82	74	95	68	76	84	58	65

33. *Writing* Use your school's library or some other reference source to find a real-life data set with the indicated cause-and-effect relationship. Write a paragraph describing each variable and explain why you think the variables have the indicated cause-and-effect relationship.

(a) *Direct Cause-and-Effect:* Changes in one variable cause changes in the other variable.

(b) *Other Factors:* The relationship between the variables is caused by a third variable.

(c) *Coincidence:* The relationship between the variables is a coincidence.

9.2 Linear Regression

Regression Lines • Applications of Regression Lines

What You Should Learn

- *How to find the equation of a regression line*
- *How to predict y-values using a regression equation*

Regression Lines

After verifying that the correlation between two variables is significant, the next step is to determine the equation of the line that best models the data. This line is called a regression line and its equation can be used to predict the value of y for a given value of x. While many lines can be drawn through a set of points, a regression line is determined by specific criteria.

Consider the scatter plot and the line shown below. For each data point, d represents the difference between the observed y-value and the predicted y-value on the line. These differences are called **residuals** and can be positive, negative, or zero. When the point is above the line, $d > 0$. When the point is below the line, $d < 0$. If the observed y-value equals the predicted y-value, $d = 0$. Of all possible lines that can be drawn through a set of points, the regression line is the line for which the sum of the squares of all the residuals, Σd^2, is a minimum.

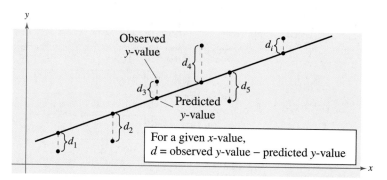

For a given x-value,
d = observed y-value − predicted y-value

DEFINITION

A **regression line**, also called a **line of best fit,** is the line for which the sum of the squares of the residuals is a minimum.

In algebra, you learned that you can write an equation of a line by finding its slope m and y-intercept b. The equation has the form $y = mx + b$. Recall that the slope of a line is the ratio of its rise over its run and the y-intercept is the y-value of the point at which the line crosses the y-axis. It is the y-value when $x = 0$.

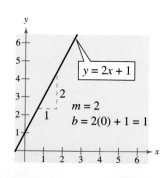

$y = 2x + 1$

$m = 2$
$b = 2(0) + 1 = 1$

A regression line allows you to use the explanatory variable x to make predictions for the response variable y.

The Equation of a Regression Line

The equation of a regression line for an independent variable x and a dependent variable y is

$$\hat{y} = mx + b$$

where $\hat{y}$ is the predicted y-value for a given x-value. The slope m and y-intercept b are given by

$$m = \frac{n\Sigma xy - (\Sigma x)(\Sigma y)}{n\Sigma x^2 - (\Sigma x)^2} \quad \text{and} \quad b = \bar{y} - m\bar{x} = \frac{\Sigma y}{n} - m\frac{\Sigma x}{n}$$

where $\bar{y}$ is the mean of the y-values in the data set and $\bar{x}$ is the mean of the x-values. The regression line always passes through the point $(\bar{x}, \bar{y})$.

▶ **EXAMPLE 1** *Finding the Equation of a Regression Line*

Find the equation of the regression line for the advertising expenditures and company sales data used throughout Section 9.1.

Advertising expenses (1000s of $), x	Company sales (1000s of $), y
2.4	225
1.6	184
2.0	220
2.6	240
1.4	180
1.6	184
2.0	186
2.2	215

SOLUTION In Example 4 of Section 9.1, you found that $n = 8$, $\Sigma x = 15.8$, $\Sigma y = 1634$, $\Sigma xy = 3289.8$, and $\Sigma x^2 = 32.44$. You can use these values to calculate the slope and y-intercept as shown.

$$m = \frac{n\Sigma xy - (\Sigma x)(\Sigma y)}{n\Sigma x^2 - (\Sigma x)^2} = \frac{8(3289.8) - (15.8)(1634)}{8(32.44) - 15.8^2} = \frac{501.2}{9.88} \approx 50.7287$$

$$b = \bar{y} - m\bar{x} = \frac{1634}{8} - (50.7287)\frac{15.8}{8} = 204.25 - (50.7287)(1.975) \approx 104.0608$$

So, the equation of the regression line is

$$\hat{y} = 50.729x + 104.061.$$

The regression line and scatter plot of the data are shown at the right. If you plot the point $(\bar{x}, \bar{y}) = (1.975, 204.25)$, you will notice that the line passes through this point.

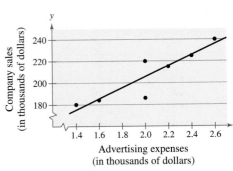

Income level (in 1000s), x	Donating percent, y
42	9
48	10
50	8
59	5
65	6
72	3

Try It Yourself 1

Find the equation of the regression line for the income level and donating percent data used throughout Section 9.1.

a. *Identify* n, Σx, Σy, Σxy, and Σx^2 from Try It Yourself 4 of Section 9.1.
b. *Calculate* the slope m.
c. *Calculate* the y-intercept b.
d. *Write* the regression line.

Answer: Page A42

Duration, x	Time, y	Duration, x	Time, y
1.80	56	3.78	79
1.82	58	3.83	85
1.88	60	3.87	81
1.90	62	3.88	80
1.92	60	4.10	89
1.93	56	4.27	90
1.98	57	4.30	84
2.03	60	4.30	89
2.05	57	4.43	84
2.13	60	4.43	89
2.30	57	4.47	86
2.35	57	4.47	80
2.37	61	4.53	89
2.82	73	4.55	86
3.13	76	4.60	88
3.27	77	4.60	92
3.65	77	4.63	91
3.70	82		

▶ **EXAMPLE 2** | *Using Technology to Find a Regression Equation*

Use a technology tool to find the equation of the regression line for the Old Faithful data used throughout Section 9.1.

SOLUTION Minitab, Excel, and the TI-83 each have features that automatically calculate a regression equation. Try using this technology to find the regression equation. You should obtain results similar to the following.

MINITAB

Regression Analysis

The regression equation is
C2 = 35.3 + 11.8 C1

Predictor	Coef	StDev	T	P
Constant	35.301	1.804	19.57	0.000
C1	11.8244	0.5178	22.84	0.000

S = 3.277   R-Sq = 94.0%   R-Sq(adj) = 93.9%

EXCEL

	A	B	C	D
1	Slope:			
2	INDEX(LINEST(known_y's,known_x's),1)			
3				11.82441
4				
5	Y-intercept:			
6	INDEX(LINEST(known_y's,known_x's),2)			
7				35.30117

TI-83

LinReg
y=ax+b
a=11.8244078
b=35.30117105
r^2=.9404868083
r=.9697869912

From the displays, you can see that the regression equation is

$$\hat{y} = 11.824x + 35.301.$$

The TI-83 display at the right shows the regression line and a scatter plot of the data.

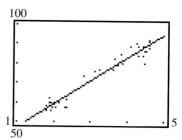

Note to Instructor

Point out the different notation used by the TI-83, Minitab, and Excel.

Men's times, x	Women's times, y
10.80	12.20
10.30	11.90
10.30	11.50
10.30	11.90
10.40	11.50
10.50	11.50
10.20	11.00
10.00	11.40
9.95	11.00
10.14	11.07
10.06	11.08
10.25	11.60
9.99	10.97
9.92	10.54
9.96	10.82
9.84	10.94

Try It Yourself 2

Use a technology tool to find the equation of the regression line for the men's and women's winning times given in the Chapter Opener.

a. *Enter* the data.
b. *Perform the necessary steps* to calculate the slope and *y*-intercept.
c. *Specify* the regression line.

Answer: Page A42

Applications of Regression Lines

After finding the equation of a regression line, you can use the equation to predict *y*-values over the range of the data. For example, an advertising executive could forecast company sales based on advertising expenditures. To predict *y*-values, substitute the given *x*-value into the regression equation, then calculate *y*.

Note to Instructor

This Picturing the World is a good place to discuss outliers.

▶ **EXAMPLE 3**   *Predicting y-Values Using Regression Equations*

The regression equation for the advertising expenditures (in 1000s of dollars) and company sales (in 1000s of dollars) data is

$$\hat{y} = 50.729x + 104.061.$$

Use this equation to predict the *expected* company sales for the following advertising expenditures.

1. 1.5 thousand dollars   2. 1.8 thousand dollars   3. 2.5 thousand dollars

SOLUTION   To predict the expected company sales, substitute each advertising expenditure for *x* in the regression equation. Then calculate *y*.

1. $\hat{y} = 50.729x + 104.061$
   $= 50.729(1.5) + 104.061$
   ≈ 180.155

   When the advertising expenditures are $1500, the company sales are about $180,155.

2. $\hat{y} = 50.729x + 104.061$
   $= 50.729(1.8) + 104.061$
   ≈ 195.373

   When the advertising expenditures are $1800, the company sales are about $195,373.

3. $\hat{y} = 50.729x + 104.061$
   $= 50.729(2.5) + 104.061$
   ≈ 230.883

   When the advertising expenditures are $2500, the company sales are about $230,883.

Prediction values are meaningful only for *x*-values in (or close to) the range of the data. The *x*-values in the original data set range from 1.4 to 2.6. So, it would not be appropriate to use the regression line $\hat{y} = 50.729x + 104.061$ to predict company sales for advertising expenditures such as 0.5 ($500) or 5.0 ($5000).

Picturing the World

The following scatter plot shows the relationship between the number of motor vehicles in a state and the number of motor vehicle deaths. *(Source: Federal Highway Admin. & National Safety Council)*

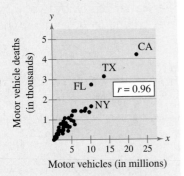

Describe the correlation between these two variables in words. Use the scatter plot to predict the number of motor vehicle deaths in a state that has 16 million motor vehicles. The regression line for this scatter plot is y = 0.053 + 0.192x. Use this equation to make your prediction. How does your algebraic prediction compare with your graphical one?

Try It Yourself 3

The regression equation for the Old Faithful data is $\hat{y} = 11.824x + 35.301$. Use this to predict the time until the next eruption for each of the following eruption durations.

1. 2 minutes
2. 3.32 minutes

a. *Substitute* each value for *x* in the regression equation.
b. *Calculate* y.
c. *Specify* the time until the next eruption for each eruption duration.

Answer: Page A42 ◀

9.2 ■ EXERCISES ■

HELP

 StatPro 9.2

 Internet Statistics 9.2

 Student Solutions Manual 9.2

 Videos 9.2

 Try It Yourself Answers 9.2

1. c

2. a

3. d

4. b

5. $\hat{y} = 0.432x - 20.297$ best fits the data.

6. $\hat{y} = 4.347x - 299.482$ best fits the data.

Basic Skills and Concepts

Matching In Exercises 1–4, match the description in the left column with a description in the right column.

1. Regression line

2. Residual

3. The y-value of a data point corresponding to x_i

4. The y-value for a point on the regression line corresponding to x_i

a. The difference between the y-value of the data point and the y-value on the line for the same x-value

b. $\hat{y}_i$

c. The line of best fit

d. y_i

Graphical Analysis In Exercises 5 and 6, a scatter plot with two lines is given. Use the equations and the least squares criteria to determine which line best fits the data.

5. The heights (in feet) and diameters (in inches) of eight trees

Height, x	70	72	75	76
Diameter, y	8.3	10.5	11.0	11.4

Height, x	85	78	77	80
Diameter, y	12.9	14.0	16.3	18.0

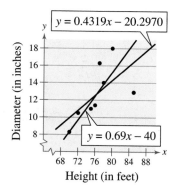

$y = 0.4319x - 20.2970$

$y = 0.69x - 40$

Height (in feet)

6. The caloric content and the sodium content (in milligrams) for 10 hot dogs *(Source: Consumer Reports)*

Calories, x	186	181	176	149	184
Sodium, y	495	477	425	322	482

Calories, x	190	158	139	175	148
Sodium, y	587	370	322	479	375

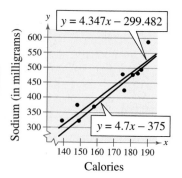

$y = 4.347x - 299.482$

$y = 4.7x - 375$

Calories

7. c

8. b

9. a

10. d

11. $\hat{y} = 1.724x + 79.733$

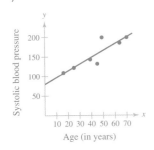

(a) 110

(b) 202

(c) 129

(d) 175

Matching In Exercises 7–10, match the regression equation with the appropriate graph. (Note that the x- and y-axes are broken.)

a.

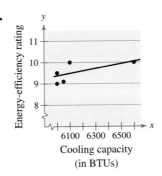

b.

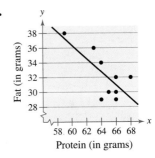

c.

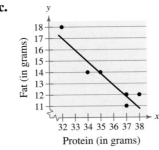

d.

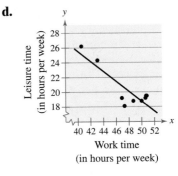

7. $y = -1.04x + 50.3$

8. $y = -0.902x + 90.5$

9. $y = 0.000114x + 2.53$

10. $y = -0.667x + 52.6$

Finding the Equation of a Regression Line In Exercises 11–16, find the equation of the regression line for the given data and graph a scatter plot of the data and the regression line. (Each pair of variables has a significant correlation.) Then use the regression equation to predict the value of *y* for each of the given *x*-values, if meaningful. If the *x*-value is not meaningful to predict the value of *y*, explain why not.

11. The ages (in years) of seven men and their systolic blood pressures

Age, x	16	25	39	45	49	64	70
Systolic blood pressure, y	109	122	143	132	199	185	199

(a) *x* = 18 years   (b) *x* = 71 years

(c) *x* = 29 years   (d) *x* = 55 years

12. See Selected Answers, page A83

13. $\hat{y} = 7.350x + 34.617$

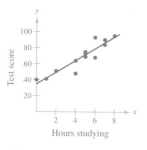

(a) 56.7

(b) 82.4

(c) It is not meaningful to predict the value of *y* for *x* = 13 because *x* = 13 is outside the range of the original data.

(d) 67.7

14. See Selected Answers, page A83

15. $\hat{y} = 1.870x + 51.360$

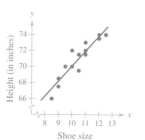

(a) 72.865

(b) 66.320

(c) It is not meaningful to predict the value of *y* for *x* = 15.5 because *x* = 15.5 is outside the range of the original data.

(d) 70.060

12. The ages (in years) of eight children and the number of words in their vocabulary

Age, x	1	2	3	4	5	6	3	5
Vocabulary size, y	3	440	1200	1500	2100	2600	1100	2000

(a) *x* = 2 years (b) *x* = 3 years
(c) *x* = 6 years (d) *x* = 12 years

13. The number of hours 13 students spent studying for a test and their scores on that test

Hours spent studying, x	0	1	2	4	4	5	5
Test score, y	40	41	51	48	64	69	73

Hours spent studying, x	5	6	6	7	7	8
Test score, y	75	68	93	84	90	95

(a) *x* = 3 hours (b) *x* = 6.5 hours
(c) *x* = 13 hours (d) *x* = 4.5 hours

14. The number of hours 12 students spent watching television during a weekend and their scores on a test on Monday

Hours spent watching TV, x	0	1	2	3	3	5
Test score, y	96	85	82	74	95	68

Hours spent watching TV, x	5	5	6	7	7	10
Test score, y	76	84	58	65	75	50

(a) *x* = 4 hours (b) *x* = 8 hours
(c) *x* = 9 hours (d) *x* = 15 hours

15. The shoe sizes and heights (in inches) for 14 men

Shoe size, x	8.5	9.0	9.0	9.5	10.0	10.0	10.5
Height, y	66.0	68.5	67.5	70.0	70.0	72.0	71.5

Shoe size, x	10.5	11.0	11.0	11.0	12.0	12.0	12.5
Height, y	69.5	71.5	72.0	73.0	73.5	74.0	74.0

(a) *x* = size 11.5 (b) *x* = size 8.0
(c) *x* = size 15.5 (d) *x* = size 10.0

16. $\hat{y} = -1.481x + 14.790$

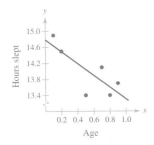

(a) 14.346

(b) It is not meaningful to predict the value of y for x = 3.9 because x = 3.9 is outside the range of the original data.

(c) 13.901   **(d)** 14.198

17. Substitute a value x into the equation of a regression line and solve for y.

18. Prediction values are meaningful only for x-values in (or close to) the range of the data.

19. (a) $\hat{y} = 1.724x + 79.733$

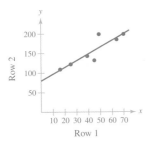

(b) $\hat{y} = 0.453x - 26.448$

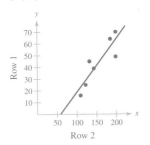

(c) The slope of the line keeps the same sign, but the values of m and b change.

20. See Selected Answers, page A83

16. The age (in years) and the number of hours slept in a day by six infants

Age, x	0.1	0.2	0.5	0.7	0.8	0.9
Hours slept, y	14.9	14.5	13.4	14.1	13.4	13.7

(a) x = 0.3 year   (b) x = 3.9 years
(c) x = 0.6 year   (d) x = 0.4 year

17. *Writing* Explain how to predict y-values using the equation of a regression line.

18. *Writing* Given a set of data and a corresponding regression line, describe all values of x that provide meaningful predictions for y.

Extending the Basics

Interchanging x and y In Exercise 19 and 20, do the following.

(a) Find the equation of the regression line for the given data, letting Row 1 represent the x-values and Row 2 the y-values. Graph a scatter plot of the data and draw the regression line with it.

(b) Find the equation of the regression line for the given data, letting Row 2 represent the x-values and Row 1 the y-values. Graph a scatter plot of the data and draw the regression line with it.

(c) What effect does switching the explanatory and response variables have on the regression line?

19.

Row 1	16	25	39	45	49	64	70
Row 2	109	122	143	132	199	185	199

20.

Row 1	0	1	2	3	3	5	5	5	6	7
Row 2	96	85	82	74	95	68	76	84	58	65

21. $\hat{y} = -1.143x + 89.256$

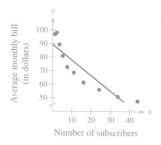

22. No

23. $r \approx -0.906$

$H_0: \rho = 0$ and $H_a: \rho \neq 0$

Critical values: $t_0 = \pm 3.355$

$$t = \cfrac{r}{\sqrt{\cfrac{1 - r^2}{n - 2}}}$$

$$= \cfrac{-0.906}{\sqrt{\cfrac{1 - (-0.906)^2}{10 - 2}}}$$

$$\approx -6.054$$

Reject H_0. There is enough evidence to conclude that a significant linear correlation exists.

24. As the number of cellular phone subscribers increases, the average monthly bill decreases.

25. Answers will vary.

Cellular Phones In Exercises 21–24, use the following information. You work for a cellular phone industry analyst and gather the data shown in the table. The table shows the number of cellular phone subscribers and the average monthly cellular phone bill in the United States for 10 years. *(Source: Cellular Telecommunications Industry Association)*

Number of subscribers (in millions), x	Average monthly bill (in dollars), y
1.2	96.83
2.1	98.02
3.5	89.30
5.2	80.90
7.6	72.74
11.0	68.68
16.0	61.48
24.1	56.21
33.8	51.00
44.0	47.70

21. Find an equation of the regression line for the data. Graph a scatter plot of the data and the regression line.

22. The analyst uses the regression line you found in Exercise 21 to predict the average monthly bill for $x = 80$ million subscribers. Is this a valid prediction? Explain your reasoning.

23. The analyst claims that the data have a significant correlation for $\alpha = 0.01$. Verify this claim.

24. Write a paragraph describing the cause-and-effect relationship between the number of cellular phone subscribers and the average monthly cellular phone bill.

25. *Writing* Use your school's library or some other reference source to find a real-life data set. Find the equation of the regression line for the data and graph a scatter plot of the data with the regression line. Then write a paragraph describing each variable and what kind of cause-and-effect relationship you think the variables have.

9 ◀ CASE STUDY

Correlation of Body Measurements

In a study published in *Medicine and Science in Sports and Exercise*, 17(2), 189, the measurements of 250 men (ages 22–81) are given. Of the 14 measurements taken of each man, some have significant correlations and others don't. For instance, the scatter plot at the right shows that the hip and abdomen circumferences of the men have a strong linear correlation ($r = 0.85$). The partial table shown here lists only the first 9 rows of the data.

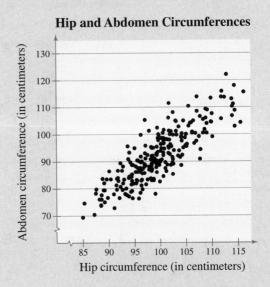

Hip and Abdomen Circumferences

Age (yr)	Weight (lb)	Height (in.)	Neck (cm)	Chest (cm)	Abdom. (cm)	Hip (cm)	Thigh (cm)	Knee (cm)	Ankle (cm)	Bicep (cm)	Forearm (cm)	Wrist (cm)	Body fat %
22	173.25	72.25	38.5	93.6	83.0	98.7	58.7	37.3	23.4	30.5	28.9	18.2	6.1
22	154.00	66.25	34.0	95.8	87.9	99.2	59.6	38.9	24.0	28.8	25.2	16.6	25.3
23	154.25	67.75	36.2	93.1	85.2	94.5	59.0	37.3	21.9	32.0	27.4	17.1	12.3
23	198.25	73.50	42.1	99.6	88.6	104.1	63.1	41.7	25.0	35.6	30.0	19.2	11.7
23	159.75	72.25	35.5	92.1	77.1	93.9	56.1	36.1	22.7	30.5	27.2	18.2	9.4
23	188.15	77.50	38.0	96.6	85.3	102.5	59.1	37.6	23.2	31.8	29.7	18.3	10.3
24	184.25	71.25	34.4	97.3	100.0	101.9	63.2	42.2	24.0	32.2	27.7	17.7	28.7
24	210.25	74.75	39.0	104.5	94.4	107.8	66.0	42.0	25.6	35.7	30.6	18.8	20.9
24	156.00	70.75	35.7	92.7	81.9	95.3	56.4	36.5	22.0	33.5	28.3	17.3	14.2

Exercises

1. Using your intuition, classify the following (x, y) pairs as having a weak correlation ($0 < r < 0.5$), a moderate correlation ($0.5 < r < 0.8$), or a strong correlation ($0.8 < r < 1.0$).

  (a) (weight, neck)   (b) (weight, height)

  (c) (age, body fat)   (d) (chest, hip)

  (e) (age, wrist)   (f) (ankle, wrist)

  (g) (forearm, height)   (h) (bicep, forearm)

  (i) (weight, body fat)   (j) (knee, thigh)

  (k) (hip, abdomen)   (l) (abdomen, hip)

2. Now, use a technology tool to find the correlation coefficient for each pair in Exercise 1. Compare your results to those obtained by intuition.

3. Use a technology tool to find the regression line for each pair in Exercise 1 that has a strong correlation.

4. Use the results of Exercise 3 to predict the following.

  (a) The weight of a man whose neck circumference is 40 centimeters.

  (b) The abdomen circumference of a man whose hip circumference is 100 centimeters.

5. Are there pairs of measurements that have stronger correlation coefficients than 0.85? Use a technology tool and intuition to reach a conclusion.

Measures of Regression and Prediction Intervals

9.3

Variation about a Regression Line • The Coefficient of Determination •
The Standard Error of Estimate • Prediction Intervals

What You Should Learn

- *How to interpret the three types of variation about a regression line*
- *How to find and interpret the coefficient of determination*
- *How to find and interpret the standard error of estimate for a regression line*
- *How to construct and interpret a prediction interval for y*

Note to Instructor

Tell students that without information about the regression line, the best predictor for any value of x is $\bar{y}$, the mean of the y-values.

Variation about a Regression Line

In this section, you will study two measures used in correlation and regression studies—the coefficient of determination and the standard error of estimate. You will also learn how to construct a prediction interval for y using a regression line and a given value of x. Before studying these concepts, you need to understand the three types of variation about a regression line.

To find the total variation, the explained variation, and the unexplained variation about a regression line, you must first calculate the **total deviation,** the **explained deviation,** and the **unexplained deviation** for each ordered pair (x_i, y_i) in a data set. These deviations are shown in the graph.

Total deviation $= y_i - \bar{y}$

Explained deviation $= \hat{y}_i - \bar{y}$

Unexplained deviation $= y_i - \hat{y}_i$

After calculating the deviations for each ordered pair, you can find the total variation, the explained variation, and the unexplained variation.

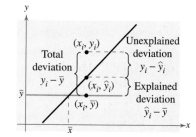

Study Tip

Consider the advertising and sales data used throughout this chapter. Using the data point (2.0, 220), you can find the total, explained, and unexplained deviations as follows.

Total deviation:

$$y_i - \bar{y} = 220 - 204.25$$
$$= 15.75$$

Explained deviation:

$$\hat{y}_i - \bar{y} = 205.518 - 204.25$$
$$= 1.268$$

Unexplained deviation:

$$y_i - \hat{y}_1 = 220 - 205.518$$
$$= 14.482$$

DEFINITION

The **total variation** about a regression line is the sum of the squares of the differences between the y-value of each ordered pair and the mean of y.

$$\text{Total variation} = \Sigma(y_i - \bar{y})^2$$

The **explained variation** is the sum of the squares of the differences between each predicted y-value and the mean of y.

$$\text{Explained variation} = \Sigma(\hat{y}_i - \bar{y})^2$$

The **unexplained variation** is the sum of the squares of the differences between the y-value of each ordered pair and each corresponding predicted y-value.

$$\text{Unexplained variation} = \Sigma(y_i - \hat{y}_i)^2$$

The sum of the explained and unexplained variations is equal to the total variation.

As its name implies, the *explained variation* can be explained by the relationship between x and y. The *unexplained variation* cannot be explained by the relationship between x and y and is due to chance or other variables.

The Coefficient of Determination

You already know how to calculate the correlation coefficient r. The square of this coefficient is called the coefficient of determination. It can be shown that the coefficient of determination is equal to the ratio of the explained variation to the total variation.

DEFINITION

The **coefficient of determination r^2** is the ratio of the explained variation to the total variation. That is,

$$r^2 = \frac{\text{Explained variation}}{\text{Total variation}}.$$

It is important that you interpret the coefficient of determination correctly. For instance, if the correlation coefficient is $r = 0.90$, then the coefficient of determination is $r^2 = 0.90^2 = 0.81$. This means that 81% of the variation of y can be explained by the relationship between x and y. The remaining 19% of the variation is unexplained and is due to other factors such as chance and sampling error.

Picturing the World

Janette Benson (Psychology Department, University of Denver) performed a study relating the age that infants crawl (in weeks after birth) with the average monthly temperature six months after birth. Her results are based on a sample of 414 infants. Janette Benson believes that the reason for the correlation in temperature to crawling age is that parents tend to bundle infants in more restrictive clothing and blankets during cold months. This bundling doesn't allow the infant as much opportunity to move and experiment with crawling.

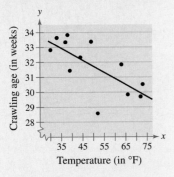

The correlation coefficient is $r = 0.70$. What percent of the variation in the data can be explained? What percent is due to chance and sampling error?

> **EXAMPLE 1** *Finding the Coefficient of Determination*

The correlation coefficient for the advertising expenditures and company sales data given in Example 1 of Section 9.1 is $r \approx 0.913$. Find the coefficient of determination. What does this tell you about the explained variation of the data about the regression line? The unexplained variation?

SOLUTION The coefficient of determination is

$$r^2 = (0.913)^2 \approx 0.834.$$

This means that about 83.4% of the variation in the company sales can be explained by the variation in the advertising expenditures. About 16.6% of the variation is unexplained and is due to chance or other variables.

Try It Yourself 1

The correlation coefficient for the Old Faithful data is $r \approx 0.970$. Find the coefficient of determination. What does this tell you about the explained variation of the data about the regression line? The unexplained variation?

a. *Identify* the correlation coefficient, r.
b. *Square* r.
c. What percent of the variation in the times is explained? What percent is unexplained? *Answer: Page A42*

The Standard Error of Estimate

When a $\hat{y}$-value is predicted from an x-value, the prediction is a point estimate. You can construct an interval estimate for $\hat{y}$, but first you need to calculate the standard error of estimate.

DEFINITION

The **standard error of estimate** s_e is the standard deviation of the observed y_i-values about the predicted $\hat{y}$-value. It is given by

$$s_e = \sqrt{\frac{\Sigma(y_i - \hat{y}_i)^2}{n - 2}}$$

where n is the number of ordered pairs in the data set.

From this formula, you can see that the standard error of estimate is the square root of the unexplained variation divided by $n - 2$. So, the closer the observed y-values are to the predicted y-values, the smaller the standard error of estimate will be.

Insight

The smaller the error of estimate, the closer the data points are to the regression line.

GUIDELINES

Finding the Standard Error of Estimate s_e

In Words	*In Symbols*
1. Make a table that includes the column headings shown at the right.	$x_i, y_i, \hat{y}_i, (y_i - \hat{y}_i)$
2. Use the regression equation to calculate the predicted y-values.	$\hat{y}_i = mx_i + b$
3. Calculate the sum of the squares of the differences between each observed y-value and the corresponding predicted y-value.	$\Sigma(y_i - \hat{y}_i)^2$
4. Find the standard error of estimate.	$s_e = \sqrt{\dfrac{\Sigma(y_i - \hat{y}_i)^2}{n - 2}}$

You can also find the standard error of estimate using the following formula.

$$s_e = \sqrt{\frac{\Sigma y^2 - b\Sigma y - m\Sigma xy}{n - 2}}$$

This formula is easy to use if you have already calculated the slope m, the y-intercept b, and several of the sums.

> **EXAMPLE 2** *Finding the Standard Error of Estimate*

The regression equation for the advertising expenditures and company sales data is

$$\hat{y} = 50.729x + 104.061.$$

Find the standard error of estimate.

SOLUTION   Use a table to calculate the sum of the squared differences of each observed y-value and the corresponding predicted y-value.

x_i	y_i	$\hat{y}_i$	$(y_i - \hat{y}_i)^2$
2.4	225	225.81	0.6561
1.6	184	185.23	1.5129
2.0	220	205.52	209.6704
2.6	240	235.96	16.3216
1.4	180	175.08	24.2064
1.6	184	185.23	1.5129
2.0	186	205.52	381.0304
2.2	215	215.66	0.4356
			$\Sigma = 635.3463$

Using $n = 8$ and $\Sigma(y_i - \hat{y}_i)^2 = 635.3463$, the standard error of estimate is

$$s_e = \sqrt{\frac{\Sigma(y_i - \hat{y}_i)^2}{n - 2}}$$

$$= \sqrt{\frac{635.3463}{8 - 2}}$$

$$\approx 10.290.$$

So, the standard error of estimate is about 10.290. That means the standard deviation of the company sales for a specific advertising expenditure is about $10,290.

Radio Ad Time	Weekly Sales
15	26
20	32
20	38
30	56
40	54
45	78
50	80
60	88

Try It Yourself 2

A researcher collects the data shown at the left and concludes that there is a significant relationship between the amount of radio advertising time (in minutes per week) and the weekly sales of a product (in hundreds of dollars). Find the standard error of estimate. Use the regression equation $\hat{y} = 1.41x + 7.31$.

a. *Use a table* to calculate the sum of the squared differences of each observed y-value and the corresponding predicted y-value.
b. *Identify* the number of ordered pairs in the data set n.
c. *Calculate* s_e.
d. *Interpret* the results.   *Answer: Page A42*

Prediction Intervals

Two variables have a **bivariate normal distribution** if for any fixed values x, the corresponding values of y are normally distributed. Because regression equations are determined using sample data and because x and y are assumed to have a bivariate normal distribution, you can construct a prediction interval for the true value of y. To construct the prediction interval, use a t-distribution with $n - 2$ degrees of freedom.

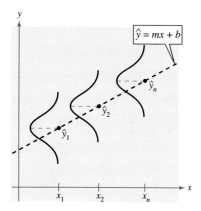

Bivariate Normal Distribution

DEFINITION

Given a linear regression equation $\hat{y} = mx + b$ and x_0, a specific value of x, a **c-prediction interval** for y is

$$\hat{y} - E < y < \hat{y} + E \quad \text{where} \quad E = t_c s_e \sqrt{1 + \frac{1}{n} + \frac{n(x_0 - \bar{x})^2}{n\Sigma x^2 - (\Sigma x)^2}}.$$

The point estimate is $\hat{y}$ and the maximum error of estimate is E. The probability that the prediction interval contains y is c.

GUIDELINES

Constructing a Prediction Interval for y for a Specific Value of x

In Words	*In Symbols*
1. Identify the number of ordered pairs in the data set, n, and the degrees of freedom.	d.f. $= n - 2$
2. Use the regression equation and the given x-value to find the point estimate $\hat{y}$.	$\hat{y}_i = mx_i + b$
3. Find the critical value, t_c, that corresponds to the given level of confidence c.	Use Table 5 in Appendix B.
4. Find the standard error of estimate s_e.	$s_e = \sqrt{\dfrac{\Sigma(y_i - \hat{y}_i)^2}{n - 2}}$
5. Find the maximum error of estimate, E.	$E = t_c s_e \sqrt{1 + \dfrac{1}{n} + \dfrac{n(x_0 - \bar{x})^2}{n\Sigma x^2 - (\Sigma x)^2}}$
6. Find the left and right endpoints and form the prediction interval.	Left endpoint: $\hat{y} - E$ Right endpoint: $\hat{y} + E$ Interval: $\hat{y} - E < y < \hat{y} + E$

Study Tip

The formulas for s_e and E use the quantities $\Sigma(y_i - \hat{y}_i)^2$, $(\Sigma x)^2$, and Σx^2. Use a table to calculate these quantities.

▶ **EXAMPLE 3**　*Constructing a Prediction Interval*

Construct a 95% prediction interval for the company sales when the advertising expenditures are $2100. What can you conclude?

SOLUTION　Because $n = 8$, there are $8 - 2 = 6$ degrees of freedom. Using the regression equation $\hat{y} = 50.729x + 104.061$ and $x_0 = 2.1$, the point estimate is

$$\hat{y} = 50.729x + 104.061$$
$$= 50.729(2.1) + 104.061$$
$$\approx 210.592.$$

From Table 5, the critical value is $t_c = 2.447$ and from Example 2, $s_e = 10.290$. Using these values, the maximum error of estimate is

$$E = t_c s_e \sqrt{1 + \frac{1}{n} + \frac{n(x_0 - \bar{x})^2}{n(\Sigma x^2) - (\Sigma x)^2}}$$

$$= (2.447)(10.290) \sqrt{1 + \frac{1}{8} + \frac{8(2.1 - 1.975)^2}{8(32.44) - (15.8)^2}}$$

$$\approx 26.857.$$

Using $\hat{y} = 210.592$ and $E = 26.857$, the confidence interval is

Left Endpoint　　　　　　　　Right Endpoint
$210.592 - 26.857 = 183.735$　　$210.592 + 26.857 = 237.449$

$183.735 < y < 237.449$

So, you can be 95% confident that when advertising expenditures are $2100, the company sales will be between $183,735 and $237,449.

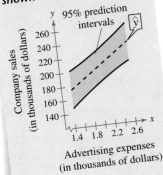

Insight

The greater the difference between x and $\bar{x}$, the wider the prediction interval is. For instance, the 95% prediction intervals for $1.4 < x < 2.6$ are shown below.

y 95% prediction intervals $\hat{y}$

Company sales (in thousands of dollars)

260
240
220
200
180
160
140

1.4　1.8　2.2　2.6　*x*

Advertising expenses (in thousands of dollars)

Try It Yourself 3

Construct a 95% prediction interval for the company sales when the advertising expenses are $2500. What can you conclude?

a. *Specify* n, d.f., t_c, s_e.
b. *Calculate* $\hat{y}$ when $x = 2.5$.
c. *Calculate* the maximum error of estimate E.
d. *Construct* the prediction interval.
e. What can you conclude?

Answer: Page A42 ◀

9.3 EXERCISES

HELP

 StatPro 9.3

 Internet Statistics 9.3

 Student Solutions Manual 9.3

 Videos 9.3

 Try It Yourself Answers 9.3

1. $\Sigma(y_i - \bar{y})^2$; the sum of the squares of the differences between the y-values of each ordered pair and the mean of the y-values of the ordered pairs.

2. See Selected Answers, page A83

3. $\Sigma(y_i - \hat{y}_i)^2$; the sum of the squares of the differences between the observed y-values and the predicted y-values.

4. See Selected Answers, page A83

5. 0.063; 6.3% of the variation is explained. 93.7% of the variation is unexplained.

6. 0.141; 14.1% of the variation is explained. 85.9% of the variation is unexplained.

7. 0.794; 79.4% of the variation is explained. 20.6% of the variation is unexplained.

8. 0.929; 92.9% of the variation is explained. 7.1% of the variation is unexplained.

9. (a) 0.817; 81.7% of the variation in proceeds can be explained by the variation in the number of issues and 18.3% of the variation is unexplained.

(b) $s_e \approx 6029.907$; the standard deviation of the proceeds for a specific number of issues is about $6,029,907,000.

Basic Skills and Concepts

In Exercises 1–3, use the graph at the right to answer the question.

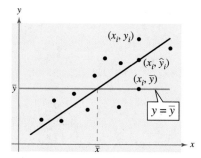

1. Use the graph to describe the total variation about a regression line in words and in symbols.

2. Use the graph to describe the explained variation about a regression line in words and in symbols.

3. Use the graph to describe the unexplained variation about a regression line in words and in symbols.

4. The coefficient of determination is the ratio of which two types of variations? What does the coefficient of determination measure?

Finding the Coefficient of Determination In Exercises 5–8, use the value of the linear correlation coefficient to calculate the coefficient of determination. What does this tell you about the explained variation of the data about the regression line? The unexplained variation?

5. $r = 0.250$

6. $r = -0.375$

7. $r = -0.891$

8. $r = 0.964$

Finding Types of Variations and the Coefficient of Determination In Exercises 9–16, find the (a) coefficient of determination and interpret the results, and (b) the standard error of estimate, s_e, and interpret the results.

9. The number of initial public offerings of stock issued in a recent 12-year period and the total proceeds of these offerings (in millions of U.S. dollars) are listed below. The equation of the regression line is

$$\hat{y} = 55.884x - 7189.033.$$

(Source: Securities Data Co.)

No. of issues, x	332	694	518	222	209	172
Proceeds, y	6284.8	17,738.8	16,745.7	6111.7	6082.0	4519.0

No. of issues, x	366	512	667	571	575	865
Proceeds, y	16,283.2	23,379.8	34,461.1	22,771.9	29,270.8	48,789.8

10. (a) 0.692; 69.2% of the variation in cigarettes exported from the United States can be explained by the variation in the number of cigarettes consumed in the United States and 30.8% of the variation is unexplained.

(b) $s_e \approx 17.285$; the standard deviation of the number of cigarettes exported for a specific number of cigarettes consumed is about 17,285,000,000.

11. (a) 0.985; 98.5% of the variation in sales can be explained by the variation in the total square footage and 1.5% of the variation is unexplained.

(b) $s_e \approx 35.652$; the standard deviation of the sales for a specific total square footage is about 35,652,000,000.

12. (a) 0.578; 57.8% of the variation in the median number of leisure hours per week can be explained by the variation in the median number of work hours per week and 42.2% of the variation is unexplained.

(b) $s_e \approx 2.013$; the standard deviation of the median number of leisure hours/week for a specific median number of work hours/week is about 2.013 hours.

13. (a) 0.998; 99.8% of the variation in the median weekly earnings of female workers can be explained by the variation in the median weekly earnings of male workers and 0.2% of the variation is unexplained.

(b) $s_e \approx 5.147$; the standard deviation of the median weekly earnings of female workers for a specific median weekly earnings of male workers is about $5.147.

10. The following table represents the number of cigarettes consumed (in billions) in the United States and the number of cigarettes exported (in billions) from the United States for seven years. The equation of the regression line is

$$\hat{y} = -1.535x + 968.999.$$

(Source: U.S. Department of Agriculture)

Cigarettes consumed in U.S., x	525	510	500	485	486	487	487
Cigarettes exported by U.S., y	164	179	206	196	220	231	244

11. The following table represents the total square footage (in billions) of retailing space at shopping centers and their sales (in billions of U.S. dollars) for 11 years. The equation of the regression line is

$$\hat{y} = 230.8x - 289.8.$$

(Source: International Council of Shopping Centers)

Total square footage, x	1.6	2.3	3.0	3.4	3.9	4.6
Sales, y	123.2	211.5	385.5	475.1	641.1	716.9

Total square footage, x	4.7	4.8	4.9	5.0	5.1
Sales, y	768.2	806.6	851.3	893.8	933.9

12. The median number of work hours per week and the median number of leisure hours per week for Americans for 10 recent years are shown below. The equation of the regression line is

$$\hat{y} = -0.646x + 50.734.$$

(Source: Louis Harris & Associates)

Median no. of work hrs. per week, x	40.6	43.1	46.9	47.3	46.8
Median no. of leisure hrs. per week, y	26.2	24.3	19.2	18.1	16.6

Median no. of work hrs. per week, x	48.7	50.0	50.7	50.6	50.8
Median no. of leisure hrs. per week, y	18.8	18.8	19.5	19.2	19.5

13. The following table represents median weekly earnings (in U.S. dollars) of full-time male and female workers for five years. The equation of the regression line is

$$\hat{y} = 0.898x - 82.291.$$

(Source: U.S. Bureau of Labor Statistics)

Median weekly earnings of male workers, x	312	419	485	538	557
Median weekly earnings of female workers, y	201	290	348	406	418

14. **(a)** 0.887; 88.7% of the variation in the turnout for federal elections can be explained by the variation in the voting age population and 11.3% of the variation is unexplained.
(b) $s_e \approx 3.747$; the standard deviation of the turnout in a federal election for a specified voting age population is about 3,747,000.

15. **(a)** 0.992; 99.2% of the variation in the money spent can be explained by the variation in the money raised and 0.8% of the variation is unexplained.
(b) $s_e \approx 16.079$; the standard deviation of the money spent for a specified amount of money raised is about $16,079,000.

16. **(a)** 0.877; 87.7% of the variation in bond and income funds can be explained by the variation in equity funds and 12.3% of the variation is unexplained.
(b) $s_e \approx 114.237$; the standard deviation of the bond and income funds for a specified equity fund is about $114,237,000,000.

17. ($17,935,784,000, $47,264,966,000); you can be 95% confident that the proceeds will be between $17,935,784,000 and $47,264,966,000 when the number of initial offerings is 712.

18. See Selected Answers, page A83

19. ($679,861,000,000, $817,739,000,000); you can be 90% confident that the sales will be between $679,861,000,000 and $817,739,000,000 when the total square footage is 4.5 billion.

20. See Selected Answers, page A83

---

14. The U.S. voting age population (in millions) and the turnout of the voting age population (in millions) for federal elections for eight recent years are listed in the table. The data can be modeled by the regression equation $\hat{y} = 0.373x + 26.473$. *(Source: Federal Election Commission)*

Voting age population, x	120.3	140.8	152.3	164.6
Turnout in federal elections, y	73.2	77.7	81.6	86.5

Voting age population, x	174.5	182.8	189.5	196.5
Turnout in federal elections, y	92.7	91.6	104.4	96.4

15. The money raised and spent (both in millions of U.S. dollars) by all congressional campaigns for eight recent years are shown in the table. The data can be modeled by the regression equation $\hat{y} = 1.020x - 25.854$. *(Source: Federal Election Commission)*

Money raised, x	354.7	397.2	472.0	477.6	471.7	659.3	740.5	790.5
Money spent, y	342.4	374.1	450.9	459.0	446.3	680.2	725.2	765.3

16. The following table represents the total assets (in billions of U.S. dollars) of equity funds and bond and income funds for nine years. The equation of the regression line is $\hat{y} = 0.689x + 68.861$. *(Source: Investment Company Institute)*

Equity funds, x	35.9	41.2	77.0	116.9	180.7
Bond and income funds, y	13.1	14	36.6	134.8	273.1

Equity funds, x	249.0	411.6	749.0	1269.0
Bond and income funds, y	304.8	441.4	761.1	798.3

Prediction Intervals   In Exercises 17–24, construct the indicated prediction interval and interpret the results.

17. Construct a 95% prediction interval for the proceeds from initial public offerings in Exercise 9 when the number of issues is 712.

18. Construct a 95% prediction interval for the cigarettes exported by the United States in Exercise 10 when the number of cigarettes consumed in the United States is 490 billion.

19. Using the results of Exercise 11, construct a 90% prediction interval for shopping center sales when the total square footage of shopping centers is 4.5 billion.

20. Using the results of Exercise 12, construct a 90% prediction interval for the median number of leisure hours per week when the median number of work hours per week is 45.1.

21. ($333.285, $400.133); you can be 99% confident that the median earnings of female workers will be between $333.285 and $400.133 when the median weekly earnings of male workers is $500.

22. (81.782 million, 112.904 million); you can be 99% confident that the voter turnout in federal elections will be between 81.782 million and 112.904 million when the voting age population is 190 million.

23. ($721.402 million, $809.522 million); you can be 95% confident that the money spent in congressional campaigns will be between $721.402 million and $809.522 million when the money raised is $775.8 million.

24. ($438.949 billion, $938.973 billion); you can be 90% confident that the total assets in bond and income funds will be between $438.949 billion and $938.973 billion when the total assets in equity funds is $900 billion.

25.

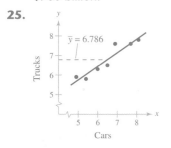

26. $\hat{y} = 0.693x + 2.280$

27. See Odd Answers, page A69

28. **(a)** 3.928 **(b)** 0.498
 (c) 4.429

29. 0.887 **30.** 0.316

31. (6.441, 8.237)

32. The slope and correlation coefficient will have the same sign because the denominators of both formulas are always positive while the numerators are always equal.

---

21. When the median weekly earnings of male workers is $500, find a 99% prediction interval for the median weekly earnings of female workers. Use the results of Exercise 13.

22. When the voting age population is 190 million, construct a 99% prediction interval for the voter turnout in federal elections. Use the results of Exercise 14.

23. A total of $775.8 million is raised in one year for congressional campaigns. Construct a prediction interval for the money spent by the campaigns. Use the results of Exercise 15 and $c = 0.95$.

24. The total assets in equity funds is $900 billion. Construct a prediction interval for the total assets in bond and income funds. Use the results of Exercise 16 and $c = 0.90$.

Extending the Basics

Old Vehicles In Exercises 25–31, use the information given at the right.

25. Construct a scatter plot of the data. Show $\bar{y}$ on the graph.

26. Find and graph the regression line.

27. Calculate the explained deviation, the unexplained deviation, and the total deviation for each data point.

28. Find the (a) explained variation, (b) unexplained variation, and (c) total variation.

29. Find the coefficient of determination. What can you conclude?

30. Find the standard error of estimate, s_e, and interpret the results.

31. Construct a 95% prediction interval for the median age of trucks in use when the median age of cars in use is 7.3.

32. ***Correlation Coefficient and Slope*** Recall that the formula for the correlation coefficient r is

$$r = \frac{n\Sigma xy - (\Sigma x)(\Sigma y)}{\sqrt{n\Sigma x^2 - (\Sigma x)^2}\sqrt{n\Sigma y^2 - (\Sigma y)^2}}$$

and the formula for the slope m of a regression line is

$$m = \frac{n\Sigma xy - (\Sigma x)(\Sigma y)}{n\Sigma x^2 - (\Sigma x)^2}.$$

Given a set of data, why must the slope m of the data's regression line always have the same sign as the data's correlation coefficient r?

Keeping cars longer.
The median age of vehicles on U.S. roads for seven different years:

Median age in years	
Cars, x	Trucks, y
8.1	7.8
7.7	7.6
6.5	6.5
6.9	7.6
6.0	6.3
5.4	5.8
4.9	5.9

Multiple Regression

Finding a Multiple Regression Equation • Predicting y-Values

What You Should Learn

- How to use technology to find a multiple regression equation
- How to use a multiple regression equation to predict y-values

Finding a Multiple Regression Equation

In many instances, a better prediction model can be found for a dependent (response) variable by using more than one independent (explanatory) variable. For example, a more accurate prediction for the company sales discussed in previous sections might be made by considering the number of employees on the sales staff as well as the advertising expenditures. Models that contain more than one independent variable are multiple regression models.

Insight

Because the mathematics associated with multiple regression is complicated, this section focuses on how to use technology to find a multiple regression equation and how to interpret the results.

> **DEFINITION**
>
> A multiple regression equation has the form
>
> $$\hat{y} = b + m_1x_1 + m_2x_2 + m_3x_3 + \cdots + m_kx_k$$
>
> where $x_1, x_2, x_3, \ldots, x_k$ are the independent variables and y is the dependent variable.

The y-intercept b is the value of y when all x_i are 0. Each coefficient m_i is the amount of change in y when the independent variable x_i is changed by one unit and all other independent variables are held constant.

▶ **EXAMPLE 1** *Finding a Multiple Regression Equation*

A researcher wants to determine how employee salaries at a certain company are related to the length of employment, previous experience, and education. The researcher selects eight employees from the company and obtains the following data.

Employee	Salary, y	Employment (in years), x_1	Experience (in years), x_2	Education (in years), x_3
A	37,310	10	2	16
B	37,380	5	6	16
C	34,135	3	1	12
D	36,985	6	5	14
E	38,715	8	8	16
F	40,620	20	0	12
G	39,200	8	4	18
H	40,320	14	6	17

Use Minitab to find a multiple regression equation that models the data.

SOLUTION Enter the y-values in C1 and the x_1-, x_2-, and x_3-values in C2, C3, and C4, respectively. Select "Regression▶Regression ..." from the Stat menu. Using the salaries as the response variable and the remaining data as the predictors, you should obtain results similar to the following.

Regression Analysis

The regression equation is
Salary, y = 29764 + 364 x1 + 228 x2 + 267 x3

Predictor	Coef	StDev	T	P
Constant	29764	1981	15.02	0.000
x1	364.41 m_1	48.32	7.54	0.002
x2	227.6 m_2	123.8	1.84	0.140
x3	266.9 m_3	147.4	1.81	0.144

S = 659.5   R-Sq = 94.4%   R-Sq(adj) = 90.2%

The regression equation is $\hat{y} = 29{,}764 + 364x_1 + 228x_2 + 267x_3$.

Try It Yourself 1

A statistics professor wants to determine how students' final grades are related to the midterm exam grades and number of classes missed. The professor selects 10 students from her class and obtains the following data.

Student	Final Grade, y	Midterm Exam, x_1	Classes Missed, x_2
1	81	75	1
2	90	80	0
3	86	91	2
4	76	80	3
5	51	62	6
6	75	90	4
7	44	60	7
8	81	82	2
9	94	88	0
10	93	96	1

Use technology to find a multiple regression equation that models the data.

a. *Enter* the data.
b. *Calculate* the regression line.   *Answer: Page A42* ◀

Minitab displays much more than the regression equation and the coefficients of the independent variables. For example, it also displays the standard error of estimate, denoted by S, and the coefficient of determination, denoted by R-Sq. In Example 1, S $= 659.5$ and R-Sq $= 94.4\%$. So, the standard error of estimate is $659.50. The coefficient of determination tells you that 94.4% of the variation in y can be explained by the multiple regression model. The remaining 5.6% is unexplained and is due to other factors or chance.

Predicting y-Values

After finding the equation of the multiple regression line, you can use the equation to predict y-values over the range of the data. To predict y-values, substitute the given value for each independent variable into the equation, then calculate y.

Use the regression equation found in Example 1 to predict an employee's salary given the following conditions.

1. 12 years of current employment, 5 years of experience, and 16 years of education

2. 4 years of current employment, 20 years of experience, and 12 years of education

SOLUTION To predict each employee's salary, substitute the values for x_1, x_2, and x_3 into the regression equation. Then calculate y.

1. $\hat{y} = 29{,}764 + 364x_1 + 228x_2 + 267x_3$
   $= 29{,}764 + 364(12) + 228(5) + 267(16)$
   $= 39{,}544$

   The employee's predicted salary is $39,544.

2. $\hat{y} = 29{,}764 + 364x_1 + 228x_2 + 267x_3$
   $= 29{,}764 + 364(4) + 228(20) + 267(12)$
   $= 38{,}984$

   The employee's predicted salary is $38,984.

Picturing the World

In a lake in Finland, 159 fish of seven species were caught and measured for weight G, length L, height H, and width W (as percents of L). The following scatter plot shows the relationship between G and L. The regression equation for this is

$$G = -459 + 32.8\,L,$$

$$r = 0.917.$$

Using all four variables, the regression equation is

$$G = -719 + 6.19L + 6.44H + 32.5W,$$

$$r = 0.932.$$

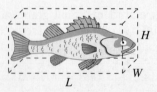

Predict the weight of a fish with the following measurements: L = 40, H = 17, and W = 11. How do your predictions vary when you use a single variable versus many variables? Which do you think is more accurate?

Try It Yourself 2

Use the regression equation found in Try It Yourself 1 to predict a student's final grade given the following conditions.

1. A student has a midterm exam score of 89 and misses 1 class.
2. A student has a midterm exam score of 78 and misses 3 classes.

a. *Substitute* the midterm score for x_1 into the regression equation.
b. *Substitute* the corresponding number of missed classes for x_2 into the regression equation.
c. *Calculate* y.
d. What is each student's final grade? *Answer: Page A42* ◀

9.4 EXERCISES

HELP

StatPro 9.4

Internet Statistics 9.4

Student Solutions Manual 9.4

Videos 9.4

Try It Yourself Answers 9.4

1. (a) 2614.6
   (b) 2298
   (c) 2680
   (d) 2233
2. (a) 6829.22
   (b) 9945.34
   (c) 7657.58
   (d) 6377.60
3. (a) 7.5
   (b) 16.8
   (c) 51.9
   (d) 62.1
4. (a) 2.335
   (b) 1.5508
   (c) 2.1977
   (d) 1.3239

Basic Skills and Concepts

Predicting y-Values In Exercises 1–4, use the multiple regression equation to predict the *y*-values for the given values of the independent variables.

1. The equation used to predict peanut yield (in pounds) is

$$\hat{y} = 6503 - 14.8x_1 + 12.2x_2$$

where x_1 is the number of acres planted (in thousands) and x_2 is the number of acres harvested (in thousands). *(Source: U.S. National Agricultural Statistics Service)*
   (a) $x_1 = 1458, \; x_2 = 1450$ (b) $x_1 = 1500, \; x_2 = 1475$
   (c) $x_1 = 1400, \; x_2 = 1385$ (d) $x_1 = 1525, \; x_2 = 1500$

2. To predict the annual rice yield (in pounds), use the equation

$$\hat{y} = 859 + 5.76x_1 + 3.82x_2$$

where x_1 is the number of acres planted (in thousands) and x_2 is the number of acres harvested (in inches). *(Source: U.S. National Agricultural Statistics Service)*
   (a) $x_1 = 2532, \; x_2 = 2255$ (b) $x_1 = 3581, \; x_2 = 3021$
   (c) $x_1 = 3213, \; x_2 = 3065$ (d) $x_1 = 2758, \; x_2 = 2714$

3. The volume (in cubic feet) of black cherry trees can be modeled by the equation

$$\hat{y} = -52.2 + 0.3x_1 + 4.5x_2$$

where x_1 is the tree's height (in feet) and x_2 is the tree's diameter (in inches).
   (a) $x_1 = 70, \; x_2 = 8.6$ (b) $x_1 = 65, \; x_2 = 11.0$
   (c) $x_1 = 83, \; x_2 = 17.6$ (d) $x_1 = 87, \; x_2 = 19.6$

4. The earnings per share (in dollars) for McDonald's Corporation are given by the equation

$$\hat{y} = -0.396 + 0.186x_1 + 0.071x_2$$

where x_1 represents total revenue (in billions of dollars) and x_2 represents total net worth (in billions of dollars). *(Source: McDonald's Corporation)*
   (a) $x_1 = 11.4, \; x_2 = 8.6$ (b) $x_1 = 8.1, \; x_2 = 6.2$
   (c) $x_1 = 10.7, \; x_2 = 8.5$ (d) $x_1 = 7.3, \; x_2 = 5.1$

Finding a Multiple Regression Equation In Exercises 5 and 6, use technology to find the multiple regression equation for the data given in the table. Then answer the following.
   (a) What is the standard error of estimate?
   (b) What is the coefficient of determination?
   (c) Interpret the results of (a) and (b).

5. $\hat{y} = -256.293 + 103.502x_1$
$\quad + 14.649x_2$

(a) 34.16

(b) 0.988

(c) The standard deviation of the predicted sales given a specific total square footage and number of shopping centers is \$34.16 billion. The multiple regression model explains 98.8% of the variation in y.

6. $\hat{y} = 0.821 + 0.092x_1 + 0.139x_2$

(a) 0.1924

(b) 0.998

(c) The standard deviation of the predicted equity given a specific net sales and total assets is \$0.1924 billion. The multiple regression model explains 99.8% of the variation in y.

7. 0.985

8. 0.997

 5. The total square footage (in billions) of retailing space at shopping centers, the number (in thousands) of shopping centers, and the sales (in billions of U.S. dollars) for shopping centers for a recent 11-year period are listed in the table. *(Source: International Council of Shopping Centers)*

Sales, y	Total square footage, x_1	Number of shopping centers, x_2
123.2	1.6	13.2
211.5	2.3	17.5
385.5	3.0	22.1
475.1	3.4	25.5
641.1	3.9	32.6
716.9	4.6	38.0
768.2	4.7	39.0
806.6	4.8	39.6
851.3	4.9	40.4
893.8	5.0	41.2
933.9	5.1	42.1

6. The following table represents the net sales (in billions of dollars), total assets (in billions of dollars), and shareholder's equity (in billions of dollars) for Wal-Mart for a recent six-year period. *(Source: Wal-Mart Annual Reports)*

Shareholder's equity, y	Net sales, x_1	Total assets, x_2
5.4	32.6	11.4
7.0	43.9	15.4
8.8	55.5	20.6
10.8	67.3	26.4
12.7	82.5	32.8
14.8	93.6	37.5

Extending the Basics

Adjusted r^2 The calculation of r^2, the coefficient of determination, depends on the number of data pairs and the number of variables. An adjusted value of r^2 can be calculated, based on the number of degrees of freedom, as follows.

$$r^2_{adj} = 1 - \left[\frac{(1 - r^2)(n - 1)}{n - k - 1} \right],$$

where n is the number of data pairs and k is the number of independent variables

In Exercises 7 and 8, after calculating r^2_{adj}, determine the percentage of the variation in y that can be explained by the relationships between variables according to r^2_{adj}. Compare this result to the one obtained with r^2.

7. Calculate r^2_{adj} for the data in Exercise 5.

8. Calculate r^2_{adj} for the data in Exercise 6.

TECHNOLOGY   MINITAB   EXCEL   TI-83

Federal Trade Commission

Tar, Nicotine, and Carbon Monoxide

Each year, the Federal Trade Commission tests the tar, nicotine, and carbon monoxide content of the various brands of cigarettes manufactured in the United States. The testing is conducted by the Tobacco Testing Institute Laboratory using methods approved by the FTC. The complete report of the more than 1200 brands tested each year is available free from the FTC.

In the table at the right, we chose 22 different brands and styles of cigarettes. We included some with high levels of tar, nicotine, and carbon monoxide and some with low levels. The numbers in the table are as follows.

T = tar in mg
N = nicotine in mg
W = weight in g
C = carbon monoxide in mg

www.FTC.gov

Brand	T	N	W	C
Alpine	16	1.0	0.99	15
Benson & Hedges	15	1.1	1.09	15
Camel	9	0.7	0.93	11
Carlton	5	0.5	0.95	3
Chesterfield	23	1.3	0.89	15
Kent	12	0.9	0.92	12
Kool	16	1.2	0.94	15
L&M	13	0.9	0.89	13
Lark	11	0.9	0.96	11
Marlboro	15	1.0	0.93	14
Merit	9	0.7	0.97	10
Newport Lights	9	0.8	0.85	10
Now	1	0.1	0.79	2
Old Gold	16	1.2	0.92	17
Pall Mall	10	0.9	1.04	12
Raleigh	15	1.0	0.96	15
Salem Ultra	4	0.4	0.91	6
Tareyton	14	1.0	1.01	14
True	5	0.5	0.98	6
Viceroy	10	0.8	0.97	10
Virginia Slims	15	1.1	0.95	13
Winston	11	0.8	1.12	13

Exercises

1. Use a technology tool to draw a scatter plot of the following (x, y) pairs in the data set.
(a) (tar, nicotine)
(b) (tar, weight)
(c) (tar, carbon monoxide)
(d) (nicotine, weight)
(e) (nicotine, carbon monoxide)
(f) (weight, carbon monoxide)

2. From the scatter plots in Exercise 1, which pairs of variables appear to have a strong correlation?

3. Use a technology tool to find the correlation coefficient for each pair of variables in Exercise 1. Which has the strongest correlation?

4. Use a technology tool to find the regression line for the following variables.
(a) (tar, nicotine)
(b) (tar, carbon monoxide)

5. Use the results of Exercise 4 to predict the following.
(a) The nicotine content of a cigarette that has a tar content of 13 mg
(b) The carbon monoxide content of a cigarette that has a tar content of 13 mg

6. Use a technology tool to find the multiple regression equations of the following form.
(a) $T = b + m_1 N + m_2 W + m_3 C$
(b) $T = b + m_1 N + m_2 C$

7. Use the results of Exercise 6 to predict the tar content of a cigarette that has 1.0 mg of nicotine and 10 mg of carbon monoxide.

Extended solutions are given in the *Technology Supplement*.
Technical instruction is provided for Minitab and Excel.

▼ **9** **CHAPTER SUMMARY**

What did you learn?

	Review Exercises
• How to find a correlation coefficient *(Section 9.1)*	*1, 2*
• How to perform a hypothesis test for a population correlation coefficient ρ *(Section 9.1)*	*3–6*
• How to find the equation of a regression line *(Section 9.2)*	*7, 8*
• How to predict *y*-values using a regression equation *(Section 9.2)*	*9, 10*
• How to find and interpret the coefficient of determination *(Section 9.3)*	*11–14*
• How to find and interpret the standard error of estimate for a regression line *(Section 9.3)*	*15, 16*
• How to construct and interpret a prediction interval for *y* *(Section 9.3)*	*17–20*
• How to use technology to find a multiple regression equation *(Section 9.4)*	*21, 22*
• How to use a multiple regression equation to predict *y*-values *(Section 9.4)*	*23, 24*

Why did you learn it? Uses and Abuses

Uses You will often want to determine whether there is a relationship between two variables. If this relationship is significant, you will be able to use one of the variables (designated as the explanatory or independent variable) to predict the value of the other variable.

For example, educators have used correlation and regression analysis to determine that there is a significant correlation between a student's SAT score and the grade point average from a student's freshman year at college. Consequently, many colleges and universities use SAT scores of high school applicants as a predictor of the applicant's initial success at college.

Abuses The most common abuse of the material in this chapter is to confuse the concepts of correlation and causation. In many cases, it is easy to distinguish these two concepts, because your intuition tells you that one variable doesn't cause the other. For instance, if you performed a study in which you found a positive correlation between children's heights and their reading ability, you would not be inclined to believe that either variable "caused" the other. But, if you performed a study in which you found a negative correlation between taking vitamin C and catching a cold, you might be tempted to conclude that taking vitamin C "causes" a person to not catch a cold. While this might be true, the point is that your study did not prove it.

9 REVIEW EXERCISES

1.

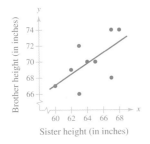

Age (in years)

$r \approx -0.939$; negative linear correlation; milk production decreases with age.

2. See Selected Answers, page A84

3. $H_0: \rho = 0$ and $H_a: \rho \neq 0$

$CV = \pm 1.711$

$t = 1.211$

Fail to reject H_0.

4. $H_0: \rho = 0$ and $H_a: \rho \neq 0$

$CV = \pm 2.086$

$t = -2.945$

Reject H_0.

5. $H_0: \rho = 0$ and $H_a: \rho \neq 0$

$CV = \pm 2.447$

$t = -6.688$

Reject H_0.

6. $H_0: \rho = 0$ and $H_a: \rho \neq 0$

$CV = \pm 4.032$

$t = 7.034$

Reject H_0.

7. $\hat{y} = 0.679x + 26.345$

Brother height (in inches)

Sister height (in inches)

$r \approx 0.625$

In Exercises 1 and 2, organize the data in a scatter plot. Then find the sample correlation coefficient, *r*. Determine whether there is a positive linear correlation, negative linear correlation, or no linear correlation between the variables. What can you conclude?

1. The ages of eight cows (in years) and their milk production (in gallons) per week

Age, x	4	4	6	7	7	8	10	11
Milk production, y	37.0	35.4	33.3	33.1	32.3	33.7	30.2	29.6

2. The annual per capita sugar consumption (in kilograms) and the average number of cavities of 11- and 12-year-old children in seven countries

Sugar, x	2.1	5.0	6.3	6.5	7.7	8.7	11.6
Cavities, y	0.59	1.51	1.55	1.70	2.18	2.10	2.43

In Exercises 3 and 4, use the given sample statistics to test the claim about the population correlation coefficient, ρ, at the indicated level of significance α for the given sample statistics.

3. Claim: $\rho = 0$, $\alpha = 0.10$. Sample statistics: $r = 0.24$, $n = 26$

4. Claim: $\rho \neq 0$, $\alpha = 0.05$. Sample statistics: $r = -0.55$, $n = 22$

In Exercises 5 and 6, test the claim about the population correlation coefficient, ρ, at the indicated level of significance α. Then interpret the decision in the context of the original claim.

5. Refer to the data in Exercise 1. At $\alpha = 0.05$, test the claim that there is a linear correlation between a cow's age and milk production.

6. Refer to the data in Exercise 2. Is there enough evidence to conclude that there is no linear correlation between sugar consumption and tooth decay? Use $\alpha = 0.01$.

In Exercises 7 and 8, use the data to find the equation of the regression line. Then construct a scatter plot of the data and draw the regression line. Can you make a guess about the sign and magnitude of *r*? Calculate *r* and check your guess.

7. The heights in inches of adult brothers and sisters from nine families

Sister, x	65	62	63	68	63	67	64	60	67
Brother, y	70	69	66	74	72	74	70	67	68

8. $\hat{y} = -0.090x + 44.675$

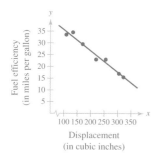

$r \approx -0.984$

9. (a) 67.764

(b) 71.159

(c) Not meaningful

10. (a) Not meaningful

(b) 26.855

(c) 18.665

(d) Not meaningful

11. 0.306

12. 0.925

13. 0.033

14. 0.548

15. (a) 0.897; 89.7% of the variation in y is explained by the model.

(b) 568.0; the standard error of the cooling capacity for a specific living area is 568.0 BTU/hr.

16. (a) 0.397; 39.7% of the variation in y is explained by the model.

(b) 101.0; the standard error of the price for a specific area is $101.

8. The engine displacement (in cubic inches) and the fuel economy (in miles per gallon) of seven automobiles

Displacement, x	170	134	220	305	109	256	322
Fuel efficiency, y	29.5	34.5	23.0	17.0	33.5	23.0	15.5

In Exercises 9 and 10, use the regression equations found in Exercises 7 and 8 to predict the value of y for each value of x, if meaningful. If not, explain why not.

9. Refer to Exercise 7. What height would you predict for a male whose sister is (a) 61 in.? (b) 66 in.? (c) 71 in.?

10. Refer to Exercise 8. What fuel efficiency rating would you predict for a car with an engine displacement of (a) 86 in.^{3}? (b) 198 in.^{3}? (c) 289 in.^{3}? (d) 407 in.^{3}?

In Exercises 11–14, use the value of the linear correlation coefficient, r, to find the coefficient of determination. Interpret the result.

11. $r = -0.553$ **12.** $r = -0.962$

13. $r = 0.181$ **14.** $r = 0.740$

In Exercises 15 and 16, use the data to (a) find the coefficient of determination, r^2, and interpret the result with regard to the regression line, and (b) find the standard error of estimate, s_e, and interpret the result.

15. The following table shows the area of eight living spaces (in square feet) and the cooling capacity (in Btu per hour) of the air conditioners used in those spaces. The regression equation is $\hat{y} = 3003.0 + 9.468x$. (*Adapted from Consumer Reports*)

Living area, x	730	485	205	420	550	590	385	630
Cooling capacity, y	10,200	7000	5300	6800	7250	9000	6900	9400

16. The following table shows the prices of 16 gas grills (in U.S. dollars) and their usable cooking area (in square inches). The regression equation is $\hat{y} = -209.5 + 1.3052x$. (*Source: Consumer Reports*)

Area, x	430	338	426	446	465	372	305	403
Price, y	480	360	570	450	350	250	175	200

Area, x	389	424	306	424	309	386	328	261
Price, y	270	270	200	200	180	200	190	150

17. $65.01 < y < 74.592$

18. $17.567 < y < 24.083$

19. $8184.33 < y < 11,455.59$

20. $88.15 < y < 537.01$

21. $\hat{y} = 6.317 + 0.8217x_1 + 0.031x_2 - 0.004x_3$

22. $s_e = 0.9139$
$r^2 = 0.942$

23. (a) 21.705
(b) 25.210
(c) 30.100
(d) 25.860

24. (a) 16.111
(b) 8.448
(c) 15.729
(d) 9.844

In Exercises 17–20, construct the indicated prediction intervals.

17. Construct a 90% prediction interval for the height of a brother in Exercise 7 whose sister is 64 inches tall.

18. Construct a 90% prediction interval for the fuel efficiency of an automobile in Exercise 8 that has an engine displacement of 265 cubic inches.

19. Construct a 95% prediction interval for the cooling capacity of an air conditioner in Exercise 15 that is used in a living area of 720 square feet.

20. Construct a 95% prediction interval for the price of a gas grill in Exercise 16 with a usable cooking area of 400 square inches.

In Exercises 21 and 22, refer to the following information. The table shows the tar, nicotine, weight, and carbon monoxide content, all in milligrams, of 13 brands of U.S. cigarettes. (*Source: Federal Trade Commission*)

Carbon monoxide, y	Tar, x_1	Nicotine, x_2	Weight, x_3
13.6	14.1	0.86	985.3
16.6	16.0	1.06	1093.8
10.2	8.0	0.67	928.0
5.4	4.1	0.40	946.2
15.0	15.0	1.04	888.5
9.0	8.8	0.76	1026.7
12.3	12.4	0.95	922.5
16.3	16.6	1.12	937.2
15.4	14.9	1.02	885.8
13.0	13.7	1.01	964.3
14.4	15.1	0.90	931.6
10.0	7.8	0.57	970.5
10.2	11.4	0.78	1124.0

21. Use technology to find the multiple regression equation from the table data.

22. Find the standard error of estimate s_e and the coefficient of determination r^2. What percentage of the variation of y can be explained by the regression equation?

In Exercises 23 and 24, use the multiple regression equation to predict the value of y for the given values of the independent variables.

23. An equation that can be used to predict fuel economy (in miles per gallon) for automobiles is $\hat{y} = 41.3 - 0.004x_1 - 0.0049x_2$, where x_1 is the engine displacement (in cubic inches) and x_2 is the vehicle weight (in pounds).
(a) $x_1 = 305, x_2 = 3750$
(b) $x_1 = 225, x_2 = 3100$
(c) $x_1 = 105, x_2 = 2200$
(d) $x_1 = 185, x_2 = 3000$

24. Use the regression equation found in Exercise 21.
(a) $x_1 = 16.5, x_2 = 0.69, x_3 = 946.4$ (b) $x_1 = 7.2, x_2 = 0.55, x_3 = 950.5$
(c) $x_1 = 16.1, x_2 = 0.88, x_3 = 961.2$ (d) $x_1 = 9.7, x_2 = 0.99, x_3 = 1118.6$

9 ▼ CHAPTER QUIZ

1.

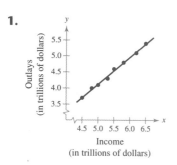

Income
(in trillions of dollars)

The data appear to have a positive correlation. The out-lays increase as the incomes increase.

2. 0.997

3. $H_0: \rho = 0$ and $H_a: \rho \neq 0$

$CV = \pm 2.447$

$t = 31.552$

Reject H_0.

4. $\hat{y} = 0.838x - 0.069$

5. 4.372

6. 0.995; $r^2 = 0.995 \rightarrow 99.5\%$ of the variation in y is explained by the regression model.

7. $0.046 trillion; the standard deviation of personal outlays for a specified personal income is $0.046 trillion.

8. ($5.16 trillion, $5.43 trillion)

9. (a) 1311.150

(b) 961.110

(c) 1120.900

(d) 1386.740

x_2 has the greatest influence on y.

Take this quiz as you would take a quiz in class. After you are done, check your work against the answers given in the back of the book.

For Exercises 1–8, refer to the data in the following table. The table lists the personal income and outlays (both in trillions of dollars) for Americans for eight recent years. *(Source: U.S. Commerce Department, Bureau of Economic Analysis)*

Personal income, x	4.5	4.8	5.0	5.3	5.5	5.8	6.2	6.5
Personal outlays, y	3.7	4.0	4.1	4.3	4.6	4.8	5.1	5.4

1. Construct a scatter plot for the data. Do the data appear to have a positive linear correlation, a negative linear correlation, or no linear correlation? Explain.

2. Calculate the correlation coefficient, r. What can you conclude?

3. Test the level of significance of the correlation coefficient, r. Use a two-tailed test with $\alpha = 0.05$.

4. Find the equation of the regression line for the data. Include the regression line in the scatter plot.

5. Use the regression line to predict the personal outlays when the personal income is 5.3 trillion dollars.

6. Find the coefficient of determination and interpret the results.

7. Find the standard error of estimate, s_e, and interpret the results.

8. Construct a 95% prediction interval for personal outlays when personal income is 6.4 trillion dollars. Interpret the results.

9. The equation used to predict sunflower yield (in pounds) is $\hat{y} = 1257 - 1.34x_1 + 1.41x_2$, where x_1 is the number of acres planted (in thousands) and x_2 is the number of acres harvested (in thousands). Use the regression equation to predict the y-values for the given values of the independent variables listed below. Then determine which variable has a greater influence on the value of y. *(Source: U.S. National Agricultural Statistics Service)*

(a) $x_1 = 2103, x_2 = 2037$ (b) $x_1 = 3387, x_2 = 3009$

(c) $x_1 = 2185, x_2 = 1980$ (d) $x_1 = 3485, x_2 = 3404$

9 CUMULATIVE TEST

Take this test as you would take a test in class. After you are done, check your work against the answers given in the back of the book.

For Exercises 1–4, refer to the following information. A rice grower's association claims that the mean consumption of rice by Americans is at least 20.1 pounds per year. A sample of 73 people has a mean consumption of rice of 18.9 pounds per year and a standard deviation of 6.7 pounds. *(Adapted from U.S. Department of Agriculture)*

1. At $\alpha = 0.01$, test the claim made by the rice grower's association. What can you conclude?

2. Describe the conditions for which a type I or type II error occurs for the hypothesis test in Exercise 1.

3. A corn grower's association studied 102 people and found that their mean consumption of corn products was 22.7 pounds and the standard deviation was 7.6 pounds. At $\alpha = 0.05$, test the claim that the mean consumption of corn products is the same as the mean consumption of rice. What can you conclude? *(Adapted from U.S. Department of Agriculture)*

4. Which distribution did you use to perform the hypothesis test in (a) Exercise 1 and (b) Exercise 3? Why?

For Exercises 5–10, use the following table. The table lists the number of acres (in thousands) of rice planted and harvested in the United States for eight years. *(Source: U.S. National Agriculture Statistics Service)*

| Acres planted, x | 2897 | 2884 | 3176 | 2920 | 3353 | 3121 | 2819 | 3056 |
| Acres harvested, y | 2823 | 2781 | 3132 | 2833 | 3316 | 3093 | 2799 | 3034 |

5. Calculate the correlation coefficient, r, and determine whether there is a positive linear correlation, negative linear correlation, or no linear correlation between the variables. What can you conclude?

6. Find the equation of the regression line for the given data. Graph a scatter plot of the data and the regression line.

7. Find the coefficient of determination and interpret the results.

8. Find the standard error of estimate, s_e, and interpret the results.

9. Construct a 95% prediction interval for the number of acres of rice harvested when the number of acres of rice planted is 3100 thousand acres. Interpret the results.

10. At $\alpha = 0.01$, test the claim that there is no linear correlation between the number of acres of rice planted and the number of acres of rice harvested.

Answers

1. H_0: $\mu \geq 20.1$ (claim)
   H_a: $\mu < 20.1$
   $z_0 = -2.33$
   $z = -1.530$
   Fail to reject H_0.

2. Type I error will occur if H_0 is rejected when $\mu \geq 20.1$. Type II error will occur if H_0 is not rejected when $\mu < 20.1$.

3. H_0: $\mu_1 - \mu_2 = 0$ (claim)
   H_a: $\mu_1 - \mu_2 \neq 0$
   $z_0 = \pm 1.96$
   $z \approx -3.496$
   Reject H_0.

4. (a) Standard normal distribution
   (b) Standard normal distribution

5. 0.989

6. $\hat{y} = 1.071x - 268.253$

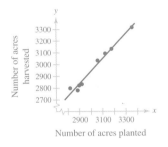

7. 0.978; $r^2 = 0.978 \rightarrow 97.8\%$ of the variation in y is explained by the model.

8. 31.46 thousand

9. (2969.4 thousand, 3134.3 thousand)

10. H_0: $\rho = 0$ and H_a: $\rho \neq 0$
    $CV = \pm 3.707$
    $t = 16.378$
    Reject H_0.

Where You've Been

As part of the New Car Assessment Program, the government buys new cars each year and crashes them into a wall at 35 miles per hour to compare how different vehicles protect passengers in a head-on collision. To measure the forces and impacts that occur during a crash test, dummies are equipped with special instruments and placed in the car. The crash test results include data on head, chest, and leg injuries. For a low crash test number, the injury potential in a 35 miles per hour frontal crash is low. If the crash test number is high, then the injury potential is high. Using the techniques of Chapter 8, you can determine if the mean chest injury potential is the same for pickups and vans. The sample statistics are as follows. *(Source: National Highway Traffic Safety Administration)*

Vehicle	Number	Mean chest injury	Standard deviation
Vans	$n_1 = 30$	$\bar{x}_1 = 54.2$	$s_1 = 12.1$
Pickups	$n_2 = 36$	$\bar{x}_2 = 50.6$	$s_2 = 8.94$

For the means of chest injury, the *P*-value for the hypothesis that $\mu_1 = \mu_2$ is about 0.177. At $\alpha = 0.05$, you fail to reject the null hypothesis. So, you do not have enough evidence to conclude that there is a significant difference in the means of the chest injury potential in a 35 miles per hour frontal crash for vans and pickups.

Federal law requires all passenger cars to pass a 30-mph frontal crash test. These tests are conducted through the New Car Assessment Program, in which the federal government buys brand new vehicles directly off a lot and crashes them. Results of these tests are classified using a one- to five-star rating, with one star indicating the least protection and five stars the most protection.

Chi-Square Tests and the *F*-Distribution

Where You're Going

In Chapter 8, you learned how to test a hypothesis that compares two populations by basing your decisions on sample statistics and their distributions. In this chapter, you will learn how to test a hypothesis that compares three or more populations.

For instance, in addition to the crash tests for vans and pickups, a third group of vehicles was also tested. The results for these light vehicles (for example, Ford Escort) are as follows.

Vehicle	Number	Mean chest injury	Standard deviation
Light	$n_3 = 35$	$\bar{x}_3 = 46.4$	$s_3 = 6.90$

From these three samples, is there evidence of a difference in chest injury potential among vans, pickups, and light vehicles in a 35-mph frontal crash?

In this chapter, you will learn that you can answer this question by testing the hypothesis that the three means are equal. For the means of chest injury, the *P*-value for the hypothesis that $\mu_1 = \mu_2 = \mu_3$ is about 0.005. At $\alpha = 0.05$, you can reject the null hypothesis. So, you can conclude that for the three types of vehicles tested, at least one of the means of the chest injury potential in a 35 miles per hour frontal crash is different from the others.

10.1

Goodness of Fit

The Chi-Square Goodness-of-Fit Test

What You Should Learn

- *How to use the chi-square distribution to test whether a frequency distribution fits a claimed distribution*

The Chi-Square Goodness-of-Fit Test

Suppose a marketing executive is planning a new advertising campaign and wants to determine the proportions of radio music listeners in a specific broadcast region who prefer each of six types of music. To determine these proportions, the executive can perform a multinomial experiment. A **multinomial experiment** is a probability experiment consisting of a fixed number of trials in which there are more than two possible outcomes for each independent trial. The probability for each outcome is fixed and each outcome is classified into **categories.** (Remember from Section 4.2 that a **binomial** experiment has only two possible outcomes.)

Now, suppose the marketing executive wants to determine whether a radio station's claim concerning the distribution of proportions of music preferences is correct. To do so, the executive could compare the distribution of proportions obtained in the multinomial experiment to the radio station's specified distribution. How can the executive compare the distributions? The answer is, perform a chi-square goodness-of-fit test.

> **DEFINITION**
>
> A **chi-square goodness-of-fit test** is used to test whether a frequency distribution fits an expected distribution.

Insight

The hypothesis tests described in Sections 10.1 and 10.2 can be used for qualitative data.

To begin a goodness-of-fit test, you must first state a null and an alternative hypothesis. Generally, the null hypothesis states that the frequency distribution fits the specified distribution and the alternative hypothesis states that the frequency distribution does not fit the specified distribution.

For example, suppose the radio station claims that the distribution of music preferences for listeners in the broadcast region is as shown at the right. To test the radio station's claim, the executive can perform a chi-square goodness-of-fit test using the following null and alternative hypotheses.

Distribution of music preferences	
Classical	4%
Country	36%
Gospel	11%
Oldies	2%
Pop	18%
Rock	29%

H_0: The distribution of music preferences in the broadcast region is 4% classical, 36% country, 11% gospel, 2% oldies, 18% pop, and 29% rock. (Claim)

H_a: The distribution of music preferences differs from the claimed or expected distribution.

To calculate the test statistic for the chi-square goodness-of-fit test, you can use observed frequencies and expected frequencies. To calculate the expected frequencies, you must assume the null hypothesis is true.

Picturing the World

How often do motorists see a driver run a red traffic light? According to the distribution in the following display, 26% of all motorists see at least one driver run a red traffic light daily.

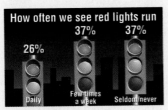

How often we see red lights run

37%   37%

26%

Daily   Few times a week   Seldom/never

Copyright 1997, USA TODAY.
Reprinted with permission.

A sample of 268 motorists is asked how often they see drivers run red traffic lights: daily, a few times per week, or seldom/never. What is the expected frequency for each response?

DEFINITION

The **observed frequency, O,** of a category is the frequency for the category observed in the sample data.

The **expected frequency, E,** of a category is the *calculated* frequency for the category. Expected frequencies are obtained assuming the specified (or hypothesized) distribution. The expected frequency for the *i*th category is

$$E_i = np_i$$

where *n* is the number of trials (the sample size) and p_i is the assumed probability of the *i*th category.

▶ **EXAMPLE 1**   *Finding Observed Frequencies and Expected Frequencies*

A marketing executive randomly selects 500 music listeners from the broadcast region and asks each whether he or she prefers classical, country, gospel, oldies, pop, or rock music. The results are listed at the right. Find the observed frequencies and the expected frequencies for each type of music.

Survey results ($n = 500$)	
Classical	8
Country	210
Gospel	72
Oldies	10
Pop	75
Rock	125

SOLUTION   The observed frequency for each type of music is the number of music listeners naming a particular type of music. The expected frequency for each type of music is the product of the number of listeners in the survey and the probability that a listener will name a particular type of music. The observed frequencies and expected frequencies are listed in the following table.

Type of music	% of listeners	Observed frequency	Expected frequency
Classical	4%	8	500(0.04) = 20
Country	36%	210	500(0.36) = 180
Gospel	11%	72	500(0.11) = 55
Oldies	2%	10	500(0.02) = 10
Pop	18%	75	500(0.18) = 90
Rock	29%	125	500(0.29) = 145

Insight

The sum of the expected frequencies always equals the sum of the observed frequencies. For instance, in Example 1 the sum of the observed frequencies and the sum of the expected frequencies are both 500.

Try It Yourself 1

Suppose the executive randomly selects 300 music listeners in the listening region. Find the expected frequencies for each type of music.

a. Multiply 300 by the probability that a listener will name a particular type of music.

Answer: Page A42

To use the chi-square goodness-of-fit test, the following must be true.

1. The observed frequencies must be obtained using a random sample.
2. Each expected frequency must be greater than or equal to 5.

The Chi-Square Goodness-of-Fit Test

If the conditions listed above are satisfied, then the sampling distribution for the goodness-of-fit test is a chi-square distribution with $k - 1$ degrees of freedom, where k is the number of categories. The test statistic for the chi-square goodness-of-fit test is

$$\chi^2 = \Sigma \frac{(O - E)^2}{E}$$

where O represents the observed frequency of each category and E represents the expected frequency of each category.

When the observed frequencies closely match the expected frequencies, the differences between O and E will be small and the chi-square test statistic will be close to 0. As such, the null hypothesis is unlikely to be rejected. However, when there are large discrepancies between the observed frequencies and the expected frequencies, the differences between O and E will be large, resulting in a large chi-square test statistic. A large chi-square test statistic is evidence for rejecting the null hypothesis. So, the chi-square goodness-of-fit test is always a right-tailed test.

GUIDELINES

Performing a Chi-Square Goodness-of-Fit Test

In Words	*In Symbols*
1. Identify the claim. State the null and alternative hypothesis.	State H_0 and H_a.
2. Specify the level of significance.	Identify α.
3. Determine the degrees of freedom.	d.f. $= k - 1$
4. Find the critical value.	Use Table 6 in Appendix B.
5. Identify the rejection region.	
6. Calculate the test statistic.	$\chi^2 = \Sigma \dfrac{(O - E)^2}{E}$
7. Make a decision to reject or fail to reject the null hypothesis.	If χ^2 is in the rejection region, reject H_0. Otherwise, do not reject.
8. Interpret the decision in the context of the original claim.	

> **EXAMPLE 2** *Performing a Chi-Square Goodness-of-Fit Test*

A radio station claims that the music preferences of the listeners in the station's broadcast region are distributed as shown in the table at the left below. You randomly select 500 radio music listeners from the broadcast region and ask each whether he or she prefers classical, country, gospel, oldies, pop, or rock music. The survey results are listed in the table at the right below. Using $\alpha = 0.01$, perform a chi-square goodness-of-fit test to test the claimed distribution. What can you conclude?

Distribution of music preferences	
Classical	4%
Country	36%
Gospel	11%
Oldies	2%
Pop	18%
Rock	29%

Survey results ($n = 500$)	
Classical	8
Country	210
Gospel	72
Oldies	10
Pop	75
Rock	125

SOLUTION The observed and expected frequencies are shown in the table at the left. The expected frequencies were calculated in Example 1. Because each expected frequency is at least 5, you can use the chi-square goodness-of-fit test to test the proposed distribution. For this test, the null and alternative hypotheses are as follows.

Type of music	Observed frequency	Expected frequency
Classical	8	20
Country	210	180
Gospel	72	55
Oldies	10	10
Pop	75	90
Rock	125	145

H_0: The distribution of music preferences in the broadcast region is 4% classical, 36% country, 11% gospel, 2% oldies, 18% pop, and 29% rock. (Claim)

H_a: The distribution of music preferences differs from the claimed or expected distribution.

Because there are six categories, the chi-square distribution has $k - 1 = 6 - 1 = 5$ degrees of freedom. Using d.f. $= 5$ and $\alpha = 0.01$, the critical value is 15.086. Using the observed and expected frequencies, the chi-square test statistic is

$$\chi^2 = \Sigma \frac{(O - E)^2}{E}$$

$$= \frac{(8 - 20)^2}{20} + \frac{(210 - 180)^2}{180} + \frac{(72 - 55)^2}{55} + \frac{(10 - 10)^2}{10}$$

$$+ \frac{(75 - 90)^2}{90} + \frac{(125 - 145)^2}{145}$$

$$\approx 22.713.$$

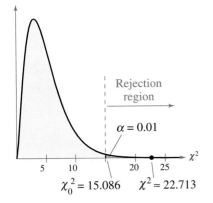

Rejection region

$\alpha = 0.01$

$\chi_0^2 = 15.086 \quad \chi^2 \approx 22.713$

The graph shows the location of the rejection region and the chi-square test statistic. Because χ^2 is in the rejection region, you should decide to reject the null hypothesis. In other words, at the 1% level, there is enough evidence to conclude that the distribution of music preferences differs from the radio station's claimed or expected distribution.

Ages	Claimed distribution	Survey results
0–9	16%	76
10–19	20%	84
20–29	8%	30
30–39	14%	60
40–49	15%	54
50–59	12%	40
60–69	10%	42
70+	5%	14

Try It Yourself 2

A sociologist claims that the age distribution for the residents of a certain city is the same as it was 10 years ago. The distribution of ages 10 years ago is shown in the table at the left. You randomly select 400 residents and record the age of each. The survey results are also listed in the table. Using $\alpha = 0.05$, perform a chi-square goodness-of-fit test to determine whether the distribution of ages has changed. What can you conclude?

a. *Identify* the claimed distribution and state H_0 and H_a.
b. *Specify* the level of significance α.
c. *Determine* the degrees of freedom.
d. *Find* the critical value and *identify* the rejection region.
e. *Find* the chi-square test statistic.
f. *Decide* whether to reject the null hypothesis. Use a graph if necessary.
g. Is there enough evidence to conclude that the distribution of ages has changed?

Answer: Page A42

EXAMPLE 3   *Performing a Chi-Square Goodness-of-Fit Test*

Men's survey results (*n* = 300)	
For irradiation	168
Against irradiation	71
No opinion	61

Irradiation is a controversial method for preserving meat. The display at the right shows several distributions describing attitudes toward the irradiation of red meat. You work for a meat-packing plant and want to test the distribution describing men's attitudes. To test the distribution, you randomly select 300 men and ask each whether

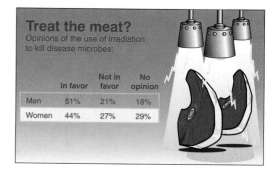

Treat the meat?
Opinions of the use of irradiation to kill disease microbes:

	In favor	Not in favor	No opinion
Men	61%	21%	18%
Women	44%	27%	29%

he is in favor of irradiation, against irradiation, or has no opinion. The results are listed in the table at the left. At $\alpha = 0.05$, test the claimed or expected distribution. What can you conclude?

SOLUTION   The observed frequencies and the expected frequencies are shown in the following table. Because each expected frequency is at least 5, you can use the chi-square goodness-of-fit test to test the claimed distribution.

Response	Observed frequency	Expected frequency
In favor of	168	300(0.61) = 183
Against	71	300(0.21) = 63
No opinion	61	300(0.18) = 54

The null and alternative hypotheses are as follows.

H_0: The distribution of men's attitudes toward the irradiation of red meat is 61% in favor, 21% against, and 18% no opinion. (Claim)

H_a: The distribution of men's attitudes toward the irradiation of red meat differs from the claimed or expected distribution.

Because there are three categories, the chi-square distribution has $k - 1 = 3 - 1 = 2$ degrees of freedom. Using d.f. $= 2$ and $\alpha = 0.05$, the critical value is 5.991. Using the observed and expected frequencies, the chi-square test statistic is as shown in the following table.

O	E	$O - E$	$(O - E)^2$	$\dfrac{(O - E)^2}{E}$
168	183	-15	225	1.229508197
71	63	8	64	1.015873016
61	54	7	49	0.9074074074
				$\chi^2 = \Sigma\dfrac{(O - E)^2}{E} \approx 3.1528$

The graph shows the location of the rejec-tion region and the chi-square test statistic. Because χ^2 is not in the rejection region, you should decide not to reject the null hypothe-sis. In other words, at the 5% level, there is not enough evidence to dispute the claimed or expected distribution of men's opinions.

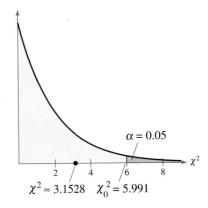

$\alpha = 0.05$

$\chi^2 \approx 3.1528 \quad \chi_0^2 = 5.991$

Try It Yourself 3

You also want to test the distribution describing women's attitudes. To test the distribution, you randomly select 200 women and ask each whether she is in favor of irradiation, against irradiation, or has no opinion. The results are listed in the table at the left. At $\alpha = 0.01$, test the claimed or expected distribution. What can you conclude?

a. *Identify* the claimed distribution and state H_0 and H_a.
b. *Specify* the level of significance α.
c. *Determine* the degrees of freedom.
d. *Find* the critical value and *identify* the rejection region.
e. Use the observed and expected frequencies to *find the chi-square test statistic*.
f. *Decide* whether to reject the null hypothesis. Use a graph if necessary.
g. Is there enough evidence to dispute the claimed distribution?

Answer: Page A42

Women's survey results $(n = 200)$	
For irradiation	100
Against irradiation	48
No opinion	52

The chi-square goodness-of-fit test is often used to determine whether a distribution is uniform. For such tests, the expected frequencies of the categories are equal. When testing a uniform distribution, you can find the expected frequency of each category by dividing the sample size by the number of categories.

10.1 EXERCISES

▶ HELP

StatPro 10.1

Internet Statistics 10.1

Student Solutions Manual 10.1

Videos 10.1

Try It Yourself Answers 10.1

1. (a) Claimed distribution:

Response	Distribution
Home	70%
Work	17%
Commuting	8%
Other	5%

H_0: Distribution of responses is as shown in table above.

H_a: Distribution of responses differs from the claimed distribution.

(b) 7.815   **(c)** 3.754

(d) Fail to reject H_0.

2. (a) Claimed distribution:

Response	Distribution
Limited advancement	41%
Lack of recognition	25%
Low salary	15%
Unhappy with mgmt.	10%
Bored/don't know	9%

H_0: Distribution of responses is as shown in table above.

H_a: Distribution of responses differs from the claimed distribution.

(b) 9.488   **(c)** 2.025

(d) Fail to reject H_0.

3. See Odd Answers, page A70

Basic Skills and Concepts

Performing a Chi-Square Goodness-of-Fit Test In Exercises 1–10, (a) identify the claim and state H_0 and H_a, (b) find the critical value and identify the rejection region, (c) find the test statistic χ^2, and (d) decide whether to reject or fail to reject the null hypothesis. Then interpret the decision in the context of the original claim.

1. Results from a survey five years ago asking where coffee drinkers typically drink their first cup of coffee are shown in the graph. To determine whether this distribution has changed, you randomly select 581 coffee drinkers and ask each where they typically drink their first cup of coffee. The results are listed in the table. Can you conclude that there has been a change in the claimed or expected distribution? Use $\alpha = 0.05$. *(Adapted from USA Today)*

Survey results	
Response	**Frequency**
At home	389
At workplace	110
While commuting	55
Restaurant/coffee bar/ other	27

2. A personnel director believes that the distribution of the reasons workers leave their jobs is different from the one shown in the graph. The director randomly selects 200 workers who recently left their jobs and asks each his or her reason for doing so. The results are shown in the table. At $\alpha = 0.05$, are the distributions different? *(Adapted from USA Today)*

Survey results	
Response	**Frequency**
Limited advancement potential	78
Lack of recognition	52
Low salary/benefits	30
Unhappy with mgmt.	25
Bored/don't know	15

3. A bicycle safety organization claims that fatal bicycle accidents are uniformly distributed throughout the week. The following table lists the day of the week for which 911 randomly selected fatal bicycle accidents occurred. At $\alpha = 0.10$, is the distribution uniform? *(Adapted from Insurance Institute for Highway Safety)*

Day	Frequency	Day	Frequency
Sunday	118	Thursday	129
Monday	119	Friday	146
Tuesday	127	Saturday	135
Wednesday	137		

4. (a) Claimed distribution:

Month	Distribution
January	8.333%
February	8.333%
March	8.333%
April	8.333%
May	8.333%
June	8.333%
July	8.333%
August	8.333%
September	8.333%
October	8.333%
November	8.333%
December	8.333%

H_0: The distribution of fatal bicycle accidents throughout the year is as shown in table above.

H_a: The distribution of fatal bicycle accidents throughout the year differs from the claimed distribution.

(b) 17.275 **(c)** 89.663

(d) Reject H_0.

5. (a) Claimed distribution:

Object struck	Distribution
Tree	28%
Embankment	10%
Utility pole	10%
Guardrail	9%
Ditch	7%
Curb	6%
Culvert	5%
Sign/Post/Fence	10%
Other	15%

H_0: Distribution of objects struck is as shown in table above.

H_a: Distribution of objects struck differs from the claimed distribution.

(b) 20.090 **(c)** 49.665

(d) Reject H_0.

6. See Selected Answers, page A84

4. A bicycle safety organization conducted a study of 996 randomly selected fatal bicycle accidents. The month each accident occurred is listed in the following table. At $\alpha = 0.10$, can you conclude that fatal bicycle accidents are not uniformly distributed by month? *(Adapted from Insurance Institute for Highway Safety)*

Month	Frequency	Month	Frequency
January	50	July	129
February	48	August	122
March	81	September	89
April	72	October	87
May	90	November	73
June	101	December	54

5. The pie chart shows the distribution of roadside hazard crash deaths with respect to the object hit. After highway warning signs were erected, a study was conducted to see if there was a change in the distribution. The results are listed in the table. Can you conclude that there is a change in the distribution? Use $\alpha = 0.01$. *(Adapted from Insurance Institute for Highway Safety)*

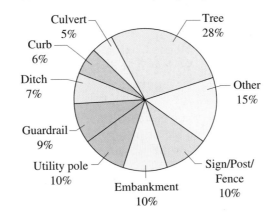

Study results	
Object struck	**Frequency**
Tree	179
Embankment	100
Utility pole	107
Guardrail	57
Ditch	36
Curb	43
Culvert	28
Sign/Post/Fence	68
Other	73

6. The pie chart shows the distribution of the time of day of roadside hazard crash deaths for a previous year. The results of a recent study of 627 randomly selected hazard crash deaths are listed in the table. At $\alpha = 0.01$, has the distribution changed? *(Adapted from Insurance Institute for Highway Safety)*

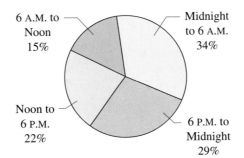

Study results	
Time of day	**Frequency**
Midnight to 6 A.M.	224
6 A.M. to Noon	128
Noon to 6 P.M.	115
6 P.M. to Midnight	160

7. (a) Claimed distribution:

Response	Distribution
Not a HS grad	33.333%
HS graduate	33.333%
College (1 yr +)	33.333%

H_0: Distribution of the responses is as shown in table above.

H_a: Distribution of the responses differs from the claimed distribution.

(b) 7.378   **(c)** 5.637

(d) Fail to reject H_0.

8. (a) Claimed distribution:

Response	Distribution
Married, husband present	25%
Married, husband absent	25%
Widowed/divorced	25%
Never married	25%

H_0: Distribution of the responses is as shown in table above.

H_a: Distribution of the responses differs from the claimed distribution.

(b) 9.348   **(c)** 10.327

(d) Reject H_0.

9. (a) Claimed distribution:

Cause	Distribution
Trans. Accidents	41%
Assaults	20%
Objects/ equipment	15%
Falls	10%
Exposure	10%
Other	4%

H_0: Distribution of the causes is as shown in table above.

H_a: Distribution of the causes differs from the claimed distribution.

(b) 11.071   **(c)** 9.493

(d) Fail to reject H_0.

7. A social service organization reports that the level of educational attainment of mothers receiving food stamps is uniformly distributed. To test this claim, you randomly select 99 mothers who currently receive food stamps and record the educational attainment of each. The results are listed in the following table. At $\alpha = 0.02$, can you conclude that the distribution is uniform? *(Adapted from U.S. Bureau of the Census)*

Response	Frequency
Not a high school graduate	37
High school graduate	40
College (1 year or more)	22

8. A social service worker believes that the marital status of mothers receiving food stamps is uniformly distributed. To test this claim, you randomly select 101 mothers who currently receive food stamps and record the marital status of each. The results are listed below. Is there enough evidence to conclude that the distribution of marital status is uniform? Use $\alpha = 0.025$. *(Adapted from U.S. Bureau of the Census)*

Response	Frequency
Married, husband present	20
Married, husband absent	19
Widowed or divorced	23
Never married	39

9. The pie chart shows the national distribution of fatal work injuries in the United States. You believe that the distribution of fatal work injuries is different in the western United States and randomly select 6231 fatal work injuries occurring in that region and record how each occurred. The results are listed in the table. At $\alpha = 0.05$, can you conclude that the distribution of fatal work injuries in the western United States is different from the national distribution? *(Adapted from U.S. Bureau of Labor Statistics)*

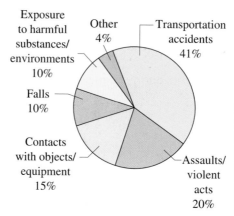

Study results: Western U.S.	
Cause	**Frequency**
Transportation accidents	2500
Assaults/violent acts	1300
Contacts with objects and equipment	985
Falls	620
Exposure to harmful substances or environments	602
Other	224

10. (a) Claimed distribution:

Response	Distribution
First marriage of bride & groom	50%
1st marriage bride remarriage groom	12%
1st marriage groom remarriage bride	14%
Remarriage of bride & groom	24%

H_0: Distribution of the responses is as shown in table above.

H_a: Distribution of the responses differs from the claimed distribution.

(b) 11.345

(c) 0.675

(d) Fail to reject H_0.

11. See Odd Answers, page A71

12. See Selected Answers, page A84

10. A marriage counselor says that 50% of all marriages are the first marriage for both the bride and the groom, 12% are the first for the bride and a remarriage for the groom, 14% are a remarriage for the bride and a first for the groom, and 24% are a remarriage for both. You randomly select 103 married couples and gather the results shown in the table. At $\alpha = 0.01$, can you support the counselor's claim?

Response	Frequency
First marriage of bride and groom	55
First marriage of bride, remarriage of groom	12
Remarriage of bride, first marriage of groom	12
Remarriage of bride and groom	24

Extending the Basics

Testing for Normality Using a chi-square goodness-of-fit test, you can decide, with some degree of certainty, whether a variable is normally distributed. In all chi-square tests for normality, the null and alternative hypotheses are as follows.

H_0: The variable has a normal distribution.

H_a: The variable does not have a normal distribution.

To determine the expected frequencies when performing a chi-square test for normality, first find the mean and standard deviation of the frequency distribution. Then use the mean and standard deviation to compute the z-score for each class boundary. Then use the z-scores to calculate the area under the standard normal curve for each class. Multiplying the resulting class areas by the sample size yields the expected frequency for each class.

In Exercises 11 and 12, (a) find the expected frequencies, (b) find the critical value and identify the rejection region, (c) calculate the test statistic x^2, and (d) decide whether to reject or fail to reject the null hypothesis. Then interpret the decision in the context of the original claim.

11. The frequency distribution shows the results of 200 test scores. Are the test scores normally distributed? Use $\alpha = 0.01$.

Class boundaries	49.5–58.5	58.5–67.5	67.5–76.5	76.5–85.5	85.5–94.5
Frequency	19	61	82	34	4

12. At $\alpha = 0.05$, can you conclude that the 400 test scores shown in the frequency distribution are normally distributed?

Class boundaries	50.5–60.5	60.5–70.5	70.5–80.5	80.5–90.5	90.5–100.5
Frequency	28	106	151	97	18

Independence

Contingency Tables • The Chi-Square Test for Independence

What You Should Learn

- *How to use a contingency table to find expected frequencies*
- *How to use a chi-square distribution to test whether two variables are independent*

Contingency Tables

In Section 3.2, you learned that two variables are **independent** if the occurrence of one variable does not affect the probability of the occurrence of the other variable. For instance, the outcomes of a roll of a die and a toss of a coin are independent. But, suppose a medical researcher wants to determine if there is a relationship between caffeine consumption and heart attack risk. Are these variables independent or are they dependent? In this section, you will learn how to use the chi-square test for independence to answer such a question. To perform a chi-square test for independence, you will use sample data that are organized in a contingency table.

DEFINITION

An *r* × *c* **contingency table** shows the observed frequencies for two variables. The observed frequencies are arranged in *r* rows and *c* columns. The intersection of a row and a column is called a **cell.**

For example, the following table is a 2 × 5 contingency table. It has two rows and five columns and shows the results of a random sample of 550 company CEOs classified by age and size of company. From the table, you can see that 108 of the CEOs between the ages of 50 and 59 direct small or midsize companies, while 85 of the CEOs in this age group direct large companies.

Company size	Age				
	39–under	40–49	50–59	60–69	70–over
Small/midsize	42	69	108	60	21
Large	5	18	85	120	22

Assuming the two variables of study in a contingency table are independent, you can use the contingency table to find the expected frequency for each cell.

Study Tip

In a contingency table, the notation $E_{r,c}$ represents the expected frequency for the cell in row *r*, column *c*. For instance, in the table at the right, $E_{1,4}$ represents the expected frequency for the cell in row 1, column 4 and is equal to 60.

Finding the Expected Frequency for Contingency Table Cells

The expected frequency for a cell, $E_{r,c}$, in a contingency table is

$$\text{Expected frequency, } E_{r,c} = \frac{\text{Sum of row } r \times \text{Sum of column } c}{\text{Sample size}}.$$

> **EXAMPLE 1** *Finding Expected Frequencies*

Find the expected frequency for each cell in the contingency table. Assume that the variables, age and company size, are independent.

Company size	Age					
	39–under	**40–49**	**50–59**	**60–69**	**70–over**	**Total**
Small/midsize	42	69	108	60	21	300
Large	5	18	85	120	22	250
Total	47	87	193	180	43	550

SOLUTION Using the formula

$$\text{Expected frequency, } E_{r,c} = \frac{\text{Sum of row } r \times \text{Sum of column } c}{\text{Sample size}},$$

you can find each expected frequency as shown.

$$E_{1,1} = \frac{300 \cdot 47}{550} \approx 25.64 \quad E_{1,2} = \frac{300 \cdot 87}{550} \approx 47.45 \quad E_{1,3} = \frac{300 \cdot 193}{550} \approx 105.27$$

$$E_{1,4} = \frac{300 \cdot 180}{550} \approx 98.18 \quad E_{1,5} = \frac{300 \cdot 43}{550} \approx 23.45 \quad E_{2,1} = \frac{250 \cdot 47}{550} \approx 21.36$$

$$E_{2,2} = \frac{250 \cdot 87}{550} \approx 39.55 \quad E_{2,3} = \frac{250 \cdot 193}{550} \approx 87.73 \quad E_{2,4} = \frac{250 \cdot 180}{550} \approx 81.82$$

$$E_{2,5} = \frac{250 \cdot 43}{550} \approx 19.55$$

Try It Yourself 1

The marketing consultant for a travel agency wants to determine whether certain travel concerns are related to travel purpose. A random sample of 300 travelers is selected and the results are classified as shown in the following contingency table. Assuming that the variables travel concerns and travel purpose are independent, find the expected frequency for each cell. (*Adapted from USA Today*)

Travel purpose	Travel concern			
	Hotel room	**Leg room on plane**	**Rental car size**	**Other**
Business	36	108	14	22
Leisure	38	54	14	14

a. *Calculate* the sum of each row.
b. *Calculate* the sum of each column.
c. *Determine* the sample size.
d. *Use the formula* to find the expected frequency for each cell.

Answer: Page A43

The Chi-Square Test for Independence

After finding the expected frequencies, you can test whether the variables are independent using a chi-square independence test.

DEFINITION

A **chi-square independence test** is used to test the independence of two variables. Using a chi-square test, you can determine whether the occurrence of one variable affects the probability of the occurrence of the other variable.

To use the chi-square independence test, the following conditions must be true.

1. The observed frequencies must be obtained using a random sample.
2. Each expected frequency must be greater than or equal to 5.

The Chi-Square Independence Test

If the conditions listed above are satisfied, then the sampling distribution for the chi-square independence test is a chi-square distribution with $(r - 1)(c - 1)$ degrees of freedom, where r and c are the number of rows and columns, respectively. The test statistic for the chi-square independence test is

$$\chi^2 = \Sigma \frac{(O - E)^2}{E}$$

where O represents the observed frequencies and E represents the expected frequencies.

To begin the independence test, you must first state a null and an alternative hypothesis. For a chi-square independence test, the null and alternative hypotheses are always some variation of the following statements.

H_0: The variables are independent.

H_a: The variables are dependent.

The expected frequencies are calculated assuming that the two variables are independent. If the variables are independent, then you can expect little difference between the observed frequencies and the expected frequencies. When the observed frequencies closely match the expected frequencies, the differences between O and E will be small and the chi-square test statistic will be close to 0. As such, the null hypothesis is unlikely to be rejected.

However, if the variables are dependent, there will be large discrepancies between the observed frequencies and the expected frequencies. When the differences between O and E are large, the chi-square test statistic is also large. A large chi-square test statistic is evidence for rejecting the null hypothesis. So, the chi-square independence test is always a right-tailed test.

GUIDELINES

Performing a Chi-Square Test for Independence

In Words	*In Symbols*
1. Identify the claim. State the null and alternative hypotheses.	State H_0 and H_a.
2. Specify the level of significance.	Specify α.
3. Determine the degrees of freedom.	d.f. $= (r - 1)(c - 1)$
4. Find the critical value.	Use Table 6 in Appendix B.
5. Identify the rejection region.	
6. Calculate the test statistic.	$\chi^2 = \Sigma \dfrac{(O - E)^2}{E}$
7. Make a decision to reject or fail to reject the null hypothesis.	If χ^2 is in the rejection region, reject H_0. Otherwise, do not reject H_0.
8. Interpret the decision in the context of the original claim.	

▶ **EXAMPLE 2** *Performing a Chi-Square Independence Test*

The following contingency table shows the results of a random sample of 550 company CEOs classified by age and size of company. The expected frequencies are displayed in parentheses. At $\alpha = 0.01$, can you conclude that the CEOs' ages are related to company size?

Company size	Age of CEOs					Total
	39–under	40–49	50–59	60–69	70–over	
Small/midsize	42 (25.64)	69 (47.45)	108 (105.27)	60 (98.18)	21 (23.45)	300
Large	5 (21.36)	18 (39.55)	85 (87.73)	120 (81.82)	22 (19.55)	250
Total	47	87	193	180	43	550

SOLUTION The expected frequencies were calculated in Example 1. Because each expected frequency is at least 5, you can use the chi-square independence test to test whether the variables are independent. The null and alternative hypotheses are as follows.

H_0: The CEOs' ages are independent of the company size.

H_a: The CEOs' ages are dependent on the company size.

Because the contingency table has two rows and five columns, the chi-square distribution has $(r - 1)(c - 1) = (2 - 1)(5 - 1) = 4$ degrees of freedom. Because d.f. = 4 and $\alpha = 0.01$, the critical value is 15.086. Using the observed and expected frequencies, the chi-square test statistic is

$$\chi^2 = \Sigma \frac{(O - E)^2}{E}$$

$$= \frac{(42 - 25.64)^2}{25.64} + \frac{(69 - 47.45)^2}{47.45} + \cdots + \frac{(120 - 81.82)^2}{81.82} + \frac{(22 - 19.55)^2}{19.55}$$

$$\approx 77.9.$$

The graph shows the location of the rejection region. Because $\chi^2 \approx 77.9$ is in the rejection region, you should decide to reject the null hypothesis. In other words, there is enough evidence at the 1% level of significance to conclude that the CEOs' ages and the company size are dependent.

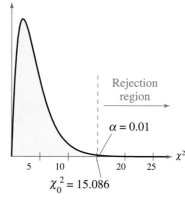

Try It Yourself 2

The marketing consultant for a travel agency wants to determine whether certain travel concerns are related to travel purpose. A random sample of 300 travelers is selected and each is asked his or her primary travel concern. The results are classified as shown in the following contingency table. At $\alpha = 0.01$, can the consultant conclude that the travel concerns depend on the purpose of travel? (The expected frequencies are displayed in parentheses.) *(Adapted from USA Today)*

Travel purpose	Travel concern				Total
	Hotel room	Leg room on plane	Rental car size	Other	
Business	36 (44.4)	108 (97.2)	14 (16.8)	22 (21.6)	180
Leisure	38 (29.6)	54 (64.8)	14 (11.2)	14 (14.4)	120
Total	74	162	28	36	300

a. *Identify* the claim and *state* H_0 and H_a.
b. *Specify* the level of significance α.
c. *Determine* the degrees of freedom.
d. *Find* the critical value and *identify* the rejection region.
e. Use the observed and expected frequencies to *find the chi-square test statistic.*
f. *Decide* whether to reject the null hypothesis. Use a graph if necessary.
g. Is there enough evidence to conclude that the travel concerns depend on the purpose of travel?   *Answer: Page A43*

> **EXAMPLE 3** *Using Technology for a Chi-Square Independence Test*

Setup

X²–Test
 Observed: [A]
 Expected: [B]
 Calculate Draw

Calculate

X²–Test
 x²=3.493357223
 p=.321624691
 df=3

Draw

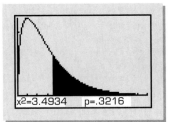

x²=3.4934   p=.3216

A health club manager wants to determine whether the number of days per week that college students spend exercising is related to gender. A random sample of 275 college students is selected and the results are classified as shown in the following table. At $\alpha = 0.05$, is there enough evidence to conclude that the number of days spent exercising per week is related to gender?

	Days per week spent exercising				
Gender	**0–1**	**2–3**	**4–5**	**6–7**	**Total**
Male	40	53	26	6	125
Female	34	68	37	11	150
Total	74	121	63	17	275

SOLUTION   The null and alternative hypotheses can be stated as follows.

H_0: The number of days spent exercising per week is independent of gender.

H_a: The number of days spent exercising per week depends on gender.

Enter the observed frequencies into matrix A. Then set up the chi-square test using a TI-83 as shown at the left.

The displays at the left show the results of selecting "Calculate" or "Draw." Because d.f. = 3 and $\alpha = 0.05$, the rejection region is $\chi^2 > 7.815$. The test statistic $\chi^2 \approx 3.49$ is not in the rejection region, so you should fail to reject the null hypothesis. There is not enough evidence to conclude that the number of days spent exercising per week is related to gender.

Study Tip

You can also use P-values to perform a chi-square test for independence. For instance, in Example 3, note that the TI-83 displays P ≈ 0.322. Because P > α, you should fail to reject the null hypothesis.

Try It Yourself 3

A researcher wants to determine whether the number of minutes adults spend online per day is related to gender. A random sample of 450 adults is selected and the results are classified as shown in the following table. At $\alpha = 0.05$, is there enough evidence to conclude that the number of minutes spent online per day is related to gender?

	Minutes spent online per day					
Gender	**0–15**	**15–30**	**30–45**	**45–60**	**60–over**	**Total**
Male	19	36	75	90	55	275
Female	21	72	45	19	18	175
Total	40	108	120	109	73	450

a. *Find* the critical value and *identify* the rejection region.
b. *Enter* the observed frequencies.
c. *Use* a technology tool to find the χ^2 test statistic or a *P*-value.
d. *Make* a decision.
e. Is there enough evidence to conclude that the number of minutes spent online per day is related to gender?   *Answer: Page A43*

10.2 EXERCISES

HELP

 StatPro 10.2

 Internet Statistics 10.2

 Student Solutions Manual 10.2

 Videos 10.2

 Try It Yourself Answers 10.2

1. (a) H_0: Skill level in a subject is independent of location.

    H_a: Skill level in a subject is dependent on location.

(b) 2; 9.210

(c) 0.297

(d) Fail to reject H_0.

2. (a) H_0: Attitudes about safety are independent of the type of school.

    H_a: Attitudes about safety are dependent on the type of school.

(b) 1; 6.635

(c) 8.691

(d) Reject H_0.

3. (a) H_0: Adults' ratings are independent of the type of school.

    H_a: Adults' ratings are dependent on the type of school.

(b) 3; 7.815

(c) 148.389

(d) Reject H_0.

Basic Skills and Concepts

Performing a Chi-Square Test for Independence In Exercises 1–10, perform the indicated chi-square test for independence by doing the following.

(a) Identify the claim and state the null and alternative hypotheses.

(b) Determine the degrees of freedom, find the critical value, and identify the rejection region.

(c) Calculate the test statistic. (If possible, use a technology tool.)

(d) Decide to reject or fail to reject the null hypothesis. Then interpret the decision in the context of the original claim.

1. Is achieving a basic skill level in a subject related to the location of the school? A random sample of students by the location of school and the number achieving basic skill levels in three subjects is shown in the following table. At $\alpha = 0.01$, test the hypothesis that the variables are independent. *(Adapted from USA Today)*

	Subject		
Location of school	**Reading**	**Math**	**Science**
Urban	43	42	38
Suburban	63	66	65

2. The results of a random sample of students by type of school and their attitudes on safety steps taken by the school staff are shown in the following table. At $\alpha = 0.01$, can you conclude that attitudes about the safety steps taken by the school staff are related to the type of school? *(Adapted from USA Today)*

	School staff has	
Type of school	**Taken all steps necessary for student safety**	**Taken some steps toward student safety**
Public	40	51
Private	64	34

3. The following contingency table shows how a random sample of adults rated their local public schools and how they rated America's public schools. At $\alpha = 0.05$, can you conclude that the adults' ratings are related to the type of school? *(Adapted from USA Today)*

	Rating			
Type of school	**Excellent**	**Good**	**Fair**	**Poor**
Local	120	405	263	151
National	41	238	481	179

4. (a) H_0: Grades are independent of the institution.

H_a: Grades are dependent on the institution.

(b) 8; 15.507

(c) 48.488

(d) Reject H_0.

5. (a) H_0: Results are independent of the type of treatment.

H_a: Results are dependent on the type of treatment.

(b) 1; 2.706

(c) 5.106

(d) Reject H_0.

6. (a) H_0: Results are independent of the type of treatment.

H_a: Results are dependent on the type of treatment.

(b) 1; 2.706

(c) 1.032

(d) Fail to reject H_0.

7. (a) H_0: Reasons are independent of the type of worker.

H_a: Reasons are dependent on the type of worker.

(b) 2; 9.210

(c) 7.326

(d) Fail to reject H_0.

4. The contingency table shows how a random sample of college freshmen graded the leaders of three types of institutions. At $\alpha = 0.05$, can you conclude that the grades are related to the institution? *(Adapted from USA Today)*

Institution	Grade				
	A	**B**	**C**	**D**	**F**
Military	25	46	19	5	3
Religious	18	44	24	7	5
Media/press	5	23	37	21	12

5. The results of a random sample of patients with obsessive-compulsive disorder treated with a drug or with a placebo are shown in the contingency table. At $\alpha = 0.10$, can you conclude that the treatment is related to the result? Based on these results, would you recommend using the drug as part of a treatment for obsessive-compulsive order? *(Adapted from The Journal of the American Medical Association)*

Result	Treatment	
	Drug	**Placebo**
Improvement	39	25
No change	54	70

6. The contingency table shows a random sample of patients with chronic fatigue syndrome treated with a drug or with a placebo. At $\alpha = 0.10$, can you conclude that the variables treatment and result are dependent? Based on these results, would you recommend using the drug as part of a treatment for chronic fatigue syndrome? *(Adapted from The Journal of the American Medical Association)*

Result	Treatment	
	Drug	**Placebo**
Improvement	20	19
No change	10	16

7. You work for a college's continuing education department and want to determine whether the reasons given by workers for continuing their education is related to job type. In your study, you collect the data shown in the contingency table. At $\alpha = 0.01$, can you conclude that the variables reason and type of worker are dependent? How could you use this information in your marketing efforts? *(Adapted from USA Today)*

Type of worker	Reason		
	Professional	**Personal**	**Professional and personal**
Technical	30	36	41
Other	47	25	30

8. (a) H_0: Blood alcohol concentration is independent of age.

   H_a: Blood alcohol concentration is dependent on age.

   (b) 2; 9.210

   (c) 10.762

   (d) Reject H_0.

9. (a) H_0: Type of crash is independent of the type of vehicle.

   H_a: Type of crash is dependent on the type of vehicle.

   (b) 2; 5.991

   (c) 106.390

   (d) Reject H_0.

10. (a) H_0: Age is independent of gender.

   H_a: Age is dependent on gender.

   (b) 5; 11.071

   (c) 2.834

   (d) Fail to reject H_0.

8. You are investigating the relationship between the ages and the blood alcohol concentration of fatally injured pedestrians. During your investigation, you collect the data shown in the contingency table. At $\alpha = 0.01$, is there enough evidence to conclude that blood alcohol concentration is related to age in nighttime pedestrian deaths? *(Adapted from Insurance Institute for Highway Safety)*

Age	Blood Alcohol Concentration		
	0.00	**0.01–0.09**	**0.10 and greater**
16–34 years	439	85	696
35 years and over	513	98	622

9. You work for an insurance company and are studying the relationship between types of crashes and the vehicles involved. As part of your study, you randomly select 3207 vehicle crashes and organize the resulting data as shown in the contingency table. At $\alpha = 0.05$, can you conclude that the type of crash depends on the type of vehicle? *(Adapted from Insurance Institute for Highway Safety)*

Type of crash	Vehicle		
	Car	**Pickup truck/ Utility vehicle**	**Cargo/Large passenger van**
Single-vehicle	895	493	45
Multiple-vehicle	1400	336	38

10. The following contingency table shows a random sample of fatally injured passenger vehicle drivers (with blood alcohol concentrations greater than or equal to 0.10) by age and gender. At $\alpha = 0.05$, can you conclude that age is related to gender in such alcohol-related accidents? *(Adapted from Insurance Institute for Highway Safety)*

Gender	Age					
	16–20	**21–30**	**31–40**	**41–50**	**51–60**	**60–over**
Male	32	51	52	43	28	10
Female	13	22	33	21	10	6

11. H_0: The proportions are equal.

H_a: At least one of the proportions is different from the others.

d.f. $= (r - 1)(c - 1) = 7$

$CV = 14.067 \rightarrow$ Reject H_0 if $\chi^2 > 14.067$

$\chi^2 \approx 3.853$

Fail to reject H_0.

12. H_0: The proportions are equal.

H_a: At least one of the proportions is different from the others.

d.f. $= (r - 1)(c - 1) = 1$

$CV = 2.706 \rightarrow$ Reject H_0 if $\chi^2 > 2.706$

$\chi^2 \approx 5.106$

Reject H_0.

Extending the Basics

Homogeneity of Proportions Test Another chi-square test that involves a contingency table is the homogeneity of proportions test. The test is used to determine if several proportions are equal when samples are taken from different populations. Before sampling the populations and making the contingency table, the sample sizes are determined. After randomly sampling different populations, you can test whether the proportion of elements in a category is the same for each population using the same guidelines in performing a chi-square independence test. The null and alternative hypotheses are always some variation of the following statements.

H_0: The proportions are equal.
H_a: At least one of the proportions is different from the others.

To perform a homogeneity of proportions test, the observed frequencies must be obtained using a random sample, and each expected frequency must be greater than or equal to 5.

11. The table shows a random sample of motor vehicle deaths by age and gender. At $\alpha = 0.05$, perform a homogeneity of proportions test on the claim that the proportions of motor vehicle deaths involving males or females are the same for each age group. *(Adapted from Insurance Institute for Highway Safety)*

	Age							
Gender	**16–24**	**25–34**	**35–44**	**45–54**	**55–64**	**65–74**	**75–84**	**85–over**
Male	80	54	41	39	39	45	73	55
Female	35	21	18	17	20	27	40	19

12. The contingency table shows the results of a random sample of patients with obsessive-compulsive disorder after being treated with a drug or with a placebo. At $\alpha = 0.10$, perform a homogeneity of proportions test on the claim that the proportions of the results for drug and placebo treatment are the same. *(Adapted from The Journal of the American Medical Association)*

	Treatment	
Result	**Drug**	**Placebo**
Improvement	39	25
No change	54	70

Traffic Safety Facts 1997

Each year, the National Highway Traffic Safety Administration (NHTSA) together with the National Center for Statistics and Analysis (NCSA) publishes *Traffic Safety Facts,* which summarizes the motor vehicle traffic crash experience for 17 states. *Traffic Safety Facts 1997* includes trend data, crash data, vehicle data, and people data.

In 1997, there were 41,967 fatalities in the United States as a result of motor vehicle crashes. The pie chart at the right shows the national distribution of traffic fatalities with respect to age group. For example, 23% of all motor vehicle fatalities were young adults aged 16–24. Using the data from the 17 NCSA states as a sample, the contingency table lists the number of motor vehicle fatalities according to age and geographic location within the United States.

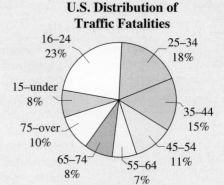

U.S. Distribution of Traffic Fatalities

Motor Vehicle Fatalities

Age	Eastern U.S.	Central U.S.	Western U.S.
	Region		
15–under	646	732	518
16–24	1907	2269	1262
25–34	1524	1583	1125
35–44	1242	1274	792
45–54	846	802	555
55–64	590	568	371
65–74	737	574	408
75–over	931	739	481

Exercises

1. In 1997, how many Americans aged 16–24 died as a result of a motor vehicle crash?

2. Assuming the variables region and age are independent, in which region did the number of motor vehicle fatalities for the 16–24 age group exceed the expected number of fatalities?

3. Assuming the variables region and age are independent, in which region did the number of motor vehicle fatalities for the 25–34 age group exceed the expected number of fatalities?

4. At $\alpha = 0.05$, perform a chi-square test to determine whether the variables region and age are independent. What can you conclude?

In Exercises 5–7, perform a chi-square goodness-of-fit test to compare the national distribution of motor vehicle fatalities with the distribution of each region of the United States. Use the national distribution as the claimed distribution. Use $\alpha = 0.05$.

5. Compare the distribution of motor vehicle fatalities for the eastern United States with the national distribution. What can you conclude?

6. Compare the distribution of motor vehicle fatalities for the central United States with the national distribution. What can you conclude?

7. Compare the distribution of motor vehicle fatalities for the western United States with the national distribution. What can you conclude?

8. In addition to the variables used in this case study, what other variables do you think are important considerations when studying the distribution of motor vehicle fatalities?

10.3

Comparing Two Variances

The *F*-Distribution • The Two-Sample *F*-Test for Variances

What You Should Learn

- *How to interpret the F-distribution and use an F-table to find critical values*
- *How to perform a two-sample F-test to compare two variances*

The *F*-Distribution

In Chapter 8, you learned how to perform hypothesis tests to compare population means and population proportions. Recall from Section 8.2 that the *t*-test for the difference between two population means depends on whether the population variances are equal. To determine whether the population variances are equal, you can perform a two-sample *F*-test.

In this section, you will learn about the *F*-distribution and how to use the *F*-distribution to compare two variances.

DEFINITION

Let s_1^2 and s_2^2 represent the sample variances of two different populations. If both populations are normal and the population variances, σ_1^2 and σ_2^2, are equal, then the sampling distribution of

$$F = \frac{s_1^2}{s_2^2}$$

is called an **F-distribution.** Several properties of the *F*-distribution are as follows.

1. The *F*-distribution is a family of curves each of which is determined by two types of degrees of freedom: the degrees of freedom corresponding to the variance in the numerator, denoted by **d.f.$_\text{N}$**, and the degrees of freedom corresponding to the variance in the denominator, denoted by **d.f.$_\text{D}$**.
2. *F*-distributions are positively skewed.
3. The total area under each curve of an *F*-distribution is equal to 1.
4. *F*-values are always greater than or equal to zero.
5. For all *F*-distributions, the mean value of *F* is approximately equal to 1.

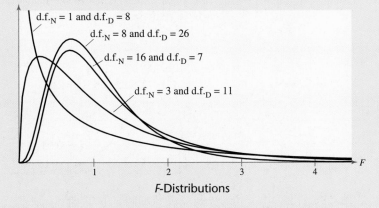

F-Distributions

Table 7 in Appendix B lists the critical values for the *F*-distribution for select-ed levels of significance α and degrees of freedom, d.f.$_N$ and d.f.$_D$.

GUIDELINES

Finding Critical Values for the *F*-Distribution

1. Specify the level of significance α.
2. Determine the degrees of freedom for the numerator, d.f.$_N$.
3. Determine the degrees of freedom for the denominator, d.f.$_D$.
4. Use Table 7 in Appendix B to find the critical value. If the hypothe-sis test is
   a. one-tailed, use the α *F*-table.
   b. two-tailed, use the $\frac{1}{2}\alpha$ *F*-table.

EXAMPLE 1   *Finding Critical F-Values for a Right-Tailed Test*

Find the critical *F*-value for a right-tailed test when $\alpha = 0.05$, d.f.$_N = 6$, and d.f.$_D = 29$.

SOLUTION   A portion of Table 7 is shown below. Using the $\alpha = 0.05$ *F*-table with d.f.$_N = 6$ and d.f.$_D = 29$, you can find the critical value as shown by the highlighted areas in the table.

d.f.$_D$: Degrees of freedom, denominator	$\alpha = 0.05$							
	d.f.$_N$: Degrees of freedom, numerator							
	1	2	3	4	5	6	7	8
1	161.4	199.5	215.7	224.6	230.2	234.0	236.8	238.9
2	18.51	19.00	19.16	19.25	19.30	19.33	19.35	19.37
26	4.23	3.37	2.98	2.74	2.59	2.47	2.39	2.32
27	4.21	3.35	2.96	2.73	2.57	2.46	2.37	2.31
28	4.20	3.34	2.95	2.71	2.56	2.45	2.36	2.29
29	4.18	3.33	2.93	2.70	2.55	2.43	2.35	2.28
30	4.17	3.32	2.92	2.69	2.53	2.42	2.33	2.27

From the table, you can see that the critical value is $F_0 = 2.43$. The graph shows the *F*-distribution for $\alpha = 0.05$, d.f.$_N = 6$, d.f.$_D = 29$, and $F_0 = 2.43$.

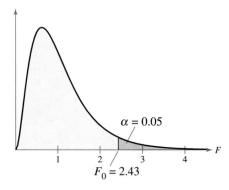

$\alpha = 0.05$

$F_0 = 2.43$

Try It Yourself 1

Find the critical F-value for a right-tailed test when $\alpha = 0.01$, d.f.$_N = 3$, and d.f.$_D = 15$.

a. *Specify* the level of significance α.
b. *Use* Table 7 in Appendix B to find the critical value.

Answer: Page A43

When performing a two-tailed hypothesis test using the F-distribution, you need only to find the right-tailed critical value. You must, however, remember to use the $\frac{1}{2}\alpha$ F-table.

▶ **EXAMPLE 2** *Finding Critical F-Values for a Two-Tailed Test*

Find the critical F-value for a two-tailed test when $\alpha = 0.05$, d.f.$_N = 4$, and d.f.$_D = 8$.

SOLUTION A portion of Table 7 is shown below. Using the $\frac{1}{2}\alpha = \frac{1}{2}(0.05) = 0.025$ F-table with d.f.$_N = 4$, and d.f.$_D = 8$, you can find the critical value as shown by the highlighted areas in the table.

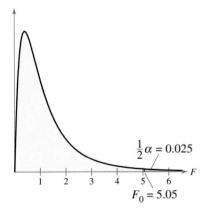

$\frac{1}{2}\alpha = 0.025$

$F_0 = 5.05$

d.f.$_D$: Degrees of freedom, denominator	$\alpha = 0.025$							
	d.f.$_N$: Degrees of freedom, numerator							
	1	2	3	4	5	6	7	8
1	647.8	799.5	864.2	899.6	921.8	937.1	948.2	956.7
2	38.51	39.00	39.17	39.25	39.30	39.33	39.36	39.37
3	17.44	16.04	15.44	15.10	14.88	14.73	14.62	14.54
4	12.22	10.65	9.98	9.60	9.36	9.20	9.07	8.98
5	10.01	8.43	7.76	7.39	7.15	6.98	6.85	6.76
6	8.81	7.26	6.60	6.23	5.99	5.82	5.70	5.60
7	8.07	6.54	5.89	5.52	5.29	5.12	4.99	4.90
8	7.57	6.06	5.42	5.05	4.82	4.65	4.53	4.43
9	7.21	5.71	5.08	4.72	4.48	4.32	4.20	4.10

From the table, the critical value is $F_0 = 5.05$. The graph shows the F-distribution for $\frac{1}{2}\alpha = 0.025$, d.f.$_N = 4$, and d.f.$_D = 8$, and $F_0 = 5.05$.

Try It Yourself 2

Find the critical F-value for a right-tailed test when $\alpha = 0.01$, d.f.$_N = 2$, and d.f.$_D = 5$.

a. *Specify* the level of significance α.
b. *Use* Table 7 in Appendix B with $\frac{1}{2}\alpha$ to find the critical value.

Answer: Page A43

The Two-Sample *F*-Test for Variances

In the remainder of this section, you will learn how to perform a two-sample *F*-test for comparing two population variances using a sample from each population. To perform such a test, two conditions must be met.

1. The samples must be independent.
2. Each population must have a normal distribution.

If these requirements are met, you can use the *F*-test to compare the population variances σ_1^2 and σ_2^2.

Two-Sample *F*-Test for Variances

A two-sample *F*-test is used to compare two population variances σ_1^2 and σ_2^2 when a sample is randomly selected from each population. The populations must be independent and normally distributed. The test statistic is

$$F = \frac{s_1^2}{s_2^2}$$

where s_1^2 and s_2^2 represent the sample variances with $s_1^2 \geq s_2^2$. The degrees of freedom for the numerator is $\text{d.f.}_N = n_1 - 1$ and the degrees of freedom for the denominator is $\text{d.f.}_D = n_2 - 1$, where n_1 is the size of the sample having variance s_1^2 and n_2 is the size of the sample having variance s_2^2.

GUIDELINES

Using a Two-Sample *F*-Test to Compare σ_1^2 and σ_2^2

In Words	*In Symbols*
1. Identify the claim. State the null and the alternative hypotheses.	State H_0 and H_a.
2. Specify the level of significance.	Specify α.
3. Determine the degrees of freedom.	$\text{d.f.}_N = n_1 - 1$ $\text{d.f.}_D = n_2 - 1$
4. Find the critical value.	Use Table 7 in Appendix B.
5. Identify the rejection region.	
6. Calculate the test statistic.	$F = \dfrac{s_1^2}{s_2^2}$
7. Make a decision to reject or fail to reject the null hypothesis.	If F is in the rejection region, reject H_0. Otherwise, do not reject H_0.
8. Interpret the decision in the context of the original claim.	

▶ **EXAMPLE 3** *Performing a Two-Sample F-Test*

A bank manager is designing a system that is intended to decrease the variance of the time customers wait in line. Under the old system, a random sample of 10 customers had a variance of 144. Under the new system, a random sample of 21 customers had a variance of 100. At $\alpha = 0.10$, is there enough evidence to convince the manager to switch to the new system? Assume both populations are normally distributed.

SOLUTION Because $144 > 100$, $s_1^2 = 144$ and $s_2^2 = 100$. Therefore, s_1^2 and σ_1^2 represent the sample and population variances for the old system, respectively. Using the claim "the variance of the waiting times under the new system is less than the variance of the waiting times under the old system," the null and alternative hypotheses are

$$H_0: \sigma_1^2 \le \sigma_2^2 \quad \text{and} \quad H_a: \sigma_1^2 > \sigma_2^2. \text{(Claim)}$$

Because the test is a right-tailed test with $\alpha = 0.10$, d.f.$_N = n_1 - 1 = 9$, and d.f.$_D = n_2 - 1 = 20$, the critical value is 1.96. Using the F-test, the test statistic is

$$F = \frac{s_1^2}{s_2^2} = \frac{144}{100} = 1.44.$$

The graph shows the location of the rejection region and the test statistic. Because F is not in the rejection region, you should fail to reject the null hypothesis. In other words, there is not enough evidence to convince the manager to switch to the new system.

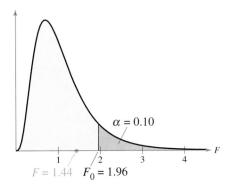

$\alpha = 0.10$

$F = 1.44 \quad F_0 = 1.96$

Picturing the World

Does location have an effect on the variance of real estate selling prices? A random sample of selling prices (in thousands of dollars) of houses sold in Albuquerque, New Mexico, is given in the following table. The first column represents the selling prices of houses in northeastern Albuquerque, and the second column lists the selling prices of houses in the remaining Albuquerque regions. *(Source: Albuquerque Board of Realtors)*

Northeast section	Other sections
205.0	129.5
208.0	97.5
215.0	93.9
215.0	82.0
199.9	78.0
190.0	77.0
180.0	70.0
156.0	62.0
145.0	54.0
144.9	107.0

Assuming the population of selling prices is normally distributed, is it possible to use a two-sample F-test to compare the population variances?

Normal solution	Treated solution
$n = 25$	$n = 20$
$s^2 = 180$	$s^2 = 56$

Try It Yourself 3

A medical researcher claims that a specially treated intravenous solution decreases the variance of the time required for nutrients to enter the bloodstream. Samples from each type of solution are randomly selected, and the results are shown in the table at the left. At $\alpha = 0.01$, is there enough evidence to support the researcher's claim? Assume the populations are normally distributed.

a. *Identify* the claim and *state* H_0 and H_a.
b. *Specify* the level of significance α.
c. *Determine* the degrees of freedom for the numerator and for the denominator.
d. *Find* the critical value and *identify* the rejection region.
e. *Use* the F-test to find the test statistic F.
f. *Decide* whether to reject the null hypothesis. Use a graph if necessary.
g. Is there enough evidence to support the claim? *Answer: Page A43* ◀

Stock A	Stock B
$n = 30$	$n = 31$
$s = 3.5$	$s = 5.7$

EXAMPLE 4   *Performing a Two-Sample F-Test*

You want to purchase stock in a company and are deciding between two different stocks. Because a stock's risk can be associated with the standard deviation of its daily closing prices, you randomly select samples of the daily closing prices for each stock to obtain the results shown at the left. At $\alpha = 0.05$, can you conclude that one of the two stocks is a riskier investment? Assume the stock closing prices are normally distributed.

SOLUTION   Because $5.7^2 > 3.5^2$, $s_1^2 = 5.7^2$ and $s_2^2 = 3.5^2$. Therefore, s_1^2 and σ_1^2 represent the sample and population variances for Stock B, respectively. Using the claim "one of the stocks is a riskier investment," the null and alternative hypotheses are

$$H_0: \sigma_1^2 = \sigma_2^2 \quad \text{and} \quad H_a: \sigma_1^2 \neq \sigma_2^2. \text{ (Claim)}$$

Because the test is a two-tailed test with $\frac{1}{2}\alpha = \frac{1}{2}(0.05) = 0.025$, d.f.$_N = n_1 - 1 = 30$, and d.f.$_D = n_2 - 1 = 29$, the critical value is 2.09. Using the *F*-test, the test statistic is

$$F = \frac{s_1^2}{s_2^2} = \frac{5.7^2}{3.5^2} \approx 2.65.$$

The graph shows the location of the rejection region and the test statistic. Because F is in the rejection region, you should reject the null hypothesis. In other words, one of the two stocks is a riskier investment.

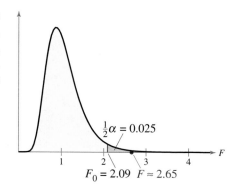

$\frac{1}{2}\alpha = 0.025$

$F_0 = 2.09 \quad F \approx 2.65$

Location A	Location B
$n = 16$	$n = 22$
$s = 0.95$	$s = 0.78$

Try It Yourself 4

A biologist claims that the pH levels of the soil in two geographic locations have equal standard deviations. Samples from each location are randomly selected, and the results are shown at the left. At $\alpha = 0.01$, is there enough evidence to reject the biologist's claim? Assume the pH levels are normally distributed.

a. *Identify* the claim and *state* H_0 and H_a.
b. *Specify* the level of significance α.
c. *Determine* the degrees of freedom for the numerator and for the denominator.
d. *Find* the critical value and *identify* the rejection region.
e. *Use* the *F*-test to find the test statistic F.
f. *Decide* whether to reject the null hypothesis. Use a graph if necessary.
g. Is there enough evidence to reject the claim?   *Answer: Page A43*

10.3 EXERCISES

HELP

StatPro 10.3

Internet Statistics 10.3

Student Solutions Manual 10.3

Videos 10.3

Try It Yourself Answers 10.3

1. Specify the level of significance α. Determine the degrees of freedom for the numerator and denominator. Use Table 7 to find the critical value F.

2. See Selected Answers, page A84

3. 2.93   4. 4.72

5. 5.32   6. 2.63

7. $H_0: \sigma_1^2 \leq \sigma_2^2$
   $H_a: \sigma_1^2 > \sigma_2^2$ (claim)
   CV = 3.52; F = 1.010
   Fail to reject H_0.

8. $H_0: \sigma_1^2 = \sigma_2^2$ (claim)
   $H_a: \sigma_1^2 \neq \sigma_2^2$
   CV = 5.12; F = 1.044
   Fail to reject H_0.

9. $H_0: \sigma_1^2 \leq \sigma_2^2$ (claim)
   $H_a: \sigma_1^2 > \sigma_2^2$
   CV = 5.26; F = 1.007
   Fail to reject H_0.

10. $H_0: \sigma_1^2 = \sigma_2^2$
    $H_a: \sigma_1^2 \neq \sigma_2^2$ (claim)
    CV = 3.08; F = 1.205
    Fail to reject H_0.

11. (a) Population 1: Company B
        Population 2: Company A
        $H_0: \sigma_1^2 \leq \sigma_2^2$
        $H_a: \sigma_1^2 > \sigma_2^2$ (claim)
    (b) 2.13   (c) 1.077
    (d) Fail to reject H_0.

12. See Selected Answers, page A84

Basic Skills and Concepts

1. Explain how to find the critical value for an *F*-test.

2. List five properties of the *F*-distribution.

Finding Critical F-Values   In Exercises 3–6, find the critical *F*-value for a right-tailed test using the indicated level of significance α and degrees of freedom d.f.$_N$ and d.f.$_D$.

3. $\alpha = 0.05$, d.f.$_N = 4$, d.f.$_D = 18$

4. $\alpha = 0.01$, d.f.$_N = 3$, d.f.$_D = 24$

5. $\alpha = 0.01$, d.f.$_N = 5$, d.f.$_D = 11$

6. $\alpha = 0.05$, d.f.$_N = 6$, d.f.$_D = 19$

Testing a Claim   In Exercises 7–10, test the claim about the differences between two population variances σ_1^2 and σ_2^2 at the given level of significance α using the given sample statistics. Assume the sample statistics are from independent samples and each population has a normal distribution.

7. Claim: $\sigma_1^2 > \sigma_2^2$, $\alpha = 0.10$.
   Sample statistics: $s_1^2 = 773$,
   $n_1 = 5; s_2^2 = 765, n_2 = 6$

8. Claim: $\sigma_1^2 = \sigma_2^2$, $\alpha = 0.05$.
   Sample statistics: $s_1^2 = 310$,
   $n_1 = 7; s_2^2 = 297, n_2 = 8$

9. Claim: $\sigma_1^2 \leq \sigma_2^2$, $\alpha = 0.01$.
   Sample statistics: $s_1^2 = 842$,
   $n_1 = 11; s_2^2 = 836, n_2 = 10$

10. Claim: $\sigma_1^2 \neq \sigma_2^2$, $\alpha = 0.05$.
   Sample statistics: $s_1^2 = 141$,
   $n_1 = 15; s_2^2 = 117, n_2 = 14$

Comparing Two Variances   In Exercises 11–18, (a) identify the claim and state H_0 and H_a, (b) find the critical value and identify the rejection region, (c) find the test statistic, and (d) decide whether to reject or fail to reject the null hypothesis. Then interpret the decision in the context of the original claim. Assume the samples are independent and each population has a normal distribution.

11. Company A claims that the variance of the life of its appliances is less than the variance of the life of Company B's appliances. A random sample of the lives of 20 of Company A's appliances has a variance of 2.6. A random sample of the lives of 23 of Company B's appliances has a variance of 2.8. At $\alpha = 0.05$, can you support Company A's claim? *(Adapted from Consumer Reports)*

12. An automobile manufacturer claims that the variance of the fuel consumption for its luxury sedans is less than the variance of the fuel consumption for the luxury sedans of a top competitor. A random sample of the fuel consumption of 19 of the manufacturer's sedans has a variance of 4.2. A random sample of the fuel consumption of 22 of its competitor's sedans has a variance of 4.5. At $\alpha = 0.05$, can you support the manufacturer's claim? *(Adapted from Consumer Reports)*

13. (a) $H_0: \sigma_1^2 = \sigma_2^2$ (claim)
$H_a: \sigma_1^2 \neq \sigma_2^2$

(b) 2.63

(c) 1.126

(d) Fail to reject H_0.

14. (a) $H_0: \sigma_1^2 = \sigma_2^2$ (claim)
$H_a: \sigma_1^2 \neq \sigma_2^2$

(b) 5.20

(c) 1.155

(d) Fail to reject H_0.

15. (a) $H_0: \sigma_1^2 \leq \sigma_2^2$ and
$H_a: \sigma_1^2 > \sigma_2^2$ (claim)

(b) 1.77

(c) 1.96

(d) Reject H_0.

16. (a) Population 1: 2nd city
Population 2: 1st city
$H_0: \sigma_1^2 = \sigma_2^2$ (claim)
$H_a: \sigma_1^2 \neq \sigma_2^2$

(b) 4.77

(c) 1.170

(d) Fail to reject H_0.

17. (a) Population 1: California
Population 2: New York
$H_0: \sigma_1^2 \leq \sigma_2^2$
$H_a: \sigma_1^2 > \sigma_2^2$ (claim)

(b) 2.35

(c) 1.616

(d) Fail to reject H_0.

18. (a) Population 1: Connecticut
Population 2: Colorado
$H_0: \sigma_1^2 \leq \sigma_2^2$
$H_a: \sigma_1^2 > \sigma_2^2$ (claim)

(b) 2.04

(c) 1.103

(d) Fail to reject H_0.

13. In a recent interview, a state school administrator stated that the standard deviations of physical science assessment test scores for eighth-grade students are the same in Districts 1 and 2. If a random sample of 12 test scores from District 1 has a standard deviation of 27.7 points and a random sample of 14 test scores from District 2 has a standard deviation of 26.1 points, can you reject the administrator's claim? Use $\alpha = 0.10$. *(Adapted from National Center for Educational Statistics)*

14. A school administrator reports that eighth-grade students are the same in District 1 and 2. As proof, the administrator gives the results of a study of test scores in each district. The study shows that a random sample of 10 test scores from District 1 has a standard deviation of 28.8 points and a random sample of 13 test scores from District 2 has a standard deviation of 26.8 points. At $\alpha = 0.01$, can you reject the administrator's claim? *(Adapted from National Center for Educational Statistics)*

15. A random sample of 25 waiting times (in minutes) before patients saw a medical professional in a hospital's minor emergency department had a standard deviation of 0.7 minute. After implementing a new admissions procedure, a random sample of 21 waiting times had a standard deviation of 0.5 minute. At $\alpha = 0.10$, can you support the hospital's claim that the standard deviation of the waiting times has decreased?

16. A travel agency's marketing brochure indicates that the standard deviations of hotel room rates for two cities are the same. If a random sample of 13 hotel room rates in one city has a standard deviation of $27.50 and a random sample of 15 hotel room rates in the other city has a standard deviation of $29.75, can you reject the agency's claim? Use $\alpha = 0.01$. *(Adapted from Smith Travel Research)*

17. The annual salaries for a random sample of 16 actuaries working in California have a standard deviation of $23,900. The annual salaries for a random sample of 17 actuaries working in New York have a standard deviation of $18,800. Using this information, can you conclude that the standard deviation of the annual salaries for actuaries is greater in California than in New York? Use $\alpha = 0.05$. *(Adapted from America's Career Infonet)*

18. An employment information service claims the standard deviation of the annual salaries for public relations managers is greater in Connecticut than in Colorado. The annual salaries for a random sample of 22 public relations managers in Connecticut have a standard deviation of $20,950. The annual salaries for a random sample of 24 public relations managers in Colorado have a standard deviation of $19,950. At $\alpha = 0.05$, can you support the service's claim? *(Adapted from America's Career Infonet)*

19. Right-tailed: 8.94
Left-tailed: 0.210

20. Right-tailed: 1.86
Left-tailed: 0.549

21. (0.366, 3.839)

22. (0.478, 5.019)

Extending the Basics

Finding Left-Tailed Critical F-values   In this section you learned that if s_1^2 is larger than s_2^2, then you only need to calculate the right-tailed critical F-value for a two-tailed test. For other applications of the F-distribution, you will need to calculate the left-tailed critical F-value. To calculate the left-tailed critical F-value, do the following.

(1) Interchange the values for d.f.$_N$ and d.f.$_D$.

(2) Find the corresponding F-value in Table 7.

(3) Calculate the reciprocal of the F-value to obtain the left-tailed critical F-value.

In Exercises 19 and 20, find the right- and left-tailed critical F-values for a two-tailed test with the given values of α, d.f.$_N$, and d.f.$_D$.

19. $\alpha = 0.05$, d.f.$_N = 6$, d.f.$_D = 3$ **20.** $\alpha = 0.10$, d.f.$_N = 20$, d.f.$_D = 17$

Confidence Interval for σ_1^2/σ_2^2 When s_1^2 and s_2^2 are the variances of independent samples from normally distributed populations, then a confidence interval for σ_1^2/σ_2^2 is as follows.

$$\frac{s_1^2}{s_2^2} F_L < \frac{\sigma_1^2}{\sigma_2^2} < \frac{s_1^2}{s_2^2} F_{R'}$$

where F_L is the left-tailed critical F-value and F_R is the right-tailed critical F-value.

In Exercises 21 and 22, construct the indicated confidence interval for σ_1^2/σ_2^2. Assume the samples are independent and each population has a normal distribution.

21. In a recent study of the cholesterol content in grilled chicken sandwiches served in fast-food restaurants, a nutritionist found that a random sample of 15 sandwiches from Arby's had a variance of $s_1^2 = 9.61$ while a random sample of 12 sandwiches from McDonald's had a variance of $s_2^2 = 8.41$. Construct a 95% confidence interval for σ_1^2/σ_2^2, where σ_1^2 and σ_2^2 are the variances of the cholesterol content of grilled chicken sandwiches from Arby's and McDonald's, respectively. *(Adapted from Fast Food Facts, Minnesota Attorney General's Office)*

22. A fast food study found that the carbohydrate content of 15 grilled chicken sandwiches from Arby's had a variance of 4.84. The study also found that the carbohydrate content of 12 grilled chicken sandwiches from McDonald's had a variance of 3.24. Construct a 95% confidence interval for σ_1^2/σ_2^2, where σ_1^2 and σ_2^2 are the variances of the carbohydrate content of grilled chicken sandwiches from Arby's and McDonald's, respectively. *(Adapted from Fast Food Facts, Minnesota Attorney General's Office)*

One-Way ANOVA

Suppose a medical researcher is analyzing the effectiveness of three types of pain relievers and wants to determine whether there is a difference in the mean length of the time it takes each medication to provide relief. To determine whether such a difference exists, the researcher can use the *F*-distribution together with a technique called *analysis of variance*. Because one independent variable is being studied, the process is called *one-way analysis of variance*.

DEFINITION

One-way analysis of variance is a hypothesis-testing technique that is used to compare means from three or more populations. Analysis of variance is usually abbreviated as **ANOVA.**

To begin a one-way analysis of variance test, you should first state a null and an alternative hypothesis. For a one-way ANOVA test, the null and alternative hypotheses are always similar to the following statements.

H_0: $\mu_1 = \mu_2 = \mu_3 = \cdots = \mu_k$ (All population means are equal.)

H_a: At least one of the means is different from the others.

When you reject the null hypothesis in an ANOVA test, you can conclude that one of the means is different from the others. Without performing more statistical tests, however, you cannot determine which of the means is different.

To use a one-way ANOVA test, the following conditions must be true.

1. Each sample must be randomly selected from a normal, or approximately normal, population.
2. The samples must be independent of each other.
3. Each population must have the same variance.

The test statistic for a one-way ANOVA test is the ratio of two variances: the variance between samples and the variance within samples.

1. The variance between samples, MS_B, measures the differences related to the treatment given to each sample and is sometimes called the **mean square between.**
2. The variance within samples, MS_W, measures the differences related to entries within the same sample. This variance, sometimes called the **mean square within,** is usually due to sampling error.

One-Way Analysis of Variance Test

If the conditions for a one-way analysis of variance test are satisfied, then the sampling distribution for the test is the F-distribution. The test statistic is

$$F = \frac{MS_B}{MS_W}.$$

The degrees of freedom for the F-test are $\text{d.f.}_N = k - 1$ and $\text{d.f.}_D = N - k$, where k is the number of samples and N is the sum of the sample sizes.

If there is little or no difference between the means, then MS_B will be approximately equal to MS_W and the test statistic will be approximately 1. Values of F close to 1 suggest that you should fail to reject the null hypothesis. However, if one of the means differs significantly from the others, MS_B will be greater than MS_W and the test statistic will be greater than 1. Values of F significantly greater than 1 suggest that you reject the null hypothesis. As such, all one-way ANOVA tests are right-tailed tests. That is, if the test statistic is greater than the critical value, H_0 will be rejected.

GUIDELINES

Finding the Test Statistic for a One-Way ANOVA Test

In Words	*In Symbols*
1. Find the mean and variance of each sample.	$\bar{x} = \dfrac{\Sigma x}{n} \quad s^2 = \dfrac{\Sigma(x - \bar{x})^2}{n - 1}$
2. Find the mean of all entries in all samples.	$\bar{\bar{x}} = \dfrac{\Sigma x}{N}$
3. Find the variance between the samples.	$MS_B = \dfrac{SS_B}{k - 1} = \dfrac{\Sigma n_i(\bar{x}_i - \bar{\bar{x}})^2}{k - 1}$
4. Find the variance within the samples.	$MS_W = \dfrac{SS_W}{N - k} = \dfrac{\Sigma(n_i - 1)s_i^2}{N - k}$
5. Find the test statistic.	$F = \dfrac{MS_B}{MS_W}$

Study Tip

The notations n_i, $\bar{x}_i$, and s_i^2 represent the sample size, mean, and variance of the ith sample, respectively. $\bar{\bar{x}}$ is sometimes called the grand mean.

The notation SS_B represents the sum of squares between groups.

$$SS_B = \Sigma n_i(\bar{x}_i - \bar{\bar{x}})^2$$

The notation SS_W represents the sum of squares within groups.

$$SS_W = \Sigma(n_i - 1)s_i^2$$

GUIDELINES

Performing a One-Way Analysis of Variance Test

In Words	*In Symbols*
1. Identify the claim. State the null and alternative hypotheses.	State H_0 and H_a.
2. Specify the level of significance.	Specify α.
3. Determine the degrees of freedom.	$\text{d.f.}_N = k - 1$ $\text{d.f.}_D = N - k$
4. Find the critical value.	Use Table 7 in Appendix B.
5. Identify the rejection region.	
6. Calculate the test statistic.	$F = \dfrac{MS_B}{MS_W}$
7. Make a decision to reject or fail to reject the null hypothesis.	If F is in the rejection region, reject H_0. Otherwise, do not reject H_0.
8. Interpret the decision in the context of the original claim.	

Tables are a convenient way to summarize the results of a one-way analysis of variance test. ANOVA summary tables are set up as shown below.

ANOVA Summary Table

Variation	Sum of squares	Degrees of freedom	Mean squares	F
Between	SS_B	d.f._N	$MS_B = \dfrac{SS_B}{\text{d.f.}_N}$	$MS_B \div MS_W$
Within	SS_W	d.f._D	$MS_W = \dfrac{SS_W}{\text{d.f.}_D}$	

> **EXAMPLE 1**   *Performing a One-Way ANOVA Test*

A medical researcher wants to determine whether there is a difference in the mean length of time it takes three types of pain relievers to provide relief from headache pain. Several headache sufferers are randomly selected and given one of the three medications. Each headache sufferer records the time (in minutes) it takes the medication to begin working. The results are listed in the following table. At $\alpha = 0.01$, can you conclude that the mean times are different?

Medication 1	Medication 2	Medication 3
12	16	14
15	14	17
17	21	20
12	15	15
	19	
$\bar{x}_1 = \frac{56}{4} = 14$	$\bar{x}_2 = \frac{85}{5} = 17$	$\bar{x}_3 = \frac{66}{4} = 16.5$
$s_1^2 = 6$	$s_2^2 = 8.5$	$s_3^2 = 7$

SOLUTION   The null and alternative hypotheses are as follows.

H_0: $\mu_1 = \mu_2 = \mu_3$
H_a: At least one mean is different from the others.

Because there are $k = 3$ samples, d.f.$_N = k - 1 = 3 - 1 = 2$. The sum of the sample sizes is $N = n_1 + n_2 + n_3 = 4 + 5 + 4 = 13$. So, d.f.$_D = N - k = 13 - 3 = 10$. Using d.f.$_N = 2$, d.f.$_D = 10$, and $\alpha = 0.01$, the critical value is 7.56. To find the test statistic, first calculate $\bar{\bar{x}}$, MS_B, and MS_W.

$$\bar{\bar{x}} = \frac{\Sigma x}{N} = \frac{56 + 85 + 66}{13} \approx 15.92$$

$$MS_B = \frac{\Sigma n_i (\bar{x}_i - \bar{\bar{x}})^2}{k - 1}$$

$$= \frac{4(14 - 15.92)^2 + 5(17 - 15.92)^2 + 4(16.5 - 15.92)^2}{3 - 1}$$

$$\approx \frac{21.92}{2} = 10.96$$

$$MS_W = \frac{\Sigma(n_i - 1)s_i^2}{N - k}$$

$$= \frac{(4 - 1)(6) + (5 - 1)(8.5) + (4 - 1)(7)}{13 - 3}$$

$$= \frac{73}{10} = 7.3$$

Using $MS_B = 10.96$ and $MS_W = 7.3$, the test statistic is

$$F = \frac{MS_B}{MS_W} = \frac{10.96}{7.3} \approx 1.50.$$

The graph shows the location of the rejection region. Because $F = 1.50$ is not in the rejection region, you should decide not to reject the null hypothesis. In other words, there is not enough evidence at the 1% level of significance to conclude that there is a difference in the mean length of time it takes the three pain relievers to provide relief from headache pain.

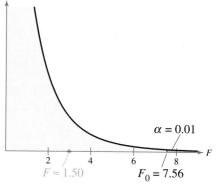

The ANOVA summary table for Example 1 is shown below.

Variation	Sum of squares	Degrees of freedom	Mean squares	*F*
Between	21.92	2	10.96	1.50
Within	73	10	7.3	

Try It Yourself 1

A sales analyst wants to determine whether there is a difference in the mean monthly sales of a company's four sales regions. Several salespersons from each region are randomly selected and each provides his or her sales amounts (in thousands of dollars) for the previous month. The results are listed in the following table. At $\alpha = 0.05$, can the analyst conclude that there is a difference in the mean monthly sales among the sales regions?

North	East	South	West
34	47	40	21
28	36	30	30
18	30	41	24
24	38	29	37
	44		23
$\bar{x}_1 = 26$	$\bar{x}_2 = 39$	$\bar{x}_3 = 35$	$\bar{x}_4 = 27$
$s_1^2 = 45.33$	$s_2^2 = 45$	$s_3^2 = 40.67$	$s_4^2 = 42.5$

a. *State* H_0 and H_a.
b. *Specify* the level of significance α.
c. *Determine* the degrees of freedom.
d. *Find* the critical value and *identify* the rejection region.
e. *Find* the test statistic F.
f. *Decide* whether to reject the null hypothesis. Use a graph if necessary.
g. Is there enough evidence to conclude that there is a difference in the mean monthly sales among the sales regions?   *Answer: Page A43*

Using technology greatly simplifies the one-way ANOVA process. When using a technology tool such as Minitab or the TI-83 to perform a one-way analysis of variance test, you can use P-values to decide whether to reject the null hypothesis. If the P-value is less than α, you should reject H_0.

▶ **EXAMPLE 2** *Using Technology to Perform ANOVA Tests*

Airline 1	Airline 2	Airline 3
122	119	120
135	133	158
126	143	155
131	149	126
125	114	147
116	124	164
120	126	134
108	131	151
142	140	131
113	136	141

Three airline companies offer flights between Corydon and Lincolnville. Several randomly selected flight times (in minutes) between the towns for each airline are shown at the left. At $\alpha = 0.01$, can you conclude that there is a difference in the means of the flight times? Use a technology tool.

SOLUTION The results obtained using the TI-83 are shown below. From the results, you can see that $P \approx 0.006$. Because $P < \alpha$, you should reject the null hypothesis. In other words, you can conclude that there is a difference in the means of the flight times.

```
TI-83
One-way ANOVA
 F=6.13023478
 p=.0063828069
 Factor
  df=2
  SS=1806.46667
↓ MS=903.233333
```

```
TI-83
One-way ANOVA
↑ MS=903.233333
 Error
  df=27
  SS=3978.2
  MS=147.340741
 Sxp=12.1383994
```

Try It Yourself 2

The data listed in the following table represent the GPAs of randomly selected freshmen, sophomores, juniors, and seniors. At $\alpha = 0.05$, can you conclude that there is a difference in the means of the GPAs? Use a technology tool.

Freshman	2.34	2.38	3.31	2.39	3.40	2.70	2.34		
Sophomores	3.26	2.22	3.26	3.29	2.95	3.01	3.13	3.59	2.84	3.00
Juniors	2.80	2.60	2.49	2.83	2.34	3.23	3.49	3.03	2.87
Seniors	3.31	2.35	3.27	2.86	2.78	2.75	3.05	3.31

a. *Enter* the data.
b. *Perform* the ANOVA test.
c. *Compare* the resulting P-value to the given level of significance α.
d. Can you conclude that there is a difference in the means of the GPAs?

Answer: Page A43 ◀

Two-Way ANOVA

When you want to test the effect of *two* independent variables, or factors, on one dependent variable, you can use a **two-way analysis of variance test.** For example, suppose a medical researcher wants to test the effect of gender *and* type of medication on the mean length of time it takes pain relievers to provide relief. To perform such an experiment, the researcher can use the following two-way ANOVA block design.

Type of medication

		I	II	III
Gender	M	Males taking type I	Males taking type II	Males taking type III
	F	Females taking type I	Females taking type II	Females taking type III

A two-way ANOVA test has three null hypotheses—two for each main effect and one for the interaction effect. A **main effect** is the effect of one independent variable on the dependent variable and the **interaction effect** is the effect of both independent variables on the dependent variable. For example, the hypotheses for the pain reliever experiment are as follows.

Hypotheses for main effects:

H_0: The type of medication has no effect on the length of time it takes a pain reliever to provide relief.

H_a: The type of medication has an effect on the length of time it takes a pain reliever to provide relief.

H_0: Gender has no effect on the length of time it takes a pain reliever to provide relief.

H_a: Gender has an effect on the length of time it takes a pain reliever to provide relief.

Hypotheses for interaction effect:

H_0: There is no interaction effect between gender and type of medication on the length of time it takes a pain reliever to provide relief.

H_a: There is an interaction effect between gender and type of medication on the length of time it takes a pain reliever to provide relief.

To test these hypotheses, you can perform a two-way ANOVA test. Using the *F*-distribution, a two-way ANOVA test calculates an *F*-test statistic for each hypothesis. As a result, it is possible to reject none, one, two, or all of the null hypotheses. The statistics involved with a two-way ANOVA test is beyond the scope of this course. You can, however, use a technology tool such as Minitab to perform a two-way ANOVA test.

Insight

The conditions for a two-way ANOVA test are the same as those for a one-way ANOVA test with the additional condition that all samples must be of equal size.

Insight

If gender and type of medication have no effect on the length of time it takes a pain reliever to provide relief, then there will be no significant difference in the means of the relief times.

10.4 EXERCISES

HELP

 StatPro 10.4

 Internet Statistics 10.4

 Student Solutions Manual 10.4

 Videos 10.4

 Try It Yourself Answers 10.4

1. (a) $H_0: \mu_1 = \mu_2 = \mu_3$
H_a: At least one mean is different from the others. (claim)

(b) d.f.$_N$ = 2
d.f.$_D$ = 27
$CV = 3.35$

(c) $F = 1.26$

(d) Fail to reject H_0.

2. (a) $H_0: \mu_1 = \mu_2 = \mu_3$
H_a: At least one mean is different from the others. (claim)

(b) d.f.$_N$ = 2
d.f.$_D$ = 13
$CV = 3.81$

(c) $F = 2.15$

(d) Fail to reject H_0.

Basic Skills and Concepts

Performing a One-Way ANOVA Test In Exercises 1–10, perform the indicated one-way ANOVA test by (a) identifying the claim and stating H_0 and H_a, (b) determining the degrees of freedom, identifying the critical value, and identifying the rejection region, (c) calculating the test statistic, and (d) deciding to reject or fail to reject the null hypothesis. Interpret the decision in the context of the original claim. Assume each sample is drawn from a normal, or approximately normal, population, that the samples are independent of each other, and that the populations have the same variances. If convenient, use technology to solve the problem.

1. The following table shows the cost per month (in dollars) for a random sample of toothpastes exhibiting moderate abrasiveness, low abrasiveness, or very low abrasiveness. At $\alpha = 0.05$, can you conclude that the mean costs per month are different? *(Source: Consumer Reports)*

Moderate abrasiveness	Low abrasiveness	Very low abrasiveness
0.75	0.74	0.44
0.46	0.96	1.40
3.16	0.65	4.00
0.97	0.70	0.91
0.72	0.72	
2.74	1.71	
0.62	1.46	
0.72	1.57	
1.00	0.77	
0.78	0.98	
1.01	0.61	
1.11	1.04	
1.45	0.61	

2. The prices (in dollars) for 16 randomly selected automobile batteries are listed in the table. The prices are classified according to battery type. At $\alpha = 0.05$, is there enough evidence to conclude that at least one of the mean battery prices is different from the others? *(Source: Consumer Reports)*

Group size 24	50	65	75	64		
Group size 58	83	63	65	63	85	65
Group size 34/78	89	84	75	90	70	60

3. (a) $H_0: \mu_1 = \mu_2 = \mu_3$ (claim)
H_a: At least one mean is different from the others.

(b) d.f.$_N$ = 2
d.f.$_D$ = 12
CV = 2.81

(c) F = 1.77

(d) Fail to reject H_0.

4. (a) $H_0: \mu_1 = \mu_2 = \mu_3 = \mu_4$ (claim)
H_a: At least one mean is different from the others.

(b) d.f.$_N$ = 3
d.f.$_D$ = 23
CV = 2.34

(c) F = 1.61

(d) Fail to reject H_0.

5. (a) $H_0: \mu_1 = \mu_2 = \mu_3 = \mu_4$ (claim)
H_a: At least one mean is different from the others.

(b) d.f.$_N$ = 3
d.f.$_D$ = 33
CV = 4.44

(c) F = 5.21

(d) Reject H_0.

3. The following table shows the price per gallon (in dollars) for a random sample of exterior deck treatments. At $\alpha = 0.10$, can you conclude that the mean prices are the same for the three types of treatments? *(Source: Consumer Reports)*

Semitransparent treatments	Lightly tinted treatments	Clear treatments
24	51	13
23	14	13
22	21	10
17	16	12
21		22
17		

4. The following table shows the annual amount spent on reading (in dollars) for a random sample of American consumers from four regions. At $\alpha = 0.10$, can you conclude that the mean annual amounts are the same in all regions? *(Adapted from U.S. Bureau of Labor Statistics)*

Northeast	Midwest	South	West
308	246	103	223
58	169	143	184
141	246	164	221
109	158	119	269
220	167	99	199
144	76	214	171
316		108	204

5. In a recent study, a health insurance company investigated the number of days patients spend at a hospital. As part of the study, the company randomly selected patients from various parts of the United States and recorded the number of days each patient spent at a hospital. The results of the study are shown below. At $\alpha = 0.01$, can the company conclude that the mean number of days patients spend in the hospital is the same for all four regions? *(Adapted from U.S. National Center for Health Statistics)*

Northeast	Midwest	South	West
8	7	3	5
6	7	5	4
9	8	6	6
4	5	6	4
5	5	3	6
6	5	6	6
8	5	4	5
10	5	6	4
11	5		6
7	7		

6. (a) $H_0: \mu_1 = \mu_2 = \mu_3 = \mu_4$
H_a: At least one mean is
different from the others.
(claim)

(b) d.f.$_N$ = 3
d.f.$_D$ = 48
CV = 2.20

(c) $F = 2.29$

(d) Reject H_0.

7. (a) $H_0: \mu_1 = \mu_2 = \mu_3 = \mu_4$
(claim)
H_a: At least one mean is
different from the others.

(b) d.f.$_N$ = 3
d.f.$_D$ = 43
CV = 2.22

(c) $F = 3.04$

(d) Reject H_0.

6. The following table shows the square footage (in thousands) for a random sample of American buildings from four regions. At $\alpha = 0.10$, can you conclude that the mean square footage for one of the regions is different? *(Adapted from U.S. National Center for Health Statistics)*

Northeast	Midwest	South	West
13.9	10.4	14.1	13.0
18.0	11.6	16.4	15.0
15.7	5.3	15.6	11.4
11.7	10.8	3.1	10.4
24.6	12.3	16.6	11.5
12.2	14.5	17.0	16.0
18.1	3.8	13.2	5.5
10.0	15.2	8.6	20.0
8.7	18.8	25.5	7.0
17.1	13.6	9.6	2.8
17.4	11.4	12.8	15.3
16.3	7.9	15.4	14.6
19.4	15.2	16.2	11.0

7. A realtor is comparing the prices of one-family houses in four cities. After randomly selecting one-family houses in the four cities and determining the price for each, the realtor organizes the prices (in thousands of dollars) in a table as shown below. At $\alpha = 0.10$, can the realtor conclude that the mean price is the same for all four cities? *(Adapted from National Association of Realtors)*

City A	City B	City C	City D
131.2	137.9	164.4	83.9
122.6	88.0	49.4	98.3
103.7	95.1	144.7	168.9
148.8	79.3	108.6	93.7
144.5	81.5	137.2	204.3
206.9	101.9	83.6	85.1
164.6	128.8	100.5	100.4
45.0	147.2	99.4	211.7
162.8	38.7	67.8	140.1
132.7	57.9	147.9	131.3
178.2	67.3	39.2	167.0
131.2		149.9	84.3

8. (a) $H_0: \mu_1 = \mu_2 = \mu_3 = \mu_4$
H_a: At least one mean is different from the others. (claim)
(b) d.f.$_N$ = 3
d.f.$_D$ = 26
CV = 2.31
(c) F = 6.36
(d) Reject H_0.

9. (a) $H_0: \mu_1 = \mu_2 = \mu_3 = \mu_4$
H_a: At least one mean is different from the others. (claim)
(b) d.f.$_N$ = 3
d.f.$_D$ = 36
CV = 4.38
(c) F = 8.46
(d) Reject H_0.

10. (a) $H_0: \mu_1 = \mu_2 = \mu_3 = \mu_4$ (claim)
H_a: At least one mean is different from the others.
(b) d.f.$_N$ = 3
d.f.$_D$ = 23
CV = 4.76
(c) F = 0.89
(d) Fail to reject H_0.

8. The following table shows the prices (in dollars) for a random sample of new mobile homes from four manufacturers. At $\alpha = 0.10$, can you conclude that at least one of the mean prices is different? *(Adapted from U.S. Bureau of the Census)*

Manufacturer A	Manufacturer B	Manufacturer C	Manufacturer D
34,918	37,223	39,029	43,176
34,904	38,079	38,711	52,844
33,971	35,646	21,774	42,936
39,404	39,420	28,836	41,685
58,000	34,732	35,535	45,320
32,710	51,223	25,185	54,841
45,049	40,630	35,791	
48,373		32,607	
		27,728	

9. The following table shows the energy consumed (in millions of Btu's) for a random sample of households from four regions. At $\alpha = 0.01$, can you conclude that, for at least one region, the mean energy consumption is different? *(Adapted from U.S. Energy Information Administration)*

Northeast	Midwest	South	West
115.2	53.0	43.6	24.7
123.2	231.1	55.7	43.4
167.3	107.9	82.7	124.9
139.5	125.6	83.5	58.6
142.7	207.2	43.3	115.6
174.0	246.2	38.2	67.0
138.3	144.9	50.1	15.7
98.9	180.4	12.5	125.0
196.6	137.8	179.7	105.8
57.3	201.8		55.5
	84.2		

10. The table at the right shows the amount spent (in dollars) on energy for a random sample of households from four regions. At $\alpha = 0.01$, can you conclude that the mean amounts spent are equal for all regions? *(Adapted from U.S. Energy Information Administration)*

Northeast	Midwest	South	West
2623	1310	1252	947
573	940	1997	1801
2142	1342	1678	1706
1146	1294	1105	1244
853	1190	1593	1345
1073	1514	1667	768
2193	689		1109

11. $CV_{\text{Scheffe}} = 13.320$

    $(1, 2) \rightarrow 4.818 \rightarrow$ No
difference

    $(1, 3) \rightarrow 12.135 \rightarrow$ No
difference

    $(1, 4) \rightarrow 10.628 \rightarrow$ No
difference

    $(2, 3) \rightarrow 2.000 \rightarrow$ No
difference

    $(2, 4) \rightarrow 1.263 \rightarrow$ No
difference

    $(3, 4) \rightarrow 0.101 \rightarrow$ No
difference

12. $CV_{\text{Scheffe}} = 6.60$

    $(1, 2) \rightarrow 4.921 \rightarrow$ No
difference

    $(1, 3) \rightarrow 0.649 \rightarrow$ No
difference

    $(1, 4) \rightarrow 4.421 \rightarrow$ No
difference

    $(2, 3) \rightarrow 1.996 \rightarrow$ No
difference

    $(2, 4) \rightarrow 0.013 \rightarrow$ No
difference

    $(3, 4) \rightarrow 1.682 \rightarrow$ No
difference

13. $CV_{\text{Scheffe}} = 6.660$

    $(1, 2) \rightarrow 7.212 \rightarrow$ Significant
difference

    $(1, 3) \rightarrow 3.519 \rightarrow$ No
difference

    $(1, 4) \rightarrow 0.260 \rightarrow$ No
difference

    $(2, 3) \rightarrow 0.724 \rightarrow$ No
difference

    $(2, 4) \rightarrow 4.782 \rightarrow$ No
difference

    $(3, 4) \rightarrow 1.866 \rightarrow$ No
difference

14. See Selected Answers, page A84

Extending the Basics

The Scheffé Test   If the null hypothesis is rejected in a one-way ANOVA test of three or more means, a Scheffé Test can be performed to find which means have a significant difference. In a Scheffé Test, the means are compared two at a time. For example, with three means you would have the following comparisons: $\bar{x}_1$ versus $\bar{x}_2$, $\bar{x}_1$ versus $\bar{x}_3$, and $\bar{x}_2$ versus $\bar{x}_3$. For each comparison, calculate

$$\frac{(\bar{x}_a - \bar{x}_b)^2}{\dfrac{SS_W}{\Sigma(n_i - 1)}\left[(1/n_a) + (1/n_b)\right]},$$

where $\bar{x}_a$ and $\bar{x}_b$ are the means being compared and n_a and n_b are the sample sizes. Then compare the value to the critical value. Calculate the critical value using the same steps as in a one-way ANOVA test and multiply the result by $k - 1$. Use this information to solve Exercises 11–14.

11. Refer to the data in Exercise 5. At $\alpha = 0.01$, perform a Scheffé Test to determine which means have a significant difference.

12. Refer to the data in Exercise 6. At $\alpha = 0.10$, perform a Scheffé Test to determine which means have a significant difference.

13. Refer to the data in Exercise 7. At $\alpha = 0.10$, perform a Scheffé Test to determine which means have a significant difference.

14. Refer to the data in Exercise 8. At $\alpha = 0.01$, perform a Scheffé Test to determine which means have a significant difference.

TECHNOLOGY   MINITAB   EXCEL   TI-83

www.nhtsa.dot.gov

Crash Tests

At the beginning of this chapter, you learned that as part of the New Car Assessment Program, the government buys new cars each year and crashes them into a wall at 35 miles per hour to compare how well different vehicles protect passengers in a head-on collision. You also learned that the dummies used in a crash test are equipped with instruments that measure the forces and impacts that occur during the crash test.

The table at the right displays the left leg injury data from the crash tests of a random sample of three vehicle types: medium (e.g., Ford Taurus), heavy (e.g., Lincoln Town Car), and multiple purpose (e.g., Toyota 4-Runner).

Vehicle Type		
Medium	**Heavy**	**Multiple Purpose**
926	541	1911
996	406	1539
332	1529	267
1353	1132	388
519	767	932
705	1224	401
611	314	1100
1657	1728	1595
571	764	430
961	260	1909
1580	1527	606
775	766	469
1132	862	430
1512	1138	1277
1500	1326	1001
1554	883	1283

Exercises

In Exercises 1–3, refer to the following samples. Use $\alpha = 0.05$.

(a) Medium and heavy vehicles
(b) Medium and multiple-purpose vehicles
(c) Heavy and multiple-purpose vehicles

1. Are the samples independent of each other? Explain.

2. Use a technology tool to determine whether the samples were selected from populations having equal variances.

3. Use a technology tool to determine whether each sample is from a normal, or approximately normal, population.

4. Using the results of Exercises 1–3, discuss whether the three conditions for a one-way ANOVA test are satisfied. If so, use a technology tool to test the claim that medium, heavy, and multiple-purpose vehicles have the same left leg injury potential in a 35 miles per hour frontal crash. Use $\alpha = 0.05$.

5. Repeat Exercises 1–4 using the data in the following table. The table displays the right leg injury data from the crash tests of a random sample of three vehicle types: medium, heavy, and multiple purpose.

Vehicle Type		
Medium	**Heavy**	**Multiple Purpose**
708	257	1629
642	985	493
611	428	613
1063	501	667
892	322	979
582	540	1264
1409	1015	1247
751	2856	855
757	821	1113
144	515	495
454	718	626
438	420	575
716	141	863
913	692	776
1049	302	1090
1107	1252	644

Extended solutions are given in the *Technology Supplement*. Technical instruction is provided for Minitab, Excel, and the TI-83.

10 ▾ CHAPTER SUMMARY

What did you learn?

Why did you learn it? Uses and Abuses

Uses As you continue in your selected field of study and on into your career, you may encounter situations in which it is necessary to test a claim about a specific distribution or test whether three or more population means are equal.

For instance, suppose you work for a large manufacturing company and part of your responsibility is to determine the distribution of your company's sales throughout the world and decide where to focus the company's efforts. Because wrong decisions will cost your company money, you want to make sure that you make the right decision. Using some of the techniques discussed in this chapter can help you.

Abuses There are several ways that the tests presented in this section can be abused. For example, it is easy to allow preconceived notions to affect the results of a chi-square goodness of fit test and a test for independence. When testing to see whether a distribution has changed, don't let the existing distribution "cloud" the study results. Similarly, when determining whether two variables are independent, don't let your intuition "get in the way." As with any hypothesis test, you must properly gather appropriate data and perform the corresponding test before you can reach a logical conclusion.

10 REVIEW EXERCISES

1. Claimed distribution:

Category	Distribution
New Pat.	25%
Old/New	25%
Old/Recur.	50%

H_0: Distribution of office visits is as shown in table above.
H_a: Distribution of office visits differs from the claimed distribution.

$CV = 5.991$
$\chi^2 = 74.101$
Reject H_0.

2. Claimed distribution:

Age	Distribution
21–29	20.5%
30–39	21.7%
40–49	18.1%
50–59	17.3%
60+	22.4%

H_0: Distribution of ages is as shown in table above.
H_a: Distribution of ages differs from the claimed distribution.

$CV = 13.277$
$\chi^2 = 279.705$
Reject H_0.

3. See Odd Answers, page A72
4. See Selected Answers, page A84

In Exercises 1 and 2, use a χ^2 goodness-of-fit test to test the claim about the population distribution. Interpret the decision in the context of the original claim.

1. A health care investigator wishes to test the following claim: Of all doctor's office visits in the United States, 25% are from new patients, 25% are from old patients with a new problem, and the remainder are old patients with a recurring problem. A random sample of various doctor's offices finds that 97 patients were new, 142 were old with a new problem, and 457 were old patients with a recurring problem. Test the investigator's claim at $\alpha = 0.05$. *(Adapted from U.S. National Center for Health Statistics)*

2. A legal researcher is studying the age distribution of juries by comparing them to the overall age distribution of available jurors. The researcher claims that the jury distribution is different from the overall distribution; that is, there is a noticeable age bias in jury selection in this area. The following table shows the number of jurors at a county court in one year and the percent of persons residing in that county, by age. Use the population distribution to find the expected juror frequencies. Test the researcher's claim at $\alpha = 0.01$.

	21–29	30–39	40–49	50–59	60 and above
Jury	45	128	244	224	359
Population	20.5%	21.7%	18.1%	17.3%	22.4%

In Exercises 3 and 4, use the given contingency table to (a) find the expected frequencies of each table element, (b) perform a χ^2 independence test, and (c) comment on the relationship between the two variables.

3. The following table shows the highest level of education of Americans by age category in a recent year. The numbers listed are in thousands of persons. Use $\alpha = 0.10$. *(Source: 1986 World Almanac and Book of Facts)*

	H.S.—did not complete	H.S. completed	College 1–3 years	College 4 or more years
25–44	10,446	18,286	14,131	17,367
45 and above	27,129	25,788	8,151	9,496

4. The contingency table shows the results of a random sample of 480 individuals classified by gender and type of vehicle owned. Use $\alpha = 0.05$.

	Type of vehicle owned			
	Car	Truck	SUV	Van
Males	85	96	45	6
Females	110	75	60	3

5. $F = 2.295$

6. $F = 4.71$

7. $F = 2.39$

8. $F = 2.01$

9. $H_0: \sigma_1^2 \geq \sigma_2^2$ (claim)
$H_a: \sigma_1^2 < \sigma_2^2$ (left-tailed test)
$CV = 3.09$
$F = 2.419$
Fail to reject H_0.

10. $H_0: \sigma_1^2 = \sigma_2^2$
$H_a: \sigma_1^2 \neq \sigma_2^2$ (claim)
$CV = 3.33$
$F = 2.273$
Fail to reject H_0.

11. $H_0: \sigma_1^2 \leq \sigma_2^2$
$H_a: \sigma_1^2 > \sigma_2^2$ (claim)
$CV = 1.92$
$F = 1.717$
Fail to reject H_0.

12. Population 1: Non-tempered
Population 2: Tempered
$H_0: \sigma_1^2 \leq \sigma_2^2$
$H_a: \sigma_1^2 > \sigma_2^2$ (claim)
$CV = 3.44$
$F = 3.759$
Reject H_0.

13. Population 1: Male
$s_1^2 = 18,486.26$
Population 2: Female
$s_2^2 = 12,102.78$
$H_0: \sigma_1^2 = \sigma_2^2$
$H_a: \sigma_1^2 \neq \sigma_2^2$ (claim)
$CV = 6.94$
$F = 1.527$
Fail to reject H_0.

In Exercises 5–8, find the critical *F*-value for a right-tailed test using the indicated level of significance α and degrees of freedom d.f.$_N$ and d.f.$_D$.

5. $\alpha = 0.05$, d.f.$_N = 6$, d.f.$_D = 50$

6. $\alpha = 0.01$, d.f.$_N = 12$, d.f.$_D = 10$

7. $\alpha = 0.10$, d.f.$_N = 5$, d.f.$_D = 12$

8. $\alpha = 0.05$, d.f.$_N = 20$, d.f.$_D = 25$

In Exercises 9 and 10, use the given sample statistics to test the claim about two population variances, σ_1^2 and σ_2^2, at the indicated level of significance α. Assume that both populations are normally distributed and the samples are independent.

9. Claim: $\sigma_1^2 \leq \sigma_2^2$, $\alpha = 0.01$. Sample statistics: $s_1^2 = 653$, $n_1 = 16$, $s_2^2 = 270$, $n_2 = 21$

10. Claim: $\sigma_1^2 \neq \sigma_2^2$, $\alpha = 0.10$. Sample statistics: $s_1^2 = 112{,}676$, $n_1 = 6$, $s_2^2 = 49{,}572$, $n_2 = 11$

In Exercises 11–14, test the claim about two population variances at the indicated level of significance α. Interpret the results in the context of the claim.

11. An agricultural analyst is comparing the wheat production in Oklahoma counties. The analyst claims that the variation in wheat production is greater in Garfield County than in Kay County. A random sample of 21 Garfield County farms yields a standard deviation of 0.76 bushels/acre; 16 Kay County farms are found to have a standard deviation of 0.58 bushels/acre. Diagnostics suggest that wheat production is normally distributed in both counties. Test the analyst's claim at $\alpha = 0.10$. *(Adapted from Environmental Verification and Analysis Center—University of Oklahoma)*

12. A steel pipe fittings company claims that the yield strength of its nontempered couplings is more variable than that of its tempered couplings. A random sample of 9 tempered couplings has a standard deviation of 13.1 megapascals, while a similar sample of 9 nontempered couplings had a standard deviation of 25.4 megapascals. From past data, it is known that the company's production process results in normally distributed yield strengths. Test the company's claim at $\alpha = 0.05$.

13. The following table shows the SAT verbal test scores for 9 female students and 14 male students. Assume that SAT verbal test scores are normally distributed. At $\alpha = 0.01$, test the claim that the test score variance for females is different than that for males.

Female	480	610	340	630	520	690	540
Male	560	680	360	530	380	460	630

Female	600	680					
Male	310	730	740	520	560	400	510

14. Population 1: Current
$s_1^2 = 0.00146$
Population 2: New
$s_2^2 = 0.00050$
H_0: $\sigma_1^2 \leq \sigma_2^2$
H_a: $\sigma_1^2 > \sigma_2^2$ (claim)
$CV \approx 2.82$
$F = 2.92$
Reject H_0.

15. H_0: $\mu_1 = \mu_2 = \mu_3 = \mu_4$
H_a: At least one mean is different from the others. (claim)
$CV = 2.29$
$F = 6.60$
Reject H_0.

16. H_0: $\mu_1 = \mu_2 = \mu_3 = \mu_4$
H_a: At least one mean is different from the others. (claim)
$CV = 3.16$
$F = 0.64$
Fail to reject H_0.

14. A plastics company that produces automobile dashboard inserts has just received a new injection mold that is supposedly more consistent than its current mold. A quality technician wishes to test whether this new mold will produce inserts that are less variable in diameter than those produced with the company's current mold. The following table shows independent random samples (of size 12) of insert diameters (in centimeters) for both the current and new molds. Assume that the variances for the current mold and the new mold are normally distributed. At $\alpha = 0.05$, test the claim that the new mold produces inserts that are less variable in diameter than the current mold produces.

New	9.611	9.618	9.594	9.580	9.611	9.597
Current	9.571	9.642	9.650	9.651	9.596	9.636

New	9.638	9.568	9.605	9.603	9.647	9.590
Current	9.570	9.537	9.641	9.625	9.626	9.579

In Exercises 15 and 16, use the given sample data to perform a one-way ANOVA test using the indicated level of significance α. What can you conclude?

15. The table at the right shows the residential energy expenditures (in dollars) of a random sample of households in four U.S. regions. Diagnostics suggest that the sample is drawn from a normally distributed population. Use $\alpha = 0.10$ to test for differences among the means for the four regions. *(Adapted from U.S. Energy Information Administration)*

Northeast	Midwest	South	West
2088	759	888	1115
1259	1346	773	898
1762	975	1141	1605
1783	1523	1232	857
1623	1233	1310	465
2175	1903	953	359
1265	1236	1005	909
1258	1176	1475	1193

16. The table at the right shows the annual income (in dollars) of a random sample of households in four U.S. regions. Diagnostics suggest that the sample is drawn from an approximately normally distributed population. Use $\alpha = 0.05$ to test for differences among the means for the four regions. *(Adapted from U.S. Census Bureau)*

Northeast	Midwest	South	West
50,533	27,175	37,348	43,970
41,798	50,788	61,090	36,378
50,661	48,847	25,393	32,587
26,789	29,602	35,098	30,665
47,620	27,152	23,261	
	42,364	47,798	
	9,078		

10 CHAPTER QUIZ

1. Population 1: San Jose
$s_1^2 = 429.984$
Population 2: Dallas
$s_2^2 = 112.779$
$H_0: \sigma_1^2 = \sigma_2^2$
$H_a: \sigma_1^2 \neq \sigma_2^2$ (claim)
$CV = 2.82$
$F = 3.813$
Reject H_0.

2. $H_0: \mu_1 = \mu_2 = \mu_3$ (claim)
H_a: At least one mean is different from the others.
$CV = 2.43$
$F = 7.39$
Reject H_0.

3. (a) Claimed distribution:

Education	25 & Over
Not a HS graduate	18.3%
HS graduate	33.6%
Some college, no degree	17.3%
Assoc. Degree	7.2%
Bach. Degree	15.8%
Advanced Degree	7.8%

(b) 0.01

(c) 15.086

(d) Reject H_0 if $\chi^2 > 15.086$.

(e) 8.522

(f) Fail to reject H_0.

(g) Fail to reject H_0. There is not enough evidence to conclude that the distribution of educational achievement differs from the claimed distribution.

4. See Odd Answers, page A73

Take this quiz as you would take a quiz in class. After you are done, check your work against the answers given in the back of the book.

For each Exercise, (a) state H_0 and H_a, (b) specify the level of significance, (c) find the critical value, (d) identify the rejection region, (e) calculate the test statistic, (f) make a decision, and (g) interpret the results in the context of the problem.

For Exercises 1 and 2, use the following table. The table lists the annual wages (in thousands of dollars) for randomly selected individuals from three metropolitan areas. Assume the wages are normally distributed. *(Adapted from U.S. Bureau of Labor Statistics, 1995)*

San Jose, CA	48.6	61.9	19.8	35.2	25.5	58.4	47.4	48.6	17.6
	57.6	81.1	26.1	76.8					
Dallas, TX	32.9	46.4	19.7	24.0	19.7	18.4	25.2	10.3	26.9
	20.5	52.6	40.7	24.4	36.5	33.9	28.0	35.3	25.5
Ann Arbor, MI	22.7	36.0	20.7	26.8	24.0	49.2	29.5	28.8	38.8
	35.8	23.1	27.6	30.8	33.5	23.3	38.7		

1. At $\alpha = 0.05$, is there enough evidence to conclude that the variances in annual wages for San Jose, CA and Dallas, TX are different?

2. Are the mean annual wages equal for all three cities? Use $\alpha = 0.10$.

For Exercises 3 and 4, use the following table. The table lists the distribution of educational achievement for Americans aged 25 and over. It also lists the results of a survey for two additional age categories. *(Adapted from U.S. Bureau of the Census)*

	25 and over	35–44	65–74
Not a H.S. graduate	18.3%	37	124
High school graduate	33.6%	102	148
Some college, no degree	17.3%	59	61
Associate degree	7.2%	27	15
Bachelor's degree	15.8%	51	37
Advanced degree	7.8%	25	22

3. Does the distribution for Americans aged 25 and over describe Americans aged 35–44? Use $\alpha = 0.01$.

4. Does the distribution for Americans aged 25 and over describe Americans aged 65–74? Use $\alpha = 0.05$.

Where You've Been

Up to this point in the text, you have studied dozens of different statistical formulas and tests that can help you in a decision-making process. Knowing how to apply various statistical tests is important. However, it is even more important that you always use critical thinking when using a statistical test. Using critical thinking when applying statistical techniques can help prevent costly mistakes and tragic errors.

The explosion of the space shuttle Challenger on January 28, 1986 is a classic example of how tragic results might have been avoided by using correct statistical techniques. Seven astronauts died because two large rubber O-rings leaked during takeoff. The rings leaked because of the low temperature at the takeoff time.

The correlation between O-ring failure and air temperature was known before the time of takeoff. In fact, an engineering group had recommended that the flight be delayed. In their argument, however, the engineers failed to present the data clearly. How would you present the following data?

Temperature (°C)	12	14	14	17	19	19	19	19	20	21	21
Damage Index	11	4	4	2	0	0	0	0	0	4	0

Temperature (°C)	21	21	21	22	23	24	24	24	26	26	27
Damage Index	4	0	0	0	0	4	0	0	0	0	0

Nonparametric Tests

Where You're Going

In this chapter, you will study additional statistical tests. Each of these has usefulness in real-life applications. Remember, however, that no statistical test, including those in this chapter, can be applied blindly. Moreover, the more important your decision, the more important it is that you look at the data from several perspectives.

With the O-ring data on the previous page, the air temperature T and the damage index D can be related by the regression line $D = 9.96 - 0.415T$. The correlation coefficient, however, is relatively weak ($r = -0.6$). The P-value is 0.003, which would indicate that the correlation is significant, but the D-values do not pass the normality requirement.

So, while a simple correlation test might indicate a relationship between air temperature and O-ring damage, one might question the results because the data do not fit the requirements for the test. Similar tests you will study in this chapter, such as Spearman's rank correlation test, will give you additional information. If you had seen the following scatter plot before the Challenger's takeoff, what decision would you have made? Is the relationship between air temperature and O-ring damage evident enough for you to have postponed the flight? (Note: The air temperature at takeoff on January 28, 1986 was 0° Celsius, and the O-ring temperature was about 6° colder.)

**Temperature and O-ring Damage
for 22 Space Shuttle Flights**

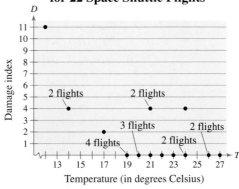

Temperature (in degrees Celsius)

11.1 The Sign Test

The Sign Test for a Population Median • The Paired-Sample Sign Test

What You Should Learn

- How to use the sign test to test a population median
- How to use the sign test to test the difference between two population medians (dependent samples)

Note to Instructor

This section can be covered along with the parametric tests of the mean found in Sections 7.2 and 7.3.

Insight

For many nonparametric tests, statisticians test the median instead of the mean.

The Sign Test for a Population Median

Many of the hypothesis tests studied so far have imposed one or more requirements for a population distribution. For example, some tests require that a population must have a normal distribution, and other tests require that population variances be equal. What if, for a given test, such requirements cannot be met? For these cases, statisticians have developed hypothesis tests that are "distribution free." Such tests are called nonparametric tests.

> **DEFINITION**
>
> A **nonparametric test** is a hypothesis test that does not require any specific conditions concerning the shape of populations or the value of any population parameters.

Nonparametric tests are usually easier to perform than corresponding parametric tests. However, they are usually less efficient than parametric tests. Stronger evidence is required to reject a null hypothesis using the results of a nonparametric test. Consequently, whenever possible, you should use a parametric test. One of the easiest nonparametric tests to perform is the sign test.

> **DEFINITION**
>
> The **sign test** is a nonparametric test that can be used to test a population median against a hypothesized value k.

The sign test for a population median can be left-tailed, right-tailed, or two-tailed. The null and alternative hypotheses for each type of test are as follows.

Left-tailed test:	H_0: median $\geq k$	and	H_a: median $< k$
Right-tailed test:	H_0: median $\leq k$	and	H_a: median $> k$
Two-tailed test:	H_0: median $= k$	and	H_a: median $\neq k$

To use the sign test, first compare each entry in the sample to the hypothesized median, k. If the entry is below the median, assign it a $-$ sign; if the entry is above the median, assign it a $+$ sign; and if the entry is equal to the median, assign it a 0. Then compare the number of $+$ and $-$ signs. (The 0's are ignored.) If there is a large difference in the number of $+$ signs and the number of $-$ signs, it is likely that the median is different from the hypothesized value and the null hypothesis should be rejected.

Table 8 in Appendix B lists the critical values for the sign test for selected levels of significance and sample sizes. When using the sign test, the sample size, n, is the total number of + and − signs. If the sample size is greater than 25, you can use the standard normal distribution to find the critical values.

Test Statistic for the Sign Test

When $n \leq 25$, the test statistic x for the sign test is the smaller number of + or − signs.

When $n > 25$, the test statistic for the sign test is

$$z = \frac{(x + 0.5) - 0.5n}{\frac{\sqrt{n}}{2}}$$

where x is the smaller number of + or − signs and n is sample size.

Because x is defined to be the smaller number of + or − signs, the rejection region is always in the left tail. Consequently, the sign test for a population median is always a left-tailed test or a two-tailed test. When the test is two-tailed, use only the left-tailed critical value. (If x is defined to be the larger number of + or − signs, the rejection region is always in the right tail. Right-tailed sign tests are presented in the exercises.)

GUIDELINES

Performing a Sign Test for a Population Median

In Words	*In Symbols*
1. Identify the claim. State the null and alternative hypotheses.	State H_0 and H_a.
2. Specify the level of significance.	Identify α.
3. Determine the sample size, n, by assigning + signs and − signs to the sample data.	n = total number of + and − signs
4. Find the critical value.	If $n \leq 25$, use Table 8 in App. B. If $n > 25$, use Table 4 in App. B.
5. Calculate the test statistic.	If $n \leq 25$, use x. If $n > 25$, use $$z = \frac{(x + 0.5) - 0.5n}{\frac{\sqrt{n}}{2}}.$$
6. Make a decision to reject or fail to reject the null hypothesis.	If x or z is less than or equal to the critical value, reject H_0. Otherwise, do not reject H_0.
7. Interpret the decision in the context of the original claim.	

▶ **EXAMPLE 1**   *Using the Sign Test*

A bank manager claims that the median number of customers per day is no more than 750. A teller doubts the accuracy of this claim. The number of bank customers per day for 16 randomly selected days are listed below. At $\alpha = 0.05$, can the teller reject the bank manager's claim?

775	765	801	742
754	753	739	751
745	750	777	769
756	760	782	789

SOLUTION   The teller must disprove the bank manager's claim that "the median number of customers per day is no more than 750." So, the null and alternative hypotheses are

$$H_0: \text{median} \leq 750 \text{ (claim)} \quad \text{and} \quad H_a: \text{median} > 750.$$

The table below shows the results of comparing each data entry to the hypothesized median 750.

+	+	+	−
+	+	−	+
−	0	+	+
+	+	+	+

From the table, you can see that there are $3 -$ signs and $12 +$ signs. So, $n = 12 + 3 = 15$. Using Table 8 with $\alpha = 0.05$ (one-tailed) and $n = 15$, the critical value is 3. Because $n \leq 25$, the test statistic x is the smaller number of $+$ or $-$ signs. So, $x = 3$. Because $x = 3$ is equal to the critical value, the teller should reject the null hypothesis. At the 5% level, the teller can reject the bank manager's claim and conclude that the median number of customers per day is more than 750.

Number of customers per day for 24 days		
2174	2491	2682
2510	2557	2418
2709	2562	2390
2467	2500	2205
2246	2054	2243
2627	1949	2500
2592	2567	2478
2348	2692	2580

Try It Yourself 1

A supermarket manager claims that the median number of customers per day is greater than 2500. A supplier wants to verify the accuracy of this claim. The number of customers per day for 24 randomly selected days are listed at the left. At $\alpha = 0.025$, can the supplier support the manager's claim?

a. *Identify* the claim and *state* H_0 and H_a.
b. *Specify* the level of significance α.
c. *Determine* the sample size, n.
d. *Find* the critical value.
e. *Determine* the test statistic x.
f. *Decide* whether to reject the null hypothesis.
g. Can the supplier support the manager's claim?   *Answer: Page A43* ◀

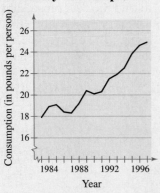
▶ EXAMPLE 2 *Using the Sign Test*

A car dealership claims to give customers a median trade-in offer of at least $6000. A random sample of 103 transactions revealed that the trade-in offer for 60 automobiles was less than $6000 and the trade-in offer for 40 automobiles was more than $6000. At $\alpha = 0.01$, can you reject the dealership's claim?

SOLUTION   To reject the dealership's claim, you must disprove the claim that "the median trade-in offer is at least $6000." The null and alternative hypotheses are

$$H_0: \text{median} \geq 6000 \text{ (claim)} \quad \text{and} \quad H_a: \text{median} < 6000.$$

Because $n \geq 25$, you should use Table 4, the Standard Normal Table, to find the critical value. Because the test is a left-tailed test with $\alpha = 0.01$, the critical value is -2.33. Of the 103 transactions, there are 60 $-$ signs and 40 $+$ signs. Ignoring the zeros, the sample size is $n = 60 + 40 = 100$, and $x = 40$. Using these values, the test statistic is

$$z = \frac{(40 + 0.5) - 0.5(100)}{\sqrt{100}/2}$$

$$= \frac{-9.5}{5}$$

$$= -1.9.$$

The graph at the right shows the location of the rejection region and the test statistic, z. Because z is greater than the critical value, it is not in the rejection region, and you should fail to reject the null hypothesis. At the 1% level of significance, you cannot reject the dealership's claim that the median trade-in offer is at least $6000.

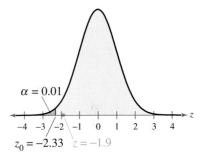

$\alpha = 0.01$

$z_0 = -2.33 \quad z = -1.9$

Try It Yourself 2

A realtor claims that the median sales price of houses sold in a certain region is $134,500. A random sample of 85 house sales reveals that 30 houses were sold for less than $134,500 and 51 houses were sold for more than $134,500. At $\alpha = 0.10$, can you reject the realtor's claim?

a. *Identify* the claim and *state* H_0 and H_a.
b. *Specify* the level of significance α.
c. *Determine* the sample size, n.
d. *Find* the critical value.
e. *Determine* the test statistic z.
f. *Decide* whether to reject the null hypothesis.
g. Can you reject the realtor's claim?   *Answer: Page A43* ◀

The Paired-Sample Sign Test

Note to Instructor

This test is often used with before-and-after data.

In Section 8.3, you learned how to use a t-test for the difference between means of dependent samples. That test required both populations to be normally distributed. If the parametric condition of normality cannot be satisfied, you can use the sign test to test the difference between two population medians. To perform the paired-sample sign test for the difference between two population medians, the following conditions must be met.

1. A sample must be randomly selected from each population.
2. The samples must be dependent (paired).

The paired-sample sign test can be left-tailed, right-tailed, or two-tailed. This test is similar to the sign test for a single population median. However, instead of comparing each data entry to a hypothesized median and recording a +, −, or 0 sign, you find the difference between corresponding data entries and record the sign of the difference. Generally, to find the difference, subtract the entry representing the second variable from the entry representing the first variable. Then compare the number of + and − signs. (The 0's are ignored.) If the number of + signs is approximately equal to the number of − signs, the null hypothesis should not be rejected. If, however, there is a significant difference between the number of + signs and the number of − signs, the null hypothesis should be rejected.

GUIDELINES

Performing a Paired-Sample Sign Test

In Words	*In Symbols*
1. Identify the claim. State the null and alternative hypotheses.	State H_0 and H_a.
2. Specify the level of significance.	Identify α.
3. Determine the sample size, n, by finding the difference for each data pair. Assign a + sign for a positive difference, a − sign for a negative difference, and a 0 for no difference.	n = total number of + and − signs
4. Find the critical value.	Use Table 8 in Appendix B.
5. Determine the test statistic.	x = lesser number of + and − signs
6. Make a decision to reject or fail to reject the null hypothesis.	If the test statistic is less than or equal to the critical value, reject H_0. Otherwise, do not reject H_0.
7. Interpret the decision in the context of the original claim.	

▶ **EXAMPLE 3** *Using the Paired-Sample Sign Test*

A psychologist claims that the number of repeat offenders will decrease if first-time offenders complete a special course. You randomly select 10 prisons and record the number of repeat offenders during a two-year period. Then after first-time offenders complete the course, you record the number of repeat offenders at each prison for another two-year period. The results are listed in the following table. At $\alpha = 0.025$, can you support the psychologist's claim?

Prison	1	2	3	4	5	6	7	8	9	10
Before	21	34	9	45	30	54	37	36	33	40
After	19	22	16	31	21	30	22	18	17	21

SOLUTION To support the psychologist's claim, you could use the following null and alternative hypotheses.

H_0: The number of repeat offenders will not decrease.

H_a: The number of repeat offenders will decrease. (claim)

The table below shows the sign of the differences between the "before" and "after" data.

Prison	1	2	3	4	5	6	7	8	9	10
Before	21	34	9	45	30	54	37	36	33	40
After	19	22	16	31	21	30	22	18	17	21
Sign	+	+	−	+	+	+	+	+	+	+

From the table, you can see that there is 1 − sign and 9 + signs. So, $n = 1 + 9 = 10$. Using Table 8 with $\alpha = 0.025$ (one tailed) and $n = 10$, the critical value is 1. Because $n \leq 25$, the test statistic x is the smaller number of + or − signs. So, $x = 1$. Because $x = 1$ is less than or equal to the critical value, you should reject the null hypothesis. At the 2.5% level, you can support the psychologist's claim that the number of repeat offenders will decrease.

Adult	Before Vaccine	After Vaccine
1	3	2
2	4	1
3	2	0
4	1	1
5	3	1
6	6	3
7	4	3
8	5	2
9	2	2
10	0	2
11	2	3
12	5	4
13	3	3
14	3	2

Try It Yourself 3

A medical researcher claims that a new vaccine will decrease the number of colds in adults. You randomly select 14 adults and record the number of colds each has in a one-year period. After giving the vaccine to each adult, you again record the number of colds each has in a one-year period. The results are listed in the table at the left. At $\alpha = 0.05$, can you support the researcher's claim?

a. *Identify* the claim and *state* H_0 and H_a.
b. *Specify* the level of significance α.
c. *Determine* the sample size, n.
d. *Find* the critical value.
e. *Determine* the test statistic x.
f. *Decide* whether to reject the null hypothesis.
g. Can you support the researcher's claim? *Answer: Page A43* ◀

11.1 ■ EXERCISES

HELP

StatPro 11.1

Internet Statistics 11.1

Student Solutions Manual 11.1

Videos 11.1

Try It Yourself Answers 11.1

1. A nonparametric test is a hypothesis test that does not require any specific conditions concerning the shape of populations or the value of any population parameters.

   A nonparametric test is usually easier to perform than its corresponding parametric test, but the nonparametric test is usually less efficient.

2. Identify the claim and state H_0 and H_a. Identify the level of significance and sample size. Find the critical value using Table 8 (if $n \leq 25$) or Table 4 ($n > 25$). Calculate the test statistic. Make a decision and interpret in the context of the problem.

3. Fail to reject H_0

4. See Selected Answers, page A85

5. (a) H_0: median $\leq 140,000$ (claim)

   H_a: median $> 140,000$

   (b) CV $= 1$

   (c) $x = 3$

   (d) Fail to reject H_0. There is not enough evidence to reject the claim.

6. See Selected Answers, page A85

Basic Skills and Concepts

1. What is a nonparametric test? How does a nonparametric test differ from a parametric test? What are the advantages and disadvantages of using a nonparametric test?

2. Explain how to use the sign test to test a population median.

Performing a Sign Test   In Exercises 3–18, (a) write the claim mathematically and identify H_0 and H_a, (b) find the critical value, (c) calculate the test statistic, and (d) decide whether to reject or fail to reject the null hypothesis. Then interpret the decision in the context of the original claim.

3. In order to estimate the median amount of new credit card charges for the previous month, a financial service accountant randomly selects 12 credit card accounts and records the amount of new charges for each account for the previous month. The amounts are listed below. At $\alpha = 0.01$, can the accountant conclude that median amount of new credit card charges for the previous month was more than $200? *(Adapted from Board of Governors of the Federal Reserve System)*

$246.71	$282.59	$155.03	$102.17	$209.80	$165.88
$199.41	$170.83	$196.54	$216.46	$145.92	$209.47

4. A meteorologist estimates that the daily median temperature for the month of July in Pittsburgh is 72° Fahrenheit. The temperatures (in degrees Fahrenheit) for 15 randomly selected July days are listed below. At $\alpha = 0.01$, is there enough evidence to reject the meteorologist's hypothesis? *(Adapted from U.S. National Oceanic and Atmospheric Administration)*

   64   72   72   75   76   70   66   73
   67   65   74   74   67   77   66

5. A real estate agent believes that the median sales price of new privately owned one-family homes sold in the past year is $140,000 or less. The sales prices of eight randomly selected homes are listed below. At $\alpha = 0.05$, is there enough evidence to reject the agent's claim? *(Adapted from U.S. Bureau of the Census and the U.S. Department of Housing and Urban Development)*

$170,000	$133,450	$89,500	$144,600
$75,800	$161,000	$149,000	$160,000

6. During a weather report, a meteorologist states that the daily median temperature for the month of January in San Diego is 57° Fahrenheit. The temperatures (in degrees Fahrenheit) for 18 randomly selected January days are listed below. At $\alpha = 0.01$, can you reject the meteorologist's claim? *(Adapted from U.S. National Oceanic and Atmospheric Administration)*

   58   62   55   55   53   52   52   59   55
   55   60   56   57   61   58   63   63   55

7. (a) H_0: median $\leq$ 1500 (claim)
H_a: median $<$ 1500

(b) CV $= -2.055$

(c) -3.040

(d) Reject H_0. There is enough evidence to reject the claim.

8. (a) H_0: median $\geq$ 22,500
H_a: median $<$ 22,500 (claim)

(b) CV $= -1.96$

(c) -1.554

(d) Fail to reject H_0. There is not enough evidence to support the claim.

9. (a) H_0: median $\leq$ 36 and
H_a: median $>$ 36 (claim)

(b) CV $= 3$

(c) $x = 8$

(d) Fail to reject H_0. There is not enough evidence to support the claim.

10. (a) H_0: median $\geq$ 31 and
H_a: median $<$ 31 (claim)

(b) CV $= 5$

(c) $x = 8$

(d) Fail to reject H_0. There is not enough evidence to support the claim.

11. (a) H_0: median $=$ 5 (claim)
and H_a: median $\neq$ 5

(b) CV $= -1.96$

(c) -2.334

(d) Reject H_0. There is enough evidence to reject the claim.

12. See Selected Answers, page A85

13. (a) H_0: median $=$ \$9.81 (claim)
and H_a: median $\neq$ \$9.81

(b) CV $= -2.575$

(c) -0.961

(d) Fail to reject H_0. There is not enough evidence to reject the claim.

7. A financial services institution reports that the median amount of credit card debt for families holding such debts is at least \$1500. In a random sample of 104 families holding debt, you see that the debt for 68 families is less than \$1500 and the debt for 36 families is greater than \$1500. At $\alpha = 0.02$, can you reject the institution's claim? *(Adapted from Board of Governors of the Federal Reserve System, Federal Reserve Bulletin)*

8. A financial services accountant estimates that the median amount of financial debt for families holding such debts is less than \$22,500. In a random sample of 70 families holding debt, the debt for 28 families was less than \$22,500 and the debt for 42 families was greater than \$22,500. At $\alpha = 0.025$, can you support the accountant's estimate? *(Adapted from Board of Governors of the Federal Reserve System, Federal Reserve Bulletin)*

9. A social sciences association conducted a study to determine the median age of recipients of social science doctorates. As part of the study, the association randomly selected 20 social service doctorates and found that 9 were conferred before age 36, 8 were conferred after age 36, and 3 were conferred at age 36. Test the association's claim that the median age of recipients of social science doctorates is greater than 36 years. Use $\alpha = 0.01$. *(Adapted from U.S. National Science Foundation)*

10. A science association claims that the median age of recipients of physical science doctorates is less than 31 years. In a random sample of 24 physical science doctorates, 8 were conferred at less than 31 years, 12 were conferred at greater than 31 years, and 4 were conferred at 31 years. At $\alpha = 0.05$, can you support the association's claim? *(Adapted from U.S. National Science Foundation)*

11. A renters' organization claims that the median number of rooms in renter-occupied units is 5. You randomly select 50 renter-occupied units and obtain the results shown below. At $\alpha = 0.05$, can you support the organization's claim? *(Adapted from U.S. Bureau of the Census)*

Unit size	Number of units
Less than 5 rooms	15
5 rooms	3
More than 5 rooms	32

Data for Exercise 11

Square footage	Number of units
Less than 1300	11
1300	2
More than 1300	9

Data for Exercise 12

12. A renters' organization believes that the median square footage of renter-occupied units is 1300 square feet. To test this claim, you randomly select 22 renter-occupied units and obtain the results shown above. At $\alpha = 0.10$, can you reject the organization's claim? *(Adapted from U.S. Bureau of the Census)*

13. A labor organization estimates that the median hourly earnings of male workers paid hourly rates is \$9.81. In a random sample of 41 male workers paid hourly rates, 16 are paid less than \$9.81 per hour, 23 are paid more than \$9.81 per hour, and 2 are paid \$9.81 per hour. At $\alpha = 0.01$, can you reject the organization's claim? *(Adapted from U.S. Bureau of Labor Statistics)*

14. (a) H_0: median $\leq$ 7.81 (claim)
H_a: median > 7.81

(b) CV = 5

(c) x = 9

(d) Fail to reject H_0. There is not enough evidence to reject the claim.

15. (a) H_0: The headache hours have not decreased.
H_a: The headache hours have decreased. (claim)

(b) CV = 1

(c) x = 3

(d) Fail to reject H_0. There is not enough evidence to support the claim.

16. (a) H_0: The headache hours have not decreased.
H_a: The headache hours have decreased. (claim)

(b) CV = 1

(c) x = 4

(d) Fail to reject H_0. There is not enough evidence to support the claim.

17. (a) H_0: The SAT scores have not improved.
H_a: The SAT scores have improved. (claim)

(b) CV = 2

(c) x = 4

(d) Fail to reject H_0. There is not enough evidence to support the claim.

14. A labor organization claims that the median hourly earnings of female workers paid hourly rates is at most $7.81. In a random sample of 23 female workers paid hourly rates, 9 are paid less than $7.81 per hour, 11 are paid more than $7.81 per hour, and 3 are paid $7.81 per hour. At α = 0.05, can you reject the organization's claim? *(Adapted from U.S. Bureau of Labor Statistics)*

15. The table shows the daily headache hours suffered by eight patients before and after receiving soft tissue therapy and spinal manipulation for seven weeks. At α = 0.05, is there enough evidence to conclude that daily headache hours were reduced after the soft tissue therapy and spinal manipulation? *(Adapted from The Journal of the American Medical Association)*

Patient	1	2	3	4	5	6	7	8
Headache hours (before)	0.8	2.4	2.8	2.6	2.7	0.9	1.2	2.2
Headache hours (after)	1.6	1.3	1.6	1.4	1.5	1.6	1.7	1.8

16. The table shows the daily headache hours suffered by 12 patients before and after receiving a new drug for seven weeks. At α = 0.01, is there enough evidence to conclude that daily headache hours were reduced after taking the new drug? *(Adapted from The Journal of the American Medical Association)*

Patient	1	2	3	4	5	6
Headache hours (before)	2.1	3.9	3.8	2.5	2.4	3.6
Headache hours (after)	2.2	2.8	2.5	2.6	1.9	1.8

Patient	7	8	9	10	11	12
Headache hours (before)	3.4	2.4	3.5	2.0	2.7	2.4
Headache hours (after)	2.0	1.6	1.5	2.1	1.8	3.0

17. A tutoring agency believes that by completing a special course, students can improve their verbal SAT skills. As part of a study, 12 students take the verbal part of the SAT, complete the special course, then take the verbal part of the SAT again. The students' scores are listed below. At α = 0.05, is there enough evidence to conclude that the students' verbal SAT scores improved?

Student	1	2	3	4	5	6
Score on first SAT	308	456	352	433	306	471
Score on second SAT	300	524	409	419	304	483

Student	7	8	9	10	11	12
Score on first SAT	538	207	205	351	360	251
Score on second SAT	708	253	399	350	480	303

18. (a) H_0: The SAT scores have not improved.
H_a: The SAT scores have improved. (claim)

(b) CV = 1

(c) $x = 3$

(d) Fail to reject H_0. There is not enough evidence to support the claim.

19. Fail to reject H_0. There is not enough evidence to reject the claim.

20. Fail to reject H_0. There is not enough evidence to reject the claim.

18. Students at a certain school are required to take the SAT twice. The table shows both verbal SAT scores for 12 students. At $\alpha = 0.01$, can you conclude that the students' scores improved the second time they took the SAT?

Student	1	2	3	4	5	6
Score on first SAT	445	510	429	452	629	453
Score on second SAT	446	571	517	478	610	453

Student	7	8	9	10	11	12
Score on first SAT	358	477	325	513	636	571
Score on second SAT	378	532	299	501	648	603

19. *Office Parties* An alcohol awareness organization conducted a survey by randomly selecting companies and asking them if they give their employees a holiday party where alcohol is served. The organization asked companies that said yes if the companies provided transportation home or offered alternatives to driving home. The results are shown in the figure.

After the Party
Companies that provide transportation home or offer other alternatives to driving home:
Don't know 1
Yes 14
No 8

(a) Use a sign test to test the null hypothesis that the proportion of companies providing transportation home or offering alternatives to driving home is equal to the proportion of companies that do not. Assign a + sign to a company that does, assign a − sign to a company that does not, and assign a 0 to a company that does not know. Use $\alpha = 0.05$.

(b) What can you conclude?

20. *Credit Cards* A financial institution conducts a survey by randomly selecting credit cardholders and asking them if they almost always pay off their credit card balances. The results are shown in the figure.

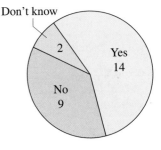

Don't know 2
Yes 14
No 9

(a) Use a sign test to test the null hypothesis that the proportion of credit cardholders almost always paying off their credit card balances is equal to the proportion of credit cardholders that do not. Assign a + sign to a credit cardholder that does, assign a − sign to a credit cardholder that does not, and assign a 0 to a credit cardholder that does not know. Use $\alpha = 0.05$.

(b) What can you conclude?

21. (a) H_0: median ≤ 418 (claim) and H_a: median > 418

(b) CV $= 2.33$

(c) 1.459

(d) Fail to reject H_0. There is not enough evidence to reject the claim.

22. (a) H_0: median ≤ 557 and H_a: median > 557 (claim)

(b) CV $= 2.33$

(c) 4.454

(d) Reject H_0. There is enough evidence to support the claim.

23. (a) H_0: median ≤ 24 and H_a: median > 24 (claim)

(b) CV $= 1.645$

(c) 1.936

(d) Reject H_0. There is enough evidence to support the claim.

24. (a) H_0: median ≤ 25.9 (claim) and H_a: median > 25.9

(b) CV $= 1.645$

(c) 1.203

(d) Fail to reject H_0. There is not enough evidence to reject the claim.

Weekly earnings	Number of workers
Less than $418	18
$418	3
More than $418	29

Data for Exercise 21

Weekly earnings	Number of workers
Less than $557	21
$557	1
More than $557	48

Data for Exercise 22

Extending the Basics

More on Sign Tests When you are using a sign test for $n > 25$ and the test is left-tailed, you know you can reject the null hypothesis if the test statistic

$$z = \frac{(x + 0.5) - \left(\frac{n}{2}\right)}{\frac{\sqrt{n}}{2}},$$

where x is the smaller number of $+$ and $-$ signs, is less than or equal to the left-tailed critical value. For a right-tailed test you can reject the null hypothesis if the test statistic

$$z = \frac{(x - 0.5) - \left(\frac{n}{2}\right)}{\frac{\sqrt{n}}{2}},$$

where x is the *larger* number of $+$ and $-$ signs, is greater than or equal to the *right-tailed* critical value.

In Exercises 21–24, (a) write the claim mathematically and identify H_0 and H_a, (b) find the critical value, (c) calculate the test statistic, and (d) decide whether to reject or fail to reject the null hypothesis. Then interpret the decision in the context of the original claim.

21. A labor organization claims that the median weekly earnings of female workers is less than or equal to $418. To test this claim, you randomly select 50 female workers and ask each to provide her weekly earnings. The results are shown at the left. At $\alpha = 0.01$, can you reject the organization's claim? *(Adapted from U.S. Bureau of Labor Statistics)*

22. A labor organization states that the median weekly earnings of male workers is greater than $557. To test this claim, you randomly select 70 male workers and ask each to provide his weekly earnings. The results are shown at the left. At $\alpha = 0.01$, can you support the organization's claim? *(Adapted from U.S. Bureau of Labor Statistics)*

23. A marriage counselor estimates that the median age of brides at the time of their first marriage is greater than 24 years. In a random sample of 65 brides, 22 are less than 24 years, 38 are more than 24 years, and 5 are 24 years. At $\alpha = 0.05$, can you support the counselor's claim? *(Adapted from U.S National Center for Health Statistics)*

24. A marriage counselor estimates that the median age of grooms at the time of their first marriage is less than or equal to 25.9 years. In a random sample of 56 grooms, 23 are less than 25.9 years, 33 are more than 25.9 years, and none are 25.9 years. At $\alpha = 0.05$, is there enough evidence to reject the counselor's claim? *(Adapted from U.S National Center for Health Statistics)*

The Wilcoxon Tests

11.2

The Wilcoxon Signed-Rank Test • The Wilcoxon Rank Sum Test

The Wilcoxon Signed-Rank Test

In this section, you will study the Wilcoxon signed-rank test and the Wilcoxon rank sum test. Unlike the sign test, the strength of these two nonparametric tests is that each considers the magnitude, or size, of the data entries.

In Section 8.3, you used a *t*-test together with dependent samples to determine whether there was a difference between two populations. To use the *t*-test to test such a difference, you must assume (or know) that the dependent samples are randomly selected from populations having a normal distribution. But, what if this assumption cannot be made? Instead of using the two-sample *t*-test, you can use the Wilcoxon signed-rank test.

Note to Instructor

This section can be covered along with the *t*-test for the difference of means using dependent samples in Section 8.3.

DEFINITION

The **Wilcoxon signed-rank test** is a nonparametric test that can be used to determine whether two *dependent* samples were selected from populations having the same distribution.

Study Tip

The absolute value of a number is its value, disregarding its sign. For example, $|3| = 3$ and $|-7| = 7$.

GUIDELINES

Performing a Wilcoxon Signed-Rank Test

In Words	*In Symbols*
1. Identify the claim. State the null and alternative hypotheses.	State H_0 and H_a.
2. Specify the level of significance.	Specify α.
3. Determine the sample size, n.	
4. Find the critical value.	Use Table 9 in Appendix B.

5. Calculate the test statistic, w_s.
  a. Complete a table using the headers listed at the right.
  b. Find the sum of the positive ranks and the sum of the negative ranks.
  c. Select the smaller of absolute values of the sums.
	Headers: **Sample 1, Sample 2, Difference, Absolute value, Rank,** and **Signed rank.**

6. Make a decision to reject or fail to reject the null hypothesis.	If w_s is less than or equal to the critical value, reject H_0. Otherwise, do not reject H_0.
7. Interpret the decision in the context of the original claim.	

▶ **EXAMPLE 1**   *Performing a Wilcoxon Signed-Rank Test*

A sports psychologist believes that listening to music affects the length of athletes' workout sessions. The length of time (in minutes) of ten athletes' workout sessions, while listening to music and while not listening to music, are listed in the table. At $\alpha = 0.05$, can you support the sports psychologist's claim?

Length of workout session, with music	45	38	28	39	41	47	62	54	33	44
Length of workout session, without music	38	40	33	36	42	41	54	47	28	35

SOLUTION   The claim is "Music affects the length of athletes' workout sessions." To test this claim, use the following null and alternative hypotheses.

H_0: There is no difference in the length of the athletes' workout sessions.
H_a: There is a difference in the length of the athletes' workout sessions.

This Wilcoxon signed-rank test is a two-tailed test with $\alpha = 0.05$ and $n = 10$. Using Table 9 in Appendix B, the critical value is 8. To find the test statistic, w_s, complete a table as shown below.

Study Tip

Do not rank any differences of zero and the sample size n should be the total number of nonzero differences. In the case of a tie between data entries, use the average of the corresponding ranks. For instance, if two data entries are tied for the fifth rank, use the average of 5 and 6, which is 5.5. If three entries are tied for the fifth rank, use the average of 5, 6, and 7, or 6.

Length of session, with music	Length of session, without music	Difference	Absolute value	Rank	Signed rank
45	38	7	7	7.5	7.5
38	40	−2	2	2	−2
28	33	−5	5	4.5	−4.5
39	36	3	3	3	3
41	42	−1	1	1	−1
47	41	6	6	6	6
62	54	8	8	9	9
54	47	7	7	7.5	7.5
33	28	5	5	4.5	4.5
44	35	9	9	10	10

The sum of the negative ranks is

$$-1 + (-2) + (-4.5) = -7.5.$$

The sum of the positive ranks is

$$(+3) + (+4.5) + (+6) + (+7.5) + (+7.5) + (+9) + (+10) = 47.5.$$

The test statistic is the smaller of the absolute value of these two sums. Because $|-7.5| < |47.5|$, the test statistic is $w_s = 7.5$.

Because the test statistic is less than the critical value, that is, $7.5 < 8$, you should decide to reject the null hypothesis. In other words, at the 5% level of significance, you have enough evidence to support the claim that music makes a difference in the length of athletes' workout sessions.

Note to Instructor

The Wilcoxon rank sum test can be covered with its parametric counterparts found in Sections 8.1 and 8.2.

Study Tip

Use the Wilcoxon signed-rank test for dependent samples and the Wilcoxon rank sum test for independent samples.

Try It Yourself 1

A quality control inspector wants to test the effectiveness of a spray-on water repellent. To test this claim, he selects 12 pieces of fabric, sprays water on each and measures the amount of water repelled (in milliliters). He then applies the water repellent and repeats the experiment. The results are listed in the table. At $\alpha = 0.01$, can he conclude that the water repellent is effective?

No repellent	8	7	7	4	6	10
Repellent applied	15	12	11	6	6	8

No repellent	9	5	9	11	8	4
Repellent applied	8	6	12	8	14	8

a. *Identify* the claim and *state* H_0 and H_a.
b. *Specify* the level of significance α.
c. *Determine* the sample size n.
d. *Find* the critical value.
e. *Calculate* the test statistic w_s by making a table, finding the sum of the positive ranks and the sum of the negative ranks, and finding the absolute value of each.
f. *Decide* whether to reject the null hypothesis. Use a graph if necessary.
g. Is there enough evidence to reject the claim? *Answer: Page A43*

The Wilcoxon Rank Sum Test

In Sections 8.1 and 8.2, you used a z-test or a t-test together with independent samples to determine whether there was a difference between two populations. To use these tests to test such a difference, you had to make several assumptions concerning the distribution of each population. But, what if these assumptions cannot be made? You can still compare the populations using the Wilcoxon rank sum test.

DEFINITION

The **Wilcoxon rank sum test** is a nonparametric test that can be used to determine whether two *independent* samples were selected from populations having the same distribution.

A requirement for the Wilcoxon rank sum test is that the sample size of both samples must be at least 10. When calculating the test statistic for the Wilcoxon rank sum test, let n_1 represent the sample size of the smaller sample and n_2 represent the sample size of the larger sample. If the two samples have the same size, it does not matter which one is n_1 or n_2.

Test Statistic for the Wilcoxon Rank Sum Test

Given two independent samples, the test statistic z for the Wilcoxon rank sum test is

$$z = \frac{R - \mu_R}{\sigma_R},$$

where

R = sum of the ranks for the smaller sample,

$$\mu_R = \frac{n_1(n_1 + n_2 + 1)}{2}, \quad \text{and}$$

$$\sigma_R = \sqrt{\frac{n_1 n_2(n_1 + n_2 + 1)}{12}}.$$

GUIDELINES

Performing a Wilcoxon Rank Sum Test

In Words	*In Symbols*
1. Identify the claim. State the null and alternative hypotheses.	State H_0 and H_a.
2. Specify the level of significance.	Specify α.
3. Find the critical value.	Use Table 4 of Appendix B.
4. Determine the sample sizes.	$n_1 \leq n_2$
5. Find the sum of the ranks for the smaller sample.	
a. List the combined data in ascending order.	
b. Rank the combined data.	
c. Add the sum of the ranks for the smaller sample.	
6. Calculate the test statistic.	$z = \dfrac{R - \mu_R}{\sigma_R}$
7. Make a decision to reject or fail to reject the null hypothesis.	If z is in the rejection region, reject H_0. Otherwise, do not reject H_0.
8. Interpret the decision in the context of the original claim.	

> **EXAMPLE 2**   *Performing a Wilcoxon Rank Sum Test*

Note to Instructor

Because ranking data with large samples can be tedious, suggest to your students that they use a stem-and-leaf plot to organize their data. If your class is using the TI-83, Minitab, or Excel, tell students they can use this technology to sort and rank data.

The table lists the earnings (in thousands of dollars) of a random sample of 10 male and 12 female salespersons. At $\alpha = 0.10$ can you conclude that there is a difference between the males' and females' earnings?

Male Earnings:	28	43	64	51	48	44	36	45	67	49		
Female Earnings:	36	27	51	43	35	48	41	37	34	47	50	40

SOLUTION   The claim is "there is a difference between the males' and females' earnings." The null and alternative hypotheses for this test are as follows.

H_0: There is no difference between the males' and the females' earnings.
H_a: There is a difference between the males' and the females' earnings.

Because the test is a two-tailed test with $\alpha = 0.10$, the critical values are -1.645 and 1.645. The rejection regions are $z < -1.645$ and $z > 1.645$. Before calculating the test statistic, you must find the values of R, μ_R, and σ_R. The table shows the combined data listed in ascending order and the corresponding ranks.

Ordered data	Sample	Rank		Ordered data	Sample	Rank
27	F	1		44	M	12
28	M	2		45	M	13
34	F	3		47	F	14
35	F	4		48	M	15.5
36	M	5.5		48	F	15.5
36	F	5.5		49	M	17
37	F	7		50	F	18
40	F	8		51	M	19.5
41	F	9		51	F	19.5
43	M	10.5		64	M	21
43	F	10.5		67	M	22

Because the smaller sample is the sample of males, R is the sum of the male rankings.

$$R = 2 + 5.5 + 10.5 + 12 + 13 + 15.5 + 17 + 19.5 + 21 + 22$$
$$= 138$$

Using $n_1 = 10$ and $n_2 = 12$ you can find μ_R and σ_R as shown.

$$\mu_R = \frac{n_1(n_1 + n_2 + 1)}{2} = \frac{10(10 + 12 + 1)}{2} = \frac{230}{2} = 115$$

$$\sigma_R = \sqrt{\frac{n_1 n_2(n_1 + n_2 + 1)}{12}} = \sqrt{\frac{(10)(12)(10 + 12 + 1)}{12}}$$

$$= \sqrt{\frac{2760}{12}} = \sqrt{230}$$

$$\approx 15.2$$

Using $R = 138$, $\mu_R = 115$, and $\sigma_R = 15.2$, the test statistic is

$$z = \frac{R - \mu_R}{\sigma_R} = \frac{138 - 115}{15.2} \approx 1.51.$$

From the graph at the right, you can see that the test statistic z is not in the rejection region. At the 10% level, you should decide to fail to reject the null hypothesis. In other words, you cannot conclude that there is a difference between the males' and females' earnings.

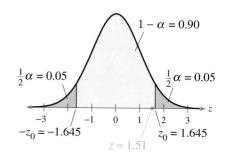

$1 - \alpha = 0.90$

$\frac{1}{2}\alpha = 0.05$ $\frac{1}{2}\alpha = 0.05$

$-z_0 = -1.645$ $z_0 = 1.645$

$z \approx 1.51$

Try It Yourself 2

You are investigating the automobile insurance claims paid (in thousands of dollars) by two insurance companies. The table lists a random sample of 12 claims paid by two insurance companies. At $\alpha = 0.05$, can you conclude that there is a difference in the claims paid by the companies?

Company A: 6.2 10.6 2.5 4.5 6.5 7.4   9.9 3.0 5.8 3.9 6.0 6.3
Company B: 7.3   5.6 3.4 1.8 2.2 4.7 10.8 4.1 1.7 3.0 4.4 5.3

a. *Identify* the claim and *state* H_0 and H_a.
b. *Specify* the level of significance α.
c. *Find* the critical value.
d. *Determine* the sample sizes n_1 and n_2.
e. *List* the combined data in ascending order, *rank* the data, and *find* the sum of the ranks of the smaller sample.
f. *Calculate* the test statistic.
g. *Decide* whether to reject the null hypothesis. Use a graph if necessary.
h. Is there enough evidence to reject the claim?   *Answer: Page A43*

11.2 EXERCISES

HELP

 StatPro 11.2

 Internet Statistics 11.2

 Student Solutions Manual 11.2

 Videos 11.2

 Try It Yourself Answers 11.2

1. (a) H_0: There is no reduction in systolic blood pressure. (claim)
H_a: There is a reduction in systolic blood pressure.

(b) Wilcoxon signed-rank test

(c) CV = 6   **(d)** $w_s = 6$

(e) Reject H_0. There is enough evidence to support the claim.

2. (a) H_0: There is no difference in salaries. (claim)
H_a: There is a difference in salaries.

(b) Wilcoxon rank sum test

(c) The critical values are ±1.645

(d) −2.306

(e) Reject H_0. There is enough evidence to reject the claim.

3. (a) H_0: There is no difference in the earnings.
H_a: There is a difference in the earnings. (claim)

(b) Wilcoxon rank sum test

(c) The critical values are ±1.96

(d) −3.873

(e) Reject H_0. There is enough evidence to support the claim.

Basic Skills and Concepts

Performing a Wilcoxon Test   In Exercises 1–6, (a) write the claim mathematically and identify H_0 and H_a, (b) decide whether to use a Wilcoxon signed-rank test or a Wilcoxon rank sum test, (c) find the critical value, (d) calculate the test statistic, and (e) decide whether to reject or fail to reject the null hypothesis. Then interpret the decision in the context of the original claim.

1. In a study testing the effects of calcium supplements on blood pressure in men, eight men were randomly chosen and given a calcium supplement for 12 weeks. The measurements listed in the table are for each subject's systolic blood pressure taken before and after the 12-week treatment period. At $\alpha = 0.10$, can you reject the claim that there was no reduction in systolic blood pressure? *(Adapted from The Journal of American Medicine)*

Patient	1	2	3	4	5	6	7	8
Before treatment	108	109	120	129	112	111	117	135
After treatment	99	115	105	116	115	117	108	122

2. A private industry analyst claims that there is no difference in the salaries earned by workers in the manufacturing and construction industries. A random sample of ten manufacturing and ten construction workers and their salaries is listed in the table. At $\alpha = 0.10$, can you reject the analyst's claim? *(Adapted from U.S. Bureau of Labor Statistics)*

Industry	Salary (in thousands of dollars)									
Manufacturing	31	38	33	33	35	47	33	29	38	45
Construction	31	30	27	32	28	34	30	33	26	35

3. A college administrator believes that there is a difference in the earnings of people with bachelor's degrees and those with associate's degrees. The table lists the earnings (in thousands of dollars) of a random sample of eleven people with bachelor's degrees and ten people with associate's degrees. At $\alpha = 0.05$, is there enough evidence to support the administrator's belief? *(Adapted from U.S. Census Bureau)*

Level of highest degree	Salary (in thousands of dollars)										
Bachelor's	37	41	55	34	56	63	40	28	43	27	34
Associate's	22	26	24	18	18	18	21	17	24	24	

4. (a) H_0: There is no difference in the number of
months mothers breast-
feed their babies. (claim)

H_a: There is a difference
in the number of months
mothers breast-feed their
babies.

(b) Wilcoxon rank sum test

(c) The critical values are
±2.575

(d) −1.723

(e) Fail to reject H_0. There
is not enough evidence
to reject the claim.

5. (a) H_0: There is not a difference in salaries.

H_a: There is a difference
in salaries. (claim)

(b) Wilcoxon rank sum test

(c) The critical values are
±1.96

(d) −1.819

(e) Fail to reject H_0. There is
not enough evidence to
support the claim.

6. (a) H_0: The new drug does
not affect the number of
headache hours.

H_a: The new drug does
affect the number of
headache hours.

(b) Wilcoxon signed-rank test

(c) 2

(d) $w_s = 6$

(e) Fail to reject H_0. There is
not enough evidence to
conclude that the drug
affects the number of
headache hours.

4. A natal health care researcher conducts a study of a random selection of
mothers under 20 years and 20–24 years. The number of weeks each mother
breastfed her baby is listed in the table. At $\alpha = 0.01$, can you reject the
researcher's claim that there is no difference in the number of months these
mothers breastfed their babies? *(Adapted from U.S. National Center for Health
Statistics)*

Age of mother	Duration (in weeks)										
Under 20 years	21	24	24	30	11	17	10	28	21	12	15
20–24 years	25	28	26	23	22	13	28	21	27	32	19	27

5. A teacher's union representative claims that there is a difference in the
salaries earned by teachers in Ohio and Pennsylvania. A random sample of
12 Ohio and 12 Pennsylvania teachers and their salaries is listed in the table.
At $\alpha = 0.05$, is there enough evidence to support the representative's
claim? *(Adapted from National Education Association)*

State	Salary (in thousands of dollars)											
Ohio	36	39	44	41	38	45	36	45	39	31	53	30
Pennsylvania	41	60	38	46	43	48	63	59	50	45	38	28

6. A medical researcher wants to determine whether a new drug affects the
number of headache hours experienced by headache sufferers. To do so, the
researcher selects seven patients and asks each to give the number of
headache hours (per day) each experiences before and after taking the
drug. The results are listed in the table. At $\alpha = 0.05$, can the researcher
conclude that the new drug affects the number of headache hours?

Patient	1	2	3	4	5	6	7
Headache hours (before)	0.8	2.4	2.8	2.6	2.7	0.9	1.2
Headache hours (after)	1.6	1.3	1.6	1.4	1.5	1.6	1.7

Extending the Basics

Wilcoxon Signed-Rank Test for n > 30 If you are performing a Wilcoxon
signed-rank test and the sample size n is greater than 30, you can use the
Standard Normal Table and the following formula to find the test statistic.

$$z = \frac{w_s - \dfrac{n(n+1)}{4}}{\sqrt{\dfrac{n(n+1)(2n+1)}{24}}}$$

In Exercises 7 and 8, perform the indicated Wilcoxon signed-rank test using
the test statistic for $n > 30$.

7. Reject H_0.

8. Reject H_0

7. A petroleum engineer wants to know whether a certain fuel additive improves a car's gas mileage. To decide, the engineer records the gas mileage of 33 cars with and without the additive. The results are listed in the table. At $\alpha = 0.10$, can the engineer conclude that the gas mileage is improved?

Car	1	2	3	4	5	6	7	8	9	10	11
Without additive	36.4	36.4	36.6	36.6	36.8	36.9	37.0	37.1	37.2	37.2	36.7
With additive	36.7	36.9	37.0	37.5	38.0	38.1	38.4	38.7	38.8	38.9	36.3

Car	12	13	14	15	16	17	18	19	20	21	22
Without additive	37.5	37.6	37.8	37.9	37.9	38.1	38.4	40.2	40.5	40.9	35.0
With additive	38.9	39.0	39.1	39.4	39.4	39.5	39.8	40.0	40.0	40.1	36.3

Car	23	24	25	26	27	28	29	30	31	32	33
Without additive	32.7	33.6	34.2	35.1	35.2	35.3	35.5	35.9	36.0	36.1	37.2
With additive	32.8	34.2	34.7	34.9	34.9	35.3	35.9	36.4	36.6	36.6	38.3

8. A petroleum engineer claims that a fuel additive improves gas mileage. The table lists the gas mileage (in miles per gallon) of 32 cars measured with and without the fuel additive. Test the claim at $\alpha = 0.05$.

Car	1	2	3	4	5	6	7	8
Without additive	34.0	34.2	34.4	34.4	34.6	34.8	35.6	35.7
With additive	36.6	36.7	37.2	37.2	37.3	37.4	37.6	37.7

Car	9	10	11	12	13	14	15	16
Without additive	30.2	31.6	32.3	33.0	33.1	33.7	33.7	33.8
With additive	34.2	34.9	34.9	34.9	35.7	36.0	36.2	36.5

Car	17	18	19	20	21	22	23	24
Without additive	35.7	36.1	36.1	36.6	36.6	36.8	37.1	37.1
With additive	37.8	38.1	38.2	38.3	38.3	38.7	38.8	38.9

Car	25	26	27	28	29	30	31	32
Without additive	37.2	37.9	37.9	38.0	38.0	38.4	38.8	42.1
With additive	39.1	39.1	39.2	39.4	39.8	40.3	40.8	43.2

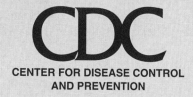

11 ◢ **CASE STUDY** ▬▬▬▬▬▬▬▬▬▬▬▬▬▬   WWW.CDC.GOV

CENTER FOR DISEASE CONTROL
AND PREVENTION

Health and Nutrition

The Recommended Dietary Allowances (RDA) are a set of nutrient standards that represent the average daily intakes of energy and nutrients considered adequate to meet the needs of most healthy Americans. For instance, for individuals ages 20–29 years, the RDA for calcium is between 800 and 1200 milligrams.

To determine how well Americans were meeting the RDA standards, the Centers for Disease Control and Prevention together with the National Center for Health Statistics conducted several three-year studies. The results of the studies are classified by age, gender, and race-ethnicity. A complete summary of the studies can be found at the Web site listed above.

The table at the right lists the calcium intake (in milligrams) for randomly selected members in various groups of individuals ages 20–29 years.

Calcium Intake (in milligrams)			
All males	Non-Hispanic white males	All females	Non-Hispanic black females
1362	819	416	887
763	1659	1187	347
1093	1264	507	378
877	944	481	1158
894	959	570	484
990	1039	710	680
796	858	1351	457
1289	1332	370	799
1687	881	1209	1042
664	1668	979	323

Exercises

1. Construct a box-and-whisker plot for the following groups. Do any of the median calcium intakes appear to be the same? Different?

   (a) All males

   (b) Non-Hispanic white males

   (c) All females

   (d) Non-Hispanic black females

In Exercises 2–5, use the sign test to test the claim. What can you conclude? Use $\alpha = 0.05$.

2. Test the claim that the median calcium intake for all males is less than or equal to 1000 milligrams.

3. Is the median calcium intake for non-Hispanic white males 1100 milligrams?

4. For all females, test the claim that the median calcium intake is greater than or equal to 700 milligrams.

5. Test the claim that the median calcium intake for non-Hispanic black females is different from 800 milligrams.

In Exercises 6 and 7, use the Wilcoxon rank sum test to test the claim. What can you conclude? Use $\alpha = 0.01$.

6. Test the claim that there is no difference in the median calcium intake for all males and the median calcium intake for non-Hispanic white males.

7. Is there a difference in the median calcium intake for all females and the median calcium intake for non-Hispanic black females?

11.3

The Kruskal-Wallis Test

The Kruskal-Wallis Test

What You Should Learn

- *How to use the Kruskal-Wallis test to determine whether three or more samples were selected from populations having the same distribution*

Note to Instructor

You can cover this test along with ANOVA in Section 10.4.

The Kruskal-Wallis Test

In Section 10.4, you learned how to use one-way ANOVA techniques to compare the means of three or more populations. When using one-way ANOVA, you should verify that each independent sample is selected from a population that is normally, or approximately normally, distributed. If, however, you cannot verify that the populations are normal, you can still compare the distributions of three or more populations. To do so, you can use the Kruskal-Wallis test.

> **DEFINITION**
>
> The **Kruskal-Wallis** test is a nonparametric test that can be used to determine whether three or more independent samples were selected from populations having the same distribution.

The null and alternative hypotheses for the Kruskal-Wallis test are as follows.

H_0: There is no difference in the distribution of the populations.

H_a: There is a difference in the distribution of the populations.

Two conditions for using the Kruskal-Wallis test are that each sample must be randomly selected and the size of each sample must be at least 5. If these conditions are met, the sampling distribution for the Kruskal-Wallis test is a chi-square distribution with $k - 1$ degrees of freedom, where k is the number of samples. You can calculate the Kruskal-Wallis test statistic using the following formula.

> **Test Statistic for the Kruskal-Wallis Test**
>
> Given three or more independent samples, the test statistic H for the Kruskal-Wallis test is
>
> $$H = \frac{12}{N(N + 1)}\left(\frac{R_1^2}{n_1} + \frac{R_2^2}{n_2} + \cdots + \frac{R_k^2}{n_k}\right) - 3(N + 1),$$
>
> where k represents the number of samples, n_i is the size of the ith sample, N is the sum of the sample sizes, and R_i is the sum of the ranks of the ith sample.

Performing a Kruskal-Wallis test consists of combining and ranking the sample data. The data are then separated according to sample and the sum of the ranks of each sample is calculated. These sums are then used to calculate the test statistic H, which is an approximation of the variance of the rank sums. If the samples are selected from populations having the same distribution, the sums of the ranks will be approximately equal, H will be small, and the null hypothesis should not be rejected. If, however, the sums of the ranks are quite different, H will be large, and the null hypothesis should be rejected.

Because the null hypothesis is rejected only when H is significantly large, the Kruskal-Wallis test is always a right-tailed test.

GUIDELINES

Performing a Kruskal-Wallis Test

In Words	*In Symbols*
1. Identify the claim. State the null and alternative hypotheses.	State H_0 and H_a.
2. Specify the level of significance.	Specify α.
3. Determine the degrees of freedom.	d.f. $= k - 1$
4. Find the critical value and identify the rejection region.	Use Table 6 in Appendix B.
5. Find the sums of the ranks for each sample.	
a. List the combined data in ascending order.	
b. Rank the combined data.	
6. Calculate the test statistic.	$H = \dfrac{12}{N(N+1)} \left(\dfrac{R_1^2}{n_1} + \dfrac{R_2^2}{n_2} + \cdots + \dfrac{R_k^2}{n_k} \right) - 3(N+1)$
7. Make a decision to reject or fail to reject the null hypothesis.	If H is in the rejection region, reject H_0. Otherwise, do not reject H_0.
8. Interpret the decision in the context of the original claim.	

▶ **EXAMPLE 1** *Performing a Kruskal-Wallis Test*

You want to compare the hourly pay rates of accountants who work in Michigan, New York, and Virginia. To do so, you randomly select ten accountants in each state and record their hourly pay rate. The hourly pay rates are listed in the table. At $\alpha = 0.01$, can you conclude that the distributions of accountants' hourly pay rates in these three states are different?

Sample hourly pay rates		
MI (Sample 1)	**NY** (Sample 2)	**VA** (Sample 3)
14.24	21.18	17.02
14.06	20.94	20.63
14.85	16.26	17.47
17.47	21.03	15.54
14.83	19.95	15.38
19.01	17.54	14.90
13.08	14.89	20.48
15.94	18.88	18.50
13.48	20.06	12.80
16.94	21.81	15.57

SOLUTION You want to test the claim that there is no difference in the hourly pay rates in Michigan, New York, and Virginia. The null and alternative hypotheses are as follows.

H_0: There is no difference in the hourly pay rates in the three states.

H_a: There is a difference in the hourly pay rates in the three states.

The test is a right-tailed test with $\alpha = 0.01$ and d.f. $= k - 1 = 3 - 1 = 2$. Using Table 6, the critical value is 9.210 and the rejection region is $\chi^2 > 9.210$. Before calculating the test statistic, you must find the sum of the ranks for each sample. The table shows the combined data listed in ascending order and the corresponding ranks.

Ordered data	Sample	Rank
12.80	VA	1
13.08	MI	2
13.48	MI	3
14.06	MI	4
14.24	MI	5
14.83	MI	6
14.85	MI	7
14.89	NY	8
14.90	VA	9
15.38	VA	10

Ordered data	Sample	Rank
15.54	VA	11
15.57	VA	12
15.94	MI	13
16.26	NY	14
16.94	MI	15
17.02	VA	16
17.47	VA	17.5
17.47	MI	17.5
17.54	NY	19
18.50	VA	20

Ordered data	Sample	Rank
18.88	NY	21
19.01	MI	22
19.95	NY	23
20.06	NY	24
20.48	VA	25
20.63	VA	26
20.94	NY	27
21.03	NY	28
21.18	NY	29
21.81	NY	30

The sum of the ranks for each sample is as follows.

$$R_1 = 2 + 3 + 4 + 5 + 6 + 7 + 13 + 15 + 17.5 + 22 = 94.5$$
$$R_2 = 8 + 14 + 19 + 21 + 23 + 24 + 27 + 28 + 29 + 30 = 223$$
$$R_3 = 1 + 9 + 10 + 11 + 12 + 16 + 17.5 + 20 + 25 + 26 = 147.5$$

Using these sums and the values $n_1 = n_2 = n_3 = 10$ and $N = 30$, the test statistic is

$$H = \frac{12}{30(30 + 1)}\left(\frac{94.5^2}{10} + \frac{223^2}{10} + \frac{147.5^2}{10}\right) - 3(30 + 1) \approx 10.76.$$

From the graph at the right, you can see that the test statistic H is in the rejection region. So, at the 1% level, you should decide to reject the null hypothesis. In other words, you can conclude that there is a difference in accountants' hourly pay rates in Michigan, New York, and Virginia.

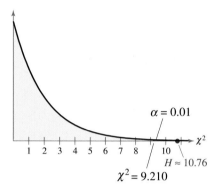

Picturing the World

To compare the water temperatures of cities bordering the Gulf of Mexico, the following data were randomly collected. *(Source: The USA Today Weather Almanac)*

Port Mansfield, TX	Eugene Island, LA	Dauphin Island, AL
62	51	56
69	55	63
77	57	51
52	63	54
60	74	60
66	82	75
75	85	80
83	60	70
65	64	78
79	76	82
83	83	84
82	86	89

At $\alpha = 0.05$, can you conclude that the temperature distributions of the three cities are different?

Try It Yourself 1

You want to compare the salaries of underwriters who work in California, Connecticut, and New Jersey. To compare the salaries, you randomly select ten underwriters in each state and record their salary. The salaries (in thousands of dollars) are listed in the table. At $\alpha = 0.10$, can you conclude that the distributions of the underwriters' salaries in these three states are different?

Sample salaries		
CA (Sample 1)	CT (Sample 2)	NJ (Sample 3)
26.42	25.57	50.16
48.46	29.86	46.72
33.68	51.03	29.73
37.18	57.07	44.57
36.55	45.04	36.35
41.33	37.39	37.24
38.36	30.00	43.26
40.31	33.68	34.29
46.55	45.29	33.91
47.17	61.46	43.89

a. *Identify* the claim and *state* H_0 and H_a.
b. *Specify* the level of significance α.
c. *Determine* the degrees of freedom.
d. *Find* the critical value and identify the rejection region.
e. *List* the combined data in ascending order, *rank* the data, and *find* the sum of the ranks of each sample.
f. *Calculate* the test statistic.
g. *Decide* whether to reject the null hypothesis. Use a graph if necessary.
h. Is there enough evidence to conclude that the salaries are different?

Answer: Page A43

11.3 **EXERCISES**

HELP

 StatPro 11.3

 Internet Statistics 11.3

 Student Solutions Manual 11.3

 Videos 11.3

 Try It Yourself Answers 11.3

---

1. (a) H_0: There is no difference in the premiums.
H_a: There is a difference in the premiums. (claim)

(b) CV = 5.991

(c) H = 14.05

(d) Reject H_0. There is enough evidence to support the claim.

2. (a) H_0: There is no difference in the premiums.
H_a: There is a difference in the premiums. (claim)

(b) CV = 5.991

(c) H = 12.55

(d) Reject H_0. There is enough evidence to support the claim.

3. (a) H_0: There is no difference in the salaries.
H_a: There is a difference in the salaries. (claim)

(b) CV = 6.251

(c) H = 6.46

(d) Reject H_0. There is enough evidence to support the claim.

Basic Skills and Concepts

Performing a Kruskal-Wallis Test   In Exercises 1–4, (a) write the claim mathematically and identify H_0 and H_a, (b) find the critical value, (c) find the sums of the ranks for each sample and calculate the test statistic, and (d) decide whether to reject or fail to reject the null hypothesis. Then interpret the decision in the context of the original claim.

1. The following table lists the annual premium for a random sample of home insurance policies in California, Florida, and Illinois. At $\alpha = 0.05$, can you conclude that the distributions of the annual premiums in these three states are different? *(Adapted from Consumer Reports)*

State	Annual Premium (in dollars)						
California	1654	553	839	777	884	753	643
Florida	1682	2067	1392	1237	1609	1550	1441
Illinois	756	496	381	437	480	566	647

2. An independent insurance representative wants to determine whether there is a difference in the annual premiums for home insurance in three states: New Jersey, New York, and Pennsylvania. To do so, the representative randomly selects several homes in each state and determines the annual premium for each. At $\alpha = 0.05$, can the representative conclude that the distributions of the annual premiums in these states are different? *(Adapted from Consumer Reports)*

State	Annual Premium (in dollars)						
New Jersey	441	420	474	411	371	470	
New York	753	684	869	719	1036	613	663
Pennsylvania	653	405	380	484	383	382	387

3. You are writing an article concerning the annual salaries of workers in four U.S. states: Alabama, Colorado, Georgia, and Iowa. The annual salaries of randomly selected workers from each state are listed in the table. Can you write in your report that the distributions of the annual salaries in these four states are different? Use $\alpha = 0.10$. *(Adapted from U.S. Bureau of Labor Statistics)*

State	Annual Salary (in thousands of dollars)							
Alabama	25.9	28.9	21.2	29.0	23.5	14.5	27.4	26.8
Colorado	25.0	19.8	10.8	28.8	25.5	26.9	23.4	35.5
Georgia	34.4	25.1	40.2	39.8	22.8	32.2	36.5	33.2
Iowa	23.4	20.3	23.3	34.1	37.5	22.5	26.1	20.9

4. (a) H_0: There is no difference in the salaries.
H_a: There is a difference in the salaries. (claim)

(b) CV = 6.251

(c) $H = 0.77$

(d) Fail to reject H_0. There is not enough evidence to support the claim.

5. (a) Fail to reject H_0.

(b) Fail to reject H_0. There is not enough evidence to support the claim. This is the same decision found in part (a) using the Kruskal-Wallis test.

6. (a) Reject H_0.

(b) Reject H_0. There is enough evidence to support the claim. This is the same decision found in part (a) using the Kruskal-Wallis test.

4. The following table lists the annual salaries for a random sample of workers in Maryland, Missouri, New Mexico, and Ohio. At $\alpha = 0.10$, can you conclude that the distributions of the annual salaries in these four states are different? *(Adapted from U.S. Bureau of Labor Statistics)*

State	Annual Salary (in thousands of dollars)						
Maryland	12.4	28.5	29.6	28.8	39.0	38.9	32.0
Missouri	25.5	45.7	28.4	25.5	23.8	43.2	24.9
New Mexico	25.3	28.9	26.3	35.1	35.2	23.2	17.8
Ohio	32.7	41.6	16.4	33.1	18.3	34.2	29.6

Extending the Basics

Comparing Two Tests In Exercises 5 and 6, perform the indicated test using (a) a Kruskal-Wallis test and (b) a one-way ANOVA test. Compare the results. If convenient, use technology to solve the problem.

5. An insurance underwriter reports that the mean number of days patients spend in a hospital differs according to the region of the United States in which the patient lives. The table lists the number of days randomly selected patients spent in a hospital. At $\alpha = 0.01$, can you support the underwriter's claim? *(Adapted from U.S. National Center for Health Statistics)*

Region	Number of Days									
Northeast	9	7	7	4	6	13	3	9	1	7
Midwest	6	5	4	10	1	5	7	4	5	8
South	5	8	1	5	8	7	5	1		
West	2	3	6	6	5	4	3	6	5	

6. The following table shows the energy consumed (in millions of Btu's) in one year for a random sample of households from four regions. At $\alpha = 0.01$, can you conclude that the mean energy consumptions are different? *(Adapted from U.S. Energy Information Administration)*

Region	Energy Consumed (in millions of Btu's)							
Northeast	72	106	151	138	104	108	95	134
	100	174						
Midwest	84	183	194	165	120	212	148	129
	113	62	97					
South	91	40	72	91	147	74	70	67
West	74	32	78	28	106	39	118	63
	70	56						

11.4

Rank Correlation

The Spearman Rank Correlation Coefficient

The Spearman Rank Correlation Coefficient

In Section 9.1, you learned how to measure the strength of the relationship between two variables using the Pearson correlation coefficient r. Two requirements for the Pearson correlation coefficient are that the variables are linearly related and that the population represented by each variable is normally distributed. If these requirements cannot be met, you can examine the relationship between two variables using the nonparametric equivalent to the Pearson correlation coefficient—the Spearman rank correlation coefficient.

The Spearman rank correlation coefficient has several advantages over the Pearson correlation coefficient. For instance, the Spearman rank correlation coefficient can be used to describe the relationship between linear or nonlinear data. The Spearman rank correlation coefficient can be used for data at the ordinal level. And, the Spearman rank correlation coefficient is easier to calculate by hand than the Pearson coefficient.

Note to Instructor

Tell students that they can calculate the Spearman rank correlation coefficient with a technology tool by replacing the given values with their corresponding ranks and then calculating r, the Pearson correlation coefficient.

> **DEFINITION**
>
> The **Spearman rank correlation coefficient,** r_s, is a measure of the strength of the relationship between two variables. The Spearman rank correlation coefficient is calculated using the ranks of paired sample data entries. The formula for the Spearman rank correlation coefficient is
>
> $$r_s = 1 - \frac{6\Sigma d^2}{n(n^2 - 1)}$$
>
> where n is the number of paired data entries and d is the difference between the ranks of a paired data entry.

Note to Instructor

To illustrate the range of values of r_s, have students calculate r_s given the following ranks of paired sample data entries.

   Set A: 2 5 1 3 4
   Set B: 2 5 1 3 4

Then have them calculate r_s for the following ranks of paired sample data entries.

   Set C: 1 2 3 4 5
   Set D: 5 4 3 2 1

The values of r_s range from -1 to $+1$. If the ranks of corresponding data pairs are exactly identical, r_s is equal to $+1$. If the ranks are in "reverse" order, r_s is equal to -1. If the ranks of corresponding data pairs have no relationship, r_s is equal to 0.

After calculating the Spearman rank correlation coefficient, you can determine whether the correlation between the variables is significant. You can do this by performing a hypothesis test for the population correlation coefficient ρ_s. The null and alternative hypotheses for this test are as follows.

H_0: $\rho_s = 0$ (There is no correlation between the variables.)
H_a: $\rho_s \neq 0$ (There is a significant correlation between the variables.)

The critical values for the Spearman rank correlation coefficient are listed in Table 10 of Appendix B. Table 10 lists critical values for selected levels of significance and for sample sizes of 30 or less. The test statistic for the hypothesis test is the Spearman rank correlation coefficient r_s.

GUIDELINES

Testing the Significance of the Spearman Rank Correlation Coefficient

In Words	*In Symbols*
1. State the null and the alternative hypotheses.	State H_0 and H_a.
2. Specify the level of significance.	Specify α.
3. Find the critical value.	Use Table 10 in Appendix B.
4. Find the test statistic.	$r_s = 1 - \dfrac{6\Sigma d^2}{n(n^2 - 1)}$
5. Make a decision to reject or fail to reject the null hypothesis.	If $|r_s|$ is greater than the critical value, reject H_0. Otherwise, do not reject H_0.
6. Interpret the decision in the context of the original claim.	

EXAMPLE 1 — *The Spearman Rank Correlation Coefficient*

The table lists the prices (in dollars per 100 pounds) received by U.S. farmers for beef and turkey from 1990 to 1996. At $\alpha = 0.10$, can you conclude that there is a correlation between the beef and turkey prices?

Year	1990	1991	1992	1993	1994	1995	1996
Beef	74.6	72.7	71.3	72.6	66.7	61.8	58.7
Turkey	39.4	38.4	37.7	39.0	40.4	41.6	43.3

SOLUTION   The null and alternative hypotheses are as follows.

H_0: $\rho_s = 0$ (There is no correlation between the beef and turkey prices.)

H_a: $\rho_s \neq 0$ (There is a correlation between the beef and turkey prices.)

Picturing the World

The table lists the number of men and women (in thousands) who have graduated from a U.S. college with a bachelor's degree from 1985 to 1995. *(Source: U.S. National Center for Education Statistics)*

Year	Male	Female
1985	483	497
1986	486	502
1987	481	510
1988	477	518
1989	483	535
1990	492	560
1991	504	590
1992	521	616
1993	533	632
1994	532	637
1995	526	634

Does a correlation exist between the number of men and women who graduate with bachelor's degrees each year? Use $\alpha = 0.05$.

Each data set has seven entries. Using Table 10 with $\alpha = 0.10$ and $n = 7$, the critical value is 0.714. Before calculating the test statistic, you must find d^2, the sum of the squares of the differences of the ranks of the data sets. You can use a table to calculate d^2 as shown below.

Beef Prices	Rank	Turkey Prices	Rank	d	d^2
74.6	7	39.4	4	3	9
72.7	6	38.4	2	4	16
71.3	4	37.7	1	3	9
72.6	5	39.0	3	2	4
66.7	3	40.4	5	-2	4
61.8	2	41.6	6	-4	16
58.7	1	43.3	7	-6	36
					$\Sigma = 94$

Using $n = 7$ and $\Sigma d^2 = 94$, the test statistic is

$$r_s = 1 - \frac{6\Sigma d^2}{n(n^2 - 1)}$$

$$= 1 - \frac{6(94)}{7(7^2 - 1)}$$

$$\approx -0.679.$$

Because $|-0.679| < 0.714$, you should fail to reject the null hypothesis. At the 10% level, you can conclude that between 1990 and 1996, there is not a significant correlation between beef and turkey prices.

Try It Yourself 1

The table lists the prices (in cents per pound) received by U.S. farmers for oat and wheat from 1989 to 1996. At $\alpha = 0.05$, can you conclude that there is a correlation between the oat and wheat prices?

Year	1989	1990	1991	1992	1993	1994	1995	1996
Oat	1.49	1.14	1.21	1.32	1.36	1.22	1.67	1.90
Wheat	3.72	2.61	3.00	3.24	3.26	3.45	4.55	4.30

a. *State* the null and alternative hypotheses.
b. *Specify* the level of significance.
c. *Find* the critical value.
d. *Use a table* to calculate d^2.
e. *Find* the standardized test statistic.
f. *Make a decision* to reject or fail to reject the null hypothesis.
g. Is there enough evidence to conclude that there is a significant correlation between oat and wheat prices between 1989 and 1996?

Answer: Page A44

11.4 ▼ EXERCISES

HELP

StatPro 11.4

Internet Statistics 11.4

Student Solutions Manual 11.4

Videos 11.4

Try It Yourself Answers 11.4

1. (a) H_0: $\rho_s = 0$ and
H_a: $\rho_s \neq 0$ (claim)

(b) CV = 0.929

(c) 0.929

(d) Reject H_0. There is enough evidence to support the claim.

2. (a) H_0: $\rho_s = 0$ and
H_a: $\rho_s \neq 0$ (claim)

(b) CV = 0.881

(c) 0.173

(d) Fail to reject H_0. There is not enough evidence to support the claim.

3. (a) H_0: $\rho_s = 0$ and
H_a: $\rho_s \neq 0$ (claim)

(b) CV = 0.497

(c) 0.568

(d) Reject H_0. There is enough evidence to support the claim.

Basic Skills and Concepts

Testing a Claim In Exercises 1–4, (a) identify the claim and state H_0 and H_a, (b) find the critical value using Table 10, (c) find the standardized test statistic r_s, and (d) decide whether to reject the null hypothesis. Then interpret the decision in the context of the original claim.

1. In an agricultural report, a commodities analyst suggests that there is a correlation between debt and income in the farming business. The table lists the total debts and total incomes for farms in seven states for a recent year. At $\alpha = 0.01$, is there enough evidence to support the analyst's claim? *(Source: U.S. Department of Agriculture)*

State	Debt (in millions of dollars)	Income (in millions of dollars)
California	14,917	23,310
Illinois	8665	9050
Iowa	11,642	12,853
Minnesota	8104	8809
Nebraska	8111	9454
North Carolina	3468	7831
Texas	9960	13,053

2. You work for a consumer product review organization and are asked to write a review on suitcases. As part of your review, you need to analyze the relationship between quality and price. The following table lists the overall scores and the prices for eight different suitcases. (The overall score represents the ease of use, features, construction, and durability of a suitcase.) At $\alpha = 0.01$, can you conclude that there is a correlation between the overall score and price? *(Adapted from Consumer Reports)*

Overall score	90	85	81	78	72	68	64	61
Price (in dollars)	495	230	190	160	350	230	260	200

3. The following table lists the overall scores and the prices for 12 different models of air conditioners. The overall score represents the air conditioner's performance and quietness. At $\alpha = 0.10$, can you conclude that there is a correlation between overall score and price? *(Adapted from Consumer Reports)*

Overall score	83	82	79	78	78	74
Price (in dollars)	320	360	360	300	230	285

Overall score	71	67	64	63	61	33
Price (in dollars)	320	300	340	295	220	280

4. (a) $H_0: \rho_s = 0$ and
$H_a: \rho_s \neq 0$ (claim)

(b) CV = 0.818

(c) 0.423

(d) Fail to reject H_0. There is not enough evidence to support the claim.

5. Fail to reject H_0

6. Fail to reject H_0

7. Fail to reject H_0

4. Is the price of a portable CD player related to its quality? To answer this question, you randomly select 11 portable CD players and determine the overall score and price of each. (The overall score represents the error correction, locate speed, battery life, and headphone quality of a CD player.) The results of the study are listed in the table. At $\alpha = 0.01$, can you conclude that there is a correlation between the overall score and the price? *(Adapted from Consumer Reports)*

Overall score	82	78	68	67	61	60
Price (in dollars)	150	100	120	140	145	100

Overall score	60	58	57	55	49
Price (in dollars)	150	80	200	80	75

Test Scores and GNP In Exercises 5–7, use the following table. The table lists the average achievement score in eighth-grade science and mathematics along with the gross national product (GNP) of nine countries for a recent year. (The GNP is a measure of a nation's total economic activity.) *(Source: IEA Third International Mathematics and Science Study, Boston College; U.S. Census Bureau)*

Country	Science average	Mathematics average	GNP (in billions of dollars)
Australia	545	530	231
Canada	531	527	542
Czech Republic	574	564	101
France	498	538	1521
Japan	571	605	5153
Portugal	480	454	103
Spain	517	487	554
Switzerland	522	545	316
USA	534	500	7247

5. At $\alpha = 0.05$, can you conclude that there is a correlation between science achievement scores and GNP?

6. At $\alpha = 0.05$, can you conclude that there is a correlation between mathematics achievement scores and GNP?

7. At $\alpha = 0.05$, can you conclude that there is a correlation between science and mathematics achievement scores?

8. Fail to reject H_0

9. Fail to reject H_0

Extending the Basics

Testing the Rank Correlation Coefficient for n > 30 If you are testing the significance of the Spearman rank correlation coefficient and the sample size n is greater than 30, you can use the Standard Normal Table and the following to find the critical value.

$$\frac{\pm z}{\sqrt{n-1}}$$

In Exercises 8 and 9, perform the indicated test.

8. The following table lists the average hours worked per week and the number of on-the-job injuries for a random sample of U.S. industries in a recent year. At $\alpha = 0.05$, can you conclude that there is a correlation between average hours worked and the number of on-the-job injuries? *(Adapted from U.S. Bureau of Labor Statistics)*

Hours worked	47.6	44.1	45.6	45.5	44.5	47.3	44.6	45.9	45.5
Injuries	16	33	25	33	18	20	21	18	21

Hours worked	43.7	44.8	42.5	46.5	42.3	45.5	41.8	43.1	44.4
Injuries	28	15	26	34	32	26	28	22	19

Hours worked	44.5	43.7	44.9	47.8	46.6	45.5	43.5	42.8	44.8
Injuries	23	20	28	24	26	29	21	28	23

Hours worked	43.5	47.0	44.5	50.1	46.7	43.1
Injuries	26	24	20	28	26	25

9. The following table lists the average hours worked per week and the number of on-the-job injuries for a random sample of U.S. construction companies in a recent year. At $\alpha = 0.05$, can you conclude that there is a correlation between average hours worked and the number of on-the-job injuries? *(Adapted from U.S. Bureau of Labor Statistics)*

Hours worked	40.5	38.3	37.8	38.2	38.6	41.2	39.0	41.0	40.6
Injuries	12	13	19	18	22	22	17	13	15

Hours worked	44.1	39.7	41.2	41.1	38.2	42.3	39.2	36.1	36.2
Injuries	10	18	19	13	24	12	12	13	15

Hours worked	38.7	36.0	37.3	36.5	37.9	38.0	36.7	40.1	35.5
Injuries	18	11	24	16	13	23	14	10	5

Hours worked	38.2	42.3	39.0	39.6	39.1	39.6	39.1
Injuries	14	13	18	15	23	15	23

TECHNOLOGY   MINITAB   EXCEL   TI-83

Selling Prices of Homes

The National Association of Realtors is the world's largest professional organization. Its members, who number over 720,000, include salespeople, brokers, appraisers, counselors, and property managers. One of the things the National Association of Realtors does is keep track of the selling prices of homes in the United States. These can be used to identify regional differences in the cost of homes.

The table at the right shows the selling prices (in thousands of dollars) of a random sample of metropolitan homes sold in 1998 in four U.S. regions: Northeast, Midwest, South, and West.

| Selling prices of metropolitan homes (in thousands of dollars) | | | |
Northeast	Midwest	South	West
107.0	106.1	115.4	138.5
112.8	92.6	120.6	152.2
84.2	146.2	98.1	124.4
212.6	102.3	86.0	128.2
188.1	90.1	122.7	120.2
89.0	120.0	107.3	158.1
98.1	166.8	120.0	147.2
124.4	116.3	88.0	121.2
89.0	121.8	134.0	125.6
110.5	121.7	97.7	133.5
139.5	102.8	104.6	175.3
138.7	106.6	128.6	102.6

Exercises

In Exercises 1–5, refer to the selling prices of metropolitan homes in the table. Use $\alpha = 0.05$ for all tests.

1. Construct a box-and-whisker plot for each region. Do the median selling prices appear to differ between regions?

2. Use a technology tool to perform a sign test to test the claim that the median selling price in the South is at least $125,000.

3. Use a technology tool to perform a Wilcoxon rank sum test to test the claim that the median selling prices in the Northeast and Midwest are the same.

4. Use a technology tool to perform a Kruskal-Wallis test to test the claim that the median selling prices for all four regions are the same.

5. Use a technology tool to perform a one-way ANOVA to test the claim that the average selling prices for all four regions are the same. How do your results compare to those in Exercise 4?

6. Repeat Exercises 1, 3, 4, and 5 using the data in the following table. The table shows the selling prices (in thousands of dollars) of a random sample of existing apartment condominiums and co-ops sold in 1998 in four U.S. regions: Northeast, Midwest, South, and West.

| Selling prices of condominiums and co-ops (in thousands of dollars) | | | |
Northeast	Midwest	South	West
94.2	103.0	90.3	171.2
161.5	127.9	79.9	103.8
107.9	116.5	69.0	108.8
83.0	151.1	60.5	126.9
110.0	65.0	45.8	146.0
104.8	95.4	82.5	130.1
99.4	112.4	101.5	105.8
78.6	123.4	55.7	86.1
115.7	84.6	71.0	155.5
100.5	91.0	77.2	147.2
95.5	106.4	65.8	122.0
114.8	90.5	90.4	151.0
129.5	108.6	67.8	96.5
79.9	99.2	120.7	111.3
106.2	124.5	95.0	148.7

Extended solutions are given in the *Technology Supplement.* Technical instruction is provided for Minitab, Excel, and the TI-83.

▼ 11 CHAPTER SUMMARY

What did you learn?

Review Exercises

- How to use the sign test to test a population median and to test the difference between two population medians (dependent samples) *(Section 11.1)*

  1–6

- How to use the Wilcoxon signed-rank test and Wilcoxon rank sum test to test the difference between two population medians *(Section 11.2)*

  7–10

- How to use the Kruskal-Wallis test to test for differences among three or more population medians *(Section 11.3)*

  11, 12

- How to use the Spearman rank correlation coefficient to determine whether the correlation between two variables is significant *(Section 11.4)*

  13, 14

The table summarizes parametric and nonparametric tests. Always use the parametric test if the conditions for that test are satisfied.

Test application	Parametric test	Nonparametric test
One-sample test	z-test for a population mean t-test for a population mean	Sign test for a population median
Two-sample tests Dependent samples	t-test for the difference between means	Paired-sample sign test Wilcoxon signed-rank test
Independent samples	z-test for the difference between means t-test for the difference between means	Wilcoxon rank sum test
Tests involving three or more samples	One-way ANOVA	Kruskal-Wallis test
Correlation	Pearson correlation coefficient	Spearman rank correlation coefficient

Why did you learn it? Uses and Abuses

Uses In previous chapters, you learned about procedures for testing hypotheses that required restrictions (such as normality) about the distribution of the population. An advantage of nonparametric tests is that little or no information about the population's distribution is required to perform the test. Therefore, if you have a sample but no information about the population's distribution, you can use a nonparametric test.

Abuses A disadvantage of a nonparametric test is that it does not use all of the sample's information and therefore is less efficient than the applicable corresponding parametric method. If you have a sample and have enough information about the population's distribution, you should use a parametric test. Otherwise, any test results and conclusions are questionable.

REVIEW EXERCISES

1. (a) H_0: median = $13,500 (claim)
H_a: median ≠ $13,500

(b) CV = 2

(c) $x = 7$

(d) Fail to reject H_0. There is not enough evidence to reject the claim.

2. (a) H_0: median ≤ $1200
H_a: median > $1200 (claim)

(b) CV = 1

(c) $x = 6$

(d) Fail to reject H_0. There is not enough evidence to support the claim.

3. (a) H_0: median ≤ 6 (claim)
H_a: median > 6

(b) CV = 1.282

(c) 2.032

(d) Reject H_0. There is enough evidence to reject the claim.

4. (a) H_0: There is no reduction in systolic blood pressure. (claim)
H_a: There is a reduction in systolic blood pressure.

(b) CV = 1

(c) $x = 4$

(d) Fail to reject H_0. There is not enough evidence to reject the claim.

In Exercises 1–6, use a sign test to test the claim by doing the following.
(a) Write the claim mathematically and identify H_0 and H_a.
(b) Find the critical value.
(c) Calculate the test statistic.
(d) Decide whether to reject or fail to reject the null hypothesis. Then interpret the decision in the context of the original claim.

1. A financial services institution estimates that the median value of stock among families that own stock is $13,500. The stock values (in thousands of dollars) among 17 randomly selected families that own stock are listed below. At $\alpha = 0.01$, can you reject the institution's claim? *(Adapted from Board of Governors of the Federal Reserve System)*

4.09	18.09	8.52	19.30	14.47	9.82	12.46	0.95	20.21
9.21	9.29	9.94	10.84	9.16	14.07	17.33	13.74	

2. A financial services institution claims that the median credit card debt among families that earn $10,000 to $24,999 is more than $1200. The credit card debts (in thousands of dollars) among 13 randomly selected families are listed below. At $\alpha = 0.01$, can you support the institution's claim? *(Adapted from Board of Governors of the Federal Reserve System)*

1.97	1.10	1.02	1.05	0.98	1.36	1.74
1.69	1.48	0.99	1.29	0.92	1.45	

3. A mail-order company believes that the median turnover time between receipt of a telephone order and packing of that order is six hours or less. Over a five-day period, 78 orders are randomly selected and their turnover time is recorded in $\frac{1}{2}$-hour increments. Eight orders took six hours, 26 orders took under six hours, and 44 orders took over six hours. At $\alpha = 0.10$, can you reject the company's claim?

4. In a study testing the effects of calcium supplements on blood pressure in men, ten men were given a calcium supplement for 12 weeks. The following measurements are for each subject's systolic blood pressure taken before and after the 12-week treatment period. At $\alpha = 0.10$, can you reject the claim that there was no reduction in systolic blood pressure? *(Adapted from The Journal of American Medicine)*

Patient	1	2	3	4	5	6	7
Before treatment	107	110	123	129	112	111	107
After treatment	100	114	105	112	115	116	106

Patient	8	9	10
Before treatment	112	136	102
After treatment	102	125	104

5. (a) H_0: There is no reduction in systolic blood pressure. (claim)
H_a: There is a reduction in systolic blood pressure.

(b) CV = 2

(c) $x = 3$

(d) Fail to reject H_0. There is not enough evidence to reject the claim.

6. (a) H_0: median = $27,900 (claim)
H_a: median ≠ $27,900

(b) CV = ±1.96

(c) −1.497

(d) Fail to reject H_0. There is not enough evidence to reject the claim.

7. (a) Dependent; Wilcoxon Signed Rank Test

(b) H_0: Producers are not under reporting the caloric content of their foods.
H_a: Producers are under reporting the caloric content of their foods. (claim)

(c) CV = 8

(d) $w_s = 2$

(e) Reject H_0. There is enough evidence to support the claim.

5. In a study testing the effects of an herbal supplement on blood pressure in men, eleven men were given an herbal supplement for 15 weeks. The following measurements are for each subject's systolic blood pressure taken before and after the 15-week treatment period. At $\alpha = 0.10$, can you reject the claim that there was no reduction in systolic blood pressure? *(Adapted from The Journal of American Medicine)*

Patient	1	2	3	4	5	6	7
Before treatment	123	109	112	102	98	114	119
After treatment	124	97	113	105	95	119	114

Patient	8	9	10	11
Before treatment	112	110	117	130
After treatment	114	121	118	133

6. The career placement office at a large university claims that the median starting salary of graduates majoring in marketing is $27,900. Of last year's graduating marketing majors, 57 were randomly surveyed about their salaries. Of the 54 graduates who were currently employed, 21 were paid less than $27,900 annually, and 33 were paid more than $27,900. At $\alpha = 0.05$, can you reject the office's claim? *(Adapted from National Association of Colleges and Employers)*

In Exercises 7–10, use a Wilcoxon test to test the claim by doing the following.

(a) Decide whether the samples are dependent or independent; then choose the appropriate Wilcoxon test.
(b) Write the claim mathematically and identify H_0 and H_a.
(c) Find the critical value.
(d) Calculate the test statistic.
(e) Decide whether to reject or fail to reject the null hypothesis. Then interpret the decision in the context of the original claim.

7. A consumer advocate group is testing the caloric content of locally produced health food. The table lists the results of calorimetric testing for the actual caloric content of nine local products and the reported values from the products' labels. At $\alpha = 0.05$, can you support the group's claim that local producers of health foods are underreporting the caloric content of their foods?

Product	1	2	3	4	5	6	7	8	9
Actual	88	82	107	171	150	140	211	172	199
Reported	60	75	75	120	135	140	170	180	185

8. (a) Independent; Wilcoxon Rank Sum Test

(b) H_0: There is no difference in the salaries. (claim)
H_a: There is a difference in the salaries.

(c) CV = ±1.96

(d) −2.659

(e) Reject H_0. There is enough evidence to reject the claim.

9. (a) Independent; Wilcoxon Rank Sum Test

(b) H_0: There is no difference in the amount of time that it takes to earn a doctorate.
H_a: There is a difference in the amount of time that it takes to earn a doctorate. (claim)

(c) CV = ±2.575

(d) −3.175

(e) Reject H_0. There is enough evidence to support the claim.

10. (a) Dependent; Wilcoxon Signed Rank Test

(b) H_0: The new drug does not affect the number of headache hours experienced.
H_a: The new drug does affect the number of headache hours experienced. (claim)

(c) CV = 4

(d) $w_s = 1$

(e) Reject H_0. There is enough evidence to support the claim.

8. A career placement advisor suggests that there is no difference in the starting salaries earned by female and male humanities graduates. A random sample of 11 female and 11 male humanities graduates and their starting salaries is listed in the table. At $\alpha = 0.05$, can you reject the advisor's claim? *(Adapted from U.S. Department of Education)*

Gender	Salary (in thousands of dollars)										
Female	20.2	20.7	21.8	20.5	20.7	20.7	20.3	20.3	20.6	20.1	20.6
Male	20.2	22.2	21.1	21.7	22.7	20.5	22.0	21.6	22.3	21.3	21.9

9. A career placement advisor estimates that there is a difference in the total time to earn a doctorate degree by female and male graduate students. A random sample of 12 female and 12 male graduate students and their total time to earn a doctorate degree is listed in the table. At $\alpha = 0.01$, can you reject the advisor's claim? *(Adapted from U.S. Department of Education)*

Gender	Total time (in years)											
Female	15	14	15	15	15	11	13	16	9	9	11	13
Male	11	8	9	11	10	8	8	10	11	9	10	8

10. A medical researcher claims that a new drug affects the number of headache hours experienced by headache sufferers. The number of headache hours (per day) experienced by eight patients before and after taking the drug are listed in the table. At $\alpha = 0.05$, can you support the researcher's claim?

Patient	1	2	3	4	5	6	7	8
Headache hours (before)	0.9	2.3	2.7	2.4	2.9	1.9	1.3	3.1
Headache hours (after)	1.4	1.5	1.4	1.8	1.3	0.6	0.7	1.9

In Exercises 11 and 12, use the Kruskal-Wallis test to test the claim by doing the following.

(a) Write the claim mathematically and identify H_0 and H_a.
(b) Find the critical value.
(c) Find the sums of the ranks for each sample and calculate the test statistic.
(d) Decide whether to reject or fail to reject the null hypothesis. Then interpret the decision in the context of the original claim.

11. (a) H_0: There is no difference in salaries between the fields of study. (claim)
H_a: There is a difference in salaries between the fields of study.

(b) CV = 5.991

(c) $H \approx 22.98$

(d) Reject H_0. There is enough evidence to reject the claim.

12. (a) H_0: There is no difference in the amount of time to earn a doctorate between the fields of study. (claim)
H_a: There is a difference in the amount of time to earn a doctorate between the fields of study.

(b) CV = 5.991

(c) $H \approx 22.2766$

(d) Reject H_0. There is enough evidence to reject the claim.

13. (a) H_0: $\rho_s = 0$ and
H_a: $\rho_s \neq 0$ (claim)

(b) CV = 0.881

(c) -0.429

(d) Fail to reject H_0. There is not enough evidence to support the claim.

14. (a) H_0: $\rho_s = 0$ and
H_a: $\rho_s \neq 0$ (claim)

(b) CV = 0.700

(c) 0.238

(d) Fail to reject H_0. There is not enough evidence to support the claim.

11. The following table lists the starting salaries for a random sample of college graduates in three fields of study. At $\alpha = 0.05$, can you conclude that the distributions of the starting salaries in these three fields of study are the same? *(Adapted from U.S. Department of Education)*

Field of study	Starting salary (in thousands of dollars)									
Education	20.4	20.5	20.4	20.2	20.4	20.2	20.1	20.1	19.4	19.9
Humanities	21.1	21.3	21.1	20.8	20.9	21.3	20.7	21.5	20.6	21.0
Natural science	22.2	22.1	22.2	21.0	21.1	21.8	22.6	22.0	22.5	21.2

12. The following table lists the total time to earn a doctorate degree for a random sample of college graduates in three fields of study. At $\alpha = 0.05$, can you conclude that the distributions of the total times in these three fields of study are the same? *(Adapted from U.S. Department of Education)*

Field of study	Total time (in years)										
Computer science	9	10	9	7	11	9	8	10	9	9	10
Natural science	8	8	7	8	7	7	8	8	8	8	7
Social science	12	13	11	11	10	9	14	10	10	11	12

In Exercises 13 and 14, use the Spearman rank correlation coefficient to test the claim by doing the following.

(a) Write the claim mathematically and identify H_0 and H_a.
(b) Find the critical value using Table 10.
(c) Find the standardized test statistic r_s.
(d) Decide whether to reject the null hypothesis. Then interpret the decision in the context of the original claim.

13. The following table lists the overall scores and the prices for eight television sets. The overall score represents the set's picture quality, sound quality, ease of use, and cable performance. At $\alpha = 0.01$, can you conclude that there is a correlation between overall score and price? *(Adapted from Consumer Reports)*

Overall score	80	79	70	65	63	62	61	58
Price (in dollars)	580	740	630	660	600	590	700	750

14. The following table lists the overall scores and the prices for nine cordless phones. The overall score represents the phone's speech clarity and handset convenience. At $\alpha = 0.05$, can you conclude that there is a correlation between overall score and price? *(Adapted from Consumer Reports)*

Overall score	81	78	72	68	66	65	67	63	57
Price (in dollars)	130	200	70	80	105	130	100	150	60

11 ▼ CHAPTER QUIZ

1. (a) H_0: There is no difference in the salaries between genders.
H_a: There is a difference in the salaries between genders. (claim)

(b) Wilcoxon Ranked Sum Test

(c) CV = ±1.645

(d) −1.722

(e) Reject H_0. There is enough evidence to support the claim.

2. (a) H_0: median = 28 (claim) and H_a: median ≠ 28

(b) Sign Test

(c) CV = 6

(d) $x = 10$

(e) Fail to reject H_0. There is not enough evidence to reject the claim.

3. (a) H_0: $\rho_s = 0$ and H_a: $\rho_s \neq 0$ (claim)

(b) Spearman Rank Correlation Coefficient Test

(c) CV = 0.881

(d) 0.095

(e) Fail to reject H_0. There is not enough evidence to support the claim.

4. (a) H_0: There is no difference in the annual premiums between the states.
H_a: There is a difference in the annual premiums between the states. (claim)

(b) Kruskal-Wallis Test

(c) CV = 5.991

(d) $H = 1.43$

(e) Fail to reject H_0. There is not enough evidence to support the claim.

Take this quiz as you would take a quiz in class. After you are done, check your work against the answers given in the back of the book.

For this quiz, do the following.
(a) Write the claim mathematically and identify H_0 and H_a.
(b) Decide which test to use.
(c) Find the critical value(s) and identify the critical region(s).
(d) Calculate the test statistic.
(e) Decide whether to reject or fail to reject the null hypothesis. Then interpret the decision in the context of the original claim.

1. A women's organization claims that there is a difference in the salaries earned by female and male employees of state and local governments. A random sample of nine female and nine male state and local government employees and their salaries is listed in the table. At $\alpha = 0.10$, can you support the organization's claim? *(Adapted from U.S. Bureau of Labor Statistics)*

Gender	Salary (in thousands of dollars)								
Female	29.2	28.8	28.4	32.0	23.8	34.3	24.8	25.6	22.8
Male	43.9	35.3	20.4	31.3	38.8	30.7	31.8	27.3	32.4

2. A government official believes that the median age in Puerto Rico is 28 years. In a random sample of 25 Puerto Ricans, 10 were less than 28 years, 13 were greater than 28 years, and 2 were 28 years. At $\alpha = 0.05$, can you support the official's claim? *(Adapted from U.S. Bureau of the Census)*

3. The following table lists the average hours worked per week and the number of on-the-job injuries for a random sample of U.S. industries in a recent year. At $\alpha = 0.01$, can you conclude that there is a correlation between average hours worked and the number of on-the-job injuries? *(Adapted from U.S. Bureau of Labor Statistics)*

Hours worked	47.3	46.7	48.7	39.6	42.3	43.6	47.5	47.9
Injuries	1	5	3	2	3	4	3	3

4. An independent insurance representative wants to determine whether there is a difference in the annual premiums for homeowner's insurance in three states: California, Florida, and Texas. To do so, the representative randomly selects several homes in each state and determines the annual homeowner's insurance premium for each. At $\alpha = 0.05$, can the representative conclude that the distributions of the annual premiums in these states are different? *(Adapted from Consumer Reports)*

State	Annual Premium (in dollars)						
California	756	429	476	427	501	512	492
Florida	677	701	573	405	604	506	458
Texas	591	490	735	546	633	502	447

11 **CUMULATIVE TEST**

1. Fail to reject H_0

2. Fail to reject H_0

3. Reject H_0

4. Fail to reject H_0

5. Reject H_0

6. Reject H_0

Take this test as you would take a test in class. After you are done, check your work against the answers given in the back of the book.

For Exercises 1–4, refer to the following table. The table lists the annual incomes (in thousands of dollars) for a random sample of households in California and Florida. *(Adapted from U.S. Bureau of the Census)*

California	62.1	44.0	45.5	37.9	40.2	26.3	48.8	49.3	31.6	44.8
Florida	44.3	37.6	28.5	17.0	22.8	15.8	34.7	23.2	23.7	31.9

1. At $\alpha = 0.05$, test the claim that the median household income in California is less than \$40,000.

2. At $\alpha = 0.05$, test the claim that the median household income in Florida is greater than \$29,000.

3. At $\alpha = 0.01$, test the claim that the median household incomes in California and Florida are the same.

4. At $\alpha = 0.01$, test the claim that the variances of the median household incomes in California and Florida are the same. (Assume each population of incomes is normally distributed.)

In Exercises 5–7, use the following table. The table lists three distributions— the percent distribution of annual incomes of households in the United States and two frequency distributions. The frequency distributions represent the results of a survey of 200 households in Kentucky and Utah. *(Adapted from U.S. Bureau of the Census)*

	Under $10,000	$10,000 to $14,999	$15,000 to $24,999	$25,000 to $34,999	$35,000 to $49,999	$50,000 to $74,999	$75,000 and over
U.S.	11.7%	8.6%	15.3%	13.7%	16.3%	18.0%	16.4%
Kentucky	5	7	52	73	59	4	0
Utah	13	16	28	35	36	61	11

5. At $\alpha = 0.10$, test the claim that the distribution of household incomes in Kentucky is the same as the U.S. distribution.

6. At $\alpha = 0.10$, test the claim that the distribution of household incomes in Utah is the same as the U.S. distribution.

APPENDIX A

In this appendix we use a 0-to-z table as an alternate development of the standard normal distribution. It is intended that this appendix be used after completing Section 5.1 in the text. If used, this appendix should replace the material in Section 5.2 except for the exercises.

Standard Normal Distribution (0-to-z)

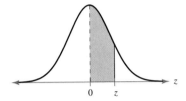

z	.00	.01	.02	.03	.04	.05	.06	.07	.08	.09
0.0	.0000	.0040	.0080	.0120	.0160	.0199	.0239	.0279	.0319	.0359
0.1	.0398	.0438	.0478	.0517	.0557	.0596	.0636	.0675	.0714	.0753
0.2	.0793	.0832	.0871	.0910	.0948	.0987	.1026	.1064	.1103	.1141
0.3	.1179	.1217	.1255	.1293	.1331	.1368	.1406	.1443	.1480	.1517
0.4	.1554	.1591	.1628	.1664	.1700	.1736	.1772	.1808	.1844	.1879
0.5	.1915	.1950	.1985	.2019	.2054	.2088	.2123	.2157	.2190	.2224
0.6	.2257	.2291	.2324	.2357	.2389	.2422	.2454	.2486	.2517	.2549
0.7	.2580	.2611	.2642	.2673	.2704	.2734	.2764	.2794	.2823	.2852
0.8	.2881	.2910	.2939	.2967	.2995	.3023	.3051	.3078	.3106	.3133
0.9	.3159	.3186	.3212	.3238	.3264	.3289	.3315	.3340	.3365	.3389
1.0	.3413	.3438	.3461	.3485	.3508	.3531	.3554	.3577	.3599	.3621
1.1	.3643	.3665	.3686	.3708	.3729	.3749	.3770	.3790	.3810	.3830
1.2	.3849	.3869	.3888	.3907	.3925	.3944	.3962	.3980	.3997	.4015
1.3	.4032	.4049	.4066	.4082	.4099	.4115	.4131	.4147	.4162	.4177
1.4	.4192	.4207	.4222	.4236	.4251	.4265	.4279	.4292	.4306	.4319
1.5	.4332	.4345	.4357	.4370	.4382	.4394	.4406	.4418	.4429	.4441
1.6	.4452	.4463	.4474	.4484	.4495	.4505	.4515	.4525	.4535	.4545
1.7	.4554	.4564	.4573	.4582	.4591	.4599	.4608	.4616	.4625	.4633
1.8	.4641	.4649	.4656	.4664	.4671	.4678	.4686	.4693	.4699	.4706
1.9	.4713	.4719	.4726	.4732	.4738	.4744	.4750	.4756	.4761	.4767
2.0	.4772	.4778	.4783	.4788	.4793	.4798	.4803	.4808	.4812	.4817
2.1	.4821	.4826	.4830	.4834	.4838	.4842	.4846	.4850	.4854	.4857
2.2	.4861	.4864	.4868	.4871	.4875	.4878	.4881	.4884	.4887	.4890
2.3	.4893	.4896	.4898	.4901	.4904	.4906	.4909	.4911	.4913	.4916
2.4	.4918	.4920	.4922	.4925	.4927	.4929	.4931	.4932	.4934	.4936
2.5	.4938	.4940	.4941	.4943	.4945	.4946	.4948	.4949	.4951	.4952
2.6	.4953	.4955	.4956	.4957	.4959	.4960	.4961	.4962	.4963	.4964
2.7	.4965	.4966	.4967	.4968	.4969	.4970	.4971	.4972	.4973	.4974
2.8	.4974	.4975	.4976	.4977	.4977	.4978	.4979	.4979	.4980	.4981
2.9	.4981	.4982	.4982	.4983	.4984	.4984	.4985	.4985	.4986	.4986
3.0	.4987	.4987	.4987	.4988	.4988	.4989	.4989	.4989	.4990	.4990
3.1	.4990	.4991	.4991	.4991	.4992	.4992	.4992	.4992	.4993	.4993
3.2	.4993	.4993	.4994	.4994	.4994	.4994.	.4994	.4995	.4995	.4995
3.3	.4995	.4995	.4995	.4996	.4996	.4996	.4996	.4996	.4996	.4997
3.4	.4997	.4997	.4997	.4997	.4997	.4997	.4997	.4997	.4997	.4998

From Frederick C. Mosteller and Robert E. K. Rourke, *Sturdy Statistics,* 1973, Addison-Wesley Publishing Co., Reading, MA. Reprinted with permission of Frederick Mosteller.

Alternate Presentation of The Standard Normal Distribution

The Standard Score • The Standard Normal Distribution

What You Should Learn

- *How to find and interpret standard z-scores and how to find the value of a variable when its standard score is given*

- *How to find areas under the standard normal curve and how to find areas under any normal curve using a table*

The Standard Score

In Section 5.1, you learned to calculate areas under a normal curve when values of the random variable x corresponded to $-3, -2, -1, 0, 1, 2,$ or 3 standard deviations from the mean. In this section, you will learn to calculate areas corresponding to other x-values. To do that you will use the standard score.

DEFINITION

The **standard score,** or **z-score,** represents the number of standard deviations a random variable, x, falls from the mean, μ. To transform the random variable to a z-score, use the following formula:

$$z = \frac{\text{value} - \text{mean}}{\text{standard deviation}} = \frac{x - \mu}{\sigma}$$

Note to Instructor

Mention that a standard score is a measure of position and can be used for any type of distribution. In theory, a z-score can be any real number. In practice, however, almost all z-scores will fall between -3 and $+3$ because almost all data values fall within 3 standard deviations of the mean.

▶ EXAMPLE 1   *Finding z-Scores*

The mean speed of vehicles along a stretch of highway is 56 mph with a standard deviation of 4 mph. You measure the speed of three cars traveling along this stretch of highway as 62 mph, 47 mph, and 56 mph. Find the z-score that corresponds to each speed. What can you conclude?

SOLUTION   The z-score that corresponds to each speed is calculated below.

$$x = 62 \text{ mph} \qquad\qquad x = 47 \text{ mph} \qquad\qquad x = 56 \text{ mph}$$
$$z = \frac{62 - 56}{4} = 1.5 \qquad z = \frac{47 - 56}{4} = -2.25 \qquad z = \frac{56 - 56}{4} = 0$$

From the z-scores, you can conclude that a speed of 62 mph is 1.5 standard deviations above the mean, a speed of 47 mph is 2.25 standard deviations below the mean, and a speed of 56 mph is equal to the mean.

Insight

A z-score can be negative, positive, or zero. If z is negative, the corresponding x value is below the mean. If z is positive, the corresponding x-value is above the mean. And if z = 0, the corresponding x-value is equal to the mean.

Try It Yourself 1

The monthly utility bills in a city have a mean of $70 and a standard deviation of $8. Find the z-scores that correspond to utility bills of $60, $71, and $92. What can you conclude?

a. *Identify* μ and σ of the nonstandard normal distribution.
b. *Transform* each value of the random variable, x, to a z-score.
c. *Interpret* the results.

Answer: Page A44 ◀

The formula on page A2 gives z in terms of x. If you solve this formula for x, you get a new formula that gives x in terms of z.

$$z = \frac{x - \mu}{\sigma} \qquad \text{Formula for } z \text{ in terms of } x$$

$$z\sigma = x - \mu \qquad \text{Multiply each side by } \sigma.$$

$$\mu + z\sigma = x \qquad \text{Add } \mu \text{ to each side.}$$

$$x = \mu + z\sigma \qquad \text{Interchange sides.}$$

Picturing the World

Each year the Centers for Disease Control and Prevention and the National Center for Health Statistics jointly publish a report summarizing the vital statistics from the previous year. According to one publication, the number of births in a recent year was 3,899,589. The weights of the newborns can be approximated by a normal distribution, as shown by the following graph.

Weights of Newborns

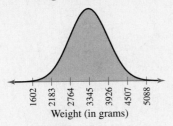

Weight (in grams)

The weights of three newborns are 2000 grams, 3000 grams, and 4000 grams. Find the z-score that corresponds to each weight. Are any of these unusually heavy or light?

Transforming a *z*-Score to an *x*-Value

To transform a standard z-score to a data value x in a given population, use the formula

$$x = \mu + z\sigma.$$

▶ **EXAMPLE 2** **Finding an x-Value**

The speeds of vehicles along a stretch of highway have a mean of 56 mph and a standard deviation of 4 mph. Find the speeds x corresponding to z-scores of 1.96, −2.33, and 0. Interpret your results.

SOLUTION The x-value that corresponds to each standard score is calculated as follows.

$z = 1.96$: $x = 56 + 1.96(4)$
$\qquad\qquad\quad = 63.84$ mph

$z = -2.33$: $x = 56 + (-2.33)(4)$
$\qquad\qquad\quad = 46.68$ mph

$z = 0$: $x = 56 + 0(4)$
$\qquad\qquad\quad = 56$ mph

You can see that 63.84 mph is above the mean, 46.68 is below the mean, and 56 is equal to the mean.

Try It Yourself 2

The monthly utility bills in a city have a mean of $70 and a standard deviation of $8. Find the *x-values* that correspond to z-scores of −0.75, 4.29, −1.82. What can you conclude?

a. *Identify* μ and σ of the nonstandard normal distribution.
b. *Transform* each z-score to an x-value.
c. *Interpret* the results.

Answer: Page A44 ◀

The Standard Normal Distribution

There are infinitely many normal distributions, each with its own mean and standard deviation. The normal distribution with a mean of 0 and a standard deviation of 1 is called **the standard normal distribution.**

If each data value of a normally distributed random variable x is transformed into a standard z-score, the result will be the standard normal distribution. When this transformation takes place, the area that falls in the interval of the nonstandard normal curve is the *same* as that under the standard normal curve within the corresponding z-boundaries.

DEFINITION

The **standard normal distribution** is a normal distribution with a mean of 0 and a standard deviation of 1.

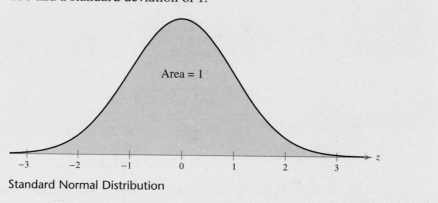

Standard Normal Distribution

It is important that you know the difference between x and z. The random variable x is sometimes called a raw score and represents values in a *nonstandard* normal distribution, while z represents values in the *standard* normal distribution.

Because every normal distribution can be transformed to the standard normal distribution, you can use z-scores and the standard normal curve to find areas under any normal curve. The Standard Normal Table (0-to-z) on page A1 lists the area under the standard normal curve between 0 and the given z-score. At first glance, the table appears to give areas for positive z-scores only. However, because of the symmetry of the standard normal curve, the table also gives areas for negative z-scores. As you examine the table, notice the following.

Properties of the Standard Normal Distribution

1. The distribution is symmetric about the mean ($z = 0$).
2. The area under the standard normal curve to the left of $z = 0$ is 0.5 and the area to the right of $z = 0$ is 0.5.
3. The area under the standard normal curve increases as the distance between 0 and z increases.

> **EXAMPLE 3** *Using the Standard Normal Table (0-to-z)*

(1) Find the area under the standard normal curve between 0 and $z = 1.15$.

(2) Find the z-scores that correspond to an area of 0.0948.

SOLUTION

(1) Find the area that corresponds to $z = 1.15$ by finding 1.1 in the left column and then moving across the row to the column under 0.05. The number in that row and column is 0.3749. So, the area between 0 and $z = 1.15$ is 0.3749.

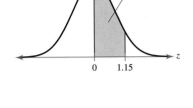

Area = 0.3749

z	.00	.01	.02	.03	.04	.05	.06
0.0	.0000	.0040	.0080	.0120	.0160	.0199	.0239
0.1	.0398	.0438	.0478	.0517	.0557	.0596	.0636
0.2	.0793	.0832	.0871	.0910	.0948	.0987	.1026
0.3	.1179	.1217	.1255	.1293	.1331	.1368	.1406

0.9	.3159	.3186	.3212	.3238	.3264	.3289	.3315
1.0	.3413	.3438	.3461	.3485	.3508	.3531	.3554
1.1	.3643	.3665	.3686	.3708	.3729	.3749	.3770
1.2	.3849	.3869	.3888	.3907	.3925	.3944	.3962
1.3	.4032	.4049	.4066	.4082	.4099	.4115	.4131
1.4	.4192	.4207	.4222	.4236	.4251	.4265	.4279

(2) Find the z-scores that correspond to an area of 0.0948 by locating 0.0948 in the table. The values at the beginning of the corresponding row and at the top of the corresponding column give the z-score. For an area of 0.0948, the row value is 0.2 and the column value is 0.04. So, the z-scores are $z = -0.24$ and $z = 0.24$.

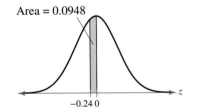

Area = 0.0948

z	.00	.01	.02	.03	.04	.05	.06
0.0	.0000	.0040	.0080	.0120	.0160	.0199	.0239
0.1	.0398	.0438	.0478	.0517	.0557	.0596	.0636
0.2	.0793	.0832	.0871	.0910	.0948	.0987	.1026
0.3	.1179	.1217	.1255	.1293	.1331	.1368	.1406
0.4	.1554	.1591	.1628	.1664	.1700	.1736	.1772
0.5	.1915	.1950	.1985	.2019	.2054	.2088	.2123

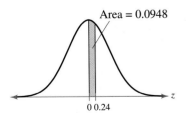

Area = 0.0948

Try It Yourself 3

(1) Find the area under the standard normal curve between 0 and $z = 2.19$.

(2) Find the z-scores that correspond to an area of 0.4850.

a. Locate the given z-score and *find the corresponding area* in the Standard Normal Table on page A1.

b. Locate the given area in the Standard Normal Table (0-to-z) and *find the corresponding z-score*.

Answer: Page A44

Use the following guidelines to find various types of areas under the standard normal curve.

GUIDELINES

Finding Areas Under the Standard Normal Curve

1. Sketch the standard normal curve and shade the appropriate area under the curve.
2. Use the Standard Normal Table (0-to-z) to find the area that corresponds to the given z-score(s).
3. Find the desired area by following the directions for each case shown.

a. Area to the left of z

   i. When $z < 0$, *subtract* the area from 0.5.

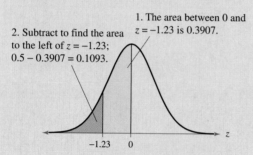

2. Subtract to find the area to the left of $z = -1.23$;
$0.5 - 0.3907 = 0.1093$.

1. The area between 0 and $z = -1.23$ is 0.3907.

   ii. When $z > 0$, *add* 0.5 to the area.

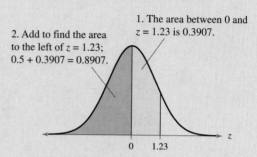

2. Add to find the area to the left of $z = 1.23$;
$0.5 + 0.3907 = 0.8907$.

1. The area between 0 and $z = 1.23$ is 0.3907.

b. Area to the right of z

   i. When $z < 0$, *add* 0.5 to the area.

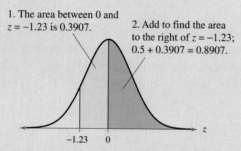

1. The area between 0 and $z = -1.23$ is 0.3907.

2. Add to find the area to the right of $z = -1.23$;
$0.5 + 0.3907 = 0.8907$.

   ii. When $z > 0$, *subtract* the area from 0.5.

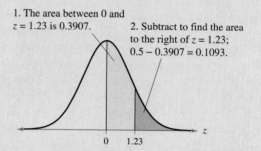

1. The area between 0 and $z = 1.23$ is 0.3907.

2. Subtract to find the area to the right of $z = 1.23$;
$0.5 - 0.3907 = 0.1093$.

c. Area between two z-scores

   i. When $z_1 < 0$ and $z_2 < 0$ *or* $z_1 > 0$ and $z_2 > 0$, *subtract* the smaller area from the larger area.

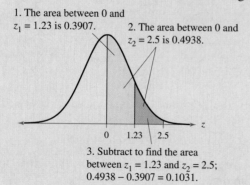

1. The area between 0 and $z_1 = 1.23$ is 0.3907.

2. The area between 0 and $z_2 = 2.5$ is 0.4938.

3. Subtract to find the area between $z_1 = 1.23$ and $z_2 = 2.5$;
$0.4938 - 0.3907 = 0.1031$.

   ii. When $z_1 < 0$ and $z_2 > 0$, *add* the areas.

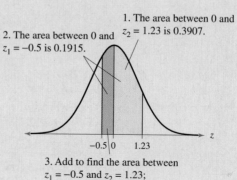

2. The area between 0 and $z_1 = -0.5$ is 0.1915.

1. The area between 0 and $z_2 = 1.23$ is 0.3907.

3. Add to find the area between $z_1 = -0.5$ and $z_2 = 1.23$;
$0.1915 + 0.3907 = 0.5822$.

> ► **EXAMPLE 4**   *Finding Area Under the Standard Normal Curve*

Find the area under the standard normal curve to the left of $z = -0.99$.

SOLUTION   The area under the standard normal curve to the left of $z = -0.99$ is shown.

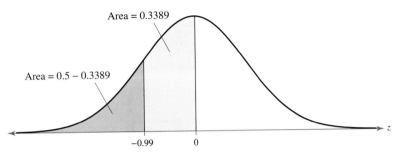

From the Standard Normal Table (0-to-z), the area corresponding to $z = -0.99$ is 0.3389. Because the area to the left of 0 is 0.5, the area to the left of $z = -0.99$ is

$$\text{Area} = 0.5 - 0.3389 = 0.1611.$$

Try It Yourself 4

Find the area under the standard normal curve to the left of $z = 2.13$.

a. *Draw* the standard normal curve and shade the area under the curve and to the left of $z = 2.13$.
b. Use the Standard Normal Table (0-to-z) to *find the area* that corresponds to $z = 2.13$.
c. *Add* 0.5 to the resulting area.

Answer: Page A44 ◄

> ► **EXAMPLE 5**   *Finding Area Under the Standard Normal Curve*

Find the area under the standard normal curve to the right of $z = 1.06$.

SOLUTION   The area under the standard normal curve to the right of $z = 1.06$ is shown.

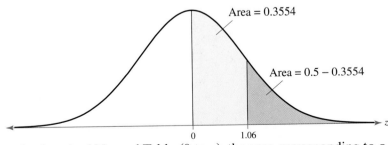

From the Standard Normal Table (0-to-z), the area corresponding to $z = 1.06$ is 0.3554. Because the area to the right of 0 is 0.5, the area to the right of $z = 1.06$ is

$$\text{Area} = 0.5 - 0.3554 = 0.1446.$$

Try It Yourself 5

Find the area under the standard normal curve to the right of $z = -2.16$.

a. *Draw* the standard normal curve and shade the area below the curve and to the right of $z = -2.16$.
b. Use the Standard Normal Table (0-to-z) to *find the area* that corresponds to $z = -2.16$.
c. *Add* 0.5 to the resulting area.   *Answer: Page A44* ◄

▶ **EXAMPLE 6**   *Finding Area Under the Standard Normal Curve*

Find the area under the standard normal curve between $z = -1.5$ and $z = 1.25$.

SOLUTION   The area under the standard normal curve between $z = -1.5$ and $z = 1.25$ is shown.

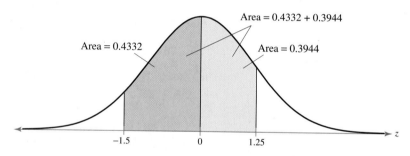

From the Standard Normal Table, the area corresponding to $z = -1.5$ is 0.4332 and the area corresponding to $z = 1.25$ is 0.3944. To find the area between these two z-scores, add the resulting areas.

$\quad$ Area $= 0.4332 + 0.3944 = 0.8276$

So, 82.76% of the area under the curve falls between $z = -1.5$ and $z = 1.25$.

Try It Yourself 6

Find the area under the standard normal curve between $z = -2.16$ and $z = -1.35$.

a. *Draw* the standard normal curve and shade the area below the curve that is between $z = -2.16$ and $z = -1.35$.
b. Use the Standard Normal Table (0-to-z) to *find the areas* that correspond to $z = -2.16$ and to $z = -1.35$.
c. *Subtract* the smaller area from the larger area.   *Answer: Page A44* ◄

Table 1—Random Numbers | APPENDIX B | **A9**

APPENDIX B

Table 1—Random Numbers

92630	78240	19267	95457	53497	23894	37708	79862	76471	66418
79445	78735	71549	44843	26104	67318	00701	34986	66751	99723
59654	71966	27386	50004	05358	94031	29281	18544	52429	06080
31524	49587	76612	39789	13537	48086	59483	60680	84675	53014
06348	76938	90379	51392	55887	71015	09209	79157	24440	30244
28703	51709	94456	48396	73780	06436	86641	69239	57662	80181
68108	89266	94730	95761	75023	48464	65544	96583	18911	16391
99938	90704	93621	66330	33393	95261	95349	51769	91616	33238
91543	73196	34449	63513	83834	99411	58826	40456	69268	48562
42103	02781	73920	56297	72678	12249	25270	36678	21313	75767
17138	27584	25296	28387	51350	61664	37893	05363	44143	42677
28297	14280	54524	21618	95320	38174	60579	08089	94999	78460
09331	56712	51333	06289	75345	08811	82711	57392	25252	30333
31295	04204	93712	51287	05754	79396	87399	51773	33075	97061
36146	15560	27592	42089	99281	59640	15221	96079	09961	05371
29553	18432	13630	05529	02791	81017	49027	79031	50912	09399
23501	22642	63081	08191	89420	67800	55137	54707	32945	64522
57888	85846	67967	07835	11314	01545	48535	17142	08552	67457
55336	71264	88472	04334	63919	36394	11196	92470	70543	29776
10087	10072	55980	64688	68239	20461	89381	93809	00796	95945
34101	81277	66090	88872	37818	72142	67140	50785	21380	16703
53362	44940	60430	22834	14130	96593	23298	56203	92671	15925
82975	66158	84731	19436	55790	69229	28661	13675	99318	76873
54827	84673	22898	08094	14326	87038	42892	21127	30712	48489
25464	59098	27436	89421	80754	89924	19097	67737	80368	08795
67609	60214	41475	84950	40133	02546	09570	45682	50165	15609
44921	70924	61295	51137	47596	86735	35561	76649	18217	63446
33170	30972	98130	95828	49786	13301	36081	80761	33985	68621
84687	85445	06208	17654	51333	02878	35010	67578	61574	20749
71886	56450	36567	09395	96951	35507	17555	35212	69106	01679
00475	02224	74722	14721	40215	21351	08596	45625	83981	63748
25993	38881	68361	59560	41274	69742	40703	37993	03435	18873
92882	53178	99195	93803	56985	53089	15305	50522	55900	43026
25138	26810	07093	15677	60688	04410	24505	37890	67186	62829
84631	71882	12991	83028	82484	90339	91950	74579	03539	90122
34003	92326	12793	61453	48121	74271	28363	66561	75220	35908
53775	45749	05734	86169	42762	70175	97310	73894	88606	19994
59316	97885	72807	54966	60859	11932	35265	71601	55577	67715
20479	66557	50705	26999	09854	52591	14063	30214	19890	19292
86180	84931	25455	26044	02227	52015	21820	50599	51671	65411
21451	68001	72710	40261	61281	13172	63819	48970	51732	54113
98062	68375	80089	24135	72355	95428	11808	29740	81644	86610
01788	64429	14430	94575	75153	94576	61393	96192	03227	32258
62465	04841	43272	68702	01274	05437	22953	18946	99053	41690
94324	31089	84159	92933	99989	89500	91586	02802	69471	68274
05797	43984	21575	09908	70221	19791	51578	36432	33494	79888
10395	14289	52185	09721	25789	38562	54794	04897	59012	89251
35177	56986	25549	59730	64718	52630	31100	62384	49483	11409
25633	89619	75882	98256	02126	72099	57183	55887	09320	73463
16464	48280	94254	45777	45150	68865	11382	11782	22695	41988

Table 2—Binomial Distribution

This table shows the probability of x successes in n independent trials, each with probability of success p.

n	x	.01	.05	.10	.15	.20	.25	.30	.35	.40	.45	.50	.55	.60	.65	.70	.75	.80	.85	.90	.95
2	0	.980	.902	.810	.723	.640	.563	.490	.423	.360	.303	.250	.203	.160	.123	.090	.063	.040	.023	.010	.002
	1	.020	.095	.180	.255	.320	.375	.420	.455	.480	.495	.500	.495	.480	.455	.420	.375	.320	.255	.180	.095
	2	.000	.002	.010	.023	.040	.063	.090	.123	.160	.203	.250	.303	.360	.423	.490	.563	.640	.723	.810	.902
3	0	.970	.857	.729	.614	.512	.422	.343	.275	.216	.166	.125	.091	.064	.043	.027	.016	.008	.003	.001	.000
	1	.029	.135	.243	.325	.384	.422	.441	.444	.432	.408	.375	.334	.288	.239	.189	.141	.096	.057	.027	.007
	2	.000	.007	.027	.057	.096	.141	.189	.239	.288	.334	.375	.408	.432	.444	.441	.422	.384	.325	.243	.135
	3	.000	.000	.001	.003	.008	.016	.027	.043	.064	.091	.125	.166	.216	.275	.343	.422	.512	.614	.729	.857
4	0	.961	.815	.656	.522	.410	.316	.240	.179	.130	.092	.062	.041	.026	.015	.008	.004	.002	.001	.000	.000
	1	.039	.171	.292	.368	.410	.422	.412	.384	.346	.300	.250	.200	.154	.112	.076	.047	.026	.011	.004	.000
	2	.001	.014	.049	.098	.154	.211	.265	.311	.346	.368	.375	.368	.346	.311	.265	.211	.154	.098	.049	.014
	3	.000	.000	.004	.011	.026	.047	.076	.112	.154	.200	.250	.300	.346	.384	.412	.422	.410	.368	.292	.171
	4	.000	.000	.000	.001	.002	.004	.008	.015	.026	.041	.062	.092	.130	.179	.240	.316	.410	.522	.656	.815
5	0	.951	.774	.590	.444	.328	.237	.168	.116	.078	.050	.031	.019	.010	.005	.002	.001	.000	.000	.000	.000
	1	.048	.204	.328	.392	.410	.396	.360	.312	.259	.206	.156	.113	.077	.049	.028	.015	.006	.002	.000	.000
	2	.001	.021	.073	.138	.205	.264	.309	.336	.346	.337	.312	.276	.230	.181	.132	.088	.051	.024	.008	.001
	3	.000	.001	.008	.024	.051	.088	.132	.181	.230	.276	.312	.337	.346	.336	.309	.264	.205	.138	.073	.021
	4	.000	.000	.000	.002	.006	.015	.028	.049	.077	.113	.156	.206	.259	.312	.360	.396	.410	.392	.328	.204
	5	.000	.000	.000	.000	.000	.001	.002	.005	.010	.019	.031	.050	.078	.116	.168	.237	.328	.444	.590	.774
6	0	.941	.735	.531	.377	.262	.178	.118	.075	.047	.028	.016	.008	.004	.002	.001	.000	.000	.000	.000	.000
	1	.057	.232	.354	.399	.393	.356	.303	.244	.187	.136	.094	.061	.037	.020	.010	.004	.002	.000	.000	.000
	2	.001	.031	.098	.176	.246	.297	.324	.328	.311	.278	.234	.186	.138	.095	.060	.033	.015	.006	.001	.000
	3	.000	.002	.015	.042	.082	.132	.185	.236	.276	.303	.312	.303	.276	.236	.185	.132	.082	.042	.015	.002
	4	.000	.000	.001	.006	.015	.033	.060	.095	.138	.186	.234	.278	.311	.328	.324	.297	.246	.176	.098	.031
	5	.000	.000	.000	.000	.002	.004	.010	.020	.037	.061	.094	.136	.187	.244	.303	.356	.393	.399	.354	.232
	6	.000	.000	.000	.000	.000	.000	.001	.002	.004	.008	.016	.028	.047	.075	.118	.178	.262	.377	.531	.735
7	0	.932	.698	.478	.321	.210	.133	.082	.049	.028	.015	.008	.004	.002	.001	.000	.000	.000	.000	.000	.000
	1	.066	.257	.372	.396	.367	.311	.247	.185	.131	.087	.055	.032	.017	.008	.004	.001	.000	.000	.000	.000
	2	.002	.041	.124	.210	.275	.311	.318	.299	.261	.214	.164	.117	.077	.047	.025	.012	.004	.001	.000	.000
	3	.000	.004	.023	.062	.115	.173	.227	.268	.290	.292	.273	.239	.194	.144	.097	.058	.029	.011	.003	.000
	4	.000	.000	.003	.011	.029	.058	.097	.144	.194	.239	.273	.292	.290	.268	.227	.173	.115	.062	.023	.004
	5	.000	.000	.000	.001	.004	.012	.025	.047	.077	.117	.164	.214	.261	.299	.318	.311	.275	.210	.124	.041
	6	.000	.000	.000	.000	.000	.001	.004	.008	.017	.032	.055	.087	.131	.185	.247	.311	.367	.396	.372	.257
	7	.000	.000	.000	.000	.000	.000	.000	.001	.002	.004	.008	.015	.028	.049	.082	.133	.210	.321	.478	.698
8	0	.923	.663	.430	.272	.168	.100	.058	.032	.017	.008	.004	.002	.001	.000	.000	.000	.000	.000	.000	.000
	1	.075	.279	.383	.385	.336	.267	.198	.137	.090	.055	.031	.016	.008	.003	.001	.000	.000	.000	.000	.000
	2	.003	.051	.149	.238	.294	.311	.296	.259	.209	.157	.109	.070	.041	.022	.010	.004	.001	.000	.000	.000
	3	.000	.005	.033	.084	.147	.208	.254	.279	.279	.257	.219	.172	.124	.081	.047	.023	.009	.003	.000	.000
	4	.000	.000	.005	.018	.046	.087	.136	.188	.232	.263	.273	.263	.232	.188	.136	.087	.046	.018	.005	.000
	5	.000	.000	.000	.003	.009	.023	.047	.081	.124	.172	.219	.257	.279	.279	.254	.208	.147	.084	.033	.005
	6	.000	.000	.000	.000	.001	.004	.010	.022	.041	.070	.109	.157	.209	.259	.296	.311	.294	.238	.149	.051
	7	.000	.000	.000	.000	.000	.000	.001	.003	.008	.016	.031	.055	.090	.137	.198	.267	.336	.385	.383	.279
	8	.000	.000	.000	.000	.000	.000	.000	.000	.001	.002	.004	.008	.017	.032	.058	.100	.168	.272	.430	.663
9	0	.914	.630	.387	.232	.134	.075	.040	.021	.010	.005	.002	.001	.000	.000	.000	.000	.000	.000	.000	.000
	1	.083	.299	.387	.368	.302	.225	.156	.100	.060	.034	.018	.008	.004	.001	.000	.000	.000	.000	.000	.000
	2	.003	.063	.172	.260	.302	.300	.267	.216	.161	.111	.070	.041	.021	.010	.004	.001	.000	.000	.000	.000
	3	.000	.008	.045	.107	.176	.234	.267	.272	.251	.212	.164	.116	.074	.042	.021	.009	.003	.001	.000	.000
	4	.000	.001	.007	.028	.066	.117	.172	.219	.251	.260	.246	.213	.167	.118	.074	.039	.017	.005	.001	.000
	5	.000	.000	.001	.005	.017	.039	.074	.118	.167	.213	.246	.260	.251	.219	.172	.117	.066	.028	.007	.001
	6	.000	.000	.000	.001	.003	.009	.021	.042	.074	.116	.164	.212	.251	.272	.267	.234	.176	.107	.045	.008
	7	.000	.000	.000	.000	.000	.001	.004	.010	.021	.041	.070	.111	.161	.216	.267	.300	.302	.260	.172	.063
	8	.000	.000	.000	.000	.000	.000	.000	.001	.004	.008	.018	.034	.060	.100	.156	.225	.302	.368	.387	.299
	9	.000	.000	.000	.000	.000	.000	.000	.000	.000	.001	.002	.005	.010	.021	.040	.075	.134	.232	.387	.630

Table 2—Binomial Distribution | APPENDIX B   **A11**

Table 2—Binomial Distribution (continued)

											p										
n	x	.01	.05	.10	.15	.20	.25	.30	.35	.40	.45	.50	.55	.60	.65	.70	.75	.80	.85	.90	.95
10	0	.904	.599	.349	.197	.107	.056	.028	.014	.006	.003	.001	.000	.000	.000	.000	.000	.000	.000	.000	.000
	1	.091	.315	.387	.347	.268	.188	.121	.072	.040	.021	.010	.004	.002	.000	.000	.000	.000	.000	.000	.000
	2	.004	.075	.194	.276	.302	.282	.233	.176	.121	.076	.044	.023	.011	.004	.001	.000	.000	.000	.000	.000
	3	.000	.010	.057	.130	.201	.250	.267	.252	.215	.166	.117	.075	.042	.021	.009	.003	.001	.000	.000	.000
	4	.000	.001	.011	.040	.088	.146	.200	.238	.251	.238	.205	.160	.111	.069	.037	.016	.006	.001	.000	.000
	5	.000	.000	.001	.008	.026	.058	.103	.154	.201	.234	.246	.234	.201	.154	.103	.058	.026	.008	.001	.000
	6	.000	.000	.000	.001	.006	.016	.037	.069	.111	.160	.205	.238	.251	.238	.200	.146	.088	.040	.011	.001
	7	.000	.000	.000	.000	.001	.003	.009	.021	.042	.075	.117	.166	.215	.252	.267	.250	.201	.130	.057	.010
	8	.000	.000	.000	.000	.000	.000	.001	.004	.011	.023	.044	.076	.121	.176	.233	.282	.302	.276	.194	.075
	9	.000	.000	.000	.000	.000	.000	.000	.000	.002	.004	.010	.021	.040	.072	.121	.188	.268	.347	.387	.315
	10	.000	.000	.000	.000	.000	.000	.000	.000	.000	.000	.001	.003	.006	.014	.028	.056	.107	.197	.349	.599
11	0	.895	.569	.314	.167	.086	.042	.020	.009	.004	.001	.000	.000	.000	.000	.000	.000	.000	.000	.000	.000
	1	.099	.329	.384	.325	.236	.155	.093	.052	.027	.013	.005	.002	.001	.000	.000	.000	.000	.000	.000	.000
	2	.005	.087	.213	.287	.295	.258	.200	.140	.089	.051	.027	.013	.005	.002	.001	.000	.000	.000	.000	.000
	3	.000	.014	.071	.152	.221	.258	.257	.225	.177	.126	.081	.046	.023	.010	.004	.001	.000	.000	.000	.000
	4	.000	.001	.016	.054	.111	.172	.220	.243	.236	.206	.161	.113	.070	.038	.017	.006	.002	.000	.000	.000
	5	.000	.000	.002	.013	.039	.080	.132	.183	.221	.236	.226	.193	.147	.099	.057	.027	.010	.002	.000	.000
	6	.000	.000	.000	.002	.010	.027	.057	.099	.147	.193	.226	.236	.221	.183	.132	.080	.039	.013	.002	.000
	7	.000	.000	.000	.000	.002	.006	.017	.038	.070	.113	.161	.206	.236	.243	.220	.172	.111	.054	.016	.001
	8	.000	.000	.000	.000	.000	.001	.004	.010	.023	.046	.081	.126	.177	.225	.257	.258	.221	.152	.071	.014
	9	.000	.000	.000	.000	.000	.000	.001	.002	.005	.013	.027	.051	.089	.140	.200	.258	.295	.287	.213	.087
	10	.000	.000	.000	.000	.000	.000	.000	.000	.001	.002	.005	.013	.027	.052	.093	.155	.236	.325	.384	.329
	11	.000	.000	.000	.000	.000	.000	.000	.000	.000	.000	.000	.001	.004	.009	.020	.042	.086	.167	.314	.569
12	0	.886	.540	.282	.142	.069	.032	.014	.006	.002	.001	.000	.000	.000	.000	.000	.000	.000	.000	.000	.000
	1	.107	.341	.377	.301	.206	.127	.071	.037	.017	.008	.003	.001	.000	.000	.000	.000	.000	.000	.000	.000
	2	.006	.099	.230	.292	.283	.232	.168	.109	.064	.034	.016	.007	.002	.001	.000	.000	.000	.000	.000	.000
	3	.000	.017	.085	.172	.236	.258	.240	.195	.142	.092	.054	.028	.012	.005	.001	.000	.000	.000	.000	.000
	4	.000	.002	.021	.068	.133	.194	.231	.237	.213	.170	.121	.076	.042	.020	.008	.002	.001	.000	.000	.000
	5	.000	.000	.004	.019	.053	.103	.158	.204	.227	.223	.193	.149	.101	.059	.029	.011	.003	.001	.000	.000
	6	.000	.000	.000	.004	.016	.040	.079	.128	.177	.212	.226	.212	.177	.128	.079	.040	.016	.004	.000	.000
	7	.000	.000	.000	.001	.003	.011	.029	.059	.101	.149	.193	.223	.227	.204	.158	.103	.053	.019	.004	.000
	8	.000	.000	.000	.000	.001	.002	.008	.020	.042	.076	.121	.170	.213	.237	.231	.194	.133	.068	.021	.002
	9	.000	.000	.000	.000	.000	.000	.001	.005	.012	.028	.054	.092	.142	.195	.240	.258	.236	.172	.085	.017
	10	.000	.000	.000	.000	.000	.000	.000	.001	.002	.007	.016	.034	.064	.109	.168	.232	.283	.292	.230	.099
	11	.000	.000	.000	.000	.000	.000	.000	.000	.000	.001	.003	.008	.017	.037	.071	.127	.206	.301	.377	.341
	12	.000	.000	.000	.000	.000	.000	.000	.000	.000	.000	.000	.001	.002	.006	.014	.032	.069	.142	.282	.540
15	0	.860	.463	.206	.087	.035	.013	.005	.002	.000	.000	.000	.000	.000	.000	.000	.000	.000	.000	.000	.000
	1	.130	.366	.343	.231	.132	.067	.031	.013	.005	.002	.000	.000	.000	.000	.000	.000	.000	.000	.000	.000
	2	.009	.135	.267	.286	.231	.156	.092	.048	.022	.009	.003	.001	.000	.000	.000	.000	.000	.000	.000	.000
	3	.000	.031	.129	.218	.250	.225	.170	.111	.063	.032	.014	.005	.002	.001	.000	.000	.000	.000	.000	.000
	4	.000	.005	.043	.116	.188	.225	.219	.179	.127	.078	.042	.019	.007	.002	.001	.000	.000	.000	.000	.000
	5	.000	.001	.010	.045	.103	.165	.206	.212	.186	.140	.092	.051	.024	.010	.003	.001	.000	.000	.000	.000
	6	.000	.000	.002	.013	.043	.092	.147	.191	.207	.191	.153	.105	.061	.030	.012	.003	.001	.000	.000	.000
	7	.000	.000	.000	.003	.014	.039	.081	.132	.177	.201	.196	.165	.118	.071	.035	.013	.003	.000	.000	.000
	8	.000	.000	.000	.001	.003	.013	.035	.071	.118	.165	.196	.201	.177	.132	.081	.039	.014	.003	.000	.000
	9	.000	.000	.000	.000	.001	.003	.012	.030	.061	.105	.153	.191	.207	.191	.147	.092	.043	.013	.002	.000
	10	.000	.000	.000	.000	.000	.001	.003	.010	.024	.051	.092	.140	.186	.212	.206	.165	.103	.045	.010	.001
	11	.000	.000	.000	.000	.000	.000	.001	.002	.007	.019	.042	.078	.127	.179	.219	.225	.188	.116	.043	.005
	12	.000	.000	.000	.000	.000	.000	.000	.000	.002	.005	.014	.032	.063	.111	.170	.225	.250	.218	.129	.031
	13	.000	.000	.000	.000	.000	.000	.000	.000	.000	.001	.003	.009	.022	.048	.092	.156	.231	.286	.267	.135
	14	.000	.000	.000	.000	.000	.000	.000	.000	.000	.000	.000	.002	.005	.013	.031	.067	.132	.231	.343	.366
	15	.000	.000	.000	.000	.000	.000	.000	.000	.000	.000	.000	.000	.000	.002	.005	.013	.035	.087	.206	.463

Table 2—Binomial Distribution (continued)

											p										
n	x	.01	.05	.10	.15	.20	.25	.30	.35	.40	.45	.50	.55	.60	.65	.70	.75	.80	.85	.90	.95
16	0	.851	.440	.185	.074	.028	.010	.003	.001	.000	.000	.000	.000	.000	.000	.000	.000	.000	.000	.000	.000
	1	.138	.371	.329	.210	.113	.053	.023	.009	.003	.001	.000	.000	.000	.000	.000	.000	.000	.000	.000	.000
	2	.010	.146	.275	.277	.211	.134	.073	.035	.015	.006	.002	.001	.000	.000	.000	.000	.000	.000	.000	.000
	3	.000	.036	.142	.229	.246	.208	.146	.089	.047	.022	.009	.003	.001	.000	.000	.000	.000	.000	.000	.000
	4	.000	.006	.051	.131	.200	.225	.204	.155	.101	.057	.028	.011	.004	.001	.000	.000	.000	.000	.000	.000
	5	.000	.001	.014	.056	.120	.180	.210	.201	.162	.112	.067	.034	.014	.005	.001	.000	.000	.000	.000	.000
	6	.000	.000	.003	.018	.055	.110	.165	.198	.198	.168	.122	.075	.039	.017	.006	.001	.000	.000	.000	.000
	7	.000	.000	.000	.005	.020	.052	.101	.152	.189	.197	.175	.132	.084	.044	.019	.006	.001	.000	.000	.000
	8	.000	.000	.000	.001	.006	.020	.049	.092	.142	.181	.196	.181	.142	.092	.049	.020	.006	.001	.000	.000
	9	.000	.000	.000	.000	.001	.006	.019	.044	.084	.132	.175	.197	.189	.152	.101	.052	.020	.006	.001	.000
	10	.000	.000	.000	.000	.000	.001	.006	.017	.039	.075	.122	.168	.198	.198	.165	.110	.055	.018	.003	.000
	11	.000	.000	.000	.000	.000	.000	.001	.005	.014	.034	.067	.112	.162	.201	.210	.180	.120	.056	.014	.001
	12	.000	.000	.000	.000	.000	.000	.000	.001	.004	.011	.028	.057	.101	.155	.204	.225	.200	.131	.051	.006
	13	.000	.000	.000	.000	.000	.000	.000	.000	.001	.003	.009	.022	.047	.089	.146	.208	.246	.229	.142	.036
	14	.000	.000	.000	.000	.000	.000	.000	.000	.000	.001	.002	.006	.015	.035	.073	.134	.211	.277	.275	.146
	15	.000	.000	.000	.000	.000	.000	.000	.000	.000	.000	.000	.001	.003	.009	.023	.053	.113	.210	.329	.371
	16	.000	.000	.000	.000	.000	.000	.000	.000	.000	.000	.000	.000	.001	.003	.010	.028	.074	.185	.440	
20	0	.818	.358	.122	.039	.012	.003	.001	.000	.000	.000	.000	.000	.000	.000	.000	.000	.000	.000	.000	.000
	1	.165	.377	.270	.137	.058	.021	.007	.002	.000	.000	.000	.000	.000	.000	.000	.000	.000	.000	.000	.000
	2	.016	.189	.285	.229	.137	.067	.028	.010	.003	.001	.000	.000	.000	.000	.000	.000	.000	.000	.000	.000
	3	.001	.060	.190	.243	.205	.134	.072	.032	.012	.004	.001	.000	.000	.000	.000	.000	.000	.000	.000	.000
	4	.000	.013	.090	.182	.218	.190	.130	.074	.035	.014	.005	.001	.000	.000	.000	.000	.000	.000	.000	.000
	5	.000	.002	.032	.103	.175	.202	.179	.127	.075	.036	.015	.005	.001	.000	.000	.000	.000	.000	.000	.000
	6	.000	.000	.009	.045	.109	.169	.192	.171	.124	.075	.037	.015	.005	.001	.000	.000	.000	.000	.000	.000
	7	.000	.000	.002	.016	.055	.112	.164	.184	.166	.122	.074	.037	.015	.005	.001	.000	.000	.000	.000	.000
	8	.000	.000	.000	.005	.022	.061	.114	.161	.180	.162	.120	.073	.035	.014	.004	.001	.000	.000	.000	.000
	9	.000	.000	.000	.001	.007	.027	.065	.116	.160	.177	.160	.119	.071	.034	.012	.003	.000	.000	.000	.000
	10	.000	.000	.000	.000	.002	.010	.031	.069	.117	.159	.176	.159	.117	.069	.031	.010	.002	.000	.000	.000
	11	.000	.000	.000	.000	.000	.003	.012	.034	.071	.119	.160	.177	.160	.116	.065	.027	.007	.001	.000	.000
	12	.000	.000	.000	.000	.000	.001	.004	.014	.035	.073	.120	.162	.180	.161	.114	.061	.022	.005	.000	.000
	13	.000	.000	.000	.000	.000	.000	.001	.005	.015	.037	.074	.122	.166	.184	.164	.112	.055	.016	.002	.000
	14	.000	.000	.000	.000	.000	.000	.000	.001	.005	.015	.037	.075	.124	.171	.192	.169	.109	.045	.009	.000
	15	.000	.000	.000	.000	.000	.000	.000	.000	.001	.005	.015	.036	.075	.127	.179	.202	.175	.103	.032	.002
	16	.000	.000	.000	.000	.000	.000	.000	.000	.000	.001	.005	.014	.035	.074	.130	.190	.218	.182	.090	.013
	17	.000	.000	.000	.000	.000	.000	.000	.000	.000	.000	.001	.004	.012	.032	.072	.134	.205	.243	.190	.060
	18	.000	.000	.000	.000	.000	.000	.000	.000	.000	.000	.000	.001	.003	.010	.028	.067	.137	.229	.285	.189
	19	.000	.000	.000	.000	.000	.000	.000	.000	.000	.000	.000	.000	.000	.002	.007	.021	.058	.137	.270	.377
	20	.000	.000	.000	.000	.000	.000	.000	.000	.000	.000	.000	.000	.000	.000	.001	.003	.012	.039	.122	.358

Table 3—Poisson Distribution | APPENDIX B   **A13**

Table 3—Poisson Distribution

x	0.1	0.2	0.3	0.4	0.5	0.6	0.7	0.8	0.9	1.0
0	.9048	.8187	.7408	.6703	.6065	.5488	.4966	.4493	.4066	.3679
1	.0905	.1637	.2222	.2681	.3033	.3293	.3476	.3595	.3659	.3679
2	.0045	.0164	.0333	.0536	.0758	.0988	.1217	.1438	.1647	.1839
3	.0002	.0011	.0033	.0072	.0126	.0198	.0284	.0383	.0494	.0613
4	.0000	.0001	.0003	.0007	.0016	.0030	.0050	.0077	.0111	.0153
5	.0000	.0000	.0000	.0001	.0002	.0004	.0007	.0012	.0020	.0031
6	.0000	.0000	.0000	.0000	.0000	.0000	.0001	.0002	.0003	.0005
7	.0000	.0000	.0000	.0000	.0000	.0000	.0000	.0000	.0000	.0001

x	1.1	1.2	1.3	1.4	1.5	1.6	1.7	1.8	1.9	2.0
0	.3329	.3012	.2725	.2466	.2231	.2019	.1827	.1653	.1496	.1353
1	.3662	.3614	.3543	.3452	.3347	.3230	.3106	.2975	.2842	.2707
2	.2014	.2169	.2303	.2417	.2510	.2584	.2640	.2678	.2700	.2707
3	.0738	.0867	.0998	.1128	.1255	.1378	.1496	.1607	.1710	.1804
4	.0203	.0260	.0324	.0395	.0471	.0551	.0636	.0723	.0812	.0902
5	.0045	.0062	.0084	.0111	.0141	.0176	.0216	.0260	.0309	.0361
6	.0008	.0012	.0018	.0026	.0035	.0047	.0061	.0078	.0098	.0120
7	.0001	.0002	.0003	.0005	.0008	.0011	.0015	.0020	.0027	.0034
8	.0000	.0000	.0001	.0001	.0001	.0002	.0003	.0005	.0006	.0009
9	.0000	.0000	.0000	.0000	.0000	.0000	.0001	.0001	.0001	.0002

x	2.1	2.2	2.3	2.4	2.5	2.6	2.7	2.8	2.9	3.0
0	.1225	.1108	.1003	.0907	.0821	.0743	.0672	.0608	.0550	.0498
1	.2572	.2438	.2306	.2177	.2052	.1931	.1815	.1703	.1596	.1494
2	.2700	.2681	.2652	.2613	.2565	.2510	.2450	.2384	.2314	.2240
3	.1890	.1966	.2033	.2090	.2138	.2176	.2205	.2225	.2237	.2240
4	.0992	.1082	.1169	.1254	.1336	.1414	.1488	.1557	.1622	.1680
5	.0417	.0476	.0538	.0602	.0668	.0735	.0804	.0872	.0940	.1008
6	.0146	.0174	.0206	.0241	.0278	.0319	.0362	.0407	.0455	.0504
7	.0044	.0055	.0068	.0083	.0099	.0118	.0139	.0163	.0188	.0216
8	.0011	.0015	.0019	.0025	.0031	.0038	.0047	.0057	.0068	.0081
9	.0003	.0004	.0005	.0007	.0009	.0011	.0014	.0018	.0022	.0027
10	.0001	.0001	.0001	.0002	.0002	.0003	.0004	.0005	.0006	.0008
11	.0000	.0000	.0000	.0000	.0000	.0001	.0001	.0001	.0002	.0002
12	.0000	.0000	.0000	.0000	.0000	.0000	.0000	.0000	.0000	.0001

x	3.1	3.2	3.3	3.4	3.5	3.6	3.7	3.8	3.9	4.0
0	.0450	.0408	.0369	.0334	.0302	.0273	.0247	.0224	.0202	.0183
1	.1397	.1304	.1217	.1135	.1057	.0984	.0915	.0850	.0789	.0733
2	.2165	.2087	.2008	.1929	.1850	.1771	.1692	.1615	.1539	.1465
3	.2237	.2226	.2209	.2186	.2158	.2125	.2087	.2046	.2001	.1954
4	.1734	.1781	.1823	.1858	.1888	.1912	.1931	.1944	.1951	.1954
5	.1075	.1140	.1203	.1264	.1322	.1377	.1429	.1477	.1522	.1563
6	.0555	.0608	.0662	.0716	.0771	.0826	.0881	.0936	.0989	.1042
7	.0246	.0278	.0312	.0348	.0385	.0425	.0466	.0508	.0551	.0595
8	.0095	.0111	.0129	.0148	.0169	.0191	.0215	.0241	.0269	.0298
9	.0033	.0040	.0047	.0056	.0066	.0076	.0089	.0102	.0116	.0132
10	.0010	.0013	.0016	.0019	.0023	.0028	.0033	.0039	.0045	.0053
11	.0003	.0004	.0005	.0006	.0007	.0009	.0011	.0013	.0016	.0019
12	.0001	.0001	.0001	.0002	.0002	.0003	.0003	.0004	.0005	.0006
13	.0000	.0000	.0000	.0000	.0001	.0001	.0001	.0001	.0002	.0002
14	.0000	.0000	.0000	.0000	.0000	.0000	.0000	.0000	.0000	.0001

Table 3—Poisson Distribution (continued)

					μ					
x	4.1	4.2	4.3	4.4	4.5	4.6	4.7	4.8	4.9	5.0
0	.0166	.0150	.0136	.0123	.0111	.0101	.0091	.0082	.0074	.0067
1	.0679	.0630	.0583	.0540	.0500	.0462	.0427	.0395	.0365	.0337
2	.1393	.1323	.1254	.1188	.1125	.1063	.1005	.0948	.0894	.0842
3	.1904	.1852	.1798	.1743	.1687	.1631	.1574	.1517	.1460	.1404
4	.1951	.1944	.1933	.1917	.1898	.1875	.1849	.1820	.1789	.1755
5	.1600	.1633	.1662	.1687	.1708	.1725	.1738	.1747	.1753	.1755
6	.1093	.1143	.1191	.1237	.1281	.1323	.1362	.1398	.1432	.1462
7	.0640	.0686	.0732	.0778	.0824	.0869	.0914	.0959	.1002	.1044
8	.0328	.0360	.0393	.0428	.0463	.0500	.0537	.0575	.0614	.0653
9	.0150	.0168	.0188	.0209	.0232	.0255	.0280	.0307	.0334	.0363
10	.0061	.0071	.0081	.0092	.0104	.0118	.0132	.0147	.0164	.0181
11	.0023	.0027	.0032	.0037	.0043	.0049	.0056	.0064	.0073	.0082
12	.0008	.0009	.0011	.0014	.0016	.0019	.0022	.0026	.0030	.0034
13	.0002	.0003	.0004	.0005	.0006	.0007	.0008	.0009	.0011	.0013
14	.0001	.0001	.0001	.0001	.0002	.0002	.0003	.0003	.0004	.0005
15	.0000	.0000	.0000	.0000	.0001	.0001	.0001	.0001	.0001	.0002

					μ					
x	5.1	5.2	5.3	5.4	5.5	5.6	5.7	5.8	5.9	6.0
0	.0061	.0055	.0050	.0045	.0041	.0037	.0033	.0030	.0027	.0025
1	.0311	.0287	.0265	.0244	.0225	.0207	.0191	.0176	.0162	.0149
2	.0793	.0746	.0701	.0659	.0618	.0580	.0544	.0509	.0477	.0446
3	.1348	.1293	.1239	.1185	.1133	.1082	.1033	.0985	.0938	.0892
4	.1719	.1681	.1641	.1600	.1558	.1515	.1472	.1428	.1383	.1339
5	.1753	.1748	.1740	.1728	.1714	.1697	.1678	.1656	.1632	.1606
6	.1490	.1515	.1537	.1555	.1571	.1584	.1594	.1601	.1605	.1606
7	.1086	.1125	.1163	.1200	.1234	.1267	.1298	.1326	.1353	.1377
8	.0692	.0731	.0771	.0810	.0849	.0887	.0925	.0962	.0998	.1033
9	.0392	.0423	.0454	.0486	.0519	.0552	.0586	.0620	.0654	.0688
10	.0200	.0220	.0241	.0262	.0285	.0309	.0334	.0359	.0386	.0413
11	.0093	.0104	.0116	.0129	.0143	.0157	.0173	.0190	.0207	.0225
12	.0039	.0045	.0051	.0058	.0065	.0073	.0082	.0092	.0102	.0113
13	.0015	.0018	.0021	.0024	.0028	.0032	.0036	.0041	.0046	.0052
14	.0006	.0007	.0008	.0009	.0011	.0013	.0015	.0017	.0019	.0022
15	.0002	.0002	.0003	.0003	.0004	.0005	.0006	.0007	.0008	.0009
16	.0001	.0001	.0001	.0001	.0001	.0002	.0002	.0002	.0003	.0003
17	.0000	.0000	.0000	.0000	.0000	.0000	.0001	.0001	.0001	.0001

					μ					
x	6.1	6.2	6.3	6.4	6.5	6.6	6.7	6.8	6.9	7.0
0	.0022	.0020	.0018	.0017	.0015	.0014	.0012	.0011	.0010	.0009
1	.0137	.0126	.0116	.0106	.0098	.0090	.0082	.0076	.0070	.0064
2	.0417	.0390	.0364	.0340	.0318	.0296	.0276	.0258	.0240	.0223
3	.0848	.0806	.0765	.0726	.0688	.0652	.0617	.0584	.0552	.0521
4	.1294	.1249	.1205	.1162	.1118	.1076	.1034	.0992	.0952	.0912
5	.1579	.1549	.1519	.1487	.1454	.1420	.1385	.1349	.1314	.1277
6	.1605	.1601	.1595	.1586	.1575	.1562	.1546	.1529	.1511	.1490
7	.1399	.1418	.1435	.1450	.1462	.1472	.1480	.1486	.1489	.1490
8	.1066	.1099	.1130	.1160	.1188	.1215	.1240	.1263	.1284	.1304
9	.0723	.0757	.0791	.0825	.0858	.0891	.0923	.0954	.0985	.1014
10	.0441	.0469	.0498	.0528	.0558	.0588	.0618	.0649	.0679	.0710
11	.0245	.0265	.0285	.0307	.0330	.0353	.0377	.0401	.0426	.0452
12	.0124	.0137	.0150	.0164	.0179	.0194	.0210	.0227	.0245	.0264
13	.0058	.0065	.0073	.0081	.0089	.0098	.0108	.0119	.0130	.0142
14	.0025	.0029	.0033	.0037	.0041	.0046	.0052	.0058	.0064	.0071
15	.0010	.0012	.0014	.0016	.0018	.0020	.0023	.0026	.0029	.0033
16	.0004	.0005	.0005	.0006	.0007	.0008	.0010	.0011	.0013	.0014
17	.0001	.0002	.0002	.0002	.0003	.0003	.0004	.0004	.0005	.0006
18	.0000	.0001	.0001	.0001	.0001	.0001	.0001	.0002	.0002	.0002
19	.0000	.0000	.0000	.0000	.0000	.0000	.0000	.0001	.0001	.0001

Table 3—Poisson Distribution | APPENDIX B   **A15**

Table 3—Poisson Distribution (*continued*)

					μ					
x	7.1	7.2	7.3	7.4	7.5	7.6	7.7	7.8	7.9	8.0
0	.0008	.0007	.0007	.0006	.0006	.0005	.0005	.0004	.0004	.0003
1	.0059	.0054	.0049	.0045	.0041	.0038	.0035	.0032	.0029	.0027
2	.0208	.0194	.0180	.0167	.0156	.0145	.0134	.0125	.0116	.0107
3	.0492	.0464	.0438	.0413	.0389	.0366	.0345	.0324	.0305	.0286
4	.0874	.0836	.0799	.0764	.0729	.0696	.0663	.0632	.0602	.0573
5	.1241	.1204	.1167	.1130	.1094	.1057	.1021	.0986	.0951	.0916
6	.1468	.1445	.1420	.1394	.1367	.1339	.1311	.1282	.1252	.1221
7	.1489	.1486	.1481	.1474	.1465	.1454	.1442	.1428	.1413	.1396
8	.1321	.1337	.1351	.1363	.1373	.1382	.1388	.1392	.1395	.1396
9	.1042	.1070	.1096	.1121	.1144	.1167	.1187	.1207	.1224	.1241
10	.0740	.0770	.0800	.0829	.0858	.0887	.0914	.0941	.0967	.0993
11	.0478	.0504	.0531	.0558	.0585	.0613	.0640	.0667	.0695	.0722
12	.0283	.0303	.0323	.0344	.0366	.0388	.0411	.0434	.0457	.0481
13	.0154	.0168	.0181	.0196	.0211	.0227	.0243	.0260	.0278	.0296
14	.0078	.0086	.0095	.0104	.0113	.0123	.0134	.0145	.0157	.0169
15	.0037	.0041	.0046	.0051	.0057	.0062	.0069	.0075	.0083	.0090
16	.0016	.0019	.0021	.0024	.0026	.0030	.0033	.0037	.0041	.0045
17	.0007	.0008	.0009	.0010	.0012	.0013	.0015	.0017	.0019	.0021
18	.0003	.0003	.0004	.0004	.0005	.0006	.0006	.0007	.0008	.0009
19	.0001	.0001	.0001	.0002	.0002	.0002	.0003	.0003	.0003	.0004
20	.0000	.0000	.0001	.0001	.0001	.0001	.0001	.0001	.0001	.0002
21	.0000	.0000	.0000	.0000	.0000	.0000	.0000	.0000	.0001	.0001

					μ					
x	8.1	8.2	8.3	8.4	8.5	8.6	8.7	8.8	8.9	9.0
0	.0003	.0003	.0002	.0002	.0002	.0002	.0002	.0002	.0001	.0001
1	.0025	.0023	.0021	.0019	.0017	.0016	.0014	.0013	.0012	.0011
2	.0100	.0092	.0086	.0079	.0074	.0068	.0063	.0058	.0054	.0050
3	.0269	.0252	.0237	.0222	.0208	.0195	.0183	.0171	.0160	.0150
4	.0544	.0517	.0491	.0466	.0443	.0420	.0398	.0377	.0357	.0337
5	.0882	.0849	.0816	.0784	.0752	.0722	.0692	.0663	.0635	.0607
6	.1191	.1160	.1128	.1097	.1066	.1034	.1003	.0972	.0941	.0911
7	.1378	.1358	.1338	.1317	.1294	.1271	.1247	.1222	.1197	.1171
8	.1395	.1392	.1388	.1382	.1375	.1366	.1356	.1344	.1332	.1318
9	.1256	.1269	.1280	.1290	.1299	.1306	.1311	.1315	.1317	.1318
10	.1017	.1040	.1063	.1084	.1104	.1123	.1140	.1157	.1172	.1186
11	.0749	.0776	.0802	.0828	.0853	.0878	.0902	.0925	.0948	.0970
12	.0505	.0530	.0555	.0579	.0604	.0629	.0654	.0679	.0703	.0728
13	.0315	.0334	.0354	.0374	.0395	.0416	.0438	.0459	.0481	.0504
14	.0182	.0196	.0210	.0225	.0240	.0256	.0272	.0289	.0306	.0324
15	.0098	.0107	.0116	.0126	.0136	.0147	.0158	.0169	.0182	.0194
16	.0050	.0055	.0060	.0066	.0072	.0079	.0086	.0093	.0101	.0109
17	.0024	.0026	.0029	.0033	.0036	.0040	.0044	.0048	.0053	.0058
18	.0011	.0012	.0014	.0015	.0017	.0019	.0021	.0024	.0026	.0029
19	.0005	.0005	.0006	.0007	.0008	.0009	.0010	.0011	.0012	.0014
20	.0002	.0002	.0002	.0003	.0003	.0004	.0004	.0005	.0005	.0006
21	.0001	.0001	.0001	.0001	.0001	.0002	.0002	.0002	.0002	.0003
22	.0000	.0000	.0000	.0000	.0001	.0001	.0001	.0001	.0001	.0001

Table 3—Poisson Distribution (continued)

x	9.1	9.2	9.3	9.4	μ 9.5	9.6	9.7	9.8	9.9	10.0
0	.0001	.0001	.0001	.0001	.0001	.0001	.0001	.0001	.0001	.0000
1	.0010	.0009	.0009	.0008	.0007	.0007	.0006	.0005	.0005	.0005
2	.0046	.0043	.0040	.0037	.0034	.0031	.0029	.0027	.0025	.0023
3	.0140	.0131	.0123	.0115	.0107	.0100	.0093	.0087	.0081	.0076
4	.0319	.0302	.0285	.0269	.0254	.0240	.0226	.0213	.0201	.0189
5	.0581	.0555	.0530	.0506	.0483	.0460	.0439	.0418	.0398	.0378
6	.0881	.0851	.0822	.0793	.0764	.0736	.0709	.0682	.0656	.0631
7	.1145	.1118	.1091	.1064	.1037	.1010	.0982	.0955	.0928	.0901
8	.1302	.1286	.1269	.1251	.1232	.1212	.1191	.1170	.1148	.1126
9	.1317	.1315	.1311	.1306	.1300	.1293	.1284	.1274	.1263	.1251
10	.1198	.1210	.1219	.1228	.1235	.1241	.1245	.1249	.1250	.1251
11	.0991	.1012	.1031	.1049	.1067	.1083	.1098	.1112	.1125	.1137
12	.0752	.0776	.0799	.0822	.0844	.0866	.0888	.0908	.0928	.0948
13	.0526	.0549	.0572	.0594	.0617	.0640	.0662	.0685	.0707	.0729
14	.0342	.0361	.0380	.0399	.0419	.0439	.0459	.0479	.0500	.0521
15	.0208	.0221	.0235	.0250	.0265	.0281	.0297	.0313	.0330	.0347
16	.0118	.0127	.0137	.0147	.0157	.0168	.0180	.0192	.0204	.0217
17	.0063	.0069	.0075	.0081	.0088	.0095	.0103	.0111	.0119	.0128
18	.0032	.0035	.0039	.0042	.0046	.0051	.0055	.0060	.0065	.0071
19	.0015	.0017	.0019	.0021	.0023	.0026	.0028	.0031	.0034	.0037
20	.0007	.0008	.0009	.0010	.0011	.0012	.0014	.0015	.0017	.0019
21	.0003	.0003	.0004	.0004	.0005	.0006	.0006	.0007	.0008	.0009
22	.0001	.0001	.0002	.0002	.0002	.0002	.0003	.0003	.0004	.0004
23	.0000	.0001	.0001	.0001	.0001	.0001	.0001	.0001	.0002	.0002
24	.0000	.0000	.0000	.0000	.0000	.0000	.0000	.0001	.0001	.0001

x	11	12	13	14	μ 15	16	17	18	19	20
0	.0000	.0000	.0000	.0000	.0000	.0000	.0000	.0000	.0000	.0000
1	.0002	.0001	.0000	.0000	.0000	.0000	.0000	.0000	.0000	.0000
2	.0010	.0004	.0002	.0001	.0000	.0000	.0000	.0000	.0000	.0000
3	.0037	.0018	.0008	.0004	.0002	.0001	.0000	.0000	.0000	.0000
4	.0102	.0053	.0027	.0013	.0006	.0003	.0001	.0001	.0000	.0000
5	.0224	.0127	.0070	.0037	.0019	.0010	.0005	.0002	.0001	.0001
6	.0411	.0255	.0152	.0087	.0048	.0026	.0014	.0007	.0004	.0002
7	.0646	.0437	.0281	.0174	.0104	.0060	.0034	.0018	.0010	.0005
8	.0888	.0655	.0457	.0304	.0194	.0120	.0072	.0042	.0024	.0013
9	.1085	.0874	.0661	.0473	.0324	.0213	.0135	.0083	.0050	.0029
10	.1194	.1048	.0859	.0663	.0486	.0341	.0230	.0150	.0095	.0058
11	.1194	.1144	.1015	.0844	.0663	.0496	.0355	.0245	.0164	.0106
12	.1094	.1144	.1099	.0984	.0829	.0661	.0504	.0368	.0259	.0176
13	.0926	.1056	.1099	.1060	.0956	.0814	.0658	.0509	.0378	.0271
14	.0728	.0905	.1021	.1060	.1024	.0930	.0800	.0655	.0514	.0387
15	.0534	.0724	.0885	.0989	.1024	.0992	.0906	.0786	.0650	.0516
16	.0367	.0543	.0719	.0866	.0960	.0992	.0963	.0884	.0772	.0646
17	.0237	.0383	.0550	.0713	.0847	.0934	.0963	.0936	.0863	.0760
18	.0145	.0256	.0397	.0554	.0706	.0830	.0909	.0936	.0911	.0844
19	.0084	.0161	.0272	.0409	.0557	.0699	.0814	.0887	.0911	.0888
20	.0046	.0097	.0177	.0286	.0418	.0559	.0692	.0798	.0866	.0888
21	.0024	.0055	.0109	.0191	.0299	.0426	.0560	.0684	.0783	.0846
22	.0012	.0030	.0065	.0121	.0204	.0310	.0433	.0560	.0676	.0769
23	.0006	.0016	.0037	.0074	.0133	.0216	.0320	.0438	.0559	.0669
24	.0003	.0008	.0020	.0043	.0083	.0144	.0226	.0328	.0442	.0557
25	.0001	.0004	.0010	.0024	.0050	.0092	.0154	.0237	.0336	.0446
26	.0000	.0002	.0005	.0013	.0029	.0057	.0101	.0164	.0246	.0343
27	.0000	.0001	.0002	.0007	.0016	.0034	.0063	.0109	.0173	.0254
28	.0000	.0000	.0001	.0003	.0009	.0019	.0038	.0070	.0117	.0181
29	.0000	.0000	.0001	.0002	.0004	.0011	.0023	.0044	.0077	.0125

Table 3—Poisson Distribution | APPENDIX B   **A17**

Table 3—Poisson Distribution *(continued)*

x	μ									
	11	12	13	14	15	16	17	18	19	20
30	.0000	.0000	.0000	.0001	.0002	.0006	.0013	.0026	.0049	.0083
31	.0000	.0000	.0000	.0000	.0001	.0003	.0007	.0015	.0030	.0054
32	.0000	.0000	.0000	.0000	.0001	.0001	.0004	.0009	.0018	.0034
33	.0000	.0000	.0000	.0000	.0000	.0001	.0002	.0005	.0010	.0020
34	.0000	.0000	.0000	.0000	.0000	.0000	.0001	.0002	.0006	.0012
35	.0000	.0000	.0000	.0000	.0000	.0000	.0000	.0001	.0003	.0007
36	.0000	.0000	.0000	.0000	.0000	.0000	.0000	.0001	.0002	.0004
37	.0000	.0000	.0000	.0000	.0000	.0000	.0000	.0000	.0001	.0002
38	.0000	.0000	.0000	.0000	.0000	.0000	.0000	.0000	.0000	.0001
39	.0000	.0000	.0000	.0000	.0000	.0000	.0000	.0000	.0000	.0001

Table 4—Standard Normal Distribution

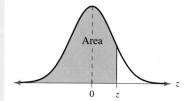

z	.09	.08	.07	.06	.05	.04	.03	.02	.01	.00
−3.4	.0002	.0003	.0003	.0003	.0003	.0003	.0003	.0003	.0003	.0003
−3.3	.0003	.0004	.0004	.0004	.0004	.0004	.0004	.0005	.0005	.0005
−3.2	.0005	.0005	.0005	.0006	.0006	.0006	.0006	.0006	.0007	.0007
−3.1	.0007	.0007	.0008	.0008	.0008	.0008	.0009	.0009	.0009	.0010
−3.0	.0010	.0010	.0011	.0011	.0011	.0012	.0012	.0013	.0013	.0013
−2.9	.0014	.0014	.0015	.0015	.0016	.0016	.0017	.0017	.0018	.0019
−2.8	.0019	.0020	.0021	.0021	.0022	.0023	.0023	.0024	.0025	.0026
−2.7	.0026	.0027	.0028	.0029	.0030	.0031	.0032	.0033	.0034	.0035
−2.6	.0036	.0037	.0038	.0039	.0040	.0041	.0043	.0044	.0045	.0047
−2.5	.0048	.0049	.0051	.0052	.0054	.0055	.0057	.0059	.0060	.0062
−2.4	.0064	.0066	.0068	.0069	.0071	.0073	.0075	.0078	.0080	.0082
−2.3	.0084	.0087	.0089	.0091	.0094	.0096	.0099	.0102	.0104	.0107
−2.2	.0110	.0113	.0116	.0119	.0122	.0125	.0129	.0132	.0136	.0139
−2.1	.0143	.0146	.0150	.0154	.0158	.0162	.0166	.0170	.0174	.0179
−2.0	.0183	.0188	.0192	.0197	.0202	.0207	.0212	.0217	.0222	.0228
−1.9	.0233	.0239	.0244	.0250	.0256	.0262	.0268	.0274	.0281	.0287
−1.8	.0294	.0301	.0307	.0314	.0322	.0329	.0336	.0344	.0352	.0359
−1.7	.0367	.0375	.0384	.0392	.0401	.0409	.0418	.0427	.0436	.0446
−1.6	.0455	.0465	.0475	.0485	.0495	.0505	.0516	.0526	.0537	.0548
−1.5	.0559	.0571	.0582	.0594	.0606	.0618	.0630	.0643	.0655	.0668
−1.4	.0681	.0694	.0708	.0722	.0735	.0749	.0764	.0778	.0793	.0808
−1.3	.0823	.0838	.0853	.0869	.0885	.0901	.0918	.0934	.0951	.0968
−1.2	.0985	.1003	.1020	.1038	.1056	.1075	.1093	.1112	.1131	.1151
−1.1	.1170	.1190	.1210	.1230	.1251	.1271	.1292	.1314	.1335	.1357
−1.0	.1379	.1401	.1423	.1446	.1469	.1492	.1515	.1539	.1562	.1587
−0.9	.1611	.1635	.1660	.1685	.1711	.1736	.1762	.1788	.1814	.1841
−0.8	.1867	.1894	.1922	.1949	.1977	.2005	.2033	.2061	.2090	.2119
−0.7	.2148	.2177	.2206	.2236	.2266	.2296	.2327	.2358	.2389	.2420
−0.6	.2451	.2483	.2514	.2546	.2578	.2611	.2643	.2676	.2709	.2743
−0.5	.2776	.2810	.2843	.2877	.2912	.2946	.2981	.3015	.3050	.3085
−0.4	.3121	.3156	.3192	.3228	.3264	.3300	.3336	.3372	.3409	.3446
−0.3	.3483	.3520	.3557	.3594	.3632	.3669	.3707	.3745	.3783	.3821
−0.2	.3859	.3897	.3936	.3974	.4013	.4052	.4090	.4129	.4168	.4207
−0.1	.4247	.4286	.4325	.4364	.4404	.4443	.4483	.4522	.4562	.4602
−0.0	.4641	.4681	.4721	.4761	.4801	.4840	.4880	.4920	.4960	.5000

Table 4—Standard Normal Distribution | APPENDIX B   **A19**

Table 4—Standard Normal Distribution *(continued)*

z	.00	.01	.02	.03	.04	.05	.06	.07	.08	.09
0.0	.5000	.5040	.5080	.5120	.5160	.5199	.5239	.5279	.5319	.5359
0.1	.5398	.5438	.5478	.5517	.5557	.5596	.5636	.5675	.5714	.5753
0.2	.5793	.5832	.5871	.5910	.5948	.5987	.6026	.6064	.6103	.6141
0.3	.6179	.6217	.6255	.6293	.6331	.6368	.6406	.6443	.6480	.6517
0.4	.6554	.6591	.6628	.6664	.6700	.6736	.6772	.6808	.6844	.6879
0.5	.6915	.6950	.6985	.7019	.7054	.7088	.7123	.7157	.7190	.7224
0.6	.7257	.7291	.7324	.7357	.7389	.7422	.7454	.7486	.7517	.7549
0.7	.7580	.7611	.7642	.7673	.7704	.7734	.7764	.7794	.7823	.7852
0.8	.7881	.7910	.7939	.7967	.7995	.8023	.8051	.8078	.8106	.8133
0.9	.8159	.8186	.8212	.8238	.8264	.8289	.8315	.8340	.8365	.8389
1.0	.8413	.8438	.8461	.8485	.8508	.8531	.8554	.8577	.8599	.8621
1.1	.8643	.8665	.8686	.8708	.8729	.8749	.8770	.8790	.8810	.8830
1.2	.8849	.8869	.8888	.8907	.8925	.8944	.8962	.8980	.8997	.9015
1.3	.9032	.9049	.9066	.9082	.9099	.9115	.9131	.9147	.9162	.9177
1.4	.9192	.9207	.9222	.9236	.9251	.9265	.9278	.9292	.9306	.9319
1.5	.9332	.9345	.9357	.9370	.9382	.9394	.9406	.9418	.9429	.9441
1.6	.9452	.9463	.9474	.9484	.9495	.9505	.9515	.9525	.9535	.9545
1.7	.9554	.9564	.9573	.9582	.9591	.9599	.9608	.9616	.9625	.9633
1.8	.9641	.9649	.9656	.9664	.9671	.9678	.9686	.9693	.9699	.9706
1.9	.9713	.9719	.9726	.9732	.9738	.9744	.9750	.9756	.9761	.9767
2.0	.9772	.9778	.9783	.9788	.9793	.9798	.9803	.9808	.9812	.9817
2.1	.9821	.9826	.9830	.9834	.9838	.9842	.9846	.9850	.9854	.9857
2.2	.9861	.9864	.9868	.9871	.9875	.9878	.9881	.9884	.9887	.9890
2.3	.9893	.9896	.9898	.9901	.9904	.9906	.9909	.9911	.9913	.9916
2.4	.9918	.9920	.9922	.9925	.9927	.9929	.9931	.9932	.9934	.9936
2.5	.9938	.9940	.9941	.9943	.9945	.9946	.9948	.9949	.9951	.9952
2.6	.9953	.9955	.9956	.9957	.9959	.9960	.9961	.9962	.9963	.9964
2.7	.9965	.9966	.9967	.9968	.9969	.9970	.9971	.9972	.9973	.9974
2.8	.9974	.9975	.9976	.9977	.9977	.9978	.9979	.9979	.9980	.9981
2.9	.9981	.9982	.9982	.9983	.9984	.9984	.9985	.9985	.9986	.9986
3.0	.9987	.9987	.9987	.9988	.9988	.9989	.9989	.9989	.9990	.9990
3.1	.9990	.9991	.9991	.9991	.9992	.9992	.9992	.9992	.9993	.9993
3.2	.9993	.9993	.9994	.9994	.9994	.9994	.9994	.9995	.9995	.9995
3.3	.9995	.9995	.9995	.9996	.9996	.9996	.9996	.9996	.9996	.9997
3.4	.9997	.9997	.9997	.9997	.9997	.9997	.9997	.9997	.9997	.9998

Table 5—*t*-Distribution

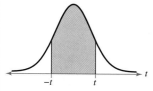
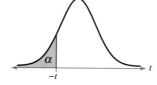
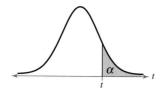
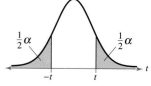

| *c* confidence interval | Left-tailed test | Right-tailed test | Two-tailed test |

d.f.	Level of confidence, *c*	0.50	0.80	0.90	0.95	0.98	0.99
	One tail, α	0.25	0.10	0.05	0.025	0.01	0.005
	Two tails, α	0.50	0.20	0.10	0.05	0.02	0.01
1		1.000	3.078	6.314	12.706	31.821	63.657
2		.816	1.886	2.920	4.303	6.965	9.925
3		.765	1.638	2.353	3.182	4.541	5.841
4		.741	1.533	2.132	2.776	3.747	4.604
5		.727	1.476	2.015	2.571	3.365	4.032
6		.718	1.440	1.943	2.447	3.143	3.707
7		.711	1.415	1.895	2.365	2.998	3.499
8		.706	1.397	1.860	2.306	2.896	3.355
9		.703	1.383	1.833	2.262	2.821	3.250
10		.700	1.372	1.812	2.228	2.764	3.169
11		.697	1.363	1.796	2.201	2.718	3.106
12		.695	1.356	1.782	2.179	2.681	3.055
13		.694	1.350	1.771	2.160	2.650	3.012
14		.692	1.345	1.761	2.145	2.624	2.977
15		.691	1.341	1.753	2.131	2.602	2.947
16		.690	1.337	1.746	2.120	2.583	2.921
17		.689	1.333	1.740	2.110	2.567	2.898
18		.688	1.330	1.734	2.101	2.552	2.878
19		.688	1.328	1.729	2.093	2.539	2.861
20		.687	1.325	1.725	2.086	2.528	2.845
21		.686	1.323	1.721	2.080	2.518	2.831
22		.686	1.321	1.717	2.074	2.508	2.819
23		.685	1.319	1.714	2.069	2.500	2.807
24		.685	1.318	1.711	2.064	2.492	2.797
25		.684	1.316	1.708	2.060	2.485	2.787
26		.684	1.315	1.706	2.056	2.479	2.779
27		.684	1.314	1.703	2.052	2.473	2.771
28		.683	1.313	1.701	2.048	2.467	2.763
29		.683	1.311	1.699	2.045	2.462	2.756
∞		.674	1.282	1.645	1.960	2.326	2.576

Table 6—Chi-Square Distribution | APPENDIX B **A21**

Table 6—Chi-Square Distribution

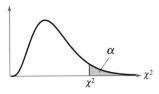

Right-tail

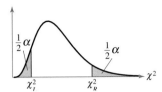

Two-tails

Degrees of freedom	α									
	0.995	**0.99**	**0.975**	**0.95**	**0.90**	**0.10**	**0.05**	**0.025**	**0.01**	**0.005**
1	—	—	0.001	0.004	0.016	2.706	3.841	5.024	6.635	7.879
2	0.010	0.020	0.051	0.103	0.211	4.605	5.991	7.378	9.210	10.597
3	0.072	0.115	0.216	0.352	0.584	6.251	7.815	9.348	11.345	12.838
4	0.207	0.297	0.484	0.711	1.064	7.779	9.488	11.143	13.277	14.860
5	0.412	0.554	0.831	1.145	1.610	9.236	11.071	12.833	15.086	16.750
6	0.676	0.872	1.237	1.635	2.204	10.645	12.592	14.449	16.812	18.548
7	0.989	1.239	1.690	2.167	2.833	12.017	14.067	16.013	18.475	20.278
8	1.344	1.646	2.180	2.733	3.490	13.362	15.507	17.535	20.090	21.955
9	1.735	2.088	2.700	3.325	4.168	14.684	16.919	19.023	21.666	23.589
10	2.156	2.558	3.247	3.940	4.865	15.987	18.307	20.483	23.209	25.188
11	2.603	3.053	3.816	4.575	5.578	17.275	19.675	21.920	24.725	26.757
12	3.074	3.571	4.404	5.226	6.304	18.549	21.026	23.337	26.217	28.299
13	3.565	4.107	5.009	5.892	7.042	19.812	22.362	24.736	27.688	29.819
14	4.075	4.660	5.629	6.571	7.790	21.064	23.685	26.119	29.141	31.319
15	4.601	5.229	6.262	7.261	8.547	22.307	24.996	27.488	30.578	32.801
16	5.142	5.812	6.908	7.962	9.312	23.542	26.296	28.845	32.000	34.267
17	5.697	6.408	7.564	8.672	10.085	24.769	27.587	30.191	33.409	35.718
18	6.265	7.015	8.231	9.390	10.865	25.989	28.869	31.526	34.805	37.156
19	6.844	7.633	8.907	10.117	11.651	27.204	30.144	32.852	36.191	38.582
20	7.434	8.260	9.591	10.851	12.443	28.412	31.410	34.170	37.566	39.997
21	8.034	8.897	10.283	11.591	13.240	29.615	32.671	35.479	38.932	41.401
22	8.643	9.542	10.982	12.338	14.042	30.813	33.924	36.781	40.289	42.796
23	9.262	10.196	11.689	13.091	14.848	32.007	35.172	38.076	41.638	44.181
24	9.886	10.856	12.401	13.848	15.659	33.196	36.415	39.364	42.980	45.559
25	10.520	11.524	13.120	14.611	16.473	34.382	37.652	40.646	44.314	46.928
26	11.160	12.198	13.844	15.379	17.292	35.563	38.885	41.923	45.642	48.290
27	11.808	12.879	14.573	16.151	18.114	36.741	40.113	43.194	46.963	49.645
28	12.461	13.565	15.308	16.928	18.939	37.916	41.337	44.461	48.278	50.993
29	13.121	14.257	16.047	17.708	19.768	39.087	42.557	45.722	49.588	52.336
30	13.787	14.954	16.791	18.493	20.599	40.256	43.773	46.979	50.892	53.672
40	20.707	22.164	24.433	26.509	29.051	51.805	55.758	59.342	63.691	66.766
50	27.991	29.707	32.357	34.764	37.689	63.167	67.505	71.420	76.154	79.490
60	35.534	37.485	40.482	43.188	46.459	74.397	79.082	83.298	88.379	91.952
70	43.275	45.442	48.758	51.739	55.329	85.527	90.531	95.023	100.425	104.215
80	51.172	53.540	57.153	60.391	64.278	96.578	101.879	106.629	112.329	116.321
90	59.196	61.754	65.647	69.126	73.291	107.565	113.145	118.136	124.116	128.299
100	67.328	70.065	74.222	77.929	82.358	118.498	124.342	129.561	135.807	140.169

Table 7—F-Distribution

$\alpha = 0.005$

d.f.$_N$: Degrees of freedom, numerator

d.f.$_D$: Degrees of freedom, denominator	1	2	3	4	5	6	7	8	9	10	12	15	20	24	30	40	60	120	∞
1	16211	20000	21615	22500	23056	23437	23715	23925	24091	24224	24426	24630	24836	24940	25044	25148	25253	25359	25465
2	198.5	199.0	199.2	199.2	199.3	199.3	199.4	199.4	199.4	199.4	199.4	199.4	199.4	199.5	199.5	199.5	199.5	199.5	199.5
3	55.55	49.80	47.47	46.19	45.39	44.84	44.43	44.13	43.88	43.69	43.39	43.08	42.78	42.62	42.47	42.31	42.15	41.99	41.83
4	31.33	26.28	24.26	23.15	22.46	21.97	21.62	21.35	21.14	20.97	20.70	20.44	20.17	20.03	19.89	19.75	19.61	19.47	19.32
5	22.78	18.31	16.53	15.56	14.94	14.51	14.20	13.96	13.77	13.62	13.38	13.15	12.90	12.78	12.66	12.53	12.40	12.27	12.14
6	18.63	14.54	12.92	12.03	11.46	11.07	10.79	10.57	10.39	10.25	10.03	9.81	9.59	9.47	9.36	9.24	9.12	9.00	8.88
7	16.24	12.40	10.88	10.05	9.52	9.16	8.89	8.68	8.51	8.38	8.18	7.97	7.75	7.65	7.53	7.42	7.31	7.19	7.08
8	14.69	11.04	9.60	8.81	8.30	7.95	7.69	7.50	7.34	7.21	7.01	6.81	6.61	6.50	6.40	6.29	6.18	6.06	5.95
9	13.61	10.11	8.72	7.96	7.47	7.13	6.88	6.69	6.54	6.42	6.23	6.03	5.83	5.73	5.62	5.52	5.41	5.30	5.19
10	12.83	9.43	8.08	7.34	6.87	6.54	6.30	6.12	5.97	5.85	5.66	5.47	5.27	5.17	5.07	4.97	4.86	4.75	4.64
11	12.73	8.91	7.60	6.88	6.42	6.10	5.86	5.68	5.54	5.42	5.24	5.05	4.86	4.76	4.65	4.55	4.44	4.34	4.23
12	11.75	8.51	7.23	6.52	6.07	5.76	5.52	5.35	5.20	5.09	4.91	4.72	4.53	4.43	4.33	4.23	4.12	4.01	3.90
13	11.37	8.19	6.93	6.23	5.79	5.48	5.25	5.08	4.94	4.82	4.64	4.46	4.27	4.17	4.07	3.97	3.87	3.76	3.65
14	11.06	7.92	6.68	6.00	5.56	5.26	5.03	4.86	4.72	4.60	4.43	4.25	4.06	3.96	3.86	3.76	3.66	3.55	3.44
15	10.80	7.70	6.48	5.80	5.37	5.07	4.85	4.67	4.54	4.42	4.25	4.07	3.88	3.79	3.69	3.58	3.48	3.37	3.26
16	10.58	7.51	6.30	5.64	5.21	4.91	4.69	4.52	4.38	4.27	4.10	3.92	3.73	3.64	3.54	3.44	3.33	3.22	3.11
17	10.38	7.35	6.16	5.50	5.07	4.78	4.56	4.39	4.25	4.14	3.97	3.79	3.61	3.51	3.41	3.31	3.21	3.10	2.98
18	10.22	7.21	6.03	5.37	4.96	4.66	4.44	4.28	4.14	4.03	3.86	3.68	3.50	3.40	3.30	3.20	3.10	2.99	2.87
19	10.07	7.09	5.92	5.27	4.85	4.56	4.34	4.18	4.04	3.93	3.76	3.59	3.40	3.31	3.21	3.11	3.00	2.89	2.78
20	9.94	6.99	5.82	5.17	4.76	4.47	4.26	4.09	3.96	3.85	3.68	3.50	3.32	3.22	3.12	3.02	2.92	2.81	2.69
21	9.83	6.89	5.73	5.09	4.68	4.39	4.18	4.01	3.88	3.77	3.60	3.43	3.24	3.15	3.05	2.95	2.84	2.73	2.61
22	9.73	6.81	5.65	5.02	4.61	4.32	4.11	3.94	3.81	3.70	3.54	3.36	3.18	3.08	2.98	2.88	2.77	2.66	2.55
23	9.63	6.73	5.58	4.95	4.54	4.26	4.05	3.88	3.75	3.64	3.47	3.30	3.12	3.02	2.92	2.82	2.71	2.60	2.48
24	9.55	6.66	5.52	4.89	4.49	4.20	3.99	3.83	3.69	3.59	3.42	3.25	3.06	2.97	2.87	2.77	2.66	2.55	2.43
25	9.48	6.60	5.46	4.84	4.43	4.15	3.94	3.78	3.64	3.54	3.37	3.20	3.01	2.92	2.82	2.72	2.61	2.50	2.38
26	9.41	6.54	5.41	4.79	4.38	4.10	3.89	3.73	3.60	3.49	3.33	3.15	2.97	2.87	2.77	2.67	2.56	2.45	2.33
27	9.34	6.49	5.36	4.74	4.34	4.06	3.85	3.69	3.56	3.45	3.28	3.11	2.93	2.83	2.73	2.63	2.52	2.41	2.29
28	9.28	6.44	5.32	4.70	4.30	4.02	3.81	3.65	3.52	3.41	3.25	3.07	2.89	2.79	2.69	2.59	2.48	2.37	2.25
29	9.23	6.40	5.28	4.66	4.26	3.98	3.77	3.61	3.48	3.38	3.21	3.04	2.86	2.76	2.66	2.56	2.45	2.33	2.24
30	9.18	6.35	5.24	4.62	4.23	3.95	3.74	3.58	3.45	3.34	3.18	3.01	2.82	2.73	2.63	2.52	2.42	2.30	2.18
40	8.83	6.07	4.98	4.37	3.99	3.71	3.51	3.35	3.22	3.12	2.95	2.78	2.60	2.50	2.40	2.30	2.18	2.06	1.93
60	8.49	5.79	4.73	4.14	3.76	3.49	3.29	3.13	3.01	2.90	2.74	2.57	2.39	2.29	2.19	2.08	1.96	1.83	1.69
120	8.18	5.54	4.50	3.92	3.55	3.28	3.09	2.93	2.81	2.71	2.54	2.37	2.19	2.09	1.98	1.87	1.75	1.61	1.43
∞	7.88	5.30	4.28	3.72	3.35	3.09	2.90	2.74	2.62	2.52	2.36	2.19	2.00	1.90	1.79	1.67	1.53	1.36	1.00

Table 7—F-Distribution | APPENDIX B   **A23**

Table 7—*F*-Distribution *(Continued)*

$\alpha = 0.01$

d.f.$_D$: Degrees of freedom, denominator	d.f.$_N$: Degrees of freedom, numerator																		
	1	2	3	4	5	6	7	8	9	10	12	15	20	24	30	40	60	120	∞
1	4052	4999.5	5403	5625	5764	5859	5928	5982	6022	6056	6106	6157	6209	6235	6261	6287	6313	6339	6366
2	98.50	99.00	99.17	99.25	99.30	99.33	99.36	99.37	99.39	99.40	99.42	99.43	99.45	99.46	99.47	99.47	99.48	99.49	99.50
3	34.12	30.82	29.46	28.71	28.24	27.91	27.67	27.49	27.35	27.23	27.05	26.87	26.69	26.60	26.50	26.41	26.32	26.22	26.13
4	21.20	18.00	16.69	15.98	15.52	15.21	14.98	14.80	14.66	14.55	14.37	14.20	14.02	13.93	13.84	13.75	13.65	13.56	13.46
5	16.26	13.27	12.06	11.39	10.97	10.67	10.46	10.29	10.16	10.05	9.89	9.72	9.55	9.47	9.38	9.29	9.20	9.11	9.02
6	13.75	10.92	9.78	9.15	8.75	8.47	8.26	8.10	7.98	7.87	7.72	7.56	7.40	7.31	7.23	7.14	7.06	6.97	6.88
7	12.25	9.55	8.45	7.85	7.46	7.19	6.99	6.84	6.72	6.62	6.47	6.31	6.16	6.07	5.99	5.91	5.82	5.74	5.65
8	11.26	8.65	7.59	7.01	6.63	6.37	6.18	6.03	5.91	5.81	5.67	5.52	5.36	5.28	5.20	5.12	5.03	4.95	4.86
9	10.56	8.02	6.99	6.42	6.06	5.80	5.61	5.47	5.35	5.26	5.11	4.96	4.81	4.73	4.65	4.57	4.48	4.40	4.31
10	10.04	7.56	6.55	5.99	5.64	5.39	5.20	5.06	4.94	4.85	4.71	4.56	4.41	4.33	4.25	4.17	4.08	4.00	3.91
11	9.65	7.21	6.22	5.67	5.32	5.07	4.89	4.74	4.63	4.54	4.40	4.25	4.10	4.02	3.94	3.86	3.78	3.69	3.60
12	9.33	6.93	5.95	5.41	5.06	4.82	4.64	4.50	4.39	4.30	4.16	4.01	3.86	3.78	3.70	3.62	3.54	3.45	3.36
13	9.07	6.70	5.74	5.21	4.86	4.62	4.44	4.30	4.19	4.10	3.96	3.82	3.66	3.59	3.51	3.43	3.34	3.25	3.17
14	8.86	6.51	5.56	5.04	4.69	4.46	4.28	4.14	4.03	3.94	3.80	3.66	3.51	3.43	3.35	3.27	3.18	3.09	3.00
15	8.68	6.36	5.42	4.89	4.56	4.32	4.14	4.00	3.89	3.80	3.67	3.52	3.37	3.29	3.21	3.13	3.05	2.96	2.87
16	8.53	6.23	5.29	4.77	4.44	4.20	4.03	3.89	3.78	3.69	3.55	3.41	3.26	3.18	3.10	3.02	2.93	2.84	2.75
17	8.40	6.11	5.18	4.67	4.34	4.10	3.93	3.79	3.68	3.59	3.46	3.31	3.16	3.08	3.00	2.92	2.83	2.75	2.65
18	8.29	6.01	5.09	4.58	4.25	4.01	3.84	3.71	3.60	3.51	3.37	3.23	3.08	3.00	2.92	2.84	2.75	2.66	2.57
19	8.18	5.93	5.01	4.50	4.17	3.94	3.77	3.63	3.52	3.43	3.30	3.15	3.00	2.92	2.84	2.76	2.67	2.58	2.49
20	8.10	5.85	4.94	4.43	4.10	3.87	3.70	3.56	3.46	3.37	3.23	3.09	2.94	2.86	2.78	2.69	2.61	2.52	2.42
21	8.02	5.78	4.87	4.37	4.04	3.81	3.64	3.51	3.40	3.31	3.17	3.03	2.88	2.80	2.72	2.64	2.55	2.46	2.36
22	7.95	5.72	4.82	4.31	3.99	3.76	3.59	3.45	3.35	3.26	3.12	2.98	2.83	2.75	2.67	2.58	2.50	2.40	2.31
23	7.88	5.66	4.76	4.26	3.94	3.71	3.54	3.41	3.30	3.21	3.07	2.93	2.78	2.70	2.62	2.54	2.45	2.35	2.26
24	7.82	5.61	4.72	4.22	3.90	3.67	3.50	3.36	3.26	3.17	3.03	2.89	2.74	2.66	2.58	2.49	2.40	2.31	2.21
25	7.77	5.57	4.68	4.18	3.85	3.63	3.46	3.32	3.22	3.13	2.99	2.85	2.70	2.62	2.54	2.45	2.36	2.27	2.17
26	7.72	5.53	4.64	4.14	3.82	3.59	3.42	3.29	3.18	3.09	2.96	2.81	2.66	2.58	2.50	2.42	2.33	2.23	2.13
27	7.68	5.49	4.60	4.11	3.78	3.56	3.39	3.26	3.15	3.06	2.93	2.78	2.63	2.55	2.47	2.38	2.29	2.20	2.10
28	7.64	5.45	4.57	4.07	3.75	3.53	3.36	3.23	3.12	3.03	2.90	2.75	2.60	2.52	2.44	2.35	2.26	2.17	2.06
29	7.60	5.42	4.54	4.04	3.73	3.50	3.33	3.20	3.09	3.00	2.87	2.73	2.57	2.49	2.41	2.33	2.23	2.14	2.03
30	7.56	5.39	4.51	4.02	3.70	3.47	3.30	3.17	3.07	2.98	2.84	2.70	2.55	2.47	2.39	2.30	2.21	2.11	2.01
40	7.31	5.18	4.31	3.83	3.51	3.29	3.12	2.99	2.89	2.80	2.66	2.52	2.37	2.29	2.20	2.11	2.02	1.92	1.80
60	7.08	4.98	4.13	3.65	3.34	3.12	2.95	2.82	2.72	2.63	2.50	2.35	2.20	2.12	2.03	1.94	1.84	1.73	1.60
120	6.85	4.79	3.95	3.48	3.17	2.96	2.79	2.66	2.56	2.47	2.34	2.19	2.03	1.95	1.86	1.76	1.66	1.53	1.38
∞	6.63	4.61	3.78	3.32	3.02	2.80	2.64	2.51	2.41	2.32	2.18	2.04	1.88	1.79	1.70	1.59	1.47	1.32	1.00

Table 7—*F*-Distribution (*Continued*)

$\alpha = 0.025$

d.f.$_D$: Degrees of freedom, denominator	d.f.$_N$: Degrees of freedom, numerator																		
	1	**2**	**3**	**4**	**5**	**6**	**7**	**8**	**9**	**10**	**12**	**15**	**20**	**24**	**30**	**40**	**60**	**120**	**∞**
1	647.8	799.5	864.2	899.6	921.8	937.1	948.2	956.7	963.3	968.6	976.7	984.9	993.1	997.2	1001	1006	1010	1014	1018
2	38.51	39.00	39.17	39.25	39.30	39.33	39.36	39.37	39.39	39.40	39.41	39.43	39.45	39.46	39.46	39.47	39.48	39.49	39.50
3	17.44	16.04	15.44	15.10	14.88	14.73	14.62	14.54	14.47	14.42	14.34	14.25	14.17	14.12	14.08	14.04	13.99	13.95	13.90
4	12.22	10.65	9.98	9.60	9.36	9.20	9.07	8.98	8.90	8.84	8.75	8.66	8.56	8.51	8.46	8.41	8.36	8.31	8.26
5	10.01	8.43	7.76	7.39	7.15	6.98	6.85	6.76	6.68	6.62	6.52	6.43	6.33	6.28	6.23	6.18	6.12	6.07	6.02
6	8.81	7.26	6.60	6.23	5.99	5.82	5.70	5.60	5.52	5.46	5.37	5.27	5.17	5.12	5.07	5.01	4.96	4.90	4.85
7	8.07	6.54	5.89	5.52	5.29	5.12	4.99	4.90	4.82	4.76	4.67	4.57	4.47	4.42	4.36	4.31	4.25	4.20	4.14
8	7.57	6.06	5.42	5.05	4.82	4.65	4.53	4.43	4.36	4.30	4.20	4.10	4.00	3.95	3.89	3.84	3.78	3.73	3.67
9	7.21	5.71	5.08	4.72	4.48	4.32	4.20	4.10	4.03	3.96	3.87	3.77	3.67	3.61	3.56	3.51	3.45	3.39	3.33
10	6.94	5.46	4.83	4.47	4.24	4.07	3.95	3.85	3.78	3.72	3.62	3.52	3.42	3.37	3.31	3.26	3.20	3.14	3.08
11	6.72	5.26	4.63	4.28	4.04	3.88	3.76	3.66	3.59	3.53	3.43	3.33	3.23	3.17	3.12	3.06	3.00	2.94	2.88
12	6.55	5.10	4.47	4.12	3.89	3.73	3.61	3.51	3.44	3.37	3.28	3.18	3.07	3.02	2.96	2.91	2.85	2.79	2.72
13	6.41	4.97	4.35	4.00	3.77	3.60	3.48	3.39	3.31	3.25	3.15	3.05	2.95	2.89	2.84	2.78	2.72	2.66	2.60
14	6.30	4.86	4.24	3.89	3.66	3.50	3.38	3.29	3.21	3.15	3.05	2.95	2.84	2.79	2.73	2.67	2.61	2.55	2.49
15	6.20	4.77	4.15	3.80	3.58	3.41	3.29	3.20	3.12	3.06	2.96	2.86	2.76	2.70	2.64	2.59	2.52	2.46	2.40
16	6.12	4.69	4.08	3.73	3.50	3.34	3.22	3.12	3.05	2.99	2.89	2.79	2.68	2.63	2.57	2.51	2.45	2.38	2.32
17	6.04	4.62	4.01	3.66	3.44	3.28	3.16	3.06	2.98	2.92	2.82	2.72	2.62	2.56	2.50	2.44	2.38	2.32	2.25
18	5.98	4.56	3.95	3.61	3.38	3.22	3.10	3.01	2.93	2.87	2.77	2.67	2.56	2.50	2.44	2.38	2.32	2.26	2.19
19	5.92	4.51	3.90	3.56	3.33	3.17	3.05	2.96	2.88	2.82	2.72	2.62	2.51	2.45	2.39	2.33	2.27	2.20	2.13
20	5.87	4.46	3.86	3.51	3.29	3.13	3.01	2.91	2.84	2.77	2.68	2.57	2.46	2.41	2.35	2.29	2.22	2.16	2.09
21	5.83	4.42	3.82	3.48	3.25	3.09	2.97	2.87	2.80	2.73	2.64	2.53	2.42	2.37	2.31	2.25	2.18	2.11	2.04
22	5.79	4.38	3.78	3.44	3.22	3.05	2.93	2.84	2.76	2.70	2.60	2.50	2.39	2.33	2.27	2.21	2.14	2.08	2.00
23	5.75	4.35	3.75	3.41	3.18	3.02	2.90	2.81	2.73	2.67	2.57	2.47	2.36	2.30	2.24	2.18	2.11	2.04	1.97
24	5.72	4.32	3.72	3.38	3.15	2.99	2.87	2.78	2.70	2.64	2.54	2.44	2.33	2.27	2.21	2.15	2.08	2.01	1.94
25	5.69	4.29	3.69	3.35	3.13	2.97	2.85	2.75	2.68	2.61	2.51	2.41	2.30	2.24	2.18	2.12	2.05	1.98	1.91
26	5.66	4.27	3.67	3.33	3.10	2.94	2.82	2.73	2.65	2.59	2.49	2.39	2.28	2.22	2.16	2.09	2.03	1.95	1.88
27	5.63	4.24	3.65	3.31	3.08	2.92	2.80	2.71	2.63	2.57	2.47	2.36	2.25	2.19	2.13	2.07	2.00	1.93	1.85
28	5.61	4.22	3.63	3.29	3.06	2.90	2.78	2.69	2.61	2.55	2.45	2.34	2.23	2.17	2.11	2.05	1.98	1.91	1.83
29	5.59	4.20	3.61	3.27	3.04	2.88	2.76	2.67	2.59	2.53	2.43	2.32	2.21	2.15	2.09	2.03	1.96	1.89	1.81
30	5.57	4.18	3.59	3.25	3.03	2.87	2.75	2.65	2.57	2.51	2.41	2.31	2.20	2.14	2.07	2.01	1.94	1.87	1.79
40	5.42	4.05	3.46	3.13	2.90	2.74	2.62	2.53	2.45	2.39	2.29	2.18	2.07	2.01	1.94	1.88	1.80	1.72	1.64
60	5.29	3.93	3.34	3.01	2.79	2.63	2.51	2.41	2.33	2.27	2.17	2.06	1.94	1.88	1.82	1.74	1.67	1.58	1.48
120	5.15	3.80	3.23	2.89	2.67	2.52	2.39	2.30	2.22	2.16	2.05	1.94	1.82	1.76	1.69	1.61	1.53	1.43	1.31
∞	5.02	3.69	3.12	2.79	2.57	2.41	2.29	2.19	2.11	2.05	1.94	1.83	1.71	1.64	1.57	1.48	1.39	1.27	1.00

Table 7—*F*-Distribution (Continued)

Table 7—*F*-Distribution | APPENDIX B **A25**

$\alpha = 0.05$

d.f._D: Degrees of freedom, denominator	d.f._N: Degrees of freedom, numerator																		
	1	2	3	4	5	6	7	8	9	10	12	15	20	24	30	40	60	120	∞
1	161.4	199.5	215.7	224.6	230.2	234.0	236.8	238.9	240.5	241.9	243.9	245.9	248.0	249.1	250.1	251.1	252.2	253.3	254.3
2	18.51	19.00	19.16	19.25	19.30	19.33	19.35	19.37	19.38	19.40	19.41	19.43	19.45	19.45	19.46	19.47	19.48	19.49	19.50
3	10.13	9.55	9.28	9.12	9.01	8.94	8.89	8.85	8.81	8.79	8.74	8.70	8.66	8.64	8.62	8.59	8.57	8.55	8.53
4	7.71	6.94	6.59	6.39	6.26	6.16	6.09	6.04	6.00	5.96	5.91	5.86	5.80	5.77	5.75	5.72	5.69	5.66	5.63
5	6.61	5.79	5.41	5.19	5.05	4.95	4.88	4.82	4.77	4.74	4.68	4.62	4.56	4.53	4.50	4.46	4.43	4.40	4.36
6	5.99	5.14	4.76	4.53	4.39	4.28	4.21	4.15	4.10	4.06	4.00	3.94	3.87	3.84	3.81	3.77	3.74	3.70	3.67
7	5.59	4.74	4.35	4.12	3.97	3.87	3.79	3.73	3.68	3.64	3.57	3.51	3.44	3.41	3.38	3.34	3.30	3.27	3.23
8	5.32	4.46	4.07	3.84	3.69	3.58	3.50	3.44	3.39	3.35	3.28	3.22	3.15	3.12	3.08	3.04	3.01	2.97	2.93
9	5.12	4.26	3.86	3.63	3.48	3.37	3.29	3.23	3.18	3.14	3.07	3.01	2.94	2.90	2.86	2.83	2.79	2.75	2.71
10	4.96	4.10	3.71	3.48	3.33	3.22	3.14	3.07	3.02	2.98	2.91	2.85	2.77	2.74	2.70	2.66	2.62	2.58	2.54
11	4.84	3.98	3.59	3.36	3.20	3.09	3.01	2.95	2.90	2.85	2.79	2.72	2.65	2.61	2.57	2.53	2.49	2.45	2.40
12	4.75	3.89	3.49	3.26	3.11	3.00	2.91	2.85	2.80	2.75	2.69	2.62	2.54	2.51	2.47	2.43	2.38	2.34	2.30
13	4.67	3.81	3.41	3.18	3.03	2.92	2.83	2.77	2.71	2.67	2.60	2.53	2.46	2.42	2.38	2.34	2.30	2.25	2.21
14	4.60	3.74	3.34	3.11	2.96	2.85	2.76	2.70	2.65	2.60	2.53	2.46	2.39	2.35	2.31	2.27	2.22	2.18	2.13
15	4.54	3.68	3.29	3.06	2.90	2.79	2.71	2.64	2.59	2.54	2.48	2.40	2.33	2.29	2.25	2.20	2.16	2.11	2.07
16	4.49	3.63	3.24	3.01	2.85	2.74	2.66	2.59	2.54	2.49	2.42	2.35	2.28	2.24	2.19	2.15	2.11	2.06	2.01
17	4.45	3.59	3.20	2.96	2.81	2.70	2.61	2.55	2.49	2.45	2.38	2.31	2.23	2.19	2.15	2.10	2.06	2.01	1.96
18	4.41	3.55	3.16	2.93	2.77	2.66	2.58	2.51	2.46	2.41	2.34	2.27	2.19	2.15	2.11	2.06	2.02	1.97	1.92
19	4.38	3.52	3.13	2.90	2.74	2.63	2.54	2.48	2.42	2.38	2.31	2.23	2.16	2.11	2.07	2.03	1.98	1.93	1.88
20	4.35	3.49	3.10	2.87	2.71	2.60	2.51	2.45	2.39	2.35	2.28	2.20	2.12	2.08	2.04	1.99	1.95	1.90	1.84
21	4.32	3.47	3.07	2.84	2.68	2.57	2.49	2.42	2.37	2.32	2.25	2.18	2.10	2.05	2.01	1.96	1.92	1.87	1.81
22	4.30	3.44	3.05	2.82	2.66	2.55	2.46	2.40	2.34	2.30	2.23	2.15	2.07	2.03	1.98	1.94	1.89	1.84	1.78
23	4.28	3.42	3.03	2.80	2.64	2.53	2.44	2.37	2.32	2.27	2.20	2.13	2.05	2.01	1.96	1.91	1.86	1.81	1.76
24	4.26	3.40	3.01	2.78	2.62	2.51	2.42	2.36	2.30	2.25	2.18	2.11	2.03	1.98	1.94	1.89	1.84	1.79	1.73
25	4.24	3.39	2.99	2.76	2.60	2.49	2.40	2.34	2.28	2.24	2.16	2.09	2.01	1.96	1.92	1.87	1.82	1.77	1.71
26	4.23	3.37	2.98	2.74	2.59	2.47	2.39	2.32	2.27	2.22	2.15	2.07	1.99	1.95	1.90	1.85	1.80	1.75	1.69
27	4.21	3.35	2.96	2.73	2.57	2.46	2.37	2.31	2.25	2.20	2.13	2.06	1.97	1.93	1.88	1.84	1.79	1.73	1.67
28	4.20	3.34	2.95	2.71	2.56	2.45	2.36	2.29	2.24	2.19	2.12	2.04	1.96	1.91	1.87	1.82	1.77	1.71	1.65
29	4.18	3.33	2.93	2.70	2.55	2.43	2.35	2.28	2.22	2.18	2.10	2.03	1.94	1.90	1.85	1.81	1.75	1.70	1.64
30	4.17	3.32	2.92	2.69	2.53	2.42	2.33	2.27	2.21	2.16	2.09	2.01	1.93	1.89	1.84	1.79	1.74	1.68	1.62
40	4.08	3.23	2.84	2.61	2.45	2.34	2.25	2.18	2.12	2.08	2.00	1.92	1.84	1.79	1.74	1.69	1.64	1.58	1.51
60	4.00	3.15	2.76	2.53	2.37	2.25	2.17	2.10	2.04	1.99	1.92	1.84	1.75	1.70	1.65	1.59	1.53	1.47	1.39
120	3.92	3.07	2.68	2.45	2.29	2.17	2.09	2.02	1.96	1.91	1.83	1.75	1.66	1.61	1.55	1.50	1.43	1.35	1.25
∞	3.84	3.00	2.60	2.37	2.21	2.10	2.01	1.94	1.88	1.83	1.75	1.67	1.57	1.52	1.46	1.39	1.32	1.22	1.00

Table 7—F-Distribution (Continued)

$\alpha = 0.010$

d.f._D: Degrees of freedom, denominator	d.f._N: Degrees of freedom, numerator																		
	1	2	3	4	5	6	7	8	9	10	12	15	20	24	30	40	60	120	∞
1	39.86	49.50	53.59	55.83	57.24	58.20	58.91	59.44	59.86	60.19	60.71	61.22	61.74	62.00	62.26	62.53	62.79	63.06	63.33
2	8.53	9.00	9.16	9.24	9.29	9.33	9.35	9.37	9.38	9.39	9.41	9.42	9.44	9.45	9.46	9.47	9.47	9.48	9.49
3	5.54	5.46	5.39	5.34	5.31	5.28	5.27	5.25	5.24	5.23	5.22	5.20	5.18	5.18	5.17	5.16	5.15	5.14	5.13
4	4.54	4.32	4.19	4.11	4.05	4.01	3.98	3.95	3.94	3.92	3.90	3.87	3.84	3.83	3.82	3.80	3.79	3.78	3.76
5	4.06	3.78	3.62	3.52	3.45	3.40	3.37	3.34	3.32	3.30	3.27	3.24	3.21	3.19	3.17	3.16	3.14	3.12	3.10
6	3.78	3.46	3.29	3.18	3.11	3.05	3.01	2.98	2.96	2.94	2.90	2.87	2.84	2.82	2.80	2.78	2.76	2.74	2.72
7	3.59	3.26	3.07	2.96	2.88	2.83	2.78	2.75	2.72	2.70	2.67	2.63	2.59	2.58	2.56	2.54	2.51	2.49	2.47
8	3.46	3.11	2.92	2.81	2.73	2.67	2.62	2.59	2.56	2.54	2.50	2.46	2.42	2.40	2.38	2.36	2.34	2.32	2.29
9	3.36	3.01	2.81	2.69	2.61	2.55	2.51	2.47	2.44	2.42	2.38	2.34	2.30	2.28	2.25	2.23	2.21	2.18	2.16
10	3.29	2.92	2.73	2.61	2.52	2.46	2.41	2.38	2.35	2.32	2.28	2.24	2.20	2.18	2.16	2.13	2.11	2.08	2.06
11	3.23	2.86	2.66	2.54	2.45	2.39	2.34	2.30	2.27	2.25	2.21	2.17	2.12	2.10	2.08	2.05	2.03	2.00	1.97
12	3.18	2.81	2.61	2.48	2.39	2.33	2.28	2.24	2.21	2.19	2.15	2.10	2.06	2.04	2.01	1.99	1.96	1.93	1.90
13	3.14	2.76	2.56	2.43	2.35	2.28	2.23	2.20	2.16	2.14	2.10	2.05	2.01	1.98	1.96	1.93	1.90	1.88	1.85
14	3.10	2.73	2.52	2.39	2.31	2.24	2.19	2.15	2.12	2.10	2.05	2.01	1.96	1.94	1.91	1.89	1.86	1.83	1.80
15	3.07	2.70	2.49	2.36	2.27	2.21	2.16	2.12	2.09	2.06	2.02	1.97	1.92	1.90	1.87	1.85	1.82	1.79	1.76
16	3.05	2.67	2.46	2.33	2.24	2.18	2.13	2.09	2.06	2.03	1.99	1.94	1.89	1.87	1.84	1.81	1.78	1.75	1.72
17	3.03	2.64	2.44	2.31	2.22	2.15	2.10	2.06	2.03	2.00	1.96	1.91	1.86	1.84	1.81	1.78	1.75	1.72	1.69
18	3.01	2.62	2.42	2.29	2.20	2.13	2.08	2.04	2.00	1.98	1.93	1.89	1.84	1.81	1.78	1.75	1.72	1.69	1.66
19	2.99	2.61	2.40	2.27	2.18	2.11	2.06	2.02	1.98	1.96	1.91	1.86	1.81	1.79	1.76	1.73	1.70	1.67	1.63
20	2.97	2.59	2.38	2.25	2.16	2.09	2.04	2.00	1.96	1.94	1.89	1.84	1.79	1.77	1.74	1.71	1.68	1.64	1.61
21	2.96	2.57	2.36	2.23	2.14	2.08	2.02	1.98	1.95	1.92	1.87	1.83	1.78	1.75	1.72	1.69	1.66	1.62	1.59
22	2.95	2.56	2.35	2.22	2.13	2.06	2.01	1.97	1.93	1.90	1.86	1.81	1.76	1.73	1.70	1.67	1.64	1.60	1.57
23	2.94	2.55	2.34	2.21	2.11	2.05	1.99	1.95	1.92	1.89	1.84	1.80	1.74	1.72	1.69	1.66	1.62	1.59	1.55
24	2.93	2.54	2.33	2.19	2.10	2.04	1.98	1.94	1.91	1.88	1.83	1.78	1.73	1.70	1.67	1.64	1.61	1.57	1.53
25	2.92	2.53	2.32	2.18	2.09	2.02	1.97	1.93	1.89	1.87	1.82	1.77	1.72	1.69	1.66	1.63	1.59	1.56	1.52
26	2.91	2.52	2.31	2.17	2.08	2.01	1.96	1.92	1.88	1.86	1.81	1.76	1.71	1.68	1.65	1.61	1.58	1.54	1.50
27	2.90	2.51	2.30	2.17	2.07	2.00	1.95	1.91	1.87	1.85	1.80	1.75	1.70	1.67	1.64	1.60	1.57	1.53	1.49
28	2.89	2.50	2.29	2.16	2.06	2.00	1.94	1.90	1.87	1.84	1.79	1.74	1.69	1.66	1.63	1.59	1.56	1.52	1.48
29	2.89	2.50	2.28	2.15	2.06	1.99	1.93	1.89	1.86	1.83	1.78	1.73	1.68	1.65	1.62	1.58	1.55	1.51	1.47
30	2.88	2.49	2.28	2.14	2.05	1.98	1.93	1.88	1.85	1.82	1.77	1.72	1.67	1.64	1.61	1.57	1.54	1.50	1.46
40	2.84	2.44	2.23	2.09	2.00	1.93	1.87	1.83	1.79	1.76	1.71	1.66	1.61	1.57	1.54	1.51	1.47	1.42	1.38
60	2.79	2.39	2.18	2.04	1.95	1.87	1.82	1.77	1.74	1.71	1.66	1.60	1.54	1.51	1.48	1.44	1.40	1.35	1.29
120	2.75	2.35	2.13	1.99	1.90	1.82	1.77	1.72	1.68	1.65	1.60	1.55	1.48	1.45	1.41	1.37	1.32	1.26	1.19
∞	2.71	2.30	2.08	1.94	1.85	1.77	1.72	1.67	1.63	1.60	1.55	1.49	1.42	1.38	1.34	1.30	1.24	1.17	1.00

From M. Merrington and C. M. Thompson (1943). Table of Percentage Points of the Inverted Beta (F) Distribution. *Biometrika* 33. pp. 74–87. Reprinted with permission from *Biometrika*.

Table 8—Critical Values for the Sign Test | APPENDIX B   **A27**

Table 8—Critical Values for the Sign Test

Reject the null hypothesis if the test statistic x is less than or equal to the value in the table.

n	One-tailed, $\alpha = 0.005$ Two-tailed, $\alpha = 0.01$	$\alpha = 0.01$ $\alpha = 0.02$	$\alpha = 0.025$ $\alpha = 0.05$	$\alpha = 0.05$ $\alpha = 0.10$
8	0	0	0	1
9	0	0	1	1
10	0	0	1	1
11	0	1	1	2
12	1	1	2	2
13	1	1	2	3
14	1	2	3	3
15	2	2	3	3
16	2	2	3	4
17	2	3	4	4
18	3	3	4	5
19	3	4	4	5
20	3	4	5	5
21	4	4	5	6
22	4	5	5	6
23	4	5	6	7
24	5	5	6	7
25	5	6	6	7

Note: Table 8 is for one-tailed or two-tailed tests. The sample size n represents the total number of $+$ and $-$ signs. The test value x is the smaller number of $+$ or $-$ signs..

Source: From *Journal of American Statistical Association* Vol. 41 (1946) pp. 557–66. W. J. Dixon and A. M. Mood.

Table 9—Critical Values for the Wilcoxon Signed-Rank Test

Reject the null hypothesis if the test statistic w_s value is less than or equal to the value given in the table.

	One-tailed, $\alpha = 0.05$	$\alpha = 0.025$	$\alpha = 0.01$	$\alpha = 0.005$
n	Two-tailed, $\alpha = 0.10$	$\alpha = 0.05$	$\alpha = 0.02$	$\alpha = 0.01$
5	1			
6	2	1		
7	4	2	0	
8	6	4	2	0
9	8	6	3	2
10	11	8	5	3
11	14	11	7	5
12	17	14	10	7
13	21	17	13	10
14	26	21	16	13
15	30	25	20	16
16	36	30	24	19
17	41	35	28	23
18	47	40	33	28
19	54	46	38	32
20	60	52	43	37
21	68	59	49	43
22	75	66	56	49
23	83	73	62	55
24	92	81	69	61
25	101	90	77	68
26	110	98	85	76
27	120	107	93	84
28	130	117	102	92
29	141	127	111	100
30	152	137	120	109

Source: From *Some Rapid Approximate Statistical Procedures.* Copyright 1949, 1964 Lerderle Laboratories, American Cyanamid Co., Wayne, N.J. Reprinted with permission.

Table 10—Critical Values for the Spearman Rank Correlation

Reject H_0: $\rho_s = 0$ if the absolute value of r_s is greater than the value given in the table.

n	$\alpha = 0.10$	$\alpha = 0.05$	$\alpha = 0.01$
5	0.900	—	—
6	0.829	0.886	—
7	0.714	0.786	0.929
8	0.643	0.738	0.881
9	0.600	0.700	0.833
10	0.564	0.648	0.794
11	0.536	0.618	0.818
12	0.497	0.591	0.780
13	0.475	0.566	0.745
14	0.457	0.545	0.716
15	0.441	0.525	0.689
16	0.425	0.507	0.666
17	0.412	0.490	0.645
18	0.399	0.476	0.625
19	0.388	0.462	0.608
20	0.377	0.450	0.591
21	0.368	0.438	0.576
22	0.359	0.428	0.562
23	0.351	0.418	0.549
24	0.343	0.409	0.537
25	0.336	0.400	0.526
26	0.329	0.392	0.515
27	0.323	0.385	0.505
28	0.317	0.377	0.496
29	0.311	0.370	0.487
30	0.305	0.364	0.478

Source: From N. L. Johnson and F. C. Leone, *Statistical and Experimental Design,* Vol. I (1964), p. 412. Reprinted with permission from the Institute of Mathematical Statistics.

CHAPTER 1

Section 1.1

1a. The population consists of the prices per gallon of regular gasoline at all gasoline stations in the U.S.

b. The sample consists of the prices per gallon of regular gasoline at the 800 surveyed stations.

c. The data set consists of the 800 prices.

2a. Population   **b.** Parameter

3a. Descriptive statistics involve the statement "76% of women and 60% of men had a physical examination within the previous year."

b. An inference drawn from the study is that a higher percentage of women had a physical examination within the previous year.

Section 1.2

1a. City population

b. City: Nonnumerical   **c.** City: Qualitative
Population: Numerical   Population: Quantitative

2. (1a) The final standings represent a ranking of hockey teams.

(1b) ordinal

(2a) The collection of phone numbers represent labels. No mathematical computations can be made.

(2b) nominal

3. (1a) The collection of body temperatures represent data that can be ordered, but makes no sense written as a ratio.

(1b) Interval

(2a) The collection of heart rates represent data that can be ordered and written as a ratio that makes sense.

(2b) Ratio

Section 1.3

1. (1a) Focus: Effect of exercise on senior citizens.
Population: Collection of all senior citizens.

(1b) Experiment

(2a) Focus: Effect of radiation fallout on senior citizens.
Population: Collection of all senior citizens.

(2b) Sampling

2a. Example: start with the first digits 92630782 . . .

b. 92|63|07|82|40|19|26

c. 63, 7, 40, 19, 26

3. (1) Convenience sampling

(2) Systematic sampling

CHAPTER 2

Section 2.1

1a. 6 classes   **b.** Min = 0   Max = 63 Class width = 11

c.   **d.** See part (e).

Lower limit	Upper limit
0	10
11	21
22	32
33	43
44	54
55	65

e.

Class	Frequency, f
0–10	27
11–21	13
22–32	16
33–43	7
44–54	11
55–65	3

2a. See part (b).

b.

Class	Frequency, f	Midpoint	Relative frequency	Cumulative frequency
0–10	27	5	0.3506	27
11–21	13	16	0.1688	40
22–32	16	27	0.2078	56
33–43	7	38	0.0909	63
44–54	11	49	0.1429	74
55–65	3	60	0.0390	77
	77		1	

c. Over 35% of the population is under 11 years old. Less than 4% of the population is over 54 years old.

3a.

Class Boundaries
−0.5–10.5
10.5–21.5
21.5–32.5
32.5–43.5
43.5–54.5
54.5–65.5

b. Use class midpoints for the horizontal scale and frequency for the vertical scale.

c.

Ages of Residents of Akhiok, Alaska

d. Most of the residents are less than 32 years old.

4a. Use class midpoints for the horizontal scale and frequency for the vertical scale.

b. See part (c).

c.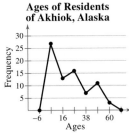

Ages of Residents of Akhiok, Alaska

d. The population of Akiok, Alaska is predominantly made up of young people.

5.

Ages of Residents of Akhiok, Alaska

6a. Use upper class boundaries for the horizontal scale and cumulative frequency for the vertical scale.

b. See part (c).

c.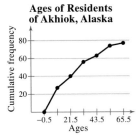

Ages of Residents of Akhiok, Alaska

d. Approximately 63 residents are less than 45 years old.

7. See the solution to Try It Yourself problem 3.

Section 2.2

1a.
```
0 |
1 |
2 |
3 |
4 |
5 |
6 |
```

b. Key: 3 | 5 = 35
```
0 | 6 3 7 1 7 5 0 3 2 1 8 6 9 2 0 4 1 6 5 5 4 6 8 2 4
1 | 7 2 5 0 1 7 0 3 6 1 1 0 2 6
2 | 8 7 1 4 7 2 5 1 5 3 9 6 8
3 | 9 3 6 2 4 0 3 1 2 1
4 | 8 7 5 6 2 9 1
5 | 0 4 3 0 2 6 5 1
6 | 3
```

c. Key: 3 | 5 = 35
```
0 | 0 1 1 1 2 2 2 2 3 3 4 4 4 5 5 5 6 6 6 6 7 7 8 8 9
1 | 0 0 0 1 1 1 2 2 3 5 6 6 7 7
2 | 1 1 2 3 4 5 5 6 7 7 8 8 9
3 | 0 1 1 2 2 3 3 4 6 9
4 | 1 2 5 6 7 8 9
5 | 0 0 1 2 3 4 5 6
6 | 3
```

d. It appears that the residents of Akhiok are a young population with most of the ages being below 40 years old.

2ab.
```
0 | 0 1 1 1 2 2 2 3 3 4 4 4
0 | 5 5 5 6 6 6 6 7 7 8 8 9
1 | 0 0 0 1 1 1 2 2 3
1 | 5 6 6 7 7
2 | 1 1 2 3 4
2 | 5 5 6 7 7 8 8 9
3 | 0 1 1 2 2 3 3 4
3 | 6 9
4 | 1 2
4 | 5 6 7 8 9
5 | 0 0 1 2 3 4
5 | 5 6
6 | 3
```

3a. Use ages for the horizontal axis.

b.

Ages of the Residents of Akhiok

c. It appears that a large percentage of the population is younger than 40 years old.

4a.

Transportation	Passengers Frequency	Relative frequency	Central angle
Bus	348	0.3460	124.6
Air	363.1	0.3610	130.0
Subway	274.6	0.2730	98.3
Amtrak	20.1	0.0200	7.2
	1005.8	1	

b.

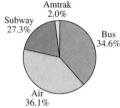

1985 Intercity Passenger Travel

Amtrak 2.0%
Subway 27.3%
Bus 34.6%
Air 36.1%

c. It appears that subway and train travel is nearly the same but approximately 4% of the 1985 bus travelers are now taking airplanes.

5a.

Cause	Frequency
Auto Dealers	14668
Auto Repair	9728
Home Furnishing	7792
Computer Sales	5733
Dry Cleaning	4649

b.

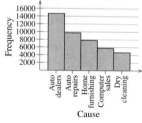

Causes of BBB Complaints

c. It appears that the auto industry (dealers and repair shops) account for the largest portion of complaints filed at the BBB.

6ab.

Salaries

c. It appears that the longer an employee is with the company, the larger his/her salary will be.

7ab.

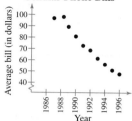

Cellular Phone Bills

c. It appears that the average monthly bill for cellular telephone subscribers has decreased significantly over the last 10 years.

Section 2.3

1a. 1745 **b.** 22.66

c. The typical age of a resident of Akhiok is 22.66 years old.

2a. 0, 1, 1, 1, 2, 2, 2, 3, 3, 4, 4, 4, 5, 5, 5, 6, 6, 6, 6, 7, 7, 8, 8, 9, 10, 10, 10, 11, 11, 11, 12, 12, 13, 15, 16, 16, 17, 17, 21, 21, 22, 23, 24, 25, 25, 26, 27, 27, 28, 28, 29, 30, 31, 31, 32, 32, 33, 33, 34, 36, 39, 41, 42, 45, 46, 47, 48, 49, 50, 50, 51, 52, 53, 54, 55, 56, 63

b. 21

c. Half of the residents of Akiok are younger than 21 and half are older than 21.

3a. 0, 1, 1, 1, 2, 2, 2, 3, 3, 4, 4, 4, 5, 5, 5, 6, 6, 6, 7, 7, 8, 8, 9, 10, 10, 10, 11, 11, 12, 12, 13, 15, 16, 16, 17, 17, 21, 21, 22, 23, 24, 25, 25, 26, 27, 27, 28, 28, 29, 30, 31, 31, 32, 32, 33, 36, 39, 41, 42, 45, 46, 47, 48, 49, 50, 50, 51, 52, 53, 54, 55, 63

b. 19

4a.

Class	Frequency	Age	Frequency	Age	Frequency
0	1	17	2	39	1
1	3	21	2	41	1
2	3	22	1	42	1
3	2	23	1	45	1
4	3	24	1	46	1
5	3	25	2	47	1
6	4	26	1	48	1
7	2	27	2	49	1
8	2	28	2	50	2
9	1	29	1	51	1
10	3	30	1	52	1
11	3	31	2	53	1
12	2	32	2	54	1
13	1	33	2	55	1
15	1	34	1	56	1
16	2	36	1	63	1

b. 6

c. The mode of the ages of the residents of Akhiok is 6 years old.

5a. Yes **b.** The mode of the responses to the survey is "Yes".

6a. 21.58; 21; 20

b. The mean in example 6 ($\bar{x} = 23.75$) was heavily influ-ened by the age 65. Neither the median nor the mode was affected as much by the age 65.

7ab.

Source	Score x	Weight w	$x \cdot w$
Test Mean	86	0.50	43
Mid-Term	96	0.15	14.4
Final	98	0.20	19.6
Computer Lab	98	0.10	9.8
Homework	100	0.05	5
		1.00	91.8

c. 91.8 **d.** The weighted mean for the course is 91.8.

8abc.

Class	Midpoint x	Frequency f	$x \cdot f$
0-10	5	27	135
11-21	16	13	208
22-32	27	16	432
33-43	38	7	266
44-54	49	11	539
55-65	60	3	180
		77	1760

d. 22.86

e. The average age of a resident of Akhiok is approxi-mately 22.86.

Section 2.4

1a. 58 and 23 **b.** 35

c. The range of the starting salaries for Corporation B is 35 or $35,000 (much larger than range of Corporation A).

2a. 41.5

bc.

Salary, x	$x - u$
23	−18.5
29	−12.5
32	−9.5
40	−1.5
41	−0.5
41	−0.5
49	7.5
50	8.5
52	10.5
58	16.5
	0

3ab.

Salary, x	$x - u$	$(x - u)^2$
23	−18.5	342.25
29	−12.5	156.25
32	−9.5	90.25
40	−1.5	2.25
41	−0.5	0.25
41	−0.5	0.25
49	7.5	56.25
50	8.5	72.25
52	10.5	110.25
58	16.5	272.25
	0	1102.5

c. 110.25 **d.** 10.5

e. The population variance is 110.25 and the population standard deviation is 10.5 or $10,500.

4a. See 3ab. **b.** 122.5 **c.** 11.07

5a. Enter data **b.** 21.64; 4.06

6a. 7, 7, 7, 7, 7, 13, 13 ,13, 13, 13 **b.** 3

7a. 1 standard deviation **b.** 34%

c. The estimated percent of the heights that are between 61.25 and 64 inches is 34%.

8a. 0 **b.** 70.6

c. At least 75% of the data lie within 2 standard deviations of the mean.

d. At least 75% of the population of Alaska is between 0 and 70.6 years old.

9a.

x	f	xf
0	10	0
1	19	19
2	7	14
3	7	21
4	5	20
5	1	5
6	1	6
	50	85

b. 1.7

c.

$x - \bar{x}$	$(x - \bar{x})^2$	$(x - \bar{x})^2 \cdot f$
−1.70	2.8900	28.9
−0.70	0.4900	9.31
0.30	0.0900	0.63
1.30	1.6900	11.83
2.30	5.2900	26.45
3.30	10.9800	10.89
4.30	18.4900	18.49
		106.5

d. 1.47

10a.

Class	x	f	xf
0	0	33	0
1-99	50	4	200
100-199	150	10	1500
200-299	250	13	3250
300-399	350	12	4200
400-499	450	11	4950
500+	650	17	11050
		100	25150

b. 251.5

c.

$x - \bar{x}$	$(x - \bar{x})^2$	$(x - \bar{x})^2 \cdot f$
-251.5	63252.25	2087324.25
-201.5	40602.25	162409
-101.5	10302.25	103022.5
-1.5	2.25	29.25
98.5	9702.25	116427
198.5	39402.25	433424.75
398.5	158802.25	2699638.25
		5602275

d. 237.9

Section 2.5

1a. 0, 1, 1, 1, 2, 2, 2, 3, 3, 4, 4, 4, 5, 5, 5, 6, 6, 6, 6, 7, 7, 8, 8, 9, 10, 10, 10, 11, 11, 11, 12, 12, 13, 15, 16, 16, 17, 17, 21, 21, 22, 23, 24, 25, 25, 26, 27, 27, 28, 28, 29, 30, 31, 31, 32, 32, 33, 33, 34, 36, 39, 41, 42, 45, 46, 47, 48, 49, 50, 50, 51, 52, 53, 54, 55, 56, 63

b. 21   **c.** 6.5, 33.5

2a. Enter data   **b.** 17, 23, 28.5

c. One quarter of the tuition costs is below $17,000 or less, one half is $23,000 or less, and three quarters is $28,500 or less.

3a. 6.5, 33.5   **b.** 27

c. The ages in the middle half of the data set vary by 27 years.

4a. 0, 6.5, 21, 33.5, 63

bc.

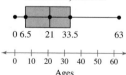

Ages of Residents of Akhiok, Alaska

0 6.5   21   33.5   63

d. It appears that half of the ages are between 6.5 and 33.5 years.

5a. 85th percentile

b. 85% of the ages are 47 years or younger.

CHAPTER 3

Section 3.1

1ab.

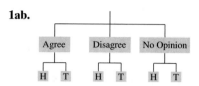

c. 6   **d.** {AH, AT, DH, DT, NH, NT}

2a. (1) 6 outcomes   (2) 1 outcome

b. (1) Not a simple event   (2) Simple event

3a. (1) 52   (2) 1   (3) 0.0192

b. (1) 52   (2) 13   (3) 0.25

c. (1) 52   (2) 52   (3) 1

4a. 4   **b.** 100   **c.** 0.04

5a. 54   **b.** 1000   **c.** 0.054

6a. Event = salmon successfully passing through a dam on the Columbia River.

b. Eperimentation   **c.** Empirical probability

7a. 0.425   **b.** 0.575   **c.** $\frac{23}{40}$ or 0.575

Section 3.2

1a. (1) 30 and 102   (2) 11 and 50

b. (1) 0.294   (2) 0.22

2a. (1) No   (2) Yes

b. (1) Independent   (2) Dependent

c. (1) A salmon successfully swimming through 1st dam does not affect the probability of successfully swimming through the 2nd dam.

(2) It has been shown in studies that exercising frequently lowers the resting rate of the heart.

3a. (1) Independent   (2) Dependent

b. (1) 0.7225   (2) 0.108

4a. (1) event   (2) compliment

b. (1) 0.729   (2) 0.999

Section 3.3

1a. (1) None are true   (2) None are true

(3) A and B cannot occur at the same time.

b. (1) Not mutually exclusive

(2) Not mutually exclusive

(3) Mutually exclusive

2a. (1) Mutually exclusive   (2) Not mutually exclusive

b. (1) $\frac{1}{6}, \frac{1}{2}$ (2) $\frac{12}{52}, \frac{13}{52}, \frac{3}{52}$ **c.** (1) 0.667   (2) 0.423

3a. $A = \{$sales between \$0 and \$24,999$\}$
$B = \{$sales between \$25,000 and \$49,000$\}$

b. A and B cannot occur at the same time
A and B are mutually exclusive

c. $\frac{3}{36}$ and $\frac{5}{36}$ **d.** 0.222

4a. (1) Mutually exclusive   (2) Not mutually exclusive

b. (1) 0.149   (2) 0.910

5a. 0.174   **b.** 0.826

Section 3.4

1a. Manufacturer: 4   **b.** 72
Size: 3
Color: 6

2a. (1) Each letter is an event (26 choices)
(2) Each letter is an event (26, 25, 24, 23, 22, and 21 choices)

b. (1) 308,915,776   (2) 165,765,600

3a. 6   **b.** 720

4a. 336

b. There are 336 possible ways that three horses can finish in first, second, and third place.

5a. $n = 12, r = 4$ **b.** 11,880

6a. $n = 20, n_1 = 6, n_2 = 9, n_3 = 5$ **b.** 77,597,520

7a. $n = 16, r = 3$ **b.** 560

c. There are 560 different possible 3 person committees that can be selected from 16 employees.

8a. 1 and 180   **b.** 0.0056

9a. 10   **b.** 220   **c.** 0.045

CHAPTER 4

Section 4.1

1a. (1) measured   (2) counted

b. (1) continuous   (2) discrete

2ab.

x	f	$P(x)$
0	16	0.16
1	19	0.19
2	15	0.15
3	21	0.21
4	9	0.09
5	10	0.10
6	8	0.08
7	2	0.02
	100	1

c.

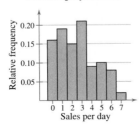

New Employee Sales

3a. Each $P(x)$ is between 0 and 1.   **b.** $\Sigma P(x) = 1$

c. Is a probability distribution.

4a. (1) Yes   (2) Yes

b. (1) No   (2) Yes

c. (1) Not a probability distribution
(2) Is a probability distribution

5ab.   **c.** $\mu = 2.60$

x	$P(x)$	$xP(x)$
0	0.16	0.00
1	0.19	0.19
2	0.15	0.30
3	0.21	0.63
4	0.09	0.36
5	0.10	0.50
6	0.08	0.48
7	0.02	0.14
	1	2.60

6ab.

x	$P(x)$	$x - \mu$	$(x - \mu)^2$	$P(x)(x - \mu)^2$
0	0.16	−2.6	6.76	1.0816
1	0.19	−1.6	2.56	0.4864
2	0.15	−0.6	0.36	0.054
3	0.21	0.4	0.16	0.0336
4	0.09	1.4	1.96	0.1764
5	0.10	2.4	5.76	0.576
6	0.08	3.4	11.56	0.9248
7	0.02	4.4	19.36	0.3872
	$\Sigma P(x) = 1$			$\Sigma P(x)(x - \mu)^2 = 3.72$

c. 1.93

7ab.   **c.** 2.44

x	f	$P(x)$	$xP(x)$
0	25	0.11	0.000
1	48	0.213	0.213
2	60	0.267	0.533
3	45	0.200	0.600
4	20	0.089	0.356
5	10	0.044	0.222
6	8	0.036	0.213
7	5	0.022	0.156
8	3	0.013	0.107
9	1	0.004	0.040
	225	1	2.440

d. You can expect an average of 2.44 sales per day.

Section 4.2

1a. Trial: Individual questions (10 trials)
Success: question answered correctly

b. Yes

c. $n = 10, p = 0.25, q = 0.75, x = 0, 1, 2, \ldots, 9, 10$

2a. Trial: 5 cards being drawn with replacement
Success: card drawn is a club
Failure: card drawn is not a club

b. $n = 5, p = 0.25, q = 0.75, x = 3$

c. 0.088

3a. Trial: 7 retirees
Success: Selecting a retiree who responded "yes"
Failure: Selecting a retiree who responded "no"

b. $n = 7, p = 0.71, q = 0.29, x = 0, 1, 2, \ldots, 6, 7$

c. 0.000172, 0.00296, 0.0217, 0.0886, 0.217, 0.319, 0.260, 0.91

d.

x	$P(x)$
0	0.0001721
1	0.00296
2	0.0217
3	0.0886
4	0.217
5	0.319
6	0.260
7	0.091

4a. Trial: 10 businessess
Success: Selecting a business with a Web site
Failure: Selecting a business with out a site

b. $n = 10, p = 0.25, x = 4$ **c.** 0.146

5a. $n = 250, p = 0.71, x = 178$ **b.** 0.056

c. The probability that exactly 178 Americans will use more than one topping on their hotdog is about 0.056.

6a. (1) $x = 2$ (2) $x = 2, 3, 4,$ or 5   (3) $x = 0$ or 1

b. (1) 0.217   (2) 0.283   (3) 0.717

c. (1) The probability that exactly two men consider fishing their favorite leisure-time activity is about 0.217.

(2) The probability that at least two men consider fishing their favorite leisure-time activity is about 0.283.

(3) The probability that fewer than two men consider fishing their favorite leisure-time activity is about 0.717.

7a. 0.042, 0.176, 0.306, 0.283, 0.148, 0.041, 0.004

b.

x	$P(x)$
0	0.042
1	0.176
2	0.306
3	0.283
4	0.148
5	0.041
6	0.004

c.

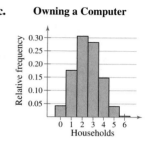

Owning a Computer

8a. Success: Selecting a clear day

b. 11.78   **c.** 7.3036   **d.** 2.703

e. On average, there are about 12 clear days during the year. The standard deviation is about 3 days.

Section 4.3

1a. 0.23, 0.177, 0.136   **b.** 0.543

c. The probability that your first sale will occur before your fourth sales call is 0.543.

2a. $P(0) \approx 0.050$
$P(1) \approx 0.149$
$P(2) \approx 0.224$
$P(3) \approx 0.224$
$P(4) \approx 0.168$

3a. 0.10   **b.** 0.10, 3   **c.** 0.0002

CHAPTER 5

Section 5.1

1a. A: 45, B: 60, C: 45   **b.** C

2a. 3.5   **b.** 3.3, 3.7; 0.2

3a. 85 is 1 standard deviation below the mean and 145 is 3 standard deviations above the mean.

b. 0.8385

Section 5.2

1a. $70, $8   **b.** -1.25; 0.125; 2.75

c. A bill of $60 is 1.25 standard deviations below the mean, a bill of $71 is 0.125 standard deviations above the mean, and a bill of $92 is 2.75 standard deviations above the mean.

2a. $70, $8 **b.** 64; 104.32; 55.44

c. $64 dollars is below the mean, $104.32 is above the mean, and $55.44 is below the mean.

3a. 0.0143 **b.** 2.17

4a. **b.** 0.9834

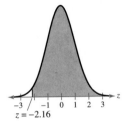

$z = 2.13$

5a. **b.** 0.0154 **c.** 0.9846

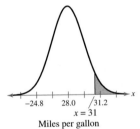

$z = -2.16$

6a. 0.0885 **b.** 0.0154 **c.** 0.0731

Section 5.3

1a. 0.92, 0.8 **b.** 0.8212, 0.7881 **c.** GRE

2a. **b.** 1.875

c. 0.9696

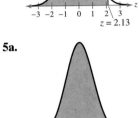

$x = 31$
Miles per gallon

d. The probability that a randomly selected Escort will get more than 31 mpg is 0.0304.

3a. **b.** $-1, 1.25$

c. 0.1587; 0.8944; 0.7357

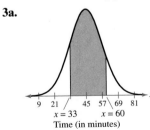

$x = 33$ $x = 60$
Time (in minutes)

4a. Read user's guide for the technology tool.

b. Enter the data. **c.** 0.4967

5a. **b.** -1.28

c. 8.512

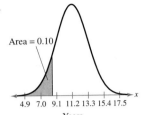

Years

d. The maximum length of time an employee could have worked and still be laid off is 8.512 years.

Section 5.4

1a.

Sample	Mean	Sample	Mean	Sample	Mean
1, 1	1	3, 1	2	6, 1	3.5
1, 2	1.5	3, 2	2.5	6, 2	4
1, 3	2	3, 3	3	6, 3	4.5
1, 5	3	3, 5	4	6, 5	5.5
1, 6	3.5	3, 6	4.5	6, 6	6
1, 7	4	3, 7	5	6, 7	6.5
2, 1	1.5	5, 1	3	7, 1	4
2, 2	2	5, 2	3.5	7, 2	4.5
2, 3	2.5	5, 3	4	7, 3	5
2, 5	3.5	5, 5	5	7, 5	6
2, 6	4	5, 6	5.5	7, 6	6.5
2, 7	4.5	5, 7	6	7, 7	7

b. 4, 2.33, 1.53 **c.** 4, 4.68, 2.16

2a. 64, 0.9

b. $n = 100$

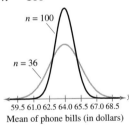

$n = 100$

$n = 36$

Mean of phone bills (in dollars)

3a. 3.5, 0.05

b.

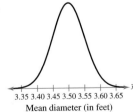

Mean diameter (in feet)

4a. 33, 0.596

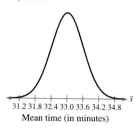

Mean time (in minutes)

b. $-10.06, 3.35$
c. $0, 0.9996$
d. 0.9990

5a. 125,000; 6500

Mean sales price (in dollars)

b. -7.03 **c.** 1

6a. 0.5, 1.58 **b.** 0.6915, 0.9429

c. There is a 69% chance an <u>individual receiver</u> will cost less than $700. There is a 94% chance that the <u>mean of a sampler of 10 receivers</u> is less than $700.

Section 5.5

1a. 70, 0.08, 0.92 **b.** 5.6, 64.4
c. Normal distribution can be used. **d.** 5.6, 2.270
2a. (1) 57, 58, . . . , 83 (2) . . . , 52, 53, 54
b. (1) $56.5 < x < 83.5$ (2) $x < 54.5$
3a. $x > 10.5$

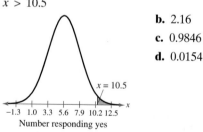

Number responding yes

b. 2.16
c. 0.9846
d. 0.0154

e. The probability that more than 10 respond yes is 0.0154.
4a. $x < 65.5$

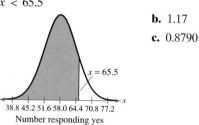

Number responding yes

b. 1.17
c. 0.8790

d. The probability that at most 65 people will say yes is 0.8790.

5a. $60.5 < x < 61.5$

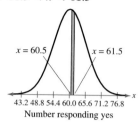

Number responding yes

b. 0.09; 0.27
c. 0.5359; 0.6064
d. 0.0705

e. The probability that exactly 61 people will respond yes is 0.0705.

CHAPTER 6

Section 6.1

1a. 14.767

b. The mean number of sentences per magazine advertisement is 14.767.

2a. 1.96, 30, 16.536 **b.** 5.917

c. You are 95% confident that the maximum error of the estimate is about 5.917 sentences per magazine advertisement.

3a. $\bar{x} = 14.767, E = 5.917$ **b.** 8.850, 20.684

c. You are 95% confident that the mean number of sentences per magazine advertisements is between 8.850 and 20.684.

4. (11.293, 18.240); (10.421, 19.113)

5a. 20, 22.9, 1.5, 1.282 **b.** 0.430 **c.** 22.47; 23.33

d. You are 80% confident that the mean age of the student is between 22.47 and 23.33 years.

6a. 1.96, 2, $s \approx 5.0$ **b.** 25

c. You should have at least 25 magazine advertisements in your sample.

Section 6.2

1a. 21 **b.** 0.90 **c.** 1.721
2a. 1.753; 4.383; 2.947; 7.368
b. (157.618, 166.383); (154.633, 169.368)
c. You are 90% confident that the mean temperature of coffee sold is between 157.618° and 166.383°.

You are 99% confident that the mean temperature of coffee sold is between 154.633° and 169.368°.

3a. 1.729; 0.162; 2.861; 0.269
b. (6.768, 7.092); (6.733, 7.127)
c. You are 90% confident that the mean mortgage interest rate is contained between 6.768% and 7.092%.

You are 99% confident that the mean mortgage interest rate is contained between 6.733% and 7.127%.

4a. No; Yes; No; Use t-distribution

Section 6.3

1a. $98, 1470$ **b.** 0.067

2a. $0.067, 0.933$ **b.** $1.645; 0.011$ **c.** $(0.056, 0.078)$

d. You are 90% confident that the proportion of adults that admired Abraham Lincoln the most is contained between 5.6% and 7.8%.

3a. $935, 0.16$ **b.** 0.84

c. $n\hat{p} = 935 \cdot 0.16 \approx 149.600 \geq 5$
$n\hat{q} = 935 \cdot 0.84 \approx 785.400 \geq 5$

Distribution of $\hat{p}$ is approximately normal.

d. 2.575 **e.** $(0.129, 0.191)$

f. You are 99% confident that the proportion of adults who think that trains are the safest mode of transportation is contained between 12.9% and 19.1%.

4a. $0.04, 0.96$ **b.** $1.645, 0.05$ **c.** 42

d. At least 42 adults should be included in the sample.

Section 6.4

1a. $24, 0.95$ **b.** $0.025, 0.975$ **c.** $39.364, 12.401$

2a. 90% CI: $42.557, 17.708$; 95% CI: $45.722, 16.047$

b. $(0.981, 2.358)$; $(0.913, 2.602)$

c. $(0.990, 1.536)$; $(0.956, 1.613)$

d. You are 90% confident that the population variance is between 0.990 and 1.536. You are 95% confident that the population variance is between 0.956 and 1.613.

CHAPTER 7

Section 7.1

1a. (1) The mean . . . is 74 months.
  $\mu = 74$

  (2) The variance . . . is less than or equal to 3.5.
  $\sigma^2 \leq 3.5$

  (3) The proportion . . . is greater than 39%.
  $p > 0.39$

b. (1) $\mu \neq 74$ (2) $\sigma^2 > 3.5$ (3) $p \leq 0.39$

c. (1) $H_0: \mu = 74$ and $H_a: \mu \neq 74$ (Claim: H_0)

  (2) $H_0: \sigma^2 \leq 3.5$ and $H_a: \sigma^2 > 3.5$ (Claim: H_0)

  (3) $H_0: p \leq 0.39$ and $H_a: p > 0.39$ (Claim: H_1)

2a. $H_0: p \leq 0.01$ and $H_1: p > 0.01$

b. Type I error will occur if the actual proportion is less than or equal to 0.01, but you decided to reject H_0.

Type II error will occur if the actual proportion is greater than 0.01, but you do not reject H_0.

c. Type II error is more serious since you would be misleading the consumer possibly causing serious injury or death.

3a. (1) $H_0: \mu = 74$ and $H_a: \mu \neq 74$

  (2) $H_0: p \leq 0.39$ and $H_a: p > 0.39$

b. (1) two-tailed   (2) right-tailed

c. (1)   (2)

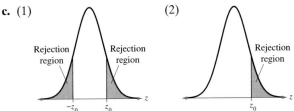

4a. There is enough evidence to reject the radio station's claim.

b. There is not enough evidence to decide that the radio station's claim is false.

5a. (No answer required)

b. (1) $\mu \leq 650$ (2) $\mu = 98.6$

6a. (1) Prove claim   (2) Disprove claim

b. (1) $H_a: \mu > 2400$ (2) $H_0: \mu \geq 2400$

Section 7.2

1a.

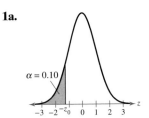

b. 0.1003 **c.** -1.28

2a.

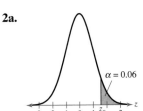

b. 0.9394 or 0.9406

c. 1.55 or 1.56

3a.

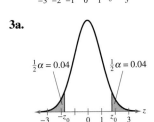

b. 0.0401 and 0.9599

c. -1.75 and 1.75

4a. $H_0: \mu \geq 8.5$ $H_a: \mu < 8.5$ (Claim: H_a)   **b.** $\alpha = 0.01$
c. $z_0 = -2.33$; Rejection region: $z \leq -2.33$
d. -3.550

e.

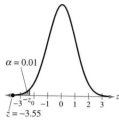

f. Reject H_0; There is enough evidence to support the claim.

5a. 0.01   **b.** ± 2.575
c. $z = -2.24$ **d.** Fail to reject H_0

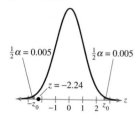

6a. (1) $P = 0.0347 > 0.01 = \alpha$
   (2) $P = 0.0347 < 0.05 = \alpha$
b. (1) Fail to reject H_0 (2) Reject H_0
7a. $P = 0.039 > 0.01 = \alpha$ **b.** Fail to reject H_0
8a. $H_0: \mu \leq 35$ and $H_a: \mu > 35$ (Claim: H_a)
b. 0.01   **c.** 2.500   **d.** P-value $= 0.0062$ **e.** Reject H_0
f. There is enough evidence to support the claim.
9a. $H_0: \mu = 150$ and $H_a: \mu \neq 150$ (Claim: H_0)
b. 0.01   **c.** -2.76 **d.** P-value $= 0.0029$ **e.** Reject H_0
f. There is enough evidence to state the claim is false.

Section 7.3

1a. 2.650   **b.** -2.650 **2a.** 1.860   **b.** 1.860
3a. 2.947   **b.** ± 2.947
4a. $H_0: \mu \geq \$875$ (Claim) $H_a: \mu < \$875$
b. 0.01 and 8   **c.** -2.896 **d.** -2.419
e. Fail to reject H_0 **f.** There is not enough evidence to reject the claim.

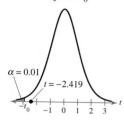

5a. $H_0: \mu = 1890$ (Claim) $H_a: \mu \neq 1890$
b. 0.01 and 18   **c.** ± 2.878 **d.** 3.798
e. Reject H_0

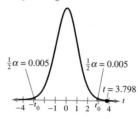

f. There is enough evidence to reject the company's claim.
6a. 0.082   **b.** $0.082 > 0.05$ **c.** Fail to reject H_0
d. There is not enough evidence to reject the claim.

Section 7.4

1a. $H_0: p \geq 0.30$; $H_a: p < 0.30$ (Claim)
b. 0.05   **c.** -1.645 **d.** -2.024 **e.** Reject H_0
f. There is enough evidence to support the claim.
2a. $H_0: p = 0.05$ (Claim); $H_a: p \neq 0.05$
b. 0.01   **c.** ± 2.575 **d.** 2.176   **e.** Fail to reject H_0
f. There is not enough evidence to reject the claim.
3a. $H_0: p \leq 0.38$; $H_a: p > 0.38$ (Claim)
b. 0.01   **c.** 2.33   **d.** 1.071   **e.** Fail to reject H_0
f. There is not enough evidence to support the claim.

Section 7.5

1a. 33.409   **2a.** 17.708   **3a.** 31.526   **b.** 8.231
4a. $H_0: \sigma^2 \leq 0.40$ (Claim); $H_a: \sigma^2 > 0.40$
b. 0.01, 30   **c.** 50.892   **d.** 56.250   **e.** Reject H_0
f. There is enough evidence to reject the claim.
5a. $H_0: \sigma \geq 3.7$; $H_a: \sigma < 3.7$ (Claim)
b. 0.05, 8   **c.** 2.733   **d.** 5.259   **e.** Fail to reject H_0
f. There is not enough evidence to support the claim.
6a. $H_0: \sigma^2 = 8.6$ (Claim); $H_a: \sigma^2 \neq 8.6$
b. 0.01, 9   **c.** 1.735, 23.589   **d.** 4.50   **e.** Fail to reject H_0
f. There is not enough evidence to reject the claim.

CHAPTER 8

Section 8.1

1a. $H_0: \mu_1 = \mu_2$; $H_1: \mu_1 \neq \mu_2$ (Claim)

b. 0.01   **c.** $z_0 = \pm 2.575$ **d.** 2.747   **e.** Reject H_0

f. There is enough evidence to support the claim.

2a. $z \approx 3.634$; P-value ≈ 0.000140

b. Rejection region is $z > 1.645$ or P-value $< 0.05 = \alpha$

c. Reject H_0

Section 8.2

1a. $H_0: \mu_1 = \mu_2$; $H_a: \mu_1 \neq \mu_2$ (Claim)

b. 0.05   **c.** 9   **d.** $t_0 = \pm 2.262$ **e.** 2.376   **f.** Reject H_0

g. There is enough evidence to support the claim.

2a. $H_0: \mu_1 \geq \mu_2$; $H_a: \mu_1 < \mu_2$ (Claim)

b. 0.10   **c.** 25   **d.** $t_0 = -1.316$ **e.** -0.90

f. Fail to reject H_0

g. There is not enough evidence to support the claim.

Section 8.3

1a. (1) Independent   (2) Dependent

2a. $H_0: \mu_d \geq 0$; $H_a: \mu_d < 0$ (Claim)

b. $\alpha = 0.05$, d.f. $= 11$ **c.** $t_0 \approx -1.796$

d. $\bar{d} = -1$; $s_d \approx 2.374$ **e.** $t \approx -1.459$

f. Fail to reject H_0

g. There is not enough evidence to support the claim.

3a. $H_0: \mu_d = 0$; $H_a: \mu_d \neq 0$ (Claim)

b. $\alpha = 0.05$, d.f. $= 6$ **c.** $t_0 = \pm 2.447$

d. $\bar{d} \approx 0.557$; $s_d \approx 0.924$ **e.** $t \approx 1.595$

f. Fail to reject H_0

g. There is not enough evidence to support the claim.

Section 8.4

1a. $H_0: p_1 = p_2$; $H_a: p_1 \neq p_2$ (Claim)

b. $\alpha = 0.05$ **c.** $z_0 = \pm 1.96$ **d.** $\bar{p} = 0.041$; $\bar{q} = 0.959$

e. $z = 5.297$ **f.** Reject H_0

g. There is enough evidence to support the claim.

2a. $H_0: p_1 \leq p_2$; $H_a: p_1 > p_2$ (Claim)

b. $\alpha = 0.05$ **c.** $z_0 = 1.645$ **d.** $\bar{p} = 0.115$; $\bar{q} = 0.885$

e. $z = 8.715$ **f.** Reject H_0

g. There is enough evidence to support the claim.

CHAPTER 9

Section 9.1

1ab.

Family income
(in thousands of dollars)

c. Yes, it appears that there is a negative linear correlation. As family income increases, the percent of income donated to charity decreases.

2ab.

Age

c. No, it appears that there is no correlation between age and subscriptions.

3ab.

c. Yes, there appears to be a positive linear relationship between men's winning time and women's winning time.

4a. $n = 6$

b.

x	y	xy	x^2	y^2
42	9	378	1764	81
48	10	480	2304	100
50	8	400	2500	64
59	5	295	3481	25
65	6	390	4225	36
72	3	216	5184	9
$\Sigma x = 336$	$\Sigma y = 41$	$\Sigma xy = 2159$	$\Sigma x^2 = 19458$	$\Sigma y^2 = 315$

c. -0.916

d. Since r is close to -1, there appears to be a strong negative linear correlation between income level and donating percent.

5a. Enter data   **b.** 0.832

c. Since r is close to 1, there appears to be a strong positive linear correlation between men's winning time and women's winning time.

6a. $H_0: \rho = 0$ and $H_a: \rho \neq 0$ **b.** 0.01   **c.** 33   **d.** ± 2.576

e. 22.921   **f.** Reject H_0

g. There is enough evidence in the sample to conclude that a significant correlation exists.

Section 9.2

1a. $n = 6$

x	y	xy	x^2
42	9	378	1764
48	10	480	2304
50	8	400	2500
59	5	295	3481
65	6	390	4225
72	3	216	5184
$\Sigma x = 336$	$\Sigma y = 41$	$\Sigma xy = 2159$	$\Sigma x^2 = 19458$

b. $m \approx -0.2134$ **c.** $b \approx 18.7837$

d. $\hat{y} = -0.213x + 18.784$

2a. Enter the data.   **b.** $m \approx 1.494$; $b \approx -3.909$

c. $\hat{y} = 1.494x - 3.909$

3a. (1) $\hat{y} = 11.824(2) + 35.301$

(2) $\hat{y} = 11.824(3.32) + 35.301$

b. (1) 58.949   (2) 74.557

c. (1) 58.949 minutes   (2) 74.557 minutes

Section 9.3

1a. 0.970   **b.** 0.941

c. 94.1% of the variation in the times is explained. 5.9% of the variation is unexplained.

2a.

x_i	y_i	$\hat{y}_i$	$(y_i - \hat{y}_i)^2$
15	26	28.392	5.721
20	32	35.419	11.689
20	38	35.419	6.662
30	56	49.473	42.602
40	54	63.527	90.764
45	78	70.554	55.442
50	80	77.581	5.851
60	88	91.635	13.214
			$\Sigma = 231.946$

b. 8   **c.** 6.218

d. The standard deviation of the weekly sales for a specific radio ad time is about $621.80.

3a. $n = 8$, d.f. $= 6$, $t_c = 2.447$, $s_e \approx 10.290$

b. 230.884   **c.** 29.236   **d.** (201.648, 260.120)

e. You can be 95% confident that the company sales will be between $201,648 and $260,120 when advertising expenditures are $2500.

Section 9.4

1a. Enter data.

b. $\hat{y} = 46.385 + 0.540x_1 - 4.897x_2$

2. (1) 89.548   (2) 73.814

CHAPTER 10

Section 10.1

1a.

Music	%of Listeners	Expected Frequency
Classical	4%	12
Country	36%	108
Gospel	11%	33
Oldies	2%	6
Pop	18%	54
Rock	29%	87

2a. Claimed Distribution:

Ages	Distribution
0–9	16%
10–19	20%
20–29	8%
30–39	14%
40–49	15%
50–59	12%
60–69	10%
70+	5%

H_0: Distribution of ages is as shown in table above.
H_a: Distribution of ages differs from the claimed distribution.

b. 0.05   **c.** 7   **d.** 14.067   **e.** 6.694   **f.** Fail to reject H_0.

g. There is not enough evidence to conclude that the distribution of ages differs from the claimed distribution.

3a. Claimed Distribution:

Response	Distribution
In favor of	44%
Against	27%
No Opinion	29%

H_0: Distribution of responses is as shown in table above.
H_a: Distribution of responses differs from the claimed distribution.

b. 0.01   **c.** 2   **d.** 9.210   **e.** 11.935   **f.** Fail to reject H_0.

g. There is not enough evidence to conclude that the distribution of responses differs from the claimed distribution.

Section 10.2

1ab.

	Hotel	Leg Room	Rental Size	Other	Total
Business	36	108	14	22	180
Leisure	38	54	14	14	120
Total	74	162	28	36	300

c. 300

d.

	Hotel	Leg Room	Rental Size	Other
Business	44.4	97.2	16.8	21.6
Leisure	29.6	64.8	11.2	14.4

2a. H_0: Travel concern is independent of travel purpose.
H_a: Travel concern is dependent on travel purpose. (claim)

b. 0.01   **c.** 3   **d.** 11.345   **e.** 8.158   **f.** Fail to reject H_0.

g. There is not enough evidence to conclude that travel concern is dependent on travel purpose.

3a. 9.488   **b.** Enter the data.   **c.** 65.619   **d.** Reject H_0.

e. Yes.

Section 10.3

1a. 0.01   **b.** 3   **c.** 15   **d.** 5.42

2a. 0.01   **b.** 2   **c.** 5   **d.** 13.27

3a. H_0: $\sigma_1^2 \le \sigma_2^2$; H_a: $\sigma_1^2 > \sigma_2^2$ (claim)

b. 0.01   **c.** 24, 19   **d.** 2.92   **e.** 3.214   **f.** Reject H_0.

g. There is enough evidence to support the claim.

4a. H_0: $\sigma_1 = \sigma_2$ (claim); H_a: $\sigma_1 \ne \sigma_2$

b. 0.01   **c.** 15, 21   **d.** 3.43   **e.** 1.483   **f.** Fail to reject H_0.

g. There is not enough evidence to reject the claim.

Section 10.4

1a. H_0: $\mu_1 = \mu_2 = \mu_3 = \mu_4$
H_a: At least one mean is different from the others.

b. 0.05   **c.** 3, 14   **d.** 3.34   **e.** 4.22   **f.** Reject H_0.

g. There is enough evidence to conclude that at least one mean is different from the others.

2a. Enter the data.   **b.** $F = 1.34$; P-value $= 0.280$

c. Fail to reject H_0

d. There is not enough evidence to conclude that at least one mean is different from the others.

Section 11.1

1a. H_0: median ≤ 2500 and H_a: median > 2500 (claim)

b. $\alpha = 0.025$ **c.** $n = 22$ **d.** The critical value is 5.

e. $x = 10$ **f.** Fail to reject H_0.

g. There is not enough evidence to support the claim.

2a. H_0: median $= 134{,}500$ (claim) and
H_a: median $\ne 134{,}500$

b. $\alpha = 0.10$ **c.** $n = 81$

d. The critical values are ±1.645.

e. $x = 30$
$$z = \frac{(x + 0.5) - 0.5(n)}{\frac{\sqrt{n}}{2}} = \frac{(30 + 0.5) - 0.5(81)}{\frac{\sqrt{81}}{2}} = -2.22$$

f. Reject H_0.

g. There is not enough evidence to reject the claim.

3a. H_0: The number of colds will not decrease.
H_a: The number of colds will decrease. (claim)

b. $\alpha = 0.05$ **c.** $n = 11$ **d.** $CV = 2$ **e.** $x = 2$

f. Reject H_0.

g. There is enough evidence to support the claim.

Section 11.2

1a. H_0: The water repellent is not effective.
H_a: The water repellent is effective. (claim)

b. $\alpha = 0.01$ **c.** $n = 11$ **d.** $CV = 5$ **e.** $w_s = 10.5$

f. Fail to reject H_0.

g. There is not enough evidence to support the claim.

2a. H_0: There is no difference in the claims paid by the companies.
H_a: There is a difference in the claims paid by the companies. (claim)

b. $\alpha = 0.05$ **c.** The critical values are ±1.96.

d. $n_1 = 12$ and $n_2 = 12$ **e.** $R = 120.5$

f. $\mu_R = 150$; $\sigma_R = 17.321$; $z = -1.703$

g. Fail to reject H_0.

h. There is not enough evidence to support the claim.

Section 11.3

1a. H_0: There is no difference in the salaries in the three states.
H_a: There is a difference in the salaries in the three states. (claim)

b. $\alpha = 0.10$ **c.** d.f. $= k - 1 = 2$

d. $CV = 4.605 \rightarrow$ Reject H_0 if $\chi^2 > 4.605$

e.

State	Salary	Rank
CT	25.57	1
CA	26.42	2
NJ	29.73	3
CT	29.86	4
CT	30.00	5
CA	33.68	6.5
CT	33.68	6.5
NJ	33.91	8
NJ	34.29	9
NJ	36.35	10
CA	36.55	11
CA	37.18	12
NJ	37.24	13
CT	37.39	14
CA	38.36	15
CA	40.31	16
CA	41.33	17
NJ	43.26	18
NJ	43.89	19
NJ	44.57	20
CT	45.04	21
CT	45.29	22
CA	46.55	23
NJ	46.72	24
CA	47.17	25
CA	48.46	26
NJ	50.16	27
CT	51.03	28
CT	57.07	29
CT	61.46	30

$R_1 = 153.5$

$R_2 = 160.5$

$R_1 = 151$

f. 0.063   **g.** Fail to reject H_0

h. There is not enough evidence to support the claim.

Section 11.4

1a. $H_0: \rho_s = 0$ and $H_a: \rho_s \neq 0$ **b.** $\alpha = 0.05$ **c.** $CV = 0.738$

d.

Oat	Rank	Wheat	Rank	d	d^2
1.49	6	3.72	6	0	0
1.14	1	2.61	1	0	0
1.21	2	3	2	0	0
1.32	4	3.24	3	1	1
1.36	5	3.26	4	1	1
1.22	3	3.45	5	-2	4
1.67	7	4.55	8	-1	1
1.9	8	4.3	7	1	1
					8

$\Sigma d^2 = 8$

e. $r_s = 1 - \dfrac{6\Sigma d^2}{n(n^2 - 1)} = 0.905$

f. Reject H_0.

g. There is enough evidence to conclude that a significant correction exists.

APPENDIX A

1a. \$70, \$8   **b.** -1.25; 0.125; 2.75

c. A bill of \$60 is 1.25 standard deviations below the mean, a bill of \$71 is 0.125 standard deviations above the mean, and a bill of \$92 is 2.75 standard deviations above the mean.

2a. \$70, \$8   **b.** 64; 104.32; 55.44

c. \$64 dollars is below the mean, \$104.32 is above the mean, and \$55.44 is below the mean.

3a. 0.4857   **b.** $z = -2.17$ and $z = 2.17$

4a.

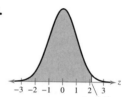

b. 0.4834

c. 0.9834

5a.

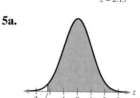

b. 0.4846

c. 0.9846

6a.

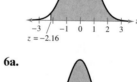

b. $z = -2.16$: Area $= 0.4846$

$z = -1.35$: Area $= 0.4115$

c. 0.0731

ODD ANSWERS

CHAPTER 1

Section 1.1   *(page 6)*

1. A sample is a subset of a population.

3. False   **5.** True   **7.** Population   **9.** Sample

11. Population: Party of registered voters in Bucks County.

Sample: Party of Bucks County voters responding to phone survey.

13. Population: Ages of adult Americans who own computers.

Sample: Ages of adult Americans who own Dell computers.

15. Population: Collection of all infants.

Sample: Collection of the 33,043 infants in the study.

17. Population: Collection of all American women.

Sample: Collection of the 546 American women surveyed.

19. Statistic   **21.** Statistic

23. The statement "56% are the primary investor in their household" is an application of descriptive statistics.

An inference drawn from the sample is that an association exists between American women and being the primary investor in their household.

25. Answers vary.

Section 1.2   *(page 12)*

1. Nominal and ordinal   **3.** True

5. False   **7.** Qualitative   **9.** Quantitative

11. Ordinal   **13.** Ratio   **15.** Interval

17. Ordinal   **19.** Nominal

21. Interval data can be ordered and differences between entries can be calculated. Ratio data has all the properties of interval data with the addition that a ratio of two data values can be formed so one data value can be expressed as a multiple of another.

Section 1.3   *(page 20)*

1. False   **3.** False   **5.** Perform an experiment.

7. Use a simulation.   **9.** Simple random sample.

11. Convenience sample.   **13.** Simple random sample.

15. Stratified sample.   **17.** Systematic sample.

19. Question is biased since it already suggests that drinking fruit juice is good for you. The question might be rewritten as "How does drinking fruit juice affect your health?"

21. The households sampled represent various locations, ethnic groups, and income brackets. Each of these variables is considered a stratum.

23. (a) Advantage: Allows respondent to express some depth and shades of meaning in the answer.

Disadvantage: Not easily quantified and difficult to compare surveys.

(b) Advantage: Easy to analyze results.

Disadvantage: May not provide appropriate alternatives and may influence the opinion of the respondent.

Review Answers for Chapter 1   *(page 25)*

1. Population: Collection of all U.S. VCR owners.

Sample: Collection of the 898 VCR owners that were sampled.

3. Population: Collection of all U.S. ATM's.

Sample: Collection of 860 ATM's that were sampled.

5. Parameter   **7.** Parameter   **9.** Quantitative

11. Quantitative   **13.** Interval   **15.** Nominal

17. Take a census.   **19.** Perform an experiment.

21. Simple random sample.   **23.** Cluster sample

25. Stratified sample

27. Telephone sampling only samples individuals who have telephones, are available, and are willing to respond.

29. The selected communities may not be representative of the entire area.

Chapter Quiz for Chapter 1   *(page 27)*

1. Population: Collection of all individuals with sleep disorders.

Sample: Collection of 163 patients in study.

2. (a) Statistic   (b) Parameter

3. (a) Qualitative   (b) Quantitative

4. (a) Nominal   (b) Ratio

5. (a) Perform an experiment.   (b) Use sampling.

6. (a) Convenience sample   (b) Systematic sample

7. (a) False   (b) False

CHAPTER 2

Section 2.1   *(page 39)*

1. By organizing the data into a frequency distribution, patterns within the data may become more evident.

3. False

5. Class width = 10

Class	Frequency	Class Boundaries	Midpoint	Cumulative frequency
20–29	10	19.5–29.5	24.5	10
30–39	132	29.5–39.5	34.5	142
40–49	284	39.5–49.5	44.5	426
50–59	300	49.5–59.5	54.5	726
60–69	175	59.5–69.5	64.5	901
70–79	65	69.5–79.5	74.5	966
80–89	25	79.5–89.5	84.5	991

7. Least frequency ≈ 10
Greatest frequency ≈ 300
Class width = 10

9. (a) 50   (b) 12.5–13.5 lbs.   (c) 24   (d) 19.5 lbs.

11. (a) Class with greatest relative frequency: 8–9 in.
Class with least relative frequency: 17–18 in.
(b) Greatest relative frequency ≈ 0.195
Least relative frequency ≈ 0.005
(c) Approximately 0.015

13. Class with greatest frequency: 500–550
Class with least frequency: 250–300 or 700–750

15.

Class	Frequency	Midpoint	Relative frequency	Cumulative frequency
0–7	8	3.5	0.32	8
8–15	8	11.5	0.32	16
16–23	3	19.5	0.12	19
24–31	3	27.5	0.12	22
32–39	3	35.5	0.12	25
	25		1	

17.

Class	Frequency	Midpoint	Relative frequency	Cumulative frequency
1000–2019	12	1509.5	0.5455	12
2020–3039	3	2529.5	0.1364	15
3040–4059	2	3549.5	0.0909	17
4060–5079	3	4569.5	0.1364	20
5080–6099	1	5589.5	0.0455	21
6100–7119	1	6609.5	0.0455	22
	22		1	

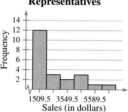

July Sales for Representatives

Class with greatest frequency: 1000–2019
Class with least frequency: 5080–6099; 6100–7119

19.

Class	Frequency	Midpoint	Relative frequency	Cumulative frequency
291–318	4	304.5	0.1818	4
319–346	3	332.5	0.1364	7
347–374	2	360.5	0.0909	9
375–402	4	388.5	0.1818	13
403–430	3	416.5	0.1364	16
431–458	3	444.5	0.1364	19
459–486	1	472.5	0.0455	20
487–514	2	500.5	0.0909	22
	22		1	

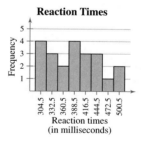

Reaction Times

Class with greatest frequency: 291–318; 375–402
Class with least frequency: 459–486

21.

Class	Frequency	Midpoint	Relative frequency	Cumulative frequency
146–169	6	157.5	0.2308	6
170–193	9	181.5	0.3462	15
194–217	3	205.5	0.1154	18
218–241	6	229.5	0.2308	24
242–265	2	253.5	0.0769	26
	26		1	

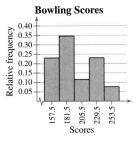

Bowling Scores

Class with greatest relative frequency: 170–193
Class with least relative frequency: 242–265

23.

Class	Frequency	Midpoint	Relative frequency	Cumulative frequency
33–35	6	34	0.2308	6
36–38	4	37	0.1538	10
39–41	6	40	0.2308	16
42–44	3	43	0.1154	19
45–47	1	46	0.0385	20
48–50	3	49	0.1154	23
51–53	3	52	0.1154	26
	26		1	

Heights of Douglas Fir Trees

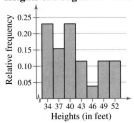

Class with greatest relative frequency: 33–35; 39–41
Class with least relative frequency: 45–47

25.

Class	Frequency	Relative frequency	Cumulative frequency
50–53	1	0.0417	1
54–57	0	0.0000	1
58–61	4	0.1667	5
62–65	9	0.3750	14
66–69	7	0.2917	21
70–73	3	0.1250	24
	24	1	

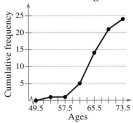

Retirement Ages

Location of the greatest increase in frequency: 62–65

27.

Class	Frequency	Relative frequency	Cumulative frequency
2–4	9	0.3214	9
5–7	6	0.2143	15
8–10	7	0.2500	22
11–13	3	0.1071	25
14–16	2	0.0714	27
17–19	1	0.0357	28
	28	1	

Gallons of Gasoline Purchased

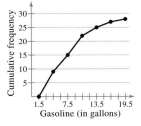

Location of the greatest increase in frequency: 2–4

29.

Class	Frequency	Midpoint	Relative frequency	Cumulative frequency
47–57	1	52	0.05	1
58–68	1	63	0.05	2
69–79	5	74	0.25	7
80–90	8	85	0.4	15
91–101	5	96	0.25	20
	20		1	

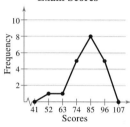

Exam Scores

Class with greatest frequency: 80–90
Classes with least frequency: 47–57 and 58–68

31. (a)

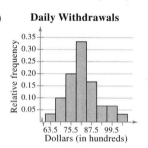

Daily Withdrawals

(b) $9,600
(c) 16.7%

33.

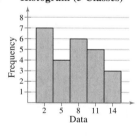

Histogram (5 Classes)

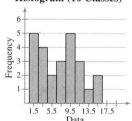

Histogram (10 Classes)

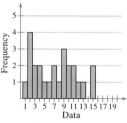

Histogram (20 Classes)

Section 2.2 *(page 51)*

1. Quantitative: Stem-and-Leaf Plot, Dot Plot, Histogram, Time Series Chart

Qualitative: Pie Chart, Pareto Chart

3. a   **5.** d

7. 27, 32, 41, 43, 43, 44, 47, 47, 48, 50, 51, 51, 52, 53, 53, 53, 54, 54, 54, 54, 55, 56, 56, 58, 59, 68, 68, 68, 73, 78, 78

Max: 78   Min: 27

9. 13, 13, 14, 14, 14, 15, 15, 15, 15, 15, 16, 17, 17, 18, 19

Max: 19   Min: 13

11. Time series chart

13. Stem-and-leaf plot or dot plot

15. (a) Key: 2|4 = 24

```
1 | 9
2 | 1112223344456667777789
3 | 0
```

(b) Key: 2|4 = 24

```
1 | 9
2 | 11122233444
2 | 566677777899
3 | 0
```

It appears that using two rows for each stem displays the data better.

17. Key: 3|3 = 33

```
3 | 233459
4 | 01134556678
5 | 133
6 | 0069
```

Most elephants tend to drink less than 55 gallons of water per day.

19. Key: 17|5 = 175

```
16 | 48
17 | 113455679
18 | 13446669
19 | 0023356
20 | 18
```

It appears that most farmers charge 17 to 19 cents per pound of apples.

21.

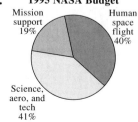

Housefly Lifespans

It appears that the lifespan of a fly tends to be between 4 and 14 days.

23. **1995 NASA Budget**

Mission support 19%

Human space flight 40%

Science, aero, and tech 41%

It appears that 40% of NASA's 1995 budget went to human space flight.

25.

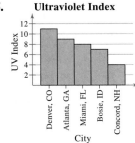

Ultraviolet Index

It appears that Denver, CO has nearly three times as much UV exposure than Concord, NH.

27.

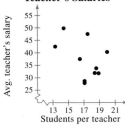

Teacher's Salaries

It appears that a teacher's average salary decreases as the number of students per teacher increases.

29.

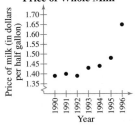

Price of Whole Milk

It appears that the price of whole milk has increased over the past 7 years.

31. When data is taken at regular intervals over a period of time, a time series chart should be used.

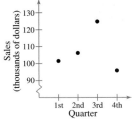

Sales for Company A

Section 2.3   *(page 62)*

1. False   **3.** False   **5.** Skewed right   **7.** Uniform

9. (7)   **11.** (8)

13. (a) $\bar{x} = 6.23$ **15.** (a) $\bar{x} = 4.57$
median = 6   median = 4.8
mode = 5   mode = 4.8

    (b) median   (b) median

17. (a) $\bar{x} = 97$ (b) median
median = 97.2
mode = 94.8, 95.4, 97.2, 103.1

19. (a) x = not possible   (b) mode
median = not possible
mode = "Worse"

21. (a) $\bar{x} = 170.63$ (b) mean
median = 169.3
mode = not possible

23. (a) $\bar{x} = 22.6$ **25.** (a) $\bar{x} = 14.11$
median = 19   median = 14.25
mode = 14   mode = 2.5

    (b) median   (b) mean

27. A = mode   **29.** 85.6   **31.** 2.8   **33.** 65.5
B = median
C = mean

35. 35.01   **37.** Positively Skewed   **39.** Symmetric

41. (a) $\bar{x} = 6.01$ (b) $\bar{x} = 5.95$
median = 6.01   median = 6.01

    (c) mean

43. (a) Mean   (b) Median   (c) Mode

45. (a) $\bar{x} = 49.23$ (b) median = 46.5

    (c) 1 | 1 3   (d) Positively skewed
        2 | 2 8
        3 | 6 6 6 7 7 7 8
        4 | 1 3 4 6 7——————— mean
        5 | 1 1 1 3
        6 | 1 2 3 4   median
        7 | 2 2 4 6
        8 | 5
        9 | 0

47. Two different symbols are needed since they describe a measure of central tendency for two different sets of data (sample is a subset of the population).

Section 2.4   *(page 78)*

1. The range is the difference between the maximum and minimum values of a data set. The advantage of the range is that it is easy to calculate. The disadvantage is that it uses only two entries from the data set.

3. 73

5. A deviation, $(x - \mu)$, is the difference between an observation, x and the mean of the data, μ. The sum of the deviations is always zero.

7. The standard deviation is the positive square root of the variance.

The standard deviation and variance can never be negative. Squared deviations can never be negative.

$$\{7, 7, 7, 7, 7\} \rightarrow n = 5, \bar{x} = 7, \text{ and } s = 0$$

9. When calculating the population standard deviation, you divide the sum of the squared deviations by n, then take the square root of that value. When calculating the sample standard deviation, you divide the sum of the squared deviations by $n - 1$, then take the square root of that value.

When given a data set, one would have to determine if it represented the population or was a sample taken from the population. If the data is a population, then σ is calculated. If the data is a sample, then s is calculated.

11. 10, 16.57, 10.25, 3.20   **13.** 19, 17.92, 59.58, 7.72

15. Company B

17. (a) 17.6, 37.35, 6.11
   8.7, 8.71, 2.95

   (b) It appears from the data that the annual salaries in LA are more variable than the salaries in Long Beach.

19. (a) 5.1, 2.95, 1.72
   4.2, 1.99, 1.41

   (b) It appears from the data that the annual salaries for public teachers are more variable than the salaries for private teachers.

21. (a) Greatest sample standard deviation: (ii)

   Data set (ii) has more entries that are farther away from the mean.

   Least same standard deviation: (iii)

   Data set (iii) has more entries that are close to the mean.

   (b) The three data sets have the same mean, but have different standard deviations.

23. (a) Similarities: Both estimate proportions of the data contained within k standard deviations of the mean.

   Difference: The Empirical Rule assumes the distribution is bell-shaped, Chebychev's Theorem makes no such assumption.

   (b) You must know that the distribution is bell-shaped.

   (c) If $k = 1$, Chebychev's Theorem would return a proportion equal to zero. If $k < 1$, it would return a negative proportion (which is not possible).

25. 47.5%   **27.** (0.05, 6.59)   **29.** 2.075, 1.328

31.

Class	Midpoint, x	f
0-4	2	19
5-13	9	36
14-17	15.5	15.8
18-24	21	26.3
25-34	29.5	37.2
35-44	39.5	44.7
45-64	54.5	61
65+	70	34.7
		274.7

33. $CV_{\text{heights}} \approx 4.73$
   $CV_{\text{weights}} \approx 9.83$
   It appears that weight is more variable than height.

35. (a) -2.61; skewed left   (b) 4.12; skewed right
   (c) 0; symmetric   (d) -8; skewed left
   (e) 4.79; skewed right

37. (a) 550, 302.765   (b) 560, 302.765   (c) 540, 302.765

   (d) By adding or subtracting a constant k to each entry, the new sample mean will be $\bar{x} + k$ with the sample standard deviation being unaffected.

Section 2.5   *(page 90)*

1. The basketball team scored more points per game than 75% of the teams in the league.

3. The student scored above 63% of the students who took the ACT placement test.

5. True

7. (a) Min = 10   **9.** (a) Min = 900
   (b) Max = 21   (b) Max = 2100
   (c) $Q_1 = 13$ (c) $Q_1 = 1250$
   (d) $Q_2 = 15$ (d) $Q_2 = 1500$
   (e) $Q_3 = 17$ (e) $Q_3 = 1950$
   (f) $IQR = 4$ (f) $IQR = 700$

11. (a) 4.5, 6, 7.5

(b)

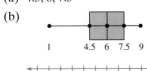

13. (a) 25, 40 , 47.5

(b) $P_{25} = Q_1 = 25$
$P_{50} = Q_2 = 40$
$P_{75} = Q_3 = 47.5$

(c) **Retirements in the House of Representatives**

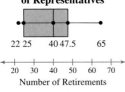

Number of Retirements

(d) Half of the retirements are between 25 and 47.5.

15. (a) 9.85, 11.2, 13.25

(b) $P_{25} = Q_1 = 9.85$
$P_{50} = Q_2 = 11.2$
$P_{75} = Q_3 = 13.25$

(c) **Automotive Mechanics**

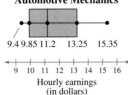

Hourly earnings (in dollars)

17. $Q_1 = B, Q_2 = A, Q_3 = C$

19. (a) 2, 4, 5

(b) **Watching Television**

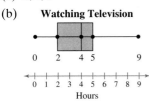

Hours

(c) Half of the hours of TV watched per day are between 2 and 5.

21. 70 inches

23. (a) 42, 49, 56

(b) **Ages of Executives**

27   42 49 56   82

25 35 45 55 65 75 85
Ages

(c) Half of the ages are between 42 and 56 years.

(d) 49

Review Answers for Chapter 2   *(page 97)*

1.

Class	Midpoint	Boundaries	Frequency	Relative frequency	Cumulative frequency
20–23	21.5	19.5–23.5	1	0.05	1
24–27	25.5	23.5–27.5	2	0.10	3
28–31	29.5	27.5–31.5	6	0.30	9
32–35	33.5	31.5–35.5	7	0.35	16
36–39	37.5	35.5–39.5	4	0.20	20
			20	1	

3. (See problem 1)

5. **Liquid Volume 12 oz Cans**

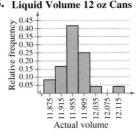

Actual volume

7. **Meals Purchased**

Number of meals

9. **Average Daily Highs**

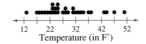

Temperature (in F°)

11. **American Kennel Club**

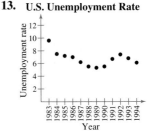

13. **U.S. Unemployment Rate**

Year

15. 30.8, 30, 29   **17.** 2.083   **19.** 87.4

21. Skewed   **23.** Skewed right   **25.** Mean

27. 3.84   **29.** 63.67, 8.11   **31.** 38653.5; 6762.2

33. 47.5%

35. The percent of the flight lengths between 0.11 and 12.59 days is at least 89%.

37. 2.44, 1.73   **39.** 70

41.

Height of Students

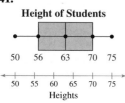

43.

Weight of Football Players

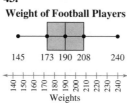

45. P$_{89}$

Chapter Quiz for Chapter 2 *(page 101)*

1. (a)

Class Limits	Midpoint	Class Boundaries	Frequency	Rel Freq	Cum Freq
101-112	106.5	100.5-112.5	3	0.12	3
113-124	118.5	112.5-124.5	11	0.44	14
125-136	130.5	124.5-136.5	7	0.28	21
137-148	142.5	136.5-148.5	2	0.08	23
149-160	154.5	148.5-160.5	2	0.08	25

(b)

(c)

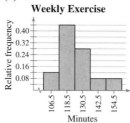

(d) Skewed

(e)

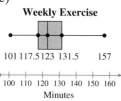

(f)

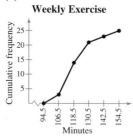

2. 125.22, 13.00

3. (a)

(b)

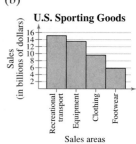

4. (a) 751.63, 784.5, none   (b) 575, 48135.13, 219.40

5. $125,000 and $185,000

6. (a) 76, 79, 88   (b) 12

(c)   **Wins for Each Team**

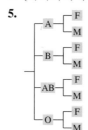

CHAPTER 3

Section 3.1 *(page 111)*

1. (a) Yes   (b) No   (c) No   (d) Yes   (e) Yes

3. {0, 1, 2, 3, 4, 5, 6, 7, 8, 9}

5.

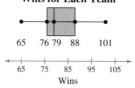

{(A, M), (A, F), (B, M), (B, F), (AB, M), (AB, F), (O, M), (O, F)} where (A, M) represents a male with blood type A, (A, F) represents a female with blood type A, etc.

7. Simple event   **9.** Empirical probability

11. 0.508   **13.** 0.159   **15.** 0.000953   **17.** 0.072

19. 0.944   **21.** (a) 0.5   (b) 0.25   (c) 0.25

23. 0.747   **25.** 0.253

27. The probability of choosing a tea drinker who does not have a college degree.

29. (a) 0.506   (b) 0.117   (c) 0

31. No, 1:5   **33.** 1:3

Section 3.2   *(page 119)*

1. Two events are independent if the occurrence of one of the events does not affect the probability of the occurrence of the other event.

If $P(B|A) = P(B)$ or $P(A|B) = P(A)$, then Events A and B are independent.

3. False. If two events are independent, $P(A|B) = P(A)$.

5. Independent   **7.** Dependent

9. (a) 0.8   (b) 0.0032   (c) Dependent

11. (a) 0.0168   (b) 0.93

13. (a) 0.109   (b) 0.382   (c) 0.618

15. (a) 0.839   (b) 0.167   (c) 0.506   (d) Dependent

17. (a) 0.0000000243   (b) 0.859   (c) 0.141

19. (a) 0.2   (b) 0.04   (c) 0.008   (d) 0.512

(e) 0.488

21. 0.954   **23.** (a) 0.444   (b) 0.4

25. (a) 0.462   (b) 0.538   (c) Yes

(d) Answers will vary.

Section 3.3   *(page 129)*

1. $P(A$ and $B) = 0$ because A and B cannot occur at the same time.

3. True   **5.** Not mutually exclusive

7. Not mutually exclusive   **9.** Mutually exclusive

11. (a) No   (b) 0.423

13. (a) Not mutually exclusive   (b) 0.126

15. (a) 0.069   (b) 0.874   (c) 0.232

17. (a) 0.014   (b) 0.226   (c) 0.774   (d) b and c

19. Answers will vary.

Conclusion: If two events, $\{A\}$ and $\{B\}$, are independent, $P(A$ and $B) = P(A) \cdot P(B)$. If two events are mutually exclusive, $P(A$ and $B) = 0$. The only scenario when two events can be independent and mutually exclusive is if $P(A) = 0$ or $P(B) = 0$.

Section 3.4   *(page 140)*

1. You are counting the number of ways two or more events can occur in sequence.

3. False, a permutation is an ordered arrangement of objects.

5. Permutation   **7.** 6240   **9.** 4500   **11.** 40,320

13. 3,628,800   **15.** 720   **17.** 32,760   **19.** 9,189,180

21. 5,586,853,480   **23.** 56

25. (a) 70   (b) 16   **27.** (a) 56   (b) 56   (c) 112

29. (a) 658,008   (b) 0.00000152   **31.** 0.00153

Review Answers for Chapter 3   *(page 145)*

1. Sample space:

{HHHH, HHHT, HHTH, HHTT, HTHH, HTHT, HTTH, HTTT, THHH, THHT, THTH, THTT, TTHH, TTHT, TTTH, TTTT}

Event: Getting three heads

{HHHT, HHTH, HTHH, THHH}

3. Empirical probability   **5.** Subjective probability

7. Classical probability   **9.** 0.71   **11.** 0.92

13. 0.60   **15.** Independent   **17.** 0.0417

19. Mutually exclusive   **21.** 0.538   **23.** 144

25. 84   **27.** 2730   **29.** 2380

31. (a) 0.955   (b) 0.000000761   (c) 0.045

(d) 0.999999239

Chapter Quiz for Chapter 3   *(page 148)*

1. (a) 0.539   (b) 0.537   (c) 0.543   (d) 0.786

(e) 0.0292

2. Not mutually exclusive; Dependent

3. (a) 518,665   (b) 32,193   (c) 550,858

4. 4500   **5.** 303,600

Cumulative Test for Chapter 3   *(page 149)*

1. Quantitative, Ratio

2. Use the sampling method of data collection. The sampling technique should be a simple random sample because it would be difficult to collect this information from the entire population of students.

3.

Class Limits	Midpoint	Freq	Boundaries	Rel Freq	Cum Freq
90-110	100	9	89.5-110.5	0.300	9
111-131	121	8	110.-131.5	0.267	17
132-152	142	3	131.5-152.5	0.100	20
153-173	163	5	152.5-173.5	0.167	25
174-195	184	5	173.5-195.5	0.167	30

4. Book Expenses

5. Book Expenses

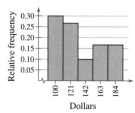

6. Key: 10|3 = 103   **7.** Skewed

```
 9 | 0 1 3 8
10 | 3 4 9
11 | 0 0 1 6 7 8 9
12 | 0 3 7
13 | 2 6
14 |
15 | 0 3 6
16 | 0 2
17 | 0 8
18 | 1 7
19 | 1 5
```

8. Book Expenses

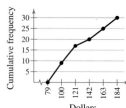

9. $\bar{x} \approx 133.7$
median = 121.5
mode = 110
Statistics

10. range = 105
$s^2 \approx 1036.185$
$s \approx 32.257$
The sample standard deviation is $32.26.

11. $Q_1 = 110$ $Q_2 = 121.5$
$Q_3 = 160$
$IQR = 150$

Book Expenses

90 110 121.5   160   195

80 100 120 140 160 180 200
Dollars

12. 0.467; 0.5   **13.** 0.7   **14.** 0.627   **15.** 142,506

CHAPTER 4

Section 4.1   *(page 159)*

1. A random variable represents a numerical value assigned to an outcome of a probability experiment.
Examples: Answers will vary.

3. False   **5.** True   **7.** Discrete   **9.** Discrete

11. Continuous   **13.** Discrete   **15.** 0.22   **17.** Yes

19. No   **21.** (a) 2.1   (b) 1.09   (c) 1.044

23. (a)

x	f	$P(x)$	$xP(x)$	$(x - \mu)^2 P(x)$
0	316	0.316	0	0.3761
1	425	0.425	0.425	0.0035
2	168	0.168	0.336	0.1388
3	48	0.048	0.144	0.1749
4	29	0.029	0.116	0.2454
5	14	0.014	0.07	0.2139
	1000	1	1.091	1.1527

(b) 1.091   (c) 1.153   (d) 1.074

(e) A household on average has 1.091 dogs with a standard deviation of 1.074.

25. (a)

x	f	$P(x)$	$xP(x)$	$(x - \mu)^2 P(x)$
0	300	0.432	0.000	0.252
1	280	0.403	0.403	0.022
2	95	0.137	0.274	0.209
3	20	0.029	0.087	0.145
	695	1	0.764	0.629

(b) 0.764   (c) 0.629   (d) 0.793

27. (a) 18.375   (b) 41.734   (c) 6.460   (d) 18.375

(e) The publisher can anticipate an average of $72,581.25 (18,375 × $3.95) per week to be generated by magazine sales.

29. (a) 0.35   (b) 0.90

31. (a) 0.741   (b) 0.259   (c) 0.245   **33.** −$0.05

Section 4.2   *(page 173)*

1. (a) $p = 0.50$ (b) $p = 0.20$ (c) $p = 0.80$

3. Is a binomial experiment.
Success: baby recovers
$n = 5, p = 0.80, q = 0.20, x = 0, 1, 2, \ldots, 5$

5. Is not a binomial experiment because there are more than 2 possible outcomes for each trial.

7. (a) 0.088   (b) 0.104   (c) 0.896

9. (a) 0.069   (b) 0.089   (c) 0.911

11. (a) 0.301   (b) 0.653   (c) 0.347

13. (a) $n = 6, p = 0.36$ (b)

Basketball Fans

x	P(x)
0	0.069
1	0.232
2	0.326
3	0.245
4	0.103
5	0.023
6	0.002

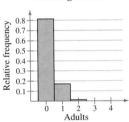

(c) 2.16   (d) 1.382   (e) 1.176

(f) On average 2.16, out of 6, women would consider themselves basketball fans. The standard deviation is 1.176 women.

$X = 0, 5$, or 6 would be uncommon due to their low probabilities.

15. (a) $n = 4, p = 0.05$ (b)

Donating Blood

x	P(x)
0	0.814506
1	0.171475
2	0.013537
3	0.000475
4	0.000006

(c) 0.2   (d) 0.19   (e) 0.436

(f) On average 0.2 eligible adults, out of every 4, give blood. The standard deviation is 0.436 adults.

$X = 2, 3$, or 4 would be uncommon due to their low probabilities.

17. $n = 7, p = 0.10$ **19.** 0.033

x	P(x)
0	0.478
1	0.372
2	0.124
3	0.023
4	0.003
5	0.000
6	0.000
7	0.000

Section 4.3   *(page 182)*

1. Geometric   **3.** Poisson

5. (a) 0.082   (b) 0.469   (c) 0.531

7. (a) 0.249   (b) 0.784   (c) 0.216

9. $\mu = 8$

(a) $P(4) = \dfrac{8^4 e^{-8}}{4!} \approx 0.057$

(b) $P(x \geq 4) = 1 - (P(0) + P(1) + P(2) + P(3))$
$\approx 1 - (0.0003 + 0.0027 + 0.0107 + 0.0286)$
$= 0.9577$

(c) $P(x > 4) = 1 - (P(0) + P(1) + P(2) + P(3) + P(4))$
$\approx 1 - (0.0003 + 0.0027 + 0.0107 + 0.0286 + 0.0573)$
$= 0.9004$

11. (a) 0.3293   (b) 0.8781   (c) 0.1219

13. (a) 1000; 999000; 999.50

On average you would have to play 1000 times until you won the lottery. The standard deviation is 999.50.

(b) 1000 times

Lose money. On average you would win $500 every 1000 times you play the lottery. Hence, the net gain would be $-\$500$

15. (a) 70; 2.0

The standard deviation is 2.0 strokes.

(b) 0.199

17. (a) 0.629   (b) 0.343   (c) 0.029

Review Answers for Chapter 4   *(page 187)*

1. Discrete   **3.** Continuous   **5.** No   **7.** Yes

9. (a)

x	Frequency	P(x)
2	3	0.005
3	12	0.018
4	72	0.111
5	115	0.177
6	169	0.260
7	120	0.185
8	83	0.128
9	48	0.074
10	22	0.034
11	6	0.009
	650	1

—CONTINUED—

9. —CONTINUED—

(b)
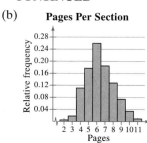

Pages Per Section

(c) 6.377
2.858
1.691

11. (a)

x	Frequency	$P(x)$
0	3	0.015
1	38	0.190
2	83	0.415
3	52	0.260
4	18	0.090
5	5	0.025
6	1	0.005
	200	1

(b)

Televisions Per Household

(c) 2.315
1.076
1.037

13. 3.37

15. Yes, $n = 12$, $p = 0.30$, $q = 0.70$, $x = 0, 1, \ldots, 12$

17. (a) 0.208 (b) 0.322 (c) 0.114

19. (a) 0.294 (b) 0.518 (c) 0.518

21. (a)

x	$P(x)$
0	0.006
1	0.050
2	0.167
3	0.294
4	0.293
5	0.155
6	0.034

(b)

Vacation Destinations

(c) 3.42, 1.4706, 1.213

(d) $P(X \leq 3) = P(1) + P(2) + P(3) = 0.816$

23. (a) 0.096 (b) 0.518 (c) 0.606

25. (a) 0.604 (b) 0.305 (c) 0.091

Chapter Quiz for Chapter 4 *(page 191)*

1. (a) Discrete (b) Continuous

2. (a)

x	Freq	$P(x)$
1	57	0.361
2	37	0.234
3	47	0.297
4	15	0.095
5	2	0.013
	158	1

(b)
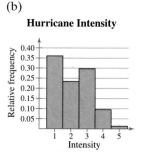

Hurricane Intensity

(c) 2.165; 1.125; 1.061
On average the intensity of a hurricane will be 2.165.
The standard deviation is 1.061.

(d) 0.108

3. (a)

x	$P(x)$
0	0.000003
1	0.000082
2	0.001147
3	0.009175
4	0.045875
5	0.146801
6	0.293601
7	0.335544
8	0.167772

(b)
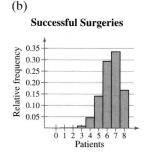

Successful Surgeries

(c) 6.4, 1.28, 1.131 (d) 0.294 (e) 0.202

4. (a) 0.1755 (b) 0.4405 (c) 0.0067

CHAPTER 5

Section 5.1 *(page 198)*

1. Answers will vary.

3. Answers will vary.

Similarities: Both curves will have the same line of symmetry.

Differences: One curve will be more spread out than the other.

5. No **7.** Yes **9.** 2 **11.** (9, 21) **13.** 0.68

15. B   **17.** 0.997   **19.** (19.86, 20.14)

21. (a)

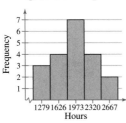

Light Bulb Lifespans

It is reasonable to assume that the lifespan is normally distributed since the histogram is nearly symmetric and bell-shaped.

(b) 1941.35, 432.385

(c) The sample mean of 1941.35 hours is less than the claimed mean, so on the average the bulbs in the sample lasted for a shorter time. The sample standard deviation of 432 hours is greater than the claimed standard deviation, so the bulbs in the sample had a greater variation in lifespan than the manufacturer's claim.

23. 0.68   **25.** (a) 320   (b) 1360   (c) 320

27.

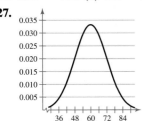

The normal distribution curve is centered at its mean (60) and has 2 points of inflection (48 and 72) representing $\mu \pm \sigma$.

29. (a) 1   (b) 0.25   (c) 0.4

Section 5.2   *(page 209)*

1. $\mu = 0, \sigma = 1$

3. "The" standard normal distribution is used to describe one specific normal distribution ($\mu = 0, \sigma = 1$). "A" normal distribution is used to describe a normal distribution with any mean and standard deviation.

5. (a) 1.2; -2.1; 0   (b) 26,800 miles

7. (a) 1.29; 2.14; -0.86; -1.29

(b) The scores seem typical because all are within 3 standard deviations of the mean. There are an equal number of scores above and below the mean so the scores do not appear to be either above or below average.

9. (a) 167.4   (b) 124.2   **11.** $-0.67, 0, 0.67$

13. 0.33   **15.** 1.29   **17.** 0.3849   **19.** 0.6247

21. 0.9382   **23.** 0.8289   **25.** 0.005   **27.** 0.05

29. 0.475   **31.** 0.437   **33.** 0.551   **35.** 0.05

37. 0.9265   **39.** 0.9744   **41.** 0.2912   **43.** 0.1469

45. 0.4798   **47.** 0.3133   **49.** 0.7540   **51.** 0.0098

53. 0.9544

Section 5.3   *(page 217)*

1. ACT   **3.** (a) 0.1357   (b) 0.6983   (c) 0.1660

5. (a) 0.1539   (b) 0.7147   (c) 0.1314

7. (a) 0.0062   (b) 0.9876   (c) 0.0062

9. (a) 2.28%   (b) 83.4   (c) 72.912   (d) 67.257

11. (a) 43.24%   (b) 10.02   (c) 31.209   (d) 21.486

13. (a) 99.87%   (b) 0.798   (c) 5.67   (d) 3.96

15. (a) 8.024   (b) 7.684   **17.** Out of control

19. Out of control

Section 5.4   *(page 230)*

1. False

3. {000, 002, 004, 006, 008, 020, 022, 024, 026, 028, 040, 042, 044, 046, 048, 060, 062, 064, 066, 068, 080, 082, 084, 086, 088, 200, 202, 204, 206, 208, 220, 222, 224, 226, 228, 240, 242, 244, 246, 248, 260, 262, 264, 266, 268, 280, 282, 284, 286, 288, 400, 402, 404, 406, 408, 420, 422, 424, 426, 428, 440, 442, 444, 446, 448, 460, 462, 464, 466, 468, 480, 482, 484, 486, 488, 600, 602, 604, 606, 608, 620, 622, 624, 626, 628, 640, 642, 644, 646, 648, 660, 662, 664, 666, 668, 680, 682, 684, 686, 688, 800, 802, 804, 806, 808, 820, 822, 824, 826, 828, 840, 842, 844, 846, 848, 860, 862, 864, 866, 868, 880, 882, 884, 886, 888}

5. 87.5, 1.804

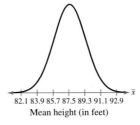

Mean height (in feet)

7. 114.7, 8.497

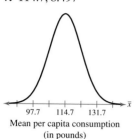

97.7   114.7   131.7
Mean per capita consumption
(in pounds)

9. 87.5, 1.042; 87.5, 1.042

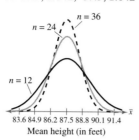

$n = 36$
$n = 24$
$n = 12$

83.6 84.9 86.2 87.5 88.8 90.1 91.4
Mean height (in feet)

11. (c)   **13.** ≈ 1 **15.** 0.6319   **17.** 0

19. Sample of 20 women with mean height less than 70 inches.

21. Yes   **23.** 0.0436   **25.** 1

Section 5.5   *(page 241)*

1. Use normal distribution. 70, 4.583

3. Cannot use normal distribution

5. d   **7.** a   **9.** a   **11.** c

13. Binomial: 0.549; Normal: 0.5463

15. (a) 0.0000199   (b) 0.000023   (c) 0.999977
    (d) 0.1635

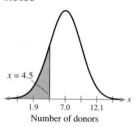

$x = 4.5$

1.9   7.0   12.1
Number of donors

17. (a) 0.0465

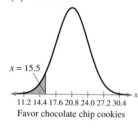

$x = 15.5$

11.2 14.4 17.6 20.8 24.0 27.2 30.4
Favor chocolate chip cookies

(b) 0.9767

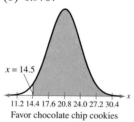

$x = 14.5$

11.2 14.4 17.6 20.8 24.0 27.2 30.4
Favor chocolate chip cookies

(c) 0.9535

$x = 15.5$

11.2 14.4 17.6 20.8 24.0 27.2 30.4
Favor chocolate chip cookies

(d) 0.1635

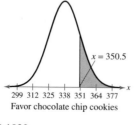

$x = 350.5$

299 312 325 338 351 364 377
Favor chocolate chip cookies

19. Highly unlikely; no   **21.** 0.1020

Review Answers for Chapter 5   *(page 245)*

1. $\mu = 15$, $\sigma = 3$ **3.** (540, 800)   **5.** 0.68

7. -2.25; 0.5; 2; 3.5   **9.** 0.2005

11. 0.3936   **13.** 0.0465   **15.** 0.4495   **17.** 0.3519

19. 0.1336   **21.** 0.8997   **23.** 0.9236   **25.** 0.0124

27. The first participant had the lower reading.

29. (a) 0.3156   (b) 0.3099   (c) 0.3446

31. (a) 1.608   (b) 1.729

33. {0 0 0, 0 0 200, 0 0 40, 0 0 600, 0 0 80, 0 200 0, 0 200 200, 0 200 40, 0 200 600, 0 200 80, 0 40 0, 0 40 200, 0 40 40, 0 40 600, 0 40 80, 0 600 0, 0 600 200, 0 600 40, 0 600 600, 0 600 80, 0 80 0, 0 80 200, 0 80 40, 0 80 600, 0 80 80, 200 0 0, 200 0 200, 200 0 40, 200 0 600, 200 0 80, 200 200 0, 200 200 200, 200 200 40, 200 200 600, 200 200 80, 200 40 0, 200 40 200, 200 40 40, 200 40 600, 200 40 80, 200 600 0, 200 600 200, 200 600 40, 200 600 600, 200 600 80, 200 80 0, 200 80 200, 200 80 40, 200 80 600, 200 80 80, 40 0 0, 40 0 200, 40 0 40, 40 0 600, 40 0 80, 40 200 0, 40 200 200, 40 200 40, 40 200 600, 40 200 80, 40 40 0, 40 40 200, 40 40 40, 40 40 600, 40 40 80, 40 600 0, 40 600 200, 40 600 40, 40 600 600, 40 600 80, 40 80 0, 40 80 200, 40 80 40, 40 80 600, 40 80 80, 600 0 0, 600 0 200, 600 0 40, 600 0 600, 600 0 80, 600 200 0, 600 200 200, 600 200 40, 600 200 600, 600 200 80, 600 40 0, 600 40 200, 600 40 40, 600 40 600, 600 40 80, 600 600 0, 600 600 200, 600 600 40, 600 600 600, 600 600 80, 600 80 0, 600 80 200, 600 80 40, 600 80 600, 600 80 80, 80 0 0, 80 0 200, 80 0 40, 80 0 600, 80 0 80, 80 200 0, 80 200 200, 80 200 40, 80 200 600, 80 200 80, 80 40 0, 80 40 200, 80 40 40, 80 40 600, 80 40 80, 80 600 0, 80 600 200, 80 600 40, 80 600 600, 80 600 80, 80 80 0, 80 80 200, 80 80 40, 80 80 600, 80 80 80}

184,218.504, 184,126.153

35. (a) 0.0485   (b) 0.8180   (c) 0.0823

37. 154.8, 8.72

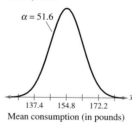

$\alpha = 51.6$

137.4   154.8   172.2
Mean consumption (in pounds)

39. (a) 0   (b) 0   **41.** Do not use normal distribution.

43. $P(x > 24.5)$

45. Use normal distribution.

0.0032

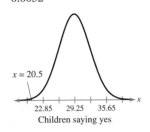

$x = 20.5$

22.85 29.25 35.65

Children saying yes

Chapter Quiz for Chapter 5 *(page 249)*

1. (a) 0.9821 (b) 0.9994 (c) 0.9802 (d) 0.8135

2. (a) 0.9198 (b) 0.1940 (c) 0.0456 **3.** 0.1292

4. 0.5759 **5.** 77.64% **6.** 1509.8 **7.** 332.688

8. 253.052 **9.** 0

10. More likely to select one student with a test score greater than 300.

11. Use normal distribution; 16.32, 2.285 **12.** 0.3594

CHAPTER 6

Section 6.1 *(page 259)*

1. You are more likely to be correct using an interval estimate since it is unlikely that a point estimate will equal the population mean exactly.

3. d **5.** 1.28 **7.** 0.47 **9.** 1.76 **11.** 0.685

13. (14.775, 15.625) **15.** (4.179, 4.361)

17. (244.928, 316.872); (238.040, 323.760)

19. (25.746, 27.854); (25.545, 28.055)

21. (94.577, 105.423)

23. (96.165, 103.835); $n = 40$ CI is wider

25. (9.719, 11.185)

27. (8.687, 12.217); $s = 5.130$ CI is wider

29. (a) An increase in the level of confidence will widen the confidence interval.

(b) An increase in the sample size will narrow the confidence interval.

(c) An increase in the standard deviation will widen the confidence interval.

31. (8.430, 9.704); (8.070, 10.064) **33.** 89

99% CI is wider.

35. (a) 121 (b) 208

99% CI requires larger sample because more information is needed from the population to be 99% confident.

37. (a) 32 (b) 87

$E = 0.15$ requires a larger sample size. As the error size decreases, a larger sample must be taken to obtain enough information from the population to ensure desired accuracy.

39. (a) 42 (b) 60

$\sigma = 0.30$ requires a larger sample size. Due to the increased variability in the population, a larger sample size is needed to ensure the desired accuracy.

41. (a) An increase in the level of confidence will increase the minimum sample size required.

(b) An increase (larger E) in the error tolerance will decrease the minimum sample size required.

(c) An increase in the population standard deviation will increase the minimum sample size required.

43. (303.498, 311.252) **45.** (13.680, 15.200)

47. (a) 0.707 (b) 0.949 (c) 0.962 (d) 0.975

(e) The finite population correction factor approaches 1 as the sample size decreases while the population size remains the same.

49. $n = \left(\dfrac{z_c\sigma}{E}\right)^2 \Rightarrow \sqrt{n} = \dfrac{z_c\sigma}{E} \Rightarrow E = \dfrac{z_c\sigma}{\sqrt{n}}$

Section 6.2 *(page 271)*

1. 1.833 **3.** 2.947 **5.** (a) 2.450 (b) 2.664

7. (a) (10.855, 14.145) (b) (11.157, 13.843); t-CI is wider.

9. (a) (4.059, 4.541) (b) (4.089, 4.511); t-CI is wider.

11. (59.482, 90.518); 15.518

13. (61.852, 88.148); 13.148; t-CI is wider.

15. (a) (3.604, 4.996) (b) (4.212, 4.388); t-CI is wider.

17. (a) 2174.75 (b) 100.341 (c) (2071.626, 2277.874)

19. (a) 909.083 (b) 305.266 (c) (635.374, 1182.792)

21. use normal distribution; (1.248, 1.252)

23. use t-distribution; (22.762, 25.238)

25. Cannot use normal or t-distribution

27. $n = 25, \bar{x} = 56.0, s = 0.25$

$\pm t_{0.99} \Rightarrow 99\%$ t-CI

$\bar{x} \pm t_c \dfrac{s}{\sqrt{n}} = 56.0 \pm 2.797\dfrac{0.25}{\sqrt{25}} \approx (55.860, 56.140)$

They are not making good tennis balls since desired bounce height of 55.5 inches is not contained between 55.850 and 56.140 inches.

Section 6.3   *(page 280)*

1. 0.080, 0.920   **3.** 0.120, 0.880   **5.** 0.066, 0.934

7. 0.691, 0.309   **9.** (0.064, 0.096); (0.058, 0.102)

11. (0.117, 0.123); (0.115, 0.125)

13. (0.053, 0.079); (0.049, 0.083)

15. (0.635, 0.747); (0.617, 0.765)

17. (a) 1068   (b) 822

(c) Having an estimate of the proportion reduces the minimum samples size needed.

19. (a) 1688   (b) 1266

(c) Having an estimate of the proportion reduces the minimum sample size needed.

21. (a) (0.554, 0.666)   (b) (0.383, 0.497)

(c) It is unlikely that the two proportions are equal because the confidence intervals estimating the proportions do not overlap.

23. (30.4%, 32.4%) is approximately a 95.2% CI.

25. If $n\hat{p} < 5$ or $n\hat{q} < 5$, the sampling distribution of $\hat{p}$ may not be normally distributed; therefore preventing the use of z_c when calculating the confidence interval.

27.

p	$q = 1 - p$	pq	p	$q = 1 - p$	pq
0.1	0.9	0.09	0.45	0.55	0.2475
0.2	0.8	0.16	0.46	0.54	0.2484
0.3	0.7	0.21	0.47	0.53	0.2491
0.4	0.6	0.24	0.48	0.52	0.2496
0.5	0.5	0.25	0.49	0.51	0.2499
0.6	0.4	0.24	0.50	0.50	0.2500
0.7	0.3	0.21	0.51	0.49	0.2499
0.8	0.2	0.16	0.52	0.48	0.2496
0.9	0.1	0.09	0.53	0.47	0.2491
1.0	0.0	0.00	0.54	0.46	0.2484
			0.55	0.45	0.2475

$\hat{p} = 0.5$ give the maximum value of $\hat{p}\hat{q}$.

Section 6.4   *(page 288)*

1. 16.919, 3.325   **3.** 35.479, 10.283   **5.** 52.336, 13.121

7. (a) (0.0000413, 0.000157)   (b) (0.00643, 0.0125)

9. (a) (0.0305, 0.191)   (b) (0.175, 0.437)

11. (a) (4.342, 44.636)   (b) (2.084, 6.681)

13. (a) (359.596, 1829.774)   (b) (18.963, 42.776)

15. (a) (6621.545, 24422.477)   (b) (81.373, 156.277)

17. Yes

Review Answers for Chapter 6   *(page 293)*

1. (a) 103.5   (b) 9.016   **3.** (10.246, 10.354)

5. 47   **7.** 1.415   **9.** 9.623   **11.** (43.177, 62.423)

13. (73.634, 86.366)   **15.** 0.420, 0.580   **17.** 0.292, 0.708

19. (0.387, 0.453)   **21.** (0.240, 0.344)   **23.** 273

25. 23.377, 4.404   **27.** 14.067, 2.167

29. (0.003, 0.013); (0.055, 0.114)

Chapter Quiz for Chapter 6   *(page 296)*

1. (a) 100.057   (b) 11.101   (c) (88.956, 111.158)

2. 34

3. (a) 6.610   (b) 3.376   (c) (4.653, 8.567)

(d) (4.789, 8.431)

4. (3231.737, 4178.263)

5. (a) 0.660   (b) (0.643, 0.677)   (c) 930

6. (a) (417.374, 1359.563)   (b) (20.430, 36.872)

Cumulative Test for Chapter 4-6   *(page 297)*

1. 0.770; (0.732, 0.808)   **2.** 2936   **3.** 0.455

4. 364.980; 83.945; 9.162

You would expect 364.98 women to say that the media have a negative effect on women's health. The standard deviation is 9.162.

5. Use normal distribution; 364.980; 9.162

6. (25.336, 25.864)

7. Normal distribution was used since $n \geq 30$ and σ was unknown.

8. 0.05548

≈ 0

You are more likely to select one woman with a BMI less than 20.

9. (a) (6.495, 18.506)   (b) (2.549, 4.302)

CHAPTER 7

Section 7.1   *(page 312)*

1. $H_0: \mu \leq 645, H_a: \mu > 645$ **3.** $H_0: \sigma = 5, H_a: \sigma \neq 5$

5. $H_0: p \geq 0.45, H_a: p < 0.45$

7. c $H_a: \mu < 3$ **9.** b $H_a: \mu \neq 3$

11. $\mu > 750$
$H_0: \mu \le 750$ and $H_a: \mu > 750$
(Claim: H_a)

13. $\sigma \le 1220$
$H_0: \sigma \le 1220$ and $H_a: \sigma > 1220$
(Claim: H_0)

15. $H_0: p = 0.44$
$H_0: p = 0.44$ and $H_a: p \ne 0.44$
(Claim: H_0)

17. Type I: Rejecting $H_0: p \ge 0.24$ when actually $p \ge 0.24$
Type II: Not rejecting $H_0: p \ge 0.24$ when actually $p < 0.24$.

19. Type I: Rejecting $H_0: \sigma \le 23$ when actually $\sigma \le 23$.
Type II: Not rejecting $H_0: \sigma \le 23$ when actually $\sigma > 23$.

21. Type I: Rejecting $H_0: p \le 0.60$ when actually $p \le 0.60$
Type II: Not rejecting $H_0: p \le 0.24$ when actually $p > 0.24$.

23. Left-tailed   **25.** Two-tailed   **27.** Two-tailed

29. (a) There is enough evidence to reject the company's claim.
(b) There is not enough evidence to decide that the company's claim is false.

31. (a) There is enough evidence to support the Dept of Labor's claim.
(b) There is not enough evidence to decide that the Dept of Labor's claim is true.

33. (a) There is enough evidence to reject the manufacturer's claim.
(b) There is not enough evidence to reject the manufacturer's claim.

35. $\mu = 10$ **37.** (a) $H_0: \mu \le 15$ (b) $H_0: \mu \ge 15$

39. If you decrease α, you are decreasing the probability that you reject H_0. Therefore, you are increasing the probability of failing to reject H_0. This could increase β, the probability of failing to reject H_0 when H_0 is false.

41. (a) Reject H_0 (b) Do not reject H_0
(c) Do not reject H_0

Section 7.2   *(page 324)*

1. Specify the level of significance, α. Decide whether the test is left-tailed, right-tailed, or two-tailed. Find the critical value(s), z_0, as follows: (a) Left-tailed: find z_0 that corresponds to an area of α. (b) Right-tailed: find z_0 that corresponds to an area of $1 - \alpha$. (c) Two-tailed: find $\pm z_0$ that corresponds to $\frac{1}{2}\alpha$ and $1 - \frac{1}{2}\alpha$.

3. 1.645   **5.** -1.88 **7.** ± 2.33

9. Right-tailed $(\alpha = 0.01)$ **11.** Two-tailed $(\alpha = 0.10)$

13. (a) Fail to reject H_0 (b) Reject H_0
(c) Fail to reject H_0 (d) Reject H_0

15. (a) Fail to reject H_0 (b) Fail to reject H_0
(c) Fail to reject H_0 (d) Reject H_0

17. Reject H_0 **19.** Reject H_0

21. (a) $H_0: \mu = 40$ $H_a: \mu \ne 40$ (Claim: H_0)
(b) ± 2.575 (c) -0.584 (d) Fail to reject H_0

23. (a) $H_0: \mu \ge 750$ $H_a: \mu < 750$ (Claim: H_0)
(b) -2.05 (c) -0.500 (d) Fail to reject H_0

25. (a) $H_0: \mu \le 28$ $H_a: \mu > 28$ (Claim: H_a)
(b) 1.55   (c) 1.318   (d) Fail to reject H_0

27. (a) Fail to reject H_0 (b) Reject H_0

29. (a) $H_0: \mu \le 260$ $H_a: \mu > 260$ (Claim: H_a)
(b) 0.838   (c) 0.2005   (d) Fail to reject H_0

31. (a) $H_0: \mu \le 7$ $H_a: \mu > 7$ (Claim: H_a)
(b) 2.996   (c) 0.0013   (d) Reject H_0

33. (a) $H_0: \mu = 15$ $H_a: \mu \ne 15$ (Claim: H_0)
(b) -0.219 (c) 0.8258   (d) Fail to reject H_0

35. Fail to reject H_0

37. Using the classical z-test, the test statistic is compared to critical values. The z-test using a P-value compares the P-value to the level of significance α.

Section 7.3   *(page 336)*

1. Identify the level of significance, α, and the degrees of freedom, $df = n - 1$. Find the critical value(s) using the t-distribution table in the row with $n - 1$ df. If the hypothesis test is:
(1) left-tailed, use "One Tail α" column with a negative sign.
(2) right-tailed, use "One Tail α" column with a positive sign.
(3) two-tailed, use "Two Tail α" column with a negative and a positive sign.

3. 1.717   **5.** -2.101 **7.** ± 2.779

9. (a) Fail to reject H_0 (b) Fail to reject H_0
(c) Fail to reject H_0 (d) Reject H_0

11. (a) Fail to reject H_0 (b) Fail to reject H_0
(c) Reject H_0 (d) Reject H_0

13. $H_0: \mu = 15$ (claim)
$H_a: \mu \ne 15$
$t_0 = \pm 4.032$
$t = -0.834$
Fail to reject H_0

15. $H_0: \mu \ge 8000$ (claim)
$H_a: \mu < 8000$
$t_0 = -2.492$
$t = -3.333$
Reject H_0

17. (a) $H_0: \mu \geq 100$; $H_a: \mu < 100$ (claim)
  (b) $t_0 = -3.747$ (c) $t = -4.472$ (d) Reject H_0
19. (a) $H_0: \mu \leq 1$; $H_a: \mu > 1$ (claim)
  (b) $t_0 = 1.796$ (c) $t = 2.309$ (d) Reject H_0
21. (a) $H_0: \mu = \$24{,}600$ (claim); $H_a: \mu \neq \$24{,}600$
  (b) $t_0 = \pm 2.262$ (c) $t = -0.572$
  (d) Fail to reject H_0
23. (a) $H_0: \mu \geq 3.0$; $H_a: \mu < 3.0$ (claim)
  (b) 0.130   (c) Fail to reject H_0
25. (a) $H_0: \mu \geq 32$; $H_a: \mu < 32$ (claim)
  (b) 0.034   (c) Fail to reject H_0
27. P-value $= 0.096 > 0.01 = \alpha$, fail to reject H_0.
29. Use the t-distribution
  $H_0: \mu \geq 21$ (claim) and $H_a: \mu < 21$
  $t = -1.118$
  P-value $= 0.163$
  Fail to reject H_0
31. Use the z-distribution
  $H_0: \mu \geq 21$ (claim) and $H_a: \mu < 21$
  $z = -0.894$
  P-value $= 0.1867$
  Fail to reject H_0
33. It is not necessary to a hypothesis test to test the repairer's claim.

$$t = \frac{\bar{x} - \mu}{\frac{s}{\sqrt{n}}} = \frac{75 - 50}{\frac{12.50}{\sqrt{5}}} = 4.472$$

Recall from #17 that:

$$t = \frac{\bar{x} - \mu}{\frac{s}{\sqrt{n}}} = \frac{75 - 100}{\frac{12.50}{\sqrt{5}}} = -4.472$$

Section 7.4   *(page 344)*

1. Verify that $np \geq 5$ and $nq \geq 5$. State H_0 and H_a. Specify the level of significance, α. Determine the critical value(s) and rejection region(s). Find the standardized test statistic. Make a decision and interpret in the context of the original claim.

3. Use normal distribution
  $H_0: p = 0.25$
  $H_a: p \neq 0.25$ (claim)
  $z_0 = \pm 1.96$
  $z = -0.260$
  Fail to reject H_0

5. Use normal distribution
  $H_0: p \geq 0.60$
  $H_a: p < 0.60$ (claim)
  $z_o = -2.33$
  $z = -0.242$
  Fail to reject H_0

7. (a) $H_0: p \geq 0.25$ (claim); $H_a: p < 0.25$
  (b) $z_0 = -2.33$ (c) $z \approx -0.163$
  (d) Fail to reject H_0.
9. (a) $H_0: p \leq 0.30$ (claim); $H_a: p > 0.30$
  (b) $z_0 = 1.88$ (c) $z \approx 1.414$
  (d) Fail to reject H_0.
11. (a) $H_0: p = 0.60$ (claim); $H_a: p \neq 0.60$
  (b) $z_0 = \pm 2.33$ (c) $z = -2.571$ (d) Reject H_0.
13. $H_0: p \geq 0.52$ (claim); $H_a: p < 0.52$
  $z_o = -1.645$
  $z = -0.439$
  Fail to reject H_0.
15. P-values are calculated in the same manner as when using the Z-test for testing the mean.
  $H_0: p \geq 0.25$ (claim)
  $H_a: p < 0.25$
  $z = -0.103$
  P-value $= 0.4602$
  Fail to reject H_0

Section 7.5   *(page 353)*

1. Specify the level of significance, α. Determine the degrees of freedom. Determine the critical values using the χ^2 distribution. If (a) right-tailed test, use the value that corresponds to df and α. (b) left-tailed test, use the value that corresponds to df and $1 - \alpha$. (c) two-tailed test, use the value that corresponds to df and $\frac{1}{2}\alpha$ and $1 - \frac{1}{2}\alpha$.
3. 38.885   **5.** 0.872   **7.** 7.261, 24.996
9. (a) Fail to reject H_0 (b) Fail to reject H_0
  (c) Fail to reject H_0 (d) Reject H_0
11. (a) Fail to reject H_0 (b) Reject H_0
  (c) Reject H_0 (d) Fail to reject H_0
13. $H_0: \sigma^2 = 0.52$ (claim); $H_a: \sigma^2 \neq 0.52$
  $\chi_L^2 = 7.564$ $\chi_R^2 = 30.191$; $\chi^2 = 16.608$
  Fail to reject H_0.
15. $H_0: \sigma \geq 40$; $H_a: \sigma < 40$ (claim)
  $\chi_0^2 = 3.053$; $\chi^2 = 11.444$
  Fail to reject H_0.
17. (a) $H_0: \sigma^2 = 3$ (claim); $H_a: \sigma^2 \neq 3$
  (b) $\chi_L^2 = 13.844$ $\chi_R^2 = 41.923$
  (c) $\chi^2 = 24.267$
  (d) Fail to reject H_0.

19. (a) H_0: $\sigma \geq 29$; H_a: $\sigma < 29$ (claim)
    (b) $\chi_0^2 = 13.240$ (c) $\chi^2 = 19.159$
    (d) Fail to reject H_0.

21. (a) H_0: $\sigma \leq 0.5$ (claim); H_a: $\sigma > 0.5$
    (b) $\chi_0^2 = 33.196$ (c) $\chi^2 = 47.040$ (d) Reject H_0.

23. (a) H_0: $\sigma^2 \leq 20{,}000$; H_a: $\sigma^2 > 20{,}000$ (claim)
    (b) $\chi_0^2 = 24.996$ (c) $\chi^2 = 16.011$
    (d) Fail to reject H_0.

25. P-value $= 0.381$
    Fail to reject H_0.

Review Answers for Chapter 7   *(page 361)*

1. H_0: $\mu \leq 1593$ (claim); H_a: $\mu > 1593$

3. H_0: $\mu = 150{,}020$ H_a: $\mu \neq 150{,}020$ (claim)

5. (a) H_0: $p = 0.85$ (claim); H_a: $p \neq 0.85$
    (b) Type I error will occur if H_0 is rejected when the actual proportion of American adults who use nonprescription pain relievers is 0.85.

        Type II error if H_0 is not rejected when the actual proportion of American adults who use nonperscription pain relievers is not 0.85.

    (c) Two-tailed
    (d) There is enough evidence to reject the claim.
    (e) There is not enough evidence to reject the claim.

7. (a) H_0: $\mu \leq 50$ (claim); H_a: $\mu > 50$
    (b) Type I error will occur if H_0 is rejected when the actual standard deviation sodium content is no more than 50 mg.

        Type II error if H_0 is not rejected when the actual standard deviation sodium content is more than 50 mg.

    (c) Right-tailed
    (d) There is enough evidence to reject the claim.
    (e) There is not enough evidence to reject the claim.

9. $z_0 = -2.05$ **11.** $z_0 = 1.96$

13. H_0: $\mu \leq 45$ (claim); H_a: $\mu > 45$
    $z_0 = 1.645$; $z = 2.128$
    Reject H_0.

15. H_0: $\mu \geq 5.500$; H_a: $\mu < 5.500$ (claim)
    $z_0 = -2.33$; $z = -1.636$
    Fail to reject H_0

17. H_0: $\mu \leq 0.05$ (claim); H_a: $\mu > 0.05$
    $z = 2.200$; P-value $= 0.0139$
    $\alpha = 0.10 \Longrightarrow$ Reject H_0
    $\alpha = 0.05 \Longrightarrow$ Reject H_0
    $\alpha = 0.01 \Longrightarrow$ Fail to reject H_0

19. $t_0 = \pm 2.093$ **21.** $t_0 = -1.345$

23. H_0: $\mu = 95$; H_a: $\mu \neq 95$ (claim)
    $t_0 = \pm 2.201$; $t = -2.038$
    Fail to reject H_0

25. H_0: $\mu \geq 0$ (claim) and H_a: $\mu < 0$
    $t_0 = -1.341$; $t = -1.304$
    Fail to reject H_0.

27. H_0: $\mu = \$25$ (claim); H_a: $\mu \neq \$25$
    $t_0 = \pm 1.740$; $t = 1.642$
    Fail to reject H_0.

29. H_0: $\mu \geq 4$ (claim); H_a: $\mu < 4$
    $t_0 = -2.539$; $t = -0.510$
    Fail to reject H_0.

31. H_0: $p = 0.15$ (claim); H_a: $p \neq 0.15$
    $z_0 = \pm 1.96$; $z = -1.063$
    Fail to reject H_0.

33. Because $np = 3.6$ is less than 5, the normal distribution cannot be used to approximate the binomial distribution.

35. H_0: $p \leq 0.40$; H_a: $p > 0.40$ (claim)
    $z_0 = 1.282$; $z = 2.628$
    Reject H_0.

37. $\chi_0^2 = 30.144$ **39.** $\chi_0^2 = 33.196$

41. H_0: $\sigma^2 \leq 2$; H_a: $\sigma^2 > 2$ (claim)
    $\chi_0^2 = 24.769$; $\chi^2 = 20.230$
    Fail to reject H_0.

43. H_0: $\sigma^2 = 1.25$ (claim); H_a: $\sigma \neq 1.25$
    $\chi_L^2 = 0.831$; $\chi_R^2 = 12.833$; $\chi^2 = 3.395$
    Fail to reject H_0.

45. H_0: $\sigma^2 \leq 0.01$ (claim); H_a: $\sigma^2 > 0.01$
    $\chi_0^2 = 49.645$; $\chi^2 = 172.800$
    Reject H_0.

Chapter Quiz for Chapter 7   *(page 365)*

1. (a) H_0: $\mu \geq 94$ (claim); H_a: $\mu < 94$
    (b) Type I error occurs if the H_0 is rejected when actually the mean consumption is at least 94 pounds.

        Type II error occurs if the H_0 has not been rejected when actually the mean consumption is less than 94 pounds.

    (c) Left tailed; z-test   (d) $z_0 = -2.05$
    (e) $z = -0.169$ (f) Fail to reject H_0.

2. (a) $H_0: \mu \geq 25$ (claim); $H_a: \mu < 25$

(b) Type I error occurs if the H_0 is rejected when actually the mean mpg is at least 25.

Type II error occurs if the H_0 has not been rejected when actually the mean mpg is less than 25.

(c) Left tailed; t-test   (d) $t_0 = -1.895$

(e) $t = -1.131$ (f) Fail to reject H_0.

3. (a) $H_0: p \leq 0.10$ (claim); $H_a: p > 0.10$

(b) Type I error occurs if the H_0 is rejected when actually the production of microwaves needing repair is no more than 0.10.

Type II error occurs if the H_0 has not been rejected when actually the production of microwaves needing repair is more than 0.10.

(c) Right tailed; z-test   (d) $z_0 = 1.75$

(e) $z = 0.755$ (f) Fail to reject H_0.

4. (a) $H_0: \sigma = 105$ (claim); $H_a: \sigma \neq 105$

(b) Type I error occurs if the H_0 is rejected when actually the standard deviation of the scores is 105.

Type II error occurs if the H_0 has not been rejected when actually the standard deviation of the scores is not 105.

(c) Two-tailed; χ^2 test

(d) $\chi_L^2 = 3.565$; $\chi_R^2 = 29.819$ (e) $\chi^2 = 15.056$

(f) Fail to reject H_0.

5. (a) $H_0: \mu = \$53{,}102$ (claim); $H_a: \mu \neq \$53{,}102$

(b) Type I error occurs if the H_0 is rejected when actually the mean salary is $53,102.

Type II error occurs if the H_0 has not been rejected when actually the mean salary is not $53,102.

(c) Two-tailed; t-test

(d) Reject H_0 if P-value $\leq \alpha = 0.05$.

(e) $t = -0.480$; P-value $= 0.640$

(f) Fail to reject H_0.

CHAPTER 8

Section 8.1   *(page 373)*

1. State the hypotheses and identify the claim. Specify the level of significance and find the critical value(s). Find the standardized test statistic. Make a decision and interpret in the context of the claim.

3. (a) 2   (b) 7.603   (c) z is in the rejection region.

(d) Reject the claim

---

5. (a) 30   (b) $z = 1.84$

(c) z is not in the rejection region.

(d) Fail to reject H_0.

7. (a) $H_0: \mu_1 = \mu_2$ (claim); $H_1: \mu_1 \neq \mu_2$

(b) $z_0 = \pm 1.645$ (c) $z \approx -2.786$ (d) Reject H_0

9. (a) $H_0: \mu_1 \geq \mu_2$; $H_1: \mu_1 < \mu_2$ (claim)

(b) $z_0 = -2.33$ (c) $z \approx -1.536$

(d) Fail to reject H_0

11. (a) $H_0: \mu_1 = \mu_2$ (claim); $H_1: \mu_1 \neq \mu_2$

(b) $z_0 = \pm 2.575$ (c) $z \approx 0.310$

(d) Fail to reject H_0

13. (a) $H_0: \mu_1 \leq \mu_2$; $H_1: \mu_1 > \mu_2$ (claim)

(b) $z_0 = 1.96$ (c) $z \approx 4.988$ (d) Reject H_0

15. (a) $H_0: \mu_1 = \mu_2$ (claim); $H_1: \mu_1 \neq \mu_2$

(b) $z_0 = \pm 2.575$ (c) $z \approx 66.172$ (d) Reject H_0

17. They are equivalent through algebraic manipulation of the equation.

$$\mu_1 = \mu_2 \Rightarrow \mu_1 - \mu_2 = 0$$

19. $H_0: \mu_1 - \mu_2 = -9$ (claim); $H_1: \mu_1 - \mu_2 \neq -9$

Fail to reject H_0. There is not enough evidence to reject the claim.

21. $H_0: \mu_1 - \mu_2 \leq 6000$; $H_1: \mu_1 - \mu_2 > 6000$ (claim)

Fail to reject H_0. There is not enough evidence to support the claim.

23. $-2.45 < \mu_1 - \mu_2 < 0.65$

25. There is not enough evidence to support the claim.

27. $H_0: \mu_1 - \mu_2 \leq 0$ and $H_1: \mu_1 - \mu_2 > 0$ (claim)

Since 0 is contained in the 95% CI for $\mu_1 - \mu_2$, fail to reject H_0. There is not enough evidence to support the claim.

Section 8.2   *(page 384)*

1. State hypotheses and identify the claim. Specify the level of significance. Determine the degrees of freedom. Find the critical value(s) and identify the rejection region(s). Find the standardized test statistic. Make a decision and interpret in the context of the original claim.

3. (a) $t_0 = \pm 1.725$ (b) $t_0 = \pm 1.833$

5. (a) $t_0 = -2.074$ (b) $t_0 = -2.306$

7. $H_0: \mu_1 = \mu_2$ (claim); $H_a: \mu_1 \neq \mu_2$

(a) -1.8 (b) $t \approx -1.199$

(c) t is not in the rejection region.

(d) Fail to reject H_0. There is not enough evidence to reject the claim.

9. $H_0: \mu_1 \leq \mu_2$ (claim); $H_a: \mu_1 > \mu_2$

(a) -55 (b) $t \approx -1.073$

(c) t is not in the rejection region.

(d) Fail to reject H_0. There is not enough evidence to reject the claim.

11. (a) $H_0: \mu_1 = \mu_2$ (claim); $H_a: \mu_1 \neq \mu_2$

(b) d.f. $= 35$; $t_0 = \pm 1.645$ (c) $t \approx -0.833$

(d) Fail to reject H_0. There is not enough evidence to reject the claim.

13. (a) $H_0: \mu_1 \geq \mu_2$; $H_a: \mu_1 < \mu_2$ (claim)

(b) d.f. $= 13$; $t_0 = -1.350$ (c) $t = -1.912$

(d) Reject H_0. There is enough evidence to support the claim.

15. (a) $H_0: \mu_1 \leq \mu_2$; $H_a: \mu_1 > \mu_2$ (claim)

(b) d.f. $= 14$; $t_0 = 1.761$ (c) $t = 2.098$

(d) Reject H_0. There is enough evidence to support the claim.

17. (a) $H_0: \mu_1 = \mu_2$; $H_a: \mu_1 \neq \mu_2$ (claim)

(b) d.f. $= 21$; $t_0 = \pm 2.831$ (c) $t \approx -6.410$

(d) Reject H_0. There is enough evidence to support the claim.

19. (a) $H_0: \mu_1 \geq \mu_2$; $H_a: \mu_1 < \mu_2$ (claim)

(b) d.f. $= 42$; $t_0 = -1.282$ (c) $t \approx -4.295$

(d) Reject H_0. There is enough evidence to support the claim and to recommend changing to the new method.

21. $-15.664 < \mu_1 - \mu_2 < -4.336$

23. $-0.849 < \mu_1 - \mu_2 < 2.849$

Section 8.3 *(page 395)*

1. Two samples are dependent if each member of one sample corresponds to a member of the other sample. Example: The weights of 22 people before starting an exercise program and the weights of the same 22 people six weeks after starting the exercise program. Two samples are independent if the sample selected from one population is not related to the sample selected from the second population. Example: The weights of 25 cats and the weights of 20 dogs.

3. Independent **5.** Dependent

7. Independent **9.** Dependent

11. $H_0: \mu_d \geq 0$; $H_a: \mu_d < 0$ (claim)

$\alpha = 0.05$, d.f. $= 9$

$t_0 = -1.833$; $t \approx 21.082$

Fail to reject H_0.

13. $H_0: \mu_d \leq 0$ (claim); $H_a: \mu_d > 0$

$\alpha = 0.10$, d.f. $= 15$

$t_0 = 1.341$; $t \approx 67.778$

Reject H_0.

15. (a) $H_0: \mu_d \geq 0$; $H_a: \mu_d < 0$ (claim) (b) $t_0 = -2.650$

(c) $\bar{d} \approx -33.714$; $s_d \approx 42.034$ (d) $t \approx -3.001$

(e) Reject H_0. There is enough evidence to support the claim that the second SAT scores are improved.

17. (a) $H_0: \mu_d \geq 0$; $H_a: \mu_d < 0$ (claim) (b) $t_0 = -1.415$

(c) $\bar{d} \approx -1.125$; $s_d \approx 0.871$ (d) $t \approx -3.653$

(e) Reject H_0. There is enough evidence to support the claim that the fuel additive improved gas mileage.

19. (a) $H_0: \mu_d \leq 0$; $H_a: \mu_d > 0$ (claim) (b) $t_0 = 1.796$

(c) $\bar{d} \approx 16.833$; $s_d \approx 6.952$ (d) $t \approx 8.388$

(e) Reject H_0. There is enough evidence to support the claim that the new drug reduces systolic blood pressure.

21. (a) $H_0: \mu_d \leq 0$; $H_a: \mu_d > 0$ (claim) (b) $t_0 = 2.764$

(c) $\bar{d} \approx 1.255$; $s_d \approx 0.441$ (d) $t \approx 9.438$

(e) Reject H_0. There is enough evidence to support the claim that soft tissue therapy and spinal manipulation help reduce the length of time patients suffer from headaches.

23. $-1.762 < \mu_d < -1.172$

Section 8.4 *(page 404)*

1. State the hypotheses and identify the claim. Specify the level of significance. Find the critical value(s) and rejection region(s). Find $\bar{p}$ and $\bar{q}$. Find the standardized test statistic. Make a decision and interpret in the context of the claim.

3. $H_0: p_1 = p_2$; $H_a: p_1 \neq p_2$ (claim)

The test is a two-tailed test. Fail to reject H_0. There is not enough evidence to support the claim.

5. $H_0: p_1 \leq p_2$ (claim); $H_a: p_1 > p_2$

The test is a right-tailed test. Fail to reject H_0. There is not enough evidence to reject the claim.

7. (a) $H_0: p_1 = p_2$ (claim); $H_a: p_1 \neq p_2$

(b) $z_0 = \pm 1.96$ (c) $z = -5.060$ (d) Reject H_0

9. (a) $H_0: p_1 \geq p_2$; $H_a: p_1 < p_2$ (claim)

(b) $z_0 = -2.33$ (c) $z = -2.859$ (d) Reject H_0

11. (a) $H_0: p_1 = p_2$ (claim); $H_a: p_1 \neq p_2$

(b) $z_0 = \pm 1.645$ (c) $z = -9.832$ (d) Reject H_0

13. $H_0: p_1 \geq p_2$; $H_a: p_1 < p_2$ (claim)

$z_0 = -2.33$; $z = -0.881$

Fail to reject H_0

15. $H_0: p_1 = p_2$ (claim); $H_a: p_1 \neq p_2$
$z_0 = \pm 1.96$; $z = 3.797$
Reject H_0

17. $0.028 < p_1 - p_2 < 0.030$

Review Answers for Chapter 8   (page 411)

1. $H_0: \mu_1 \geq \mu_2$ (claim); $H_1: \mu_1 < \mu_2$
$z_0 = -1.645$; $z = -1.862$
Reject H_0

3. $H_0: \mu_1 \geq \mu_2$; $H_1: \mu_1 < \mu_2$ (claim)
$z_0 = -1.282$; $z = -2.060$
Reject H_0

5. $H_0: \mu_1 \geq \mu_2$; $H_1: \mu_1 < \mu_2$ (claim)
$z_0 = -1.645$; $z = -2.713$
Reject H_0

7. $H_0: \mu_1 = \mu_2$ (claim); $H_a: \mu_1 \neq \mu_2$
$t_0 = \pm 1.96$; $t = 1.121$
Fail to reject H_0

9. $H_0: \mu_1 \leq \mu_2$ (claim); $H_a: \mu_1 > \mu_2$
$t_0 = 1.711$; $t = -1.460$
Fail to reject H_0

11. (a) $H_0: \mu_1 \leq \mu_2$; $H_a: \mu_1 > \mu_2$ (claim)
(b) $t_0 = 1.645$ (c) $t = 2.266$ (d) Reject H_0

13. Independent

15. $H_0: \mu_d = 0$ (claim); $H_a: \mu_d \neq 0$
$t_0 = \pm 1.96$; $t = 8.065$
Reject H_0

17. $H_0: \mu_d \leq 6$ (claim) and $H_a: \mu_d > 6$
$t_0 = 1.282$; $t = 19.921$
Reject H_0

19. (a) $H_0: \mu_d \leq 0$ and $H_a: \mu_d > 0$ (claim)
(b) $t_0 = 1.383$ (c) $\bar{d} = 5$; $s_d \approx 8.743$
(d) $t \approx 1.808$ (e) Reject H_0.
(f) There is enough evidence to support the claim.

21. $H_0: p_1 = p_2$; $H_a: p_1 \neq p_2$ (claim)
$z_0 = \pm 1.96$; $z = -1.198$
Fail to reject H_0

23. $H_0: p_1 \leq p_2$; $H_a: p_1 > p_2$ (claim)
$z_0 = 1.282$; $z = -1.971$
Fail to reject H_0

25. (a) $H_0: p_1 = p_2$ (claim); $H_a: p_1 \neq p_2$ (b) $z_0 = \pm 1.645$
(c) $z = -0.776$ (d) Fail to reject H_0
(e) There is not enough evidence to reject the claim.

Chapter Quiz for Chapter 8   (page 415)

1. (a) $H_0: \mu_1 \leq \mu_2$; $H_1: \mu_1 > \mu_2$ (claim)
(b) Right tailed z-test   (c) $z_0 = 1.645$
(d) $z = 28.387$ (e) Reject H_0

2. (a) $H_0: \mu_1 = \mu_2$ (claim); $H_a: \mu_1 \neq \mu_2$
(b) Two tailed t-test (assume vars are equal)
(c) $t_0 = \pm 2.779$ (d) $t = 4.285$ (e) Reject H_0

3. (a) $H_0: p_1 \leq p_2$; $H_a: p_1 > p_2$ (claim)
(b) Right tailed z-test   (c) $z_0 = 1.282$
(d) $z \approx 158.471$ (e) Reject H_0

4. (a) $H_0: \mu_d \leq 0$; $H_a: \mu_d > 0$ (claim)
(b) Dependent t-test   (c) $t_0 = 1.796$
(d) $t = 9.016$ (e) Reject H_0

CHAPTER 9

Section 9.1   (page 373)

1. Positive linear correlation

3. No linear correlation (but there is a nonlinear correlation between the variables)

5. c   **7.** b

9. Explanatory variable: Amount of water consumed.
Response variable: Weight loss.

11. (a)

(b) 0.883   (c) Strong positive linear correlation

13. (a)

(b) 0.923   (c) Strong positive linear correlation

15. (a)

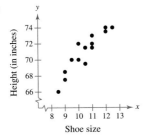

(b) 0.926   (c) Strong positive linear correlation

17. (a)

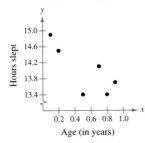

(b) -0.789 (c) Negative linear correlation

19. $r = -0.84$

21. State the null and alternative hypotheses. Specify the level of significance and determine the degrees of freedom. Identify the rejection regions and calculate the standardized test statistic. Make a decision and interpret in the context of the original claim.

23. Fail to reject H_0. There is not enough evidence to support the claim a significant linear correlation exists.

25. Reject H_0. There is enough evidence to conclude that a significant linear correlation exists.

27. (a) $H_0: \rho = 0$ and $H_a: \rho \neq 0$
   (b) $t_0 = \pm 1.796$ (c) $t \approx 7.955$
   (d) Reject H_0. There is enough evidence to conclude that a significant linear correlation exists.

29. (a) $H_0: \rho = 0$ and $H_a: \rho \neq 0$
   (b) $t_0 = \pm 2.179$ (c) $t \approx 8.497$
   (d) Reject H_0. There is enough evidence to conclude that a significant linear correlation exists.

31. The correlation coefficient remains unchanged when the x-values and y-values are switched.

33. Answers will vary.

Section 9.2   *(page 436)*

1. c   **3.** d   **5.** $\hat{y} = 0.432x - 20.297$ best fits the data.
7. c   **9.** a

11. $\hat{y} = 1.724x + 79.733$

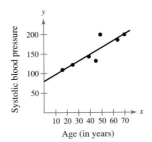

(a) 110   (b) 202   (c) 129   (d) 175

13. $\hat{y} = 7.350x + 34.617$

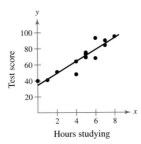

(a) 56.7   (b) 82.4
(c) It is not meaningful to predict the value of y for $x = 13$ because $x = 13$ is outside the range of the original data.
(d) 67.7

15. $\hat{y} = 1.870x + 51.360$

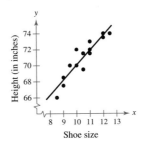

(a) 72.865   (b) 66.320
(c) It is not meaningful to predict the value of y for $x = 15.5$ because $x = 15.5$ is outside the range of the original data.
(d) 70.060

17. Substitute a value x into the equation of a regression line and solve for y.

19. (a) $\hat{y} = 1.724x + 79.733$

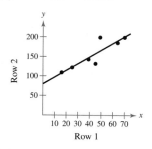

(b) $\hat{y} = 0.453x - 26.448$

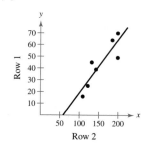

(c) The slope of the line keeps the same sign, but the values of m and b change.

21. $\hat{y} = -1.143x + 89.256$

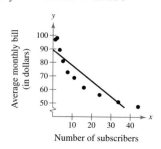

23. $r \approx -0.906$
$H_0: \rho = 0$ and $H_a: \rho \neq 0$
Critical values: $t_0 = \pm 3.355$

$$t = \frac{r}{\sqrt{\dfrac{1 - r^2}{n - 2}}} = \frac{-0.906}{\sqrt{\dfrac{1 - (-0.906)^2}{10 - 2}}} \approx -6.054$$

Reject H_0. There is enough evidence to conclude that a significant linear correlation exists.

25. Answers will vary.

Section 9.3   *(page 448)*

1. $\Sigma(y_i - \bar{y})^2$; the sum of the squares of the differences between the y-values of each ordered pair and the mean of the y-values of the ordered pairs.

3. $\Sigma(y_i - \hat{y}_i)^2$; the sum of the squares of the differences between the observed y-values and the predicted y-values.

5. 0.063; 6.3% of the variation is explained. 93.7% of the variation is unexplained.

7. 0.794; 79.4% of the variation is explained. 20.6% of the variation is unexplained.

9. (a) 0.817; 81.7% of the variation in proceeds can be explained by the variation in the number of issues and 18.3% of the variation is unexplained.

(b) $s_e \approx 6029.907$; the standard deviation of the proceeds for a specific number of issues is about $6,029,907,000.

11. (a) 0.985; 98.5% of the variation in sales can be explained by the variation in the total square footage and 1.5% of the variation is unexplained.

(b) $s_e \approx 35.652$; the standard deviation of the sales for a specific total square footage is about 35,652,000,000.

13. (a) 0.998; 99.8% of the variation in the median weekly earnings of female workers can be explained by the variation in the median weekly earnings of male workers and 0.2% of the variation is unexplained.

(b) $s_e \approx 5.147$; the standard deviation of the median weekly earnings of female workers for a specific median weekly earnings of male workers is about $5.147.

15. (a) 0.992; 99.2% of the variation in the money spent can be explained by the variation in the money raised and 0.8% of the variation is unexplained.

(b) $s_e \approx 16.079$; the standard deviation of the money spent for a specified amount of money raised is about $16,079,000.

17. ($17,935,784,000, $47,264,966,000); you can be 95% confident that the proceeds will be between 17,935,784,000 and $47,264,966,000 when the number of initial offerings is 712.

19. ($679,861,000,000, $817,739,000,000); you can be 90% confident that the sales will be between $679,861,000,000 and $817,739,000,000 when the total square footage is 4.5 billion.

21. ($333.285, $400.133); you can be 99% confident that the median earnings of female workers will be between $333.285 and $400.133 when the median weekly earnings of male workers is $500.

23. ($721.402 million, $809.522 million); you can be 95% confident that the money spent in congressional campaigns will be between $721.402 million and $809.522 million when the money raised is $775.8 million.

25.

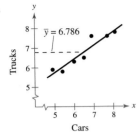

27.

x_i	y_i	$\hat{y}_i$	$\hat{y}_i - \bar{y}$	$y_i - \hat{y}_i$	$y_i - \bar{y}$
8.1	7.8	7.893	1.107	−0.093	1.014
7.7	7.6	7.616	0.830	−0.016	0.814
6.5	6.5	6.785	−0.002	−0.285	−0.286
6.9	7.6	7.062	0.276	0.538	0.814
6.0	6.3	6.438	−0.348	−0.138	−0.486
5.4	5.8	6.022	−0.764	−0.222	−0.986
4.9	5.9	5.676	−1.11	0.224	−0.886

29. 0.887   **31.** (6.441, 8.237)

Section 9.4   *(page 455)*

1. (a) 2614.6   (b) 2298   (c) 2680   (d) 2233
3. (a) 7.5   (b) 16.8   (c) 51.9   (d) 62.1
5. $\hat{y} = -256.293 + 103.502x_1 + 14.649x_2$
   (a) 34.16   (b) 0.988
   (c) The standard deviation of the predicted sales given a specific total square footage and number of shopping centers is $34.16 billion. The multiple regression model explains 98.8% of the variation in y.
7. 0.985   **8.** 0.997

Review Answers for Chapter 9   *(page 459)*

1.

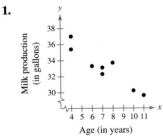

$r \approx -0.939$; negative linear correlation; milk production decreases with age.
3. $H_0: \rho = 0$ and $H_a: \rho \neq 0$; $CV = \pm 1.711$; $t = 1.211$
   Fail to reject H_0.
5. $H_0: \rho = 0$ and $H_a: \rho \neq 0$; $CV = \pm 2.447$; $t = -6.688$
   Reject H_0.

7. $\hat{y} = 0.679x + 26.345$

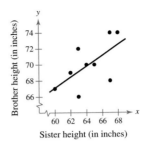

$r \approx 0.625$
9. (a) 67.764   (b) 71.159   (c) Not meaningful
11. 0.306   **13.** 0.033
15. (a) 0.897; 89.7% of the variation in y is explained by the model.
   (b) 568.0; the standard error of the cooling capacity for a specific living area is 568.0 BTU/hr.
17. $65.01 < y < 74.592$ **19.** $8184.33 < y < 11,455.59$
21. $\hat{y} = 6317 + 0.8217x_1 + 0.031x_2 - 0.004x_3$
23. (a) 21.705   (b) 25.210   (c) 30.100   (d) 25.860

Chapter Quiz for Chapter 9   *(page 462)*

1.

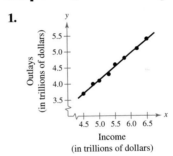

The data appear to have a positive correlation. The outlays increase as the incomes increase.
2. 0.997
3. $H_0: \rho = 0$ and $H_a: \rho \neq 0$; $CV = \pm 2.447$; $t = 31.552$
   Reject H_0.
4. $\hat{y} = 0.838x - 0.069$ **5.** 4.372
6. 0.995; $r^2 = 0.995 \to$ 99.5% of the variation in y is explained by the regression model.
7. $0.046 trillion; the standard deviation of personal outlays for a specified personal income is $0.046 trillion.
8. ($5.16 trillion, $5.43 trillion)
9. (a) 1311.150   (b) 961.110   (c) 1120.900
   (d) 1386.740
   x_2 has the greatest influence on y.

Cumulative Test for Chapter 9 *(page 463)*

1. H_0: $\mu \geq 20.1$ (claim); H_a: $\mu < 20.1$

$z_0 = -2.33$; $z = -1.530$; Fail to reject H_0.

2. Type I error will occur if H_0 is rejected when $\mu \geq 20.1$. Type II error will occur if H_0 is not rejected when $\mu < 20.1$.

3. H_0: $\mu_1 - \mu_2 = 0$ (claim); H_a: $\mu_1 - \mu_2 \neq 0$

$z_0 = \pm 1.96$; $z \approx -3.496$; Reject H_0.

4. (a) Standard normal distribution

(b) Standard normal distribution

5. 0.989

6. $\hat{y} = 1.071x - 268.253$

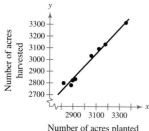

7. 0.978; $r^2 = 0.978 \to 97.8\%$ of the variation in y is explained by the model.

8. 31.46 thousand

9. (2969.4 thousand, 3134.3 thousand)

10. H_0: $\rho = 0$ and H_a: $\rho \neq 0$; $CV = \pm 3.707$; $t = 16.378$ Reject H_0.

CHAPTER 10

Section 10.1 *(page 472)*

1. (a) Claimed distribution:

Response	Distribution
Home	70%
Work	17%
Commuting	8%
Other	5%

H_0: Distribution of responses is as shown in table above.

H_a: Distribution of responses differs from the claimed distribution.

(b) 7.815   (c) 3.754

(d) Fail to reject H_0.

3. (a) Claimed distribution:

Day	Distribution
Sunday	14.286%
Monday	14.286%
Tuesday	14.286%
Wednesday	14.286%
Thursday	14.286%
Friday	14.286%
Saturday	14.286%

H_0: The distribution of fatal bicycle accidents throughout the week is as shown in the table above.

H_a: The distribution of fatal bicycle accidents throughout the week differs from the claimed distribution.

(b) 10.645   (c) 4.648

(d) Fail to reject H_0.

5. (a) Claimed distribution:

Object struck	Distribution
Tree	28%
Embankment	10%
Utility pole	10%
Guardrail	9%
Ditch	7%
Curb	6%
Culvert	5%
Sign/Post/Fence	10%
Other	15%

H_0: Distribution of objects struck is as shown in table above.

H_a: Distribution of objects struck differs from the claimed distribution.

(b) 20.090   (c) 49.665

(d) Reject H_0.

7. (a) Claimed distribution:

Response	Distribution
Not a HS grad	33.333%
HS graduate	33.333%
College (1yr+)	33.333%

H_0: Distribution of the responses is as shown in table above.

H_a: Distribution of the responses differs from the claimed distribution.

(b) 7.378   (c) 5.637

(d) Fail to reject H_0.

9. (a) Claimed distribution:

Cause	Distribution
Trans. Accidents	41%
Assaults	20%
Objects/equipment	15%
Falls	10%
Exposure	10%
Other	4%

H_0: Distribution of the causes is as shown in table above.

H_a: Distribution of the causes differs from the claimed distribution.

(b) 11.071   (c) 9.493

(d) Fail to reject H_0.

11. (a) Frequency distribution: $\mu = 69.435$; $\sigma \approx 8.337$

Lower Boundary	Upper Boundary	Lower z-score	Upper z-score	Area
49.5	58.5	−2.39	−1.31	0.0867
58.5	67.5	−1.31	−0.23	0.3139
67.5	76.5	−0.23	0.85	0.3933
76.5	85.5	0.85	1.93	0.1709
85.5	94.5	1.93	3.01	0.0255

Class Boundaries	Distribution	Frequency	Expected	$\dfrac{(O-E)^2}{E}$
49.5–58.5	8.67%	19	17	0.235
58.5–67.5	31.39%	61	63	0.063
67.5–76.5	39.33%	82	79	0.114
76.5–85.5	17.09%	34	34	0
85.5–94.5	2.55%	4	5	0.2
		200		0.612

H_0: Variable has a normal distribution

H_a: Variable does not have a normal distribution

(b) 13.277   (c) 0.612   (d) Fail to reject H_0.

Section 10.2   *(page 482)*

1. (a) H_0: Skill level in a subject is independent of location.

H_a: Skill level in a subject is dependent on location.

(b) 2; 9.210   (c) 0.297   (d) Fail to reject H_0.

3. (a) H_0: Adults' ratings are independent of the type of school.

H_a: Adults' ratings are dependent on the type of school.

(b) 3; 7.815   (c) 148.389   (d) Reject H_0.

5. (a) H_0: Results are independent of the type of treatment.

H_a: Results are dependent on the type of treatment.

(b) 1; 2.706   (c) 5.106   (d) Reject H_0.

7. (a) H_0: Reasons are independent of the type of worker.

H_a: Reasons are dependent on the type of worker.

(b) 2; 9.210   (c) 7.326   (d) Fail to reject H_0.

9. (a) H_0: Type of crash is independent of the type of vehicle.

H_a: Type of crash is dependent on the type of vehicle.

(b) 2; 5.991   (c) 106.390   (d) Reject H_0.

11. H_0: The proportions are equal.

H_a: At least one of the proportions is different from the others.

d.f. $= (r-1)(c-1) = 7$

$CV = 14.067 \rightarrow$ Reject H_0 if $\chi^2 > 14.067$

$\chi^2 \approx 3.853$

Fail to reject H_0.

Section 10.3   *(page 493)*

1. Specify the level of significance α. Determine the degrees of freedom for the numerator and denominator. Use Table 7 to find the critical value F.

3. 2.93   **5.** 5.32

7. H_0: $\sigma_1^2 \leq \sigma_2^2$; H_a: $\sigma_1^2 > \sigma_2^2$ (claim)

$CV = 3.52$; $F = 1.010$

Fail to reject H_0.

9. H_0: $\sigma_1^2 \leq \sigma_2^2$ (claim); H_a: $\sigma_1^2 > \sigma_2^2$

$CV = 5.26$; $F = 1.007$

Fail to reject H_0.

11. (a) Population 1: Company B
Population 2: Company A

H_0: $\sigma_1^2 \leq \sigma_2^2$; H_a: $\sigma_1^2 > \sigma_2^2$ (claim)

(b) 2.13   (c) 1.077   (d) Fail to reject H_0.

13. (a) H_0: $\sigma_1^2 = \sigma_2^2$ (claim); H_a: $\sigma_1^2 \neq \sigma_2^2$

(b) 2.63   (c) 1.126   (d) Fail to reject H_0.

15. (a) H_0: $\sigma_1^2 \leq \sigma_2^2$ and H_a: $\sigma_1^2 > \sigma_2^2$ (claim)

(b) 1.77   (c) 1.96   (d) Reject H_0.

17. (a) Population 1: California
Population 2: New York

H_0: $\sigma_1^2 \leq \sigma_2^2$; H_a: $\sigma_1^2 > \sigma_2^2$ (claim)

(b) 2.35   (c) 1.616   (d) Fail to reject H_0.

19. Right-tailed: 8.94   **21.** (0.366, 3.839)
Left-tailed: 0.210

Section 10.4 *(page 503)*

1. (a) $H_0: \mu_1 = \mu_2 = \mu_3$

H_a: At least one mean is different from the others. (claim)

(b) d.f.$_n$ = 2; d.f.$_d$ = 27; $CV = 3.35$

(c) $F = 1.26$ (d) Fail to reject H_0.

3. (a) $H_0: \mu_1 = \mu_2 = \mu_3$ (claim)

H_a: At least one mean is different from the others.

(b) d.f.$_n$ = 2; d.f.$_d$ = 12; $CV = 2.81$

(c) $F = 1.77$ (d) Fail to reject H_0.

5. (a) $H_0: \mu_1 = \mu_2 = \mu_3 = \mu_4$ (claim)

H_a: At least one mean is different from the others.

(b) d.f.$_n$ = 3; d.f.$_d$ = 33; $CV = 4.44$

(c) $F = 5.21$ (d) Reject H_0.

7. (a) $H_0: \mu_1 = \mu_2 = \mu_3 = \mu_4$ (claim)

H_a: At least one mean is different from the others.

(b) d.f.$_n$ = 3; d.f.$_d$ = 43; $CV = 2.22$

(c) $F = 3.04$

(d) Reject H_0.

9. (a) $H_0: \mu_1 = \mu_2 = \mu_3 = \mu_4$

H_a: At least one mean is different from the others. (claim)

(b) d.f.$_n$ = 3; d.f.$_d$ = 36; $CV = 4.38$

(c) $F = 8.46$ (d) Reject H_0.

11. $CV_{\text{Scheffe}} = 13.320$

$(1, 2) \rightarrow 4.818 \rightarrow$ No difference

$(1, 3) \rightarrow 12.135 \rightarrow$ No difference

$(1, 4) \rightarrow 10.628 \rightarrow$ No difference

$(2, 3) \rightarrow 2.000 \rightarrow$ No difference

$(2, 4) \rightarrow 1.263 \rightarrow$ No difference

$(3, 4) \rightarrow 0.101 \rightarrow$ No difference

13. $CV_{\text{Scheffe}} = 6.660$

$(1, 2) \rightarrow 7.212 \rightarrow$ Significant difference

$(1, 3) \rightarrow 3.519 \rightarrow$ No difference

$(1, 4) \rightarrow 0.260 \rightarrow$ No difference

$(2, 3) \rightarrow 0.724 \rightarrow$ No difference

$(2, 4) \rightarrow 4.782 \rightarrow$ No difference

$(3, 4) \rightarrow 1.866 \rightarrow$ No difference

Review Answers for Chapter 10 *(page 510)*

1. Claimed distribution:

Category	Distribution
New Patients	25%
Old/New	25%
Old/Recurring	50%

H_0: Distribution of office visits is as shown in table above.

H_a: Distribution of office visits differs from the claimed distribution.

$CV = 5.991$; $\chi^2 = 74.101$

Reject H_0.

3. (a) Expected frequencies:

	HS-Did not Complete	HS Complete	College 1-3 years	College 4+ years	Total
25-44	17,303.105	20,295.862	10,260.752	12,370.281	60,230
45+	20,271.895	23,778.138	12,021.248	14,492.719	70,564
Total	37,575	44,074	22,282	26,863	130,794

(b) H_0: Education is independent of age.

H_a: Education is dependent on age.

$CV = 6.251$; $\chi^2 = 11852.71$; Reject H_0

(c) There is enough evidence to conclude that education is dependent on age.

5. $F = 2.295$ **7.** $F = 2.39$

9. $H_0: \sigma_1^2 \geq \sigma_2^2$ (claim); $H_a: \sigma_1^2 < \sigma_2^2$ (left-tailed test)

$CV = 3.09$; $F = 2.419$

Fail to reject H_0.

11. $H_0: \sigma_1^2 \leq \sigma_2^2$; $H_a: \sigma_1^2 > \sigma_2^2$ (claim)

$CV = 1.92$; $F = 1.717$

Fail to reject H_0.

13. Population 1: Male; $s_1^2 = 18{,}486.26$

Population 2: Female; $s_2^2 = 12{,}102.78$

$H_0: \sigma_1^2 = \sigma_2^2$; $H_a: \sigma_1^2 \neq \sigma_2^2$ (claim)

$CV = 6.94$; $F = 1.527$

Fail to reject H_0.

15. $H_0: \mu_1 = \mu_2 = \mu_3 = \mu_4$

H_a: At least one mean is different from the others. (claim)

$CV = 2.29$; $F = 6.60$

Reject H_0.

Chapter Quiz for Chapter 10   *(page 513)*

1. Population 1: San Jose; $s_1^2 = 429.984$
Population 2: Dallas; $s_2^2 = 112.779$

$H_0: \sigma_1^2 = \sigma_2^2$; $H_a: \sigma_1^2 \neq \sigma_2^2$ (claim)

$CV = 2.82$; $F = 3.813$

Reject H_0.

2. $H_0: \mu_1 = \mu_2 = \mu_3$ (claim)

H_a: At least one mean is different from the others.

$CV = 2.43$; $F = 7.39$

Reject H_0.

3. (a) Claimed distribution:

Education	25 & Over
Not a HS graduate	18.3%
HS graduate	33.6%
Some college, no degree	17.3%
Associate Degree	7.2%
Bachelor Degree	15.8%
Advanced Degree	7.8%

H_0: Distribution of educational achievement is as shown in table above.

H_a: Distribution of educational achievement differs from the claimed distribution.

(b) 0.01   (c) 15.086   (d) Reject H_0 if $\chi^2 > 15.086$.

(e) 8.522   (f) Fail to reject H_0.

(g) Fail to reject H_0. There is not enough evidence to conclude that the distribution of educational achievement differs from the claimed distribution.

4. (a) Claimed distribution:

Education	25 & Over
Not a HS graduate	18.3%
HS graduate	33.6%
Some college, no degree	17.3%
Associate Degree	7.2%
Bachelor Degree	15.8%
Advanced Degree	7.8%

H_0: Distribution of educational achievement is as shown in table above.

H_a: Distribution of educational achievement differs from the claimed distribution.

(b) 0.05   (c) 11.071   (d) Reject H_0 if $\chi^2 > 15.086$.

(e) 49.390   (f) Reject H_0.

(g) There is enough evidence to conclude that the distribution of educational achievement differs from the claimed distribution.

CHAPTER 11

Section 11.1   *(page 472)*

1. A nonparametric test is a hypothesis test that does not require any specific conditions concerning the shape of populations or the value of any population parameters.

A nonparametric test is usually easier to perform than its corresponding parametric test, but the nonparametric test is usually less efficient.

3. Fail to reject H_0

5. (a) H_0: median $\leq 140{,}000$ (claim)

H_a: median $> 140{,}000$

(b) $CV = 1$ (c) $x = 3$

(d) Fail to reject H_0. There is not enough evidence to reject the claim.

7. (a) H_0: median ≤ 1500 (claim)

H_a: median < 1500

(b) $CV = -2.055$ (c) -3.040

(d) Reject H_0. There is enough evidence to reject the claim.

9. (a) H_0: median ≤ 36 and H_a: median > 36 (claim)

(b) $CV = 3$ (c) $x = 8$

(d) Fail to reject H_0. There is not enough evidence to support the claim.

11. (a) H_0: median $= 5$ (claim) and H_a: median $\neq 5$

(b) $CV = -1.96$ (c) -2.334

(d) Reject H_0. There is enough evidence to reject the claim.

13. (a) H_0: median $= \$9.81$ (claim) and

H_a: median $\neq \$9.81$

(b) $CV = -2.575$ (c) -0.961

(d) Fail to reject H_0. There is not enough evidence to reject the claim.

15. (a) H_0: The headache hours have not decreased.

H_a: The headache hours have decreased. (claim)

(b) $CV = 1$ (c) $x = 3$

(d) Fail to reject H_0. There is not enough evidence to support the claim.

17. (a) H_0: The SAT scores have not improved.

H_a: The SAT scores have improved. (claim)

(b) $CV = 2$ (c) $x = 4$

(d) Fail to reject H_0. There is not enough evidence to support the claim.

19. Fail to reject H_0. There is not enough evidence to reject the claim.

21. (a) H_0: median ≤ 418 (claim) and H_a: median > 418
   (b) CV $= 2.33$ (c) 1.459
   (d) Fail to reject H_0. There is not enough evidence to reject the claim.

23. (a) H_0: median ≤ 24 and H_a: median > 24 (claim)
   (b) CV $= 1.645$ (c) 1.936
   (d) Reject H_0. There is enough evidence to support the claim.

Section 11.2   *(page 533)*

1. (a) H_0: There is no reduction in systolic blood pressure. (claim)
   H_a: There is a reduction in systolic blood pressure.
   (b) Wilcoxon signed-rank test
   (c) CV $= 6$ (d) $w_s = 6$
   (e) Reject H_0. There is enough evidence to support the claim.

3. (a) H_0: There is no difference in the earnings.
   H_a: There is a difference in the earnings. (claim)
   (b) Wilcoxon rank sum test
   (c) The critical values are ± 1.96 (d) -3.873
   (e) Reject H_0. There is enough evidence to support the claim.

5. (a) H_0: There is not a difference in salaries.
   H_a: There is a difference in salaries. (claim)
   (b) Wilcoxon rank sum test
   (c) The critical values are ± 1.96 (d) -1.819
   (e) Fail to reject H_0. There is not enough evidence to support the claim.

7. Reject H_0.

Section 11.3   *(page 541)*

1. (a) H_0: There is no difference in the premiums.
   H_a: There is a difference in the premiums. (claim)
   (b) CV $= 5.991$ (c) $H = 14.05$
   (d) Reject H_0. There is enough evidence to support the claim.

3. (a) H_0: There is no difference in the salaries.
   H_a: There is a difference in the salaries. (claim)
   (b) CV $= 6.251$ (c) $H = 6.46$
   (d) Reject H_0. There is enough evidence to support the claim.

5. (a) Fail to reject H_0.
   (b) Fail to reject H_0. There is not enough evidence to support the claim. This is the same decision found in part (a) using the Kruskal-Wallis test.

Section 11.4   *(page 546)*

1. (a) H_0: $\rho_s = 0$ and H_a: $\rho_s \neq 0$ (claim)
   (b) CV $= 0.929$ (c) 0.929
   (d) Reject H_0. There is enough evidence to support the claim.

3. (a) H_0: $\rho_s = 0$ and H_a: $\rho_s \neq 0$ (claim)
   (b) CV $= 0.497$ (c) 0.568
   (d) Reject H_0. There is enough evidence to support the claim.

5. Fail to reject H_0 **7.** Fail to reject H_0

9. Fail to reject H_0

Review Answers for Chapter 11   *(page 551)*

1. (a) H_0: median $= \$13,500$ (claim) H_a: median $\neq \$13,500$
   (b) CV $= 2$ (c) $x = 7$
   (d) Fail to reject H_0. There is not enough evidence to reject the claim.

3. (a) H_0: median ≤ 6 (claim) H_a: median > 6
   (b) CV $= 1.282$ (c) 2.032
   (d) Reject H_0. There is enough evidence to reject the claim.

5. (a) H_0: There is no reduction in systolic blood pressure.(claim) H_a: There is a reduction in systolic blood pressure.
   (b) CV $= 2$ (c) $x = 3$
   (d) Fail to reject H_0. There is not enough evidence to reject the claim.

7. (a) Dependent; Wilcoxon Signed Rank Test
   (b) H_0: Producers are not under reporting the caloric content of their foods. H_a: Producers are under reporting the caloric content of their foods. (claim)
   (c) CV $= 8$ (d) $w_s = 2$
   (e) Reject H_0. There is enough evidence to support the claim.

9. (a) Independent; Wilcoxon Rank Sum Test

(b) H_0: There is no difference in the amount of time that it takes to earn a doctorate.

H_a: There is a difference in the amount of time that it takes to earn a doctorate. (claim)

(c) CV = ±2.575   (d) −3.175

(e) Reject H_0. There is enough evidence to support the claim.

11. (a) H_0: There is no difference in salaries between the fields of study. (claim)

H_a: There is a difference in salaries between the fields of study.

(b) CV = 5.991   (c) $H \approx 22.98$

(d) Reject H_0. There is enough evidence to reject the claim.

13. (a) H_0: $\rho_s = 0$ and H_a: $\rho_s \neq 0$ (claim)

(b) CV = 0.881   (c) −0.429

(d) Fail to reject H_0. There is not enough evidence to support the claim.

Chapter Quiz for Chapter 11   (page 555)

1. (a) H_0: There is no difference in the salaries between genders.

H_a: There is a difference in the salaries between genders. (claim)

(b) Wilcoxon Ranked Sum Test

(c) CV = ±1.645   (d) −1.722

(e) Reject H_0. There is enough evidence to support the claim.

2. (a) H_0: median = 28 (claim) and H_a: median ≠ 28

(b) Sign Test   (c) CV = 6   (d) $x = 10$

(e) Fail to reject H_0. There is not enough evidence to reject the claim.

3. (a) H_0: $\rho_s = 0$ and H_a: $\rho_s \neq 0$ (claim)

(b) Spearman Rank Correlation Coefficient Test

(c) CV = 0.881   (d) 0.095

(e) Fail to reject H_0. There is not enough evidence to support the claim.

4. (a) H_0: There is no difference in the annual premiums between the states.

H_a: There is a difference in the annual premiums between the states. (claim)

(b) Kruskal-Wallis Test

(c) CV = 5.991   (d) $H = 1.43$

(e) Fail to reject H_0. There is not enough evidence to support the claim.

Cumulative Test for Chapter 11

(page 556)

1. Fail to reject H_0 2. Fail to reject H_0
3. Reject H_0 4. Fail to reject H_0
5. Reject H_0 6. Reject H_0

SELECTED ANSWERS

CHAPTER 2

Section 2.1

6. Class width = 5

Class	Frequency	Class Boundaries	Midpoint	Cumulative Frequency
16-20	100	15.5-20.5	18	100
21-25	122	20.5-25.5	23	222
26-30	900	25.5-30.5	28	1122
31-35	207	30.5-35.5	33	1329
36-40	795	35.5-40.5	38	2124
41-45	568	40.5-45.5	43	2692
46-50	322	45.5-50.5	48	3014

16.

Class	Frequency	Midpoint	Relative Frequency	Cumulative Frequency
30-113	5	71.5	0.1724	5
114-197	7	155.5	0.2414	12
198-281	8	239.5	0.2759	20
282-365	2	323.5	0.0690	22
366-449	3	407.5	0.1034	25
450-533	4	491.5	0.1379	29
	29		1	

18.

Class	Frequency	Midpoint	Relative Frequency	Cumulative Frequency
32-35	2	33.5	0.1250	2
36-39	6	37.5	0.3750	8
40-43	5	41.5	0.3125	13
44-47	2	45.5	0.1250	15
48-51	1	49.5	0.0625	16
	16		1	

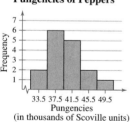

Pungencies of Peppers

Pungencies (in thousands of Scoville units)

Class with greatest frequency: 36-39

Class with least frequency: 48-51

20.

Class	Frequency	Midpoint	Relative Frequency	Cumulative Frequency
2456-2542	7	2499	0.28	7
2543-2629	3	2586	0.12	10
2630-2716	2	2673	0.08	12
2717-2803	4	2760	0.16	16
2804-2890	9	2847	0.36	25
	25		1	

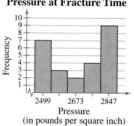

Pressure at Fracture Time

Pressure (in pounds per square inch)

Class with greatest frequency: 2804-2890

Class with least frequency: 2630-2716

22.

Class	Frequency	Midpoint	Relative Frequency	Cumulative Frequency
10-23	11	16.5	0.3438	11
24-37	9	30.5	0.2813	20
38-51	6	44.5	0.1875	26
52-65	2	58.5	0.0625	28
66-80	4	72.5	0.1250	32
	32		1	

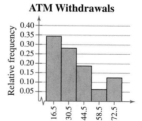

ATM Withdrawals

Dollars

Class with greatest relative frequency: 10-23

Class with least relative frequency: 52-65

24.

Class	Frequency	Midpoint	Relative Frequency	Cumulative Frequency
7-8	7	7.5	0.28	7
9-10	8	9.5	0.32	15
11-12	6	11.5	0.24	21
13-14	3	13.5	0.12	24
15-16	1	15.5	0.04	25
	25		1	

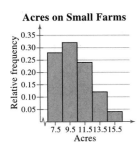

Acres on Small Farms

Class with greatest relative frequency: 9-10

Class with least relative frequency: 15-16

26.

Class	Frequency	Relative Frequency	Cumulative Frequency
16-24	3	0.15	3
25-33	8	0.40	11
34-42	7	0.35	18
43-51	0	0.00	18
52-60	2	0.10	20
	20	1	

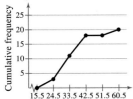

Daily Saturated Fat Intake

Location of the greatest increase in frequency: 25-33

28.

Class	Frequency	Relative Frequency	Cumulative Frequency
1-5	5	0.2083	5
6-10	9	0.3750	14
11-15	3	0.1250	17
16-20	4	0.1667	21
21-25	2	0.0833	23
26-30	1	0.0417	24
	24	1	

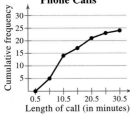

Length of Long Distance Phone Calls

Location of the greatest increase in frequency: 6-10

30.

Class	Frequency	Midpoint	Relative Frequency	Cumulative Frequency
0-2	17	1	0.4146	17
3-5	17	4	0.4146	34
6-8	5	7	0.1220	39
9-11	1	10	0.0244	40
12-14	0	13	0.0000	40
15-17	1	16	0.0244	41
	41		1	

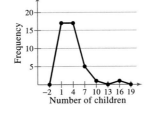

Number of Children of First 41 Presidents

Class with greatest frequency: 0-2   3-5

Class with least frequency: 12-14

Section 2.2

16. (a) Key: 49 | 2 = 492

```
47 | 45
48 | 4599
49 | 026
50 | 78
51 | 789
52 | 159
53 | 18
54 |
55 |
56 | 0
```

(b) Key: 49 | 2 = 492

```
47 | 4
47 | 5
48 | 4
48 | 599
49 | 02
49 | 6
50 |
50 | 78
51 |
51 | 789
52 | 1
52 | 59
53 | 1
53 | 8
54 |
54 |
55 |
55 |
56 | 0
```

It appears that the data is displayed better using one row for each stem. Using two rows for each stem tends to spread the data out too much.

18. Key: 31 | 9 = 319

```
29 | 8
30 | 5
31 | 9
32 | 7
33 |
34 | 5
35 | 1
36 |
37 |
38 |
39 | 03
40 | 39
41 | 059
42 |
43 |
44 | 689
45 | 05
46 | 05
47 | 99
48 |
49 | 1
50 | 3
```

It appears that the majority of the elephants eat between 390 and 480 lbs. of hay each day.

24.

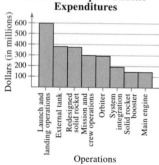

1995 NASA Space Shuttle Expenditures

It appears that the launch and landing operations of the shuttle are nearly twice as much as the next largest expenditure (external tank).

26.

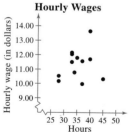

Hourly Wages

It appears that hourly wage increases as the number of hours worked increases.

30.

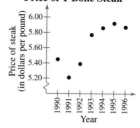

Price of T-Bone Steak

It appears that the price of T-bone steak has increased over the past 7 years.

32.

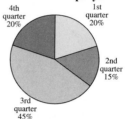

Sales for Company B

The pie chart should be displaying all four quarters, not just the first three.

Section 2.4

30.

Class	Midpoint, x	Frequency
3-4	3.5	5
5-6	5.5	6
7-8	7.5	6
9-10	9.5	7
11-13	11.5	6
		30

$\mu = 7.7, \sigma \approx 2.75$

Section 2.5

8. (a) Min = 100   (b) Max = 320
(c) $Q_1 = 130$ (d) $Q_2 = 205$ (e) $Q_3 = 270$
(f) IQR = 140

10. (a) Min = 25   (b) Max = 85
(c) $Q_1 = 50$ (d) $Q_2 = 65$ (e) $Q_3 = 70$
(f) IQR = 20

12. (a) $3, 5, 8$

(b)

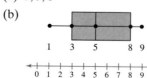

16. (a) $28, 29, 32$

(b) $P_{25} = Q_1 = 28$
$P_{50} = Q_2 = 29$
$P_{75} = Q_3 = 32$

(c)

Tenure for Teachers

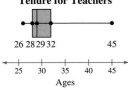

Review Exercises for Chapter 2

6.

Class	Midpoint	Frequency
79-93	86	9
94-108	101	12
109-123	116	5
124-138	131	3
139-153	146	2
154-168	161	1
		32

CHAPTER 3

Section 3.1

6.

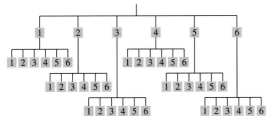

$\{(1, 1), (1, 2), (1, 3), (1, 4), (1, 5), (1, 6), (2, 1), (2, 2), (2, 3),$
$(2, 4), (2, 5), (2, 6), (3, 1), (3, 2), (3, 3), (3, 4), (3, 5), (3, 6),$
$(4, 1), (4, 2), (4, 3), (4, 4), (4, 5), (4, 6), (5, 1), (5, 2), (5, 3),$
$(5, 4), (5, 5), (5, 6), (6, 1), (6, 2), (6, 3), (6, 4), (6, 5), (6, 6)\}$

CHAPTER 4

Section 4.1

24. (a)

x	f	$P(x)$	$xP(x)$	$(x - \mu)^2 P(x)$
0	273	0.273	0	0.5482
1	349	0.349	0.349	0.0607
2	203	0.203	0.406	0.0690
3	78	0.078	0.234	0.1955
4	57	0.057	0.228	0.3803
5	40	0.04	0.2	0.5135
	1000	1	1.417	1.7671

(b) 1.417 (c) 1.767 (d) 1.329

(e) A household has an average of 1.417 cats with a standard deviation of 1.329.

26. (a)

x	f	$P(x)$	$xP(x)$	$(x - \mu)^2 P(x)$
0	260	0.152	0.000	0.527
1	500	0.292	0.292	0.217
2	425	0.249	0.498	0.005
3	305	0.178	0.534	0.231
4	175	0.102	0.408	0.466
5	45	0.026	0.130	0.256
	1710	1	1.862	1.701

(b) 1.862 (c) 1.701 (d) 1.304

(e) The average number of accidents per student is 1.862 with a standard deviation of 1.304.

Section 4.2

14. (a)

x	$P(x)$
0	0.237305
1	0.395508
2	0.263672
3	0.087891
4	0.014648
5	0.000977

(b)

Trouble Sleeping at Night

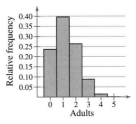

(c) 1.25 (d) 0.9375 (e) 0.968

—CONTINUED—

14. —CONTINUED—

(f) On average 1.25 adults, out of every 5, have difficulty sleeping at night. The standard deviation is 0.968 adults.

$x = 5$ would be uncommon due to its low probability.

16. (a) $n = 5, p = 0.38$

x	$P(x)$
0	0.092
1	0.281
2	0.344
3	0.211
4	0.065
5	0.008

(b)

Blood Type

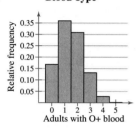

(c) 1.9   (d) 1.178   (e) 1.085

(f) On average 1.9 adults, out of every 5 has O+ blood. The standard deviation is 1.085 adults.

$x = 5$ is uncommon due to its low probability.

Review Exercises for Chapter 4

10. (a)

x	Freq	$P(x)$
0	7	0.219
1	8	0.250
2	10	0.313
3	3	0.094
4	3	0.094
5	1	0.031
	32	1

(b)

Goals Per Game

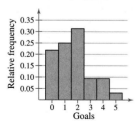

(c) 1.688, 1.777, 1.333

12. (a)

x	Freq	$P(x)$
15	76	0.134
30	445	0.786
60	30	0.053
90	3	0.005
120	12	0.021
	566	1

(b)

Advertising Sales

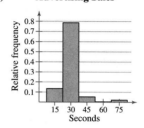

(c) 31.802, 265.480, 16.294

CHAPTER 5

Section 5.4

6. 80, 25.820

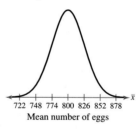

Mean number of eggs

8. 51.2, 3.42

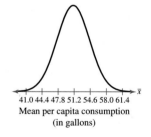

Mean per capita consumption (in gallons)

Section 5.5

16. (a) 0.1347

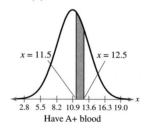

Have A+ blood

(b) 0.4090

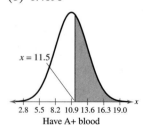

Have A+ blood

(c) 0.5910

(d) 0.9292

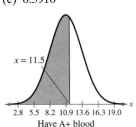

Have A+ blood

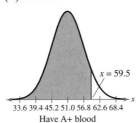

Have A+ blood

CHAPTER 7

Section 7.1

8. d $H_a: \mu > 3$

10. a $H_a: \mu < 2$

12. $\sigma < 3$

$H_0: \sigma \geq 3$ and $H_a: \sigma < 3$ (Claim: H_a)

14. $p = 0.09$

$H_0: p = 0.09$ and $H_a: p \neq 0.09$ (Claim: H_0)

16. $\mu = 24$

$H_0: \mu = 24$ and $H_a: \mu \neq 24$ (Claim: H_0)

18. Type I: Rejecting $H_0: p = 0.21$ when actually $p = 0.21$.

Type II: Not rejecting $H_0: p = 0.21$ when actually $p \neq 0.21$.

30. (a) There is enough evidence to reject the Postal Service's claim.

(b) There is not enough evidence to reject the Postal Service's claim.

32. (a) There is enough evidence to reject the manufacturer's claim.

(b) There is not enough evidence to reject the manufacturer's claim.

34. (a) There is enough evidence to reject the soft-drink maker's claim.

(b) There is not enough evidence to reject the soft-drink maker's claim.

Section 7.2

2. State the claim mathematically. Identify the null and alternative hypotheses. Specify the level of significance. Sketch the sampling distribution. Determine the critical value(s). Determine the rejection region(s). Find the standardized test statistic. Make a decision to reject or fail to reject the null hypothesis. Interpret the decision in the context of the original claim.

Section 7.3

2. Identify the claim. State H_0 and H_a. Specify the level of significance. Identify the degrees of freedom and sketch the sampling distribution. Determine the critical value(s) and rejection region(s). Find the standardized test statistic. Make a decision and interpret it in the context of the original claim. The population must be normal or nearly normal.

10. (a) Fail to reject H_0 (b) Reject H_0

(c) Reject H_0 (d) Fail to reject H_0

12. (a) Fail to reject H_0 (b) Reject H_0

(c) Fail to reject H_0 (d) Reject H_0

20. (a) $H_0: \mu \leq 4$; $H_a: \mu > 4$ (claim)

(b) $t_0 = 1.833$ (c) $t \approx 0.791$ (d) Fail to reject H_0.

Section 7.4

4. Use normal distribution

$H_0: p \leq 0.30$ (claim); $H_a: p > 0.30$

$z_0 = 1.645$; $z = 2.440$

Reject H_0.

6. Use normal distribution

$H_0: p \leq 0.125$ (claim); $H_a: p > 0.125$

$z_0 = 2.33$; $z = 2.180$

Fail to reject H_0.

8. (a) $H_0: p \leq 0.55$ (claim); $H_a: p > 0.55$

(b) $z_0 = 2.33$ (c) $z \approx 0.445$ (d) Fail to reject H_0.

10. (a) $H_0: p \leq 0.50$; $H_a: p > 0.50$ (claim)

(b) $z_0 = 1.282$ (c) $z = 0.6$ (d) Fail to reject H_0.

Section 7.5

2. State H_0 and H_a. Specify the level of significance. Determine the degrees of freedom. Determine the critical value(s) and rejection region(s). Find the standardized test statistic. Make a decision and interpret in the context of the original claim.

10. (a) Fail to reject H_0 (b) Fail to reject H_0

(c) Reject H_0 (d) Reject H_0

12. (a) Fail to reject H_0 (b) Fail to reject H_0

(c) Fail to reject H_0 (d) Reject H_0

20. (a) $H_0: \sigma \geq 30$; $H_a: \sigma < 30$ (claim)

(b) $\chi_0^2 = 2.088$ (c) $\chi^2 = 8.294$

(d) Fail to reject H_0.

Review Exercises for Chapter 7

6. (a) H_0: $\mu \geq 30{,}000$ (claim); H_a: $\mu < 30{,}000$

(b) Type I error will occur if H_0 is rejected when the actual mean tire life is at least 30,000 miles.

Type II error if H_0 is not rejected when the actual mean tire life is less than 30,000 miles.

(c) Left-tailed

(d) There is enough evidence to reject the claim.

(e) There is not enough evidence to reject the claim.

8. (a) H_0: $\mu \geq 20$; H_a: $\mu < 20$ (claim)

(b) Type I error will occur if H_0 is rejected when the actual mean number of fat calories is at least 20.

Type II error if H_0 is not rejected when the actual mean number of fat calories is less than 20.

(c) Left-tailed

(d) There is enough evidence to support the claim.

(e) There is not enough evidence to support the claim.

14. H_0: $\mu = 0$; H_a: $\mu \neq 0$ (claim)

$z_0 = \pm 1.96$; $z \approx -2.040$

Reject H_0

16. H_0: $\mu = 7450$ (claim); H_a: $\mu \neq 7450$

$z_0 = \pm 1.96$; $z \approx 1.926$

Fail to reject H_0

26. H_0: $\mu = 4.20$ (claim); H_a: $\mu \neq 4.20$

$t_0 = \pm 2.896$; $t = 2.423$

Fail to reject H_0

28. H_0: $\mu \leq 10$ (claim); H_a: $\mu > 10$

$t_0 = 1.397$; $t = 1.810$

Reject H_0

CHAPTER 8

Section 8.1

4. (a) -10 (b) -2.887

(c) z is not in the rejection region.

(d) Fail to reject H_0

Section 8.2

2. (1) The samples must be independent.

(2) Each population must have a normal distribution.

(3) The size of at least one of the samples is less than 30.

8. H_0: $\mu_1 \geq \mu_2$ (claim); H_a: $\mu_1 < \mu_2$

(a) 0.04   (b) $t \approx 0.331$

(c) t is not in the rejection region.

(d) Fail to reject H_0. There is not enough evidence to reject the claim.

12. (a) H_0: $\mu_1 = \mu_2$ (claim); H_a: $\mu_1 \neq \mu_2$

(b) d.f. = 11; $t_0 = \pm 2.201$ (c) $t \approx 0.403$

(d) Fail to reject H_0. There is not enough evidence to reject the claim.

Section 8.4

4. H_0: $p_1 \geq p_2$; H_a: $p_1 < p_2$ (claim)

The test is a left-tailed test. Reject H_0. There is enough evidence to support the claim.

6. H_0: $p_1 \leq p_2$ (claim); H_a: $p_1 > p_2$

Fail to reject H_0. There is not enough evidence to reject the claim.

8. (a) H_0: $p_1 = p_2$ (claim); H_a: $p_1 \neq p_2$

(b) $z_0 = \pm 1.645$ (c) $z = -2.866$ (d) Reject H_0

CHAPTER 9

Section 9.1

14. (a)

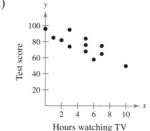

(b) -0.831 (c) Strong negative linear correlation

16. (a)

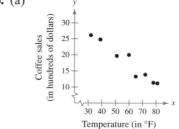

(b) -0.971 (c) Strong negative linear correlation

18. (a)

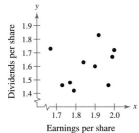

(b) 0.279   (c) Weak positive linear correlation

22. r = sample correlation coefficient

ρ = population correlation coefficient

Section 9.2

12. $\hat{y} = 513.943x - 495.170$

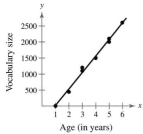

(a) 533   (b) 1047   (c) 2588

(d) It is not meaningful to predict the value of y for $x = 12$ because $x = 12$ is outside the range of the original data.

14. $\hat{y} = -4.067x + 93.970$

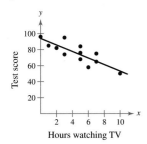

(a) 77.7   (b) 61.4   (c) 57.4

(d) It is not meaningful to predict the value of y for $x = 15$ because $x = 15$ is outside the range of the original data.

20. (a) $\hat{y} = -4.297x + 94.200$

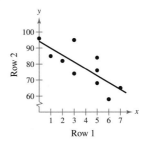

(b) $\hat{y} = -0.1413x + 14.763$

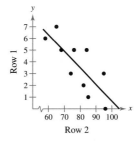

(c) The slope of the line keeps the same sign, but the values of m and b change.

Section 9.3

2. $\Sigma(\hat{y}_i - \bar{y})^2$; the sum of the squares of the differences between the predicted y-values and the mean of the y-values of the ordered pairs.

4. $r^2 = \dfrac{\Sigma(\hat{y}_i - \bar{y})^2}{\Sigma(y_i - \bar{y})^2}$; r^2 is the ratio of the explained variation to the total variation and is the percent of variation of y that is explained by the relationship between x and y.

18. (168,603,000,000, 265,095,000,000); you can be 95% confident that the number of cigarettes exported will be between 168,603,000,000 and 265,095,000,000 when the number of cigarettes consumed is 490 billion.

20. (17.573, 25.625); you can be 90% confident that the median number of leisure hours/week will be between 17.573 and 25.625 when the median number of work hours/week is 45.1.

Review Exercises for Chapter 9

2.

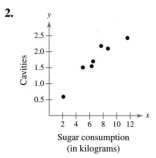

Sugar consumption
(in kilograms)

$r \approx 0.953$; positive linear correlation; the average number of cavities increases as the annual per capita sugar consumption increases.

CHAPTER 10

Section 10.1

6. (a) Claimed distribution:

Time of Day	Distribution
Midnight–6 A.M.	34%
6 A.M.–Noon	15%
Noon–6 P.M.	22%
6 P.M.–Midnight	29%

H_0: Distribution of the time of day of roadside hazard crash deaths is as shown in the table above.

H_a: Distribution of the time of day of roadside hazard crash deaths differs from the claimed distribution.

(b) 11.345 (c) 19.358 (d) Reject H_0.

12. (a) Frequency distribution: $\mu = 74.775$; $\sigma = 9.822$

Lower Boundary	Upper Boundary	Lower z-score	Upper z-score	Area
50.5	60.5	−2.47	−1.45	0.0668
60.5	70.5	−1.45	−0.44	0.2564
70.5	80.5	−0.44	0.58	0.3891
80.5	90.5	0.58	1.60	0.2262
90.5	100.5	1.60	2.62	0.0504

Class Boundaries	Distribution	Frequency	Expected	$\frac{(O - E)^2}{E}$
50.5–60.5	6.68%	28	27	0.037
60.5–70.5	25.64%	106	103	0.087
70.5–80.5	38.91%	151	156	0.160
80.5–90.5	22.62%	97	90	0.544
90.5–100.5	5.04%	18	20	0.2
		400		1.028

H_0: Variable has a normal distribution

H_a: Variable does not have a normal distribution

(b) 9.488 (c) 1.015 (d) Fail to reject H_0.

Section 10.3

2. (1) The F-distribution is a family of curves determined by two types of degrees of freedom, $d.f._N$ and $d.f._D$.

(2) F-distributions are positively skewed.

(3) The area under the F-distribution curve is equal to 1.

(4) F-values are always greater than or equal to zero.

(5) For all F-distributions, the mean value of F is approximately equal to 1.

12. (a) Population 1: Competitor

Population 2: Auto Manufacturer

H_0: $\sigma_1^2 \leq \sigma_2^2$; H_a: $\sigma_1^2 > \sigma_2^2$ (claim)

(b) 2.18 (c) 1.071 (d) Fail to reject H_0.

Section 10.4

14. $CV_{Scheffe} = 6.930$

$(1, 2) \rightarrow 0.148 \rightarrow$ No difference

$(1, 3) \rightarrow 7.842 \rightarrow$ Significant difference

$(1, 4) \rightarrow 2.581 \rightarrow$ No difference

$(2, 3) \rightarrow 5.312 \rightarrow$ No difference

$(2, 4) \rightarrow 3.677 \rightarrow$ No difference

$(3, 4) \rightarrow 17.877 \rightarrow$ Significant difference

Review Exercises for Chapter 10

4. (a) Expected frequencies:

	Car	Truck	SUV	Van	Total
Males	94.25	82.65	50.75	4.35	232
Females	100.75	88.35	54.25	4.65	248
Total	195	171	105	9	480

(b) H_0: Type of vehicle is independent of gender.

H_a: Type of vehicle is dependent on gender.

$CV = 7.815$; $\chi^2 = 8.403$; Reject H_0

(c) There is enough evidence to conclude that type of vehicle owned is dependent on gender.

CHAPTER 11

Section 11.1

4. (a) H_0: median = 72 (claim) and H_a: median ≠ 72
   (b) CV = 1   (c) $x = 6$
   (d) Fail to reject H_0. There is not enough evidence to reject the claim.

6. (a) H_0: median = 57 (claim) and H_a: median ≠ 57
   (b) CV = 2   (c) $x = 8$ (d) Fail to reject H_0.

12. (a) H_0: median = 1300 (claim) and H_a: median ≠ 1300
    (b) CV = 5   (c) $x = 9$
    (d) Fail to reject H_0. There is not enough evidence to reject the claim.

Chapter 1, page 0, Chicago, Illinois, skyline. Doug Segal, Panoramic Images; page 0, Manhattan. Colin Paterson, PhotoDisc, Inc.; page 0, New York City Skyline. PhotoDisc, Inc.; page 0, Los Angeles Skyline. Larry Brownsten, PhotoDisc, Inc.; page 1, Houston, Texas. M. Mastrorillo, The Stock Market; page 1, Aerial view of Philadelphia, Pennsylvania. Lien/Nibauer. Liaison Agency, Inc.

Chapter 2, page 28, Akhiok resident, David Eluska. Roy Corral Photography; page 28, Akhiok resident with sea urchin harvest. Roy Corral Photography; page 28, Akhiok woman. Roy Corral Photography; page 28, Akhiok resident with drying salmon. Roy Coral Photography; page 28, Akhiok resident (smiling man). Roy Corral Photography; page 28, Akhiok children. Roy Corral Photography; page 28, Akhiok child. Roy Corral Photography; page 29, Akhiok resident, young girl. Roy Corral Photography; page 29, Town of Akhiok. Roy Corral Photography; page 56, Fishing village—Akhiok, Alaska. Roy Corral Photography.

Chapter 3, page 102, Dam. Billie Johnson, U.S. Army Corps of Engineers, Washington; page 103, Sockeye salmon in water. Natalie B. Fobes; page 102, Chinook or King Salmon migrating, (Oncorhynchus tshawytschal). Tom and Pat Leeson Photography; page 102, Person removing fish with nets. Natalie B. Fobes; page 103, Sunset in the Gorge. Jay Carroll Photo/Grafix; page 132, Logo, Institute for Operations Research and the Management Sciences (INFORMS). Reprinted by permission, The Institute for Operations Research and the Management Sciences (INFORMS), 901 Elkridge Landing Road, Suite 400, Linthicum, Maryland 21090-2909 USA.

Chapter 4, page 150, Mountain Climatic, Weather Station. National Center for Atmospheric Research, Boulder, Colorado; page 150, Storm over road. Rob Atkins, The Image Bank; page 150, Cumulonimbus cloud, Painted Desert, Arizona. Tom Bean; page 151, Hay (Reeds). SuperStock, Inc.; page 151, View from mouth of ice cave past massive icicles, Michigan. G. Ryan & S. Beyer, Tony Stone Images.

Chapter 5, page 192, Woman working out with dumbbells, close-up. David Madison, Tony Stone Images; page 192, Middle Age/ Individual-Outdoor. SuperStock, Inc.; page 192, Man on Treadmill. Keith Brofsky, PhotoDisc, Inc.; page 192, Swimming Laps. PhotoDisc, Inc.; page 193, Jogging. Sean Thompson, PhotoDisc. Inc.

Chapter 6, page 250, Better not best. Chuck Kimmerle, Grand Forks Herald; page 250, Wheat at sunset. U. S. Wheat Associates; page 250, Men standing by combines and machinery. U. S. Wheat Associates; page 251, Wheatfield with combines. U. S. Wheat Associates; page 250, Grain pouring into truck. U. S. Wheat Associates; page 251, Close up of wheat. Chuck Kimmerle, Grand Forks Herald; page 265, Loggerhead sea turtle. Zig Leszczunski, Animals Animals/Earth Scenes; page 266, William Sealy Gosset, 1876-1937. English statistician. Brewer for Guinness beer.

(TDRS). An accident 73 seconds after lift-off claimed both crew and vehicle. NASA Headquarters; page 514, Kennedy Space Center, Florida—Main engine exhaust. Solid Rocket Booster plume and an expanding ball of gas from the external tank is visible seconds after the Space Shuttle *Challenger* Accident on January 28, 1986. NASA Headquarters; page 514, Woman astronaut, Christa McAuliffe. NASA/Lyndon B. Johnson Space Center; page 514, A 9'7" x 16' segment of *Challenger*'s right wing is unloaded at the logistics facility after being off-loaded from the rescue and salvage ship USS *Opportune.* NASA/Lyndon B. Johnson Space Center; page 515, Kennedy Space Center, Florida—Crew members of Space Shuttle Mission 51-L walk out of the Operations and Checkout Building on their way to Pad-39B where they will board the orbiter *Challenger*. Crew members from front to back are: Commander Francis R. Scobee; Mission Specialists Judith A. Resnik and Ronald E. McNair; Pilot Michael J. Smith; and Payload Specialist Gregory B. Jarvis. NASA Headquarters; page 515, Memorial of Space Shuttle *Challenger*. Smithsonian photo by Dr. Bella J. May. Copyright 1995, Smithsonian Institution, Washington D.C.

TABLES

Table 1 (Random Numbers). Reprinted from A Million Random Digits with 100,000 Normal Deviates by the Rand Corporation (New York: The Free Press, 1955). Copyright 1955 and 1983 by the Rand Corporation. Used by permission.

Table 2 (Binomial Probability Distribution). Binomial Probability Distribution, reprinted from Understanding Statistics 6/e by Brase and Brase. Copyright 1999 by Houghton Mifflin. Reprinted by permission of Houghton Mifflin.

Table 3 (The Poisson Distribution). Reprinted with permission from W. H. Beyer, Handbook of Tables for Probability and Statistics, 2nd ed., CRC Press, Boca Raton, Florida, 1986.

Table 4 (Standard Normal Distribution). Table A-3, pp. 681–682 from Probability and Statistics for Engineers and Scientists 6/e by Watpole, Myers and Myers. Copyright 1997. Reprinted by permission of Prentice-Hall, Inc., Upper Saddle River, NJ.

Table 5 (The *t*-Distribution). Adapted from W. H. Beyer, Handbook of Tables for Probability and Statistics, 2nd ed., CRC Press, Boca Raton, Florida, 1986. Reprinted with permission.

Table 6 (Chi-Square Distribution). D. B. Owen, Handbook of Statistics Tables (table A.5). Copyright 1962 by Addison-Wesley Publishing Company, Inc. Reprinted by permission of Addison Wesley Longman.

▼ **INDEX** ████████████

Index of Data Sets included on the Data Disk

Data sets in the chapter opener and in examples have descriptive names as shown in the table below. For other data sets, the file name uses the type (e.g. Exercise, Try It Yourself, etc.) and chapter and section umber (where appropriate). For example, Exercise 15 in section 2.1 is named **Ex2_1-15** and the Case Study in chapter 2 is named **CS2**.

Chapter or Section	Chapter Opener Name, (page)	Example number, Name (page)	Try It Yourself number (page)	Exercise number	Case Study, Technology	Review, Quiz, Test
CHAPTER 1	Census (1)					
CHAPTER 2	Akhiok (28)				CS6, Tech 2	Review: 1, 4, 6, 8, 13 Quiz: 1,6
Section 2.1		1 Internet (28)		15, 16, 17, 18, 19, 20, 21, 22, 23, 24, 25, 26, 27, 28, 29, 30, 31, 32, 33		
Section 2.2		1 AL_RBIs (44) 7 Cellphone (50)	TIY 6 (49)	15, 16, 17, 18, 19, 20, 21		
Section 2.3		6 Ages		17, 18, 37, 38, 39, 40, 45		
Section 2.4		5 Atlanta (67) 9 children (76)	TIY 5 (72)	30, 33		
Section 2.5		2 Tuition (86)		11, 12, 19, 20, 23		
CHAPTER 3						Test: 3
CHAPTER 4					CS4	
CHAPTER 5					Tech5	
Section 5.1				21, 22		
Section 5.2				7		
CHAPTER 6					CS6	Review: 1, 2 Quiz: 1
Section 6.1		1 Sentence (252)	TIY 1 (252)	43, 44, 45, 46		
CHAPTER 7					CS7	
Section 7.2		9 Franchise (323)		25, 26, 33, 34		
Section 7.3				23, 24		
CHAPTER 8						Review: 11, 19, 20 Quiz: 4
Section 8.1				13, 14, 15, 16		
Section 8.2				17, 18, 19, 20		
Section 8.3		2 Golfer (392) 3 Voter (393)	TIY 2 (393)	15, 19, 20, 21, 22, 23, 24		
CHAPTER 9	Olympics (416)				CS9, Tech9	Review: 1, 16, 21
Section 9.1		3 OldFaithful (420)		13, 14, 15, 18, 27, 28, 29, 30		
Section 9.2				6, 13, 14, 15, 21		
Section 9.3				9, 11, 12		
Section 9.4		1 Salary (452)	TIY 1 (453)	4, 5		
CHAPTER 10					CS10, Tech 10_1, Tech 10_b	Review: 13, 14, 15, 16 Quiz: 1
Section 10.1				14		
Section 10.4		2 Airline (501)	TIY 2 (501)	1, 2, 4, 5, 6, 7, 8, 9, 10		
CHAPTER 11	Challenger (514)				CS11, Tech 11_a, Tech 11_b,	Review: 4, 5, 7, 8, 9, 11, 12 Quiz: 4 Test: 1, 5
Section 11.1		3 Prison (521)	TIY 1 (518) TIY 3 (521)	11, 16		
Section 11.2		1 Music (528) 2 Earnings (531)	TIY 1 (529) TIY 2 (532)	2, 3, 4, 5, 7, 8		
Section 11.3		1 Payrates (539)	TIY 1 (540)	1, 2, 3, 4, 5, 6		
Section 11.4				1, 3, 4, 5, 8, 9		